Physical Rehabilitation:

Assessment and Treatment

Physical Rehabilitation:
Assessment and Treatment

Third Edition

SUSAN B. O'SULLIVAN, EdD, PT
Associate Professor
Department of Physical Therapy
College of Health Professions
University of Massachusetts Lowell
Lowell, Massachusetts

THOMAS J. SCHMITZ, PhD, PT
Associate Professor
Division of Physical Therapy
School of Health Professions
Brooklyn Campus
Long Island University
New York, New York

 F. A. DAVIS COMPANY • **Philadelphia**

F. A. Davis Company
1915 Arch Street
Philadelphia, PA 19103

Printed in the United States of America
Last digit indicates print numbers: 10 9 8 7 6 5 4 3

Publisher: Jean-François Vilain
Production Editor: Marianne Fithian
Cover Design: Donald B. Freggens, Jr.

As new scientific information becomes available through basic and clinical research, recommended treatments and drug therapies undergo changes. The author(s) and publisher have done everything possible to make this book accurate, up to date, and in accord with accepted standards at the time of publication. The authors, editors, and publisher are not responsible for errors or omissions or for consequences from application of the book, and make no warranty, expressed or implied, in regard to the contents of the book. Any practice described in this book should be applied by the reader in accordance with professional standards of care used in regard to the unique circumstances that may apply in each situation. The reader is advised always to check product information (package inserts) for changes and new information regarding dose and contraindications before administering any drug. Caution is especially urged when using new or infrequently ordered drugs.

Library of Congress Cataloging-in-Publication Data

O'Sullivan, Susan B.
　　Physical rehabilitation: assessment and treatment /
Susan B. O'Sullivan, Thomas J. Schmitz. — 3rd ed.
　　　　p.　cm.
　　Includes bibliographical references and index.
　　ISBN 0-8036-6699-3 (alk. paper)
　　1. Physical therapy.　I. Schmitz, Thomas J.　II. Title.
　　[DNLM: 1. Physical Therapy—methods.　2. Disability Evaluation.
3. Orthopedic Equipment.　WB 460 O86p　1994]
RM700.O88　1994
615.8'2—dc20
DNLM/DLC
for Library of Congress　　　　　　　　　　94-955
　　　　　　　　　　　　　　　　　　　　　　　CIP

Preface

We have been gratified at the wide acceptance by both entry level physical therapy faculty and students of *Physical Rehabilitation: Assessment and Treatment*. Designed as a comprehensive text on the rehabilitation management of adult patients, it also serves as a valuable reference for practicing physical therapists inexperienced in the rehabilitation setting as well as for other rehabilitation professionals. This third edition recognizes the continuing growth of the field and strives to integrate current research in basic and clinical sciences with physical therapy assessment and treatment procedures.

The conceptual basis of *Physical Rehabilitation: Assessment and Treatment* is established at the outset with three chapters examining clinical decision making, psychosocial aspects of adjustment to physical disability, and the influence of values on patient care. Thus, the reader is directed early on to develop an understanding of the whole patient and to build effective problem-solving skills.

Chapters 4 through 12 focus on procedures used in assessment of patients with physical dysfunction. Chapters 13 and 14 outline general strategies for improving motor control and gait. Subsequent chapters, 15 through 29, examine common disabilities encountered in general clinical practice and appropriate assessment and treatment strategies. Chapters on special rehabilitation topics of prosthetics, orthotics, wheelchairs, and biofeedback are also included (Chapters 20, 30 through 32). New to the third edition are chapters on the rehabilitation management of chronic pulmonary dysfunction (chapter 15), on chronic pain (chapter 27), and on communication disorders (chapter 29).

This third edition has benefited from the input of numerous readers who have used this text in either an academic or a clinical setting and are dedicated to improve patient care. In response to their constructive criticisms, we have attempted to expand and update content, correct errors, rectify omissions, and delete material as deemed appropriate.

We continue to utilize a format designed to facilitate and reinforce the learning of key concepts. To that end, every chapter of *Physical Rehabilitation: Assessment and Treatment* includes an initial set of learning objectives, an introduction, summary, study questions for self-assessment, glossary, and extensive references. In addition, chapters provide supplemental reading lists and resources for further investigation of the theories and management strategies presented. Numerous photographs and illustrations have been included to reinforce the concepts and techniques presented in the text. Summary tables, assessment tools, and treatment protocols are provided to assist the learner in organizing vast amounts of information.

We recognize the primary strength of this text comes from the input from our talented contributors, recognized authorities from different clinical specialties with unique perspectives, knowledge, and skills. Their integration of current research and clinical experience has immeasurably strengthened this text.

Because physical therapy is a growing profession with frequent and often rapid advances, we will always consider this book a "work in progress." With this in mind, we welcome the continuing suggestions for improvement from our colleagues and students.

Susan B. O'Sullivan
Thomas J. Schmitz

Acknowledgments

A project of this scope would not be possible without the valuable contributions of many individuals throughout the development of its three editions. We offer our gratitude to all our contributors (listed separately). Our gratitude, too, goes to the various individuals who have reviewed portions of the manuscript at one stage or the other. Their constructive comments greatly enhanced the contents of each edition:

Debbie Alton, PT; Lucien Côté, MD; Chad L. Deal, MD; Ruth Dickinson, MA, PT; Jeffrey E. Falkel, PhD, PT; Adele C. Germain, MS, OTR; Meryl R. Gersh, MMSc, PT; Margaret A. Henly, MA, PT; Hollis Herman, MS, PT; Rosalind Hickenbottom, PhD, PT; John M. Hovde, MA, PT; Timothy L. Kauffman, MS, PT; Alice Lewis, PT; Phyllis A. Lisanti, RN, PhD; Prudence D. Markos, MS, PT; Robert F. Meenan, MD, MPH; Carolee Moncur, PhD, PT; Arthur J. Nelson, PhD, PT; Charles R. Noback, PhD; Cynthia C. Norkin, EdD, PT; Frank Pierson, PT; Reginald L. Richard, MS, PT; Gay Rosenberg, MA, PT; Thomas Shaw, PT; Marlys J. Staley, MS, PT; Bonnie Teschendorf, MHA, PT; Catherine A. Trombly, MA, OTR; Anne E. Veazey, MS, PT; Douglas J. Westphal, MS, PT; Catherine Perry Wilkinson, EdD, PT.

We wish to thank the following individuals who contributed their time, energy and talent to the completion of the photographs: Christopher M. Powers, MS, PT; Gay Rosenberg, MA, PT; Curtis Sullenger, BA; Terry Futrell, MEd; Raymond Manson, BFA; Kathleen Nordahl, MEd; Alice Lewis, PT; and Kathy Ryan, PT. Our grateful thanks go also to the individuals whose photographs appear throughout the text.

We also extend our thanks to the staff at F. A. Davis, in particular Marianne Fithian, Production Editor; Herbert J. Powell, Director of Production; and Jean-François Vilain, Publisher; for their encouragement, expertise, and advice throughout.

Contributors

Donna Wolf Behr, PT
Graduate Program in Physical Therapy
MGH Institute of Health Professions
Boston, Massachusetts

Adrienne Falk Bergen, PT
Seating Specialist
Dynamic Medical Equipment, Ltd.
Westbury, New York

Carol M. Davis, EdD, PT
Associate Professor
Division of Physical Therapy
Department of Orthopaedics and Rehabilitation
University of Miami School of Medicine
Coral Gables, Florida

Daniel A. Dyrek, MS, PT
Director
MGH Physical Therapy Associates
Assistant Professor
MGH Institute of Health Professions
Massachusetts General Hospital
Boston, Massachusetts

Joan E. Edelstein, MA, PT
Associate Professor of Clinical Physical Therapy
Director, Program in Physical Therapy
Columbia University
New York, New York

Jeffrey E. Falkel, PhD, PT
South West Physical Therapy
Littleton, Colorado

Andrew A. Guccione, PhD, PT
Director of Quality Assurance, Research, and Education
Physical Therapy Services
Massachusetts General Hospital
Boston, Massachusetts
Lecturer in Orthopaedics
Harvard Medical School
Cambridge, Massachusetts

Barbara J. Headley, MS, PT
President
Innovative Systems for Rehabilitation
St. Paul, Minnesota

David E. Krebs, PhD, PT
Professor and Director
MGH Biomotion Laboratory
Graduate Program in Physical Therapy
MGH Institute of Health Professions
Harvard Medical School
Boston, Massachusetts

Patricia Leahy, MS, PT, NCS
Assistant Professor
Department of Physical Therapy
Philadelphia College of Pharmacy and Science
Philadelphia, Pennsylvania

Aaron Lieberman, DSW
Associate Professor
Wurzweler School of Social Work
Yeshiva University
Diplomate
American Academy of Social Work
American Academy of Pain Management
Administrative Director
Psychological Consulting Associates
New York, New York

Bilha Reichberg Lieberman, RN, MS, MSW
Fellow
American Orthopsychiatric Association
American Academy of Pain Management
Clinical Member
American Association of Marriage and Family
Therapists
Clinical Director
Psychological and Consulting Associates
New York, New York

Morris B. Lieberman, PhD
Professor
Long Island University
Diplomate in Behavioral Medicine
International Academy of Behavioral Medicine
Diplomate
American Academy of Pain Management
Director, Psychological Service
Psychological and Consulting Associates
New York, New York

Bella J. May, EdD, PT, FAPTA
Professor
Department of Physical Therapy
Medical College of Georgia
Co-Director
PhysioTherapy International PC
Augusta, Georgia

Joseph M. McCulloch, PhD, PT
Professor and Head
Department of Physical Therapy and Rehabilitation
Louisiana State University Medical Center
Shreveport, Louisiana

Cynthia Clair Norkin, EdD, PT
Director and Associate Professor
Ohio University School of Physical Therapy
Athens, Ohio

Susan B. O'Sullivan, EdD, PT
Associate Professor
Department of Physical Therapy
College of Health Professions
University of Massachusetts Lowell
Lowell, Massachusetts

Leslie Gross Portney, PhD, PT
Assistant Professor
Graduate Program in Physical Therapy
MGH Institute of Health Professions
Boston, Massachusetts

Reginald L. Richard, MS, PT
Burn Clinical Specialist
Miami Valley Hospital Regional Adult Burn Center
Dayton, Ohio

Martha Taylor Sarno, MA, MD
Professor
Clinical Rehabilitation Medicine
New York University School of Medicine
Director
Speech-Language Pathology Department
Rusk Institute of Rehabilitation Medicine
New York University Medical Center
New York, New York

Thomas J. Schmitz, PhD, PT
Associate Professor
Division of Physical Therapy
School of Health Professions
Brooklyn Campus
Long Island University
New York, New York

Marlys J. Staley, MS, PT
Supervisor
Occupational and Physical Therapy
Shriners Burns Institute
Cincinnati, Ohio

Julie Ann Starr, MS, PT
Department of Physical Therapy
Sargent College of Allied Health Professions
Boston University
Boston, Massachusetts

Chaye Lamm Warburg, MA, OTR
Assistant Professor
Programs in Occupational Therapy
Columbia University
New York, New York

Contents

Clinical Decision Making: Planning Effective Treatments

Susan B. O'Sullivan

OBJECTIVES

1. Describe the key steps in the clinical decision-making process.
2. Define the major responsibilities of the therapist in planning effective treatments.
3. Identify potential problems that could adversely affect the therapist's planning and delineate remediation strategies.
4. Describe two different models currently applied to clinical decision making.

INTRODUCTION

Clinical decision making involves a series of interrelated steps that enable the physical therapist to plan an effective treatment compatible with the needs and goals of the patient and members of the health care team. These steps include (1) collection of data, (2) analysis of data and problem identification, (3) establishment of goals and priorities, (4) formulation of an appropriate treatment plan, (5) implementation of the treatment plan, and (6) evaluation of the patient and treatment outcome. Important components of each step of the process include appropriate knowledge and clinical skills, effective decision-making skills, accurate documentation, and effective communication with the patient and other members of the health care team (Fig. 1–1).

STEP 1. COLLECT DATA

This step involves recognizing and defining the patient's problem(s) and identifying the resources available for treatment. It includes the gathering of both subjective and objective data. Assessment begins with patient referral or initial entry and continues as an ongoing process throughout the course of rehabilitation. The medical record provides an important early source of information about the history of the patient's illness and the patient's present status. An understanding of disease processes, medical terminology, differential diagnosis using laboratory and other diagnostic tests, and medical

management, including pharmacology, is essential. This may require the use of resource material or professional consultation in order to ensure a complete understanding of the data. Effective use of the medical record should also include a review of the professional reports of other members of the health care team.

An interview is another preliminary measure that is used to obtain information about the patient. An interview reveals information about the patient's primary complaint, the history of the present illness or injury, premorbid lifestyle, personal goals and expectations, motivation, and knowledge of the medical condition. Health habits, including exercise likes and dislikes, and frequency and intensity of regular activity, will also prove helpful in planning an effective treatment program. Pertinent information about the patient's home and work environments also should be obtained. During the interview, listen carefully to what the patient says. Observe the patient closely, noting present mental and physical function. Finally, the interview can be used to establish rapport, effective communication, and mutual trust. Patient cooperation serves to make the therapist's observations more valid and becomes crucial to the success of the rehabilitation program.

Once this preliminary information is gathered, a determination of the pertinent assessment procedures needed can be made through the use of screening examinations. Screening exams allow the therapist to quickly scan through data from the body systems, noting areas of deficit. Screening exams indicate areas where more detailed assessments are warranted. More definitive assessments are then used to provide objective data to accurately determine the degree of specific function and

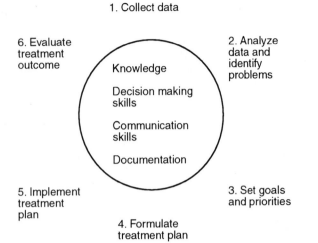

Figure 1–1. Steps in clinical decision making.

dysfunction (e.g., manual muscle test, range of motion test, oxygen consumption, and so forth). Adequate training and skill in performing these procedures is crucial in ensuring both validity and reliability of the tests. Failure to correctly perform a procedure can lead to the gathering of inaccurate data and the formation of an inappropriate treatment plan. Later chapters will focus on specific assessment procedures and will discuss issues of validity and reliability. Use of a standardized evaluation protocol can facilitate the process but may not always be appropriate for each individual patient. The unique problems of patients require the careful attention of the therapist and a determination of the appropriateness of a protocol. Therapists should resist the tendency to gather excessive and extraneous data under the mistaken belief that more information is better. Unnecessary data will only confuse the picture, rendering the clinical decision making more difficult while unnecessarily raising the cost of care. If the data are inconsistent, additional tests or assessment by another therapist may be warranted.

STEP 2. ANALYZE DATA AND IDENTIFY PROBLEMS

The assessment data must then be organized and analyzed. Terminology of the World Health Organization's *International Classification of Impairments, Disabilities, and Handicaps* (ICIDH)[1] provides an appropriate framework to categorize clinical observations systematically. **Impairments** are the result of pathology (disease or insult) and consist of the specific alterations in anatomic, physiologic, or psychologic structures or functions. For a patient with stroke, example of impairments that are the direct result of pathology might include sensory loss, motor loss, and abnormal motor planning and coordination. Schenkman and Butler[2] expand on this model with the addition of indirect and composite categories of impairments. **Indirect impairments** occur as

sequelae or secondary complications. They are the clinical manifestations of expanding multisystem dysfunction and result from prolonged inactivity, poor management, or lack of rehabilitation intervention. Examples of indirect impairments that might affect the same stroke patient include disuse atrophy, contracture, decubitus ulcers, or pneumonia. **Composite impairments** refer to those impairments that have multiple underlying causes, both direct and indirect. Faulty balance is an example of an impairment that can have both direct and indirect causes. Physical therapists routinely evaluate impairments. Analysis can be facilitated by the identification and classification of these impairments into direct, indirect, and composite categories. According to the ICIDH, **disability** is an inability to perform an activity in the manner or range considered normal for that individual, and results from an impairment. Four main categories of function are defined: (1) physical, (2) mental, (3) social, and (4) emotional. **Handicap** is used to describe the social disadvantage that results when an impairment or disability prevents an individual from fulfilling his or her normal role. An inability to return to work is an example of a handicap. Clinical applications and variations of this model are present in the literature.[3–7]

Therapeutic decisions must be based on a thorough understanding of pathology, the problems identified, the needs of the patient, and the services available. Impairments and disabilities must be analyzed to identify causal relationships. For example, shoulder pain in the patient with hemiplegia may be due to several factors, including hypotonicity and immobility (direct impairments) or soft tissue damage (an indirect impairment). Determining which of these factors is the primary cause of the problem can be a difficult yet critical step in determining an appropriate treatment and resolving the patient's pain. Some impairments may not be related to the patient's functional limitations and therefore need not become a focus of treatment.[7] Treatment decisions must focus on the skills the patient will need to achieve maximum functional independence. Finally, not all impairments can be remediated by physical therapy. Some impairments are permanent, the direct result of unrelenting pathology. Therapists need to recognize the scope of physical therapy intervention. A primary emphasis on reducing the number and severity of indirect impairments and functional disabilities is a more realistic goal in these situations.[6]

The generation of an asset list is also an important part of the clinical decision-making process. The therapist analyzes the assessment data and determines patient strengths and abilities. These areas are then supported and emphasized during therapy, providing the patient with the opportunity for positive and successful learning experiences. Improved motivation and compliance are the natural outcomes of this planning.

The development of a classification scheme of diagnostic categories unique to physical therapy is a natural outcome of the evaluation process and has been the subject of increasing attention in physical therapy literature.[8–11] The use of diagnostic categories has the potential benefit of clarifying the body of knowledge in physical therapy and the role of physical therapists (PTs) in the health care system. In a market of increasingly direct access to physical therapy services, use of specific categories could also facilitate reimbursement. Sahrmann[8] suggests the focus of such a classification system should be on the primary dysfunction identified in the physical therapy evaluation. Jette[10] suggests that diagnostic categories should include physical impairments and functional disabilities based on the ICIDH classification. The American Physical Therapy Association has affirmed that "physical therapists may establish a diagnosis within the scope of their knowledge, experience, and expertise,"[12] and progress toward specific diagnostic categories is ongoing. Therapists should keep abreast of current developments in this area.

STEP 3. SET GOALS AND PRIORITIES

Determining appropriate treatment goals assists the therapist in planning, prioritizing, monitoring, and measuring the effectiveness of treatment. It is a difficult process, requiring skill in the interpretation of assessment data, professional judgment, and skill in facilitating patient participation in the process.

Involvement of the patient is critical in achieving patient compliance.[13] Many rehabilitation plans have failed miserably simply because the patient did not see the relevance of the professionals' goals or because the patient had established a very different set of goals for themselves. Payton et al.[14] address this issue in an excellent reference entitled *Patient Participation in Program Planning: A Manual for Therapists,* which assists in the mutual planning process. These authors suggest including such questions for the patient as:

- What are your concerns?
- What is your greatest concern?
- What do you want to see happen? What would make you feel that you are making progress?
- What are your goals (long-term goals)?
- What is your first goal (short-term goal)?

The therapist then integrates this information obtained from the patient with the objective and subjective assessment data. A goal statement is generated with the patient's full cooperation and understanding.

Long-term goals (LTGs) define the patient's expected level of performance at the end of the rehabilitation process. They describe the functional outcomes of therapy and should specify

1. Who will perform the behavior—for example, patient, family, or both.
2. What is the specific behavior—that is, what the person will do.
3. Under what conditions the behavior will be performed—for example, what help is needed to accomplish the behavior; the level of independence, assistance, or supervision involved; the type of assistive device or other equipment needed; the

type of environment needed (controlled or closed, open).
4. How the outcome (attainment of the goal) will be measured—for example, degrees of range of motion, manual muscle test grades, number of feet ambulated, number of repetitions performed, amount of time on task.[15,16]

Long-term goals usually assume functional level at the time of discharge or, in instances of long-term care, are specified in terms of a specific time frame, generally 2 to 3 months. For example:

- The patient will be independent in ambulation using an ankle-foot orthosis and a quad cane on level surfaces for unlimited distances and for all daily activities.
- The patient will require close supervision in wheelchair propulsion and maximum assistance of one person in all transfer activities.

Long-term goals are established by the rehabilitation team and reflect mutual agreement that all members of the team will work toward assisting the patient to reach these goals. They become the focus of the discharge summary.

Once long-term goals have been established, the next step is to determine the component skills that will be needed to attain these goals. Each component skill then becomes the objective of a **short-term goal** (STG). The therapist should determine the appropriate sequence of subskills (STGs) and prioritize them accordingly. The written goal includes the same four elements, though they generally do not have the same functional emphasis. They also specify a shorter time span, i.e., generally 2 to 3 weeks, or a specific number of treatments. Examples of STGs related to an LTG appear following:

Long-term goal. The patient will be independent in ambulation with bilateral knee-ankle orthoses and Loftstrand crutches for unlimited distances on all surfaces.

Short-term goals.

1. The patient will increase strength in shoulder depressor muscles and elbow extensor muscles in both upper extremities from good to normal within 2 weeks.
2. The patient will increase range of motion 10 degrees in knee extension bilaterally to within normal limits within 2 weeks.
3. The patient will be independent in the application of lower extremity orthoses within 1 week.
4. The patient will perform sit-to-stand activities from wheelchair to crutches with moderate assistance of one person within 2 weeks.
5. The patient will ambulate with bilateral knee-ankle orthoses in parallel bars using a swing-through gait and supervision, for 25 ft within 2 weeks.
6. The patient will be independent in ambulation with bilateral knee-ankle orthoses and Loftstrand crutches using a swing-through gait for 50 ft on level surfaces within 3 weeks.

The patient advances through this sequence of STGs until he or she achieves the final end point or LTG. Each treatment plan usually has several LTGs, and a STG may be part of more than one sequence. Thus STGs are often interrelated, and the final outcome of several LTGs may be dependent on the achievement of one component skill. In formulating a treatment plan, the therapist needs to accurately identify component skills and their relationship to treatment outcomes. Estimating outcome and the time frame needed to attain a goal is a skill that may be difficult at first for the inexperienced therapist. Consultation with experienced professionals can often assist in this process.

STEP 4. FORMULATE TREATMENT PLAN

Once appropriate goals have been formulated, the next step is to determine the therapeutic procedures that can be used to achieve each goal. The therapist may choose from a wide variety of procedures, many of which will be discussed in this text. It is important to identify all possible treatment alternatives, to carefully weigh those alternatives, and to decide on those procedures that have the best probability of success with that patient. Using a protocol approach—for example, exercises for the hip fracture patient—standardizes care but may not be suitable for the individual needs of the patient. Henry[17] points out that protocols foster a separation of evaluation findings from the selection of treatments. In addition, an overdependence on the use of protocols may demonstrate a therapist's difficulty in problem solving. Therapists need to remain open to new treatment options and keep abreast of recent professional literature. An integrated treatment approach that provides multiple treatment options is often the one that has the greatest chance for success. Narrowly adhering to one treatment approach reduces the available options and may limit or preclude success. Available clinical information should be carefully assessed and additional information should be sought if needed. Watts[18] suggests that clinical judgment "is clearly an elegant mixture of art and science." Professional consultation with expert clinicians may be an effective means of helping a therapist sort through the complex issues involved in decision making, especially when the patient is chronically ill, or has multiple disease processes or complications.

Decisions need to be formulated on the basis of a number of considerations, such as the patient's general health, communication with the rehabilitation team, and financial costs and projected length of hospitalization. A general outline of the treatment plan can be constructed using the **FITT** (Frequency, Intensity, Time, Type) **equation.** An estimate should be made of the frequency (number of times per day or week treatment will be given), intensity (number of repetitions or activities), time (duration of the treatment session), and type. This last component includes specific modalities, therapeutic exercise procedures, gait training procedures, assistive devices, and other specialized equipment needs. The plan should also include the strategies selected to meet the educational needs of the patient and family. The

therapist is responsible for effective time management, and the treatment plan should include delegation of appropriate responsibilities of treatment to assistants or aides. The general outline may also consider potential discharge plans, including plans for a home visit, a home program, and home modifications or potential equipment needs.

Specific treatment procedures may then be outlined. A classification schema that identifies specific components of the treatment is often helpful, especially to the inexperienced therapist. For example, components of a therapeutic exercise procedure can be delineated by a description of the activity (specific posture and movement), the technique (type of contraction and mode of therapist intervention: guided, assisted, or resisted movement), and elements (verbal commands, sensory inputs).[19] Procedures should be selected to reach individual STGs. The therapist should ideally choose procedures that accomplish more than one goal and should sequence the procedures effectively to address key problems first. Procedures should also be sequenced to achieve optimum motivational effects, interspacing the more difficult or uncomfortable procedures with easier ones. The therapist should include tasks that ensure success during the session and, whenever possible, should end each treatment session on a positive note. This helps the patient retain a positive feeling of success and look forward to the next treatment.

STEP 5. IMPLEMENT TREATMENT PLAN

The therapist must take into account a number of factors in structuring an effective treatment session. The treatment area should be properly arranged to respect the patient's privacy, with adequate draping and positioning. The environment should be structured to reduce distractions and focus attention on the task at hand. In applying exercise procedures the therapist should consider good body mechanics, effective use of gravity and position, and correct application of techniques and modalities. Equipment should be gathered prior to treatment and be in good working order. All safety precautions must be observed. The patient's pretreatment level of function or initial central state should be carefully assessed. General state organization of the central nervous system and homeostatic balance of the somatic and autonomic systems are important determinants of how a patient may respond to treatment. Stockmeyer[20] points out that a wide range of influences, from emotional to cognitive to organic, may affect how a patient reacts to a particular treatment. Patients with altered homeostatic mechanisms cannot be expected to react to treatment in predictable ways. Responses to treatment should be carefully monitored. Treatment modifications should be implemented as soon as needed to ensure successful performance. Therapists develop the "art of clinical practice" by learning to adjust their input (voice commands, manual contacts, and so on) in response to the patient's movements.[18]

Treatment thus becomes a dynamic and interactive process between patient and therapist. Shaping of behavior can be further enhanced by careful orientation to the purpose of the tasks and how they meet the patient's needs, thereby ensuring optimal cooperation and motivation.

STEP 6. EVALUATE TREATMENT OUTCOME

This last step is ongoing and involves continuous reevaluation of the patient and efficacy of treatment. The patient's abilities are evaluated in terms of the specific goals set forth in the treatment plan. A determination as to whether a patient has achieved the desired level of competence for each skill must be made. Two outcomes are possible: the patient reaches the stated goal or the patient does not reach the goal. If the goal was reached, was it the result of the treatment intervention or the result of natural improvement? In either case, new STGs can be written and appropriate treatment procedures selected. When LTGs are reached or are close to being reached, discharge planning and plans for follow-up care can be initiated. If the goal has not been reached, the therapist must determine why this is so. Was the goal realistic, given the database? Was the treatment selected at an appropriate level to challenge the patient or was it too easy or too difficult? Was the patient sufficiently motivated? Were all the treatment uncertainties and constraining variables identified? With either outcome, the therapist must consider modification of the treatment plan. If the treatment was not appropriate, additional information may be sought, different treatment alternatives selected, and treatment goals modified. Long-term goals are revised if the patient progresses more rapidly or slowly than expected. Each modification in the program is evaluated in terms of its effect on the overall treatment plan. Thus the treatment plan becomes a fluid statement of how the patient is progressing and where he is going. Its overall success is dependent upon the therapist's clinical decision-making skills and on engaging the patient's cooperation and motivation. Wolf[21] cautions against empiricism, that is, continuing to use a treatment simply because it has worked in the past. Rather therapists should strive to develop a concrete database through research on which the validity of treatment can be substantiated. Expansion of the body of knowledge with the continued development of sound theories of action and continued professional development are the responsibility of every therapist.

CLINICAL DECISION-MAKING MODELS

Models for clinical decision making assist the practitioner in identifying problems, recognizing relevant data, synthesizing material, and formulating conclusions. This chapter synthesizes several models, including a systems approach for treatment planning, the problem-oriented system, and clinical decision analysis.

Schematically, the **systems model** is represented by the flow chart shown in Figure 1–2. This model uses a step-by-step approach in which the solution at each step is dependent on the information derived from the preceeding one.[22–25]

In the problem-oriented system originally developed by Weed[26–27] and adopted by many institutions, the patient-treatment process is divided into four phases:

Phase 1: The formation of a database, including history, physical examination, and laboratory and other assessment results.

Phase 2: The identification of a specific problem list from the interpretation of the database, including specific impairment of function (physical, psychologic, social, and vocational) resulting from the disease process or from secondary impairments.

Phase 3: The identification of a specific treatment plan for each of the problems described. Evaluative and progress notes are written for each problem (using a problem-oriented medical record or POMR).

Phase 4: The assessment of the effectiveness of each of the plans and subsequent changes in these plans as a result of patient progress.

Computerization of the POMR is available to store vast amounts of data and relate it to the range of possible diagnoses and the management options available. Computerization also serves to decrease the dependence on a memory-based system, and highlight the decision-making capabilities of clinicians.[28]

The reader will recognize many similarities between the systems model and the problem-oriented model. Both represent an organized approach for gathering data and determining an appropriate treatment plan. A third model for consideration involves clinical decision analysis.

Decision analysis is a formal discipline that was developed by Howard Raiffa at the Harvard Business School.[29] Its application to operations research, management science, systems analysis, and medicine is widespread.[29–32] It is designed to consider choice in the face of uncertainty, allowing the decision maker to integrate variables and calculate relevant probabilities and out-

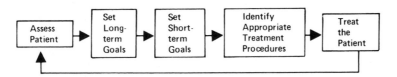

Figure 1–2. Flow chart illustrating the Systems Approach.

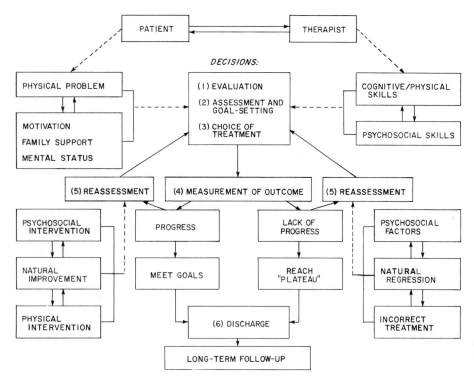

Figure 1–3. Flow chart illustrating the decision-making model. (From Wolf,[21] p 172, with permission.)

comes. The key steps in decision analysis are (1) define or structure the decision problem, (2) define successful and unsuccessful outcomes, (3) determine alternative approaches and their consequences, (4) estimate and analyze probabilities, (5) estimate costs in terms of tangible and intangible resources, and (6) select a preferred strategy. Decision analysis recognizes a series of choices, the timing of these choices, the key uncertainties or risks, and the potential benefits of each strategy. The final outcome is arrived at only after a series of "if . . . then" decisions that allow the choices to be considered individually. Thus, the final decision best represents a realistic balance between the necessary resources and expected outcomes.[33]

The generation of a **decision tree** or flow diagram allows the components of the decision process to be displayed in a sequence that embodies both temporal and logical structure. Each tree may have several branching pathways (strategies) that include decision points (interventions) and chance points (events that represent the consequences or results of an evaluative or therapeutic action). A tree is, therefore, progressively built from a database that includes the patient problem, alternative treatment paths, results of actions, and possible outcomes. Statistical probabilities of various possible outcomes, when known, are entered at appropriate points. Decisions can then be formed based on the probability of achieving a successful outcome. One of the drawbacks to using this system in physical therapy is that currently there are limited, reliable, standardized databases of outcomes on which to base decisions. Many of the decisions reached in physical therapy are based on the practical experience of individual therapists and are largely unpublished.[34] Decision trees do serve to highlight various different strategies without, as Weinstein et

al. point out, losing sight of the whole problem.[30] They also highlight the critical trade-offs between the benefits and risks of treatment, and potential biases, distortions, or omissions in planning[35] (Fig. 1–3). The final step in this quantitative analysis is the selection of an action most likely to lead to a successful outcome. The therapist needs to balance factors of both cost and effectiveness.

Watts[33] states that this is a time-consuming method, which should be used selectively. She suggests formal analyses for frequently made treatment decisions, those with important consequences, or those with significant controversy or uncertainty. Wolf's *Clinical Decision Making in Physical Therapy*[21] and *Clinical Decision Analysis* by Weinstein et al.[30] are excellent references to aid in further understanding of this model. Several computer programs are also available to assist health professionals in constructing and analyzing decision trees and in probability calculations.[36–38]

DOCUMENTATION AND COMMUNICATION

Data included in the medical record should be meaningful (important, not just nice to have), accurate (valid and reliable), timely (recorded promptly), and systematic (regularly recorded).[39] Written documentation is formally done at the time of admission and at discharge from the program and at periodic intervals during the course of rehabilitation. The format and timing of notes may vary according to institutional policy or the needs of third party payers. In the POMR, the medical record is divided into four sections, representing each of the four phases. Each member of the health care team records his or her findings and plans, according to the specific problem list. Progress notes are written in the **SOAP format** (subjective, objective, assessment, plan). The subjective findings are what the patient and his or her family tell you. The objective findings are what you observe, test, or measure. The assessment includes professional judgments about the subjective and/or objective findings and formulated into both long-term and short-term goals. The plan includes both general and specific aspects of treatment. Thus the POMR highlights the relationship of the database to the treatment plan and allows the specific patient problems to become the central focus of planning.[15]

Computer-assisted data management systems are becoming readily available to many therapists. Software programs permit data storage and retrieval, as well as statistical manipulation. The format is variable and may be consistent with the POMR system or others. An understanding of the software capabilities and of the data management system is essential in learning to use these programs.[40]

The therapist's plans should include goals written in objective, measurable terms. Plans and notes should be current, dated, neat, and legible. Acceptable medical terminology should be used and confusing abbrevia-tions avoided. Physical therapy notes should be understandable to all who read and use the medical record. Throughout the treatment planning process, the therapist should regularly communicate with other health professionals and with the patient and family. Effective communication provides an open chain of dialogue and allows for full cooperation and understanding. Communication should be appropriately modified for patients of different ages, cultural backgrounds, and educational levels and for patients with language differences, and communication or cognitive impairments.[19]

SUMMARY

An organized process of clinical decision making allows the therapist to systematically plan effective treatments. The steps identified in this process are as follows: (1) collect data, (2) analyze the data and identify problems, (3) set goals and priorities, (4) formulate a treatment plan, (5) implement the treatment plan, and (6) evaluate the treatment outcome. Inherent in this process are an appropriate knowledge base, skills in decision making, clinical practice, communication, and documentation.

QUESTIONS FOR REVIEW

1. What are the key steps in the clinical decision-making process?

2. What are the sources of information in assessing patient function and dysfunction?

3. What is the difference between a long-term goal and a short-term goal? How may they be interrelated? Practice writing examples of both.

4. How are treatment plans formulated? What factors are important to consider?

5. In evaluating treatment outcome, why might a patient have failed to reach a stated goal? What actions could you as the therapist take?

6. Compare and contrast two different models for decision making: the problem-oriented system and clinical decision analysis. What are the advantages and disadvantages of each?

7. What are the four components of the SOAP format of written documentation?

REFERENCES

1. International Classification of Impairments, Disabilities, and Handicaps. World Health Organization, Geneva, Switzerland, 1980.
2. Schenkman, M and Butler, R: A model for multisystem evaluation, interpretation, and treatment of individuals with neurologic dysfunction. Phys Ther 69:538, 1989.
3. Harris, B and Dyrek, D: A model of orthopaedic dysfunction for clinical decision making in physical therapy practice. Phys Ther 69:548, 1989.
4. Schenkman, M and Butler, R: A model for multisystem evaluation and treatment of individuals with Parkinson's disease. Phys Ther 69:932, 1989.
5. Wagstaff, S: The use of the International Classification of Impairments, Disabilities and Handicaps in rehabilitation. Physiother 68:233, 1982.
6. Guccione, A: Physical therapy diagnosis and the relationship between impairments and function. Phys Ther 71:499, 1991.
7. Nagi, S: Disability and Rehabilitation. Ohio State University Press, Columbus, OH, 1969.
8. Sahrmann, S: Diagnosis by the physical therapist—a prerequisite for treatment. Phys Ther 68:1703, 1988.
9. Rose, S: Diagnosis: defining the term. Phys Ther 69:162, 1989.
10. Jette, A: Diagnosis and classification by physical therapists: a special communication. Phys Ther 69:967, 1989.
11. Behr, D, Katz, M, and Krebs, D: Diagnosis enhances, not impedes boundaries of physical therapy practice. Orthop Sports Phys Ther 13:218, 1991.

12. APTA: Diagnosis by physical therapists (HOD 06-84-19-78). In: Applicable House of Delegates Policies. American Physical Therapy Association, Alexandria, VA, 1989, p 28.
13. DiMatteo, M and DiNicola, D: Achieving Patient Compliance. Pergamon Press, New York, 1982.
14. Payton, O, Nelson, C, and Ozer, M: Patient Participation in Program Planning: A Manual for Therapists. FA Davis, Philadelphia, 1990.
15. Kettenbach, G: Writing S.O.A.P. Notes. FA Davis, Philadelphia, 1990.
16. Zimmerman, J: Goals and Objectives for Developing Normal Movement Patterns. Aspen Publishing, Rockville, MD, 1988.
17. Henry, J: Identifying problems in clinical problem solving. Phys Ther 65:1071, 1985.
18. Watts, N: Decision analysis: a tool for improving physical therapy education. In Wolf, S (ed): Clinical Decision Making in Physical Therapy. FA Davis, Philadelphia, 1985, p 8.
19. Sullivan, P, Markos, P, and Minor, M: An Integrated Approach to Therapeutic Exercise. Reston Publishing, Reston, VA, 1982.
20. Stockmeyer, S: Clinical decision making based on homeostatic concepts. In Wolf, S (ed): Clinical Decision Making in Physical Therapy. FA Davis, Philadelphia, 1985, p 79.
21. Wolf, S: Clinical Decision Making in Physical Therapy. FA Davis, Philadelphia, 1985.
22. Day, D: A systems diagram for teaching treatment planning. Am J Occup Ther 27:239, 1973.

23. May, B and Newman, J: Developing competence in problem solving. Phys Ther 60:1140, 1980.
24. Olsen, S: Teaching treatment planning—a problem solving approach. Phys Ther 63:526, 1983.
25. Payton, O: Clinical reasoning process in physical therapy. Phys Ther 65:924, 1985.
26. Weed, LL: Medical Records, Medical Education and Patient Care. The Press of Case Western Reserve University, Cleveland, OH, 1969.
27. Hill, J: Problem Oriented Approach to Physical Therapy Care-Programmed Instruction. American Physical Therapy Association, Alexandria, VA, 1977.
28. Weed, L and Zimny, N: The problem-oriented system, problem-knowledge coupling, and clinical decision making. Phys Ther 69:565, 1989.
29. Raiffa, H: Decision Analysis: Introductory Lectures on Choices under Uncertainty. Addison-Wesley, Reading, MA, 1968.
30. Weinstein, M, et al: Clinical Decision Analysis. WB Saunders, Philadelphia, 1980.
31. Keeney, R: Decision analysis: an overview. Operations Research 30:803, 1982.
32. Watts, N: Eighteenth Mary McMillan lecture: the privilege of choice. Phys Ther 63:1802, 1983.
33. Watts, N: Clinical decision analysis. Phys Ther 69:569, 1989.
34. Shewchuk, R and Francis, K: Principles of clinical decision making—an introduction to decision analysis. Phys Ther 68:357, 1988.
35. Eraker, S and Politser, P: How decisions are reached: physician and patient. Ann Intern Med 97:262, 1982.
36. Pauker, S and Kassirer, J: Clinical decision analysis by personal computer. Arch Intern Med 141:1831, 1981.
37. Silverstein, M: A clinical decision analysis program for the Apple computer. Med Decis Making 3:29, 1983.
38. Lau, J, Kassirer, J and Pauker, S: Decision maker 3.0 improved decision analysis by personal computer. Med Decis Making 3:39, 1983.
39. Johnson, G: Bases for clinical decision making: assimilating data and marketing skills. In Wolf, S (ed): Clinical Decision Making in Physical Therapy. FA Davis, Philadelphia, 1985, p 61.
40. Hislop, H: Clinical decision making: educational data and risk factors. In Wolf, S (ed): Clinical Decision Making in Physical Therapy. FA Davis, 1985, p 25.

GLOSSARY

Composite impairment: An impairment whose underlying cause includes both direct and indirect effects of the original pathology or insult.

Decision analysis: A systematic approach to decision making under conditions of uncertainty. Decision analysis focuses on structuring and diagramming over time the problem, the management alternatives and consequences, the uncertainties, and the preferences of the decision makers.

Decision tree: A flow diagram that allows the components of the decision analysis process to be displayed in a sequence that embodies both temporal and logical structure.

Disability: An inability to perform an activity in the manner or range considered normal for that individual; the result of an impairment.

FITT equation: A general formula for outlining a treatment plan, including frequency, intensity, time, and type of therapeutic intervention.

Handicap: The social disadvantage for an individual that results when an impairment or disability prevents an individual from fulfilling his or her normal role.

Impairment: Any loss or abnormality of anatomic, physiologic, or psychologic structure or function; a direct and natural consequence of pathology or insult.

Indirect impairments: The sequelae or secondary complications occurring in systems other than the system affected by the original pathology or insult; the clinical manifestations of expanding multisystem dysfunction.

Long-term goals (LTGs): Statements that define the patient's expected level of performance at the end of rehabilitation; the functional outcome of therapy. Goals specify (1) who will perform the behavior, (2) what the specific behavior is, (3) under what conditions the behavior will be performed, and (4) how the outcome will be measured.

Problem-oriented system: An organized approach to the patient-treatment process characterized by four phases: (1) formation of a database, (2) identification of a specific problem list, (3) identification of a specific treatment plan, and (4) evaluation of the effectiveness of treatment plans.

Short-term goals (STGs): Statements which define the interim steps or component skills required to attain long-term goals. The structure of STGs is the same as that of LTGs.

SOAP format (subjective, objective, assessment plan): Progress note format utilized in the POMR; delineation is made among subjective findings, objective findings, assessment results, and plan of care.

Systems model: A step by step model of treatment planning; the solution to each problem is dependent on information obtained in the preceding step.

Psychosocial Aspects of Physical Rehabilitation

Aaron Lieberman
Morris B. Lieberman
Bilha Reichberg Lieberman

OBJECTIVES

1. Develop an awareness of the psychologic impact of disablement on the patient.
2. Gain an understanding of the human adaptation process.
3. Realize the inseparability of the physical from the psychologic aspects of functioning.
4. Understand the interplay between the internal and external realities of one's life space.
5. Realize that the physical cause of disability is but one factor among a myriad of other contributory aspects of disability.
6. Understand the importance of the "self-concept" and its implications for rehabilitation.
7. Gain knowledge of the impact of values and learning on adaptive and maladaptive coping.
8. Understand the role played by cognition and perception on disability and its outcome.
9. Consider the role played by the premorbid personality structure and its effect on the outcome of a disablement.
10. Gain an understanding of the general adaptation syndrome, its aims, uses, and potential dangerous side effects.
11. Realize the subjectivity of the meaning of disablement and disability to the patient.
12. Appreciate the interactive role of the various causal factors on health, disease, and disability.
13. Understand the impact of psychologic functioning and social interaction on health, disease, and accident proneness.
14. Learn the significance of "role" in adjustment to life changes and disablement.
15. Understand the significance of the stages of psychologic adjustment to loss and disability outcome.
16. Recognize the danger signs that might indicate psychopathologic adjustment of a patient.
17. Gain knowledge of what can be expected as "normal" during the post-traumatic adjustment period.
18. Develop an understanding of the contributions that physical rehabilitation clinicians and mental health professionals can make to each other's clinical work.
19. Enhance the physical rehabilitation specialist's therapeutic impact by use of the elements of psychosocial understanding and intervention methods.
20. Recognize the importance of psychosocial adjustment, without which rehabilitation cannot be successful.

INTRODUCTION

A comprehensive offering of state-of-the-art physical rehabilitation cannot limit itself to the administration of physical methods alone. As the editors state in their preface to the third edition of this book, the materials presented should be of service to all health care professionals involved with rehabilitation. In keeping with this mandate, the authors have invited contributions involving various aspects of rehabilitation for the benefit of the reader.

The psychosocial sciences are being progressively recognized as an essential resource for understanding the patient population, the rehabilitation process, and the significance of interaction between the two; they are crucial to effective treatment and the alleviation of suffering.

Of necessity, as broad as the scope of this text is, the focus had to be limited to the adult population. Thus, this presentation of psychosocial aspects of rehabilitation refrains from elaborating on specific populations, including the special considerations involved with the pediatric population.

Likewise, for the sake of brevity, the emphasis in this chapter is on physical disability and rehabilitation. This should not be seen as excluding the nondisabled client whose need is limited to the alleviation of pain and suffering. The emphasis on the disabled client and on rehabilitation should be seen as an inclusive rather than an exclusive approach because the material presented will hopefully contribute to a better understanding of all clients referred for physical rehabilitation.

DISABILITY AND ADJUSTMENT

Disability can be likened to the proverbial iceberg: the onlooker can see only the tip, whereas the entity itself contains more hidden aspects of its being than are revealed on the surface. An expression of physical pain or the absence of normal sense experiences, the lack of sensory input or motor output, a missing or dysfunctional limb or structure, and other such reflections of loss are just the surface structure of physical disability. Yet, these are the major domains that traditionally have been addressed when dealing with physical disability.

At best, our understanding of what an individual who is disabled might feel about the state he or she is in can only be an approximation of their unique **perceptions** or feelings. All of those uniquely combined thoughts and feelings that the individual has gathered during a lifetime of personal experiences shape that individual's perception of **disablement.**

The factors that shape individual reactions include the set of values, directions, and prohibitions taken on by the individual. These combine with **innate** and acquired drives, needs, and experiences to create an individual unique perceptual mode and form an individualized cognitive base. It is through this that the individual has learned to see the **self** and the surrounding world. The resultant **self-image,** whether conscious or unconscious, organizes the stage and creates a set of values and expectations by which one measures oneself and one's worth. It becomes the compass with which one steers through life and guides relationships, and the framework that structures the goals and foundations of one's individualized world.

Through this process, a method of **coping** and functioning emerges—the **style of coping** through which one recognizes the self. Then suddenly, or gradually, depending on the nature and extent of a disablement, the lifelong foundation and structure of that "self" become damaged and weakened by the impact of the disability, oftentimes to the point of total collapse. The disabling condition as well as the perception of it disrupts the structure that had been so carefully erected. Rules and roles change; relative independence and the ability to perform the essential tasks of living are gone, or perceived as such. The ability to give and take love, care, affection, and support is diminished or lost. Relative financial stability and security may vaporize into thin air.

Intellectually, we the "healers" can understand the trauma; we may even be sensitive enough to feel some of it. We may associate our patient's suffering with recollections of some pain or loss experiences we have personally experienced. The physical therapist, working towards the goal of rehabilitating a client, needs to be cognizant of the possibility that **adjustment** to the actual physical disability may not be the most difficult adjustment for the patient. The individual will most likely have a more difficult task adjusting to new perceptions about him- or herself and the societal attitudes toward the disability. These factors and the individual's reactions to the new situation will most likely impact on the overall adjustment, the rehabilitation treatment process, and its outcome.

Ignoring this probability may lead to a serious level of interference with or complication of the therapeutic outcome. An awareness of these issues can prevent or minimize their interference and enable the clinician to mobilize the very same factors in the service of the rehabilitative effort.

This chapter presents an overview of these issues and will attempt to suggest some practical guidelines that should enhance the therapeutic impact.

ADAPTATION: A SURVIVAL MODALITY

Living is a constant ongoing adjustment and **adaptation** process encompassing different operating levels of an organism and its life space. This process is active at the physiologic, physical, psychologic, and social levels. Although there are indeed significant differences among these aspects of functioning, we should keep in mind that they are but part of an entity that functions as an integrated whole. Any separation between levels and parts of an individual's system is an artificial convenience, because no part within the person is independent of the rest of that individual. **Psychologic adjustment** is accordingly part and parcel of overall adjustment in general, rather than a separate independent entity. There are many aspects of the dynamic, interactive, and ongoing process of an individual's adaptation within the context of total life space. This life space includes, among others

1. The body total with its various genetic, electrochemical, hormonal, and neurologic configurations.
2. Innate instinctual drives, as well as conditioned mental mechanisms.
3. Sociocultural, spiritual, and ethnic beliefs and value systems as well as socioeconomic realities of the time and place in which a person interacts.
4. The historic-mythologic, philosophic-ideologic, or even imagined-delusional image that one feels part of and is influenced by.

NATURE AND NURTURE

As we grow and age, various sets of expectations change and evolve. The nature or direction of these changes depends on our species-specific and individual, genetically inherited developmental capacities, as well as the **proscribed roles** and the ethnic and social status we are born into. Other aspects, such as the prevailing political-ideological climate and religious beliefs, the historic period with its economic and technologic systems, and family idiosyncrasies and structure, are among the contributing factors to the individual's adaptive and adjusting style. They are part and parcel of the mold from which the unique individual emerges and creates an idiosyncratic style of adaptive (or **maladaptive**) perceptual and conceptual functioning, a response repertoire, and a **personality structure,** through which the individual negotiates the surrounding environment.

The evolving self is in no way a passive target of the above-mentioned factors. As that self evolves it combines and channels innate drives and needs with learned or reinforced behaviors and values. These, in turn, are shaped by one's ongoing development and experience; real and imagined personal competence, vulnerability, and perception; an internalized ideology, value system, and social channeling. Coping is an ongoing learning process that is constantly affected by a variety of social and environmental influences.

As a result, the individual's interaction with the internal and external reality becomes selective, subjective, and idiosyncratic. This process can be seen as the sum total of an interactional history of one's **nature** and **nurture.** The chronology of this interactional history includes the genetic evolution specific to one's species and ancestry, and the cultural and environmental forces that shape the world into which the individual was born. This interaction then shapes the individual's unique subjective perception of the world and of the self. It likewise shapes an intricate mental defense and adaptation system, a unique response repertoire that is, and will be, utilized in present and future coping and adjustment. This adjustment process is therefore an ongoing learning and relearning experience unique to the individual. Accordingly, an individual's adjustments will depend on the "ego" (or self) and its **defense** structure. It will depend on the relative strength or vulnerability of the ego and the adjustment style one has adopted. Oftentimes catering to these conflicting biologic, psychologic, and social needs requires the balancing of internal and external resources. We will call this balancing act "coping" even though, depending on one's theoretical preference, many other names have been used to describe the same concept. Coping is, accordingly, a combination of innate and learned behaviors that are utilized by individuals attempting to deal with the demands of internal and external conditions, conditions that oftentimes conflict with each other. It is an active process aimed at creating a state of biologic and psychologic equilibrium. The attempt to bring about such a balance, and to satisfy or mediate between internal and external pressures is what adjustment is all about. This is an ongoing process without which life would be difficult, if not impossible. Because adaptation and coping are significantly affected by conflicting inputs, coping may at times differ from accepted values or inner needs and result in a failure to serve the best interest of the individual or society. When one's coping is contrary to environmental standards or one's own best interest, it will most likely be termed **"deviant"** in the first

instance and "maladaptive" in the second. Maladaptive adjustment might develop as the result of faulty perception, learned rejection of the self, misguided values, or misinterpretations of reality; while the deviant adjustment might be due to justified or unjustified disagreement with the surrounding set of values. Either way the coping response of an individual is part of an adaptation process that aims at survival, even though the individual's coping responses may not lead to this goal. The reader should be cognizant that it is the perception of the responding individual that determines the selected response. The physician will frequently encounter patient behaviors that are contrary to the client's best interest. An understanding of this may be helpful in eliciting better cooperation and compliance with the therapeutic regimen prescribed.

It becomes clear that psychologic adjustment is an intricate interactive process; that it dictates to, while being dictated by, the body mechanism and the idiosyncratic, perceived, real or fictitious, external world one lives in. It represents the consciously perceived self, as well as unconscious motivations, emotions, drives, values, and perceptual functioning. Psychologic adjustment is therefore of paramount importance in any consideration of the individual. It includes a need to maintain and develop a **self-identity** within the biologic and social structure of which one is a part. Psychologic adjustment of an individual might be considered crucial to what life is all about to that individual; it will determine its quality, and sometimes may even bring about its destruction. Psychologic adjustment can significantly enhance the utilization of one's resources for rehabilitation from a physical disability, or be a major contributing factor to the disability itself.

REACTION TO INJURY AS AN ADJUSTMENT PROCESS

For the purpose of differentiation between objective loss of function and the ensuing subjective state, we chose to call the objective and actual loss a disablement. Thus the loss of a leg is, within this context, a disablement (impairment). An individual's reaction to injury, illness, or loss of function can be a psychologic impairment, which contributes towards the ensuing physical disability. Reaction to **disability** can therefore be considered an adjustment process to a disruptive event that impinged on and interrupted the "normal mode" of functioning of that individual. This implies that when an individual is confronted with a disablement, various adjustments are attempted in order to cope with the newly created situation. The elicited response to the disablement may encompass most, if not all, levels of the individual's functioning. This would include, among others, the vegetative process, the autonomous nervous system and cortical responses, the hormonal and autoimmune response, as well as the intra- and interpersonal reactions. Above all, the response to disablement and rehabilitation would depend on what the disabling condition means to its victim.

The response thus triggered by the various aspects of

one's functioning and coping style might optimize or, conversely, minimize the rehabilitative efforts. Acceptance of the resultant objective limitations, the development of compensatory functioning, and adjusting to a different mode of life and different societal roles that are called for by the newly created conditions, will usually be adaptive. Unwarranted retreats to lower-level functioning, isolation, rejection of oneself, loss of self-appreciation, or ultimately an escape into nihilism or death would obviously be considered maladaptive. For some individuals who have experienced coping difficulties prior to a disablement, disability may be utilized as an escape from responsibility or a tool for manipulations. In others, it may bring about further deterioration, or it may have just the opposite effect and become an opportunity to turn a stagnant life around. Engel[1] reports that in some instances of emotionally dysfunctional individuals, disability may contribute positively to their overall adjustment. Moos[2] sees in such findings a provocative challenge; he claims that most researchers tend to accentuate the negative reactions to disability, a viewpoint that obscures any positive compensations some individuals resort to when faced with a disabling condition. Ehrenteil[3] also stresses the possible positive reaction to disability and suggests that disability may have an ego-integrative role. As one example, a doctoral student of ours utilized her crippling neurologic disease as a chance to change her premorbid, mundane life as a secretary into a professional one. Becoming confined to a wheelchair and dependent on unemployment and disability income enabled her to pursue doctoral level study in psychology, a dream that could not be realized while being in good health and self-supporting. She, for one, gladly used her disability as an entry into a professional career.

SUBJECTIVITY OF DISABILITY

A person's disability is to a large extent directly related to the way that he or she perceives the condition. The extent of a disability will increase if the focus is on deficiencies rather than assets. Much of such focusing depends on the premorbid makeup of an individual, his or her coping repertoire, and on the cultural perception of the disabling situation. The interaction of these factors will determine the adjustment to the disablement. It is our task as clinicians to assist our clients in making a favorable adjustment to their disablement and to prevent unfavorable adaptations to their conditions.

Adjustments are attempts to develop a fit between two or more variables. In living organisms, adjustment usually implies adapting for the sake of survival, though under certain circumstances individual survival is sacrificed for the survival of the species. The same holds true for the human species albeit distorted at times.

To effectively serve the complicated survival needs of the human species we have developed various mental mechanisms, also called **ego defense** or defense mechanisms, which assist us in this task. These mechanisms are utilized to alleviate the pressures and conflicting demands that we encounter in life. Even though these defenses are aimed at survival, oftentimes the pressures and conflicts are such that we will utilize these defenses for the sake of alleviating immediate or short-term pressures at the cost of what is indeed best for our survival. To accomplish this we will turn a blind eye to the encountered reality. These defense mechanisms will invariably create faulty perceptions, which will trigger behaviors that may alleviate the pressures we feel. We create these faulty perceptions, and resort to them, in order to mitigate the felt pressures, all the while denying or being unaware of their inappropriateness.

Our aim as clinicians is to prevent maladaptive adjustment in our patients. We will usually consider the acceptance of a life spent in a wheelchair for a patient who has the capacity to learn to ambulate on his or her own as maladaptive adjustment; yet we have to understand that the patient's choice is an adjustment that may nevertheless be the best choice from that person's vantage point. As already stated, the terms adjustment, coping, and adaptation are given to value interpretation and do not imply a positive outcome. For the purpose of convenience, we will use the term "maladaptive" for faulty adaptation and the term "adaptive" for its opposite.

When a maladaptive response is the result of faulty reality testing, value judgments, misinformation, or defective neuronal brain activity, it becomes the duty of "responsible others" to enable that individual to shift to a more appropriate and adaptive one. Parents, spouses, teachers, clinicians, and at times society, will take on the role of the "responsible other." Yet who really knows best? We have to respect the individual's right to make his or her own life decisions unless there is objective evidence that judgmental faculties are diminished. And let us always make sure that our own information is correct and that our own judgment is not clouded. We carry a professional obligation to make every conceivable effort to understand the individual's covert reasons for his or her functioning before passing judgment as to its appropriateness. This takes special skills, objectivity, and an ability to put our own values and interests aside. If we do not do this, then our judgments may be the ones that need correction.

We have discussed the adjustment process in detail because of its significance to the process of rehabilitation. Most of life's adjustments become routine and almost automatic. Nonroutine but expected events have much more of an impact, whereas those that are both unexpected and disruptive can have a catastrophic impact, at times out of proportion to the actual damage sustained.

ADJUSTMENT TO DISABLEMENT

Among the factors contributing to adjustment are the extent of the injury or illness, the onset mode, the prognosis, cortical involvement, the social, medical, psychologic, and economic support systems, and the subjective perception of the situation, as well as the **premorbid** coping capacity of the patient. Also of significance is the realistic degree of interference the disability may have in the vocational and personal mode of life of a given individual. A loss of one finger should objectively have little effect on a professional singer but will most likely bring an end to much more than just the career of a concert pianist. Good psychologic adjustment may drive the latter into becoming a successful conductor, whereas a bad adjustment might cripple the same individual for life.

Adjustment is obviously more dramatic during a major disabling condition and is therefore the focus of this discussion. Let us remember that what makes a condition major or minor is subjective, and therefore even minor physical conditions are major to most of their owners. What is discussed here is applicable to most patients in need of physical rehabilitation. Pain and reaction to injury are subjective and not in direct proportion to the actual extent of injury. The difference in the need for adjustment is due to personal perception. Obviously an injury that ceases to impact on the injured person within a relatively short period, or that does not require any special attention or changes in one's functioning, will leave few, if any, scars. When the subjective reaction to a disablement is disproportionate to the level of actual damage, it can be assumed that the response is most likely triggered by some emotional factor and/or personality structure rather than by the precipitating injury or illness.

Successful adjustment would imply the restoration of, or some approximation to, the premorbid condition of the disabled function, and compensation for the loss by the utilization of other assets. We have previously implied that disability in physical functioning is usually accompanied by disruptions of psychologic and social functioning. Compensating the physical loss by itself does not necessarily bring with it a correction of the other losses a patient experiences. Ignoring those other perceived losses may interfere with the physical rehabilitation and increase the level of the physical disability.

Psychologic adjustment to injury or disablement can be divided into three phases. The first of these is the immediate period of the injury or disablement; this is followed by the second phase, which lasts until a relatively stable adjustment has been made. The third period is the one where a relative equilibrium has been reached, either by a return to premorbid functioning to the extent possible, or by having reached a level of functioning and coping that is optimal in view of the nature of the disablement. For the purpose of our discussion we will refer to these as the **traumatic reaction period,** the **posttraumatic adjustment period,** and the stabilization period, respectively.

The Traumatic Reaction Period and the General Adaptation Syndrome

During a catastrophic event, whether due to accident or to acute, severe illness, an individual's response will be primarily at the physiologic level. When a body perceives itself to be in danger it will trigger its own emergency responses. Likewise, the medical emergency team will occupy itself with the immediate life-saving attempts necessary for physical survival. Evaluation of psychologic adjustment would most likely not be possible until later and therefore would not be an early focus of intervention.

When the trauma is relatively mild or the disability has a gradual onset, as happens during evolving illness, the psychologic reaction may be the most noticeable one. In either case an interactive feedback loop would appear between the physiologic and emotional functioning of the victim as a result of the ensuing **stress reaction.**

During an extreme catastrophic reaction an organism would most likely respond with what Selye[4] termed the **general adaptation syndrome** (GAS). Selye described GAS as an organism's defensive adaptation attempt that expresses itself through physiologic and emotional interactions of responses aimed at dealing with real or perceived emergency situations. During this reaction there is a hormonal release of corticotropin (ACTH), which sets into motion an increase in specific physiologic activity aimed at maximizing the body's defense capacity and minimizes physiologic activities that are not essential during the emergency. While such corticosteroid increase serves the defensive stance, its inhibitory effect on other body needs such as the production of insulin and calcium is undesirable in the long run. When such inhibition is prolonged, additional undesirable effects such as hypertension, digestive problems, and interference with the immune system will result. Selye has been able to document the devastating effect that the prolongation of this response has on human mental and physical functioning. Therefore, situations that activate the sympathetic system through repeated alarms, traumas, or chronic stress may alter synaptic transmission and lead to anxiety and depression of normal function.

It should be noted that physiologic and pyschologic interaction in response to stress is not limited to catastrophic conditions. An extensive body of research shows stress reactions to be present in individuals under conditions that would hardly affect the average person. Everyday life frustrations, internal and external conflict situations, and changes in life conditions are major causes of stress reaction that may have a devastating effect on an individual's functioning and health. The rehabilitation specialist should accordingly be cognizant of the fact that even though his or her patient's objective emergency situation is over, stress reaction may still be easily triggered, and that the stress reaction is not limited to the traumatic reaction period or to the primary injury or illness. The patient may develop increasing awareness of the trauma and experience the everyday frustrations in interacting with the newly created physical, social, and emotional realities; activities that were previously performed almost automatically and effortlessly become difficult and oftentimes impossible to perform. These become compounded with readjustment needs of daily life activities and a new and usually lower self-image. Guilt feelings or blame are interlaced with anger towards the real or imagined causal agents of the condition the patient experiences. This extra load of stress may lead to a chronic stress level that will interfere with rehabilitation efforts.

The Posttraumatic Period

The posttraumatic period is usually the time during which much, if not most, of the rehabilitative effort takes place; it is also the period during which the psychologic effects of the traumatic experience are felt by the patient. Mann and Gold[5] claim that the psychologic problems after injury are as disabling as the physical ones, and found this to be even more pronounced when the physical injury was less evident. It seems as if most of the psychologic defenses and reactions that took second place during the traumatic period start emerging as the physical injury is diminished. These repressed reactions seem to interact with the growing awareness of the aftereffects of the disablement and create perceptions, fears, anxieties, and behaviors that the rehabilitation specialist has to confront, be aware of, and deal with. Of particular interest to the rehabilitation worker at this stage is the emergence of **posttraumatic stress disorder (PTSD)**. Knowledge of the nature of this secondary disorder and its prevalence will aid the therapist to better understand the patient's reactions and feelings at this stage of rehabilitation. Posttraumatic stress disorder, as a common psychological response to a wide variety of traumatic experiences, has been the object of increasing interest and will be discussed later in this chapter.

The Stabilization Period

The stabilization period is the third and last phase of psychologic adjustment. During this phase the role of the clinical team is usually phased out or minimized as the patient enters into a relatively adjusted and balanced state of living. It should be noted, however, that stabilization is a relative term and does not imply optimal adaptation. Adaptation is a relative term that indicates a comparatively good functioning within the environment and can be either beneficial or adverse. For example, the *New York Times* (October 7, 1987) described an individual weighing over 1000 pounds who had been confined to bed in a prone position for over a decade as a result of his weight, which did not allow him any mobility. The disability was reportedly due to his enormous appetite. This individual adjusted to his food craving and stabilized his life to the ensuing body weight. His enormous weight and size made it impossible for his body to support itself or for him to exit the confinement of his bed and room. He reportedly was content with the confined condition created by his eating habit. It can be said that this bedridden, immobilized person was living a stabilized and adjusted life: adjusted to an imprisoned state, without any activity except the frequent intake of food, staring at television, and getting attention from his caretaking kin. It can be said that this is a severe case of maladaptation, which nevertheless can be considered an adjustment, albeit a self-destructive one.

This case illustrates the importance of the quality of the stabilization period. It is during this latter period that the patient may accept or reject the quality or value of the life that the disablement affords him or her. Likewise, it is during the stabilization period that life can become meaningful, or meaningless, for the given individual. Being alert to all the needs of the patient as well as to the signs and symptoms of maladaptation during the posttraumatic adjustment period is therefore vital. We emphasize the need for an integrated holistic approach, which must essentially include the psychosocial aspect of disability as well as the physical one. A primary goal of this chapter is to alert the clinician to the emotional wounds that illness and injury create and to underscore the importance of interacting with the other clinical team members in meeting the needs of the patient as an integrated human being.

THE ROLE OF COGNITION

One of the psychologic factors that exerts a major impact on patients' rehabilitative functioning is their cognitive makeup. Present-day psychology regards **cognition** as one of the most significant factors in determining an individual's way of dealing with the world. Dollard and Miller[6] claimed that cognition and motivation are the major determinants of individual functioning. Subsequent psychologic research confirmed this view, and considered emotions and stress to be the result of the individual's cognitive functioning. This view has since been supported by numerous studies, and indicates the important role played by perception in dealing with the situations with which an individual is confronted.[7-10] Selye stated, "It is not what happens to you that matters, but how you take it."[11]

Accordingly, the traumatic severity of a noxious stimulus depends, to a great degree, on the individual's perception of an event, and the subjective value assigned to the factors affected by it. Likewise the ability to cope with the situation as perceived is significantly dependent on the individual's perception of his or her coping ability, rather than on the actual resources available. This indicates that an individual's perception of a given situation, and the ability to cope with it effectively, is significantly determined by his or her psychologic makeup. Thus, the choice of any adjustment to loss of function and illness is dictated from within the personal world of an individual's belief and value system as well as the ensuing perception. Faulty reality appraisal or misguided coping strategies will create maladaptation. Conversely, confidence in one's resources and a positive set of values will help overcome disability through actualizing untapped or dormant assets. Experience shows that identical physical or physiologic damage will result in different levels of disability when affecting different individuals.[12]

THE SUBJECTIVITY OF PHYSICAL DISABILITY

It becomes clear that the clinician's understanding of the psychologic adjustment of a given patient is paramount. The seasoned therapist knows that an amputated limb is not a discarded anatomic part but rather an inseparable part of the patient even after its loss. The patient will not only feel the (phantom) sensation in the lost limb but may also perceive life as worthless without it, regardless of the actual and objective significance of the loss and its physical effect. The prosthesis replacing a limb may enable physical ambulation quite effectively but fail its owner emotionally. Without that limb the patient may feel impotent, worthless, estranged, punished, guilty, unloved, frightened, and crippled, even though physical functioning has been restored.

Considering the above, it becomes doubtful that an individual can lose some essential function or an anatomical part without losing part of the psychologic self. The lack of a visible catastrophic response to such a loss most likely indicates a defensive stance rather than the absence of such a reaction. Thus a therapist will fail such a patient by ignoring the lost anatomic part or by addressing treatment exclusively to the physical dysfunction.

It therefore becomes imperative to consider a client's psychologic makeup as a major prognostic determinant. We cannot isolate the physical body from the totality of the person and expect to treat it successfully. Of no less importance is the effect the individual's psychologic functioning has on the disabling condition itself. For a better understanding of the interaction between psychologic functioning and physical disability we will attempt to differentiate between the contributing causative factors of the disability and the disability itself.

THE INTERACTION OF CAUSAL AND AFFECTED FACTORS IN DISABILITY

Traditionally the causative factor of physical disablement was considered to be the external or internal agent that disrupts an individual's physical or physiologic functioning. Examples of these would be a foreign body intrusion, an ingested poison or microorganism that causes organ damage, a degenerative disease or genetic flaw that destroys or interferes with body functions, and other such physiochemical assaults. These would be considered the primary causal factors of the disability. The ensuing psychologic response state would accordingly be considered a secondary impairment and a complicating or contributing factor to the disability.

Disability is the end result of both primary and secondary impairments, which shape the response of the individual afflicted by them. Accordingly, the disability is not necessarily in direct proportion to the physical damage, but rather represents the end result of the synergistic effect of the physical loss and the individual's perception and mental attitude towards this loss. Just like pain, disability is very much dependent on the experiencing individual. This does not imply that the physical loss itself is dependent on the mental state of the victim; but rather that the extent of the disability depends on that state. A positive mental outlook will not remove a disablement but will most likely improve chances of healing. A limb will not regrow by wishing for it or by having a positive mental attitude; yet without the latter, the chances of a prosthesis replacing the lost limb and improving function will significantly diminish.

PSYCHOLOGIC FACTORS IN PHYSICAL DISABILITY

Physical factors are not always the primary cause of a physical disability. The psychologic and medical literature is replete with evidence indicating the presence of emotional factors and emotional disruption as primary contributors to accidents and debilitating disease.[13-16] Charcot and Freud demonstrated the undeniable role psychologic factors play in the development of disease.[17]

One of the earlier theories considering emotionality as the cause of illness was the psychosomatic model presented by Alexander.[13]

The psychosomatic theory posits that physical illness may be secondary to an emotional condition and should be treated as such. Neglect in dealing with the psychologic causal agent will accordingly result in a continuation of its malevolent effect on the victim and interfere with rehabilitation of the resultant disability. What is suggested is that the disablement, whether due to accident or illness, may at times have psychopathologic origins.

In the previous discussion of Selye's general adaptation syndrome, we mentioned the interaction of perception and cognitive functioning with physiologic reactions. It follows that faulty perception and cognition, resulting in stress, will expose one to increased risks of injury and illness.[18,19] We do not wish to elaborate on this but feel that the nonpsychologic clinician has to be aware of the role played by mental functioning in reinforcing physical illness and injury, and at times, even in their creation. Such beliefs are shared by most psychologic theories and are increasingly accepted by medical science. Psychodynamic theorists and practitioners consider much of physical disease and accidental injury as the outcome of repressed, displaced, or somatosized mental energy.[20] Freud[21] posited the idea of "thanatos," described as a destructive, inborn drive, needed for survival. Freud believed that under certain psychopathologic conditions this drive turns towards the self and may express itself in conscious suicidal attempts or in unconscious self-destructive behaviors.

The third revised edition of the *Diagnostic and Statistical Manual of Mental Disorders* (*DSM-III R*) of the American Psychiatric Association[22] has assigned a special diagnostic category to the psychologic factors affecting physical conditions. The predominant symptomatology of "psychological factors affecting physical conditions" (DSM-III code 316.00) is described in the ***DSM-III R*** and its revised edition as any physical condition or disorder that has been triggered by a psychosocial **stressor.** The manual then states that the physical disturbance will eventually remit after the stressor ceases or may be replaced by a different type of adaptation (*DSM III R,* pp. 303–304).

The way psychopathology contributes to physical ailments and accidents is obviously dependent on the type of emotional disturbance that exists. While it is beyond the aim of this chapter to review these, we will mention some general characteristics that might affect disability.

It is obvious that in psychotic functioning, when lack of reality testing or states of confusion are prevalent, risks of accidents and disease states are increased. Similarly, emotionally troubled individuals may be preoccupied with their problems or exhaust their capacity for coping with life to a degree that will interfere with their alertness, and obviously their ability to properly take care of their own safety and health.

Some emotional disorders and personality types find their expression in dangerous behaviors such as aggression against others and the self, or in impulsive behaviors that may result in serious injury. These disorders would include the sociopathic, the antisocial, the impulsive, and the inadequate personality type, as well as pyromaniacs, psychotics, and depressed patients. Their compliance with rehabilitative efforts would likewise be hindered by their emotional state. Under such circumstances the affected physical dysfunctions are rather an indirect outcome of the emotional state.

STRESS AND DISEASE

Individuals suffering from some of the various types of neuroses and certain personality characteristics will be more prone to somatic or stress-induced physical illness, because stress is constantly produced by many if not most of these conditions. Constant stress is not limited to those suffering from emotional dysfunction. All of us are at times given to stressful situations. We have already discussed how the prolongation of stress will eventually create physical as well as emotional dysfunction and result in illness.

Research links stress to a variety of medical, social and psychologic dysfunctions.[23,24] Stress can be defined as a state induced by a stimulus that manifests itself by virtue of one's cognitive interpretation.[24,25] The stimulus itself is considered a stressor. Thus, a stressor is any stimulus that evokes stress, and stress reactions are the observable consequences of the stressor.

We will present an analysis of stress from an adaptation point of view. The stress response, like other adaptation mechanisms, is aimed at survival. This response is, accordingly, an attempt to deal with a real, or imagined, stimulus that is perceived as a threat to the self or to one's homeostatic balance. The stress response consists of the mobilization of the body's resources to ward off the perceived enemy. An appropriate analogy can be found in the mobilization of a nation's military and civilian resources against a perceived "enemy threat," which may or may not exist. By shifting its peacetime manpower and productivity towards the "war effort," a nation attempts to strengthen its defensive and aggressive powers at the cost of everyday maintenance of the country. If prolonged, such a state of affairs may impov-

erish the nation to the point of collapse, rebellion, or a weakened condition that may indeed bring about its dissolution. An appropriate analogy can be seen in the dissolution of the Soviet Union, which wasted most of its resources on military buildup to the point of economic collapse. Mobilization for defense, although taxing, is an appropriate response in the face of realistic danger. When stress is the result of prolonged or repetitive faulty perception, the resulting exhaustion of limited resources may endanger survival. An imaginary perceived danger will create a genuine stress situation, just as a real one would. Because falsely perceived danger is not reality based, it does not end with changes in reality and tends to linger. Prolonged stress will endanger survival by depriving the individual of the resources needed for "peaceful" life. Woolfolk and Lehrer[23] illustrate this as follows:

> the individual is not a passive recipient in stressful transactions between the person and the environment, but . . . (is an active interacting participant who may even) . . . generate stress through maladaptive beliefs, attitudes and patterns of action. (p. 348)

Others similarly postulate that stress is caused by the appraisal of an event by the individual, rather than by actual circumstances, and conclude that the cognitive appraisal of a problem will determine an ensuing coping pattern.[26,27] This development in cognitive psychology was instrumental in a gradual movement from normative research to an emphasis on individual differences.

Lazarus[28,29] and Serban[30] considered stress to be a cause of pathologic modes of adaptation leading to impairment of human functioning, and to cognitive and behavioral disturbances. For the sake of rehabilitative intervention it is important to view the interaction of personal characteristics with the external situation as perceived by the patient. The stress level can be considered the outcome of a reciprocal interaction between the individual and the environment. Such interaction plays a significant role in any strategy the individual utilizes to manage one's world and oneself. Faulty coping will result in an abundance of stressors that will diminish coping ability. Because much of what constitutes a stressor depends on one's perceptual functioning, psychologic and emotional guidance and support may diminish the number and intensity of stressors perceived and created. Such support from the therapeutic environment would most likely result in improved adaptation to **"life events"**; those major changes which confront the newly disabled patient.

Much of the literature on stress and coping in general has identified major life events as stressors. Life events refer to major changes in life-style, status, **role,** or situation. This view is consistent with the notion that stress, though individually mediated, is to some degree environmentally based or exacerbated by environmental and social conditions. Various life event measures have been developed and are used in assessing potential environmental stress. One of the better known and more widely used assessment instruments is the **Holmes-Rahe Social Readjustment Rating Scale** (Appendix A), which quantifies the effects of life changes on stress and health. Such measures of life events assume a relatively global impact, and take into account only the listed ones. Although there is validity in such an approach, a potentially more sensitive and valid measure,[31] the **Hassles Scale** (Appendix B), suggested by Kanner[32] and his associates, is being recognized in recent literature.

This scale requires subjects to identify the irritating and frustrating demands of everyday transactions with the environment. The approach takes into account the individual's perception, or cognitive mediation, of events by which they feel threatened, and is consistent with the theoretical assumption that struggle with chronic difficulties may tax coping abilities and lead to greater difficulties in attempting to manage events encountered in daily life. Empirical evidence indicates a more direct association with and a greater predictability of health and emotional outcome through the use of daily hassles measures. It has long been established that "major alterations in social circumstances can produce deleterious effects on mental and physical well-being."[33]

With all the changes engendered in almost every aspect of functioning when disability strikes, patients are more likely to find an increase in daily hassles and a relative increase in the number and intensity of stressors confronting them. Dealing with life becomes more taxing when disabling circumstances block one's coping style and result in a poorer fit of the person within his or her world; this contributes more stress to an already overstressed situation. The stress becomes even more profound when one of the aspects in need of adjusting is the core of the self, the self-image.

In our introduction, the evolving "self" was shown to be part of a unitary integrated life space. Included in that self-image are the body and the roles one plays within one's world. These can be profoundly affected by disablement. A brief discourse as to the implications of these inevitable changes of the self-image may help the clinician gain a better understanding of the disabled patient.

Role and status changes, as part of our developmental growth, are expected and accepted. In our early life we start a process of maturation, become more independent, and gradually move into the various roles that maturation brings about. These changes are rather rapid during the early stages in life and slow down as the years pass. Even though most of these changes are biosocially guided and anticipated, they still become stressors as evidenced by the Holmes-Rahe study. It should therefore be of no surprise that unanticipated changes, generated by disruptive, accidental events rather than by one's natural biologic and social flow, will assume a much higher stress level. Berger[34] states that the ensuing emotional devastation can assume dangerous proportions. Such a situation might even lead to emotional suicide, a triggering of a slow kind of physical self-destruction and oftentimes actual suicide.

Durkheim,[33] the "father of sociology" and one of the first to conduct a scientific study of suicide, stated that one of the major factors in suicide is the "discrepancy between the expected and the achieved." We can indeed see that it is not so much the condition people

are in but where they think they ought to be that shapes their disappointments. It follows that the more an individual expects out of life the more likely it is that he or she will experience disappointment when such expectations are cut short by a traumatic event. It seems that a child who has not built up expectations of independence can find it easier to adapt to a disability than a person who achieved, or was about to achieve independent status. A **congenital** disability or one that develops gradually may not be as emotionally devastating as one that disrupts prior realistic expectations. It is clear that the type of onset and the stage of life that a person with a disability is in will have important implications for the patient.

ROLE THEORY

Role theory appears to have significant predictive value in explaining human interaction. Berger notes, "Role theory, when pursued to its logical conclusions, does far more than provide us with a convenient shorthand for the description of various social activities. It gives us . . . a view of man based on his existence in society."[34] Berger defines role as "a typified response to a typified expectation." A role, then, analogous to that of an actor in a play, is the "part" played by an individual in interaction with another individual(s) playing another part. These related parts have in them a **script** that defines the general behaviors, feelings, and acts that belong to each "part." Lebovitz[35] correctly expands the notion to point out that roles are both the collection of rights and duties and the behavior attached to a position. It is the "pattern according to which the individual is to act in the particular situation."[35] Simply put, a role is a specified cluster of behaviors and expectations attached to each distinct, identified relationship with another person or persons. Some example of roles are male, female, athlete, patient, paraplegic, brother, wife, professor, policeman, and so forth. Each role carries certain expectations of behavior such as dress, attitude, and the like, and each of these forms part of the individual's makeup and identity. Each individual takes on, or is assigned, many different roles in the course of a lifetime and these may be enacted individually or simultaneously. Roles provide the individual with an identity, with predictability in social intercourse, and with parameters of behavioral expectations, both his or hers and those of others. By delimiting and defining how each individual must behave, roles help society and the individual put order and predictability into his or her world and into personal interactions with others.

A role, then, is a script for behavioral limits in social interaction, a social artifact in which analogous roles differ from culture to culture. It is, however, a powerful and important artifact in that it defines and prescribes status, social behavioral and interactional patterns, social identity vis-à-vis the self and others, and, in so doing, organizes and adds predictability to daily life. Roles are shaped and defined by the culture or society and have internal and interrelated meanings and relationships with each other within the culture that defines them. Role theory holds that these roles are not innate, but are rather learned. They are social manifestations and are defined socially. As MacCandless[36] notes, "through implicit and explicit codes, most of which have a moral, or right-wrong overtone, societies set up standards of behavior for their members."

From the point of view of the individual, learning or fulfilling a role, whether **ascribed** or attained, is largely an unconscious, unreflective process. The powerful impact of this process on the individual lies in its unconscious nature. "The role forms, shapes, patterns both action and actor."[34] Accepting the role of "female," which is difficult not to accept, because it is an ascribed role, implies accepting the identity of a female, the behaviors, dress, activities, preferences, and feelings of a female. With the role of "female," for example, comes all of that which society accepts or decrees as being female, including feelings, proclivities, interests, dress, and so forth. Roles, as Berger notes, "carry with them both certain actions and the emotions and attitudes which belong to these actions."[34] Mead,[37] a progenitor of role theory, asserted that the genesis of the self is the same as the individual's discovery of society. That is to say, that in discovering and defining the self, the individual is representing his or her society in him- or herself, and is the reflection of how society shaped and defined him or her. This notion seems analogous to Cooley's **"looking glass self,"** whereby the child begins to define the self and develops his or her identity from the way others treat and interact with the child.[38] Even the recent reversals of some of the previously proscribed roles can be viewed as "ascribed" by some of the current "subcultures."

Many proponents of role theory, such as Goffman[39] and Blumer[40] view self-identity as developing in a negotiation process that takes place with two or more people as they establish their social roles. The self, and self-identity are derived from the social roles assumed, and through the evaluative and comparative process vis-à-vis others in the social and interactive universe. One's self is defined in regard to one's roles.

All this illustrates the significance of roles and what a role change might mean to an individual: what an individual might be going through after having sustained a severe loss of function and relative independence, change of life-style and self-image, social interaction, financial and vocational upheaval, and body comfort. How then does one adjust to these upsetting changes?

Obviously such adjustment will be quite individualistic and is affected by any or all of the following: preexisting coping style and conditions, the responsibility or blame one feels about the illness or injury, the value a person sets on the self and the meaning of the loss, the reality of the conditions that have changed as a result of the situation, the messages received from within and without, the support-rejection balance of circumstances, and the functioning capacity of the body and mind.

ADJUSTMENT AS A FUNCTION OF ROLE, SOCIETAL VALUES, AND SELF-IMAGE

Lebovitz,[35] in discussing the interrelation between roles, self-identity, self-perception, and the way these either aid or interfere with adjustment, states:

it is largely through the process of 'role taking' that one's self-identity (or personality) develops . . . it is assumed that self identity, self image, or personality emerge from socialization. . . .

It can be assumed that any change of status as well as any change in abilities or physical attributes brings along with it an impact in this interactional negotiating process. Through this process we constantly adjust our own view of ourselves and internalize the positive or negative value messages we receive from these interactions.

Though this process is not fully determinative and depends on how these messages are filtered through our own perceptions, nonetheless, changes in the responses of others interact with changes in ourselves in the negotiating processes of social interactions. This everchanging interaction process constantly adjusts and shapes our view, further interactions with our surrounding world, and the fit between our world and ourselves.

Messages of assurance and support enable forward positive movement towards stable and vital adjustment. Studies have shown that even drastic and encompassing disablement can be incorporated as part of a self-image that is positive, adjusted, and stable. Weinberg[41] found that 50 percent of those disabled early in life would chose not to revert to their predisabled state. The need to reestablish self-identity when there is a change in physical looks or abilities can work against lifelong patterns and developed images, as well as internalized societal values. In Western society, the image of disablement most often carries a negative value. Livneh[42] classified the sources of the negative values as follows: sociocultural conditioning, childhood influences, psychodynamic mechanisms, disability as a punishment for sin, anxiety-provoking unstructured situations, aesthetic aversion, threats to body image integrity, minority group comparability, disability as a reminder of death, as well as prejudice-inviting behaviors. Indeed, the disabled tend to view themselves as different in both psychologic and physical dimensions. In a study about the introjection of societies' negative views by the disabled, Weinberg-Asher[43] found no difference, when comparing views towards the disabled, between the able-bodied and the disabled themselves. Identical findings were also reported by Gokhals[44] and others. Wright[45] tells us that positive life attitudes will not thrive when the focus is on the disabling aspects of a disability.

Constructive views within a coping framework can be an excellent venue for providing positive attitudes. The ability to see the person as a whole with particular strengths and weaknesses—particular attributes of which the disablement is only one factor—is realistic and constructive. Though conveying such a message may seem implicit to the rehabilitation worker, the need to verbally reinforce and restate this viewpoint to the client and the family is a crucial yet simple tool in facilitating cooperation and positive adjustment.

SOCIAL SUPPORT

The psychosocial perspective holds that the extent of a disability is, in large part, dependent on the nature and extent of the physical and social resources available to those afflicted. Evidence abounds to suggest that social support plays a strong preventative and palliative role in a wide range of physical and medical conditions. The treating clinician will have a large role in determining which of the physical resources under his or her control can and should be made available, and will advise regarding prosthetics and environmental devices to smooth out life for the client with a disability. Yet he or she can also encourage and be cognizant of the social supports available to the client. Social support is defined as the availability of other persons in the environment who can potentially offer either instrumental or emotive support—financial or material help, a listening ear, advice, or encouragement. Macklprang and Hepworth[46] state that the availability of social support exerts a direct impact on the speed and adequacy of adjustment and the overall happiness and quality of life. Similar findings are reported by numerous investigators.[47-56] These studies confirm the palliative benefit that a social support network exerts on the recovery and adjustment process as well as its potential impact on patient management.

Considering that withdrawal and depression are one of the commonly found initial reactions of a patient to his or her condition and that social exposure is also generally diminished, it becomes clear that the beneficial effect of social support has to be part and parcel of treatment planning.

STAGES OF ADJUSTMENT

Depending on the interactive intensity of all the above factors, adjustment will be relatively rapid or prolonged, adaptive or maladaptive. The literature reviewed indicates the prevalence of a "stage" type of emotional adjustment to physical traumatization. The described stages seem to indicate that after an initial shock and anxiety reaction, most individuals go into the **denial stage,** which may last from several days to a couple of weeks. During this stage the individual may believe that the loss will be restored or may not even exist. Repression, daydreaming, or fantasy are other expressions of this stage. Denial may at times mask the depression or anxiety that is expected to be an outcome of the condition the patient is in. When **denial** eventually lifts, the next reaction stage of grief (**grief reaction stage**) may exhibit itself in forms such as depression or mourning; it may become complicated by exaggerated self-blame,

which may or may not be realistic. The symptoms of this grief reaction will be similar to those found in the mourning following the loss of a loved one. The grief reaction, as is true in the mourning reaction, needs to be resolved by the client in order to be able to move on with life. Anger (**anger reaction stage**), the following reaction stage, usually assumes the form of projections or externalization of blame, anger, and hostility. Negativity, rebellion, opposition, and noncompliance are other forms of expressing this anger. Resolution of this stage, which should preferably culminate in an eventual, **adaptive reconciliation** with the newly created reality, may instead end up in a maladaptive retreat and **regression.** Oftentimes patients will experience posttraumatic stress disorder.

These emotional response stages are expected reactions that help individuals with disabling conditions deal with the severity of the abnormal state they find themselves in. Siller[57] considers such reactions essential for the process of living through the traumatic period and the working through of a reconstitution of a personality structure. Accordingly, unbearable affects are "displaced, delayed, or disguised suggesting a clinical picture of their absence."[57] These are obvious generalizations, which might be used as guidelines but have to be compromised by the reality of each individual case. Although the stages might be quite similar, the content of individual reactions may differ significantly from person to person. As is true for the rest of the population, the handicapped are different from each other in their personal preferences. Whereas some patients may feel vulnerable and ashamed about their helplessness and dependency, others will feel secure and may even savor being taken care of. Some will show resiliency and others will not.

POSTTRAUMATIC STRESS AND EMOTIONAL COMPLICATIONS

Apart from the less common lapses into a severe psychotic state, the more common psychopathologic reaction is posttraumatic stress disorder. The *DSM-III R* lists two subtypes of posttraumatic stress disorder. The first one is the acute type (code 308.30) and the second is the chronic or delayed type (code 309.81). The disorder is considered acute if its appearance is within the first half year after the traumatic event and its duration is limited to a maximum of 6 months. The chronic type may be delayed in its appearance and lasts well over 6 months. For the diagnosis of posttraumatic stress disorder to be applicable, the reaction has to be the result of a "stressor (which) would evoke significant symptoms of distress in most people and is generally outside the range of common experiences."[22]

Among the symptoms exhibited are one or more of the following: reexperiencing the traumatic event; **numbing** of responsiveness to, or reduced involvement with, the external world; or a variety of autonomic, **dysphoric,** or cognitive symptoms. The reexperiencing of the event is described as consisting of recurrent, painful, **intrusive recollections,** dreams, and nightmares about it and, on rare occasions, dissociative-like states during which the victim may act as if reliving the actual traumatic event. The latter may take only several minutes but may last hours and even days.

The numbing of responsiveness, also called psychic numbing or emotional anesthesia, is expressed by complaints of feeling detached or estranged from others, a loss of ability or interest in previously enjoyable activities, or the lack of any emotions or feelings. The other possible symptoms are excessive autonomic arousal, hyperalertness, exaggerated startle response, and difficulty falling asleep."[22] Also listed in the *DSM-III R* are other types of sleep dysfunctions; recurrent nightmares; impairment of memory, concentration or task completion ability; and survival guilt in those cases where others were also affected during a catastrophic event. Horowitz[58] describes the latter two types of symptoms as the intrusive and the denial states, respectively. The first is a superalert type of reaction expressed in anticipatory anxiety, excessive alertness, and constant scanning to a point of perceiving things that are not there (hallucinations). The denial reaction is in direct contrast with the superalert reaction in that it exhibits itself in a diminution of responsiveness to the condition.

Additional associated features that should alert the rehabilitation worker to the presence of posttraumatic stress disorder are increased irritability, hostile behavior, constant tension, and somatic stress symptom. Other emotional disabilities specific to the sudden onset of a disabling condition are brief reactive psychoses immediately following the event. The emotional turmoil and the delusions exhibited may diminish after several hours or may last a couple of weeks. Modlin[59] found that about one third of the trauma patients he assessed exhibited a chronic type of free-floating anxiety, concentration and memory difficulties, nightmares and muscle tension, sexual and social difficulties.

These are the typical posttraumatic psychopathologies found among the patients whose disability was due to a catastrophic or sudden onset. Many disabilities are more gradual or are anticipated as a result of an expected outcome of illness. Patients with such conditions may also succumb to similar emotional disruptions and dysfunctions. Because their condition progresses at a slower pace the adjustment requirements are not as intense. But like the proverbial straw that breaks the camel's back, a point may be reached that tips the balance. Such balance loss may be triggered indirectly and by stressors other than the disability—by a spouse who can no longer bear the engendered difficulties, or a boss who will not accept the productivity loss, or other such conditions; the outcome may be an emotional avalanche no less devastating in its effect than a sudden accident.

Whether sudden or gradual, the loss can, and will, leave psychologic wounds and scars on the individual. We all have our breaking point and a limitation of personal resources. At periods when the stress level goes beyond what an individual's coping repertoire is capable of dealing with a variety of maladaptive reactions will usually set in. This is certainly true in disablement;

the aforementioned reaction stages the patient goes through do not always ward off the severe onslaught of the trauma, the pain, the dramatic life changes, or the losses experienced. Instead of the possible positive attempts at an eventual reconstruction of personality, faulty coping, severe depression, regression, and even psychosis or suicide may ensue.

Other severe forms of psychopathology may gradually develop after the trauma or appear right at the beginning. These pathologic reactions predominantly fall within the depressive and anxiety disorder categories. Less debilitating reactions still affecting every aspect of life would include phobic avoidance, **lability,** guilt, addictions, and other self-defeating behaviors, as well as suicide attempts. Any signs of severe reaction or inappropriate lack of reaction should be seen as indicators of a need to consult the mental health professional. Similarly any protraction over periods beyond what is considered typical for mourning, anger, depression, anxiety, withdrawal, and other such behaviors should not be ignored. Prolonged depression will usually indicate a process depression, which is a more serious type than what may be called a reactive depression; the latter can be expected to appear during times of emotional upset. Lack of rehabilitative progress in patients expected to do better should not be ignored. Other signs to look for are an increase in alcohol intake or smoking, accident proneness, suicidal ideation, and excessive use of tranquilizers, sedatives, and other drugs, as well as changes in sleep and food patterns. A breakdown of cognitive functioning, confusion, disorientation, illogical thinking, lack of reality testing, childlike dependencies or exaggerated fears are all danger signals that require immediate attention. Most of these described reactions are usually ignored, mistakenly considered to be minor problems, or stay unnoticed altogether. The visible absence of emotional problems is no guarantee of their absence, and even minor problems should not be considered as such unless clinically confirmed.

PHYSICAL REHABILITATION AND EMOTIONAL FUNCTIONING

It is imperative that the clinical staff should be alert to the implications of emotional disorders and the adjustment process. The rehabilitation worker should be able to differentiate between those emotional reactions expected as a result of a given illness or injury, and the appearance of a process of pathology. Such malevolent awareness can have significant implications for the rehabilitation process and the future survival of the patient.

In dealing with disabling trauma and disease the physical therapist stands out as the frontline clinician in the rehabilitative effort. The patient will usually spend more time and be more intimately involved with a particular physical therapist than with most other health professionals. Consequently, the physical therapist is more apt to notice and effect changes in the emotional state of a given patient than the rest of the team. The therapist who is alert to the psychologic dynamics of adjustment, maladjustment, and how these interact with each other and with the rehabilitative effort, can be expected to have a healing effect beyond that of the physical modality he or she administers. In many instances such alertness to the emotional state of the patient will enhance the patient's satisfactory life adjustment by bringing about the maximization of dormant potentials.

Accordingly, rehabilitation should be considered as much more than physical restoration, replacement, or the acceptance of physical loss. Trieshman[60] deems rehabilitation as being a process "of learning to live with one's disability in one's own environment." We add here that such learning should include the utilization and shifting of one's premorbid, underutilized, or unrealized potentials. As aptly stated by Trieshman, the learning process dynamic is one "that starts at the moment of injury and continues for the remainder of the person's life."[60] There is no definable end point that can be labeled "rehabilitated" or "adjusted" because, as with all people in all areas of life, disabled people are continually learning to adapt to their environment. Like everyone else, the person with a disability has to be able to gain some rewards and fulfillment in order to "continue to endure the fatigue and frustration that life with a physical disability may include."[60]

STABILIZATION AND REINTEGRATION

It becomes imperative that the physical and medical treatment objectives contain the restoration of the "secondary impairment" created by the trauma of the physical disability. Restoration of physical function, activities of daily living (ADL) training, and vocational retraining by themselves will go only so far and no more. Even successful psychotherapy within the walls of the hospital will not assure the successful reintegration of the client on his or her return to the premorbid environment. Until the hospitalized client is prepared for reintegration to the outside life, discharge may be counterproductive. The client, as well as his or her family, have to be prepared for the social, emotional, sexual, and financial adjustments they will have to face within the home and community environment. Until then, rehabilitation should not be considered complete. The change from the **patient-role** to the giving up of that role can be as devastating as the original change to patient-role, and may result in significant levels of depression, anxiety, and lack of social integration, as exhibited in the studies by Berk and Feibel,[61] and Udin and Keith.[62] Most of what has been discussed so far has addressed the posttraumatic adjustment period, during which the major involvement of rehabilitation takes place. The stabilization period was described as the third and final stage, during which the patient is expected to enter into a relatively adjusted and stabilized state of living. As stated previously, adjustment and stabilization do not imply beneficial adaptation. Hopefully such stabilization will not be of the maladaptive type.

All of this points to the importance of the quality that the stabilization period takes on. It is during this period that our patient is experiencing the quality, and even the value of the life towards which our clinical efforts are aimed. It is easy to lose sight of the fact that the operational period within which the rehabilitation worker is exerting professional efforts to rehabilitate a patient is similar to the gestation period of pregnancy. It is the preparation for the life after birth when life takes on its real meaning. Likewise, it is during the stabilization period following the posttraumatic adjustment when life becomes again meaningful (or meaningless) for the given individual, with the clinician acting as the "midwife" whose input can indeed make a difference.

Being alert to all the needs of the patient as well as to the signs and symptoms of maladaptation during the posttraumatic adjustment period is therefore vital for a good "delivery." It points again to the need for an integrated holistic approach, which has to include the psychosocial aspects of disability together with physical rehabilitation. This is the aim of this chapter: to alert clinicians to all that the wounds, illness, and injury open up—a period pregnant with dangers as well as opportunities. Interacting with the other members of the clinical team becomes therefore paramount for the clinician, regardless of one's specialty.

INTERACTIVE CLINICAL TEAM APPROACH

Having considered the enormity of the problem and the uniqueness of each case, it becomes clear that the task of rehabilitation demands as deep an understanding as a clinician can possibly gain. Insight into a patient's background, status, spiritual and other values, the perception of the handicapping condition by the patient, as well as the patient's philosophy of life will enhance the clinician's capacity as a healer. Above all, skills in observing and listening to what the patient says, either in words, in expressions, in his or her joking or crying demeanor are important for this process. A patient's interaction with others and any differences exhibited, whether these interactions occur with other patients, staff, friends, or family, are the clues to which the therapist has to be alert.

Collecting all this data and becoming familiar with the scientific findings about human psychosocial functioning will help develop the tools needed to enhance therapeutic efforts. It will enable the therapist to turn emotional disruptions around and put these in the service of the rehabilitation process.

To this end, a cooperative effort between the many clinical disciplines in the rehabilitative effort is essential. Such integration of the methodology of the physical therapies with those of the other health professionals, combined with an awareness of each profession's boundaries and limitations, will engender team work and give the patient a better chance for maximizing compensatory functioning within his or her place in the world.

Again we underscore the importance of the team

approach of clinicians from the various disciplines. Rehabilitation is an encompassing term that includes many disciplines and techniques, each one of which specializes in different aspects of the rehabilitative effort. It may therefore be tempting for one therapist to let the other therapists "do their thing" independent of his or her own efforts. The return of physical functioning can seldom, if ever, succeed unless the emotional aspects of the client's functioning are considered or enhanced and psychologic techniques are incorporated into the treatment.

This is not to say that a therapist should go beyond the boundaries of one's profession or specialization when treating clients. The psychologist should not do physical therapy per se and neither should the physical therapist treat or diagnose emotional illness; but the utilization of some psychologic techniques and an alertness to emotional problems have to be considered in order to optimize physical therapy intervention.

The interactive team approach can enhance rehabilitation work by a sharing of each other's expertise in a cooperative effort. The mental health professional can hardly be effective without the physical therapist's communication of his or her observations of the patient. In return, the mental health worker can help the physical therapist through evaluation of the patient's intellectual capacity, motivation, and emotional functioning. The mental health professional can advise about patient management and the use of psychologic techniques for direct or indirect intervention with problem patients and in problems with patients. Likewise the mental health professional can provide and assist in the utilization of specific techniques for stress and pain management. Another area that some members of the mental health team are specialized in is discharge planning, family therapy, and the use and enhancement of social and natural support networks (environmental support systems).

EVALUATION AND PSYCHOLOGIC TESTING

A thorough evaluation of the patient's psychologic and social functioning can significantly contribute to a better understanding of needs, fears, anxieties, and capacities that may be utilized in the rehabilitative efforts. It may guide the therapeutic effort towards a more rapid and appropriate recovery effort and may prevent unnecessary, frustrating attempts towards less realistic goals. The importance of psychologic and cognitive evaluation is exemplified by a case in which ambulation training was successfully achieved in a patient who was cognitively limited. That patient, once able to ambulate again after his cerebrovascular accident, failed to see a stairway and viewed it as a continuation of the floor. The resultant broken hip and injuries to his head would have been prevented if his cognitive functioning had been assessed prior to ambulation training. Proper evaluation of psychologic rehabilitative capacity will minimize frustration and any eventual loss of motivation shared by the patient, the family, and the staff when rehabilitative efforts are exerted beyond the capacity of the patient.

Such assessment furnishes essential information about the client's emotional adjustment to the disablement, assets and liabilities, personality structure, perceptual-motor and cognitive functioning. These can then be utilized to better understand coping barriers and behavioral difficulties, and to develop strategies for dealing with overt or covert interpersonal and intrapersonal difficulties. Beals and Hickman[63] showed that psychologic assessment of the return to work of back-injured workers was more predictive than that of physicians. Psychoneurologic testing such as the Halstead-Reitan Neuropsychological Battery has been shown to detect brain damage better than electroencephalography, radiographs, the brain scan, or neurologic evaluations.[64]

Tsushima and Wedding[65] found the Halstead-Reitan Neuropsychological Battery to be as accurate as that of a computerized axial tomography (CAT) scan. These authors also found **neuropsychologic assessment** to be more sensitive in detecting subtle brain damage than clinical medical assessment. Such subtle damage may have no gross medical implications but would prove of great importance for rehabilitation because the damage may seriously interfere with the client's learning capacity.

Psychologic assessment is especially helpful in assessing subjective symptomatology, and hypochondriasis or malingering, and can be especially useful when dealing with such complaints as pain, headaches, or vertigo. Such assessments require the specialized expertise of the psychologist and neuropsychologist. Psychologists, psychiatrists, clinical social workers, occupational therapists and counselors are also specialized in other assessment methods that can reveal personality and social problem areas, and educational, vocational, and learning capacity. These assessments are geared toward individual patient needs. Although not inclusive, the following list highlights the major areas of consideration in a mental health assessment.

1. Present and premorbid intellectual, emotional, and coping functioning.
2. Present and premorbid psychopathologies and personality structure, and diagnosis of levels of depression, anxiety, and other mental disabilities.
3. Evaluation of suicidal, decompensation, and other risks.
4. Degree of organicity and cognitive disability, and its relationship to the patient's rehabilitative capacity.
5. Symbolic meaning of the disability and loss, and the compensatory reserves that can be elicited.
6. Frustration tolerance, motivation, and secondary gain interference.
7. Pain, stress, and tolerance evaluation.
8. Assessment of vocational interests and background, and present functioning capacity.
9. Sexual attitudes and dysfunction.
10. Assessment of the present and premorbid family structure and interaction, social and economic status, and the natural support network (environmental support systems).

This list is rather limited and emphasizes what the authors consider most significant for the process of rehabilitation. The findings derived from these evaluations can direct the rehabilitative efforts towards the areas that can most benefit from therapeutic intervention.

DISABILITY AND MENTAL HEALTH PRACTICE

Within the constraints of this discussion we will mention some intervention methods aimed at overcoming psychologic disruptions and maladaptive defense mechanisms, and enhancing of motivation towards recovery. In addition to direct intervention by the mental health clinician, the latter can consult and assist the rehabilitation team in the utilization of psychologic and behavior modification principles available for patient management and the rehabilitation effort. The results of psychosocial assessment can highlight strengths that should be taken advantage of and weaknesses that should be corrected or compensated for. In order to maximize the benefits that can be derived from the mental health team it is important to be aware of the different specializations that make it up. A brief description follows:

1. The psychiatrist is a medically trained physician specializing in mental disorders and their treatment.
2. The psychologist has a doctorate in one of the psychologic specialties. The one most involved in the rehabilitation process would be the clinical psychologist specifically trained in diagnostic assessment and treatment of personality and emotional dysfunctions. Additional specializations would include neuropsychology and **behavioral medicine,** as well as health and counseling psychology. For certain patient populations child psychology, as well as school, educational, or industrial psychology, can assume great importance.
3. Clinical, psychiatric, and social case workers are trained to assess and intervene where environmental, social, and family dysfunction and their interaction affect the individual's adjustment and functioning.
4. The occupational therapist is trained in assessment of psychosocial and cognitive function. Emphasis is on relationships between deficits in these areas and associated functional impairments.
5. Other counselors, such as speech pathologists, art therapists, dance and movement therapists, vocational counselors, rehabilitation counselors, psychiatric nurses, and pastoral counselors specialize in their distinctive support areas.

Within these professions there are multiple subspecialties. These include neuropsychology and neuropsychiatry, psychoanalysis, behavioral medicine and behavior modification, forensic psychiatry and psychology, geriatrics, group therapy, family and marital therapy, sex therapy, stress and pain reduction, **biofeedback,** and hypnotherapy.

Mental health clinicians can render significant help in dealing with special problems: such as discharge planning and the use of environmental support groups, which have proven to be invaluable in mainstreaming patients to a comparative integrated life. The significance of self-help groups as a most effective resource for reintegration into society has been documented by Lieberman and Borman.[66]

Another area of great concern is the sexual functioning, or the lack of it, during disability. This is an area that needs elaboration but is beyond the scope of this writing. Of necessity we have left out all issues relating to the family of the disabled individual, including the family's own reactions to the disability and its victim. According to Hartman, Macintosh, and Englehardt, these reactions run the whole range of human feelings.[67] We can only touch on this, as well as on the other important areas mental health workers deal with, such as family and marital therapy. These interventions can play a major role in the rehabilitative effort. In addition, with the guidance of the mental health care worker, the methods of intervention can be used by other team members.

SUMMARY

Psychologic and social adjustment to illness and physical trauma is a uniquely personal experience, dependent on innate and acquired characteristics, as well as the many environmental factors impinging on that individual. The interplay between the physical damage, the physiologic resources, and the emotional self only partly determine the outcome of illness or injury. Social pressures and social support systems are important forces to be considered. These then facilitate or hinder the treatment effort and the eventual rehabilitation of the patient. Beyond the techniques available for treatment, the personality structure that has evolved during a lifetime of innate and external conditioning, the acquired input of values and roles and, the individual's coping capacity are all considerations of the rehabilitation specialist. Furthermore, the social milieu surrounding the patient— the hospital, family, finances, bias, sexual needs and pressures, and available support systems—are all factors that shape the course of healing.

A most important factor any rehabilitation worker is constantly confronted with is the patient's personality. The understanding of the uniqueness of each and every individual therefore becomes mandatory. The knowledge that personality structure is the sum total of lifelong experience and a conglomeration of a very unique temperament, perceptual selectivity, a set of ego defenses, and a perceptual structure of the self and the world, clarifies the idiosyncratic nature of individuals. These then shape an individual's adaptive or maladaptive adjustment process.

Coping skills combine both innate and learned adaptive behaviors and allow an individual to balance internal and external resources in the presence of conflicting biologic, psychologic, and social needs. Ultimately, coping responses allow for survival of the individual, even though the outcome may be contrary to what seems best for the individual. Thus psychologic adjustment is an intricate interactive process incorporating the body mechanism and the external world, conscious perceptions of self and unconscious perceptions, motivation, emotions, drives, and values.

Reactions to disability are influenced by the extent of the injury, or illness, its mode of onset, the prognosis, affected brain mechanisms, support systems, and subjective perceptions. The initial reaction to a catastrophic event or illness is primarily physiologic and has been described by Selye as the general adaptation response. During the posttraumatic period, the psychologic aspect of functioning assumes major importance. Such a response is defined as an attempt to cope with a real or imagined stimulus—a stressor—which is perceived as a threat to one's self or one's homeostatic balance. The disabled person is more likely to experience increases in the number and intensity of daily stressors. Role and status changes are also important parts of the disablement experience.

Adjustment may be rapid or prolonged, adaptive or maladaptive. Stages in the process of adjustment to loss and disability have been identified. Initial shock or anxiety is followed by progression through stages of denial, depression, and anger. The end result of this process may be the final acceptance of the newly created reality or, instead, a maladaptive retreat and regression. Adjustment may also be characterized by posttraumatic stress syndrome or other pathology. Therapists need to recognize characteristic danger signs of pathology.

The rehabilitation specialist who considers these factors and makes them part of the methods and techniques of treatment intervention can increase the chances for recuperation. It would be an insurmountable task for a rehabilitation worker to become specialized in all that is significant to a patient, and in all the methods to know and treat these. This is why we have the various specialties. Yet there is a dire need for every one of these specialists to become cognizant of the rudiments of those areas that impinge on their effectiveness. Such knowledge can only improve the understanding of a patient's level of cooperation, compliance, and attitude towards rehabilitation. The psychologic dynamic of adjustment can be facilitated by an interactive team approach in which the contribution of all members is maximized. Rehabilitation should be complete only when the patient and family are prepared for the social, emotional, and sexual adjustment they will have to face when the patient returns to home and community.

QUESTIONS FOR REVIEW

1. How does the general adaptation syndrome serve the body during a catastrophic event and at what cost?

2. Describe how an individual's attempt to best serve his or her survival needs may result in maladaptation.

3. In what conscious or unconscious ways might a disablement serve the needs of an individual to the degree that he or she might prefer to stay disabled?

4. Describe the difference in the needs for intervention comparing the traumatic reaction phase and the posttraumatic adjustment period.

5. Explain the meaning of psychic numbing and give the reasons for its development.

6. What is the importance of the role one plays in life in regard to disability?

7. Name five stages of adjustment to loss or disablement.

8. What are some of the features that should alert the physical therapist to the presence of posttraumatic stress disorder?

9. At what point can one consider rehabilitation completed?

10. Name some of the contributions a mental health clinician can make towards physical rehabilitation.

11. Describe the role of perception in the formation of disability.

12. How can emotional factors create disability?

REFERENCES

1. Engel, GL: Guilt, pain and success. Psychosom Med 24:37, 1962.
2. Moos, RH: Coping with physical illness. Plenum, New York, 1977.
3. Ehrenteil, OF: Common medical disorders rarely found in psychotic patients. Arch Neurol Psychiatry 77:1957, 1957.
4. Selye, H: The general adaptation syndrome and the disease of adaptation. J Clin Endocrinol Metab 6:117–230, 1946.
5. Mann, AM and Gold, EM: Psychological sequelae of accident injury: a medico-legal quagmire. Can Med Assoc J 95:1359–1363, 1966.
6. Dollard, J and Miller, NE: Personality and Psychotherapy: An Analysis in Terms of Learning, Thinking and Culture. McGraw-Hill, New York, 1950.
7. Ellis, A: Humanistic Psychology: The Rational-Emotive Approach. Julian, New York, 1973.
8. Lazarus, R: Psychological Stress and the Coping Process. McGraw-Hill, New York, 1966.
9. Malmo, RB: Overview. In Greenfield, N and Sternbach, R (eds): Handbook of Pyschophysiology. Holt, Rinehart & Winston, New York, 1972.
10. Kirtz, S and Moos, RH: Physiological effects of social environments. Psychosom Med 36:96–114, 1974.
11. Selye, H: Stress in Health and Disease. Butterworth & Co., Reading, MA, 1976.
12. Bourestom, N, and Howard, M: Personality characteristics of three personality groups. Arch Phys Med Rehabil 46:626–632, 1965.
13. Alexander, F: Studies in Psychosomatic Medicine. Ronald Press, New York, 1948.
14. Alexander, F: Psychosomatic Medicine: Its Principles and Applications. Norton, New York, 1950.
15. Engel, GL and Schmale, S: Psychoanalytic theory of somatic disorder: conversion, specificity, and the disease onset situation. J Am Psychoanal Assoc 15:344–365, 1967.
16. Wittkower, ED, et al: A global survey of psychosomatic medicine. Int J Psychiatry 7:576–591, 1969.
17. Dunbar, F: Emotions and Bodily Changes, ed. 3. Columbia University Press, New York, 1947.
18. Henry, JP and Stephens, P: Stress, Health and the Social Environment. Springer-Verlag, New York, 1977.
19. Eisler, R and Polak, P: Social stress and psychiatric disorder. J Ment Nerv Dis 153:227–233, 1971.
20. Wollf, HG and Itace, CC (eds): Life Stress and Bodily Disease. William & Wilkins, Baltimore, 1950.
21. Freud, S: Civilization and Its Discontents, in The Standard Edition of the Complete Psychological Works of Sigmund Freud. Vol. 21. pp 64–145, 1930.

22. American Psychiatric Association: Diagnostic and Statistical Manual of Mental Disorders, ed 3 revised. American Psychiatric Association, Washington, DC, 1987.
23. Woolfolk, RL and Lehrer, PM: Principles and practice of Stress Management. The Guilford Press, New York, 1984.
24. Kirtz, S and Moos, RH: Physiological effects of social environments. Psychosom Med 36:96–114, 1974.
25. Ellis, A: Humanistic Psychology: The Rational-Emotive Approach. Julian, New York, 1973.
26. Lazarus, RS: Patterns for Adjustment. McGraw-Hill, New York, 1976.
27. Malmo, RB: Overview. In Greenfield, N and Sternbach, R (eds): Handbook of Psychophysiology. Holt, Rinehart & Winston, New York, 1972.
28. Lazarus, RS: Psychological Stress and the Coping Process. McGraw-Hill, New York, 1966.
29. Lazarus, RS: The Concept of Stress and Disease. In Levi, L (ed): Society, Stress and Disease, vol 1. Oxford University Press, London, 1971.
30. Serban, G: Stress in schizophrenics and normals. Br J Psychiatry 126:397–407, 1975.
31. Holmes, T and Rahe, R: The social readjustment scale. J Psychosom Res 11:213–218, 1967.
32. Kanner, AD, et al: Comparison of two modes of stress management: daily hassles and uplifts versus major life events. J Behav Med 4:1, 1981.
33. Durkheim, E: Suicide. Free Press, Glenkove, IL, 1951.
34. Berger, PL: Invitation to Sociology: A humanistic perspective. Anchor Books, New York, 1963.
35. Lebovitz, S: An Introduction to Sociological Concepts. John Wiley & Sons, New York, 1977.
36. MacCandless, BR: The socialization process. In Seidman, JM (ed): The Child: A Book of Readings. Holt, Rinehart & Winston, New York, 1969, pp 42–50.
37. Mead, GH: Mind, Self, and Society. University of Chicago Press, Chicago, 1934.
38. Cooley, CH: Human Nature and the Social Order, rev. ed. Scribner's, New York, 1922.
39. Goffman, E: The Presentation of Self in Everyday Life. Doubleday Anchor, New York, 1959.
40. Blumer, H: Symbolic Interactionism: Perspective and Method. Prentice-Hall, Englewood Cliffs, NJ, 1969.
41. Weinberg, N: Physically disabled people assess the quality of their lives. Rehabilitation Literature 42:12–15, 1984.
42. Livneh, H: On the origins of negative attitudes toward people with disabilities. Rehabilitation Literature 43:338–347, 1982.
43. Weinberg-Asher, N: The effect of physical disability on self perception. Rehabilitation Counseling Bulletin 20:15–20, 1976.
44. Gokhals, SD: Dynamics of attitude change. International Social Work 28:31–39, 1985.
45. Wright, BA: Developing constructive views of life with a disability. Rehabilitation Literature 41:274–279, 1980.
46. Macklprang, RW, and Hepworth, DH: Ecological factors in rehabilitation of patients with severe spinal cord injuries. Soc Work Health Care 13:23–38, 1987.
47. Flaherty, J: The role of social support in the functioning of patients with unipolar depression. Am J Psychiatry 140:473–476, 1983.
48. Dean, A, Lin, N, and Ensel, W: The epidemiological significance of social support systems on depression. Research in Community and Mental Health 2:77–109, 1981.
49. Gallo, F: Social support networks and the health of elderly persons. Social Work Research and Abstracts 20:13–19, 1984.
50. Maddox, G: Persistence of life style among the elderly: a longitudinal study of patterns of social activity in relation to life satisfaction. In Neugarten, B (ed): Middle Age and Aging. University of Chicago Press, Chicago, 1968, p 181.
51. MacMahon, B and Pugh, TF: Epidemiology: Principles and Method. Little Brown, Boston, 1970.
52. Schultz, NR and Moore, D: Loneliness: correlates, attributes, and coping among older adults. Personality and Social Psychology Bulletin 75, 1984.
53. Maguire, G: An exploratory study of the relationship of valued activities to the life satisfaction of elderly persons. Occupational Therapy Journal of Research 3:164, 1983.
54. Ward, RA, Sherman, SR, and LaGory, M: Informal networks and knowledge of services for older persons. J Gerontology 39:216–233, 1984.
55. Quam, J: Older women and informal supports: impact on prevention. Prevention and Human Services 3:119–133, 1983.
56. Clark, A: Personal and social resources as correlates of coping behavior among the aged. Psychol Rep 51:577–578, 1982.
57. Siller, J: Psychological situation of the disabled with spinal cord injuries. Rehabilitation Literature 30:290–296, 1969.
58. Horowitz, MJ: Stress-response syndromes: post-traumatic and adjustment disorders. In Cooper, AM, Frances, AJ, and Sacks, MH (eds): The Personality Disorders and Neuroses. JB Lippincott, Philadelphia, 1986, pp 409–424.
59. Modlin, HC: The post-accident and anxiety syndrome: the psychosocial aspects. Am J Psychiatry 123:1008–1012, 1967.
60. Trieshman, RB: Spinal Injuries: Psychological, Social and Vocational Adjustment. Pergamon Press, Elmsford, NY, 1980.
61. Berk, S and Feibel, J: The unmet psychological and family needs of stroke survivors. In Trieshman, RB (ed): Spinal Injuries: Psychological, Social and Vocational Adjustment. Pergamon Press, Elmsford, NY, 1980.
62. Udin, H and Keith, R: Patients' daily activites after discharge from a rehabilitation hospital. In Trieshman, RB (ed): Spinal Injuries: Psychological, Social and Vocational Adjustment. Pergamon Press, Elmsford, NY, 1980.
63. Beals, RK and Hickman, NW: Industrial injuries of the back and extremities. J Bone Joint Surg [Am] 54A:1593–1611, 1972.
64. Filskov, SB and Goldstein, SG: Diagnostic validity of the Halstead-Reitan Neuropsychological Battery. J Consult Clin Psychol 42:382–388, 1974.
65. Tsushima, WT and Wedding, D: A comparison of the Halstead-Reitan Neuropsychological Battery and computerized tomography in the identification of brain disorder. American Journal of Nervous and Mental Disease 167:704–707, 1979.
66. Lieberman, M and Borman, L: Self help groups for coping with crises. Jossey-Bass, San Francisco, 1979.
67. Hartman, C, Macintosh, B, and Englehardt, B: The neglected and forgotten sexual partner of the physically disabled. Soc Work 28:370–374, 1983.

SUPPLEMENTAL READINGS

Adamson, JD and Schmale, AH Jr: Object loss, giving up, and the object of psychiatric disease. Psychonomic Medicine 27:557–576, 1965.
Ader, R (ed): Psychoneuroimmunology. Academic Press, New York, 1981.
Anderson, TR and Cale, TM: Sexual counseling of the physically disabled. Postgrad Med 58:117–123, 1975.
Burstein, A: Posttraumatic stress disorder in victims of motor vehicle accidents. Hosp Community Psychiatry 40:295–297, 1989.
Cannon, WB: Bodily Changes in Pain, Hunger, Fear and Rage. Charles T. Branford, 1950.
Chigier, E: Sexual Adjustment of the Handicapped. Proceeding Preview of the 12th World Congress of Rehabilitation International, Sydney, Australia, 1972.
Chigier, E (ed): Sex and the Disabled. The Israel Rehabilitation Annual, 1977.
Clark, A: Personal and social resources as correlates of coping behavior among the aged. Psychol Rep 51:577–578, 1982.
Cook, R: Sex education program service model for the multihandicapped adult. Rehabilitation Literature 35:264–267, 1974.
Costella, CG: The adaptive function of depression. Canada's Mental Health 25:20–21, 1977.
Davidson, LM and Baum, A: Chronic stress and posttraumatic stress disorders. J Consult Clin Psychol 54:303–308, 1986.
Eisenberg, MG and Falconer, J: Current trends in sex education programming for the physically disabled: some guidelines for implementation and evaluation. Sexual Disabilities 1:6–15, 1978.
Ford, AB and Orfirer, AP: Sexual behavior and the chronically ill patient. Med Aspects Hum Sex 1:51–61, 1967.
Hartman, C, Macintosh, B, and Englehardt, B: The neglected and forgotten sexual partner of the physically disabled. Soc Work 28:370–374, 1983.

Krantz, DS and Glass, DC: Personality, behavior patterns, and physical illness: conceptual and methodological issues. In Gentry, DW (ed): Behavioral Medicine. Guilford Press, New York, 1984.

Lazarus, RS and Folkman, S: Coping and adaptation. In Gentry, DW (ed): Behavioral Medicine. Guilford Press, New York, 1984.

Lieberman, MA: Adaptive process in late life. In Datan, N and Ginsberg, LH (eds): Life-span Developmental Psychology. Academic Press, New York, 1975.

MacMahon, B and Pugh, TF: Epidemiology: Principles and Methods. Little Brown, Boston, 1970.

Madakasira, S and O'Brien, KF: Acute posttraumatic stress disorder in victims of natural disaster. J Nerv Ment Dis 175:286–290, 1987.

Maguire, G: An exploratory study of the relationship of valued activities to the life satisfaction of elderly persons. Occupational Therapy Journal of Research 3:164–172, 1983.

Mcfarlane, AC: The phenomenology of posttraumatic stress disorders following a natural disaster. J Nerv Ment Dis 176:22–29, 1988.

Menninger, K: The Vital Balance: The Life Process in Mental Health and Illness. Viking, New York, 1963.

Patrick, GD: Comparison of Novice and Veteran Wheelchair Athletes' Self-Concept and Acceptance of Disability, Rehabilitation Counseling Bulletin 27:186–188, 1984.

Platt, J and Husband, SD: Posttraumatic stress disorder and the motor vehicle accident victim. American Journal of Forensic Psychology 5:35–42, 1987.

Plutchik, R and Kellerman, H (eds): Theories of Emotion. Academic Press, New York, 1980.

Quam, J: Older women and informal supports: impact on prevention. Prevention and Human Services 3:119–133, 1983.

Russell, RA: Concepts of adjustment to disability: an overview. Rehabilitation Literature 42:330–338, 1981.

Shuchter, S and Zisook, S: Psychological reactions to the PSA crash. Int J Psychiatry Med 14:293–301, 1984.

Schulz, R and Decker, S: Long-term adjustment to physical disability. J Pers Soc Psychol 48:1162–1172, 1985.

Schultz, NR and Moore, D: Loneliness: correlates, attributes, and coping among older adults. Personality and Social Psychology Bulletin, 75, 1984.

Schweitzer, NJ: Coping with stigma: an integrated approach to counseling physically disabled persons. Rehabilitation Counseling Bulletin 25:204–211, 1982.

Sigelman, CK, Vengroff, LP, and Spanhel, CH: Disability and the concept of life functions. Rehabilitation Counseling Bulletin 23:103–113, 1979.

Sloan, P: Posttraumatic stress in survivors of an airplane crash-landing: a clinical and exploratory research intervention. Journal of Traumatic Stress 1:211–229, 1988.

Syme, LS: Sociocultural factors in disease etiology. In Gentry, DW (ed): Behavioral Medicine. Guilford Press, New York, 1984.

Thorn-Gray, BE and Kern, LH: Sexual dysfunction associated with physical disability: a treatment guide for the rehabilitation practitioner. Rehabilitation Literature 44:138–144, 1983.

Versluys, HP: Physical rehabilitation and family dynamics. Rehabilitation Literature 41:58–65, 1980.

Ward, RA, Sherman, SR, and LaGory, M: Informal networks and knowledge of services for older persons. J Gerontol 39:216–233, 1984.

Weinberg, N: Physically disabled people assess the quality of their lives. Rehabilitation Literature 42:12–15, 1984.

Weinberg-Asher, N: The effect of physical disability on self perception. Rehabilitation Counseling Bulletin 20:15–20, 1976.

Wright, BA: Value laden beliefs and principles for rehabilitation. Rehabilitation Literature 42:266–269, 1981.

Zeitlin, S and Williamson, GG: Coping characteristics of disabled and nondisabled young children. American J Orthopsychiatry 60:404–411, 1990.

GLOSSARY

Adaptation (adaptive): The ongoing active process through which an individual adjusts to changing environmental life situations.

Adaptive reconciliation (acceptance): The fifth and final reaction stage of adjustment to physical disablement or loss. During this stage the loss is no longer considered an obstacle to be overcome but as one of many personal characteristics; approaches to meeting personal needs with respect to realities of the life situation have been reconciled. In some instances, acceptance has failed and the patient may instead end up in a maladaptive retreat and regression.

Adjustment: Alignment of one's inner needs with the realities of personal capabilities, and/or environment; may be adaptive or maladaptive.

Anger reaction stage (and hostility): The fourth emotional reaction stage of adjustment to physical disablement or loss; manifested by animosity, negativism, rebelliousness, opposition, antagonism, and noncompliance.

Ascribed role: Implies the identity that one is born into, such as gender; requires accepting the behaviors, dress, activities, preferences and feelings, and all that society accepts or decrees for that identity.

Behavioral medicine: A subspecialty in mental health that addresses the interaction of psychologic factors with those of medical intervention and the disease process.

Biofeedback. A method of treatment and diagnostics that utilizes the measurements of physiologic reactions through instrumentation to increase patient awareness and control of those reactions.

Cognition: The process by which an organism becomes knowledgeable. It is influenced by one's personality characteristics, emotional factors, and subjectivity. It is one of the most significant factors in determining an individual's way of dealing with his or her world.

Congenital: A condition which an individual was born with, not necessarily genetic.

Coping: The process through which individuals deal with the variety of social and environmental factors encountered in life.

Coping style: An individual evolved response repertoire that is relatively solidified and predictable.

Defense mechanisms: See "ego defense."

Denial: An ego defense mechanism that is utilized to deny an unacceptable actuality or situation.

Denial stage: The second reaction stage of psychologic adjustment to physical disablement or loss; an unconscious defense mechanism in which existence of unpleasant realities is blocked from conscious awareness.

Deviant: A term used to describe an individual's coping that is contrary to environmental standards.

Disability: Within this text the term is used to describe a reduction or loss of function that is directly or indirectly due to a real or imagined incapacity to function.

Disablement: Within this text the term is used to describe the actual, objective loss of function as a result of illness or accident.

DSM-III R: The revised third edition of the *Diagnostic Statistical Manual of the American Psychiatric Association,* which is the accepted manual for categorizing emotional disorders and their diagnostic indicators.

Dysphoria (dysphoric): Exaggerated feelings of depression; may be accompanied by anxiety.

Ego defense (defense mechanism): The ego utilizes unconscious defense mechanisms to protect itself from real or imagined dangers, pressures, and conflictual demands through a process by which unpleasant realities are blocked from conscious awareness. Among these defensive mechanisms are rationalizations, projection, overcompensation, reaction formation, repression, and peceptual distortion.

General adaptation syndrome (GAS): An organism's immediate reaction to an extreme catastrophe; a defensive adaptation response aimed at dealing with real or perceived emergency situations.

Grief reaction stage: The third emotional reaction stage of adjustment to physical disablement or loss; distinguished by mental suffering, sorrow, and regret; may become complicated by exaggerated self-blame, which may or may not be realistic. The grief reaction, as is true for the mourning reaction, needs to be resolved by the client in order to move on with life.

Hassles Scale: An instrument measuring the irritating and frustrating demands of everyday transactions an individual feels faced with.

Holmes-Rahe Social Readjustment Rating Scale: One of the better known and more commonly used assessment instruments that quantifies the effects of life changes on stress and health.

Innate: Determined by heredity.

Intrusive recollections: The experiencing of dreams and nightmares about disturbing events of the past; often experienced during the posttraumatic stress disorder stage.

Lability: Emotional instability; manifested by alterations or fluctuations in emotional state.

Life events: A term used to describe major changes in an individual's life and considered to be a source of stress.

Looking glass self: A term suggested by Cooley to describe the way in which a child begins to define him- or herself and develops his or her identity from the way others treat and interact with the child.

Maladaptive: A term used to describe coping that is contrary to an individual's own best interest or survival; usually the result of faulty perception, learned rejection of the self, misguided values, or misinterpretations of reality.

Mental defense: Same as ego defense mechanisms, or defense mechanisms.

Nature and nurture: The first term describes inherited characteristics while the second one is reserved for those attributes developed as a result of environmental input.

Neuropsychologic assessment: An evaluation system utilizing the measurement of behavioral and psychologic expressions that seem to reveal subtle brain damage that may or may not be revealed by other neurologic instruments.

Numbing or **psychic numbing (emotional anesthesia):** Feelings of being detached or estranged from others, a loss of ability to enjoy or feel interest in previously enjoyable activities, or the lack of any emotions or feelings.

Patient role: According to role theory an individual will tend to grow into this role when becoming a patient; usually a painful transition, which once adjusted to may create difficulties in returning to the premorbid role.

Perception: A response repertoire through which the individual combines information input with his or her personality structure.

Personality structure: The characteristics of a given individual and the respective internalized ideology, value system, and behavioral tendencies the individual has accumulated.

Posttraumatic adjustment period: The second reaction stage of adjustment to physical disablement or loss; this is usually the time during which psychologic effects of the traumatic experience are most felt by the patient.

Posttraumatic stress disorder (PTSD): Psychopathologic reaction to a traumatic event; symptoms exhibited may include reexperiencing the traumatic event; numbing of responsiveness to, or reduced involvement with, the external world; and/or a variety of autonomic, dysphoric, or cognitive symptoms.

Premorbid: The functioning and condition of a patient prior to the present pathologic state; a reference point of the level of loss and deterioration.

Proscribed roles: The ethnic and social status roles one is born into.

Psychologic adjustment: The intricate interactive process dictated by conscious and unconscious motivations, emotions, drives, values, and perceptual functioning.

Regression: A return or retreat to a former state; a defense mechanism elicited by illness or life frustration and characterized by appearance of less mature behaviors, which were successful during earlier periods of the individual's life.

Role: Describes a specified cluster of behaviors and expectations attached to each distinct, identified, relationship to another person or persons; typified response to a typified expectation, or a part played by an individual interacting with other individuals.

Script: A term within role theory that defines the general behaviors, feelings, and acts which belong to each part of the various roles an individual plays out in life.

Self and self-identity: Concepts derived from the social roles assumed through the evaluative and comparative process vis-à-vis others in the social and interactive universe.

Self-image: A term used to describe the individual's self-perception as a part of a unitary integrated life space; includes the body, as well as the roles one plays within one's world.

Stress reaction: The observable consequences of the stressor; accompanied by symptoms such as palpitations, cold sweat, faint feelings, dilated pupils, pallor, fear, and a host of other complaints.

Stressor: Any stimulus that evokes stress.

Style of coping: A unique style of coping and functioning characteristic of an individual's personality and developed during a lifetime.

Traumatic reaction period or stage: The first emotional reaction stage of adjustment to physical disablement or loss; characterized by disbelief, tension, and an inability to acknowledge that the traumatic event took place.

APPENDIX A   HOLMES-RAHE
SOCIAL READJUSTMENT SCALE

Rank	Life Event	Mean Value	Rank	Life Event	Mean Value
1	Death of spouse	100	23	Son or daughter leaving home	29
2	Divorce	73	24	Trouble with in-laws	29
3	Marital separation	65	25	Outstanding personal achievement	28
4	Jail term	63	26	Wife begin or stop work	26
5	Death of close family member	63	27	Begin or end school	26
6	Personal injury or illness	53	28	Change in living conditions	25
7	Marriage	50	29	Revision of personal habits	24
8	Fired at work	47	30	Trouble with boss	23
9	Marital reconciliation	45		Change in work hours or	
10	Retirement	45	31	conditions	20
11	Change in health of family member	44	32	Change in residence	20
12	Pregnancy	40	33	Change in schools	20
13	Sex difficulties	39	34	Change in recreation	19
14	Gain of new family member	39	35	Change in church activities	19
15	Business readjustment	39	36	Change in social activities	18
16	Change in financial state	38	37	Mortgage or loan less than $10,000	17
17	Death of close friend	37	38	Change in sleeping habits	16
18	Change to different line of work	36		Change in number of family get-	
	Change in number of arguments		39	togethers	15
19	with spouse	35	40	Change in eating habits	15
20	Mortgage over $10,000	31	41	Vacation	13
21	Foreclosure of mortgage or loan	30	42	Christmas	12
22	Change in responsibilities at work	29	43	Minor violations of the law	11

From Holmes and Rahe, with permission.[31]

APPENDIX B   THE HASSLES SCALE

Directions: Hassles are irritants that can range from minor annoyances to fairly major pressures, problems, or difficulties. They can occur few or many times.

Listed in the center of the following pages are a number of ways in which a person can feel hassled. First, circle the hassles that have happened to you *in the past month.* Then look at the numbers on the right of the items you circled. Indicate by circling a 1, 2, or 3 how SEVERE each of the *circled* hassles has been for you in the past month. If a hassle did not occur in the last month, do NOT circle it.

Hassles	Severity 1. Somewhat severe 2. Moderately severe 3. Extremely severe		
(1) Misplacing or losing things	1	2	3
(2) Troublesome neighbors	1	2	3
(3) Social obligations	1	2	3
(4) Inconsiderate smokers	1	2	3
(5) Troubling thoughts about your future	1	2	3
(6) Thoughts about death	1	2	3
(7) Health of a family member	1	2	3
(8) Not enough money for clothing	1	2	3
(9) Not enough money for housing	1	2	3
(10) Concerns about owing money	1	2	3
(11) Concerns about getting credit	1	2	3
(12) Concerns about money for emergencies	1	2	3
(13) Someone owes you money	1	2	3
(14) Financial responsibility for someone who doesn't live with you	1	2	3
(15) Cutting down on electricity, water, etc.	1	2	3
(16) Smoking too much	1	2	3
(17) Use of alcohol	1	2	3
(18) Personal use of drugs	1	2	3
(19) Too many responsibilities	1	2	3
(20) Decisions about having children	1	2	3
(21) Non-family members living in your house	1	2	3
(22) Care for pet	1	2	3
(23) Planning meals	1	2	3
(24) Concerned about the meaning of life	1	2	3
(25) Trouble relaxing	1	2	3
(26) Trouble making decisions	1	2	3
(27) Problems getting along with fellow workers	1	2	3
(28) Customers or clients give you a hard time	1	2	3

APPENDIX B   THE HASSLES SCALE (*Continued*)

Hassles	Severity 1. Somewhat severe 2. Moderately severe 3. Extremely severe		
(29) Home maintenance (inside)	1	2	3
(30) Concerns about job security	1	2	3
(31) Concerns about retirement	1	2	3
(32) Laid-off or out of work	1	2	3
(33) Don't like current work duties	1	2	3
(34) Don't like fellow workers	1	2	3
(35) Not enough money for basic necessities	1	2	3
(36) Not enough money for food	1	2	3
(37) Too many interruptions	1	2	3
(38) Unexpected company	1	2	3
(39) Too much time on hands	1	2	3
(40) Having to wait	1	2	3
(41) Concerns about accidents	1	2	3
(42) Being lonely	1	2	3
(43) Not enough money for health care	1	2	3
(44) Fear of confrontation	1	2	3
(45) Financial security	1	2	3
(46) Silly practical mistakes	1	2	3
(47) Inability to express yourself	1	2	3
(48) Physical illness	1	2	3
(49) Side effects of medication	1	2	3
(50) Concerns about medical treatment	1	2	3
(51) Physical appearance	1	2	3
(52) Fear of rejection	1	2	3
(53) Difficulties with getting pregnant	1	2	3
(54) Sexual problems that result from physical problems	1	2	3
(55) Sexual problems other than those resulting from physical problems	1	2	3
(56) Concerns about health in general	1	2	3
(57) Not seeing enough people	1	2	3
(58) Friends or relatives too far away	1	2	3
(59) Preparing meals	1	2	3
(60) Wasting time	1	2	3
(61) Auto maintenance	1	2	3
(62) Filling out forms	1	2	3
(63) Neighborhood deterioration	1	2	3
(64) Financing children's education	1	2	3
(65) Problems with employees	1	2	3
(66) Problems on job due to being a woman or man	1	2	3
(67) Declining physical abilities	1	2	3
(68) Being exploited	1	2	3
(69) Concerns about bodily functions	1	2	3
(70) Rising prices of common goods	1	2	3
(71) Not getting enough rest	1	2	3
(72) Not getting enough sleep	1	2	3
(73) Problems with aging parents	1	2	3
(74) Problems with your children	1	2	3
(75) Problems with persons younger than yourself	1	2	3
(76) Problems with your lover	1	2	3
(77) Difficulties seeing or hearing	1	2	3
(78) Overloaded with family responsibilities	1	2	3
(79) Too many things to do	1	2	3
(80) Unchallenging work	1	2	3
(81) Concerns about meeting high standards	1	2	3
(82) Financial dealings with friends or acquaintances	1	2	3
(83) Job dissatisfactions	1	2	3
(84) Worries about decisions to change jobs	1	2	3
(85) Trouble with reading, writing, or spelling abilities	1	2	3
(86) Too many meetings	1	2	3
(87) Problems with divorce or separation	1	2	3
(88) Trouble with arithmetic skills	1	2	3
(89) Gossip	1	2	3
(90) Legal problems	1	2	3
(91) Concerns about weight	1	2	3
(92) Not enough time to do the things you need to do	1	2	3
(93) Television	1	2	3
(94) Not enough personal energy	1	2	3
(95) Concerns about inner conflicts	1	2	3

APPENDIX B   THE HASSLES SCALE (*Continued*)

Hassles	Severity 1. Somewhat severe 2. Moderately severe 3. Extremely severe		
(96) Feel conflicted over what to do	1	2	3
(97) Regrets over past decisions	1	2	3
(98) Menstrual (period) problems	1	2	3
(99) The weather	1	2	3
(100) Nightmares	1	2	3
(101) Concerns about getting ahead	1	2	3
(102) Hassles from boss or supervisor	1	2	3
(103) Difficulties with friends	1	2	3
(104) Not enough time for family	1	2	3
(105) Transportation problems	1	2	3
(106) Not enough money for transportation	1	2	3
(107) Not enough money for entertainment and recreation	1	2	3
(108) Shopping	1	2	3
(109) Prejudice and discrimination from others	1	2	3
(110) Property, investments or taxes	1	2	3
(111) Not enough time for entertainment and recreation	1	2	3
(112) Yardwork or outside home maintenance	1	2	3
(113) Concerns about news events	1	2	3
(114) Noise	1	2	3
(115) Crime	1	2	3
(116) Traffic	1	2	3
(117) Pollution	1	2	3

HAVE WE MISSED ANY OF YOUR HASSLES? IF SO, WRITE
    THEM IN BELOW.

(118) _____

ONE MORE THING: HAS THERE BEEN A CHANGE IN YOUR
LIFE THAT AFFECTED HOW YOU ANSWERED THIS
SCALE? IF SO, TELL US WHAT IT WAS.

From Kanner, et al.[32] with permission.

Influence of Values on Patient Care: Foundation for Decision Making

Carol M. Davis

OBJECTIVES

1. Identify what a value is and how it directs human behavior.
2. Recognize how humans acquire values.
3. Identify how values influence the choices of patients and health professionals.
4. Distinguish between value-directed behavior that enhances healing and value-directed behavior that is likely to interfere with healing.

Initially, one might question the logic of including a chapter on values in a text related to management of adult rehabilitation patients. The fact is, the entire book is devoted to educating the reader about the proper decisions to make in the rehabilitation process. Values play a critical role in most decision making, and to omit this aspect of decision making would be unwise.

Providing an operating definition of a *value* poses something of a challenge. Many interpretations have been made and several authors have provided a variety of definitions.[1-6] For the purposes of this chapter, a value is defined as an inner force that provides the standards by which patterns of choice are made. For example, if people value the safety of their lives, among other acts they will probably choose to wear a seatbelt when driving or riding in an automobile. That choice is guided by the importance they place on their safety, or by their value of safety.

Because values are internal and difficult to measure, they have not been studied as vigorously as other aspects of human behavior. One cannot see a value; one can only feel it working. Values play a particularly important role in influencing our choices. The importance of this influence is emphasized when one considers that *knowing* the right thing to do and *doing* it are two separate phenomena. The first has to do with knowledge or cognition, the second with values or attitudes. This text is aimed at teaching the "knowing" aspect; this chapter, however, is devoted to elucidating the value aspect in choosing.

Most choices are value based; some decisions seem more difficult to make than others. Difficulty may arise when the therapist must resolve a value dilemma, when two seemingly equal goals or choices compete with one another. Difficulty also may arise when the therapist's values conflict with the values of the patient, the patient's family, colleagues, the larger health care system, or society. This chapter further defines values, describes how we acquire our values, and illustrates the influence values have on decisions. In addition, the influence that patient's values have on therapist's decisions is explored; examples of common difficult decisions in rehabilitation are provided. Finally, the role communication plays in the process of making difficult choices is discussed.

PROCESS OF DECISION MAKING

How choices are made is different from what choices are made. The latter can be viewed as the answer or the solution, the former describes a process. Decision making or choosing in rehabilitation is sometimes composed of nothing more than a reactive, instinctive stimulus-response effort, or haphazard trial-and-error guessing. But more often, making the right decision, choosing the best alternative, results from professionally educated problem solving. One type of problem solving in health care is termed **clinical reasoning.** When a therapist first sees a patient, the process of clinical reasoning begins. Various questions are asked in sequence to assess the patient's problem fully and, inevitably, to decide on the most appropriate treatment for this particular person at this point in time.

The greater part of professional education in health care is devoted to developing good clinical reasoners. The best instructors bravely refuse to give the "right" answer and encourage students to learn the process of discovery. In this way, students rise above the technical level of training. They are encouraged to become professionals capable of responding to complex patient situations by carefully reading the literature, questioning, touching, testing, and listening with the "third ear" to what is said as well as to what is left unsaid.

Problem solving is fundamental to our daily lives as human beings. We often do not realize we are problem solving because the process is so habitual, so subconscious. Just deciding what to have for breakfast can involve an intricate multistep process:

What shall I have for breakfast?
What's in the kitchen?
Cereal, eggs, bacon, pancakes, juice, toast
How hungry am I?
Starved!
How much time do I have?
Thirty minutes.
What did the scale say?
5 pounds over
That does it; juice and dry toast!

The answer to this problem-solving process was based on identifying the importance of one value over others. The fact that the scale revealed 5 excess pounds became the determining factor for making the final choice. Another person might have made the same choice but for a different reason:

How much time do I have?
5 minutes.
No time to eat! I'll have toast and juice and eat it on the way!

Most choices result from prioritizing values. The more we know about our values, the more we learn and understand our science, and the more we know about the facts of the situation, the easier it is to make a decision that seems best.[1]

Deciding what to eat for breakfast is a decision-making process of a different sort than deciding whether a patient is a good candidate to receive an above-knee prosthesis. The differences are important. The first, what to eat, is a personal choice; the second, whether to recommend a prosthesis, is a professional decision. The first is a choice that bears little consequence for the chooser if the less-than-best decision is made. However, the decision about the prosthesis has profound consequence for another person if the less-than-best decision is made. The first example, what to eat for breakfast, is more accurately viewed as a value preference or a **nonmoral value** choice; the prosthesis decision is made up largely of several moral-value-laden decisions. **Moral values,** such as **justice,** honesty, compassion, integrity, all reflect a way of relating to human beings, and thus moral values carry more importance than value preferences, because humans are more important than food, or music, or what we wear.[2]

When we study to become professionals, part of the professional socialization process involves the adoption of values that usually overlap with our personal values.

At times, however, they might conflict with them. Professional responsibility, we learn, requires that we put the patient's needs before our own and act in ways that show we deserve the patient's trust.[3] Let us take a closer look at what a value is and how we obtain our personal and professional values.

VALUES AND VALUING

A **value** cannot be seen directly, and it cannot be measured. Values are constructs (moral schemes) that are made up of beliefs, emotions, and attitudes about what is best and what is not good. We can view values only indirectly by asking a person what he or she values, or, even more important, by watching another person's behavior. Values are reflected in our actions, especially the pattern of our actions over a period of time. Thus one might say, "I value honesty," but we might wonder how much when he or she knowingly cheats on income tax returns over a period of 5 years. Another value obviously has priority over honesty for this person.

Values, at times, cooperate and, at times, conflict with each other. A dilemma exists when we have difficulty choosing which value should have priority. For example, respect for life is the central value for advocates of a woman's right to choose abortion as well as for those opposed to abortion. The difference in opinion and belief of these two groups is not the value of life, but the importance of the mother's life over the fetus' life above all considerations; the reproductive-freedom advocates claim the primacy of the mother's choice for the quality of her life and resist outside interference with her right to choose.

People are not born with values, but they are born with instincts and needs. Values are acquired from social interactions, primarily with parents and family, and, for many, with religion. The initial learning of values takes the form of "following the rules" that parents believe will minimize personal pain and conflict, maximize pleasure and meaning, and promote harmony and peace in the home.

Adolescents, as a part of natural maturation, test the values of the home by breaking rules and trying out forbidden behavior. This process marks the beginning of a transformation in which value-based rules followed to avoid punishment become internalized and, on reflection, are adopted as one's own. Most people end up with a set of values very similar to that of their parents. However, for some, the difference in the way they prioritize their values causes a distancing between themselves and certain family members. One example of children prioritizing their values differently from their parents is the son who is the first in four generations not to study law.

The values of health professionals take on different priorities from the values of people in other careers whose primary satisfaction in work comes not from helping people directly but largely from working with ideas or inanimate objects. Likewise, although physical therapists as a group seem to display a consistent set of values, it might be conjectured that one of the key differences that distinguishes profoundly different specialists—for example, sports physical therapists who care for those who are well but injured, from those devoted to caring for seriously ill, brain-injured patients—is the way in which the specialist prioritizes values. The sports physical therapist expresses different interests in and focuses professional goals on a population with needs very different from those of brain-injured patients. The different choices made in preferred patient populations may stem from different values as well as different needs and interests.

We make our most meaningful choices based on what attracts us and leads us to growth and self-fulfillment, a life of pleasure and meaning.[4] Being aware of our values helps us make informed and consistent choices that lead to personal and professional satisfaction. This is part of the process physical therapists undergo as they search out a specialty area of interest following their first few years in clinical practice.

CODE OF ETHICS

The set of moral norms adopted by a professional group to direct value-laden choices in a way consistent with professional responsibility is termed a **code of ethics** (Fig. 3–1). One might follow the code without internalizing it, just as small children follow the "rules of the house." For the code of ethics to function as a set of professional values, one must reflect on it and decide that it, indeed, forms a values complex around which one is willing to organize professional choices. Thus, as was previously stated, reflection is necessary to the internalization of values to make them truly one's own.[5,6] The choices that then follow this internalization are likely to be consistent with one's basic beliefs, show coherence, be authentic or genuine, and adequate to the task of decision making. Those who make the smoothest transitions into professional practice are likely to be those whose personal values and priorities greatly overlap with the values inherent in their chosen professional practice. Given that one's basic human survival needs are met, the more one reflects on one's choices and on which choices result in the good and meaningful life, the more one is apt to experience consistent reward from opportunities.

THE VALUES OF PATIENTS AS A FACTOR IN CARE

Patients come to physical therapy as whole persons in need of professional help and guidance. All people can be viewed as possessing four quadrants of need that comprise the whole: the physical, the psychologic, the intellectual, and the spiritual. It could be said that a more meaningful and peaceful life results when choices are made that respond equally to the demands of all four

---

CODE OF ETHICS

PREAMBLE

This Code of Ethics sets forth ethical principles for the physical therapy profession. Members of this profession are responsible for maintaining and promoting ethical practice. This Code of Ethics, adopted by the American Physical Therapy Association, shall be binding on physical therapists who are members of the Association.

PRINCIPLE 1

Physical therapists respect the rights and dignity of all individuals.

PRINCIPLE 2

Physical therapists comply with the laws and regulations governing the practice of physical therapy.

PRINCIPLE 3

Physical therapists accept responsibility for the exercise of sound judgment.

PRINCIPLE 4

Physical therapists maintain and promote high standards in the provision of physical therapy services.

PRINCIPLE 5

Physical therapists seek remuneration for their services that is deserved and reasonable.

PRINCIPLE 6

Physical therapists provide accurate information to the consumer about the profession and the services they provide.

PRINCIPLE 7

Physical therapists accept the responsibility to protect the public and the profession from unethical, incompetent, or illegal acts.

PRINCIPLE 8

Physical therapists participate in efforts to address the health needs of the public.

Adopted by the House of Delegates
June 1981
Amended June 1987

Figure 3–1. Code of ethics of the American Physical Therapy Association (From the American Physical Therapy Association, with permission.)

---

quadrants of need. Central to the work of Carl Jung is the belief that a healthy personality results from obtaining a *balance* between thinking and feeling and between intuition and sensation.[7]

Patients come to physical therapy at various stages in their lives and with a unique history of having made thousands of choices. Over time, the therapist comes to realize that some patients display a life pattern of meaningful, consistent, well-thought-out choices; others reveal a life of capricious, noncentered, unorganized value-based behavior. Often patients' risky choices have directly or indirectly brought them to therapy; for example, the young patient with quadriplegia who drove into a tree while drunk. Many patient problems in movement and function that are encountered in rehabilitation are not the result of "fate," but result from a lifetime of choices that gave other values a higher priority than the physical, or than the prevention of illness and injury. The more physical therapists become aware of how much control people actually have over their state of wellness and health, the more difficult it becomes for some therapists to remain nonjudgmental about their patients. It is exceedingly difficult for some clinicians, for example, to remain nonjudgmental when treating a chronic smoker for emphysema or a tremendously obese patient for hip and knee joint problems.

It is important, however, to remember that we are morally and ethically bound to give the highest quality of care, as free from judgment and bias as possible, to all patients. This is where balance in all four of our quadrants helps us. If our needs are being met in all four areas, physical, intellectual, emotional, and spiritual, we feel less frustrated and irritated by personal stress, can remain centered and better able to remain nonjudgmental, and can set boundaries with compassion. Patients, with all their frailties can be seen as separate from us, doing the best for themselves that they can.

To be "centered" is to experience one's energy concentrated in the middle and balanced so that no one quadrant's needs predominate. When we feel centered, we feel balanced, just as the balanced karate expert stands with his or her weight so distributed that blows coming in any direction can be absorbed and pushed away without loss of balance. If, for example, our emotional needs are not getting met, we often feel unbalanced or uncentered. We either spend energy repressing or expressing energy in the stress of loneliness, need for attention, or irritability. On the other hand, when our four quadrants are equally attended, we feel centered and thus can feel the whole in every part. Centered energy, centered consciousness then allows us to free our attention away from our needs and toward the patients' needs, and we can be therapeutically present to the other.

When we need nothing more than to assist our patients to heal, whatever they choose to do can be viewed with greater objectivity. When we, ourselves, "need" our patients to get better, to thank us, to praise us, to acknowledge our skill and intellect because those common human emotional needs are not getting met outside the clinic, we are more likely to judge our patients when they fail to meet our needs.

THE INFLUENCE OF VALUES ON THE PRIMARY GOAL OF PATIENT CARE

When a feeling of criticism and negative judgment of a patient occurs within health practitioners, they must be aware of it and consciously work not to let it affect their behavior. The primary goal of health practitioners is to help *all* people recover or maintain their health so they may function at the highest, most independent, most **autonomous** level possible day to day. If the primary goal is to achieve optimal health and healing, certain values seem to promote that goal more than others. One way to ascertain values that promote health and healing is to describe behavior between a therapist and patient that does the very opposite, or that interferes with health and healing. Putting yourself in the place of the patient, what therapist behaviors would *interfere* with your progress toward getting well or healing? Table 3–1 presents a sample list of very obvious behaviors that would detract from a patient's ability to function optimally in a

Table 3–1 THERAPIST BEHAVIORS AND POSSIBLE UNDERLYING VALUES THAT DETRACT FROM THE HEALING PROCESS

Therapist Behaviors that Interfere or Detract from the Healing Process	Negative Values that Might Underlie Each Behavior
1. Acting cool or aloof, obviously paying more attention to other patients.	1. a. Prejudice: to prejudge or to classify a person as belonging to a larger group and thus to believe things about that person that one believed about the larger group. b. Indifference: lack of interest or concern: aloofness, detachment.
2. Overly criticizing you (the patient) so that you feel as if nothing you do is right.	2. a. Prejudice. b. Perfectionism: the doctrine that the perfection of moral character is a person's highest good and that freedom from imperfection is attainable. c. Lack of flexibility.
3. Treating you as an object rather than as a person with feelings of pain and worry and insecurity.	3. Depersonalization: to detract from an individual's uniqueness: to fail to honor a person's individuality.
4. Treating you as if you were a child, incapable of really understanding anything that is said.	4. Patronizing: to adopt an air of condescension.
5. Being unable or unwilling to help you in your exercises; leaving you alone most of the time.	5. a. Indifference. b. Prejudice.
6. Making fun of you in your presence and behind your back.	6. Depersonalization.
7. Telling others things you've shared in confidence.	7. Breaking confidentiality: not keeping another person's trust private and secret.
8. Not letting you work on your own.	8. Fostering dependence.
9. More often than not guessing about what is best for you. Admitting he or she "is not sure" what to do, but "let us not let that stop us."	9. Failure to recognize and to act on one's limits of knowledge.
10. Always fitting you in as if everything else in the therapist's life is more important than you are.	10. Placing selfish interest over patient's needs.

Table 3-2 THERAPIST BEHAVIORS AND POSSIBLE UNDERLYING VALUES THAT FACILITATE THE HEALING PROCESS

Therapist Behaviors that Facilitate or Promote the Healing Process	Positive Values that Might Underlie Each Behavior
1. Offering you (the patient) the same amount of attention offered other patients, so it balances out from day to day.	1. Justice: the quality of impartiality or fairness.
2. Accepting your weaknesses along with your strengths and verbally reinforcing the desired behaviors.	2. Unconditional positive regard; acceptance.
3. Always treating you as a person with feelings and being sensitive to those feelings each day.	3. a. Respect: the act of giving particular attention to a person; worthy of high regard. b. Compassion: sympathetic consciousness of another's situation and the desire to be of effective help in relieving a painful situation.
4. Explaining things at your level, not oversimplifying or making things too complex.	4. a. Respect. b. Accurate and sensitive communication.
5. Always reachable yet never fostering dependence; encouraging independent activity.	5. a. Autonomy: a quality or state of self-governance; independence. b. Dignity: the quality of being worthy, honored, esteemed; to have distinction as a person.
6. Never using humor inappropriately, never laughing *at* you, but encouraging you to be able to laugh, sometimes even at yourself.	6. Appropriate humor, nondefensive humor.
7. Always keeping your confidence.	7. Confidentiality: keeping another person's trust private and secret.
8. Fostering your own independent activity without letting you feel stranded.	8. Autonomy.
9. Realizing when he or she needs the advice of someone else and asking for help in a timely fashion.	9. Recognizing the limits to one's knowledge, knowing when to get help or to refer; honesty.
10. Making you feel special, cherished, and unique; showing individual concern for you and your progress.	10. a. Compassion. b. Sensitivity to your uniqueness.

therapeutic setting. Also included are a list of possible negative values that might underlie each of these behaviors.

Behaviors and underlying values that *facilitate* healing might be described as the exact opposite of those that detract from healing (Table 3-2). These therapist behaviors, it seems, would obviously help restore a patient's hope, promote progress toward recovery, and assist with achieving the highest possible level of independent function.

Many of us who would read the list of negative behaviors (Table 3-1) that detract from healing would respond, "I'd never behave in such a way with my patients!" But, in fact, a huge gap exists between knowing the right thing to do, wanting to do it, and actually doing it.

Essential to a "therapeutic use of self" is the capacity to feel **compassion** for those who suffer. Compassion is quite different from **pity**, wherein a person feels sorry for those who are less fortunate. The compassion of the mature health professional is fueled with imagination, or the ability to envision what is possible from the other person's perspective. Imaginative understanding involves **self-transposal** (a cognitive attempt to put one's self in the place of another) at the least and **empathy** (a complex type of identification with another's experience) at the most. As healers, therapists must not block but, rather, must allow empathy to occur, a momentary "crossing over" into the patient's frame of reference. Thus compassion is a very personal, intimate experience that is built on "trust, honesty, and the time and willingness to listen."[8]

Let us examine some patient care situations that require professional choice and that may result in a less-than-optimal prioritizing of our professional and personal values.

VALUE-LADEN SITUATIONS IN REHABILITATION

What would you do, and *why,* if this situation happened to you?

Joyce, a 22-year-old college student, was referred to physical therapy following surgical removal of her left leg owing to osteogenic sarcoma. Other than generalized weakness from chemotherapy, surgery, and bedrest, and incisional pain and soreness, she was in "good health" on her arrival to the rehabilitation center.

You have been treating her for 6 weeks, having begun therapy from her admission to the rehabilitation center. Preoperative training was given in the acute setting: you have assisted her with preprosthetic training, strengthening, prosthetic training and acceptance, and gait training. She has been progressing well.

Joyce is intelligent and inquisitive, yet somewhat stubborn. Two weeks before discharge you notice an increasing tendency on her part to be careless and to take unnecessary risks, like hopping on one foot rather than donning her prosthesis. In addition, she admits to thinking that her daily strengthening exercises are stupid and that, after discharge, she may just throw the prosthesis away and depend on a wheelchair. Even crutches are too much bother.

You feel confused and frustrated. You've invested a great deal of energy into the successful rehabilitation of this person and her behavior at this point seems ignorant and manipulative. Her refusal to cooperate with your suggestions angers you; you feel that her basic laziness in requesting a wheelchair existence represents settling for a quality of life that is less than optimal and selfish. You feel as if you've failed to help her realize her full adult potential.

You feel overstressed with the demands of your work.

Once the patient-care day has begun, therapists seldom find or take the time to reflect on the larger issues, those that hover on the fringe of the work consciousness. Instead, therapists tend to focus on the immediate situation in front of them, quickly gathering data and problem solving as they go. Joyce's growing problem of reluctance could be viewed as a peripheral issue at first, one the therapist hoped would pass without needing to be confronted. But as her discharge date comes closer, the therapist is forced to respond to what appears to be regressive behavior.

The therapist's responses may reveal one or more of several thoughts and feelings. Especially when under stress, one may become impatient and angry and lecture Joyce to "grow up." The therapist may feel personal failure and frustration and, in a condescending way, let her know he or she expected far more reward for the efforts placed in her successful rehabilitation. These are often automatic, emotion-based responses based on a value of spontaneous honesty and the right to express feelings regardless of the impact that expression may have on others. The therapist is unhappy and wants the situation to change but does not know how to change it, so the therapist displays poor impulse control and aggressively "lets off steam."

As "human" as this choice may seem, more mature behavior is required of health professionals. No longer may they claim the luxury of spontaneous outburst, for the impact of the therapists' outbursts rarely solves value-based problems and often creates larger ones. Obviously, this is not conducive to healing.

On reflection, one realizes that Joyce's regressive behavior may likely reveal inner conflict, fear, or depression. If one puts oneself in her place, it is not difficult to come to some understanding that a person under these circumstances might be afraid and might see a safer existence in a wheelchair. The value of compassion, funded by empathy and self-transposal, elevates the problem-solving process to a professional choice to sit down and to discuss this issue comprehensively with Joyce, referring her to the social worker for psychologic support and counseling, if necessary. Nonjudgmental concern and understanding are foundational to healing. In addition, health professionals caring for adults must accept that occasionally they will encounter a patient who is unwilling to cooperate with their suggestions and who resists their attempts to offer therapeutic care and advice. With the value of patient autonomy in mind, the professional's role is not to assume a paternalistic stance indicating "I know what is better for you than you do," but instead to outline as clearly, creatively, and accurately as possible the predictable results of the choices the patient is making. Patients must have control over their own lives to the greatest extent possible.

These guidelines exist in their purest sense when therapists are treating adult patients who are not suffering from confusion, mental or intellectual disorders, or significant depression. With children, or with adults who do suffer the conditions mentioned, therapists must aim for the greatest extent of autonomous choice possible and focus appropriate attention on parents and family care givers.

Reactive care, characterized by on-the-spot problem solving and decision making, is an unavoidable part of rehabilitation. However, the greater the number of our decisions that are based on reaction rather than on proaction or well-thought-out alternatives, the more idiosyncratic, inconsistent, and erratic our behavior will seem. Part of professional responsibility is to anticipate possible problems and to think through alternatives in advance. Likewise, the more that therapists base their decisions on scientific evidence and the more that they reflect on the values behind alternative choices, the more apt they are to make consistent, scientifically based decisions reflective of the highest professional care. These decisions are inevitably more conducive to healing.

Triage situations always elicit value priorities. A decision as simple as who to see first of three new inpatient referrals requires a value-based choice. What factors seem important in making that decision among these three new patients?

1. An 80-year-old, frail elderly woman with osteoporosis admitted following surgery to repair a fractured hip. Room 300.
2. A 30-year-old man with severe low back pain secondary to possible herniated disk. Room 201.
3. A 53-year-old woman who had a mild heart attack 3 weeks ago, admitted for cardiac rehabilitation. Room 302.

How would you decide, at 8 AM, which of these three patients to see first? What facts seem to make a difference? The patient's age? His or her location in the hospital (closest versus farthest away from where you are now)? Your existing patient load and schedule? Your subconscious or conscious aversion to certain patients, such as those with low back pain or the elderly? If our primary goal in rehabilitation is to help patients recover their health so that they might function at the highest, most independent level possible, how can we use this goal to help direct our choices?

Putting the patient's needs first seems to be critical to this decision. The therapist's choice should not be based solely on personal convenience. What additional facts are needed? Putting oneself in the place of the patient, one comes to realize that the existence of certain factors calls forth our immediate attention. One factor that readily comes to mind that demands our immediate consideration is responding to patients in pain. Pain can totally consume one's attention and will take immediate priority in our choices. Responding first to patients in severe discomfort seems very important in sequencing the order of treatments. The therapist needs to find out which of these three individuals may have had a difficult night and is most in need of attention for relief of pain.

SUMMARY

Professional rehabilitative care requires problem solving that is proactive, based on scientific data, and demonstrates a consistent, conscious value of choosing behavior that is conducive to healing. Clinicians must become "informed reasoners,"[2] who have systematically gathered the facts, have recognized potential choices and values dilemmas, and have taken the time to weigh which choice is most conducive to the healing process.

Central to this process is the courage to confront seemingly peripheral factors that therapists are tempted to hope will go away. Likewise, central to this process is the willingness to put oneself in the place of the patient. Pellegrino[9] cautions us not to be so egocentric as to treat others simply as we would like to be treated. Instead, he suggests that the Golden Rule of health care should be to give each patient the opportunity to tell you what his or her needs or wants are, as you would want them to give you.

Finally, sensitive and accurate communication is required. In health, people feel alive by their connection to the world, and in illness they feel cut off, fragmented, and uninterested in the world. As healers, the therapists' role then becomes one of entering the patient's context of meaning. By using human-to-human skills of listening accurately to words and feelings; by communicating trust, truth, respect, interest, and caring; by explaining in ways that are relevant and intelligible to the patient; and by being sensitive to the patient's values, the therapist facilitates the patient's hope and strong belief that he or she is the patient's advocate in the world. In other words, the therapist helps the patient do what is necessary to feel once more alive in the world, connected, and hopeful of recovery to a meaningful life. Even in the face of chronic debilitating disease, terminal illness, or irreversible paralysis there is a sense that the therapist can help patients feel reconnected to the possibility of a life with meaning.

The behaviors that enhance the therapeutic moment flow out of placing the person and his or her meaning of what is wrong central to any and all attempts to offer help. Behaviors that emerge from valuing a patient's humanity—sensitive and accurate listening, respect, trust, compassion, and problem solving, to name a few—work to reinforce autonomy and dignity and to restore a patient's hope and personal control of his or her life as therapists simultaneously apply their scientific knowledge and skill.[10]

This is what is required of health care professionals in day-to-day patient care. To do less is to render less than compassionate, professional help. Reflecting, coming to better know the right thing to do, and consistently doing it, result in a professional life of growth and meaning.

QUESTIONS FOR REVIEW

1. A person's values are difficult to identify. How can one know what a person values?

2. How are values related to behavior?

3. A belief is not a value, but beliefs direct our values. If a person believes fairness is good, what values can you predict the individual will hold?

4. What is the difference between a moral and a nonmoral value?

5. Give an example of a nonmoral value choice; of a moral value choice.

6. What is the difference between behavior that agrees with a code of ethics and behavior that is value based?

7. What is our obligation as health professionals when a patient refuses to take our suggestions and recommendations for healing?

8. What role does communication play in making value-based decisions in rehabilitation?

REFERENCES

1. Purtilo, RB and Cassel, CK: Ethical Dimensions in the Health Professions. WB Saunders, Philadelphia, 1981.
2. Wehlage, G and Lockword, AL: Moral relativism and values education. In Purpel, D and Ryan, K (eds): Moral Education—It Comes with the Territory. McCutchen, Berkeley, CA, 1976.
3. Pelligrino, ED: What is a profession? J Allied Health 12:161, 1983.
4. Morrill, RL: Teaching Values in College. Jossey-Bass, San Francisco, 1980.
5. Beck, C: A philosophical view of values and value education. In Hennessy, T (ed): Values and Moral Development, Paulist Press, New York, 1976.
6. Raths, LE, Harmin, M, and Simon, SB: Values and Teaching. Charles E Merrill, Columbus, OH, 1966.
7. Jung, CG: The Structure and Dynamics of the Psyche. Pantheon, New York, 1960.
8. Pence, GE: Can compassion be taught? J Med Ethics 9:189, 1983.
9. Pellegrino, ED and Tomasma, DC: A Philosophical Basis of Medical Practice. Oxford University Press, New York, 1981.
10. Davis, CM: The influence of values on patient care. In Payton OD (ed): Psychosocial Aspects of Clinical Practice. Churchill Livingston, New York, 1986, p 119.

SUPPLEMENTAL READINGS

Brammer, LM: The Helping Relationship, ed 3. Prentice-Hall, Englewood Cliffs, NJ, 1985.
Cassell, E: The Healer's Art. JB Lippincott, Philadelphia, 1976.
Collins, M: Communication in Health Professions. Phys Ther 61:1587, 1981.
Davis CM: Patient Practitioner Interaction/An Experiential Manual for Developing the Art of Health Care. Slack, Thorofare, NJ, 1989.
Frankena, W: Ethics, ed 2. Prentice-Hall, Englewood Cliffs, NJ, 1973.
Henerson, ME, Morris, LL, and Fitzgibbon, M: How to Measure Attitudes. Sage Publications, Beverly Hills, CA 1978.
Howard, J and Strauss, A: Humanizing Health Care. John Wiley & Sons, New York, 1975.
Kestenbaum, V (ed): The Humanity of the Ill. University of Tennessee Press, Knoxville, TN, 1982.
Payton, OD (ed): Psychosocial Aspects of Clinical Practice. Churchill Livingston, New York, 1986.
Pence, GE: Ethical Options in Medicine. Medical Economics, Oradell, NJ, 1980.
Purtilo, RB and Cassel, CK: Ethical Dimensions in the Health Professions. WB Saunders, Philadelphia, 1981.
Purtilo, RB: Health Professional/Patient Interaction. WB Saunders, Philadelphia, 1984.
Ramsey, P: The Patient as Person. Yale University Press, New Haven, 1970.

GLOSSARY

Association: Strong feelings of identification with another person.

Autonomy (autonomous): A quality or state of self-governance; independence.

Clinical reasoning: A problem-solving process based on identifying the importance of one value over others; process of prioritizing values in formulating a response to a situation.

Code of ethics: A set of moral norms adopted by a professional group to direct value-laden choices in a way consistent with professional responsibility.

Compassion: Sympathetic consciousness of another's situation and the desire to alleviate pain or suffering.

Confidentiality: Keeping another person's trust private and secret.

Depersonalization: To detract from an individual's dignity or worth; failure to honor a person's uniqueness.

Dignity: The quality of being worthy, honored, esteemed; to have distinction as a person.

Empathy: A three-stage process that includes (1) identification with another's experience or situation, (2) a shared experience with another person, and (3) a reclaiming of one's individuality separate from the shared moment.

Identification: Close personal association with another person leading to a feeling of sameness.

Indifference: Lack of interest or concern; aloofness, detachment.

Justice: The quality of impartiality or fairness.

Moral values: Values that dictate how one interacts with or treats another human being, which reflect a person's basic uniqueness, dignity, and worth.

Nonmoral values: Values that do not reflect how one treats another person but reflect esthetic, political, intellectual, personal, or social choices.

Patronizing: To adopt an air of condescension.

Perfectionism: The doctrine that the perfection of moral character is a person's highest good and that freedom from imperfection is attainable.

Pity: Sympathetic heartfelt sorrow; shared feeling wherein the individual pitied is deemed "less than" the one pitying.

Prejudice: To prejudge or to classify a person as belonging to a larger group and thus to believe things about that person that one believes about the larger group.

Respect: The act of giving particular attention to a person; worthy of high regard.

Self-transposal: The attempt to put oneself cognitively in the place of the other; to "walk in another person's shoes."

Sympathy: Feeling at one with another's feelings.

Value: An inner force that provides the standards by which patterns of choice are made.

CHAPTER 4

Vital Signs

Thomas J. Schmitz

OBJECTIVES

1. Identify the reasons for monitoring vital signs.
2. Explain the importance of monitoring vital signs in establishing a database of patient information.
3. Recognize the importance of monitoring vital signs as a method of assessing patient response to selected treatment activities.
4. Describe the common techniques for monitoring temperature, pulse, respiration, and blood pressure.
5. Identify normative values or ranges for each vital sign.
6. Describe the normal variations in vital signs and the factors that influence these changes.
7. Describe methods for recording data obtained from monitoring vital signs.

The ability to monitor vital signs accurately is an important component of general physical therapy assessment skills. Although frequently considered a nursing responsibility, results from a vital signs assessment have important implications for physical therapy management.

The **vital signs,** also referred to as the cardinal signs, generally include temperature, pulse, respiration, and blood pressure. These signs are important indicators of the body's physiologic status and reflect the function of internal organs. Variations in vital signs are a clear indicator that some change in the patient's physiologic status has occurred.

The purposes of obtaining information related to vital signs include

1. Establishing a database of values for an individual patient.
2. Assisting in goal setting and treatment planning.
3. Assisting with assessment of patient response to treatment.
4. Contributing to assessment of effectiveness of treatment activities.

In assessing vital signs it is important to note that "normal" values are specific to an individual. Although average or normative values have been established, some individuals will typically or "normally" display higher or lower values than those represented by these normative figures. This addresses the importance of monitoring vital signs as a serial process. Vital sign measurements yield the most useful information when performed and recorded at periodic intervals rather than as a one-time assessment. This type of serial recording allows changes in patient status or response to treatment to be monitored over time as well as indicating an acute change in physiologic status at a specific point in time.

An additional factor to consider is that many variables influence the vital signs. These may include time of day, time of the month, exercise, age, sex, weight, metabolic conditions, general health status, pain, and drug intake.[1,2]

BODY TEMPERATURE

Body temperature represents a balance between the heat produced or acquired by the body and the amount lost. Because humans are warm-blooded, or **homoiothermic,** body temperature remains relatively constant, despite changes in the external environment. This is in contrast to cold-blooded, or **poikilothermic,** animals (such as reptiles) in which body temperature varies with that of their environment.

The Thermoregulatory System

The purpose of the thermoregulatory system is to maintain a relatively constant internal body temperature. This system monitors and acts to maintain temperatures that are optimal for normal cellular and vital organ function. The thermoregulatory system consists of three primary components: the thermoreceptors, the regulating center, and the effector organs (Fig. 4–1).[3]

THERMORECEPTORS

The thermoreceptors provide input to the temperature-regulating center located in the hypothalamus. The regulating center is dependent on information from thermoreceptors to achieve constant temperatures. Once this information reaches the regulatory center, it

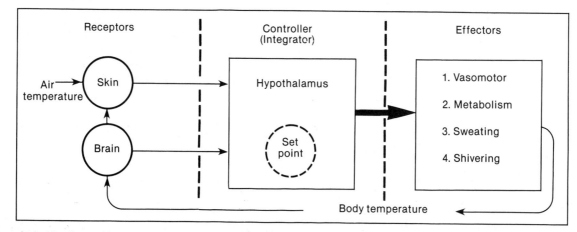

Figure 4–1. The three primary elements of the thermoregulatory system: the receptors, which provide input regarding body temperature; the hypothalamic control center, which coordinates heat production and loss processes; and the effector organs, which regulate heat loss, conservation, and dissipation mechanisms. (From Judy,[5] p 536, with permission.)

is compared with a "set point" standard or optimal temperature value. Depending on the contrast between the "set" value and incoming information, mechanisms may be activated either to conserve or to dissipate heat.[3]

Afferent temperature input is provided to the regulating center by both *peripheral* and *central* thermoreceptors. The peripheral receptors, composed primarily of free nerve endings, have a high distribution in the skin (cutaneous thermoreceptors). However, thermoreceptors also have been located in the spinal cord and abdomen, and may possibly be present in other deep structures not yet identified.[3,4] The cutaneous thermoreceptors demonstrate a larger distribution of cold to warmth receptors and are sensitive to rapid changes in temperature.[5] Signals from these receptors enter the spinal cord through afferent nerves and travel to the hypothalamus via the lateral spinothalamic tract.[3,6]

The central thermoreceptors are located in the hypothalamus. These thermoreceptors are sensitive to temperature changes in blood perfusing the hypothalamus. These cells also can initiate responses to either conserve or dissipate heat. They are particularly sensitive to core temperature changes and monitoring body warmth.[5,6]

REGULATING CENTER

The temperature-regulating center of the body is located in the hypothalamus. The hypothalamus functions to coordinate the heat production and loss processes, much like a thermostat, ensuring an essentially constant and stable body temperature. By influencing the effector organs, the hypothalamus achieves a relatively precise balance between heat production and heat loss. In a healthy individual, the hypothalamic thermostat is set and carefully maintained at 37°C ± 1°C (98.6°F ± 1.8°F).[5] In situations in which input from thermoreceptors indicates a drop in temperature below the "set" value, mechanisms are activated to conserve heat. Conversely, a rise in temperature will activate mechanisms to dissipate heat (Fig. 4–2). These responses are activated through hypothalamic control over the effector organs. Input to the effector organs is transmitted through nervous pathways of both the somatic and autonomic nervous systems.[3,6,7]

EFFECTOR ORGANS

The effector organs respond to both increases and decreases in temperature. The primary effector systems include vascular, metabolic, skeletal muscle (shivering) responses, and sweating. These effector systems function either to increase or to dissipate body heat.

Conservation and Production of Body Heat

When body temperature is lowered, mechanisms are activated to conserve heat and to increase heat produc-

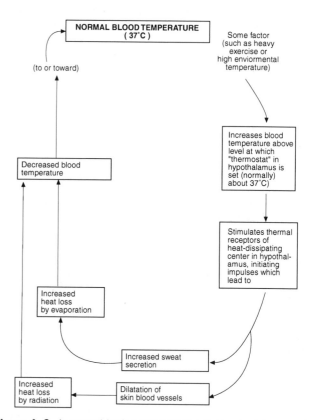

Figure 4–2. Increased body temperature activates heat loss mechanisms to maintain normal internal temperature. (From Anthony and Thibodeau,[7] p 633, with permission.)

tion. Following are descriptions of heat conservation and production mechanisms.

Vasoconstriction of blood vessels. The hypothalamus activates sympathetic nerves, an action that results in vasoconstriction of cutaneous vessels throughout the body. This significantly reduces the lumen of the vessels and decreases blood flow near the surface of the skin where the blood would normally be cooled. Thus the amount of heat lost to the environment is decreased.

Decrease in or abolition of sweat gland activity. To reduce or to prevent heat loss by evaporation, sweat gland activity is diminished. Sweating is totally abolished with cooling of the hypothalamic thermostat below approximately 37°C (98.6°F).[4]

Cutis anserina or piloerection. Also a response to cooling of the hypothalamus, this heat conservation mechanism is commonly described as "gooseflesh." The term *piloerection* means "hairs standing on end." Although of less significance in man, in lower mammals with greater hair covering, this mechanism functions to trap a layer of insulating air near the skin and decrease heat loss.

The body also responds to decreased temperature with several mechanisms designed to produce heat. These mechanisms are activated when the body thermostat falls below approximately 37°C (98.6°F).[4] Following are descriptions of heat production mechanisms.

Shivering. The primary motor center for shivering is located in the posterior hypothalamus. This area is activated by cold signals from the skin and spinal cord. In response to cold, impulses from the hypothalamus activate the efferent somatic nervous system and result in increased tone of skeletal muscles. As the tone gradually increases to a certain threshold level, shivering (involuntary muscle contraction) is initiated and heat is produced. This reflex shivering can be at least partially inhibited through conscious cortical control.[6]

Hormonal regulation. The function of hormonal influence in thermal regulation is to increase cellular metabolism, which subsequently increases body heat. Increased metabolism occurs through circulation of two hormones from the adrenal medulla: *norepinephrine* and *epinephrine.* Circulating levels of these hormones, however, are of greater significance in maintaining body temperature in infants than in adults. Heat production by these hormones can be increased in an infant by as much as 100 percent, as opposed to 10 to 15 percent in an adult.[4]

A second form of hormonal regulation involves increased output of thyroxine by the thyroid gland. Thyroxine increases the rate of cellular metabolism throughout the body. This response, however, occurs only as a result of prolonged cooling, and heat production is not immediate.[5] The thyroid gland requires several weeks to hypertrophy before increased demands for thyroxine can be achieved.

Loss of Body Heat

Excess heat is dissipated from the body through four primary methods: radiation, conduction, convection, and evaporation.

Radiation is the transfer of heat by electromagnetic waves from one object to another. This heat transfer occurs through the air between objects that are not in direct contact. Heat is lost to surrounding objects that are colder than the body (e.g., loss of heat to a wall or surrounding room objects).

Conduction is the transfer of heat from one object to another through a liquid, solid, or gas. This type of heat transfer requires direct molecular contact between two objects, as when a person is sitting on a cold surface, or when heat is lost in a cool swimming pool. Heat is also lost by conduction to air.

Convection is the transfer of heat by movement of air or liquid (water). This form of heat loss is accomplished secondary to conduction. Once the heat is conducted to the air, the air is then moved away from the body by convection currents. Use of a fan or a cool breeze provides convection currents. Heat loss by convection is most effective when the air or liquid surrounding the body is continually moved away and replaced.

Evaporation is the conversion of a liquid to a vapor. This form of heat loss occurs on a continual basis through the respiratory tract and through perspiration from the skin. Evaporation provides the major mechanism of heat loss during heavy exercise. Profuse sweating provides a significant cooling effect on the skin as it evaporates. In addition, this cooling of the skin functions to further cool the blood as it is shunted from internal structures to cutaneous areas.

Abnormalities in Body Temperature

INCREASED BODY TEMPERATURE

An elevation in body temperature is generally believed to assist the body in fighting disease or infection. **Pyrexia** is the elevation of normal body temperature, more commonly referred to as **fever. Hyperpyrexia** and **hyperthermia** are terms that describe an extremely high fever, generally above 41.1°C (106°F).[8]

Pyrexia occurs when the "set" value of the hypothalamic thermostat rises. This elevation is caused by the influence of fever-producing substances called **pyrogens.** Pyrogens are secreted primarily from toxic bacteria or are released from degenerating body tissue.[4] The effects of these pyrogens result in fever during illness. As a result of the new, higher thermostat value, the body responds by activating its heat conservation and production mechanisms. These mechanisms raise body temperature to the new, higher value over a period of several hours. Thus a fever, or **febrile** state, is produced.

The clinical signs and symptoms of a fever vary with the level of disturbance of the thermoregulatory center, and with the specific stage of the fever (onset, course, or termination). These signs and symptoms may include general malaise, headache, increased pulse and respiratory rate, chills, piloerection, shivering, loss of appetite (**anorexia**), pale skin that later becomes flushed and hot to the touch, nausea, irritability, restlessness, constipation, sweating, thirst, coated tongue, decreased urinary output, weakness, and insomnia.[1,9,10] With higher elevations in temperature (hyperpyrexia), disorientation, confusion, convulsions, or coma may occur. These latter symptoms are more common in children under the age of 5 years and are believed to be related to the immaturity of the nervous system.[10]

Three specific stages have been identified describing the course of a fever:

1. *Invasion* or *onset* is the period from either gradual or sudden rise until the maximum temperature is reached.
2. *Fastigium* or *stadium* (course) is the point of highest elevation of the fever. Once maximum temperature is reached, it remains relatively stable.
3. *Difervescence* (termination) identifies the period during which the fever subsides and temperatures move toward normal. This drop in temperature can occur suddenly (crisis) or gradually (lysis).

LOWERED BODY TEMPERATURE

Exposure to extreme cold produces a lowered body temperature called **hypothermia.** With prolonged exposure to cold there is a decrease in metabolic rate, and body temperature gradually falls. As cooling of the brain occurs, there is a depression of the thermoregulatory center. The function of the thermoregulatory center becomes seriously impaired when body temperature falls below approximately 34.4°C (94°F) and is completely lost with temperatures below 29.4°C (85°F).[4] The body's heat regulatory and protection mechanism is therefore lost.

Symptoms of hypothermia include decreased pulse and respiratory rates, cold and pale skin, **cyanosis,** decreased cutaneous sensation, depression of mental and muscular responses, and drowsiness, which may eventually lead to coma.[1,4,10] If left untreated, the progression of these symptoms may lead to death.

Factors Influencing Body Temperature

A statistical average or normal temperature of 37°C (98.6°F) taken orally has been established for body temperature in an adult population. However, body temperature is most accurately presented as a range. A range of values is more representative of normal body temperature as certain everyday circumstances (e.g., time of day) or activities (e.g., exercise) influence the body's temperature. In addition, some individuals typically run a slightly higher or lower body temperature than the statistical average. Therefore, deviations from the average will be apparent from individual to individual, as well as between measures taken from a single subject under varying circumstances.

TIME OF DAY

The term **circadian rhythm** describes a 24-hour cycle of normal variations in body temperature. Certain predictable and regular changes in temperature occur on a daily basis. Body temperature tends to be lowest in the early morning hours, between 4 AM and 6 AM, and highest in the late afternoon and early evening hours, between 4 PM and 8 PM.[9] These regular changes in body temperature are influenced significantly by both digestive processes and the level of skeletal muscle activity.

For individuals who work at night, this pattern is usually inverted.[10]

AGE

Compared with adults, infants demonstrate a higher normal temperature because of the immaturity of the thermoregulatory system. Infants are particularly susceptible to environmental temperature changes, and their body temperature will fluctuate accordingly. Young children also average higher normal temperatures because of the heat production associated with increased metabolic rate and high physical activity levels. Elderly populations tend to demonstrate lower than average body temperatures. Lower temperatures in elderly populations are associated with a variety of factors, including lower metabolic rates, decreased subcutaneous tissue mass (which normally insulates the body against heat loss), decreased physical activity levels, and inadequate diet.

EMOTIONS

Extremes in emotions will increase body temperature due to increased glandular secretions and a subsequent increase in metabolic rate.[1]

EXERCISE

The effects of exercise on body temperature are an important consideration for physical therapists. Strenuous exercise significantly increases body temperature because of increased metabolic rate. Active muscle contractions are an important and potent source of heat production. During exercise, body temperature increases are proportional to the relative intensity of the work load.[5] Vigorous exercise can increase the metabolic rate by as much as 20 to 25 times that of the basal level.[5]

MENSTRUAL CYCLE

Increased levels of progesterone during ovulation cause body temperature to rise 0.3°C to 0.5°C (0.5°F to 0.9°F). This slight elevation is maintained until just prior to the initiation of menstruation, at which time it returns to normal levels.[10]

PREGNANCY

Because of increased metabolic activity, body temperature remains elevated approximately 0.5°C (0.9°F). Temperature returns to normal after parturition.

EXTERNAL ENVIRONMENT

Generally, warm weather tends to increase body temperature, and cold weather decreases body temperature. Environmental conditions influence the body's ability to maintain constant temperatures. For example, in hot, humid environments the effectiveness of evaporative cooling is severely diminished because the air is already heavily moisture laden. Other forms of heat dissipation are also dependent on environmental factors such as movement of air currents (convection). Clothing also can be an important external consideration because it can function both to conserve and to facilitate release of body heat. The amount and type of clothing is important. To dissipate heat, absorbent, loose-fitting, light-colored clothing is most effective. To conserve heat, several layers of lightweight clothing to trap air and to insulate the body are recommended.

LOCATION OF MEASUREMENT

Rectal temperatures are from 0.3°C to 0.5°C (0.5°F to 0.9°F) higher than oral temperatures; axillary temperatures are approximately 0.6°C (1.1°F) lower than oral temperatures.[11]

INGESTION OF WARM OR COLD FOODS

Oral temperatures will be affected by oral intake, including smoking. Patients should refrain from smoking or eating for at least 15 minutes (preferably 30 minutes) prior to an oral temperature reading.

Assessing Body Temperature

TYPES OF THERMOMETERS
Electronic Thermometers

This type of thermometer provides a rapid (several-second) measure of body temperature. Standard oral electronic thermometers consist of a portable battery-operated unit, an attached probe, and plastic disposable probe covers (Fig. 4–3). The units provide a flashed, digital display of body temperature, or a stationary scale and needle marker.[1] An important advantage of these thermometers is the low chance of cross-infection, inasmuch as the probe covers are used only once.

Hand-held electronic oral thermometers are also commercially available. These units are typically about 6 inches in length with a tapered design (Fig. 4–4). One end of the device is narrow and serves as the probe. The opposite end is broad and houses the battery. These

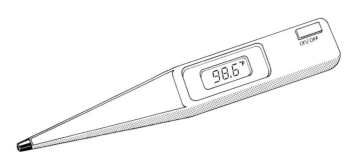

Figure 4–4. Hand-held electronic oral thermometer.

thermometers also provide a flashed, digital display of body temperature. A few models allow use with disposable covers.

Electronic thermometers are also available that measure body temperature from the external ear (Fig. 4–5). These battery-operated hand-held units include an ear probe (with disposable covers) and provide a rapid, digital readout of body temperature. Other types of electronic thermometers include both earlobe clips and finger sleeve or clip sensors. Nipple-shaped, passifier designs are also available for monitoring oral temperatures of infants.

Clinical Glass Thermometer

Traditionally, temperatures have been taken by a glass thermometer, which consists of a glass tube with a bulbous tip filled with mercury. Once the bulb is in contact with body heat, the mercury expands and rises in the glass column to register body temperature. Reflux of mercury down the tube is prevented by a narrowing of the base. The device must be shaken vigorously to return the mercury to the bulb before the next use.

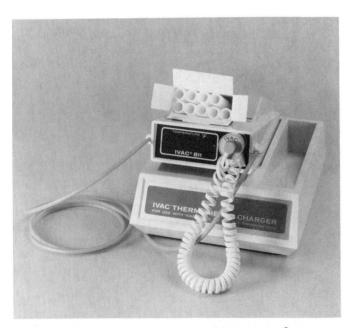

Figure 4–3. Standard electronic oral thermometer. Components include a battery-powered unit with a digital display, a probe, and disposable probe covers. (Courtesy of IVAC Corporation, San Diego, CA.)

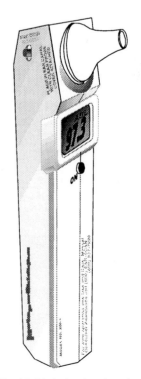

Figure 4–5. Hand-held electronic external ear thermometer.

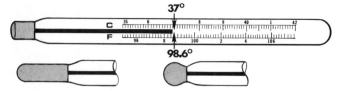

Figure 4–6. Clinical glass thermometer illustrating the three shapes of bulbous ends. The blunt end (*top*) can be used for both oral and rectal temperatures. The elongated end (*bottom left*) is for oral measures, and the rounded end (*bottom right*) is for rectal measures. (From Saperstein and Frazier,[1] p 456, with permission.)

Glass thermometers are calibrated in either (or both) Celsius and Fahrenheit scales. The range is from approximately 34°C (93°F) to 42.2°C (108°F), with slight variations among different manufacturers. The calibrations are in degrees and tenths of a degree. As such, each long line represents a full degree and each short line indicates 0.1 degrees on the Celsius thermometer and 0.2 degrees on the Fahrenheit thermometer. When recording temperatures it is common practice to round the fractions of degrees to the nearest whole number.

There are three different shapes of bulbous ends on glass thermometers, depending on their intended use (Fig. 4–6). A blunt tip can be used for both oral and rectal temperatures. The elongated end is for oral or axillary measures, and the rounded tip is for rectal measures.

Chemical Thermometers

These instruments are used in a similar fashion to a clinical glass thermometer because they are placed under the patient's tongue. They consist of a series of calibrated dots impregnated with a temperature-sensitive chemical. After removal, the dots are examined for color changes to determine the temperature reading. They are disposed of after use.

Temperature-Sensitive Tape

Heat-sensitive tape or disks respond to body temperature by changing color. They are frequently used with pediatric patients. The forehead and abdomen are common placement sites. The temperature readings are nonspecific and are usually confirmed with a more precise measure if deviations are noted.

PROCEDURE FOR ASSESSING BODY TEMPERATURE

For purposes of establishing baseline data and assessing response to treatment, physical therapists generally use oral monitoring. However, in situations in which oral temperatures may be contraindicated and an electronic unit with an alternative sensor is unavailable, an axillary measure may substitute. Both procedures will be described.

Electronic Thermometer for Assessing Oral Temperature

A. Wash hands.
B. Assemble equipment.
 1. An electronic thermometer unit.

2. Disposable probe cover.
 3. Worksheet and pen or pencil to record collected data.
C. Procedure.
 1. Explain procedure and rationale in terms appropriate to the patient's understanding.
 2. Assure patient comfort.
 3. Turn on power unit (some units require a warm-up period).
 4. Place disposable cover over probe.
 5. Ask patient to open mouth, and place the covered probe at the posterior base of the tongue to the right or left of the frenulum. Instruct patient to close the lips (not teeth) around the probe and hold it in place.
 6. Electronic thermometer probes should be left in place following manufacturer's instructions for that particular unit (frequently between 10 and 45 seconds).
 7. Remove prove and dispose of cover.
 8. Temperature reading is obtained from digital readout or scale.
 9. Record results.

Clinical Glass Thermometer for Assessing Oral Temperature

A. Wash hands.
B. Assemble equipment.
 1. An oral thermometer.
 2. Soft tissue to wipe thermometer.
 3. Worksheet and pen or pencil to record collected data.
C. Procedure.
 1. Explain procedure and rationale in terms appropriate to the patient's understanding.
 2. Assure patient comfort.
 3. The thermometer should be held firmly between the thumb and forefinger at the end opposite the bulb.
 4. If the thermometer has been soaked in a disinfectant solution, rinse under cold water.
 5. Dry the thermometer using a clean tissue, wiping from the bulb toward the fingers in a rotating fashion.
 6. Hold the thermometer at eye level and rotate until the column of mercury is clearly visible. Note the level of the column.
 7. If necessary, shake the thermometer until the mercury is below 35°C (95°F). While holding the thermometer securely, use quick, downward motions of the wrist, which will effectively lower the column.
 8. Ask patient to open mouth, and place thermometer at the posterior base of the tongue to the right or left of the frenulum. Instruct patient to close the lips (not teeth) around thermometer to hold it in place.
 9. Leave the clinical glass thermometer in place for 7 to 8 minutes. It should be noted that considerable discrepancy exists in the literature regarding the length of time the thermometer should be left in place. Times vary from 5 to 10 minutes.

10. Remove the thermometer.
11. Using a clean tissue, wipe the thermometer away from the fingers in a rotating fashion.
12. Hold the thermometer at eye level, rotate until the mercury is clearly visible, and read the highest point on the scale to which the mercury has risen.
13. Record results.
14. Return the thermometer to an appropriate area for disinfecting.

Assessing Axillary Temperature

Although less accurate, axillary temperatures are used when oral temperatures are contraindicated and an electronic unit with an alternative sensor is unavailable. Contraindications for taking an oral temperature might include **dyspnea,** surgical procedures involving the mouth or throat, very young children, and delirious or irrational patients. In these circumstances axillary measures are considered safer. Axillary temperatures are approximately 0.6°C (1.1°F) lower than oral.[11] The following procedure should be used.

A. Wash hands.
B. Assemble equipment.
1. An oral clinical glass thermometer is usually used.
2. Soft tissue to wipe thermometer.
3. A towel to dry axillary region (moisture will conduct heat).
4. Worksheet and pen or pencil to record collected data.
C. Procedure.
1. Follow procedure, steps 1 through 7, for assessing oral temperature with a clinical glass thermometer.
2. Expose axillary region. If any moisture is present, the area should be gently towel dried with a patting motion (vigorous rubbing will increase temperature of the area).
3. Place the thermometer in the axillary region between the trunk and upper arm (Fig. 4–7). The patient's arm should be placed tightly across the chest to keep the thermometer in place (asking the patient to move his or her hand toward the opposite shoulder is often a useful direction). If the

patient is disoriented or very young, the thermometer must be held in place.
4. Leave thermometer in place for 10 minutes.
5. Remove thermometer.
6. Using a clean tissue, wipe the thermometer away from the fingers in a rotating fashion.
7. Holding the thermometer at eye level, rotate it until the mercury is clearly visible, and read the highest point on the scale to which the mercury has risen.
8. Record results. Generally, a temperature reading is assumed an oral measure unless otherwise noted. An axillary temperature is designated by a circled A after the temperature (e.g., 95°F Ⓐ). Similarly a circled R indicates a rectal measure (e.g., 99°F Ⓡ).
9. Return the thermometer to appropriate area for disinfecting.

PULSE

The **pulse** is the wave of blood in the artery created by the contraction of the left ventricle during the cardiac cycle (one complete cycle of cardiac muscle contraction and relaxation). With each contraction, blood is pumped into an already full aorta. The inherent elasticity of the aortic walls allows expansion and acceptance of the new supply. The blood is then forced out and surges through the systemic arteries. It is this wave or surge of blood that is felt as the pulse.

Pressure changes in the large arteries during the cardiac cycle are reflected in the arterial waveform (Fig. 4–8). The lowest point of pressure occurs during ventricular **diastole;** the highest point occurs during ventricular **systole** (peak ejection). The dicrotic notch represents closure of the aortic valve.[12] A healthy adult heart beats an average of 70 times per minute, a rate which

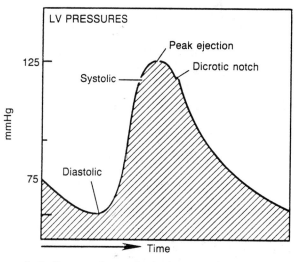

Figure 4–8. Pressure changes in the large arteries during a cardiac cycle. Peak pressure occurs during ventricular systole (peak ejection); low pressure is evident during ventricular diastole. Closure of aortic valve is represented by the dicrotic notch. (From Dolan,[12] p 759, with permission.)

Figure 4–7. Positioning for monitoring axillary temperature.

provides continuous circulation of approximately 5 to 6 liters of blood through the body.

The pulse can be palpated wherever a superficial artery can be stabilized over a bony surface. In monitoring the pulse, specific attention is directed toward assessing three parameters: rate, rhythm, and volume.

The *rate* is the number of beats per minute. A pulse range of 60 to 80 beats per minute is considered normal for an adult. However, multiple factors will influence the pulse rate, including age, sex, emotional status, and physical activity level. Body size and build also influence pulse rate.[2,11] Tall, thin individuals generally have a slower pulse rate than those who are obese or have stout frames.

The *rhythm* describes the intervals between beats. In a healthy individual, the rhythm is *regular* or *constant* and indicates that the time intervals between beats are essentially equal.

The *volume* (force) refers to the amount of blood pushed through the artery during each ventricular contraction. The quantity (volume) of blood within the vessel produces the force of the pulse. Normally, the force of each beat is equal. With a higher blood volume, the force of the pulse is greater and with lower volumes it is weaker. The volume is assessed by how easily the pulse can be obliterated. With an increased volume the pulse is large, difficult to obliterate and is termed a **bounding** or **full** pulse; a feeling of high tension is noted. With lower volumes, the pulse is small, is easily obliterated and termed **weak** or **thready.**

Several other important terms are used to describe variations in pulse.[12,13] An **alternating** pulse (pulsus alterans) is a fluctuation between a weak and a strong beat with no change in overall cycle time. The term **bigeminal** is used to describe two regular pulse beats followed by a long pause. A **paradoxical pulse** (pulsus paradoxus) is a decreased amplitude of the pressure wave with inspiration and return to full amplitude on expiration; it is often associated with restrictive pericarditis. Figure 4–9 presents a schematic presentation of common arterial pulse waveforms.

In addition to rate, rhythm, and volume, the *quality* or *feel* of the arterial wall should be assessed. Typically, a vessel will feel smooth, elastic, soft, flexible, and relatively straight. With advancing age, vessels may demonstrate sclerotic changes. These changes frequently cause the vessels to feel twisted, hard, or cordlike with decreased elasticity and smoothness.

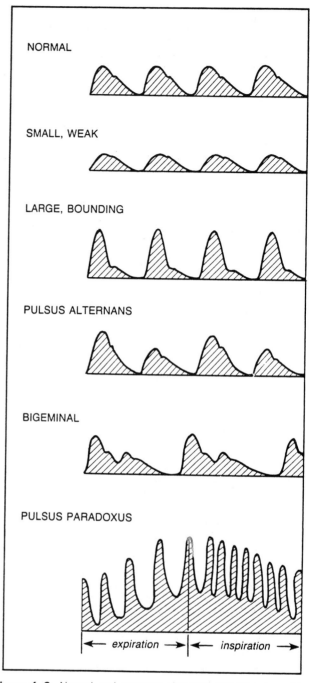

Figure 4–9. Normal and common abnormal arterial pulses. (From Bates,[13] p 297, with permission.)

Factors Influencing Pulse

Essentially, any factor that alters the metabolic rate will also influence heart rate. Several factors are of particular importance when considering pulse rate.

AGE

Fetal pulse rates average 120 to 160 beats per minute.[1] The pulse rates for a newborn range between 70 and 170, with an average of 120 beats per minute. Pulse rate gradually decreases with age until it stabilizes in adulthood. The average adult pulse rate is generally considered to be between 60 and 80 beats per minute; however, much wider variations, from 50 to 100 beats per minute, are considered within a normal range for adults.

SEX

Men and boys typically have slightly lower pulse rates than women and girls.

EMOTIONS

Responses to a variety of emotions (e.g., grief, fear, anxiety, or pain) activate the sympathetic nervous system, with a resultant increase in pulse rate.

EXERCISE

Oxygen demands of skeletal muscles are significantly increased during physical activity. At rest, only 20 to 25 percent of the available muscle capillaries are open.[4] During vigorous exercise, extensive vasodilation causes all capillaries to open. The heart rate increases to provide additional blood flow to the muscle and to meet the increased oxygen requirement. For physical therapists, monitoring a patient's pulse rate is an important method of assessing response to exercise. Typically, the pulse rate will increase as a function of the intensity of the activity. A linear relationship exists between pulse rate and intensity of work load. To use the pulse rate effectively, both the patient's resting and predicted maximal heart rates must be determined.[14] Maximum heart rate values are determined by an exercise stress test or by using the formula for age-adjusted maximum heart rate: maximum heart rate equals 220 minus age (see Chapter 16, Coronary Artery Disease). Generally, pulse rates during a 15- to 30-minute therapeutic exercise program for a healthy individual should not exceed 60 to 70 percent of predicted maximum heart rate.[15]

In assessing pulse rate response to exercise, level of aerobic fitness also must be considered. Both resting and submaximal exercise heart rates are typically lower in trained subjects. In response to an identical exercise intensity, a sedentary person's heart rate will demonstrate greater acceleration when compared with a trained individual. Although the metabolic requirements of an activity are the same, the lower heart rate response in a trained subject occurs as a result of a more efficient (increased) stroke volume. The linear relationship between pulse rate and work load exists for both trained and untrained subjects. However, the rate of rise will differ. When compared with a sedentary person, the trained individual will achieve a higher work output and greater oxygen consumption before reaching a specified submaximal heart rate.[5]

SYSTEMIC OR LOCAL HEAT

During periods of fever, the heart rate will increase. The body will attempt to dissipate heat by vasodilation of peripheral vessels. Heart rate will increase to shunt blood flow to cutaneous areas for cooling. Local applications of thermal modalities (such as a hot pack) also will elevate heart rate to provide increased circulation to cutaneous areas secondary to arteriolar and capillary dilation.

Assessing the Pulse

A peripheral pulse can be monitored at a variety of sites on the body. Superficial arteries located over a bony surface are easiest to palpate and are referred to as "pulse points." Following, these pulse sites, their locations, and some common indications for use are described.

1. Temporal: superior and lateral to the outer canthus of the eye; used when the radial pulse is inaccessible.
2. Carotid: on either side of the anterior neck below the earlobe and between the sternocleidomastoid muscle and the trachea, used in cardiac arrest, in infants, and to monitor blood flow to brain.
3. Brachial: medial aspect of the antecubital fossa; used to monitor blood pressure.
4. Radial: radial aspect of the wrist at the base of the thumb; easily accessible, used for routine pulse monitoring.
5. Femoral: inguinal region; used in cardiac arrest and to monitor lower extremity circulation.
6. Popliteal: behind the knee (usually easier to palpate with slight knee flexion); used to monitor lower extremity circulation and blood pressure.
7. Pedal (dorsalis pedal): dorsal, medial aspect of foot; used to monitor lower extremity circulation.

In addition to the peripheral sites, the apical pulse may be monitored by auscultation (listening), using a stethoscope directly over the apex of the heart. Apical pulses are used when other sites are inaccessible (e.g., medical or surgical contraindications) or difficult to locate and to palpate, such as in newborns and some cardiac patients. Pulse locations are illustrated in Figure 4–10.

PROCEDURES FOR ASSESSING PULSE

A site should be selected that will not cause discomfort and consequently alter the pulse rate.[2] Additionally, site location will be influenced by the specific patient diagnosis or the reasons for pulse monitoring. Peripheral pulses are monitored by palpation, using the tips of the first three fingers. Pulse rates obtained from the apex of the heart require use of a stethoscope.

Assessing Peripheral Pulses
A. Wash hands.
B. Assemble equipment.
　1. A watch with a second hand.
　2. Worksheet and pen or pencil to record collected data.
C. Procedure.
　1. Explain procedure and rationale to patient in terms appropriate to his or her understanding.
　2. Assure patient comfort.
　3. Select the pulse point to be monitored.
　4. Place the first three fingers squarely and firmly over the pulse site; use only enough pressure to feel the pulse accurately (if the pressure is too great it will occlude the artery).
　5. Count the pulse for 30 seconds and multiply by 2; if any irregularities are noted, a full 60-second count should be taken; note the rhythm, volume, and quality or feel of the vessel.
　6. Record results.

Assessing Apical Pulse
A. Wash hands.
B. Assemble equipment.
　1. A stethoscope.
　2. Antiseptic wipes for cleaning ear pieces and diaphragm of stethoscope before and after use.
　3. A watch with a second hand.

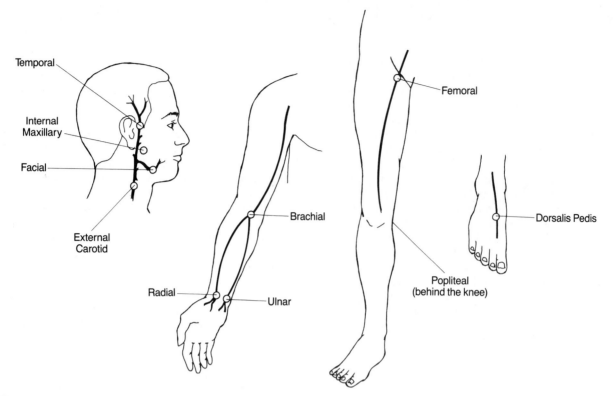

Figure 4–10. Common sites for monitoring peripheral pulses. Site selection will be influenced by patient condition and reasons for monitoring pulse.

4. Worksheet and pen or pencil to record collected data.
C. Procedure.
1. Explain procedure and rationale to patient in terms appropriate to his or her understanding.
2. Assure patient comfort.
3. Use antiseptic wipe to clean the ear pieces and diaphragm of the stethoscope.
4. Locate the site where pulse will be monitored; the apical pulse is located approximately 3.5 inches (8.9 cm) to the left of the midsternum, in the fifth intercostal space, within an inch of the midclavicular line drawn parallel to the sternum.[8] These landmarks are guides to locating the apical pulse. In some individuals a stronger pulse may be noted by altering placement of the stethoscope (e.g., placement in the fourth or sixth intercostal space).
5. Warm the diaphragm of the stethoscope in the palm of hand.
6. Place stethoscope in ears so that the ear attachments are tilted forward.
7. Place diaphragm over the apex of heart. Count the pulse for 60 seconds; the pulse will be heard as a "lubb-dubb." The "lubb" represents closure of the atrioventricular (tricuspid and mitral) valves. The "dubb" represents closure of the semilunar (aortic and pulmonic) valves.[9,11]
8. Record results.
9. If the same examiner is using the stethoscope again, it is not necessary to clean the ear pieces; the diaphragm should always be cleaned.

Assessing the Apical-Radial Pulse

Typically, the apical and radial pulse valves are the same. However, in some situations (e.g., cardiac disease or vascular occlusion) blood pumped from the left ventricle may not be reaching the peripheral site or may be producing a weak or imperceptible pulse. The apical pulse in such cases would be stronger than the radial.

To monitor the apical-radial pulse, two people are needed to simultaneously monitor each of the two pulses for 60 seconds. The results from the two assessments are then compared. The difference between the two counts is called the **pulse deficit.** This type of monitoring provides additional information regarding the status of the cardiovascular system.

Electronic Pulse Monitoring

Electronic pulsemeters (Fig. 4–11) use sensors to detect the pulse. Pulsemeters have gained expanded use in prescribed exercise and training programs because they provide a practical, accurate method of continual pulse monitoring. The devices consist of small, battery-operated units that can be strapped to the patient's wrist or waist, or bracketed to a piece of exercise equipment. Most units incorporate a lead wire with a distal sensor. The sensors are typically housed in a finger sleeve, earlobe clip, or chest strap attachment. The sensors transmit heart rate information back to the monitors. Many of the units allow programming target heart rate zones and storage of exercise information over a variable number of entries. Some of the newer units can transfer exercise

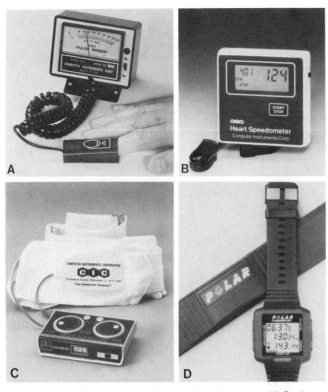

Figure 4-11. Sample models of electronic pulsemeters. (A) Stationary scale and needle marker readout with finger sleeve sensor, (B) earlobe clip sensor with digital display, (C) chest strap sensor with digital display, and (D) wireless chest strap sensor with wristwatch display. (Courtesy of Computer Instruments Corporation, Port Washington, New York.)

information directly to a computer for storage and later analysis. This provides a permanent record and serial data on exercise performance.

Some pulsemeters are equipped with more than one type of sensor. This feature allows selection of a sensor appropriate to the activity (e.g., an earlobe clip or chest strap would be preferable to a finger sleeve for monitoring an activity that involved upper extremity movement). Pulse values are provided by a digital display or stationary scale and needle marker.

Some pulsemeters provide wireless transmission from a chest sensor strap to a wristwatch display. Other units provide pulse values by placing the thumb firmly against a flat metal sensor. Various additional options are available on these units and differ with the model and manufacturer. Among the more common features are the ability to preset the upper and lower limits of the pulse rate for a specific activity and an auditory signal when pulse values move outside the target range.

Leger and Thivierge[16] examined the validity of 13 commercially available heart rate monitors by comparing findings with electrocardiogram (ECG) readings. A high correlation ($r = 0.93$) was found between ECG readings and heart rate values obtained with conventional chest electrodes. Lower correlations were obtained using other types of electrodes. Findings from this study suggest some unconventional electrodes will yield unreliable results and are inadequate for clinical use.

RESPIRATION

The primary function of respiration is to supply the body with oxygen for metabolic activity and to remove carbon dioxide. The respiratory system, consisting of a series of branching tubes, brings atmospheric oxygen into contact with the gas exchange membrane of the lungs in the alveoli. Oxygen is then transported throughout the body via the cardiovascular system.

The Respiratory System

Air enters the body by way of the nose and pharynx, where it is warmed, filtered, and humidified. It is then moved to the larynx, trachea, bronchi, and bronchioles (Fig. 4-12). The terminal bronchioles then branch into the respiratory bronchioles. Attached to their walls is the functional gas exchange unit of the lungs, the alveolus.

INSPIRATION

Inspiration is initiated by contraction of the diaphragm and intercostal muscles. During contraction of these muscles, the diaphragm moves downward and the intercostals lift the ribs and sternum up and outward. The thoracic cavity is thus increased in size and allows for lung expansion.

EXPIRATION

During relaxed breathing, expiration is essentially a passive process. Once the respiratory muscles relax, the thorax returns to its resting position, and the lungs recoil. This ability to recoil occurs due to the inherent elastic properties of the lungs.

Regulatory Mechanisms

Regulation of respiratory function is a complex process. It involves multiple components of both neural and chemical control and is closely integrated with the cardiovascular system.

Breathing is controlled by the *respiratory center,* which lies bilaterally in the pons and medulla.[17,18] The respiratory muscles are controlled by motor nerves whose cell bodies are located in this area. This respiratory center provides control of both the rate and the depth of breathing in response to the metabolic needs of the body.

Both *central* and *peripheral* chemoreceptors influence respiration. *Central* chemoreceptors located in the respiratory center are sensitive to changes in either carbon dioxide or hydrogen ion levels of arterial blood. An increase in either carbon dioxide levels or hydrogen ions will stimulate breathing.[4] *Peripheral* chemoreceptors are located at the bifurcation of the carotid arteries (carotid bodies) and in the arch of the aorta (aortic bodies). These receptors are sensitive to the partial pressure of oxygen (PaO_2) in the arterial blood. When PaO_2 levels in arterial blood drop, afferent impulses carry this

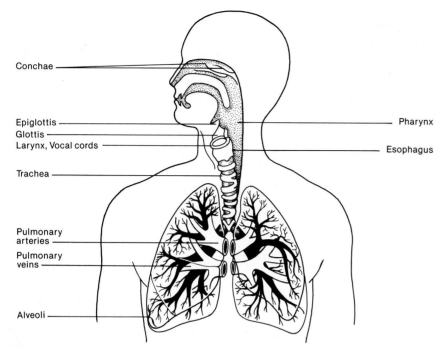

Conchae

Epiglottis
Glottis
Larynx, Vocal cords

Trachea

Pulmonary
arteries
Pulmonary
veins

Alveoli

Pharynx

Esophagus

Figure 4–12. The respiratory pathways. (From Guyton,[4] p 299, with permission.)

information to the respiratory center. Motor neurons to the respiratory muscles are stimulated to increase tidal volume (amount of air exchanged with each breath) or, with very low oxygen levels, to also increase the respiratory rate.[6] These peripheral chemoreceptors cause an increase in respiration only when PaO_2 levels fall to approximately 60 mmHg (from a normal level of about 90 to 100 mmHg).[17] This is because the receptors are sensitive only to PaO_2 levels in plasma and not to the total oxygen in blood.[6]

Respiration also is influenced by a protective stretch mechanism called the *Hering-Breuer reflex.* Stretch receptors throughout the walls of the lungs monitor the amount of entering air. When overstretched, these receptors send impulses to the respiratory center to inhibit further inhalation. Impulses stop at the end of expiration so that another inspiration can be initiated.[4,17,18] Respiration is also stimulated by vigorous movements of joints and muscle (exercise) and is strongly influenced by voluntary cortical control.

Factors Influencing Respiration

Multiple factors can alter normal, relaxed, effortless respiration. As with temperature and pulse, any influence that increases the metabolic rate also will increase the respiratory rate. Increased metabolism and subsequent demand for oxygen will stimulate increased respiration. Conversely, as metabolic demands diminish, respirations also will decrease. Several influencing factors are of particular importance when assessing respiration. These include age, body size, stature, exercise, and body position.

AGE

The respiratory rate of a newborn is between 30 and 60 breaths per minute. The rate gradually slows until adulthood, when it ranges between 12 and 18 breaths per minute.[19] In elderly people the respiratory rate increases owing to decreased elasticity of the lungs and decreased efficiency of gas exchange.[9]

BODY SIZE

Men generally have a larger vital capacity than women; adults larger than adolescents and children.

STATURE

Tall, thin individuals generally have a larger vital capacity than stout or obese individuals.

EXERCISE

Respiratory rate and depth will increase as a result of increased oxygen consumption and carbon dioxide production.

BODY POSITION

The supine position can significantly affect respiration and predispose the patient to stasis of fluids. The two influential factors are compression of the chest against the supporting surface and increased volume of intrathoracic blood.[9] Both these factors will limit normal lung expansion.

In addition to the above-mentioned factors, respiration also may be affected by drug intake, certain disease states, and the patient's emotional status.

Parameters of Respiratory Assessment

In assessing respiration, four parameters are considered: rate, depth, rhythm, and character.

The *rate* is the number of breaths per minute. Either inspirations or expirations should be counted, but not both. The normal adult respiratory rate is 12 to 18 per minute. The rate should be counted for 30 seconds and multiplied by two. If any irregularities are noted, a full 60-second count is indicated.

The *depth* of respiration refers to the amount (volume) of air exchanged with each breath. Normally, the depth of respirations are the same, producing a relatively even, uniform movement of the chest. The normal adult tidal volume is approximately 500 ml of air. The depth of respiration is assessed by observation of chest movements. It is usually described as deep or shallow, depending on whether the amount of air exchanged is greater or less than normal.[2] With deep respirations, a large volume of air is exchanged; with shallow respirations, a small amount of air is exchanged, with minimal lung expansion or chest wall movement.

The *rhythm* refers to the regularity of inspirations and expirations. Normally, there is an even time interval between respirations. The respiratory rhythm is described as regular or irregular.

The *character* of respirations refers to deviations from normal, quiet, effortless breathing. Two important deviations that alter the character of breathing are the amount of effort required and the sound produced during respiration.

Difficult or labored breathing is called **dyspnea.** Dyspneic patients require increased, noticeable effort to breathe. This is frequently evident by increased activity noted in accessory respiratory muscles such as the intercostals and abdominals. Use of these muscles helps increase effectiveness of respiration. The intercostals assist in raising the ribs to expand the thoracic cavity; the abdominals assist function of the diaphragm. Additional muscles that may provide accessory functions in respiration are the sternocleidomastoid, pectoralis major and minor, scalene, and the subclavius.

The sound of breathing is also important in assessing the character of respirations. Following, several relevant terms related to respiratory sounds are described:

1. Wheezing: a whistling sound produced by air passing through a narrowed bronchi or bronchiole; it may be heard on both inspiration and expiration but is more prominent on expiration; apparent with emphysema and asthmatic patients.
2. Stridor: a harsh, high-pitched crowing sound that occurs with upper airway obstructions caused by narrowing of the glottis or trachea (e.g., tracheal stenosis, presence of a foreign object).
3. Rales: rattling, bubbling, or crackling sounds that occur owing to secretions in the air passages of the respiratory tract. They may be heard with the ear but are most accurately assessed by use of a stethoscope.
4. Sigh: a deep inspiration followed by a prolonged, audible expiration; occasional sighs are normal and function to expand alveoli. Frequent sighs are abnormal and may be indicative of emotional stress.
5. Stertorous: a snoring sound owing to secretions in the trachea and large bronchi.

In addition to the rate, depth, rhythm, and character, several distinctive *patterns* of respiration have been described. The more common include the following:

1. **Tachypnea:** an increased respiratory rate, greater than 24 breaths per minute; associated with high fever (attempt to eliminate body heat), respiratory insufficiency, and lesions in the respiratory control center.
2. **Bradypnea:** a decreased respiratory rate, less than 10 breaths per minute; apparent with dysfunction of the respiratory control center, metabolic disorders, and drug or alcohol abuse.
3. **Apnea:** absence of respirations, usually temporary in duration; most frequently caused by an airway obstruction or disorder of the central respiratory mechanism.
4. **Hyperventilation:** increase in the rate and depth of respiration; associated with acute anxiety or emotional stress, central nervous system dysfunction, and drug overdose.
5. **Cheyne-Stokes respirations:** a pattern characterized by a gradual increase in rate and depth followed by a gradual decrease. Periods of apnea occur between cycles. Considered a serious symptom, this respiratory pattern is often noted as death approaches. This pattern is also associated with severe congestive heart failure, renal failure, drug overdose, meningitis, and unaccustomed exposure to high altitudes.[8,20]
6. **Biot's respirations:** pattern that alternates between periods of apnea and hyperpnea (increased rate and depth).[8] Associated with meningitis and central nervous system disorders that cause increased intracranial pressure.[8,20]
7. **Kussmaul's respirations:** a gasping, labored pattern with both increased rate and depth; rapid and deep respirations without pauses;[21] associated with metabolic acidosis and renal failure.
8. **Apneustic breathing:** prolonged inspiration with short, ineffective expiration; seen in lesions of the pons.[8]
9. **Paradoxical respirations:** lung inflation occurs on expiration, and deflation occurs on inspiration; may occur in open pneumothorax or in paralysis of diaphragm.[8]

Figure 4–13 presents a schematic illustration of common respiratory patterns.

Assessing Respiration

Because respiration is under both voluntary (cortical) and involuntary control, it is important that the patient is unaware that respiration is being assessed. Once aware of the assessment, usual breathing characteristics may be altered. Therefore, it is often recommended that respirations be observed immediately after taking the pulse. After monitoring the pulse, the fingers can remain in place at the pulse site, and respiration can be assessed. With the use of this technique the patient's conscious attention will not be drawn to the respiratory assessment. Ideally, respiration should be assessed with the chest exposed. If this is not possible, or if respirations cannot be easily observed through clothing, maintain fingers on the radial pulse site and place the patient's arm across the chest. This will allow limited

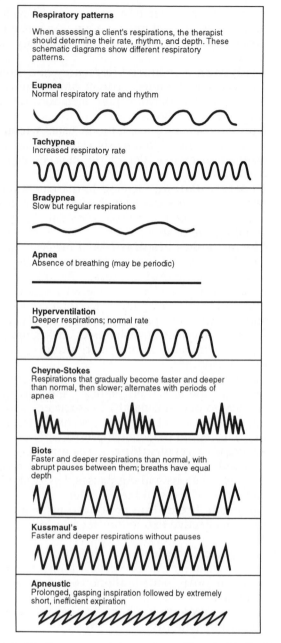

Respiratory patterns

When assessing a client's respirations, the therapist should determine their rate, rhythm, and depth. These schematic diagrams show different respiratory patterns.

Eupnea
Normal respiratory rate and rhythm

Tachypnea
Increased respiratory rate

Bradypnea
Slow but regular respirations

Apnea
Absence of breathing (may be periodic)

Hyperventilation
Deeper respirations; normal rate

Cheyne-Stokes
Respirations that gradually become faster and deeper than normal, then slower; alternates with periods of apnea

Biots
Faster and deeper respirations than normal, with abrupt pauses between them; breaths have equal depth

Kussmaul's
Faster and deeper respirations without pauses

Apneustic
Prolonged, gasping inspiration followed by extremely short, inefficient expiration

Figure 4–13. Common respiratory patterns. (From Grable,[21] p 98, with permission.)

palpation without drawing conscious input from the patient.

PROCEDURE FOR ASSESSING RESPIRATION
A. Wash hands.
B. Assemble equipment.
  1. A watch with a second hand.
  2. Worksheet and pen or pencil to record collected data.
C. Procedure.
  1. Assure patient comfort.
  2. Expose chest area if possible; if area cannot be exposed and respirations are not readily observable, place patient's arm across chest and keep your

fingers positioned as if continuing to monitor the radial pulse.
3. Count the respirations (either inspirations or expirations, but not both) for 30 seconds and multiply by two; if any irregularities are noted, count for a full 60 seconds.
4. Observe the depth, rhythm, character, and pattern of respiration.
5. Return clothing if chest has been exposed.
6. Record results.

BLOOD PRESSURE

Blood pressure refers to the force the blood exerts against a vessel wall. Because liquid flows only from a higher to a lower pressure, the pressure is highest in the arteries, lower in the capillaries, and lowest in veins.[22] Inasmuch as the heart is an intermittent pulsatile pump, pressure is measured at both the highest and lowest points of the pulse. These points are represented by the systolic (ventricular contraction) and diastolic (ventricular relaxation) pressures. The systolic pressure is the highest pressure exerted by the blood against the arterial walls. The diastolic pressure (which is constantly present) is the lowest pressure. The difference between the two pressures is called the **pulse pressure.**

Regulatory Mechanisms

The *vasomotor center* is located bilaterally in the lower pons and upper medulla. It transmits impulses through sympathetic nerves to all vessels of the body.[6] The vasomotor center is tonically active, producing a slow, continual firing in all vasoconstrictor nerve fibers. It is this slow, continual firing that maintains a partial state of contraction of the blood vessels and provides normal *vasomotor tone.*[4] The vasomotor center assists in providing a stable arterial pressure required to maintain blood flow to body tissue and organs. This occurs because of its close connection to the cardiac controlling center in the medulla (because changes in cardiac output will influence blood pressure). Additionally, the vasomotor and cardiac controlling centers require input from afferent receptors.

AFFERENT RECEPTORS
Input regarding blood pressure is provided primarily by *baroreceptors* and *chemoreceptors*. The *baroreceptors* (pressoreceptors) are stimulated by stretch of the vessel wall from alterations in pressure. These receptors have a high concentration in the walls of the internal carotid arteries above the carotid bifurcation and in the walls of the arch of the aorta. The areas where baroreceptors are located in the carotid arteries are called *carotid sinuses* and monitor blood pressure to the brain. Their locations on the aortic arch are called *aortic sinuses* and are responsible for monitoring blood pressure throughout the body.

In response to an increase in blood pressure the baroreceptor input to the vasomotor center results in an inhibition of the vasoconstrictor center of the medulla and excitation of the vagal center.[4] This results in a decreased heart rate, decreased force of cardiac contraction, and vasodilation, with a subsequent drop in blood pressure. The baroreceptor input during a lowering of blood pressure would produce the opposite effects.

The *chemoreceptors* are stimulated by reduced arterial oxygen concentrations, increases in carbon dioxide tension, and increased hydrogen ion concentrations.[23] These receptors lie close to the baroreceptors. Those located in the carotid artery are called *carotid bodies,* and on the aortic arch they are termed *aortic bodies.*

Impulses from these receptors travel to the brain (cardioregulatory and vasomotor centers) via afferent pathways in the vagus and glossopharygneal nerves. Efferent impulses from these centers, in response to alterations in blood pressure, will alter heart rate, strength of cardiac contractions and size of blood vessels.[23]

Factors That Influence Blood Pressure

Many factors influence pressure. As with all vital signs, blood pressure is represented by a range of normal values and will yield the most useful data when monitored over a period of time. Several important factors that should be considered when assessing blood pressure include blood volume, diameter and elasticity of arteries, cardiac output, age, exercise, and arm position.

BLOOD VOLUME

The amount of circulating blood in the body directly affects pressure. Blood loss (e.g., hemorrhage) will cause pressure to drop. Conversely, an increased blood volume (e.g., blood transfusion) will cause the pressure to rise.

DIAMETER OR ELASTICITY OF ARTERIES

The size (diameter) of the vessel lumen will provide either increased peripheral resistance (vasoconstriction) or decreased resistance (vasodilation) to cardiac output. The elasticity of the vessel wall also influences resistance. Normally the expansion and recoil properties of the arterial walls provide a continuous, smooth flow of blood into the capillaries and veins between heartbeats. With age, these properties are diminished. Thus, there is a higher resistance to blood flow with resultant increase in systolic pressure. Because the flexibility and recoil properties are diminished, there is a lower diastolic pressure.

CARDIAC OUTPUT

When increased amounts of blood are pumped into the arteries, the walls of the vessels distend, resulting in a higher blood pressure. With lower cardiac output, less blood is pushed into the vessel, and there is a subsequent drop in pressure.

AGE

Blood pressure varies with age (Table 4–1). It normally rises after birth and reaches a peak during early puberty. By age 17 or 18 years, the adult blood pressure has been reached. The normal, average adult blood pressure is usually considered 120/80 mmHg (the top number indicates systolic pressure; the bottom, diastolic pressure).

EXERCISE

Physical activity will increase cardiac output, with a consequent linear increase in blood pressure. Greater increases are noted in systolic pressure owing to proportional changes in pressure gradient of peripheral vessels during vasodilation. Blood pressure increases are proportional to the intensity of the work load.

VALSALVA MANEUVER

The **Valsalva maneuver** is an attempt to exhale forcibly with the glottis, nose, and mouth closed. It causes an increase in intrathoracic pressure with an accompanying collapse of the vein of the chest wall. There is a subsequent decrease in blood flow to the heart, a decreased venous return, and a drop in arterial blood pressure. This maneuver serves to internally stabilize the abdominal and chest wall during periods of rapid and maximum exercise such as weight lifting. Although the Valsalva maneuver can temporarily enhance muscle function via this stabilization, it has a direct effect on blood pressure and should be avoided by individuals with vascular impairment.[5]

ARM POSITION

Blood pressure may vary as much as 20 mmHg by altering arm position.[24] For consistency of measures, the patient should be sitting with the arm in a horizontal-supported position at heart level.[24] If patient condition or the type of activity precludes these positions, alterations should be carefully documented. As with other vital signs, factors such as fear, anxiety, or emotional stress also will cause an increase in blood pressure.

Table 4–1 VARIATIONS IN BLOOD PRESSURE WITH AGE

Age	Normal Blood Pressure (mmHg)
Newborn	40 to 70 systolic
1 month	80 systolic, 45 diastolic
6 months	90 systolic, 60 diastolic
2 years	80 to 90 systolic, 55 to 65 diastolic
4 years	100 to 115 systolic, 55 to 75 diastolic
6 years	105 to 125 systolic, 60 to 80 diastolic
8 years	105 to 125 systolic, 65 to 80 diastolic
10 years	110 to 135 systolic, 65 to 80 diastolic
12 years	115 to 135 systolic, 65 to 80 diastolic
14 years	120 to 140 systolic, 70 to 85 diastolic
Adult	110 to 140 systolic, 60 to 80 diastolic
Elderly	Same as for an adult, or slightly higher systolic and slightly lower diastolic

From Kozier and Erb,[25] p 487, with permission of the publisher.

Assessing Blood Pressure

EQUIPMENT

The equipment required for taking blood pressure includes a *blood pressure cuff,* a *sphygmomanometer,* and a *stethoscope* (Fig. 4–14). The blood pressure cuff is an airtight, flat rubber bladder that can be inflated with air. The bladder is covered with cloth that extends beyond the length of the bladder. There are two tubes that extend from the cuff. One is attached to a rubber bulb that has a valve used to maintain or to release air from the cuff. The second tube is attached to a manometer (portion of sphygmomanometer that registers the pressure reading).

The cuffs may be secured on the patient's extremity by Velcro, snaps, or hooks, and many are wrapped to keep them in place.[25] They come in a variety of sizes.

Obtaining a cuff of appropriate size is important. The cuff should cover approximately one-half to two-thirds of the patient's upper arm or leg and should be long enough to encircle the limb.[25] Cuffs that are too narrow will show inaccurately high readings, and cuffs that are too wide, inaccurately low. Generally, the cuff width should be 20 percent wider than the diameter of the limb. A typical adult cuff width is 4.5 to 5.5 inches (12 to 14 cm) with a bladder length of 9 inches (23 cm).[2]

The sphygmomanometer registers the blood pressure reading. There are two types: *aneroid manometers* and *mercury manometers* (Fig. 4–14). The aneroid manometer registers the blood pressure by way of a circular calibrated dial and needle. The mercury manometer registers blood pressure on a mercury-filled calibrated cylinder. At the uppermost portion of the mercury column is a convex curve called the *meniscus.* A reading is

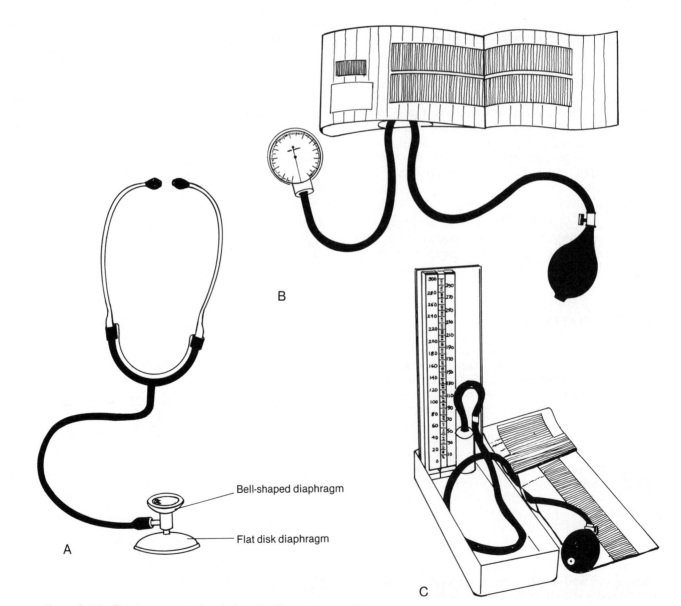

B

Bell-shaped diaphragm

Flat disk diaphragm

A

C

Figure 4–14. Blood pressure equipment includes (*A*) a stethoscope (this stethoscope has a combination of both a bell-shaped and a flat disk diaphragm) and either (*B*) an aneroid manometer and cuff or (*C*) mercury manometer and cuff.

obtained by viewing the meniscus at *eye level*. If not observed directly at eye level, an inaccurate reading will be obtained.

The stethoscope is used to listen to the sounds over the artery as pressure is released from the cuff. It includes an amplifying mechanism (diaphragm) and earpieces connected by rubber tubing. There are two types of diaphragms: a bell-shaped and a flat disk shape. Stethoscopes may have a single type of diaphragm or a combination of the two (Fig. 4–14). The bell-shaped diaphragms are generally recommended for assessing blood pressure.[26] By a combination of listening through the stethoscope and watching the manometer, the blood pressure reading is obtained.

Electronic sphygmomanometers are also commercially available. They contain a microphone and transducer built into the cuff.[11] Thus the need for a stethoscope is eliminated. A flashing light or audible "beep" indicates both the systolic and diastolic pressures. Some electronic units also have a built-in paper printer to provide a hard copy of data (Fig. 4–15).

KOROTKOFF'S SOUNDS

When assessing blood pressure, a series of sounds are heard through the stethoscope called Korotkoff's sounds. Initially when pressure is applied in the cuff, the blood flow is occluded and no sound is heard through the stethoscope. As the pressure is gradually released, a series of five phases or sounds have been identified.[26]

Phase 1: the first clear, faint, rhythmic tapping sound that gradually increases in intensity; period when blood initially flows through the artery; systolic pressure.

Phase 2: a murmur or swishing sound is heard.

Phase 3: sounds become crisp and louder.

Phase 4: sound is distinct, abrupt muffling; soft blowing quality; first diastolic pressure.

Phase 5: sounds disappear; second diastolic pressure.

Controversy exists as to the point of true diastolic pressure (phase 4 versus phase 5). The American Heart Association recommends use of the fifth phase as the most accurate index of diastolic pressure in adult populations.[25] Recording only one diastolic pressure (phase 5) is common practice in most clinical settings. For example, a blood pressure reading with a systolic pressure of 120 and a second diastolic reading of 76 would

be recorded as 120/76. In facilities where both diastolic pressures are routinely documented, three numbers are recorded. For example, a systolic pressure of 120, a first diastolic reading of 80 and a second of 76 would be recorded as 120/80/76.

PROCEDURE FOR ASSESSING BLOOD PRESSURE

A primary consideration in assessing blood pressure is that it should be done in a minimal amount of time. The blood pressure cuff acts as a tourniquet. As such, venous pooling and considerable discomfort to the patient will occur if the cuff is left in place too long.

The brachial artery is the most common site for blood pressure monitoring and an assessment at this site will be described in detail. A description for monitoring lower extremity blood pressure is also presented.

Assessing Brachial Artery Pressure

A. Wash hands.
B. Assemble equipment.
  1. A stethoscope.
  2. A sphygmomanometer with a blood pressure cuff (size of cuff should be appropriate for size of extremity).
  3. Antiseptic wipes for cleaning earpieces and diaphragm of stethoscope before and after use.
  4. Worksheet and pen and pencil to record collected data.
C. Procedure.
  1. Explain procedure and rationale to patient in terms appropriate to his or her understanding.
  2. Assist the patient to the desired position (the sitting position is recommended);[24] assure patient comfort.
  3. Expose the arm, and place at heart level with the elbow extended.
  4. Wrap the blood pressure cuff around the arm approximately 2.5 to 5 cm (1 to 2 inches) above the antecubital fossa; the center of cuff should be in line with the brachial artery (Fig. 4–16).
  5. Check that the sphygmomanometer registers zero.
  6. Use an antiseptic wipe to clean the earpieces and diaphragm of the stethoscope.
  7. Place the earpieces of the stethoscope (tilting forward) into ears; the tubes of the stethoscope should not be crossed and should hang freely.
  8. Locate and palpate the brachial artery in the antecubital fossa; place the diaphragm of the stethoscope over the artery (Fig. 4–16).
  9. Close the valve of the blood pressure cuff (turn clockwise).
  10. Pump the blood pressure cuff until the manometer registers approximately 20 mmHg above the anticipated systolic pressure.
  11. Release the valve carefully, allowing air out slowly; air should be released at a rate of 2 to 3 mmHg per heartbeat.
  12. Watch the manometer closely and note the point at which the first sound is heard (a mercury manometer must be viewed at eye level); this is

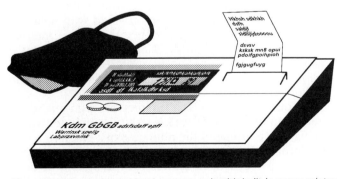

Figure 4–15. Electronic blood pressure unit with built-in paper printer and digital display.

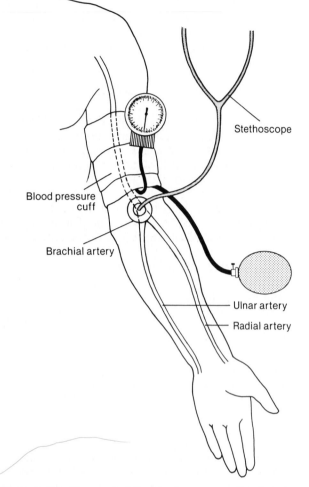

Figure 4–16. Placement of the blood pressure cuff and stethoscope for monitoring brachial artery pressure.

sures are contraindicated, such as following trauma or surgery.

Essentially, the procedure is the same as that for assessing pressure at the brachial artery, with the following variations:

1. The patient is placed in a prone position with slight knee flexion.
2. The popliteal artery is used to monitor pressure; in comparison with the brachial artery, the popliteal artery usually yields higher systolic and lower diastolic values.
3. A wide cuff is used (approximately 18 cm [17 inches]). This is placed around the lower third of the thigh. The center of the cuff should be in line with the popliteal artery.

RECORDING RESULTS

For purposes of physical therapy documentation, many therapists include vital signs data directly within the narrative format of their note. The most important element in recording this information is that it allows easy comparison from one entry to the next. The date, time of day, patient position, examiner's name, and equipment used should all be clearly indicated.

Traditionally, nursing personnel have used graph sheets to record vital sign information. For the therapist practicing in a facility where such forms are used, they will be useful in providing recent vital sign data. Familiarity with the specific recording system is important. Several methods are used; they generally include some variation of open and closed circles, connecting lines and/or color codes. A sample of such a sheet is presented in Figure 4–17. Modifications of this type of form also may be useful for documenting response to physical therapy treatment.

SUMMARY

Values obtained from monitoring vital signs provide the physical therapist with important information about the patient's physiologic status. Results from these measures assist in establishing a database of values for an individual patient. They also assist in goal setting, treatment planning, assessment of patient response to treatment, and periodic reassessment to determine the effectiveness of treatment interventions.

The procedure for assessing each vital sign has been presented. Because multiple factors influence vital signs, the most useful data are obtained with measures taken at periodic intervals rather than at a one-time assessment. This will allow changes in patient status or response to treatment to be monitored over time, as well as indicate an acute change in status at a specific point in time.

For purposes of physical therapy assessments, documentation of vital sign data is typically included within the narrative format of the note. Use of a graph to record this information may prove a useful adjunct to the physical therapy record. Regardless of the system of documentation selected, of critical importance is that it allow easy comparison of serial entries over time.

the point where blood first begins to flow through the artery and represents the **systolic pressure;** deflections in the dial or column of mercury will now be noted.

13. Continue to release air carefully. Note the point on the manometer when the sound first becomes muffled; this is the first **diastolic pressure.**
14. Continue to release air gradually.
15. Note the point on the manometer when the sound disappears and deflection ceases; this is recorded as the *second diastolic pressure.*
16. Allow remainder of air to release quickly.
17. If the same examiner is using the stethoscope again, it is not necessary to clean the earpieces; however, the diaphragm of the stethoscope should always be cleaned between patients.
18. Record results.

Assessing Popliteal (Thigh) Stethoscope Pressure

Lower extremity readings are indicated in situations in which comparisons between the upper and lower extremities is warranted, such as peripheral vascular disease. They also are used when upper extremity pres-

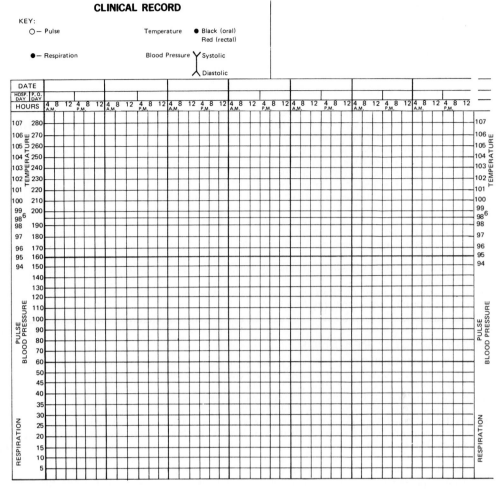

Figure 4–17. Graphic record sheet for recording vital signs. (From Saperstein and Frazier,[1] p 483, with permission.)

QUESTIONS FOR REVIEW

1. Identify the reasons for monitoring vital signs.

2. Why are vital sign values more significant when monitored as a serial process rather than as a one-time assessment?

3. Describe the primary mechanisms by which the body conserves and produces heat.

4. Differentiate the four primary heat loss mechanisms: radiation, conduction, convection, and evaporation.

5. Describe daily occurrences that can either increase or decrease body temperature.

6. Describe the procedure for assessing oral temperature using a standard clinical glass thermometer.

7. Describe the procedure for assessing axillary temperatures using a standard clinical glass thermometer.

8. Define pulse rate, rhythm, and volume.

9. What factors influence the pulse?

10. Describe the procedure for assessing both radial and apical pulses.

11. What parameters are addressed during a respiratory assessment? Define each.

12. What factors will influence respiration?

13. Describe the following respiratory patterns: Cheyne-Stokes, Kussmal's, apneustic breathing, and paradoxical breathing.

14. Describe the procedure for assessing respiration.

15. What factors influence blood pressure?

16. What are the five phases of Korotkoff's sounds?

17. What changes will be noted in blood pressure readings if an inappropriate size cuff is used?

18. Describe the procedure for assessing blood pressure using a stethoscope and sphygmomanometer.

REFERENCES

1. Saperstein, AB and Frazier, MA: The assessment of vital signs. In Saperstein, AB and Frazier, MA (eds): Introduction to Nursing Practice. FA Davis, Philadelphia, 1980, p 452.

2. Wolf, L, Weitzel, MH, and Fuerst, EL: Fundamentals of Nursing, ed 6. JB Lippincott, Philadelphia, 1979.

3. Judy, WJ: Energy metabolism, temperature regulation and exercise. In Selkurt, EE (ed): Basic Physiology for the Health Sciences, ed 2. Little Brown, Boston, 1982, p 513.

4. Guyton, AC: Human Physiology and Mechanisms of Disease, ed 5. WB Saunders, Philadelphia, 1992.

5. McArdle, WD, Katch, FI, and Katch, VL: Exercise Physiology: Energy, Nutrition, and Human Performance, ed 3. Lea & Febiger, Philadelphia, 1991.
6. Berger, RA: Applied Exercise Physiology. Lea & Febiger, Philadelphia, 1982.
7. Anthony, CP and Thibodeau, GA: Textbook of Anatomy and Physiology. CV Mosby, St. Louis, 1983.
8. Thomas, CL (ed): Taber's Cyclopedic Medical Dictionary, ed 16. FA Davis, Philadelphia, 1989.
9. Kozier, B and Erb, G: Fundamentals of Nursing: Concepts and Procedures, ed 3. Addison-Wesley, Menlo Park, CA, 1987.
10. Watson, JE (ed): Medical-Surgical Nursing and Related Physiology, ed 2. WB Saunders, Philadelphia, 1979.
11. DuGas, BW: Introduction to Patient Care: A Comprehensive Approach to Nursing, ed 4. WB Saunders, Philadelphia, 1983.
12. Dolan, JT: Cardiovascular assessment. In Dolan, JT (ed): Critical Care Nursing: Clinical Management Through the Nursing Process. FA Davis, Philadelphia, 1991, p 751.
13. Bates, B: A Guide to Physical Examination, ed 4. JB Lippincott, Philadelphia, 1988.
14. Lunsford, BR: Clinical indicators of endurance. Phys Ther 58:704, 1978.
15. Amundsen, LR: Assessing exercise tolerance: a review. Phys Ther 59:534, 1979.
16. Leger, L and Thivierge, M: Heart rate monitors: validity, stability, and functionality. Physician Sports Med 16, 1988.
17. Wilson, LM: Normal respiratory function. In Price, SA and Wilson, LM (eds): Pathophysiology: Clinical Concepts of Disease Processes, ed 4. McGraw-Hill, New York, 1992, p 515.
18. Selkurt, EE: Respiration. In Selkurt, EE (ed): Basic Physiology for the Health Sciences, ed 2. Little Brown, Boston, 1982, p 324.
19. Jarvis, CM: Assessing pulse, respiration and blood pressure. In Sorensen, KC and Luckmann, J (eds): Basic Nursing: A Psychophysiologic Approach, ed 2. WB Saunders, Philadelphia, 1986, p 525.
20. Jarvis, CM: Vital signs: how to take them more accurately and understand them more fully. Nursing 76:31, 1976.
21. Grable, L: Physical assessment. In Morton, PA (ed): Health Assessment in Nursing, ed 2. Springhouse, Springhouse, PA.
22. Diekelmann, N, et al: Fundamentals of Nursing. McGraw-Hill, New York, 1980.
23. Ford, PJ: Anatomy of the cardiovascular system. In Price, SA and Wilson, LM (eds): Pathophysiology: Clinical Concepts of Disease Processes, ed 4. McGraw-Hill, New York, 1992, p 371.
24. Webster, J, et al: Influence of arm position on measurement of blood pressure. BMJ 288:1574, 1984.
25. Kozier, B and Erb, G: Techniques in Clinical Nursing: A Comprehensive Approach. Addison-Wesley, Menlo Park, CA, 1982.
26. Kirkendall, WM, et al: Recommendations for Human Blood Pressure Determination by Sphygmomanometers. American Heart Association, Dallas, 1980.

SUPPLEMENTAL READINGS

Andzel, WD and Busuttil, C: Metabolic and physiological responses of college females to prior exercise, varied rest intervals and a strenuous endurance task. J Sports Med 22:113, 1982.
Astrand, P-O and Rodahl, K: Textbook of Work Physiology: Physiological Bases of Exercise, ed 3. McGraw-Hill, New York, 1986.
Baruch, IM and Mossberg, KA: Heart-rate response of elderly women to nonweight-bearing ambulation with a walker. Phys Ther 63:1782, 1983.
Britten, MX: Monitoring body temperature and understanding its significance. In Sorensen, KC and Luckmann, J (eds): Basic Nursing: A Psychophysiologic Approach. WB Saunders, Philadelphia, 1979, p 626.
Bye, PTP, Farkas, GA, and Roussos, CH: Respiratory factors limiting exercise. Ann Rev Physiol 45:439, 1983.
Carlson, KK and Snyder, ML: Vital sign assessment. In Craven, RF and Hirnle, CJ (eds): Fundamentals of Nursing: Human Health and Function. JB Lippincott, Philadelphia, 1992, p 348.
Davis, C and Lentz, M: Circadian rhythms: charting oral temperatures to spot abnormalities. J Gerontol Nurs 15:34, 1989.
Dewitt, S: Nursing assessment of the skin and dermatological lesions. Nurs Clin North Am 25:235, 1990.
Driscoll, DJ, et al: Functional single ventricle: cardiorespiratory response to exercise. J Am Coll Cardiol 4:337, 1984.
Erickson, R and Yount, S: Comparison of tympanic and oral temperatures in surgical patients. Nurs Res 40:90, 1991.
Fraser, C and Filler, MJ: The assessment factor most nurses forget. RN 52:32, 1989.
Green, JF: Fundamental Cardiovascular and Pulmonary Physiology, ed 2. Lea & Febiger, Philadelphia, 1987.
Greer, M, Dimick, S, and Burns, S: Heart rate and blood pressure response to several methods of strength training. Phys Ther 64:179, 1984.
Giuffre, M, Heidenreich, T, Carney-Gersten, P, Dorsch, J, and Heidenreich, E: The relationship between axillary and core body temperatures. Appl Nurs Res 3:52, 1990.
Grabbe, L: Physical assessment skills. In Morton, PG (ed): Health Assessment in Nursing, ed 2. Springhouse, Springhouse, PA, 1993, p 71.
Guyton, AC: Textbook of Medical Physiology, ed 8. WB Saunders, Philadelphia, 1991.
Hanson, M: Drug fever: remember to consider it in diagnosis. Postgrad Med 89:167, 1991.
Hedemark, LL and Kronenberg, RS: Chemical regulation of respiration: normal variations and abnormal responses. Chest 82:488, 1982.
Hill, M and Grim, C: How to take a precise blood pressure. Am J Nurs 91:38, 1991.
Hollerbach, AD and Sneed, NV: Accuracy of radial pulse assessment by length of counting interval. Heart Lung 19:258, 1990.
Iveson-Iveson, J: Students' forum-vital signs 4: blood pressure. Nurs Mirror 154:41, 1982.
Iveson-Iveson, J: Students' forum-vital signs 2: pulse taking. Nurs Mirror 154:28, 1982.
Iveson-Iveson, J: Students' forum-vital signs 3: respiration. Nurs Mirror 154:31, 1982.
Jennett, S, Lamb, JF, and Travis, P: Sudden large and periodic changes in heart rate in healthy young men after short periods of exercise. BMJ 285:1154, 1982.
Jette, DU: Physiological effects of exercise in the diabetic. Phys Ther 64:339, 1984.
Metzger, B and Therrien, B: Effect of position on cardiovascular response during the Valsalva maneuver. Nurs Res 39:198, 1990.
Rebenson-Piano, M, et al: An evaluation of two indirect methods of blood pressure measurements in ill patients. Nurs Res 39:42, 1989.
Shangold, M and Mirkin, G: Women and exercise: physiology and sports medicine. FA Davis, Philadelphia, 1988.
Sulzbach, LM: Measurement of pulsus paradoxus. Focus Crit Care 16:142, 1989.
Wenger, NK (ed): Exercise and the Heart. FA Davis, Philadelphia, 1985.
Vander, AJ, Sherman, JH, and Luciano, DS: Human Physiology: The Mechanisms of Body Function, ed 5. McGraw-Hill, New York, 1990.

GLOSSARY

Anorexia: Loss of appetite.
Apnea: Absence of respirations, usually temporary in duration.
Biot's respirations: Breathing pattern that alternates between periods of apnea and hyperapnea (increased rate and depth).
Blood pressure: Tension exerted by the blood on the walls of a vessel.
Bradycardia: Abnormally slow (low) pulse rate; below approximately 50 beats per minute.
Bradypnea: Decreased respiratory rate; less than 10 breaths per minute.

Cheyne-Stokes respiration: Breathing pattern characterized by a gradual increase in rate and depth followed by a gradual decrease; periods of apnea occur between cycles.

Circadian rhythm: Variations in vital sign values that occur on a regular and predictable 24-hour cycle.

Cyanosis: Dusky, bluish, gray, or dark purple tinge of the skin and mucous membranes; caused by abnormally high amounts of reduced hemoglobin in the blood.

Diastole: Period of relaxation of the ventricles of the heart; the muscle fibers lengthen and the heart dilates.

Diastolic pressure: The pressure of the blood during relaxation (diastole) of the ventricles.

Dyspnea: Difficult or labored breathing, sometimes accompanied by pain; normal following vigorous physical activity.

Eupnea: Normal, effortless breathing.

Febrile: Pertaining to a fever; state of elevated body temperature.

Fever: Elevated body temperature.

Fever, types of
1. **Intermittent fever:** Temperatures alternate between pyrexia and normal or subnormal temperatures within a 24-hour period; an intermittent fever with fluctuations between high and low temperatures is termed a hectic fever.
2. **Relapsing (recurrent) fever:** Periods of pyrexia that alternate with normal temperatures; periods may last for a day or more.
3. **Remittent fever:** Fluctuations in temperature above normal without returning to normal between fluctuations.
4. **Sustained (constant) fever:** Consistently elevated temperature with little or no fluctuation.

Homoiotherm (homoiothermic): An animal whose body temperature remains relatively constant regardless of the temperature of the external environment; a warm-blooded animal.

Hyperpnea: Increased rate and depth of respiration.

Hyperpyrexia: Extremely high fever; temperature reading of 41.1°C (106°F) or greater.

Hypertension: Higher than normal blood pressure.

Hyperthermia: Extremely high fever; temperature reading of 41.1°C (106°F) or greater.

Hyperventilation: Increase in the rate and depth of respiration.

Hypopnea: Abnormal decrease in both rate and depth of respiration.

Hypotension: Lower than normal blood pressure.

Hypothermia: Body temperature below average normal range.

Hypoventilation: Decrease in the rate and depth of respiration.

Orthopnea: Difficulty breathing in positions other than upright sitting and standing.

Poikilotherm (poikilothermic): An animal whose body temperature varies with that of the external environment; a coldblooded animal.

Pulse, common terms used to describe
1. **Alternating (pulsus alterans):** Fluctuation between a weak and a strong beat.
2. **Bigeminal:** Two regular pulse beats followed by a long pause.
3. **Bounding:** A pulse that is difficult to obliterate; usually owing to high blood volume within a vessel; artery has a feeling of tension on palpation (SYN: full, high-tension).
4. **Dicrotic:** A pulse that feels double on palpation; caused by prolonged ending of the pulse wave; also may be perceived as a weak wave between two beats.
5. **Intermittent:** Pulse that occasionally skips a beat.
6. **Irregular:** Pulse that varies in both force and rate.
7. **Paradoxical (pulsus paradoxus):** Decreased amplitude of the pressure wave with inspiration and return to full amplitude on expiration.
8. **Thready:** Fine and barely perceptible pulse; easily obliterated (SYN: filiform, weak).
9. **Trigeminal:** Three regular pulse beats followed by a pause.
10. **Waterhammer:** Strong, jerky pulse of short duration that suddenly collapses (SYN: Corrigan's pulse).
11. **Weak:** Fine and barely perceptible pulse; easily obliterated (SYN: filiform, thready).

Pulse deficit: The difference between the apical and radial pulses.

Pulse pressure: The difference between the diastolic and systolic pressures.

Pyrexia: Increased body temperature; fever.

Pyrogen: Fever-producing substance.

Systole: Period during which the ventricles of the heart are contracting.

Systolic pressure: The pressure of the blood during contraction (systole) of the ventricles.

Tachycardia: Abnormally rapid (high) pulse rate; over approximately 100 beats per minute.

Tachypnea: Increased respiratory rate; greater than 24 breaths per minute.

Tidal volume: Volume or amount of air exchanged with a single breath.

Vital signs: The signs of life; that is, pulse, body temperature, respiration, and blood pressure (SYN: cardinal signs).

Valsalva maneuver: An attempt to exhale forcibly with the glottis, nose, and mouth closed; causes increased intrathoracic pressure, slowing of the pulse, decreased return of blood to the heart, and increased venous pressure.

Assessment and Treatment Planning Strategies for Musculoskeletal Deficits

Daniel A. Dyrek

OBJECTIVES

1. Provide a conceptual definition of musculoskeletal dysfunction as a foundation for therapeutic intervention.
2. Describe a brief rationale for the onset of musculoskeletal dysfunction and its relationship to pain, tissue dysfunction, and functional impairment.
3. Identify the principles of the musculoskeletal assessment process.
4. Define the type of forces used to provoke tissues and structures during a musculoskeletal assessment.
5. Describe techniques for provocation of selected tissues and structures.
6. Describe the components of the generic assessment process for upper and lower quarter musculoskeletal pain and dysfunction.
7. Describe three classification schemes for musculoskeletal pain and dysfunction and the applicable treatment strategy for each scheme.
8. Describe the individual goals of a generic treatment strategy for musculoskeletal pain and tissue dysfunction.

This chapter presents principles and strategies of musculoskeletal assessment and treatment planning. The material is relevant to any patient with a deficit of musculoskeletal origin. Orthopedic or musculoskeletal problems exist with any type of movement dysfunction regardless of which body system might be initially or primarily responsible for the patient's problem. The musculoskeletal component may be primarily responsible for the chief complaint, the contributing factor to it, or perhaps a result of it. The physical therapist must be knowledgeable and skilled in performing a thorough orthopedic screening assessment. Therefore, material in this chapter is appropriate for the therapist working with any type of patient population, including patients with burns, neurologic, cardiopulmonary, or musculoskeletal conditions, or any other condition in which movement dysfunction is present.

This chapter begins by identifying the goals of the musculoskeletal assessment and introduces the concept of the prerequisite knowledge base that the therapist must possess prior to assessing the patient. The forces applied during assessment and their effects, the differential assessment of tissue, and types of mobility deficits are discussed. A generic screening examination outline and assessment section serve to further illustrate the assessment process. The chapter concludes with a discussion of treatment goals and strategies.

PRINCIPLES OF ASSESSMENT

Purpose of the Assessment

The three primary purposes of the musculoskeletal physical therapy assessment are (1) to identify the specific lesion responsible for the patient's chief complaint of pain and functional impairment, (2) to assess the integrity and performance of the involved tissues and structures, and (3) to determine the patient's functional ability during daily, occupational, and recreational activities.

The first purpose of the assessment stems from the fact that pain is commonly the primary reason a patient seeks treatment. The initial goal is to identify the source of the pain by performing **provocation tests** (application of controlled external forces to impose an internal load) to isolated tissues and structures known to be capable of causing the patient's symptoms. Maitland[1] describes this process, in relation to examining joints, as identifying a **comparable sign.** The sign is the result of the provocation test, that is, pain, tenderness, restricted motion, or muscle spasm. The sign must correspond to the patient's symptoms. It is used as an indicator of treatment efficacy by reexamining it after treatment.

The second purpose of the examination is to assess the integrity and functional status of the involved tissues and structures. The tissues of the body combine to form a structure that performs a function. The clinician examines the structure to assess its ability to perform its role. For example, muscle fibers and collagen tissue compose the structure of the myotendon unit. Its function is to provide movement and stability of body parts. The clinician assesses the strength of the myotendon unit. The muscle is examined for its torque-producing capacity and the tendon is examined for its load-transmitting capacity. The clinician continues by examining other structures that ultimately combine with the myotendon unit to provide a means of function for the body as a whole.[2]

The third purpose is to assess the functional abilities of the patient during activities of daily living, occupational tasks, and leisure activities. The ultimate goal of physical therapy practice is to restore the maximal functional status of the patient as permitted by the integrity and performance of the tissues and structures of the body. The parameters of clinical testing to assess function must be based initially in the assessment of the individual tissues and structures of the body. Because the individual body components will ultimately combine to permit integrated function, these components must be assessed in the examination process. The attention to this level of assessment will permit a more realistic prognosis and secondarily determine the sequence for treatment. In addition, it will allow enhanced classification of patients for research purposes to determine the efficacy of treatment. For example, the patient with a balance disorder who also possesses dysfunction of the talocrural joint and weakness of the flexors of the first metatarsophalangeal joint will require a prognosis for improving balance, which incorporates the potential to resolve the musculoskeletal dysfunction in the foot and ankle complex. The sequence of treatment suggests addressing the musculoskeletal dysfunction prior to, or simultaneously with, depending on the degree of the findings, treating the balance disorder. The prognosis and projected duration of required treatment will be different for this patient compared to the patient with a balance disorder but without accompanying musculoskeletal dysfunction. Specific classification of dysfunction in patients will enhance the practice of physical therapy, for example, during clinical decision making, research on treatment efficacy, and interaction with the third party payers of patient care.

Periodic reexamination of the comparable sign, the functional status of the tissues, and the overall functional abilities of the patient provides a more objective measure of progress than measurement of a patient's symptoms. Symptoms can fluctuate widely in frequency, intensity, location, and correlation with activity. The patient's psychologic, cultural, and environmental influences can affect the perception of symptom behavior and intensity. The symptoms alone can be a misleading indicator of treatment success in dealing with mechanical lesions of the musculoskeletal system.

This concept is illustrated in the following example. A wheelchair-dependent patient with a spinal cord injury complains of diffuse shoulder pain. The musculoskeletal assessment of the shoulder complex reveals that the specific lesion causing the pain is tendonitis of a rotator cuff. The assessment of the functional status of the tissues and structures reveals diminished strength and abnormal glenohumeral capsular length and flexibility. These factors result in impairment of joint mobility. All of the above deficits culminate in functional loss: the patient is unable to propel a wheelchair. Several comparable signs may be identified in this example. The first is reproduction of the patient's pain from application of manual resistance augmented by palpation loads to the involved myotendon unit, with resulting tensile stress to the lesion. The second is the elicitation of pain by passive range of motion toward internal rotation to stretch the involved tissue, again to cause a tensile load. The third sign is restricted shoulder abduction, resulting in pain from impingement of the rotator cuff. A fourth sign is the restricted anteroinferior glide of the humeral head on the glenoid fossa owing to capsular fiber shortening, which results in reduced abduction. Throughout a course of treatment, these four signs, identified in the initial exam, are reassessed periodically to measure the effect of treatment.

Establishing the Provisional Assessment

The clinical decision-making process involved in assessing musculoskeletal tissues as the source of pain is often unclear territory. Although clinical tests are based on the applied sciences of physiology, anatomy, and biomechanics, and are coupled with the knowledge of the natural course of signs and symptoms for generic and specific orthopedic lesions, many of the individual musculoskeletal tests are unreliable in incriminating a specific tissue as the cause of pain or dysfunction. This makes the first goal of the orthopedic examination a difficult task. A single positive test does not confirm the presence of a lesion. Confirmation may be obtained by correlating the results of multiple tests, and by performing multiple tests administered over a period of time to test the variability of a test response. Several repetitions may be made during a single examination session or during subsequent sessions with the patient.[3] Refer to Chapter 1 for further reading on the process of making clinical decisions.

Because of the lack of clear and immediate confirmation of the patient's problem, the clinician may have to establish a provisional assessment on which to plan treatment. The patient's response to treatment is continually monitored by the therapist; if progress is occur-

EXAMINATION PROCESS FOR THE PATIENT WITH A MUSCULOSKELETAL DEFICIT

1. Clinician requires knowledge of:
   - Anatomy
   - Kinesiology
   - Pathokinesiology
   - Physiology
   - Pathophysiology

   - Symptomatology of musculoskeletal disorders
   - Clinical manifestation of musculoskeletal disorders
   - Conceptual models of musculoskeletal dysfunction

2. Clinician acquires knowledge of principles of the musculoskeletal examination

Training Stage

3. Clinician acquires skill in musculoskeletal examination techniques

- -

Performance Stage

4. Patient presents with unknown lesion as cause of primary complaint, i.e., pain and/or dysfunction resulting in functional limitation

5. Clinician conducts examination

   a. History of condition and behavior of symptoms is obtained

   b. Examination test is administered to identify or provoke an isolated tissue structure.

   c.1. Positive finding suggests involvement of one or more tissues or structures

   c.2. Negative finding temporarily diminishes suspicion of tissue involvement.

   d.1. Administer further tests to isolate a specific tissue

   d.2. Administer further tests to provoke tissue to ensure no involvement

   e. Lesion identified; etiology of primary complaint is known

   f. Evaluate effect of lesion on the functional status of tissues "and Structures" (range of motion, strength, soft tissue flexibility, joint mobility)

   g. Evaluate the functional ability of the patient

6. Assessment obtained by correlating information

7. Goals identified

8. Treatment plan initiated

9. Clinician monitors effect of treatment (repeat steps 5–8)

Figure 5–1. Examination process for the orthopedic patient.

ring, treatment should continue based on the initial provisional assessment. If, however, no benefit is being derived, the therapist must reexamine the patient and establish an alternative plan of care. The assessment of a patient's condition may sometimes be confirmed only after treatment is successful (Fig. 5–1).

Skill is required to choose the necessary tests while avoiding the loss of valuable time with irrelevant tests. This process is promoted by performing a thorough patient interview so that a provisional assessment of the patient's condition can be made prior to the actual physical examination. Subsequently, the physical therapist selects tests that correlate with the suspected etiologies of the patient's primary complaint.

Musculoskeletal Dysfunction

The model of orthopedic dysfunction presented in Figure 5–2 provides a framework that is used throughout this chapter.[4] It is an alternative to the traditional medical model that focuses on the etiology and treatment of disease. It provides an outline for the etiology of tissue dysfunction, impairment of musculoskeletal structures, and functional disability of the patient. The model recognizes the static and dynamic qualities of tissue dysfunction. The following definition establishes a concep-

tual framework for use in clinical decision making and in studying common and divergent components of different treatment techniques and supporting rationale. It expands on an existing definition of dysfunction as "abnormal function."[5]

Musculoskeletal dysfunction is a pathophysiologic and pathokinesiologic condition of tissues and structures in the musculoskeletal system.[6] The condition can alter the properties and function of periarticular and extraarticular soft tissue, resulting in symptoms, signs, impairment, disability, and handicap. The tissues of the body involved in this process are referred to as the "soft tissues" and consist of the dermis, muscle, tendon, ligament, capsule, nerve, blood vessel, fascia, periosteum, and such unique structures as the intervertebral disc and pubic symphysis. It may be useful, under certain circumstances, to think of bone and cartilage as "soft tissues" also, because of their ability to deform and respond over time.

Dysfunction of soft tissue implies induration, shortening, weak tissue strength, lengthening, or a combination of these (Fig. 5–3) that results in altered mechanical, nutritional, and neurophysiologic states. Dysfunction of extraarticular and periarticular tissue results in premature, latent, absent, diminished, or excessive loading of tissues and structures, subsequently impairing normal function.

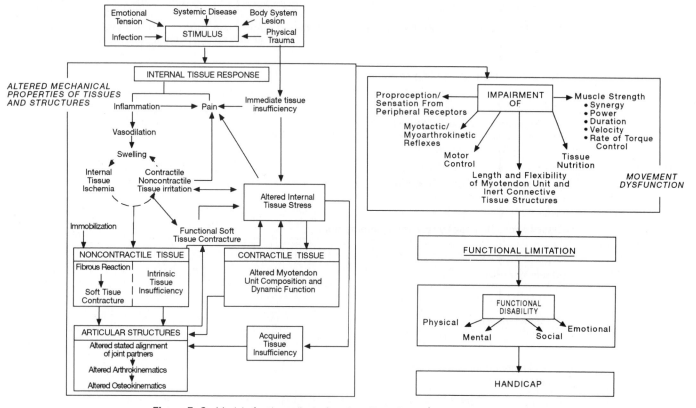

Figure 5–2. Model of orthopedic dysfunction. (From Dyrek,[4] p 5, with permission.)

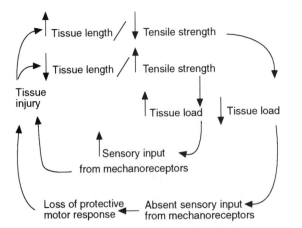

Figure 5–3. Sequelae of altered internal tissue stress resulting from length and strength deficits. (From Dyrek,[6] p 2, with permission.)

Soft tissue dysfunction is one condition producing four general categories of problems that form the basis of intervention in physical therapy practice. The categories are
1. Pain
   • Chemical origin
   • Mechanical origin
2. Contracture, tissue induration
3. Instability, tissue insufficiency
4. Weakness
   • Motor control
   • Tissue weakness

This definition addresses the fundamental level at which the physical therapist intervenes during patient management.[7] Numerous physiologic implications of orthopedic dysfunction impact on clinical decision making during examination and management of the patient.[6]

Prerequisite Knowledge Base

Prior to conducting a musculoskeletal assessment, the clinician must possess a thorough knowledge of anatomy, kinesiology, pathokinesiology, physiology, pathophysiology, and symptomatology and physical presentation of musculoskeletal disorders (Fig. 5–1). With this knowledge, the examiner has the information to effectively plan and execute the assessment process. For example, as a patient relates his or her history to the skilled therapist, the therapist can mentally prepare a list of possible disorders, pathophysiologic or pathokinesiologic in nature, that could exist as the primary cause of the patient's problem. The tests necessary to provoke the tissues of the body segment under consideration are dictated by the list of possible abnormal conditions. The clinician can focus the examination process based on each individual patient's history of problems and present symptoms. The clinician also can eliminate specific tests as inappropriate, given a thorough history and report of symptoms. Objectivity, however, must be exercised to avoid biased suspicion of a specific pathology as the cause of the patient's problem. Inexperienced ther-

apists may look and test for what they expect to be present instead of remaining objective during the examination. The experienced examiner will continually compare physical findings with the established mental list of suspected conditions and will readily add or delete such conditions as the examination proceeds. Payton,[3] and Barrows and Tamblyn,[8] provide further insight into the reasoning process used in clinical practice. The physical therapist should have prerequisite knowledge of the areas of musculoskeletal assessment, described in the following discussion, to promote a thorough examination process.

CLINICAL MANIFESTATIONS OF GENERAL MUSCULOSKELETAL CONDITIONS

Many common musculoskeletal conditions may be found during the examination of different lesions. Muscle spasm, soft tissue density abnormalities, tenderness in various portions of contractile and noncontractile tissue, effusion, and edema are a few examples of common musculoskeletal conditions. The clinician must be knowledgeable of the generic signs and symptoms the patient will describe in each case and learn to recognize the manner of clinical presentation for each condition.

For example, swelling as described by the patient can present two ways, as either edema or effusion. **Edema** is the presence of excessive fluid in the soft tissues of the body and is external to the joint capsule. **Effusion** is excessive fluid within the joint. The therapist must learn to differentiate between these two types of swelling to effectively manage the course of treatment.

CLINICAL MANIFESTATIONS OF SPECIFIC MUSCULOSKELETAL CONDITIONS

The physical signs and symptoms of the numerous possible lesions in the body segment under consideration must be known. Given this knowledge, the therapist can clarify the patient's report of symptoms through careful and meticulous interviewing, thereby compiling a concise list of conditions as the possible causes of the patient's problem.

For example, the therapist must know the signs and symptoms for various lesions that may be responsible for pain in the elbow region. Then the therapist can mentally compare the patient's signs and symptoms with the possible lesions capable of transmitting pain to the elbow. The tissues and structures and related body parts must be considered during this comparison process. From this process, the most probable causes of the patient's complaint can be identified, and an assessment process can be planned and carried out that will narrow the possibilities to a single clear assessment.

NATURAL COURSE OF GENERAL AND SPECIFIC MUSCULOSKELETAL CONDITIONS

Once the patient's problem has been identified, clinical treatment planning proceeds. The natural course of a lesion is the path that it will follow if no clinical intervention occurs. Basically, the clinician must decide whether the condition and its sequelae can heal optimally without treatment or if it requires a therapeutic program.

For example, a diagnosis of an isolated muscle strain may not require any treatment other than rest. Rest diminishes the physical stress to the lesion and promotes healing of the muscle tissue. The patient is scheduled for reexamination after the estimated time period necessary to allow the lesion to heal. This reexamination allows the therapist to examine for residual deficits that may impair function and elicit pain in the future.

A second example illustrates the need to alter the natural course of a lesion through an aggressive treatment program. The patient with hemiplegia found to have chronic effusion of the talocrural joint due to a contracture may have permanent and progressive symptoms. Permanent damage to soft tissue and joint structures of the talocrural joint and surrounding area can occur due to the weight-bearing force imposed on the altered joint. Secondarily, pain and reflex inhibition of neighboring musculature may occur in this patient. Therefore, intensive restorative musculoskeletal treatment should be implemented as a component of the total rehabilitation program.

Awareness of the natural course for a known condition also allows the clinician to determine the potential efficacy of treatment measures. A realistic prognosis can then be formulated for the patient, and appropriate treatment goals and an appropriate treatment plan can be established.

ELEMENTS OF THE EXAMINATION PROCESS

Types of Force Applied During the Examination Process

The musculoskeletal examination process seeks to provoke isolated tissues and structures of the musculoskeletal system, including peripheral nerves, to determine their role in the patient's pain and dysfunction. Tissue provocation is accomplished by the examiner applying a controlled external force to impose an internal load on the tissue. This internal load is called **stress.** The mechanical effect of the stress, that is, deformation of the tissue, is referred to as **strain.** The application of stress, and its resultant effect of strain, is the primary method by which the examiner can reproduce the patient's pain and identify abnormal tissue responses and integrity.

Different types of tissue demonstrate unique stress-strain curves based on their physical composition. Figure 5–4 illustrates the relative behavior of three different types of tissue. The clinician must acquire the skill to determine the normalcy of the response for numerous tissues. (The reader is referred to the Supplemental Readings for further information on the mechanical behavior of connective tissue.)

During the examination process, the clinician controls the variables of applying an external force while palpating and observing the response of the tissue. The external force can be modified by altering the

1. magnitude of the force
2. duration of force application
3. velocity of application
4. frequency of application

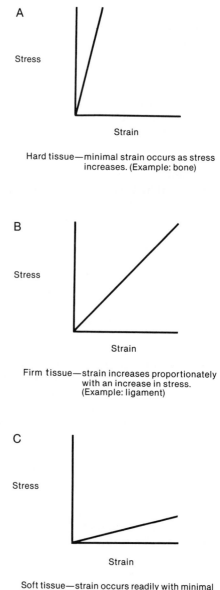

A

Stress

Strain

Hard tissue—minimal strain occurs as stress increases. (Example: bone)

B

Stress

Strain

Firm tissue—strain increases proportionately with an increase in stress. (Example: ligament)

C

Stress

Strain

Soft tissue—strain occurs readily with minimal stress. (Example: muscle)

Figure 5–4. Relative stress-strain curves for three different tissue types.

5. location of force application and the degree of pretest tension in the tissue
6. direction of force(s) application

Each of these variables can be manipulated by the examiner to thoroughly assess a specific tissue.

Following are several examples that illustrate this concept:

1. A low-magnitude stretching force may be insufficient to elicit pain in a tissue with a low-grade inflammatory process; however, a higher-magnitude force may elicit a patient's symptom.
2. A short duration load on internal tissue caused by stretching may not yield a pain response in a condition of chronic scar tissue, whereas a prolonged duration of load may elicit pain.
3. A slow velocity of force application may fail to elicit signs and symptoms, whereas a high rate of force application may yield positive findings.
4. A single application of a force may not elicit pain but repetitive applications of the same magnitude of force may then elicit the patient's pain.
5. The importance of the location of force application and the degree of pretest tension in the tissue can be illustrated by considering the condition of patellar tendonitis. A positive finding of tenderness may be found only at the tendoperiosteal attachments, a weak link in the force transmission system, rather than in the body of the tendon. Also the degree of knee flexion, which alters the degree of tendon stretch, will affect the level of load in the tendon prior to adding additional stress by palpation. For example, palpation of the tendon may not elicit tenderness with the knee in full extension with the tendon in a relatively slack position; but palpation may reveal tenderness in a position of 90-degree knee flexion where the tendon is more tense.
6. The direction of force applied by the examiner will affect how the tissue is loaded and, therefore, the result of the test. For example, referring again to a case of patellar tendonitis, a palpation force applied perpendicular to the anterior tendon in the sagittal plane may be negative, whereas a "shear" force applied perpendicular to the medial or lateral edge of the tendon in the coronal plane may elicit a positive pain response. (Points 5 and 6 illustrate the concept of assessing tissue flexibility and its ability to resist tissue-deforming loads in the sagittal, coronal, and horizontal planes and along the long axis of the tissue.)

The therapist must consider each of the variables and their combinations during the application of a force to the tissue for the purpose of examination. Only then can the clinician eliminate the tissue as a source of the patient's complaint. The types of tissue response and their clinical significance are discussed in this chapter in the section on tissue response.

COMPRESSION

Compression is a load that pushes the fibers of a material together along its long axis; it results in, or tends to cause, a shortening and widening of the material (Fig. 5–5A).[9,10] Clinically, the application of a com-

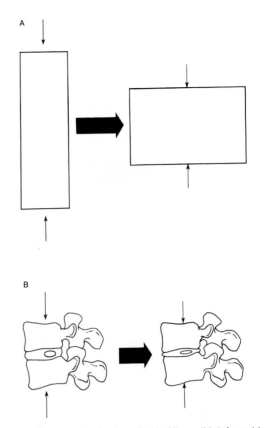

Figure 5–5. Compression load applied to (A) a solid deformable object and applied to (B) a vertebral segment, resulting in deformation of the intervertebral disk.

pression load can approximate two tissues or structures, creating an abnormal location or intensity of force and subsequently eliciting tissue irritation and pain. Examples are the loading of articular cartilage in the weight-bearing joints of the lower extremity while standing, or a component of the load imposed on the intervertebral disc while sitting (Fig. 5–5B). During examination, compression loads are applied to joint surfaces to elicit pain and to determine the quality of the joint surface.[11]

TENSION

Tension occurs when an internal load imposed by forces acting in opposite directions results in the tendency to elongate or in the actual elongation of the fibers in a material. The elongation is accompanied by narrowing of the fiber (Fig. 5–6A). Tension is imposed on the quadriceps mechanism when it is passively stretched during simultaneous hip extension and knee flexion. Tension also occurs while applying resistance to the contraction of a muscle. Clinically, tension imparted to a joint will distract the joint surfaces (see Fig. 5–6B). The capsuloligamentous component of the joint will be subject to a tensile load. The application of this load can be used diagnostically to determine the presence of tissue inflammation in the fibers of the capsule, as indicated by the elicitation of pain. The clinical application of this type of load can be used for therapeutic purposes to restore the length of capsular fibers in the presence of a contracture.

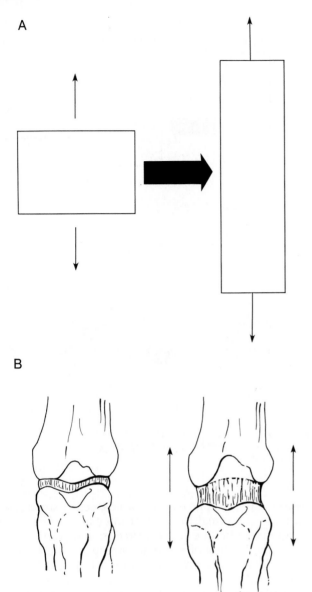

Figure 5–6. Tension load applied to (*A*) a solid deformable object and applied to (*B*) the capsuloligamentous tissue of a joint, resulting in elongation of the tissue and distraction of the joint surfaces.

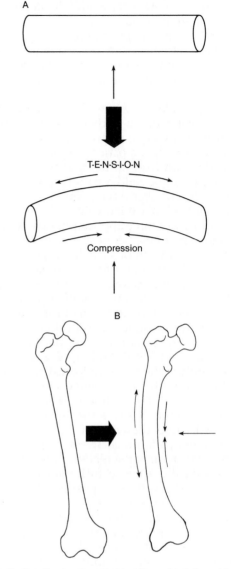

Figure 5–7. Bending load applied to (*A*) a solid deformable object and applied to (*B*) the femur. A force applied medially to the thigh creates a laterally directed load, resulting in bending of the femur.

BENDING

Bending occurs when the application of a load imposed along the length of a tissue or structure causes deformation around an axis perpendicular to the long axis of the material. The bending effect will occur at an unsupported point in the material. A pattern of deformation occurs characterized by the creation of a tension load on the convex surface and a compression load on the concave side of the material (Fig. 5–7A). For example, a force imposed medially on the thigh creates a laterally directed load, resulting in bending of the femur (see. Fig. 5–7B). A high magnitude load that exceeds the intrinsic strength of the bone would result in a fracture. A load applied for a long duration would result in remodeling of the bone until it assumed a static curved contour.

TORSION

Torsion is a force that creates a twisting of the material around its long axis (Fig. 5–8). For example, rotation of one vertebral segment imposes a torsional load on the intervertebral disc. Repetitive high-magnitude torsional loading to the disc can result in tissue failure or tears of its outer ring, the annulus fibrosis. Subsequently the vertebral segment can develop an altered degree and pattern of motion allowing the segment to become a source of symptoms.

Clinically, the loads applied are often a combination of the forces described previously. Through the skillful application of these forces, the examiner attempts to selectively load skin-fascia, muscle, tendon, myotendon and tendoperiosteal junctions, capsule, ligament, bursa, joint surfaces, and select peripheral nerves. The ability to isolate the force to a specific tissue or structure is

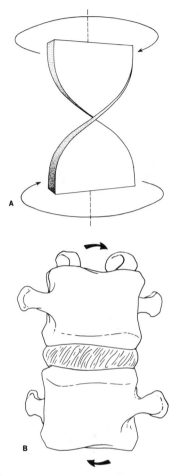

Figure 5–8. Torsion load applied to (*A*) a solid deformable object and applied to (*B*) an intervertebral disk.

influenced by accessibility; therefore, some body parts, such as the spine, are more difficult to examine than others.

Tissue Responses

The application of external force to tissue of the musculoskeletal system permits the therapist to detect the tissue in which pain originates, tenderness exists, and to determine the quantity and quality of tissue resistance.

TISSUE REACTIVITY

The external force applied by the clinician imposes an internal load on the tissue. Inflamed tissue subjected to such load can evoke the perception of pain by the stimulation of peripheral nociceptors and mechanoreceptors. As will be explained in the next section, active, passive, and resisted motions will impose an internal tissue load. Normal healthy tissue will not evoke pain when subjected to a load, unless a force of sufficient magnitude or duration is applied to exceed the load-bearing characteristics of the tissue. The clinician assesses the degree of **tissue reactivity** during the examination.

This information will assist in categorizing the lesion, that is, acute, subacute, or chronic, and secondarily to determine the appropriate level of force the patient could sustain during treatment without aggravating symptoms and the condition of the tissue. The degree of tissue reactivity also should be considered when advising the patient on safe levels of participation in activities of daily living and occupational tasks.

In addition to monitoring the patient's report of pain, the quality of resistance during passive motion imparted by the tissue to the palpating fingers is assessed by the clinician. Several characteristics of the resistance should be considered:

1. the presence of pain accompanying the resistance
2. the point in the range where resistance is felt
3. the type of resistance

TISSUE RESISTANCE

Tissue resistance, the stiffness perceived by the clinician, while performing passive motion or loading may be felt at several points in the range of motion: premature, normal, latent, or absent. A predicted range of motion exists for the tested body segment in comparison with the opposite extremity, other joints of the body, and in regard to the general population. If the end point of resistance is met prematurely, then the tissue or joint is restricted. Similarly, when the resistance occurs at some point beyond the predicted range, the tissue has excessive length or the joint is hypermobile. The anticipated resistance to motion can be absent, as in the case of a total rupture of a ligament. The appropriate treatment plan is dictated by the individual finding. If restricted tissue is found during examination, stretching techniques should be performed to restore tissue length and flexibility. In the presence of articular tissue elongation resulting in a hypermobile joint or elongated soft tissue, suitable treatment would be to provide stability to the joint via strengthening-stabilizing exercises, an orthosis, or surgical repair.

Tissue Density Assessment

Localized changes in tissue density can occur as sequelae of orthopedic dysfunction. The clinical significance of these deficits is described earlier in the chapter. Assessment of density is performed via palpation. The palpation should be performed in a three-dimensional or triplanar manner under conditions of rest; various lengths as controlled by passive motion; and tension as created by active contraction. For example, tissue induration may be palpable only when a myotendon unit is elongated, or tenderness at a myotendon junction may be present when palpation of the junction is performed during an isometric contraction, whereas the tenderness is absent at rest. A thorough exam requires screening for soft tissue abnormalities with a full spectrum of tissue-loading parameters.

Pain

The pattern of pain accompanying resistance during passive range of motion yields valuable diagnostic and prognostic information. Cyriax[12] describes three patterns that can occur:

1. *Pain before resistance.* Pain occurs prior to reaching the extreme of available motion. This pattern is suggestive of an acute inflammatory lesion of either extraarticular or articular origin.
2. *Pain simultaneous with resistance.* Suggestive of a subacute inflammatory process.
3. *Resistance prior to pain.* Pain is not elicited at the point of resistance, rather, overpressure must be applied to elicit pain; that is, a greater force to passively stretch the tissues beyond the physiologic range. A normal synovial joint can tolerate overpressure without eliciting pain. This pattern is indicative of a mild or chronic lesion that could tolerate aggressive treatment.

Thorough assessment of a joint requires that the pattern of pain and resistance be correlated with the point where the normal resistance to motion is expected to occur.

Type of Resistance: End-Feels

The type of resistance, that is, the **end-feel,** felt by the examiner when passively stretching a joint and its associated soft tissues provides important diagnostic and prognostic information. The end-feel is felt at the extreme of the available range of motion as the clinician imposes **overpressure** to the joint and tissues. Numerous authors have described various end-feels.[12–14] Both physiologic and pathologic end-feels exist in peripheral and spinal joints.

Normal end-feels. Kaltenborn[13] describes three normal physiologic end-feels that possess an elastic quality of varying degrees:

1. *Soft.* Limitation is due to soft tissue approximation (e.g., knee flexion) or soft tissue stretching (e.g., ankle dorsiflexion with knee extension).
2. *Firm.* Limitation of action is due to soft tissue stretching of the less resilient capsule and ligament (e.g., external rotation of the humerus).
3. *Hard.* Limitation is due to bone-on-bone approximation (e.g., elbow extension).

Table 5–1 presents a summary of normal end-feels.

Pathologic or abnormal end-feels. A pathologic end-feel may be the normal type of resistance anticipated for the joint under examination but occurring prematurely or late in the range of motion, or it could be an abnormal type of resistance for the joint.

Following are examples of pathologic end-feels:

1. *Muscle spasm.* Characterized by a fairly abrupt stop with a mild "rebounding" sensation.
2. *Boggy.* Soft, "mushy" resistance (e.g., effusion).
3. *Springy.* A "rubbery" rebound with firm, unyielding resistance (e.g., displaced meniscus at the tibiofemoral joint).
4. *Empty.* The patient voluntarily prevents the passive motion or requests the motion to cease secondary to severe pain. No tissue resistance is felt by the examiner.
5. *Capsular.* Firm limitation, yet resilient with maintained force; occurs prematurely in the range of motion.
6. *Bony block.* A sudden, abrupt limitation of motion; no "giving" sensation occurs with prolonged pressure (e.g., osteophyte limiting joint motion).
7. *Laxity.* Loose; excessive mobility beyond the normal anatomic range of motion.

Differential Assessment of Soft Tissue Lesions by Motion

Three types of motion—active, passive, and resistive—provide valuable information by isolating the source of the patient's symptoms and assessing the functional status of tissues and structures. The results of each motion test are compared to reveal the

1. location, type, and intensity of pain
2. type of tissue responsible for the reproduction of pain
3. location of the lesion
4. strength
5. willingness and ability of the patient to perform a motion

Cyriax[12] developed the following scheme to assess soft tissue lesions. He classified tissues as either inert or contractile and explained how they reacted to the three types of motion. **Contractile tissues** make up the myotendinous unit and its attachments—specifically muscle, tendon, periosteum, and the bursa. These tissues can elicit pain when internal tension is produced by a muscle contraction during active and resistive motion, and by the stretch imposed on the tissue during passive motion. **Noncontractile tissues,** also known as **inert tissues,** are those that are not capable of a contraction and therefore are not inherently capable of producing their own internal load: the load must be applied by a passive force external to the tissue. The inert tissues are the joint capsule, ligaments, fascia, bursa, nerves (peripheral and root), dura mater, blood vessels, articular cartilage, and bone.

Subsequently, Cyriax[12] elucidated the following results of selectively applying tension to the two types of tissue by each motion.

1. *Active movement.* Active movement involves the loading of inert and contractile tissue simultaneously, so a specific type of tissue cannot be incriminated as

Table 5–1 NORMAL END-FEELS[1,15–18]

Type	Anatomic Limitation to Motion	Joint Motion Example
1. Hard	Bone in contact with bone	Elbow extension
2. Soft	Soft tissue approximation	Elbow and knee flexion
3. Firm	Joint capsule	Shoulder and hip rotation
	Muscle	Hip flexion with the knee extended (straight leg raise)
	Ligaments	Forearm supination

Adapted from Norkin, CC and White, JD: *Measurement of Joint Motion: A Guide to Goniometry.* FA Davis, Philadelphia, 1985.

the location of the lesion. However, this motion does serve a useful purpose. It can grossly identify

   a. the body segment where pain is originating

   b. the patient's ability and willingness to move

   c. where in the range of motion the pain occurs

   d. the effect of movement on the intensity of pain

   e. the pattern of motion—normal or abnormal

   f. the amount of functional movement available to the patient to execute activities of daily living (ADL) and occupational tasks

2. *Passive movement.* Passive movement tests the inert structures. The clinician controls which structure is loaded and then applies overpressure at the extreme of the available range of motion. The pattern of pain accompanying the onset of resistance should be noted. Passive motion provides a gross assessment of the length of extraarticular and periarticular soft tissue.

3. *Active and passive motion combinations.* Two specific patterns of active and passive motions exist to identify further the type of tissue responsible for the symptoms.

   a. Active and passive motions are restricted or painful in the same direction. This pattern is indicative of a capsular or arthrogenic lesion.

   b. Active and passive actions are restricted or painful in opposite directions. This pattern is indicative of a contractile tissue lesion. Resistive motion is indicated to further incriminate the tissue.

4. *Resistive movement.* The manual application of resistance to motion performed by the patient permits the clinician to assess strength and to isolate contractile tissue as a source of pain.

Strength is assessed as a gross indicator of the contractile tissue's ability to produce torque. The clinician uses the information for diagnostic purposes and as a predictor of functional ability.

Strength is assessed by resisting an isometric contraction performed midway between the available ranges of motion. This point is chosen to avoid simultaneously loading inert tissue, which could result in pain and impair the patient's ability to produce maximal resistance. A grading system is provided in Table 5–2 for clinical recording of the strength assessment. Specific positions are utilized to isolate individual muscles for testing.[15]

Table 5–2 NUMERICAL GRADING SYSTEM FOR STRENGTH ASSESSMENT

0	No palpable or observable contraction.
1	Trace muscle contraction is palpable; no body part motion is observed.
2	Full range of motion with gravity eliminated; minimal range of motion is present against gravity.
3	Full range of motion is present against gravity.
4	Full range of motion is present against gravity with considerable resistance to motion provided by examiner.
5	Full range of motion is present against gravity with strong resistance to motion provided by examiner.

(+) and (−) symbols can be used to provide finer discrimination between the above criteria.

Following a gross assessment of strength as described previously, the clinician can test for strength under various conditions to more adequately assess the contractile tissue function. A determination can be made of the effect of myotendon length on strength by examining it in shortened and lengthened positions. Other variables of manual testing such as velocity of resistance, duration, and repetitions can be manipulated by the examiner. Advanced strength assessment using equipment such as an isokinetic dynamometer permits testing of the variables already discussed under concentric, isometric, and eccentric conditions.

Resistance to motion also can be used to test the contractile tissue as a source of pain. The controlled application of resistance to contractile tissue creates an internal load to the tissue. The load can reproduce the patient's typical pain when an inflammatory lesion is present. This is what Maitland describes as a "comparable sign."[1]

Resisted motion is used to aid in the assessment of tissue reactivity. The technique is identical to the strength testing consideration addressed above. When assessing for tissue reactivity, it is of critical importance to ensure that the isometric contraction is resisted at the midpoint of a joint's range of motion. This will prevent the loading of inert tissue, which must be avoided. The force created by the resisted contraction will compress the articular surfaces; however, articular cartilage, an inert tissue, is not innervated, so it cannot elicit pain.

Four patterns of pain and strength exist to provide additional information regarding the tissue:

1. Painful and strong indicates a minor lesion.
2. Painful and weak indicates a major lesion.
3. Painless and weak indicates a lesion of neurologic origin or a total rupture of a myotendinous unit.
4. Painless and strong indicates normal function.

Capsular and Noncapsular Patterns of Restricted Motion

When testing the patient's range of motion, the clinician must be aware of the possible capsular and noncapsular patterns of restricted motion that can occur in a joint. The assessment of the patient's lesion and its therapeutic management are dependent on the therapist's ability to differentiate between these two sources of restricted mobility.

Cyriax[12] has described a **capsular pattern** as a characteristic pattern of restricted motion owing to a diffuse arthrogenic etiology. The length and flexibility of capsular fibers are impaired in this pattern secondary to an intraarticular inflammatory process. Fibrosis of the capsular tissue occurs as a natural sequela of the healing process in inflamed tissue. The resulting capsular pattern of restriction is specific for each joint, regardless of the initial cause or underlying disease generating the inflammation. Table 5–3 lists capsular patterns of the upper and lower extremity joints as identified by Cyriax.[12]

The capsular pattern must be contrasted with a pattern

Table 5–3 CAPSULAR PATTERNS OF EXTREMITY JOINTS

Shoulder (glenohumeral joint)	Maximum loss of external rotation
	Moderate loss of abduction
	Minimum loss of internal rotation
Elbow complex	Flexion loss is greater than extension loss
Forearm	Full and painless
	Equally restricted in pronation and supination in presence of elbow restrictions[13]
Wrist	Equal restrictions in flexion and extension
Hand	
Carpometacarpal joint I	Abduction and extension restriction
Carpometacarpal joints II–V[13]	Equally restricted in all directions
Upper extremity digits	Flexion loss is greater than extension loss
Hip	Maximum loss of internal rotation, flexion, abduction
	Minimal loss of extension
Knee (tibiofemoral joint)	Flexion loss is greater than extension loss
Ankle (talocrural joint)	Plantarflexion loss is greater than extension loss
Subtalar joint	Restricted varus motion
Midtarsal joint	Restricted dorsiflexion, plantarflexion, abduction and medial rotation
Lower extremity digits	
Metatarsalphalangeal joint I	Extension loss is greater than flexion
Metatarsalphalangeal joints II–V	Variable, tend toward flexion restriction
Interphalangeal joints	Tend toward extension restriction

of limitation resulting from reasons other than a capsular contracture. The **noncapsular pattern** can be caused by random ligamentous adhesions, internal joint derangement, and extraarticular lesions such as a shortened muscle. Diffuse arthritis, that is, circumferential inflammation of the joint, and its sequelae, are not present in this pattern. So, unlike the capsular pattern for a given joint, the noncapsular pattern is variable. For example, two noncapsular patterns of restricted knee motion can occur in directly opposite directions. The pattern for the knee joint owing to internal derangement caused by a torn meniscus can be a loss of extension; however, a lack of flexion is demonstrated in the presence of a shortened quadriceps mechanism.

The two patterns are not mutually exclusive. The clinician must examine for both and design treatment strategies to address all components of restricted motion.

Accessory Joint Motion

This topic is included in the chapter to acquaint the reader with a fundamental, but sometimes overlooked, level of the physical examination. It is not intended to emphasize the topic over other components of the exam process.

Extremity and spinal synovial joints and some cartilaginous joints possess accessory joint motion. This type of motion is the necessary "slack" in a mechanical system, whether it is in a person or in a constructed system. For example, a kitchen drawer is capable of sliding on its tracts; however, on closer inspection one finds that some play in the sliding mechanism permits a degree of side-to-side and up-and-down movement. The play is essential for normal operation of the drawer. The joints of the body require the same "slack" or joint play.

The joint play exists because
1. Articular surfaces are not perfectly congruent; that is, the shape of the opposing joint surfaces are not symmetrical.
2. Strict degrees of freedom of motion do not exist. The concept of a joint complex moving around another to a maximum of three axes is a basic but inadequate explanation of joint mechanics. Innumerable axes exist in a joint during the range of motion of bone shafts.

Accessory joint motion is a prerequisite for normal, full asymptomatic and friction-free movement. It is not under voluntary control. The term **arthrokinematics** refers to this accessory joint motion, that is, the intrinsic, intracapsular motion occurring between adjacent joint surfaces. A loss of accessory joint motion (i.e., joint dysfunction) can result in a loss of range of motion and **osteokinematics,** the rotatory motion of a bone shaft. Normal accessory joint motion cannot be restored by the muscle activity of active or resisted motion nor by passive rotatory motion. An exception to this situation would be when the soft tissue restriction responsible for the joint dysfunction possesses low tensile strength. In most cases, the intrinsic mechanics of a joint must be passively restored by the clinician. The techniques of joint mobilization are used for examination and treatment of accessory joint motion.

Attempts to restore osteokinematic range of motion or strength prior to restoring the accessory joint motion can result in joint inflammation, pain, effusion, hemarthrosis, capsuloligamentous laxity, and fracture. It is hypothesized that the prolonged use of an extremity demonstrating joint dysfunction can result in degenerative joint disease.

An example to illustrate this is the observable lack of digit mobility in a patient 2 months after tissue trauma to the finger. The restricted motion may be accompanied by pain, effusion, and impaired function. On closer examination, the second metacarpophalangeal joint exhibits an osteokinematic restriction of flexion. An accessory joint motion assessment demonstrates impaired anterior gliding and distraction of the proximal phalanx on the metacarpal. The first goal of treatment is to restore the anterior glide and distraction of the phalanx. In the absence of extracapsular contributions to restricted motion, achievement of this goal may restore the joint flexion, reduce the pain, permit the effusion to resolve, and improve the functional use of the hand. The need for additional treatment measures would be assessed on an individual basis.

Screening Assessment

The following sections pertain to the process of conducting a screening assessment of the upper and lower quarters of the body. The concept of structuring an assessment process by body quadrants is clinically appropriate because

1. Pain is commonly referred from a lesion site to another location.
2. Multiple tissues and structures of a body quadrant are capable of referring pain to the same location.
3. A regional examination permits differential assessment of the tissues and structures for identification of the actual lesion site.

The upper quarter consists of all structures and soft tissues superior to the third thoracic segment; that is, the craniocervicomandibular complex, the cervicothoracic spine, tissues of the superior thorax, and the entire upper extremity. Neck motions require the participation of the superior thoracic vertebrae, hence the inclusion of the first three thoracic vertebrae in the upper quarter. The lower quarter consists of the inferior thoracic spine and the associated soft tissues and structures, the entire lumbopelvic region, and one of the lower extremities. The inferior thoracic region (to approximately T-10) is included in the lower quarter because of its neurologic sensory contribution to the lumbopelvic region and its facet joint alignment, which permits it to function like an extension of the lumbar spine (Table 5–4).

Exceptions exist to a strict dichotomy between the upper and lower quarters of the body; for example, a total body postural assessment is indicated in the examination of either quarter. The relative importance of the midthoracic area to the patient's symptoms will determine the depth of the assessment to be conducted in this region.

For purposes of this discussion, only the major points of a screening assessment for either body quarter will be addressed. The reader is encouraged to consult the Supplemental Readings for further examination techniques.

PATIENT INTERVIEW FOR HISTORY AND SUBJECTIVE REPORT

A thorough interview of the patient permits the therapist to establish a mental list of provisional diagnoses that aids in carrying out a coordinated and logical examination sequence. The physical examination will either support or contravene the possible diagnoses until one is identified as the primary etiology. Throughout the examination process the therapist continually adds or deletes provisional diagnoses as the source of the patient's symptoms.

The examiner must acquire skill in guiding an interview so that contradictory or vague information can be clarified without eliciting responses that the patient feels are expected to occur. The interviewer must remain objective, for only without bias to any particular diagnosis can the patient be examined adequately.

The initial step in the interview is obtaining the history of the patient's primary complaint, which establishes a background to better understand present symptoms. The evolution of the problem—its behavior over time, the effect of previous treatment, and so forth—allows various lesions to be suspected as the etiology of the complaint. Next, the subjective report is conducted, in which the patient describes current symptoms. The symptoms and their behavior are noted, to permit a comparison with those of known problems; this aids in establishing and refining a mental list of possible lesions. Symptoms can fluctuate over time and with activity or different postures, so it is the responsibility of the examiner to obtain a thorough understanding of the patient's symptoms. If symptoms appear to fluctuate widely, then the clinician needs to question the patient about them over a longer duration of morbidity until a clear pattern is determined. Similarly, the therapist must consider the effect of a wide scope of activities and postures when symptoms initially appear to be either erratic or unaffected by the patient's present activity level.

The documentation of symptoms at the time of the initial examination establishes a baseline from which the effect of treatment can be monitored. However, it should be noted that the success of initial treatment measures is not based solely on the status of symptoms. During early stages of intervention, the effect of treatment may be based on the status of neuromusculoskeletal tissues and the integrated mechanics of soft tissues and joint structures, with an anticipated change in symptoms to follow.

History of Present Condition

The following outline can guide the examiner in obtaining a thorough history of the present condition and a subjective report of symptoms from the patient. The information is appropriate for the examination of the upper or lower body regions.

1. Patient's age and sex.
2. If the patient has been referred by a physician or dentist, obtain the physician's assessment and the reason for the referral to physical therapy.

Table 5–4 COMPONENTS OF THE UPPER AND LOWER QUARTERS OF THE BODY

Upper Quarter*
1. Cranium
2. Temperomandibular joints
3. Cervical spine
4. Superior thoracic spine (to approximately T3–4)
5. Ribs
6. Sternum
7. Upper extremity†—clavicle, scapula, brachium, antebrachium, wrist, hand, digits

Lower Quarter
1. Inferior thoracic spine‡ (from approximately T10)
2. Lumbar spine
3. Pelvis—sacrum and ilia
4. Lower extremity—thigh, leg, ankle, foot, digits

---

*Includes the bone, articular cartilage, capsuloligamentous complex, muscles, tendon, periosteum, nerves, dura, blood vessels, and fascia.

†The body quarter is referred to as left or right by the side of the extremity under examination.

‡The relative importance of the midthoracic region to the patient's symptoms will determine the extent of the examination to be conducted in this region.

3. Briefly delineate the patient's primary complaint.
4. Obtain the history of the present condition.
   a. Date of initial onset and any related exacerbations.
   b. Mode of onset—traumatic, acquired, or congenital. Identify the specific precipitating event whenever a traumatic onset is reported by the patient.
   c. Dates and results of previous examinations by other health care practitioners, medical tests, and medical imaging studies.
   d. Dates and results of previous treatment measures. Inquire about the effect of rest, physical modalities, medication, manual treatment, exercise, orthotics, injection, and surgery (include date, procedure, and postoperative course).
5. Past medical history—obtain information regarding any problems or events related to the primary complaint.
   a. Musculoskeletal or neurologic trauma, disease, or dysfunction of a local or related body part.
   b. Any known congenital anomalies.
   c. Previous surgery on a related body segment.
6. Secondary medical problems—the clinician must be aware of disease processes that mimic signs and symptoms attributable to the musculoskeletal system.[19] The following body systems should be screened for any deficits:
   a. Cardiac
   b. Respiratory
   c. Neurologic
   d. Vascular
   e. Metabolic
   f. Dermatologic
   g. Visual
   h. Gastrointestinal/genitourinary
   i. Endocrine
7. Medication—type, frequency, dosage, and effect. The examiner should be aware that
   a. Present use of analgesic or antiinflammatory agents may reduce the level of symptoms during the initial examination.
   b. Prolonged use of corticosteroid drugs is associated with osteopenia and reduced tensile strength of connective tissue, that is, ligaments. These adverse effects of medication must be considered as possible contributing factors to the patient's complaint. If these problems are suspected, the examiner should avoid applying excessive force over the lever of a long bone shaft to prevent a fracture or ligament tear.
   c. The use of anticoagulant medication may render the patient susceptible to contusions and hemarthrosis. Consequently, the clinician should monitor the application site and magnitude of force applied during both examination and treatment when the patient is using this type of medication.
8. Occupation—obtain an ergonomic description of the work environment, tasks, activities, and postures. Inquire about the level of psychologic tension perceived by the patient related to occupational responsibilities (when appropriate to the primary complaint).

9. Social situation.
   a. Marital and family status.
   b. Home architecture (see Chapter 12: Environmental Assessment).

Subjective Report of Symptoms

The goal of this section is to obtain a description of the patient's pain or physical problem through information provided voluntarily by the patient and elicited by the therapist during the interview. The following lists some of this information:
1. Anatomic location of primary and secondary pain sites (Fig. 5–9).
2. Description of pain sensation(s).
3. Frequency and duration of pain.
4. The effect of time, rest, activities of daily living, and occupational demands on the pain or problem. Generic questions useful in obtaining this information follow:
   • Where is your pain? Does it ever "travel?" Has your pain always been in the present location?
   • What does your pain feel like? Is it always the same? If not, what changes it?
   • Do you always have pain? If so, does it fluctuate, and what causes it to do so? If you don't continually have pain, when are you free of pain? Full of pain?
   • Has your pain or problem been getting worse, staying the same, or getting better since it started?
   • If activity affects your pain, then describe which activities worsen or improve your symptoms.
   • Do you experience joint swelling? Spasm? Joint clicking or crepitus? If so, is pain associated with it?
5. Motor or sensory symptoms—obtain information suggestive of upper or lower neuron deficits. Questions useful in obtaining this information include:
   • Do you experience any weakness? If so, where and when? Is it constant or intermittent?

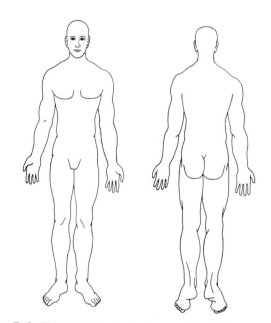

Figure 5–9. This type of body chart can supplement the patient's verbal description of the location of the pain.

- Do you experience numbness, tingling, burning, shooting pain, or any patches of sensitive skin? If so, where and when?
- Do you experience hot or cold sensations in your arms or legs?
- Do you experience any muscle twitching?
- Do you sometimes drop objects?
- Do your arms or hands shake when you reach to pick up an object? When you are at rest?

6. Vascular symptoms or signs.
    - Do you experience constant or intermittent discoloration of your hands and feet? If so, when?
    - Do you experience hot or cold sensations in your arms or legs?
    - Do you experience swelling in your arms or legs?

7. Functional assessment—identify the patient's past and present levels of function and the effect of functional activity on the behavior of symptoms (see Chapter 11: Functional Assessment).
    a. Activities of daily living
        - Hygiene
        - Dressing
        - Food acquisition
        - Food preparation
        - Household maintenance
        - Ability to use transportation services
        - Ambulation
    b. Occupational tasks—identify the effect of the occupational demands (as identified in the section on history of the present condition, mentioned previously) on the patient's symptoms.
    c. Recreational activity—identify the type and frequency of activity.

    The therapist should correlate the physical requirements of functional tasks with the patient's symptoms and physical status. This comparison allows recommendations for safe and asymptomatic levels of activity.

8. Obtain the physiologic and functional goals the patient wishes to derive from treatment.

The information above must be supplemented with additional questions based on suspected etiologies. Comprehension of the knowledge base, described earlier in this chapter as being prerequisite to the performance of an examination, is essential to interview the patient adequately.

Musculoskeletal Examination

The purpose of this section of the assessment process is to examine for normal and abnormal findings of the musculoskeletal and peripheral neurologic systems. The information already provided in this chapter should be applied during the examination process.

The components of the screening examination are outlined below.

1. *Vital signs.* When appropriate, assess heart rate, blood pressure, and respiratory rate (see Chapter 4: Assessment of Vital Signs).
2. *Mental Status.* Assess the patient's orientation to time, place, and person.
3. *Inspection.*
    a. Posture. Conduct a total body postural assessment. Perform this with the patient in a standing position to impose a weight-bearing load on the body. A triplanar assessment is conducted for all body segments, joints, and bone shafts. Triplanar assessment refers to visual inspection of body parts in the sagittal, coronal, and horizontal planes. Inspection should be performed from anterior, posterior, and lateral views.

        A plumb line should be used to establish a central reference point for inspection from each view. Following are the proximal fixation points for the plumb line:
        - Mental protuberance of the mandible for the anterior view
        - Anterior margin of the mastoid process on the temporal bone for the lateral view
        - External occipital protuberance (inion) on the occipital bone for the posterior view

        The therapist should compare the observed findings with normal postural alignment.
    b. Extremity girth. Measure to assess for muscle atrophy or hypertrophy and swelling. The circumference of the limb should be measured at regular intervals along the long axis of the body part. A prominence of bone is used as a reproducible landmark for reassessment of the patient's status.
    c. Soft tissue edema. Assess for extraarticular soft tissue swelling.
    d. Joint effusion. Assess for intracapsular joint swelling.
    e. Skin condition. Observe for dry or moist skin, callus formation, flaking, color changes, hair distribution, and uniformity of appearance.
    f. Nail condition. Observe for broken or ridged nails; the size, color, and any abnormal shape such as club-shape (convex) or spoon-shape (concave) should also be noted. Conditions of the nail are indicative of its nutritional status.
    g. Muscle spasm, guarding, and protective splinting. Each is characterized by abnormal timing, degree, or duration of isolated muscle contraction. Spasm is present when a constant contraction exists with the body part in both weight-bearing and non-weight-bearing positions. Muscle guarding is characterized by constant contraction while the body part is weight-bearing, voluntarily moved, or subject to external forces, but is absent in a non-weight-bearing position. Protective splinting is a brief reflexive contraction of muscle that occurs during movement.
    h. Observe general body movement during the interview portion of the examination. Inspect and observe for postures used by the patient to relieve symptoms, and for postures capable of contributing to symptoms.
4. *Palpation.*
    a. Assess for soft tissue tenderness, flexibility, and density—including skin, fascia, muscle, ligament, and tendon. Apply palpatory forces parallel and perpendicular to the long axis of the structure.

b. Examine for joint line tenderness and masses.

c. Swelling should be noted, and a differentiation made between edema and effusion.

d. Temperature of the skin should be assessed, using the back of the palpating hand over a lesion or the distal extremities.

5. *Range of motion.*

a. Active and passive range of motion is assessed for the joint(s) primarily and secondarily contributing to the problem.[16] Note the presence of capsular versus noncapsular patterns of restricted motion.

b. Note end-feel and pain response during passive range of motion with overpressure (see section on tissue response).

c. Assess accessory joint motion, its end-feel and pain response.[1,13]

6. *Muscle strength.*

a. Conduct a thorough assessment of strength by manual resistance to the body segment under examination.[15] Note the elicitation of pain from manual resistance applied to contractile tissues.

b. Conduct a gross assessment of strength for body segments related to the area possessing the primary lesion. If deficits are identified, then conduct a more thorough assessment.

c. Observe for compensatory trunk or limb movements in the presence of muscle weakness.

d. When appropriate, assess muscle torque capabilities at a higher level of function by conducting an isokinetic dynamometry assessment of strength under concentric and eccentric loading conditions at varying velocities of movement.[17,18,20]

7. *Neurologic assessment.*

a. Sensation. Basic forms of sensation to be routinely assessed are superficial tactile sensation (light touch), superficial pain (pin prick), temperature, and vibration (see Chapter 6: Sensory Assessment).

b. Motor. Conduct an upper or lower quadrant myotomal assessment, depending on the body region under examination. A positive finding of weakness may indicate involvement of a specific nerve level (Table 5–5).

c. Deep tendon reflexes. Test the muscle stretch reflex as elicited by a rapid striking of the muscle's tendon. The deep tendon reflexes routinely assessed in each quarter are found in Table 5–6.

d. Pathologic reflexes. Assess for upper motor neuron disease or lesions of the corticospinal tracts. For example, the Babinski reflex is elicited by stroking the lateral plantar surface of the foot. A positive response is extension of the first digit and fanning of the other digits.

e. Proprioception. Assess for passive motion sense and static position sense. *Passive motion sense* (kinesthesia) is the ability of the patient to perceive the direction of passive limb or digit movement without visual stimuli. The patient can be asked to describe verbally the commencement, direction, or cessation of motion or to mimic the direction and degree of motion with the contralateral body part. *Static position sense* is the ability of

the patient to mimic the position of a body part after the therapist has passively moved the part.

f. Peripheral nerve provocation tests. The examiner imposes an external force on a peripheral nerve, thereby creating internal load in the nerve. A positive finding of pain or paresthesia can be elicited in a compressed or inflamed nerve. For example, to elicit the ulnar nerve Tinel sign, the nerve is palpated within the groove between the medial epicondyle of the humerus and the ulna bone of the medial elbow region. A positive finding is local tenderness and referred pain, and/or paresthesia along the distal route of the nerve.

8. *Specific tests.* An important section of the examination involves the execution of select musculoskeletal tests. The type of tests and extent of testing are dependent on the nature of the chief complaint, symptoms, and previous physical examination results. Some examples are:

a. In the presence of spinal pain, the therapist should elect to perform passive intervertebral mobility testing (PIVM). This procedure assesses the quantity of motion at a vertebral segment. The quality of accompanying tissue responses, as dis-

Table 5–5 MYOTOMES

Upper Quarter Myotomes

Level	Action to Be Tested	Muscle
C-5	Shoulder abduction	Deltoid
C-5, C-6	Elbow flexion	Biceps
C-7	Elbow extension	Triceps
C-8	Ulnar deviation	Flexor carpi ulnaris
		Extensor carpi ulnaris
T-1	Digit abduction/adduction	Interossei

Lower Quarter Myotomes

Level	Action to Be Tested	Muscle
L-2, L-3	Hip flexion	Iliopsoas
L-3, L-4	Knee extension	Quadriceps
L-5	Ankle dorsiflexion	Anterior tibialis
	Extension of great toe	Extensor hallucis longus
S-1	Plantarflexion	Gastrocnemius

Table 5–6 DEEP TENDON REFLEXES

	Root Level	Muscle	Peripheral Nerve
Upper quarter:	C5-6	Biceps	Musculocutaneous
	C5-6	Brachioradialis	Radial
	C-7	Triceps	Radial
Lower quarter:	L3-4	Quadriceps	Femoral
	S1	Gastrocnemius	Sciatic (tibial)

The degree of reflex activity is graded on a 0 to 4 scale. Grades are awarded based on a predicted response and comparison of responses between body halves.

0 = no reflex response
1 = minimal response
2 = moderate response } normal range
3 = brisk, strong response
4 = clonus

cussed earlier in this chapter, is important to monitor.

b. Ligament stress tests use the application of varus and valgus stress to the elbow complex to assess the medial and lateral collateral ligaments. The degrees of varus and valgus motion, joint gapping and pain are compared with the contralateral extremity.

These tests are performed routinely for a few joints but for others would be dependent on earlier examination results.

c. When the therapist suspects the presence of a thoracic outlet syndrome, a full battery of tests would be performed. The tests attempt to differentiate between vascular and neurogenic causes of thoracic outlet syndrome. Representative tests include Adson's test, the pectoralis minor test, the costoclavicular test, and the quadrant maneuver.

9. *Gait.* Conduct a triplanar assessment of each body region (see Chapter 10: Gait Analysis).

10. *Function.* Conduct an interview regarding, and when feasible assess, the patient's ability to perform activities of daily living, occupational tasks, and recreational activities. Assess for limitations secondary to pain, endurance, strength, or mobility restrictions. Assess for modifications in the method of task performance, assistive devices, or home and/or work environment that the patient may have made to facilitate functional abilities.

Assessment Summary

The examination process is completed with the formulation of a determination of the patient's chief complaint and its contributing factors. The completed assessment is a summary of all pertinent historical, subjective, and physical findings. It is a correlation of normal and abnormal findings to establish a specific identification of the patient's primary complaint, that is, pain and/or dysfunction. The examination findings are compared against known pathologies for the body segment under consideration. As mentioned earlier in this chapter, the therapist must develop a thorough knowledge base of musculoskeletal and peripheral neurologic pathologies. The symptoms and clinical manifestations of these pathologies must be known before they can be used for comparison in the examination process. The completed assessment will dictate the goals and course of treatment.

The primary factors to be included are

1. The mode of onset—traumatic, acquired, or congenital
2. The primary etiology of the chief complaint, that is, pain or functional limitation: a diagnosis
3. The stage of symptoms
4. Contributing factors to the primary etiology
5. Prognosis from physical therapy measures
6. Duration and frequency for the course of treatment

The mechanism of onset for the patient's symptoms assists the therapist in determining the prognosis, goals, and treatment plan. The prognosis for restoring a patient's comfort and functional capacity can be limited by the presence of congenital deficits of the musculoskeletal system. For example, a patient who suffers a sprain of the medial collateral ligament in the knee can experience a delay in healing secondary to the presence of a congenital valgus deformity, which imposes excessive mechanical stress to the medial tissues of the knee. The prognosis is more favorable if the sprain is unaccompanied by congenital deficits. Generally, a patient who reports a specific recent event as the initial cause of symptoms may have a more favorable prognosis than the patient with an insidious onset. Naturally, all the variables of duration of symptoms, mechanism of onset, extent of tissue involvement, effect of previous treatment, and the clarity in delineating the effect of activity and static postures on symptoms will influence the prognosis.

The assessment should establish the stage of the patient's condition. The basic classifications of acute, subacute, and chronic conditions provide valuable information regarding the patient's ability to tolerate mechanical loads such as those imposed by daily activity or by a therapist during treatment. The classification of a patient's condition is assisted by considering the duration of symptoms since the time of initial onset. An acute stage of symptoms may exist for 48 to 72 hours after onset, whereas the subacute stage may persist from 2 weeks to several months after the onset of initial symptoms. Symptoms can be considered chronic after approximately 3 to 6 months. The significance of the duration of symptoms, however, may not allow a clear assessment of the patient's condition. For example, the patient may be experiencing an acute exacerbation of a chronic lesion at the time of the initial examination. The classification of the condition implies the degree of reactivity of involved tissues to forces applied during routine activities of daily living, occupational tasks, and recreational activity. Similarly, it permits the clinician to estimate the amount of force, frequency, and duration of a treatment plan that would not exceed the tolerance of the tissue and subsequently aggravate the symptoms. The physical therapist involved in treatment of musculoskeletal pain and dysfunction must acquire the skill to determine the reactivity of tissue, inasmuch as the basis of treatment often is to impose physical force. For example, a patient with a spinal cord injury who reports the onset of shoulder pain only after propelling a wheelchair over a 5-mile racecourse obviously has a shoulder that is less reactive to mechanical stresses than the patient who develops acute shoulder pain after performing a transfer from bed to a wheelchair. The former patient can be expected to tolerate a more aggressive treatment approach than the latter patient.

Another reason for classifying the reactivity of a lesion is to assist the clinician in establishing a prognosis. The acute lesion can be expected typically to demonstrate more spontaneous improvement than the chronic lesion. Conversely, chronic symptoms of low intensity and that are mildly reactive to mechanical loads imposed by daily activities can be expected to respond less dramatically to treatment.

In addition to formulating a prognosis for recovery,

classification of the lesion allows the clinician to determine the goals of treatment for the patient. A goal of obtaining a pain-free functional status for the patient with a 2-year history of shoulder pain and dysfunction may be inappropriate, whereas it would be feasible to expect the industrial worker with a recent initial episode of shoulder pain to achieve such a goal.

Treatment also can be based appropriately on the stage of the lesion. The methods, frequency, duration, and intensity of treatment are chosen with the knowledge of the patient's ability to tolerate the effects of these variables on his or her tissues and perception of pain.

A treatment approach should be formulated to address specific problems in the diagnosis. Treatment must address a specific lesion, since the treatment on the basis of symptoms alone can result in frustration for both the patient and the therapist. Symptoms are unreliable as a sole indicator for the effect of treatment because they are subject to variability in intensity, location, and behavior. For example, glenohumeral joint dysfunction, which can occur in the patient with hemiplegia secondary to a central nervous system disorder, commonly refers pain to the lateral brachium. Ultrasound treatment administered to the site of pain may yield minimal or temporary results under the best of conditions. The ultrasound could be directed, however, at the *underlying source* of pain. Rather than for pain relief, it could be used instead to promote collagen extensibility by application to the anteroinferior capsule of the joint in the axilla. Ultrasound can assist in the restoration of tissue length and flexibility, which permits normal glenohumeral arthrokinematics and osteokinematics and subsequently relief from pain.

A clear cause-and-effect relationship between a lesion and symptoms cannot always be made during an initial examination. Instead, the assessment may establish a provisional diagnosis, subject to confirmation only after treatment has succeeded in resolving the symptoms. In this case, the effects of treatment must be monitored continually and modified as appropriate, and flexibility must be exercised by the therapist to modify the provisional assessment. In the realm of musculoskeletal dysfunction, the therapist may be confronted with the inability to develop a "comparable sign" and instead must develop a hypothesis for treatment based on identified tissue and lesions.

TREATMENT GOALS AND STRATEGIES

The treatment goals and strategies should correlate with the deficits identified by the clinician in the assessment section of the examination. The therapist must be aware of all possible treatment goals that can be established for any patient who possesses a musculoskeletal problem. Table 5–7 lists nine generic treatment goals that should be considered during the treatment planning process.

The promotion of soft tissue healing by improving the

Table 5–7 GENERIC TREATMENT GOALS

1. Promote healing by improving the nutritional status of tissue.
2. Restore or prevent the loss of soft tissue flexibility and length for contractile and noncontractile tissue.
3. Restore or prevent the loss of normal joint alignment.
4. Restore or prevent the loss of normal joint mobility.
5. Promote normal myotactic and myoarthrokinetic reflexes.
6. Promote normal motor control.
7. Resolve pain and associated symptoms.
8. Prevent recurrence of the lesion.
9. Restore the functional ability of the patient.

nutritional status of the involved body part is fundamental to any treatment plan, whether acute or chronic problems are present. The nutritional status is improved by altering the circulatory status of a tissue site, and it may be altered for different purposes. One approach is to increase circulation to an area exhibiting reduced vascularity. For example, the ischemia produced by a muscle spasm causes the retention of metabolites which act as a chemical irritant to the tissue and further promote the spasm (Fig. 5–2). The application of modalities or manual techniques to increase circulation can reduce the tissue ischemia. Another method of improving the tissue's nutritional status is to decrease the circulation to an inflamed area. The purpose is to prevent excessive coagulation of blood and the resulting fibrotic reaction. Excessive fibrosis results in a loss of tissue and structural length and flexibility, as in the contracture of a myotendon unit. The clinician must be aware of the need to consider this latter method, not only in the acute lesion but also in the acute exacerbation of tissues in an underlying chronic condition.

The restoration of soft tissue flexibility and prevention of deficits are key elements in the treatment of musculoskeletal dysfunction. Healing by fibrosis is the normal response to tissue trauma. Because fibrosis causes shortening of the collagenous structure inherent in musculoskeletal soft tissue, the therapist must continually be aware of preventing this shortening or restoring the flexibility of soft tissue. Soft tissue is a three-dimensional structure, and its pliability must be examined and treated in each dimension. Theoretically, for each dimension of length, width, and depth, the flexibility must be assessed in a plane parallel to that dimension. However, in the body the examination and treatment of all three dimensions cannot always be performed, owing to limited access to some tissues. Manual techniques can be used to restore flexibility by applying mechanical forces to impose tensile and shear loads on contractile and noncontractile tissues. The techniques also can be used to elicit neurophysiologic responses to facilitate the lengthening of innervated contractile soft tissue. Modalities can be used prior to the application of manual techniques to prepare the tissues for stretching; for example, the application of ultrasound to increase collagen extensibility.[21] The restoration of flexibility will enable the tissue to tolerate physical stress, thereby reducing the internal load and the subsequent inflammatory reaction and stimulation of nociceptors.

Normal static joint alignment should be restored to ensure an initial proper axis from which motion can be initiated. Absence of joint alignment permits excessive loading of neighboring soft tissue and articular surfaces and impairment of arthrokinesia and osteokinesia. Examples of joint malalignment are the anterior displacement of the humeral head relative to the glenoid fossa as observed in the patient with laxity of the anterior glenohumeral joint capsule, and the posterior tibial subluxation on the femur as seen in a patient after prolonged immobilization of the knee.

The restoration of joint mobility—that is, normal arthrokinesia and osteokinesia—is necessary to prevent abnormal soft tissue loading of the joint capsule, ligaments, synovial lining, and articular surfaces. Excessive or abnormally directed loading can lead to pain, capsular laxity, effusion, hemarthrosis, and eventually degenerative joint disease. Subsequently, the patient's level of function is impaired.

The promotion of normal **myoarthrokinetic reflexes**[22] is achieved through goals 1, 2, 3, and 4 listed in Table 5–7. For example, joint effusion causes an inhibitory effect on surrounding musculature,[23] and ligamentous laxity is purported to decrease the normal protective response muscle imparts to a joint when it is subjected to physical stress,[24] the latter occurring secondary to a sensory loss from the ligament.

The restoration of normal motor control involves multiple factors of strength, mobility, controlled mobility, stability, and skill. Chapters 8 and 13 provide a detailed discussion of motor control; however, there are some points relevant to the musculoskeletal system that should be included here. Strength involves the production of torque with sufficient magnitude and duration at functional velocities during concentric and eccentric modes of muscle contraction. Strength is a result of peripheral contractile tissue and structural capabilities linked with central neural control. Joint stability is obtained through passive tissue tension by an intact ligament of normal length and tensile strength, and through dynamic contraction of agonistic and antagonistic muscle groups throughout the range of motion. Treatment is aimed at obtaining optimum stability of joints and mobility of the body's lever arms. The physical therapist should be concerned with the peripheral and central aspects of motor control for the total rehabilitation of the patient.

The reduction of pain and associated symptoms is accomplished primarily by achieving the goals already described. However, when these goals are unattainable, the clinician may elect to alter the perception of pain through the neuromodulation of peripheral sensory information, such as the use of transcutaneous electrical nerve stimulation (TENS). The clinician must consider other factors that affect the perception of pain. In addition to the physiologic factors described in the generic goals, emotional, social, psychologic, cultural, and environmental influences can alter the perception of pain. When the clinician recognizes that multiple factors are influencing the patient's pain, consideration should be given to referring the patient to other health care practitioners for a team approach to pain management.

The patient must assume the major role in preventing a recurrence of the problem. It is the responsibility of the therapist to educate the patient regarding the nature of the lesion. The patient should be aware of the effect of mechanical stresses imposed on the body part under consideration by daily activity and occupational tasks. This information enables the patient to prevent recurring pain through altering the method of executing tasks, modifying the environment, and using equipment to assist in performing the task.

The functional status of the patient is improved or restored by achieving the goals already described. In addition, the therapist seeks to improve the patient's functional status by conducting training sessions in which the patient practices the proper biomechanical execution of daily and occupational tasks in a simulated environment.

The nine generic goals are applied to three categories of musculoskeletal lesions in Table 5–8. The three plans function as a strategy for treatment of musculoskeletal tissue and structural deficits. They are provided to serve as

1. A treatment planning guide for the clinician.
2. A framework on which new knowledge and skills can be added during the professional development of a therapist.
3. A basis for the analysis of the rationale for various treatment techniques and modalities.

Table 5–8 TREATMENT STRATEGIES

1. Soft tissue lesion without a mechanical deficit.

Promote tissue nutrition.
↓
Alter mechanical tissue load.
↓
Prevent formation of soft tissue restrictions or insufficiency.
↓
Promote motor control.
↓
Restore previous or maximal functional status.

2. Soft tissue flexibility or length deficit without an articular component.

(The first two steps below are appropriate if soft tissue inflammation is present.)

Pomote tissue preparation.
↓
Restore contractile and noncontractile tissue flexibility, length, and load-bearing capacity. ·
↓
Promote motor control.
↓
Restore previous or maximal functional status.

3. Articular deficit with soft tissue lesion and/or length and flexibility deficit.

Promote tissue nutrition.   Promote tissue preparation.
↓   ↓
Alter mechanical tissue load.   Restore tissue flexibility and length.
↓
Prevent formation of soft
tissue restrictions.
↘
Restore proper static joint alignment.
↓
Restore normal joint mobility.
↓
Restore motor control.
↓
Restore previous or maximal functional status.

The order of the goals under each category provides a sequential treatment plan.[6] However, based on the needs of the individual patient, the clinician should modify the plan as necessary.

SUMMARY

The goal of this chapter has been to promote an understanding of the principles, content, and strategies of the assessment and treatment planning process for the patient with musculoskeletal dysfunction. The areas with which the therapist must become familiar in order to perform a thorough examination were discussed. The therapist must know and understand the etiology, symptoms, physical manifestations, and natural course of musculoskeletal conditions. The application and effect of the tools used for the examination process and the wide realm of tissue responses to physical tests also must be understood. With this knowledge base, the clinician can begin to test components and identify deficits of the musculoskeletal system.

Treatment planning for the patient with musculoskeletal deficits begins with the formation of goals based on the assessment. Identification of strategies for achieving these goals is the next step. This chapter provides the reader with generic goals and strategies for consideration in treating a wide variety of musculoskeletal conditions.

QUESTIONS FOR REVIEW

1. Outline a conceptual model of musculoskeletal tissue dysfunction and its sequelae.

2. Outline the generic steps of an examination process.

3. Describe how active, passive, and resistive motion can be used as an assessment tool.

4. Describe the possible responses of soft tissue and structures to provocation tests conducted during a physical examination.

5. Define and provide three examples of a capsular pattern.

6. Define "end-feel" and list five characteristic types.

7. Provide three reasons for thoroughly interviewing a patient to obtain a history of the problem and a subjective report of the symptoms.

8. List the components of a screening examination for the musculoskeletal system.

9. Describe the purpose and components of the assessment section of a musculoskeletal examination.

10. List nine generic treatment goals appropriate for treatment of the patient with musculoskeletal pain and dysfunction.

11. Provide a sequential treatment plan using the goals identified in question #10 for the following:

    a. A soft tissue lesion without a mechanical deficit.

    b. A soft tissue restriction without an articular deficit.

    c. An articular deficit with soft tissue lesion and/or length and flexibility deficit.

REFERENCES

1. Maitland, GD: Peripheral Manipulation. Butterworths, Boston, 1977.
2. Cailliet, R: Soft Tissue Pain and Disability. FA Davis, Philadelphia, 1977.
3. Payton, CD: Clinical Reasoning Process in Physical Therapy. Phys Ther 65:924, 1985.
4. Dyrek, DA, Harris, BA, Riegger, C: A model of orthopaedic dysfunction: implications for examination and treatment (abstract). Phys Ther 67:740, 1987.
5. Terminology of Orthopedic Physical Therapy. Orthopedic Section, American Physical Therapy Association, LaCrosse, WI, 1987.
6. Dyrek, DA: Management of the individual with musculoskeletal dysfunction. In O'Sullivan, SB (ed): Topics in Physical Therapy. American Physical Therapy Association, Alexandria, VA, 1990.
7. Harris, BA and Dyrek, DA: A model of orthopaedic dysfunction for clinical decision making in physical therapy practice. Phys Ther 69:548–552, 1989.
8. Barrows, HS and Tamblyn, RM: Problem-Based Learning: An Approach to Medical Education. Springer-Verlag, New York, 1980.
9. Rodgers, MM and Cavanagh, PR: Glossary of biomechanical terms, concepts and units. Phys Ther 64:1886, 1984.
10. White, AA and Panjabi, MM: Clinical Biomechanics of the Spine. JB Lippincott, Philadelphia, 1978.
11. Maitland, GD: The hypothesis of adding compression when examining and treating synovial joints. J Orthop Sports Phys Ther 2:7, 1980.
12. Cyriax, J: Textbook of Orthopaedic Medicine, Vol 1, Diagnosis of Soft Tissue Lesions, ed 8. Bailliere Tindall, London, 1983.
13. Kaltenborn, FM: Mobilization of the Extremity Joints: Examination and Basic Treatment Techniques. Olaf Norlis Bokhandel, Oslo, Norway, 1980.
14. Grieve, GP: Mobilization of the Spine, ed 3. Churchill Livingstone, New York, 1979.
15. Daniels, L and Worthingham, C: Muscle Testing Techniques of Manual Examination. WB Saunders, Philadelphia, 1980.
16. Joint Motion: Method of Measuring and Recording. American Academy of Orthopedic Surgeons, Chicago, 1985.
17. Moffroid, M and Whipple, R: Specificity of speed of exercise. Phys Ther 50:1699, 1970.
18. Perrine, J and Edgerton, VR: Muscle force-velocity and power velocity relationships under isokinetic loading. Med Sci Sports 10:159, 1978.
19. Boissonnault, WG: Examination in Physical Therapy Practice: Screening for Medical Disease. Churchill Livingstone, New York, 1991.
20. Winter, DA, Wells, RP, and Orr, GW: Errors in the use of isokinetic dynamometers. Eur J Appl Physiol 46:397, 1981.
21. Lehman, JF, Masock, AJ, Warren, CG, et al: Effects of therapeutic temperatures on tendon extensibility. Arch Phys Med Rehabil 51:481, 1970.
22. Wyke, B: The neurology of joints. Ann Roy Coll Surg Engl 41:35, 1967.
23. Spencer, JD, Hayes, KC, and Alexander, IJ: Knee joint effusion and quadriceps reflex inhibition in man. Arch Phys Med Rehabil 65:171, 1984.
24. Kennedy, JC, Alexander, IJ, and Hayes, KC: Nerve supply of the human knee and its functional importance. Am J Sports Med 10:329, 1982.

SUPPLEMENTAL READINGS

Akeson, WH, Grood, ES, Noyes, FR, Zernicke, RF: Collagen cross linking alterations in joint contractures: changes in periarticular connective tissue collagen after nine weeks of immobilization. Connect Tissue Res 5:15–19, 1977.

Bowling, RW and Erhard, R: Letter to the editor. Bull Orthop Sports Med APTA 4:8, 1979.

Brodin, H: Principles of examination and treatment in manual medicine. Scand J Rehabil Med 11:181, 1979.

Butler, DL, et al: Biomechanics of ligaments and tendons. Exerc Sports Sci Rev 6:126–282, 1979.

Coates, H and King, A: The Patient Assessment: A Handbook for Therapists. Churchill Livingstone, New York, 1982.

Cohen, S and Viellion, G: Patient assessment: examining joints of the upper and lower extremities. Am J Nurs 81:763, 1981.

Corrigan, B and Maitland, GD: Practical Orthopaedic Medicine. Butterworths, Boston, 1983.

Currier, DP and Nelson, RM (eds): Dynamics of Human Biologic Tissues. FA Davis, Philadelphia, 1992.

Curwin, S and Stanish, WD: Tendonitis: Its Etiology and Treatment. DC Heath, Lexington, MA, 1984.

Cyriax, JH and Cyriax, PH: Illustrated Manual of Orthopaedic Medicine. Butterworths, London, 1983.

Darnell, MW: A proposed chronology of events for forward head posture. J Cranioman Prac 1:49, 1983.

Davies, GJ, Malone, T, and Bassett, FH: Knee examination. Phys Ther 60:1565, 1980.

DonTigny, R: Letter to the editor. Bull Orthop Sports Med APTA 4:8, 1979.

Ebner, M: Connective Tissue Massage: Theory and Therapeutic Application. Robert E Krieger, Huntington, NY, 1975.

Eddy, DM and Clanton, CH: The art of diagnosis: solving the clinicopathological exercise. N Engl J Med 30:1263, 1982.

Erhard, R and Bowling, R: The recognition and management of the pelvic component of low back and sciatic pain. Bull Orthop Sec APTA 2:4, 1977.

Friedman, MH and Weisberg, J: Application of orthopaedic principles in evaluations of the temporomandibular joint. Phys Ther 62:597, 1982.

Fulkerson, JP: Awareness of the retinaculum in evaluating patellofemoral pain. Am J Sports Med 10:147, 1982.

Garrett, WE and Duncan, PW: Muscle injury and rehabilitation. In Malone TR (ed): Sports Injury Management. Williams & Wilkins, Baltimore, MD, 1988, pp 1–76.

Goodridge, JP: Muscle energy technique: definition, explanation, methods of procedure. J Am Osteopath Assoc 81:249, 1981.

Gould, JA and Davies, GJ: Orthopaedic and Sports Physical Therapy. CV Mosby, St. Louis, 1985.

Gozna, ER and Harrington, IJ: Biomechanics of Musculoskeletal Injury. Williams & Wilkins, Baltimore, 1982.

Grieve, EFM: Mechanical dysfunction of the sacroiliac joint. Int Rehabil Med 5:46, 1983.

Grieve, GP: The sacroiliac joint. Physiotherapy 62:384, 1976.

Grieve, GP: Common Vertebral Joint Problems. Churchill Livingstone, New York, 1981.

Harms-Ringdahl, K, Brodin, H, Eklund, L, et al: Discomfort and pain from loaded passive joint structures. Scand J Rehabil Med 15:205–211, 1983.

Hoke, B, Howell, D, and Stack, ML: The relationship between isokinetic testing and dynamic patellofemoral compression. J Orthop Sports Phys Ther 4:150, 1983.

Hoppenfield, S: Physical Examination of the Spine and Extremities. Appleton-Century-Crofts, New York, 1976.

Hubbard, RP: Mechanical behavior of connective tissue. In Greeman, PE (ed): Concepts and Mechanisms of Neuromuscular Functions. Springer-Verlag, New York, 1984.

Janda, V: Muscle Function Testing. Butterworth, Boston, 1983.

Kapandji, IA: The Physiology of the Joints, Vol 1, Upper Limb, 1982. Vol 2, Lower Limb, 1971. Vol 3, The Trunk and Vertebral Column, 1984. Churchill Livingstone, New York.

Kessler, RM and Hertling, D: Management of Common Musculoskeletal Disorders: Physical Therapy Principles and Methods. Harper & Row, Philadelphia, 1983.

Kirkaldy-Willis, WH and Hill, RJ: A more precise diagnosis for low back pain. Spine 4:102, 1979.

Lamb, D: The neurology of spinal pain. Phys Ther 59:971, 1979.

Little, RW: Biomechanics modeling and concepts. In Greenman, PE (ed): Concepts and Mechanisms of Neuromuscular Functions. Springer-Verlag, New York, 1984.

Magee, DJ: Orthopaedic Physical Assessment. WB Saunders, Philadelphia, 1987.

Maigne, R: Low back pain of thoracolumbar origin. Arch Phys Med Rehabil 61:389, 1980.

Maitland, GD: Vertebral Manipulation. Butterworth & Co, Boston, 1977.

Maitland, GD: Examination of the cervical spine. Aust J Physiother 25:29, 1979.

Maitland, GD: Musculo-skeletal Examination and Recording Guide, ed 3. Launderdale Press, Glen Osmond, South Australia, 1981.

McKenzie, RA: The Lumbar Spine: Mechanical Diagnosis and Therapy. Spinal Publications. Waikanae, New Zealand, 1981.

Mennell, JM: Joint Pain. Little, Brown & Co, Boston, 1964.

Mitchell, FL, Moran, PS, and Pruzzo, NA: An Evaluation and Treatment Manual of Osteopathic Muscle Energy Procedures. Mitchell, Moran, and Pruzzo, Valley Park, MO, 1979.

Moll, JMH, Liyanange, SP, and Wright, V: An objective clinical method to measure lateral spinal flexion. Rheum Phys Med 11:225, 1972.

Nelson, MA, Allen P, Clamp, SE, de Dombal, FT: Reliability and reproducibility of clinical findings in low back pain. Spine 4:97, 1979.

Paris, SB: Anatomy as related to function and pain. Orthop Clin North Am 14:475, 1983.

Polley, HF and Hunder, GG: Pneumatologic Interviewing and Physical Examination of the Joints. WB Saunders, Philadelphia, 1978.

Radakovich, M and Malone, T: The superior tibiofibular joint: the forgotten joint. J Orthop Sports Phys Ther 3:129, 1982.

Ritter, MA and Gosling, C: The Knee: A Guide to the Examination and Diagnosis of Ligament Injuries. Charles C Thomas, Springfield, IL, 1979.

Rocabado, M: Biomechanical relationship of the cranial, cervical and hyoid regions. J Cranioman Prac 1:61, 1983.

Smidt, GL and Rogers, MW: Factors contributing to the regulation and clinical assessment of muscular strength. Phys Ther 62:1283, 1982.

Steindler, A: Kinesiology of the Human Body under Normal and Pathological Conditions. Charles C Thomas, Springfield, IL, 1955.

Tank, R and Halbach, J: Physical therapy evaluation of the shoulder complex in athletes. J Orthop Sports Phys Ther 3:108, 1982.

Taylor, DC, Dalton, JD, Seaber, AV, and Garrett, WE: Viscoelastic properties of muscle-tendon nits: the biomechanical effects of stretching. Am J Sports Med 18:300–309, 1990.

Tomberlin, JP, Eggart, JS, and Callister, L: The use of standardized evaluation forms in physical therapy. J Orthop Sports Phys Ther 5:348, 1984.

Travell, JG and Simons, DG: Myofascial Pain and Dysfunction: The Trigger Point Manual. Williams & Wilkins, Baltimore, 1983.

Urban, LM: The straight-leg-raising test: a review. J Orthop Sports Phys Ther 2:117, 1981.

Vidik, A: Functional properties of collagenous tissue. Rev Connect Tis Res 6:127–215, 1981.

Wadsworth, GT: Wrist and hand examination and interpretation. J Orthop Sports Phys Ther 5:108, 1983.

Weismantel, A: Evaluation and treatment of sacroiliac joint problems. Bull Orthop Sports Med APTA 3:5, 1978.

Woerman, AL and Binder-Macleod, SA: Leg length discrepancy assessment: accuracy and precision in five clinical methods of evaluation. J Orthop Sports Phys Ther 5:230, 1984.

Wolf, SL: Clinical Decision Making in Physical Therapy. FA Davis, Philadelphia, 1984.

Woo SI-Y, Gomez, MA, Woo Y-K, et al: Mechanical properties of tendons and ligaments: the relationship between immobilization and exercise on tissue remodeling. Biorheology 19:397–408, 1982.

Young, A, Stokes, M, Iles, JF, et al: Effects of joint pathology on muscle. Clin Orthop 219:21–27, 1987.

Zohn, DA and Mennell, JM: Musculoskeletal Pain: Diagnosis and Physical Treatment. Little, Brown, & Co, Boston, 1976.

GLOSSARY

Arthrokinematics: The intrinsic, usually intracapsular, articular motion occurring between adjacent joint surfaces; a prerequisite for normal, pain-free osteokinematics.

Bending: A deformation around an axis perpendicular to the long axis of a material caused by the imposition of a load along the length of a tissue; results in a tension load on the convex surface and a compression load on the concave surface.

Capsular pattern: A characteristic pattern of restricted osteokinematics secondary to fibrosis of the joint capsule, resulting in loss of capsuloligamentous flexibility and length; accompanied by an impairment of arthrokinematics.

Comparable sign: A term advocated by Maitland[7] to describe a positive finding—that is, restricted movement, pain, or muscle spasm—found during assessment; the sign relates to or is "comparable to" the patient's symptoms.

Compression: A load that pushes the fibers of a material together along its long axis; it results in, or tends to cause, a shortening and widening of the material.

Contractile tissue: The myotendonous unit, that is, muscle, tendon, and tendoperiosteal attachment; transmits the internal load created during contraction of a muscle.

Edema: In an orthopedic context, refers to extraarticular soft tissue swelling.

Effusion: In an orthopedic context, refers to intracapsular swelling of a joint.

End-feel: The characteristic quality of resistance imparted to the examiner's hands when applying passive overpressure to a joint and its associated soft tissues; can be normal or abnormal.

Flexibility: Sufficient three-dimensional or triplanar deformation to permit the normal function of extensibility and recoil with adequate strength and at appropriate velocity, and the ability to return to a normal length. The deformation can occur parallel, perpendicular, or rotatory to the long axis of the structure.

Myoarthrokinetic reflex: Neurophysiologic reflexes elicited by loading of the joint capsule and ligaments; can either facilitate or inhibit the musculature.

Noncapsular pattern: A limitation of joint motion that results from other than a capsular pattern of restriction; for example, internal derangement of the knee.

Noncontractile (inert) tissue: Tissue incapable of contraction; includes the joint capsule, ligaments, fascia, bursa, nerves (peripheral and root), dura mater, blood vessels, articular cartilage, and bone; can be loaded only by internal passive force.

Osteokinematics: The movement occurring between two bones; involves rotatory motion of bone around an axis; the extracapsular motion of one bone moving in relation to another stable bone.

Overpressure: The passive force applied to a joint and its associated soft tissues to stress the joint partners beyond the physiologic range of motion; used to determine the type of end-feel, the status of soft tissue and joint structures, and the presence of pain in response to mechanical deformation of tissue.

Provocation test: The application of controlled external forces to impose an internal load on isolated tissues and structures.

Strain: The deformation that occurs to a material subject to loading, that is, stress; can cause lengthening or shortening of the structure.

Stress: The internal load produced in a structure by an external force.

Tension: An internal load imposed by forces acting in opposite directions and resulting in a tendency to elongate, or the actual elongation of the fibers in a material.

Tissue reactivity: The tolerance of tissue to an internal load created by the external force of the examiner; indicated by the patient's perception of pain intensity.

Torsion: A force that creates a twisting of the material around its long axis.

CHAPTER

Sensory Assessment 6

Thomas J. Schmitz

> **OBJECTIVES**
>
> 1. Identify the purposes of performing a sensory assessment.
> 2. Describe the classification and function of the receptor mechanisms involved in the perception of sensation.
> 3. Identify the spinal pathways that mediate sensation.
> 4. Identify the general guidelines for completing a sensory assessment.
> 5. Describe the testing protocol for assessment of each sensory modality.

Disturbances of the sensory system pose significant functional implications for the patient. Impairment of sensation may be associated with any disease or trauma affecting the nervous system.[1] This impairment can result from dysfunction at any point within the sensory system, from the receptor, or the peripheral nerve, to the spinal cord, nuclei, sensory tracts, brainstem, thalamus, or sensory cortex.[1-3] The resultant sensory dysfunction frequently presents as an inability to cortically interpret external sensory stimuli. Examples of diagnoses that generally demonstrate some level of sensory impairment include disease or injury to the peripheral nerves or spinal cord, burns, hemiplegia, arthritis, multiple sclerosis, fractures, and head trauma or disease. This list, which is not all-inclusive, indicates the wide variety of disorders that may present with some element of sensory deficit and the importance of a thorough knowledge of techniques for assessing sensation.

Alterations in sensory function also occur during the normal aging process. Decreased acuity of many sensations occurs or is a characteristic finding with normal aging.[4-6] The exact morphology of diminished sensation with age has not been clearly established. However, several neurologic changes have been identified and suggest potential explanations. The average weight of the brain declines with age and is believed to be related to a degeneration of neurons and replacement gliosis.[7] There is also a decrease in the number of enzymes responsible for dopamine and norepinepherine synthesis,[8] as well as depletion of the neuronal dendrites in the aging brain.[9]

Several authors have reported reduced conduction velocity of sensory nerves with advancing age, and this may be reflective of a loss of sensory axons.[7,10] Others have found no significant change in conduction velocity with age.[11] A reduction in the number of Meissner's corpuscles, responsible for touch detection,[12] and decreased concentrations of pacinian corpuscles,

responsive to rapid tissue movement (e.g., vibration), has been reported.[13] Degeneration of some myelinated fibers of the spinal cord[14] and a decrease in distance between the nodes of Ranvier in peripheral nerves have also been associated with advancing age.[15,16] This later finding may be related to a slowing of saltatory conduction identified by some authors.[7,10]

Documented changes in sensory function with aging include changes in response to tactile[17] and vibratory stimuli,[18] decreased two-point discrimination,[12,19] decreased kinesthetic awareness,[4] and minimal alterations in the perception of pain.[20] These changes frequently appear in the presence of age-related visual or hearing losses that impair compensatory capabilities. In addition, some medications may influence further the distortion of sensory input.[6] This combination of sensory changes may present in a variety of functional impairments for the elderly individual, including postural instability, exaggerated body sway, balance problems, wide-based gait, tendency to drop items held in the hand, and difficulty in recognizing body positions in space.[21]

Considering the close relationship between sensory input and motor output, detailed information related to sensory status is a critical factor in treatment planning. For example, a patient who has decreased awareness of where a limb is in space may be unable to execute appropriate motor responses during a program of therapeutic exercise or to safely accomplish some functional activities. Sensory deficits also interfere with acquisition of new motor skills as motor learning is highly dependent on sensory information and feedback mechanisms. Consequently, treatment designed for a patient with impaired sensation must be adjusted either to improve or to accommodate the sensory deficit.[1] Additionally, insensitive body parts, particularly the hands and feet, are often subjected to injury. This is evident by the frequent occurrence of burns, cuts, lacerations, and bruises on insensitive limbs.[22] Knowledge of the patient's sensory deficit will guide the therapist in appropriately educating the patient about the impairment and precautions that should be taken to avoid injury.

Sensory testing is usually a component of the overall initial examination. Because sensory deficits will influence motor performance, the sensory assessment is completed prior to tests that involve elements of active motor function (such as manual muscle testing, active range of motion, functional assessments, and so forth). Sensory tests are also an important component of periodic reassessment to determine the effectiveness of the rehabilitation program.[23]

The purposes of performing a sensory assessment are to

1. Determine the level of sensory feedback affecting movement (including influence of sensory deficits on performance of functional activities or use of adaptive equipment and prosthetics or orthotics).
2. Provide a basis for initiating a program of desensitization (use of tactile stimuli to decrease hypersensitivity) or sensory retraining (learning the sensation of a movement or sensory stimuli).
3. Determine the need for instruction in techniques to compensate for the sensory loss, such as use of visual cues during movement.[1,24]
4. Assure patient safety and prevent secondary complications (for example, prevention of burns during application of heating modalities, prevention of decubitus ulcers, and so forth).
5. Formulate goals and plan for appropriate therapeutic intervention.
6. Help determine, over a period of time, the effects of rehabilitation, or surgical or medical management.[25]

Prior to a discussion of specific testing protocol, a brief review of the sensory system is warranted. The following section presents an overview of the approaches to classification of the sensory system: divisions and types of sensory receptors, and the pathways that mediate sensory signals.

CLASSIFICATION OF THE SENSORY SYSTEM

Portions of the sensory system have been classified for both descriptive and functional purposes. In 1920, Henry Head[26] grossly divided tactile sensations into two systems, the **protopathic** and **epicritic** systems. Head theorized that the protopathic system was designed for protection, to warn or to defend the organism against potential harm.[27] This system was concerned with unpleasant sensations such as pain; extreme changes in temperature;[28] and diffuse, unpleasant light touch sensations such as itching or tingling.[27]

The epicritic system, believed to be a phylogenetically newer system, was considered to exert a controlling function over the protopathic system.[29] The epicritic system was described as concerned with highly discriminative sensations such as localization of cutaneous stim-

uli, object recognition,[27] two-point discrimination, and subtle changes in temperature.[28] Although both systems could mediate the perception of pain, it was the protopathic system that was identified as being most concerned with pain messages, often producing a motor response.[29]

Another classification system divides sensation into three categories on the basis of the type or location of the receptor that responds to a particular stimulus. The three divisions include the superficial, deep, and combined sensations.[28] **Exteroceptors** are the sensory receptors responsible for the superficial sensations. They receive stimuli from the external environment via the skin and subcutaneous tissue.[30] Exteroceptors are responsible for the perception of pain, temperature, light touch, and pressure.[28,30] **Proprioceptors** are the sensory receptors responsible for deep sensations. These receptors receive stimuli from muscles, tendons, ligaments, joints, and fascia,[28,30] and are responsible for position sense, movement **(kinesthesia)** sense, and vibration.

The combination of both the superficial and deep sensory mechanisms makes up the third category of combined, or cortical sensations.[31] These sensations require information from both the exteroceptive and proprioceptive receptors, as well as intact function of cortical sensory association areas. The combined (cortical) sensations include stereognosis, two-point discrimination, barognosis, graphesthesia, tactile localization, recognition of texture, and bilateral simultaneous stimulation.[1,28,31]

Sensations also have been classified according to the system by which they are mediated to higher centers. Sensations are mediated by either the *anterolateral spinothalamic* or the *dorsal column-medial lemniscal system*.[2,27,29,30,32] The anterolateral spinothalamic system responds to stimuli that are potentially harmful in nature. This is similar to Head's protopathic classification.[26] It contains slow-conducting fibers of small diameter, some of which are unmyelinated.[32,33] The system is concerned with transmission of thermal and nociceptive information,[30] and mediates pain, temperature, crudely localized touch,[2,32,33] tickle, itch, and sexual sensations.[34] The dorsal column-medial lemniscal system (also referred to as the dorsal column system) is considered to be involved with responses to more discriminative sensations. This is analogous to Head's epicritic system.[26] It contains faster-conducting fibers of large diameter with greater myelination.[2] This system mediates the sensations of discriminative touch and pressure sensations, vibration, movement, and position sense.[2,30,33,34] The two systems are not independent but integrated so as to function together.

Classification of Sensory Receptors

The sensory receptors frequently are divided according to their structural design and the type of stimulus to which they preferentially respond.[2] These divisions include (1) *mechanoreceptors,* which respond to mechanical deformation of the receptor or surrounding area; (2) *thermoreceptors,* which respond to changes in temperature; (3) *nocioceptors,* which respond to noxious stimuli and result in the perception of pain; (4) *chemoreceptors,* which respond to chemical substances and are responsible for taste, smell, oxygen levels in arterial blood, carbon dioxide concentration and osmolality of body fluids; and (5) *photic (electromagnetic) receptors,* which respond to light within the visible spectrum.[2,34]

It is important to note that pain is not limited to stimuli received from nocioceptors, because other types of receptors and nerve fibers contribute to this sensation. High intensities of stimuli to any type of receptor may be perceived as pain (for example, extreme heat or cold, and high-intensity mechanical deformation).[2]

TYPES OF SENSORY RECEPTORS

A composite list of the general classification of sensory receptors is presented in Table 6–1. Note that this

Table 6–1 CLASSIFICATION OF SENSORY RECEPTORS

I. Mechanoreceptors
  A. Cutaneous sensory receptors
    1. Free nerve endings
    2. Hair follicle endings
    3. Merkel's disks
    4. Ruffini endings
    5. Krause's end-bulbs
    6. Meissner's corpuscles
    7. Pacinian corpuscles
  B. Deep sensory (joint) receptors
    1. Muscle spindles
    2. Golgi tendon organs
    3. Free nerve endings
    4. Pacinian corpuscles
    5. Joint receptors
      a. Golgi-type endings
      b. Free nerve endings
      c. Ruffini endings
      d. Paciniform endings
II. Thermoreceptors
  A. Cold
    1. Cold receptors
  B. Warmth
    1. Warmth receptors
III. Nocioceptors
  A. Pain
    1. Free nerve endings
    2. Extremes of stimuli to other sensory receptors
IV. Electromagnetic receptors
  A. Vision
    1. Rods
    2. Cones
V. Chemoreceptors
  A. Taste
    1. Receptors of taste buds
  B. Smell
    1. Receptors of olfactory nerves in olfactory epithelium
  C. Arterial oxygen
    1. Receptors of aortic and carotid bodies
  D. Osmolality
    1. Probably neurons of supraoptic nuclei
  E. Blood CO_2
    1. Receptors in or on surface of medulla and in aortic and carotid bodies
  F. Blood glucose, amino acids, fatty acids
    1. Receptors in hypothalamus

Adapted from Guyton.[34]

list also includes the receptors responsible for electromagnetic (visual) and chemical stimuli.

Cutaneous Sensory Receptors

Cutaneous receptors are located at the terminal portion of the afferent fiber.[2] These include free nerve endings, hair follicle endings, Merkel's disks, Ruffini endings, Krause's end-bulbs, Meissner's corpuscles, and pacinian corpuscles. The density of these sensory receptors varies for different areas of the body. For example, there are many more tactile receptors in the fingertips than in the back. These areas of higher receptor density correspondingly display a higher cortical representation in somatic sensory area I.[35] Receptor density is a particularly important consideration in interpreting the results of a sensory assessment for a given body surface. Figure 6–1 presents a diagram of the cutaneous sensory receptors and their respective locations within the various layers of skin.

  1. *Free nerve endings.* These receptors are found throughout the body. Stimulation of free nerve endings results in the perception of pain, temperature, touch,[2] pressure, tickle, and itch sensations.[34]
  2. *Hair follicle endings.* At the base of each hair follicle a free nerve ending is entwined. The combination of the hair follicle and its nerve provides a sensitive receptor. These receptors are sensitive to mechanical movement and touch.[2]
  3. *Merkel's disks.* These receptors are located below the epidermis in hairy and glabrous skin. They are sensitive to low-intensity touch, as well as to the velocity of touch. They provide for the ability to perceive continuous contact of objects against the skin and are believed to play an important role in

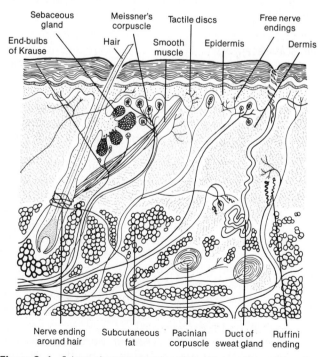

Figure 6–1. Schematic representation of the skin and its receptors. The receptors are located in the three layers of skin: the epidermis, dermis, and the subcutaneous layer. (From Gardner,[30] p 222, with permission.)

both two-point discrimination and localization of touch.[34]

4. *Ruffini endings.* Located in the deeper layers of the dermis, these encapsulated endings are involved with the perception of touch and pressure. They are particularly important in signaling continuous states of skin deformation.[36]

5. *Krause's end-bulb.* These receptors are located in the dermis. They are believed to have a contributing role in the perception of touch and pressure (C.R. Noback, personal communication, August 12, 1985).

6. *Meissner's corpuscles.* Located in the dermis, these encapsulated nerve endings contain many nerve filaments within the capsule. They are in high concentration in the fingertips, lips, and toes—areas that require high levels of discrimination. These receptors play an important role in discriminative touch and the recognition of texture.[2,36]

7. *Pacinian corpuscles.* These receptors are located in the subcutaneous tissue layer of the skin and in deep tissues of the body (including tendons and soft tissues around joints). They are stimulated by rapid movement of tissue and are quickly adapting. They play a significant role in the perception of deep touch and vibration.[2,30,34]

Deep Sensory Receptors

The deep sensory receptors are located in muscles, tendons, and joints.[2,32,34,36] They include both muscle and joint receptors. They are concerned primarily with posture, position sense, proprioception, muscle tone and speed, and direction of movement. The deep sensory receptors include the muscle spindle, Golgi tendon organs, free nerve endings, pacinian corpuscles, and joint receptors.

Muscle Receptors

1. *Muscle spindles.* The muscle spindle fibers (intrafusal fibers) lie in a parallel arrangement to the muscle fibers (extrafusal fibers). They monitor changes in muscle length as well as velocity of these changes. The muscle spindle plays a vital role in position and movement sense and in motor learning.

2. *Golgi tendon organs.* These receptors are located in series at both the proximal and distal tendinous insertions of the muscle. The Golgi tendon organs function to monitor tension within the muscle. They also are considered to provide a protective mechanism by preventing structural damage to the muscle in situations of extreme tension. This is accomplished by inhibition of the contracting muscle and facilitation of the antagonist.

3. *Free nerve endings.* These receptors are within the fascia of the muscle. They are believed to respond to pain and pressure.

4. *Pacinian corpuscles.* Located within the fascia of the muscle, these receptors respond to vibratory stimuli and deep pressure.

Joint Receptors

1. *Golgi-type endings.* These receptors are located in the ligaments, and function to detect the rate of joint movement.

2. *Free nerve endings.* Found in the joint capsule and ligaments, these receptors are believed to respond to pain and crude awareness of joint motion.

3. *Ruffini endings.* Located in the joint capsule and ligaments, Ruffini endings are responsible for the direction and velocity of joint movement.

4. *Puciniform endings.* These receptors are found in the joint capsule and primarily monitor rapid joint movements.

Transmission of Sensory Signals

Somatic sensory information enters the spinal cord through the dorsal roots. Sensory signals are then carried to higher centers via ascending pathways from one of two systems: the *anterolateral spinothalamic system* or the *dorsal column-medial lemniscal system.*

ANTEROLATERAL SPINOTHALAMIC SYSTEM

The spinothalamic tracts are diffuse pathways concerned with nondiscriminative sensations such as pain, temperature, tickle, itch, and sexual sensations. This system is activated primarily by mechanoreceptors, thermoreceptors, and nocioceptors, and is composed of afferent fibers that are small and slowly conducting. Sensory signals transmitted by this system do not require discrete localization of signal source or precise gradations in intensity.[2,28,34]

After originating in the dorsal roots, the fibers of the spinothalamic system cross to the opposite anterolateral segment of the white matter (Fig. 6–2) and ascend diffusely in the anterior and lateral white columns. They demonstrate a diffuse pattern of termination at all levels of the lower brainstem as well as at the thalamus.[2,28,36]

Compared with the dorsal column-medial lemniscal system, the anterolateral spinothalamic pathways make up a cruder, more primitive system. The spinothalamic tracts are capable of transmitting a wide variety of sensory modalities. However, their diffuse pattern of termination results in only crude abilities to localize the source of a stimulus on the body surface, and poor intensity discrimination.[36]

The three major tracts of the spinothalamic system include the (1) *anterior (ventral) spinothalamic tract,* which carries the sensations of crudely localized touch and pressure; (2) the *lateral spinothalamic tract,* which carries pain and temperature; and (3) the *spinoreticular tract,* which is involved with diffuse pain sensations.[2,28,34]

DORSAL COLUMN-MEDIAL LEMNISCAL SYSTEM

This system is responsible for the transmission of discriminative sensations received from specialized mechanoreceptors. Sensory modalities that require fine gra-

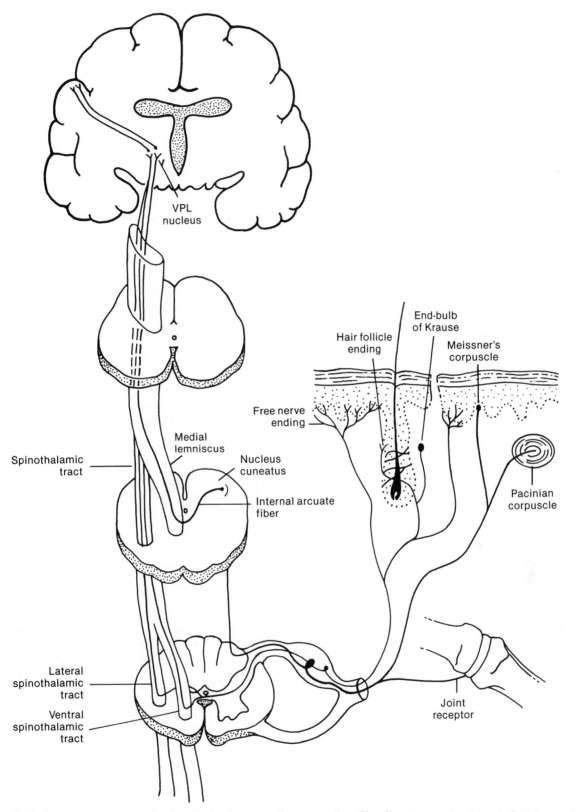

Figure 6–2. Cutaneous receptors and major spinal pathways mediating sensations. The afferents conveying the superficial (protopathic) sensations are small, slow conducting, and travel via the spinothalamic tracts. The afferents conveying the discriminative sensations are larger, faster conducting, and travel via the dorsal-lemniscus pathway. Branches for reflexes, pain, and temperature have been omitted. (From Brown,[2] p 230, with permission. Originally adapted from Netter, F: The CIBA Collection of Medical Illustrations. I. The Nervous System. CIBA Chemical Co, Summit, NJ, 1972.)

dations of intensity and precise localization on the body surface are mediated by this system. Sensations transmitted by the dorsal column-medial lemniscal pathway include discriminative touch, **stereognosis,** tactile pressure, **barognosis, graphesthesia,** recognition of texture, kinesthesia, **two-point discrimination,** proprioception, and vibration.[2,28,34]

This system is composed of large, rapidly conducting fibers. After entering the dorsal column the fibers ascend to the medulla and synapse with the dorsal column nuclei (nuclei gracilis and cuneatus). From here they cross to the opposite side and pass up to the thalamus through bilateral pathways called the *medial lemnisci.* Each medial lemniscus terminates in the ventral posterolateral thalamus. From the thalamus, third-order neurons project to the somatic sensory cortex (Fig. 6–2).[2,28,34]

GENERAL GUIDELINES FOR SENSORY ASSESSMENTS

The testing procedure consists of two components: (1) application of the stimulus and (2) patient response to the stimulus. During the sensory assessment, the following information should be gathered.

1. The type of sensation affected.
2. The quantity of involvement or body surface areas affected.
3. The degree of involvement (e.g., absent, impaired, delayed responses, hyperesthesia, and so forth).
4. Localization of the exact boundaries of the sensory impairment (this will assist in determining location of the lesion).
5. The patient's subjective feelings about changes in sensation.

The patient's ability to comprehend instructions and to communicate responses is crucial to accurate sensory testing. As such, general knowledge of the patient's cognitive status and hearing and visual acuity is required. Several simple preliminary tests may be warranted to make these determinations if the therapist is unfamiliar with the patient.

Rapid tests for mental orientation typically involve asking the patient questions related to *time* (date, day of the week, or season of the year), *place* (present location, home address, name of the city or state) and *person* (the patient's own name and age, identification of family members or other individuals known to the patient). Simple tests for memory might involve requests for information related to both long-term and short-term recall; for example, requesting information pertaining to place of birth or historic facts as well as what was eaten for breakfast or repetition of a series of numbers. A gross hearing assessment can be made by observing the patient's response to conversation. The therapist also should note how alterations in volume and tone of verbal directions influence patient response. Finally, a gross assessment of visual acuity may be necessary. This can be assessed quickly by asking the patient to read a standard eye chart or to identify the time from a wall clock. Peripheral field vision can be tested by sitting

directly in front of the patient with outstretched arms. The index fingers should be extended and gradually brought toward midline of the patient's face. The patient is asked to identify when the therapist's approaching finger(s) is first seen. Differences between right and left visual field acuity should be noted carefully. Depth perception may be grossly checked by holding two pencils or fingers in front of the patient. The patient is asked to identify the foreground object.

Findings from these gross assessments will guide the therapist in preparation for formal sensory testing. Because the sensory tests require a patient response to the stimulus, disoriented patients generally cannot be accurately tested. However, vision, hearing, or speech deficits will not adversely affect test results if appropriate adaptations are made in providing instructions and indicating responses. Such modifications include use of increased visual cues or manual contacts.

Patient instruction prior to the sensory assessment is also an important consideration. A full explanation of the purpose and goals of the testing should be provided. The patient also should be informed that his or her cooperation is necessary in order to obtain accurate test results. It is of considerable importance that the patient be instructed not to guess if he or she is uncertain of the correct response.

During the assessment, the patient should be in a comfortable, relaxed position in a quiet room. If full body testing is indicated, both prone and supine positions will be required in order to assess each side of the body.[37] Preferably, the tests should be performed when the patient is well rested. Considering the high level of concentration required, it is not surprising that fatigue has been noted to affect results of some sensory tests adversely.[38] A "trial run" or demonstration of each procedure should be performed just prior to the actual test. This will orient and inform the patient regarding the procedure and exactly what to anticipate during the testing.

Some method of occluding the patient's vision during the testing should be used (vision should not be occluded during the explanation and demonstration). Visual input is prevented because it may compensate for a sensory deficit and thus decrease the accuracy of test results. The traditional methods of occluding vision are by use of a blindfold (a small folded towel can be used effectively) or by asking the patient to keep the eyes closed. These methods are practical in most instances. However, in situations of central nervous system dysfunction, a patient may become anxious[24] or disoriented[1] if vision is occluded for a long period of time. In these situations a small screen[1,24] or folder[24] may be preferable to restrict visual input. Whatever method is used, it should be removed between the tests while directions and demonstrations are provided.

The superficial (exteroceptive) sensations are usually assessed first, inasmuch as they consist of more primitive responses, followed by the deep (proprioceptive), and then combined (cortical) sensations. If a test indicates impairment of the superficial responses, it is likely that some impairment of the more discriminative (deep and combined) sensations also will be noted.

The tests should be carried out following the main sensory nerves and their segmental (dermatome) supply. The **dermatomes** are the cutaneous areas that correspond to the spinal segments that provide their innervation (Fig. 6–3). Dermatome charts do not represent discrete boundaries because some overlap of innervation exists at the borders of adjacent dermatomes. However, the charts are useful as a reference during testing, and they provide a basis for recording results.[1]

Sensory tests are usually performed in a distal to proximal direction. This progression will conserve time, particularly when dealing with localized lesions involving a single extremity, where deficits tend to be more severe distally. It is generally not necessary to test every segment of each dermatome; testing general body areas is sufficient. However, once a deficit area is noted, testing must become more discrete and the exact boundaries of the impairment should be identified. A skin pencil may be useful to mark the boundaries of sensory change directly. This information should be transferred later to a gross sensory assessment form (Table 6–2) and graphically presented on the dermatome chart (Fig. 6–3) for inclusion in the medical record. Most often the dermatome charts are completed using a color code (i.e., each color represents a different sensation). The colors used to plot each sensation are then coded at the bottom of the page. In some instances hatch marks of varying density are used to represent gradations in sensory impairment (i.e., the closer together, the greater the sensory impairment). With this method, a completely colored-in area indicates no response to a given sensation. With varied or "spotty" sensory loss it is not uncommon that more than one dermatome chart is required to completely depict all test findings.

During testing, the application of stimuli should be applied in a random, unpredictable manner with variation in timing.[1] This will improve accuracy of the test results by avoiding a consistent pattern of application, which might provide the patient with "clues" to the correct response. During application of stimuli, consideration must be given also to skin condition. Scar tissue or callused areas are generally less sensitive and will demonstrate a diminished response to sensory stimuli.

Equipment

To perform a sensory assessment the following equipment and materials are required:

1. A large-headed pin or a large paper clip that has one segment bent open (providing one sharp and one dull end). The sharp end of either instrument should not be sharp enough to risk puncturing the skin. If a large-headed pin is used, the sharp end may be made more blunt by a light sanding.
2. Two test tubes with stoppers.
3. A camel hair brush, a piece of cotton, or a tissue.
4. A variety of small commonly used articles such as keys, coins, pencils, and so forth.
5. An aesthesiometer or an electrocardiogram (ECG) caliper[38] with the tips sanded to blunt the ends[39] and a small ruler.
6. A series of small weights of the same dimension but representing graduated increments in weight.
7. Samples of fabrics of various textures such as cotton, wool, or silk (approximately 4 × 4 inches [10 × 10 cm]).
8. Tuning fork and earphones (to reduce auditory clues).

Reliability of Sensory Testing

As with all assessment procedures, the reliability of sensory testing is an important consideration for physical therapists. Currently, there are few systematic reports of data collection related to the reliability of sensory tests. In a study by Kent,[40] the upper limbs of 50 adult patients with hemiplegia were tested for sensory and motor deficits. Three sensory tests were administered and then repeated by the same examiner within 1 to 7 days. Results revealed a high reliability for both stereognosis ($r = 0.97$) and position sense ($r = 0.90$). A low reliability was reported for two-point discrimination, with correlation coefficients ranging from 0.59 to 0.82, depending on the body area tested.

Although limited published data are available related to reliability measures, several approaches can be used to improve this aspect of the tests. These include (1) use of consistent guidelines for completing the tests; (2) administration of the tests by trained, skillful examiners; and (3) subsequent retests performed by the same indi-

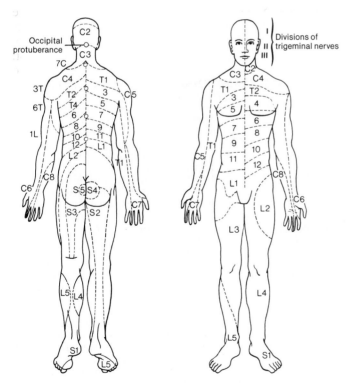

Figure 6–3. The dermatome chart represents the cutaneous areas supplied by a single dorsal root and its ganglia. The trunk demonstrates a sequential, segmental pattern of innervation, and the extremities present an irregular pattern as segmental innervation migrates distally. (From Gilroy and Meyer,[37] p 58, with permission.)

Table 6–2 GROSS SENSORY ASSESSMENT FORM

This form provides a general record of the type, severity, and location of the sensory impairment(s). It should be used in conjunction with one or more dermatome charts that graphically outline the exact boundaries of the deficit. The designations P and D may be added to the grading key to indicate either a proximal (P) or a distal (D) location of the deficit on the limb or body part.

Name: _____ Date: _____
Examiner: _____

Key to Grading*
1. Intact: normal, accurate response
2. Decreased: delayed response
3. Exaggerated: increased sensitivity or awareness of the stimulus after it has ceased
4. Inaccurate: inappropriate perception of a given stimulus
5. Absent: no response
6. Inconsistent or ambiguous: response inadequate to assess sensory function accurately

Sensations	Upper Extremity		Lower Extremity		Trunk		Comments
	Right	Left	Right	Left	Right	Left	
Superficial							
Pain (sharp/dull discrimination)	_____	_____	_____	_____	_____	_____	
Temperature	_____	_____	_____	_____	_____	_____	
Light touch	_____	_____	_____	_____	_____	_____	
Pressure	_____	_____	_____	_____	_____	_____	
Deep (Proprioceptive)							
Movement sense	_____	_____	_____	_____	NA	NA	
Position sense	_____	_____	_____	_____	NA	NA	
Vibration	_____	_____	_____	_____	_____	_____	
Combined (Cortical)							
Tactile localization	_____	_____	_____	_____	_____	_____	
Two-point discrimination	_____	_____	_____	_____	_____	_____	
Bilateral simultaneous stimulation	_____	_____	_____	_____	_____	_____	
Stereognosis	_____	_____	_____	_____	_____	_____	
Barognosis	_____	_____	NA	NA	NA	NA	
Graphesthesia	_____	_____	NA	NA	NA	NA	
Recognition of texture	_____	_____	NA	NA	NA	NA	

* Separate notation should be made for assessment of the face. Abnormal responses should be briefly described in the comments section. NA indicates that the test is not appropriate for the given body area.

vidual. It also should be noted that the reliability of sensory tests will be further influenced by the patient's understanding of the test procedure and the patient's ability to communicate results.[1]

The studies by Nolan[23,25,41] have generated some renewed interest in both the reliability and the validity of sensory testing in general. Additional research related to standardization of testing protocols, development of quantitative approaches to collecting information, and establishment of additional normative data for various age groups will improve the reliability, validity, and future clinical application of test results.

Testing Protocol

This section presents the individual tests for assessment of sensation. The tests are subdivided for superficial, deep, and combined sensations. Table 6–3 provides the terminology used to describe common sensory deficits.

SUPERFICIAL SENSATIONS
Pain (Sharp/Dull Discrimination)
Test. A large-headed pin or reshaped paper clip is used (providing one sharp end and one dull end). Both stim-

Table 6–3 TERMINOLOGY DESCRIBING COMMON SENSORY DEFICITS

Abarognosis	Inability to recognize weight.
Allesthesia	Sensation experienced at a site remote from point of stimulation.
Analgesia	Complete loss of pain sensibility.
Anesthesia	Loss of sensation.
Astereognosis	Inability to recognize the form and shape of objects by touch (SYN: tactile agnosia).
Causalgia	Painful, burning sensations, usually along the distribution of a nerve.
Hypalgesia	Decreased sensitivity to pain.
Hyperalgesia	Increased sensitivity to pain.
Hyperesthesia	Increased sensitivity to sensory stimuli.
Hypesthesia	Decreased sensitivity to sensory stimuli.
Paresthesia	Abnormal sensation such as numbness, prickling, or tingling, without apparent cause.
Thalamic syndrome	Vascular lesion of the thalamus resulting in sensory disturbances and partial or complete paralysis of one side of the body, associated with severe, boring-type pain. Sensory stimuli may produce an exaggerated, prolonged, or painful response.
Thermanalgesia	Inability to perceive heat.
Thermanesthesia	Inability to perceive sensations of heat and cold.
Thermhyperesthesia	Increased sensitivity to temperature.
Thermhypesthesia	Decreased temperature sensibility.

uli (sharp and dull ends of pin) are applied in random fashion. To avoid summation of impulses, the stimuli should not be applied too close to each other or in rapid succession. In order to maintain a uniform pressure with each successive application of stimuli, the pin or reshaped paper clip should be held firmly and the fingers allowed to "slide" down the pin or paper clip once in contact with the skin. This will avoid the chance of gradually increasing pressure during application. It should again be noted that the instrument used to test sharp/dull discrimination should not be sharp enough to puncture the skin, since this would carry the subsequent risk of transmitting a blood-borne infection.

Response. The patient is asked to indicate when a stimulus is felt and to reply "sharp," "dull," or "unable to tell." All areas of the body should be tested.

Temperature

Test. Two test tubes with stoppers are required for this assessment; one should be filled with hot water and the other with crushed ice. Ideal temperatures for cold are between 41°F (5°C) and 50°F (10°C) and for hot, between 104°F (40°C) and 113°F (45°C). Caution should be exercised to remain within these ranges, because exceeding these temperatures may elicit a pain response and consequently inaccurate test results. The test tubes are randomly placed in contact with the skin area to be tested. All skin surfaces should be tested.

Response. The patient is asked to indicate when a stimulus is felt and to reply "hot," "cold," or "unable to tell."

It should be noted that clinical usefulness of thermal testing may be problematic. Nolan[38] points out that the tests are extremely difficult to duplicate on a day-to-day basis because of rapid changes in temperature once the test tubes are exposed to room air. Although it is a simple test to perform, assessing changes over time is not practical unless a method of monitoring the temperature of the test tubes is used.[38]

Light Touch

Test. For this test a camel hair brush, piece of cotton, or a tissue is used. The area to be tested is lightly touched or stroked.

Response. The patient is asked to indicate when he or she recognizes that a stimulus has been applied by responding "yes" or "now."

Pressure

Test. The therapist's thumb or fingertip is used to apply a firm pressure on the skin surface. This pressure should be firm enough to indent the skin[1,24] and to stimulate the deep receptors.[1]

Response. The patient is asked to indicate when he or she recognizes that a stimulus has been applied by responding "yes" or "now."

DEEP (PROPRIOCEPTIVE) SENSATIONS

The **proprioceptive** sensations include both **position sense** and **movement sense** (kinesthesia) as well as **vibration.** Position sense is the awareness of the position of joints at rest. Movement sense or kinesthesia is the awareness of movement. Vibration refers to the ability to perceive a rapidly oscillating or vibratory stimuli. Although these sensations are closely related, they should be assessed individually.

Movement Sense (Kinesthesia)

Test. This test assesses the *perception of movement.* The extremity or joint(s) to be assessed is moved passively through a relatively small range of motion. Small increments in range of motion are used as joint receptors fire at specific points throughout the range. The therapist should identify the range of motion being assessed (e.g., initial, mid, or terminal range). As discussed earlier, a trial run or demonstration of the procedure should be performed prior to actual testing. This will ensure that the patient and the therapist agree on terms to describe the direction of movements.

Response. The patient is asked to indicate verbally the direction of movement *while the extremity is in motion.* The patient is asked to describe the direction and range of movement in terms previously discussed with the therapist (i.e., "up," "down," "in," "out," and so forth). The patient may also respond by simultaneously duplicating the movement with the opposite extremity. This second approach, however, is usually impractical with proximal lower extremity joints, owing to potential stress on the low back. During testing, movement of larger joints is usually discerned more quickly than that of smaller joints. The therapist's grip should remain constant, preferably over bony prominences, to reduce tactile stimulation.

Position Sense

Test. This test assesses *joint position sense.* The extremity or joint(s) to be assessed is moved through a range of motion and held in a static position. Again, small increments in range of motion are used and the range of motion being assessed should be identified (e.g., initial, mid, or terminal range). As with movement sense, caution should be used with hand placements to avoid excessive tactile stimulation.

Response. While the extremity or joint(s) under assessment is held in a static position by the therapist, the patient is asked to describe the position verbally or duplicate the position of the extremity or joint(s) with the opposite extremity.

Vibration

Test. The test for vibration assesses the ability to perceive a vibratory stimulus. The base of a vibrating tuning fork is placed on a bony prominence (such as the sternum, elbow, or ankle). If intact, the patient will perceive the vibration. If there is impairment, the patient will be unable to distinguish between a vibrating and nonvibrating tuning fork. Therefore, there should be a random application of vibrating and nonvibrating stimuli. Earphones may be used for this test procedure to reduce auditory clues from the vibrating fork. It should be noted that the tuning fork provides only a gross assessment of the ability to perceive a vibrating stimuli as the frequency of vibration cannot be held constant during the test procedure.

Response. The patient is asked to respond by verbally identifying the stimulus as vibrating or nonvibrating each time the base of the fork is placed in contact with a bony prominence.

COMBINED (CORTICAL) SENSATIONS
Stereognosis

Test. Testing for object recognition will require use of items of differing size and shape. A variety of small, easily obtainable and culturally familiar objects are used for this assessment. These objects may include keys, coins, combs, safety pins, pencils, and so forth. Individual objects are placed in the patient's hand. The patient is allowed to manipulate the object and is asked to identify the item verbally. The patient should be allowed to handle several sample test items during the explanation and demonstration of the procedure.

Response. The patient is asked to name the object verbally. For patients with speech deficits the items can be selected from a group after each test.

Tactile Localization

Test. This test assesses the ability to localize touch sensation on the skin. Using a fingertip, the therapist touches different skin surfaces. After each application of a stimulus the patient is given time to respond.

Response. The patient is asked to identify the location of the stimuli by touch or verbal description. The patient's eyes may be open during the response component of this test.[1] Tactile localization may be tested separately or included with other tests[1] (e.g., localization of sharp/dull or light-touch sensations). The distance between the application of the stimulus and the site indicated by the patient should be measured and recorded.

Two-Point Discrimination

Test. This test assesses the ability to perceive two points applied to the skin simultaneously. It is a measure of the smallest distance between two stimuli (applied simultaneously and with equal pressure) that can still be perceived as two distinct stimuli.[38] This assessment is among the most practical and easily duplicated test for cutaneous sensation. Two-point discrimination has been the subject of a series of important studies by Nolan.[23,25,41] The purpose of his research was to establish normative data on two-point discrimination for young adults. His sample consisted of 43 college students ranging in age from 20 to 24 years. Values from Nolan's studies are presented in Table 6–4 for the upper extremity, Table 6–5 for the lower extremity, and Table 6–6 for the face and trunk. These findings are consistent with earlier, less extensive studies on two-point discrimination in the upper limb.[40,42] Normative values are extremely useful in interpreting test results from sensory assessments, as well as from other types of assessments. However, the results from these studies[23,25,41] must be used cautiously, inasmuch as they relate to a specific population. They should not be generalized for interpreting data from older or younger patients.

Several instruments have been described for use in measuring two-point discrimination. These include a reshaped paper clip,[43] a Boley gauge,[39] and an aesthe-

Table 6–4 TWO-POINT DISCRIMINATION VALUES FOR THE UPPER EXTREMITY (n = 43)

Skin Region	$\overline{X}$ (mm)	s
Upper—lateral arm	42.4	14.0
Lower—lateral arm	37.8	13.1
Mid—medial arm	45.4	15.5
Mid—posterior arm	39.8	12.3
Mid—lateral forearm	35.9	11.6
Mid—medial forearm	31.5	8.9
Mid—posterior forearm	30.7	8.2
Over 1st dorsal interosseous muscle	21.0	5.6
Palmar surface—distal phalanx, thumb	2.6	0.6
Palmar surface—distal phalanx, long finger	2.6	0.7
Palmar surface—distal phalanx, little finger	2.5	0.7

From Nolan,[41] with permission of the American Physical Therapy Association.

siometer.[1,38] The ECG caliper (a compass-type device) has been identified as a particularly practical, inexpensive, and easily obtained tool for measuring two-point discrimination.[38] Prior to use for two-point discrimination testing, the tips of the ECG caliper should be lightly sanded to form blunt ends.[39] This will ensure that the tactile stimulus will not be perceived as painful.

During the test procedure the two ends are applied to the skin simultaneously. With each successive application, the two ends are gradually brought closer together until the stimuli are perceived as one. The smallest distance between the stimuli that is still perceived as two distinct points is measured with a ruler and recorded. To increase the validity of the test it is appropriate to alternate the application of two stimuli with the random application of only a single stimulus. It is also important to consider that perception of two-point discrimination varies considerably for different individuals and body parts, being most refined in the distal upper extremities. Nolan[23] also noted a high level of two-point discrimination in the great toe. In testing for two-point discrimination, both intraindividual[23] and interindividual[23,25,41] variations in perception of the stimulus must be considered.

Response. The patient is asked to identify the perception of "one" or "two" stimuli.

Table 6–5 TWO-POINT DISCRIMINATION VALUES FOR THE LOWER EXTREMITY (n = 43)

Skin Region	$(\overline{X})$ mm	s
Proximal—anterior thigh	40.1	14.7
Distal—anterior thigh	23.2	9.3
Mid—lateral thigh	42.5	15.9
Mid—medial thigh	38.5	12.4
Mid—posterior thigh	42.2	15.9
Proximal—lateral leg	37.7	13.0
Distal—lateral leg*	41.6	13.0
Medial leg	43.6	13.5
Tip of great toe	6.6	1.8
Over 1–2 metatarsal interspace	23.9	6.3
Over 5th metatarsal	22.2	8.6

* $n = 41$.

From Nolan,[23] with permission of the American Physical Therapy Association.

Table 6–6 TWO-POINT DISCRIMINATION VALUES FOR THE FACE AND TRUNK (n = 43)

Skin Region	$\overline{X}$ (mm)	s
Over eyebrow	14.9	4.2
Cheek	11.9	3.2
Over lateral mandible	10.4	2.2
Lateral neck	35.2	9.8
Medial to acromion process	51.1	14.0
Lateral to nipple	45.7	12.7*
Lateral to umbilicus	36.4	7.3†
Over iliac crest	44.9	10.1‡
Lateral to C7 spine	55.4	20.0†
Over inferior angle of scapula	52.2	12.6†
Lateral to L3 spine	49.9	12.7†

* n = 26.
† n = 42.
‡ n = 33.
From Nolan,[25] with permission of the American Physical Therapy Association.

Bilateral Simultaneous Stimulation

Test. This test assesses the ability to perceive a simultaneous touch stimulus on opposite sides of the body; proximally and distally on a single extremity; or proximally and distally on one side of the body. The therapist simultaneously (and with equal pressure) (1) touches identical locations on opposite sides of the body, (2) touches proximally and distally on opposite sides of the body, and (3) touches proximal and distal locations on the same side of the body. The term *extinction phenomena* is used to describe a situation in which only the proximal stimulus is perceived, with "extinction" of the distal.

Response. The patient verbally states when he or she perceives a touch stimulus and the number of stimuli felt.

Several additional tests for the combined (cortical) sensations include barognosis, graphesthesia, and recognition of texture. However, these tests are usually not performed if stereognosis and two-point discrimination are found to be intact.[31]

Barognosis

Test. To assess for recognition of weight, a series of small objects of the same size but of graduated weight is used. The therapist may choose to place a series of different weights in the same hand one at a time, or to place a different weight in each hand simultaneously.

Response. The patient is asked to identify the comparative weight of objects in a series (i.e., to compare the relative weight of the object with the previous one); or when the objects are placed in both hands simultaneously the patient is asked to compare the weight of

the two objects. The patient responds by indicating that the object is "heavier" or "lighter."

Graphesthesia

Test. The recognition of letters, numbers, or designs traced on the skin is assessed by the use of the eraser end of a pencil. A series or combination of letters, numbers, or designs is traced on the palm of the patient's hand (with the bottom of the figure at the base of the patient's hand). Between each separate drawing the palm should be gently wiped with a soft cloth to clearly indicate a change in figures to the patient. This test is also a useful substitute for stereognosis when paralysis prevents grasping an object.

Response. The patient is asked to identify verbally the figures drawn on the skin. For patients with speech deficits the figures can be selected (pointed to) from a series of line drawings.

Recognition of Texture

Test. This test assesses the ability to differentiate among various textures. Suitable textures may include cotton, wool, or silk. The items are placed individually in the patient's hand. The patient is allowed to manipulate the sample texture.

Response. The patient is asked to identify the individual textures as they are placed in the hand. They may be identified by name (e.g., silk, cotton) or by texture (e.g., rough, smooth).

SUMMARY

Sensory assessments provide important information related to the status of the sensory system. Results from these tests assist in goal setting, treatment planning, and periodic reassessment to determine the effectiveness of treatment intervention. Individual tests for assessment of each sensation have been presented. Reliability of these test procedures can be improved by careful adherence to consistent guidelines, administration of tests by trained individuals, and subsequent retests performed by the same examiner. Documentation of test results should address the type(s) of sensation affected, the quantity and degree of involvement, and localization of the exact boundaries of the sensory deficits. Finally, it should be emphasized again that additional research related to sensory testing is warranted. The development of standardized protocols, reliability measures, and additional normative data will significantly improve the clinical applications of data obtained from sensory assessments.

QUESTIONS FOR REVIEW

1. Describe the purposes of performing a sensory assessment. Identify when a sensory assessment should be completed (in terms of sequencing with respect to other initial examinations such as manual muscle testing, functional tests, and so forth). Identify four patient groups or diagnoses that would routinely warrant a sensory assessment.

2. Identify
   a. The five classifications of sensory receptors and the types of stimuli to which they respond.

b. The cutaneous and joint receptors, their location, and types of stimuli to which they respond.

c. The spinal pathways and the sensations they mediate.

3. Describe

a. The type of information that should be gathered during a sensory assessment.

b. The materials required to complete the assessment.

c. How you would prepare the patient for the sensory testing.

d. The sequence or progression of testing you would follow.

4. For each of the three groups of sensations—superficial, deep, and combined—describe each sensory test, providing both the test procedure and directions for patient response.

5. Describe the method(s) you would use to record the results of your assessment.

REFERENCES

1. Trombly, CA and Scott, AD: Evaluation and treatment of somatosensory sensation. In Trombly, CA (ed): Occupational Therapy for Physical Dysfunction, ed 3. Williams & Wilkins, Baltimore, 1989, p 41.
2. Brown, DR: Neurosciences for Allied Health Therapies. CV Mosby, St Louis, 1980.
3. Minor, MAD and Minor, SD: Patient Care Skills, ed 2. Appelton & Lange, Norwalk, CT, 1990.
4. Colavita, FB: Sensory Changes in the Elderly. Charles C Thomas, Springfield, MA, 1978.
5. Corso, JF: Aging Sensory Systems and Perception. Praeger, New York, 1981.
6. Jackson, O: Brain function, aging, and dementia. In Umphred, DA (ed): Neurological Rehabilitation. CV Mosby, St Louis, 1990, p 661.
7. Adams, RD and Victor, M: Principles of Neurology, ed 5. McGraw-Hill, New York, 1993.
8. Goldman, J and Cote, L: Aging of the brain: dementia of the Alzheimer's type. In Kandel, ER, Schwartz, JH, and Jessel, TM (eds): Principles of Neural Science, ed 3. Appleton & Lange, Englewood Cliffs, NJ, 1991.
9. Scheibel, M, Lindsay, RD, Tomiyasu, U, and Scheibel, AB: Progressive dendritic changes in aging human cortex. Exp Neurol 47:392, 1975.
10. Dorfman, LJ and Bosley, TM: Age related changes in peripheral central nerve conduction in man. Neurology 29:38, 1979.
11. Merchut, MP and Toleikis, SC: Aging and quantitative sensory thresholds. Electromyogr Clin Neurophysiol 30:293, 1990.
12. Bolton, CF, Winkelmann, RK, and Dyck, PJ: A quantitative study of Meissner's corpuscles in man. Neurology 16:1, 1966.
13. Schmidt, RF, Wahren, LK, and Hagbarth, KE: Multiunit neural responses to strong finger pulp vibration, I. Relationship to age. Acta Physiol Scand 140:, 1990.
14. Mufson, EJ and Stein, DG: Degeneration in the spinal cord of old rats. Exp Neurol 70:179, 1980.
15. Lascelles, RG and Thomas, PK: Changes due to age in internodal length in the sural nerve of man. J Neurol Neurosurg Psychiatry 29:40, 1966.
16. Vizoso, AD: The relationship between internodal length and growth in human nerves. J Anat 84:342, 1950.
17. Thornbury, JM and Mistretta, CM: Tactile sensitivity as a function of age. J Gerontol 36:34, 1981.
18. Verrillo, RT: Age related changes in the sensitivity to vibration. J Gerontol 35:185, 1980.
19. Gellis, M and Pool, R: Two-point discrimination distances in the normal hand and forearm. Plast Reconstr Surg 59:57, 1977.
20. Harkins, SW, Price, DD, and Martelli, M: Effects of age on pain perception: thermonociception. J Gerontol 41:58, 1986.
21. Maguire, GH: The changing realm of the senses. In Lewis, CB (ed): Aging: The Health Care Challenge, ed 2. FA Davis, Philadelphia, 1990, p 116.
22. Wood, H: Prevention of deformity in the insensitive hand: the role of the therapist. Am J Occup Ther 23:487, 1969.
23. Nolan, MF: Limits of two-point discrimination ability in the lower limb in young adult men and women. Phys Ther 63:1424, 1983.
24. Pedretti, LW: Evaluation of sensation and treatment of sensory dysfunction. In Pedretti, LW and Zoltan, B (eds): Occupational Therapy: Practice Skills for Physical Dysfunction, ed 3. CV Mosby, St Louis, 1990, p 177.
25. Nolan, MF: Quantitative measure of cutaneous sensation: two-point discrimination values for the face and trunk. Phys Ther 65:181, 1985.
26. Head, H: Studies in Neurology, vol 2. Oxford University Press, London, 1920.
27. Ayers, AJ: Sensory Integration and Learning Disorders. Western Psychological Services, Los Angeles, 1972.
28. Chusid, JG: Correlative Neuroanatomy and Functional Neurology, ed 19. Lange Medical Publications, Los Altos, CA, 1985.
29. Ayers, AJ: Tactile functions: their relation to hyperactive and perceptual motor behavior. Am J Occup Ther 18:6, 1964.
30. Gardner, E: Fundamentals of Neurology: A Psychophysiological Approach, ed 6. WB Saunders, Philadelphia, 1975.
31. Paine, RS and Oppe, TE: Neurological Examination of Children. Clinics in Developmental Medicine, Vols 20–21. Spastics Society Medical Education and Information Unit in Association with William Heinemann Medical Books, London, 1966.
32. Werner, JK: Neuroscience: A Clinical Perspective. WB Saunders, Philadelphia, 1980.
33. Farber, SD: Neurorehabilitation: A Multisensory Approach. WB Saunders, Philadelphia, 1982.
34. Guyton, AC: Human Physiology and Mechanisms of Disease, ed 5. WB Saunders, Philadelphia, 1992.
35. Guyton, AC: Basic Neuroscience: Anatomy and Physiology, ed 2. WB Saunders, Philadelphia, 1991.
36. Guyton, AC: Textbook of Medical Physiology, ed 8. WB Saunders, Philadelphia, 1991.
37. Gilroy, J and Meyer, JS: Medical Neurology, ed 3. Macmillan, New York, 1979.
38. Nolan, MF: Clinical assessment of cutaneous sensory function. Clin Manage Phys Ther 4:26, 1984.
39. Werner, JL and Omer, GE: Evaluating cutaneous pressure sensation of the hand. Am J Occup Ther 24:347, 1970.
40. Kent, BE: Sensory-motor testing: the upper limb of adult patients with hemiplegia. J Am Phys Ther Assoc 45:550, 1965.
41. Nolan, MF: Two-point discrimination assessment in the upper limb in young adult men and women. Phys Ther 62:965, 1982.
42. Moberg, E: Evaluation of sensibility in the hand. Surg Clin North Am 40:357, 1960.
43. Moberg, E: Emergency Surgery of the Hand. E & S Livingstone, London, 1967.

SUPPLEMENTAL READINGS

Adams, JH, Corsellis, JAN, and Duchen, LW (eds): Greenfield's Neuropathology, ed 4. John Wiley & Sons, New York, 1984.

Albe-Fessard, D and Fessard, A: Recent advances on the neurophysiological bases of pain sensation. Acta Neurobiol Exp (Wars 3) 35:715, 1975.

Appel, SH (ed): Current Neurology, vol 5. John Wiley & Sons, New York, 1984.

Asbury, AK, McKhann, GM, and McDonald, WI (eds): Diseases of the Nervous System, vol 1. WB Saunders, Philadelphia, 1986.

Asbury, AK, McKhann, GM, and McDonald, WI (eds): Diseases of the Nervous System, vol 2. WB Saunders, Philadelphia, 1986.

Bender, MB, Stacy, C, and Cohen, J: Agraphesthesia: a disorder of directional cutaneous kinesthesia or a disorientation in cutaneous space. J Neurol Sci 53:531, 1982.

Burgess, PR, et al: Signaling of kinesthetic information by peripheral sensory receptors. Annu Rev Neurosci 5:171, 1982.

Dannenbaum, R and Dykes, RW: Evaluation of cutaneous sensation in myelodysplastic children, using electrical stimulation. Dev Med Child Neurol 26:184, 1984.

Dellon, AL: Evaluation of Sensibility and Re-education of Sensation in the Hand. Williams & Wilkins, Baltimore, 1981.

Dellon, AL, Curtis, RM, and Edgerton, MT: Evaluating recovery of sensation in the hand following nerve injury. The Johns Hopkins Medical Journal 130:235, 1972.

Dyck, PJ, et al: Clinical versus quantitative evaluation of cutaneous sensation. Arch Neurol 33:651, 1976.

Dyck, PJ, Schultz, PW, and O'Brien, PC: Quantitation of touch-pressure sensation. Arch Neurol 26:465, 1972.

Dykes, RW: Parallel processing of somatosensory information: a theory. Brain Res Rev 6:47, 1983.

Elfant, IL: Correlation between kinesthetic discrimination and manual dexterity. Am J Occup Ther 31:23, 1977.

Fisher, AG, Murray, EA, and Bundy, AC: Sensory integration: theory and practice. FA Davis, Philadelphia, 1991.

Huss, AJ: Sensorimotor and neurodevelopmental frames of reference. In Hopkins, HL and Smith, HD (eds): Willard and Spackman's Occupational Therapy, ed 7. JB Lippincott, Philadelphia, 1988, p 114.

Iggo, A and Andres, KH: Morphology of cutaneous receptors. Annu Rev Neurosci 5:1, 1982.

McCloskey, DI: Kinesthetic sensibility. Physiol Rev 58:763, 1978.

Merzenich, MM and Kaas, JH: Principles of organization of sensory-perceptual systems in mammals. Prog Psychobiol Physiol Psychol 9:1, 1980.

Moberg, E: Criticism and study of methods for examining sensibility in the hand. Neurology 12:8, 1962.

Mulder, DW, et al: Motor neuron disease (ALS): evaluation of detection thresholds of cutaneous sensation. Neurology 33:1625, 1983.

Norrsell, U: Behavioral studies of the somatosensory system. Physiol Rev 60:327, 1980.

Russell, EW: Tactile sensation—an all-or-none effect of cerebral damage. J Clin Psychol 36:858, 1980.

Schmidt, RF (ed): Fundamentals of Sensory Physiology, ed 3. Springer Verlag, New York, 1986.

GLOSSARY

Abarognosis: Inability to recognize weight.

Allesthesia: Sensation experienced at a site remote from point of stimulation.

Analgesia: Complete loss of pain sensibility.

Anesthesia: Loss of sensation.

Astereognosis: Inability to recognize the form and shape of objects by touch (SYN: tactile agnosia).

Barognosis: Ability to recognize weight.

Causalgia: Painful, burning sensations, usually along the distribution of a nerve.

Dermatome: Cutaneous areas that correspond to the spinal segments providing their innervation.

Epicritic system: Division of sensory system described by Head (1920); refers to highly discriminative nerve fibers that allow perception of fine sensory stimuli.

Exteroceptors: Sensory receptors that provide information from the external environment.

Graphesthesia: Recognition of numbers, letters, or symbols traced on the skin.

Hypalgesia: Decreased sensitivity to pain.

Hyperalgesia: Increased sensitivity to pain.

Hyperesthesia: Increased sensitivity to sensory stimuli.

Hypesthesia: Decreased sensitivity to sensory stimuli.

Interoceptor: Sensory receptors that provide information about the body's internal environment (such as oxygen levels and blood pressure).

Kinesthesia (movement sense): Sensation and awareness of active or passive movement.

Pallesthesia: Ability to perceive or to recognize vibratory stimuli.

Paresthesia: Abnormal sensation such as numbness, prickling, or tingling, without apparent cause.

Position sense: Sensation and awareness of static positions of a joint or body segment.

Proprioception (proprioceptive): Sensation and awareness of body position and movements.

Proprioceptors: Sensory receptors responsible for deep sensations; found in muscles, tendons, ligaments, joints, and fascia.

Protopathic system: Division of sensory system described by Head (1920); refers to nerve fibers that allow perception of crude, nondiscriminative, poorly localized sensations such as pain and temperature.

Reliability: The level of consistency of either a measuring instrument or a testing method.

Sensation: The appreciation of stimuli through the organs of special sense (e.g., eyes, ears, nose), the peripheral cutaneous sensory system (e.g., temperature, taste, touch), or internal receptors (e.g., muscle, joint receptors).

Stereognosis: The ability to recognize the form of objects by touch.

Thalamic syndrome: Vascular lesion of the thalamus resulting in sensory disturbances and partial or complete paralysis of one side of the body, associated with severe, boring-type pain. Sensory stimuli may produce an exaggerated, prolonged, and/or painful response.

Thermanalgesia: Inability to perceive heat.

Thermanesthesia: Inability to perceive sensations of heat and cold.

Thermesthesia: Ability to perceive heat and cold sensations, temperature sensibility.

Thermhyperesthesia: Increased sensitivity to temperature.

Thermhypesthesia: Decreased temperature sensibility.

Two-point discrimination: Ability to distinguish two blunt points applied to the skin simultaneously.

Validity: The degree to which an instrument or tool measures what it is designed to measure; the degree to which an assessment instrument or tool is able to predict future behavior.

CHAPTER 7

Coordination Assessment

Thomas J. Schmitz

OBJECTIVES

1. Identify the purposes of performing a coordination assessment.
2. Describe the common coordination deficits associated with lesions of the cerebellum, basal ganglia, and dorsal columns.
3. Define the major areas of movement capabilities tested during a coordination assessment.
4. Describe the specific tests used to assess both nonequilibrium and equilibrium coordination deficits.
5. Describe the testing protocol for performing a coordination assessment.

Coordination is the ability to execute smooth, accurate, controlled movements. The ability to produce these movements is a complex process, which is dependent on a fully intact neuromuscular system. Coordinated movements are characterized by appropriate speed, distance, direction, rhythm, and muscle tension. In addition, they involve appropriate synergist influences, easy reversal between opposing muscle groups, and proximal fixation to allow distal motion or maintenance of a posture. *Incoordination* and *coordination deficit* are general terms used to describe abnormal motor function characterized by awkward, extraneous, uneven, or inaccurate movements.[1]

Physical therapists are frequently involved in management of coordination deficits. These deficits are often related to, and indicative of, the area of central nervous system (CNS) involvement of a particular diagnosis. Some locations of CNS involvement present very classic and stereotypical deficits, but others are much less predictable. Several examples of diagnoses that typically demonstrate coordination deficits related to CNS involvement include **parkinsonism,** multiple sclerosis, **Huntington's disease,** cerebral palsy, **Sydenham's chorea,** cerebellar tumors[2] and some learning disabilities.[3-5]

The purposes of performing a coordination assessment include the following:

1. To assess the ability of muscles or groups of muscles to work together to perform a task or functional activity.
2. To assist with goal setting and formulation of treatment plans.
3. To provide a basis for developing a program of therapeutic exercise designed to improve coordination.
4. To assist in determining methods to teach, to simplify, or to adapt an activity.[4]
5. To assist in selection of adaptive equipment that

may facilitate performance or improve safety of an activity.
6. Over time, to determine the effects of therapeutic intervention or drug therapy on coordinated movement.

COORDINATION DEFICITS AND CENTRAL NERVOUS SYSTEM INVOLVEMENT

Several areas of the CNS provide input to, and act together with, the cortex in the production of coordinated movement. These include the cerebellum, basal ganglia, and dorsal (posterior) columns. Although it is incorrect to assign *all* problems of incoordination to one of these sites, lesions in these areas are responsible for many characteristic motor deficits seen in adult populations. The following sections present a brief overview of the normal function of the cerebellum, basal ganglia, and posterior columns, as well as common clinical features associated with lesions in each of these areas.

Cerebellum

The primary function of the cerebellum is coordination of motor activity, equilibrium, and muscle tone. Although all of the mechanisms of cerebellar function are not clearly understood, lesions of this area have been noted to produce typical patterns of incoordination, impaired balance, and decreased muscle tone.

Several theories of function of the cerebellum in motor activity have been established. Among the more widely held is that the cerebellum functions as a *comparator* and *error-correcting mechanism.*[6-9] The cerebellum compares the *commands for movement* transmitted from the motor cortex with the *actual motor performance* of the body segment. This occurs by a comparison of information received from the cortex with that obtained from peripheral feedback mechanisms. The motor cortex and brainstem motor structures provide the commands for the intended motor response.[10] Peripheral feedback during the motor response is provided by muscle spindles, Golgi tendon organs, joint and cutaneous receptors, the vestibular apparatus,[11] and the eyes and ears. This feedback provides continual input regarding posture and balance, as well as position, rate, rhythm, and force of slow movements of peripheral body segments.[8] If the input from the feedback systems does not compare appropriately (i.e., movements deviate from the intended command), the cerebellum supplies a corrective influence. This effect is achieved by corrective signals sent to the cortex, which, via motor pathways, modifies or "corrects" the ongoing movement (e.g., increasing or decreasing the level of activity of specific muscles).[8] The cerebellum also functions to modify cortical commands for subsequent movements.[7]

This CNS analysis of movement information, determination of level of accuracy, and provision for error correction is referred to as a **closed-loop system.**[12] It should be noted that not all movements are controlled by this system. Stereotypical movements (e.g., gait activities) and rapid, short duration movements, which do not allow sufficient time for feedback to occur, are believed to be controlled by an **open-loop system.** In this system, control originates centrally from a **motor program,** which is a "memory" or preprogrammed pattern of information for coordinated movement. The motor system then follows the established pattern independent of feedback or error-detection mechanisms.[12]

CLINICAL FEATURES OF CEREBELLAR DYSFUNCTION

Specific clinical findings are associated with cerebellar disease. Many of these findings either directly or indirectly influence the ability to execute accurate, smooth, controlled movements. The clinical features identified emphasize the crucial influence of the cerebellum on equilibrium, posture, muscle tone, and initiation and force of movement. The following clinical signs are manifestations of cerebellar lesions.

1. **Hypotonia** is a decrease in muscle tone. It is believed to be related to the disruption of afferent input from stretch receptors and/or lack of the cerebellum's facilitory efferent influence on the fusimotor system.[13] A diminished resistance to passive movement will be noted, and muscles may feel abnormally soft and flaccid.[14] Diminished deep tendon reflexes also may be noted.
2. **Dysmetria** is a disturbance in the ability to judge the distance or range of a movement. It may be manifested by an overestimation (**hypermetria**) or an underestimation (**hypometria**) of the required range needed to reach an object or goal.
3. **Dysdiadochokinesia** is an impaired ability to perform rapid alternating movements. This deficit is observed in movements such as rapid alterna-

tion between pronation and supination of the forearm. Movements are irregular, with a rapid loss of range and rhythm.[11]

4. **Tremor** is an involuntary oscillatory movement resulting from alternate contractions of opposing muscle groups. Two types of tremors are associated with cerebellar lesions. An **intention,** or **kinetic, tremor** occurs during voluntary motion of a limb and tends to increase as the limb nears its extended goal.[7] Intention tremors are diminished or absent at rest.[6] **Postural,** or **static, tremors** may be evident by back-and-forth oscillatory movements of the body while the patient maintains a standing posture. They also may be observed as up-and-down oscillatory movements of a limb when it is held against gravity.[11]
5. **Movement decomposition** describes a movement performed in a sequence of component parts rather than as a single, smooth activity. For example, when asked to touch the index finger to the nose, the patient might first flex the elbow, then adjust the position of the wrist and fingers, further flex the elbow, and finally flex the shoulder.
6. **Disorders of gait** involve ambulatory patterns that typically demonstrate a broad base of support. The arms may be held away from the body to improve balance. Initiation of forward progression of a lower extremity may start slowly, and then the extremity may unexpectedly be flung rapidly and forcefully forward and audibly hit the floor.[15] Gait patterns tend to be generally unsteady, irregular, and staggering, with deviations from an intended forward line of progression.
7. **Ataxia** is a general, comprehensive term used to describe the combined influence of cerebellar dysfunction (especially dysmetria and decomposition of movement)[16] on gait, posture, and patterns of movement.
8. **Dysarthria** is a disorder of the motor component of speech articulation. The characteristics of cerebellar dysarthria are referred to as *scanning speech.* This speech pattern is typically slow, and may be slurred, hesitant, with prolonged syllables[7] and inappropriate pauses.[6] Word use, selection, and grammar remain intact,[7,11] but the melodic quality of speech is altered.[11]
9. **Nystagmus** is a rhythmic, oscillatory movement of the eyes. Several deficits related to eye movements are associated with cerebellar lesions. Nystagmus is the most common and causes difficulty with accurate fixation. It is typically apparent as the eyes move away from a midline resting point to fix on a peripheral object. An involuntary drift back to the midline position is observed.[15] Nystagmus is believed to be linked to the cerebellum's influence on synergy and tone of the extraocular muscles.[13]
10. The **rebound phenomenon** was originally described by Gordon Holmes. It is the loss of the check reflex,[15] or check factor,[17] which functions to halt forceful active movements. Normally, when application of resistance to an isometric contraction is suddenly removed, the limb will remain in

approximately the same position by action of the opposing muscle(s). With cerebellar involvement, the patient is unable to "check" the motion, and the limb will move suddenly when resistance is released. The patient may strike himself or herself or other objects when the resistance is removed.

11. **Asthenia** is a generalized muscle weakness associated with cerebellar lesions.

In addition to these characteristic clinical features of cerebellar involvement, a greater length of time may also be required to initiate voluntary movements. Difficulty also may be observed in stopping or changing the force, speed, or direction of movement.[14]

Basal Ganglia

The basal ganglia are a group of nuclei located at the base of the cerebral cortex. The three main nuclei of the basal ganglia include the *caudate,* the *putamen,* and the *globus pallidus.* These nuclei have close anatomic and functional connections with two other subcortical nuclei that are also frequently considered as part of the basal ganglia: the *subthalmic nucleus* and the *substantia nigra.*[9,16]

Although the influences of the basal ganglia on movement are not understood as clearly as those of the cerebellum, there is evidence that the basal ganglia play an important role in several complex aspects of movement and postural control. These include the initiation and regulation of gross intentional movements and the ability to accomplish automatic movements and postural adjustments. In addition, the basal ganglia play an important role in maintaining normal background muscle tone.[18,19] This is accomplished by the inhibitory effect of the basal ganglia on both the motor cortex and lower brainstem. The basal ganglia also are believed to influence some aspects of both perceptual[20] and cognitive functions.[20,21]

Clinical observation indicates that patients with lesions of the basal ganglia typically demonstrate several characteristic motor deficits. These are (1) poverty and slowness of movement; (2) involuntary, extraneous movement; and (3) alterations in posture and muscle tone.[18,21] Common diagnostic groups that demonstrate basal ganglia involvement are parkinsonism, **Wilson's disease,** and Huntington's disease.

CLINICAL FEATURES OF LESIONS OF THE BASAL GANGLIA

Disorders of the basal ganglia present a unique pattern of deficits, with characteristic involuntary movements, disturbances of muscle tone and posture, and diminished postural reactions. The following clinical signs are manifestations of basal ganglia lesions.

1. **Bradykinesia** is slowed or decreased movement. It may be demonstrated in a variety of ways, such as a decreased arm swing; slow, shuffling gait; difficulty initiating or changing direction of movement; lack of facial expression; or difficulty stopping a movement once begun.

2. **Rigidity** is an increase in muscle tone causing greater resistance to passive movement. Two types of rigidity may be seen: *lead pipe* and *cogwheel.* Lead pipe rigidity is a uniform, constant resistance felt by the examiner as the extremity is moved through a range of motion. Cogwheel rigidity is considered a combination of the lead pipe type with tremor. It is characterized by a series of brief relaxations or "catches" as the extremity is passively moved.

3. **Tremor** is an involuntary, rhythmic, oscillatory movement observed at rest (resting tremor). Resting tremors typically disappear or decrease with purposeful movement but may increase with emotional stress. Tremors associated with basal ganglion lesions (e.g., parkinsonism) are frequently noted in the distal upper extremities in the form of a "pill-rolling" movement, where it looks as if a pill is being rolled between the first two fingers and the thumb. Motion of the wrist, and pronation and supination of the forearm, may be evident. Tremors also may be apparent at other body parts as well, such as the head.[6]

4. **Akinesia** is an inability to initiate movement and is seen in the late stages of parkinsonism. This deficit is associated with assumption and maintenance of fixed postures.[20] A tremendous amount of mental concentration and effort is required to perform even the simplest motor activity.[8]

5. **Chorea** is a characteristic movement disorder associated with Huntington's disease. Features of chorea include involuntary, rapid, irregular, and jerky movements, also referred to as *choreiform movements.*

6. **Athetosis** is characterized by slow, involuntary, writhing, twisting, "wormlike" movements. Frequently, greater involvement in the distal upper extremities is noted; this may include fluctuations between hyperextension of the wrist and fingers and a return to a flexed position, combined with rotary movements of the extremities. Many other areas of the body may be involved, including the neck, face, tongue,[8] and trunk. The phenomena are also referred to as *athetoid movements.* Pure athetosis is relatively uncommon and most often presents in combination with spasticity, tonic spasms, or chorea.[22] Athetosis is a clinical feature of cerebral palsy.

7. **Choreoathetosis** is a term used to describe a movement disorder with features of both chorea and athetosis.

8. **Hemiballismus** is characterized by sudden, jerky, forceful, wild, flailing motions of the arm and leg of one side of the body. Primary involvement is in the axial and proximal musculature of the limb. Hemiballismus results from a lesion of the contralateral subthalmic nucleus.[14–16]

9. **Dystonia** involves twisting, sometimes bizarre, movements caused by involuntary contractions of the axial and proximal muscles of the extremities.[15] Torsion spasms also are considered a form of dystonia, with spasmotic torticollis being the most common.[15] If the contraction is prolonged at the end of the movement, it is termed a *dystonic posture.*[20]

Dorsal (Posterior) Columns

The dorsal (posterior) columns play an important role in both coordinated movement and posture. The dorsal columns are responsible for mediating proprioceptive input from muscles and joint receptors. Proprioceptive input includes both position sense (awareness of the position of a joint at rest) and kinesthesia (awareness of movement).

Coordination deficits associated with dorsal column lesions are somewhat less characteristic than those produced by other CNS lesions. However, they typically result in equilibrium and motor control disturbances related to the patient's lack of proprioceptive feedback. Because vision assists in both guiding movements and maintaining balance, visual feedback can be an effective mechanism to compensate partially for a proprioceptive loss. Thus, coordination and/or balance problems will be exaggerated in poorly lit areas, or when the patient's eyes are closed. In addition, some noticeable slowing of voluntary movements may be observed. This occurs because visually guided motions are generally more accurate when speed of movement is reduced.

Disturbances of gait are a common finding in dorsal column lesions. The gait pattern is usually wide-based and swaying, with uneven step lengths and excessive lateral displacement. The advancing leg may be lifted too high and then dropped abruptly with an audible impact. Watching the feet during ambulation is typical[15] and is indicative of a proprioceptive loss.

Another common deficit seen with dorsal column dysfunction is dysmetria. As mentioned earlier, this is an impaired ability to judge the required distance or range of movement and may be noted in both the upper and lower extremities. It is manifested by the inability to place an extremity accurately or to reach a target object. For example, in attempting to lock a wheelchair brake, the patient may inaccurately judge (overestimate, or underestimate) the required movement needed to reach the brake handle. As with other coordination deficits associated with dorsal column lesions, visual guidance will reduce the manifestations of dysmetria.

Changes in Coordinated Movement with Age

When assessing elderly persons, consideration must be given to the effects of aging on several aspects of movement abilities. The following are typical changes associated with aging and may present either as primary or secondary components of a coordination deficit.

1. *Decreased strength.* Several peripheral factors are believed to contribute to decreased muscle hypertrophy and diminished function. These include a loss of alpha motor neurons, atrophy of type I and II myofibers, diminished oxidative capacity of exercising muscle, and a subsequent reduction in ability to produce torque.[23,24]
2. *Slowed reaction time.* The time interval between application of a stimulus and initiation of movement is increased.[25] This finding is also linked to degenerative changes in the motor unit. In addition, *premotor time* (time interval between application of a stimulus and initiation of electromyographic [EMG] activity), and *motor time* (time interval between onset of EMG activity and initiation of movement) is lengthened with normal aging.[23,26]
3. *Loss of flexibility.* Increased tightness of joints is particularly evident toward the end range of motion and may influence the overall skill in coordinated movement. Loss of flexibility has been linked to degenerative changes in collagen fibers, dietary deficiencies, general paucity of movement, and arthritic joint changes.[27]
4. *Faulty posture.* Diminished strength and flexibility are precursors to poor postural alignment.[26] Faulty posture is further influenced by inactivity and prolonged sitting. Of particular importance is the potential loss of ability to accomplish preparatory postural adjustments prior to execution of a movement.[28]
5. *Impaired balance.* Decreased balance[29,30] and increased postural sway[30,31] (the small oscillating movements of the body over the feet during relaxed standing) both occur with advancing age. As a result, coordinated movements within the limits of stability for an elderly person will be altered (i.e., the magnitude of displacement that will disrupt stability will be decreased).

These changes may be accentuated further by alterations in sensation, perceptual skills, and visual acuity. Knowledge of these anticipated changes will improve the therapist's ability to interpret results of coordination assessments for older patients. Several recent texts[32,33] provide important references and further details of the physiologic, neurologic, and musculoskeletal changes associated with advancing age.

TESTING PROCEDURES

Preliminary Considerations

Accurate and careful observation is an important preliminary to performing a coordination assessment. Inasmuch as treatment activities will be geared toward improving functional activity levels, initial observations should focus here. Prior to specific testing procedures, the patient should first be observed performing a variety of functional activities. These may include bed mobility, self-care routines (dressing, combing hair, brushing teeth), transfers, eating, writing, changing position from lying or sitting to standing, maintaining a standing position, walking, and so forth.

During the initial observation, general information can be obtained that will assist in localizing specific areas of deficit. This information will include

1. Level of skill in each activity (including amount of assistance or assistive devices required).
2. The occurrence of extraneous movements, oscillations, swaying, or unsteadiness.
3. Number of extremities involved.

4. Distribution of coordination impairment: proximal and/or distal musculature.
5. Situations or occurrences that alter (increase or decrease) coordination deficits.
6. Amount of time required to perform an activity.
7. Level of safety.

From this initial observation the therapist will be guided in selecting the most appropriate tests for the deficit areas noted. An initial screening of strength, sensation, and range of motion prior to the coordination assessment will improve validity because weakness, tactile deficits, and decreased range of motion all may influence coordinated movement. It is also important to note that coordination deficits may occur in the presence of normal muscle strength and intact sensation.

Coordination tests generally can be divided into two main categories: *gross motor activities* and *fine motor activities*. Gross motor tests involve assessment of body posture, balance, and extremity movements involving large muscle groups. Examples of gross motor activities include crawling, kneeling, standing, walking, and running. Fine motor tests involve assessment of extremity movements concerned with utilization of small muscle groups. Examples of fine motor activities include manipulating objects with the hands, and finger dexterity, which involves skillful, controlled manipulation of tiny objects.

Coordination tests can be subdivided into *nonequilibrium* and *equilibrium* tests. Nonequilibrium coordination tests assess both static and mobile components of movements when the body *is not* in an upright (standing) position. These tests involve both gross and fine motor activities. Equilibrium tests assess both static and dynamic components of posture and balance when the body is in an upright (standing) position. They involve primarily gross motor activities and require observation of the body in both static (stationary) and mobile (body in motion) postures.

Coordination tests focus on assessment of movement capabilities in five main areas: (1) *alternate* or *reciprocal motion*, which tests the ability to reverse movement between opposing muscle groups; (2) *movement composition*, or *synergy*, which involves movement control achieved by muscle groups acting together; (3) *movement accuracy*, which assesses the ability to gauge or to judge distance and speed of voluntary movement; (4) *fixation* or *limb holding*, which tests the ability to hold the position of an individual limb or limb segment; and (5) *equilibrium and posture holding*, which assesses the ability to maintain balance and upright body posture.

Table 7–1 presents a sample of tests appropriate for nonequilibrium coordination testing, and Table 7–2 presents suggested tests for assessing equilibrium coordination. It should be noted that a single test is often appropriate to assess several different deficit areas, and areas may be tested simultaneously to conserve time. The tests contained here are intended as samples and are not all-inclusive. Other activities may be developed that are equally effective in assessing a particular deficit and may be more appropriate for an individual patient. It also should be emphasized that careful observation during performance of functional activities (e.g., self-care routines, wheelchair propulsion, transfers, and so forth) often provide an effective means for assessing many coordination deficits.

The two subdivisions of coordination tests presented here (nonequilibrium and equilibrium) have traditionally been used for providing structure and organization to administration of the tests. However, it should be noted that the "nonequilibrium" division presents something of a misnomer, inasmuch as elements of posture and balance are required during these tests. Although each subdivision places particular emphasis on certain components of movement, *there will clearly be overlap between assessment findings from the two subdivisions.*

Table 7–3 includes selected coordination deficits and suggested tests that would be appropriate to assess the given problem.

Testing Protocol

The following progression should be used in performing a coordination assessment.

1. *Gather equipment.*
   a. Coordination assessment form.
   b. Pen or pencil to record data.
   c. Stopwatch (for timed performance).
   d. Two chairs.
   e. Mat or treatment table.
   f. Method of occluding vision (if needed).
2. *Select location.* The most appropriate setting is a quiet, well-lit room, free of distractions.
3. *Test selection.* Tests should be selected (see Tables 7–1 and 7–2) to assess the specific components of movement appropriate for the individual patient. This activity will be guided by an initial observation of functional activities completed prior to formal coordination testing.
4. *Patient preparation.* Preferably, testing should be conducted when the patient is well rested. The testing procedures should be fully explained to the patient. Each coordination test should be described and demonstrated by the therapist prior to actual testing. Because testing procedures require mental concentration and some physical activity, fatigue, apprehension or fear may adversely influence test results.
5. *Testing.* Generally, nonequilibrium tests are completed first, followed by the equilibrium tests. Attention should be given to carefully guarding the patient during testing; use of a safety belt may be warranted. During the testing activities the following questions can be used to help direct the therapist's observations. The findings should be included in the comment section of the assessment form.
   a. Are movements direct, precise, and easily reversed?
   b. Do movements occur within a reasonable or normal amount of time?
   c. Does increased speed of performance affect level (quality) of motor activity?
   d. Can continuous and appropriate motor adjustments be made if speed and direction are changed?
   e. Can a position or posture of the body or specific

Table 7–1 NONEQUILIBRIUM COORDINATION TESTS[3,15,17]*

1. Finger to nose	The shoulder is abducted to 90 degrees with the elbow extended. The patient is asked to bring the tip of the index finger to the tip of the nose. Alterations may be made in the initial starting position to assess performance from different planes of motion.
2. Finger to therapist's finger	The patient and therapist sit opposite each other. The therapist's index finger is held in front of the patient. The patient is asked to touch the tip of the index finger to the therapist's index finger. The position of the therapist's finger may be altered during testing to assess ability to change distance, direction, and force of movement.
3. Finger to finger	Both shoulders are abducted to 90 degrees with the elbows extended. The patient is asked to bring both hands toward the midline and approximate the index fingers from opposing hands.
4. Alternate nose to finger	The patient alternately touches the tip of the nose and the tip of the therapist's finger with the index finger. The position of the therapist's finger may be altered during testing to assess ability to change distance, direction, and force of movement.
5. Finger opposition	The patient touches the tip of the thumb to the tip of each finger in sequence. Speed may be gradually increased.
6. Mass grasp	An alternation is made between opening and closing fist (from finger flexion to full extension). Speed may be gradually increased.
7. Pronation/supination	With elbows flexed to 90 degrees and held close to body, the patient alternately turns the palms up and down. This test also may be performed with shoulders flexed to 90 degrees and elbows extended. Speed may be gradually increased. The ability to reverse movements between opposing muscle groups can be assessed at many joints. Examples include active alternation between flexion and extension of the knee, ankle, elbow, fingers, and so forth.
8. Rebound test	The patient is positioned with the elbow flexed. The therapist applies sufficient manual resistance to produce an isometric contraction of biceps. Resistance is suddenly released. Normally, the opposing muscle group (triceps) will contract and "check" movement of the limb. Many other muscle groups can be tested for this phenomenon, such as the shoulder abductors or flexors, elbow extensors, and so forth.
9. Tapping (hand)	With the elbow flexed and the forearm pronated, the patient is asked to "tap" the hand on the knee.
10. Tapping (foot)	The patient is asked to "tap" the ball of one foot on the floor without raising the knee; heel maintains contact with floor.
11. Pointing and past pointing	The patient and therapist are opposite each other, either sitting or standing. Both patient and therapist bring shoulders to a horizontal position of 90 degrees of flexion with elbows extended. Index fingers are touching or the patient's finger may rest lightly on the therapist's. The patient is asked to fully flex the shoulder (fingers will be pointing toward ceiling) and then return to the horizontal position such that index fingers will again approximate. Both arms should be tested, either separately or simultaneously. A normal response consists of an accurate return to the starting position. In an abnormal response, there is typically a "past pointing," or movement beyond the target. Several variations to this test include movements in other directions such as toward 90 degrees of shoulder abduction or toward 0 degrees of shoulder flexion (finger will point toward floor). Following each movement, the patient is asked to return to the initial horizontal starting position.
12. Alternate heel to knee; heel to toe	From a supine position, the patient is asked to touch the knee and big toe alternately with the heel of the opposite extremity.
13. Toe to examiner's finger	From a supine position, the patient is instructed to touch the great toe to the examiner's finger. The position of finger may be altered during testing to assess ability to change distance, direction, and force of movement.
14. Heel on shin	From a supine position, the heel of one foot is slid up and down the shin of the opposite lower extremity.
15. Drawing a circle	The patient draws an imaginary circle in the air with either upper or lower extremity (a table or the floor also may be used). This also may be done using a figure-eight pattern. This test may be performed in the supine position for lower extremity assessment.
16. Fixation or position holding	Upper extremity: The patient holds arms horizontally in front. Lower extremity: The patient is asked to hold the knee in an extended position.

*Tests should be performed first with eyes open and then with eyes closed. Abnormal responses include a gradual deviation from the "holding" position and/or a diminished quality of response with vision occluded. Unless otherwise indicated, tests are performed with the patient in a sitting position.

extremity be maintained without swaying, oscillations, or extraneous movements?

f. Are placing movements of both upper and lower extremities exact?

g. Does occluding vision alter quality of motor activity?

h. Is there greater involvement proximally or distally? On one side of body versus the other?

i. Does the patient fatigue rapidly? Is there a consistency of motor response over time?

6. *Documentation.* The results of each test activity should be recorded.

Table 7–2 EQUILIBRIUM COORDINATION TESTS

1. Standing in a normal, comfortable posture.
2. Standing, feet together (narrow base of support).
3. Standing, with one foot directly in front of the other (toe of one foot touching heel of opposite foot).
4. Standing on one foot.
5. Arm position may be altered in each of the above postures (i.e., arms at side, over head, hands on waist, and so forth).
6. Displace balance unexpectedly (while carefully guarding patient).
7. Standing, alternate between forward trunk flexion and return to neutral.
8. Standing, laterally flex trunk to each side.
9. Walking, placing the heel of one foot directly in front of the toe of the opposite foot.
10. Walk along a straight line drawn or taped to the floor, or place feet on floor markers while walking.
11. Walk sideways and backward.
12. March in place.
13. Alter speed of ambulatory activities (increased speed will exaggerate coordination deficits).
14. Stop and start abruptly while walking.
15. Walk in a circle, alternate directions.
16. Walk on heels or toes.
17. Normal standing posture. Observe patient both with patient's eyes open and with patient's eyes closed (or vision occluded). If patient is able to maintain balance with eyes open but not with vision occluded, it is indicative of a proprioceptive loss. This inability to maintain an upright posture without visual input is referred to as a *positive Romberg sign*.

RECORDING TEST RESULTS

Protocol for assessing and recording results from coordination tests vary considerably among institutions and individual therapists. Owing to the nature of the assessment and the wide variation in types and severity of deficits, observational coordination assessments are not highly standardized. However, a number of standardized tests are available for upper extremity assessment. These tests assess specific components of manual dexterity through the use of functional or work-related tasks. Many of these tests were developed originally to assess personnel for recruitment to various employment activities. Several examples of these tests are discussed later in this chapter.

Several options are available for recording results from a coordination assessment. A coordination assessment form is frequently useful to provide a composite picture of the deficit areas noted. These forms are often developed within clinical settings. They may be general (a sample is included in the appendix to this chapter), or they may be specific to a given group of patients, such as those with head injuries.[34] Generally, these forms tend to lack reliability testing. However, they do provide a systematic method of data collection and documentation. These forms frequently include some type of rating scale in which level of performance is weighted using an arbitrary scale. An example of such a scale follows:

4-Normal performance.
3-Movement accomplished with only slight difficulty.
2-Moderate difficulty is demonstrated in accomplishing activity, movements are arrhythmic, and performance deteriorates with increased speed.

Table 7–3 SAMPLE TESTS FOR SELECTED MOTOR DEFICITS CONTRIBUTING TO COORDINATION PROBLEMS

Deficit	Sample Test
1. Dysdiadochokinesia	Finger to nose Alternate nose to finger Pronation/supination Knee flexion/extension Walking with alternations in speed
2. Dysmetria	Pointing and past pointing Drawing a circle or figure eight Heel on shin Placing feet on floor markers while walking
3. Movement decomposition	Finger to nose Finger to therapist's finger Alternate heel to knee Toe to examiner's finger
4. Hypotonia	Passive movement Deep tendon reflexes
5. Tremor (intention)	Observation during functional activities (tremor will typically increase as target is approached) Alternate nose to finger Finger to finger Finger to therapist's finger Toe to examiner's finger
6. Tremor (resting)	Observation of patient at rest Observation during functional activities (tremor will diminish significantly or disappear)
7. Tremor (postural)	Observation of normal standing posture
8. Asthenia	Fixation or position holding (upper and lower extremity) Application of manual resistance to assess muscle strength
9. Rigidity	Passive movement Observation during functional activities Observation of resting posture(s)
10. Bradykinesia	Walking, observation of arm swing Walking, alter speed and direction Request that a movement or gait activity be stopped abruptly Observation of functional activities
11. Disturbances of posture	Fixation or position holding (upper and lower extremity) Displace balance unexpectedly in sitting or standing Standing, alter base of support Standing, one foot directly in front of the other Standing on one foot
12. Disturbances of gait	Walk along a straight line Walk sideways, backward March in place Alter speed of ambulatory activities Walk in a circle

1-Severe difficulty noted; movements are very arrhythmic; significant unsteadiness, oscillations, and/or extraneous movements are noted.
0-Unable to accomplish activity.

A score from the rating scale would then be assigned to each component of the coordination assessment. An advantage of using rating scales is that they provide a mechanism for qualitatively describing patient performance. However, several inherent limitations exist in using such scales. Often the descriptions are not reflective of exact patient performance. Or the rating scale may not be defined adequately or detailed appropriately, thus decreasing reliability of repeated or interexaminer testing. Frequently, coordination forms include a *comments* section. This component of the form allows for additional narrative descriptions of patient performance. Using a combination of a rating scale and narrative comments or summary will ensure that all deficit areas are adequately documented.

The use of a series of *timed tests* is another approach to assessing coordination. Because accomplishing an activity in a reasonable amount of time is a component of performance, the length of time required to accomplish certain activities is recorded by use of a stopwatch. A few standardized measurement tools have been developed based on timed activities. However, specific timed performance measures may be incorporated into a more general assessment form as well.

Computer assisted force-plates also have been used to measure one component of equilibrium coordination. This approach provides a qualitative assessment of sway (a measure of postural stability).[35,36] The force-plates are capable of monitoring fluctuations in vertical pressure exerted by the feet. They offer the important advantage of providing an objective measure of postural stability.

Finally, *videotape recordings* have been used effectively for periodic assessment of coordination deficits. Videotapes provide a permanent, visual record of patient performance. They are particularly useful for assessing treatment and/or drug management via preintervention and postintervention recordings.

Although several options for documenting results are available, a written record using some type of assessment form is most common. An important consideration in establishing a protocol for recording test results is that each therapist is interpreting the form and/or rating scale in the same manner. This will require developing an instrument that is well defined, with distinct rating scale categories. Training sessions for new staff members and periodic reviews for the entire staff will improve inter-rater reliability.

STANDARDIZED INSTRUMENTS FOR ASSESSING MANUAL DEXTERITY AND COORDINATION

Several standardized tests have been developed to assess upper extremity coordination and hand dexterity through the use of functional activities. Many of these tests include normative data to assist with interpretation of test results. Strict adherence to the prescribed method of administration is imperative when using standardized tests. Any deviations from the established protocol will affect the validity and reliability of the measures and consequently make comparisons with published norms invalid. The skill of the examiner is another important consideration. The tests should be administered by an individual specifically trained in administration and interpretation of results. Subsequent retests should be performed by the same individual. These standardized tests are particularly useful in providing objective measures of patient progress over time. Several examples of these tests are described below.

The *Jebsen-Taylor Hand Function Test*[37] measures hand function using seven subtests of functional activities: writing; card turning; picking up small objects; simulated feeding; stacking; picking up large, lightweight objects; and picking up large, heavy objects. The test is easy to construct, to administer, and to score. Normative data are included relating to age, sex, maximum time, and hand dominance. It allows assessment of hand function in seven common activities of daily living.

The *Minnesota Rate of Manipulation Test*[38,39] was originally designed to select personnel for jobs requiring arm and hand dexterity. This test assesses ability in five operations: placing, turning, displacing, one-hand turning and placing, and two-hand turning and placing. The test requires use of a form board with wells and round disks.

The *Purdue Pegboard*[39,40] test assesses dexterity by placement of pins in a pegboard and assembly of pins, washers, and collars (Fig. 7–1). There are several subtests, including right-hand prehension, left-hand prehension, prehension test with both hands, and assembly. The test has been used to select personnel for industrial jobs that require manipulative skills. Normative values are available, and both unilateral and bilateral dexterity

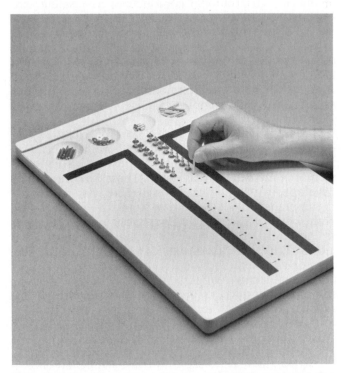

Figure 7–1. Purdue pegboard. (Courtesy of North Coast Medical, San Jose, CA.)

can be assessed. This test requires use of a testing board, pins, collars, and washers.

The *Crawford Small Parts Dexterity Test*[1,39] uses the manipulation of small tools as a component of the test. The test uses pins, collars, and screws as well as a board into which these small objects fit. Use of tweezers is required both to place the pins in holes and to place a collar over the pin. The screws must be placed with the fingers and screwed in using a screwdriver. This test has been useful in prevocational testing. Normative data are available. This test is scored by time.

There are a variety of other standardized and commercially distributed tests available. Selection should be based on the individual needs of a given facility and the diagnostic groups most frequently seen. Additionally, careful assessment should be made of criteria used for standardization of the testing instrument.

SUMMARY

Coordination assessments provide the physical therapist with important information related to motor performance. They assist in identifying the source of motor deficits (although some clinical findings may not be attributable to a single area of CNS involvement). They also assist in goal setting and treatment planning and with periodic reassessment to determine the effectiveness of treatment interventions. Because observational coordination tests are not highly standardized, the potential for error and misinterpretation of results exists. Sources of potential error can be reduced by use of well-defined rating scales, administration of tests by skilled examiners, and subsequent retesting performed by the same therapist.

A variety of observational coordination assessments have been presented. The majority of these tests can be used to assess more than one type of motor deficit. Documentation should include the type, severity, and location of the deficit as well as factors that alter the quality of performance. It is evident that multiple influences affect movement capabilities. As such, the results of coordination tests must be carefully considered with respect to data obtained from other assessments such as sensation, muscle strength, tone, and range of motion.

QUESTIONS FOR REVIEW

1. Describe the clinical features of coordination deficits associated with lesions of the cerebellum, basal ganglia, and dorsal columns.

2. Explain the purpose of an initial observation of the patient prior to a formal coordination assessment. What type of activities should be observed? What information should be gathered?

3. Identify and describe the five general areas of movement capabilities assessed during a coordination assessment.

4. Differentiate between the types of activities included in equilibrium versus nonequilibrium coordination tests.

5. What questions related to patient performance should be considered during a coordination assessment to help direct the examiner's observations?

6. Define each of the following terms. Identify at least two coordination tests that would be appropriate for assessing each deficit. Explain the testing protocol you would use for each.
   a. Dysdiadochokinesia
   b. Dysmetria
   c. Movement decomposition
   d. Tremor (i.e., intention, resting, postural)
   e. Rigidity
   f. Bradykinesia

REFERENCES

1. Trombly, CA and Scott, AD: Evaluation of motor control. In Trombly, CA (ed): Occupational Therapy for Physical Dysfunction, ed 3. Williams & Wilkins, Baltimore, 1989, p 55.

2. Lombardo, MC: Central nervous system tumors. In Price, SA and Wilson, LM (eds): Pathophysiology: Clinical Concepts of Disease Processes, ed 4. Mosby Year Book, New York, 1992, p 817.

3. Clark, F, Mailloux, Z, and Parham, D: Sensory integration and children with learning disabilities. In Pratt, PN and Allen, AS (eds): Occupational Therapy for Children, ed 2. CV Mosby, St Louis, 1989, p 457.

4. Johnson, JH: Children with physical and orthopedic disabilities. In Pratt, PN and Allen, AS (eds): Occupational Therapy for Children, ed 2. CV Mosby, St Louis, 1989, p 510.

5. Kendrick, KA and Hanten, WP: Differentiation of learning disabled children from normal children using four coordination tasks. Phys Ther 60:784, 1980.

6. Brown, DR: Neurosciences for Allied Health Therapies. CV Mosby, St Louis, 1980.

7. Ghez, C: The cerebellum. In Kandel, ER, Schwartz, JH and Jessell, TM (eds): Principles of Neural Science, ed 3. Appleton & Lange, East Norwalk, CT, 1991, p 626.

8. Guyton, AC: Human Physiology and Mechanisms of Disease, ed 5. WB Saunders, Philadelphia, 1992.

9. Lavine, RA: Neurophysiology: The Fundamentals. DC Heath, Lexington, MA, 1983.

10. Ghez, C: The control of movement. In Kandel, ER, Schwartz, JH, and Jessell, TM (eds): Principles of Neural Science, ed 3. Appleton & Lange, East Norwalk, CT, 1991, p 533.

11. Urbscheit, NL: Cerebellar dysfunction. In Umphred, DA (ed): Neurological Rehabilitation, ed 2. CV Mosby, St Louis, 1990, p 597.

12. Schmidt, RA: Motor Control and Learning: A Behavioral Emphasis, ed 2. Human Kinetics, Champaign, IL, 1988.

13. Werner, JK: Neuroscience: A Clinical Perspective. WB Saunders, Philadelphia, 1980.

14. Nolte, J: The Human Brain: An Introduction to Its Functional Anatomy. CV Mosby, St Louis, 1981.

15. Chusid, JG: Correlative Neuroanatomy and Functional Neurology, ed 19. Lange Medical Publications, Los Altos, CA, 1985.

16. Gilman, S and Newman, SW: Manter and Gatz's Essentials of Clinical Neuroanatomy and Neurophysiology, ed 8. FA Davis, Philadelphia, 1992.

17. DeJong, RN: The Neurologic Examination, ed 3. Harper & Row, New York, 1970.

18. Henneman, E: Motor functions of the brainstem and basal ganglia. In Mountcastle, VB (ed): Medical Physiology, vol 1, ed 14. CV Mosby, St Louis, 1980, p 787.

19. Guyton AC: Basic Human Neurophysiology, ed 3. WB Saunders, Philadelphia, 1981.
20. Melnick, ME: Basal ganglia disorders: metabolic, hereditary, and genetic disorders in adults. In Umphred, DA (ed): Neurological Rehabilitation. CV Mosby, St Louis, 1990, p 551.
21. Cote, L and Crutcher, MD: The basal ganglia. In Kandel, ER, Schwartz, JH and Jessell, TM (eds): Principles of Neural Science, ed 3. Appleton & Lange, East Norwalk, CT, 1991, p 647.
22. Schanzenbacher, KE: Diagnostic problems in pediatrics. In Pratt, PN and Allen, AS (eds): Occupational Therapy for Children. CV Mosby, St Louis, 1989, p 77.
23. Craik, RL: Sensorimotor changes and adaptation in the older adult. Guccione, AA (ed): Geriatric Physical Therapy. Mosby Year Book, St Louis, 1993, p 71.
24. Murray, P: Strength of isometric and isokinetic contractions in knee muscles of men aged 20 to 86. Phys Ther 60:4, 1980.
25. Stelmach, GE and Worringham, CJ: Sensorimotor deficits related to postural stability. Clin Geriatr Med 1:679, 1985.
26. Welford, AT: Between bodily changes and performance: some possible reasons for slowing with age. Exp Aging Res 10:73, 1984.
27. Lewis, BC and Bottomley, JM: Musculoskeletal changes with age: clinical implications. In Lewis, BC (ed): Aging: The Health Care Challenge, ed 2. FA Davis, Philadelphia, 1990, p 135.
28. Mankovskii, N, Mints, YA, and Lysenyuk, UP: Regulation of the preparatory period for complex voluntary movement in old and extreme old age. Hum Physiol 6:46, 1980.
29. Bohannon, RW, et al: Decrease in timed balance test scores with aging. Phys Ther 64:1067, 1984.
30. Daleiden, S and Lewis, CB: Clinical implications of neurologic changes in the aging process. In Lewis, BC (ed): Aging: The Health Care Challenge, ed 2. FA Davis, Philadelphia, 1990, p 162.
31. Brocklehurst, JC, Robertson, D, and James-Groom, P: Clinical correlates of sway in old age-sensory modalities. Age Ageing 11:1, 1982.
32. Guccione, AA (ed): Geriatric Physical Therapy. Mosby Year Book, St Louis, 1993.
33. Lewis, BC (ed): Aging: The Health Care Challenge, ed 2. FA Davis, Philadelphia, 1990.
34. Cruz, VW: Evaluation of coordination: a clinical model. Clinical Management in Physical Therapy 6:6, 1986.
35. Thyssen, HH, et al: Normal ranges and reproducibility for the quantitative Romberg's test. Acta Neurol Scand 66:100, 1982.
36. Jansen, EC, Larsen, RE, and Olesen, MB: Quantitative Romberg's test: measurement and computer calculation of postural stability. Acta Neurol Scand 66:93, 1982.
37. Jebsen, RH, et al: An objective and standardized test of hand function. Arch Phys Med Rehabil 50:311, 1969.
38. Fess, EE: Documentation: Essential elements of an upper extremity assessment battery. In Hunter, JM, et al (eds): Rehabilitation of the Hand, ed 2. CV Mosby, St Louis, 1984, p 49.
39. Smith, HD: Assessment and evaluation: an overview. In Hopkins, HL and Smith, HD (eds): Willard and Spackman's Occupational Therapy, ed 8. JB Lippincott, Philadelphia, 1993, p 169.
40. Baxter, PL and Ballard, MS: Evaluation of the hand by functional tests. In Hunter, JM, et al (eds): Rehabilitation of the Hand, ed 2. CV Mosby, St Louis, 1984, p 91.

SUPPLEMENTAL READINGS

Adams, JH, et al (eds): Greenfield's Neuropathology, ed 5. Oxford University Press, New York, 1992.
Adams, RD and Victor, M: Principles of Neurology, ed 5. McGraw-Hill, New York, 1993.
Asbury, AK, McKhann, GM, and McDonald, WI (eds): Diseases of the Nervous System, vol 1, ed 2. WB Saunders, Philadelphia, 1992.
Asbury, AK, McKhann, GM, and McDonald, WI (eds): Diseases of the Nervous System, vol 2, ed 2. WB Saunders, Philadelphia, 1992.
Bohannon, RW, et al: Decrease in timed balance test scores with aging. Phys Ther 64:1067, 1984.
Crutchfield, CA, Shumway-Cook, A, and Horak, FB: Balance and coordination training. In Scully, RM and Barnes, MR (eds): Physical Therapy. JB Lippincott, Philadelphia, 1989, p 825.
Glick, TH: Neurologic Skills. Blackwell Scientific Publications, Boston, 1993.
Kauffman, TL: Well elderly. In Scully, RM and Barnes, MR (eds): Physical Therapy. JB Lippincott, Philadelphia, 1989, p 1226.
Keshner, EA: Reevaluating the theoretical model underlying the neurodevelopmental theory. Phys Ther 61:1035, 1981.
Kornse, DD, et al: Developmental apraxia of speech and manual dexterity. J Commun Disord 14:321, 1981.
Kottke, FJ: From reflex to skill: The training of coordination. Arch Phys Med Rehabil 61:551, 1980.
Kottke, FJ: Therapeutic exercise to develop neuromuscular coordination. In Kottke, FJ and Lehmann, JF (eds): Krusen's Handbook of Physical Medicine and Rehabilitation, ed 4. WB Saunders, Philadelphia, 1990, p 452.
Mayo Clinic and Mayo Foundation: Clinical Examinations in Neurology, ed 6. Mosby Year Book, St. Louis, 1991.
Nolte, J: The Human Brain: An Introduction to its Functional Anatomy, ed 3. Mosby Year Book, Boston, 1993.
Martin, JH: Neuroanatomy: Text and Atlas. Appleton & Lange, Norwalk, CT, 1989.
Schmahmann, JD: An emerging concept: the relationship of the cerebellum to behavior and mental processes. Arch Neurol 48:1178, 1991.
Simon, RP, Aminoff, MJ, and Greenberg, DA: Clinical Neurology. Appleton & Lange, Norwalk, CT, 1989.
Thomas, JR: Acquisition of motor skills: information processing differences between children and adults. Res Q Exerc Sport 51:158, 1980.
Wilson, LM: The nervous system. In Price, SA and Wilson, LM (eds): Pathophysiology: Clinical Concepts of Disease Processes, ed 4. Mosby Year Book, St. Louis, 1992, p 771.

GLOSSARY

Akinesia: An inability to initiate movement; seen in the late stages of parkinsonism.

Asthenia: A generalized muscle weakness associated with cerebellar lesions.

Asynergia: Loss of ability to associate muscles together for complex movements.

Ataxia: A general term used to describe uncoordinated movement; may influence gait, posture, and patterns of movements.

Athetosis: Slow, involuntary, writhing, twisting, "wormlike" movements; clinical feature of cerebral palsy (SYN: athetoid movements).

Bradykinesia: Abnormally slow movements.

Chorea: Involuntary, rapid, irregular, jerky movements; clinical feature of Huntington's disease (SYN: choreiform movements).

Choreoathetosis: Movement disorder with features of both chorea and athetosis; frequently seen in cerebral palsy.

Closed-loop system (servomechanism, servo): A movement control process that employs feedback against a reference for correctness for computation of error and subsequent movement correction.

Dysarthria: Disorder of the motor component of speech articulation.

Dysdiadochokinesia: Impaired ability to perform rapid alternating movements.

Dysmetria: Impaired ability to judge the distance or range of a movement.

Dyssynergia: Impaired ability to associate muscles together for complex movement; decomposition of movement.

Dystonia: Impaired or disordered tonicity; tone fluctuates in an unpredictable manner from low to high.

Hemiballismus: Sudden, jerky, forceful, wild, flailing motions of one side of the body.

Huntington's disease: A degenerative disease of the basal ganglia and cerebral cortex with hereditary transmission as an autosomal dominant trait. Onset is usually after the age of 30 and is frequently fatal within 5 to 15 years after onset. The disease is characterized by choreiform movements; disturbances of tone, posture, and gait; and dementia.

Hyperkinesia: A general term used to describe abnormally increased muscle activity or movement; restlessness.

Hypermetria: Excessive distance or range of a movement; an overestimation of the required motion needed to reach a target object.

Hypokinesia: A general term used to describe decreased motor responses (especially to a specific stimulus); sluggishness, listlessness.

Hypometria: Shortened distance or range of a movement; an underestimation of the required motion needed to reach a target object.

Hypotonia (hypotonus): Reduced muscle tension below normal resting levels.

Motor program: A set of prestructured commands that when initiated results in the production of a coordinated movement sequence.

Movement decomposition: Performance of a movement in a sequence of component parts rather than as a single smooth activity.

Nystagmus: Rhythmic, oscillatory movement of the eyes.

Open-loop system: A control mechanism that uses preprogrammed instructions to regulate movement independent of a feedback and error-detection process.

Parkinsonism: A degenerative disease with primary involvement of the basal ganglia; characterized by tremors, rigidity, bradykinesia, and impairments of posture, balance, and gait. Onset is typically in the fifth or sixth decade of life (SYN: paralysis agitans).

Rebound phenomenon: Absence of a check reflex; when resistance to an isometric contraction is suddenly removed, the body segment moves forcibly in the direction in which effort was focused.

Rigidity: Increase in muscle tone; results in greater resistance to passive movement. Resistance is felt as constant and uniform (lead-pipe rigidity), or as jerky "catches" (cogwheel rigidity).

Romberg sign: Inability to maintain standing balance when vision is occluded.

Sydenham's chorea: Childhood disease associated with rheumatic fever. The disease is self-limiting, and recovery is usually complete; characterized by involuntary, abrupt, jerky, extraneous movements and disturbances of balance and gait; impairments of speech and memory also may be apparent.

Tremor: An involuntary oscillatory movement resulting from alternate contractions of opposing muscle groups.

Tremor, types of intention (kinetic) tremor: Occurs during voluntary motion.

Postural (static) tremor: Back-and-forth oscillatory movements of the body while patient maintains a standing posture.

Resting tremor: Present when involved body segment is at rest; typically disappears or decreases with purposeful movement.

Wilson's disease: A hereditary disease associated with faulty copper metabolism; characterized by degenerative changes in the brain, cirrhosis of the liver, a greenish-brown pigmentation of the cornea (Kayser-Fleischer ring), personality changes, festinating gait, flexed postures, dystonia, tremors, involuntary movements, and dysphagia (SYN: hepatolenticular degeneration).

APPENDIX A   SAMPLE COORDINATION ASSESSMENT FORM

Name: _____

Examiner: _____ Date _____

PART I NONEQUILIBRIUM TESTS

Key to Grading

5. Normal performance.
4. Minimal impairment: able to accomplish activity with slightly less than normal speed and skill.
3. Moderate impairment: able to accomplish activity, but coordination deficits very noticeable; movements are slow, awkward and unsteady.
2. Severe impairment: able only to initiate activity without completion.
1. Activity impossible.

Grade:Left	Coordination Test	Grade:Right	Comments
	Finger to nose		
	Finger to therapist's finger		
	Finger to finger		
	Alternate nose to finger		
	Finger opposition		
	Mass grasp		
	Pronation/supination		
	Rebound test of Holmes		
	Tapping (hand)		
	Tapping (foot)		
	Pointing and past pointing		
	Alternate heel to knee; heel to toe		
	Toe to examiner's finger		
	Heel on shin		
	Drawing a circle (hand)		
	Drawing a circle (foot)		
	Fixation/position holding (upper extremity)		
	Fixation/position holding (lower extremity)		

Additional comments:

PART II EQUILIBRIUM TESTS

Key to Grading

4. Able to accomplish activity.
3. Can complete activity; minor physical contact guarding required to maintain balance.
2. Can complete activity; significant (moderate to maximal) contact guarding required to maintain balance.
1. Activity impossible.

Grade	Coordination Test	Comments
	Standing: normal comfortable posture	
	Standing: normal comfortable posture with vision occluded	
	Standing: feet together	
	Standing on one foot	seconds L( ); R( )
	Standing: forward trunk flexion and return to neutral	
	Standing: lateral trunk flexion	
	Walk: place heel of one foot in front of toe of the opposite foot	
	Walk: along a straight line	

Grade	Coordination Test	Comments
	Walk: place feet on floor markers	
	Walk: sideways	
	Walk: backward	
	Walk: in a circle	
	Walk: on heels	
	Walk: on toes	

Additional comments:

NOTE: Notations should be made under comments section if
1. Lack of visual input renders activity impossible or alters quality of performance.
2. Verbal cuing is required to accomplish activity.
3. Alterations in speed affect quality of performance.
4. An excessive amount of time is required to complete activity.
5. Changes in arm position influence equilibrium tests.
6. Any extraneous movements, unsteadiness, or oscillations are noted in head, neck, or trunk.
7. Fatigue alters consistency of response.

CHAPTER 8

Motor Control Assessment

Susan B. O'Sullivan

OBJECTIVES

1. Identify the purposes and components of a motor control assessment.
2. Identify the central nervous system control mechanisms associated with motor control.
3. Describe common motor control deficits.
4. Describe specific procedures and tests used to assess motor control deficits.
5. Identify complicating factors that may influence the results of a motor control assessment.

Motor control evolves from a complex set of neurologic and mechanical processes that govern posture and movement. Some movements are genetically predetermined and become apparent through processes of normal growth and development. Examples of these include the **reflex** patterns that predominate during much of our early life. Other movements, termed motor skills, are learned through interaction and exploration of the environment. Practice and experience are important variables in defining motor learning and motor skill development. Sensory information about movement is used to guide and shape the development of the **motor program.** A motor program is a set of commands that, when initiated, results in the production of a coordinated movement sequence.[1] **Motor plans** combine several motor programs into an action strategy while subprograms are smaller subroutines of coordinated muscle action. **Motor memory** involves the storage of motor programs or subprograms and includes information on how the movement felt (sense of effort), movement components, and movement outcome. Memory allows for continued access of this information for repeat performance or modification of existing patterns of movement.

Both reflex patterns and motor skills are subject to control by the central nervous system (CNS), which organizes vast amounts of sensory information and produces the commands necessary for coordinated movement. Several levels of CNS command hierarchies can be identified (Fig. 8–1). The highest level includes the association cortex and basal ganglia (caudate loop), which organize sensory information and elaborate the overall motor plan. The middle level includes the sensorimotor cortex, cerebellum, basal ganglia (putamen loop), and brainstem. These areas shape and define the

specific motor programs and initiate commands. The lowest level is the spinal cord, which executes the commands, translating them into the final muscle actions.[2] These CNS levels do not function in a rigid top-down hierarchic manner, as once thought, but rather appear flexible. Control commands operate through numerous feedback loops and proceed in both ascending and descending manner. Systems theory suggests a distributed mode of motor control. A basic concept of this theory is that units of the CNS are organized around specific task demands (termed task systems). The entire CNS may be necessary for complex tasks, while only small portions may be needed for simple tasks. Command levels vary depending upon the specific task executed. Thus the highest level of command may not be required in the execution of some simple movements.[3,4]

Damage to the central nervous system interferes with motor control processes. Lesions affecting specific areas of the CNS can produce specific, recognizable deficits that are consistent among patients, e.g., patients with stroke typically demonstrate abnormal synergistic patterns. Integrated action of the CNS is also impaired and this may account for individual differences in CNS adaptation and movement outcomes. In conditions with widespread damage to the CNS (e.g., traumatic head injury) the resultant problems in motor control are numerous, complex, and difficult to delineate.

The selection of motor control assessments is dependent upon several factors. Specific parameters of control need to be identified and an appropriate tool selected. If the tool accurately measures the parameter of performance being examined, it is said to have validity. The reliability of an instrument is reflected in the consistency of results obtained by an examiner over repeat trials (intra-rater reliability) or by multiple examiners

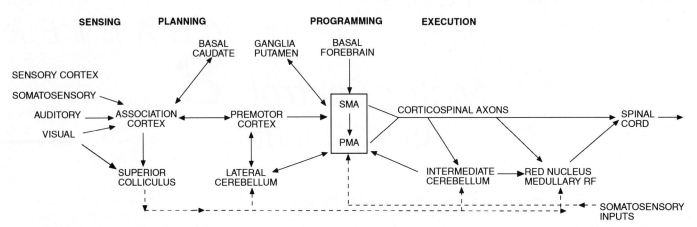

Figure 8–1. Major directions of information flow, during a voluntary movement, to and from the primary motor areas (PMA) and supplementary motor areas (SMA). Only some of the connections of the superior colliculus are shown. (RF = reticular formation.) (From Brooks,[2] p 199, with permission.)

(inter-rater reliability). Therapists should select standardized tools with established validity and reliability whenever possible. Assessments can be qualitative, focusing on a subjective estimation of performance, or quantitative, using objective measures. Documentation constraints imposed by the health care system and third party payers increasingly emphasize objective, quantitative assessments as proof of the need for services and the effectiveness of services.

FACTORS INFLUENCING MOTOR CONTROL ASSESSMENT

Cognition

In patients with CNS lesions, mental status may be affected. Cognitive deficits can range from loss of consciousness to memory deficits, poor judgment, short attention span, distractibility, or difficulties in information processing and learning, to name just a few. A detailed assessment by a clinical neuropsychologist may be necessary to obtain a complete and accurate picture of these deficits.[5] Lack of attention to cognitive problems by the physical therapist can render an assessment of motor control in a patient with brain damage invalid and unreliable.

The patient's ability to follow directions and understand the task should be ascertained. If memory and short-term learning are impaired, instructions should be kept to brief, concise phrases. New tasks may pose greater problems for the patient than tasks which are familiar. Complex tasks can be broken down into component parts to simplify them and ensure successful performance. Arranging the environment by reducing distractors may also be necessary to ensure maximum performance during assessment. Demonstration and positive feedback can assist the patient to understand what is expected, and can be used to improve performance. Whenever modifications and cognitive strategies are necessary, they should be recorded in the patient's chart.

Communication

Communication disorders may occur in patients with CNS lesions. The speech and language pathologist has the primary role in assessment, diagnosis, and treatment of these deficits. Problems can range from articulation deficits, dysarthria, to receptive and expressive language dysfunction, aphasia. A speech and language assessment generally includes an examination of cognitive skills (tests of attention, memory, and thought processing) and language skills (speaking, reading, and writing). See Chapter 29 for a thorough discussion of this topic.

Auditory or visual receptive problems can significantly impair performance on a physical therapy assessment. It is crucial to identify an appropriate means of communicating with the patient. This may include simplifying verbal or written instructions, or using alternate forms of communication such as gestures, pantomime, or communication boards. A common error is to assume that the patient understands the task at hand when he or she really has no idea what is expected. To ensure accuracy of testing, frequent checks for comprehension should be performed throughout the assessment. For example, the use of message discrepancies (saying one thing and gesturing another) can be used to test the patient's level of understanding.[6,7]

Arousal (Central State)

An assessment of **arousal** level or central state is important in determining the degree to which an individual is able to respond. Low arousal is associated with sleep or drowsiness, whereas high arousal is associated with extreme excitement. The autonomic nervous system (ANS) functions to establish baseline values for a number of body functions, maintain equilibrium (homeostasis), and to initiate actions designed to adapt and protect the individual under varying circumstances. Autonomic and somatic systems interact and influence each other through the action of the brainstem and more specifically the reticular formation (RF). Sensory stimuli influence the RF and initiate arousal responses, while motor systems become engaged in carrying out the commands of the RF in producing "fight or flight" responses. Balanced interaction of the autonomic and somatic systems allows for reactive yet stable responses of an individual.[8]

An imbalance in the ANS, with the sympathetic system dominant, results in an individual with high arousal. Specific responses include hyperalertness, increased heart rate (HR), increased blood pressure (BP), increased respiratory rate (RR), dilated pupils, and sweating. Whereas a certain level of arousal is necessary for optimal motor performance, high levels cause a deterioration in performance. This is referred to as the **inverted-U theory** or the **Yerkes-Dodson law.**[9] Excess levels of arousal can also yield unexpected responses. This theory was originally proposed by Wilder as the **Law of Initial Value (LIV).**[10] Patients at either end of an arousal continuum (either very high or very low) may not respond at all or may respond in an unpredictable manner. Stockmeyer[11] suggests that this may explain the reactions of labile patients who seem to lack the homeostatic controls for normal function. Assessment of baseline levels of central state should, therefore, precede other aspects of a motor control assessment in the patient suspected of autonomic instability (e.g., brain injury). Critical factors in obtaining a baseline assessment include: (1) a representative sampling of ANS responses, including HR, BP, RR, pupil dilation and sweating; (2) a determination of patient reactivity, including the degree of response, rate of response to sensory stimulation; and (3) a determination of compensatory mechanisms in response to physiologic stressors.[11] Careful monitoring during motor performance can also assist in defining homeostatic stability. More specific guidelines for assessment of vital functions can be found in Chapter 4.

Sensation

Sensory information is a critical component of motor control because it provides the necessary feedback used to monitor and shape performance. This is termed a **closed-loop system** and is defined as "a control system employing feedback, a reference of correctness, computation of error, and subsequent correction in order to maintain a desired state of the environment."[12] A variety of feedback sources are used to monitor movement including visual, vestibular, proprioceptive, and tactile inputs. The CNS analyzes all available movement information, determines error, and institutes appropriate corrective action when necessary. Thus a thorough sensory examination of each of these systems is an important preliminary step in a motor control assessment (see Chapter 6).

The primary role of closed-loop systems in motor control appears to be the monitoring of constant states such as posture and balance, and the control of slow movements or those requiring a high degree of accuracy. Feedback information is also essential for the learning of new motor tasks. Patients who have deficits in any movement-monitoring sensory system may be able to compensate with other sensory systems. For example, the patient with major proprioceptive losses can use vision as an error-correcting system to maintain a stable posture. When vision is occluded, however, postural instability becomes readily apparent (e.g., positive Romberg test). Significant sensory losses and inadequate compensatory shifts to other sensory processes may result in severely disordered movement responses. The patient with proprioceptive losses and severe visual disturbances, such as diplopia (commonly seen in the multiple sclerosis patient), may be unable to maintain a stable posture at all. An accurate assessment, therefore, requires that the therapist not only look at each individual sensory system but also at the overall interaction of these systems and compensatory adjustments. Postural tasks, balance, slow (ramp) movements, tracking tasks, or new motor tasks provide the ideal challenge in which to monitor feedback control and closed-loop processes.

Perception

Perceptual function is defined as the selection, integration, and interpretation of sensory stimuli from the body and the surrounding environment. It is critical to motor performance, motor learning, and successful interaction with the environment. Deficits can frequently go undetected, produce ineffectual behaviors, and influence the results of a motor control assessment. Perceptual problems should always be suspected when the patient has great difficulty in accomplishing a task, although specific causes (e.g., spasticity, weakness) cannot be identified. Perceptually impaired patients also display difficulty in doing simple tasks independently and safely, in completing tasks, and in switching from one task to another. These patients tend to make the same mistakes over and over again and often show a diminished capacity to visually locate or identify objects that seem necessary for task completion. They also experience difficulty in following simple instructions even though comprehension is good. Perceptually impaired individuals are often impulsive, distractible, and frustrated, and exhibit poor motor planning ability. Patients who are inattentive to one side of the body or deny the presence or extent of disability must also be suspected of perceptual dysfunction.[13] The occupational therapist has a primary role in the assessment, diagnosis, and treatment of these deficits. See Chapter 28 for a thorough discussion of this topic.

MOTOR CONTROL ASSESSMENT

The assessment of motor control dysfunction is a multifaceted process that seeks to identify areas of deficit in peripheral and/or central function. Thus a number of assessments are discussed.

Flexibility

Available range of motion (ROM) at specific joints is an important element of functional movement. Limitations restrict the normal action of muscles as well as the biomechanical alignment of body parts. Longstanding immobilization results in contracture, a fixed resistance resulting from fibrosis of tissues surrounding a joint. There is considerable variability in ROM among normal individuals. Factors influencing this variability include age, sex, and other factors. Average ranges of motion are available from the American Academy of Orthopedic Surgeons[14] and from other texts.[15] These averages should be viewed with caution because the populations used are not specifically defined and the test positions and instruments are not identified.

Assessment includes active ROM, passive ROM, end-feel, and tests for flexibility. **Active range of motion (AROM)** refers to the amount of joint motion obtained with unassisted voluntary joint motion. Muscle strength and coordination are some of the factors that can influence active ROM. Usually the therapist visually judges available active movement, although a goniometer can be used if comparisons with passive ROM are to be made. Additionally the therapist should determine: (1) the presence of pain with motion (when pain appears, how severe is the pain, what is the patient's reaction to the pain), (2) the pattern and quality of the movement, (3) movement of associated joints or substitutions, and (4) the cause of limitation if present.[16] As a general rule, if a patient is able to perform full active ROM, without pain or discomfort, passive ROM testing is not necessary.[17]

Passive range of motion (PROM) is the amount of joint motion available when an examiner moves the joint through the range without assistance from the patient. Normally passive ROM is slightly greater than active ROM, the result of **joint play** motion. This is the small amount of joint motion that occurs at the end range and is not under voluntary control. Passive ROM is always tested with a goniometer. The reliability and validity of goniometric measurements can be influenced by a number of factors, including motions tested, passive versus active ROM, methods of application and variations among different patient types.[18] Clinical measurement can be improved through the use of standardized testing procedures, which have been described in detail. Norkin and White's *Measurement of Joint Motion* is an excellent text.[15] In addition to goniometric measurements, the therapist should determine the cause of limitation (e.g., pain, spasm, adhesion, etc.) and the quality of the movement observed (e.g., jerky, hypertonic, rigid, etc.).[16]

End-feel refers to the characteristic feel each specific joint has at the end range of motion. Some joints are limited by the joint capsule, while other joints are limited by ligaments, joint surfaces, muscle tension, or soft tissue approximation. Determination of normal end-feels (soft, firm, and hard) and pathologic end-feels (soft, firm, hard, empty) is enhanced by the use of standardized descriptions[15] and requires practice and sensitivity.

Special tests are available to assess any involved joint. Generally these tests assist in the determination of joint ligamentous integrity and/or muscle flexibility. The results of these tests, when considered with all other assessments can be used to detect specific injuries, diseases, or conditions. Hoppenfeld's *Physical Examination of the Spine and Extremities*[17] and Magee's *Orthopedic Physical Assessment*[16] are two excellent references which describe these numerous tests.

Tone

Muscle **tone** is defined as the resistance of muscle to passive elongation or stretch. Resistance may be due to (1) physical inertia, (2) intrinsic mechanical-elastic stiffness of muscle and connective tissues, and (3) reflex muscle contraction (tonic stretch reflexes).[19] Since muscles rarely work in isolation, the term postural tone is preferred by some clinicians to describe a pattern of muscular tension that exists throughout the body and affects groups of muscles.[20] Tone is categorized as **hypertonia** (increased above normal resting levels), **hypotonia** (decreased below normal resting levels), or **dystonia** (impaired or disordered tonicity).

TONAL ABNORMALITIES
Spasticity

In **spasticity,** there is a velocity-dependent increase in tonic stretch reflexes with exaggerated tendon jerks (phasic stretch reflexes). The term velocity-dependent implies that the quicker the stretch, the stronger the resistance of the spastic muscle. Spasticity results from both disordered spinal mechanisms (altered synaptic activity, changes in the intrinsic electrical properties of the neuron) and disordered supraspinal mechanisms (gamma efferent hyperexcitability of the stretch reflex).[19,21] Spasticity is one component of **upper motor neuron (UMN) syndrome.** Upper motor neuron syndrome is a term used to describe the motor dysfunction observed in patients with lesions of cortical, subcortical, or spinal cord structures. Additional symptoms include abnormal reflex behaviors, loss of precise autonomic control, impaired muscle activation, paresis, decreased dexterity, and fatigability.[19,22]

Passive stretch of a spastic muscle may produce an initial high resistance, followed by a sudden inhibition or letting go of resistance, termed the **clasp-knife reflex. Clonus,** characterized by cyclical, spasmodic hyperactivity of antagonistic muscles occurring at a regular frequency, may occur with sustained stretch to a spastic muscle. Clonus is common in the calf muscles but may also occur in other areas of the body such as the jaw or wrist. The Babinski reflex, dorsiflexion of the great toe with fanning of the other toes on stimulation of the lateral sole of the foot, is a common finding with spastic hypertonia.[19]

Brainstem lesions can produce either decerebrate rigidity or decorticate rigidity. **Decerebrate rigidity** refers to sustained contraction and posturing of the trunk and limbs in a position of full extension. **Decorticate rigidity** refers to sustained contraction and posturing of the trunk and lower limbs in extension, and the upper limbs in flexion. Both decerebrate and decorticate rigidity result from an alteration in control of the stretch reflex arc, and can be viewed as an exaggerated and severe form of spasticity.

Rigidity

In **rigidity,** resistance is uniformly increased in both agonist and antagonist muscles, rendering body parts stiff and immoveable. Rigidity is relatively constant and independent of the velocity of a stretch stimulus. Lesions of the nigrostriatal dopamine system of the basal ganglia produce the rigidity commonly seen in Parkinson's disease. While the etiology is not well understood, it appears the rigidity is the result of excessive supraspinal drive acting on a normal spinal mechanism.[23] Patients may demonstrate either **cogwheel rigidity** or **leadpipe rigidity.** Cogwheel rigidity is a rachetlike response to passive movement characterized by an alternate letting go and increasing resistance to movement, while leadpipe rigidity is a constant rigidity. Bradykinesia, tremor, and loss of postural stability are motor deficits associated with rigidity in patients with Parkinson's disease.[22]

Flaccidity

Hypotonia and **flaccidity** are the terms used to define decreased or absent muscular tone. Resistance to passive movement is diminished, stretch reflexes are dampened, and limbs are easily displaced (floppy) with frequent hyperextensibility of joints. Movements are generally impaired, with weakness (paresis) or paralysis. Hypotonia can be produced by upper motor neuron lesions affecting the cerebellum or pyramidal tracts. Hypotonia can also occur as a temporary state, termed **spinal shock** or **cerebral shock,** depending upon the location of the injury to the central nervous system. The duration of the CNS depression that occurs with shock is highly variable and typically is followed by an emerging hyperreflexic, hypertonic state. Lower motor neuron lesions affecting the peripheral nervous system can produce symptoms of muscle weakness or paralysis, fasciculations, hypotonia, hyporeflexia, and atrophy.[24]

Dystonia

Dystonia is a hyperkinetic movement disorder characterized by impaired or disordered tone, and sustained and twisting involuntary movements. Muscle contractions may be slow or rapid, and are repetitive and patterned (writhing). Tone fluctuates in an unpredictable manner from low to high. **Dystonic posturing** refers to a sustained twisting deformity that may last for several minutes or permanently. Dystonia results from a central deficit and can be inherited (primary idiopathic dystonia), associated with other neurodegenerative disorders (Wilson's disease, Parkinson's disease), or metabolic disorders (amino acid or lipid disorders). Dystonia is also seen in dystonia musculorum deformans or spasmodic torticollis (wry neck).[24]

TONAL ASSESSMENT

Tone can be influenced by a number of factors including (1) position and interaction of tonic reflexes, (2)

stress and anxiety, (3) volitional effort and movement, (4) medications, (5) general health, (6) environmental temperature, and (7) state of CNS arousal or alertness. In addition, bladder state (full or empty), fever and infection, and metabolic and/or electrolyte imbalance can also influence tone. The therapist should consider the impact of each of these factors in arriving at a determination of tone. Tonal assessment requires repeat examinations and a highly consistent testing approach in order to improve the reliability of test results.

Initial Observation

Initial observation of the patient can reveal abnormal posturing of the limbs or body. Stereotyped movement patterns (abnormal synergies) are suggestive of the presence of tone abnormalities. Involuntary fluctuating movements may be indicative of dystonia, while complete absence of spontaneous movements may be indicative of flaccidity. Careful clinical assessment should be made regarding the effect of the patient's body and head positions on tone. For example, the patient who is supine with the lower limb stiffly held in extension and plantarflexion can be suspected of having increased extensor tone due to the tonic labyrinthine reflex. Symmetrical and asymmetrical tonic neck reflexes and supporting reactions also commonly influence tone. Posturing in fixed, antigravity positions, for instance, with the arm held fixed against the body in flexion, adduction, and supination, is also suggestive of spasticity. Limbs that appear floppy and lifeless, for example, a leg rolled out to the side in external rotation, may be indicative of a low tone condition. Palpation may yield information about the resting state of muscles. Consistency, firmness, and turgor can be examined and the responsiveness to touch noted.

Deep tendon reflexes. Tapping the tendon directly with the tips of the therapist's fingers or with a standard reflex hammer is used to assess the deep tendon reflexes (DTRs). The resulting muscle contraction is subjectively graded using a scale of 0–4. A normal response is graded a 2+. In spastic hypertonia the reflexes will be exaggerated (3+) or clonic (4+), while in hypotonic states the reflexes will be decreased (1+) or absent (0). Typical reflexes examined include the jaw, biceps, brachioradialis, triceps, patellar, hamstring, and ankle (see Table 8–1). Use of standardized positions also allows the therapist to accurately isolate and examine radicular integrity of muscles. If DTRs are difficult to elicit, responses can be usually enhanced by specific reinforcement maneuvers. In the **Jendrassik maneuver,** the patient hooks together the fingers of the hands and attempts to pull them apart. While this pressure is maintained, the reflex is tested. Additional maneuvers include clenching the teeth or making a contralateral fist when upper extremity reflexes are being tested.[25]

Passive Motion Testing

Assessment of passive motion reveals subjective information about the responsiveness of muscles to a stretch stimulus. Since these responses should be examined in the absence of voluntary control, the patient is instructed to relax, letting the therapist support and

Table 8–1 REFLEX ASSESSMENT—MYOTATIC REFLEXES*

Myotatic Reflexes (Stretch)	Stimulus	Response
Jaw (trigeminal n)	Patient is sitting, with jaw relaxed and slightly open. Place finger on top of chin; tap downward on top of finger in a direction which causes the jaw to open.	Jaw rebounds.
Biceps (C5, C6)	Patient is sitting with arm flexed and supported. Place thumb over the biceps tendon in the cubital fossa, stretching it slightly. Tap thumb or directly on tendon.	Slight contraction of muscle normally occurs (elbow flexes).
Triceps (C7, C8)	Patient is sitting with arm supported in abduction, elbow flexed. Palpate triceps tendon just above olecranon. Tap directly on tendon.	Slight contraction of muscle normally occurs (elbow extends).
Hamstrings (L5, S1, S2)	Patient is prone with knee semiflexed and supported. Palpate tendon at the knee. Tap on finger or directly on tendon.	Slight contraction of muscle normally occurs (knee flexes).
Patellar (L2, L3, L4)	Patient is sitting with knee flexed, foot unsupported. Tap tendon of quadriceps muscle between the patella and tibial tuberosity.	Contraction of muscle normally occurs (knee extends).
Ankle (S1, S2)	Patient is prone with foot over the end of the plinth or sitting with knee flexed and foot held in slight dorsification. Tap tendon just above its insertion on the calcaneus. Maintaining slight tension on the gastrocnemius-soleus group improves the response.	Slight contraction of muscle normally occurs (foot plantarflexes).

*Scoring key for myotatic reflexes: 0 = no response; 1+ = decreased response; 2+ = normal response; 3+ = exaggerated response; 4+ = clonus.

move the limb. All movements are assessed, with particular attention given to those identified as problematic in the initial observation period. During a passive motion test, the therapist should maintain firm and constant manual contacts, moving the limb randomly and at a continuous rate. When tone is normal, the limb moves easily and the therapist is able to alter direction and speed without feeling abnormal resistance. The limb is responsive and feels light. Hypertonic limbs generally feel stiff and resistant to movement, while flaccid limbs feel heavy and unresponsive. Older adults may find it difficult to relax; their stiffness should not be mistaken for spasticity.[26] Varying the speed of movement is important. Faster movements intensify the response and increase the amount of resistance offered by a spastic muscle. Clonus, a phasic stretch response, is assessed using a quick stretch stimulus. For example, ankle clonus is tested by sudden dorsiflexion of the foot. The clasp-knife phenomena should also be assessed.

A qualitative determination of the degree of tone should be made. Therapists need to be familiar with the wide range of normal responses in order to develop an appropriate frame of reference to evaluate abnormality. In cases of localized or unilateral dysfunction (e.g., hemiplegia), comparison to the unaffected, "normal" limbs is common. These comparisons may not be reliable, however, since abnormal findings have been reported on these supposedly normal extremities.[27]

A general clinical scale used to evaluate tone is

0 No response (flaccidity)
1 Decreased response (hypotonia)
2 Normal response
3 An exaggerated response (mild to moderate hypertonia)
4 A sustained response (severe hypertonia)

A clinical scale developed to assess spastic hypertonia is the Ashworth Scale, a five-point ordinal scale.[28] A later modification created an additional intermediate grade to reduce the clustering effect around the middle grades and it has been shown to have high inter-rater reliability.[29] See Table 8–2 for a description of the modified Ashworth scale.

Pendulum test. A **pendulum test** can be used to assess spasticity. With the patient seated or lying with knees flexed over the end of a table, the patient's knee is fully extended and allowed to drop and swing like a pendulum. A normal and hypotonic limb will swing freely for several oscillations. Hypertonic limbs are resistant to the swinging motion and will quickly return to the initial dependent starting position. Movements can be quantified using an electrogoniometer (ROM oscillations) and an electromyograph (EMG) (motor unit activity).[30] The pendulum test has also been performed on an isokinetic dynamometer with high test-retest reliability.[31]

Drop arm test. In a **drop arm test,** the therapist tests the integrity of automatic proprioceptive reactions by suddenly dropping a limb that has been held. A normal limb falls momentarily, then catches and maintains the position as intact proprioceptors react to prevent it from falling. Hypotonic limbs fall abruptly, while hypertonic limbs demonstrate a delay and resistance to falling.[20]

Table 8–2 MODIFIED ASHWORTH SCALE FOR GRADING SPASTICITY

Grade	Description
0	No increase in muscle tone.
1	Slight increase in muscle tone, manifested by a catch and release or by minimal resistance at the end of the ROM when the affected part(s) is moved in flexion or extension.
1+	Slight increase in muscle tone, manifested by a catch, followed by minimal resistance throughout the remainder (less than half) of the ROM.
2	More marked increase in muscle tone through most of the ROM, but affected part(s) easily moved.
3	Considerable increase in muscle tone, passive movement difficult.
4	Affected part(s) rigid in flexion or extension.

From Bohannon and Smith,[29] p 207, with permission from the APTA.

Voluntary Movement Control

Assessment of voluntary movement control can reveal additional information about the influence of tonal abnormalities on motor control. During functional assessment, movements should be carefully observed and analyzed for tonal interference. Strong efforts are likely to produce increased arousal and hypertonic responses. Quantitative scoring systems, based on the time it takes to complete an activity, can be used. Scoring systems have been developed that attempt to evaluate the influence of spasticity on voluntary control, ranging from the absence of voluntary movement to normal voluntary control.[20,32–34] These assessments allow objective measurement of function but provide only an indirect estimation of tone. Since other problems may be the cause of poor functional performance (e.g., decreased ROM, altered recruitment patterns), the therapist must use this information as an adjunct to other tonal assessments.[35]

Assessment should also focus on automatic postural tone (APT) or postural set. The preparatory (feed forward) adjustments in postural tone needed in advance of voluntary movement or anticipated displacements in the body's center of gravity are analyzed. Specific activities can include (1) the assumption of upright positioning (e.g., sitting up) and (2) self-initiated arm movements (e.g., reaching forward) in sitting or standing. Postural control deficits (e.g., increased sway and instability or excessive stiffness) can reveal important information about CNS tonal control.[36,37]

Other Measures

Biomechanical investigations that examine torque and electromyography (EMG) have been used in the clinical assessment of tone and movement (see Chapter 9). Specifically, investigation has focused on reflex stiffness and velocity sensitivity, and phasic and tonic stretch reflex dysfunction in spasticity.[19]

Electrophysiologic reflex testing has also been used to assess tone. The Hoffman (H) reflex is elicited by an electrical stimulus, usually to the tibial nerve. The large Ia afferent fiber (an artificially induced DTR) is stimulated. Increased H-reflex responsiveness is present in spastic hemiplegia and spinal cord injury.[19] The **tonic vibration reflex** (TVR) is a sustained contraction of the muscle in response to the application of an electrically driven vibrator. Normal individuals are able to voluntarily inhibit the TVR while those with spasticity are not. In moderate and severe spasticity, vibratory suppression of the deep tendon reflexes is considerably less than normal. Vibration in spastic hypertonia may also produce timing abnormalities (sudden or jerky onset) and an irradiation or spreading of the tonic contraction to other muscles, including antagonists.[38]

Reflexes and Reactions

SUPERFICIAL CUTANEOUS REFLEXES

Superficial reflexes are elicited with a noxious stimulus, usually a light scratch. Some reflexes which are commonly tested are the plantar reflex, confirming toe signs (Chaddock), and superficial abdominal reflexes. The plantar reflex is tested for the presence of a Babinski response. A noxious stroking stimulus is applied on the sole of the foot along the lateral surface of the foot and up across the ball of the foot. A normal response consists of flexion of the big toes, sometimes the other toes, or no response at all. An abnormal response (positive Babinski) consists of extension (dorsiflexion) of the big toe, sometimes with fanning of the other toes. In adults, it is always indicative of corticospinal dysfunction. The Chaddock sign is elicited by stroking around the lateral ankle and up the lateral aspect of the foot. It also produces extension of the big toe and is considered a confirmatory toe sign. The superficial abdominal reflex is elicited with quick, light strokes over the skin of the abdominals. A localized contraction under the stimulus is produced, with a resultant deviation of the umbilicus toward the area stimulated. An abnormal response consists of no response or a strong, delayed response.[25] Examples of superficial reflex tests are summarized in Table 8–3.

DEVELOPMENTAL REFLEXES AND REACTIONS

Information about the function and integration of the developmental reflexes and reactions is obtained through a systematic examination. Assessment begins with the primitive and tonic reflexes. These reflexes are

Table 8–3 REFLEX ASSESSMENT—SUPERFICIAL REFLEXES

Superficial Reflexes (Cutaneous)	Stimulus	Response
Plantar (S1, S2)	With a large pin or fingertip, stroke up the lateral side of the foot, moving from the heel to the base of the little toe and then across the ball of the foot.	Normal response is plantarflexion of the great toe, and sometimes the other toes, with slight inversion and flexion of the distal foot. Abnormal response, termed a + Babinski, is extension of the great toe with fanning of the four other toes (typically seen in upper motor neuron lesions).
Chaddock	Stroke around lateral ankle and up lateral aspect of foot to the base of the little toe.	Same as for plantar.
Abdominal (T7–12)	Position patient in supine position, relaxed. Make quick, light stroke with a large pin or fingertip over the skin of the abdominals from the periphery to the umbilicus (test each abdominal quadrant separately).	Localized contraction under the stimulus, causing the umbilicus to move toward the quadrant stimulated.

normally present during gestation or infancy and become integrated by the CNS at an early age. Once integrated, these reflexes are not generally recognizable in their pure form. They do continue, however, as adaptive fragments of behavior, underlying normal motor control and aiding volitional movement.[39] In adults, they are apparent under some conditions of fatigue or effort,[40,41] or following damage to the CNS.[32,42] Adult patients who present with developmental reflexes demonstrate a limitation of freedom of the normal selection of movements and postures. Reflexes in this category include (1) spinal level or elemental reflexes—flexor withdrawal, extensor thrust, crossed extension and (2) brainstem level or tuning reflexes—tonic neck, tonic labyrinthine, and associated reactions. Spinal level reflex responses are generally the simplest to observe and are typically judged by their appearance as part of an overt movement response. Brainstem reflexes on the other hand serve to bias the musculature and may not be visible through movement responses. In fact, movement is rarely produced but rather posture is more typically influenced through tonal adjustments. Thus the term "tuning reflexes" is an appropriate description of their function.

To obtain an accurate assessment, the therapist must be concerned with several factors. The patient must be postioned appropriately to allow for the predicted movement response. An adequate test stimulus is essential, including both an adequate magnitude and duration of stimulation. Keen observation skills are needed to detect what may be subtle movement changes and to distinguish normal from abnormal responses. Obligatory and sustained responses which dominate motor behavior are always considered abnormal in the adult patient. Palpation skills can assist in identifying tonal changes not readily apparent to the eye. Objective scoring of responses is essential. A sample reflex scoring key suggested by Capute et al.[43,44] is as follows:

0   Absent
1 + Tone change: slight, transient with no movement of the extremities
2 + Visable movement of extremity
3 + Exaggerated, full movement of extremities
4 + Obligatory and sustained movement, lasting for more than 30 seconds

Higher level reactions (righting, equilibrium, protective) are controlled by centers in the midbrain and cortex and are important components of normal postural control and movement. The term **reaction** is commonly used to refer to those reflexes that appear during infancy or early childhood and remain throughout life. **Righting reactions** (RR) serve to maintain the head in its normal upright posture (face vertical, mouth horizontal) or to maintain the normal alignment of the head and trunk. Assessment procedures focus on positioning or manipulating the body and observing the automatic adjustments necessary to restore normal alignment and head position. **Equilibrium reactions** (ER) serve to maintain balance in response to alterations in the body's center of gravity (COG) and/or base of support (BOS). They can be tested by using a movable surface that alters the patient's base of support with respect to the body's

center of gravity (termed tilting reactions). Equilibrium boards or gymnastic balls are commonly used to assess tilting reactions. Equilibrium reactions can also be tested by altering the patient's position through voluntary movements or by perturbation (manual displacement). Protective reactions (PR, protective extension reactions) serve to stabilize and support the body in response to a displacing stimulus when the center of gravity exceeds the base of support. Thus the arms or legs extend in an effort to support the body weight as the body falls toward the support surface.

Reflex testing procedures have been effectively described by a number of authors.[43-46] These assessment procedures are outlined in Table 8–4.

Muscle Strength

Strength refers to the ability of muscle to produce force. The resultant force can be used in the production of movement (isotonic contraction) or in resistance to movement (isometric contraction). Current methods used to measure strength include manual muscle testing (MMT) and dynamometry. Standardized methods and protocols have been developed to address issues of validity and reliability.

Patients with central nervous system dysfunction present with deficits that pose additional challenges for the validity and reliability of strength testing. Therapists have for some time cautioned against using manual muscle testing in these patients. Bobath[20] cautioned that weakness of muscles in patients with CNS deficits may not be actual muscle weakness but may be the result of opposition by spastic antagonists, the presence of mass patterns of movements, sensory deficit, and/or lack of synergistic fixation. Spasticity in the agonist muscle can also interfere with force production.[35,47-49] Individual joint movements, mandated by standardized MMT procedures, may not be possible in the presence of stereotypical movement patterns. The mandated test positions may also be influenced by the presence of abnormal reflex activity.[32,50] The generalizability of strength measurements taken in one position to performance of tasks in other positions is also problematic.[51] Despite these limitations, clinical measurement of strength in patients with CNS lesions has been the focus of increasing attention in the literature. Investigators have utilized strength measures to assess paresis and have reported significant results in terms of reliability[52-55] and correlations between strength and functional capacity.[56,57] Rothstein et al.[51] conclude that many of these studies have serious methodological problems, which cast doubt on their validity. Patients with CNS lesions are a diverse group with many different problems and subcategories of function. Strength testing may be appropriate for some patients while not for others. Appropriate criteria for the use of strength tests are therefore critical in determining whether the standards of validity and reliability are met.

MANUAL MUSCLE TESTING

Two standardized approaches to manual muscle testing have been used in practice for a number of years.

Table 8–4 REFLEX ASSESSMENT—DEVELOPMENTAL REFLEXES

Primitive/Spinal Reflexes	Stimulus	Response
Flexor withdrawal	Noxious stimulus (pinprick) to sole of foot. Tested in supine or sitting position.	Toes extend, foot dorsiflexes, entire leg flexes uncontrollably. Onset: 28 weeks gestation. Integrated: 1–2 months.
Crossed extension	Noxious stimulus to ball of foot of extremity fixed in extension; tested in supine position.	Opposite lower extremity flexes, then adducts and extends. Onset: 28 weeks gestation. Integrated: 1–2 months.
Traction	Grasp forearm and pull up from supine into sitting position.	Grasp and total flexion of the upper extremity. Onset: 28 weeks gestation. Integrated: 2–5 months.
Moro	Sudden change in position of head in relation to trunk; drop patient backward from sitting position.	Extension, abduction of upper extremities, hand opening, and crying followed by flexion, adduction of arms across chest. Onset: 28 weeks gestation. Integrated: 5–6 months.
Startle	Sudden loud or harsh noise.	Sudden extension or abduction of arms, crying. Onset: birth. Integrated: persists.
Grasp	Maintained pressure to palm of hand (palmer grasp) or to ball of foot under toes (plantar grasp).	Maintained flexion of fingers or toes. Onset: palmer, birth; plantar, 28 weeks gestation. Integrated: palmer, 4–6 months; plantar, 9 months.

Tonic/Brainstem Reflexes	Stimulus	Response
Asymmetrical tonic neck (ATNR)	Rotation of the head to one side.	Flexion of skull limbs, extension of the jaw limbs, "bow and arrow" or "fencing" posture. Onset: birth. Integrated: 4–6 months.
Symmetrical tonic neck (STNR)	Flexion or extension of the head.	With head flexion: flexion of arms, extension of legs; with head extension: extension of arms, flexion of legs. Onset: 4–6 months. Integrated: 8–12 months.
Symmetrical tonic labyrinthine (TLR or STLR)	Prone or supine position.	With prone position: increased flexor tone/flexion of all limbs; with supine: increased tone/extension of all limbs. Onset: birth. Integrated: 6 months.
Positive supporting	Contact to the ball of the foot in upright standing position.	Rigid extension (co-contraction) of the lower extremities. Onset: birth. Integrated: 6 months.
Associated reactions	Resisted voluntary movement in any part of the body.	Involuntary movement in a resting extremity. Onset: birth–3 months. Integrated: 8–9 years.

Midbrain/Cortical Reflexes	Stimulus	Response
Neck righting action on the body (NOB)	Passively turn head to one side; tested in supine.	Body rotates as a whole (log rolls) to align the body with the head. Onset: 4–6 months. Integrated: 5 years.
Body righting acting on the body (BOB)	Passively rotate upper or lower trunk segment; tested in supine.	Body segment not rotated follows to align the body segments. Onset: 4–6 months. Integrated: 5 years.
Labyrinthine head righting (LR)	Occlude vision; alter body position by tipping body in all directions.	Head orients to vertical position with mouth horizontal. Onset: birth–2 months. Integrated: persists.
Optical righting (OR)	Alter body position by tipping body in all directions.	Head orients to vertical position with mouth horizontal. Onset: birth–2 months. Integrated: persists.
Body righting acting on head (BOH)	Place in prone or supine position.	Head orients to vertical position with mouth horizontal. Onset: birth–2 months. Integrated: 5 years.
Protective extension (PE)	Displace center of gravity outside the base of support.	Arms or legs extend and abduct to support and to protect the body against falling. Onset: arms, 4–6 months; legs, 6–9 months. Integrated: persists.
Equilibrium reactions—tilting (ER)	Displace the center of gravity by tilting or moving the support surface (e.g., with a movable object such as an equilibrium board or ball).	Curvature of the trunk toward the upward side along with extension and abduction of the extremities on that side; protective extension on the opposite (downward) side. Onset: prone 6 months; supine 7–8 months; sitting 7–8 months; quadruped 9–12 months; standing 12–21 months. Integrated: persists.
Equilibrium reactions—postural fixation	Apply a displacing force to the body, altering the center of gravity in its relation to the base of support; can also be observed during voluntary activity.	Curvature of the trunk toward the external force with extension and abduction of the extremities on the side to which the force was applied. Onset: prone 6 months; supine 7–8 months; sitting 7–8 months; quadruped 9–12 months; standing 12–21 months. Integrated: persists.

Table 8–5 MANUAL MUSCLE TESTING GRADES

Daniels and Worthingham	Kendall		
0 (zero)	0	0	No contraction felt.
T (trace)	5%	1	Muscle can be felt to tighten, but has no visible movement.
P (poor)	20%	2	Produces movement with gravity eliminated, but cannot function against gravity.
F (fair)	50%	3	Can move or hold against gravity.
G (good)	80%	4	Can move or hold against moderate resistance and gravity.
N (normal)	100%	5	Can move or hold against maximum resistance and gravity.

These include the Daniels and Worthingham[58] and Kendall[59] methods. Both use standardized positions, which attempt to isolate muscle function. In the Daniels and Worthingham method, resistance is applied throughout the range of motion, or alternately resistance is given at the end of the range (break test). In the Kendall method, maximum resistance is applied in the mid-range. Grading is based on the original work of Dr. Robert Lovett[60] and uses both gravity and manual resistance. Daniels and Worthingham use letter grades (after Lovett) to designate muscle strength, while Kendall uses percentages. Alternately, numerical grades have also been used (Table 8–5). Pluses and minuses are used to designate further graduations in the measurements. In order to ensure validity, therapists must carefully observe, palpate, and utilize correct positioning. Substitutions, muscle actions that compensate for specific muscle weakness, should be identified and eliminated. Limited ROM and lack of adequate stabilization are also factors that can influence muscle performance and grading, and should be noted. Reliability of manual muscle testing in the clinical setting has been low. In one study the investigators found the percentage of therapists, obtaining the same muscle grade, only ranged from 50 to 60 percent.[61] Factors that influence the reproducibility of the results include difficulty with determining the magnitude of resistive force (subjectivity of good and normal grades), differences in testing method, differences in force application (point, line of force, speed), duration of the contraction, patient factors (cooperation, fatigue), therapist factors (experience, instructions, volume of commands, interactions with patient), and environment (distracting influences).[61]

DYNAMOMETRY
Hand-held Dynamometry

Hand-held dynamometers are small portable devices that measure mechanical force; they have been incorporated clinically into manual muscle testing procedures. The therapist reads the exact amount of force applied to the muscle during tests for good and normal grades instead of estimating the amount of resistance.

High intra-tester and inter-tester reliability scores have been reported.[53,62,63] Limitations in their use include difficulty in stabilizing the limb and device, controlling the rate of muscle tension development, and applying sufficient force for a break test.[64] These may be factors in reports that the portable dynamometer is less reliable for testing lower extremity muscle groups.[65]

Isokinetic Dynamometry

An **isokinetic dynamometer** is an instrument that controls the velocity of a moving limb, keeping it at a constant rate, while accommodating resistance to match the patient's force as the part moves through the range. For example, the speed control on a Cybex II Isokinetic Dynamometer can be set between 0 and 300 degrees per second, while the range of torque output monitored is between 0 and 448 newton meters.[66] The use of an isokinetic dynamometer during a motor control assessment allows the therapist to monitor important characteristics of performance, including peak torque at varying speeds, and range of motion or arc of excursion as a function of time. Rate of tension development (time to peak torque) and shape of the torque curve have also been described. Since they are subject to a wide range of variability, they may not provide meaningful clinical measures.[67,68] Reciprocal contractions (agonist–antagonist relationships) have been analyzed. Corrections for weight of the limb (gravity effects) are necessary in order to arrive at an accurate relationship. Comparison with reciprocal actions in functional patterns of movement may not be valid as these two modes of action are very dissimilar.[67] Endurance (muscle fatigue) can also be measured. One commonly used method is percentage decrement, the time it takes for peak torque to drop by a certain percentage (e.g., 50%). Equipment also allows for testing of static measures (isometric peak torques) and eccentric torques. In order to ensure the validity of the measurements, calibration of the equipment is necessary and should be performed each day testing is done. Proper alignment of the joint axis and machine axis is required. Isokinetic testing has been shown to have high reliability for testing maximum torque production.[69–73] At least one practice session is recommended to acquaint the patient with the equipment and testing protocol. Repeat test sessions should utilize an identical protocol.

Patients with CNS involvement demonstrate a variety of deficits including decreased torque development, decreased limb excursion, extended times to peak torque development and the time peak torque is held, increased time intervals between reciprocal contractions, and/or problems in torque development at higher speeds.[27,74,75] For example, many patients with hemiplegia are unable to develop tension above 70 to 80 degrees per second. When this value is compared to the speed needed for normal walking (100 degrees per second), reasons for gait difficulties become readily apparent. Normative data, when available, can provide an appropriate reference for evaluating and interpreting patient data.[76–79] Watkins et al.[27] studied a group of patients with hemiplegia and found, in addition to many of the above changes, diminished torque values on the supposedly normal extremities. These findings cast doubt as to the validity of using the uninvolved side as a reference for normal control in patients with hemiplegia. Isokinetic dynamometry has provided useful and objective information about the movement problems of selected neurologic patients with high test-retest reliability.[54,75,80,81] Continued application of dynamometry in the area of motor control assessment is needed.

Movement Patterns

Most motor tasks are achieved through a combination of both open-loop and closed-loop processes. A central program defines the movement, while feedback functions to monitor and modify the movement as needed. Assessment should focus on both modes of control. Thus novel tasks and well-learned tasks should be included. The therapist needs to ascertain the balance between feedback guidance and motor programming. For example, in performing *learned tasks,* how much feedback control is needed to complete the movement? If an unexpected load or challenge to the movement is introduced, how quickly does the patient respond with the appropriate adjustment?

SYNERGISTIC ORGANIZATION

Synergy is the cooperative action of muscles working together to produce movement. These patterns of muscle actions operate with fixed spatial and temporal relationships. In normal movement, different synergies are selected and interwoven to produce coordinated movement. Testing of coordination is discussed fully in Chapter 7.

Synergistic organization of movement may be disturbed in cases of injury to the CNS. Mass patterns of movement dominate behavior, while selective movement control becomes disordered or disappears completely. Often primitive reflexes (e.g., asymmetrical tonic neck, tonic labyrinthine reflex, positive support) reemerge. **Abnormal synergies,** stereotyped patterns of flexion (flexion, abduction, external rotation) and extension (extension, adduction, internal rotation), are also typically present. Patients are firmly locked into these synergy patterns and cannot isolate individual joint movements. This loss of selective motor control is the result of impaired control by the higher centers and is not due to the presence of spasticity (a coexisting phenomena). In some patient populations, for instance, those with stroke, the abnormal synergies are highly predictable and characteristic of the middle stages of recovery.[20,32,33] Synergistic organization may also be temporally impaired. Patients may demonstrate a variety of movement patterns but have significant timing deficits.

Assessment of synergistic patterns is qualitative. The therapist observes movement in a variety of positions, and determines if movement is available, stereotypic, or normal. If the movement is stereotypic, what muscle groups are associated? How strong are the linkages between muscle groups? Are the movements influenced by primitive reflexes? For example, do elbow, wrist, and finger flexion always occur when shoulder flexion is initiated. Therapists also need to identify when these patterns occur, under what circumstances, and what variations are possible. As CNS recovery progresses, synergies become more variable and may only reemerge under certain conditions such as stress or fatigue. Lessening of synergy dominance and more variation of available movements thus become hallmarks of sequential recovery in patients with stroke. Some tests, Brunnstrom's Hemiplegic Classification and Progress Record[32] and Fugl-Meyer's Sensorimotor Assessment[33] assess control by using both in-synergy and out-of-synergy movements. Brunnstrom scored the test using available joint range completed, while Fugl-Meyer modified the original work of Brunnstrom and developed an ordinal rating scale, which rates whether the movement was minimally, partially, or maximally completed. Bobath[20] and Davies[50] focus hemiplegic assessment on the degree to which movements deviate from synergy patterns. Specific test items focus on selective movement control and scoring is on a simple yes-no basis.

Balance

Normal postural control involves the control of relative positions of body parts by skeletal muscles, with respect to gravity and to each other. **Balance** can be defined as the stability produced on each side of a vertical axis. The center of mass (COM) is maintained over the base of support (BOS). The overall goals of the balance control system are safety and function, achieved through multiple CNS inputs and outputs. Components include (1) sensory elements responsible for the detection of body motion, (2) sensory interaction processes, and (3) musculoskeletal elements. Assessment of balance should focus on each of these areas of function.

SENSORY ELEMENTS

The visual system detects the relative orientation of the body parts and the orientation of the body with reference to the environment (termed visual proprioception). It also relays information about the organization of the external environment. Motor functions include righting reactions of the head, trunk, and limbs (optical righting reactions), and visually guided movement. Visual acuity should be assessed using a Snellen eye chart. A distance acuity poorer than 20/50 will have a significant effect on postural stability.[82] Visual field defects (e.g., hemianopsia) can also affect balance.

Somatosensory inputs consist of the cutaneous sensations from body parts in contact with the support surface (e.g., feet) and muscle and joint proprioceptors. They detect the relative orientation and movement of body parts and orientation of the support surface. Motor functions include the stretch reflexes (myotatic and inverse myotatic reflexes), flexor withdrawal and crossed extensor reflexes, and automatic postural reactions. Assessment should include a sensory examination of the extremities and trunk. Cutaneous function (touch and pressure) and proprioceptive responses, particularly of the foot and ankle, are critical in ascertaining somatosensory contributions to balance.

The vestibular system detects angular and linear acceleration and deceleration forces acting on the head, and the orientation of the head with reference to gravity. Its primary motor functions include the stabilization of gaze during head movements (vestibulo-ocular reflex, VOR), righting reactions of the head, trunk, and limbs (labyrinthine righting reactions), and regulation of muscle tone and postural muscle activation. Tests for vestibular function include positional and movement testing, use of rotary chair (Barany test) and the caloric test. These tests stimulate the semicircular canals, either through movement or temperature changes, and the patient is observed for symptoms of vertigo and nystagmus (VOR effects).[83]

SENSORY INTERACTION

Sensory organization by the CNS is flexible; the CNS weights and uses the inputs as needed. All contribute to a sense of equilibrium, which is a sense of the position of the COM in relation to the support surface. Under most conditions, a stable support surface and surroundings, upright posture is primarily maintained by somatosensory inputs. If the support surface becomes disturbed, vision becomes the dominant input. If both the support surface and vision are disturbed, vestibular inputs, which are referenced to gravity, become dominant and resolve the sensory conflict.[84] Balance responses are therefore context dependent and are triggered by specific sensory inputs. Because these inputs are redundant, stable balance can be maintained in the absence of vision, on unstable surfaces, or in sensory conflict situations. If more than one sensory system is deficient however, lack of balance control will be evident.[85]

The **Clinical Test for Sensory Interaction in Balance (CTSIB)** is a simple, inexpensive test that can be used to assess sensory organization.[86] This test, also known as the foam and dome method, assesses standing balance under six different sensory conditions. The support surface varies from normal to standing on dense foam, which distorts orientational information. Visual inputs vary from eyes open, to eyes closed (similiar to a Romberg test), to wearing a dome that provides visually incorrect information by moving in phase with the patient's head movement. Condition 1 provides the baseline reference, while each of the other 5 conditions systematically varies the sensory inputs, increasing the level of sensory conflict. Condition 6 (altered somatosensory and visual inputs) is the most difficult. Each condition is maintained for 30 seconds. The CTSIB is scored by observing changes in the amount and direction of postural sway. A numerical scoring system (1 = minimal sway, 2 = mild sway, 3 = moderate sway, 4 = fall) can be used. Alternatively, the time in balance can be scored using a stopwatch, or the amount of sway can be estimated using a plumb line and postural grid. Subjective complaints of the patient (e.g., nausea, dizziness) and changes in movement strategy should be noted during each of the test conditions.

Dynamic posturography can give objective measures of balance responses using more sophisticated, computerized equipment. NeuroCom's Equitest is an example.[87] This equipment can be used to evaluate sensory organization (using the same six sensory conditions as the CTSIB) as well as the patient's motor performance. A visual surround is used instead of the dome head piece (Fig. 8-2). Both the surround and forceplate are referenced to the patient by means of hydraulic mechanisms. A printed bar graph tells how well the patient did during each of the six conditions. Ratios comparing one condition to another can provide information regarding reliance on one sensory system over another.

MUSCULOSKELETAL ELEMENTS

Musculoskeletal responses vary from the simple monosynaptic stretch reflex to functional stretch reflexes and postural synergies, and full-scale equilibrium reactions. **Limits of stability (LOS)** refers to the maximum angle from vertical that can be tolerated without a loss of balance. In adults, Nashner has found the LOS to be 12 degrees in an anteroposterior direction and 16 degrees in a medial-lateral direction.[84] As the LOS are reached with a COM disturbance, the magnitude of the postural response increases. Specific **automatic pos-**

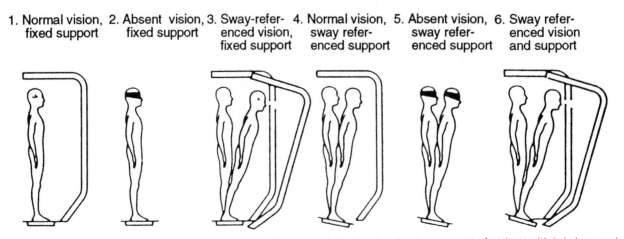

1. Normal vision, fixed support 2. Absent vision, fixed support 3. Sway-referenced vision, fixed support 4. Normal vision, sway referenced support 5. Absent vision, sway referenced support 6. Sway referenced vision and support

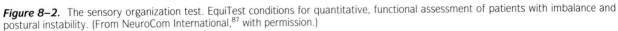

Figure 8–2. The sensory organization test. EquiTest conditions for quantitative, functional assessment of patients with imbalance and postural instability. (From NeuroCom International,[87] with permission.)

SAMPLE BALANCE EXERCISES FOR SPECIFIC GOALS

Training Ankle Strategy
- Standing on BAPS board with large dome
- Standing sway exercise
- Slow, small perturbations of balance
- Reaching for objects

Training Hip Strategy
- Standing on foam or a wedge or BAPS board w/ smaller dome
- Standing sway – client bows at waist
- Moderate, rapid perturbations of balance
- Reaching for objects at lower heights

Training Stepping Strategy
- Standing on foam/wedge and reaching for objects beyond hand's reach
- Stepping over obstacles
- Large, rapid perturbations of balance – predictable and unpredictable
- Step-ups and step-downs

Improving Center of Gravity Control
- Sitting
  - Sit on an unstable surface – wedge, mats, BAPS board, therapy ball
  - Alter upper extremity support on the seating surface – one hand, no hands, etc.
  - Incorporate reaching/throwing to challenge limits of stability
- Standing
  - Spell the alphabet in the air with one leg
  - Sit to and from standing
  - Elastic band exercises for lower extremities

Improving responses to changing Base of Support
- Standing
  - Feet together
  - Tandem standing
  - Single Limb
- Add upper extremity activities, making surface less compliant, causing perturbations

Training Gait
- Walk with narrower bases of support
- Walk backward, sideways or with sudden turns/stops/starts
- Add obstacles – on ground or at level requiring ducking

Training Visual system (by disadvantaging the vestibular and proprioceptive systems)
- Standing on compliant surfaces
- Teach how to fixate vision on specific objects

Training the Vestibular system (by disadvantaging the vision and proprioceptive systems)
- Standing on compliant surfaces with eyes closed or with vision distorted

Training the Proprioceptive system (by disadvantaging the visual system)
- Standing on noncompliant surfaces with eyes closed or vision distorted

tural synergies have been described by Nashner and others.[88-90] These are discrete patterns of leg and trunk muscle contractions that are characterized by consistency in muscle combinations, timing, and intensity and are used to preserve standing balance. The **ankle strategy** involves shifting the COM forward and back by rotating the body as a relatively rigid mass about the ankle joints. Muscle activation patterns occur in a distal to proximal sequence. The ankle strategy is most effective when there are small disturbances within the limits of stability. The **hip strategy** involves shifts in the COM by flexing or extending at the hips. It has a proximal to distal pattern of muscle activation and is utilized with larger disturbances of the COM and higher frequency sway. The **stepping strategy** realigns the BOS under the COM by using rapid steps in the direction of the displacing force. This strategy is elicited when the limits of stability are reached in response to fast, large postural perturbations. Ankle or hip strategies are no longer sufficient to maintain balance (Fig. 8-3). Accompanying these postural synergies, there is also a simultaneous descending pattern of activation of the head and trunk.[91] In sitting, postural synergies to regain balance include movement of the trunk about the hips, with thigh and abdominal muscles acting to maintain the seated position. Postural synergies can function in either a feedback mode (as a reaction to a specific stimulus) or in a feedforward mode (in preparation for voluntary movement which requires a balance adjustment). The term equilibrium reaction is used to denote a total body compensatory reaction involving automatic movements of the limbs and trunk. The initial response recruits the postural synergies. As the limits of stability are reached, compensatory arm, head, and trunk movements are added (see Table 8-4). Postural synergies and reactions

are influenced by previous experience, currently available sensory inputs, the specific parameters of a disturbing stimulus, and the position of the body at the time of imbalance.

The assessment of musculoskeletal components of balance should first include a determination of ROM, tone, and strength. Weakness and limited ROM in the ankles will affect successful use of an ankle strategy, while weakness and limited ROM about the hips will influence the hip strategy. Limitations of neck ROM can be expected in patients with primary vestibular disorders.

Traditional methods of balance assessment have focused on the maintenance of posture (static balance), balance during weight shifting or movement (dynamic balance), and responses to perturbation.[92-94] Both the sitting and standing positions can be used for static balance tests. Tests in standing include double limb support, single limb support, tandem (heel-toe position), and eyes open and eyes closed (Romberg test). Dynamic tests can include standing up, walking, turning, stopping, and starting. Subjective grading scales are typically used and can range from a simple three-point scale (absent, impaired, present) to a more definitive scale of functional balance grades (see Table 8-6) Reliability measures are lacking for most subjective scales. Time maintained in balance using a stopwatch for a 30-second trial has also been utilized with static tests.[95]

Postural synergies and reactions should be investigated. The therapist needs to determine if the synergies are (1) present and normal, (2) present but limited, (3) present but inappropriate for the particular context or situation, (4) abnormal, or (5) absent. Differences can be detected by systematically varying support surface characteristics and the size of postural perturbations. Both feedback and feedforward modes of control should be assessed. Balance control is therefore observed in response to a displacing force or perturbation (feedback mode). Both expected and unexpected forces should be used. Responses are then observed in response to a self-initiated movement task (e.g., reaching forward).[96] Duncan et al.[97] have developed a standing reach test that uses a simple yardstick to reliably measure balance control during functional reach.

The **postural stress test** (PST) by Wolfson et al.[98] is a useful clinical measure of motor responses to specified weight disturbances during standing. Weights (equal to

Ankle In-place strategies   Hip   Stepping strategy

Figure 8-3. Strategies for correcting balance perturbations. (From Nashner,[84] pp 6, 8, with permission.)

Table 8-6 FUNCTIONAL BALANCE GRADES

Normal	Patient is able to maintain balance without support. Accepts maximal challenge and can shift weight in all directions.
Good	Patient is able to maintain balance without support. Accepts moderate challenge and can shift weight, although limitations are evident.
Fair	Patient is able to maintain balance without support. Cannot tolerate challenge. Cannot maintain balance while shifting weight.
Poor	Patient requires support to maintain balance.
Zero	Patient requires maximal assistance to maintain balance.

From Leahy,[127] p 75, with permission.

1.5%, 3%, and 4% of body weight) are applied through a pulley system to a waist belt which is, in turn, attached to the patient. The subject's responses to these disturbances are videotaped over three trials and analyzed. A balance strategy score (BSS) is determined based on the postural synergies with nine different scores possible. High inter-rater reliability has been reported.[99] The maximal load test of Lee et al.[91] is another test that uses a weight and pulley system to apply a specific load to challenge balance.

Dynamic posturography can also provide valuable, objective information about motor performance. Equitest's[87] movement coordination test provides information about postural movements, including symmetry of weight bearing and forces generated, latency of postural responses, amplitude of response in relation to the stimulus size, and strategy utilized (ankle or hip). Optional EMG monitoring can reveal specific muscle activation patterns and latencies. The Equitest system is expensive and usually found in research settings or clinics that specialize in vestibular disorders. A number of systems have been developed for clinical use for both evaluation and training. A graphic representation of COM distribution during stance and weight shifting and limits of stability is typically provided. Dynamic posturographic equipment is relatively recent, and research is needed to establish the reliability of both sensory interaction and motor performance measures.[100]

Postural sway can be measured simply by visual inspection against a postural grid[96] or with more sophisticated instrumentation. Optical and mechanical sensing devices have been used to determine COM shifts.[91] Alternately, sway can be measured by shifts in the COM while standing on a computerized force platform. The shifts are detected as changes in pressure (vertical loading). A graph is printed out with information on center of pressure changes including initial stance position, mean sway path, total excursion and the zone of stability.[101]

Gait

An investigation of walking skills includes an assessment of the determinants of gait during level walking, as well as stepping movements and all walking variations including stopping, starting, varying speeds; walking sideways, backwards, with crossed legs; and stairclimbing, and walking on uneven terrains. Since walking represents a continuous movement sequence, the ability to sustain a consistent walking pattern over time should be noted. Use of assistive devices, and the type of gait pattern and/or the amount of assistance a patient requires are also important to describe. Examination of postural control during ambulation focuses on an observation of the base of support (step width and step length) and the position and movement of the upper extremities. Widely spaced steps and arms held out to the side or elevated in a high guard position are indicative of decreased balance control. A skilled gait pattern includes a normal heel-toe sequence with trunk coun-

terrotation and reciprocal arm swing. A complete description of normal gait parameters and gait analysis can be found in Chapter 10.

Functional Abilities

Patients with motor control deficits often seek rehabilitative services because of a loss of function. Analysis of function focuses on the measurement and classification of functional abilities and the identification of functional limitations. Testing can focus on any of four dimensions of function: physical, mental, affective/social. Physical function tests can yield important information about motor control. Numerous instruments are available. The selection of an appropriate tool will depend upon specific patient characteristics and treatment focus and may vary with practice setting. This topic is discussed fully in Chapter 11: Functional Assessment.

DEVELOPMENTAL PERSPECTIVE

A developmental perspective is also utilized for the assessment of motor skills. Characteristics of motor skill development in children have been described in detail by number of authors.[102–109] Select motor tasks were incorporated into a theoretic model by Rood[110] and Stockmeyer,[111] termed skeletal function sequence. Progression through an intertask sequence was focused on four basic stages of control: (1) mobility, (2) stability, (3) controlled mobility, and (4) skill. These levels of control have been applied to assessment and treatment of a wide variety of patients (both children and adults) with motor dyscontrol.[112,113] Neurodevelopment treatment (NDT) also utilizes a developmental approach to the motor assessment and treatment of children and adults with neurologic disabilities.[20] Assessment includes a descriptive analysis of specific motor patterns with particular emphasis on movement transitions between postures, rotational patterns, antigravity control, and normal postural reactions.

Current evidence suggests that there is considerable variability in motor development and performance. Rigid adherence to a developmental sequence of events, for instance, creeping must occur before standing and walking, is not accurate.[114,115] Skills may be acquired at different times and rates and vary in overall composition. Application of developmental sequences to the assessment and treatment of adult populations is fraught with issues of validity. Changes in movement patterns across the lifespan can be influenced by such factors as changing body dimensions, age, and level of physical activity.[116] Thus the activity of rolling over and sitting up may vary considerably between two adults of different size and/or age. Though there is some evidence of a progression, recovery of function in adult patients does not duplicate processes of normal motor development.[117,118]

Patterns of movement acquired during early development can be used as part of an assessment of motor control, since many remain an integral part of physical independence across the lifespan. Skills such as rolling over, sitting up, standing up, kneeling, and so on, are important components of daily life. Inability to perform these skills would severely impair an individual's functional ability within the environment. Developmental activities also allow focus on a specific area of body control, for example, prone on elbows activities emphasize upper trunk and head control while bridging activities emphasize lower trunk control. Because upright antigravity control is acquired gradually, many developmental activities are also inherently safe due to proximity to the ground (low COG, wide BOS).[117]

Developmental terminology can be used as a qualitative framework for the description of functional patterns. **Mobility** is a term used to describe initial movement in a functional pattern. There is adequate range of motion for movement to occur and sufficient motor unit activity to initiate muscle contraction. Movements are not sustained or well coordinated, and have a large reflexive, protective base. Antigravity control is not well developed. **Stability** is used to describe the ability to maintain a steady position in a weight-bearing, antigravity posture (also referred to as static postural control).[20] **Tonic holding** describes stability control achieved during holding in the shortened range of contraction (shortened held resisted contraction, SHRC) while **co-contraction** is used to describe control achieved during midrange holding in antigravity postures. Stabilization is achieved largely by proximal segments. **Controlled mobility** (CM) describes the ability to alter a position or move into a new position while maintaining postural stability (also termed dynamic postural control).[20] Thus an individual is able to shift weight or rock in a weight-bearing position. Full range of motion and balanced control in all directions are expected. Independent assumption of a posture (movement transition) is also an example of controlled mobility function. This is a more difficult activity as it requires the patient to move through a greater range of movement and against maximum effects of gravity. The patient must assume the posture (e.g., sit up from supine) without assistance or support. If assistance is required, the type and amount is noted. A major distinguishing factor between normal and abnormal CM responses is the degree to which rotation is incorporated into the movement transition.[20] **Static-dynamic control,** a variation of controlled mobility, is defined as the ability to shift weight onto one side and free the opposite limb for non-weight-bearing, dynamic activities. Unilateral weight bearing places even greater demands for dynamic stability than seen with rocking because the support limb assumes the full weight-bearing load while the dynamic limb constantly challenges control. Balance responses are essential for success in controlled mobility and skill level activities. **Skill** is highly coordinated movement that allows for investigation and interaction with the physical and social environment. Proximal segments stabilize while distal segments are free for function, for example, manipulation and transport. Movements are consistent, with an economy of effort, and regulated with precise timing and direction. Skilled movements can be discrete, continuous, or serial. Kicking a ball is an example of a discrete skill, with a recognizable beginning and end. Swimming is a continuous skill (no recognizable beginning and end) while playing a piano represents a serial skill (a series of discrete actions put together). Movements are shaped to the specific environments in which they occur: movement in a stable environment is called a **closed skill,** while movement in a changing environment is called an **open skill.** Skilled movements are task specific; skill in one task does not necessarily carry over to another. A skilled individual is able to perform single or simultaneous movement sequences. Thus the skilled individual is able to move with precise control (e.g., feeding or dressing), to maintain movement sequences for extended periods (e.g., walking or running), to perform equally well in different types of environments (e.g., in the clinic or at home), and to combine different movement sequences (e.g., walking while reaching for an object).[109,119,120] Table 8–7 includes a motor control checklist that utilizes several different functional activities structured according to this descriptive framework.

VIDEOTAPE ANALYSIS

The qualitative analysis of movement can be assisted by the use of video equipment. Patient responses recorded on videotape provide a permanent record of motor performance and allow the therapist the opportunity to compare responses over time. Recordings made at 3, 6, and 9 months of recovery can be compared easily without complete reliance on the therapist's memory or written notes. Accuracy of observations can be improved. A therapist who is closely involved in assisting or guarding during performance may not be attentive enough to observe all movement parameters. Videotapes can also be viewed repeatedly at different speeds to thoroughly investigate motor control during different activities and at different body segments. For example, a patient's performance in a task such as sitting up from supine can be observed first at regular speeds, then at slow motion speeds. Stop-action or freezing a frame can also be used to isolate a problematic point in the movement sequence. This may be helpful, particularly for the inexperienced therapist, in improving both the quality and reliability of observations. Direct assessment of patient performance without video capabilities does not permit this detailed analysis. Moreover, repeated trials may needlessly tire the patient while yielding a significant decrease in performance. Videotapes can be used to provide feedback for the patient, increasing awareness of a particular motor problem and teaching an appropriate corrective action. Sequential video recordings over the course of rehabilitation provide visual documentation of patient progress and can be important motivational tools in therapy. This equipment can also be a valuable tool in educating family members and other staff.[121–124] Reliability of taping for intersession comparisons can be improved by the following measures. Placement of equipment should be planned in advance to achieve the best location and should be consistently placed over subsequent sessions. Use of a tripod can improve the stability of the pictures. During the session, repeat trials of the same task (e.g.,

Table 8–7 MOTOR CONTROL RECORDING FORM

Patient's name: _____   Patient's number: _____

Physician _____   Diagnosis: _____

Therapist: _____   Date: _____

Score: N = level of control normal; P = level of control present but of poor quality; O = level of control absent

| | Stage of Motor Control | | | | | | |
| | Mobility | | Stability | | Controlled Mobility | | |
Posture	ROM	Initiate Motion	Tonic Holding	Co-contraction	Weight Shifting	Static/Dynamic	Skill
Sidelying/rolling							
Sitting							
Pivot prone							
Prone on elbows							
Quadruped							
Hooklying/ lower trunk rotation							
Kneeling							
Half kneeling							
Modified plantigrade							
Standing/ walking							
Comments:							

at least three trials) will provide information about the consistency of performance. Descriptions of the performance during each trial can be edited onto the tape or documented in a written summary.[125]

LEARNING FACTORS

Learned skills comprise a large part of our movement repertoire. Individual differences in sensorimotor experiences account for a significant part of the variation that exists between individuals with regard to underlying motor abilities and skill acquisition. An assessement of motor control must, therefore, consider sources of individual differences in order to arrive at an accurate starting point for treatment planning. Important elements include preferential learning style, interests, personality characteristics, problem-solving abilities and other pre-existing psychosocial behavioral patterns. These elements can best be determined by talking with the patient and family and using careful listening and observation skills. The medical chart also provides an important source of information concerning relevant premorbid history.

Individual differences are also based upon prefer-ences for sensory processing. For example, an individual may rely heavily on visual processing and demonstration in order to perform a task. Another may depend more upon auditory processing, talking themselves through a movement task. Task experience also structures the type of sensory processing preferred. Fitts[126] identified three distinct phases of motor learning: (1) early or cognitive phase, (2) associated or intermediate phase, and (3) the final or autonomous phase of learning. The predominance of sensory processing mechanisms varies according to the stage of learning. In the early stage, visual demonstration, auditory instructions, and manual guidance can contribute to learning the general idea or cognitive map of the task. For most individuals visual-spatial processing appears to predominate. During the middle stage, organization of the movement pattern is accomplished more through concentration on proprioceptive feedback, with less emphasis on visual or verbal guidance. During the last stage, refinement of the movement task occurs through more automatic and less cognitive processing of kinesthetic cues. Thus preferential modes of sensory processing vary according to task experience and stage of motor learning. The term preferential is used here to indicate a preferred mode of processing and not the total exclusion of other forms of processing.

A thorough understanding of each of these factors allows the therapist to appropriately structure the therapeutic environment and therapist–patient interaction. Successful motor performance during assessment may depend less on underlying patient motor ability than on overall interest, cooperation, and motivation.

SUMMARY

Assessment of motor control is a difficult process, critically related to the therapist's ability to accurately observe, analyze, and categorize behavior. An understanding of normal motor control mechanisms is essential to this process. Determining the causative factors responsible for abnormal movement patterns must be based upon a comparison of expected or normal responses (norm-referenced behaviors) with the patient's abnormal ones. This can best be achieved by a systematic and thorough approach to assessment with emphasis on the use of valid and reliable tools. A number of different factors are analyzed, ranging from peripheral factors of range of motion, muscle power, and sensation, to more central ones of tone, reflexes, and overall patterns of recruitment, timing, and organization within the CNS. Classical clinical testing of individual sensorimotor systems can yield valuable information about the integrity of these components. However, normal motor control is achieved through the integrated action of CNS systems. Assessment must therefore also focus on integrated function. Our theoretical understanding of the CNS and its control processes is both incomplete and imperfect. Therapists must, therefore, be constantly aware of the changing knowledge base in neuroscience in order to incorporate new ideas into their therapeutic approach to both assessment and treatment.

QUESTIONS FOR REVIEW

1. What types of movement patterns comprise our normal movement repertoire? How does the assessment of each differ? In normal patients? In patients with motor control deficits?

2. How can mental status, sensation, perception, communication ability, and arousal influence a motor control assessment?

3. Define closed-loop processes of motor control. How do they differ from open-loop processes? How can you structure a motor assessment to yield information about each?

4. Describe the procedures used to assess tonal abnormalities. In what order would you sequence them and why? What influences may affect an assessment of tone?

5. Describe the reasons, both pro and con, for using strength testing (MMT) in patients with neurologic deficit.

6. Describe the six different conditions used to test sensory organization in both the "foam and dome" and Equitest methods. Which is the most difficult balance task to perform and why?

7. In a person with normal balance, which postural strategy is likely to be elicited with a mild disturbance in the center of mass? With a moderate disturbance that approaches the limits of stability? With a significant disturbance that exceeds the limits of stability?

8. Describe developmental terminology that can be used to qualitatively describe a functional movement pattern. Use the activity of sitting as a frame of reference.

9. What are synergistic patterns of movement? What are the differences between normal and abnormal synergies? How can it be assessed?

10. What role do learning factors have in motor performance? How can they be assessed?

11. Describe the role of videotapes in the assessment of motor control.

12. What are the major difficulties in arriving at an accurate assessment of motor control? How can the assessment be structured to improve validity and reliability?

REFERENCES

1. Schmidt, R: Motor Control and Learning, ed 2. Human Kinetics, Champaign, IL, 1988, p 225.
2. Brooks, V: The Neural Basis of Motor Control. Oxford University Press, New York, 1986.
3. Bernstein, N: The Coordination and Regulation of Movements. Pergamon Press, New York, 1967.
4. Gelfand, I, Gurfinkel, V, Tomlin, S, and Tsetlin, M: Models of Structural-Functional Organization of Certain Biological Systems. MIT Press, Cambridge, MA, 1971.
5. Beh-Yishay, Y and Diller, L: Cognitive deficits. In Rosenthal, M, Griffith, E, Bond, M, and Miller, J (eds): Rehabilitation of the Head Injured Adult. FA Davis, Philadelphia, 1983.
6. Fowler, R and Fordyce, W: Stroke: Why Do They Behave That Way? American Heart Association, Dallas, 1974.
7. Smith, R: Speech and language assessment. In Rosenthal, M, Griffith, E, Bond, M, and Miller, J (eds): Rehabilitation of the Head Injured Adult. FA Davis, Philadelphia, 1983.
8. Dell, P: Reticular homeostasis and critical reactivity. In Moruzzi, B, Fessard, A, and Jasper, HH (eds): Progress in Brain Research, vol 1, Brain Mechanisms. Elsevier, New York, 1963.
9. Yerkes, R and Dodson J: The relation of strength of stimulus to rapidity of habit-formation. J Comp Neurol Psychol 18:459, 1908.
10. Wilder, J: Basimetric approach (law of initial value) to biological rhythms. Ann N Y Acad Sci 98:1211, 1961.

11. Stockmeyer, S: Clinical decision making based on homeostatic concepts. In Wolf, S (ed): Clinical Decision Making in Physical Therapy. FA Davis, Philadelphia, 1985.

12. Schmidt, R: Motor Control and Learning, ed 2. Human Kinetics, Champaign, IL, 1988, p 184.

13. Siev, E, Freishtat, B, and Zoltan, B: Perceptual and Cognitive Dysfunction in the Adult Stroke Patient, ed 2. Slack, Thorofare, NJ, 1986.

14. American Academy of Orthopaedic Surgeons: Joint Motion: Method of Measuring and Recording. American Academy of Orthopaedic Surgeons, Chicago, 1965.

15. Norkin, C and White D: Measurement of Joint Motion: A Guide to Goniometry. FA Davis, Philadelphia, 1985.

16. Magee, D: Orthopedic Physical Assessment, ed 2. WB Saunders, Philadelphia, 1992.

17. Hoppenfeld, S: Physical Examination of the Spine and Extremities. Appleton-Century-Crofts, Norwalk, CT, 1976.

18. Gajdosik, R and Bohannon R: Clinical measurement of range of motion: review of goniometry emphasizing reliability and validity. Phys Ther 67:1867, 1987.

19. Katz, R and Rymer, Z: Spastic hypertonia: mechanisms and measurement. Arch Phys Med Rehabil 70:144, 1989.

20. Bobath, B. Adult Hemiplegia: Evaluation and Treatment, ed 2. Heinemann Medical Books, London, 1978.

21. Burke, D: Spasticity as an adaptation to pyramidal tract injury. In Waxman, S (ed): Advances in Neurology, 47: Functional Recovery in Neurological Disease. Raven Press, New York, 1988.

22. Dimitrijevic, M: Spasticity and Rigidity. In Jankovic, J and Tolosa E (eds): Parkinson's Disease and Movement Disorders. Urban & Schwarzenburg, Baltimore, 1988.

23. Jankovic, J: Pathophysiology and clinical assessment of motor symptoms in Parkinson's disease. In Koller, W (ed): Handbook of Parkinson's Disease. Marcel Dekker, New York, 1987.

24. Jankovic, J and Fahn, S: Dystonic syndromes. In Jankovic, J and Tolosa, E (eds): Parkinson's Disease and Movement Disorders. Urban & Schwarzenburg, Baltimore, 1988.

25. Barrows, H. Guide to Neurological Assessment. JB Lippincott, Philadelphia, 1980.

26. Weiner, W and Goetz, C (eds): Neurology for the Non-Neurologist. Harper & Row, Philadelphia, 1981.

27. Watkins, M, Harris, B, and Kozlowski, B: Isokinetic testing in patients with hemiparesis. Phys Ther 64:184, 1984.

28. Ashworth, B: Preliminary trial of carisoprodol in multiple sclerosis. Practitioner 192:540, 1964.

29. Bohannon, R and Smith, M: Interrater reliability of a modified Ashworth scale of muscle spasticity. Phys Ther 67:206, 1987.

30. Bajd, T and Vodovnik, L: Pendulum testing of spasticity. J Biomed Eng 6:9, 1984

31. Bohannon, R: Variability and reliability of the pendulum test for spasticity using a Cybex II Isokinetic Dynamometer. Phys Ther 67:659, 1987.

32. Brunnstrom, S: Movement Therapy in Hemiplegia. Harper & Row, New York, 1970.

33. Fugl-Meyer, A: The post-stroke hemiplegic patient, I. A method for evaluation of physical performance. Scand J Rehabil Med 7:13, 1975.

34. Ashburn, A: A physical assessment for stroke patients. Physiotherapy 68:109, 1982.

35. Sahrmann, S and Norton, B: The relationship of voluntary movement to spasticity in the upper motor neuron syndrome. Ann Neurol 2:460, 1977.

36. Badke, M and DiFabio, R: Effects of postural bias during support surface displacements and rapid arm movements. Phys Ther 65:1490, 1985.

37. Horak, F: Clinical measurement of postural control in adults. Phys Ther 67:1881, 1987.

38. Bishop, B: Vibratory stimulation, II. Vibratory stimulation as an evaluation tool. Phys Ther 55:28, 1975.

39. Easton, T: On the normal use of reflexes. Am Sci 60:591, 1972.

40. Hellebrandt, F, Schade, M, and Carns, M: Methods of evoking the tonic neck reflexes in normal human subjects. Am J Phys Med 35:144, 1956.

41. Hellebrandt, F and Waterland, J: Expansion of motor patterning under exercise stress. Am J Phys Med 41:56, 1962.

42. Bobath, B: Abnormal Postural Reflex Activity Caused by Brain Lesions. Heinemann Medical Books, London, 1965.

43. Capute, A, Accardo, P, Vining, E, et al: Primitive Reflex Profile. University Park Press, Baltimore, 1978.

44. Capute, A, Accardo, P, Vining, E, et al: Primitive reflex profile: a pilot study. Phys Ther 58:1061, 1978.

45. Barnes, M, Crutchfield, C, and Heriza, C: The Neurophysiological Basis of Patient Treatment, vol II, Reflexes in Motor Development. Stokesville Publishing, Atlanta, 1978.

46. Fiorentino, M: Reflex Testing Methods for Evaluating C.N.S. Development, ed 2. Charles C Thomas, Springfield, IL, 1973.

47. Knuttsson, E and Martensson, A: Dynamic motor capacity in spastic paresis and its relation to prime mover dysfunction, spastic reflexes and antagonist co-activation. Scand J Rehabil Med 12:93, 1980.

48. Rosenfalck, A and Andreassen, S: Impaired regulation of force and firing pattern of single motor units in patients with spasticity. J Neurol Neurosurg Psychiatry 43:907, 1980.

49. Bohannon, R, et al: Relationship between static muscle strength deficits and spasticity in stroke patients with hemiparesis. Phys Ther 67:1068, 1987.

50. Davies, P: Steps to Follow. Springer-Verlag, New York, 1985.

51. Rothstein, J, Riddle, D, and Finucane, S: Commentary. Is the measurement of muscle strength appropriate in patients with brain lesions? Phys Ther 69:230, 1989.

52. Hamrin, E, Eklund, G, Hillgren, A, et al: Muscle strength and balance in post-stroke patients. Ups J Med Sci 87:11, 1982.

53. Riddle, D, Finucane, S, Rothstein, J, and Walker, M: Intrasession and intersession reliability of hand-held dynamometer measurements taken on brain-damaged patients. Phys Ther 69:182, 1989.

54. Tripp, E and Harris, S: Test-retest reliability of isokinetic knee extension and flexion torque measurements in persons with spastic hemiparesis. Phys Ther 71:390, 1991.

55. Bohannon, R: Is the measurement of muscle strength appropriate in patients with brain lesions? Phys Ther 69:225, 1989.

56. Nakumura, R, Hosokawa, T, Tsuji, I: Relationship of muscle strength for knee extension to walking capacity in patients with spastic hemiparesis. Tohoku J Exp Med 145:335, 1985.

57. Bohannon, R and Andrews, W. Correlation of knee extensor muscle torque and spasticity with gait speed in patients with stroke. Arch Phys Med Rehabil 71:330, 1990.

58. Daniels, L and Worthingham, C: Muscle Testing: Techniques of Manual Examination, ed 4. Philadelphia, WB Saunders, 1980.

59. Kendall, F and McKreary, E: Muscles: Testing and Function. Williams & Wilkins, Baltimore, 1983.

60. Lovett, R: The Treatment of Infantile Paralysis. Blakiston's Son & Co., Philadelphia, 1917.

61. Frese, E, Brown, M, Norton, B: Clinical reliability of manual muscle testing: middle trapezius and gluteus medius muscles. Phys Ther 67:1072, 1987.

62. Bohannon, R: Test-retest reliability of hand-held dynamometry during a single session of strength assessment. Phys Ther 66:206, 1986.

63. Bohannon, R and Andrews, A: Interrater reliability of handheld dynamometry. Phys Ther 67:931, 1987.

64. Kloos, A: Measurement of muscle tone and strength. Neurology Report 16:9, 1992.

65. Agre, J, Magness, J, Hull, S, et al: Strength testing with a portable dynamometer: reliability for upper and lower extremities. Arch Phys Med Rehabil 68:454, 1987.

66. Isolated Joint Testing and Exercise: A Handbook for Using the Cybex II and U.B.X.T. Cybex, Ronkonkoma, NY, 1981.

67. Rothstein, J, Lamb, R, Mayhew, T: Clinical uses of isokinetic measurements. Phys Ther 67:1840, 1987.

68. Moffroid, M: Principles of isokinetic instrumentation. In O'Sullivan, S (ed): Topics in Physical Therapy. American Physical Therapy Association, Alexandria, VA, 1990.

69. Mawdsley, R and Knapik, J: Comparison of isokinetic measurements with test repetitions. Phys Ther 62:169, 1982.

70. Moffroid, M, Whipple, R, Hofkosh, J, et al: A study of isokinetic exercise. Phys Ther 49:735, 1969.

71. Farrell, M and Richards, J: Analysis of the reliability and validity of the isokinetic communicator exercise device. Med Sci Sports Exerc 18:44, 1986.

72. Johnson, J and Siegal, D: Reliability of an isokinetic movement of the knee extensors. Research Quarterly 49:88, 1978.

73. Tredinnick, T and Duncan, P: Reliability of measurements of concentric and eccentric isokinetic loading. Phys Ther 68:656, 1988.

74. Armstrong, L, Winant, D, Swasey, P, et al: Using isokinetic dynamometry to test ambulatory patients with multiple sclerosis. Phys Ther 63:1274, 1983.

75. McCrory, M, et al: Reliability of concentric and eccentric measurements on the Lido Active Isokinetic Rehabilitation System. Med Sci Sports Exerc (Suppl) 21:52, 1989.

76. Watkins, M and Harris, B: Evaluation of isokinetic muscle performance. Clin Sports Med 2:37, 1983.

77. Holmes, J and Gordon, J: Isokinetic strength characteristics of the quadriceps femoris and hamstring muscles in high school students. Phys Ther 64:914, 1984.

78. Goslin, B and Charteris, J: Isokinetic dynamometry: normative data for clinical use in lower extremity (knee) cases. Scand J Rehabil Med 11:105, 1979.

79. Murray, M, Gardner, G, Mollinger, L, et al: Strength of isometric and isokinetic contractions: knee muscles of men aged 20 to 86. Phys Ther 60:412, 1980.

80. Griffin, J, McClure, M, and Bertorini, T: Sequential isokinetic and manual muscle testing in patients with neuromuscular disease: a pilot study. Phys Ther 66:32, 1986.

81. Kozlowski, B: Reliability of isokinetic torque generation in chronic hemiplegic subjects. Phys Ther 64:714, 1984.

82. Brandt, T, Paulus, W, Straube, V: Visual acuity, visual field and visual scene characteristics affect postural balance. In Igarash, M and Black, F (eds): Vestibular and Visual Control on Posture and Locomotor Equilibrium. Karger, Basel, 1985.

83. Herdman, S: Assessment and treatment of balance disorders in the vestibular-deficient patient. In Duncan, P (ed): Balance. American Physical Therapy Association, Alexandria, VA, 1990.

84. Nashner, L: Sensory, neuromuscular, and biomechanical contributions to human balance. In Duncan, P (ed): Balance. American Physical Therapy Association, Alexandria, VA, 1990.

85. Horak, F, et al: Postural strategies associated with somatosensory and vestibular loss. Exp Brain Res 82:167, 1990.

86. Shumway-Cook, A and Horak, F: Assessing the influence of sensory interaction on balance: suggestion from the field. Phys Ther 66:1548, 1986.

87. Nashner, L: A Systems Approach to Understanding and Assessing Orientation and Balance. NeuroCom International, Clackamas, OR, 1987.

88. Nashner, L: Adaptive reflexes controlling human posture. Exp Brain Res 26:59, 1976.

89. Nashner, L and McCollum, G: The organization of human postural movements: a formal basis and experimental synthesis. Behavioral and Brain Sciences 8:135, 1985.

90. Horak, F and Nashner, L: Central programming of postural movements: adaptation to altered support-surface configuration. J Neurophysiol 55:1369, 1986.

91. Keshner, E: Reflex, voluntary, and mechanical processes in postural stabilization. In Duncan, P (ed): Balance. American Physical Therapy Association, Alexandria, VA, 1990.

92. Lee, W, Deming, L, Sahgal, V: Quantitative and clinical measures of static standing balance in hemiparetic and normal subjects. Phys Ther 68:970, 1988.

93. Carr, J, Shepherd, R, Nordholm, L, et al: Investigation of a new motor assessment scale for stroke patients. Phys Ther 65:175, 1985.

94. Goldie, P, Matyas, T, Spencer, K: Postural control in standing following stroke: test-retest reliability of some quantitative clinical tests. Phys Ther 70:234, 1990.

95. Bohannon, R, Larkin, P, Cook, A, et al: Decrease in timed balance test scores with aging. Phys Ther 64:1967, 1984.

96. Horak, F: Clinical measurement of postural control in adults. Phys Ther 67:1881, 1987.

97. Duncan, P, Weiner, D, Chandler, J, et al: Functional reach: a new clinical measure of balance. J Gerontol 85:529, 1990.

98. Wolfson, L, Whipple, R, Amerman, P, et al: Stressing the postural response: a quantitative method for testing balance. J Am Geriatr Soc 34:845, 1986.

99. Chandler, J, Duncan, P, Studenski, S: Balance performance on the postural stress test: comparison of young adults, healthy elderly, and fallers. Phys Ther 70:410, 1990.

100. Flores, A: Objective measurement of standing balance. Neurology Report 16:17, 1992.

101. Murray, M, Seireg, A, Sepie, S: Normal postural stability and steadiness. J Bone Joint Surg 57:510, 1975.

102. Bayley, N: The development of motor abilities during the first three years. Monographs of the Society for Research in Child Development 1 (1, serial no 1), 1935.

103. Gesell, A and Amatruda, C: Developmental Diagnosis. Harper, New York, 1941.

104. McGraw, M: The Neuromuscular Maturation of the Human Infant. Hafner Press, New York, 1945.

105. Peiper, A: Cerebral Function in Infancy and Childhood. Consultants Bureau Enterprises, New York, 1963.

106. Milani-Comparetti, A and Gidone, E: Pattern analysis of motor development and its disorders. Dev Med Child Neurol 9:631, 1967.

107. Connolly, K (ed): Mechanisms of Motor Skill Development. Academic Press, New York, 1970.

108. Illingworth, R: The Development of the Infant and Young Child. Normal and Abnormal. E & S Livingstone, London, 1975.

109. Keogh, J and Sugden, D: Movement Skill Development. Macmillan, New York, 1985.

110. Rood, M: The use of sensory receptors to activate, facilitate, and inhibit motor response, autonomic and somatic in developmental sequence. In Sattely, C (ed): Approaches to Treatment of Patients with Neuromuscular Dysfunction. William Brown, Dubuque, 1962.

111. Stockmeyer, S: An interpretation of the approach of Rood to the treatment of neuromuscular dysfunction. Am J Phys Med 46:900, 1967.

112. Sullivan, P, Markos, P and Minor, M: An Integrated Approach to Therapeutic Exercise. Reston, Reston, VA, 1982.

113. Voss, D, Ionta, M, Myers, B: Proprioceptive Neuromuscular Facilitation, ed 3. Harper & Row, Philadelphia, 1985.

114. Horowitz, L and Sharby, N: Development of prone extension postures in healthy infants. Phys Ther 68:32, 1988.

115. Fishkind, M and Haley, S: Independent sitting development and the emergence of associated motor components. Phys Ther 66:1509, 1986.

116. VanSant, A: Life span development in functional tasks. Phys Ther 70:788, 1990.

117. Barnes, M and Crutchfield, C: Reflex and Vestibular Aspects of Motor Control, Motor Development and Motor Learning. Stokesville, Atlanta, 1990.

118. Gordon, J: Assumptions underlying physical therapy intervention: theoretical and historical perspectives. In Carr, J, Shepherd, R, Gordon, J, et al: Movement Science Foundations for Physical Therapy Rehabilitation. Aspen, Rockville, MD, 1987.

119. Gentile, A, Higgins, J, Miller, E, and Rosen, M: The structure of motor tasks. Movement 7:11, 1975.

120. Gentile, A: Skill acquisition: action, movement and neuromotor processes. In Carr, J, Shepherd, R, Gordon J, et al: Movement Science: Foundations for Physical Therapy in Rehabilitation. Aspen, Rockville, MD, 1987.

121. Stichbury, J: Assessment of disability following severe head injury. Physiotherapy 61:268, 1975.

122. Turnbull, G and Wall, J: The development of a system for the clinical assessment of gait following stroke. Physiotherapy 71:294, 1985.

123. Pink, M: High speed video applications in physical therapy. Clinical Management 5:14, 1985.

124. VanSant, A: Rising from a supine position to erect stance; description of adult movement and a developmental hypothesis. Phys Ther 68:185, 1988.

125. Lewis, A: Documentation of movement patterns used in the performance of functional tasks. Neurology Report 16:13, 1992.

126. Fitts, P and Posner, M: Human Performance. Brooks/Cole, Belmont, CA, 1969.

127. Leahy, P: Motor control assessment. In Montgomery, P and Connolly, B (eds): Motor Control and Physical Therapy: Theoretical Framework and Practical Applications. Chattanooga Group, Hixson, TN, 1991.

128. Minor, M and Minor, S: Patient Evaluation Methods for the Health Professional. Reston, Reston, VA, 1985.

GLOSSARY

Active range of motion (AROM): The amount of joint motion obtained with unassisted voluntary joint motion.

Arousal: An internal state of alertness or excitement.

Automatic postural synergies: Discrete patterns of leg and trunk muscle contractions characterized by consistency in muscle combinations, timing, and intensity; they are used to preserve standing balance.

Ankle strategy: The center of mass shift forward and backward by rotating the body as a relatively rigid mass about the ankle joints.

Hip strategy: The center of mass shift by flexing or extending at the hips.

Stepping strategy: The realignment of the base of support under the center of mass by using rapid steps in the direction of the displacing force.

Balance: The stability produced on each side of a vertical axis. The center of gravity is maintained over the base of support.

Cerebral shock: Transient hypotonia following injury to the brain.

Clasp-knife reflex: A sudden relaxation or letting go of a spastic muscle in response to a stretch stimulus.

Clinical Test for Sensory Interaction in Balance (CTSIB) (foam and dome method): A test that assesses standing balance under six different sensory conditions.

Clonus: Cyclic hyperactivity of antagonistic muscles occurring at a regular frequency.

Closed-loop system: A control system employing feedback as a reference for correctness, commutation of error, and subsequent correction in order to maintain a desired state.

Closed skills: Motor skills performed in a stable, predictable environment.

Co-contraction: Stability control achieved by the contraction of antagonistic muscles around a joint; provides stabilization during weight-bearing activities.

Controlled mobility (dynamic postural control, dynamic equilibrium): The ability to maintain postural control during weight shifting and movement.

Decerebrate rigidity: Sustained contraction of extensor muscles resulting from a lesion in the brainstem between the superior colliculi and vestibular nuclei.

Decorticate rigidity: Sustained contraction of extensor muscles in the lower limbs and flexor muscles in the upper limbs as a result of a brainstem lesion.

Drop arm test (placing test): A test used to assess the integrity of automatic proprioceptive reactions; the limb is raised to a new position and suddenly dropped.

Dynamic posturography: A computerized test of sensory organization and movement coordination during standing balance.

Dystonia: A hyperkinetic movement disorder characterized by impaired or disordered tone, and sustained and twisting involuntary movements.

Dystonic posturing: Sustained twisting deformity that may last for several minutes or permanently.

End-feel: The characteristic feel each specific joint has at the end of its range of motion.

Equilibrium reactions: Total body automatic responses that serve to maintain or regain balance during posture and movement.

Flaccidity: Absence of muscle tone.

Hypertonia: State of increased tone above normal resting levels.

Hypotonia: State of decreased tone below normal resting levels.

Inverted-U theory (Yerkes-Dodson law): There is an optimal level of arousal for performance; too much or too little arousal can cause marked deterioration in performance.

Isokinetic dynamometer: An exercise device that controls the velocity of a limb movement, keeping it at a constant rate while offering accommodating resistance through the range of motion.

Joint play: The small amount of joint motion that occurs at the end range and is not under voluntary control.

Jendrassik maneuver: Method used to facilitate eliciting the deep tendon reflexes of the lower extremities; the patient hooks together the fingers of the hands and attempts to pull them apart. While the pressure is maintained, the reflex is tested.

Law of Initial Value (LIV) of Wilder: A law describing the relationship between a stimulus and a change in a function from its prestimulus level: the higher the initial value of a function, the less change will occur in response to a function-increasing stimulus, and the lower the initial value of a function, the less change will occur in response to a function-decreasing stimulus.

Limits of stability (LOS): The maximum angle from vertical that can be tolerated without a loss of balance; normally 12 degrees in an anteroposterior direction and 16 degrees in a mediolateral direction.

Mobility: Initial movement in a functional pattern; range of motion is available for movement to occur and there is sufficient motor unit activity to indicate muscle contraction.

Motor memory: The storage of motor programs or subprograms for later retrieval and use.

Motor program: A set of commands that, when initiated, results in the production of a coordinated movement sequence.

Motor plan: The combination of several motor programs into an action strategy.

Open skills: Motor skills performed in a constantly changing, unpredictable environment.

Passive range of motion (PROM): The amount of joint motion available when an examiner moves the joint through the range without assistance from the patient.

Pendulum test: A test used to assess spasticity. A limb (usually the leg) is extended and allowed to drop and swing like a pendulum; normal and hypotonic limbs swing freely, while spastic limbs are resistant to the motion.

Postural control: The control, by skeletal muscles, of the relative positions of body parts with respect to gravity and to each other.

Postural stress test (Wolfson): A clinical measure of

motor responses to specified weight disturbances during standing.

Reaction: An involuntary movement response to a stimulus; it appears in infancy and remains throughout life.

Reflex: A genetically defined involuntary movement response to a stimulus.

Righting reaction: An involuntary movement response to a stimulus; it serves to maintain the normal alignment of the head and body in space.

Rigidity: Stiffness; inability to bend or be bent.

Cogwheel rigidity: A rachetlike response to passive movement characterized by an alternate giving and increased resistance to movement.

Leadpipe rigidity. A constant resistance to movement.

Skill: Highly coordinated movement that allows for investigation and interaction with the physical and social environment.

Spasticity: Increased tone or resistance of muscle causing stiff awkward movements; the result of an upper motor neuron lesion.

Spinal shock: Transient hypotonia following injury to the spinal cord.

Stability: The ability to maintain a steady position in a weight-bearing, antigravity posture.

Tonic holding: Stability control of postural extensor muscles holding in the shortened range of motion.

Static-dynamic control: The ability to shift weight onto one side and free the opposite limb for non-weight-bearing dynamic activities.

Synergy: Normal association of functionally linked muscles that produce coordinated movement.

Abnormal synergy: A stereotyped mass pattern of movement in which muscles are abnormally linked together in predictable movement patterns; seen in some neurologic conditions.

Tone (muscle): The resistance of muscles to passive elongation or stretch.

Tonic vibration reflex: A sustained contraction of muscle in response to a vibratory stimulus.

Upper motor neuron (UMN) syndrome: Motor dysfunction observed in patients with lesions of cortical, subcortical, or spinal cord structures. Characterized by spasticity, abnormal reflex behaviors, loss of precise autonomic control, impaired muscle activation, paresis, decreased dexterity, and fatigability.

Electromyography and Nerve Conduction Velocity Tests

Leslie Gross Portney

OBJECTIVES

1. Describe the instrumentation system used to record electromyographic (EMG) data for clinical and kinesiologic uses.
2. Describe the general methodology used to perform an EMG and nerve conduction velocity (NCV) examination.
3. Describe the characteristics of normal and abnormal EMG potentials.
4. Describe the EMG and NCV findings typically seen with neuromuscular disorders.
5. Discuss the implications of clinical EMG findings for goal setting and treatment planning in rehabilitation.
6. Discuss the relationship between EMG and force with different types of contractions.
7. Discuss procedural, technical and physiologic considerations for interpreting clinical and kinesiologic electromyographic data.
8. Describe the uses of kinesiologic EMG for clinical evaluation and treatment of patients with neuromuscular or musculoskeletal dysfunction.

Luigi Galvani presented the first report on electrical properties of muscles and nerves in 1791.[1] He demonstrated that muscle activity followed stimulation of neurons and recorded potentials from muscle fibers in states of voluntary contraction in frogs. This information was disregarded for close to a century, as conflicting theories were accepted, and did not become part of medical technology until the early part of this century, when instrumentation was developed to make recording such activity reliable and valid. Today **electromyography (EMG)** is used to evaluate the scope of neuromuscular disease or trauma, and as a kinesiologic tool to study muscle function.

As an assessment procedure, *clinical electromyography* involves the detection and recording of electrical potentials from skeletal muscle fibers. **Nerve conduction velocity (NCV)** tests determine the speed with which a peripheral motor or sensory nerve conducts an impulse. Together with other clinical assessments, these two electrodiagnostic procedures can provide information about the extent of nerve injury or muscle disease, and the prognosis for surgical intervention and rehabilitation. These data can be valuable for diagnosis and determination of rehabilitation goals for patients with musculoskeletal and neuromuscular disorders.

Kinesiologic EMG is used to study muscle activity and to establish the role of various muscles in specific activities. Although the concepts are the same, the focus of kinesiologic EMG is quite different from that of clinical EMG, in terms of instrumentation requirements and data analysis techniques. Basmajian and De Luca[2] have provided a thorough review of literature in this area.

CONCEPTS OF ELECTROMYOGRAPHY

Electromyography is, in essence, the study of motor unit activity. Motor units are composed of one anterior horn cell, one axon, its neuromuscular junctions, and all the muscle fibers innervated by that axon (Fig. 9–1). The single axon conducts an impulse to all its muscle fibers, causing them to depolarize at relatively the same time. This depolarization produces electrical activity that is manifested as a **motor unit action potential (MUAP)** and recorded graphically as the *electromyogram.* It is often reassuring to a patient to realize that EMG only records electrical activity already present in contracting muscle, as opposed to introducing electrical energy into the body. The reader is encouraged to review the anatomy and physiology of the neuromuscular system as a basis for further discussion of electromyographic data.

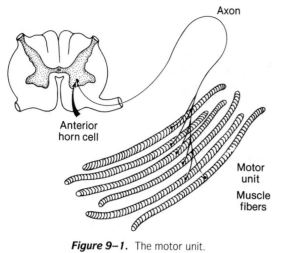

Figure 9–1. The motor unit.

Instrumentation

Recording the EMG requires a system that includes **electrodes** to pick up electrical potentials from contracting muscle (input phase); an amplifier, which processes the small electrical signal (processor phase); and a display (output phase), which converts the electrical signal to visual and/or audible signals so that the data can be analyzed (Fig. 9–2).

INPUT PHASE
Electrodes
Several types of electrodes can be used to monitor the myoelectric signal. **Surface electrodes** are used to test nerve conduction velocity and in kinesiologic investigations. They are generally considered adequate for monitoring large superficial muscles or muscle groups. They are not considered selective enough to record activity accurately from individual **motor units** or from specific small or deep muscles.[3] **Fine-wire indwelling electrodes** can be used for kinesiologic study of small and deep muscles. *Needle electrodes* are necessary to record single motor unit potentials for clinical EMG.

In addition to the **recording electrodes** (either surface or needle), a **ground electrode** must be applied to provide a mechanism for cancelling out the interference effect of external electrical noise such as that caused by fluorescent lights, broadcasting facilities, diathermy equipment, and other electrical apparatus. The ground electrode is a surface plate electrode that is attached to the skin near the recording electrodes, but usually not over muscle.

Surface electrodes are small metal discs, most commonly made of silver/silver chloride,[4] that are applied to the skin overlying the appropriate muscle (Fig. 9–3). They are typically 3 to 5 mm in diameter (effective surface area), and are often contained within a casing that can be affixed to the surface of the skin with adhesive collars or tape. In a *bipolar arrangement,* two electrodes are placed over one muscle, usually over the belly, in a longitudinal direction parallel to the muscle fibers.[5,6]

Electrode gel is applied beneath surface electrodes to facilitate the conduction of electrical potentials. Often, some skin preparation is necessary to reduce **skin resistance,** which can interfere with the quality of recording. This may include washing, rubbing with alcohol, and abrading the superficial skin layer to remove dead, dry skin cells. However, with advances in instrumentation technology, **amplifiers** may have sufficient input **impedance** and electrodes may be of sufficient conductivity, so that skin preparation may not be necessary.

Fine-wire indwelling electrodes were introduced in the early sixties for kinesiologic study of small and deep muscles.[7] They are made using two strands of small-diameter wire (approximately 100 μm). These are coated with a polyurethane or nylon insulation and threaded through a hypodermic needle. The tips of the wires are bared for 1 to 2 mm and bent back against the needle shaft (Fig. 9–4). The needle is inserted into the muscle belly and immediately withdrawn, leaving the wires embedded in the muscle. Because of the small diameter of these wires, which are as thin as a hair, subjects cannot feel the presence of the wires in the muscle. The wires form a bipolar electrode configuration that can record from a localized area and is capable of picking up single motor unit potentials. Fine-wire electrodes are necessary when monitoring activity from deep mus-

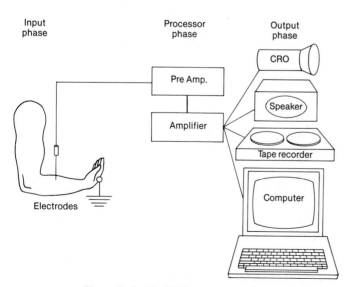

Figure 9–2. The EMG recording system.

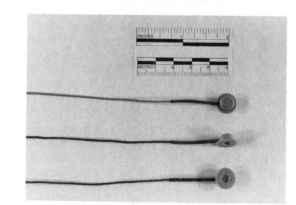

Figure 9–3. Silver-silver chloride surface electrodes (Beckman type).

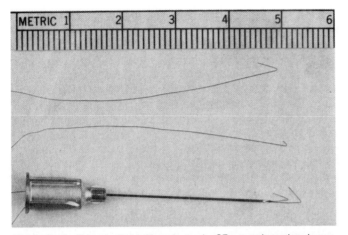

Figure 9-4. Fine-wire indwelling electrode: 27 gauge hypodermic needle through which two strands of polyurethane coated wire are threaded. Insulation is removed from the tips of the wires, and hooks are created to keep the wires imbedded while the needle is removed from the muscle. (From Soderberg and Cook,[10] p 1814, with permission.)

cles, such as the soleus, or small or narrow muscles, such as the finger flexors. They may not be as useful for larger muscles because they sample motor unit activity from such a small area of the muscle.

A *needle electrode* is required for clinical EMG, so that single motor unit potentials can be recorded from different parts of a muscle. The first studies of motor unit activity were done by Adrian and Bronk in 1929 using a **concentric (coaxial) needle electrode.**[8] This electrode consists of a stainless steel cannula, similar to a hypodermic needle, through which a single wire of platinum or silver is threaded (Fig. 9-5A). The cannula shaft and wire are insulated from each other, and only their tips are exposed. The wire and the needle cannula act as electrodes, and the difference in potential between them is recorded. A *bipolar concentric needle electrode* can also be used, with two wires threaded through the cannula (Fig. 9-5B). The bared tips of both wires act as the two electrodes, the needle serving as the ground.

Another commonly used approach for clinical EMG involves the use of a **monopolar needle electrode,**

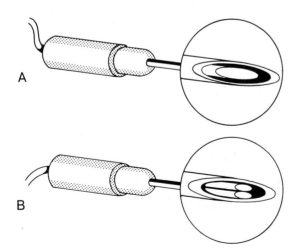

Figure 9-5. Concentric needle electrodes, showing single (*A*) and bipolar (*B*) wire configurations.

which is composed of a single fine needle, insulated except at the tip. A second surface electrode, placed on the skin near the site of insertion, serves as the **reference electrode.** These electrodes are less painful than concentric electrodes because they are much smaller in diameter. Because monopolar configurations record much larger potentials than bipolar, the type of electrode must be specified to avoid misinterpretation of data relative to the size of potentials and the area of pickup. Clinical EMG can also be used to record from single muscle fibers. *Single-fiber needle electrodes* are concentric, but have wires 25 μm in diameter (as compared to 0.1 mm for standard concentric electrode wires).

Any one of these types of needle electrodes can be used for a clinical EMG examination. Needle electrodes are not useful for kinesiologic study because of the discomfort caused by the needle remaining in the muscle during contraction. Fine wire electrodes are not appropriate for use in clinical EMG because the examiner does not have good control over placement of the electrode, or the ability to move the electrode within the muscle once it is placed. Guidelines for insertion of electrodes have been published[9] and anatomical references should always be consulted to assure accurate and safe placement when using needles. Because they pierce the skin, all needle and fine-wire electrodes must be sterilized.

The Myoelectric Signal

An electrode is a transducer, a device for converting one form of energy into another. Electrodes convert the bioelectric signal resulting from muscle or nerve depolarization into an electrical potential capable of being processed by an amplifier. It is the *difference in electrical potential* between the two recording electrodes that is processed.

The unit of measurement for difference of potential is the **volt** (V). The **amplitude,** or height, of potentials is usually measured in microvolts (10^{-6} V). The greater the difference in potential seen by the electrodes, the greater the amplitude, or voltage, of the electrical potential. The amplitude of a MUAP is usually measured peak-to-peak, that is, from the highest to the lowest point. The **duration** of the potential is a measure of time from onset to cessation of the electrical potential.

It is of interest to analyze the process by which a motor unit potential is transmitted to an amplifier in order to understand how such potentials can be interpreted. Because of the dispersion of the fibers in a single motor unit, the muscle fibers from several motor units may be interspersed with one another (Fig. 9-6). Therefore, when one motor unit contracts, the depolarizing fibers are not necessarily close together. Consequently, a needle or surface electrode cannot be situated precisely within or over any one motor unit.

All the fibers of a single motor unit contract almost synchronously, and the electrical potentials arising from them travel through body fluids, as a result of the excellent conducting properties of the electrolytes surrounding the fibers. This process is called **volume conduction.** The electrical activity will flow through the conducting medium, the *volume conductor,* in all direc-

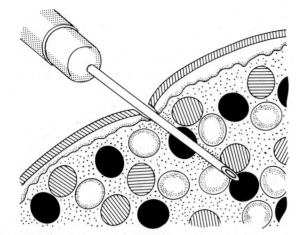

Figure 9–6. Cross-section view of muscle belly with needle electrode inserted. Differently shaded fibers represent different motor units.

tions—not just in the direction of the inserted needle electrode or the surface electrodes on the skin. Fibrous tissue, fat, and blood vessels act as insulation against the flow. Therefore, the actual pattern of the flow of electrical activity within the volume conductor is not predictable. The signals that do reach the electrode are transmitted to the amplifier. All others are simply not recorded, although they are present. The activities produced by all the individual fibers contracting at any one time are summated since they reach the electrode almost simultaneously. Electrodes only record potentials they pick up, without differentiating their origin. Therefore, if two motor units contract at the same time, from the same or adjacent muscles, the activity from fibers of both units will be summated and recorded as one large potential.

What variables, then, influence how much electrical activity is seen by the electrodes, and consequently, the size and shape of the recorded potential? First, the proximity of the electrodes to the fibers that are firing will affect the *amplitude* and *duration* of the recorded potential. Fibers that are further away will contribute less to the recorded potential. Second, the number and size of the fibers in the motor unit will influence the potential's size. A larger motor unit will produce more activity. Third, the distance between the fibers will affect the output, because if the fibers are very spread out, less of their total activity is likely to reach the electrodes. The size of the electrodes may also be a consideration. If the recording surface is larger, the electrodes will pick up from a larger area, making the size of the recorded signal greater. Therefore, to record from smaller muscles, a smaller electrode should be used.

The distance between the electrodes is another major factor affecting the size of the recorded potential. Greater electrode spacing will increase the surface, width and depth of the recording area. Because voltage is dependent on the difference in potential between the electrodes, the greater the distance, the greater the voltage, or amplitude. There is, of course, a critical limit to this distance, above which the electrodes will not be able to record a valid signal. Some surface electrode assemblies have been developed where the two electrodes are fixed within a casing, so that interelectrode

distance is standardized.[2,10] Needle electrodes have a fixed distance between the wires and the needle shaft; this distance never changes, even when the electrode is moved. Fine-wire indwelling electrodes are the least reliable in this aspect, since there is little control over the interwire distance within the muscle. The wires are often prone to change position within the muscle after repeated contractions, a situation that compromises the validity of the signals.

The effect of interelectrode distance explains the higher amplitude potentials seen with monopolar recording. The reference electrode is usually a significant distance away from the active recording electrode on a neutral area, thereby recording zero potential. The difference in potential, then, between the reference and active recording electrodes is much larger than that seen between two electrodes placed over the muscle. It should be clear, however, that this greater EMG signal does not represent a greater amount of motor unit activity. It is artifactually of greater voltage, and potentially distorted because of the greater interelectrode distance.

The shape, size, and duration of the recorded motor unit potential is actually a graphic representation of the electrical activity being picked up by the electrodes, relative to the structure of the motor unit and the electrode placement (Fig. 9–7). Therefore, with a given electrode placement, each motor unit potential will look distinctly different. The implications of this process for repeated EMG testing should be evident. It is impossible to recognize a motor unit potential as the same one if electrodes have been reinserted or moved because the spatial and temporal relationships between the electrodes and the muscle fibers cannot be validly duplicated. This holds true for surface electrodes as well, although reapplication of surface electrodes has been shown to be more reliable than reinsertion of wire electrodes.[11]

Another important consideration is the ability of elec-

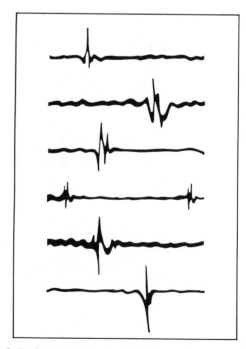

Figure 9–7. Single motor unit potentials as seen on an oscilloscope.

trodes to selectively record activity from a single muscle. Because of volume conduction, electrical activity from nearby contracting muscles, other than the muscle of interest, may reach the electrodes and be processed simultaneously. There is no way to distinguish this activity by looking at the output signal. Careful electrode placement and spacing, and choice of size and type of electrode will help control such "**cross talk**" or electrical "overflow."[2]

Artifacts

The EMG signal should be a true representation of motor unit activity occurring in the muscle of interest. Unfortunately, many excess signals, or **artifacts** can be recorded and processed simultaneously with the EMG. These artifacts can be of sufficient voltage to distort the output signal markedly. Electromyographers will usually observe the output signal on an oscilloscope to monitor artifacts.

Movement artifact. All electrodes are composed of a metallic detecting surface that is in contact with an electrolyte. This electrolyte may be the conductive electrode gel placed between a surface electrode and the skin, or it may be the tissue fluids surrounding an inserted needle or fine-wire electrode. An ion exchange occurs at the interface between the electrode and electrolyte, and this is recorded as a bioelectric event when a difference of potential exists between the two electrodes.[12] If no muscle activity is present, therefore, and the ionization that exists at each electrode–electrolyte interface is stable, then no difference of potential exists, resulting in **electrical silence.**

If, however, some disturbance occurs at one or both electrode–electrolyte interfaces, so as to produce a difference of potential, a low-frequency signal will be recorded that does not represent EMG activity. This signal is called **movement artifact.** It may result from movement of the skin beneath a surface electrode, pressure on or movement of the electrodes, or it may be caused by movement of a needle or fine-wire electrode within a contracting muscle. For example, if hamstring muscle activity is being monitored during an activity in the sitting position, pressure on the electrodes on the posterior aspect of the thigh may cause movement artifact. Some form of padding under the thigh, placed proximal and distal to the electrodes can help alleviate this pressure. Most movement artifact occurs at **frequencies** below 10 to 20 Hz, causing minimal interference with the amplitude of the signal, but creating a wavy baseline. These artifacts can usually be eliminated with firm fixation of the electrodes and proper filtering of the signal (see discussion of frequency response in the next section).

Movement of electrode cables can also cause a high-voltage, high-frequency artifact, as a result of disturbance in the electromagnetic field that surrounds the conducting lead wires. These artifacts produce wide, large-amplitude spikes, and are not easily filtered. Some recording systems have small preamplifiers that attach directly to the electrode sites so as to eliminate lengthy cables. Care must be taken to reduce these artifacts and not to interpret such signals as motor unit activity. For activities requiring broad movements, electrode cables should be taped down as much as possible, either to a table or chair, or along the limb itself, to avoid artifacts caused by cable movement.

Power line interference. The human body acts as an antenna, attracting electromagnetic energy from the surrounding environment. This energy is most commonly drawn from power lines and electrical equipment operating under an alternating current at 60 cycles per second (60 Hz). An artifact caused by this interference current resembles a sine wave and can cause a constant hum in the recorded signal if it is not eliminated through appropriate amplification techniques. A 60 Hz signal can occur if electrode attachments become loose, or if electrodes are broken or frayed. Electrode wires often break beneath the protective tubing that connects the electrode itself to the lead wire. If raw data are not monitored, this condition may not be noticed. Other equipment in the area also may be the source of electrical interference. Diathermy equipment, electrical stimulators, and vibrators are examples of devices that generate electrical noise. Sometimes, using isolated power lines will help with this situation.

Electrocardiogram (ECG). A third type of artifact, from ECG, can occur when electrodes are placed on the trunk, upper arm, or upper thigh. Correct application of the ground electrode and use of an amplifier with appropriate characteristics should help reduce these potentials, but may not be able to eliminate them. Their amplitude will vary depending on placement of electrodes. Electrocardiogram artifacts are generally regular, however, and their effect may be successfully cancelled out. If the EMG is being analyzed for frequency characteristics this signal will provide significant interference.

PROCESSOR PHASE

Differential Amplifier

Before the graphic motor unit potential can be visualized, it is necessary to amplify the small myoelectric signal. An amplifier converts the electrical potential seen by electrodes to a voltage signal large enough to be displayed. This electrical potential is composed of the EMG signal from muscle contraction and unwanted **noise** from static electricity in the air and power lines. To control for the unwanted signals, the recording electrodes each transmit electrical potentials to two sides of a **differential amplifier,** each electrode supplying input to one side. The *difference in potential* between each input and ground is processed in opposite directions. The difference between these signals is amplified and recorded, hence the name of the amplifier. If the two electrodes receive equal signals, no activity is recorded. Noise is transmitted to both ends of the amplifier as a *common mode signal.* The noise, being equal at both ends of the amplifier, is cancelled out when the difference of potential between the two sides is recorded.

Common Mode Rejection Ratio

In reality, however, the noise is not eliminated completely in a differential amplifier. Some of the recorded voltage will reflect noise. The **common mode rejection ratio (CMRR)** is a measure of how much the desired signal voltage is amplified relative to the unwanted signal.[4] A CMRR of 1000:1 indicates that the wanted signal is amplified 1000 times more than the noise. The CMRR may also be expressed in decibels (dB) (1000:1 = 60 dB). The higher this value the better. A good differential amplifier should have a common mode rejection ratio exceeding 100,000:1.

Signal-to-Noise Ratio

Noise also can be internally generated by the electronic components of an amplifier, including resistors, transistors, and integrated circuits. This noise is often manifested as a hissing sound on an **oscilloscope.** The factor that reflects the ability of the amplifier to limit this noise relative to the amplified signal is the **signal-to-noise ratio,** or the ratio of the wanted signal to the unwanted signal.

Gain

This characteristic refers to the amplifier's sensitivity, that is, its ability to amplify signals. The *gain* refers to the ratio of the output signal level to the input level. A higher gain will make a smaller signal appear larger on the display. A greater sensitivity is required for clinical EMG where individual motor units must be distinctly visible and their amplitude measured.

Input Impedance

Impedance is a resistive property, opposing current flow, that occurs in alternating current circuits (such as an amplifier). It is analogous to resistance, which is exhibited by direct circuits. Electrodes provide one source of impedance and are affected by such variables as electrode material, size of the electrode, length of the leads, and the electrolyte. If the electrode impedance is too great, the signal will be attenuated. Electrode impedance can be reduced by using larger electrodes of good conductivity with shorter leads. Fine-wire and needle electrodes generally have much greater impedance than surface electrodes, due to their much smaller surface area.

Body tissues, including adipose tissue, blood, and skin, also provide a source of resistance to the electrical field. Resistance and impedance are measured in units called ohms (Ω). Skin impedance can be measured with an ohmmeter and its value reduced by proper preparation. Most researchers have reported acceptable skin impedance under 20,000 Ω, although with proper preparation and good electrodes, resistance can usually be reduced to between 1000 and 5000 Ω. Some skin areas, such as those with darker pigments, or those that are more exposed, generally have higher impedance. Skin impedance obviously is only a concern with surface electrodes.

Impedance is also present at the input of an amplifier. The muscle action potential is effectively divided into voltage changes at the electrode and amplifier input terminals. Due to the direct relationship between voltage and impedance (based on Ohm's law), if the impedance at the amplifier is greater than the impedance at the electrode, the voltage drop will be greater at the amplifier (the recorded potential) and more accurately represent the true signal voltage. If the electrode impedance is too great, the voltage will drop at the source of the signal and less of the electrical energy will be transmitted to the amplifier. Therefore, the amplifier input impedance should be substantially greater (at least 1000 times) than the impedance recorded at the electrodes. An input impedance of 1 megohm is acceptable for surface electrodes, but should be greater with fine-wire and needle electrodes.[10] Because skin resistance contributes to the impedance measured at the electrodes, greater input impedance decreases the need for skin preparation with surface electrodes.

Frequency Response

The EMG waveforms processed by an amplifier are actually the summation of signals of varying frequencies, measured in **hertz** (1 Hz = 1 cycle per second). A MUAP can be likened to a piano chord, which is composed of many notes, each at a different frequency (sound). If we vary the notes, the chord will sound different. Similarly, the shape and amplitude of an action potential are, in part, a function of the frequencies that compose the waveform.

Amplifiers usually have variable filters that can be adjusted to limit the range of frequencies they will process. The **frequency bandwidth** delineates the highest and lowest frequency components that will be processed, or the upper and lower cutoff frequencies. If the full range of frequencies that make up the major portion of a waveform are not processed, the potential will be distorted. Amplifiers should be able to respond to signals between 10 and 10,000 Hz in order to accurately record nerve and muscle potentials for clinical EMG.[13,14,15] For kinesiologic purposes, however, where specific waveform characteristics are not of major interest, a bandwidth of 10 to 1000 Hz is adequate for surface electrodes, and 20 to 2000 Hz for fine-wire electrodes.[10] Limiting signals to these frequency ranges is also helpful for reducing the effects of low- and high-frequency artifacts.

OUTPUT PHASE

The amplified signals must be displayed in a useful fashion. The type of output used is dependent on the type of information desired and instrumentation available.

Clinical Electromyograph Displays

A cathode ray oscilloscope (CRO) is usually used for visual display in clinical EMG. A loudspeaker transforms the myoelectric signals into sound. Tape recorders have been used to record both the CRO image and the sound, to be played back at a later time for review. Many newer units incorporate computers that provide for digitizing the signal for storage, and converting back to analog signals for later display. Ink pen-writers are not appropriate for electrodiagnostic purposes because the pens have inherent frequency limitations that do not allow faithful reproduction of the motor unit potentials.

The cathode ray oscilloscope contains a cathode ray tube (Fig. 9–8). An electron gun in the rear of the tube

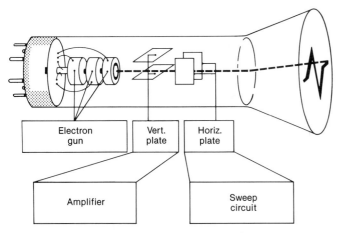

Figure 9–8. The cathode ray tube.

projects an electron beam toward the interior of the screen, which is coated with a phosphorescent material. Two sets of plates, vertical and horizontal, control the vertical deflection and horizontal *sweep* of the beam across the screen. The vertical excursion displays the signal voltage in microvolts (μV) and the speed of the horizontal sweep reflects the signal duration in milliseconds (msec). By convention, a negative deflection goes above the baseline, and a positive vertical deflection moves below the baseline.

The exterior front of the oscilloscope screen is usually covered with a grid, forming vertical and horizontal divisions. The value of these divisions, relative to the displayed signal, can be manipulated so that a given signal can look larger or smaller, or move faster or slower across the screen. When trying to display very small potentials, the sensitivity must be high, although this will cause artifacts and noise to increase in size as well.

An oscilloscope may have a storage capability, allowing potentials to remain on the screen for indefinite periods. Alternatively, a camera can be connected to the oscilloscope with its shutter triggered by the sweep of the oscilloscope. Photographs can then be made of the test results for a permanent record. Some electromyographs have a built-in camera that can transpose the image on the screen onto photosensitive paper. Electromyographs can also be interfaced with computers that perform complex analyses of motor unit potentials and send results to a printer.

A loudspeaker displays the sound of the motor unit potential. The signal relayed from the amplifier can be transformed into sound in the same way that any radio signal is processed. For the same reason that every motor unit potential will look different, it will also sound different. Normal and abnormal potentials have distinctive sounds that are helpful in distinguishing them. These will be described in the next section.

Electromyographs historically have been equipped with an FM magnetic tape recorder, which enabled the electromyographer to maintain a permanent recording of the test results, both sound and image, to be played back on the oscilloscope for detailed analysis and reference. With the onset of computerization, this addition is not seen as often today.

Kinesiologic Electromyograph Displays

Several types of recorders are used in kinesiologic study. The pen or chart recorder has been used historically, providing a permanent written record of the output. These recorders have limitations in terms of frequency response, and are only useful when integrated or averaged waveforms are generated. An oscilloscope is often used in conjunction with a pen recorder to allow visual inspection of raw signals for artifacts.

Recorders also are available with a mechanism for focusing light beams, instead of pens, across photosensitive paper, creating an image of the EMG signal. These light beams are not subject to the same frequency limitations as pens, and can record raw EMG at frequencies adequate for kinesiologic and clinical study.

Present technology allows the recording of raw and integrated EMG signals on magnetic tape, or sampling using a computer and printer. Several inexpensive analog-to-digital convertors are available for use with microcomputers, as well as the software needed to perform motion analysis using EMG data.

CLINICAL ELECTROMYOGRAPHY

The Electromyographic Examination

An EMG examination assesses the integrity of the neuromuscular system, including upper and lower motor neurons, the neuromuscular junction, and muscle fibers. The test usually involves observation of muscle action potentials from several muscles in different stages of muscle contraction. The specific muscles to be tested are determined by the examiner according to the identified clinical problem and the results of a physical exam. If a peripheral nerve lesion is suspected, the muscles innervated by that nerve will be studied. Examiners can test muscles whose innervations arise from a single nerve root to determine the site of injury. When the extent of injury is questioned, muscles that appear unaffected may be examined as well. Each patient's case must be studied and the test planned accordingly.

RECORDING TECHNIQUES

Initially, the patient is asked to relax the muscle to be examined during insertion of the needle electrode. Insertion into a contracting muscle is uncomfortable, but bearable. At this time, the electromyographer will observe a spontaneous burst of potentials, which is possibly caused by the needle breaking through muscle fiber membranes. This is called **insertion activity** and normally lasts less than 300 msec.[13,14] This activity is also seen during examination as the needle is repositioned in the muscle. It usually stops when the needle stops moving. Insertion activity can be described as normal, reduced, or increased, in part depending on the magnitude and speed of movement of the needle in the muscle. It is considered a measure of muscle excitability and may be markedly reduced in fibrotic muscles or exag-

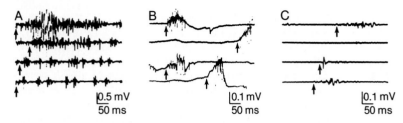

Figure 9–9. Increased (*A*), normal (*B*), and decreased (*C*) insertion activity induced by movements of the needle electrode (indicated by arrows). The tracings were obtained from the first dorsal interosseus in a patient with tardy ulnar palsy (*A*), tibialis anterior in a control subject (*B*), and fibrotic deltoid of a patient with severe dermatomyositis (*C*). (From Kimura,[14] p 231, with permission.)

gerated when denervation or inflammation is present (Fig. 9–9).

Following cessation of insertion activity, a normal relaxed muscle will exhibit electrical silence, which is the absence of electrical potentials. The baseline recorded will usually be slightly wavy as a result of the high amplifier sensitivity, which causes the baseline to reflect electrical noise from external and internal sources. These wavy deflections are readily distinguished from muscle potentials. Observation of silence in the relaxed state is an important part of the EMG examination. Potentials arising spontaneously during this period are significant abnormal findings. It is often difficult for a patient to relax sufficiently to observe complete electrical silence. However, the potentials seen will be distinct motor unit potentials, whereas **spontaneous potentials** can be differentiated by their low amplitude, shape, and sound. Sedation of a patient in order to achieve this relaxation is not practical because voluntary movement will be hampered.

One exception to finding no activity in normal resting muscle occurs when the needle is in the end-plate region. Such activity may be reflected as constant low-amplitude noise or high-amplitude intermittent spikes. It usually disappears by repositioning the needle slightly. *End-plate potentials* may be excessive in denervated muscle.[14]

After observing the muscle at rest, the patient is asked to contract the muscle minimally (Fig. 9–10). This weak voluntary effort should cause individual motor units to fire. These motor unit potentials are evaluated with respect to *amplitude, duration, shape, sound,* and *frequency* (Fig. 9–11). These five parameters are the essential characteristics that will distinguish normal and abnormal potentials. Finally, the patient is asked to increase levels of contraction progressively to a strong effort, allowing evaluation of recruitment patterns.

Normal Motor Unit Action Potentials

A motor unit potential is actually the summation of electrical potentials from all the fibers of that unit close enough to the electrodes to be recorded. The voltage amplitude is affected by the number of fibers involved. The duration and shape are functions of the distance of the fibers from the electrodes, the more distant fibers contributing to terminal phases of the potential.

In normal muscle, the amplitude of a single motor unit action potential may range from $300\mu V$ to 5mV, peak-to-peak, recorded with a concentric needle. The amplitude is primarily determined by a limited number of fibers located close to the electrode tip. Therefore, motor units must be sampled from different sites in order to determine their amplitude accurately.

The total duration, measured from initial baseline deflection to return to baseline, will normally range from 3 to 16 msec. Duration is a function of the synchrony with which individual muscle fibers fire within a

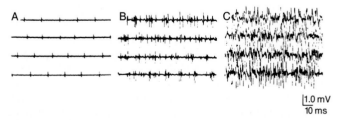

Figure 9–10. Normal recruitment of the triceps brachii in a 44-year-old healthy man. Activity was recorded during minimal contraction (*A*) where single motor unit activity is evident, during moderate contraction (*B*) when motor units are recruited, and during maximal contraction (*C*) when an interference pattern is visible. (From Kimura,[14] p 241, with permission.)

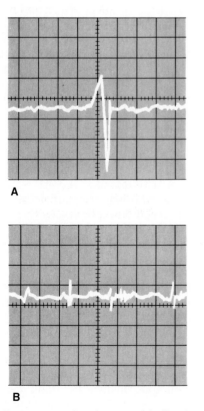

Figure 9–11. Single motor unit action potentials. The characteristics of amplitude, duration, and shape are examined by the electromyographer. (*A*) Normal biphasic potential, (*B*) Normal triphasic potentials. (From Yanof, HM: Biomedical Electronics, ed 2. FA Davis, Philadelphia, 1972, p 438, with permission.)

motor unit. This is affected by the length and conduction velocity of the axon terminals and muscle fibers. Duration can be affected significantly by electrical activity originating in fibers distant to the electrode. The *rise time* of the potential, measured from the initial positive peak to the following negative peak, provides an indication of the distance between the electrode and the contracting motor unit. A normal unit close to the electrode should have a rise time between 100 and 200 μsec. Distant discharges will have a longer rise time, and will not be useful for assessing motor unit properties.

The typical shape of a MUAP is diphasic or triphasic, with a **phase** representing a section of a potential above or below the baseline. It is not abnormal to observe small numbers of **polyphasic potentials,** having four or more phases, in normal muscle. However, when polyphasic potentials represent more than 10 percent of a muscle's output, it may be an abnormal finding.

The normal motor unit will fire up to 15 times per second with strong contraction. The identifying sound is a clear, distinct thump.[13] Gradually increasing the force of contraction will allow the electromyographer to observe the pattern of *recruitment* in the muscle. With greater effort, increasing numbers of motor units fire at higher frequencies, until the individual potentials are summated and can no longer be recognized, and an **interference pattern** is seen (Fig. 9–10). This is the normal finding with a strong contraction. Highest amplitudes for interference patterns typically vary between 2 mV and 5 mV.

One of the disadvantages of conventional assessment methods is that the examination of single motor unit potentials can only be made during weak voluntary effort, essentially restricting the analysis to low-threshold Type I motor units. An interesting alternative involves the use of *automatic quantitative assessment,* which further analyzes the interference pattern by assessing the number of directional changes of the waveform that do not necessarily cross the baseline.[16,17] These data are processed by a computer to display the number of reversals and the intervals between reversals within a given time period. Such ratios can vary between normal and pathologic conditions, allowing for greater diagnostic precision in the differentiation of primary muscle disease and neurogenic lesions.[18–21] This approach allows the electromyographer to observe the behavior of motor units even during maximal effort, when individual potentials cannot be delineated.

An electromyographer, therefore, evaluates insertion activity, as well as activity with the muscle at rest and in states of minimal, moderate, and maximal contraction. The needle electrode is moved to different areas and depths of each muscle to sample different muscle fibers and motor units. This is necessary because of the small area from which a needle electrode will pick up electrical activity, and because the effects of pathology may vary within a single muscle. Up to 25 different points within a muscle may be examined by moving and reinserting the needle electrode.

ABNORMAL POTENTIALS
Spontaneous Activity

Because a normal muscle at rest exhibits electrical silence, any activity seen during the relaxed state can be considered abnormal. Such activity is termed *spontaneous* because it is not produced by voluntary muscle contraction. Four types of spontaneous potentials have been identified: **fibrillation potentials, positive sharp waves, fasciculation potentials,** and **repetitive discharges.**

Fibrillation potentials. Fibrillation potentials are believed to arise from spontaneous depolarization of a single muscle fiber.[13,14] This theory is supported by the small amplitude and duration of the potentials. They are not visible through the skin. Fibrillation potentials may result from spontaneous discharges of denervated muscle fibers as a result of hypersensitivity to small quantities of circulating acetylcholine.[22,23,24] Fibrillation potentials are classically indicative of lower motor neuron disorders, such as peripheral nerve lesions, anterior horn cell disease, radiculopathies, and polyneuropathies with axonal degeneration. They are also found to a lesser extent in myopathic diseases such as muscular dystrophy, dermatomyositis, polymyositis, and myasthenia gravis.

Fibrillation potentials may have up to three phases, and their spikes may vary in amplitude from 20 to 300 μV, with an average duration of 2 msec (Fig. 9–12).[24,25] Their sound is a high-pitched click, which has been likened to rain falling on a roof or wrinkling tissue paper.[25] Fibrillation potentials have been recorded at frequencies of up to 30 per second.[24]

Positive sharp waves. Positive sharp waves have been observed in denervated muscle at rest, usually accompanied by fibrillation potentials. However, they are also reported in primary muscle disease, especially muscular dystrophy and polymyositis.[13,26] The waves are typically diphasic, with a sharp initial positive deflection (below baseline) followed by a slow negative phase (Fig. 9–12). The negative phase is of much lower amplitude than the positive phase, and of much longer duration—sometimes up to 100 msec.[13,27] The peak-to-peak amplitude may be variable, with voltages approaching 1 mV. The discharge frequency may range from 2 to 100 per second. The sound has been described as a dull thud. Positive sharp waves may be the result of single fiber discharges near the electrode tip or a synchronized discharge of several denervated fibers.[13,28] They are probably recorded from damaged areas of muscle fiber,[13] or they may be initiated by mechanical stimulation by the electrode within the muscle itself.[28]

Evidence indicates that fibrillation potentials and positive sharp waves may also be present with upper motor neuron lesions, creating a need for alternative explanations for their occurrence.[29–32] Spielholz observed both types of potentials in patients with spinal cord lesions and attributed their occurrence to the lack of some trophic factor from higher centers to the anterior horn cell.[33] This connection is lost with peripheral denervation. In upper motor neuron lesions the anterior horn cell itself is denervated, resulting in similar EMG find-

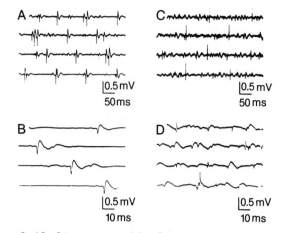

Figure 9–12. Spontaneous activity of the anterior tibialis in a 68-year-old woman with amyotrophic lateral sclerosis. Positive sharp waves (*A*, *B*) have a consistent configuration with a sharp positive deflection followed by a long duration low amplitude negative deflection (*B*). Fibrillation potentials (*C, D*) are low amplitude biphasic spikes. (From Kimura,[14] p 256, with permission.)

ings. Speilholz suggests that these findings may explain the observation of fibrillations and positive sharp waves with myopathies, and that the presence of these potentials indicates that muscle disease also affects the neuron. Johnson et al. proposed a similar hypothesis to explain finding spontaneous potentials in patients following cerebral vascular accident.[30]

Bilateral slowing of nerve conduction velocities in the ulnar and peroneal nerves has also been documented in patients with hemiplegia, supporting the hypothesis of lower motor neuron involvement.[34] Similar findings were not obtained, however, in a study of patients with cerebral palsy.[35] These findings have also been disputed by others, who have not confirmed the presence of spontaneous EMG activity in patients with hemiplegia,[36,37] or who argue that such spontaneous potentials are due to secondary disease of lower motor neurons.[38] Further study is obviously needed to clarify the effect of upper motor neuron involvement on lower motor neuron function.

Investigators have also demonstrated spontaneous potentials in normal muscles of healthy subjects, primarily in muscles of the feet.[39] They suggest that pathologic changes involving axonal loss, segmental demyelination, and collateral sprouting may be associated with aging or mechanical trauma to the feet. Their findings have important clinical implications in that interpretation of the pattern of EMG and other assessments is necessary in order to accurately evaluate pathology.

Fasciculations. Fasciculations are spontaneous potentials seen with irritation or degeneration of the anterior horn cell, nerve root compression, and muscle spasms or cramps. They are believed to represent the involuntary asynchronous contraction of a bundle of muscle fibers or a whole motor unit. While their origin is not clearly known, there is evidence that the spontaneous discharge originates in the spinal cord or anywhere along the path of the peripheral nerve, causing contraction of the muscle fibers.[40]

Fasciculations are often visible through the skin, seen

as a small twitch. They are not by themselves a definitive abnormal finding, however, since they are also seen in normal individuals, particularly in calf muscle, eyes, hands, and feet. When seen with other abnormal factors, such as fibrillations and positive sharp waves, fasciculations do contribute information relative to pathology. The amplitude and duration of these potentials may be similar to a motor unit potential (Fig. 9–13). They may be diphasic, triphasic, or polyphasic. Their firing rate is usually irregular, up to 50 per second. Their sound has been described as a low-pitched thump.[13]

Repetitive discharges. Repetitive discharges, also called *bizarre high frequency discharges,* are seen with lesions of the anterior horn cell and peripheral nerves, and with myopathies. The discharge is characterized by an extended train of potentials of various form (Fig. 9–14). The feature that distinguishes these discharges from other spontaneous potentials is their frequency, which usually ranges from 5 to 100 impulses per second. The amplitude can vary from 50 μV to 1 mV, and duration may be up to 100 msec.[14] Repetitive discharges that increase and decrease in amplitude in a waxing and waning fashion are typical of myotonias, and sound like a "dive-bomber." High-frequency discharges are probably triggered by movement of the needle electrode within unstable muscle fibers, or by volitional activity.[13]

Abnormal Voluntary Potentials

Polyphasic potentials are generally considered abnormal, but they are elicited on voluntary contraction, not at rest. They are typical of myopathies and peripheral nerve involvement. In primary muscle disease, these potentials are generally of smaller amplitude than normal motor units, and of shorter duration. These multiphasic changes occur because of the decrease in the number of active muscle fibers within the individual motor units due to pathology. Although the entire unit will fire during voluntary contraction, fewer fibers are available in each unit to contribute to the total voltage and the duration of the potential. The polyphasic configuration is a result of the slight asynchrony of muscle fibers within a motor unit. This phenomenon is probably due to the difference in the length of the terminal branches of the axon extending to each individual fiber. The effects of this are normally not seen because the

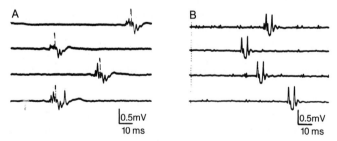

Figure 9–13. Fasciculation potentials in two patients with polyneuropathy. Recordings were obtained from the tibialis anterior in both patients, showing a very polyphasic potential of long duration (*A*) and a double-peaked complex discharge (*B*). Fasciculation potentials are not always abnormal in waveform as shown here and are usually indistinguishable in shape from voluntarily activated motor unit potentials. (From Kimura,[14] p 260, with permission.)

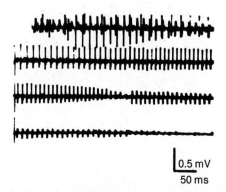

Figure 9–14. Repetitive discharge from the right anterior tibialis in a 39-year-old man with myotonic dystrophy. The waxing and waning quality of these discharges is evident. (From Kimura,[14] p 254, with permission.)

time differences are so slight. However, when some fibers are no longer contracting, these differences become more apparent, resulting in a fragmentation of the motor unit potential (Fig. 9–15).[13]

Polyphasic potentials may also be seen following regeneration of a peripheral nerve. As some muscle fibers become reinnervated they will generate action potentials with voluntary contraction. However, there are significantly fewer fibers acting than were present in the original unit, and these fibers will clearly reflect asynchronous depolarization. These polyphasic potentials are also much smaller in amplitude and duration than normal units. They have been termed nascent motor units. Although they are considered abnormal potentials, they are a positive finding with peripheral nerve lesions.

Some forms of neuropathic involvement, such as anterior horn cell disease, will result in hypertrophy of an intact motor unit by collateral sprouting of axons to fibers of denervated motor units, forming **giant motor units.** Because these sprouts are of small diameter and

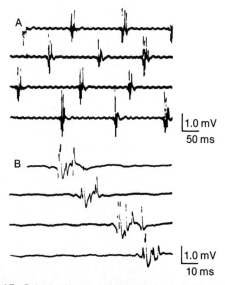

Figure 9–15. Polyphasic motor unit potentials from the anterior tibialis in a 52-year-old man with amyotrophic lateral sclerosis, recorded at fast (A) and slow (B) sweep speeds. (From Kimura,[14] p 265, with permission.)

have slow conduction velocities, there is a dispersion in the recorded potential, which increases the amplitude and duration and results in a polyphasic shape. If this situation is sufficiently prevalent, the interference pattern may be increased in amplitude.

Sources of Error in Clinical Electromyography

The subjective techniques used for electromyographic examination leave several avenues for error in performing and reporting the tests.[41,42] An understanding of potential errors will facilitate valid and reliable interpretation of test results.

Interpretation of when insertion activity is reduced or increased is dependent upon electrode position as well as subjective estimation. When the muscle is supposedly at rest, a trained observer must be able to distinguish spontaneous potentials from single motor unit potentials generated out of anxiety. The examiner must be able to judge the level of the patient's effort in order to validly determine if recruitment is normal and an interference pattern is achieved.[42] The electromyographer must also be able to distinguish different motor unit potentials, evaluating their amplitude, duration, and shape.

In terms of technique, it is obvious that inaccurate electrode placement will distort the recorded potentials. In EMG examinations, great care must be taken to ensure appropriate placement of the needle electrode within the muscle. Anatomical anomalies must be considered. This becomes especially important because of volume conduction, when small or thin muscles are tested, such as those in the hand. Electrodes can be inserted too far, penetrating deeper muscles and thereby providing false information.

The interpretation of EMG potentials also provides opportunity for error. In EMG, an experienced eye is needed to accurately identify abnormal potentials. It is also important to report them in appropriate terminology so that they are properly communicated. Fibrillation potentials and positive sharp waves were once called "denervation potentials." This did not distinguish the two types of potentials, nor is it an accurate expression in many cases. Similarly, an experienced examiner must also be able to judge when the percentage of polyphasic potentials is above normal.

Nerve Conduction Velocity Tests

Hodes, Larabee, and German[43] first developed the technique for calculating the conduction velocity of the ulnar nerve in 1948. Dawson and Scott[44] further refined the procedure a year later, recording nerve potentials from the ulnar and median nerves through the skin at the wrist. This EMG technique has since become a valuable tool for evaluating abnormalities and lesions of peripheral nerves, as well as localizing the site of involvement.

Nerve conduction velocity tests involve direct stimulation to initiate an impulse in motor or sensory nerves. The **conduction time** is measured by recording evoked potentials either from the muscle innervated by the motor nerve or from the sensory nerve itself. Nerve conduction velocity can be tested on any peripheral nerve that is superficial enough to be stimulated through the skin at two different points. Most commonly it is performed on the ulnar, median, peroneal, and posterior tibial nerves; less commonly on the radial, femoral, and sciatic nerves. Complete guidelines for performing nerve conduction velocity tests are available in several references.[45-47]

INSTRUMENTATION

Although EMG records the spontaneous or volitional potentials of motor units, nerve conduction measurements involve **evoked potentials,** produced by direct electrical stimulation of peripheral nerves. The instrumentation, therefore, includes a stimulator in addition to all the components of the electromyograph already described (Fig. 9–16).

The stimulating electrode is typically a two-pronged bipolar electrode with the **cathode** ($-$) and the **anode** ($+$) extending from a plastic casing (Fig. 9–17). A single cathodal stimulating electrode can also be used in conjunction with an inactive electrode. A needle electrode can be used to stimulate the nerve. The stimulus is provided by a square-wave generator, with pulses typically delivered at a duration of 0.1 msec and a frequency of 1 pulse per second (up to 20 pulses per second). The intensity needed will vary with the nerve and the individual patient, usually between 100 and 300 V, or 5 and 40 mA.[14] Diseased nerves with decreased excitability may require as much as 500 V or 75 mA. These intensities are considered safe for an ordinary patient. However, with a cardiac pacemaker, grounding should be checked and stimulation should be a sufficient distance from the pacemaker.[48] With indwelling cardiac catheters or central venous pressure lines, nerve conduction studies are contraindicated, as the electrical current may directly reach the cardiac tissue.

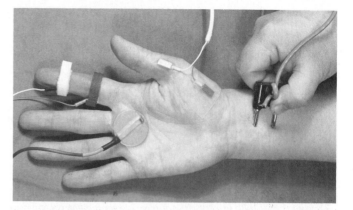

Figure 9–17. Set up for motor and sensory conduction velocity tests of the median nerve. Recording electrodes are placed over the muscle belly of the abductor pollicis brevis for motor conduction, and ring electrodes are placed over the proximal and distal interphalangeal joints of the second digit for sensory conduction. The ground electrode is located between the stimulating and recording electrodes on the hand. The nerve is stimulated at the wrist (shown) and at the elbow to obtain motor latencies. Only stimulation at the wrist is necessary for sensory latency. (From Kimura,[14] p 106, with permission.)

A trigger mechanism is incorporated into the recording system, so that the oscilloscope sweep is triggered by the stimulator. This means that the sweep begins when the stimulus is delivered, producing a **stimulus artifact** on the screen with each successive stimulus. This allows the measurement of time from stimulus onset to response. The sweep makes one complete excursion across the screen for each pulse put out by the stimulator.

MOTOR NERVE CONDUCTION VELOCITY

Stimulation and Recording

Recording potentials directly from a peripheral nerve makes monitoring of purely sensory or motor fibers impossible. Therefore, to isolate the potentials conducted by motor axons of a mixed nerve, the evoked potential is recorded from a distal muscle innervated by the nerve. Although the stimulation of the nerve will evoke sensory and motor impulses, only the motor fibers will contribute to the contraction of the muscle. For the ulnar nerve the test muscle is the abductor digiti minimi; for the median nerve the abductor pollicis brevis; for the peroneal nerve, the extensor digitorum brevis; and for the posterior tibial nerve, the abductor hallicus or abductor digiti minimi.

Surface electrodes are usually used to record the evoked potential from the test muscle, although needle electrodes may be used when responses are very weak. The surface electrodes should be small, less than 1 cm in diameter. One recording electrode, the *active electrode,* (sometimes called the *pickup electrode*) is placed over the belly of the test muscle. Accurate location of this electrode is important to the accuracy of the test, and the belly of the muscle should be carefully palpated, preferably against slight resistance. The second

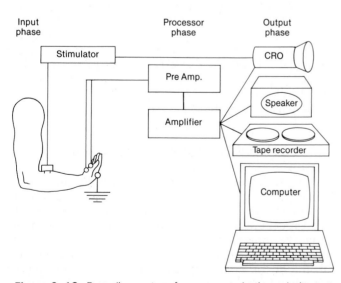

Figure 9–16. Recording system for nerve conduction velocity test, showing addition of the stimulator. Note the connection between the stimulator and the CRO, which is the triggering mechanism.

recording electrode, the *reference electrode,* is taped over the tendon of the muscle, distal to the active electrode. The skin should be cleaned with alcohol to reduce skin resistance before applying electrodes. A *ground electrode* is placed over a neutral area between the *recording electrodes* and the stimulation sites, usually over the dorsum of the hand or foot, or over the wrist or ankle. The skin over the stimulation sites should also be cleaned with alcohol to decrease resistance to the stimulus pulse, making the procedure more comfortable for the patient.

For purposes of illustration, the test procedure for the MNCV of the median nerve will be described. The technique is basically the same for all nerves, except for the sites of stimulation and placement of the recording electrodes. The active electrode is taped over the belly of the test muscle, the abductor pollicis brevis, and the reference electrode is taped over the tendon just distal to the metacarpophalangeal joint. The stimulating electrode is placed over the median nerve at the wrist, just proximal to the distal crease on the volar surface, with the cathode directed toward the recording electrodes (Fig. 9–17). The **cathode** is the stimulating electrode (usually black) and the **anode** is the inactive electrode (usually red). It is important that the cathode be directed toward the recording electrodes to stimulate depolarization toward the muscle **(orthodromic conduction).**

At the moment the stimulus is produced, the **stimulus artifact** is seen at the left of the screen. The trigger mechanism controls this and it will, therefore, always appear in the same spot on the screen, facilitating consistent measurements. This spike is purely mechanical and does not represent any muscle activity (Fig. 9–18).

The stimulus intensity starts out low and is slowly increased until the *evoked potential* is clearly observed. When the stimulating electrode is properly placed over the nerve, all muscles innervated distal to that point will contract, and the patient will see and feel his hand "jump." The intensity is then increased until the evoked response no longer increases in size. At that time the intensity is increased further by about 25 percent to be sure that the stimulus is *supramaximal.* Because the intensity must be sufficient to reach the threshold of all motor fibers in the nerve, a supramaximal stimulus is required. It is also essential that the cathode be properly placed over the nerve trunk so that the stimulus reaches all the motor axons.

As in the electromyogram, the potentials seen on the oscilloscope represent the electrical activity picked up by the recording electrodes. The signal will represent the difference of electrical potential between the active and reference electrodes. When the supramaximal stimulus is applied to the median nerve at the wrist, all the axons in the nerve will depolarize and begin conducting an impulse, transmitting the signal across the motor end plate, initiating depolarization of the muscle fibers. During these events the two recording electrodes do not record a difference in potential because no activity is taking place beneath the electrodes. When the muscle fibers begin to depolarize, the electrical potentials are transmitted to the electrodes through the volume conductor, and a deflection is seen on the oscilloscope. This

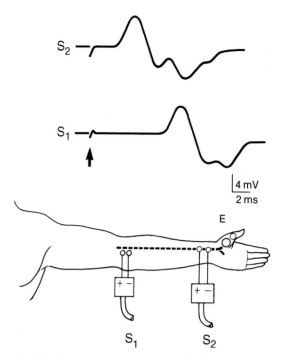

Figure 9–18. Illustration of the recording of median nerve motor conduction velocity, with recording electrodes (E) over the thenar muscles. The M wave is recorded following stimulation at the wrist (S2) and elbow (S1). Nerve conduction time from the elbow to the wrist is determined as the difference between the latencies recorded from the distal (S₂) and proximal (S₁) stimulations. Latency is measured from stimulus artifact (*arrow*) to onset of M wave. The motor nerve conduction velocity is then calculated by dividing the surface distance between the two points by the conduction time.

is the *evoked potential,* which is called the **M wave** (Fig. 9–18). The M wave represents the summated activity of all motor units in the muscle that respond to stimulation of the nerve trunk. The amplitude of this potential is, therefore, a function of the total voltage produced by the contracting motor units. The initial deflection of the M wave is the negative portion of the wave, above the baseline.

Nerve conduction velocity tests can be performed on more proximal segments of the nerve trunk by stimulating at more proximal points, such as Erb's point and the axilla (Fig. 9–18). However, this procedure is used less frequently.

Calculation of Motor Conduction Velocity

The point at which the M wave leaves the baseline indicates the time elapsed from the initial propagation of the nerve impulse to the depolarization of the muscle fibers beneath the electrodes. This is called the response **latency.** The latency is measured in milliseconds from the stimulus artifact to the onset of the M wave. This time alone is not a valid measurement of nerve conduction because it incorporates other events besides pure nerve conduction, namely, transmission across the myoneural junction and generation of the muscle action potential. There is also evidence that the distal segments and terminal branches of nerves conduct at much slower rates than the main axon.[49] Therefore, these extraneous factors must be eliminated from the calculation of the nerve conduction velocity, so that the measurement reflects only the speed of conduction within the nerve trunk.

To account for these distal variables, the nerve is stimulated at a second, more proximal point. This will produce a response similar to that seen with distal stimulation (Fig. 9–18). The stimulus artifact will appear in the same spot on the screen, but the M wave will originate in a different place because the time for the impulses to reach the muscle would, obviously, be longer. Subtraction of the **distal latency** from the **proximal latency** will determine the **conduction time** for the nerve trunk segment between the two points of stimulation. **Conduction velocity (CV)** is determined by dividing the distance between the two points of cathodal stimulation (measured along the surface) by the difference between the two latencies (velocity = distance/time).

$$CV = \frac{\text{Conduction distance}}{\text{Proximal latency} - \text{distal latency}}$$

Conduction velocity is always expressed in meters per second, although distance is usually measured in centimeters and latencies in milliseconds. These units must be converted during calculation.

To compute the motor nerve conduction velocity for the test illustrated in Fig. 9–19, the proximal and distal latencies are determined by measuring the time from the stimulus artifact to the initial M wave deflection, according to the calibration scale, or sweep speed. The conduction time is calculated by taking the difference between these latencies. **Conduction distance** is then determined by measuring the length of the nerve between the two points of stimulation. For example,

Proximal latency	7 msec
Distal latency	2 msec
Conduction distance	30 cm

$$CV = \frac{30 \text{ cm}}{7 \text{ msec} - 2 \text{ msec}} = \frac{30 \text{ cm}}{5 \text{ msec}} = 60 \text{ m/s}$$

Interpretation of the motor nerve conduction velocity is made in relation to normal values, which are usually expressed as mean values, standard deviations, and ranges. Norms have been determined by many investigators in different laboratories. Even so, average values seem to be fairly consistent. The motor nerve conduction velocity for the upper extremity has a fairly wide range, with values reported from 45 to 70 m/s. The average normal value is about 60 m/s. For the lower extremity, the average value is about 50 m/s. Distal latencies and average normal amplitudes of M waves are also found in such tables, but these must be viewed with caution, since technique, electrode setup, instrumentation, and patient size can affect these values. The reader is referred to more comprehensive discussions for complete tables of normal values.[13,46,50]

It is important to note that the value calculated as the conduction velocity is actually a reflection of the speed of the fastest axons in the nerve. Although all axons are stimulated at the same point in time, and supposedly fire at the same time, their conduction rates vary with their size. Not all motor units will contract at the same time, since some receive their nerve impulse later than others. Therefore, the initial M wave deflection represents the contraction of the motor unit, or units, with the fastest conduction velocity. The curved shape of the M wave is reflective of the progressively slower axons reaching their motor units at a later time.

The M wave can also provide useful information about the integrity of the nerve or muscle. Three parameters should be evaluated: amplitude, shape, and duration. Any change occurring in these characteristics is called **temporal dispersion.** These parameters reflect the summated voltage over time produced by all the contracting motor units within the test muscle. Therefore, if the muscle is partially denervated, fewer motor units will contract following nerve stimulation. This will cause the M wave amplitude to decrease. Duration may change depending on the conduction velocity of the intact units. Similar changes may also be evident in myopathic conditions, in which all motor units are intact, but fewer fibers are available in each motor unit.

The shape of the M wave can also be variable. Deviation from a smooth curve need not be abnormal, and it is often useful to compare the proximal and distal M waves with each other as well as with the contralateral side. They should be similar. In abnormal conditions, changes in shape may be the result of a significant slowing of conduction in some axons, repetitive firing, or asynchronous firing of axons following a single stimulus.

SENSORY NERVE CONDUCTION VELOCITY

Sensory neurons demonstrate the same physiologic properties as motor neurons, and conduction velocity can be measured in a similar way. However, some differences in technique are necessary to differentiate between sensory and motor axons. Although sensory fibers can be tested using orthodromic conduction (physiologic direction) or **antidromic conduction** (opposite to normal conduction), orthodromic measurements appear to be more common. For the same reason that motor axons are examined by recording over

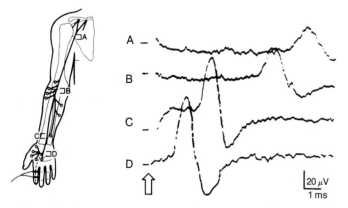

Figure 9–19. Sensory nerve conduction study of the median nerve. The sites of stimulation shown include axilla (*A*), elbow (*B*), wrist (*C*), and palm (*D*). Digital potentials are recorded antidromically, using ring electrodes placed around the second digit. The arrow indicates the stimulus artifact. (From Kimura,[14] p 105, with permission.)

muscle, sensory axons are either stimulated or recorded from digital sensory nerves. This eliminates the activity of the motor axons from the recorded potentials.

Stimulation and Recording

The **stimulating electrode** used for motor conduction velocity tests can be used for sensory tests, or the stimulus may be provided by ring electrodes placed around the base of the middle of the digit innervated by the nerve (Fig. 9–17). The recording electrodes can be surface or needle electrodes. Surface electrodes are placed over the nerve trunk where it is superficial to the skin. The active electrode is placed distally, and a ground electrode is usually set between the stimulating and recording electrodes.

The electrode positions can be reversed, measuring antidromic conduction. If electrode sites are consistent, the latencies should be essentially equivalent in both directions. Orthodromic stimulation of fingertips appears to be more uncomfortable than stimulation of the nerve trunk.[13]

Sensory potentials for the median and ulnar nerves can be recorded at the wrist and elbow. The ulnar nerve can also be monitored at the axilla, although it is rather unreliable and difficult to differentiate between median and ulnar nerves. In lower extremities, the toes can be stimulated and sensory potentials recorded at various sites along the tibial and sciatic nerves. Sensory examination has been reported to be more difficult in the lower extremities because of anatomic variations.[13] The path of the main nerve trunk can often be determined by electrical stimulation and observation of motor responses.

Calculation of Sensory Conduction Velocity

Latencies are usually measured from the stimulus artifact to the peak of the evoked potential, rather than to the initial deflection, because of the uneven baseline seen with sensory tests (Fig. 9–18). The baseline is more uneven because sensory tests require much greater amplifier sensitivity than do motor tests, and this allows more noise to interfere with recording. Although sensory conduction velocity can be determined in the same way as motor conduction velocity (dividing distance by difference between latencies), often latencies are sufficient measurements, because terminal branching does not seem to be a significant limitation. Therefore, the latency essentially represents sensory nerve conduction activity only.

Normal SNCV ranges between 45 and 75 m/s. Amplitude, measured with surface electrodes, may be 10 to 60 μV, and duration should be short, less than 2 msec. Sensory evoked potentials are usually sharp, not rounded like the M wave. Sensory nerve conduction velocities have been found to be slightly faster than motor nerve conduction velocities because of the larger diameter of sensory nerves.[51]

Because the amplitude of sensory potentials can be so low, even under normal conditions, the potential can be hidden in the erratic baseline, making it difficult to distinguish from the noise. Dawson and Scott, in their early studies, used photographic superimposition to overlay 100 sweeps.[44] Because the stimulus artifact and the evoked potential will appear in the same place with each sweep, the random background noise looks dispersed and the evoked response is brighter on film. More sophisticated instrumentation has been developed that can process repetitive sweeps; by averaging only the signals that appear in the same time frame, the noise can be cancelled out and the response reinforced. Electronic averagers then display the evoked potential clearly. Today, these systems are often computerized, allowing the potential to be clearly delineated from the random noise.

SOURCES OF ERROR IN CONDUCTION VELOCITY TESTS

For nerve conduction measurements, proper placement of both recording and stimulating electrodes is essential for reliable measurement. The active electrode should be directly over the muscle belly so that the M wave will be an accurate representation of full motor unit activity. Some leeway exists, however, before conduction velocity values are significantly affected.

When patients are not able to voluntarily contract the test muscle, the electromyographer must be able to accurately locate the muscle belly. The electrodes may also record volume-conducted potentials from neighboring muscles, resulting in misinterpretation of the output. If the stimulating electrode is not directly over the nerve trunk, all axons may not be stimulated, or axons from adjacent nerves may be stimulated instead. Consideration must be given to the possibility of anomalous innervation for the same reason.

In addition to placement concerns, the intensity of the stimulus is important. A submaximal stimulus may not be sufficent to reach the threshold of all axons in the nerve. This will significantly increase the latency obtained. The supramaximal stimulus that is required may also be of great enough intensity to cause spread of the stimulus pulse to other nerves.

Errors can occur in the calculation of the conduction velocity. The measurement of the distance between stimulation sites (conduction distance) must be accurate. This is of special concern when the nerve trunk does not follow a perfectly straight path, as with the ulnar and radial nerves. The position of the limb will greatly affect these measurements as well. When measuring latencies, the location of the initial deflection of the M wave may be somewhat subjective. In addition, the actual determination of the latency time must be exact. A permanent recording of some kind, such as film or computer printout, is preferable to reading off the oscilloscope, where parallax errors are readily made. It is also easy to make errors in calculation of the nerve conduction velocity. Omission of distal latencies and distance between electrodes can also be considered an error in reporting, since these values are necessary to the evaluation of normal versus abnormal results.

In sensory nerve conduction velocity tests, care must be taken when placing electrodes, so that antidromic motor responses or volume-conducted activity is not recorded with the sensory potentials. If this occurs, the latency, shape and duration of the evoked sensory potential will be significantly affected.

Other factors must also be considered when interpreting test results. Age and temperature are the two most influential factors that can cause variations in conduction velocity. Nerve conduction is slowed considerably in infants, young children, and elderly individuals. At birth the motor nerve conduction velocity is approximately half normal adult values, gradually increasing until reaching adult rates at 5 years of age.[52,53] Motor and sensory conduction velocities have been shown to decrease slightly following age 35, with larger, significant differences noted after age 70.[54,55]

Lower temperature can also decrease motor and sensory conduction velocities significantly.[56] Drops of 1°C (34°F) in intramuscular temperature have been correlated with changes of 2 to 2.4 m/s in conduction velocity. It is advisable to warm a cool limb prior to examination to stabilize the limb's temperature.

Echternach has thoroughly discussed measurement issues related to EMG and NCV that will be helpful to anyone interested in these test procedures.[42]

Reporting the Results of the Clinical Electromyograph Examination

The performance of reliable and valid EMG examinations requires extensive experience and expertise with biomedical instrumentation, as well as neuromuscular anatomy and pathology. The material presented here, however brief, is intended to provide sufficient background for the reader to intelligently utilize information from an electromyographic report and to apply these data to other aspects of patient care specifically related to prognosis, goal setting, and treatment planning. With this in mind, it seems appropriate to review how such reports are presented.

The EMG report is typically found in a patient's chart or medical record. The essential data include (1) the specific muscle or muscles tested, including side of the body and the innervation of these muscles; (2) the response seen during electrode insertion; (3) the response at rest (spontaneous activity, specifying type of potentials or electrical silence); and (4) responses with voluntary contraction (motor unit potentials and recruitment) (Fig. 9–20). The data provided should relate to the five parameters of electrical potentials previously described: amplitude, duration, shape, sound, and frequency.

Reports of nerve conduction measurements should include (1) location of recording and stimulating electrodes; (2) the calculated velocity, in meters per second; (3) the distal latency and distance between recording and stimulating electrodes; and (4) the amplitude and duration of the M wave or evoked sensory potential (Fig. 9–21). Comments should follow the data, stating the impression or implications of findings.

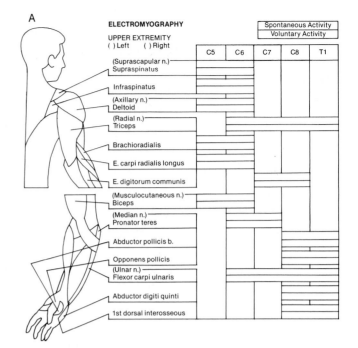

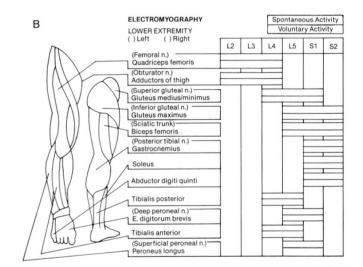

Figure 9–20. Sample report form for EMG. This pictorial form demonstrates the relative position and peripheral nerve and root innervation of the commonly tested upper extremity and lower extremity muscles. Information about spontaneous and voluntary activity can be recorded for each muscle. (From Brumback, RA, et al: Pictorial report form for needle electromyography. Phys Ther 63:224, 1983, with permission.)

It is extremely important to stress here that diagnoses should not be made solely on the basis of electromyographic data. All other appropriate assessment procedures performed on the patient are used to provide a complete picture of the patient's disorder. These include a history and laboratory tests, as well as physical therapy evaluations, such as the manual muscle test, sensory tests, a range of motion test, and so forth. Electrodiagnostic findings will often provide objective evidence to support clinical observations.

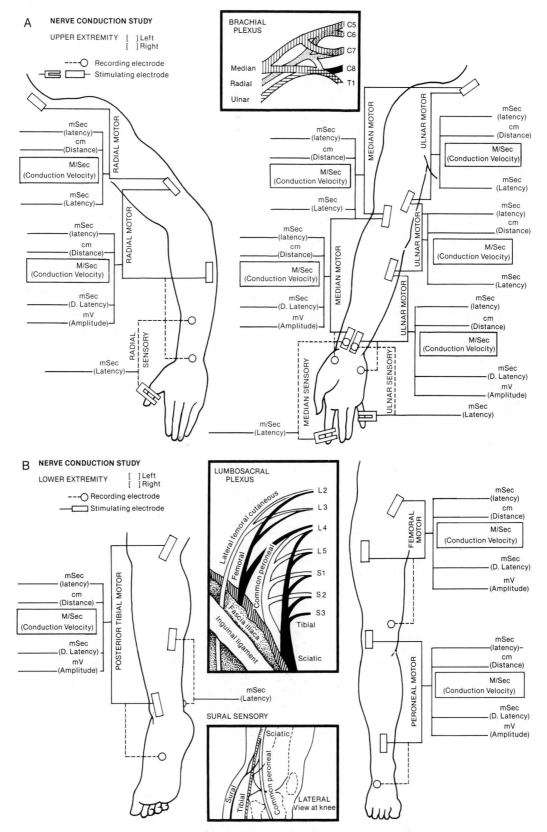

Figure 9–21. Sample report form for nerve conduction studies, containing listings of latencies, electrode distances, potential amplitudes, and calculated conduction velocities, followed by interpretation. Forms for upper and lower extremity show relationship of anatomy to nerve conduction velocity data. (From Brumback, RA, et al: Pictorial report form for nerve conduction studies. Phys Ther 61:1457, 1981, with permission.)

CLINICAL IMPLICATIONS OF ELECTROMYOGRAPH TESTS

Typical findings with neurogenic or myogenic disorders can be described. The following discussion will focus on selected disorders that typify EMG and NCV results, and their implications for evaluation and treatment planning.

Disorders of Peripheral Nerve

Electrophysiologic findings usually correlate with clinical signs in patients with neuropathic involvement.[57] Some differences exist between types of neuropathies in terms of relative onset of sensory and motor symptoms and nerve conduction changes. Electromyographic findings are usually significant only if axonal damage is a factor. Often electrophysiologic changes are seen before clinical manifestations, with sensory nerves being affected before motor; this makes the electromyogram unremarkable. The sensory nerve conduction velocity test may then provide the most helpful information. Clinicians will find such information useful in following progression or remission of the existing condition.

PERIPHERAL NERVE LESIONS

Lesions of the peripheral nerve fall into three categories: neurapraxia, axonotmesis, and neurotmesis. They may be due to traumatic injury or entrapment. Such disorders typically cause weakness and atrophy of all muscles innervated distal to the lesion. Sensory findings often occur first, but may not be as definitive as motor deficits in localizing the site of the lesion.[14] Electromyographic data can assist in the identification and prognosis of such cases.

Neurapraxia

A neurapraxia involves some form of local blockage, which stops or slows conduction across that point in the nerve. Conduction above and below the blockage is usually normal. Compression disorders are the most common types of neurapraxic lesions, such as Bell's palsy (facial nerve), Saturday night palsy (radial nerve compression in spiral groove), pressure over the peroneal nerve at the fibula head, and carpal tunnel syndrome (median nerve entrapment). Nerve conduction velocity tests can detect evidence of demyelinization prior to axonal degeneration, which may occur with long-standing compression. Nerve conduction measurements will usually reveal increased latencies across the compressed area, but normal conduction velocity above and below. In acute conditions with no denervation, the EMG will be normal at rest. This should be considered a positive prognostic sign. The interference pattern may be decreased or absent if there is severe blockage.

Axonotmesis

With axonotmesis the neural tube is intact, but axonal damage has occurred. This may be a progressive condition as a result of long-standing neurapraxia, or it may occur from a traumatic lesion. The deficit in nerve con-duction velocity will depend partly on the number of axons affected. If the larger diameter fibers remain intact, the conduction velocity may be normal. However, M wave amplitude will be decreased because fewer motor units are contracting. Fibrillation potentials and positive sharp waves are typically seen on EMG 2 to 3 weeks following denervation, depending on the distance of the axon from the cell body.

Neurotmesis

Neurotmesis involves total loss of axonal function, with disruption of the neural tube. Conduction ceases below the lesion. A conduction velocity test cannot be performed because no evoked response can be elicited. Recovery is dependent on proper orientation of axons as they regenerate. Spontaneous potentials will appear with the muscle at rest, and no activity is produced with attempted voluntary contraction.

Regeneration of peripheral nerves will be signaled by the presence of small polyphasic potentials (nascent units) with voluntary contraction. These may be seen before clinical recovery is evident through the results of clinical assessments such as the manual muscle test. After clinical recovery is established, polyphasic potentials may persist, often as giant potentials, due to collateral sprouting. Rehabilitation goals for patients with peripheral nerve injuries can be influenced by results of serial EMG findings. Evidence of regeneration will suggest that motor function is improving and treatment plans should address minimal exercise for the weak and easily fatigued muscles. Positive signs of regeneration will also help in setting realistic long-term goals for functional recovery.

POLYNEUROPATHIES

Polyneuropathies typically result in sensory changes, distal weakness, and hyporeflexia. Neuropathies can be related to general medical conditions, such as diabetes, alcoholism, renal disease, or malignancies; they may result from infections, such as leprosy or Guillain-Barre syndrome; and they may be associated with metabolic abnormalities, such as malnutrition or the toxic effects of drugs or chemicals.[14]

Neuropathic conditions may be manifested as axonal damage or demyelination of axons. With *axonal lesions,* recruitment will be severely affected. A partial interference pattern may be observed with maximal effort, or single motor unit potentials may still be identifiable (Fig. 9–22). The motor unit duration and amplitude may be decreased. Fibrillation potentials, positive sharp waves, and fasciculations are typical (Fig. 9–12).

With *demyelinization,* nerve conduction measurements will often provide the most useful data. Sensory fibers are often affected before motor fibers, and significant slowing of sensory conduction velocity may be seen. The evoked potential will typically be reduced in amplitude.

Motor Neuron Disorders

Motor neuron disorders most commonly involve degenerative diseases of the anterior horn cells. These

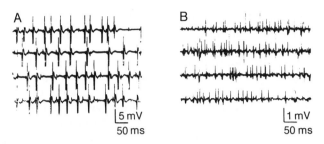

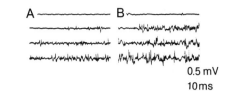

0.5 mV

10ms

Figure 9–22. Large amplitude, long duration motor unit potentials from the first dorsal interosseus (*A*) compared with relatively normal motor unit potentials from orbicularis oculi (*B*) in a patient with polyneuropathy. Note discrete single unit interference pattern during maximal voluntary contraction. (From Kimura,[14] p 267, with permission.)

Figure 9–23. Low-amplitude, short-duration motor unit potentials recorded during minimal voluntary contraction from the biceps brachii (*A*) and tibialis anterior (*B*) in a 7-year-old boy with Duchenne dystrophy. A high number of discharging motor units during minimal contraction reflects early recruitment. (From Kimura,[14] p 268, with permission.)

include poliomyelitis, syringomyelia, and some diseases that are characterized by degeneration of both upper and lower motor neurons, such as amyotrophic lateral sclerosis, progressive muscular atrophy, and progressive bulbar palsy.[58] Spinal muscular atrophies are another classification of motor neuron disease.[59] The reader is referred to comprehensive texts to review clinical features of these diseases.[14,60]

Diseases of the anterior horn cell are classically indicated by fibrillation potentials and positive sharp waves at rest (Fig. 9–12), and by reduced recruitment with voluntary contraction, due to loss of motor neurons. Single motor unit action potentials that can still be seen with maximal effort are called a **single motor unit pattern.** Polyphasic motor unit potentials of increased amplitude and duration are typically seen later in the course of the disease (Fig. 9–15), due to reinnervation and collateral sprouting.[61] Motor nerve conduction velocity may be slowed, depending on the distribution of degeneration among motor fibers, but sensory evoked potentials are unaffected.

Myopathies

In primary muscle diseases, such as the dystrophies or polymyositis, the motor unit remains intact, but degeneration of muscle fibers is evident. Therefore, the number of fibers innervated by one axon is diminished. Motor nerve conduction is typically normal, although the amplitude of the M wave will be decreased because fewer fibers are responding to stimulation. Sensory nerve potentials and neuromuscular transmission are normal. In the early stages, the EMG examination shows prolonged insertion activity, perhaps due to the instability of muscle fibers or of the muscle membrane itself. Fibrillations and positive sharp waves are also seen, sometimes with repetitive discharges. Voluntary contraction typically elicits short-duration, low-amplitude polyphasic potentials, reflecting random loss of muscle fibers. Less than maximal effort will require early recruitment and an interference pattern is evoked because more motor units are needed to create the necessary tension within the muscle (Fig. 9–23). The total amplitude of the interference pattern, however, will be diminished.

In advanced stages of polymyositis and muscular dystrophy, when contractile tissue is replaced by fibrous tissue and other tissues, no electrical potentials may be seen at all. On insertion, the needle will meet some resistance as it enters the fibrotic tissue. Motor nerve conduction measurements will also be impossible under such conditions because no evoked potential can be elicited.

Since most myopathies are progressive, clinicians will find EMG and MNCV findings helpful in documenting the extent of deterioration over time. Electromyography will help delineate the distribution of the involvement, assisting the therapist in focusing treatment and planning adaptations for functional activities.

Myotonia

Myotonia is a disorder characterized by delayed relaxation of previously contracted muscle.[13] It results in a pathologic muscle stiffness. Myotonia dystrophica exhibits EMG changes typical of myopathy as well. Myotonic disorders do not have a known etiology, although recent studies suggest that a defect in the sarcolemmal membrane causes after-depolarization following activation of the muscle membrane.[62]

As a part of the generalized membrane abnormality, myotonia may result in mildly slowed motor nerve conduction velocity,[63] and a marked reduction in motor unit activity.[64] However, the typical EMG response in myotonia is the persistence of high-frequency repetitive discharges with alternately increasing and decreasing amplitude (Fig. 9–14). This "waxing and waning" is a distinctive feature, producing the classic "dive-bomber" sound. These trains of potentials can discharge at frequencies up to 150 pulses per second. The **myotonic discharge** follows voluntary contraction or may be provoked by needle insertion or movement. Myotonic symptoms can be abolished or lessened pharmacologically.[13]

Myasthenia Gravis

Myasthenia gravis and myasthenic syndrome are disorders of neuromuscular transmission characterized by weakness following repetitive contractions, and recovery following rest or administration of an anticholinesterase. Myasthenia gravis is thought to be an autoimmune disorder,[65] often associated with other immunologic diseases.[14] It is characterized by weakness and excessive fatigability, often confined to ocular muscles, or palatal and pharyngeal muscles.[66]

Myasthenic syndrome often is associated with small

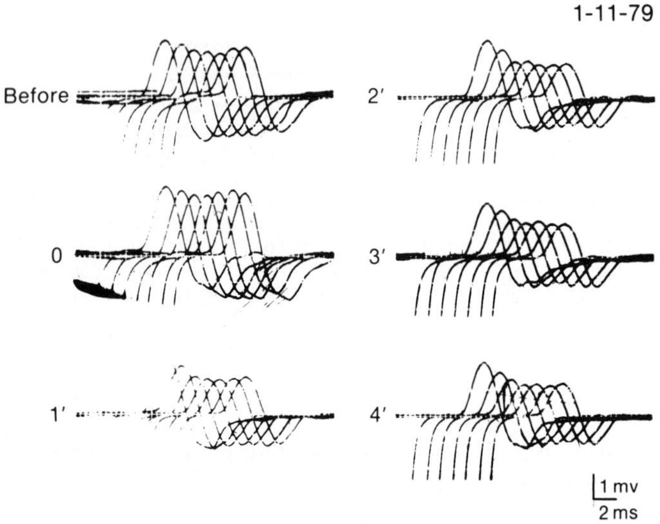

1-11-79

Figure 9–24. Decremental evoked motor responses before and after voluntary exercise in a patient with generalized myasthenia gravis. The median nerve was stimulated at the rate of three shocks per second for seven shocks in each train. The M wave was recorded from the thenar muscles. Comparing the amplitude of the last response with the amplitude of the first, the decrement was 25 percent at rest. (From Kimura,[14] p 191, with permission.)

cell carcinoma of the bronchus, and is more prevalent in males. Weakness and fatigability primarily affect the lower extremities, particularly the pelvic girdle and thigh muscles.[14]

Myasthenic disorders demonstrate a normal EMG at rest, although fibrillation potentials and positive sharp waves may be present in severely affected muscles, indicating loss of innervation. Motor unit potentials will appear normal at first and then progressively decrease in amplitude with continued effort. Repetitive stimulation during a motor nerve conduction test will cause progressive decreases in the amplitude of the M wave (Fig. 9–24). Pharmacologic intervention often will normalize the response.

Radiculopathy

Nerve root involvement, or radiculopathy, is not an uncommon condition at all spinal levels. Electromyography can often assist in identifying this condition, determining the etiology for radiating pain, persistent weakness, hyporeflexia, and fasciculations. Sensory symptoms accompany motor signs, and may range from mild paresthesias to complete loss of sensation.

The fundamental feature in the determination of motor nerve root involvement is the delineation of the distribution of abnormal findings within muscles receiving their peripheral innervation from the same myotome. For example, abnormal potentials seen in the extensor muscles of the hand may suggest involvement of the radial nerve. However, if the biceps brachii is examined (musculocutaneous nerve), as well as the opponens pollicis (median nerve), and these muscles also exhibit some abnormal electromyographic potentials, the common feature could be considered the C-6

nerve root. These findings would have significant implications for treatment planning in terms of addressing the cause of muscle weakness or fatigue.

Electromyographic abnormalities are those typical of neuropathic involvement. Compression of a nerve root can result in irritation or degeneration of nerve fibers. If the lesion is of sufficient severity and duration, the electromyogram will show increased insertion activity, fibrillation potentials, and positive sharp waves at rest, and low-amplitude polyphasic potentials. In later stages high-amplitude polyphasic potentials may appear, reflecting reinnervation. Electromyography is especially valuable in differentiating between disorders of the peripheral nerve trunk and more proximal involvement. It may be more useful than nerve conduction velocity studies, which may not show any remarkable changes at distal segments of these peripheral nerves unless diffuse degeneration has occurred.

KINESIOLOGIC ELECTROMYOGRAPHY: USE IN THE CLINIC

In addition to being a standard tool for neuromuscular evaluation, electromyography can be an extremely useful adjunct to clinical practice. Physical therapists have become increasingly involved in the use of kinesiologic EMG to examine muscle function during specific purposeful tasks or therapeutic regimens.[67] For this purpose, therapists are no longer concerned with examining single motor unit potentials, but instead look at patterns of muscle response, onset and cessation of activity, and the level of muscle response in relation to effort, type of muscle contraction, and position. Therapists can use EMG to assess the ability of exercises to facilitate or inhibit specific muscle activity, and thereby determine if treatment goals are being realized.[68,69] With the growing need for validation of treatment effectiveness, EMG presents an objective means for scientific documentation.

A wealth of kinesiologic literature exists, much of it involving the use of EMG. Professional journals include many articles concerned with clinical questions and techniques. The therapist should have a basic understanding of kinesiologic EMG in order to critically evaluate methods and data analysis procedures in kinesiologic EMG studies.

While the principles of recording and instrumentation are the same for clinical and kinesiologic EMG, several additional factors must be considered in order to interpret kinesiologic EMG data.

Instrumentation

ELECTRODES

As described earlier, surface and fine-wire, indwelling electrodes are used in kinesiologic study, although surface electrodes are used more often in clinical situations. Once a muscle is chosen for study, its size and location must be considered in choosing and applying or inserting electrodes. Based on previous discussions of volume conduction and the factors affecting the motor unit potential, the following determinations must be made: (1) electrode size, (2) interelectrode distance, (3) location of electrode sites (including the ground), and (4) skin preparation (for surface electrodes).

Smaller muscles obviously require the use of smaller electrodes, with a small interelectrode distance. If electrodes are too far apart, even on larger muscles, activity from nearby muscles may be recorded. This cross talk would confound interpretation of the output by making activity look greater than it actually was. If electrodes are located poorly, levels of activity recorded with strong contractions may not accurately indicate the muscle's activity. Electromyographers will often use manual muscle testing procedures to verify that the recordings are being obtained from the desired muscles. The ground electrode should be located reasonably close to the recording electrodes, preferably on the same side of the body. Skin should be prepared to reduce impedance, although newer amplifiers may have sufficient input impedance to make this unnecessary.

Criteria for location of electrode sites are not universally accepted. Fine-wire electrodes should be inserted into the muscle belly using guidelines similar to those used for clinical EMG. For surface electrodes, Basmajian and DeLuca[2] suggest that the greatest EMG amplitude can be obtained by attaching electrodes in the region halfway between the center of the innervation zone and the further tendon. Many investigators and clinicians have found it efficient to use palpation for locating surface electrode sites over the muscle belly, if the subject can voluntarily contract the muscle to facilitate this process. However, if repeated measurements are attempted, requiring reapplication of surface electrodes, this method may be unreliable. When electrodes are not oriented to the muscle in the same way with repeated testing, the output will look different even with identical levels of contraction. Some investigators have used electrical stimulation of motor points to locate optimal electrode sites. Some have marked the skin with indelible solutions to be able to relocate electrodes. Still others have used body landmarks and measured specific distances to standardize application sites (Fig. 9–25). Basmajian and Blumenstein[70] have provided guidelines for placement of surface electrodes for use with biofeedback that can be useful for kinesiologic study as well, but do not adjust locations for variation in body parameters and muscle bulk. Zipp[71] has provided a set of recommendations that include a mechanism to accomodate differences in body dimensions.

Verification of surface electrode placement is usually attempted using manual muscle testing procedures to see if the EMG responds when appropriate resistance is applied. The technique is only partially effective, however, because muscles cannot effectively be isolated.

The distance between electrodes must also be standardized so that repeated analysis of EMG is valid. If electrodes are further apart at a second session, the same level of contraction may produce higher-amplitude readings. Recommendations have been made that 2 to

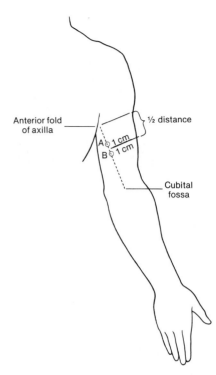

Figure 9–25. Example of standardized electrode placement for the biceps brachii. A line is drawn from the anterior axillary fold to the center of the cubital fossa, and a point marked at the center of this line. Electrodes are then placed 1 cm above and below this point along the line.

10 mm should separate electrode centers.[6] When placement criteria are specified, researchers have shown fairly good test-retest reliability for surface electrodes,[11,72] although submaximal contractions have demonstrated better reproducibility than maximal contractions.[73] Reapplication of indwelling electrodes is less reliable than that of surface electrodes[11,74] because of the difficulty in consistently locating a needle within muscle tissue on reinsertion.

When using surface electrodes, the therapist must also consider problems related to the displacement of skin overlying muscle during movement. The spatial relationship between the electrodes and the muscle can change greatly as a muscle contracts through its range. This will, of course, affect the EMG signal. The electrode sites should be determined with this in mind. Such problems are often seen when monitoring the biceps brachii, sternocleidomastoid, or scapula muscles, for instance. Electrodes should be applied to the skin with the limb or body part positioned as it will be during the procedure.

SIGNAL CONDITIONING

For clinical EMG the *raw signal* is displayed to allow visual examination of the size and shape of individual muscle and nerve potentials. For kinesiologic EMG, however, the therapist is generally interested in looking at overall muscle activity during specific activities, and quantification of the signal is often desired in order to describe and compare changes in the magnitude and pattern of muscle response.

Several forms of output can be useful for this purpose.

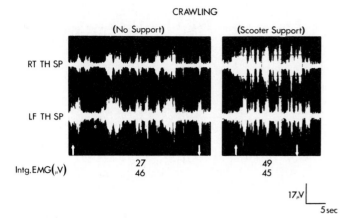

Figure 9–26. The EMG activity recorded from the right and left thoracic paraspinal regions (RT TH SP, LF TH SP) during floor and scooter crawling. *Arrows* indicate duration of EMG sampling, and numbers refer to integrated EMG values of upper and lower traces, respectively. (From Wolf, et al.[69] p 223, 1986, with permission.)

Computer processed raw data can be displayed on a monitor or printout. Raw EMG can be displayed on an oscilloscope (Fig. 9–26) or ink-chart recorder at a gain and sweep speed that allows visualization of the total muscle activity. Remember, however, that the raw EMG signal cannot be faithfully reproduced on an ink-chart recorder because of the inertia of the pens, which prevents them from being able to process high-frequency components. Pens generally cut off signals above 70 to 100 Hz. Even with these limitations, however, the raw data can be examined for general patterns and changes. Fiber optic recorders operate without such limitations, and can faithfully reproduce the myoelectric signal.

The EMG signal can also be manipulated electronically in several ways to facilitate quantification, and to eliminate problems of processing raw data (Fig. 9–27). Through a process called **rectification,** both the negative and positive portions of the raw signal appear above the baseline; the signal is then *full-wave rectified.* The rectified signal is then put through a series of circuits and filters to be presented in a "smoothed" format. One format is a *linear envelope,* which describes a curve outlining the peaks of the full-wave rectified signal.[15] Many authors and electronic equipment companies call this an "integrated" signal, but that is a misnomer, as the linear envelope is a moving average of the EMG output over time.

Another type of circuit provides mathematical **integration** of the EMG signal through accumulation of

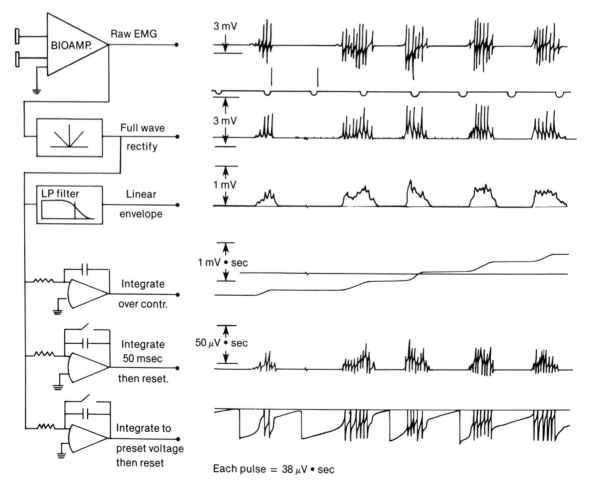

Figure 9–27. Illustration of the raw EMG and several methods of signal processing. The raw EMG was full-waved rectified and expressed as a linear envelope and integrated data. (From Winter DA: Biomechanics of Human Movement. John Wiley & Sons, New York, 1979, p 140, with permission.)

electrical energy on a capacitor, or condensor. *Integrated EMG* (IEMG) results from summation of the area under the curve.[15] These curves can be processed in several ways (Fig. 9–27). The simplest method is integration throughout the period of muscular activity. The total accumulated activity can be determined for a series of contractions or a single contraction. The slope of the curve, or ramp, is a direct function of the amount of electrical energy being processed.

Alternatively, the condensor can be set to discharge at predetermined intervals based on time or voltage amplitude. Time intervals can be set so that the capacitor resets to zero on a regular basis, within periods as small as 200 msec or as long as 10 seconds. The height of each peak, or ramp, then represents the accumulated activity over that time interval. Integration can also be based on a preset voltage level. When the condensor reaches this voltage, it resets to zero, without regard to time. If the EMG signal is very weak, the condensor may continue to collect electrical energy for indefinite periods until its discharge threshold is finally reached. The frequency with which the condensor resets is an indication of the level of EMG activity. Each ramp can also be depicted as a pulse and the frequency of pulses can be counted to determine the level of activity (Fig. 9–27).

A third method is determination of the *root-mean-square (RMS),* an electronic average, representing the square root of the average of the squares of the current or voltage over the whole cycle. Root-mean-square provides a nearly instantaneous output of the power of the EMG signal,[10,15] and is considered a preferable output form by some researchers.[2] These averaged or integrated signals can also be displayed by a meter, light bar, or speaker, as they are in most biofeedback devices. An analysis of the *frequency spectra* that comprise the motor unit waveform (called Fourier analysis) is a fourth method used to interpret changes in motor unit activity. Variations in frequency characteristics can be identified with fatigue,[75] and abnormalities of the neuromuscular system.[76]

Technology has advanced sufficiently today that microcomputers are now readily applied to the processing of conditioned signals, including integration and display. Personal computers can be easily adapted to interface with electromyographs of all types. The EMG signal can be stored, averaged, and sampled in a variety of ways to permit detailed and complete analysis.

QUANTIFYING ELECTROMYOGRAPHY

Many clinicians have access to instrumentation that will monitor the EMG signal. Most biofeedback devices can be used for kinesiologic monitoring of EMG signals, as can a clinical electromyograph with an oscilloscope. Sometimes chart recorders will be available; polygraphs designed for use with an electroencephalograph (EEG) will often be able to monitor EMG signals. The therapist should be aware of the input impedance, frequency bandwidth, and gain of an amplifier, so that a reasonable portion of the EMG signal can be validly recorded.

Although amplifiers that provide an integrated output display are easier to use (such as those on most biofeedback devices), raw data viewed on an oscilloscope can

still be useful.[69] The major disadvantage of using raw data is that it is not quantitative, and it may be difficult to discern small changes in amplitude. However, many clinicians find the raw signal helpful because it allows them to better visualize the bursts of activity and periods of silence.

In its simplest form, the raw EMG signal can be analyzed in relation to the onset and cessation of activity, without regard to amplitude. The timing of a muscle's response is often of interest to determine the latency of responses between different muscles, or relative to some other parameter, such as the command to move, or specific task components.

Quantification of raw EMG signals can be difficult because the signals are often erratic. Subjective rating scales have been used to grade the relative amplitude of the raw signal, using numerical gradings from 0 to 4 (Fig. 9–28). Readings of 0 and 1 indicated no or insignificant activity; grade 2, moderate activity; and grades 3 and 4, major or marked contraction of the test muscle. These scales are useful for making gross comparisons of one muscle's EMG level during activities within a single test session. The level of grade 4 should be determined by obtaining a reading during a maximal contraction. All further comparisons are then made relative to that level. This method is reasonably useful with isometric contractions, when the level of EMG stays fairly consistent within a contraction. However, with movement, the variation in level of EMG throughout the contraction can make this form of analysis very difficult.

Integrated EMG (IEMG), recorded on a chart recorder, can be quantified by using a planimeter to measure the area under the curve, which is often expressed in arbitrary units for comparison. Cumulative IEMG can be analyzed by measuring the total voltage accumulated over a set time interval, relative to a known signal. Computer analysis allows sampling either raw or integrated data at specific intervals (such as 100 or 1,000 samples/s).

More subjective quantification can be accomplished with biofeedback devices that have a meter or light bar that allows monitoring of the voltage level of the output. While permanent recordings of these values may not be available, the therapist can use the readings to approximate the level of activity. Because these values tend to change rapidly, it is often helpful to observe the highest or lowest value or the range of values achieved during a

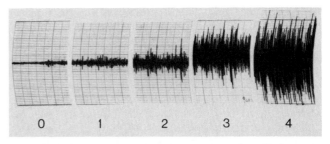

Figure 9–28. One scheme for subjective grading of raw EMG, showing a five grade basis for data analysis of one muscle's activity. Grade 0 indicates zero to nil activity; Grade 1 minimal activity; Grade 2 moderate activity; Grade 3 marked activity; Grade 4 maximal activity.

particular activity, and to use these scores for comparison purposes. Trying to get more specific than that may be misleading, unless the levels of contraction are very uniform and values can be easily determined from the display.

NORMALIZATION

The purpose of quantifying the EMG signal is usually to compare activity between sessions, muscles, or subjects. Because of the variability inherent in EMG procedures, and the interindividual differences in anatomy and movement characteristics, some form of *normalization* is necessary in order to validate these comparisons. This is usually done by first recording the EMG of a muscle during a maximal voluntary contraction (MVC), or some known submaximal level of contraction,[73,77] and then expressing all other EMG values as a percentage of this contraction. This "control" value serves as a standard against which all comparisons can be made, even if test values exceed the control. In this way subjects and muscles can be compared, and activity on different days can be correlated by repeating the control contraction at each test session. This helps eliminate some of the problems related to reapplication of electrodes as well.

Other methods of normalization have included using a series of submaximal contractions,[3,77] or contractions during defined reference tasks[78] or one of the tasks being tested.[79] Although no standard method has been developed for this normalization, most investigators use manual muscle test positions, resisting isometric contractions either manually or against some fixed resistance. Others have used isotonic contractions against a known weight, or maximal isokinetic efforts.

The Relationship between Electromyography and Force

The relationship between EMG and muscle tension has been studied since 1952,[80,81] and continues to be the subject of many investigations. It is generally accepted that a direct relationship exists between EMG and muscular effort, but this relationship must be discussed in terms of muscle length and type of contraction.

ISOMETRIC CONTRACTIONS

Several early studies have demonstrated that when muscle maintains a constant length, EMG varies directly with muscle tension. Many investigators have documented a linear relationship between muscle tension and integrated EMG.[81,82,83] Others have reported curvilinear relationships.[82,84,85] The linear slope or the degree of nonlinearity seems to vary with the muscle tested, with the joint position or muscle length, with electrode placements, and with the method of measurement of force.[82,84,86] Even though the use of different methods makes comparisons of these studies difficult, they all support the general conclusion that an increase in EMG output is observed with increasing muscle tension, as long as the muscle length does not change, that is, during an isometric contraction.[84,87] This relationship exists with spasticity as well, although the slope of the rela-

tionship appears greater than normal, indicating that more motor units are recruited at higher tension levels than in the normal muscle.[88]

When muscle length is varied, however, this relationship does not hold. Generally, less EMG is seen with greater tension as a muscle is lengthened and, conversely, greater EMG is seen with decreased tension as a muscle is shortened (Fig. 9–29).[81] Theoretically, therefore, we can assume that fewer motor units are needed to produce the same level of tension in the lengthened position.

ISOTONIC CONTRACTIONS

The relationship between EMG and force is further confounded during isotonic contractions, which are defined as contractions producing average constant force or torque.[15] When muscle length continually changes during movement, several factors must be considered. The force–length relationship of the muscle varies throughout the contraction, thereby constantly altering the motor unit activity in proportion to tension. The axis of rotation of the joint changes as the limb moves through its range, so as to change the moment arm and resulting force components. The movement of the skin over the muscle and the variation in shape of the muscle as it contracts will also affect the spatial relationship between the electrodes and muscle fibers, and change the amount of electrical activity actually recorded at different muscle lengths. It is difficult, therefore, to validly quantify muscle activity when movement is occurring.

The EMG–force relationship has also been examined in terms of eccentric and concentric contractions. Eccentric, or lengthening, contractions utilize elastic elements and metabolic processes more efficiently than concentric contractions.[89,90] Therefore, for the same amount of muscle tension, an eccentric contraction will require fewer motor units, that is, less overall EMG activity, than a concentric contraction.

The rate of muscle shortening is another consideration. Studies have shown that during eccentric contractions the level of EMG activity remains constant for a given load, independent of the velocity of the contraction.[87,91] Concentric EMG activity, on the other hand, is greater, for a given force, as velocity is increased, and probably reflects a need for greater recruitment to accommodate for a faster contraction time. However, only when velocity is kept constant is the EMG proportional to tension.[91] Therefore, with isotonic movement at uncontrolled velocity, EMG will not be a direct reflection of muscle tension. This is an important point when we consider clinical applications of EMG.

FATIGUE

When a muscle exhibits localized fatigue following repeated contractions, one might expect to see a decrease in overall EMG output. The opposite is generally observed, however. We typically see an increase in EMG amplitude as a muscle fatigues.[83] In an attempt to maintain the level of active tension in the muscle, additional motor units are recruited and active motor units fire at increasing rates to compensate for the decreased

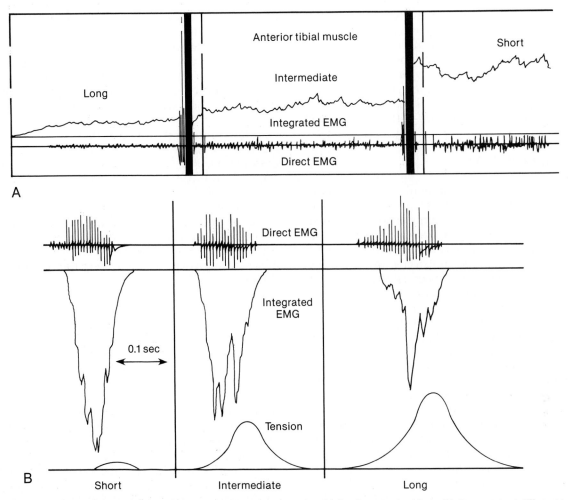

Figure 9–29. (A) Maximal voluntary isometric contraction of the anterior tibialis of a normal subject with the muscle at different lengths. Note the rise in EMG activity as the muscle is progressively shortened. The integrated EMG is really a linear envelope. (B) EMG activity of the triceps brachii of a cineplastic amputee, illustrating the same effect. (From Inman, et al.[81] p 193, with permission.)

force of contraction of the fatigued fibers. This has been substantiated in many studies using submaximal contractions.[83,92-94] Following maximal contraction, when the entire motor unit pool is supposedly recruited, force declines and EMG activity stays constant.[95] This suggests that fatigue is occurring within the muscle, but that the maximal number of motor units is still contracting. Eventually, however, as the contraction continues, the contractile elements within the muscle will fail and simultaneously EMG activity will start to decrease.[92] Electromyographic indications of fatigue can occur very quickly, within the first 60 seconds of both submaximal and maximal contractions.[92,93,95,96]

Researchers have observed both linear[83,84,92,95] and nonlinear[82,97] EMG–force relationships during fatiguing contractions. The slope of this relationship varies with the degree of fatigue.[98] Studies have also demonstrated a relationship between predominance of fiber type within a muscle and its EMG fatigue characteristics.[82,93] Muscles composed of primarily Type I (slow twitch) fibers fatigue at a slower rate and demonstrate only small increases in EMG.[82]

Electromyographic evidence of local muscle fatigue may also be demonstrated by frequency analysis of motor unit potentials. Because a myoelectric signal is actually composed of potentials firing at different frequencies, an interference pattern can be decomposed into its different frequency components. In a fatigued state, an analysis of the frequency spectrum can reveal a decrease in the higher-frequency components and a gradual increase in low-frequency components.[99] The shifts in frequency characteristics may be due to several factors, such as synchronization of motor units, changes in recruitment patterns, or changes in the shape of motor unit potentials.[75] The median frequency is usually used to quantify such changes.

As a clinical research tool, shifts in median frequency can be used to identify if a muscle is exhibiting evidence of local fatigue. Several researchers have been able to document muscle fatigue during specific tasks using this technique.[100-103] By measuring frequency shifts in the electrical potentials of an impaired muscle during treatment, a therapist can determine if the muscle is being sufficiently exercised.[2,99] If the frequency spectrum does not change over time, then synergists may be responsible for the force being generated, rather than the involved muscle. If a decrease in the frequency is seen at first, and the frequency then abruptly levels off without a decrease in output force, the involved muscle may have stopped participating, and other muscles may have taken over to generate the force. Such a technique could be helpful in discriminating which muscles are truly contributing the force output that is measured over a joint. Of course, appropriate instrumentation for recording and analysis must be available. This type of data will not be analyzed using conventional EMG units or biofeedback devices.

ELECTROMYOGRAPHY AND STRENGTH

The above factors are of great significance for interpreting EMG amplitude during activities that require muscles to operate at different lengths or speeds, or that utilize different types of contractions. Those who use EMG to study muscle function during activities are often tempted to make statements regarding the muscle's "strength." Although this term is used clinically, it must be used with caution. Strength is a construct that must be defined as torque or force produced under a specific set of conditions. Clinicians must be very careful, therefore, about concluding that a muscle is "working harder" or that a muscle is "stronger" just because the EMG activity is greater. Within a single session, when electrode positions remain constant, the position of the limb, the type of contraction, and the speed of movement will affect the level of EMG activity recorded.

The significance of these factors becomes apparent when comparisons are made between isometric exercises performed at different joint angles. The recorded EMG activity from a single muscle positioned at different points in the range may have varied amplitudes, but may in fact represent contractions of similar tension levels. Therefore, the EMG, which records motor unit activity, must be distinguished from muscle tension, which is a function of contractile processes. Therapists often use the term "optimal" to describe a biomechanically advantageous position for a muscle. However, EMG could be lower at this optimal position because fewer motor units are required to create a given level of force. Greater EMG activity may actually indicate that a muscle's efficiency is decreased.

Therapists should also be cognizant of the fact that EMG can record activity of individual muscles, while the force or torque measured across a joint may represent the resultant interaction of agonists, antagonists, and synergists. Adjacent muscles make differential contributions to the strength, stability, and coordination of a contraction. The EMG of the agonist may not necessarily be a valid representation of activity around a joint. Therefore, EMG data cannot be expected to provide direct information about an individual muscle's "strength."

Therapists must also resist the temptation to make inferences about *muscle tone* based on EMG activity. Normal muscle "tonus" refers to resting tension within a muscle due to the elastic and viscoelastic properties of muscle fibers.[104] Tone also reflects the reflex responsiveness or readiness of a muscle to contract. Essential to a definition of tone is the fact that even though a relaxed muscle shows no electrical activity on EMG, it still maintains a passive state of tone.[105] Therefore, tone is not a

function of motor unit activity, and cannot be measured with EMG. This means that when the term spasticity is used to indicate a state of hypertonus, it actually refers to the potential for an overactive muscle response to a stimulus,[105] and not motor unit activity, per se. Just as in a normal muscle at rest, a "relaxed" spastic muscle will exhibit electrical silence. This is true of spastic and rigid muscles of patients with parkinsonism as well.[106]

Although there is evidence that lower motor neuron changes are evident on EMG with upper motor neuron dysfunction,[30,31,33] such activity is not consistently seen,[36,37] and would not be of sufficient amplitude to be picked up with surface electrodes. We can, for kinesiologic purposes, consider a spastic muscle "normal" in terms of peripheral innervation. When a muscle contracts, be it normal or hypertonic, a normal motor unit pattern will be recorded on EMG. The level of motor unit activation will directly affect the amplitude of the signal.

Clinical Applications

Therapists can use EMG in a wide variety of applications, in both assessment and treatment, as an adjunct to observation and palpation. With an appreciation for the concepts of recording and of the limitations of interpretation previously discussed, the therapist will find EMG a valuable clinical tool to help validate intervention. This approach should be differentiated from EMG biofeedback, where EMG is used to provide information to the patient, to allow the patient to learn to control his or her own neuromuscular responses. Kinesiologic applications involve the use of EMG to provide information to the therapist, to identify activity that would otherwise go undetected, to allow for adjustment of technique or position, and to provide information about the effectiveness of a specific procedure.

The following discussion illustrates a few examples of the clinical applications of electromyography.

SELECTING A MUSCLE

Because activities or functional movements are generally performed by muscle groups, decisions about which muscle or muscles to monitor can be difficult. Therapists are often limited to one or two recording channels, and must, therefore, choose muscles that are representative of the group, or that are considered prime movers. One must be careful not to assume an active muscle is "responsible" for a movement, however, when all participants are not monitored. It may be necessary to repeat the activity several times, each time monitoring a different set of muscles, in order to get a better sense of what is happening around a joint.

If muscles are closely situated, such as finger flexors or intrinsic hand muscles, electrodes can be placed to record from the entire muscle group. The therapist must determine which muscles combine to perform the movement, and interpret output in terms of a general pattern of muscle activity. Of course, the EMG cannot then be attributed to any one muscle, and it is not possible to determine which muscle contributed more or less to the total output. When the activity of a single muscle is of interest, surface electrodes should be placed as close together as possible over the muscle belly, to avoid recording overflow activity from adjacent musculature.

MOTOR CONTROL

It has been established that it is not possible to "measure" tone with surface electrodes. It is possible, however, to monitor the level of motor unit activity facilitated by a stimulus such as passive stretch,[107] by a treatment modality, or with changes in position (assuming that the muscle length has not changed significantly). Clinicians must be aware, however, that the EMG cannot distinguish voluntary contraction from reflex activity, and the output could be a function of both.[108]

Associated reactions, or exercise overflow, can also be monitored with EMG. Exercise overflow refers to EMG activity recorded in unexercised muscles during contraction in another body part. Overflow activity to ipsilateral or contralateral muscles or body parts can be observed on EMG even when overt movement does not occur.[109] Such muscle activity can be monitored while adjusting an applied load, during position changes, or during resistive exercise.

Even though some authors have concluded that exercise overflow does not occur to any appreciable degree in normals,[2,110] others have clearly demonstrated such activity in this population.[111,112] Discrepancies exist because some investigators have based their conclusions on a limited amount of data, monitoring only selected muscles. One must be careful not to make broad generalizations about directions of overflow or primary sites of overflow unless many muscles are tested. Even if the muscle chosen to be monitored is not active, others may be.

Studies of patients with spasticity have consistently shown, however, that overflow does indeed occur to a marked degree,[113] often with reactions occurring in predictable patterns on the involved side.[114] Investigators who have stabilized the overflow extremity, so that the overflow muscles were resisted, have demonstrated much higher levels of activity[115] than those who have left the overflow limb free.[110] Electromyography can help the therapist judge the level of response, although caution must be exercised in interpreting why the overflow activity is present. In addition to neurophysiologic responses, some overflow may be occurring as a function of stabilization requirements. These issues are hard to separate, and EMG will not discriminate between them.

Many techniques are used to influence muscle activity. Equipment such as electrical stimulators and vibrators can be problematic when used in conjunction with EMG because they can cause 60-Hz interference. These instruments generally need to be turned off in order to monitor the EMG response following application. Tapping may be effectively performed over a tendon without much interference, but tapping over the muscle belly can cause movement artifact. Other techniques, such as cryotherapy, resistance, positioning, and so on, will generally not interfere with valid EMG recording, although the therapist must always be concerned with movement artifacts in setting up procedures.

ASSESSMENTS
Manual muscle test

Electromyography can be used to evaluate the degree of effort during isometric break tests. It can also assist in identifying substitutions. However, caution must be exercised in interpreting a muscle as "substituting" for a prime mover when it is a synergist or stabilizer. Silence should not be expected in muscles surrounding the "tested muscle." Overflow electrical activity from adjacent muscles may also be recorded at the electrodes of the test muscle, and the output will then be interpreted incorrectly. Putting electrodes on several surrounding muscles allows for some differentiation. If muscles are close together, however, surface electrodes may not be able to provide sufficient differentiation, even if they are spaced close together.

Equilibrium Reactions

Electromyography can be used to assess amplitude and timing of onset of the activity of supporting muscle groups in order to describe patterns of response. This can be done sitting or standing. Weight-bearing patterns can be objectively examined by monitoring lower extremity musculature, particularly hip and ankle muscles.[116] Treatment strategies may address facilitation or inhibition of specific muscle groups to enhance balance reactions and weight shifting. Therapists are encouraged to read the literature describing normal EMG patterns[2] and to use EMG in the clinic to clarify the effect of intervention. For example, do muscles respond in consistent patterns? Is activity sporadic or constant? This may be most useful in tests where balance is purposely perturbed, because in normal standing or sitting, supporting musculature is minimally active.[117]

Gait

Electromyography can be useful to assess muscle activity during gait if instrumentation allows simultaneous and coordinated tracking of the activity, for example, film, videotape, electrogoniometers, or contact foot switches to delineate swing and stance phases. Speed of walking must be considered in terms of the effect on EMG activity. Therapists can refer to many studies that report normal patterns of EMG during gait,[118,119] while recognizing that these "norms" are ideal models, and that an individual patient will probably not match them. Gait is a prime example of a situation where functional performance must be the major consideration, and EMG only used for information purposes. A patient may ambulate without functional difficulty, even though his EMG pattern at the knee is not "normal." The complex interactions between muscles in an activity like gait must also be considered, and recognition given to the varied patterns that may result in normal functional movement.

Procedurally, length of electrode leads can limit the distance walked, and in many cases will result in cable artifacts. Telemetry has been used with some success to allow free walking. Many biofeedback units have straps that allow patients to carry them while walking, and use of such units also helps limit this problem. Electrode assemblies with preamplifiers that are attached over the muscle will protect against cable artifact as well.

Passive Movement

Electromyography can help identify whether movements are truly passive. In this situation EMG can act as a feedback device to both the therapist and patient. Electrode placement need not be specific to monitor general activity around the joint. Passive stretch to a normal, relaxed muscle does not elicit appreciable EMG activity, regardless of speed of movement,[120,121] indicating that patients can voluntarily relax to allow full passive motion to occur.

MOVEMENT PATTERNS

Therapists can use EMG to observe the effect of treatment on patterns of muscle response.[109] When movement cannot be observed, EMG can be particularly useful as a measurement tool. For example, agonist-antagonist relationships can be examined, and co-contraction or reciprocal inhibition can be documented. Specific therapeutic procedures, such as traction[122] or approximation, and activities such as mat exercises or PNF patterns,[123] can be studied, and the pattern of muscle activity can be more objectively determined than by visual observation alone. Muscle interactions can be examined during isokinetic exercise as well,[124] where velocity of movement can be controlled and range of motion easily tracked.

Therapeutic concepts must be operationally defined, however. For example, how much activity must be present in a group of muscles around a joint for "co-contraction" to be present? Must all the muscles be equally active? Must an antagonistic muscle be totally silent for reciprocal inhibition to have occurred? Is a muscle an antagonist by virtue of being attached on the opposite side of a joint, or is it defined by its action? Can a muscle normally considered an antagonist be a synergist? The answers to these questions are not clear, and how a therapist defines them for clinical use will be important in the setup and interpretation of the EMG. Using a maximal voluntary contraction as a reference, or control contraction, for interpreting muscle activity can help with this issue.

Looking at patterns of timing can also be useful in many situations. Levels of skill, coordination, and balance are often determined by evaluating timing of onset of muscle activity as well as amplitude. Researchers have seen changes in antagonist-synergist activity with improvements in these parameters.[125] Some form of permanent output is helpful for measurement, since timing differences can often be less than 1 second. Some authors have used EMG changes as evidence of motor learning, showing distinct patterns emerging in agonist-antagonist activity with practice.[126]

When two-joint muscles are a part of a movement pattern, their activity will reflect action at one or both joints, depending on biomechanical and functional parameters. The interpretation of the EMG can become tentative when one is not clear what contribution a muscle is making at each joint. Muscles such as the hamstrings and rectus femoris are major examples. When the length-tension relationships are affected by changes at both ends of a muscle, it can be difficult to judge whether the EMG is adequately representing the muscle's function. Therapists should make every effort to limit movement to one joint and stabilize the other when movement is necessary. This consideration should also be given to muscles whose function is primarily at one joint, but whose tendons cross two joints, such as finger and wrist flexors, the long head of biceps femoris or triceps femoris, and gastrocnemius.

SUMMARY

Electromyography provides a powerful tool for documenting the role of muscle in physical activity, and for assessing the integrity of the neuromuscular system. Despite its common use in movement research, however, therapists must use EMG wisely, recognizing its limitations as a measurement tool. Interpretation of EMG must account for the effect of velocity and acceleration, type of muscle contraction, instrumentation, and a host of anatomic, physiologic, and neurogenic factors that can influence the output signal.[127] Electromyography can show that a muscle is working, but not *why* it is working, and it can only be interpreted as a measure of motor unit activity. Electromyography cannot determine that a treatment is "effective" in the sense of achieving predicted functional outcomes. Electromyography by itself cannot provide information as to whether a muscle has gotten stronger or weaker, or if it is hypertonic or hypotonic. Under most circumstances, with repeated testing over short time periods, small changes will be hard to evaluate. These must be determined through clinical assessment. But the EMG can provide information that may increase efficacy during treatment or assessment. It is a form of feedback for the therapist that can be invaluable in situations where overt movement or muscle contraction is not observable.

Kinesiologic literature abounds with studies concerning the use of EMG to evaluate muscle function under different conditions.[2] Therapists should be familiar with this body of literature in order to interpret and utilize EMG data. These studies can also be used as guides for setting up EMG as part of treatment plans. One must be critical of EMG studies, however, since many of them demonstrate methodological faults that can invalidate findings. In addition, the results of EMG studies may not always be generalized to a specific patient, and should not be considered the "correct" responses in all cases. Obviously, the therapist's clinical judgment must prevail when observing responses of individual patients.

The clinician is encouraged to explore the uses of EMG in any situation where response of superficial muscles is of interest. As long as the limitations of interpretation of EMG are kept in mind, this tool can be a major adjunct to therapeutic intervention and assessment.

QUESTIONS FOR REVIEW

1. What are the basic components of a recording system for electromyography and nerve conduction velocity tests?

2. What characteristics should be considered when choosing an amplifier for monitoring EMG?

3. What are the stages in a clinical EMG examination?

4. Describe how motor and sensory nerve conduction velocities are calculated.

5. What are the typical EMG and NCV findings with peripheral nerve lesions, myopathy, and motor neuron disease?

6. What are the possible causes of movement artifact? How can these effects be reduced or eliminated?

7. Describe four types of signal conditioning for EMG.

8. Describe a method for quantifying raw EMG.

9. What is the effect of changing muscle length on the relationship between EMG and force?

10. What type of changes are seen in the EMG signal when a muscle fatigues?

11. Assume you are including EMG to monitor muscle response as a component of a treatment program. What considerations are important for setting up your procedure in terms of

    a. Choice and placement of electrodes?

    b. Type of contractions?

    c. Patient position?

    d. Timing of activities?

    e. How the EMG will be interpreted?

REFERENCES

1. Green, RM: Commentary on the Effect of Electricity on Muscular Motion. Elizabeth Licht, Cambridge, 1953.
2. Basmajian, JV and De Luca, CJ: Muscles Alive, ed 2. Williams & Wilkins, Baltimore, 1985.
3. Perry, J, Easterday, CS, and Antonelli, DJ: Surface versus intramuscular electrodes for electromyography of superficial and deep muscles. Phys Ther 61:7, 1981.
4. Strong, P: Biophysical Measurements. Tektronix, Beaverton, OR, 1973, p 295.
5. Zuniga, EM, Truong, XT, and Simons, DG: Effects of skin electrode position on averaged electromyographic potentials. Arch Phys Med Rehabil 50:264, 1969.
6. Loeb, GE and Gans, C: Electromyography for Experiments. University of Chicago Press, Chicago, 1986.
7. Basmajian, JV and Stecko, G: A new bipolar electrode for electromyography. J Appl Physiol 17:849, 1962.
8. Adrian, ED and Bronk, DW: The discharge of impulses in motor nerve fibers. J Physiol (Lond) 67:119, 1929.
9. Goodgold, J: Anatomical Correlates of Clinical Electromyography. Williams & Wilkins, Baltimore, 1974.
10. Soderberg, GL and Cook, TM: Electromyography in biomechanics. Phys Ther 64:1813, 1984.
11. Komi, PV and Buskirk, ER: Reproducibility of electromyographic measurements with inserted wire electrodes and surface electrodes. Electromyography 4:357, 1970.
12. Geddes, LA: Electrodes and the Measurement of Bioelectric Events. John Wiley, New York, 1972.
13. Goodgold, J and Eberstein, A: Electrodiagnosis of Neuromuscular Diseases, ed 2. Williams & Wilkins, Baltimore, 1978.
14. Kimura, J: Electrodiagnosis in Diseases of Nerve and Muscle: Principles and Practice, ed 2. FA Davis, Philadelphia, 1989.
15. Units, Terms and Standards in the Reporting of EMG Research. Montreal, Canada, Ad Hoc Committee of the International Society of Electrophysiological Kinesiology. Department of Medical Research, Rehabilitation Institute of Montreal, August, 1980.
16. Hayward, M: Automatic analysis of the electromyogram in healthy subjects of different ages. J Neurol Sci 33:397, 1977.
17. McGill, KC and Dorfman, LJ: Automatic decomposition electromyography (ADEMG): Validation and normative data in brachial biceps. Electroencephalogr Clin Neurophysiol 61:453, 1985.
18. Fuglsang-Frederiksen, A, Dahl, K, and Monaco, ML: Electrical muscle activity during a gradual increase in force in patients with neuromuscular diseases. Electroencephalogr Clin Neurophysiol 57:320, 1984.
19. Hausmanowa-Petrusewicz, I and Kopec, J: EMG parameter changes in the effort pattern at various load in dystrophic muscle. Electromyogr Clin Neurophysiol 24:121, 1984.
20. Hayward, M and Willison, RG: Automatic analysis of the electromyogram in patients with chronic partial denervation. J Neurol Sci 33:415, 1977.
21. Martinez, AC, Ferrer, MT, and Perez Conde, MC: Automatic analysis of the electromyogram, II. Studies in patients with primary muscle disease and neurogenic involvement: Comparison of diagnostic yields versus individual motor unit potential parameters. Electromyogr Clin Neurophysiol 24:17, 1984.
22. Daube, JR: Needle Examination in Electromyography. American Association of Electromyography and Electrodiagnosis, Minimonograph #11, Rochester, MN, 1979.
23. Denny-Brown, D and Pennybacker, JB: Fibrillation and fasciculation in voluntary muscle. Brain 61:311, 1938.
24. Thesleff, S: Fibrillation in denervated mammalian skeletal muscle. In Culp, WJ and Ochoa, J (eds): Abnormal Nerves and Muscle as Impulse Generators. Oxford University Press, Oxford, 1982, pp 678–694.
25. Buchthal, F and Rosenfalck, A: Spontaneous electrical activity of human muscle. Electroencephalogr Clin Neurophysiol 20:321, 1966.
26. Pearson, CM: Polymyositis. Annu Rev Med 17:63, 1966.
27. Eisen, AA: Electromyography and nerve conduction as a diagnostic aid. Orthop Clin North Am 4:885, 1973.
28. DeLisa, JA, Kraft, GH, and Gans, BM: Clinical electromyography and nerve conduction studies. Orthop Rev 7:75, 1978.
29. Brandstater, ME and Dinsdale, SM: Electrophysiological studies in the assessment of spinal cord lesions. Arch Phys Med Rehabil 57:70, 1976.
30. Johnson, EW, Denny, ST, and Kelly, JP: Sequence of electromyographic abnormalities in stroke syndrome. Arch Phys Med Rehabil 56:468, 1975.
31. Taylor, RG, Kewalramani, LS, and Fowler, WM: Electromyographic findings in lower extremities of patients with high spinal cord injury. Arch Phys Med Rehabil 55:16, 1974.
32. Cruz Martinez, A: Electrophysiological study in hemiparetic patients: electromyography, motor conduction velocity, and response to repetitive nerve stimulation. Electromyogr Clin Neurophysiol 23:139, 1983.
33. Spielholtz, NI, Sell, GH, Goodgold, J, et al: Electrophysiological studies in patients with spinal cord lesions. Arch Phys Med Rehabil 53:558, 1972.
34. Takebe, K, Narayan, MG, Kukulka, C, et al: Slowing of nerve conduction velocity in hemiplegia: Possible factors. Arch Phys Med Rehabil 56:285, 1975.
35. Takebe, K and Basmajian, JV: Motor and sensory nerve conduction velocities in cerebral palsy. Arch Phys Med Rehabil 57:158, 1976.
36. Chokroverty, S and Median, J: Electrophysiological study of hemiplegia. Arch Neurol 35:360, 1978.
37. Alpert, S, Idarraga, S, Orbegozo, J, et al: Absence of electromyographic evidence of lower motor neuron involvement in hemiplegic subjects. Arch Phys Med Rehabil 52:179, 1971.
38. Chokroverty, S and Medina, J: Electrophysiological study of hemiplegia. Arch Neurol 35:360, 1978.
39. Falck, B and Alaranta, H: Fibrillation potentials, positive sharp waves and fasciculation in the intrinsic muscles of the foot in healthy subjects. J Neurol Neurosurg Psychiatry 46:681, 1983.
40. Wettstein, A: The origin of fasciculations in motorneuron disease. Ann Neurol 5:295, 1979.

41. Johnson, EW, Fallon, TJ, and Wolfe, CV: Errors in EMG reporting. Arch Phys Med Rehabil 57:30, 1976.

42. Echternach, JL: Measurement issues in nerve conduction velocity and electromyographic testing. In Rothstein, JM (ed): Measurement in Physical Therapy. Churchill Livingstone, New York, 1985, p 281.

43. Hodes, R, Larrabee, MG, and German, W: The human electromyogram in response to nerve stimulation and the conduction velocity of motor axons. Arch Neurol Psychiatry 60:340, 1948.

44. Dawson, GD and Scott, JW: The recording of nerve action potentials through the skin in man. J Neurosurg Psychiatry 12:259, 1949.

45. Smorto, MP and Basmajian, JV: Clinical Electroneurography: An Introduction to Nerve Conduction Tests. Williams & Wilkins, Baltimore, 1972.

46. DeLisa, JA and MacKenzie, K: Manual of Nerve Conduction Velocity Techniques. Raven Press, New York, 1982.

47. Ma, DM and Liveson, JA: Nerve Conduction Handbook. FA Davis, Philadelphia, 1983.

48. AEEE: Guidelines in Electrodiagnostic Medicine. Professional Standard Committee, American Association of Electromyography and Electrodiagnosis. Rochester, MN, 1984.

49. Trojaborg, W: Motor nerve conduction velocities in normal subjects with particular reference to the conduction in proximal and distal segments of median and ulnar nerves. Electroencephalogr Clin Neurophysiol 17:314, 1964.

50. Sutherland, S: Nerve and Nerve Injuries. Williams & Wilkins, Baltimore, 1968.

51. Dawson, GD: The relative excitability and conduction velocity of sensory and motor nerve fibers in man. J Physiol (Lond) 131:436, 1956.

52. Thomas, JE and Lambert, EH: Ulnar nerve conduction velocity and H-reflex in infants and children. J Appl Physiol 15:1, 1960.

53. Gamstorp, I: Normal conduction velocity of ulnar, median and peroneal nerves in infancy, childhood and adolescence. Acta Paediatrica (Suppl 146)68, 1963.

54. Buchthal, F and Rosenfalck, A: Evoked action potentials and conduction velocity in human sensory nerves. Brain Res 3:1, 1966.

55. Norris, AH, Shock, NW, and Wagman, IH: Age changes in the maximum conduction velocity of motor fibers of human ulnar nerves. J Appl Physiol 5:589, 1953.

56. Halar, EM, DeLisa, JA, and Soine, TL: Nerve conduction studies in upper extremities: skin temperature corrections. Arch Phys Med Rehabil 64:412, 1983.

57. Braddom, RL, Hollis, JB, and Castell, DO: Diabetic peripheral neuropathy: a correlation of nerve conduction studies and clinical findings. Arch Phys Med Rehabil 58:308, 1977.

58. Rose, FC: Clinical aspects of motor neuron disease. In Rose, FC (ed): Motor Neuron Disease. Grune & Stratton, New York, 1977, p 1.

59. Gardner-Medwin, D and Walton, JN: A classification of the neuromuscular disorders and a note on the clinical examination of the voluntary muscles. In Walton, JN (ed): Disorders of Voluntary Muscle, ed 2. Little Brown, Boston, 1969, p 411.

60. Brooke, MH: A Clinician's View of Neuromuscular Diseases. Williams & Wilkins, Baltimore, 1977.

61. Wohlfart, G: Collateral regeneration from residual motor nerve fibers in amyotrophic lateral sclerosis. Neurology 7:124, 1957.

62. Rowland, LP: Pathogenesis of muscular dystrophies. Arch Neurol 33:315, 1976.

63. Caccia, MR, Negri, S, and Parvis, VP: Myotonic dystrophy with neural involvement. J Neurol Sci 16:253, 1972.

64. McComas, AJ, Campbell, MJ, and Sica, REP: Electrophysiological study of dystrophia myotonica. J Neurol Neurosurg Psychiatry 34:132, 1971.

65. Simpson, JA: Myasthenia gravis: A new hypothesis. Scott Med J 5:419, 1960.

66. Perlo, VP, et al: Myasthenia gravis: Evaluation of treatment in 1355 patients. Neurology 16:431, 1966.

67. Physical Therapy Advanced Clinical Competencies: Clinical Electrophysiology. Clinical Electrophysiology Council, Board for Certification of Advanced Clinical Competence, Chapel Hill, NC, 1984.

68. Soderberg, GL and Cook, TM: An electromyographic analysis of quadriceps femoris muscle setting and straight leg raising. Phys Ther 63:1434, 1983.

69. Wolf, SL, Edwards, DI, and Shutter, LA: Concurrent assessment of muscle activity (CAMA): A procedural approach to assess treatment goals. Phys Ther 66:218, 1986.

70. Basmajian, JV and Blumenstein, R: Electrode Placement for EMG Biofeedback. Williams & Wilkins, Baltimore, 1980.

71. Zipp, P: Recommendations for the standardization of lead positions in surface electromyography. Eur J Appl Physiol 50:41, 1982.

72. Graham, GP: Reliability of electromyographic measurements after surface electrode removal and replacement. Percept Mot Skills 49:215, 1979.

73. Yang, JF and Winter, DA: Electromyography reliability in maximal and submaximal isometric contractions. Arch Phys Med Rehabil 64:417, 1983.

74. Kadaba, MP, Wooten, ME, Gainey, J, et al: Repeatability of phasic muscle activity: performance of surface and intramuscular wire electrodes in gait analysis. J Orthop Res 3:350, 1985.

75. Lindstrom, L and Petersen, I: Power spectrum analysis of EMG signals and its application. In Desmedt, JE (ed): Computer-Aided Electromyography: Progress in Clinical Neurophysiology, vol 10. Karger, Basel, Switzerland, 1983.

76. Muro, MM, Nagata, A, Murakami, K, et al: Surface EMG power spectral analysis of neuro-muscular disorders during isometric and isotonic contractions. Am J Phys Med 61:244, 1982.

77. Perry, J and Bekey, GA: EMG-force relationships in skeletal muscle. Crit Rev Biomed Eng 7:22, 1981.

78. Winkel, J and Bendix, T: Muscular performance during seated work evaluated by two different EMG methods. Eur J Appl Physiol 55:167, 1986.

79. Janda, DH, Geiringer, SR, Hankin, FM, et al: Objective evaluation of grip strength. J Occup Med 29:569, 1987.

80. Lippold, OCJ: The relation between integrated action potentials in a human muscle and its isometric tension. J Physiol (Lond) 117:492, 1952.

81. Inman, VT, Ralston, HJ, Saunders, CM, et al: Relation of human electromyogram to muscular tension. Electroencephalogr Clin Neurophysiol 4:187, 1952.

82. Woods, JJ and Bigland-Ritchie, B: Linear and non-linear surface EMG/force relationships in human muscles. Am J Phys Med 62:287, 1983.

83. Edwards, RG and Lippold, OCJ: The relation between force and integrated electrical activity in fatigued muscle. J Physiol (Lond) 132:677, 1956.

84. Vredenbregt, J and Rau, G: Surface electromyography in relation to force, muscle length and endurance. In Desmedt, JE (ed): New Developments in Electromyography and Clinical Neurophysiology, vol 1. Karger, Basel, Switzerland, 1973, p 606.

85. Zuniga, EN and Simons, DG: Nonlinear relationship between averaged electromyogram potential and muscle tension in normal subjects. Arch Phys Med Rehabil 50:613, 1969.

86. Lawrence, JH and De Luca, CJ: Myoelectric signal vs. force relationship in different human muscles. J Appl Physiol 54:1653, 1983.

87. Heckathorne, CW and Childress, DS: Relationships of the surface electromyogram to the force, length, velocity, and contraction rate of the cineplastic human biceps. Am J Phys Med 60:1, 1981.

88. Tang, A and Rymer, WZ: Abnormal force-EMG relations in paretic limbs of hemiparetic human subjects. J Neurol Neurosurg Psychiatry 44:690, 1981.

89. Doss, WS and Karpovich, PV: A comparison of concentric, eccentric and isometric strength of elbow flexors. J Appl Physiol 20:351, 1965.

90. Knuttgen, HG, Peteresen, FB, and Klausen, K: Exercise with concentric and eccentric muscle contractions. Acta Paediat Scand Suppl 217, 1971.

91. Bigland, B and Lippold, OCJ: The relation between force, velocity and integrated electrical activity in human muscles. J Physiol (Lond) 123:214, 1954.

92. Currier, DP: Measurement of muscle fatigue. Phys Ther 49:724, 1969.

93. Hakkinen, K and Komi, PV: Electromyographic and mechanical characteristics of human skeletal muscle during fatigue under voluntary and reflex conditions. Electroencephalogr Clin Neurophysiol 55:436, 1983.

94. deVries, HA: Method for evaluation of muscle fatigue and endurance from electromyographic fatigue curves. Am J Phys Med 47:125, 1968.

95. Bigland-Ritchie, B, Jones, DA, Hosking, GP, et al: Central and

peripheral fatigue in sustained maximum voluntary contractions of human quadriceps muscle. Clin Sci Mol Med 54:609, 1978.

96. Hagberg, M: Electromyographic signs of shoulder muscular fatigue in two elevated arm positions. Am J Phys Med 60:111, 1981.
97. Petrofsky, JS, Glaser, R, Phillips, C, et al: Evaluation of the amplitude and frequency components of the surface EMG as an index of muscle fatigue. Ergonomics 25:213, 1982.
98. Lenman, JAR: Quantitative electromyographic changes associated with muscular weakness. J Neurol Neurosurg Psychiatry 22:306, 1959.
99. DeLuca, CJ: Myoelectrical manifestations of localized muscular fatigue in humans. Crit Rev Biomed Eng 11:251, 1985.
100. Kuorinka, I: Restitution of EMG spectrum after muscular fatigue. Eur J Appl Physiol 57:311, 1988.
101. Baidya, KN and Stevenson, MG: Local muscle fatigue in repetitive work. Ergonomics 31:227, 1988.
102. Okada, M: Effect of muscle length on surface EMG wave forms in isometric contractions. Eur J Appl Physiol 56:482, 1987.
103. Huijing, PA, Adelerbof, A, Giesberger, R, et al: Triceps source EMG spectrum changes during sustained submaximal isometric contractions at different muscle lengths. Electromyogr Clin Neurophysiol 26:181, 1986.
104. Griffith, ER: Spasticity. In Rosenthal, M, Griffith, ER, Bond, MR, et al (eds): Rehabilitation of the Head Injured Patient. FA Davis, Philadelphia, 1983, p 125.
105. Basmajian, JV: New views on muscular tone and relaxation. Can Med Assoc J 77:203, 1957.
106. Shimazu, H, Hongo, T, Kubota, K, et al: Rigidity and spasticity in man: electromyographic analysis with reference to the role of the globus pallidus. Arch Neurol 6:10, 1962.
107. Sahrmann, SA and Norton, BJ: Stretch reflex of the biceps and brachioradialis muscles in patients with upper motor neuron syndrome. Phys Ther 58:1191, 1978.
108. Nelson, AJ: Motor assessment. In Rosenthal, M, Griffith, ER, Bond, MR, et al (eds): Rehabilitation of the Head Injured Adult. FA Davis, Philadelphia, 1983, p 241.
109. Sullivan, PE, Markos, PD, and Minor, MAD: An Integrated Approach to Therapeutic Exercise: Theory and Clinical Application. Reston Publishing, Reston, VA, 1982.
110. Gregg, RA, Mastellone, AF, and Gersten, JW: Cross exercise—a review of the literature and study utilizing electromyographic techniques. Am J Phys Med 36:269, 1957.
111. Devine, KL, LeVeau, BF, and Yack, HJ: Electromyographic activity recorded from an unexercised muscle during maximal isometric exercise of the contralateral agonists and antagonists. Phys Ther 61:898, 1981.
112. Markos, PD: Ipsilateral and contralateral effects of proprioceptive neuromuscular facilitation techniques on hip motion and electromyographic activity. Phys Ther 59:1366, 1979.

113. Hopf, HC, Schlegel, HJ, and Lowitzch, K: Irradiation of voluntary activity to the contralateral side in movements of normal subjects and patients with central motor disturbances. Eur Neurol 12:142, 1974.
114. Russell, AS: Electromyographic activity during proprioceptive neuromuscular facilitation in normal and hemiplegic patients. Master's thesis. Stanford University, Palo Alto, CA, 1971.
115. Portney, LG, Sullivan, PE, and Bachelder, ME: Analysis of exercise overflow to preferred and nonpreferred limbs (abstract). Phys Ther 64:749, 1984.
116. Nelson, AJ: Strategies for improving motor control. In Rosenthal, M, Griffith, ER, Bond, MR, et al (eds): Rehabilitation of the Head Injured Adult. FA Davis, Philadelphia, 1983.
117. Basmajian, JV and Bentzon, JW: An electromyographic study of certain muscles of the leg and foot in the standing posture. Surg Gynecol Obstet 98:662, 1954.
118. Waters, RL and Morris, JM: Electrical activity of muscles of the trunk during walking. J Anat 111:191, 1972.
119. Shiavi, R, Champion, S, Freeman, F, et al: Variability of electromyographic patterns for level-surface walking through a range of self-selected speeds. Bull Prosthet Res 10:5, 1981.
120. Leavitt, LA and Beasley, WC: Clinical application of quantitative methods in the study of spasticity. Clin Pharmacol Ther 5:918, 1964.
121. Bierman, W and Ralston, HJ: Electromyographic study during passive and active flexion and extension of the knee of the normal human subject. Arch Phys Med Rehabil 46:71, 1965.
122. Svendsen, DA and Matyas, TA: Facilitation of the isometric maximum voluntary contraction with traction: a test of PNF prediction. Am J Phys Med 62:27, 1983.
123. Sullivan, PE and Portney, LG: Electromyographic activity of shoulder muscles during unilateral upper extremity proprioceptive neuromuscular facilitation patterns. Phys Ther 60:283, 1980.
124. Osternig, LR, Hamill, J, Corcos, DM, et al: Electromyographic patterns accompanying isokinetic exercise under varying speed and sequencing conditions. Am J Phys Med 63:289, 1984.
125. Brunt, D, Andersen, JC, and Huntsman, B: Postural responses to lateral perturbation in healthy subjects and ankle sprain patients. Med Sci Sports Exerc 24:171, 1992.
126. Hobart, DJ, Kelly, DL, and Bradley, LS: Modification occurring during acquisition of a novel throwing task. Am J Phys Med 54:1, 1975.
127. Gerleman, DG and Cook, TM: Instrumentation. In Soderberg, GL (ed): Selected Topics in Surface Electromyography for Use in the Occupational Setting: Expert Perspectives. U.S. Department of Health and Human Services, Public Health Service, Centers for Disease Control, NIOSH, Publication No. 91-100, US Government Printing Office, Washington, DC, 1992, pp 44–68.

SUPPLEMENTAL READINGS

Basmajian, JV and Blumenstein, R: Electrode Placement for EMG Biofeedback. Williams & Wilkins, Baltimore, 1980.

Basmajian, JV and De Luca, CJ: Muscles Alive, ed 5. Williams & Wilkins, Baltimore, 1985.

Echternach, JL: Measurement issues in nerve conduction velocity and electromyographic testing. In Rothstein, JM (ed): Measurement in Physical Therapy. Churchill Livingstone, New York, 1985, p 281.

Goodgold, J and Eberstein, A: Electrodiagnosis of Neuromuscular Diseases, ed 2. Williams & Wilkins, Baltimore, 1978.

Kimura, J: Electrodiagnosis in Diseases of Nerve and Muscle: Principles and Practice, ed 2. FA Davis, Philadelphia, 1989.

Soderberg, GL: Kinesiology: Application to Pathological Motion. Williams & Wilkins, Baltimore, 1986, p 100.

Soderberg, GL and Cook, TM: Electromyography in biomechanics. Phys Ther 64:1434, 1984.

Units, Terms and Standards in the Reporting of EMG Research. Montreal, Canada, Ad Hoc Committee of the International Society of Electrophysiological Kinesiology. Department of Medical Research, Rehabilitation Institute of Montreal, August, 1980.

United States Department of Health and Human Services: Selected Topics in Surface Electromyography for Use in the Occupational Setting: Expert Perspectives. National Institute for Occupational Safety and Health, Publication No. 91-100, US Government Printing Office, Washington, DC, 1992.

GLOSSARY

Amplifier: A device used to process an electrical signal, converting it to a voltage output which can be displayed.

Amplitude: Of an action potential, the maximum voltage difference between two points, usually measured baseline to peak, or peak to peak; expresses the level of the signal activity.

Anode: The positive terminal of a source of electrical current.

Antidromic conduction: Propagation of an action

potential in a direction opposite to the normal (orthodromic) direction for that fiber, that is, conduction along motor fibers toward the spinal cord, and conduction along sensory fibers away from the spinal cord.

Artifact: A voltage signal generated by a source other than the one of interest. See stimulus artifact, movement artifact.

Cathode: The negative terminal of a source of electrical current.

Common mode rejection ratio (CMRR): A ratio expressing an amplifier's ability to reject unwanted noise while amplifying the wanted signal, for example, a ratio of 1000:1 indicates the wanted signal will be amplified 1,000 times more than noise, can also be expressed in decibels (1000:1 equals 60 dB).

Conduction distance: Distance measured (in centimeters) between two points of stimulation along a nerve in a nerve conduction velocity test.

Conduction time: Time difference (in milliseconds) between the distal and proximal latencies in a nerve conduction velocity test, that is, the time it takes for an impulse to travel between the two points of stimulation along a nerve trunk.

Conduction velocity: Speed of propagation of an action potential along a nerve or muscle fiber. Calculated in meters per second by dividing the conduction distance by the conduction time. The calculated velocity represents the conduction velocity of the fastest axons in the nerve.

Cross talk: Activity seen at one electrode site that is generated by a muscle other than the one being monitored.

Differential amplifier: An amplifier that processes the voltage difference between two input terminals, effectively rejecting common mode voltages that appear between each input terminal and the common ground.

Duration: The duration of an action potential is measured as the interval from the first deflection from the baseline to its final return to the baseline.

Electrical silence: The absence of measurable electromyographic activity, typically recorded at rest in normal muscles.

Electrode: A device capable of recording electrical potentials or conducting electricity to provide a stimulus.

Concentric (coaxial) needle electrode: Recording electrode consisting of a steel cannula through which is threaded a single platinum wire that is insulated from the needle shaft. The wire and shaft are bared at the tip and the potential difference between them is recorded in the presence of electrical activity. The electrode can also be configured with two wires (bipolar) threaded through the cannula, recording the difference of potential between these wires.

Fine-wire indwelling electrode: Small-diameter insulated wires inserted into the muscle belly by means of a hypodermic needle.

Ground electrode: An electrode connected to a common source, used to reduce the effect of electrical noise in a recording system; an arbitrary zero potential reference point.

Monopolar needle electrode: A solid wire, usually of stainless steel, coated, except at its tip, with insulating material. Voltage is measured between the tip of the needle and some other electrode, usually placed on the skin (reference electrode).

Recording electrode (active electrode): Needle or surface electrode used to record electrical activity from nerve and muscle.

Reference electrode: In motor nerve conduction velocity test, the electrode placed over the tendon of the test muscle. In monopolar recording of EMG, the inactive electrode placed over a neutral area.

Stimulating electrode: Device used to apply electrical current to stimulate propagation of a nerve impulse or muscle contraction; requires positive (anode) and negative (cathode) terminals.

Surface electrode: Small metal disks, most commonly made of silver/silver chloride, applied to the skin overlying the appropriate muscle and used to monitor EMG signals from large, superficial muscles.

Electromyography (EMG): The recording and study of the electrical activity of muscle. It is commonly used to refer to nerve conduction studies as well. The electromyograph is the instrument used to record and display the electromyogram.

Evoked potential: Waveform elicited by a stimulus.

Fasciculation potential: A random, spontaneous twitching of a group of muscle fibers which may be visible through the skin. The amplitude, configuration, duration, and frequency are variable.

Fibrillation potential: Electrical activity associated with fibrillating muscle and reflecting the activity of a single muscle fiber; associated with denervation and myopathy. Classically, these potentials are biphasic spikes of short duration (<5 msec), with a peak-to-peak amplitude less than 1 mV, a firing rate ranging from 1 to 50 Hz, and a high-pitched regular sound likened to "rain on the roof."

Frequency: Number of complete cycles of a repetitive waveform in 1 second. Measured in hertz (Hz).

Frequency bandwidth: Frequency response of an amplifier, referring to the limits on the range of signal frequencies processed; for example, 10 to 1000 Hz.

Giant motor unit: A motor unit potential with a peak-to-peak amplitude and duration much greater than normal ranges. Often seen following collateral sprouting with regeneration of peripheral nerves.

Hertz (Hz): Unit of frequency representing cycles per second.

Impedance: A form of resistance to current flow in an alternating current circuit. Skin, electrodes, and amplifier input terminals provide sources of impedance to EMG potentials.

Insertion activity: Electrical activity caused by insertion or movement of a needle electrode in a muscle. Can be described as normal, reduced, increased, or prolonged.

Integration: Mathematical processing of a rectified electromyographic signal that allows quantification. Integration can be performed over set time intervals or within preset voltage threshold levels.

Interference pattern: Electrical activity, recorded from a muscle during maximal voluntary effort, in which identification of each of the contributing motor unit potentials is not possible.

Latency: In nerve conduction velocity tests, the interval between onset of a stimulus and the onset of a response, measured from the stimulus artifact to the onset of the M wave.

Distal latency: The time (in milliseconds) for an action potential to travel from the distal point of stimulation along a nerve to the recording electrode.

Proximal latency: The time (in milliseconds) for an action potential to travel from the proximal point of stimulation along a nerve to the recording electrode.

Motor unit: The anatomical unit of an anterior horn cell, its axon, the neuromuscular junctions, and all the muscle fibers innervated by that axon.

Motor unit action potential (MUAP): Action potential reflecting the electrical activity of a single motor unit capable of being recorded by an electrode. Characterized by its amplitude, configuration, duration, frequency, and sound.

Movement artifact: An electrical signal resulting from the movement of the recording electrodes or their cables.

M wave: A compound action potential evoked from muscle by a single electrical stimulus to its motor nerve.

Myotonic discharge: A high-frequency discharge, characterized by repetitive firing (20–80 Hz) of biphasic or monophasic potentials recorded after needle insertion or after voluntary muscle contraction, with a waxing and waning amplitude and frequency and a sound likened to a "dive-bomber."

Nerve conduction velocity (NCV): The speed with which a peripheral motor or sensory nerve conducts an impulse.

Noise: An unwanted electrical signal that is detected along with the desired signal.

Orthodromic conduction: Propagation of an action potential in the same direction as physiologic conduction, that is, motor nerve conduction away from the spinal cord and sensory nerve conduction toward the spinal cord.

Oscilloscope: A device for displaying electronic signals on a screen, composed of a cathode ray tube (CRT) within which horizontal and vertical beams strike a phosphorescent surface, allowing visualization of the signal. Control of the values for vertical and horizontal divisions permits quantification of the amplitude and duration of signals.

Phase: That portion of a wave between the departure from and the return to the baseline.

Polyphasic potential: An action potential having five or more phases.

Positive sharp wave: A form of electrical potential associated with fibrillating muscle fibers, recorded as a biphasic, positive-negative action potential initiated by needle movement and recurring in uniform patterns. The initial positive phase is of short duration (< 5 msec) and large amplitude (up to 1 mV); the second negative phase is of long duration (10–100 msec) and low amplitude.

Rectification: A process whereby the negative portion of an electromyographic wave is inverted and superimposed on the positive portion, so that the signal is seen only above the baseline. This allows further processing and integration.

Repetitive discharges (bizarre high-frequency discharges): An extended train of potentials, generally 5 to 100 impulses per second, commonly seen in lesions of the anterior horn cell and peripheral nerves, and with some myopathies.

Sensitivity: Characteristic of a system, expressing its ability to record and display signals of different sizes, usually expressed as a range, for example, 20 μV to 30 mV.

Signal-to-noise ratio: The relationship (proportion) between the signal power and the power of the noise.

Single motor unit pattern: An interference pattern, recorded at maximal effort, when single motor unit potentials can still be identified.

Skin resistance: The opposition to electrical conduction offered by skin cells and other substances on the skin, usually necessitating some form of skin preparation prior to application of surface electrodes.

Spontaneous potentials: Action potentials recorded from muscle or nerve at rest after insertional activity has subsided and when there is no voluntary contraction or external stimulus.

Stimulus artifact: A potential recorded at the time the stimulus is applied.

Temporal dispersion: Distortion of duration, amplitude, or shape of the M wave potential in a motor nerve conduction velocity test.

Volt (V): The difference of potential between two points; the unit of measurement for EMG amplitude.

Volume Conduction: Spread of current from a potential source through a conducting medium, such as body tissues.

CHAPTER 10

Gait Analysis

Cynthia Clair Norkin

OBJECTIVES

1. Define the terms used to describe normal gait.
2. Define reliability and validity in relation to gait analysis.
3. Describe the variables that are assessed in each of the following types of gait analyses: kinematic qualitative analysis, kinematic quantitative analysis, and kinetic analysis.
4. Describe and give examples of some of the most commonly used types of observational gait analysis.
5. Compare and contrast the advantages and disadvantages of kinematic qualitative and kinematic quantitative gait analyses.

INTRODUCTION

One of the major purposes of the rehabilitative process is to help patients achieve as high a level of functional independence as possible, within the limits of their particular disabilities. Human locomotion or gait is one of the basic components of independent functioning that is commonly affected by either disease processes or injury. Therefore, the goal of many physical therapy treatment programs is to restore or to improve a patient's ambulatory status.

Content of Gait Analysis

In order to set realistic treatment goals and to develop and implement a treatment plan directed toward improving or restoring a patient's gait, the physical therapist must be able to assess ambulatory status. The assessment should include

1. An accurate description of gait pattern and gait variables.
2. An identification and description of all gait deviations.
3. An analysis of the deviations and identification of the mechanisms responsible for producing abnormalities in gait.
4. Assessment of energy expenditure and endurance.
5. Determination of the functional ambulation capabilities of the patient in relation to functional ambulation demands of the home and community environment.

The assessment should provide objective data that can be used as a basis for formulating realistic treatment goals and assessing progress toward these goals.

Selection of a Gait Analysis

Gait is a complex activity, and a large amount of the physical therapy literature is devoted to methods of analyzing gait.[1-22] The type of gait analysis the clinician selects depends on the purpose of the analysis, the type of equipment available, and the knowledge, skills, and experience of the clinician.

The purpose of a gait analysis may include, but is not limited to, the following: assessment of the fit of a lower extremity prosthesis,[1] comparison of the effects of different types of assistive devices,[2] determination of either the need for or the effectiveness of an orthotic device,[3,4] assessment of the need for surgical interventions, assessment of the need for increasing endurance or gait velocity, and assessment of the need for reducing energy expenditure. To determine the need for either a prosthetic or an orthotic adjustment, the therapist may need to assess the forces acting during gait. To determine if a patient should increase ambulating endurance, the therapist needs to assess time and distance variables, as well as physiologic parameters such as energy expenditure.

The type of equipment necessary for performing a gait analysis depends on the purpose of the analysis, equipment availability, and the amount of time that the therapist can expend. Equipment used in a gait analysis may be as simple as a pencil and paper[5] or as complex as an electronic imaging system with force plates embedded in the floor.[6,7]

The knowledge, skills, and experience of the therapist are essential ingredients in any gait analysis. The therapist must be aware of the types of analyses available and which assessment methods are reliable and valid so that the appropriate method may be selected. The therapist must have a knowledge and understanding of the kinematics, kinetics, and neural control of normal and pathologic human locomotion in order to analyze and to interpret the data obtained from an assessment. Familiarity with the terminology used to describe gait is an essential first step.

Gait Terminology

To assess gait a therapist must be familiar with the terminology used to describe gait. Usually gait is described in reference to the activities of one extremity. The largest unit used to describe gait is called a *gait cycle*. In normal walking a gait cycle commences when the heel of the reference extremity contacts the supporting surface. The gait cycle ends when the heel of the same extremity contacts the ground again. The gait cycle is divided into two phases, **stance** and **swing,** and two periods of **double support.** In normal gait the stance phase, which constitutes 60 percent of the gait cycle, is defined as the interval in which the foot of the reference extremity is in contact with the ground. The swing phase, which constitutes 40 percent of the gait cycle, is that portion in which the reference extremity does not contact the ground. The term double support refers to the two intervals in a gait cycle in which body weight is being transferred from one foot to the other and both right and left feet are in contact with the ground at the same time (Fig. 10–1).

Step and **stride** are considered to be quantitative variables and will be discussed in the kinematic quantitative gait section. However, a definition of these variables is necessary for a comprehensive overview of gait terminology. Two steps, a *right step* and a *left step,* comprise a stride, and a stride is equal to a gait cycle. A step may be defined in two dimensions: distance and time. **Step length** is the distance from the point of heel strike of one extremity to the point of heel strike of the opposite

extremity, whereas **stride length** is the distance from the point of heel strike of one extremity to the point of heel strike of the same extremity. **Stride time** and **step time** refer to the length of time required to complete a step and a stride, respectively (Fig. 10–2).

Traditionally, each phase of gait (stance and swing) has been divided into the following units: stance (*heel strike, footflat, midstance, heel off,* and *toe off*) and swing (*acceleration, midswing,* and *deceleration*). However, the subdivisions within phases have been redefined, and a more recent terminology has been developed at Los Amigos Research and Education Institute at the Rancho Los Amigos Medical Center (RLA). In this terminology the subdivisions are named as follows: stance (*initial contact, loading response, midstance, terminal stance,* and *preswing*) and swing (*initial swing, midswing,* and *terminal swing*).[22,23] The similarities and differences between the two terminologies are presented in Table 10–1.

Angular rotations at the joints in each portion of both swing and stance phases, as well as muscle activity and function, are presented in Tables 10–2 to 10–6. The clinician should be familiar with ranges and patterns of motion associated with normal gait in order to identify deviations from published standards. The clinician also should be familiar with the muscle activity and function associated with normal gait in order to perform an analysis of the causes of the deviations.

Types of Analyses

The types of gait analyses in use today can be classified under two broad categories: kinematic and kinetic. Kinematic gait analyses are used to describe movement patterns without regard for the forces involved in producing the movement.[5] A kinematic gait analysis consists of a description of movement of the body as a whole or body segments in relation to each other during gait. Kinematic gait analyses can be either qualitative or quantitative. Kinetic gait analyses are used to determine

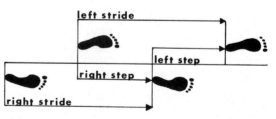

Figure 10–2. A right stride and a left stride. Right stride length is the distance between the point of contact of the right heel (at the lower left corner of the diagram) and the next contact of the right heel. Left stride length is the distance between the point of contact of the left heel (at the top left of the diagram) to the point of contact of the next left heel. Each stride contains two steps, but only both steps in the left stride are labeled. The left stride contains a right step and a left step. The right step length (shown in the middle of the diagram) is the distance between left heel contact to the point of right heel contact. Left step length is the distance between right heel contact and the next left heel contact. Step and stride times refer to the amount of time required to complete a step and to complete stride, respectively.

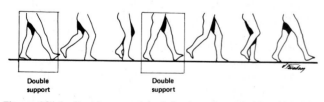

Figure 10–1. Double support is defined as the period in which some portion of the feet of both extremities are in contact with the supporting surface at the same time. Two periods of double support occur within a single gait cycle. One period occurs early in the stance phase of the reference extremity and the other occurs late in the stance phase of the reference extremity. (From Norkin, and Levangie,[32] p 452, with permission.)

Table 10–1 GAIT TERMINOLOGY

Traditional	Rancho Los Amigos	Traditional	Rancho Los Amigos
Stance Phase		**Swing Phase**	
Heel Strike: The beginning of the stance phase when the heel contacts the ground. The same as initial contact.	Initial contact: The beginning of the stance phase when the heel or another part of the foot contacts the ground.	Acceleration: The portion of beginning swing from the moment the toe of the reference extremity leaves the ground to the point when reference extremity is directly under the body.	Initial swing: The portion of swing from the point when the reference extremity leaves the ground to maximum knee flexion of the same extremity.
Foot flat: Occurs immediately following heel strike, when the sole of the foot contacts the floor. This event occurs during loading response.	Loading response: The portion of the first double support period of the stance phase from initial contact until the contralateral extremity leaves the ground.	Midswing: Portion of the swing phase when the reference extremity passes directly below the body. Midswing extends from the end of acceleration to the beginning of deceleration.	Midswing: Portion of the swing phase from maximum knee flexion of the reference extremity to a vertical tibial position.
Midstance: The point at which the body passes directly over the reference extremity.	Midstance: The portion of the single limb support stance phase that begins when the contralateral extremity leaves the ground and ends when the body is directly over the supporting limb.	Deceleration: The swing portion of the swing phase when the reference extremity is decelerating in preparation for heel strike.	Terminal swing: The portion of the swing phase from a vertical position of the tibia of the reference extremity to just prior to initial contact.
Heel off: The point following midstance at which time the heel of the reference extremity leaves the ground. Heel off occurs prior to terminal stance.	Terminal stance: The last portion of the single limb support stance phase that begins with heel rise and continues until contralateral extremity contacts the ground.		
Toe off: The point following heel off when only the toe of the reference extremity is in contact with the ground.	Preswing: The portion of stance that begins the second double support period from the initial contact of the contralateral extremity to lift off of the reference extremity.		

Table 10–2 ANKLE AND FOOT: STANCE PHASE, SAGITTAL PLANE ANALYSIS

Portion of Phase	Normal Motion[24]	Normal Moment	Normal Muscle Activity	Result of Weakness	Possible Compensation
Heel strike to foot flat	0°–15° plantarflexion	Plantarflexion	Pretibial group acts eccentrically to oppose plantarflexion moment and thereby to prevent foot slap by controlling plantarflexion.	Lack of ability to oppose the plantarflexion moment causes the foot to slap the floor.	To avoid foot slap and to eliminate the plantarflexion moment, the foot may be placed flat on the floor or placed with the toes first at initial contact.
Foot flat through midstance	15° plantarflexion to 10° dorsiflexion	Plantarflexion to dorsiflexion	Gastrocnemius and soleus act eccentrically to oppose the dorsiflexion moment and to control tibial advance.	Excessive dorsiflexion and uncontrolled tibial advance.	To avoid excessive dorsiflexion, the ankle may be maintained in plantarflexion.
Midstance to heel off	10°–15° dorsiflexion	Dorsiflexion	Gastrocnemius and soleus contract eccentrically to oppose the dorsiflexion moment and control tibial advance.	Excessive dorsiflexion and uncontrolled forward motion of tibia.	The ankle may be maintained in plantarflexion. If the foot is flat on the floor, the dorsiflexion moment is eliminated and a step-to gait is produced.
Heel off to toe off	15° dorsiflexion to 20° plantarflexion	Dorsiflexion	Gastrocnemius, soleus, peroneus brevis, peroneus longus, flexor hallucis longus contract to plantarflex the foot.	No roll off. Decreased contralateral step.	Whole foot is lifted off the ground.

Table 10–3 ANKLE AND FOOT: SWING PHASE, SAGITTAL PLANE ANALYSIS

Portion of Phase	Normal Motion	Normal Moment	Normal Muscle Action	Result of Weakness	Possible Compensation
Acceleration to midswing	Dorsiflexion to neutral	None	Dorsiflexors contract to bring the ankle into neutral and to prevent the toes from dragging on the floor.	Foot drop and/or toe dragging.	Hip and knee flexion may be increased to prevent toe drag, or the hip may be hiked or circumducted. Sometimes vaulting on the contralateral limb may occur.
Midswing to deceleration	Neutral	None	Dorsiflexion.	Foot drop and/or toe dragging.	Hip and knee flexion may be increased to prevent toe drag. The swing leg may be circumducted, or vaulting may occur on the contralateral side.

Table 10–4 KNEE: STANCE PHASE, SAGITTAL PLANE ANALYSIS

Portion of Phase	Normal Motion	Normal Moment	Normal Muscle Action	Result of Weakness	Possible Compensation
Heel strike to foot flat	Flexion 0°–15°	Flexion	Quadriceps contracts initially to hold the knee in extension and then eccentrically to oppose the flexion moment and control the amount of flexion.	Excessive knee flexion because the quadriceps cannot oppose the flexion moment.	Plantar flexion at ankle so that foot flat instead of heel strike occurs. Plantarflexion eliminates the flexion moment. Trunk lean forward eliminates the flexion moment at knee and therefore may be used to compensate for quadriceps weakness.
Foot flat through midstance	Extension 15°–5°	Flexion to extension	Quadriceps contracts in early part, and then no activity is required.	Excessive knee flexion initially.	Same as above in early part of midstance. No compensation required in later part of phase.
Midstance to heel off	5° of flexion to 0° (neutral)	Flexion to extension	No activity required.		None required.
Heel off to toe off	0°–40° flexion	Extension to flexion	Quadriceps required to control amount of knee flexion.		

Table 10–5 KNEE: SWING PHASE, SAGITTAL PLANE ANALYSIS

Portion of Phase	Normal Motion	Normal Moment	Normal Muscle Action	Result of Weakness	Possible Compensation
Acceleration to midswing	40°–60° flexion	None	Little or no activity in quadriceps. Biceps femoris (short head), gracilis, and sartorius contract concentrically.	Inadequate knee flexion.	Increased hip flexion, circumduction, or hiking.
Midswing	60°–30° extension	None			
Deceleration	30°–0° extension	None	Quadriceps contracts concentrically to stabilize knee in extension, in preparation for heel strike.	Inadequate knee extension.	

Table 10–6 HIP: STANCE PHASE, SAGITTAL PLANE ANALYSIS

Portion of Phase	Normal Motion	Normal Moment	Normal Muscle Action	Result of Weakness	Possible Compensation
Heel strike to foot flat	30° flexion	Flexion	Erector spinae, gluteus maximus, hamstrings.	Excessive hip flexion and anterior pelvis tilt owing to inability to counteract flexion moment.	Trunk leans backward to prevent excessive hip flexion and to eliminate the hip flexion moment. (See Fig. 10–5.)
Foot flat through midstance	30° flexion to 5° (neutral)	Flexion to extension	Gluteus maximus at beginning of period to oppose flexion moment, then activity ceases as moment changes from flexion to extension.	At the beginning of the period, excessive hip flexion and anterior pelvic tilt owing to inability to counteract flexion moment.	At beginning of the period, subject may lean trunk backward to prevent excessive hip flexion; however, once the flexion moment changes to an extension moment, the subject no longer needs to incline the trunk backward.
Midstance to heel off		Extension	No activity.	None.	None required.
Heel off to toe off	10° of hyperextension to neutral	Extension	Illiopsoas, adductor, magnus, and adductor longus.	Undetermined.	Undetermined.

the forces that are involved in gait.[24] In some instances, kinematic and kinetic gait variables may be assessed in one analysis. The most comprehensive gait analysis is one that includes kinematic, kinetic, and physiologic variables.

KINEMATIC QUALITATIVE GAIT ANALYSIS

The most common method used in the clinic is a **qualitative gait analysis.** This method usually requires only a small amount of equipment and a minimal amount of time.

Definition of Variables

The primary variable that is assessed in a qualitative kinematic analysis is **displacement,** which includes a description of patterns of movement, deviations from normal body postures, and joint angles at specific points in the gait cycle. **Linear displacement** is measured in meters, whereas rotational displacement is measured in degrees. An example of **rotational displacement** is the amount of knee flexion and extension that occurs during the gait cycle. Four different reference systems are used in describing displacement:

1. Absolute spatial system: the environment is used as a reference.
2. Relative system: the position of one body segment is described in relation to another body segment.
3. Absolute reference system: the body segment is

described in reference to the vertical or horizontal position.
4. Relative reference system: the excursion of a body segment from one position to another is described (e.g., the ankle passes through a 35-degree excursion from relative dorsiflexion to relative plantarflexion).[24]

Observational Gait Analysis

The most common method of performing a kinematic qualitative analysis is through observation. Some of the most well-known observational gait analysis schemes have been developed by Brunnstrom,[25] at New York University Post-Graduate Medical School Prosthetics and Orthotics,[26] Temple University,[27] and at Rancho Los Amigos Medical Center.[22,23] Daniels and Worthingham[28] included a procedure for observational gait analysis at the end of their manual muscle testing text, and the first edition of this text included a worksheet for observational gait analysis.[29] In general, these protocols provide the therapist with a systematic approach to observational gait analysis by directing the therapist's attention to a specific joint or body segment during a given point in the gait cycle. Most of these methods use checklists or profiles in which the examiner notes the presence or absence of a particular deviation or critical event at a particular point in the patient's gait cycle.

The Temple University method uses a scoring system that consists of the following seven descriptive terms: present, inconsistent, borderline, occurs throughout, absent, limited, and exaggerated. This system is used to rate 48 gait deviations. The Temple system also includes a section for assessing time and distance measures, that is, velocity, step length, step time, and width of base of support. The observational gait analysis method formulated by New York University Post-Graduate Medical School Prosthetics and Orthotics includes 13 gait deviations, which are rated on a three-point scale: 0—not noticeable, +—noticeable, and + +—very noticeable. The Rancho Los Amigos technique involves a systematic assessment of the movement patterns of the following body segments at each point in the gait cycle: ankle, foot, knee, hip, pelvis, and trunk. The Rancho Los Amigos form consists of 48 descriptors of common gait deviations such as toe drag, excessive plantarflexion and dorsiflexion, excessive varus or valgus at the knee or foot, hip hiking, and trunk flexion. The observing therapist must decide whether or not a deviation is present and note the occurrence and timing of the deviation on the form.[23]

Considerable training and constant practice are necessary to develop the observational skills that are needed for performing any observational gait analysis. Therapists who wish to learn the Rancho method may elect to attend a workshop or the therapist can learn by studying the Rancho Los Amigos Observational Gait Analysis Handbook.[23] Forms for recording an assessment are included in the handbook and a sample form is included in this chapter (Fig. 10–3). Practice gait filmstrips useful for learning how to use the recording forms may be obtained by writing to Rancho Los Amigos.[23] However, prior to selecting a particular assessment method the therapist should attempt to obtain information regarding the method's reliability and validity.

Reliability

Reliability as applied to gait analysis refers to the level of consistency of either a measuring instrument (footswitches, forceplates, and electrogoniometers) or a method of analysis (observational gait checklists and formulas for measuring stride length). To determine if a measuring instrument is reliable, the measurements obtained from successive and repeated use of the instrument must be consistent. For example, if an electrogoniometric measurement of a known angle of 60 degrees measures 60 degrees on every Monday morning for 2 months, the instrument is said to be reliable. If, however, the measurement obtained is 60 degrees on the first Monday, 30 degrees on the second Monday, and 40 degrees on the third Monday, the instrument would have very low reliability.

To make a definitive determination of the reliability of an instrument, one must make certain that factors other than the instrument that could influence the measurement are ruled out (e.g., that a subject has not injured his or her knee between successive measurements or that the placement of the instrument had not changed).

To determine whether an assessment method is reliable, two different forms of reliability need to be determined: *intra-tester and inter-tester reliability*. The *intra-tester reliability* of an assessment method can be determined by examining the consistency of the results

obtained when one individual uses a particular method repeatedly. For example, Sue Jones, PT, uses a particular method to assess a student physical therapist's gait. Sue repeats her assessment at 2-week intervals for 8 weeks and obtains the same results during each analysis. In this instance the method would be considered as having high intra-tester reliability because the results obtained by the same person are consistent over time. (The preceding example is a hypothetical one because factors other than the therapist's skill such as patient fatigue, time of day, and other variables may affect the patient's performance and must be controlled in any analysis.)

Inter-tester reliability is determined by looking at the consistency of the data obtained from repeated analyses performed by a number of different persons. If the results obtained by the numerous examiners are in agreement, and no significant differences in the results exist among testers, the method has high inter-tester reliability.

Generally the reliability of existing observational gait analyses is low or moderate because of difficulties involved in trying to observe and make accurate judgments about the motions occurring at numerous body segments. Also, therapists differ in their observational skills. Only moderate reliability between therapists (inter-tester reliability) was found when a modification of the New York University (NYU) orthotic gait analysis method was used to assess the gait of 10 patients with hemiplegia. The authors suggested that training therapists in gait analysis was necessary to improve reliability.[30] In another study only moderate inter-rater and intra-rater reliability was found when three physical therapists with at least 5 years' experience used an observational gait form created from the NYU, Temple, and Rancho forms to evaluate the gaits of 15 disabled children with knee-ankle-foot orthoses (KAFOs).[31] The reliability of the Rancho Los Amigos observational gait analysis technique has not been published. Gronley and Perry[6] reported that differences among raters were resolved through discussion and consensus.

Validity

The other aspect of gait analysis that must be considered is *validity*. *Validity* refers to the degree that a measurement reflects what it is supposed to measure. If a test instrument purports to measure functional ambulation ability, one would expect the test to predict the patient's performance on functional ambulation skills. If the test does not predict a patient's functional ambulation skills, the test may not be considered valid. An instrument such as an electrogoniometer can be tested for validity by comparing angle measurements with computer generated angles. Unfortunately, many of the methods used for observational gait analysis have not been tested for reliability and validity.

The reader should attempt to determine if the reliability and validity of an instrument or method of analysis has been determined by either looking in the literature or by contacting other investigators who are using the particular method or instrument. If an instrument or

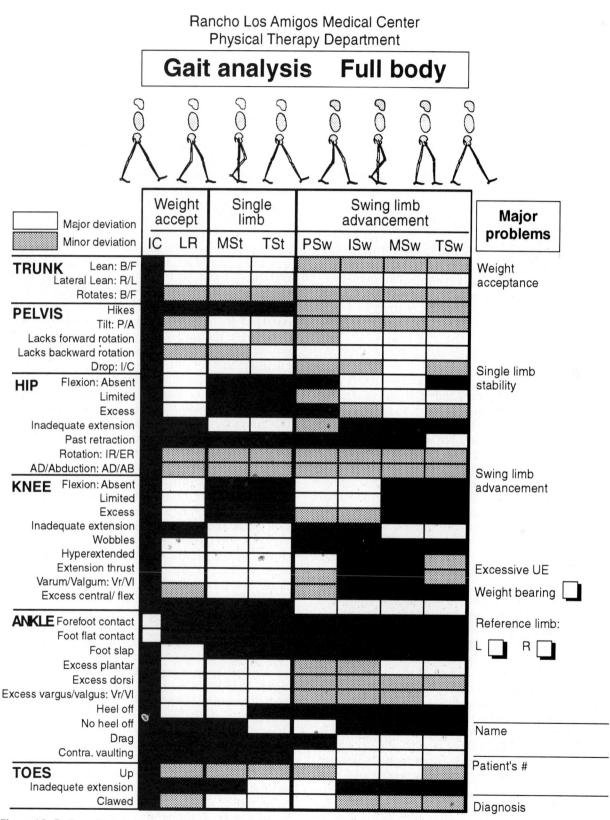

Figure 10–3. Form for full body observational gait analysis. (From Los Amigos Research and Education Institute of Rancho Los Amigos Medical Center,[23] p 55, with permission.)

method has not been tested, therapists may wish to perform their own tests for reliability and validity.

Advantages and Disadvantages

The advantages of observational gait analyses are that they require little or no instrumentation, are inexpensive to use, and can yield general descriptions of gait variables. The disadvantages are that the technique, being dependent on both the therapist's training and observational skills, is subjective and has only moderate reliability.

When using any type of observational gait analysis, therapists should seriously consider either cinematography or videography. A visual record is especially important when using the Rancho format because of the time involved in assessing a large number of variables at six different body parts. Most patients cannot walk continuously for the length of time required to complete a detailed full-body observational analysis. Videotape records of a patient's initial assessment and reassessment can be used to provide evidence of progress and as a means of determining the reliability of the assessment instrument.

Although the use of videotape may increase the reliability of observational gait analysis, unless therapists are knowledgeable about normal gait parameters and variables and are adequately trained in observation, reliability will probably remain in the low to moderate range. Eastlack[20] found only low to moderate inter-rater reliability among 54 practicing physical therapists who rated ten gait variables while observing the videotaped gait of three patients. These therapists reported that they were comfortable performing observational gait analyses. However, more than half of the therapists (32) were unfamiliar with any of the following three commonly used observational gait analysis formats: (1) New York University's Child Prosthetic-Orthotic Studies Observational Analysis Form, (2) Temple University's The Visual Examination of Pathologic Gait, and (3) Rancho Los Amigos' Observational Gait Analysis Handbook. The greatest number (13) of the 22 therapists who were familiar with one of the three observational gait analysis methods indicated exposure to the Rancho Los Amigos format.[20] The lack of agreement among raters that was found in this study as well as the lack of knowledge of normal gait parameters and terminology have serious implications for patient treatments that are based on the results of observational gait analyses.

Observational gait analysis is a useful tool for determining the quality of a patient's gait and for identifying common deviations, but it should be used in conjunction with quantitative measures. Videotape or film can provide a permanent record of the patient's gait. Also videography or cinematography may be used to assess joint range of motion at the hip, knee, and ankle by taking goniometric measurements directly from the screen. Stuberg[17] found no significant differences between goniometric measurements taken from videotaped gait and measurements taken from film for 10 children with

cerebral palsy and 9 normal children. Examples of the process involved in an observational gait analysis will be presented in the following section.

Kinematic Gait Analysis and Assessment of Variables

The first step in observational gait analysis is the identification and accurate description of the patient's gait pattern and any deviations. The second step involves a determination of the causes. To identify and to describe a patient's gait, the therapist must have an accurate mental picture of normal gait postures and normal displacements of the body segments in each portion of the two phases of gait and in each plane of analysis (saggital and frontal), and a good knowledge of gait terminology. To determine the causes of a patient's gait pattern and specific deviations, the therapist must understand the normal roles and functions of muscles in gait and the normal forces involved.[32] A patient's deviations from normal occur because of an inability to perform the tasks of walking in a normal fashion. For example, a patient with paralysis of the dorsiflexors (which causes a foot drop) cannot use the dorsiflexors to attain the normal neutral position of the ankle necessary to complete the task of clearing the floor during the swing phase. Therefore, the patient must find some other method of clearing the floor. The patient could compensate for the inability to dorsiflex the ankle by some method such as increasing the amount of hip and knee flexion above the normal amount; by **circumduction** of the entire limb (Fig. 10–4) or by *hiking* the hip (Fig. 10–5). The type of compensation that a particular individual selects depends on the specific disability. Increased hip and knee flexion may be used if the patient has an isolated problem in the ankle and adequate muscle strength and range of motion in the extremity. Circumduction or hip hiking may be used if the patient has a stiff knee or an extensor thrust, either of which might prevent use of increased knee flexion to raise the plantarflexed foot above the floor. The therapist needs to be aware that patients may use a variety of methods to compensate for joint or muscle deficits.

Tables 10–2 to 10–7 provide a review of the normal sagittal plane joint displacements, moments of force, and muscle activity and function, as well as the results of isolated muscle weaknesses and possible compensations. Tables 10–8 to 10–14 present a few of the common deviations observed in a sagittal plane analysis, along with probable causes for the deviations. Tables 10–15 and 10–16 provide sample gait analysis recording forms. If the reader decides to use the gait analysis recording forms presented in this text, reliability tests should be conducted because these forms are presented only as guides and have not been evaluated.

In Tables 10–2 to 10–7, the phase of gait, normal joint displacements, moments of force, and muscle activity are presented in the first four columns, and the effects of muscle weakness and possible compensations are presented in the last two columns. (The reader should be

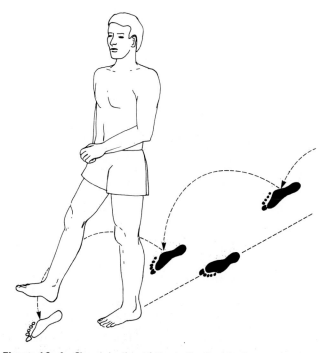

Figure 10–4. Circumduction of the patient's right lower extremity is used as a mechanism for advancing the swing leg. The patient uses a combination of external rotation and abduction to move the limb away from the body. This combination of motions is followed by adduction and internal rotation to bring the leg back toward the body. Circumduction may be used as a method of advancing the limb in the absence of hip flexors or in the case of a stiff knee.

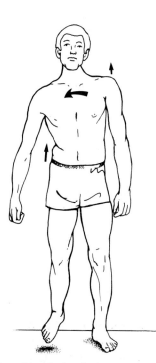

Figure 10–5. The subject in the diagram is using a contraction of the quadratus lumborum to hike his right hip. Hip hiking elevates the extremity so that the foot can clear the floor during the swing phase.

aware that only the effects of isolated muscle weaknesses and associated compensations are presented.) The intent of the tables is to identify factors of normal gait that must be considered when observing gait and to give an example of how to proceed with an analysis of the causes of an atypical gait pattern or particular deviation.

Tables 10–8 to 10–14 present some of the common gait deviations, as well as possible causes and analyses. Notice that the sample recording form presented in Table 10–16 has the same format as Tables 10–8 to 10–14 so that the clinician can use the sample analyses presented in the tables as guides.

Observational Gait Analysis Procedure

Following are directions for performing an observational gait analysis:

1. Select the area in which the patient will walk, and measure the distance that you want the patient to cover.
2. Position yourself to allow an unobstructed view of the patient. For filming, the camera should be positioned to view the patient's lower extremities and feet as well as the head and trunk from both the sagittal and frontal perspectives.
3. Select the joint or segment to be assessed first (e.g., ankle and foot), and mentally review the normal displacement patterns and muscle functions.

Table 10–7 HIP: SWING PHASE, SAGITTAL PLANE ANALYSIS

Portion of Phase	Normal Motion	Normal Moment	Normal Muscle Activity	Result of Weakness	Possible Compensation
Acceleration to midswing	20–30° flexion	None	Hip flexor activity to initiate swing illiopsoas, rectus, femoris, gracilis, sartorius, tensor fascia lata.	Diminished hip flexion causing an inability to initiate the normal forward movement of the extremity and to raise the foot off the floor.	Circumduction and/or hip hiking may be used to bring the leg forward and to raise the foot high enough to clear the floor.
Midswing to deceleration	30° flexion to neutral	None	Hamstrings.	A lack of control of the swinging leg. Inability to place limb in position for heel strike.	

Table 10–8 COMMON DEVIATIONS, ANKLE AND FOOT: STANCE PHASE, SAGITTAL PLANE ANALYSIS

Portion of Phase	Deviation	Description	Possible Causes	Analysis
Initial contact	Foot slap	At heel strike, forefoot slaps the ground.	Flaccid or weak dorsiflexors or reciprocal inhibition of dorsiflexors; atrophy of dorsiflexors.	Look for low muscle tone at ankle. Look for steppage gait (excessive hip and knee flexion) in swing phase.
	Toes first	Toes contact ground instead of heel. The tiptoe posture may be maintained throughout the phase, or the heel may contact the ground.	Leg length discrepancy; contracted heel cord; plantarflexion contraction; spasticity of plantarflexors; flaccidity of dorsiflexors; painful heel.	Compare leg lengths and look for hip and/or knee flexion contractures. Analyze muscle tone and timing of activity in plantarflexors. Check for pain in heel.
	Foot flat	Entire foot contacts the ground at heel strike.	Excessive fixed dorsiflexion; flaccid or weak dorsiflexors; neonatal/proprioceptive walking.	Check range of motion at ankle. Check for hyperextension at the knee and persistence of immature gait pattern.
Midstance	Excessive positional plantarflexion	Tibia does not advance to neutral from 10° plantarflexion.	No eccentric contraction of plantarflexors; could be due to flaccidity/weakness in plantarflexors; surgical overrelease, rupture, or contracture of Achilles tendon.	Check for spastic or weak quadriceps; hyperextension at the knee; hip hyperextension; backward- or forward-leaning trunk. Check for weakness in plantarflexors or rupture of Achilles tendon.
	Heel lift in midstance	Heel does not contact ground in midstance.	Spasticity of plantarflexors.	Check for spasticity in plantarflexors, quadriceps, hip flexors, and adductors.
	Excessive positional dorsiflexion	Tibia advances too rapidly over the foot, creating a greater than normal amount of dorsiflexion.	Inability of plantarflexors to control tibial advance. Knee flexion or hip flexion contractures.	Look at ankle muscles, knee and hip flexors, range of motion, and position of trunk.
	Toe clawing	Toes flex and "grab" floor.	Could be due to a plantar grasp reflex that is only partially integrated; could be due to positive supporting reflex; spastic toe flexors.	Check plantar grasp reflex, positive supporting reflexes, and range of motion of toes.
Push-off (heel off to toe off)	No roll off	Insufficient transfer of weight from lateral heel to medial forefoot.	Mechanical fixation of ankle and foot. Flaccidity or inhibition of plantarflexors, inverters, and toe flexors. Rigidity/cocontraction of plantarflexors and dorsiflexors. Pain in forefoot.	Check range of motion at ankle and foot. Check muscle function and tone at ankle. Look at dissociation between posterior foot and forefoot.

Table 10–9 COMMON DEVIATIONS, ANKLE AND FOOT: SWING PHASE, SAGITTAL PLANE ANALYSIS

Portion of Phase	Deviation	Description	Possible Causes	Analysis
Swing	Toe drag	Insufficient dorsiflexion (and toe extension) so that forefoot and toes do not clear floor.	Flaccidity or weakness of dorsiflexors and toe extensors. Spasticity of plantarflexors. Inadequate knee or hip flexion.	Check for ankle, hip, and knee range of motion. Check for strength and muscle tone at hip, knee, and ankle.
	Varus	The foot is excessively inverted.	Spasticity of the invertors. Flaccidity or weakness of dorsiflexors and evertors. Extensor pattern.	Check for muscle tone of invertors and plantarflexors. Check strength of dorsiflexors and evertors. Check for extensor pattern of the lower extremity.

**Table 10–10 COMMON DEVIATIONS, KNEE: STANCE PHASE,
SAGITTAL PLANE ANALYSIS**

Portion of Phase	Deviation	Description	Possible Causes	Analysis
Initial contact (heel strike)	Excessive knee flexion	Knee flexes or "buckles" rather than extends as foot contacts ground.	Painful knee; spasticity of knee flexors or weak or flaccid quadriceps. Short leg on contralateral side.	Check for pain at knee; tone of knee flexors; strength of knee extensors; leg lengths; anterior pelvic tilt.
Foot flat	Knee hyperextension (genu recurvatum); see Fig. 10–6	A greater than normal extension at the knee.	Flaccid/weak quadriceps and soleus compensated for by pull of gluteus maximus. Spasticity of quadriceps. Accommodation to a fixed ankle plantarflexion deformity.	Check for strength and muscle tone of knee and ankle flexors, and range of motion at ankle.
Midstance	Knee hyperextension (genu recurvatum)	During single limb support, tibia remains in back of ankle mortice as body weight moves over foot. Ankle is plantarflexed.	Same as above.	Same as above.
Push-off (heel off to toe off)	Excessive knee flexion	Knee flexes to more than 40° during push-off.	Center of gravity is unusually far forward of pelvis. Could be due to rigid trunk, knee/hip flexion contractures; flexion-withdrawal reflex; dominance of flexion synergy in middle recovery from CVA.	Look at trunk posture, knee and hip range of motion, and flexor synergy.
	Limited knee flexion	The normal amount of knee flexion (40°) does not occur.	Spastic/overactive quadriceps and/or plantarflexors.	Look at tone in hip, knee, and ankle muscles.

CVA = cardiovascular accident.

4. Select either a sagittal plane observation (view from the side) or a frontal plane observation (view from the front or back).
5. Observe the selected segment during the initial part of the stance phase and make a decision about the position of the segment. Note any deviations from the normal pattern.
6. Observe either the same segment during the next part of the stance phase or another segment at the initial part of the stance phase. Progress through the same process as in step five.
7. Repeat the process described in step six, until you have completed an assessment of all segments in the sagittal and frontal planes. Remember to concentrate on one segment at a time in one part of the gait cycle. Do not jump from one segment to another, or from one phase to another.

8. Always perform observations on both sides (right and left). Although only one side may appear to be involved, the other side of the body may be affected.

Observational Gait Analysis in Neuromuscular Disorders

The gait patterns of individuals with neuromuscular deficits are influenced primarily by abnormalities in muscle tone and synergistic organization, influences of nonintegrated early reflexes, diminished influence of righting and equilibrium reactions, diminished dissociation among body parts, and diminished coordination. If proximal stability (co-contraction of the postural muscles of the trunk) is threatened by atypically low or high

**Table 10–11 COMMON DEVIATIONS, KNEE: SWING PHASE, SAGITTAL PLANE
ANALYSIS**

Portion of Phase	Deviation	Description	Possible Causes	Analysis
Acceleration to midswing	Excessive knee flexion	Knee flexes more than 65°	Diminished preswing knee flexion, flexor-withdrawal reflex, dysmetria.	Look at muscle tone in hip, knee, and ankle. Test for reflexes and dysmetria.
	Limited knee flexion	Knee does not flex to 65°	Pain in knee, diminished range of knee motion, extensor spasticity. Circumduction at the hip.	Assess for pain in knee and knee range of motion. Test muscle tone at knee and hip.

Table 10–12 COMMON DEVIATIONS, HIP: STANCE PHASE, SAGITTAL PLANE ANALYSIS

Portion of Phase	Deviation	Description	Possible Causes	Analysis
Heel strike to foot flat	Excessive flexion	Flexion exceeding 30°.	Hip and/or knee flexion contractures. Knee flexion caused by weak soleus and quadriceps. Hypertonicity of hip flexors.	Check hip and knee range of motion and strength of soleus and quadriceps. Check tone of hip flexors.
Heel strike to foot flat	Limited hip flexion	Hip flexion does not attain 30°.	Weakness of hip flexors. Limited range of hip flexion. Gluteus maximus weakness.	Check strength of hip flexors and extensors. Analyze range of hip motion.
Foot flat to midstance	Limited hip extension	The hip does not attain a neutral position.	Hip flexion contracture, spasticity in hip flexors.	Check hip range of motion and tone of hip muscles.
	Internal rotation	An internally rotated position of the extremity.	Spasticity of internal rotators. Weakness of external rotators. Excessive forward rotation of opposite pelvis.	Check tone of internal rotators and strength of external rotators. Measure range of motion of both hip joints.
	External rotation	An externally rotated position of the extremity.	Excessive backward rotation of opposite pelvis.	Assess range of motion at both hip joints.
	Abduction	An abducted position of the extremity.	Contracture of the gluteus medius. Trunk lateral lean over the ipsilateral hip.	Check for abduction pattern.
	Adduction	An adducted position of the lower extremity.	Spasticity of hip flexors and adductors such as seen in spastic diplegia. Pelvic drop to contralateral side.	Assess tone of hip flexors and adductors. Test muscle strength of hip abductors.

muscle tone, or muscle tone that fluctuates, controlled mobility is lost. In gait, a loss of control over the sequential timing of muscular activity may result in asymmetrical step and stride lengths. In addition, deviations from normal posture and motion may occur, such as forward or backward trunk leaning (Fig. 10–6), excessive flexion or extension at the hip and knee in the stance phase, and diminished dorsiflexion or excessive plantarflexion.

In the presence of multiple muscle involvement or neurologic deficits that affect balance, coordination, and muscle tone, the deviations observed and the analysis of these deviations will be more complex than indicated in the tables. Examples of gait patterns observed in association with spasticity and with hypotonus follow.

An individual with hypertonic diplegic cerebral palsy may have a posteriorly tilted pelvis, forward flexion of the upper trunk, protracted scapulae, and somewhat excessive neck extension. Excessive hip flexion, adduction and internal rotation may be observed during stance and may be accompanied by either excessive knee flexion or hyperextension. If excessive knee flexion occurs during stance, dorsiflexion at the ankle may be exaggerated during late stance and/or preswing in order to advance the tibia over the ankle and to clear the toes and forefoot from the ground after push-off (heel off to toe off).

In other individuals, hyperextension at the knee occurs in stance and may be accompanied by plantarflexion and inversion at the ankle and foot (Fig. 10–7). Electromyographic recordings may show prolonged activity in the quadriceps and in the gastrocnemius-soleus muscle groups. The hamstrings, and the gluteal

Table 10–13 COMMON DEVIATIONS, HIP: SWING PHASE, SAGITTAL PLANE ANALYSIS

Portion of Phase	Deviation	Description	Possible Causes	Analysis
Swing	Circumduction	A lateral circular movement of the entire lower extremity consisting of abduction, external rotation, adduction, and internal rotation.	A compensation for weak hip flexors or a compensation for the inability to shorten the leg so that it can clear the floor.	Check strength of hip flexors, knee flexors, and ankle dorsiflexors. Check range of motion in hip flexion, knee flexion, and ankle dorsiflexion. Check for extensor pattern.
	Hip hiking	Shortening of the swing leg by action of the quadratus lumborum.	A compensation for lack of knee flexion and/or ankle dorsiflexion. Also may be a compensation for extensor spasticity of swing leg.	Check strength and range of motion at knee, hip, and ankle. Also check muscle tone at knee and ankle.
	Excessive hip flexion	Flexion greater than 20–30°.	Attempt to shorten extremity in presence of foot drop. Flexor pattern.	Check strength and range of motion at ankle and foot. Check for flexor pattern.

Table 10–14 COMMON DEVIATIONS, TRUNK: STANCE, SAGITTAL PLANE ANALYSIS

Portion of Phase	Deviation	Description	Possible Causes	Analysis
Stance	Lateral trunk lean	A lean of the trunk over the stance extremity (gluteus medius gait/Trendelenberg gait). See Figure 10–7.	A weak or paralyzed gluteus medius on the stance side cannot prevent a drop of the pelvis on the swing side, so a trunk lean over the stance leg helps compensate for the weak muscle. A lateral trunk lean over the affected hip also may be used to reduce force on the hip if a patient has a painful hip.	Check strength of gluteus medius and assess for pain in the hip.
	Backward trunk lean	A backward leaning of the trunk, resulting in hyperextension at the hip (gluteus maximus gait).	Weakness or paralysis of the gluteus maximus on the stance leg. Anteriorly rotated pelvis.	Check for strength of hip extensors. Check pelvic position.
	Forward trunk lean	A forward leaning of the trunk, resulting in hip flexion.	Compensation for quadriceps weakness. The forward lean eliminates the flexion moment at the knee. Hip and knee flexion contractures.	Check for strength of quadriceps.
		A forward flexion of the upper trunk.	Posteriorly rotated pelvis.	Check pelvic position.

Table 10–15 GAIT ANALYSIS RECORDING FORM

Fixed Postures Observed During Gait

Patient's Name		Age	Sex
Head	Tilt	To the right _____	To the left _____
		Forward _____	Backward _____
Trunk	Lean	To the right _____	To the left _____
		Forward _____	Backward _____
Pelvis	Tilt	To the right _____	To the left _____
		Anterior _____	Posterior _____
Hip	Flexion	On the right _____	On the left _____
		Bilateral _____	
	Extension	On the right _____	
		Bilateral _____	
	Abduction	On the right _____	On the left _____
		Bilateral _____	
	Adduction	On the right _____	On the left _____
		Bilateral _____	
	External rotation	On the right _____	
		Bilateral _____	
	Internal rotation	On the right _____	On the left _____
		Bilateral _____	
Knee	Flexion	On the right _____	On the left _____
		Bilateral _____	
	Extension	On the right _____	On the left _____
		Bilateral _____	
	Hyperextension	On the right _____	On the left _____
		Bilateral _____	
	Valgum	On the right _____	On the left _____
		Bilateral _____	
	Varum	On the right _____	On the left _____
		Bilateral _____	
Ankle/foot	Dorsiflexion	On the right _____	On the left _____
		Bilateral _____	
	Plantarflexion	On the right _____	On the left _____
		Bilateral _____	
	Varus	On the right _____	On the left _____
		Bilateral _____	
	Valgus	On the right _____	On the left _____
		Bilateral _____	
	Pes planus	On the right _____	On the left _____
		Bilateral _____	
	Pes cavus	On the right _____	On the left _____
		Bilateral _____	

Table 10–16 RECORDING FORM FOR OBSERVATIONAL GAIT ANALYSIS

Patient's name _____ Age _____ Sex _____ Height _____ Weight _____
Diagnosis _____
Footware _____ Assistive devices _____
Date _____ Therapist _____
DIRECTIONS: Place a check in the space opposite the deviation if the deviation is observed.

Body Segment	Deviation	HS		FF		MST		HO		TO		ACC		MSW		DEC		Possible Cause	Analysis
		R	L	R	L	R	L	R	L	R	L	R	L	R	L	R	L		
Ankle and foot	None																		
Observations	Foot flat																		
In the sagittal plane	Foot slap																		
	Heel off																		
	No heel off																		
	Excessive plantarflexion																		
	Excessive dorsiflexion																		
	Toe drag																		
	Toe clawing																		
	Contralateral vaulting																		
Observations in the frontal plane	Varus																		
	Valgus																		
Knee	None																		
Observations in the sagittal plane	Excessive flexion																		
	Limited flexion																		
	No flexion																		
	Hyperextension																		
	Genu recurvatum																		
	Diminshed extension																		
Observations in the frontal plane	Varum																		
	Valgum																		
Hip	None																		
Observations in the sagittal plane	Excessive flexion																		
	Limited flexion																		
	No flexion																		
	Diminished extension																		
Observations in the frontal plane	Abduction																		

Stance columns: HS, FF, MST, HO, TO. *Swing* columns: ACC, MSW, DEC.

Table 10–16 RECORDING FORM FOR OBSERVATIONAL GAIT ANALYSIS *(continued)*

| Body Segment | Deviation | Stance | | | | Swing | | | | Possible Cause | Analysis |
		HS	FF	MST	HO	TO	ACC	MSW	DEC		
	Adduction										
	External rotation										
	Internal rotation										
	Circumduction										
	Hiking										
Pelvis	None										
Observations in sagittal plane	Anterior tilt										
	Posterior tilt										
	Increased backward rotation										
	Increased forward rotation										
	Limited backward rotation										
	Limited forward rotation										
	Drops on contralateral side										
Trunk	None										
Observations in frontal plane	Backward rotation										
	Lateral lean										
	Forward rotation										
	Backward lean										
	Forward lean										

ACC = acceleration; DEC = deceleration; FF = foot flat; HO = heel off; HS = heel strike; MST = midstance; MSW = midswing; TO = toe off.

and dorsiflexor muscle groups may be reciprocally inhibited.

In each of the previous cases, there is insufficient dissociation between the pelvic and shoulder girdles, as evidenced by markedly decreased longitudinal trunk rotation. Weight shift is accomplished by lateral flexion, and slight extension of the weight-bearing side of the body is accomplished by lateral extension. The ground reaction force application lines are excessively displaced from the centers of rotation at the hips and knees (Fig. 10–8).

In individuals with low muscle tone in the trunk, proximal stability (tonic extension and co-contraction of axial muscles) is diminished. The pelvis may be anteriorly tilted so that the upper trunk is slightly extended.

The scapulae may be retracted and the head may be forward. The hip may be flexed during stance, and the knee may be hyperextended, with plantarflexion at the ankle. The foot may be pronated, with the majority of the body weight being borne on the medial border. Frequently these individuals show diminished longitudinal trunk rotation and sluggish equilibrium reactions in the trunk. They tend to rely on protective extension reactions of the limbs to maintain balance. The staggering reactions of the lower extremities may be pronounced. Stride length and step length may be uneven. Gait may be wide-based and unsteady. Although the gait patterns in neurologic gait may be complex and an analysis of the causes may be difficult, a detailed observational gait analysis can provide valuable data.

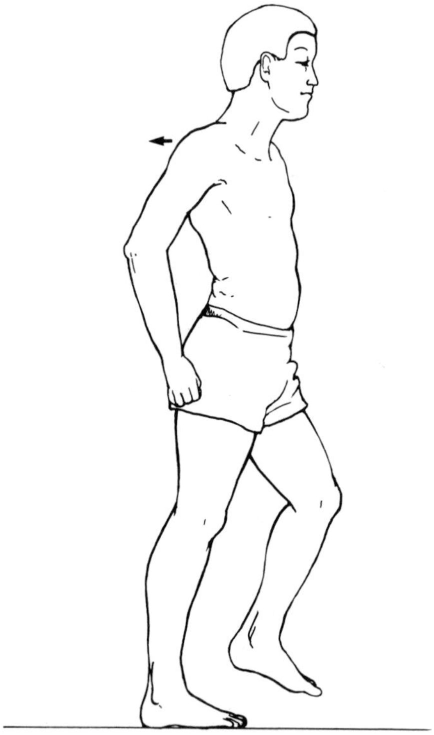

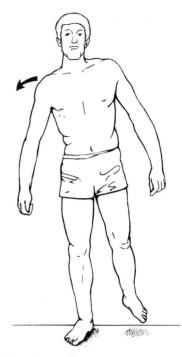

Figure 10–8. The patient is leaning his trunk over the right hip in an attempt to compensate for a weak gluteus medius on the right. This type of gait is often called a gluteus medius gait.

Generally, in order to analyze gait patterns in persons who have sustained neurologic damage, the following preliminary questions need to be asked:

1. How does the position of the head influence muscle tone in the trunk and the limbs?
2. How does weight bearing influence muscle tone and synergistic activity in the upper and lower extremities?
3. What is the position of the pelvis, trunk, and shoulder?
4. Are balance reactions impaired?

KINEMATIC QUANTITATIVE GAIT ANALYSIS

Kinematic **quantitative gait analyses** are used to obtain information on time and distance gait variables as well as motion patterns. The data obtained through these analyses are quantifiable and therefore provide the therapist with baseline data that can be used both to plan treatment programs and to assess progress toward goals or goal attainment. The fact that the data are quantifiable is important because third party payers are demanding that therapists use measurable parameters when they are assessing patient function, setting goals, and documenting the effects of a treatment program. However, data derived from qualitative observations may be necessary to classify degrees of motor impairment and to check the validity of the quantitative variables measured. Therefore both qualitative and quantitative gait analyses should be performed to provide a comprehensive picture of an individual's gait.

Figure 10–6. The subject leans or lurches his trunk posteriorly to eliminate the flexion moment at the hip. This type of deviation during gait is often referred to as a gluteus maximus gait because the trunk lean backward is used as a compensation in patients with a weak gluteus maximus.

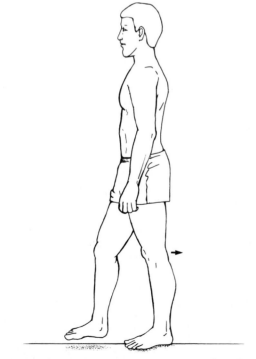

Figure 10–7. The patient's knee is thrust into a hyperextended position during single limb support. The tibia remains in back of the ankle mortise as the body weight moves over the foot.

Distance and Time Variables

The variables measured in a quantitative gait analysis are listed and described in Table 10–17. Because distance and time variables are affected by a number of factors such as age, sex, height,[33-38] weight, level of physical activity,[39-41] level of maturation,[42] and type of foot gear, attempts have been made to take these factors into account. Ratios such as stride length divided by functional lower extremity length are used to normalize for differences in patient's leg lengths. Step length divided by the subject's height is used in an attempt to normalize differences among patients' heights. Other ratios are used to assess symmetry; for example, right swing time divided by left swing time, or swing time divided by stance time. Sutherland et al.[42] list the ratio of pelvic span to ankle spread as one of the determinants of mature gait in children.

In a situation in which a patient cannot ambulate independently (either with or without assistive devices),

Table 10–17 GAIT VARIABLES: QUANTITATIVE GAIT ANALYSIS

Variable	Description
Speed	A scalar quantity that has magnitude but not direction.
Free speed	A person's normal walking speed.
Slow speed	A speed slower than a person's normal speed.
Fast speed	A rate faster than normal.
Cadence	The number of steps taken by a patient per unit of time. Cadence may be measured in centimeters as the number of steps per second $$\text{Cadence} = \frac{\text{number of steps}}{\text{time}}$$ A simple method of measuring cadence is by counting the number of steps taken by the patient in a given amount of time. The only equipment necessary is a stopwatch, paper, and pencil.
Velocity	A measure of a body's motion in a given direction.
Linear velocity	The rate at which a body moves in a straight line.
Angular velocity	The rate of motion in rotation of a body segment around an axis.
Walking velocity	The rate of linear forward motion of the body. This is measured in either centimeters per second or meters per minute. To obtain a person's walking velocity, divide the distance traversed by the time required to complete the distance. $$\text{Walking velocity} = \frac{\text{distance}}{\text{time}}$$ Walking velocity may be affected by age, level of maturation, height, sex, type of footwear, and weight. Also, velocity may affect cadence, step, stride length, and foot angle as well as other gait variables.
Acceleration	The rate of change of velocity with respect to time. Body acceleration has been defined by Smidt and Mommens[2] as the rate of change of velocity of a point posterior to the sacrum. Acceleration is usually measured in meters per second per second (m/s^2).
Angular acceleration	The rate of change of the angular velocity of a body with respect to time. Angular acceleration is usually measured in radians per second per second (radians/s^2).
Stride time	The amount of time that elapses during one stride: that is, from one foot contact (heel strike if possible) until the next contact of the same foot (heel strike). Both stride times should be measured. Measurement is usually in seconds.
Step time	The amount of time that elapses between consecutive right and left foot contacts (heel strikes). Both right and left step times should be measured. Measurement is in seconds.
Stride length	The linear distance between two successive points of contact of the same foot. It is measured in centimeters or meters. The average stride length for normal adult men is 1.46 m. The average stride length for adult women is 1.28 m.
Swing time	The amount of time during the gait cycle that one foot is off the ground. Swing time should be measured separately for right and left extremities. Measurement is in seconds.
Double support time	The amount of time spent in the gait cycle when both lower extremities are in contact with the supporting surface. Measured in seconds.
Cycle time (stride time)	The amount of time required to complete a gait cycle. Measured in seconds.
Step length	The linear distance between two successive points of contact of the right and left lower extremities. Usually a measurement is taken from the point of heel contact at heel strike of one extremity to the point of heel contact of the opposite extremity. If a patient does not have a heel strike on one or both sides, the measurement can be taken from the heads of the first metatarsals. Measured in centimeters or meters.
Width of walking base (step width)	The width of the walking base (base of support) is the linear distance between one foot and the opposite foot. Measured in centimeters or meters.[7]
Foot angle (degree of toe out or toe in)	The angle of foot placement with respect to the line of progression. Measured in degrees.[7]
Bilateral stance time	The length of time up to 30 seconds that a person can stand upright in the parallel bars bearing weight on both lower extremities.
Uninvolved stance time	The length of time up to 30 seconds that an individual can stand in the parallel bars while bearing weight on the uninvolved lower extremity (involved extremity is raised off the supporting surface).
Involved stance time	The length of time up to 30 seconds that an individual can stand in the parallel bars on the involved lower extremity (uninvolved lower extremity is raised off the supporting surface).
Dynamic weight transfer rate	The rate at which an individual standing in the parallel bars can transfer weight from one extremity to another. Measured in seconds from the first lift-off to the last lift-off.
Parallel bar ambulation	Length of time required for an individual to walk the length of the parallel bars as rapidly as possible. Two trials are averaged to obtain this measurement. Measurement is in seconds.

subordinate locomotor variables may be assessed using the Functional Ambulation Profile (FAB).[43] In this profile the following five variables are evaluated by using a stopwatch to determine the amount of time required either to accomplish a task or to maintain a position:

1. Bilateral stance time.
2. Uninvolved stance time.
3. Involved stance time.
4. Dynamic weight transfer rate.
5. Parallel bar ambulation.

The National Institute of Handicapped Research funded a project to develop a uniform data system for medical rehabilitation. An instrument called the Functional Independence Measure (FIM) Locomotion Scale is one of the first parts of the system to be published. The FIM scale of functional levels for locomotion includes the following four levels of primary categories:

4.0—Complete independence
3.0—Modified independence
2.0—Modified dependence
1.0—Complete dependence

Three subcategories are included under 3.0—modified independence (supervision, minimal assistance, and moderate assistance).[44]

Methods Used for Measuring Variables

The physical therapy literature contains a number of studies describing techniques for measuring time and distance gait variables,[10–15] as well as studies investigating the uses and reliability of different methods of measurement.[45] Two types of variables (time and distance) are frequently included in a kinematic quantitative gait analysis and are necessary for the interpretation of kinetic and electromyographic (EMG) data. The techniques and equipment required for measurement of these variables range from simple to complex. The time requirements also vary, and the therapist must be familiar with different methods of assessing these variables in order to select the method most appropriate to each situation. Prior to selecting a method of measurement, the therapist should understand the variable in question and how that variable is related to the patient's gait.

DISTANCE VARIABLES

Variables such as degree of foot angle, width of base of support, step length, and stride length can be assessed simply and inexpensively in the clinic by recording the patient's footprints during gait. Many different methods for recording footprints have been described in the literature: for example, the absorbent paper method;[9] commercially available carbon paper system;[5] painting,[8] inking,[45] or chalking of the feet; and felt-tipped markers attached to the shoes.[14] Other more expensive methods for assessing these variables include imaging systems, gait mats, foot switches, cinematography, videotaping, and time-lapse photography.

Walkways for recording footprints may be created either by the application of various materials to the floor or by using an uncarpeted floor or hallway. A few of the materials used to create walkways include absorbent paper,[9] commercially produced carbon paper, and aluminum.[15] In the absorbent paper method, three layers of material are placed over a carpeted floor to form a walkway. The first layer is brown paper, the second layer is moistened paper or terry cloth, and the third layer is absorbent paper such as a paper tablecloth. When the patient walks along the walkway, the pressure of the body weight causes the water from the second layer to be absorbed by the dry top layer. The therapist outlines the footprints with a felt-tipped pen immediately following the walking trial. The resulting record permits measurement of step and stride lengths, stride width, and foot angle. The commercially made carbon paper and aluminum paper provide a similar type of footprint record.

Other simple methods of recording footprints require the application of paints, ink, or chalk to the bottom of the patient's foot or shoe or the attachment of inked pads or other markers. For example, the bottoms of a patient's feet may be covered with tempera paint[8] prior to walking along a paper-covered walkway, or a felt-tipped marker may be taped to the back of a patient's shoe.[14] In both methods, measurements of step length, stride length, step width, and foot angle may be obtained.

Another way of obtaining step length and stride length data is by placing a grid pattern on the floor.[11] A strip of masking tape about 30 cm wide and 10 meters long is laid down in a straight line. The tape is marked off in 3-cm increments for its entire length, and the segments are numbered consecutively so that the patient's heel strikes can be identified. The therapist calls out the heel strike locations from the numbers on the grid pattern and the numbers are recorded by a tape recorder. Cadence and velocity as well as step and stride lengths may be obtained from this method.

TEMPORAL VARIABLES

In all of the above listed methods of assessing stride and step lengths, temporal variables such as cadence, velocity, and stride times may be calculated. The distance that the patient walks, and the time taken to complete the distance from the first heel strike on the measured distance to the last heel strike, can be assessed. Cadence can be determined by dividing the number of steps taken during the walking trial by the elapsed time between the first and last heel strikes. Velocity can be calculated by taking the total distance between the first and last heel strikes and dividing it by the elapsed time for the distance. In order to obtain a normal walking speed, the patient should be allowed to take a few steps prior to the beginning of any measurements.

Todd et al.,[46] who tested 84 normal children (41 girls and 43 boys) ages 13 months to 12 years, and analyzed data from over 200 other children ages 11 months to 16 years, have developed a two-dimensional gait graph that provides a visual record of a child's walking performance. The gait graph is similar in appearance to graphs used for height and weight; however the gait graph shows norms for gait dimensions of cadence, and stride length adjusted by height (Fig. 10–9).

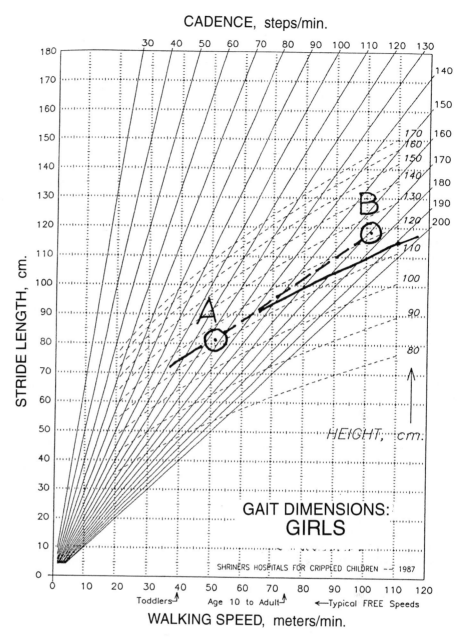

Figure 10–9. The *solid line* on the gait graph represents normal parameters for height. The *dashed line* represents data plotted for a normal 6-year-old girl whose height was 114 cm. A similar chart is available for boys. (From Todd, et al.[46] p 201, with permission.)

INSTRUMENTED SYSTEMS

Joint displacement can be measured with goniometry. Two types of goniometers are available: a polarized light goniometer, called a polgon,[47] and an electrogoniometer, which is called an elgon.[13] The polgon is composed of sensors containing photoelectric cells with polarized gratings in front of the cells. These sensors are placed on the body segments being assessed. An optical projector illuminates the subject as he or she walks, and the sensors emit electrical signals as the sensors move relative to each other. The electrogoniometer is a potentiometer that converts movement into an electrical signal that is proportional to the degree of movement.

Data obtained from both the polgon and the elgon can be displayed either as angle/angle diagrams[47] or on a strip chart recorder. Angle-angle diagrams are produced by plotting the angular sagittal plane displacements of adjacent joints against each other. Strip chart recorders provide a record of the displacement patterns of gait. According to Perry, electrogoniometers, which cost approximately $3000.00, are the "most convenient and least expensive" means of measuring knee and ankle motion during walking.[22]

Instrumented methods of assessing temporal and distance measures include gait mats and foot switches. **Gait mats** have a series of switches embedded in them that can be scanned by a microprocessor to yield temporal data. The pressure switches under the patient's foot close and release as the subject walks along the mat. The opening and closing of the switches provide information on step length, step time, and average walking speed. The accuracy of the gait mat produced by Eq., Philadelphia, PA, has been reported as ± 1.5 cm for location and ± 20 msec for timing.[41] **Foot switches** of various types can be purchased and placed either inside or outside a patient's shoes. The foot switches consist of transducers and a semiconductor and are used to signal such events as heel strike. One type of foot switch device that has been used to assess both temporal and loading variables is the Krusen Limb Load Monitor.[10] Originally this device was designed to monitor the amount of weight a patient placed on an affected extremity. When the weight exceeded a predetermined magnitude, the instrument emitted a warning signal. Recently, the device has been modified and used to obtain data on temporal and loading gait variables. This device consists of a pressure-sensitive force plate that can be worn within a patient's shoe. It can be connected to a strip chart recorder to yield a permanent record of temporal and distance gait variables.[10]

Imaging systems such as the **light-emitting diode (LED)** system for assessing sagittal-plane motion and temporal and distance variables have been used at the University of Iowa. The system consists of LEDs, foot switches, and a 35-mm single-frame color-slide photographic technique.[12]

Electromyography is used to analyze the timing and peak activity of muscle activity during gait.[48-50] It is usually used in combination with other instrumentation to identify the particular portion of the gait cycle in which the muscle activity occurs.[51] Automated motion analysis systems that feed data directly into a computer can provide information on time and distance measures as well as joint range of motion. Detailed information on automated systems may be obtained by contacting one of the following: Northern Digital Incorporated, Selspot Systems Limited, Ariel Performance Analysis System Incorporated, Motion Analysis Corporation, Oxford Metrics, Vicon, Whatsmart, Optitrack, and Peak Performance Technologies. These systems have various advantages and disadvantages and are extremely expensive.[21]

RELIABILITY AND VALIDITY

Reliability of the absorbent paper and felt-tipped pen methods has not been reported. In a study of 61 neurologically impaired patients, Holden et al.[45] used ink footprints on a paper-covered walkway. High inter-rater and test-retest reliability was reported using the inked footprint method to determine the following variables: velocity, cadence, step length, and stride length. These investigators also found a strong linear relationship between the variables tested and a Functional Ambulation Classification test protocol that was developed at Massachusetts General Hospital.[45] The grid pattern method of gait analysis is reported to be a feasible clinical research tool as well as a good method for quantitative analysis of temporal and distance measures.[11] Soderberg and Gabel[12] report that the LED system has high inter-rater and intra-rater reliability for temporal and distance measures. Test-retest reliability coefficients for Nelson's functional ambulation profile also are reported to be high.[43] Stuberg[17] found no significant differences in measurements of stride length and walking velocity using cinematography and measurements using moleskin foot markers on a paper walkway and a stopwatch. Subjects in the study were 10 children with cerebral palsy and 9 normal children.

ADVANTAGES AND DISADVANTAGES

The primary advantages of assessing temporal and distance measures are that these measures can be assessed simply and inexpensively in the clinic and that they yield an objective and reliable baseline on which to formulate goals and to assess progress or lack of progress toward goals. For example, gait patterns displayed by patients with arthritis often are characterized by a reduced rate and range of knee motion compared with those of normal subjects, and they have a slower than normal gait velocity. Brinkmann and Perry[52] found that following joint replacement the rate and range of knee motion and gait velocity increased above preoperative levels but did not reach normal levels. Usually increases in measures such as cadence and velocity indicate improvement in a patient's gait. However, comparisons with normal standards are appropriate only if the goal of treatment is to restore a normal gait pattern (e.g., for a patient recovering from a meniscectomy). Comparisons with normal standards may not be appropriate for a patient who has had a cerebral vascular accident. The appropriate norms for a hemiplegic patient's gait may be either a hemiplegic population of similar age, sex, and involvement, or the patient's pretreatment gait.

Therapists need to be extremely cautious when selecting a norm or standard by which to measure patient progress. Significant age, sex, weight, and activity-level-related differences have been found in temporal and distance measures.[33-42,53,54] Hinman et al.[36] in a study involving 289 men and women aged 19 to 102 years found that the oldest group (63 years and older) had a significantly slower self-selected walking speed and smaller step length in comparison with the younger group. Age was a significant determinant of walking speed after age 62 but height was a significant determinant prior to age 62.[36] In a study of 15 healthy elderly, ages 62 to 78 (10 men, 5 women) the authors found that step length was significantly shorter and the double-support stance period significantly increased in this sample, compared with a data base of young adults.[38] Leiper and Craik,[41] in a study designed to compare the effects of physical activity level on gait variables in 81 women (64.0–94.5 years), found that the normal walking speeds of all the women tested were slower than values reported for younger women.

Therefore, one way to determine if the standard is appropriate is to compare the characteristics of the population used to establish the norm with the patient's characteristics. For example, is the age of the patient in the same range as the sample population? Is the patient's sex the same as that of the sample population? Holden and colleagues[45] have recommended that gait performance goals for patients with neurologic problems should not only be based upon norms derived from patients with the same diagnosis but should also consider etiologic factors, type of ambulation aid, and functional category.

Temporal and distance measures may be critical factors in determinations of a patient's independence in ambulation. For example, a patient may need to attain a certain velocity of gait in order to cross a local street within the limit of the time allotted by a crossing light.

A patient may need to walk a certain distance in order to shop in the local supermarket. Changes in velocity may affect step length, cadence, and other gait variables. Therapists need to survey the patient's community to determine the distances and time requirements for accessing stores and public buildings prior to making a judgment about a patient's functional ambulation status.[55] Robinett found that target goals on a sample of gait assessment forms were low compared to distance and velocity requirements found in a community survey. For example, the fastest walking velocity found on the forms was 18.2 m/min whereas the minimum safe street crossing velocity that the investigators found in a survey of rural and urban communities was 30 m/min with a range of 30 to 82.5 m/min.[56]

Few disadvantages exist regarding quantitative gait analysis except for the expense involved in instrumentation and the fact that a certain amount of uncertainty exists about how to normalize for leg length, height, age, sex, weight, level of maturation, and disability.[57]

Table 10–18 GAIT ANALYSIS RECORDING FORM: TEMPORAL AND DISTANCE MEASURES

Patient's name _____   Age _____   Sex _____

Height _____   Weight _____

Diagnosis: _____

Ambulatory aids: Yes _____   No _____

Type: Crutch(es) _____   Cane(s):R _____   Walker: _____

L _____

Other: _____

Date										
Therapist's initials										
Distance walked (distance from first to last heel strike)										
Elapsed time (time from first to last heel strike)										
Walking velocity (distance walked divided by elapsed time)										
Left stride length (distance between two consecutive left heel strikes)*										
Right stride length (distance between two consecutive right heel strikes)*										
Left step length (distance between a right heel strike and the next consecutive left heel strike)*										
Right step length (distance between a left heel strike and the next consecutive right heel strike)*										
Step length difference (difference between right and left step lengths)										
Cadence (total number of steps taken divided by the elapsed time)										
Width of walking base (perpendicular distance between right and left heel strike)*										
Left foot angle (angle formed between a line bisecting the left foot and the line of progression)*										
Right foot angle (angle formed between a line bisecting the right foot and the line of progression)*										
Right stride length to right lower extremity length (right stride length divided by right lower extremity length)										
Left stride length to left lower extremity length (left stride length divided by left lower extremity length)										

*The therapist may wish to obtain averages for stride and step lengths, width of walking base, and foot angles.

Temporal and distance assessments should be used as an integral part of or in conjunction with both observational and kinetic assessments to provide a complete picture of gait. A sample recording form for time and distance variables is presented in Table 10–18.

KINETIC GAIT ANALYSIS

Kinetic gait analyses are directed toward assessment and analysis of the forces involved in gait, that is, ground reaction forces, joint torques, center of pressure, and intrinsic foot pressure. Although kinetic gait analyses have been used primarily for research purposes, they may be used clinically in the future. A complete review of kinetic gait analysis methods is beyond the scope of this chapter, but a few of the major variables are presented and described in Table 10–19.

The instrumentation required to assess kinetic variables is complex and expensive. Force plates are usually used as part of or in combination with a motion analysis system. Systems cost in the range of $50,000 to $150,000.[58] If a therapist wishes to use an instrumented system, he or she should contact one of the many facilities that are using these systems, such as the Mayo Clinic in Minnesota, Newington Childrens Hospital in Newington, Connecticut, or Rancho Los Amigos Medical Center in California.

Energy Cost During Ambulation

Generally, conditions that affect either the motor control of gait and posture and/or conditions that affect joint and muscle structure and function will increase the energy cost of gait.[59-63] The use of assistive devices and speed of gait also affect energy expenditure.[64] Therefore energy expenditure is an important consideration in any gait analysis. The two parameters usually measured to determine energy expenditure are oxygen cost and oxygen rate.[22] The oxygen cost or energy expenditure per unit of distance walked (milliliters per kilogram of body weight per meter: ml/kg/m) defines the physiologic work involved in the task.[59] The oxygen rate or energy expenditure per unit of time (millimeters per kilogram of body weight per minute: ml/kg/min) defines the power requirement.[59,60] The preferred method of measuring oxygen uptake is called open spirometry. The Douglas bag technique in which expired air is collected during walking and subsequently analyzed has been the classic method of analysis.[22,62] Modifications of this technique, including metabolic carts, are in use today.[22,64]

The relative energy cost of gait can be estimated by monitoring heart rate during ambulation. Heart rate is directly and linearly related to oxygen consumption during exercise[59] and can provide information as to how the patient's cardiovascular system is adapting to the stress of ambulation. Relative energy consumption has been found to correlate strongly with heart rate, and absolute level of energy consumption has been found to correlate strongly with heart rate and maximum walking speed. Simple measures of heart rate and maximum ambulatory velocity allowed accurate prediction ($r = 0.89$) of energy consumption in 35 children with myelomeningocele.[60]

The most accurate way to assess heart rate is to use a telemetry system that produces beat-by-beat information as well as electrocardiographic activity. The intensive care or cardiac care units in many hospitals have telemetry systems that could be utilized for monitoring a patient during gait. If the therapist does not have access to telemetry monitoring, heart-rate responses to ambulation can be assessed by palpation of the radial or carotid arteries. A pulse measurement should be taken at rest, just prior to ambulation, immediately after ambulation, and at various intervals after ambulation (1 minute, 3 minutes, and 5 minutes). The palpation method allows the therapist to determine how hard the heart had to work to accomplish a given gait activity and how long the heart takes to return to resting level.

Table 10–19 GAIT VARIABLES: KINETIC GAIT ANALYSIS

Variable	Description
Ground (floor) reaction forces	Vertical, anterior-posterior, and medial-lateral forces created as a result of foot contact with the supporting surface. These forces are equal in magnitude and opposite in direction to the force applied by the foot to the ground. Ground reaction forces are measured with force platforms in newtons (N) or pound force.
Torque (moment of force)	The turning or rotational effect produced by the application of a force. The greater the perpendicular distance of the point of application of a force from an axis of rotation, the greater the turning effect, or torque, produced. Torque is calculated by multiplying the force by the perpendicular distance from the point of application of the force and the axis of rotation. Torque = force × perpendicular distance or moment arm Measurement is in newton meters.
Joint forces	The forces between articular surfaces that are created by muscle, gravity, and inertial forces. These forces are measured in newtons.
Work	Work is the product of the force applied and the distance the object moves in the direction of the force. Work = force × distance

SUMMARY

An overview of some methods for kinematic and kinetic gait analyses have been presented in this chapter. Many of the common variables that can be assessed in gait analyses have been described. Observational gait analysis and time and distance variables have been emphasized because they appear to be the most commonly used in the clinical setting. Clinicians and educators are urged to adopt a systematic method for performing gait analyses and to test the reliability and validity of the method so that gait analyses become more reliable and valid assessment tools than they are at the present time. Readers are encouraged to consult references such as Perry's Gait Analysis[22] and the Rancho Los Amigos Handbook[23] for more detailed information.

The ability to perform a meaningful gait analysis that accurately describes a patient's gait will provide important quantifiable information necessary for adequate treatment planning. This chapter introduced the kinematic gait variables that the physical therapist can assess inexpensively and easily in a clinical setting and provided a model for performing an observational gait analysis.

For most purposes, kinematic analysis and heart-rate monitoring will yield the information necessary for routine clinical use. The most comprehensive analysis includes kinematic, kinetic, and physiologic variables.

QUESTIONS FOR REVIEW

1. Describe each of the three different types of gait analyses (kinematic qualitative, kinematic quantitative, and kinetic).

   a. List the variables assessed in each of the three types of gait analysis.

   b. Select one variable from each type of analysis and describe a method of assessment.

2. Explain the difference between intra-tester and inter-tester reliability and give examples of how a test might be set up for each form of reliability.

3. Compare the advantages of a kinematic qualitative gait analysis with the advantages of a kinematic quantitative analysis.

4. Using the model presented in Tables 10–1 to 10–11, perform an observational gait analysis that includes both identification of observed deviations and an analysis to determine the causes of the deviations.

5. What factors must be considered when assessing time and distance variables?

6. What distances must people in your community walk in order to get into stores, banks, and post offices?

7. How quickly must one walk to cross a street before the light changes?

REFERENCES

1. Ogg, LH: Gait analysis for lower-extremity child amputees. Phys Ther 45:940, 1965.
2. Smidt, GL and Mommens, MA: System of reporting and comparing influence of ambulatory aids on gait. Phys Ther 60:551, 1980.
3. Zachazewski, JE, Eberle, ED, and Jefferies, ME: Effects of tone-inhibiting casts and orthoses on gait. Phys Ther 62:453, 1982.
4. McCulloch, M, Brunt, D, and Van der Linden, D: The effect of foot orthotics and gait velocity on lower limb kinematics and temporal events. J Orthop Sports Phys Ther 17:2, 1993.
5. Craik, RL and Otis, CA: Gait assessment in the clinic. In Rothstein, JM (ed): Measurement in Physical Therapy. Churchill Livingstone, London, 1985.
6. Gronley, JK and Perry, J: Gait analysis techniques. Rancho Los Amigos Hospital Gait Laboratory. Phys Ther 64:1831, 1984.
7. Laughman, RK, et al: Objective clinical evaluation of function. Phys Ther 64:35, 1984.
8. Shores, M: Footprint analysis in gait documentation: an instructional sheet format. Phys Ther 60:1163, 1980.
9. Clarkson, BH: Absorbent paper method for recording foot placement during gait. Phys Ther 63:345, 1983.
10. Wolf, SL and Binder-Macleod, SA: Use of the krusen limb load monitor to quantify temporal and loading measurements of gait. Phys Ther 62:976, 1982.
11. Robinson, JL and Smidt, GL: Quantitative gait evaluation in the clinic. Phys Ther 61:351, 1981.
12. Soderberg, GL and Gabel, RH: A light emitting diode system for the analysis of gait: A method and selected clinical examples. Phys Ther 58:426, 1978.
13. Little, H: Gait analyses for physiotherapy departments: A review of current methods. Physiotherapy 67:334, 1981.
14. Cerny, K: A clinical method of quantitative gait analysis. Phys Ther 63:1125, 1983.
15. Chodera, JD: Analysis of gait from footprints. Physiotherapy 60:179, 1974.
16. Cerny, K: Pathomechanics of stance: clinical concepts for analysis. Phys Ther 64:1851, 1984.
17. Stuberg, WA, et al: Comparison of a clinical gait analysis method using videography and temporal-distance measures with 16-mm cinematography. Phys Ther 68:1221, 1988.
18. Gunderson, LA, et al: Bilateral analysis of the knee and ankle during gait: an examination of the relationship between lateral dominance and symmetry. Phys Ther 69:640, 1989.
19. Stanerson, B, Norton, BJ, and Sahrmann, SA: Reliability of a system to measure gait variables in children with cerebral palsy (abstract). Phys Ther (suppl) 17:1990.
20. Eastlack, ME, et al: Interrator reliability of videotaped observational gait-analysis assessments. Phys Ther 71:465, 1991.
21. Rose, SSA, Ounpuu, S, and Deluca, PA: Strategies for the assessment of pediatric gait in the clinical setting. Phys Ther 71:961, 1991.
22. Perry, J: Gait Analysis: Normal and Pathological Function. Slack, Thorofare, NJ, 1992.
23. Pathokinesiology Service and Physical Therapy Department: Observational Gait Analysis Handbook, Professional Staff Association of Rancho Los Amigos Medical Center. Downey, CA, 1989.
24. Rodgers, MM and Cavanagh, PR: Glossary of biomechanical terms, concepts, and units. Phys Ther 64:82, 1984.
25. Brunnstrom, S: Movement Therapy in Adult Hemiplegia. Harper & Row, New York, 1970.
26. Lower Limb Prosthetics. New York University Medical Center Post-Graduate Medical School Prosthetics and Orthotics, New York, 1981.
27. Bampton, S: A Guide to the Visual Examination of Pathological Gait. Temple University Rehabilitation Research and Training Center 8, Moss Rehabilitation Hospital, Philadelphia, 1979.
28. Daniels, L and Worthingham, C: Muscle Testing: Techniques of Manual Examination, ed 5. WB Saunders, Philadelphia, 1986.
29. O'Sullivan, S, Cullen, K, and Schmitz, T: Physical Rehabilitation:

Evaluation and Treatment Procedures, FA Davis, Philadelphia, 1981.
30. Goodkin, R and Diller, L: Reliability among physical therapists in diagnosis and treatment of gait deviations in hemiplegics. Percept Mot Skills 37:727, 1973.
31. Krebs, D, Edelstein, J, and Fishman, S: Observational gait analysis reliability in disabled children (abstract). Phys Ther 64:741, 1984.
32. Norkin, C and Levangie, P: Joint Structure and Function: A Comprehensive Analysis, ed 2. FA Davis, Philadelphia, 1992.
33. Finley, FR, Cody, K, and Finizie, R: Locomotive patterns in elderly women. Arch Phys Med Rehabil 50:140, 1969.
34. Murray, M, et al: Walking patterns in normal men. J Bone Joint Surg (Am) 46A:335, 1964.
35. Murray, M, Kory, R, and Sepic, S: Walking patterns of normal women. Arch Phys Med Rehabil 51:637, 1970.
36. Hinmann, JE, et al: Age-related changes in speed of walking. Med Sci Sports Exerc 20:161, 1988.
37. Blanke, DJ and Hageman, PA: Comparison of gait of young men and elderly men. Phys Ther 69:144, 1989.
38. Winter, DA, et al: Biomechanical walking pattern changes in the fit and healthy elderly. Phys Ther 70:340, 1990.
39. Hills, AP and Parker, AW: Gait characteristics of obese children. Arch Phys Med Rehabil 72:403, 1991.
40. Spyropoulos, P et al: Biomechanical gait analysis in obese men. Arch Phys Med Rehabil 72:1065, 1991.
41. Leiper, CI and Craik, RL: Relationship between physical activity and temporal-distance characteristics of walking in elderly women. Phys Ther 71:791, 1991.
42. Sutherland, DH, et al: The development of mature gait. J Bone Joint Surg 61A:336, 1980.
43. Nelson, AJ: Functional ambulation profile. Phys Ther 54:1059, 1974.
44. Morton, T: Uniform data system for rehab begins: first tool measures dependence level. Progress Report, American Physical Therapy Association 15:14, October 1986.
45. Holden, MK, et al: Clinical gait assessment in the neurologically impaired, reliability and meaningfulness. Phys Ther 64:35, 1984.
46. Todd, FN, et al: Variations in the gait of normal children: a graph applicable to the documentation of abnormalities. J Bone Joint Surgery (Am) 71A:196, 1989.
47. Grieve, DW, Leggett, D, and Wetherstone, B: The analysis of normal stepping movements as a possible basis for locomotor assessment of the lower limbs. J Anat 127:515, 1978.
48. Lyons, K, et al: Timing and relative intensity of hip extensor and abductor muscle action during level and stair ambulation. Phys Ther 64:1597, 1983.
49. Waters, RL, et al: Electromyographic gait analysis before and after operative treatment for hemiplegic equinus and equinovarus deformity. J Bone Surg (Am) 64A:284, 1982.
50. Peat, M, et al: Electromyographic temporal analysis of gait: Hemiplegic locomotion. Arch Phys Med Rehabil 57:421, 1976.
51. Sutherland, DH, Cooper, L, and Daniel, D: The role of ankle plantar flexors in normal walking. J Bone Joint Surg (Am) 62A:355, 1980.
52. Brinkmann, JR and Perry, J: Rate and range of knee motion during ambulation in healthy and arthritic subjects. Phys Ther 65:7, 1985.
53. Hageman, PA and Blanke, DJ: Comparison of gait of young women and elderly women. Phys Ther 66:1382, 1986.
54. Holden, MK, Gill, JM, and Magliozzi, MR: Impaired patients. Phys Ther 66:1530, 1986.
55. Lerner-Frankiel, MB, et al: Functional community ambulation: What are your criteria? Clinical Management 6:12, 1986.
56. Robinett, CS and VonDran, MA: Functional ambulation velocity and distance requirements in rural and urban communities: a clinical report. Phys Ther 63:1371, 1988.
57. Inman, VT, Ralston, HJ, and Todd, F: Human Walking. Williams & Wilkins, Baltimore, 1981.
58. Yack, HJ: Techniques for clinical assessment of human movement. Phys Ther 64:17, 1984.
59. Astrand, PO and Rodahl, K: Textbook of Work Physiology. McGraw-Hill, New York, 1977, p 617.
60. Findley, TW and Agre, JC: Ambulation in the adolescent with spina bifida, II. Oxygen cost of mobility. Arch Phys Med Rehabil 69:855, 1988.
61. Waters, RL, et al: Comparable energy expenditure after arthrodesis of the hip and ankle. J Bone Joint Surg (Am) 70A:1032, 1988.
62. Gussoni, M, et al: Energy cost of walking with hip joint impairment. Phys Ther 70:295, 1990.
63. Olgiati, R, Burgunder, JM, and Mumenthaler, M: Increased energy cost of walking in multiple sclerosis: Effect of spasticity, ataxia and weakness. Arch Phys Med Rehabil 69:846, 1988.
64. Marsolais, MD and Edwards, BG: Energy costs of walking and standing with functional neuromuscular stimulation and long leg braces. Arch Phys Med Rehabil 69:243, 1988.

GLOSSARY

Acceleration: The rate of change of velocity with respect to time. Body acceleration has been defined by Smidt and Mommens[2] as the rate of change of velocity of a point posterior to the sacrum. Acceleration is usually measured in meters per second per second (m/s^2).

Accelerometer: A device used to measure the vertical, anterior-posterior, and medial-lateral accelerations of body segments.

Angle-angle diagrams: Diagrams in which angular displacements of adjacent joints in the sagittal plane are plotted against each other.

Angular acceleration: The rate of change of the angular velocity of a body segment with respect to time. Angular acceleration is usually measured in radians per second per second (radians/s^2).

Angular velocity: The rate of motion in rotation of a body segment around an axis.

Bilateral stance time: The length of time (up to 30 seconds) that a subject can stand upright in the parallel bars bearing weight on both lower extremities.

Cadence: Number of steps per unit of time; may be measured in centimeters as the number of steps per second (**cadence** = number of steps/time). A simple method of measuring cadence is by counting the number of steps taken by the patient in a given amount of time. The only equipment necessary is a stopwatch, paper, and pencil.

Circumduction: A circular motion of the swinging leg that includes the hip motions of abduction, external rotation, adduction, and internal rotation. This gait deviation may be used to compensate for inadequate hip or knee flexion and/or insufficient dorsiflexion.

Cycle time (stride time): The amount of time required to complete a gait cycle; measured in seconds.

Displacement: The change in position of the body as a whole (**linear, or translational, displacement**) or its segments (**rotational displacement**). **Linear,** or **translational, displacement** is measured in meters, whereas **rotational displacement** is measured in degrees.

Double support time: The period of the gait cycle when both lower extremities are in contact with the supporting surface (double support); measured in seconds.

Dynamic weight transfer rate: The speed at which an

individual standing in the parallel bars can transfer weight from one extremity to another; measured in seconds from the first lift off to the eighth lift off.

Foot angle: Degree of toe out or toe in; the angle of foot placement with respect to the line of progression; measured in degrees.

Free speed: Defined as an individual's normal walking speed.

Ground (floor) reaction forces: Vertical, anterior-posterior, and medial-lateral forces created as a result of foot contact with the supporting surface. These forces are equal in magnitude and opposite in direction to the force applied by the foot to the ground. Ground reaction forces are measured with force platforms in newtons (N) or pound force.

Involved stance time: The length of time (up to 30 seconds) that an individual can stand in the parallel bars on the involved lower extremity (uninvolved lower extremity is raised off the supporting surface).

Joint forces: The forces between articular surfaces that are created by muscle, gravity, and inertial forces; measured in newtons.

Kinematics: A description of the type, amount, and direction of motion; does not include the forces producing the motion.

Kinetics: The study of the forces that cause motion.

Light-emitting diode (LED): System for assessing sagittal-plane motion and temporal and distance variables. The system consists of LEDs, foot switches, and a 35-mm single-frame color-slide photographic technique.

Linear velocity: The rate at which a body moves in a straight line.

Parallel bar ambulation: Length of time required for an individual to walk the length of the parallel bars as rapidly as possible. Two trials are averaged to obtain this measurement; measured in seconds.

Qualitative gait analysis: The identification and description of gait patterns.

Quantitative gait analysis: The measurement in distance and time of gait variables.

Speed: A scalar quantity; it has magnitude but not direction. **Slow speed** is a speed slower than an individual's normal speed; **fast speed** is a rate faster than normal.

Stance phase: The portion of gait in which one extremity is in contact with the ground. The phase is divided into the following segments: heel strike, foot flat, midstance, heel off, and toe off. The Rancho Los Amigos divisions are initial contact, loading response, midstance, terminal stance, and preswing.

Step: Consists of two dimensions; a distance (**step length**) and time (**step time**); two steps comprise a stride.

Step length: The linear distance between two successive points of contact of the right and left lower extremities. Usually a measurement is taken from the point of heel contact at heel strike on one extremity to the point of heel contact of the opposite extremity. If a patient does not have a heel strike on one or both sides, the measurement can be taken from the heads of the first metatarsals; measured in centimeters or

meters. Both right and left step lengths should be obtained. When the right foot is leading, it is a right step. When the left foot is leading, it is a left step.

Step time: The number of seconds between consecutive right and left foot contacts; both right and left step times should be measured.

Stride: Consists of two dimensions; a distance (**stride length**) and a time (**stride time**).

Stride length: The linear distance between two consecutive foot contacts of the same lower extremity. Usually a measurement is taken from the point of one heel contact at heel strike and the next heel contact of the same extremity. However, stride length may be measured by using other events such as two consecutive toe offs; measured in centimeters or meters. Both right and left stride lengths should be measured.

Stride time: The number of seconds that elapses during one stride (from one foot contact until the next contact of the same foot). Stride time is synonymous with **cycle time.** Both right and left stride times should be measured.

Swing phase: The phase of gait during which the reference limb is not in contact with the supporting surface.

Swing time: The number of seconds during the gait cycle that one foot is off the ground. Swing time should be measured separately for right and left extremities.

Torque (moment of force): The turning of rotational effect produced by the application of a force. The greater the perpendicular distance of the point of application of a force from an axis of rotation, the greater the turning effect or torque produced. Torque is calculated by multiplying the force by the perpendicular distance from the point of application of the force and the axis of rotation.

Torque = f × perpendicular distance
or moment arm

Measurement is in newton meters.

Uninvolved stance time: The length of time (up to 30 seconds) that an individual can stand in the parallel bars while bearing weight on the uninvolved lower extremity (involved extremity is raised off the supporting surface).

Velocity: A measure of a body's motion in a given direction.

Walking velocity: The rate of linear forward motion of the body; measured in either centimeters per second or meters per minute.

Walking velocity = distance/time

Walking velocity may be affected by age, level of maturation, height, sex, type of footwear, and weight. Also, velocity may affect cadence, step, stride length, and foot angle, as well as other gait variables.

Width of walking base (step width, base of support): The linear distance between one foot and the opposite foot; measured in centimeters or meters.

Work: The application of a force through a distance; accomplished whenever a force moves an object through a distance.

Work = force × distance

CHAPTER 11

Functional Assessment

Andrew A. Guccione

OBJECTIVES

1. Discuss the concepts of health status, impairment, functional limitation, disability, and handicap.
2. Define functional activity, and discuss the purposes and components of a functional assessment.
3. Select activities and roles appropriate to an individual's particular characteristics and condition to guide a functional assessment.
4. Compare and contrast characteristics of various formal tests of function, including physical function tests and multidimensional functional assessment instruments.
5. Identify factors to be considered in the selection of formal instruments for testing function.
6. Compare and contrast various scoring methods used in functional assessment.
7. Discuss the issues of reliability and validity as they relate to functional assessment.

The ultimate objective of any rehabilitation program is to return the individual to a life-style that is as close to the premorbid level of function as possible or, alternatively, to actualize the current potential for function and maintain it. For an otherwise healthy patient with a fractured arm, this may be a reasonably simple process: improving range of motion and strength will reestablish skills in dressing and feeding. For the patient with a stroke, the task is much more complex because the problems are much more extensive, complicated, and interwoven. The two cases, however, are broadly similar. In both instances, the therapist begins with a description of the patient's problem in functional terms and a systematic assessment of each body system, plans treatments to reduce or to eliminate the problems identified, and measures the progress of those treatments towards the desired functional outcome.

Every individual values the ability to live independently. Functional activities encompass all those tasks, activities, and roles that identify a person as an independent adult or as a child progressing toward adult independence. These activities require the integration of both cognitive and affective abilities with motor skills. Functional activity is a patient-referenced concept and is dependent on what the individual identifies as essential to support physical and psychologic well-being, as well as to create a personal sense of meaningful living. Function is not totally individualistic, however, for there are certain categories of activities that are common to everyone. Eating, sleeping, elimination, and hygiene are major components of survival and protection common to all animals. Particular to humans are the evolutionary advancements of bipedal locomotion and complex hand activities that permit independence in the personal environment. Work and recreation are functional activities in a social context.

This chapter presents a conceptual framework for assessing functional status and introduces the reader to terminology used in the field. It presents an overview of the purposes of functional assessment and the range and rigor of formal test instruments currently available to clinicians and researchers. Considerations in test selection and principles of administration are also presented.

A CONCEPTUAL FRAMEWORK

Chronically ill and disabled persons represent a large segment of the population in this country. Approximately 35 million individuals suffer from physical or mental impairments that limit their capacity to perform some daily functional activity.[1] Traditionally, these individuals have been categorized or classified according to their medical diseases or conditions. Medical assessment procedures such as physical examination and laboratory tests are the primary tools to delineate the problems created by disease. Focus on a biomedical model, with emphasis on the characteristics of disease (etiology, pathology, manifestations), may result in the medical labeling of individuals: for example, referring to people as amputees, paraplegics, arthritics, or CVAs (cardiovascular accidents) rather than as individuals with these conditions. This model virtually ignores the equally important social, psychologic, and behavioral dimensions of the **illness** that accompanies the **disease.** Illness refers to the personal behaviors that emerge when the reality of having a disease is internalized and

193

experienced by an individual.[2] Factors related to illness often play a key role in determining the success or failure of rehabilitation efforts and may lie well beyond the nature of the medical condition that prompted a patient's referral to physical therapy. In helping the individual with a disease, physical therapists come to understand each person's illness as well.

A broad conceptual framework is necessary to fully understand the concept of health and its relationship to functional disability. Terms such as well-being, quality of life, and functional status are often used interchangeably to describe health status. The most global definition of **health** has been provided by the World Health Organization (WHO). This organization defined health as "a state of complete physical, mental, and social well-being, and not merely the absence of diseases and infirmity."[3] Although such global definitions are useful as philosophic statements, they lack the precision necessary for a clinician or researcher. Factors that are often used to define health in more measurable terms include (1) *physical signs,* (2) *symptoms,* and (3) *functional disability.*[4] Full consensus on the meaning of these terms, however, has not been reached. The WHO adopted an International Classification of Impairments, Disability, and Handicaps (ICIDH)[5] with the goal of promoting the use of consistent terminology and to provide a framework for discourse among health professionals. This classification system, however, has not been generally adopted by rehabilitation specialists.[6]

Nagi[7-9] has been particularly influential in developing a model that explicates health status and the relationship among the various terms used to describe health status (Fig. 11–1). The conceptual framework, developed by Nagi and used in this chapter for understanding health status, begins with the pathology or disease process that mobilizes the body's defenses and response mechanisms. Physical signs and symptoms set the individual's clinical presentation apart as abnormal and indicate the body's attempts to cope with this attack on its normal functioning. **Physical signs** are the directly observable or measurable changes in an individual's organs or systems. **Symptoms** are the more subjective reactions to the changes experienced by the individual. Thus the individual demonstrates an elevated blood pressure (a physical sign) and reports feeling dizzy (a symptom). Many medical conditions are, in fact, not labels for a single pathologic entity, but clusters of signs and symptoms that designate a syndrome. Two common examples of "diseases" that are really syndromes are congestive heart failure and AIDS. Although the definition of disease presented previously implies an active condition,

many of the physical signs and symptoms that are important to physical therapy evaluation and treatment are not associated with active or ongoing medical conditions. For example, a resolved myocardial infarction is a fixed lesion with great importance for physical therapists, but is not an active disease process in itself.

Impairments, as described within Nagi's model, evolve as the natural consequence of pathology or disease and are defined as any alteration or deviation from normal in anatomic, physiologic, or psychologic structures or functions.[7-9] The partial or complete loss of a limb or an organ, or any disturbance in body part, organ, or system function are examples of impairments. Physical therapists are primarily concerned with impairments of the musculoskeletal, neuromuscular, and cardiopulmonary systems—for example, loss of range of motion, strength or endurance. Impairments may be temporary or permanent, and represent an overt manifestation of the disease or pathologic state. Some impairments are themselves sequelae of other impairments. For example, the patient with a swollen and stiff joint may eventually develop muscle weakness in those muscles surrounding the joint. Therefore, impaired muscle strength would be the result of impaired joint mobility, rather than a specific disease or pathological process.[10,11]

A **functional limitation** is the inability of an individual to perform a task or activity in the way it is done by most people, usually as the result of an impairment.[7,8,9] Accurate judgment about the relationship between impairments and functional limitations is at the heart of all physical therapy evaluation and treatment.[12] Three main categories of function have been delineated: **physical function, psychological function,** and **social function.** *Physical function* refers to those sensorimotor skills necessary for the performance of usual daily activities. Getting out of bed, walking, climbing stairs, and bathing are examples of physical functions. Physical therapists are traditionally most involved with this category of functional assessment and treatment. Tasks concerned with daily self-care such as feeding, dressing, hygiene, and physical mobility are called **basic activities of daily living (BADL).** Advanced skills that are considered vital to an individual's independent living in the community are termed **instrumental activities of daily living (IADL).** These include a wide range of high-level skills such as managing personal affairs, cooking and shopping, home chores, and driving. *Psychological function* has two components: mental and affective. **Mental function** refers to the intellectual or cognitive abilities of an individual. Factors such as initiative, attention, concentration, memory, problem solving, or judgment are important components of normal mental function. **Affective function** refers to the affective skills and coping strategies needed to deal with the everyday "hassles," as well as the more traumatic and stressful events each person encounters over the course of a lifetime. Factors such as self-esteem, attitude toward body image, anxiety, depression, and the ability to cope with change are examples of affective functions. Finally, *social function* refers to an individual's performance of social roles and obligations. Categories of roles and activities that

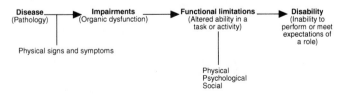

Figure 11–1. Schematic representation of Nagi's model of the process of disablement.

are relevant to assessing an individual's social function include social activity, including participation in recreational activities and clubs; social interaction, such as telephoning or visiting relatives or friends; and social roles created and sustained through interpersonal relationships specific to one's personal life and occupation.

Although deficits in behavioral or motor skills, or limitations in function, may typically exist in certain disease categories, the exact empirical relationship between a particular set of impairments and a specific functional disability is not yet known. The "cause-and-effect" relationship between an impairment and a functional limitation is most often demonstrated empirically in the clinic. For example, physical therapists may assume that the fact that a patient can not bathe independently is causally linked to the fact that the individual has lost upper extremity range of motion. The return of function following remediation of the impairment of joint mobility is then considered clinical evidence of a causal relationship between the impairment and the functional limitation. To be clinically meaningful, functional assessment must be linked to the other tests and measurements that are used by a physical therapist to assess a patient.

When an individual is limited in a number of functional activities and unable to engage in critical social roles (e.g., a worker), this person may be regarded as **disabled.**[7-9] Disability is characterized by a discordance between the actual performance of an individual in a particular role and the expectations of the community regarding what is "normal" for an adult. Thus, disability is a term that takes its meaning from the community in which the individual lives and the criteria for "normal" within that social group. Many factors can influence the connections among disease, impairment, and function, not the least of which will be the individual's personal response. Patients with the same disease and the same impairments may not always have the same functional limitations. Furthermore, although an individual may perform functional activities differently than is "normal," this person may successfully accomplish expected social roles and escape the label of being "disabled." Physical therapists most often think of "normal" adulthood in terms of independence in self-care activities, competence and autonomy in decision making, and productivity. In some cultural subgroups, social expectations may be quite different, particularly if the individual has certain impairments or functional limitations. Physical therapists should account for the effects of culture and social expectations in determining what is "normal" function for an individual, especially when the therapist and the patient do not share the same social backgrounds.

The term **handicap** describes the social disadvantage of an impairment, a functional limitation, or a disability.[13] A handicap reflects the cultural, social, economic, and environmental consequences of a disability. The negative value placed by others on an impairment, functional limitation, or disability makes a person handicapped. In some instances, even a person who is functioning independently may still be handicapped by the

social stigma of using an assistive device such as a wheelchair. Physical therapists can help change social attitudes and environmental restrictions like architectural barriers that stigmatize individuals as "handicapped."

ASSESSMENT OF FUNCTION

Purpose of Functional Assessment

Analysis of function focuses on the measurement and classification of **functional activities** and an individual's ability to successfully engage in them. In essence, functional assessment measures how a person does certain tasks or fulfills certain roles in the various dimensions of living, previously described. Functional assessment is accomplished via a test or battery of tests, the results of which can be used as

1. Baseline information for setting function-oriented treatment goals
2. Indicators of a patient's initial abilities and progression toward more complex functional levels
3. Criteria for decisions on admission and discharge from a rehabilitation or extended care facility, or to determine needs for community services
4. Guidelines for determining the safety of an individual in performing a particular task, and the risk of injury with continued performance
5. Evidence of the effectiveness of a specific treatment intervention (rehabilitative, surgical, or medical) on function.

General Considerations

Physical therapists possess a unique body of knowledge related to the identification, remediation, and prevention of movement dysfunction. Thus, they have traditionally been actively involved in the assessment of physical function by watching a patient perform the activity and grading its performance. More recently, physical therapists have begun to incorporate self-report data into functional assessments. Other members of the rehabilitation team, including the occupational therapist, nurse, rehabilitation counselor, and recreational therapist, are also typically involved in administering and interpreting functional assessments. Some formal instruments for functional assessment are designed to be completed collectively by the team. Other tests are compiled in separate sections by specific health professionals and housed together in the patient's chart. Where teams exist, physical therapists are typically responsible for the assessment of bed mobility, transfers, balance, and locomotion (wheelchair, ambulation, and negotiation of graded elevations). Occupational therapists are typically involved in the assessment of feeding, bathing, dressing, homemaking, and use of adaptive devices for upper extremity activities. Overlap among team members exists, however. For example, the assessment of toilet transfers may be done by the physical therapist, occupational therapist, or the nurse as a component of a general bowel and bladder program. In these instances, testing should be coordinated to reduce duplication and unnecessary patient stress. In noninstitutional settings or where there is no team, the physical therapist may be responsible for all items on a physical function test.

Types of Instruments

A **performance-based assessment** functional assessment may be administered by a therapist who observes the patient during the performance of an activity. Relevant data also may be collected by **self-assessment,** either directly from the patient or by a trained interviewer. Irrespective of the particular instrument used, there are several basic considerations to be kept in mind. The setting chosen must be conducive to the type of testing and free of distractions. If a performance-based evaluation is chosen, the setting should be as similar as possible to the actual environment in which the patient usually performs the tasks and activities assessed. Instructions should be precise and unambiguous. Assessments may be biased by fatigue. If a patient performs best in the morning, but tires by afternoon, an accurate assessment of functional ability must consider the variation in the patient's performance. Therapists should be aware of patients whose endurance fluctuates during the day, and interpret the data accordingly. Also, a patient should be told if the testing will take several sessions.

PERFORMANCE-BASED ASSESSMENTS

A *performance-based assessment* may be used initially to describe the patient's current level of function and ultimately as an indicator of the success of the rehabilitation program. This assessment should be administered in conjunction with the initial assessment of impairments (e.g., testing of sensation, range of motion, strength, motor control, and coordination). Retesting should occur at regular intervals to document progress, and at discharge.

During the administration of the test, each task is presented, and the patient is asked to perform: for example, "Push your wheelchair over to that red chair and stop." The patient is given no other instructions or assistance unless he or she is unable or unsure of how to perform, then only as much direction or assistance as is needed is given. Appropriate safety precautions should be taken during the session so that the patient does not attempt tasks that are potentially dangerous.

SELF-ASSESSMENTS

In contrast to performance-based measures, useful data on how a person functions may also be gathered by asking the patient directly, or through a trained interviewer. The critical issue in the ability of a *self-assessment* to capture function correctly and completely lies in providing clearly worded questions without language bias, concise directions on completing the questions, and a format that encourages accurate reporting of answers to all questions. Self-assessments should be designed so that questions are asked in a standard format and answers are recorded as specified by the predetermined choices. Long paper-and-pencil tests may be difficult for those with upper extremity disability.

Interviewers must be taught to administer a questionnaire and should practice until they have reached a high degree of agreement with expert assessors of the same cases. Periodic retraining may be necessary if interviewers do not have frequent practice administering the instrument. The interview should be scheduled with the patient in advance and conducted in an environment conducive to complete concentration. Interviews may be conducted by phone or in person, but the mode of administration should be kept consistent if comparisons of the data are to be made. Ad lib prompting by the interviewer or caregivers for answers is discouraged because these intrusions into the patient's *self*-assessment tend to bias results. If the patient has had help in filling out a form, or responding to questions, this should be noted. Similarly, if the data have been provided by a spouse, family member, or caregiver, this should be documented as well.

It is extremely important to distinguish between questions that indicate a person's habitual performance (e.g., "*Do* you cook your own meals?") and those that identify a person's perceived capacity to perform a task (e.g., "If you had to, *could* you cook your own meals?"). Understanding the differences between what a person actually does, would be willing to do, and what that person potentially could do, is an essential component of designing realistic, and achievable, functional goals of treatment. For example, even though a person might have the capacity to climb stairs, there may not be any willingness to do so.

The time-frame reference of self-assessment is also a relevant consideration. A therapist should decide in advance if the relevant "window" on a person's functional level is the past 24 hours, last week, last month, or the previous year. One can easily imagine how the same person might respond differently regarding the same functional activity depending on frame of reference. Instruments that assess only short-term objectives may not relate well to the long-term objectives of a rehabilitation program.

Instrument Parameters and Formats

Performance-based and self-assessment instruments grade performance on a number of different criteria, using a variety of formats. There is no one parameter or format that is perfect for every type of clinical encounter or research need. It is particularly important that documentation of a patient's progress not be blunted by "floor" or "ceiling" effects of various descriptors. For example, if a therapist wishes to measure changes in function among generally well elderly patients and the most advanced functional activity on a instrument measures "independent ambulation on level surfaces," there would be no room to demonstrate either progression or decline except around ambulation on level surfaces. Similarly, a severely debilitated patient might improve in transfers from needing the maximum assistance of two persons to maximum assistance of one. If the instrument only measures change from "maximum assistance" to "moderate assistance," this patient's real improvement will not be recorded.

DESCRIPTIVE PARAMETERS

Therapists should use descriptive terms that are well-defined and unambiguous. Meanings of descriptive terms should be clear to all others using the medical record. Table 11–1 provides a sample set of acceptable terms and definitions. Additional terms used to qualify function include **dependence, difficulty,** and **endurance.** Most often, the term *dependence* means human assistance and not reliance on devices and aids. However, the use of equipment during the performance of a functional task should be noted; for example, the patient is independent in ambulation with axillary crutches, or independent in dressing with adapted clothing and long-handled shoe-horn.

Difficulty is a hybrid term that suggests that an activity poses an extra burden for the patient, regardless of dependence level. It is unclear whether it is a measure of overall perceptual motor skill, coordination, efficiency, or a combination of measures. Difficulty can be measured in two ways. One approach assumes that difficulty is likely to be present and quantifies the degree of difficulty that the individual experiences while performing the activity, for example, "How much difficulty do you have while doing household chores? None, some, or a great deal?" The other approach quantifies the frequency that the difficulty is encountered, for example, "How often do you have difficulty putting on your shoes? Never, sometimes, very often, or always?"

Often it is helpful to qualify functional status by linking a person's performance to categorical impairments. *Endurance* refers to the energy consumption required to complete the functional task and the degree to which patients must exert themselves to engage in the activity. Simple measurements of endurance generally include heart rate, respiratory rate, and blood pressure, both at rest (baseline measurements) and during the most stressful elements of the functional task: for example, "heart rate increased to 120 per minute with independent ambulation on stairs: no significant increase in respiratory rate." In addition, the patient's perception of exertion and overt signs of fatigue, such as shortness of breath, also should be noted. These notations may assist the therapist in a quick determination of some obvious impairments that limit function.

Additional factors that are frequently used to describe functional performance include (1) pain, (2) variations in the time of day, (3) medication level, and (4) environmental influences.

Table 11–1 FUNCTIONAL ASSESSMENT AND IMPAIRMENT TERMINOLOGY

DEFINITIONS
1. **Independent:** patient is able consistently to perform skill safely with no one present.
2. **Supervision:** patient requires someone within arm's reach as a precaution; low probability of patient having a problem requiring assistance.
3. **Close guarding:** person assisting is positioned as if to assist, with hands raised but not touching patient; full attention on patient; fair probability of patient requiring assistance.
4. **Contact guarding:** therapist is positioned as with close guarding, with hands on patient but not giving any assistance; high probability of patient requiring assistance.
5. **Minimum assistance:** patient is able to complete majority of the activity without assistance.
6. **Moderate assistance:** patient is able to complete part of the activity without assistance.
7. **Maximum assistance:** patient is unable to assist in any part of the activity.

DESCRIPTIVE TERMINOLOGY
A. Bed mobility
  1. Independent—no cuing* is given
  2. Supervision
  3. Minimum assistance
  4. Moderate assistance } may require cues
  5. Maximum assistance
B. Transfers: ambulation
  1. Independent—no cuing is given
  2. Supervision
  3. Close guarding
  4. Contact guarding } may require cues
  5. Minimum assistance
  6. Moderate assistance
  7. Maximum assistance
C. Balance
  1. Normal: patient is able to maintain position with therapist maximally disturbing balance.
  2. Good: patient is able to maintain position with moderate disturbance from therapist.
  3. Fair: patient is able to maintain position for short periods of time unsupported.
  4. Poor: patient attempts to assist but requires assistance from other person to maintain position.
  5. No balance: patient is unable to assist in maintaining position.

*Types of cues: verbal, visual, or tactile. In some instances (e.g., a person with a memory deficit, short attention, learning disability, visual loss), a decrease in the number of cues may represent treatment progress, even though the level of dependence remains the same. Interim progress notes can denote these changes by citing frequencies (e.g., 2 out of 3 tries) or an arbitrarily defined rank order scale (e.g., always/occasionally/rarely).

QUANTITATIVE PARAMETERS

The timing of a series of functional activities is often used when a given speed of performance is required or an improvement in performance speed is expected. One of the most common examples of timed assessments is found in premedication and postmedication assessments of individuals with Parkinson's disease who are placed on levodopa therapy. Examples of activities that may be timed include (1) walking a set distance, (2) writing one's signature, (3) donning an article of clothing, and (4) crossing a street during the time of a "Walk" light. Scores of timed tests should not be taken as absolute, but rather as one dimension of performance. Although the ability to complete a particular activity in a specified period of time does provide important data on a patient's overall ability, it may not always be clear as to what is being measured. For example, the patient may get dressed quickly, within seconds, but do so with poorly coordinated movements and a haphazard outcome. When the task is slowed down, the movements become more coordinated, with a more satisfactory and functional end result, but the time taken to do the task increases. Time also can be used as a measure of endurance. It provides objective evidence of the ability of the cardiopulmonary system to support sustained activity. However, certain medical conditions that affect energy expenditure may require that the patient properly pace a functional activity in order to complete it successfully. Thus, time scores alone do not always yield the complete functional picture. When interpreted in light of other aspects of the patient's clinical presentation, they do provide an added dimension to the assessment.

CHECKLIST FORMAT

One of the simplest formats in functional assessment is a *checklist* with a description of various functional tasks on which the patient is simply scored as able to do/not able to do, independent/dependent, completed/incomplete, etc. The results are not particularly descriptive of exact nature of an individual's limitations and require further interpretation.

NUMERIC OR LETTER-GRADE FORMAT

A few tests use numeric or letter grades that are assigned to describe qualitatively the degree to which a person can perform the task. Most commonly, the scales are **ordinal** or **rank-order** scales (e.g., no difficulty, some difficulty, unable to do, or on a scale of 1 to 5 rate your ability to . . .). Scales may be graded in ascending or descending order. Letter grades are awarded in the same way. Standard manual muscle testing is an example of an ordinal scale that uses letter grades. The primary drawback in using such a system to score function is that these grades do not define categories that are separated by equal intervals. For example, it is not possible to tell whether the patient who went from maximal assistance to moderate assistance changed as much as a patient who also went one level between moderate assistance and minimal assistance.

SUMMARY OR ADDITIVE SCALE FORMAT

The **summary,** or **additive scale** grades a specific series of skills, awards points for part or full performance, and sums the subscores as a proportion of the total possible points, such as 60/100 or 6/24 and so forth. One common example, which is well-known to physical therapists is the Barthel Index (Table 11-2).[14] Some formal, standardized instruments for assessing function summarize detailed information about a complex area of function into an overall index score. Use of these instruments facilitates the interpretation of complex data and enables the clinician to perform cross-disease, cross-program, and cross-population comparisons of function. Caution must be exercised in considering only summated scores, however, because potentially important individual differences in functional ability can

Table 11-2 BARTHEL INDEX*

Date _____
Initial _____

FEEDING
10 = Independent. Able to apply any necessary device. Feeds in reasonable time.
 5 = Needs help (e.g., for cutting).   _____
BATHING
 5 = Independent   _____
PERSONAL TOILET
 5 = Independently washes face, combs hair, brushes teeth, shaves (manages plug if electric).   _____
DRESSING
10 = Independent. Ties shoes, fastens fasteners, applies braces.
 5 = Needs help, but does at least half of work in reasonable time.   _____
BOWELS
10 = No accidents. Able to use enema or suppository, if needed.
 5 = Occasional accidents or needs help with enema or suppository.   _____
BLADDER
10 = No accidents. Able to care for collecting device if used.
 5 = Occasional accidents or needs help with device.   _____
TOILET TRANSFERS
10 = Independent with toilet or bedpan. Handles clothes, wipes, flushes or cleans pan.
 5 = Needs help for balance, handling clothes or toilet paper.   _____
TRANSFERS—CHAIR AND BED
15 = Independent, including locking of wheelchair, lifting footrests.
10 = Minimum assistance or supervision.
 5 = Able to sit, but needs maximum assistance to transfer.   _____
AMBULATION
15 = Independent for 50 yards. May use assistive devices, except for rolling walker.
10 = With help, 50 yards.
 5 = Independent with wheelchair for 50 yards if unable to walk.   _____
STAIR CLIMBING
10 = Independent. May use assistive devices.
 5 = Needs help or supervision.   _____

                                                    Totals _____

*A score of zero (0) is given in any category in which the patient does not achieve the stated criterion. (From Mahoney and Barthel,[14] pp 62–65, with permission.)

be masked.[15] A patient who is limited in only a few of the many tasks covered on a functional assessment will most likely score well, despite what could be substantial limitations in function which are pertinent to the physical therapy treatment plan. Similarly, two patients with the same numeric score might be quite different in their functional deficits, having gained (or lost) their points on different activities.

VISUAL ANALOG SCALE FORMAT

Visual or **linear analog scales** attempt to represent measurement quantities in terms of a straight line

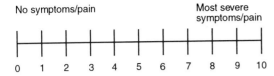

Figure 11–2. A visual analog scale for measuring pain or other symptoms. The patient is instructed to mark the line at the point that corresponds to the degree of pain or severity of symptoms that is experienced.

placed horizontally or vertically on paper (Fig. 11–2). The endpoints of the line are labeled with descriptive terms to anchor the extremes of the scale and to give reference to any point in the continuum between them. Some scales will also use descriptors between the endpoints to assist the individual in grading. Commonly the lines are 10 cm in length, but distances of 15 and 20 cm are also used. The patient is asked to bisect the line at a point representing his or her position on the scale. The score is then obtained by measuring from the zero mark to the mark bisecting the scale.

VISUAL RECORDING FORMAT

With ever-increasing technology, new tools are available to clinicians and researchers for recording changes in function. Although they are more costly than traditional methods, videotaping or filming can be a valuable adjunct to functional assessment. Visual recordings are appropriate methods for assessing and validating the effectiveness of new drugs or treatment approaches and are useful to patients in depicting the true extent of their disability. They are also useful in training staff to score tasks reliably by reaching agreement on observed performance.

Interpreting Test Results

Clearly, the single most important consideration in functional assessment is using the test results correctly to establish and to revise treatment goals and the treatment plan. The therapist should carefully delineate the contributing factors that result in the functional deficit. When diminished ability is evident, the therapist must attempt to ascertain the cause of the problem. Some important questions to ask include:

1. What are the normal movements necessary to perform the task?
2. Which impairments inhibit performance or completion of the task? For example, do factors such as poor motor planning and execution, decreased strength, decreased range of motion, or altered tone impair function?
3. Are the patient's problems the result of communication or perceptual, visual, auditory, or cognitive involvement? Does poor memory or fatigue impair functional ability?

Examples of the kinds of questions a therapist must pose to assess function and integrate findings into a comprehensive treatment program are found in the case vignettes that follow:

Case A	Case B
36-year-old male construction worker	72-year-old female homemaker
Diagnosis traumatic right below-knee amputation; post fracture left femur	Diagnosis CVA; right hemiplegia with global aphasia

Partial Assessment Findings

Strength and motor control: decreased in all extremities following prolonged immobilization	Strength and motor control: flaccid paralysis right extremities
Functional limitation: unable to transfer from bed to wheelchair	Functional limitation: unable to transfer from bed to wheelchair

Although the functional limitation in each case is in fact identical, the contributing factors, short-term and long-term goals, and the treatment approach would be markedly different. In Case A, the patient's inability to transfer can reasonably be attributed to decreased strength. When ameliorated, it is likely that the patient will go on to achieve a long-term goal of independent ambulation with a prosthesis. The patient in Case B has factors that can not be addressed solely through physical therapy. In addition, it may be difficult to determine whether it is the paralysis or the aphasia that compromises efforts to assess and to improve function. Although a similar goal of independence in wheelchair mobility and transfers may be proposed, frequent reassessment may demonstrate that functional deficits persist, despite improvement in motor function. In that case, the impairments in comprehension and language function may be the more important contributing factors. Thus the design of rehabilitation programs is based on the impairments that presumably underlie the functional deficits. If remediation of the impairment does not solve the functional problem, the therapist needs to reexamine the initial clinical impression by looking for other potentially causative factors.

Some functional tasks may need to be analyzed more precisely. Activities can be broken down into subordinate parts, or subroutines. A **subordinate part** is defined as an element of movement without which the task can not proceed safely or efficiency. For example, bed mobility includes the following subordinate parts: (1) scooting in bed (changing position for comfort or skin care and getting to the edge), (2) rolling onto the side, (3) lowering the legs, (4) sitting up, and (5) balancing over the edge of the bed. A functional loss of independent bed mobility may result from an inability to perform any or all of these subroutines. These are not only checkpoints for assessing patients, but they also later form the basis of a treatment program. The more involved the patient, the slower the learner, or the more complex the task, the more the functional task may need to be broken down into subordinate parts.

Assessing the Quality of Instruments

Within the rehabilitation setting, many tools have been developed primarily for in-house use and may have spread from facility to facility as staff have moved.

In most instances, the instruments underwent many modifications and the original sources have been lost. Other tests have been designed more rigidly and tested in clinical trials, assessing the instrument's psychometric properties and providing documentation of its **reliability** and **validity** in the literature. If the reliability and validity of an instrument is not established, little faith can be put in the results obtained or in the conclusions drawn from the results.[16] A poorly constructed instrument can produce data that are questionable, if not worthless. In light of the fact that the viability of physical therapy as a reimbursable service rests on the demonstration of functional outcomes, the importance of these concepts to functional assessment becomes clear. Some of the more recently developed instruments have undergone extensive testing of their measurement properties.

RELIABILITY

A reliable instrument measures a phenomenon dependably, time after time, accurately, predictably, and without variation. If a functional assessment or any test is not reliable, the patient's initial baseline status or the true effect of treatment can be concealed. Assessments performed by the same therapist of the same performance should be highly correlated *(intra-rater reliability)*. Instruments should also have strong *inter-rater reliability,* or agreement among multiple observers of the same event. If a particular patient is assessed by several therapists in the course of treatment, or reassessed over time to determine long-term change, the reliability of the functional assessment tool must be known.

A flaw in the clinical use of most types of functional tests is the tendency to disregard inter-rater reliability. To use functional assessments with maximum accuracy, (1) scoring criteria must be defined clearly and must be mutually exclusive, (2) criteria must be strictly applied to each clinical situation, and (3) all therapists in a facility must be retrained periodically in the use of the instrument to ensure similarity.

VALIDITY

Validity is a multifaceted concept. Questions of an instrument's validity attempt to determine (1) whether an instrument designed to measure function truly does just that, (2) what are appropriate applications of the instrument, and (3) how should the data be interpreted. First, the valid instrument should, on the face of it, appear to measure what it purports to measure *(face validity)*.[16] Through the use of various statistical procedures, it is also possible to demonstrate the degree to which items on the instrument group together to measure concepts that can be labeled as "physical mobility" or "social interaction" *(construct validity)*. There are different types of validity. Another critical component is whether the assessment instrument measures all the important or specified dimensions of function *(content validity)*. If there were a **gold standard,** that is, an unimpeachable measure of a phenomenon, such as a laboratory test with normative values, then a new instrument could be tested against the results of this standard. Such a "gold standard" does not exist for functional assessment instruments. New functional assessment tools can, however, be compared with existing ones that

are accepted measures of the same functional activities. The degree to which the two instruments agree establishes *concurrent validity.* Cross comparisons between these instruments have established concurrent validity. This issue is particularly relevant for self-assessment instruments. The concurrent validity of some self-assessment instruments has been determined by comparison with clinician ratings.

OTHER FACTORS

In addition to reliability and validity, a measure of functional status should be (1) sufficiently sensitive to reflect changes in patient status, (2) reasonably stable, so that it indicates no change when none has occurred, and (3) concise enough to be clinically useful.

Considerations in Selection of Instruments

A large number of instruments have been developed to assess and to classify functional ability. Given the plethora of instruments that currently exist, it is quite reasonable to ask how these instruments compare with one another. It is important to remember that no instrument is perfect for all patients or all situations. No instrument can assess all the items potentially relevant to a particular individual and provide the perfect composite picture. For example, one instrument may provide an extensive assessment of BADL but not deal with psychologic or social dimensions of function. Another instrument may investigate social functioning while omitting some **activities of daily living (ADL)** tasks. Many items overlap from instrument to instrument. For example, a question on the ability to ambulate is a common item found in most physical function instruments. Although instruments may cover the same kind of activity, the questions posed about the performance of the same activity may be quite different. For example, one instrument may investigate the degree of difficulty and of human assistance required to "dress yourself, including handling of closures, buttons, zippers, snaps." Another may ask, "How much help do you need in getting dressed?" As discussed above, differences also may exist in the time frames sampled in the various instruments.

Critical questions to ask, therefore, in selecting an instrument include:

1. What are the domains or categories that the assessment instrument focuses on?
2. How adequately does the instrument measure the domain or domains being sampled?
3. What areas of physical function are included? Does the instrument measure BADL? IADL?
4. What aspect of function is being measured? Is the level of dependence-independence considered? Length of time required to complete the functional task? Degree of difficulty? Influence of pain?
5. What is the time frame sampled in the assessment?
6. What is the mode of administration?
7. What type of scoring system is used?
8. Are multiple instruments necessary to provide a more complete assessment? Extrapolating items

from a variety of instruments may provide the kind of data desired but should be considered with extreme caution, inasmuch as this process usually results in a loss of reliability or validity.

Factors such as the theoretic orientation of the user, the purpose for using the instrument, and the relevance of particular functional items to certain patient populations all enter into the decision-making process. In the final analysis, the choice of instrument may be dictated by practical considerations. For example, self-report instruments, which rely on information from the patient, are limited in use to mentally competent individuals. Time and resources for administration also may influence test selection. In any case, there are many suitable instruments available for assessing functional status.

Selected Instruments Assessing Physical Function

BARTHEL INDEX

The Barthel Index specifically measures the degree of assistance required by an individual on 10 items of mobility and self-care ADL[14] (Table 11-2). Levels of measurement are limited to either complete independence or needing assistance. Each performance item is assessed on an ordinal scale with a specified number of points assigned to each level or ranking. Variable weightings were established by the developers of the Barthel Index for each item, based on clinical judgment or other implicit criteria. An individual who uses human assistance in eating, for example, would receive five points: independence in eating would receive a score of 10 points. A single global score, ranging from zero to 100, is calculated from the sum of all weighted individual item scores, so that a zero equals complete dependence in all 10 activities, and 100 equals complete independence in all 10 activities. The Barthel Index has been used widely to monitor functional changes in individuals receiving inpatient rehabilitation, particularly in the arena of predicting the functional outcomes associated with stroke.[17,18] Although its psychometric properties have not been fully assessed, the Barthel Index has achieved high correlations (0.74 to 0.80) with other measures of physical disability. An analysis of test-retest reliability (0.89) and inter-rater reliability (0.95) demonstrated very strong characteristics as well.[19]

KATZ INDEX OF ACTIVITIES OF DAILY LIVING

The Katz Index of ADL focuses on patient performance and the degree of assistance required in six categories of basic ADL: bathing, dressing, toileting, transferring, continence, and feeding[20,21] (Table 11-3). Using both direct observation and patient self-report over a 2-week period, the examiner scores one point for each activity that is performed without human help. A zero score is given if the activity is performed with human assistance or is not performed. Activity scores are combined to form a cumulative scale in letter grades (A through G) in order of increasing dependency. An individual's global letter score indicates an exact pattern of responses to the list of items. A score of B in the Katz Index, for example, means that the individual is independent in performing all but one of the six basic ADL categories. On the other hand, a score of D means that the individual is independent in all but bathing, dressing, and one additional function. The combination of categoric deficits in the Katz Index represents its developers' theoretic orientation. The developers of the Katz Index assumed a developmental and hierarchic organization of function in constructing their instrument. This organizational model is based on the empirically noted integration of neurologic and locomotor responses that is seen in children. One version of the scale demonstrated agreement ratios of 0.68 and 0.98 between different professional raters. The test-retest reliability of respondent self-reports produced intraclass correlation coefficients ranging from 0.61 to 0.78.[22] The Katz Index, originally developed for use with institutionalized patients, has been adapted for use in community-based populations.[23] A major disadvantage of using the Katz Index in rehabilitation settings is its failure to include an item on ambulation. The predictive validity of the instrument for long-term survival also has been reported.[21]

SUMMARY OF PHYSICAL FUNCTION TESTS

No single physical functional assessment instrument covers all areas of physical function (Table 11-4). Even items that appear to assess the same function may, depending on how the item is worded, be concerned with a different aspect of performance.[24] Therefore, instruments should be chosen to match the specific needs of the clinician and the likely functional limitations of the clinical population served.

Multidimensional Functional Assessment Instruments

Further research has resulted in the emergence of newer health status instruments to measure the components of health more comprehensively. Most concentrate on two or three dimensions of a patient's function, and record little about a person's disease or impairments. Therefore, to some degree the term *health status* frequently used to describe these instruments is a misnomer, inasmuch as these instruments actually measure multiple dimensions of function and not "health." Used in conjunction with traditional clinical methods of assessing signs and symptoms, multidimensional functional status instruments can add an important comprehensive view of a patient's function to the overall health assessment process. In this respect they add a crucial, and previously missing, component in assessing the health of individuals. A few of these instruments representative of the current "state of the art" are discussed below.

THE SICKNESS IMPACT PROFILE

The Sickness Impact Profile (SIP) was developed to address the need for an instrument that was precise enough to detect changes in perceived function.[25,30] Intended for use across types and severities of illness, it

Table 11–3 THE KATZ INDEX OF ADL

Name _____ Day of evaluation _____

For each area of functioning listed below, check description that applies. (The word "assistance" means supervision, direction, or personal assistance.)

Bathing—either sponge bath, tub bath, or shower.

□	□	□
Receives no assistance (gets in and out of tub by self if tub is usual means of bathing).	Receives assistance in bathing only one part of the body (such as back or a leg).	Receives assistance in bathing more than one part of the body (or not bathed).

Dressing—gets clothes from closets and drawers—including underclothes, outer garments and using fasteners (including braces if worn).

□	□	□
Gets clothes and gets completely dressed without assistance.	Gets clothes and gets dressed without assistance except for assistance in tying shoes.	Receives assistance in getting clothes or in getting dressed, or stays partly or completely undressed.

Toileting—going to the "toilet room" for bowel and urine elimination, cleaning self after elimination, and arranging clothes.

□	□	□
Goes to "toilet room," cleans self, and arranges clothes without assistance (may use object for support such as cane, walker, or wheelchair and may manage night bedpan or commode, emptying same in morning).	Receives assistance in going to "toilet room" or in cleansing self or in arranging clothes after elimination or in use of night bedpan or commode.	Doesn't go to room termed "toilet" for the elimination process.

Transfer

□	□	□
Moves in and out of bed as well as in and out of chair without assistance (may be using object for support such as cane or walker).	Moves in and out of bed or chair with assistance.	Doesn't get out of bed.

Continence

□	□	□
Controls urination and bowel movement completely by self.	Has occasional "accidents."	Supervision helps keep urine or bowel control; catheter is used, or is incontinent.

Feeding

□	□	□
Feeds self without assistance.	Feeds self except for getting assistance in cutting meat or buttering bread.	Receives assistance in feeding or is fed partly or completely by using tubes or intravenous fluids.

The Index of Independence in Activities of Daily Living is based on an evaluation of the functional independence or dependence of patients in bathing, dressing, going to toilet, transferring, continence, and feeding. Specific definitions of functional independence and dependence appear below the index.

A—Independent in feeding, continence, transferring, going to toilet, dressing, and bathing.
B—Independent in all but one of these functions.
C—Independent in all but bathing and one additional function.
D—Independent in all but bathing, dressing, and one additional function.
E—Independent in all but bathing, dressing, going to toilet, and one additional function.
F—Independent in all but bathing, dressing, going to toilet, transferring, and one additional function.
G—Dependent in all six functions.
Other—Dependent in at least two functions, but not classifiable as C, D, E, or F.

Independence means without supervision, direction, or active personal assistance, except as specifically noted below. This is based on actual status and not on ability. A patient who refuses to perform a function is considered as not performing the function, even though he is deemed able.

Bathing (sponge, shower, or tub)
Independent: assistance only in bathing a single part (as back or disabled extremity) or bathes self completely
Dependent: assistance in bathing more than one part of body; assistance in getting in or out of tub or does not bathe self

Dressing
Independent: gets clothes from closets and drawers; puts on clothes, outer garments, braces; manages fasteners; act of tying shoes is excluded
Dependent: does not dress self or remains partly undressed

Going to toilet
Independent: gets to toilet; gets on and off toilet; arranges clothes; cleans organs of excretion (may manage own bedpan used at night only and may or may not be using mechanical supports)
Dependent: uses bedpan or commode or receives assistance in getting to and using toilet

Transfer
Independent: moves in and out of bed independently and moves in and out of chair independently (may or may not be using mechanical supports)
Dependent: assistance in moving in or out of bed and/or chair; does not perform one or more transfers

Continence
Independent: urination and defecation entirely self-controlled
Dependent: partial or total incontinence in urination or defecation; partial or total control by enemas, catheters, or regulated use of urinals and/or bedpans

Feeding
Independent: gets food from plate or its equivalent, into mouth (precutting of meat and preparation of food, as buttering bread, are excluded from evaluation)
Dependent: assistance in act of feeding (see above); does not eat at all or parenteral feeding

From Katz, S, et al: Progress in the development of the Index of ADL. The Gerontologist/The Journal of Gerontology. 10:20, 1970, with permission.

Table 11–4 ITEMS COVERED IN SELECTED PHYSICAL FUNCTION INSTRUMENTS

Characteristics	Barthel	Katz
Mobility		
Bed activities	No	No
Transfers	Yes	Yes
Ambulation	Yes	No
Inclines/stairs	Yes	No
Basic ADL		
Bathing	Yes	Yes
Grooming	Yes	No
Dressing	Yes	Yes
Feeding	Yes	Yes
Toileting	Yes	Yes

ADL = activities of daily living.

is designed to detect small impacts of illness. The SIP contains 136 items in 12 categories of activities. These include sleep and rest, eating, work, home management, recreation, ambulatory mobility, body care and movement, social interaction, alertness, emotional behavior, and communication. A sample SIP measure of affective functioning specific to emotional behavior is found in Table 11–5. The entire test can be either self-administered or administered by an interview in 20 to 30 minutes. The scores are percentage ratings based on the ratio of the summed scale scores to the summed values of all SIP items. Higher scores indicate greater dysfunction.

The SIP test-retest reliability coefficients range from 0.75 to 0.92 for the overall score and from 0.45 to 0.60 for items checked.[27] Validity has been assessed using subjective self-assessment, clinician assessment, and subject's scores on other instruments. Correlations that are relevant to establishing multiple forms of validity range from a low of 0.35 to a high of 0.84.[26] The SIP has been used to describe the physical and psychosocial functions of individuals in an outpatient setting in relation to the duration of disease,[31] and the efficacy of using transcutaneous electrical nerve stimulation (TENS) with low back pain patients.[32] There are, however, some con-

Table 11–5 SICKNESS IMPACT PROFILE (SIP): AFFECTIVE FUNCTION

Please respond to (check) *only* those statements that you are *sure* describe you today and are related to your state of health.

1. I say how bad or useless I am; for example, that I am a burden on others. _____
2. I laugh or cry suddenly. _____
3. I often moan and groan in pain or discomfort. _____
4. I have attempted suicide. _____
5. I act nervous or restless. _____
6. I keep rubbing or holding areas of my body that hurt or are uncomfortable. _____
7. I act irritable and impatient with myself; for example, talk badly about myself, swear at myself, blame myself for things that happen. _____
8. I talk about the future in a hopeless way. _____
9. I get sudden frights. _____

CHECK HERE WHEN YOU HAVE READ ALL STATEMENTS ON THIS PAGE ☐

Reprinted by permission of Marilyn Bergner, PhD.

cerns regarding its use and suitability in certain kinds of studies. In assessing disability, SIP focuses only on ability versus inability to perform an activity; for example, "I am not going into town." It neglects the range of performance in between, with some potential loss of precision. The SIP also combines many functional activities into a single item, which may also reduce its discriminatory ability, such as "I have difficulty doing handwork; for example, turning faucets, using kitchen gadgets, sewing, carpentry." A few investigators have noted that the SIP may be more sensitive to detecting deterioration of status than to improvement, which may diminish its suitability as an instrument for monitoring individuals over time.[33]

THE HEALTH STATUS QUESTIONNAIRE (HSQ) 2.0

The Health Status Questionnaire (HSQ) 2.0 contains 36 items that are similar to questions used in the Rand Health Insurance Study, and were known for several years as the SF (short form)-36. The HSQ 2.0 also contains another three questions that screen for depression. Specifically, the questions of the HSQ were culled from the 113 questions used in the Medical Outcomes Study (MOS) to examine the relationship between physician practice styles and patient outcomes.[34] The MOS has provided important data on the functional status of adults with chronic conditions[35] and on the well-being of depressed patients compared to subjects with a chronic medical condition.[36] In an earlier version, the HSQ demonstrated exceptional reliability and validity (correlation coefficients ranging from 0.81 to 0.88).[37] Normative data for these self-report items have been collected.[38]

The HSQ forms eight different scales using 35 questions: physical function, social function, physical role function, emotional role function, mental health, energy/fatigue, bodily pain, and general health perceptions. The last question considers self-perceived change in health during the past year. Items are scored on nominal (yes/no) or ordinal scales. Each possible response to an item on a scale is assigned a number of points. The total points for all items within a scale are then added and transformed mathematically to yield a percentage score, with 100% representing optimal health. Sample items on physical function and role function are presented in Table 11–6.

THE MULTILEVEL ASSESSMENT INSTRUMENT (MAI)

Based on their research at the Philadelphia Geriatric Center, the Multilevel Assessment Instrument (MAI) was developed by Lawton and coworkers[39,40] as a model for assessment of older individuals; it was based on competence or ability to perform in the areas traditionally recognized as components of health status. These include physical health, cognition, activities of daily living (ADL), time use or formal social activity, and social interaction and support. Psychologic well-being is understood as personal adjustment in terms of morale and psychiatric symptoms and, unlike many other instruments, recognizes this as distinct from cognitive func-

Table 11–6 THE HEALTH STATUS QUESTIONNAIRE (HSQ): 2.0 PHYSICAL AND ROLE FUNCTION

The following questions are about activities you might do during a typical day. Does *your health* limit you in these activities? If so, how much? (Mark one box on each line.)	Yes, limited a lot	Yes limited a little	No, not limited at all
a. *Vigorous activities,* such as running, lifting heavy objects, participating in strenuous sports	1□	2□	3□
b. *Moderate activities,* such as moving a table, pushing a vacuum cleaner, bowling, or playing golf	1□	2□	3□
c. Lifting or carrying groceries	1□	2□	3□
d. Climbing *several* flights of stairs	1□	2□	3□
e. Climbing *one* flight of stairs	1□	2□	3□
f. Bending, kneeling or stooping	1□	2□	3□
g. Walking *more than a mile*	1□	2□	3□
h. Walking *several blocks*	1□	2□	3□
i. Walking *one block*	1□	2□	3□
j. Bathing or dressing yourself	1□	2□	3□

During the *past 4 weeks,* have you had any of the following problems with your work or other regular daily activities *as a result of your physical health?* (Mark one box on each line.)	Yes	No
a. Cut down the *amount of time* you spent on work or other activities	1□	2□
b. *Accomplished less* than you would like	1□	2□
c. Were limited in the *kind* of work or other activities	1□	2□
d. Had *difficulty* performing the work or other activities (for example, it took extra effort)	1□	2□

tioning. This is a relevant distinction in geriatric populations in which deficits in mental processes such as memory or calculation may exist separate from factors related to morale or psychologic outlook. This instru-

Table 11–7 THE MULTILEVEL ASSESSMENT INSTRUMENT: INSTRUMENTAL ACTIVITIES OF DAILY LIVING

Can you use the telephone
  without help   □
  with some help   □
  Are you completely unable to use the telephone?   □
Can you get to places out of walking distance
  without help   □
  with some help   □
  Are you completely unable to travel unless special arrangements are made?   □
Can you go shopping for groceries
  without help   □
  with some help   □
  Are you completely unable to do any shopping?   □
Can you prepare your own meals
  without help   □
  with some help   □
  Are you completely unable to prepare any meals?   □
Can you do your own housework
  without help   □
  with some help   □
  Are you completely unable to do any housework?   □
Can you do your own handyman work
  without help   □
  with some help   □
  Are you completely unable to do any handyman work?   □
Can you do your own laundry
  without help   □
  with some help   □
  Are you completely unable to do any laundry at all?   □
If you had to take medicine, can you do it
  without help (in the right doses at the right time)   □
  with some help (take medicine if someone prepares it for you and/or reminds you to take it)   □
  Are you/would you be completely unable to take your own medicines?   □
Can you manage your own money
  without help   □
  with some help   □
  Are you completely unable to handle money?   □

Reprinted by permission of Powell Lawton, PhD.

ment also investigates the perceived quality of the individual's residential environment and the adequacy of economic resources. Taken in their entirety, these domains represent the interests of the entire health care team. The IADL battery from the MAI is found in Table 11–7.

The subscale properties of the MAI have been fully investigated and do not depend on an interviewer's summary judgments, as do a few other multidimensional instruments. Because it was developed expressly to

Table 11–8 ITEMS COVERED IN SELECTED MULTIDIMENSIONAL FUNCTIONAL ASSESSMENT INSTRUMENTS

Items	SIP	HSQ	MAI
Symptoms	Yes	Yes	Yes
Physical function			
Bed activities	No	No	No
Transfers	No	No	Yes
Ambulation	Yes	Yes	Yes
Dexterity	No	No	No
Mobility restriction/confinement	Yes	Yes	Yes
BADL			
Bathing	Yes	Yes	Yes
Grooming	No	No	Yes
Dressing	No	Yes	Yes
Feeding	No	No	Yes
Toileting	No	No	Yes
IADL			
Indoor home chores	Yes	Yes	Yes
Outdoor home chores/shopping	Yes	Yes	Yes
Community travel/drive car	Yes	Yes	Yes
Work/school	Yes	Yes	No
Affective function			
Anxiety	No	Yes	Yes
Depression	No	Yes	Yes
Emotional behavior	Yes	No	No
General health perceptions	No	Yes	Yes
Social function			
Interaction	Yes	Yes	Yes
Support/network	No	No	Yes
Activity/leisure	Yes	Yes	Yes

BADL = basic activities of daily living; HSQ = Health Status Questionnaire; IADL = instrumental activities of daily living; MAI = Multilevel Assessment Instrument; SIP = Sickness Impact Profile.

address the salient characteristics of the elderly and was tested a significant number of times in comparisons with other instruments, it is extensively used, particularly for studies assessing psychologic well-being among the elderly.[41-46] All of its scales have been tested and may be used as modular assessment batteries either separately or together.

The MAI scales are currently available in long, middle, and short versions. The long forms of the scales have all been validated by comparison with clinicians' ratings. These versions of the MAI scales also have the highest reported test-retest correlations, ranging from 0.73 to 0.95. Intraclass correlations between interviewer and clinician administrations ranged from 0.58 to 0.88 on the various subscales. The full MAI administered by an interviewer takes approximately 50 minutes.

SUMMARY OF MULTIDIMENSIONAL FUNCTIONAL ASSESSMENT INSTRUMENTS

For the purposes of illustration, three multidimensional instruments have been presented. Choice of a multidimensional instrument carries the same caveats mentioned for instruments assessing physical function.[47] No instrument assesses all potentially relevant items. Table 11–8 presents a comparison of items covered. In the physical function area, questions on the ability to ambulate and on mobility restrictions and/or confinement are the only items these instruments have in common. Aspects of physical function not covered in any of these instruments include bed activities and dexterity. The MAI includes more BADL items than the SIP or the HSQ. The SIP and the HSQ investigate work performance, whereas the MAI does not. Anxiety and depression are explicitly addressed as areas of psychologic function in the HSQ and the MAI. Finally, only the MAI explores social support and social network as a component of social function.

SUMMARY

This chapter has presented a conceptual framework for understanding health status and functional assessment. The traditional medical model with its narrow focus on disease and its symptoms fails to consider the broader social, psychologic, and behavioral dimensions of illness. All these factors have impact on an individual's function. Functional assessment, therefore, must be viewed as a broad, multidimensional process. Three main categories of function have been delineated: physical, psychological, and social. Instrumentation has been presented that addresses the physical dimension, the area of assessment that physical therapists are traditionally most involved with, as well as many other dimensions. Finally, specific aspects of functional assessment have been discussed, including purpose, selection of instruments, aspects of test administration, interpretation of test results, and assessment of instrument quality.

QUESTIONS FOR REVIEW

1. How do functional status and functional assessment relate to health status?

2. Your rehabilitation facility has decided to use the Barthel Index. How can reliability be ensured so that the results can be used with confidence in both treatment planning and research?

3. What criteria can be used in the selection of a functional instrument?

4. Discuss the uses, advantages, and disadvantages of performance-based assessments, interviewer assessments, and self-administered assessments.

5. Explain how environment and fatigue and other related issues affect a functional assessment. Suggest ways to control these factors in the clinic.

6. Identify the major types of scoring systems used in functional assessments. What are some common errors in interpretation of testing results?

7. Review Tables 11–2 through 11–8. Hypothesize a caseload in a rehabilitation facility and indicate how and when you could use each of these instruments with your proposed population. Describe the advantages and disadvantages of each.

8. Using one of the instruments, develop a set of results and use them to set treatment goals and to formulate a treatment plan.

9. For each of the following, identify particular physical tasks relevant to that individual's functional status.
   a. A 22-year-old female file clerk.
   b. A 31-year-old male physical therapist.
   c. A 39-year-old female homemaker with children.
   d. A 45-year-old male construction worker.
   e. A 56-year-old female school teacher.
   f. A 65-year-old male journalist.

10. Discuss the relationships between disease, impairment, functional limitations, disability, and handicap.

REFERENCES

1. Pope, AM and Tarlov, AR (eds): Disability in America: Toward a National Agenda for Prevention. National Academy Press, Washington, DC, 1991.
2. Duckworth, D: The need for a standard terminology and classification of disablement. In Granger, C and Gresham, G (eds): Functional Assessment in Rehabilitation Medicine. Williams & Wilkins, Baltimore, 1984.
3. World Health Organization (WHO): The First Ten Years of the World Health Organization, World Health Organization, Geneva, 1958.
4. Jette, A: Concepts of health and methodological issues in functional assessment. In Granger, C and Gresham G (eds): Functional Assessment in Rehabilitation Medicine. Williams & Wilkins, Baltimore, 1984.
5. World Health Organization (WHO): International Classification of Impairments, Disabilities, and Handicaps. World Health Organization, Geneva, 1980.
6. Guccione, AA: Physical therapy diagnosis and the relationship between impairments and function. Phys Ther 71:499, 1991.
7. Nagi, S: Disability concepts revisited. In Pope, AM and Tarlov, AR

(eds): Disability in America: Toward a National Agenda for Prevention. National Academy Press, Washington, DC, 1991.

8. Nagi, S: Disability and Rehabilitation. Ohio State University Press, Columbus, OH, 1969.

9. Nagi, S: Some conceptual issues in disability and rehabilitation. In Sussman, M (ed): Sociology and Rehabilitation. Ohio State University Press, Columbus, OH, 1965.

10. Schenkman, M and Butler RB: A model for multisystem evaluation, interpretation, and treatment of individuals with neurologic dysfunction. Phys Ther 69:538, 1989.

11. Schenkman, M and Butler RB: A model for multisystem evaluation and treatment of individual's with Parkinson's disease. Phys Ther 69:932, 1989.

12. Guccione, AA: Physical therapy diagnosis and the relationship between impairments and function. Phys Ther 71:499, 1991.

13. Granger, C: A conceptual model for functional assessment. In Granger, C and Gresham, G (eds): Functional Assessment in Rehabilitation Medicine. Williams & Wilkins, Baltimore, 1984.

14. Mahoney, FI and Barthel, DW: Functional evaluation: the Barthel Index. Md State Med J 14:61, 1965.

15. Guccione, AA, Felson, DT, and Anderson, JJ: Defining arthritis and measuring functional status in elders: methodological issues in the study of disease and disability. Am J Public Health 80:949, 1990.

16. Rothstein, JM: Measurement and clinical practice: theory and application. In Rothstein, JM (ed): Measurement in Physical Therapy. Churchill Livingstone, New York, 1985.

17. Granger, CV, Hamilton, BB, and Gresham, GE: The Stroke Rehabilitation Outcome Study, I. General description. Arch Phys Med Rehabil 69:506, 1988.

18. Granger, CV, Hamilton, BB, Gresham, GE, and Kramer, AA: The Stroke Rehabilitation Outcome Study, II. Relative merits of the total Barthel Index score and a four-item subscore in predicting patient outcomes. Arch Phys Med Rehabil 70:100, 1989.

19. Granger, C, Albrecht, G, and Hamilton, B: Outcome of comprehensive medical rehabilitation: measurement by Pulses profile and the Barthel index. Arch Phys Med Rehabil 60:145, 1979.

20. Katz, S, Ford, AB, Moskowitz, RW, et al: Studies of illness in the aged. The Index of ADL: a standardized measure of biological and psychosocial function. JAMA 185:914, 1963.

21. Katz, S, Downs, TD, Cash, HR, et al: Progress in the development of the Index of ADL. Gerontologist 10:20, 1970.

22. Liang, M and Jette, A: Measuring functional ability in chronic arthritis. Arthritis Rheum 24:80, 1981.

23. Branch, L, Katz, S, Kniepmann, K, et al: A prospective study of functional status among community elders. Am J Public Health 74:266, 1984.

24. Guccione, AA and Jette, AM: Assessing limitations in physical function in patients with arthritis. Arthritis Care Res 1:170, 1988.

25. Gilson, BS, Gilson, JS, Bergner, M, Bobbitt, RA, Bergner, M, et al: The Sickness Impact Profile: development of an outcome measure of health care. Am J Public Health 65:1304, 1975.

26. Bergner, M, Bobbitt, RA, Pollard, WE, et al: The Sickness Impact Profile: validation of a health status measure. Med Care 14:57, 1976.

27. Pollard, WE, Bobbitt, RA, Bergner, M, et al: The Sickness Profile: reliability of a health status measure. Med Care 14:146, 1976.

28. Carter, WB, Bobbitt, RA, Bergner, M, et al: Validation of an interval scaling: the Sickness Impact Profile. Health Serv Res 11:516, 1976.

29. Bergner, M, Bobbitt, RA, Carter, WB, et al: The Sickness Impact Profile: development and final revision of a health status measure. Med Care 19:787, 1981.

30. Deyo, RA, Inui, TS, Leininger, JD, et al: Measuring functional outcomes in a chronic disease: a comparison of traditional scales and a self-administered health status questionnaire in patients with rheumatoid arthritis. Med Care 21:180, 1983.

31. Deyo, R, Inui, TS, Leininger, J, et al: Physical and psychosocial function in rheumatoid arthritis. Clinical use of a self-administered health status instrument. Arch Intern Med 142:870, 1982.

32. Deyo, RA, Walsh, NE, Martin, DC, et al: A controlled trial of transcutaneous electrical stimulation (TENS) and exercise for chronic low back pain. N Engl J Med 322:1627, 1990.

33. MacKenzie, CR, Charlson, ME, DiGioa, D, et al: Can the Sickness Impact Profile measure change: an example of scale assessment. J Chronic Dis 39:429, 1986.

34. Tarlov, AR, Ware, JE, Jr, Greenfield, S, et al: The Medical Outcomes Study: an application of methods for monitoring the results of medical care. JAMA 262:925, 1989.

35. Stewart, AL, Greenfield, S, Mays, RD, et al: Functional status and well-being of patients with chronic conditions: results from the Medical Outcomes Study. JAMA 262:907, 1989.

36. Wells, KB, et al: The functioning and well-being of depressed patients: results from the Medical Outcomes Study. JAMA 262:914, 1989.

37. Stewart, AL, Hays, RD, and Ware, JE, Jr: The MOS short general health survey: reliability and validity in a patient population. Med Care 26:724, 1988.

38. Wetzler, HP and Radosevich, DM: Health Status Questionnaire (SF-36) technical report. Interstudy, Excelsior, MN, 1992.

39. Lawton, MP, Moss, M, Fulcomer, M, et al: A research and service oriented multilevel assessment instrument. J Gerontol 37:91, 1982.

40. Lawton, M: Environment and other determinants of well-being in older people. Gerontologist 23:349, 1983.

41. Hinrichsen, G: The impact of age-concentrated, publicly assisted housing on older people's social and emotional well-being. J Gerontol 40:758, 1985.

42. Scheidt, R: A taxonomy of well-being for small-town elderly: a care for rural diversity. Gerontology 24:84, 1984.

43. Ward, R, Sherman, S, and LaGory, M: Informal networks and knowledge of services for older persons. J Gerontol 39:216, 1984.

44. Weinberger, M, Darnell, JC, Martz, BL, et al: The effects of positive and negative life changes on the self-reported health status of elderly adults. J Gerontol 41:114, 1986.

45. Windley, P and Scheidt, R: Service utilization and activity participation among psychologically vulnerable and well elderly in rural small towns. Gerontologist 23:283, 1983.

46. Wolinsky, FD, Coe, RM, Miller, RK, et al: Measurement of the global and functional dimensions of health status in the elderly. J Gerontol 39:88, 1984.

47. Guccione, AA and Jette, AM: Multidimensional assessment of functional limitations in patients with arthritis. Arthritis Care Res 3:44, 1990.

GLOSSARY

Activities of daily living (ADL): Activities necessary for daily self-care, personal maintenance, and independent community living.

Affective function: Mental and emotional skills and coping strategies needed to perform everyday tasks and stresses, as well as the more traumatic events each person encounters over the course of a lifetime; includes such factors as self-esteem, body image, anxiety, depression, and the ability to cope with change.

Basic activities of daily living (BADL): Tasks concerned with daily self-care, such as feeding, dressing, hygiene, and physical mobility.

Checklist: Assessment tool format in which a description of various tasks is simply scored dichotomously (e.g., present or absent; completed or not completed).

Dependence: A state requiring some level of human assistance.

Difficulty: Hybrid term that suggests that an activity poses an extra burden for an individual, regardless of dependence level.

Disability (disabled): Inability to perform social roles typical of independent adults, taking into account age, sex, social, and cultural factors.

Disease: Pathologic condition of the body that presents

a group of characteristic signs and symptoms that sets the condition apart as abnormal.

Endurance: Energy consumption required to complete a functional task.

Functional activities: Activities identified by an individual as essential to support physical and psychologic well-being, as well as to create a personal sense of meaningful living.

Functional limitation: Deviation from normal in the way an individual performs a task or activity, usually as the result of impairment.

Gold standard: Accepted, accurate measure of a particular phenomenon that can serve as the normative standard for other measures.

Handicap: Social disadvantage for a given individual of impairment, functional limitation, or disability.

Health: State of complete physical, mental, and social well-being, and not merely the absence of disease and infirmity.

Illness: Forms of personal behavior that emerge as the reality of having a disease is internalized and experienced by an individual.

Impairments: Any loss or abnormality of anatomic, physiologic, or psychologic structure or function; the natural consequence of pathology or disease.

Instrumental activities of daily living (IADL): Advanced skills considered vital to an individual's independent living in the community, including managing personal affairs, cooking and shopping, and home chores.

Interviewer assessment: Process in which the assessor interviews or questions a subject and records answers.

Mental function: Intellectual or cognitive abilities of an individual, including initiative, attention, concentration, memory, problem solving, and judgment.

Ordinal scale (or rank order): Classification scheme that rates observations in terms of the relationship between items (e.g., less than, equal to, or greater than).

Performance-based assessment: Assessment of a particular skill based on observation of an actual attempt, as opposed to acceptance of a self-report of skill level.

Physical function: Sensory-motor skills necessary for the performance of usual daily activities.

Physical signs: Directly observable or measurable changes in an individual's organs or systems as a result of pathology or disease.

Psychological function: Ability to use mental and affective resources effectively in response to the requirements of a particular situation.

Reliability: Degree to which an instrument can consistently measure the same parameter under specific conditions.

Self-administered assessment (self-assessment): Survey or series of questions constructed to be answered directly by the respondent without additional input or direction.

Social function: Ability to interact successfully with others in the performance of social roles and obligations; includes social interactions, roles, and networks.

Subordinate part: Element of movement without which the task cannot proceed safely or efficiently.

Summary (or additive) scale: Approach to grading a specific series of skills by awarding points for each task or activity; totals the score as a percentage of 100 or as a fraction.

Symptoms: Subjective reactions to the changes experienced by an individual as a result of pathology or disease.

Validity: The degree to which data or results of a study are correct or true.

Visual (or linear) analog scale: Linear rating designed to capture a subject's judgment of his or her position on a continuum. A line is presented horizontally or vertically on paper, with the endpoints anchored with descriptive words representing the extremes in terms of the parameter of interest.

CHAPTER 12

Environmental Assessment

Thomas J. Schmitz

OBJECTIVES

1. Describe the purposes of an environmental assessment.
2. Describe the activities involved in preparation for an on-site visit.
3. Identify the components of an environmental assessment.
4. Describe the significance of environmental accessibility for individuals with mobility impairments.
5. Value the importance of an environmental assessment as an integral part of overall rehabilitation planning.

A primary goal of rehabilitation is for the patient to return to a former environment and life-style. In order to achieve this goal, continuity of accessibility must exist among forms of transportation, building entrances, and building interiors. The value of any one of these components is diminished without access to the others. An accessible building is useless if suitable transportation to and from the facility is not available. With total accessibility as a goal, environmental assessments must address the multiple but individual requirements of each patient. These include the housing, social, recreational, educational, and employment needs of the patient.

The purposes of an environmental assessment are multiple and serve to

1. Assess the degree of safety, level of function, and comfort of the patient in the home, community, and work environment.
2. Make realistic recommendations to the patient, family, employer, and/or government agencies and third party payers regarding **environmental accessibility.**
3. Assess the patient's need for additional **adaptive equipment.**
4. Assist in preparing the patient and family for discharge from the hospital and to help determine whether further services may be required (i.e., outpatient treatment, home health services, and so forth).

The environmental assessment may be done through either an on-site visit or an interview. The on-site visit is preferable because it allows assessment of performance in the actual environment in which the activities must be accomplished. On-site visits are often useful in reducing patient, family, and employer apprehension concerning

the patient's ability to function independently. The on-site visit also provides an excellent opportunity for the therapist to make recommendations regarding altering, coping with, or adapting specific **environmental barriers.** Considering the time and costs involved with on-site visits, an on-site visit preceded by an interview is often the best way to assess the patient's environment.

Although the therapist may want to visit the patient's home and workplace, if applicable, an interview with the patient and family may be all that is needed to provide suggestions and guidelines for some aspects of the environmental assessment (e.g., general community access). Because it is usually not feasible for the therapist to assess all aspects of the patient's total environment, family involvement is particularly important in assuring that the goal of maximum accessibility is met. Prior to the patient's discharge, the therapist should guide and encourage the family in an investigation of access to community recreational and educational facilities, the availability of public transportation, and the accessibility of local shopping facilities.

ON-SITE ASSESSMENT

Preparations for the On-Site Visit

During the patient's hospitalization, the family should be encouraged to make several visits to the physical and occupational therapy departments. These visits serve several functions. They provide the family an opportunity to become familiar with the patient's capabilities and limitations. They give the family time to learn safe methods of assisting with ambulation, transfers, exercise, and functional activities. During these visits the therapist will have an opportunity to instruct the family in the use of adaptive equipment. The time spent in family education will facilitate the patient's transition from the hospital to the home and community. When realistic, weekend passes for the patient should be encouraged prior to the on-site assessment. During these visits problems not previously anticipated by the therapist or family may be uncovered. Emphasis can then be placed on solving these problems prior to actual discharge.

Preceding the on-site assessment, information should be gathered about several important areas that will influence both the preparation for and the types of suggestions made during the visit. This information should include

1. Knowledge of the family's interrelations (especially the family's attitude toward the patient and the extent of their desire to have the patient return home).
2. The family's attitude toward the hospital and staff, which may influence receptivity to suggested modifications to the home.
3. Knowledge of the projected prognosis for the patient's disability (e.g., whether the disability is static or progressive, and what long-term functional capabilities are expected).
4. General knowledge of the physical structure of the living space (house, apartment, number of levels, stairs, railings, and so forth).
5. Detailed information about the patient's present level of function as judged by all disciplines working with the patient (occupational therapy, physical therapy, speech, and so forth).
6. Information about the patient's insurance coverage and financial situation (in terms of capacity to modify environment).
7. Knowledge of the patient's future plans (gainful employment, school, vocational training, and so forth).

This information can be gathered from interviews with the patient, family conferences, medical records, social service interviews, and specific assessment procedures. Once this information is gathered, decisions can be made concerning the amount of adaptive equipment required for the on-site visit, whether an assessment of the patient's work environment will be required, and the appropriate team members to accompany the patient on the visit.

Home Assessment

Ideally, the physical and occupational therapists should accompany the patient on the home visit. They assume shared responsibility for assessing the patient's functional level at home. Depending on the specific needs of the patient and/or family, a speech therapist, social worker, or nurse also may be included on the home visit. The visit should be broken into two components. The first portion should deal with accessibility of the dwelling's exterior, and the second half should be concerned with an assessment of the home's interior. A tape measure and home assessment form are valuable tools during the visit. Many rehabilitation departments develop their own home assessment forms to meet the particular needs of their patient population. The forms help organize the visit and are useful in directing attention to all necessary details. A variety of home assessment forms are available. A sample is provided in Appendix A. This form can be expanded or modified, depending on the specific needs of the individual or patient population.

One method of accomplishing the interior assessment is to begin with the patient in bed as though it were morning. Simulation of all daily activities, including dressing, grooming, bathroom activities, and preparation of meals can ensue. The patient should attempt to perform all transfer, exercise, ambulation, self-care, and homemaking activities as independently as possible to facilitate the assessment. This will provide an additional opportunity to teach the family how and when to assist the patient.

Upon arrival at the home for the on-site visit, the patient may need to rest for a short while before beginning the assessment. This is an important consideration, because many patients become very excited or emotional when returning home after a lengthy absence. This may be true even if previous passes were issued for weekend home visits.

The following considerations are offered as suggestions for home assessments. This list is neither exhaustive nor inclusive for every diagnosis. It is intended to direct attention to some of the most common concerns encountered during home visits.

EXTERIOR ACCESSIBILITY: GENERAL CONSIDERATIONS

1. It is important to note whether the house or apartment is owned or rented. The type and ownership of the home may preclude any modifications the patient or family may require.
2. The relative permanence of the dwelling should be considered. If the patient plans to move in the near future, it will influence the type of modifications recommended (e.g., installing permanent ramps versus removable ones, or paving a gravel driveway).

EXTERIOR ACCESSIBILITY: SPECIFIC CONSIDERATIONS
Route of Entry

1. If there is more than one entry to the dwelling, the most accessible should be selected (closest to driveway, most level walking surface, least amount of stairs, available handrails, and so forth).
2. Ideally, the driveway should be a smooth, level surface with easy access to the home. Walking surfaces to the entrance should be carefully assessed. Cracked and uneven surfaces should be repaired or an alternate route selected.
3. The entrance should be well lighted and provide adequate cover from adverse weather conditions.

4. The height, number, and condition of stairs should be noted. Ideally, steps should not be greater than 7 inches (17.5 cm) high with a depth of 11 inches (27.9 cm).[1] **Nosings,** or ''lips,'' on the stairs are often problematic and should be removed or reduced, if possible. The steps also should have a nonslip surface.

5. Handrails should be installed, if needed. In general, the handrails should measure 32 inches (81.3 cm) in height, and at least one handrail should extend 18 inches (45.7 cm) beyond the foot and top of the stairs.[1] Modifications in height measurements will be required for particularly tall or short individuals.

6. If a ramp is to be installed, there should be adequate space. The recommended **grade** for wheelchair ramps is 12 inches of ramp length for every inch of threshold height.[2] Ramps should be a minimum of 48 inches (121.9 cm) wide, with a nonslip surface.[3] Handrails also should be included on the ramp (32 inches [81.3 cm] in height) and extend 12 inches (30.5 cm) beyond the top and bottom of the ramp.[2]

Entrance

1. For wheelchair users, the entrance should have a platform large enough to allow the patient to rest and to prepare for entry. This platform area is particularly important when a ramp is in use. It provides for safe transit from the inclined surface to the level surface. If a wheelchair user is required to open a door that swings out, this area should be at least 5 feet × 5 feet (153 cm × 153 cm). If the door swings away from the patient, a space at least 3 feet (91.5 cm) deep and 5 feet (153 cm) wide is required.[1]

2. The door locks should be accessible to the patient. The height of the locks should be assessed as well as the amount of force required to turn the key. Alternative lock systems (e.g., voice- or card-activated or push buttons) may be an important consideration for some patients.

3. The door handle should be turned easily by the patient. Rubber doorknob covers or lever-type handles (slip-on models are available) are often easier to use for patients with limited grip strength.

4. The door should open and close in a direction that is functional for the patient. A cane may be hung outside the door to help the wheelchair user close the door when leaving.

5. If there is a raised **threshold** in the doorway, it should be removed. If removal is not possible, the threshold should be lowered to no greater than one half inch (1.27 cm) in height, with **beveled** edges.[1] If needed, weatherstripping the door will help prevent drafts.

6. The doorway width should be measured. Generally, 32 inches (81.3 cm)[2] to 34 inches (86.3 cm)[1] is an acceptable doorway width to accommodate most wheelchairs.

7. If the door is weighted to aid in closing, the pressure should not exceed 8 pounds in order to be functional for the patient.[1]

8. **Kick plates** may be added to doors subject to frequent use by wheelchair users or individuals using ambulatory assistive devices. The kick plate should measure 12 inches (30.5 cm) in height from the bottom of the door.[1]

INTERIOR ACCESSIBILITY: GENERAL CONSIDERATIONS
Furniture Arrangement

1. Sufficient room should be made available for maneuvering a wheelchair or ambulating with an assistive device.

2. Clear passage must be allowed from one room to the next.

3. Unrestricted access should be provided to electrical outlets, telephones, and wall switches. Outlets may need to be raised and wall switches lowered.

Floors

1. All floor coverings should be glued or tacked to the floor. This will prevent bunching or rippling under wheelchair use. When carpeting is used, a dense, low pile generally provides for easiest movement of a wheelchair or ambulatory assistive device.

2. Scatter rugs should be removed.

3. Use of nonskid waxes should be encouraged.

4. For patients with visual deficits, lines of brightly colored tape can be placed on the floor surface to assist mobility in poorly lighted areas.

Doors

1. Raised thresholds should be removed to provide a flush, level surface.

2. Doorways may need to be widened to allow clearance for a wheelchair or assistive device. In instances in which this is not possible, wheelchair users may benefit from a narrowing device attached directly to the chair. This allows the width of the chair to be temporarily reduced by turning a crank handle.

3. Doors may have to be removed, reversed, or replaced with curtains, folding doors, or a door of lighter weight.

4. As mentioned earlier in regard to exterior doors, handles inside the home should also be assessed. Rubber doorknob covers or lever-type handles may be important considerations. **Knurled surface** door handles are used on interiors of buildings and dwellings when frequented by visually impaired persons. These abrasive, knurled surfaces indicate that the door leads to a hazardous area and alerts the individual to danger.

Stairs

1. All indoor stairwells should have handrails and should be well lighted (battery-operated wall lamps are a practical supplement to electrical light sources).

2. For patients with decreased visual acuity or age-

related visual changes, contrasting textures on the surface of the top and bottom stair(s) will alert them that the end of the stairwell is near. Circular bands of tape also can be placed at the top and bottom of the handrail for the same purpose.

3. Many patients with visual impairment will benefit also from bright, contrasting color tape on the border of each stair. The warm colors (reds, oranges, and yellows) are generally easier to see than the cool colors (blues, greens, and violets).

Heating Units

1. All radiators, heating vents, and hot-water pipes should be appropriately screened off to prevent burns, especially for patients who have sensory impairments.
2. Adaptations may be required to allow patient access to heat controls (e.g., use of reachers or enlarged, extended, or adapted handles on heat-control valves).

INTERIOR ACCESSIBILITY: SPECIFIC CONSIDERATIONS

Bedroom Area

1. The bed should be stationary and positioned to provide ample space for transfers. Stability may be improved by placing the bed against a wall or in the corner of the room (except when the patient plans to make the bed). Additional stability may be achieved by placing rubber suction cups under each leg.
2. The height of the sleeping surface must be considered to facilitate transfer activities. The height of the bed may be raised by use of wooden blocks with routed depressions to hold each leg. The use of another mattress or box spring also will provide additional height to the bed. Blocks may be used to raise the height of chairs.
3. The mattress should be carefully assessed. It should provide a firm, comfortable surface. If the mattress is in relatively good condition, a bed board inserted between the mattress and box spring may suffice to improve the sleeping surface adequately. If the mattress is badly worn, a new one should be suggested.
4. A bedside table or cabinet might be suggested; it will be useful to hold a lamp, a telephone, necessary medications, and a call bell if assistance is needed.
5. The closet clothes bar may require lowering to provide wheelchair accessibility. The bar should be lowered to 52 inches (132 cm) from the floor.[1] Wall hooks also may be a useful addition to the closet area and should be placed between 40 inches (101.6 cm) and 56 inches (142.2 cm) from the floor.[1] Shelves also can be installed at various levels in the closet (Fig. 12–1). The highest shelf should not exceed 45 inches (114.3 cm) in height.[1] Clothing and grooming articles frequently used by the patient should be placed in the most easily accessible bureau drawer.

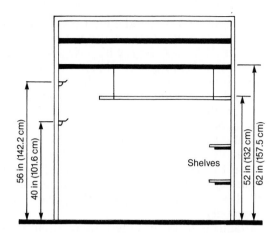

Figure 12–1. Closet modifications to provide accessibility for a wheelchair user. (From Cotler and DeGraff,[1] p 57, with permission.)

6. A portable commode, urinal, or bedpan also may be an appropriate consideration.

Figure 12–2 illustrates the basic components and dimensions of a wheelchair-accessible bedroom.

Bathroom Area

1. If the door frame prohibits passage of a wheelchair, the patient may transfer at the door to a chair with **casters** attached. As mentioned earlier, another solution to this problem may be to order a wheelchair adaptor that allows the width of the chair to be narrowed.
2. An elevated toilet seat will facilitate transfer activities.
3. **Grab bars** (securely fastened to a reinforced wall) will assist in both toilet and tub transfers. Grab bars should be 1.5 inches (3.8 cm)[1,2] in diameter and be knurled. For use in toilet transfers, the bars should be mounted horizontally 33 inches (83.8 cm) to 36 inches (91.4 cm)[2] from the floor (Fig. 12–3). The length of the grab bars should be between 24 inches (61 cm) and 36 inches (91.4 cm) on the back wall and 42 inches (106.7 cm) on the side wall.[2] For use in tub transfers they should be mounted horizontally 24 inches (61 cm) high, measured from the floor of the tub.[3]
4. A tub seat may be recommended for bathing. Many types of commercially produced tub seats are available. In selecting a tub seat, function and safety are primary considerations. The tub seat should provide a wide base of support with suction feet, a back rest, and a relatively long seating surface to facilitate transfers in and out of the tub (Fig. 12–4).
5. A bathmat or nonskid adhesive strips may be placed on the floor of the tub (these are easily attainable at most hardware stores).
6. Additional bathroom considerations may include handspray attachment to the bathtub faucet, a governor to regulate the hot-water temperature, enlarged faucet handles on the tub or sink, and a towel rack and toilet articles that are within easy reach of the patient.

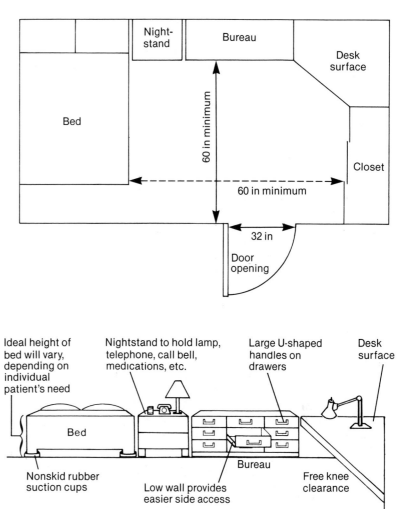

Figure 12–2. Sample dimensions and features of a bedroom area, providing access for an individual using a wheelchair.

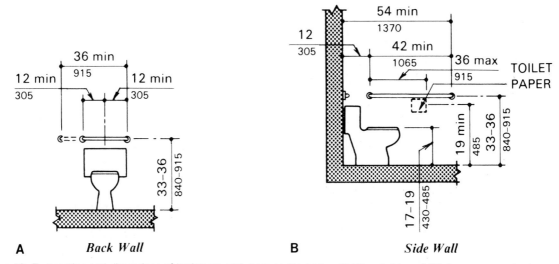

A   *Back Wall*   **B**   *Side Wall*

Figure 12–3. Location and dimensions of bathroom grab bars on the back wall (A) and side wall (B). Larger numerals denote inches, smaller numerals denote millimeters. (From American National Standards Institute,[2] p 46, with permission.)

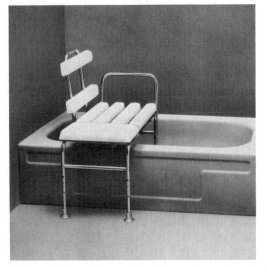

Figure 12–4. A tub seat that provides a wide base of support with suction feet, a back rest, and a long seating surface to facilitate transfers. (Courtesy of Lumex, Bay Shore, NY.)

7. An enlarged mirror over the sink also may be useful. A wall mirror with an adjustment hinge to tilt the top away from the wall facilitates use from a sitting position. Hinged-wall, gooseneck, or accordion fold-up mirrors (with one side magnified) are also helpful for close work.
8. Any exposed hot-water pipes under the sink should be insulated to avoid burns.

Figure 12–5 illustrates the basic components and minimum space requirements of a wheelchair-accessible bathroom.

Kitchen
1. The height of counter tops (work space) should be appropriate for the wheelchair user; the armrests should be able to fit under the working surface. The ideal height of counter surfaces should be no greater than 31 inches (79 cm) from the floor with a knee clearance of 27.5 inches (69.8 cm) to 30 inches (76.2 cm).[1] Counter space should provide a depth of at least 24 inches (61 cm).[1] All surfaces should be smooth to facilitate sliding of heavy items from one area to another. Slide-out counter spaces are useful in providing an over-the-lap working surface. For ambulatory patients, stools (preferably with back and foot rests) may be placed strategically at the main work area(s).
2. A small cart with casters may be suggested to improve ease of movement of articles from refrigerator to counter and other such activities.
3. The height of tables also should be checked and the tables may have to be raised or lowered.
4. Equipment and food storage areas should be selected with optimum energy conservation in mind. All frequently used articles should be within easy reach, and unnecessary items should be eliminated. Additional storage space may be achieved by installation of open shelving or use of peg

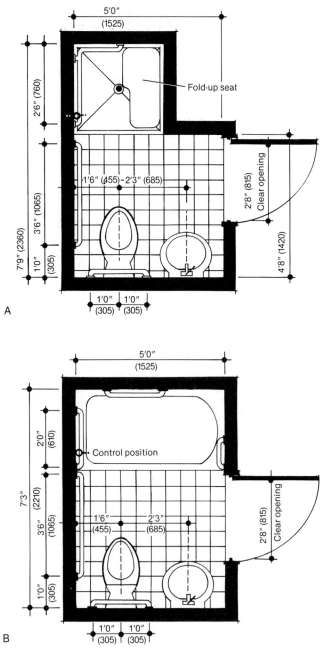

Figure 12–5. Sample features and minimum space requirements of a residential bathroom with (*A*) a shower stall and (*B*) a bathtub. The dotted line indicates lengths of wall that require reinforcement to receive grab bars or supports. (From Nixon, V: Spinal Cord Injury: A Guide to Functional Outcomes in Physical Therapy Management. Aspen Systems Corporation, Rockville, MD, 1985, p 186, with permission.)

boards for pots and pans. If shelving is added, adjustable shelves are preferable and should be placed 16 inches (41 cm)[3] above the countertop.
5. Electric stoves are generally preferable to open-flame gas burners. Controls may require adaptation and should be located on the front border of the stove (to eliminate the need for reaching across the burners). Burners that are placed beside each other provide a safer arrangement than those placed one behind the other. A burn-proof counter

surface adjacent to the burners will facilitate movement of hot items once cooking is completed. Smooth, ceramic cooktop surfaces also reduce the amount of lifting required while cooking. If cooktops provide knee clearance beneath, exposed or potential contact surfaces must be insulated.[2]

6. A split-level cooking unit is generally more easily accessible than a single, low-level combined oven and burner unit.
7. A countertop microwave oven also may be an important consideration for some patients.
8. The sink may be equipped with large bladetype handles, and a spray-hose fixture often provides improved function. Shallow sinks 5 to 6 inches (12.7 cm to 15.2 cm)[1,3] in depth will improve knee clearance below. As in the bathroom, hot-water pipes under the kitchen sink should be insulated to prevent burns.
9. Dishwashers should be front loading, with pull-out shelves.
10. Access to the refrigerator will be enhanced by use of a side-by-side (refrigerator-freezer) model.
11. A smoke detector and one or more easily accessible, portable fire extinguishers should be available. For patients with hearing impairments, the smoke detector can be attached to a strobe light to signal danger visually.

Figure 12–6 presents sample features of a kitchen designed for a wheelchair user.

Workplace Assessment

An investigation of the workplace is an important component of the environmental assessment. The most effective means of assessing the patient's work environment is an on-site visit. The specificity of the patient's job will dictate many of the types of functional activities that will be needed to perform the required tasks. When assessing level of function in the work environment, the principles of energy conservation and ergonomics are of prime importance in prevention of injury and in maximizing the worker's efficiency and comfort. Capabilities should be weighed against the physical demands of the work environment, and the therapist, using knowledge of adaptive equipment and applied biomechanics, may suggest changes appropriate to the situation.

Intervention in the workplace is an expanding area of interest within physical therapy. The on-site evaluation of the workplace typically includes (1) a *job analysis* to identify the specific components of the work task and features of the environment in which they must be accomplished; (2) an *ergonomic assessment* to identify the immediate or predicted risks of musculoskeletal injury for an individual worker; (3) a *plan for risk reduction* that provides recommendations to eliminate the potential for injury; and (4) a *plan to optimize function* that includes suggestions for adaptive equipment and recommendations for improving performance within the work environment.[4]

Many of the assessments and adaptive strategies employed in the home will be used in the work environment as well. Several considerations specific to the work setting are described below.

EXTERNAL ACCESSIBILITY

1. A parking space should be available within a short distance of the building if the patient plans to drive to and from work. Parking spaces should be a minimum of 96 inches (243.8 cm) wide, with an adjacent access aisle 60 inches (152.4 cm) wide.[2] The location should be clearly marked as a handicapped parking area.
2. External accessibility of the building should be addressed using guidelines similar to those presented for home exteriors.

INTERNAL ACCESSIBILITY

1. Initially, the component requirements of the work task must be identified. This will include determination of mobility required (movement within and outside the primary work area), as well as determination of demands or skill required in each of the following areas: strength (trunk, upper versus lower extremities), posture, endurance, manual dexterity, eye-hand coordination, vision, hearing, and communication.
2. The immediate work area should be carefully examined. This will include lighting, temperature, seating surface (if other than a wheelchair), the height and size of the work counter (some patients may benefit from a variable height or tilting work surface) and exposure to noise, vibration, or fumes. Access to supplies, materials, or equipment should be considered with respect to the patient's vertical and horizontal reaching capabilities. From an upright wheelchair sitting position, the vertical range (Fig. 12–7) of reach is from 20 inches (50.8 cm) to 48 inches (121.9 cm).[1] The maximum functional horizontal reach is considered 18 inches (45.7 cm) from the edge of a desk or work surface.[1] For patients with good trunk control, reaching capacity will be increased.
3. Access to public telephones, drinking fountains, and bathrooms should be addressed.

Alpert[4] suggests four potential approaches to facilitating optimum function in the work environment. These include (1) modification in the work space design or tools and equipment; (2) administrative changes such as rotation of job assignments, staggered breaks, lower production rates, and limited overtime; (3) education on effective work habits (e.g., correct posture, altered size of handled tools, and frequent equipment maintenance); and (4) use of protective or adaptive equipment.

A variety of building survey forms have been developed to facilitate the on-site assessment of the workplace. These forms assist with attending to all necessary details during the visit. A sample of such a form is provided in Appendix B.

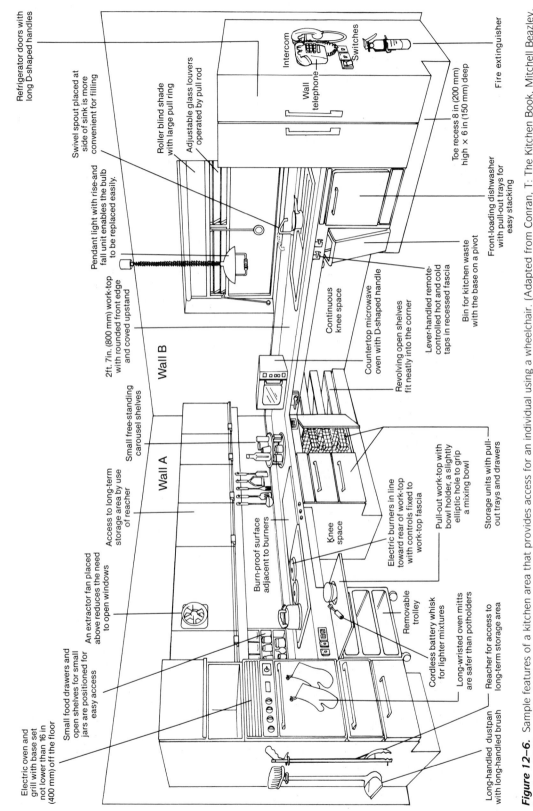

Refrigerator doors with long D-shaped handles

Swivel spout placed at side of sink is more convenient for filling

Roller blind shade with large pull ring

Adjustable glass louvers operated by pull rod

Intercom

Switches

Wall telephone

Fire extinguisher

Toe recess 8 in (200 mm) high × 6 in (150 mm) deep

Front-loading dishwasher with pull-out trays for easy stacking

Pendant light with rise-and fall unit enables the bulb to be replaced easily.

2ft. 7in. (800 mm) work-top with rounded front edge and coved upstand

Wall B

Continuous knee space

Countertop microwave oven with D-shaped handle

Revolving open shelves fit neatly into the corner

Lever-handled remote-controlled hot and cold taps in recessed fascia

Bin for kitchen waste with the base on a pivot

Small free-standing carousel shelves

Wall A

Access to long-term storage area by use of reacher

Burn-proof surface adjacent to burners

Knee space

Electric burners in line toward rear of work-top with controls fixed to work-top fascia

Pull-out work-top with bowl holder, a slightly elliptic hole to grip a mixing bowl

Storage units with pull-out trays and drawers

An extractor fan placed above reduces the need to open windows

Small food drawers and open shelves for small jars are positioned for easy access

Removable trolley

Cordless battery whisk for lighter mixtures

Long-wristed oven mitts are safer than potholders

Reacher for access to long-term storage area

Electric oven and grill with base set not lower than 16 in (400 mm) off the floor

Long-handled dustpan with long-handled brush

Figure 12–6. Sample features of a kitchen area that provides access for an individual using a wheelchair. (Adapted from Conran, T: The Kitchen Book, Mitchell Beazley, London, 1977, pp 118–119.)

216

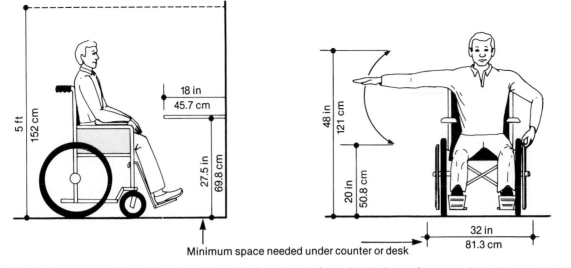

Minimum space needed under counter or desk

Figure 12–7. Maximum available unilateral vertical and horizontal reach for a wheelchair user from an upright sitting position. (From Cotler and DeGraff,[1] p 9, with permission.)

Community Assessment

To attain the goal of full accessibility for the patient, the availability of community resources, services, and facilities must be investigated. As mentioned earlier, when direct involvement by the therapist is not possible, this may best be accomplished by providing the family with guidelines for exploring access to local facilities. Another important consideration is to refer the patient and/or the family to community organizations such as the Arthritis Foundation, National Easter Seal Society, Multiple Sclerosis Society, Chamber of Commerce, or the Veterans Administration. These groups can provide information on services available to disabled residents of the community. Individuals who are returning to school should be encouraged to contact the campus disabled student services office. Information will be offered on housing, disabled student services, and general campus resources.

Two important areas that warrant attention when investigating community resources are the availability of appropriate transportation and accessibility of area social, religious, educational, cultural, and shopping facilities.

TRANSPORTATION

Currently the availability of accessible public transportation varies considerably among geographic areas. As such, careful exploration by the patient and family will be needed to determine what resources are obtainable in specific locales. Some communities provide part-time service of partially or completely accessible buses. These include the so-called kneeling buses equipped with a hydraulic unit that lowers the entrance to curb level for easier boarding. Some buses, although fewer in number, are designed with hydraulic lifts to allow direct entry by a wheelchair user. In communities where these buses are available, they typically operate on specific time schedules and are frequently limited to highly traf-

ficked routes. Careful planning is usually necessary to benefit from such service.

Unfortunately, the majority of public transportation systems in the United States do not allow use by non-ambulatory individuals or by those with limited ambulatory capacity. Most urban transit systems are virtually inaccessible to individuals with mobility impairments. As an alternative, many areas provide door-to-door van transportation to disabled residents of the community. Again, availability of such services may be scarce in some locations.

Some patients will want to master driving an adapted automobile or van. This, of course, will improve opportunities for community travel significantly. Motor vehicle adaptations are selected based on the physical capabilities of the individual. Common adaptive equipment includes *hand controls* to operate the brakes and the accelerator; *steering wheel attachments,* such as knobs or universal cuffs, for individuals with limited grip strength; *lifting units* to assist with placement of the wheelchair into the vehicle; and, for patients with quadriplegia or high-level paraplegia, *self-contained lifting platforms* for entry to a van while remaining seated in a wheelchair.

For patients whose capacity for long-distance ambulation is limited and/or whose endurance is low, commercially available city-going electric carts (Fig. 12–8) may be a practical alternative for travel within a reasonable proximity of the home.

ACCESS TO COMMUNITY FACILITIES

A few elements considered for workplace assessment warrant attention for general community access, as well. Briefly, these area facilities should be assessed for the availability of appropriate parking areas, beveled curbs, external and internal structural accessibility of buildings, availability of accessible public telephones, drinking fountains, bathrooms, and restaurants. Theaters, auditoriums, and lecture halls must be considered with

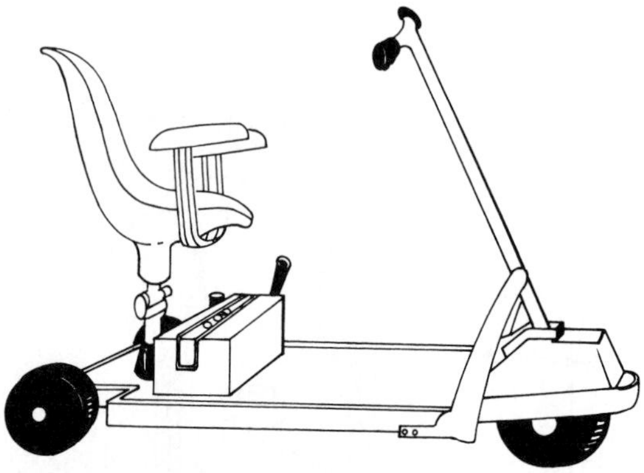

Figure 12–8. Motorized cart suitable for outdoor travel.

respect to accessible seating areas. Locations of emergency exits also should be noted for all facilities. In addition to these general considerations, stores and shopping areas should also be inspected for access to merchandise (especially for wheelchair users), appropriate aisle widths, and adequate space at checkout counters.

Another useful source of information on community access are the guidebooks offered by many larger cities. These books provide information on accessibility of hotels, restaurants, transportation, and cultural and recreational facilities.[5] These publications usually can be obtained from the city's chamber of commerce, the mayor's office for the handicapped, or the office of tourism. Combined use of such guides and phoning ahead for details of accessibility will facilitate travel both within and outside the local community.

Follow-up Report

Upon completion of the environmental assessment, a final combined report should be compiled. This report consists of information obtained from the home and, if applicable, the workplace assessment. Information should be included about the measures taken to explore general community accessibility.

Documentation of the on-site visit should incorporate a completed home assessment or building survey form. Additional information that should be provided includes

1. A description of the methods used to assist the patient in ambulation or functional activities.
2. A description of the type and quantity of adaptive equipment required (including source and cost).
3. Suggested structural modifications with precise specifications.
4. Recommended changes in furniture arrangements, floor coverings, and so forth.

Documentation related to community access entails a verification that the patient is aware of available community resources. The sources of this information, as well as whether the therapist was directly or indirectly involved in assessment, should be documented.

The completed report should then be included as part of the patient's medical record. Copies of the report should be submitted to the patient's family, the physi-

cian, third party payer(s), and any community-based health care or social service agencies that will be providing care upon discharge.

FUNDING FOR ENVIRONMENTAL MODIFICATIONS

The patient and family may require assistance in locating appropriate financial resources to achieve environmental accessibility. Typically, the social service department within the rehabilitation facility will provide direction in this area. Potential sources of funding include private insurance companies, Veterans Administration Housing Grants, the Division of Vocational Rehabilitation (DVR), and the Worker's Compensation Commission.

An important consideration is that not all patients will have current housing that is amenable to modification (e.g., an individual who previously lived in a third-floor walk-up apartment and is now a wheelchair user). In such instances, the local Housing and Urban Development (HUD) office will be an important resource. This office can provide a listing of accessible housing within the community. Because there are often waiting lists for such dwellings, early application is warranted.

Finally, some "creative funding" for specific items (such as specialized adaptive equipment not covered by other resources) may be available through private organizations or foundations. Considerable time, research, and perseverance may be required in locating a receptive organization. General suggestions the patient and family might consider in seeking assistance include contacting local businesses or corporate-giving offices, civic or service clubs, churches or synagogues, labor unions, Jaycees, and the Knights of Columbus.[6]

LEGISLATIVE ACTION RELATED TO ENVIRONMENTAL ACCESS

In recent years much attention has been focused on the importance of environmental accessibility. Through legislation and a variety of private organizations, significant strides have been made in this area. The Architectural Barrier Act of 1968 (P.L. 90-480) provided that certain buildings that were financed by federal funds be designed and constructed "to insure that physically handicapped persons will have ready access to, and use of, such buildings [p 719]."[7] The Rehabilitation Act of 1973 provided that access must be established in all federally funded buildings and transportation facilities constructed since 1968.[8] Because many federally funded institutions provided low compliance with the 1973 Rehabilitation Act, an amendment was passed in 1978.[9] The Comprehensive Rehabilitation Services Amendments (P.L. 95-602) of 1978 strengthened the enforcement of the original 1973 Rehabilitation Act.[9] The Architectural and Transportation Barriers Compliance Board is the governing body responsible for enforcing this legislation.[4]

Another important item of legislation related to environmental accessibility is the Public Buildings Act of 1983, which functioned to establish public building policies for the federal government. This act (section 307) provided several amendments to the Architectural Barrier Act of 1968 to further strengthen and delineate the importance of accessibility. The term *fully accessible* in this act was defined as

> the absence or elimination of physical and communications barriers to the ingress, egress, movement within, and use of a building by handicapped persons and the incorporation of such equipment as is necessary to provide such ingress, egress, movement, and use and, in a building of historic, architectural, or cultural significance, the elimination of such barriers and the incorporation of such equipment in such a manner as to be compatible with the significant architectural features of the building to the maximum extent possible.[10] (p 373)

In 1990 the Americans with Disabilities Act (ADA) was signed into law. This recent legislation is among the most comprehensive of the civil rights laws enacted for individuals with disabilities. It guarantees civil rights protection and equal opportunity in the areas of government services, employment, public transportation, privately owned transportation available to the public, telephone service, and public accommodations.[11] This law requires that by 1993, all "public places of accommodation" be made accessible to disabled people unless it imposes "undue hardship" to the business. This law includes compliance by restaurants, movie theaters, hotels, professional offices, and retail stores.

In the ADA of 1990 *disability* is defined as "a physical or mental impairment that substantially limits one or more major life activities; a record of such impairment or being regarded as having such impairment."[12] A definition of "undue hardship" is not stipulated. However, such hardship would likely include excessive direct cost of adapting the environment, limited resources of the business, and the effect of these changes on daily operation of a business.[13] Connolly[13] suggests that the cost of changes can not be used as a defense during litigation unless the financial burden would threaten the very existence of the business. The ADA also provides a federal tax credit incentive for measures taken by businesses to comply with this law.

Despite the recent gains made in architectural accessibility, many barriers continue to exist. Inasmuch as most public transportation systems were built before 1968, accessibility is not required by law.[4] However, effective in 1990, the ADA indicates that all concerns that offer public transit along a fixed route must also provide buses that are accessible to individuals with disabilities, including access by wheelchairs.[11,12] Other areas that continue to be problematic include revolving doors, the design of many supermarkets and shopping areas (barrier imposed by checkout areas and items displayed on high shelves),[9] lack of available parking spaces, multiple levels of stairs at the entrance to some buildings, and the design of many theaters and auditoriums that do not have specifically designated areas for wheelchair users.[5]

In response to recent legislation related to accessibility, several important publications have been developed to assist in the planning and/or modification of existing facilities.[2,3,14-17] These publications provide answers to frequently asked questions and offer specifications for making facilities accessible to and usable by people with mobility impairments.

Although increasing numbers of buildings are being designed to provide accessibility, this area warrants further involvement from therapists. Both physical and occupational therapists are equipped to provide leadership in compliance with existing and new laws. They have important knowledge and skills to enable them to provide valuable input into the modification and/or initial planning of barrier-free designs.

SUMMARY

Information obtained from an environmental assessment is an important factor in facilitating the patient's transition from the rehabilitation setting to the home and community. Such assessments assist in determining the level of patient access, safety, and function within specific components of the environment. They also assist in determining the need for additional treatment interventions, environmental modifications, outpatient services, and adaptive equipment. Additionally, they assist in preparing the patient, family, and/or colleagues for the individual's return to a given setting.

This chapter has presented a sample approach to environmental assessment. Common environmental features that typically warrant consideration have been highlighted. Inasmuch as a return to a former environment is often a primary goal of rehabilitation, early consideration of these issues is warranted. Collaboration among team members, the patient, and family will ensure an optimum and highly individualized approach to community reintegration.

QUESTIONS FOR REVIEW

1. Identify the purposes of an environmental assessment.

2. What information should be obtained prior to an on-site visit? Identify possible sources of this information.

3. Who should be involved in the on-site visit?

4. Identify the components of a home assessment (i.e., what specific aspects of the dwelling's interior and exterior should be assessed?).

5. Explain the importance of an environmental assessment in overall rehabilitation planning.

6. Describe the information that should be included in the follow-up report once the environmental assessment is complete.

7. What civil rights of individuals with disabilities are protected by the 1990 Americans with Disabilities Act?

REFERENCES

1. Cotler, SR and DeGraff, AH: Architectural Accessibility for the Disabled of College Campuses. New York State University Construction Fund, Albany, NY 1976.
2. American National Standards Institute: American National Standard for Buildings and Facilities—Providing Accessibility and Usability for Physically Handicapped People. American National Standards Institute, New York, NY, 1986.
3. Building Design Requirements for the Physically Handicapped, rev ed. Eastern Paralyzed Veterans Association, New York, NY, undated.
4. Alpert, J: The physical therapist's role in job analysis and on site education. Orthop Phys Ther Pract 5:8, 1993.
5. Trombly, CA and Versluys, HP: Environmental evaluation and community reintegration. In Trombly, CA (ed): Occupational Therapy for Physical Dysfunction, ed 3. Williams & Wilkins, Baltimore, 1989, p 427.
6. Corbet, B (ed): National Resource Directory: An Information Guide for Persons with Spinal Cord Injury and Other Physical Disabilities. National Spinal Cord Injury Association, Newton, MA, 1985.
7. Architectural Barriers Act, Public Law 90-480, 1968.
8. Silver, M: Federal compliance board under fire. Accent on Living 22:24, 1977.
9. Ross, EC: New rehabilitation law. Accent on Living 23:23, 1978.
10. Public Buildings Act, 98th Congress, 1st session, 1983.
11. Eastern Paralyzed Veterans Association: Understanding the Americans with Disabilities Act. Eastern Paralyzed Veterans Association, Jackson Heights, NY.
12. United States Department of Justice: Americans with Disabilities Act: Information Bulletin. United States Department of Justice, Civil Rights Division, Coordinator and Review Section, Washington, DC, 1990.
13. Connolly, JB: Understanding the ADA. Clinical Management 12:40, 1992.
14. Matheson, LN: Americans with Disabilities Act of 1990—effective strategies for compliance. Industrial Rehabilitation Quarterly Winter: 5, 1992.
15. Equal Opportunity Commission and the United States Department of Justice: The ADA—Questions and Answers. Equal Opportunity Commission and the United States Department of Justice, Civil Rights Department, Washington, DC, 1991.
16. Equal Employment Opportunity Commission: The ADA—Your Responsibilities as an Employer. Equal Employment Opportunity Commission, Washington, DC, 1991.
17. Equal Employment Opportunity Commission and the United States Department of Justice: Americans with Disabilities Act Handbook. Equal Opportunity Commission and the United States Department of Justice, Civil Rights Department, Washington, DC, 1991.

SUPPLEMENTAL READINGS

Austill-Clausen, R: Adaptive equipment for the home. In May, BJ (ed): Home Health and Rehabilitation. FA Davis, Philadelphia, 1993, p 193.
Berube, B: Barrier-free design—making the environment accessible to the disabled. Can Med Assoc J 124:68, 1981.
Colvin, ME and Korn, TL: Eliminating barriers to the disabled. Am J Occup Ther 38:748, 1984.
Francis, RA: The development of federal accessibility law. J Rehabil 49:29, 1983.
Frieden, L: Independent living models. Rehabil Lit 41:169, 1980.
Jirovec, RL, Jirovec, MM, and Bosse, R: Environmental determinants of neighborhood satisfaction among urban elderly men. Gerontologist 24:261, 1984.
May, BJ: The home environment. In May, BJ (ed): Home Health and Rehabilitation, FA Davis, Philadelphia, 1993, p 173.
Neistadt, ME and Marques, K: An independent living skills training program. Am J Occup Ther 38:671, 1984.
Randall, M: Locating rehabilitation product information through ABLE-DATA. Occupational Therapy in Health Care 1:747, 1984.

Raschko, BB: Housing Interiors for the Disabled and Elderly. Van Nostrand Reinhold, New York, 1982.
Speidel, LK: Air transportation and the disabled: current and future trends. Occup Ther Health Care 1:55, 1984.
Symington, DC and MacLean, J: Environmental control systems in chronic care hospitals and nursing homes. Arch Phys Med Rehabil 67:322, 1986.
Taira, ED: An occupational therapist's perspective on environmental adaptations for the disabled elderly. Occup Ther Health Care 1:25, 1984.
Van Iderstine, C: Home environment analysis. In Scully, R and Barnes, ML (eds): Physical Therapy. JB Lippincott, Philadelphia, 1989.
Wamboldt, JJ: Computer environmental control units for the severely physically disabled: a guide for the occupational therapist. Occupational Therapy in Health Care 1:155, 1984.
West, J (ed): Americans with Disabilities Act: From Policy to Practice. Milbank Memorial Fund, New York, NY, 1991.
Wister, A: Environmental adaptation by persons in their later life. Aging 11:267, 1989.

GLOSSARY

Adaptive equipment: Devices or equipment designed and fabricated to improve performance in activities of daily living.

Beveled: Smooth, slanted angle between two surfaces; for example, a slant or inclination between two uneven surfaces to allow easier passage of a wheelchair.

Casters: Small revolving wheels on the legs of a chair; such a chair may allow mobility in an area that is unable to accommodate a wheelchair; term also refers to the small front wheels of a wheelchair.

Environmental accessibility: Absence or removal of physical barriers from the entrance and within a building or dwelling to allow use by individuals with different physical abilities.

Environmental barrier: Any component of a dwelling, structure, or vehicle that prevents use of the facility or service by individuals with different physical abilities (e.g., revolving doors, stairways, narrow doorways).

Grab bars: Wall supports used to assist a person in both toilet and tub transfers; can be mounted vertically, horizontally, or diagonally.

Grade, gradient: Degree of inclination or slope of a ramp.

International symbol of access: Symbol widely used to indicate that a building and its facilities are accessible.

Kick plate: Metal guard plate attached to the bottom of a door.

Knurled surface: Roughened area, often in a criss-crossed pattern; used on either doorknobs or grab bars. On doorknobs it is used to provide tactile clues to visually impaired persons to indicate that passage leads to an area of danger. On grab bars it is used to improve grasp and to prevent slipping.

Nosing: Edge or brim of a step that projects out over the lower stair surface.

Threshold: Elevated surface on floor of doorway; a doorsill.

APPENDIX A   HOME ASSESSMENT FORM

TYPE OF HOME
_____ Apartment
          Is elevator available? _____
          What floor does patient live on? _____
_____ One floor home.
_____ Two or more floors.
_____ Does patient live on first floor, second floor, or use all floors of home?
_____ Basement. Does patient have or use basement area?

ENTRANCES TO BUILDING OR HOME
Location   Front   Back   Side (Circle one)
    Which entrance is used most frequently or easily? _____
    Can patient get to entrance? _____
Stairs
    Does patient manage outside stairs? _____
    Width of stairway _____
    Number of steps _____ Height of steps _____
    Railing present as you go up. R _____ L _____
    Both _____
    Is ramp available for wheelchair patient? _____
Door
    Can patient unlock, open, close, lock door? (Circle for yes)
    If doorsill is present, give height _____ and material _____
    Width of doorway _____
    Can patient enter _____ leave _____ via door?
Hallway
    Width of hallway _____
    Are any objects obstructing the way? _____

APPROACH TO APARTMENT OR LIVING AREA
    (Omit if not applicable)
Hallway
    Width _____
    Obstructions? _____
Steps
    Does patient manage? _____
    Width of stairway _____
    Number of steps _____ Height of steps _____
    Railing present as you go up? R _____ L _____
    Both _____
    Is ramp available? _____
Door
    Can patient unlock, open, close, lock door? (Circle one)
    Doorsill? Give height _____ material _____
    Width of doorway _____
    Can patient enter _____ leave _____ via door?
Elevator
    Is elevator present? _____ Does it land flush with door? _____
    Width of door opening _____
    Height of control buttons _____
    Can patient manage elevator alone? _____

INSIDE HOME
Note width of hallways and of door entrances.
Note presence of doorsills and height.
Note if patient must climb stairs to reach room.
Can patient move from one part of the house to another?
    Hallways _____
    Bedroom _____
    Bathroom _____
    Kitchen _____
    Living room _____
    Others _____

Can patient move safely?
    Loose rugs _____
    Electrical cords _____
    Faulty floors _____
    Highly waxed floors _____
    Sharp-edged furniture _____
Note areas of particular danger for patient.
    Hot-water pipes _____
    Radiators _____
BEDROOM
    Is light switch accessible? _____
    Can patient open and close windows? _____
Bed
    Height _____ Width _____
    Both sides of bed accessible? _____ Headboard present? _____
        footboard? _____
    Is bed on wheels? _____ Is it stable? _____
    Can patient transfer from wheelchair to bed? _____
        and bed to wheelchair? _____
    Is night table within patient's reach from bed _____
        Is telephone on it? _____
Clothing
    Is patient's clothing located in bedroom? _____
    Can patient get clothes from dresser? _____ closet? _____
        elsewhere? _____

BATHROOM
Does patient use wheelchair _____ walker _____ in bathroom?
Does wheelchair _____ walker _____ fit into bathroom?
Light switch accessible? _____ Can patient open and close window? _____
What material are bathroom walls made of? _____
    If tile, how many inches does it extend from the floor beside the toilet? _____
How many inches from the top of the rim of the bathtub? _____
Does patient use toilet? _____
    Can patient transfer independently to and from toilet? _____
    Does wheelchair wheel directly to toilet for transfers? _____
    What is height of toilet seat from floor? _____
    Are there bars or sturdy supports near toilet? _____
    Is there room for grab bars? _____
Can patient use sink? _____ What is height of sink? _____
    Is patient able to reach and turn off faucets? _____
    Is there knee space beneath sink? _____
    Is patient able to reach necessary articles? _____ mirror? _____
        electrical outlet? _____
Bathing
    Does patient take tub bath? _____ shower? _____
        sponge bath? _____
    If using tub, can patient safely transfer without assistance? _____
    Bars or sturdy supports present beside tub? _____
    Is equipment necessary? (tub seat, handspray attachment, tub rail, no-skid strips, grab rails, other _____)
    Can patient manage faucets and drain plug? _____
    Height of tub from floor to rim _____
    Is tub built-in _____ or on legs _____ ?
    Width of tub from the inside _____
    If uses separate shower stall, can patient transfer independently and manage faucets? _____
    If patient takes sponge bath, describe method. _____
    _____
    _____

APPENDIX A   HOME ASSESSMENT FORM (*Continued*)

LIVING ROOM AREA
Light switch accessible? _____ Can patient open and close
   window? _____
Can furniture be rearranged to allow manipulation of wheelchair?_____
Can patient transfer from wheelchair to and from sturdy chair? _____
   Height of chair _____
Can patient transfer from wheelchair to and from sofa? _____
   Height of sofa _____
Can ambulatory patient transfer to and from chair? _____ sofa? ____
Can patient manage television and radio? _____

DINING ROOM
Light switch accessible? _____
Is patient able to use table? _____ Height of table _____

KITCHEN
What is the table height? _____ Can wheelchair fit under? _____
Can patient open refrigerator door and take food? _____
Can patient open freezer door and take food? _____
Sink
   Can patient be seated at sink? _____
   Can patient reach faucets? _____ Turn them on and off? _____
   Can patient reach bottom of basin? _____
Shelves and cabinets
   Can patient open and close? _____
   Can patient reach dishes, pots, silver, and food? _____
Comments:

Transport
   Can patient carry utensils from one part of kitchen to another? _____
Stove
   Can patient reach and manipulate controls? _____
   Light pilot on oven? _____
   Manage oven door? _____
   Place food in oven and remove? _____
   Manage broiler door? _____
   Put food in and remove? _____
Other Appliances
   Can patient reach and turn on appliances? _____
   Can patient use outlets? _____
Counter space: Is there enough for storage and work area?

Diagram (include stove, refrigerator, sink, table, counters, others if
   applicable)

LAUNDRY
If patient has no facilities, how will laundry be managed?
Location of facilities in home or apartment and description of facilities
   present:

Can patient reach laundry area? _____
Can patient use washing machine and dryer? _____
   Load and empty? _____
   Manage doors and controls? _____
Can patient use sink? _____
   What is height of sink? _____
   Able to reach and turn on faucets? _____
   Knee space beneath sink? _____
   Able to reach necessary articles? _____
Is laundry cart available? _____
Can patient hang clothing on line? _____
Ironing board
   Location:
      Is it kept open? _____
      If not kept open, can patient set up and take down ironing board?
      _____
      Can patient reach outlet? _____

CLEANING
Can patient remove mop, broom, vacuum, pail from storage? _____
Use equipment? (mop, broom, vacuum and so forth) _____

EMERGENCY
Location of telephone in house:

Could patient use fire escape or back door in a hurry if alone? _____
Does patient have numbers for neighbors, police, fire and physician?
_____

OTHER
Will patient be responsible for child care? _____
   If so, give number of children _____ and ages: _____
Will patient do own shopping? _____
   Is family member or friend available? _____
   Is delivery service available? _____
Does family have automobile? _____
Is family member or friend available to help with lawn care, changing
   high light bulbs, and so forth? _____

APPENDIX B   BUILDING SURVEY FORM

Name of building: _____ Date of survey: _____
Location: _____ Surveyor: _____

	Yes	No
PARKING AREA		
1. Are handicapped parking spaces with adequate wheelchair transfer space designated?	_____	_____
2. Are curb cutouts available and appropriately labeled?	_____	_____
3. Are parking spaces easily accessible to walkway without requiring negotiating behind parked cars?	_____	_____
4. Indicate number of available handicapped parking spaces. _____		
ENTRANCES TO BUILDING		
1. Is at least one major entrance available for use by the handicapped?	_____	_____
2. Does the entrance provide access to a level where elevators are available?	_____	_____
ELEVATORS		
1. Is a passenger elevator available?	_____	_____
2. Does the elevator reach all levels of the building?	_____	_____
3. Are control buttons (both inside and outside of the elevator) no more than 48 in (122 cm) from the floor?	_____	_____
4. Are control buttons raised and easy to push?	_____	_____
5. Is an emergency telephone accessible?	_____	_____
PUBLIC TELEPHONES		
1. Are an appropriate number of phones available and accessible to handicapped individuals?	_____	_____
2. Are they dial or pushbutton? _____		
3. Is the height of the dial mechanism no more than 44 in (112 cm) from the floor?	_____	_____
4. Is a receiver volume control available?	_____	_____

	Yes	No
FLOOR SURFACES		
1. Are surfaces nonslip?	_____	_____
2. If carpeting is present, is it tightly woven and securely glued to floor (to prevent rippling under wheelchair)?	_____	_____
REST ROOMS		
1. Is there an adequate number of rest rooms available and accessible to the handicapped?	_____	_____
2. Is there at least 48 in (122 cm) between inside wall and partitions enclosing toilet?	_____	_____
3. Is entrance to cubicle at least 48 in (122 cm) wide?	_____	_____
4. Are grab bars present and securely mounted?	_____	_____
5. Is height of seat not more than 17.5 in (44.5 cm)?	_____	_____
6. Is toilet paper holder within easy reach?	_____	_____
7. Is adequate turning space (6 ft × 6 ft [183 cm × 183 cm]) available in main area of rest room?	_____	_____
8. Is there adequate space for clearance of knees under sink?	_____	_____
9. Are drain and hot-water pipes covered or shielded to avoid burns?	_____	_____
10. Are faucet handles large (blade-type) and accessible?	_____	_____
WATER FOUNTAINS		
1. Is the fountain height appropriate for use by someone in a wheelchair?	_____	_____
2. Are controls pushbutton or blade-type?	_____	_____
3. Is a foot control available?	_____	_____
4. Is adequate space (at least 3 ft [92 cm] provided near fountain to permit wheelchair mobility?	_____	_____

From Cotler and DeGraff,[1] with permission.

Strategies to Improve Motor Control and Motor Learning

Susan B. O'Sullivan

OBJECTIVES

1. Describe a clinical decision-making model that incorporates factors of normal motor control, motor learning, and developmental task goals.
2. Identify appropriate treatment strategies to improve each of the following: cognition, attention, arousal, sensation, flexibility, strength, tone, and patterns of movement.
3. Identify factors critical to motor learning and describe a training strategy designed to optimize learning.
4. Identify appropriate treatment techniques to attain the task goals of mobility, stability, controlled mobility, and skill.

Developing strategies to improve motor control and motor learning requires a thorough understanding of the neural processes involved in producing movement. In addition, a knowledge of normal development can help provide a focus for overall task goals. A conceptual model that ties these three areas together provides a useful framework for planning and allows the therapist to approach clinical problem solving in a systematic manner. Patients frequently demonstrate deficits of varying intensities, and in more than one area of function. Careful assessment of motor behaviors, and the environmental contexts in which they occur, provides an appropriate base for initiating therapeutic intervention. Many of these assessment procedures are discussed in preceding chapters. In physical therapy, a number of different treatment approaches and techniques have been developed to address a multiplicity of problems. Use of a clinical decision-making model based upon normal function allows the blending of therapeutic approaches and the development of an optimal treatment plan designed to meet the individual needs of the patient (Fig. 13–1).[1–3]

COMPONENTS OF MOTOR CONTROL

Motor control involves the complex interaction of many body systems; it allows the processing of sensory information, integration, and decision making by neural control centers, and the execution of appropriate motor responses. Individuals first perceive the need to move; they identify stimuli, attend to environmental conditions, and develop the idea for movement (ideation phase). A motor plan is then determined and elaborated (planning phase). The programming phase includes the structuring of specific motor programs (coordinative structures) necessary to run the plan. Specific elements are determined including range of motion (ROM), strength, muscle tone, and sensation. Finally, the execution phase involves engaging the selected muscles necessary for movement, and the feedback monitoring systems necessary for control. A model of the neural processes involved in movement is provided in Figure 8–1.[1] Successful motor performance depends on intact functioning of each of the component parts.

Perception

Perceptual processes allow the sorting out and organization of incoming sensory stimuli into meaningful data. Sage[2] defines the essential steps of perception as the "detection, discrimination, recognition, and identification of incoming information for an interpretation." Perceptual processes thus require interaction of sensory systems with memory processes. Long-term memory stores are searched and meaning is attached on the basis

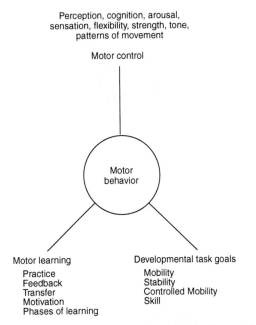

Perception, cognition, arousal,
sensation, flexibility, strength, tone,
patterns of movement

Motor control

Motor
behavior

Motor learning

Practice
Feedback
Transfer
Motivation
Phases of learning

Developmental task goals

Mobility
Stability
Controlled Mobility
Skill

Figure 13–1. A conceptual model for clinical problem solving.

of past sensorimotor experiences. The clarity and the intensity of the stimulus can affect the duration of information processing during this phase. Individual differences exist in preferred modes of perceptual processing (visual versus auditory learners), in processing abilities (slow versus fast reaction times), and in consistency of response over time. Intraindividual differences may also result from the inability of an individual to adapt to different environmental situations. Perceptual deficits and therapeutic strategies for remediation are discussed fully in Chapter 28.

Cognition

Response selection follows stimulus identification and is the result of decision processing in the central nervous system (CNS). During the cognitive phase, an individual must determine the idea of the movement. A **motor plan** is formulated that attends to the known task demands and specific environmental conditions. Components of the motor plan are assembled. These include motor programs (also called coordinative structures[3]) and subprograms. A **motor program** is defined as an abstract code or set of prestructured commands that, when initiated, results in the production of a coordinated movement sequence.[4] A **subprogram** is a smaller learned subroutine. Learning a new movement is made easier by the existence of motor programs and subprograms that reduce the degrees of freedom problem; that is, they free the executive level from having to decide on all aspects of a particular movement. Stored programs can be called up, modified, or reassembled in different orders, to form the new motor pattern. Strategies to improve the cognitive phase are discussed in a later section in this chapter (see section on motor learning: cognitive phase).

Attention

Selective attention mechanisms allow an individual to attend to relevant cues of both the task and the environment while screening out irrelevant ones. Information selected for processing is augmented, while other irrelevant information is inhibited. Control of attention mechanisms is influenced by stimulus intensity, novelty, past experience or memory, motivation, and expectancy. Ongoing processing of sensory information also influences attention mechanisms and enhances continued neural transmission. Thus the sensations that immediately precede a sensory cue can make it easier for subsequent sensations to be received. In treatment, consistency and emphasis on the sensations of movement may make succeeding movements easier and enhance the development of motor control.[5] The complexity of task demands or fatigue can also influence attentiveness and substantially decrease performance.

STRATEGIES TO IMPROVE ATTENTION

It is important to carefully structure and limit information presented to the patient with attention deficits. Good verbal commands, using adequate volume and inflection, can provide an effective means of directing attention.[6] The therapist can ensure that the important parts of the skill are attended to by focusing on key task elements.[4,5]

Patients with attention deficits are unable to attend to important stimuli and often appear erratic in thought and action. Consistency must become the hallmark of treatment. The treatment schedule, setting, procedures, verbal instructions, and staff should be consistent from day to day. Activities should be planned that work within the limitations of the patient's attention span. Thus short periods of treatment and simple repetitive activities are more beneficial than longer and more complex ones. Familiar activities and activities of special interest to the patient are generally more successful than novel tasks. Instructions should also be kept short and simple. Combining instructions with demonstration is frequently a more effective strategy to engage the patient's attention than instructions alone. Key factors in achieving success in treatment are controlling the environment (eliminating distractors), establishing a consistent daily routine, and prompt rewarding of desired behaviors.[7–10]

Patients who **perseverate** appear to get stuck on a thought or action and persist in repeating themselves over and over again. These patients should be gently guided into a new activity. Use of interesting activities can help refocus attention, while use of well-defined sequences of activities can help limit perseveration episodes. Successful completion of a task or sequence of movements should be positively rewarded.

Arousal

Arousal (central set) refers to the overall level of alertness of the central nervous system. Low arousal is associated with sleep or drowsiness, whereas high arousal is associated with extreme excitement. The autonomic nervous system (ANS) functions to establish baseline values for a number of body functions, to maintain equilibrium (homeostasis), and to initiate actions designed to adapt and protect the individual under varying conditions (fight-or-flight responses). The arousal system (reticular activating system [RAS]) maintains the body in a general state of readiness and prepares sensory and motor systems for upcoming stimuli or tasks. A number of factors can influence central set, including emotions, medications, time of day, or fatigue. Stimulus-specific arousal responses are activated by cortical activity (thinking) and by novel, unexpected, or threatening stimuli.[11]

A certain level of arousal is necessary for optimal motor performance. High states of arousal cause a deterioration in performance, whereas low states fail to yield the necessary responsiveness needed for effective performance. This is referred to as the **inverted U hypothesis** (Yerkes-Dodson law).[12] Excess levels of arousal can also yield unexpected or paradoxical responses.[13] For example, a patient with a head injury who is extremely agitated may not appear to respond to the addition of a new environmental stimulus. Because the patient is already hyperkinetic, an increase in motor activity is not observed. With further stimulation, the patient may respond by lapsing into decreased consciousness (a reversal of response). Thus the state of the CNS affects the reaction of somatic systems to external stimuli.[14]

Poor selectivity of sensory cues can be found with low levels of arousal, whereas increased distractibility and poor decision making are characteristic of excessive arousal levels. Performance and learning are impaired in both situations. Different motor tasks may require different levels of arousal. For example, high arousal levels improve performance on rapid, power activities. However, the same level of arousal decreases performance on precision or fine motor tasks. Tasks that require a high degree of steadiness or decision processing are also impaired by high arousal levels. Examples of these include postural holding responses and complex motor skills. **Open skills** are more impaired by high arousal levels than are **closed skills.** Optimal arousal levels also vary according to the stage of learning, with the higher arousal levels being more disruptive during early learning.[4]

STRATEGIES TO IMPROVE AROUSAL LEVELS

Patients with brain damage may show decreased alertness and arousal levels (vegetative or low-level states). These patients may benefit from an organized stimulation program designed to improve generalized response levels, sometimes called **coma stimulation** or early recovery management programs. Two different types of stimulation have been used: environmental stimulation and structured sensory stimulation. Environmental stimulation involves structuring the patient's environment to provide ongoing stimuli such as music in the room, visual targets, or mobiles. Structured sensory stimulation involves presenting stimuli to the patient in a direct fashion, and uses tactile, visual, vestibular, auditory, olfactory, and gustatory stimuli.[15] Table 13–1 presents some of the stimuli typically used. Sensitivity to the patient's responses helps to determine the optimal times for treatment, general length of the session, and the type of stimulation that proves most beneficial. Premorbid interests often provide an important source of information in determining which stimuli are most meaningful to the patient. Overstimulation should be avoided. Stimuli should be carefully presented, one at a time, and extraneous environmental stimuli minimized. Verbal explanations, focusing the patient on the specific stimulus, should be kept brief and to the point. Once responsiveness increases, the therapist should have the patient begin to discriminate particular types of stimuli and respond to them with specific motor responses.

Table 13–1 SENSORY STIMULI USED IN MODIFYING AROUSAL LEVELS

Low Arousal State Sensory Stimuli Are High Intensity, High Frequency Intermittent, Phasic	Response Is One of Generalized Arousal; Brief, Phasic

Auditory
    Verbal commands
    Brisk music
    Different sounds
	Orientation to sound

Visual
    Stationary targets
    Tracking targets (horizontal and vertical)
    Bright colors
	Orientation to objects

Cutaneous
    Light, moving touch
    Different textured, shaped materials
	Activation of total withdrawal patterns

Kinesthetic
    Upright positioning (wheelchair, tilt table)
    ROM, ADL tasks
	Orientation to environment and body

Vestibular
    Fast movements: angular or transient linear acceleration
    Mobile surfaces (large ball, bolster, equilibrium board)
	Increased tone Increased postural reactions

Olfactory/gustatory
    Different scents, tastes
    Noxious odors
	Orientation to stimuli

High Arousal State Sensory Stimuli Are Low Intensity, Low Frequency Maintained, Tonic	Response Is One of Generalized Calming; Maintained, Tonic

Auditory
    Soft, soothing voice
    Soft music
    Quiet environment
Visual
    Soft, low lights
Cutaneous
    Maintained touch
    Neutral warmth
    Slow stroking down back
	Decreased tone, decreased activity

Kinesthetic Highly structured activity	Organized responses

ADL = activities of daily living; ROM = range of motion.

Thus, touching two different textured objects, discriminating between them, and then holding the one selected, requires the patient to make choices and initiate actions. Response times are frequently delayed so extra time should be allowed for the patient to respond.[7,10] The effectiveness of stimulation programs in influencing recovery from head injury is inconclusive. Available research is flawed with methodologic problems and more definitive research is needed.[15]

Agitated patients who demonstrate excess levels of arousal also benefit from control of sensory stimuli. Frequently, sources of stimulation from the environment precipitate bouts of agitation and disorganization. The patient is generally unable to effectively process stimuli and is similarly unable to control his or her responses, which are often bizarre and combative. Careful assessment can distinguish the offending stimuli and those that have a calming influence. The environment should be modified to eliminate or reduce irritative stimuli. Thus treatment can be given in a quiet room rather than in a noisy gym. Because unexpected surprises often precipitate outbursts, consistency in total management is very important. Establish a daily routine and provide an overall structure. Each new activity should be carefully explained before the activity is attempted. During the execution of the task, verbal reassurances and manual guidance are often helpful to the patient. When agitated outbursts occur, the therapist should calmly redirect the patient's attention away from the cause of irritation. Often selection of a task over which the patient has some control will help the patient regain composure. The therapist should provide a model for calm, controlled behavior and reward each successful effort with positive reinforcement.[32,33]

Therapeutic stimuli can be selected that attempt to restore homeostatic balance by promoting generalized relaxation. These include maintained touch, slow stroking, neutral warmth, slow vestibular stimulation, or inverted positioning (Tables 13–2 and 13–3). In general, they are applied in a slow, maintained manner and are thought to produce a calming effect by influencing brainstem activity and parasympathetic outflow.

Sensation

Several general concepts are important to an understanding of the role of sensation in movement. Sensory inputs are used to guide the execution of ongoing movement. Sensory inputs are also used to modify successive movements and shape motor programs through corrective actions. Variability and adaptability of movements to the environment is made possible by the use of sensory inputs. Interaction of sensory and motor systems occurs throughout the CNS. Spinal level interactions are largely reflexive in nature, whereas supraspinal centers modulate higher levels of motor behavior. Overall, the CNS is viewed as a flexible hierarchy with multiple control sites and interactions.[1]

Sensory stimulation of movement patterns is an important part of neurotherapeutic approaches.[16-21] Movements are elicited through the use of specific stimuli (e.g., stretching, tapping). Because these movements rely on external inputs, their greatest use is as a temporary bridge between absent or severely disordered control and voluntary control. Once a desired motor response is obtained, active movements that utilize naturally occurring intrinsic sensory information will serve to reinforce and strengthen the response. Active movements also allow the use of feedforward movement adjustments, rather than strictly feedback adjustments. Sensory stimulation can be used to assist early attempts at movement but should be withdrawn as soon as possible to encourage voluntary movement control. Repeated use of sensory stimulation long after it is necessary can result in movements that become stimulus-dependent, and can further limit the patient's ability to regain normal control.[22]

The various types of sensory receptors demonstrate differential sensitivity. Each receptor is highly sensitive to a preferential stimulus while being relatively insensitive to other stimuli at normal intensities. Use of appropriate intensities of sensory stimulation is important to ensure that the desired receptors are stimulated. Excess stimulation can activate unwanted sensory receptors and produce undesired responses, including generalized arousal and sympathetic "fight-or-flight" reactions. Another special characteristic of sensory receptors is their adaptation to stimuli over time. Generally, they can be divided into two categories, slow- or fast-adapting receptors. In treatment, fast-adapting or phasic receptors such as touch receptors are generally more effective in initiating movement sequences, whereas slow-adapting, tonic receptors such as joint receptors, Golgi tendon organs, and muscle spindles are used more in monitoring and regulating movement responses (e.g., postural corrections). Velocity of movement is also a consideration. At slow velocities, afferent stimuli can contribute to movement responses, while at high velocities there is not sufficient time to allow for afferent information to effect motor control. Certain body segments such as the face, palms of the hands, and soles of the feet demonstrate both high concentrations of tactile receptors and increased representation in the sensory cortex. These areas are highly responsive to stimulation and are closely linked to both protective and exploratory functions.[23,24]

Damage to the central nervous system can produce deficits in sensory function. Alterations in tactile, proprioceptive, visual, or vestibular systems can affect a patient's ability to move and learn new activities. Deafferentiation in animals and in humans is associated with nonuse of a limb, although movement is possible under forced situations. Thus the therapist needs to focus training on movement of sensory-deficient limbs even though the patient may have little interest in moving the limb. The movements obtained should not be expected to be normal, however, since significant deficits have been noted in fine motor control in deafferentiated limbs.[4]

FACILITATION TECHNIQUES

Physical therapists have a number of therapeutic techniques that can be used to facilitate, activate, or inhibit

Table 13–2 EXTEROCEPTIVE STIMULATION TECHNIQUES

Stimulus	Response	Considerations
Light Touch	Initiates phasic, protective withdrawal Increased arousal Emotional reactions	Low threshold response Accommodates rapidly Effective in initially mobilizing muscles Apply resistance to maintain contraction Areas of high receptor density (hands, feet, lips) are more receptive to stimuli *Adverse effects* Increased arousal; *contraindicated* in patients demonstrating generalized arousal, autonomic instability
Activates Fast adapting skin receptors *Techniques* Manually applied: brief, light stroke; brief swipe with ice cube; light pinch or painful stimulus		
Maintained Touch (maintained pressure)	Calming effect; generalized inhibition	Useful with aroused patients, patients hypersensitive to sensory experiences Apply to hypersensitive areas to normalize responses Avoid brief touch stimuli Use with other maintained stimuli
Activates Tactile receptors ANS (parasympathetic responses) *Techniques* Firm manual contacts Pressure to midline abdomen, back Firm pressure to lips, palms, soles		
Slow Stroking (applied paravertebrally to posterior primary rami)	Calming effect; generalized inhibition	Useful with aroused, sympathetic patients Position patient in relaxed, supported position: prone, sitting tipped forward, resting on table and pillow
Activates ANS (parasympathetic responses) *Technique* With flat hand apply firm, alternate strokes paravertebrally for 3 to 5 min		
Manual Contacts	Facilitates agonist muscle contraction Manual cueing; gives direction to movement Provides security and support to unstable body segments	
Activates Skin receptors *Techniques* Firm, direct contact over contracting muscle or body part		
Prolonged Icing	Inhibition of muscle tone Inhibition of pain	Adverse effects Sympathetic arousal and withdrawal; monitor carefully *Contraindicated* in patients with sensory deficits; generalized arousal, autonomic instability, vascular problems
Activates Decreases neural and/or spindle firing Decreases metabolic rate of tissues *Techniques* Ice chips and/or ice wraps Icepack Immersion in cold water		
Neutral Warmth (retention of body heat)	Generalized inhibition of tone Calming effect; relaxation Decreased pain	Useful for aroused, sympathetic patients Spasticity Avoid overheating; may see rebound effects
Activates Thermoreceptors ANS (parasympathetic responses) *Techniques* Wrapping body or body part with ace wraps, towels Application of snug-fitting clothing, gloves, socks, tights Tepid baths Air splints Duration: 10–20 min		

muscle contraction. These have been collectively called facilitation techniques, although this term is a misnomer, because they also include techniques used for inhibition. The term **facilitation** refers to the enhanced capacity to initiate a movement response through increased neuronal activity and altered synaptic poten-tial. An applied stimulus may lower the synaptic threshold of the alpha motor neuron but may not be sufficient to produce an observable movement response. **Activation** on the other hand refers to the actual production of a movement response and implies reaching a critical threshold level for neuronal firing. **Inhibition** refers to

Table 13–3 VESTIBULAR STIMULATION TECHNIQUES (*Continued*)

Stimulus	Response	Considerations
Slow Maintained Vestibular		

Activates
Otolith organs, tonic receptors
Less effect on semicircular canals
Techniques
Slow, repetitive rocking movements
  Rocking chair
  Gymnastic ball
  Equilibrium board
  Hammock
Slow, rolling movements
  Passive initially, then active
	Generalized inhibition of tone
	Decreased arousal; calming effect
		Low-intensity stimulation
		Useful with hypertonic, hyperactive aroused
		  patients; tactile defensiveness
		Teach self-relaxation

Fast, Irregular Vestibular		

Activates
Semicircular canals phasic receptors
Less effect on otoliths
Techniques
Fast spinning with
  Mesh net or hammock
  Scooter board and/or ramps
  Spinning chair
Fast rolling, spinning movements
	Generalized facilitation of tone
	Improved motor coordination
	Improved retinal image stability
	Decreased postrotatory nystagmus
		High-intensity stimulation with irregular
		  components: acceleration and
		  deceleration
		Useful with
		  hypotonic patients (e.g., Down's
		    syndrome)
		  sensory integrative dysfunction
		  stroke, cerebral palsy
		  helps overcome akinesia (e.g.,
		    parkinsonism)
		Adverse effects
		Behavioral changes
		Seizures
		Sleep disturbances
		Contraindicated in
		  patients with recurrent seizures or
		  intolerant to stimulation

Inverted Positioning Tonic labyrinthine response		

Activates
Vestibular
Carotid sinus
Technique
Tip patient's head down in relation to trunk
  Prone over large ball, stool
  Inverted positioning apparatus
  Sitting, head tipped
	Generalized activation of postural extensors
	Depressor effect on medullary centers
	Decreased heart rate, respiratory rate, blood
	  pressure
	Calming effect
		Requires careful monitoring
		Useful with hyperactive, aroused patients
		Postural extensors assisted by adding
		  vibration
		Contraindicated in
		  patients with unstable blood pressure,
		  intracranial pressures

the decreased capacity to initiate a movement response through altered synaptic potential. The synaptic threshold is raised, making it more difficult for the neuron to fire and produce movement. The combination of spinal inputs and supraspinal inputs acting on the alpha moto neuron (final common pathway) will determine whether a muscle response is facilitated or inhibited.

Several general guidelines are important. First, facilitative techniques can be additive. That is, several inputs applied simultaneously, such as quick stretch, resistance, and verbal commands that are commonly combined in proprioceptive neuromuscular facilitation (PNF) patterns, may produce the desired motor response, whereas use of a single stimulus may not. This demonstrates the property of spatial summation within the CNS. Repeated application of the same stimulus (e.g., repeated quick stretches) may also produce the desired motor response due to the property of temporal summation within the CNS, whereas a single stimulus does not. The application of a given facilitation technique does not always produce the predicted response. The response to stimulation or inhibition is unique to each patient and dependent upon a number of different factors, including level of intactness of the CNS, central set, and the specific level of activity of the motoneurons in question.[11,13] For example, a depressed, hypoactive patient may require large amounts of stimulation to achieve the desired response, whereas a hyperactive patient requires very little stimulation, if any, to generate a movement response. The intensity, duration, and frequency of simulation need to be adjusted to meet the individual needs of the patient. Unpredicted responses can also be the result of poorly applied or incorrect techniques. For example, an inadequate vibrator that produces a low-frequency vibratory discharge (5 to 50 Hz) can stimulate low-frequency receptors in the skin and cause a withdrawal response. The normal high-frequency stimulus produces selective activation of spindle primary endings and reflex contraction of the muscle that is vibrated.

Very little controlled research is available to guide the therapist in the application of facilitation techniques. Therefore it is critical that keen observation skills and good judgment be applied to each clinical situation. Initial selection of stimuli should be based on a careful assessment of the patient and the environment. The selection and application of a specific stimulus requires an accurate knowledge of predicted responses. Careful observation during application can be compared with the therapist's knowledge of expected responses. If the responses are not as expected, adjustment in either stimulus intensity, duration, or frequency may be necessary to improve the response. If no response is obtained or the opposite of what is expected emerges, continued stimulation is generally not indicated.[19]

Facilitation techniques can be grouped according to the sensory system and receptors that are preferentially activated during application of the stimuli. Thus techniques are classified as extereoceptive (Table 13–2), vestibular (Table 13–3), proprioceptive (Table 13–4), or special (affecting the special senses of vision, hearing, or smell). Stimulus-response mechanisms, application techniques, and special considerations are presented in these tables.

Flexibility

Joint range of motion and muscle flexibility must be adequate to allow biomechanical alignment and functional excursions of muscle. Deficiencies can lead to changes in muscle activity, movement control, and postural adjustments. In addition, secondary impairments can develop, for example, muscle atrophy, fibrosis, contracture, and ankylosis. Both static and dynamic flexibility are required for normal motor control. Early therapeutic intervention is critical in maintaining full and pain-free range of motion (ROM), joint integrity, flexibility, and function. Additional benefits include increased circulation to the limbs and temporary relief of pain and spasticity.

Joint ranging techniques include traction, mobilization, manipulation, and ROM exercises.[25–27] The use of a preliminary therapeutic heat modality (hot pack or ultrasound) can be helpful to increase tissue temperature and collagen extensibility.[28] Cold modalities can be used to cool muscles and decrease muscle spasm and splinting.[29] Hypertonic patients will also benefit from prolonged icing and relaxation techniques (e.g., **rhythmic rotation**) before ranging. Range of motion exercises should be performed with the limb well supported to prevent joint trauma. Movements should be slow and smooth, with a prolonged stretch, and moderate resistance should be applied at the end of the physiologic range. Short, repeated stretches with high resistance are generally contraindicated as they can result in joint trauma.[30]

Techniques to increase muscle flexibility include static, ballistic, or facilitation (PNF) stretching techniques. **Static stretching** involves maintaining a position of maximum length of the muscles and connective tissues with a low-load stretch applied for an extended period of time. Therapists can use manual techniques, positioning with mechanical pulleys and weights, splinting, inhibitory casting, or a tilt table with wedges and straps. The benefits of static stretching with low loads include less danger of tearing the tissues, less muscle soreness, and decreased energy requirements. **Ballistic stretching** involves quick stretching of the muscles and tissues through bobbing or bouncing movements involving active antagonist muscle contractions. This type of stretch can also improve flexibility but is associated with higher rates of microtrauma and injury. Ballistic stretch is generally viewed as inappropriate for the sedentary or elderly patient.[29] Proprioceptive neuromuscular facilitation techniques include **contract-relax (CR)** and **hold-relax (HR)**.[18] Both are specifically designed to improve muscle flexibility through the use of intrinsic mechanisms that produce autogenic inhibition of the tight muscles via Golgi tendon organ (GTO) mechanisms. Maximal contraction of the tight muscles in the agonist (range-limiting) pattern is followed by voluntary relaxation and passive movement into the antagonist pattern. Hold-relax utilizes isometric contraction of agonist muscles, while contract-relax utilizes isotonic contraction of the rotators accompanied by isometric contraction of all other muscles in the agonist pattern. In a variation, **contract-relax-active motion (CRAM)**, active movement into the antagonist pattern is elicited following the contract-relax phase and adds the effects of reciprocal inhibition (antagonist contraction further inhibits the tight agonist). A number of researchers have demonstrated the effectiveness and superiority of these techniques over static and ballistic techniques.[31–35]

A program of flexibility exercises should be done regularly in order to optimize benefits. Whenever possible, a warm-up period should be included. The use of an aerobic activity, for example, calisthenics or low-resistance cycling, will gradually raise the tissue temperature and enhance the safety of the stretching program. A cool-down period should include a gradual reduction of the level of activity with maintenance of the newly gained stretched position. Icing can also be added, if necessary, to reduce tissue inflammation. Flexibility exercises should always be followed by active functional movements that maximize the mobility gained in the new range. Patients and/or their families should be taught flexibility exercises in order to maintain carryover outside of the clinic setting.

Strength

An essential component of motor control is muscular strength. **Strength** is the ability of muscle to produce the tension necessary for the initiation of movement, control of movement, or maintenance of posture. Strength is regulated by a number of factors, including motor unit recruitment, motoneuron firing patterns, muscle fiber composition, type of contraction, length of muscle, velocity of contraction, and movement arm.[36]

Table 13–4 PROPRIOCEPTIVE STIMULATION TECHNIQUES

Stimulus	Response (+ Facilitates; − Inhibits)	Considerations
Quick Stretch		

Activates
 Muscle spindles
    Ia endings (velocity and length sensitive)
    Input to higher centers
 Techniques
 Quick stretch to muscle
 Tapping over muscle belly or tendon
	Peripheral reflex support;
	    + + agonist
	 Reciprocal innervation effects;
	    − antagonists, − synergists
		Low threshold response
		 Relatively short-lived
		 Apply resistance to maintain
		 Typically applied in lengthened range to initiate contraction (PNF)
		 Adverse effects
		 May increase spasticity

Prolonged Stretch		
Activates Muscle spindles, Ia and II (length) Golgi tendon organs (Ib) Joint receptors Input to higher centers *Techniques* Slowly applied maintained stretch especially in lengthened ranges Inhibitory splinting, casting Reflex-inhibiting patterns (NDT) Mechanical: low load weight	Primarily inhibition Dampens muscle contraction Dampens tone	Higher threshold response May be more effective in extensors than flexors (added II inhibition) To maintain inhibitory effects, activate antagonist muscles
Resistance (maintained stretch)		

Recruits both alpha and gamma motoneuron
 Activates
 Muscle spindles
 Input to higher centers
 Techniques
 Manual resistance
 Use of body weight and/or gravity
 Mechanical: weights
	Recruits motor units
	 Hypertrophies extrafusal fibers
	 Peripheral reflex support;
	    + + agonist
	 Reciprocal innervation effects;
	    − antagonists, − synergists
	 Enhances stretch sensitivity of spindle
	 Enhances kinesthetic awareness
		In weak hypotonic muscles see enhanced effects with eccentric and isometric contractions (less spindle unloading)
		 Maximal resistance: may see irradiation to other muscles (overflow)
		 Adverse effects
		 May increase spasticity

Joint Approximation		
Activates Joint receptors (static) *Techniques* Joint compression—manual Mechanical—weight cuffs or belts Bouncing and/or gymnastic ball	Facilitates postural extensors/ stabilizers Enhances joint awareness	Use in extensor patterns (PNF) weight-bearing positions, mid to shortened ranges for extensor muscles *Contraindicated* in inflamed joints
Joint Traction		
Activates Joint receptors (phasic) *Techniques* Manual distraction	Facilitates flexors Enhances movement, joint awareness	Used in flexor patterns (PNF) Slow, sustained traction to painful joints relieves muscle spasm, pain (joint mobilization)
Inhibitory Pressure		

Activates
 Tactile receptors
 Muscle spindles
 GTOs
 Techniques
 Firm pressure to long tendons applied manually or through positioning at end ranges
 Mechanical: firm objects (cones) in hand
 Inhibitory splints, casts
	Inhibition; dampens muscle tone	*Considerations:*
		 Weight-bearing postures used to provide inhibition:
		    Quadruped, kneeling for quadriceps
		    Sitting, extended arm support or quadruped for long finger flexors

Vibration High-frequency (100–200 Hz)		

Activates
 Muscle spindles
    + + Ia fibers
 TVR supported by higher centers
 Also activates Pacinian corpuscles
	Tonic vibration reflex (TVR)
	    + + agonist, − antagonist
	 Nonadapting; fires as long as vibrator applied
	 Brief after discharge effects
		Apply with slight pressure (too much pressure will dampen vibrator)
		 Duration: brief, 1–2 min moving vibrator over muscle

Table 13–4 PROPRIOCEPTIVE STIMULATION TECHNIQUES (*Continued*)

Stimulus	Response (+ Facilitates; − Inhibits)	Considerations
Vibration		
Technique Electric vibrators, (battery-driven vibrators may provide ineffective stimulus) *To enhance responses* Apply with active contraction, resistance in lengthened range, at myotendinous junction, with slight cooling	Inhibition of monosynaptic stretch reflexes Can suppress cutaneous sensations and pain via gate mechanism	*Clinical indications* Activation weak hypotonic muscles, postural extensors; useful to facilitate tonic holding Decreases tactile hypersensitivity in peripheral nerve injury, pain *Contraindicated* in hypertonicity, tremor, ataxia, seizure disorders, very young children
Low-frequency (5 to 50 Hz)	Produces a flutter response or alarming reaction; protective withdrawal, nausea, vertigo	Battery powered vibrators may provide ineffective (low frequency) stimulation.

Techniques that optimize these factors yield maximum strength gains.

TECHNIQUES TO INITIATE CONTRACTION

The initiation of movement requires several key factors: (1) appropriate ideation and/or motivation to move, (2) adequate production of force to overcome gravity, (3) adequate ROM, and (4) appropriate timing of force production throughout the movement. For the patient with disordered motor control who has difficulty initiating a contraction, eccentric movements should ideally be practiced before concentric. The tension produced in an eccentric contraction is greater with a lower demand for motor unit activity than that produced in a concentric contraction.[37] The muscle spindle is also stretched throughout eccentric movement, thereby providing additional peripheral reflex support of contraction, whereas in concentric movement spindle unloading occurs. Similar benefits of maintaining spindle support of contraction can be seen with isometric contraction. Control is therefore relearned more easily if eccentric and isometric contractions are practiced before progressing to concentric movements.

The therapist needs to consider the length-tension relationship. Prestretching the muscle by starting contraction in the lengthened range optimizes tension development through increased use of viscoelastic forces. For example, a patient may be unable to flex the hip when sitting, while flexion of the hip when supine, with the knee flexed over the side of the mat, is possible. This concept of starting contraction in the lengthened range is one that is maximized in PNF.[18]

Velocity of contraction is a consideration. In concentric contractions total tension decreases as velocity increases. Thus patients may have difficulty generating contractions at high speeds, while at low speeds contraction is possible. For example, stroke patients have difficulty recruiting fast-twitch motor units and generating force at high velocities of movement.[38] Effective strategies to gain strength would therefore begin with slow velocities and gradually progress to faster speeds.

Increased demands are placed on the patient in movements with fluctuating velocities, for example, movements with acceleration segments. Patients may be unable to generate the forces needed during the different phases of movement. An example is the difficulty many stroke patients have during gait, as they are unable to generate the necessary forces within the right time frame. Training thus needs to focus on timing, to obtain adequate velocity of movement along with adequate force.

The therapist may chose to use any one of a number of facilitation techniques (previously discussed) that enhance muscle contraction through motor unit recruitment and/or peripheral reflex support. These include quick stretch, tapping, vibration, resistance, manual contacts, or light touch. Electrical stimulation[39-41] and biofeedback[42-43] are also effective tools in enhancing initial contraction and maintaining contractile properties. These techniques should be viewed as a temporary measure to be withdrawn as soon as voluntary control is possible. Continued practice will reinforce and strengthen neuromuscular associations.[44]

STRENGTH TRAINING

Strength training methods have been well described and documented.[45,46] These include isometric, isotonic, and isokinetic training sequences. Free weights, pulley systems, gravity, and body weight all provide sources of external load on muscle. The exercise prescription includes consideration of intensity, frequency, duration, and type of exercise. Overall, the effectiveness of a strengthening program is dependent upon achieving an adequate training stimulus. The loads placed on muscle must be greater than those normally incurred during activities of living (overload principle).[45] Selection of a particular training sequence must be based on the specific needs of the patient and the potential benefits of a particular method. Isometric training will result in gains in static strength without added joint motion. This may be important during early rehab when protection of an injured part is necessary. Isometric gains are specific to the range exercised, and multiple angle positions have to be used in order to achieve widespread strength gains. Isotonic gains in strength and endurance can be obtained through a series of progressive resistive exercises (PRE) by using either concentric or eccentric contractions. A major disadvantage of this type of training is that the weight selected is determined by the amount that can be lifted by the muscle at the weakest point of the range (fixed resistance). Isokinetic training offers the additional advantages of providing accommodating resistance throughout the range, while maintaining a predetermined speed. Movement control can be practiced at varying speeds. These are important considerations for training of the patient with disordered motor control.

Strength gains can also be achieved in patients with significant disuse atrophy and weakness, through the use of a functional training program (e.g., mat activities, diagonal patterns of motion). Resistance to the activity is provided by gravity, body weight, and by manual resistance of the therapist. There are several advantages of this type of program. For example, these movements are naturally occurring patterns of motion and very different from the straight planes of motion commonly employed in many machine setups. The practice of specific functional tasks also maximizes relearning of "real-life" skills and translates more easily into independence. Gains in functional independence are highly motivating to patients.

Tone

Tone is the resistance of muscle to passive elongation or stretch. Disorders of tone (e.g., spasticity) affect movement control and are a major focus in rehabilitation management of many patients. If left untreated, spasticity can lead to the development of secondary impairments such as joint impairments, abnormal patterns of movement, postural asymmetries.

Numerous therapeutic techniques have been developed to address hypertonicity—some with a neurophysiologic basis and some empirically. These include
1. Prolonged icing
2. Prolonged stretch and/or elongation of the shortened muscle group
3. Inhibitory pressure
4. Slow stroking
5. Slow vestibular stimulation
6. Rhythmic rotation
7. Inverted positioning
8. Neutral warmth
9. Vibration of the antagonist muscle
10. Inhibitory splinting or casting.

Biofeedback has also been used to reduce electromyographic (EMG) levels in spastic muscles.[47] The effectiveness of these techniques varies and is dependent on a number of factors—the patient's central state of arousal, medications, fatigue, or speed of movement, to name just a few. Reduction in tone is largely temporary. Patients may report changes—for example, feeling less stiff or moving easier—that last for minutes or hours. Changes are most often documented through improvements in range. Improvement does not necessarily carry over to active control of movement or changes in function.[48]

Active exercise is necessary in order to enhance carryover of tone reduction into active movement control. The following guidelines can be used. First, all unnecessary muscle activity should be eliminated, with the primary focus on muscle contraction of the antagonist muscles. Agonist (spastic muscle) contraction is not allowed. Movements should be slow and well controlled, and should emphasize increasing control over newly gained range and direction. Assistance (active assistive movement) can be given initially and should be withdrawn as soon as the patient is able to move on his or her own. Once active movement in the antagonist pattern is possible, reciprocal actions can be attempted. Agonist (spastic muscle) contractions are initiated in small ranges, with emphasis on reversing movement and moving back into the antagonist pattern. Smooth, reciprocal movements are practiced while relaxation is maintained. Highly stressful activities, for example, intense effort, may reinforce abnormal tone and are contraindicated.[19,20,49,50]

Movement Patterns

Coordinated movement is the harmonious working together of various muscles resulting in the production of skilled movement. Actions at two or more joints are linked together with a synergistic muscle activity that is highly organized, with appropriate sequencing, timing, and force production. Movements are performed against a background of postural adjustments that serve to maintain upright balance. The regulation of postural control during voluntary movement is largely automatic and is carefully matched to control the destabilizing forces that result from movement. Neural control centers responsible for organizing and controlling movement and posture are varied. The three main higher centers include the cortex, the cerebellum, and the basal ganglia. The cortex, through its connections with the brainstem motor regions and spinal cord, selects and initiates voluntary motor patterns and postural synergies. The basal ganglia and cerebellum closely modulate cortical output and translate motor plans into specific motor programs. Motor programs can be run off virtually without the influence of peripheral feedback. This is referred to as an **open-loop control** process (Fig. 13–2). Examples of movements controlled in this manner include well-learned or rapid movement sequences (e.g., playing a piano). **Closed-loop control** is defined as movement control that employs feedback against a reference for correctness (Fig. 13–3).[4] The plan for the intended movement is checked and integrated with feedback about movement success and postural stability. Any discrepancy between the two immediately results in modification of movement and posture. Feedback processes play a critical role in the learning of new motor skills and in the maintenance of body posture and balance.

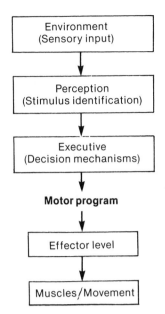

Figure 13–2. Open-loop motor control system.

The complexity of human movement negates any simplistic model of movement control. Both open-loop and closed-loop processes operate together as part of the larger system. Motor programs provide the generalized code for motor events, and feedback mechanisms refine and perfect movement. Either may assume a dominant role, depending upon the task at hand. Both may operate within a given movement but at different times and with different functions. This has been described as an **intermittent control hypothesis.**[4] Movement experiences lead to the development of an overall CNS model of body dynamics, which then serves as a reference for additional movement. Patients with motor control defi-

cits may demonstrate impairments in voluntary movement patterns or in the postural adjustments that accompany movement.[51-53]

STEREOTYPIC PATTERNS OF MOVEMENT

Stereotypic movement synergies are evidenced by muscles that are firmly linked together in limited synergistic patterns. There is a loss of selective movement and individual joint control.[49] They are common in patients with neurologic dysfunction (e.g., stroke, traumatic head injury). The alterations in synergistic control may arise from deficits in central programming, altered peripheral inputs, or both. Reduced firing rates, muscle fiber atrophy (predominately Type II), and abnormal firing patterns may also contribute to the problem. In addition, the deficits may be related to alterations in biomechanical properties (e.g., increased muscle and joint stiffness).

The primary goal of treatment is to break up stereotypic synergies by altering and reorganizing the movement components. Strong linkages are identified and modified first. For example, elbow flexion is typically strongly associated with shoulder flexion and abduction (flexion synergy). An early treatment activity can be to practice elbow extension with shoulder flexion. Generally training begins in a supported position with control of small ranges, and progresses to full range control and more challenging movement combinations. Once strong elements are broken up, focus can be shifted to weaker elements. Gradually more and more varieties of movements are introduced.[19-21, 49] The main task of rehabilitation is to rebuild functional patterns of movement. Practice must therefore be specific to the movement combinations needed for functional skills, for example, knee flexion with hip extension is needed for toe-off during gait and is not normally part of the stereotypic synergies seen in the patient with stroke.

COORDINATION TRAINING

Patients may demonstrate deficits in the coordination of movement. Overall composition of the movement (synergistic organization) may be impaired. Control may be difficult if speed and direction are changed. Alternate or reciprocal movements may be disorganized and movement steadiness (fixation) impaired. Swaying, tremors, or extra movements may accompany intended movements. Reaction times may be delayed and movement times slowed. Increased variability of performance is also common.[53] Treatment must focus on an accurate identification of the deficits (see Chapter 7: Coordination Assessment). The treatment programs selected must focus on specific deficits. If the problem is in speed control, then practice must include movements in which the speed of movement is varied. If the problem is with reciprocal movements, then these must become the focus of treatment. Thus practice of missing components is essential in achieving successful treatment outcomes. Training should include different types of functional

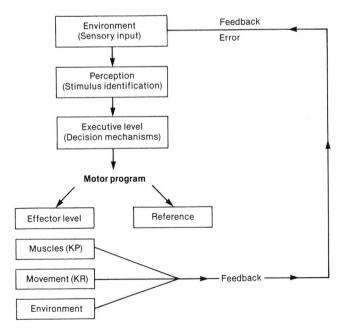

Figure 13–3. Closed-loop motor control system.

activities practiced in specific environmental contexts so as to allow for the flexible modification of motor programs.[52,53]

BALANCE

A training program to improve balance must be based on an accurate assessment of deficits (see Chapter 8: Motor Control Assessment). Patients may present with deficits in biomechanical alignment and weight distribution. They may lack the musculoskeletal control to execute appropriate responses (e.g., ankle, hip, or stepping strategies, automatic postural reactions). They may lack adequate sensory orientation information (e.g., somatosensory, visual, or vestibular inputs). Or they may select sensory orientation information or motor patterns that are inappropriate for the specific conditions of the task.[54,55]

Biomechanical Alignment and Weight Distribution

Abnormal alignment of body segments can limit postural strategies for balance. Effective physical therapy management includes ROM, strengthening, and postural exercises to correct diagnosed alignment problems. Early training should help the patient to correct body alignment and identify his or her **limits of stability** (LOS). The patient is instructed to slowly sway forward and back, side to side. The outer point at which the center of mass (COM) is still able to be maintained within the base of support (BOS) is termed the LOS. Loss of balance occurs when the LOS has been exceeded, for example, when the COG extends beyond the BOS. Practice of volitional body sway is important to assist the patient in developing accurate perceptual awareness of stability limits, an important part of an overall CNS internal model of body dynamics. Patients may present with specific directional instabilities, such as weight bearing more on one side than the other (e.g., after a stroke). Practice should be directed toward achieving symmetrical stance and improving sway in the direction of the instability. Instruction and feedback can be effective aids in reducing the problem. Mirrors can be used to visually guide the patient to midposition. Postural sway biofeedback (center of pressure biofeedback using a computerized platform) can be used to improve symmetrical weight distribution and to decrease lateral postural sway.[56-59] Standing balance training can also be achieved with less sophisticated equipment such as a set of bathroom scales or limb load monitors. Both have been used effectively to provide weight distribution feedback and improve sway.[60-62]

Reeducation of Postural Patterns

Use of appropriate **automatic postural synergies** is an important focus of treatment. Extraneous movements should be eliminated. Compensatory strategies that are nonfunctional and do not contribute to effective balance control should also be eliminated. Focus should be on achieving appropriate muscle activity specific to the demands of the balance task. For example, small shifts in the COM alignment and/or slow body sway motions are normally achieved by an ankle strategy.[54] Adequate

ROM and strength in ankle dorsiflexors and plantarflexors is essential. The patient should be encouraged to contract ankle muscles during standing balance tasks of small-range, slow-velocity shifts. Larger shifts in the COM, which approach the LOS, and/or faster body sway motions, normally recruit a hip strategy. Attention should be directed to normalizing ROM and strength in hip muscles. The patient should practice hip motions (flexion and extension) during balance tasks that normally recruit the hip strategy. If the COM exceeds the LOS, stepping strategies are recruited. Practice should focus on encouraging stepping movements (forwards-backwards stepping, sidestepping). Deficits of neuromuscular components can be assisted through a variety of measures. Timing of synergistic components can be improved through the use of electromyographic (EMG) biofeedback, isokinetic exercise, or functional electrical stimulation. Tone reduction techniques can be used to improve abnormalities of tone that interfere with postural responses.[63]

Automatic postural reactions (righting and equilibrium reactions) are used to right the head and readjust the body to regain equilibrium. Compensatory movements in the head, trunk, and upper extremities all assist lower extremity postural synergies in readjusting the COM within the base of support (BOS). Therapists generally use two methods to initiate these reactions: (1) perturbation (a displacing force), in which the COM is displaced outside of the BOS, and (2) a moveable surface (gymnastic ball, equilibrium board, standing tilt board) to displace the BOS. A number of different postures (e.g., sitting, standing, kneeling, half-kneeling) can be utilized.[19-21] Considerations in the selection of postures should include patient safety and level of control. Support may be given initially to reduce fear if using a new posture but should be quickly withdrawn to allow focus on active control by the patient. Challenges to balance should be appropriate to the patient's range and speed of control. Progression can achieved by (1) varying the amount and speed of the challenge, (2) varying the posture (increasing the level of difficulty by using more upright postures requiring greater antigravity control), (3) varying the complexity of the task (e.g., weight shifting to picking up objects off the floor), and (4) varying the degree of the patient's attention (redirecting attention during the balance task, e.g., ball throwing and/or catching). Anticipatory postural adjustments should also be practiced, since the feedforward mode of control is operational during postural control. The patient can be provided with advance information about an upcoming perturbation (e.g., direction or amount of force). The postural responses that are initiated are generally improved with prior instructions. Prior knowledge may serve as an important source of information in initiating correct postural patterns.[64]

An important goal of balance training is to promote overall postural awareness and safety education. Prevention of falls in the balance-deficient patient is a primary concern of therapy. Since the LOS changes with different tasks, a variety of functional activities and environmental settings should be practiced.[63] Training should include emphasis on maintaining an adequate base of support (e.g., feet slightly apart) during ADLs. For example, many falls occur as the patient turns to sit down because the feet become crossed and the BOS narrows. Proper body alignment should similarly be stressed. If a force is expected, patients should widen their base of support in the direction of the expected force. If greater stability is needed, patients should learn to lower their BOS (e.g., crouch down). Greater stability can also be achieved if friction is increased between the body and the support surface (e.g., wearing rubber-soled shoes).

Sensory Organization Issues

An important focus of a balance-training program is the utilization and integration of appropriate sensory monitoring systems. Normally three sources of inputs are utilized to maintain balance: somatosensory inputs (i.e., proprioceptive and tactile inputs from the feet and ankles), visual inputs, and vestibular inputs.[54] Careful assessment can identify the patient's preferred sensory mode to maintain balance. Treatment can then use varying sensory conditions (e.g., Clinical Test for Sensory Interaction and Balance, CTSIB) to challenge the patient.[65] For example, patients who depend on vision can practice balance tasks with eyes open and eyes closed, in reduced lighting, or in situations of inaccurate vision (petrolatum coated or prism glasses). Patients who depend on somatosensory inputs can practice balance on varying surfaces (floor versus carpet, foam, outside terrain, moving surfaces). Challenges to the vestibular system can be introduced by reducing both visual and somatosensory inputs or introducing a conflict situation, for example, when a patient is blindfolded while standing on foam. Repetition and practice are important factors in assisting in CNS modification and compensation.[63]

Patients with significant deficits in any of the sensory systems will need to be assisted in shifting toward the other systems in order to monitor and adjust balance. For example, the patient with proprioceptive losses must learn to shift focus onto the visual system in order to monitor balance. Thus the bilateral amputee learns to rely heavily on visual inputs in order to maintain standing balance. If deficits exist in more than one of the major sensory systems, compensatory shifts are generally inadequate and balance deficits will be more pronounced.[66] Other patients must be encouraged to ignore distorted information (e.g., impaired proprioception accompanying stroke) in favor of more accurate sensory information (e.g., vision). Life-style counseling is important to help patients recognize potentially dangerous situations and reduce the likelihood of falls. Augmented feedback can also be used to provide additional sensory information (e.g., verbal commands, biofeedback devices with auditory signals, or visual monitors).

MOTOR LEARNING

Motor learning has been defined as "a set of internal processes associated with practice or experience leading to relatively permanent changes in the capability for skilled behavior."[67] Learning a motor skill is a complex process that requires spatial, temporal, and hierarchic organization of the central nervous system. Central nervous system changes are not directly observable but rather are inferred from changes in motor behavior. Improvements in performance occur as a result of practice, for instance, appropriate sequencing of movement components, reduced effort and concentration, improved timing and speed control. Performance, however, is not always an accurate reflection of the amount of learning that has taken place. Factors such as fatigue, poor motivation, or drugs may cause performance to deteriorate while learning may still occur. **Retention** is another parameter used to assess learning. The learner is able to demonstrate the skill over time and after a period of no practice (a retention interval). Performance after a retention interval may decrease slightly but should return to original performance levels within relatively few practice trials. For example, riding a bike is a well-learned skill that is generally retained after long intervals, even though an individual may not ride a bike for years. The ability to apply a learned skill to the learning of other similar tasks is termed **generalizability** and can also be used to assess learning. Individuals who learn to transfer from wheelchair to mat can apply that learning to other types of transfers (e.g., wheelchair to car, wheelchair to tub). The time and effort required to organize and learn these new types of transfers should be reduced. Finally, learning can be measured by resistance to contextual change. This is the **adaptability** required to perform a motor task in altered environmental situations.[68] Thus an individual who has learned a skill (e.g., walking with a cane) should be able to apply that learning to new and variable situations (e.g., walking outdoors, walking downtown on a busy street). Motor learning is the direct result of practice and experience and is highly dependent upon sensory information and feedback processes. The relative importance of the different types of sensory information varies according to task and to the phase of learning. Individual differences exist and may influence both the rate and degree of learning possible. Differences in learning capability also exist for the patient with CNS dysfunction.

Phases of Motor Learning

The process of motor learning has been described by Fitts[69,70] as occurring in relatively distinct phases, termed cognitive, associated, and autonomous. These phases provide a useful framework for describing the learning process and for organizing strategies. Table 13–5 provides a summary of this information.

COGNITIVE OR EARLY PHASE

During the initial **cognitive phase** of learning, the major task at hand is to develop an overall understanding of the skill, termed the cognitive map or cognitive plan. This decision-making phase of "what to do" requires a high level of cognitive processing as the learner performs successive approximations of the task,

Table 13–5 STAGES OF MOTOR LEARNING AND TRAINING STRATEGIES

Cognitive Phase	Associated Phase	Autonomous
Learner develops an understanding of task: cognitive mapping	Learner practices movement	Learner practices and refines movement
Knows task demands	Spatial and temporal components of movement are organized	Spatial and temporal components become highly organized
Assesses abilities	Extraneous movements, errors decrease	Movement becomes increasingly autonomous, requiring little cognitive monitoring
Develops strategies	Dependence on visual feedback decreases; on proprioceptive feedback increases	
Performs successive approximations of task	Cognitive monitoring decreases	Control is shifted from higher to lower centers
Involves stimulus selection, discrimination, perceptual organization, development of a motor program	Motor program becomes refined	*"How to succeed" decision*
Dependence on visual feedback	*"How to do" decision*	
"What to do" decision		
Training Strategies:	*Training Strategies:*	*Training Strategies:*
Highlight purpose of task in functionally relevant context	Organize practice	Organize practice/high levels of practice are used
Demonstrate task accurately, at ideal performance speed	Identify movement errors, intervene when errors become consistent	Identify movement errors, prescribe corrections as needed
Break complex tasks down into component parts; teach parts and whole	Give feedback:	Stress refinement of skill, consistency of performance in varied environment (open skills)
Have patient verbalize task components and requirements performance	Correct early in movement or immediately after	Repeat practice conditions at least two times to allow learner to correct errors
Use manual guidance to assist	Emphasize proprioceptive feedback, "feel of movement"/internal reference of correctness	Beyond that vary environment to challenge learner
Direct attention to critical task elements	Modify environment:	Provide distractors
Point out similarities to other learned tasks	Gradually progress toward open environment	Assess need for conscious attention
Select appropriate sensory channels to provide feedback	Help learner develop own decision-making mechanisms:	
Have patient look at movement; vision important	Allow brief period of introspection	
Organize practice	Facilitation techniques, guidance may be counterproductive	
Stress slow, controlled movements	Encourage consistency of performance	
Structure environment for development of closed skills		
Use reinforcements (praise) for correct performance		
Provide feedback: do not cue on errors, which are largely inconsistent at this time		
Avoid verbal bombardment		

discarding strategies that are not successful and retaining those that are.[71] The resulting trial-and-error process initially yields a performance that is uneven. Processing of sensory cues and perceptual-motor organization eventually leads to the selection of a motor program that proves reasonably successful. Since the learner progresses from an initially disorganized and often clumsy pattern to more organized movements, improvements in performance can be readily observed during this acquisition phase. The learner relies primarily on visually guided movement during this initial phase of learning.

ASSOCIATIVE OR INTERMEDIATE PHASE

During the middle or **associative phase** of learning, refinement of the motor program is achieved through practice. Spatial and temporal aspects become organized as the movement develops into a coordinated pattern. Performance improves, with greater consistency and fewer errors and extraneous movements. The learner is now concentrating on "how to do" the movement rather than on what movement to do. Proprioceptive cues become increasingly important, while depen-

dence on visual cues decreases. The learning process takes varying lengths of time depending on a number of factors. The nature of the task, the prior experience and motivation of the learner, and the organization of practice and teaching strategies used can all influence learning.

AUTONOMOUS OR FINAL PHASE

The final or **autonomous stage** of learning is characterized by motor performance that after considerable practice is largely automatic. There is only a minimal level of cognitive monitoring of movement, with motor programs so refined they can almost "run themselves." The spatial and temporal components of movement are highly organized, and the learner is capable of coordinated motor patterns. The learner is now free to concentrate on other aspects, such as "how to succeed" at a competitive sport. Movements are virtually error-free with little interference from environmental distractions. Thus the learner can perform the movements equally well in a closed, stable environment or in an open, changing one.

Strategies to Improve Motor Learning

Motor learning can be facilitated through the use of effective training strategies.[4,50] Practice and feedback are critical to the learning process.

PRACTICE

Practice is essential for motor learning and the development of motor programs. In general, increased practice leads to increased learning. The organization of a practice schedule will depend upon several factors, including the patient's motivation, attention span, concentration, and endurance. Additional factors include the type of movement task and the frequency of allowable therapy sessions; the latter is often dependent upon in-hospital scheduling and availability of services and payment. For outpatients, practice at home is highly dependent upon motivation, family support, and suitable environment. Clinical decisions about practice focus on (1) duration of practice versus rest periods (massed versus distributed practice), (2) number and/or type of tasks practiced (constant versus variable practice), (3) practice order of tasks, and (4) environmental context.

Massed practice consists of continuous, unspaced sessions in which the practice time is greater than rest time. Fatigue may be a factor in decreasing performance levels. **Distributed practice** consists of spaced practice intervals in which the rest time equals or exceeds the practice time. While learning is possible with both, distributed practice is preferrable for many rehabilitation patients with limited performance capabilities. With adequate rest periods, performance can be improved without the interfering effects of fatigue. Distributed practice is also of benefit if motivation is low or if the learner has a short attention span, poor concentration, or motor planning deficits (dyspraxia). Distributed practice should also be considered if the task itself is complex, long, or has a high energy cost. Massed practice can be used when motivation or skill level are high and when the patient has adequate attention and concentration.

Constant practice refers to practice organized around one task and performed repeatedly, while **variable practice** refers to the practice of several variations of the same task or within the same category of movements. While both allow motor skill acquisition, variable practice is superior in producing retention and generalizability. For example, if independence in functional mobility and transfers is desired, optimal function can be achieved if several different types of transfers are practiced during therapy. The constant challenge of varying the task demands increases the depth of processing, and forces the patient to be a more active learner. The acquired problem-solving skills can then be applied to other variations or novel situations that have not yet been attempted. Practice of only one type of transfer would not achieve the same level of results.[72-74]

The third area for clinical decision making involves *practice order*, the sequence in which tasks are practiced. *Blocked order* refers to the repeated practice of a task or group of tasks in a predictable order (three trials of task 1, three trials of task 2, three trials of task 3: 111222333). *Serial order* refers to a predictable but non-repeating order (practice of multiple tasks in the following order: 123123123). *Random order* refers to a non-repeating and nonpredictable order (123321312). While skill acquisition can be achieved with all three, differences have been found. Blocked order produces improved early performance while random and serial order produce better retention and generalizability. This is due to contextual interference, which results in increased depth of cognitive processing, and retrieval practice, where the program is retrieved from memory.[73,75,76] The key element here is the degree to which the learner is actively involved in problem solving. For example, a treatment session can be organized to include several variations of the same skill (e.g., pelvic rotation) practiced in different activities (bridging, kneeling, plantigrade walking). Random ordering of the tasks may initially delay acquisition of the desired movement (performance) but over the long term will enhance learning (retention, generalizability).[77]

Altering the environmental context is an important consideration in structuring practice sessions. Since learning is task-specific within specific environments, tasks must be practiced in the environments in which they naturally occur. Practicing walking only within the physical therapy clinic might lead to successful performance in that setting but does little to prepare the patient for ambulation at home or in the community. The therapist should begin to gradually modify the environment as soon as performance becomes consistent.

Mental practice is the cognitive rehearsal of a motor performance and has been found to improve performance and learning.[78] The patient is instructed to mentally rehearse the movement before attempting actual performance. This activity reinforces the cognitive mapping phase. It is important to make sure the patient is actively rehearsing the correct movement steps. This can be assessed by having the patient initially verbalize aloud the steps he or she is rehearsing.

FEEDBACK

The vast body of motor learning and therapeutic literature stresses the importance of feedback in promoting learning. Feedback can be either **intrinsic,** occurring as a natural result of the movement, or **augmented,** by extrinsic sensory cues not typically received in the task. Proprioceptive, visual, vestibular, and cutaneous signals are examples of types of intrinsic feedback, while verbal commands are an effective form of augmented feedback. During therapy, both intrinsic and augmented feedback can be manipulated to enhance motor learning. It is important to use precise, accurate feedback and to assist the learner in perceiving and classifying the sensory cues necessary for movement.

The overall goal of therapy is to have the patient achieve the desired movement outcome with the most efficient pattern possible. Feedback about the nature or quality of the movement pattern produced is termed **knowledge of performance (KP).** Information about the end result or overall outcome of the movement is termed **knowledge of results (KR).** While both KP and KR are important for motor learning and performance, research indicates that accurate KR is critical with regard to learning.[79,80] The learner should be assisted in perceiving and classifying movement cues that highlight final outcome. Performance cues should focus on key task elements that lead to a successful final outcome. Augmented feedback can be used to provide error information as well as motivational support and reinforcement. Clinical decisions about feedback focus on (1) the selection of which sensory systems to employ, (2) how much feedback to use, and (3) when to give the feedback.

The selection of sensory systems depends upon specific assessment findings and on the stage of learning. The sensory systems selected must provide accurate information. If intrinsic mechanisms are impaired and provide distorted or incomplete information, then alternate sensory systems and/or augmented feedback should be emphasized.[77]

Decisions about frequency and scheduling of feedback (when and how much) must be reached. Frequent feedback (e.g., given after every performance trial) quickly guides the learner to the correct performance. Too little feedback will delay or preclude learning, while too much feedback is also detrimental, as it fosters feedback dependence. In this last situation, the patient may be able to perform a movement task but only when feedback is present (e.g., the therapist's verbal commands). Research demonstrates that variations in feedback delivery (varied feedback schedules) slow the acquisition of a skill but are more beneficial to long-term learning and retention. Examples of varied feedback schedules include (1) *summed feedback,* feedback given after a set number of trials (e.g., after every third trial); (2) *faded feedback,* feedback given at first after every trial and then less frequently (e.g., after every second trial, progressing to every fifth trial); and (3) *delayed feedback,* feedback given after a time delay (e.g., a 3-second delay); and (4) *bandwidth feedback,* feedback given only when performance is outside a given error range.[81-85] The beneficial effects noted are again due to the increased depth in cognitive processing of relevant response and task information. In contrast, the therapist who bombards a patient with frequent and continuous verbal feedback stressing accurate performance precludes the learner from focusing attention on the naturally occurring intrinsic signals and internal processing. The patient's own problem-solving skills are minimized, while the therapist's skills predominate. Winstein[86] points out that this may well explain why many studies on the effectiveness of therapeutic approaches cite minimal "carry-over" and limited retention of newly acquired motor skills.[86]

TRANSFER

Practice of related or similar movement skills may improve performance in other desired skills. This has been termed **transfer of learning** and can be a useful strategy in promoting learning. The most frequently used application of this principle is practicing component parts of a motor activity in order to learn the whole activity, what is known as **parts-to-whole transfer.** This is not always a successful strategy, however, and is dependent upon the nature of the learner and the task. If the task is complex, with highly independent parts, or if the learner has a limited memory or attention span, then learning can be enhanced through this method of practice. If the task has highly integrated, dependent parts or is relatively simple, then practice of the integrated whole will be more successful. If the parts-to-whole method is used, it is important to alternately practice both the parts and then the whole in order to insure adequate transfer. Thus, within the same session the patient should practice the component parts, then the integrated whole. Delaying practice of the integrated whole for days or weeks can interfere with transfer effects and learning.[4]

The integration of motor programs is made easier by practice that includes appropriate timing. In tasks that require speed and accuracy, both should be emphasized. Stressing accuracy first and then speed may not result in adequate transfer of learning, since accuracy tasks involve feedback processing while speed tasks involve feedforward processing. For example, when gait movements are practiced at very slow speeds stressing accuracy, the timing needed for normal or fast walking may then be difficult to achieve. Transfer effects can also be incorporated into treatment by having the patient practice the desired movements using the **contralateral transfer** of extremities. For example, in hemiplegia the more normal extremities (uninvolved side) can be engaged in practice of the desired movement patterns first. This enhances formation of the necessary motor program, which can then be used to control the same movements on the opposite, involved extremities. This method cannot, however, substitute for lack of movement potential of the affected extremities. Transfer can be improved if the number of practice trials of the contralateral extremities is increased and actual training of those limbs is promoted. Transfer of training is greatest between similar parts (arm to arm), and with similar tasks having identical stimuli and responses (arm flexion pattern to arm flexion pattern). Contralateral movements are also used to test understanding of the movement requested.

MOTIVATION

Motivation is the internal state that directs the system towards a goal.[4] The patient must fully understand the purpose of the task at hand and want to master it. Planning that involves the patient and family in mutual goal setting can greatly enhance the desire to achieve those goals. Continued motivation can also be enhanced by the effective use of feedback during treatment. Treatment successes are important and can be highlighted through the use of carefully planned positive reinforcements. Balancing the more difficult tasks with easier ones allows the patient to experience feelings of success interspersed with frustrations. The therapist should also plan each therapy session to end on a positive, successful note. The patient can then feel positive about his overall efforts and eager to continue therapy.

Strategies also vary according to the specific phase of learning. Thus the plan to facilitate motor learning in the early cognitive phase differs from training in the later stages (see Table 13–5). It is important to recognize that overlapping exists and that patients in transitional phases may benefit from a combination of training strategies.

TRAINING STRATEGIES FOR THE COGNITIVE PHASE

The overall goal during this phase of learning is to facilitate task understanding and organize early practice. The therapist should highlight the purpose of the action in a context that is functionally relevant. The task should seem important, desirable, and realistic to learn. The therapist should demonstrate the task exactly as it should be done (i.e., smoothly, completely, and at ideal performance speeds). This helps the patient develop an internal cognitive map or reference of correctness. Attention should be directed to key aspects of the task. Features of the environment critical to performance should be highlighted, and the therapist should point out similarities to other learned tasks so that subroutines that are part of other motor programs can be recruited.

Feedback, particularly visual feedback, is important to stress during the early phase of learning. The patient should be directed to watch the movements closely. Augmented visual feedback can be provided through the use of mirrors and videotaped demonstration. The patient's initial performance trials can be recorded for later review, or audiovisual materials such as videotapes or films of other patients can be used for demonstration. Highly skilled patients (e.g., rehab graduates) can be called upon for demonstration. Demonstration has also been shown to be effective in producing learning, even with unskilled models. In this situation the observer/patient benefits from the cognitive processing and problem solving he or she uses while watching the unskilled model attempt to correct errors and arrive at the desired movement.[74]

If the patient has visual-spatial deficits, techniques emphasizing visual feedback and demonstration may be problematic. Facilitation techniques (tapping, stretch, etc.) can be used initially to activate missing synergic elements and focus attention on movement components. Verbal feedback should be directed toward KR. Since there are many movement errors during this phase and they are largely inconsistent, they should not be emphasized. To do so would create an impossible situation, in which there is interference to learning from a steady stream of verbal corrections. Instead, KP feedback should focus on providing information on key task elements. Following the completion of a trial, allow the patient a brief period to think through the movement and analyze the outcome before providing feedback. This provides a time for introspection, organization of intrinsically available feedback, and problem solving. The therapist can then provide feedback and assistance in the decision-making process for the next practice trial. If the patient is successful, encourage him or her to repeat the performance. If not, reexamine the movement and/or the environment and assist the patient in analyzing and modifying the strategy. Finally, use reinforcements effectively, giving praise to encourage and motivate. Frustration levels are at the highest during this early acquisition phase.

Initial performance during early learning can be improved by manually guiding the patient through the movement. Guidance allows the patient to preview the stimuli inherent in the movement pattern, that is, to learn the "sensations of movement" as described by the Bobaths.[19] Manual guidance can also be effective in situations when vision or hearing are impaired. The supportive use of hands can allay patient fears and instill confidence. The therapist's hands can be used to effectively substitute for the missing elements and ensure correct performance. The key to success in using manually guided movements is providing only as much assistance as needed and removing the assistance as soon as possible. Active movements promote learning, while passively dragging the patient through the movements does little to ensure learning and may actually increase dependence on the therapist. In some patients, guided movement becomes a "crutch" that prevents the development of independent movement. Clinically we see the patient who cannot move unless assisted by "my therapist" and whose performance is markedly reduced when assistance is removed. The therapist needs to promote independence and active control. Guided movement is most effective for slow postural responses (positioning tasks) and least effective for rapid or ballistic tasks.

Initial practice efforts during this phase should be controlled. Low to moderate effort enhances voluntary control, while intense effort can result in overflow to muscles not directly involved in the activity and in incorrect movements. Structuring practice sessions during the cognitive phase involves minimizing fatigue (both physical and mental) and keeping the environmental distractors to a minimum.

TRAINING STRATEGIES FOR THE ASSOCIATIVE PHASE

The overall goal during this phase of learning is improving the organization of the motor program. Frequent practice allows the spatial and temporal components of movement to become organized into a coordinated pattern. The therapist should identify movement errors only as they become consistent and should suggest appropriate interventions. Corrections given early in the movement or immediately after are more effective than a continuous verbal barrage. Demonstration also continues to be very useful during this phase of learning to reaffirm a reference of correctness. Focus on major task elements and the necessary corrections will frequently result in significant improvement of the whole task. Practice should continue to be carefully structured. Encourage consistency. As learning progresses, the environment can be gradually modified to introduce some variations in the environment.

Performance can be improved through the use of feedback. During this stage it is appropriate to focus the patient's attention on proprioceptive feedback, the "feel of the movement." Thus the patient is directed to attend to the sensations intrinsic to the movement itself and to associate those sensations with the motor plan. Facilitation techniques may be counterproductive at this stage, since they maintain dependence on initiation and control of movement by the therapist and preclude the learning of intrinsic sensations of active movement. Guided movement may also be counterproductive, as it alters the normal feel of active movement. Error detection and problem solving should begin to shift from therapist to patient. Self-analysis of videotaped performance can be a useful way to accomplish this goal.

TRAINING STRATEGIES FOR THE AUTONOMOUS PHASE

The patient is directed to continue with high levels of practice. Errors are infrequent and when they are identified corrections should be initiated. The therapist should stress refinement of skills and movement consistency in a variety of environmental contexts; this will promote an overall range of movement patterns that are adaptable and fit the changing circumstances of the environment. It is important to repeat the same practice conditions at least twice in order to allow the learner the opportunity to analyze the movement and correct errors. Beyond that, the therapist should vary the practice conditions. Focus should be on the patient's movement analysis and decision-making skills. With fast, open-loop skills this can occur upon completion of the movement, when responses can be compared to the learned reference of correctness. With slower, closed-loop tasks that are performed with the benefit of ongoing feedback, error detection and correction can also occur during the movement action. The use of distractors such as ongoing conversation or simultaneous tasks (e.g., ball skills during standing and walking) can yield important evidence of the autonomous nature of the patient's movements. Finally, it is important to remember that many patients with motor control deficits do not reach this final skill level of learning. For example, in patients with traumatic head injury, performance may reach consistent levels within structured environments, while performance in more open environmental settings is not possible.

Schmidt[87] makes the point that learning is an ongoing process and is never completed. He proposes a **schema theory** in which rules, concepts, or relationships (e.g., sequencing, phasing, and relative forces of elements) for movement are stored in memory. The recall of these schema allows the movements required in novel situations to be structured and reasonably successful even if they have not been attempted previously. Schema theory highlights the need for patients to be active learners. They need to be involved in processing information in order to utilize feedback cues, detect errors, and generate their own solutions for movement problems. The role of the therapist using a motor learning model is primarily one of facilitator of learning.

DEVELOPMENTAL PERSPECTIVE

Control of posture and movement is a continuously evolving process that proceeds throughout life. While the fundamentals of movement are learned as a child, acquisition of new motor skills continues throughout the life span. Since many of the adaptive components of movement, postural sets, or motor programs already exist in the adult patient, they can be called up to relearn a motor skill or form a new one. This is a very different situation from that of the child who has not yet developed these skills. Motor patterns vary across the life span. Thus a child performs the activity of sitting up quite differently than does the adult, whose skills are modified by the CNS as it adapts to a number of factors. These include changes in body dimensions, effects of aging, levels of physical fitness, and disease processes.[88] For example, adults alter the way they roll over and sit up as they increase in body size and decrease in overall strength and fitness.

Use of developmental theory,[89-93] which focuses on the acquisition of motor control, is common in some therapeutic approaches, for example, Bobath's neurodevelopmental treatment,[19-21] Rood's developmental sequence,[16,17] Voss's developmental mat activities.[18] Treatment incorporates different positions and patterns of movement (frequently termed developmental mat activities) such as prone on elbows, quadruped, sitting up, plantigrade, walking, and so on. Some of these activities are more functional for the adult patient than others (e.g., sitting up versus quadruped). Developmental activities may also be utilized because they allow focus on a specific area of body control; for example, prone on elbows emphasizes shoulder, upper trunk, and head control. They may also be utilized because of safety factors; for example, the low center of gravity and wide base of support found in kneeling as opposed to standing. It is clear that the selection of activities should not be based on a rigid application of a predetermined developmental sequence; for example, the patient learns head control in prone on elbows before learning head control in sitting. Actually in this example the reverse sequence is probably easier because of the decreased effects of gravity acting on the head in sitting.

Guidelines that are generally applied in the developmental approaches include the reestablishment of motor control in

1. Cephalo–caudal and proximal–distal directions
2. Isometric movements (holding in a posture) before isotonic control (moving in a posture)
3. Eccentric control (moving out of a posture) before concentric control (moving into a posture)
4. Symmetrical movement patterns before asymmetrical
5. Discrete movements before continuous movement sequences

These guidelines arise from developmental research literature. While they may be helpful in structuring treatment for some patients, they should not be rigidly applied. It is clear that considerable variability exists in the development of children and in the recovery of adult patients from insult or injury, and treatments should reflect this individuality.

Developmental Strategies to Improve Motor Control

A developmental perspective utilizing the overall task goals of mobility, stability, controlled mobility, and skill can be helpful in assisting the therapist to identify problems and organize treatments (see discussion on developmental perspective in Chapter 8). For example, following a stroke, a patient may be unable to move the upper extremity at all. This can be categorized as a problem in initial mobility (initiation of movement). This same patient may be unable to maintain unsupported sitting for more than a few seconds and may sit with a slumped, poorly aligned posture (a problem with impaired stability). The patient loses balance and falls over when asked to make the slightest movement adjustment in any direction (impaired controlled mobility). One would reasonably expect that this patient's ability to perform a skill level function such as dressing in unsupported sitting would also be severely impaired or impossible.

STRATEGIES TO IMPROVE MOBILITY

Initial mobility can be elicited through the use of low-threshold, phasic stimuli. As previously mentioned, these can include quick stretch, light touch, quick icing, or light pinching to elicit withdrawal responses. Associated reactions and reflexes have also been used in some therapeutic approaches to bridge the gap between complete lack of movement and early movement attempts.[18,49] These strategies should be considered only a temporary measure to facilitate movement. The movements should be immediately reinforced with resistance and voluntary efforts. The movements can also be reinforced with dynamic verbal commands, which focus the patient's attention on gaining control through voluntary effort.

Specific exercise techniques that can be used to assist patients in initiating movements include active assisted movement, rhythmic initiation, repeated contractions, and hold-relax active motion. **Active assisted movement (AAM)** involves both manual assistance and active movements. The therapist first guides the patient through the correct movement pattern to ensure that the patient has the correct idea of the desired movement. The patient is then asked to actively participate in the movement pattern. The therapist provides assistance only during those parts of the pattern that require assistance, while stressing active control by the patient. **Rhythmic initiation (RI)** is a PNF technique that involves voluntary relaxation followed by passive, active-assistive, and finally mildly resisted movements of the agonist pattern. Transition into the next stage is dependent upon the patient's ability to (1) relax and be moved passively before attempting active movement, and (2) participate in the movement actively before attempting mildly resisted movement. Rhythmic initia-

tion was developed for use with hypertonic patients (e.g., the patient with Parkinson's disease), although it can be used during the initial stages of motor learning to guide and stimulate correct motor patterns (e.g., for the patient with dyspraxia or receptive aphasia). **Repeated contraction (RC)** is another PNF technique that involves repeated isotonic contractions of the agonist pattern. The movements are resisted, and repeated stretch is added to reinforce voluntary contraction during the weak parts of the range. **Hold-relax active motion (HRA)** involves first obtaining an isometric contraction in the shortened range, followed by active relaxation and passive movement into the lengthened range. The patient is instructed to move isotonically back through the range against resistance and repeated stretch if needed. The technique of HRA is applied in one direction only and can be used to enhance stretch sensitivity and contraction of a weak or hypotonic agonist.

STRATEGIES TO IMPROVE STABILITY

Stability can be enhanced through the use of maintained types of stimuli. These include vibration, resistance, joint approximation, tapping, and manual contacts. The stimuli are maintained in order to enhance sustained contraction. Weight cuffs or Theraband can also be added to increase proprioceptive loading. Stimuli should be applied while patients are holding against gravity in weight-bearing postures. Prone on elbows, quadruped, sitting, or modified plantigrade postures can be used to develop upper trunk and/or upper extremity stability, while quadruped, bridging, kneeling, half-kneeling, plantigrade, or standing postures can be used to develop trunk and/or lower extremity stability.

Specific exercise techniques that can be utilized to assist patients in gaining stability include placing and holding, alternating isometrics, rhythmic stabilization, or slow reversal-hold (see below). **Placing and holding** (hold-after-positioning) consists of placing a patient in a position or posture and asking the patient to hold actively against the resistance of gravity. **Alternating isometrics (AI)** consists of alternate isometric contractions of first the agonist, then antagonist, muscles. The patient is instructed to hold and the therapist resists the hold first in one direction, then in the other. The holding can be challenged in all directions, that is, flexion-extension, abduction-adduction, diagonally, or rotationally.[94] **Rhythmic stabilization (RS)** similarly employs isometric contractions of antagonist patterns but differs from AI in that it attempts to apply the resistance simultaneously to alternate muscle groups. For example, in standing, resistance can be applied simultaneously to the trunk flexors at the shoulders and to the trunk extensors at the pelvis. The therapist's hands are then switched to the opposite surfaces and the resistance is applied to shoulder extensors and pelvic flexors. This occurs without any distinct relaxation phase between opposing contractions. **Slow reversal-hold (SRH)** is a technique that involves alternate isometric and isotonic contractions of both agonists and antagonists. The patient is instructed to hold (agonist contraction) followed by stretch and resisted movement in the opposite direction ending with a corresponding hold of the antagonists. When SRH is used as a stability technique, the isometric components are stressed and the range of movement becomes progressively more limited. Slow reversal-hold applied through a decreasing range (decrements of range) can be effective in helping hyperkinetic patients achieve stability.

STRATEGIES TO IMPROVE CONTROLLED MOBILITY

Activities to improve controlled mobility (CM) include rocking or weight shifting in any of the previously mentioned weight-bearing postures. The movements can occur in any direction, that is, flexion-extension, abduction-adduction, diagonally, or rotationally. Diagonal movements are generally more efficient since they represent a combination of both flexion-extension and abduction-adduction movement components. Thus in a quadruped position the patient can rock forward and diagonally over one shoulder and backward and diagonally over the opposite leg. The range of movement is gradually expanded through an increasing range while the patient works to achieve smooth, well-controlled movement transitions. A more advanced CM activity is static-dynamic work. Here the patient shifts his or her weight onto an extremity and frees the opposite extremity for non-weight-bearing activities. For example, in quadruped position the patient shifts weight onto the right arm and the legs and lifts the left arm up off the mat. Additional movements, such as PNF extremity patterns, can be added to the non-weight-bearing limb to increase the level of difficulty. Controlled mobility activities challenge the patient by superimposing control of dynamic movements on stability control. Gymnastic ball activities can also be used to focus on controlled mobility function and balance reactions. Manual contacts, stretch, resistance, and verbal commands are effective stimuli in enhancing these responses.

Specific exercise techniques that can be used to assist patients in gaining controlled mobility include slow reversals, slow reversal-hold, repeated contractions, and agonist reversals. **Slow reversals** (SR) consist of alternating isotonic contractions of first agonist, then antagonist, patterns. The movements are reversed without any relaxation phase and are resisted throughout. During the movements the patient is directed toward gaining full range of motion. Thus SRH can be used to promote either stability (as previously mentioned) or controlled mobility. When used as a CM technique, it progresses through increments of range. It is appropriate to use *repeated contractions* (RC) as a controlled mobility technique when muscle imbalances exist and the movements are stronger in one direction than the other. Repeated contractions are applied if weakness exists in any part of the range. **Agonist reversal (AR)** is a technique that incorporates resistance to both concentric and eccentric contractions of the agonists. For example, in bridging, the assumption of the posture involves concentric contraction of the hip extensor muscles, while getting back down involves a controlled eccentric letting go. Thus AR works on control of agonist muscles by using two types of contraction patterns. Common activities that require eccentric control include sitting down, descending stairs, and moving from kneeling to heel-sitting.

STRATEGIES TO IMPROVE SKILL

Progression to skill-level activities occurs normally after control in stability and controlled-mobility activities has been achieved. Examples of activities that demonstrate skilled function include locomotion (reciprocal creeping or walking), skilled hand function (grasp and manipulation), and oral-motor function. Highly coordinated patterns of movement such as the PNF extremity patterns also represent skill-level function when performed correctly.

Specific exercise techniques that can be used to enhance skilled function include slow reversals, slow reversal-hold, timing for emphasis, and resisted progression. **Timing for emphasis (TE)** promotes normal timing of pattern components by reinforcing or resisting the stronger components to augment the weaker ones. Completion of a diagonal pattern of motion (PNF pattern) emphasizes all components with normal distal to proximal timing. When an imbalance exists, the stronger components are maximally resisted to create overflow and enhance contractions of the weaker segments. The stronger components can also be isometrically "locked in" at a point in the range where they are the strongest, while repeated contractions are then applied simultaneously to improve contraction of the weaker components. **Resisted progression (RP)** involves the use of stretch and resistance to enhance locomotion. The therapist's manual contacts are positioned to resist both the forward progression and pelvic rotation. Locomotion patterns can be resisted in any direction, that is, forwards-backwards, sideways, diagonally. Crossed-step walking or PNF **braiding** (a PNF activity) can also be used to develop skilled-level function. Manual contacts, stretch, resistance, and verbal commands are effective in facilitating coordinated responses.

SUMMARY

This chapter has outlined a conceptual framework based on normal processes of motor control, motor learning, and motor development. Clinical decision making for patients with motor control deficits must be based upon a comparison of normal and abnormal function in each of these areas. The therapist must be able to recognize, categorize, and sequence motor behaviors appropriately in order to develop effective treatment goals and strategies. The unique problems of each patient also require that the therapist recognize a number of interrelated factors, including individual needs, motivations, concerns, and potential for response. Movements must be evaluated and undertaken within the context in which they normally occur. Peripheral inputs can be used to initiate and enhance motor patterns. Given the tremendous variability in central nervous system function, however, it is unrealistic to expect that individual techniques can produce identical responses in different patients or even in the same patient under different environmental circumstances. Techniques must therefore be chosen carefully and monitored closely during treatment. The basic components of control must be addressed; these include flexibility, strength, tone, and patterns of movement. Functional changes can result only from active participation of the patient and repeated practice of the desired activity. Early, frequent, and consistent practice provides the best chance for optimal treatment results. Meaningful progress may be painstakingly slow, especially in the presence of multiple and complex motor control problems. Frustrations frequently run high for both patient and therapist alike. Physical therapists have many skills and techniques available to assist patients. The adoption of a standardized or single approach to patient care can blind the clinician to the full range of treatment options available and should be avoided.

QUESTIONS FOR REVIEW

1. What types of techniques can be used to modify arousal levels? What factors need to be considered when working with patients with low arousal levels? High arousal?

2. Clinically how would you decide if a sensory stimulation technique was indicated? What parameters would you use to decide on continued use of the technique? How would you monitor outcomes?

3. Describe a sequence of exercises that could be used to assist a patient with disordered motor control to initiate muscle contraction.

4. Your patient demonstrates significant sensorimotor deficits in balance following a stroke to the right side. What training activities would you consider? How would you determine which ones would be appropriate for this patient?

5. Differentiate between the three different phases of motor learning. How should training strategies differ during each stage?

6. Developmental strategies form the basis of several neurotherapeutic approaches in physical therapy. How should these strategies be applied to management of the adult patient as compared to the pediatric patient?

7. Identify three therapeutic techniques that can be used for patients with deficits in the mobility stage of motor control. Do the same for stability, controlled mobility, and skill stages.

8. Your patient is 22 years old and is recovering from a severe head injury. List three procedures that could be used to decrease the moderate to severe spasticity present in the trunk and proximal extremities.

9. Discuss motor learning training strategies designed to improve retention and generalizability. How do they differ from strategies that optimize performance?

REFERENCES

1. Brooks, V: The Neural Basis of Motor Control. Oxford University Press, New York, 1986.
2. Sage, G: Introduction to Motor Behavior: A Neuropsychological Approach, ed 2. Addison-Wesley, 1977.
3. Bernstein, N: The Coordination and Regulation of Movements. Pergamon Press, Oxford, 1967.
4. Schmidt, R: Motor Control and Learning, ed 2. Human Kinetics, Champaign, IL, 1988.
5. Bobath, B: The treatment of neuromuscular disorders by improving patterns of coordination. Physiotherapy 55:1, 1969.
6. Johansson, C, Kent, B, and Shepard, K: Relationship between verbal command volume and magnitude of muscle contraction. Phys Ther 63:1260, 1983.
7. Malkmus, D, Booth, B, and Kodimer, C: Rehabilitation of the Head Injured Adult: Comprehensive Cognitive Management. Professional Staff Association of Rancho Los Amigos Hospital, Downey, CA, 1980.
8. Malkmus, D: Integrating cognitive strategies into the physical therapy setting. Phys Ther 63:1952, 1983.
9. Reinhart, M: Considerations for functional training in adults after head injury. Phys Ther 63:1975, 1983.
10. Howard, M and Bleiberg, J: A Manual of Behavior Management Strategies for Traumatically Brain-Injured Adults. Rehabilitation Institute of Chicago, Chicago, 1983.
11. Dell, P: Reticular homeostasis and critical reactivity. In Moruzzi, G, Fessard, A, and Jasper, H (eds): Progress in Brain Research, Vol 1, Brain Mechanisms. Elsevier, New York, 1963.
12. Yerkes, R and Dodson, J: The relationship of strength of stimulus to rapidity of habit-formation. J Comp Neurol Psychol 18:459, 1908.
13. Wilder, J: Stimulus and Response: The Law of Initial Value. John Wright & Sons, Bristol, UK, 1967.
14. Stockmeyer, S: Clinical decision making based on homeostatic concepts. In Wolf, S (ed): Clinical Decision Making in Physical Therapy. FA Davis, Philadelphia, 1985.
15. Zasler, N, Kreutzer, J, and Taylor, D: Coma stimulation and coma recovery. Neurorehabilitation 1:33, 1991.
16. Rood, M: The use of sensory receptors to activate, facilitate, and inhibit motor response, autonomic and somatic, in developmental sequence. In Satterly, C (ed): Approaches to the Treatment of Patients with Neuromuscular Dysfunction. Wm C Brown, Dubuque, IA, 1962.
17. Stockmeyer, S: An interpretation of the approach of Rood to the treatment of neuromuscular dysfunction. Am J Phys Med 46:950, 1967.
18. Voss, D, Ionta, M, and Myers, B: Proprioceptive Neuromuscular Facilitation, ed 3. Harper & Row, Philadelphia, 1985.
19. Bobath, B: Adult Hemiplegia: Evaluation and Treatment, ed 2. Wm Heinemann Medical Books, London, 1978.
20. Davies, P: Steps to Follow: A Guide to the Treatment of Adult Hemiplegia. Springer-Verlag, New York, 1985.
21. Davies, P: Right in the Middle: Selective Trunk Activity in the Treatment of Adult Hemiplegia. Springer-Verlag, New York, 1990.
22. Gordon, J: Assumptions underlying physical therapy intervention: theoretical and historical perspectives. In Carr, J, Shepherd, R, Gordon, J, et al (eds): Movement Science Foundations for Physical Therapy Rehabilitation. Aspen, Rockville, MD, 1987.
23. Guyton, A: Neuroscience: Anatomy and Physiology, ed 2. WB Saunders, Philadelphia, 1991.
24. Mountcastle, V (ed): Medical Physiology, Vol 1, ed 14. CV Mosby, St Louis, 1980.
25. Kaltenborn, F: Mobilization of the Extremity Joints, ed 3. Harper & Row, Philadelphia, 1980.
26. Maitland, G: Vertebral Manipulation, ed 5. Butterworth, Boston, 1986.
27. Zachazewski, J: Improving flexibility. In Scully, R and Barnes, M (eds): Physical Therapy. JB Lippincott, Philadelphia, 1989.
28. Wessling, K, DeVane, D, and Hylton, C: Effects of static stretch versus static stretch and ultrasound combined on triceps surae muscle extensibility in healthy women. Phys Ther 67:674, 1987.

29. Cornelius, W and Jackson, A: The effects of cryotherapy and PNF techniques on hip extensor flexibility. Athletic Training 19:183, 1984.

30. Kottke, F, Parley, D, Ptak, D: The rationale for prolonged stretching of shortened connective tissue. Arch Phys Med Rehabil 47:345, 1982.

31. Sady, S, Wortman, M, Blanke, D: Flexibility training: ballistic, static or proprioceptive neuromuscular facilitation. Arch Phys Med Rehabil 63:261, 1982.

32. Markos, P: Ipsilateral and contralateral effects of proprioceptive neuromuscular facilitation techniques on hip motion and electromyographic activity. Phys Ther 59:1366, 1979.

33. Odeen I: Reduction of muscular hypertonus by long-term muscle stretch. Scand J Rehabil Med 13:93, 1981.

34. Hubley, C, et al: The effect of static stretching exercises and stationary cycling on range of motion at the hip joint. J Orthop Sports Phys Ther 6:104, 1984.

35. Moore, M and Hutton, R: Electromyographic investigation of muscle stretching techniques. Med Sci Sports 12:322, 1980.

36. Smidt, G and Rogers, M: Factors contributing to the regulation and clinical assessment of muscular strength. Phys Ther 62:1283, 1982.

37. Astrand, P and Rodahl, K: Textbook of Work Physiology. McGraw-Hill, New York, 1977.

38. Harro, C: Implications of motor unit characteristics to speed of movement in hemiplegia. Neurol Rep 9:55, 1985.

39. Draper, V and Ballard, L: Electrical stimulation versus electromyographic biofeedback in the recovery of quadriceps femoris muscle function following anterior cruciate ligament surgery. Phys Ther 71:455, 1991.

40. Soo, D, Currierk, D, and Threlkeld, A: Augmenting voluntary torque of healthy muscle by optimization of electrical stimulation. Phys Ther 68:333, 1988.

41. Selkowitz, D: Improvement in isometric strength of the quadriceps femoris muscle after training with electrical stimulation. Phys Ther 65:186, 1985.

42. Wolf, S, LeCraw, D, and Barton, L: Comparison of motor copy and targeted biofeedback training techniques for restitution of upper extremity function among patients with neurologic disorders. Phys Ther 69:719, 1989.

43. Krebs, D: Biofeedback in neuromuscular re-education and gait training. In Schwartz, M (ed): Biofeedback: A Practitioner's Guide. Guilford Press, New York, 1987.

44. Duncan, P and Badke, M: Therapeutic strategies for rehabilitation. In Duncan, P and Badke, M (eds): Stroke Rehabilitation. Year Book Medical Publishers, Chicago, 1987.

45. Mangine, R, Heckmann, T, Eldridge, V: Improving strength, endurance, and power. In Scully, R and Barnes, M (eds): Physical Therapy. JB Lippincott, Philadelphia, 1989.

46. Kisner, C and Colby, L: Therapeutic Exercise Foundations and Techniques, ed 2. FA Davis, Philadelphia, 1990.

47. DeBacher G: Biofeedback in spasticity control. In Basmajian, J (ed): Biofeedback: Principles and Practice for Clinicians, ed 2. Williams & Wilkins, Baltimore, 1983.

48. Sahrmann, S and Norton, B: The relationship of voluntary movement to spasticity in the upper motoneuron syndrome. Ann Neurol 2:460, 1977.

49. Brunnstrom, S: Movement Therapy in Hemiplegia. Harper & Row, New York, 1970.

50. Carr, J and Shepherd, R: A Motor Relearning Programme for Stroke, ed 2. Aspen, Rockville, MD, 1987.

51. Frank, J and Earl, M: Coordination of posture and movement. Phys Ther 70:855, 1990.

52. Keshner, E: Controlling stability of a complex movement system. Phys Ther 70:844, 1990.

53. Corcos, D: Strategies underlying the control of disordered movement. Phys Ther 71:25, 1991.

54. Nashner, L: Sensory, neuromuscular, and biomechanical contributions to human balance. In Duncan, P (ed): Balance. American Physical Therapy Association, Alexandria, VA, 1990.

55. Nashner, L and McCollum, B: The organization of human postural movements: a formal basis and experimental synthesis. Behavioral and Brain Sciences 8:135, 1985.

56. Hocherman, S, Dickstein, R, and Pillar, T: Platform training and postural stability in hemiplegia. Arch Phys Med Rehabil 65:588, 1984.

57. Shumway-Cook, A, Anson, D, and Haller, S: Postural sway biofeedback: its effect on reestablishing stance stability in hemiplegic patients. Arch Phys Med Rehabil 69:395, 1988.

58. Winstein, C, Gardner, E, McNeal, D, et al: Standing balance training: effect on balance and locomotion in hemiparetic adults. Arch Phys Med Rehabil 70:755, 1989.

59. Winstein, C: Balance retraining: Does it transfer? In Duncan, P (ed): Balance. American Physical Therapy Association, Alexandria, VA, 1990, p 95.

60. Wannstedt, F and Herman, R: Use of augmented sensory feedback to achieve symmetrical standing. Phys Ther 58:553, 1978.

61. Gapsis, J, Menken, S, Kelly, M: Limb load monitor: evaluation of a sensory feedback device for controlling weight bearing. Arch Phys Med Rehabil 63:38, 1982.

62. Gauthier-Gagnon, C, St. Pierre, D, Drouin, G, et al: Augmented sensory feedback in the early training of standing balance of below-knee amputees. Physiotherapy Canada 38:137, 1986.

63. Shumway-Cook, A and McCollum G: Assessment and treatment of balance deficits. In Montgomery, P and Connolly, B (eds): Motor Control and Physical Therapy. Chattanooga Group, Hixson, TN, 1991.

64. Badke, M and DeFabio, R: Balance deficits in patients with hemiplegia: considerations for assessment and treatment. In Duncan, P (ed): Balance. Proceedings of the APTA Forum. American Physical Therapy Association, Alexandria, VA, 1990.

65. Shumway-Cook, A and Horak, F: Assessing the influence of sensory interaction on balance. Phys Ther 66:1548, 1986.

66. Herdman, S: Assessment and treatment of balance disorders in the vestibular-deficient patient. In Duncan, P (ed): Balance. American Physical Therapy Association, Alexandria, VA, 1990.

67. Schmidt, R: Motor Control and Learning, ed 2. Human Kinetics, Champaign, IL, 1988, p 346.

68. Adams, J: Historical review and appraisal of research on the learning, retention, and transfer of human motor skills. Psychol Bull 101:41, 1987.

69. Fitts, P and Posner, M: Human Performance. Brooks/Cole, Belmont, CA, 1967.

70. Fitts, P: Perceptual-motor skills learning. In Melton, A (ed): Categories of Human Learning. Academic Press, New York, 1964, p 243.

71. Lee, T, Swanson, L, Hall, A: What is repeated in a repetition? Effects of practice conditions on motor skill acquisition. Phys Ther 71:150, 1991.

72. Wulf, G and Schmidt, R: Variability in practice facilitation in retention and transfer through schema formation or context effects? J Mot Behav 20:133, 1988.

73. Shea, J and Morgan, R: Contextual interference effects on the acquisition, retention, and transfer of a motor skill. J Exp Psychol [Hum Learn] 3:179, 1979.

74. Lee, T and Swanson, L: What is repeated in a repetition? Effects of practice conditions on motor skill acquisition. Phys Ther 71:150, 1991.

75. Gentile, A: Skill acquisition: action, movement, and neuromotor processes. In Carr, J, Shephard, R, Gordon, J, et al (eds): Movement Science Foundations for Physical Therapy Rehabilitation. Aspen, Rockville, MD, 1987, p 93.

76. Battig, W: The flexibility of human memory. In Cermak, L and Craik, F (eds): Levels of Processing in Human Memory. Lawrence Erlbaum Associates, Hillsdale, NY, 1979, p 23.

77. Winstein, C: Motor learning considerations in stroke rehabilitation. In Duncan, P and Badke, M (eds): Stroke Rehabilitation: The Recovery of Motor Control. Yearbook Medical, Chicago, 1987.

78. Feltz, D and Landers, D: The effects of mental practice on motor skill learning and performance: a meta-analysis. J Sports Psychol 5:25, 1983.

79. Salmoni, A, Schmidt, R, Walter, C: Knowledge of results and motor learning: a review and critical appraisal. Psychol Bull 95:355, 1984.

80. Lee, T, White, M, Carnahan, H: On the role of knowledge of results in motor learning: exploring the guidance hypothesis. J Mot Behav 22:191, 1990.

81. Sherwood, D: Effect of bandwidth knowledge of results on movement consistency. Percept Mot Skills 66:535, 1988.

82. Swinnen, S, Schmidt, R, Nicholson, D, et al: Information feedback for skill acquisition: instantaneous knowledge of results degrades learning. J Exp Psychol 16:706, 1990.

83. Bilodeau, E and Bilodeau, I: Variable frequency knowledge of

results and the learning of a simple skill. J Exp Psychol 55:379, 1958.

84. Ho, L and Shea, J: Effects of relative frequency of knowledge of results on retention of a motor skill. Percept Mot Skills 46:859, 1978.

85. Winstein, C and Schmidt, R: Reduced frequency of knowledge of results enhances motor skill learning. J Exp Psychol (Learn Mem Cogn) 16:677, 1990.

86. Winstein, C: Knowledge of results and motor learning: implications for physical therapy. Phys Ther 71:140, 1991.

87. Schmidt, R: A schema theory of discrete motor skill learning. Psychol Rev 82:225, 1975.

88. VanSant, A: Life-span development in functional tasks. Phys Ther 70:788, 1990.

89. Bayley, N: The development of motor abilities during the first three years. Monographs of the Society for Research in Child Development 1 (1, serial no 1), 1935.

90. Gesell, A and Amatruda, C: Developmental Diagnosis. Harper, New York, 1941.

91. McGraw, M: The Neuromuscular Maturation of the Human Infant. Hafner Press, New York, 1945.

92. Keogh, J and Sugden, D: Movement Skill Development. Macmillan, New York, 1985.

93. Gentile, A: A working model of skill acquisition with application to teaching. Quest 17:3, 1972.

94. Sullivan, P, Markos, P, and Minor, M: An Integrated Approach to Therapeutic Exercise. Reston, Reston, VA, 1982.

SUPPLEMENTAL READINGS

Barnes, M and Crutchfield, C: Reflex and Vestibular Aspects of Motor Control, Motor Development and Motor Learning. Stokesville, Atlanta, 1990.

Bishop, B: Vibration stimulation, I. Neurophysiology of motor responses evoked by vibratory stimulation. Phys Ther 54:1273, 1974.

Fiebert, I and Brown, E: Vestibular stimulation to improve ambulation after a cerebral vascular accident. Phys Ther 59:423, 1979.

Kukula, C, Fellows, W, Oehlertz, J, and Vanderwilt, S: Effect of tendon pressure on alpha motoneuron excitability. Phys Ther 65:595, 1985.

Montgomery, P and Connolly, B: Motor Control and Physical Therapy. Chattanooga Group, Hixson, TN, 1991.

Mulder, T and Hulstyn, W: Sensory feedback therapy and theoretical knowledge of motor control and learning. Am J Phys Med 63:226, 1984.

Ottenbacher, K: Developmental implications of clinically applied vestibular stimulation: a review. Phys Ther 63:338, 1983.

Pederson, D: The soothing effect of rocking as determined by the direction and frequency of movement. Can J Behav Sci 7:237, 1975.

Ratliffe, K, Alba, B, Hallum, A, et al: Effects of approximation on postural sway in healthy subjects. Phys Ther 67:502, 1987.

Rheault, W, Derleth, M, Casey, M, Czarnik, C, Kania, D, and Nagel, G: Effects of inverted position on blood pressure, pulse rate, and deep tendon reflexes of healthy young adults. Phys Ther 65:1358, 1985.

Spicer, S and Matyas, T: Facilitation of TVR by cutaneous stimulation. Am J Phys Med 59:223, 1980.

Sullivan, P and Markos, P: Clinical Procedures in Therapeutic Exercise. Appleton & Lange, Norwalk, CT, 1987.

Twist, D: Effects of wrapping technique on passive range of motion in a spastic upper extremity. Phys Ther 65:299, 1985.

GLOSSARY

Activation: An internal state characterized by potential for action; the attainment of a critical threshold level of neuronal firing for movement.

Active assisted movement (AAM): Manual assistance of active movement.

Adaptability: The capacity to perform a task in altered environmental contexts; resistance to contextual change.

Agonist reversal (AR): A proprioceptive neuromuscular facilitation (PNF) technique involving resisted contractions, both concentric and eccentric, of the agonist pattern.

Alternating isometrics (AI): A proprioceptive neuromuscular facilitation (PNF) technique involving alternate isometric contractions, first of agonists, then antagonists.

Arousal (central set): A central nervous system (CNS) state of alertness or excitement.

Associative phase (motor learning): The middle phase of learning in which refinement of the motor program is achieved through continued practice.

Automatic postural synergies: Discrete patterns of leg and trunk muscle contractions characterized by consistency in muscle combinations, timing, and intensity and used to perserve standing balance.

Autonomous phase (motor learning): The final stage of learning in which the spatial and temporal aspects of movement become highly organized through practice.

Ballistic stretching: Quick stretching of muscles and tissues through bobbing or bouncing movements involving active antagonist muscle contractions.

Braiding: A proprioceptive neuromuscular facilitation (PNF) gait activity consisting of sidewards crossed stepping (one leg moves across and in front of the other leg followed by a side step of the other leg; the cycle is repeated with a step across and behind followed by a side step of the other leg).

Closed-loop control: A control system that employs feedback, a reference of correctness, a computation of error, and subsequent correction in order to maintain a desired state.

Closed skill: Motor skill performed in an unchanging, predictable environment (closed environment).

Cognitive phase (motor learning): The initial phase of learning in which the cognitive plan for the task is developed.

Coma stimulation: An organized program of sensory stimulation designed to improve the overall level of alertness and arousal of brain-injured (comatose) patients.

Contract-relax (CR): A proprioceptive neuromuscular facilitation (PNF) technique involving a maximally resisted contraction of the range-limiting antagonist pattern followed by active relaxation and movement into the agonist pattern. Rotators are allowed to contract isotonically while all other muscles contract isometrically.

Contract-relax-active-motion (CRAM): The addition of active movement into the newly gained range following the contract-relax phase.

Contralateral transfer: Practice of a motor skill by a contralateral extremity first.

Facilitation: Increased capacity to initiate a movement response through increased neuronal activity and altered synaptic potential.

Feedback: Sensory information provided to the central nervous system (CNS) from the production of movement. Two general types exist:

   Augmented feedback (extrinsic feedback): Feedback that is added to that normally received during a movement task.

   Intrinsic feedback: The feedback normally received during the execution of movement.

Generalizability: The ability to apply a learned skill to the learning of other similar tasks.

Hold-relax (HR): A proprioceptive neuromuscular facilitation (PNF) technique involving a maximally resisted isometric contraction of the range-limiting antagonist pattern followed by active relaxation and movement into the agonist pattern.

Hold-relax active motion (HRA): A proprioceptive neuromuscular facilitation (PNF) technique involving maximal isometric contraction in the shortened range, followed by active relaxation, passive movement into the lengthened range, and resisted movement back to the shortened range.

Inhibition: Decreased capacity to initiate a movement response through decreased neuronal activity and altered synaptic potential.

Intermittent control hypothesis: A theory of motor control that specifies the interaction between closed-loop and open-loop processes in controlling movement.

Inverted U hypothesis (Yerkes-Dodson law): Increasing arousal level improves performance up to a point. Further increases in the intensity of arousal result in a decrease in performance.

Knowledge of performance (KP): Feedback that occurs during movement and allows for error detection and movement modification.

Knowledge of results (KR): Feedback that occurs at the conclusion of movement and allows the appraisal of the overall success of the movement response.

Limits of stability (LOS): The maximum angle from vertical that can be tolerated without a loss of balance.

Motor learning: A set of internal processes associated with practice or experience and leading to relatively permanent changes in the capability for skilled behavior.[4]

Motor plan: An idea or plan for purposeful movement that is made up of component motor programs.

Motor program: An abstract code or set of prestructured commands that, when initiated, results in the production of a coordinated movement sequence.[4]

   Subprogram: A smaller learned subroutine.

Open-loop control: A control system that uses preprogrammed instructions and does not use feedback information and error-detection processes.[4]

Open skills: Motor skills performed in a changing, unpredictable environment (open environment).

Perseveration (perseverate): Continued repetition of a word or act not related to successive instructions or commands.

Placing and holding: A neurodevelopment treatment (NDT) technique in which the body or part is placed in a posture or position and the patient is asked to hold actively against the resistance of gravity.

Practice: Repeated performance trials.

   Constant practice: Practice organized around one task performed repeatedly.

   Distributed practice: An alternating sequence of rest and practice sessions in which the rest time equals or exceeds the practice time.

   Massed practice: A prolonged period of practice with infrequent rest periods.

   Variable practice: Practice of several variations of the same task or within the same category or class of movements.

Repeated contraction (RC): A proprioceptive neuromuscular facilitation (PNF) technique involving repeated stretch and resisted isotonic contractions of an agonist muscle.

Resisted progression (RP): A proprioceptive neuromuscular facilitation (PNF) technique involving the use of stretch and resistance to enhance patterns of locomotion.

Retention: The ability to demonstrate a skill over time and after a period of no practice.

Rhythmic initiation (RI): A proprioceptive neuromuscular facilitation (PNF) technique involving voluntary relaxation followed by passive, active-assistive, and finally mildly resisted movements of the agonist pattern.

Rhythmic rotation (RRo): A relaxation technique used in proprioceptive neuromuscular facilitation (PNF) and NDT that involves repeated, passive rotational movements of a limb or the trunk followed by movement into the lengthened range; may be therapist-directed (passive motion) or patient-directed (active motion). Verbal commands for voluntary relaxation assist the relaxation effort.

Rhythmic stabilization (RS): A proprioceptive neuromuscular facilitation (PNF) technique involving isometric contractions of antagonist patterns while resistance is applied simultaneously to both agonists and antagonists.

Schema theory: A theory of motor control in which rules, concepts, or relationships for movement are stored in memory and recalled in the structuring of motor acts.

Slow reversals (SR): A proprioceptive neuromuscular facilitation (PNF) technique involving alternating isotonic contractions of first agonist, then antagonist, patterns.

Slow reversal-hold (SRH): A proprioceptive neuromuscular facilitation (PNF) technique involving alternate isometric and isotonic contractions of both agonist and antagonist patterns: a holding response of the agonist is followed by a resisted isotonic contraction of the antagonist pattern and progresses to an isometric hold of the antagonist in the shortened range.

Static stretching: Use of a low-load maintained stretch applied for extended periods of time.

Stereotypic movement synergies: Muscles activated in an abnormal synergistic unit and firmly linked together; movement variations and isolated joint movements are not possible.

Strength: The ability of muscle to produce tension necessary for the initiation of movement, control of movement, or maintenance of posture.

Timing for emphasis (TE): A proprioceptive neuromuscular facilitation (PNF) technique involving an isometric hold and resistance of the stronger components of a pattern while repeated contractions are applied to the weaker components.

Tone: The resistance of muscle to passive elongation or stretch.

Transfer of learning: Practice of related or similar movement skills that results in improved performance of other desired skills.

Parts-to-whole transfer: Practice of component parts before practice of the integrated whole.

Preambulation and Gait Training

Thomas J. Schmitz

OBJECTIVES

1. Identify the purposes of a preambulation exercise program.
2. Identify the components of a general gait-training program.
3. Describe the guidelines for measuring assistive devices.
4. Describe the common gait patterns used with assistive devices.
5. Describe the techniques for guarding the patient during gait training in the parallel bars, on level surfaces, and on stairs.

Ambulation is a primary functional goal for many patients. Physical therapists need to be able to identify problems that limit or prevent ambulation, to determine their causes, and to plan appropriate therapeutic intervention. This intervention typically includes preambulation exercises and gait training. The purpose of gait-training activities is to provide the patient with a method of ambulation that allows maximum functional independence and safety at a reasonable energy cost.

This chapter presents a general discussion of preambulation exercises, and gait training with assistive devices, that can be modified to meet the needs of individual patients. Several factors will be of major influence in determining the extent and type of gait-training activities required. These factors include the patient's primary diagnosis, medical history, and weight-bearing status, as well as data obtained from the physical therapist's assessment, and input from the patient regarding ambulatory goals. For example, the progression of gait-training activities indicated for an otherwise healthy individual with a non-weight-bearing tibial fracture would be very different from those developed for a patient with paraplegia.

The major elements of a gait-training program are outlined in Table 14–1. It should be noted that the entire sequence will not be indicated for each patient. Depending on individual patient need, multiple segments may be accomplished concurrently (i.e., a more rapid progression may be indicated), or portions may be completely omitted.

PREPARATION FOR STANDING

Preambulation Mat Program

Preambulation exercises prepare the patient for assuming the upright position and typically involve a large component of mat work. Many of these mat activities are based on a developmental framework and progress from initial activities with a large base of support (BOS) and a low center of gravity (COG) through later activities which have a smaller BOS and high COG. The techniques utilized within each posture of the mat program are sequenced according to the four stages of motor control and progress from (1) *mobility,* which incorporates initiation of movement techniques, including *assist to position* in which the therapist manually assists the patient to achieve a given posture; to (2) *stability,* characterized by the ability to maintain a posture against gravity; to (3) *controlled mobility,* which is the ability to maintain postural control during weight shifting and movement; and finally to (4) *skill,* which is the highest level, characterized by discrete motor control superimposed on proximal stability. The techniques used within each posture typically progress from assisted or guided movement to active movement to resisted movement.

These mat or lead-up activities (the term *lead-up* implies that the activities are preparatory for or "lead up" to ambulation) have important functional carryover

Table 14–1 GENERAL OUTLINE OF GAIT-TRAINING PROGRAM

A. PREAMBULATION MAT PROGRAM: Activities and techniques to
  1. Improve strength, coordination, and range of motion.
  2. Facilitate proprioceptive feedback.
  3. Develop postural stability.
  4. Develop controlled mobility in movement transitions.
  5. Develop dynamic balance control and skills.
B. PARALLEL BAR PROGRESSION: Instruction and training in
  1. Moving from sitting to standing and reverse.
  2. Standing balance and weight-shifting activities.
  3. Use of appropriate gait pattern, forward progression, and turning.
  *4. Moving from sitting to standing, and reverse, with assistive device.
  *5. Standing balance and weight-shifting activities with assistive device.
  *6. Use of assistive device (with selected gait pattern) for forward progression and turning.
C. ADVANCED PARALLEL BAR ACTIVITIES
  1. Walking sideward (sidewalking).
  2. Walking backward.
  3. Braiding.
  4. Resisted ambulatory activities.
D. INDOOR PROGRESSION: Instruction and training in
  1. Use of assistive device for ambulation on level surfaces.
  2. Elevation activities, including climbing stairs and, if available indoors, negotiating ramps and curbs.
  3. Opening doors and passing through doorways (including elevators) and over thresholds.
  4. Falling techniques (generally included for active ambulators requiring long-term use of assistive devices).
E. OUTDOOR PROGRESSION: Instruction and training in
  1. Opening doors and passing through thresholds that lead outdoors.
  2. Use of assistive device for ambulation on outdoor surfaces and uneven terrain.
  3. Elevation activities including stair climbing and negotiating ramps and curbs.
  4. Crossing a street within the time allocated by a traffic light.
  5. Entering an automobile and/or public transportation.

*Because of limited space, use of the parallel bars may not be possible. However, when adjustable-width bars are available, they provide added security for preliminary use of the assistive device. An alternative approach would be to begin use of the device *outside and next to* the parallel bars.

to other daily activities as well, such as relieving pressure, dressing, and bed mobility. The development of successful mat programs will require the therapist to draw on several different exercise approaches. The work of Voss,[1] Sullivan,[2] and coworkers is particularly helpful in this regard. Additionally, many other more traditional forms of exercise provide important components of an overall program of preambulation exercises (e.g., progressive resistive exercises, sling/spring suspension techniques, and coordination exercises).

Depending on the level of patient involvement, the goals of a preambulation exercise program will be to
  1. Improve strength.
  2. Improve or maintain range of motion.
  3. Improve coordination.
  4. Facilitate proprioceptive feedback.
  5. Instruct the patient in handling and moving the affected extremity or extremities.
  6. Develop postural stability in sitting and standing.
  7. Develop controlled mobility function as evidenced by the ability to move within postures.

  8. Develop controlled mobility function in movement transitions such as rolling and moving from a supine position to a sitting position.
  9. Improve trunk and pelvic control.
  10. Develop static and dynamic balance control, including righting, equilibrium, and protective reactions.

A general outline of suggested preambulation mat exercises follows. The activities should be ordered from easiest to most difficult and should reflect the spiral nature of the development of motor control; that is, total mastery of one activity *is not necessary* before moving to the next higher level. Sequences may be planned in such a fashion that multiple postures may be overlapped and used in a mat program concurrently. Although the activities are described here in a general order of easiest to more difficult, it is not uncommon for the order to be changed, or for several activities to be worked on simultaneously. With adult patients it is common to work on several levels of activities concurrently. The specific activities and techniques selected, as well as the sequence, will be determined by goals established for the individual patient. Chapter 13 (Strategies to Improve Motor Control and Motor Learning) should be consulted for descriptions of the individual techniques and additional treatment suggestions. The mat sequence that follows uses a number of activities and postures, including rolling, prone-on-elbows (and prone-on-hands), hooklying and bridging, quadruped, sitting, kneeling and half-kneeling, modified plantigrade, and, finally, standing.

ROLLING

Rolling may be the initial starting point for a preambulation mat program for some patients. This activity provides a large BOS and low COG without bearing weight through the joints. Mat work may begin in a *sidelying* position at first, particularly if initiation of rolling is difficult. Resisted isometric contractions in shortened ranges (termed *shortened held resisted contraction*) are a useful early technique in sidelying. This technique uses sustained isometric contractions of the postural extensors. Manual contacts are posteriorly on the shoulder and pelvis. The patient is asked to "hold" maximally against the resistance of the therapist through increments of range. Additionally, the proprioceptive neuromuscular facilitation (PNF) techniques of *hold-relax-active movement* and *rhythmic stabilization* (1) also may be used in sidelying to facilitate contraction and proximal *stability*.

Rolling activities generally progress from *log rolling* to *segmental rolling*. **Log rolling** produces movement of the entire trunk as a unit around the longitudinal axis of the body. **Segmental rolling** is a progression from log rolling. In segmental rolling either the upper or the lower segment of the trunk moves independently while the other segment is stabilized. As the progression continues, **counterrotation** will develop. *Counterrotation* involves simultaneous movement of the upper and lower segments of the trunk in opposite directions. Several suggested activities follow that can be used and/or combined to facilitate rolling.

1. Flexion of the head and neck with rotation may be used to assist movement from supine to prone positions.
2. Extension of the head and neck with rotation may be used to assist movement from prone to supine positions.
3. Bilateral upper extremity activities that cross the midline will produce a pendular motion and can be used to rock the body from a supine position toward a prone position. To create this momentum, both elbows are extended and the shoulders are flexed to approximately 110 degrees with the hands clasped together. The upper extremities are then swung from side to side.
4. Crossing the ankles will also facilitate rolling. The ankles are crossed so that the upper leg is toward the direction of the roll (e.g., the right ankle would be crossed over the left when rolling toward the left).
5. Several PNF patterns are useful during early rolling activities.[1-3] The upper extremity PNF patterns of D_1 flexion, D_2 extension, chop, and lift will facilitate rolling. The lower extremity pattern of D_1 flexion will also facilitate rolling.[3]

PRONE-ON-ELBOWS POSITION

In the prone-on-elbows position there continues to be a large BOS and low COG. This position provides weight bearing on the elbows and forearms. The posture is useful to facilitate proximal stability of the glenohumeral and scapular musculature; this is an important prerequisite for using the upper extremities in weight bearing. Although head and neck control is required to assume a prone-on-elbows position, it can be further improved in this posture. The prone-on-elbows position must be used cautiously because some patients will find it difficult to tolerate the increased **lordotic** curve. Additionally, this position may be problematic for patients with shoulder or elbow pathology, cardiac or respiratory impairment, or hip flexor tightness.

To assist in initial assumption of the prone-on-elbows position, the patient should be in the following starting position:[4] prone, both lower extremities extended, the shoulders abducted, elbows flexed, forearms pronated, palms flat on supporting surface, and the head in a neutral position (or turned to one side for comfort). The therapist is positioned to the side of the patient or, if the supporting surface permits, straddling the patient's trunk with one foot on either side of the patient's body. The therapist's hips and knees should be flexed and manual contacts placed over the pectoral muscles with fingers pointing toward the sternum. The therapist then assists the patient to assume the position by lifting and supporting the upper trunk as the patient adducts the shoulders to allow weight bearing on the elbows (Fig. 14–1). Several suggested activities that can be used as a progression within this posture follow.

1. Initial activities should include assisted assumption and maintenance of the posture.

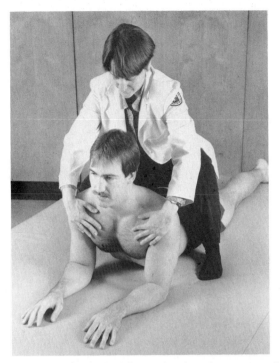

Figure 14–1. Method for assisting patient into the prone-on-elbows position.

2. Manually applied approximation force can be used to facilitate *holding* of proximal musculature. Rhythmic stabilization or alternating isometrics may be used to increase stability of head, neck, and scapula.[2]
3. A progression can be made to independent maintenance of the posture while altering head position and depressing the scapula.
4. Weight shifting in this position will improve dynamic stability through increased *joint approximation*.[5] Weight shifting is usually easiest in a lateral direction but may also be accomplished in an anterior or posterior direction (Fig. 14–2).
5. Activities that require resisted grasp in this position such as squeezing a ball or a cone[5] will reinforce *cocontraction* at the shoulder.[5,6]
6. Controlled mobility activities of the scapula can be used to promote proximal dynamic stability (e.g., prone-on-elbows push-ups).
7. Static-dynamic activities should be included in the prone-on-elbows position. This involves unilateral weight bearing on the static limb while the dynamic limb is freed. This will further facilitate cocontraction in the weight-bearing limb.
8. Movement within this posture can be achieved by an on-elbows forward-and-backward progression.
9. Movement into and out of the posture should be a final component of the prone-on-elbows sequence.

PRONE-ON-HANDS POSITION

This position is considered an intermediate step between the prone-on-elbows and quadruped positions.[5] In the prone-on-hands position a smaller BOS and higher COG is achieved. Weight is now borne

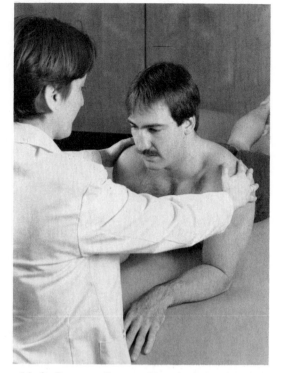

Figure 14–2. Prone-on-elbow position. Lateral weight shifting will improve dynamic stability secondary to increased joint approximation.

through the elbows to the hands and wrists. As with the prone-on-elbows position, this position also will be inappropriate for many patients owing to the excessive lordosis required to assume and to maintain the position. However, this position has several important functional implications. The functional carryover of the prone-on-hands position includes development of the initial hyperextension of the hips and low back for patients requiring this type of postural alignment during ambulation (e.g., patients with paraplegia), and standing from a wheelchair or rising from the floor with crutches and bilateral knee-ankle orthoses.

To assist to the prone-on-hands position, the patient should first assume the prone-on-elbows position. The therapist's position and manual contacts are the same as for assisting to prone-on-elbows. Initially, work in this position often requires starting with the patient's supporting hand placement further away from the body (i.e., with greater than 90 degrees of shoulder flexion) until the patient becomes accustomed to the position. This type of early positioning may require contact guarding from the therapist to allow maintenance of the position. Several suggestions follow for activities that may be completed while the patient is in the prone-on-hands position.

1. Initial activities should include assisted assumption and assisted maintenance of the posture.
2. Additional approximation force can be applied through manual contacts to further facilitate tonic holding of proximal musculature.
3. Independent maintenance of the posture should be practiced; a progression can be made to maintain-

ing the posture with alterations in head position and during scapular depression.
4. Lateral weight shifting with weight transfer between hands will increase joint approximation.
5. Resisted scapular depression and prone-on-hands push-ups may be used as strengthening exercises in this position.
6. A progression can be made to movement within this posture in both forward and lateral directions. This activity has useful functional implications for patients with paraplegia. An important example is floor-to-stand transitions. The prone-on-hands position provides the functional skills to allow the patient to reposition the body and the crutches to prepare for standing.

HOOKLYING

In this posture the patient is supine with hips and knees flexed and feet flat on the mat. This position provides a large BOS and low COG. Lower trunk rotation can be facilitated by movement of the lower extremities across the midline. It is useful in activating both the lower abdominals and low back extensors as well as increasing range of motion in the low back and hips.[2] Activities within this posture are initiated with assisted or guided movement. A progression is then made to application of resistance applied in each direction away from the midline. Manual contacts at the knees must be altered from the medial to lateral surfaces as the direction of movement is changed. Several suggestions that may be used and/or combined in the hooklying position follow.

1. Tonic holding activities within a shortened range will improve stability (shortened held resisted contraction).
2. Rhythmic stabilization may be used with manual contacts at the knees to facilitate co-contraction and stability.[1]
3. Active assisted, guided, or resisted movement in each direction away from the midline may be used to increase range of motion (Fig. 14–3).

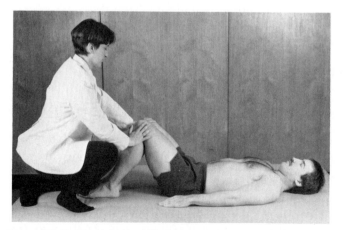

Figure 14–3. Hooklying. In this position lower trunk rotation and range of motion is facilitated by movement of the lower extremities in each direction from the midline.

4. Hip abduction and adduction can be facilitated by use of alternating isometrics with manual contacts at the knees.

5. The level of difficulty of this activity may be increased by decreasing the amount of hip and knee flexion and moving manual contacts for application of resistance to the ankles.[2]

BRIDGING

This activity is a progression from hooklying. It places the lower extremities in a weight-bearing position and is an important precursor to assuming the kneeling position and in developing sit-to-stand control. For this activity the patient is in a hooklying position and elevates the pelvis off the mat (Fig. 14–4). The BOS is thus reduced and the COG is raised. This activity is particularly useful for facilitating pelvic motions and strengthening the low back and hip extensors in preparation for the stance phase of gait. In addition, bridging has several important functional implications, including bed mobility, use of a bedpan, pressure relief, lower extremity dressing, and movement from a sitting to a standing position. Specific pelvic motions (e.g., pelvic forward motion, rotation, and lateral shift) required during gait also can be initiated and facilitated in this position. Several suggestions that can be used as a progression within this posture follow.

1. Initial activities will involve assisted assumption and assisted maintenance of the position. Manual contacts to assist to position are at the pelvis. Assistance during early bridging activities also can be provided by having the patient abduct the arms on the mat to provide a larger BOS.

2. The ability to maintain, or to hold, the posture can be facilitated by use of isometric contractions. The techniques of alternating isometrics and rhythmic stabilization can be used to promote stability.

3. Independent maintenance of the posture should be practiced with a progressive decrease in the BOS

provided by the upper extremities (i.e., moving arms closer to body).

4. The techniques of slow reversal and slow reversal-hold can be used to facilitate pelvic rotation and lateral shifting.[2]

5. Strengthening can be accomplished during bridging by application of resistance with manual contacts at the anterior superior iliac spines. Resistance also can be applied diagonally (greater emphasis of resistance to one side) to facilitate pelvic rotation and/or to increase range of motion selectively on one side.[1,7]

6. Bridging also can be used to facilitate hip abduction and adduction. This can be accomplished either symmetrically (resistance applied against the same motion in each extremity) or asymmetrically (resistance applied against opposing motions) by use of alternating isometrics with manual contacts at the knees.[7]

7. Unassisted or resisted (e.g., using agonist reversal) movement into and out of the posture should be practiced.

8. Several modifications to bridging can be made to make the activity more demanding by altering the BOS. These modifications include (a) performing the activity with support from only one lower extremity in preparation for weight acceptance during the stance phase of gait, and (b) decreasing the angle of hip and knee flexion (i.e., moving the feet distally).

QUADRUPED POSITION

This on-all-fours position further decreases the BOS and raises the COG with weight bearing through multiple joints. The **quadruped** position is the first position in the mat progression that allows weight bearing through the hips. This posture is particularly useful for facilitating initial control of the musculature of the lower trunk and hips.

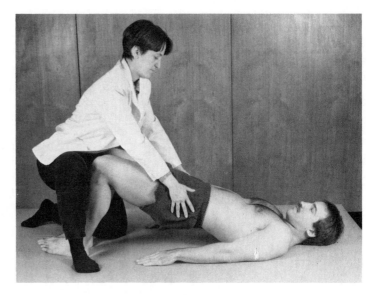

Figure 14–4. Bridging. Manual contacts at the pelvis can be used to assist or to resist pelvic elevation.

Assumption of the quadruped position can be achieved from two positions. If the patient is able to sit, the patient may be guided into sidesitting by rotating the trunk to allow weight bearing on the hands with the elbows extended. The therapist then guides the lower trunk into the quadruped position, with manual contacts on the pelvis to assist movement of the pelvis over the knees.

The quadruped position also may be assumed from a prone-on-elbows position. Using this technique the therapist straddles the patient's lower extremities with one foot placed parallel to each thigh. With the therapist's hips and knees bent, he or she then lifts and guides the pelvis over the knees as the patient "walks" backward on elbows. Once the pelvis is positioned over the knees, the patient assumes or is assisted into weight bearing on hands with full elbow extension. Several suggested techniques and activities that can be incorporated into the quadruped position follow.

1. Initial activities involve assisted assumption and assisted maintenance of the position. If these activities are difficult, a gymnastic ball can first be used to support the patient's trunk during the movement transition from sidesitting to the quadruped position and then during maintenance of the position. The ball can be placed centrally under the trunk or moved toward the upper or lower extremities, depending on the area of greatest weakness.

2. Rhythmic stabilization or alternating isometrics will facilitate co-contraction of shoulder, hip, and trunk musculature.[1]

3. Weight shifting can be used in a forward, backward, and side-to-side direction to increase weight bearing over two extremities simultaneously to improve dynamic stability.

4. Manual application of approximation force can be used to facilitate co-contraction through both upper and lower extremities.

5. For patients with spasticity, this position can be used to provide inhibitory pressure to the quadriceps and long finger flexors (using an open-hand position) to diminish tone.

6. Rocking through increments of range (forward, backward, side-to-side, and diagonally) will facilitate equilibrium and proprioceptive responses as well as increase range of motion at the proximal weight-bearing joints.[1,2]

7. Static-dynamic activities, such as freeing one or more extremities from a weight-bearing position, may be used in the quadruped position. A progression is frequently made from unweighting one upper extremity to unweighting one lower extremity to unweighting opposite upper and lower extremities simultaneously. This activity will provide greater joint approximation forces on the supporting extremities and increase dynamic holding of postural muscles (Fig. 14–5).

8. Unassisted movement into and out of the quadruped posture can be practiced.

9. Movement within the quadruped position (*creeping*) has several important implications for ambulation. It is typically the first activity that requires

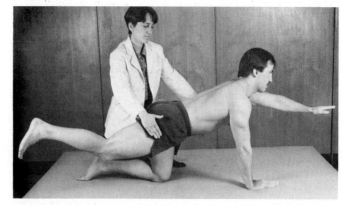

Figure 14–5. Quadruped. Static-dynamic activities facilitate dynamic holding of postural muscles by increasing weight-bearing demands on the static limbs.

trunk counterrotation, an important prerequisite for ambulation. Creeping can also be used to improve strength (resisted progression), facilitate dynamic balance reactions, and improve coordination and timing.

SITTING

A program of mat activities typically includes work in the sitting position. Sitting can be used effectively to develop balance, trunk control, and weight bearing on the upper extremities. In addition, improved stability of the head and neck can be achieved in this position. Two types of sitting are often incorporated into a preambulation mat program:

1. **Short sitting.** In this position the patient's hips and knees are flexed with the feet flat on the floor.
2. **Long sitting.** In this position the hips are flexed and the knees are extended on the supporting surface. The sitting position provides a small BOS and high COG. However, it should be noted that the BOS for the two types of sitting is different and may influence selection for an individual patient. For example, the long sitting position provides a relatively large BOS as compared with the short sitting position. This larger BOS in long sitting is provided by placement of the lower extremities in contact with the supporting surface.

Another factor that warrants consideration in selection of a sitting posture is the range of motion required to assume the position. The long sitting position will be difficult for some patients, owing to limited range of motion in the low back and/or hamstrings. Hamstring tightness in the long sitting position may also result in alterations in pelvic position, causing the patient to "sit back" on the ischia.

The BOS in sitting may be altered by changing the position of upper extremity support. Upper extremity support may be placed posterior to the pelvis (large BOS), lateral to the pelvis (small BOS), or anterior to the pelvis (intermediate BOS). Several suggestions that can be incorporated into a progression of activities used in the sitting positions follow.

1. Initial activities will focus on assisted assumption and assisted maintenance of the position. For

patients with proprioceptive loss, use of a mirror during sitting activities may provide important visual feedback.

2. Manual application of approximation force may be used at the shoulders to promote co-contraction.

3. A variety of PNF techniques may be used. Specifically, alternating isometrics and rhythmic stabilization are important in promoting early stability in this posture.[1]

4. For patients with spasticity, sitting with extended arm support and with the hand open and flat will provide inhibitory input to the long finger flexors to dampen tone.

5. The position of upper extremity support may be altered with subsequent transfer of weight in each position (e.g., posteriorly, anteriorly, and laterally). This activity also will promote co-contraction as well as alter the BOS.

6. Unassisted maintenance of the posture should be included with a gradual reduction and then elimination of upper extremity support.

7. Balancing activities may be practiced in sitting position without upper extremity support. The position of the upper extremities may be altered by having the patient move into shoulder flexion, abduction, and so forth while maintaining trunk balance. A progression may be made to movement of the trunk (forward, backward, and side-to-side) without upper extremity support. As a component of these activities the patient's balance may be manually challenged at the trunk or by passive movement of the lower extremities. Balance also may be challenged by asking the patient to practice throwing and catching a ball to and from various directions, or by completing functional activities such as putting on a pair of socks, tying shoes, and so forth.

8. Unassisted movement into and out of the sitting position should be practiced.

9. When indicated, the sitting position is often used for partial instruction in self-range-of-motion exercises. Both long sitting and tailor sitting ("Indian style" sitting, which places the hips in flexion, abduction and external rotation, with the knees flexed and the ankles crossed) can be used for this purpose. Forward flexion of the trunk with the knees extended in long sitting will maintain length of the low back and hamstring muscles. The tailor sitting position facilitates range of motion in hip external rotation, abduction, and knee flexion, and allows easier access to the ankle and foot.

10. Sitting push-ups are an important preliminary activity for transfers and ambulation as well as for improving ability in positional changes. This activity is accomplished by placing arms at sides, extending the elbows, and depressing the shoulders to lift the buttock from the mat. The activity can be initiated with bearing weight on the base of the hands placed directly on the mat and progressed to the use of push-up blocks with graded increments in height. A modification of the sitting push-up is placement of both hands on one side of the body in a long sitting position (sidesitting). The patient then pushes down on both upper extremities to lift the buttocks off the mat. This facilitates lower trunk rotation in preparation for gait. The functional implications of this activity are also related to movement transitions from sitting to quadruped positions. In addition, it is an important preliminary activity prior to sit-to-stand activities for patients with paraplegia (initial trunk rotation is often required before standing).

11. Movement within this posture has direct functional carryover to transfers, ambulation, and positional changes. However, these activities require good bilateral upper extremity strength (e.g., patients with paraplegia). Many of these activities are included in a mat program for patients with spinal cord injury and may incorporate the use of mat crutches. For patients with spinal cord injury, movement within sitting can be accomplished by using a seated push-up in combination with movement from the head and upper body. Momentum is created by throwing the head and shoulders forcefully in the direction opposite to the desired direction of motion. For example, while performing a push-up on the mat from the long sitting position, simultaneous rapid and forceful extension of the head and shoulders will move the lower extremities forward; movement in a posterior direction can be achieved by use of a sitting push-up with simultaneous rapid and forceful flexion of the head and trunk. This same progression of movement is used with the **swing-to** and **swing-through gait** patterns. Movement in the sitting position also may be accomplished by hiking one hip and shifting weight forward or backward and then repeating with the opposite hip.

12. A number of additional exercises may be included in the sitting position. With manual contacts at the shoulder, resistance may be applied to trunk extension, flexion, and rotation. Combining PNF patterns of the head, trunk, and extremities in sitting (e.g., chopping or lifting activities) can be used to improve strength, as well as to assist the patient in achieving functional goals related to this posture.[2]

KNEELING

The kneeling position further decreases the BOS, raises the COG, and provides weight bearing at the hips and knees. This position is particularly useful for establishing lower trunk and pelvic control and further promoting upright balance control. The position also facilitates the lower extremity pattern (initiated during bridging) of combined hip extension with knee flexion necessary for gait activities.

It is usually easiest to assist the patient into a kneeling position from a quadruped position. From the quadruped position, the patient moves or "walks" the hands backward until the knees further flex and the pelvis drops toward the heels. The patient will be "sitting" on the heels. From this position the patient may be assisted to kneeling by using the upper extremities to climb stall bars while the therapist guides the pelvis. Another method is for the therapist to assume a heel-sitting position directly in front of the patient. The patient's upper extremities are supported on the therapist's shoulders while the therapist manually guides the pelvis. Several suggested techniques and activities that can be utilized during kneeling follow.

1. Initial activities concentrate on assisted assumption and assisted maintenance of the position.
2. Approximation force may be used at the hips to facilitate co-contraction.
3. The PNF technique of slow reversal or slow reversal-hold is effective in facilitating pelvic forward motion, lateral shifting, and rotation.[2]
4. Eccentric hip control can be facilitated by agonist reversals. This technique uses a smooth reversal between concentric and eccentric contractions. With manual contacts at the pelvis, the hips are moved into increments of flexion with a return to extension. The excursion of movement is gradually increased. This technique also improves ability to move from heel-sitting to the kneeling position.
5. Transfer of weight from one knee to the other will facilitate co-contraction on the supporting limb.
6. Balancing activities may be practiced, progressing from support with one upper extremity to balancing without upper extremity support. The patient's balance may be challenged in this position. Throwing and catching a ball from various directions also can be used as a component of these balance activities.
7. Unassisted assumption of the posture can be facilitated by use of reverse chop or lift-trunk patterns.[1]
8. Hip hiking and forward progression, or "kneel walking," while the upper extremities are supported on the therapist's shoulder can be included in this position. A resisted progression can be used to facilitate forward movement. A progression is then made to a resisted progression with the upper extremities freed.
9. A variety of mat crutch activities can be used in the kneeling position (most commonly used with individuals who have sustained spinal cord injuries). Examples include weight shifting anteriorly, posteriorly, and laterally with emphasis on lower trunk and pelvic control, by placing the crutches forward, backward, and to the side with weight shifts in each direction; alternately raising one crutch at a time and returning it to the mat; hip hiking; instruction in selected gait patterns and forward progression using crutches.
10. Kneeling can be used to provide inhibition to the quadriceps muscle and thus to dampen tone in patients with spasticity. Reduction of extensor tone may be an important preparatory activity to standing and walking for some patients.

HALF-KNEELING

In half-kneeling (Fig. 14–6) the COG is the same as in kneeling; however, the BOS is widened. Greater

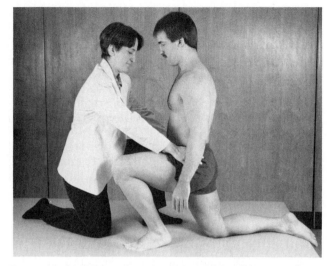

Figure 14–6. Half-kneeling. Anterior weight shifting onto forward limb.

demands are now placed on the posterior weight-bearing limb in preparation for weight acceptance during the stance phase of gait. Weight on the forward limb is now borne through the ankle. This position allows facilitation of hip extension, lateral pelvic control, and ankle movements, and it increases proprioceptive input through the foot.[8] The following techniques and activities are appropriate for use in the half-kneeling position.

1. Initial activities will include assisted assumption and assisted maintenance of the posture.
2. Rhythmic stabilization or alternating isometrics may be used in this position to improve stability. Several combinations of manual contacts may be used:[2] shoulder and pelvis; shoulder and anterior knee; and pelvis and anterior knee.
3. Anterior–posterior diagonal weight shifting in this position will facilitate range of motion of the hip, knee, and especially the ankle (Fig. 14–6).
4. Resistance may be introduced with manual contacts at the pelvis during weight shifting (e.g., slow reversal or slow reversal-hold).

MODIFIED PLANTIGRADE

Modified plantigrade (Fig. 14–7) is an early weight-bearing posture that can be used in preparation for erect standing and walking. In this position there is a relatively small BOS and high COG. This posture inherently promotes stability because weight-bearing demands are placed on all joints of all four extremities. Modified plantigrade posture is an important precursor to walking inasmuch as it superimposes close to full weight bearing on an advanced lower extremity pattern. This pattern, required during gait, combines hip flexion with knee extension and ankle dorsiflexion.

Initial assist-to-position activities are usually easiest from a sitting position, using a chair with arms. The chair is positioned directly in front of a treatment table or other stable surface of appropriate height. A guarding belt is warranted during early transitions from sitting to plantigrade positions. The patient is asked or assisted to move forward in the chair. The feet should be flat on the

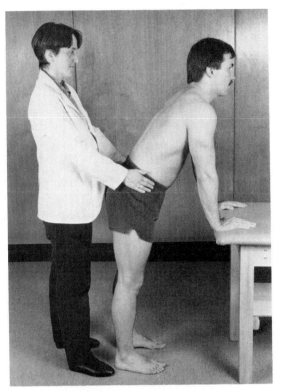

Figure 14–7. Modified plantigrade.

floor and the hands placed on the armrests of the chair. The patient then pushes down on the armrests and moves toward the modified plantigrade posture (placing one hand at a time onto the supporting surface). The therapist provides the needed level of assistance by use of the guarding belt and/or manual contacts. Several suggested activities and techniques that can be used in this posture follow.

1. Initial activities involve assisted assumption and assisted maintenance of the posture.
2. Stability can be enhanced by use of manual approximation force at both the shoulders and the pelvis. Rhythmic stabilization and alternating isometrics also can be used to promote stability in this position. Manual contacts are at the pelvis, shoulders, or shoulders and pelvis.
3. Range of motion can be increased and dynamic stability further enhanced by controlled mobility techniques such as rocking through increments of range. Rocking can be used in multiple directions (e.g., forward, backward, diagonally) and is effective in increasing weight bearing over one or more extremities. Guided weight shifting is effectively accomplished by the therapist standing behind the patient with manual contacts at the pelvis.[2]
4. A progression can be made to static-dynamic activities. Freeing one extremity will place increased demands on the three remaining weight-bearing limbs. Lower extremity positions can be altered by stepping with the dynamic limb in both forward and backward directions. Body weight is then shifted over the dynamic limb while the static limb remains stationary. This will facilitate pelvic motion and lateral shifting. Rotation of the lower trunk also can be emphasized during static-dynamic lower extremity activities.

STANDING

In erect standing the BOS is small with a high COG, requiring greater balance control. Standing activities are most often initiated in the parallel bars (described in the next section). However, for many patients these activities can be initiated next to a treatment table or other supporting surface. Some patients may demonstrate sufficient stability to maintain a standing posture prior to being able to assume the position independently.

It should be noted that achieving a specific level of motor control within a posture *does not guarantee translation of gains to standing.* Subcomponents (e.g., hip stability in quadruped) do not translate into ambulatory function without practice within a specific context. Motor learning relies on sensory information and feedback provided by practice and experience to shape specific functions. Components of the lead-up activities must be incorporated in upright standing to ensure transfer of subcomponents into a functional whole. The amount of practice required and the rate of learning vary among patients.

The following activities and techniques can be used in the standing position.

1. Initial activities involve assisted assumption (described under parallel bar progression) and assisted maintenance of the position.
2. The ability to maintain the posture can be promoted by stability techniques such as rhythmic stabilization and alternating isometrics with manual contacts at the pelvis, scapula, or both scapula and pelvis.[1]
3. Guided weight shifting onto alternate lower extremities with manual contacts on the pelvis also will improve stability. Additional support may be provided by placement of the patient's hands on the therapist's shoulders. As stability improves, upper extremity support should be reduced or eliminated.
4. Controlled-mobility activities of the trunk can be practiced in standing with the feet symmetrical or in stride. Anterior-posterior, lateral, and rotational movements of the trunk can be emphasized.[2]
5. Static-dynamic activities will promote weight acceptance by advancing the dynamic limb forward and moving body weight over the advanced limb. This activity also will promote forward rotation and lateral shift of the pelvis (Fig. 14–8).
6. Walking represents the final and highest level of motor control (skill). Manual contacts can be placed at the pelvis to guide and to assist with control of pelvic movement. Upper extremity support should be gradually decreased and then eliminated. The sequence of activities in standing typically includes resisted progression; walking backward, sidestep, cross-step; and PNF braiding. These activities are described in the following section.

This section presented a sample of mat activities to improve control. The incremental emphasis of control from proximal to distal body segments is summarized in

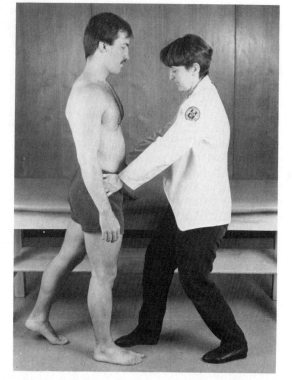

Figure 14–8. Standing. Static-dynamic activities will promote weight acceptance on the dynamic limb, forward pelvis rotation, and lateral shift.

Table 14–2. It should be noted that this basic sequence will require adaptation and modification, depending on the unique needs of each individual patient. In addition to the preambulation mat activities outlined, a program of strengthening and coordination exercises are important concurrent activities during preparation for ambulation. Transfer training and wheelchair management also can be initiated in conjunction with mat activities once the patient has begun work on movement within the sitting position. Table 14–3 presents a summary of the preambulation exercise program.

Parallel Bar Progression

Upright activities in the parallel bars can be initiated as soon as adequate motor control is achieved. All mat activities may not be warranted or feasible before initiating upright activities. Prior to standing, two important

Table 14–2 FOCUS OF CONTROL WITHIN EACH POSTURE OF THE PREAMBULATION MAT PROGRESSION

Posture	Focus of Control
Rolling	Trunk
	Segmental rotation
	Counterrotation
Prone-on-elbows	Head
	Neck
	Upper trunk
	Scapula
	Shoulders
Prone-on-hands	Elbows (intermediate control of upper extremities)
Hooklying	Lower trunk
	Proximal lower extremities
Bridging	Lower trunk
	Hips/pelvis
	Lower extremities
Quadruped	Trunk
	Proximal and intermediate upper extremities
	Proximal lower extremities
Sitting	Trunk
	Proximal and intermediate upper extremities
Kneeling	Trunk
	Pelvis
	Proximal lower extremities
Half-kneeling	Trunk
	Pelvis
	Proximal and distal lower extremities (knee and ankle)
	Reciprocal control of lower extremities
Plantigrade	Trunk
	Proximal and intermediate control of lower extremities
Standing	Trunk
	Lower extremities

preliminary activities include fitting the patient with a guarding belt and adjusting the parallel bars. The initial adjustment of the parallel bars is an estimate based on the patient's height. Ideally the bars should be adjusted to allow 20 to 30 degrees of elbow flexion and come to about the level of the greater trochanter. Considering individual variations in body proportions and arm length, the elbow measurement is usually most accurate. Once the patient is standing, the height of the bars can be checked. If adjustments are required, the patient should be returned to a sitting position. Prior to beginning work in the parallel bars, two important preparatory activities include *wheelchair positioning* and *placement of the guarding belt.*

Table 14–3 PREAMBULATION EXERCISE PROGRAM: SAMPLE PROGRESSION OF PREPARATORY ACTIVITIES

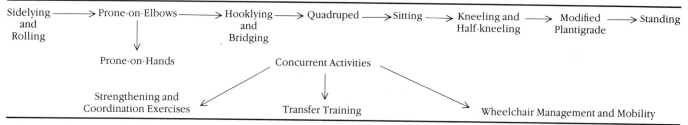

Sidelying and Rolling ⟶ Prone-on-Elbows ⟶ Hooklying and Bridging ⟶ Quadruped ⟶ Sitting ⟶ Kneeling and Half-kneeling ⟶ Modified Plantigrade ⟶ Standing

Prone-on-Elbows ⟶ Prone-on-Hands

Concurrent Activities

Prone-on-Hands ⟶ Strengthening and Coordination Exercises

Concurrent Activities ⟶ Transfer Training

Concurrent Activities ⟶ Wheelchair Management and Mobility

The patient's wheelchair should be positioned at the end of the parallel bars. The brakes should be locked, the footrests placed in an upright position, and the patient's feet should be flat on the floor. The guarding belt should be fastened securely around the patient's waist. Guarding belts provide several critical functions. They increase the therapist's effectiveness in controlling or preventing potential loss of balance; they improve patient safety; they facilitate the therapist's use of proper body mechanics in untoward circumstances; and finally, they are an important consideration regarding issues of liability. The safety implications of the guarding belt should be explained to the patient carefully. A sequence of activities for use in the parallel bars follows.

1. *Initial instruction/demonstration.* In initiating instruction in parallel bar activities, the entire progression should be presented before breaking it into component parts. This will include instruction and demonstration in how to assume a standing position in the parallel bars, guarding techniques to be used by the therapist, the components of initial standing balance activities, the gait pattern to be used, how to turn in the parallel bars, and how to return to a sitting position. Demonstrating these activities by assuming the role of the patient during verbal explanations will facilitate learning. Each component of the parallel bar progression should then be reviewed prior to the patient's actual performance of the activity.

2. *Assuming the standing position.* To prepare for standing, the patient should be instructed to move forward in the chair. The therapist is positioned directly in front of the patient. A method of guarding should be selected that does not interfere with the patient's use of the upper extremities while moving to standing. One useful approach is to grasp the guarding belt anteriorly (an "underhand" grasp will provide the most security). With unilateral involvement, the therapist's opposite wrist should be placed on the lateral trunk near the axillary region on the patient's stronger or unaffected side with the hand at the lateral border of the scapula. Care should be taken not to exert any upward pressure into the axilla. Although the correct position for guarding is typically on the patient's weaker side, the therapist may stand closer to the unaffected side in order to brace or to guard the patient's sound lower extremity and to ensure one strong supporting limb. For example, this approach would be indicated in situations in which one lower extremity requires a non-weight-bearing status. If bilateral involvement exists, the therapist should be positioned more centrally in order to brace both of the patient's knees. If necessary, the patient's feet may be braced (by the therapist's feet) to prevent sliding. An alternate hand placement particularly useful with bilateral involvement is one hand at the posterior hip, the opposite hand on the lateral aspect of the guarding belt or lateral trunk below the axilla. Having moved forward in the chair with the supporting foot or feet flat on the floor, the patient should be instructed to come to a standing position by leaning forward and pushing down on the armrests of the wheelchair. The patient should *not* be allowed to

stand by pulling up on the parallel bars. As the patient nears an erect posture, the hands should be released from the armrests one at a time and placed on the parallel bars. The patient's COG should be guided over the BOS to promote a stable standing posture.

3. *Initial parallel bar activities.* During parallel bar activities, the therapist usually stands inside the bars facing the patient or outside the bars on the patient's weaker side. In guarding the patient from inside the bars, one hand should grasp the guarding belt anteriorly, and the opposite hand should be in front of, *but not touching,* the patient's shoulder. From outside the bars one hand should grasp the belt posteriorly with the opposite hand in front of, *but not touching,* the patient's shoulder. This method of guarding provides effective hand placement for an immediate response should the patient's balance be lost. It also eliminates the patient's feeling of being "held back" or "pushed forward," which may occur with manual contacts at the shoulders. The following initial balancing activities in the parallel bars can be modified relative to the patient's weight-bearing status and the specific requirements of a treatment (e.g., use of a prosthesis or orthosis). Guarding techniques are maintained by the therapist during these activities.

a. *Standing balance.* Initially, the patient should be allowed time to become acclimated to the upright posture. During initial standing activities, the therapist should be alert to complaints of nausea or lightheadedness, which may indicate an onset of **orthostatic (postural) hypotension** caused by a drop in blood pressure. These symptoms typically disappear as tolerance to the upright posture improves. However, if the patient has been confined to bed and/or a wheelchair for a prolonged period, these symptoms may be severe. In these situations a gradual progression of tilt-table activities and careful monitoring of vital signs is warranted prior to standing.

b. *Limits of stability.* Exploration of limits of stability involves determining how far the patient's COG can be displaced while balance is maintained. Early exploration is accomplished by use of *anterior-posterior* and *lateral weight shifts* and *alteration in hand placement* on the parallel bars.

   1. *Lateral weight shift.* The patient shifts weight from side to side without altering the BOS; hand placement on the parallel bars is not altered.

   2. *Anterior-posterior weight shift.* The patient shifts weight forward and backward without altering the BOS; hand placement on the parallel bars is not altered.

   3. *Anterior-posterior hand placement and weight shift.* The patient moves the hands forward on the bars and shifts weight anteriorly. This is alternated with a posterior hand placement, and weight is shifted backward.

   4. *Single-hand support.* The patient balances with support from only one hand on the parallel bars; hands are alternated. A progression of this activity involves gradual changes in position of the freed hand and upper extremity. For example,

begin the activity by moving the freed hand several inches above the bar and gradually progress to alternate positions such as shoulder flexion, abduction, crossing the midline, and so forth. A progression can be made to balancing with both hands freed from the bars.

c. *Hip hiking.* The patient maintains the BOS and alternately hikes one hip at a time; hand placement on the parallel bars is maintained. Resistance can be applied by manual contacts at the pelvis.

d. *Standing push-ups.* The patient's hands are placed just anterior to the thighs on the parallel bars. Body weight is lifted by simultaneous elbow extension and shoulder depression. Additional height may be gained by forward flexion of the head. Return to the starting position is made by a controlled lowering of the body. This activity requires significant upper extremity strength and builds on the controlled mobility developed in preambulation activities. It is usually reserved for younger patient groups, such as those with paraplegia, and selected patients with lower extremity amputation.

e. *Stepping forward and backward.* The patient steps forward with one leg, shifts weight anteriorly, and returns to the starting position (normal BOS). This is alternated with stepping backward with one leg, shifting the weight posteriorly, and returning to the starting position. Resistance can be applied with manual contacts at the pelvis.

f. *Forward progression.* The patient begins ambulation in the parallel bars using the selected gait pattern and appropriate weight bearing on the affected lower extremity. The patient should be instructed to push down rather than to pull on the parallel bars while ambulating, inasmuch as this is the motion that eventually will be required with an assistive device. This will be easier if the patient is instructed to use a loose or open grip on the bars rather than a tight grip; the loose or open grip facilitates correct use of the parallel bars and, ultimately, the assistive device.

g. *Turning.* Once the desired distance in the parallel bars has been reached, the patient should be instructed to turn toward the stronger side. For example, with a non-weight-bearing left lower extremity, the turn should be toward the right. The patient should be instructed to turn by stepping in a small circle and not to pivot on a single extremity. This technique will carry over to ambulation outside the bars, when pivoting will always be discouraged because of the potential loss of balance by movement on a small BOS. Guarding while turning in the parallel bars can be accomplished two ways. The therapist can remain in front of the patient, maintain the same hand positions, and turn with the patient. This will keep the therapist positioned in front of the patient. A second method is not to turn with the patient but, rather, to guard from behind on the return trip. In this method hand placements will change during the turn. Hand placement is changed gradually by first placing

both hands on the guarding belt as the patient initiates the turn. One hand then remains on the posterior aspect of the belt and the freed hand is placed anterior to, *but not touching,* the shoulder on the patient's weaker side for the return trip toward the chair. Although both techniques are acceptable, the latter is probably more practical, considering the limited space available in the parallel bars.

As mentioned earlier, guarding also may be accomplished from outside the parallel bars. This positioning of the therapist is particularly useful during later stages of gait training. However, it presents several inherent problems for early training. If unilateral involvement exists, it is frequently difficult to remain close to the patient's weaker side (especially if the patient is not able to ambulate the full length of the parallel bars). In addition, the distance between the therapist and patient imposed by the intervening bar renders the therapist less effective in guarding and in using appropriate, safe body mechanics to help support the patient during periods of unsteadiness or loss of balance.

h. *Returning to the seated position.* When reaching the chair the patient should again turn as described earlier. Once completely turned, patients are typically instructed to continue backing up until they feel the seat of the chair on the back of their legs (this will require substitution with visual or auditory clues for patients with impaired sensation). At this point the patient releases the stronger hand from the parallel bar and reaches back for the wheelchair armrest. Once this hand has securely grasped the armrest, the patient should be instructed to bend forward slightly, release the opposite hand from the parallel bar and place it on the other armrest. Keeping the head and trunk forward the patient gently returns to a seated position.

4. *Advanced parallel bar activities.* Although not appropriate for every patient, several more advanced activities also can be incorporated into gait training in the parallel bars. These include the following.

a. *Resisted forward progression.* Resistance can be applied through manual contacts at the pelvis and/or shoulder as the patient walks forward.

b. *Walking backward.* Walking backward can be initiated actively and can progress to application of resistance through manual contacts at the pelvis. This activity also combines hip extension with knee flexion and is particularly useful for patients with hemiplegia with synergy influence in the lower extremities.

c. *Walking sidestep.* Initially, this activity is performed actively. A progression can then be made to application of resistance with manual contacts at the pelvis and thigh. Walking sidestep (sidewards) facilitates active abduction of the moving limb, combined with controlled mobility and weight bearing of the opposite supporting extremity.

d. *PNF braiding.* This activity requires a crossed and sidestep progression with one limb advancing alternately anteriorly and posteriorly across the other while the second limb sidesteps. It incorporates lower trunk rotation as well as crossing the midline.

ASSISTIVE DEVICES AND GAIT PATTERNS

Before continuing with the progression of gait training activities outside the parallel bars, consideration will be given to (1) selection and measurement of assistive devices, and (2) selection and description of gait patterns used with each ambulatory device.

Selection, Measurement, and Gait Patterns for Use of Ambulatory Assistive Devices

There are three major categories of ambulatory assistive devices: canes, crutches, and walkers. Each has several modifications to the basic design, many of which were developed to meet the needs of a specific patient problem or diagnostic group. Assistive devices are prescribed for a variety of reasons, including problems of balance, pain, fatigue, weakness, joint instability, excessive skeletal loading, and cosmesis.[9] Another primary function of assistive devices is to eliminate weight bearing fully or partially from an extremity. This unloading occurs by transmission of force from the upper extremities to the floor by downward pressure on the assistive device.

CANES

The function of a cane is to *widen the BOS* and *to improve balance.* Canes are not intended for use with restricted weight-bearing gaits (such as non- or partial-weight-bearing). Patients are typically instructed to hold a cane in the hand *opposite the affected extremity.* This positioning of the cane most closely approximates a normal reciprocal gait pattern with the opposite arm and leg moving together. It also widens the BOS with less lateral shifting of the COG than when the cane is held on the ipsilateral side.[10]

Contralateral positioning of the cane is particularly important in reducing forces created by the abductor muscles acting at the hip. During normal gait, the hip abductors of the stance extremity contract to counteract the gravitational moment at the pelvis on the contralateral side during swing. This prevents tilting of the pelvis on the contralateral side but results in a compressive force acting at the stance hip. Use of a cane in the upper extremity opposite the affected hip will reduce these forces. The floor (ground) reaction force created by the downward pressure of body weight on the cane counterbalances the gravitational movement at the affected hip.[11,12] Thus the need for tension in the abductor muscles is reduced, with a subsequent decrease in joint compressive forces.

Several components of floor reaction forces that create joint compression at the hip can be reduced by use of a cane. In a study by Ely and Smidt,[13] contralateral use of a cane was found to decrease the vertical and posterior components of the floor reaction force produced by the affected foot. They noted that the reductions in vertical floor reaction peaks were probably due to a shifting of body weight toward the cane, which was a contributing factor in reducing contact force at the affected hip.

Other authors also have advocated the use of canes to reduce forces acting at the hip.[10,12,14] This concept is particularly important for activities such as stair climbing, when the forces generated at the hip are significantly increased.[11] Clearly, use of a cane has important implications for hip disorders such as joint replacements or degenerative joint disease.

In addition to altering the forces on the affected extremity, canes are selected on the basis of their ability to improve gait by providing increased dynamic stability and improving balance. This is achieved by the increased BOS provided by the additional point of floor contact. The level of stability provided by canes is on a continuum. The greatest stability is provided by the broad-based canes and the least by a standard cane. The following section presents several of the more common types of canes in clinical use and identifies their advantages and disadvantages.

Standard Cane

This assistive device also is referred to as a regular or conventional cane (Fig. 14–9A). It is made of wood or plastic and has a half circle ("crook") handle. The distal rubber tip is at least 1 inch in diameter or larger.

Advantages. This cane is inexpensive and fits easily on stairs or other surfaces where space is limited.

Disadvantages. The standard cane is not adjustable and must be cut to fit the patient. Its point of support is anterior to the hand and not directly beneath it.

Standard Adjustable Aluminum Cane

This assistive device (Fig. 14–9B) has the same basic design as the regular or standard cane. It is made of aluminum tubing and has a half-circle handle with a molded plastic covering. The telescoping design of this cane enables the height to be adjusted by placing the locking-pin mechanism into the proper notch. Variations in available height range differ slightly with manufacturers. However, they are generally adjustable within the range of approximately 27 to 38.5 inches (68 to 98 cm). The distal rubber tip is at least 1 inch in diameter or larger. (*Note:* Most adjustable aluminum assistive devices use a push-button pin or notch mechanism to alter height; many include a reinforcing cuff that is tightened by a thumbscrew or a rotation sleeve.)

Advantages. This cane is quickly adjustable, facilitating ease of determining appropriate height. It is particularly useful for measurement prior to altering the length of a standard cane. It is lightweight and fits easily on stairs.

Disadvantages. The point of support is anterior to the hand and not directly beneath it. This cane is also more costly than a standard cane.

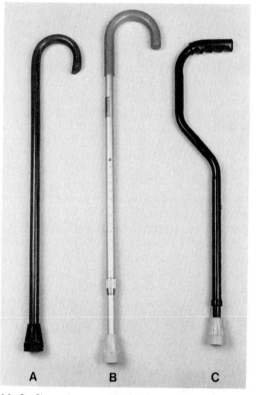

Figure 14–9. Shown here are (A) standard wooden cane, (B) standard adjustable aluminum cane, and (C) adjustable offset cane.

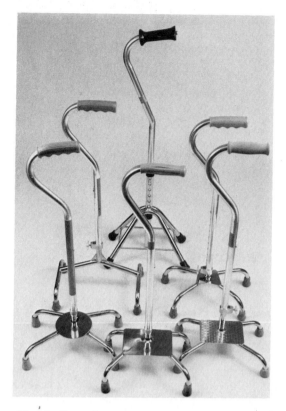

Figure 14–10. Shown here are a variety of large-based quadruped canes.

Adjustable Aluminum Offset Cane

The proximal component of the body of this cane is offset anteriorly. It is made of aluminum tubing with a plastic or rubber molded grip-shaped handle (Fig. 14–9C). The telescoping design allows the height to be adjusted from approximately 27 to 38.5 inches (68 to 98 cm) by a pin or notch mechanism. The diameter of the distal rubber tip is at least 1 inch or larger.

Advantages. The design of this cane allows pressure to be borne over the center of the cane for greater stability. This cane also is quickly adjusted, lightweight, and fits easily on stairs.

Disadvantages. This cane is more costly than standard or adjustable aluminum canes.

Quad (Quadruped) Cane

This assistive device is constructed of aluminum and aluminum tubing. It is available in a variety of designs and base sizes, depending on the manufacturer (Figs. 14–10 and 14–11). The characteristic feature of these canes is that they provide a broad base with four points of floor contact. Each point (leg) is covered with a rubber tip. The legs closest to the patient's body are generally shorter and may be angled to allow foot clearance. On some designs the proximal portion of the cane is offset anteriorly. The handpiece is usually one of a variety of contoured plastic grips. A telescoping design allows for height adjustments. Quad canes are generally adjustable from approximately 28 to 38 inches (71 to 91 cm).

Advantages. This cane provides a broad-based sup-

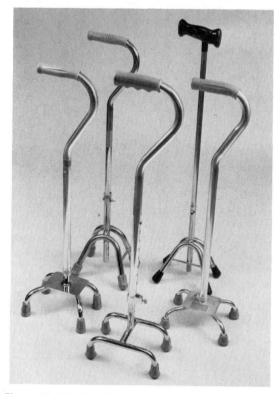

Figure 14–11. A variety of small-based quadruped canes.

port. Bases are available in several different sizes. This cane is also easily adjustable.

Disadvantages. Depending on the specific design of the cane, the pressure exerted by the patient's hand may not be centered over the cane and may result in patient complaints of instability. As a result of the broad BOS, quad canes often are not practical for use on stairs. Another disadvantage of broad-based canes is that they warrant use of a slower gait pattern. If a faster forward progression is used, the cane often "rocks" from rear legs to front legs, which decreases effectiveness of the cane. Patients should be instructed to place all four legs of the cane on the floor simultaneously to obtain maximum stability.

Walk Cane

This cane also is constructed of aluminum and aluminum tubing (Fig. 14–12). It provides a very broad base with four points of floor contact. Each point (leg) is covered with a rubber tip. The legs farther from the patient's body are angled to maintain floor contact and to improve stability. The handgrip is molded plastic around the uppermost segment of aluminum tubing. Walk canes fold flat and are adjustable in height from approximately 29 to 37 inches (73 to 94 cm).

Advantages. Walk canes provide a very broad-based support and are more stable than a quad cane. These canes also fold flat for travel or storage.

Disadvantages. As with the quad canes, the specific design of a walk cane or handgrip placement may not

Figure 14–12. Walk cane.

allow pressure to be centered over the cane. Walk canes cannot be used on most stairs. They require use of a slow forward progression and are generally more costly than quad canes.

Hand Grips

A general consideration relevant to all canes is the nature of the handgrip. There are a variety of styles and sizes available. The type of handgrip should be judged and selected primarily on the basis of patient comfort and on the grip's ability to provide adequate surface area to allow effective transfer of weight from the upper extremity to the floor. It is useful to have several styles available for assessment with individual patients.

Measuring Canes

In measuring cane height, the cane (or center of a broad-based cane) is placed approximately 6 in from the lateral border of the toes. Two landmarks typically are used during measurement: the greater trochanter and the angle at the elbow. The top of the cane should come to approximately the level of the greater trochanter, and the elbow should be flexed to about 20 to 30 degrees. Because of individual variations in body proportion and arm lengths, the degree of flexion at the elbow is a more important indicator of correct cane height. This elbow flexion serves two important functions:[10] It allows the arm to shorten or to lengthen during different phases of gait, and it provides a shock-absorption mechanism. Finally, as with all assistive devices, the height of the cane should be assessed with regard to patient comfort and the cane's effectiveness in accomplishing its intended purpose.

Gait Pattern for Use of Canes

As discussed earlier, the cane should be held in the upper extremity opposite the affected limb. For ambulation on level surfaces, the cane and the involved extremity are advanced simultaneously (Fig. 14–13). The cane should remain relatively close to the body and should not be placed ahead of the toe of the involved extremity. These are important considerations, because placing the cane too far forward or to the side will cause lateral and/or forward bending, with a resultant decrease in dynamic stability.

When bilateral involvement exists, a decision must be made as to which side of the body the cane will be held. This question is most effectively resolved by a problem-solving approach with input from both the patient and therapist. Questions to be considered include

1. On which side is the cane most comfortable?
2. Is one placement superior in terms of improving balance and/or ambulatory endurance?
3. If gait deviations exist, is one position more effective in improving the overall gait pattern?
4. Is safety influenced by cane placement (e.g., during transfers, stair climbing, or ambulation on outdoor surfaces)?
5. Is there a difference in grip strength between hands?
6. Are two canes needed for stability?

(4) Cycle is repeated.

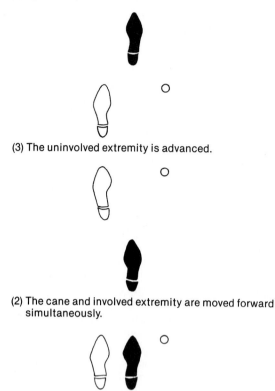

(3) The uninvolved extremity is advanced.

(2) The cane and involved extremity are moved forward simultaneously.

(1) Starting position. In this example, the left lower extremity is the involved limb.

Figure 14–13. Gait pattern for use of cane.

Consideration of these questions will generally provide sufficient information to determine the most effective cane placement when bilateral involvement exists.

CRUTCHES

Crutches are used most frequently to improve balance and to either relieve weight bearing fully or partially on a lower extremity. They are typically used bilaterally, and function to *increase the base of support, to improve lateral stability,* and to allow the upper extremities *to transfer body weight to the floor.* This transfer of weight through the upper extremities permits functional ambulation while maintaining a restricted weight-bearing status. There are two basic designs of crutches in frequent clinical use: *axillary* and *forearm* crutches.

Axillary Crutches

These assistive devices also are referred to as regular or standard crutches (Fig. 14–14A). They are made of lightweight wood or aluminum. Their design includes an axillary bar, a handpiece, and double uprights joined distally by a single leg covered with a rubber suction tip (which should have a diameter of 1.5 to 3 inches). The single leg allows for height variations. Height adjustments for wooden and some aluminum crutches are accomplished by altering the placement of screws and wing bolts in predrilled holes. The height of the handgrips is adjusted in the same manner. Some types of alu-

minum crutches use a push-button pin or notch mechanism for height adjustments similar to those found on aluminum canes. Others also have patient height markers adjacent to the notches to assist in adjustment. Axillary crutches are generally adjustable in adult sizes from approximately 48 to 60 inches (122 to 153 cm), with children's and extra-long sizes available.

A modification to this basic design is the ortho crutch (Fig. 14–14B). This type of axillary crutch is made of aluminum. Its design includes a single upright, an axillary bar covered with sponge-rubber padding, and a handgrip covered with molded plastic. The crutch adjusts both proximally (to alter elbow angle) and distally (to alter height of crutch). Adjustments are made using a push-button pin or notch mechanism. The distal end of the crutch is covered with a rubber suction tip.

The body of research available comparing the two designs of axillary crutches is limited. One study compared the level of energy expended during non-weight-bearing ambulation using each type of crutch.[15] The results indicated that less energy was expended with the ortho crutches than with standard axillary crutches for short periods over short distances. Although the findings of a single study have limited clinical application, the authors suggest that the results have implications regarding crutch selection for patients with cardiovascular involvement for short-distance ambulation.

Advantages. Axillary crutches improve balance and lateral stability and provide for functional ambulation

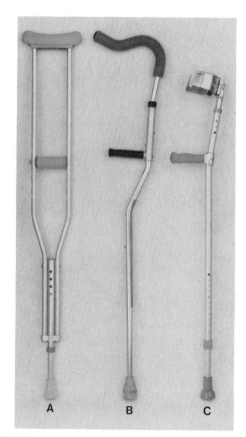

Figure 14–14. An (A) axillary crutch, (B) ortho crutch, and a (C) forearm crutch.

with restricted weight bearing. They are easily adjusted, inexpensive when made of wood, and can be used for stair climbing.

Disadvantages. Because of the tripod stance required to use crutches and the resultant large BOS, crutches are awkward in small areas. For the same reason, the safety of the user may be compromised when ambulating in crowded areas. Another disadvantage is the tendency of some patients to lean on the axillary bar. This pressure creates the potential for damage to nervous and vascular structures in the axilla.

Platform attachments. These attachments (Fig. 14–15) are also referred to as forearm rests or troughs. Although they are described here, they also are used with walkers. Their function is to allow transfer of body weight through the forearm to the assistive device. A platform attachment is used when weight bearing is contraindicated through the wrist and hand (e.g., some patients with arthritis). The forearm piece is usually padded, has a dowl or handgrip, and has Velcro straps to maintain the position of the forearm. Trough crutches are also commercially available.

Forearm Crutches

These assistive devices are also known as Lofstrand and Canadian crutches (Fig. 14–14C). They are constructed of aluminum. Their design includes a single upright, a forearm cuff, and a handgrip. This crutch adjusts both proximally to alter position of the forearm cuff and distally to alter the height of the crutch. Adjustments are made using a pin or notch mechanism. The available heights of forearm crutches are indicated from handgrip to floor and are generally adjustable in adult sizes from 29 to 35 inches (74 to 89 cm), with children's and extra-long sizes available. The distal end of the crutch is covered with a rubber suction tip. The forearm cuffs are available with either a medial or anterior opening. The cuffs are made of metal and can be obtained with a plastic coating.

Advantages. The forearm cuff allows use of hands

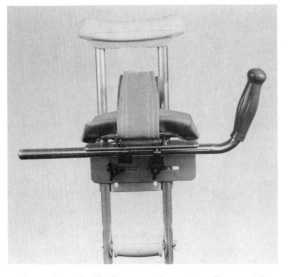

Figure 14–15. Platform attachment to axillary crutch.

without the crutches becoming disengaged. They are easily adjusted and allow functional stair-climbing activities. Many patients feel they are more cosmetic and they fit more easily into an automobile owing to the overall decreased height. They are also the most functional type of crutch for stair-climbing activities for individuals wearing bilateral knee-ankle-foot orthoses.

Disadvantages. Forearm crutches provide less lateral support owing to the absence of an axillary bar. The cuffs may be difficult to remove. These crutches are more costly than wooden axillary crutches.

Measuring Crutches

Axillary crutches. Several methods are available for measuring axillary crutches. The most common use a standing or a supine position. Measurement from standing is most accurate and is the preferred approach.

Standing. From the standing position in the parallel bars, crutches should be measured from a point approximately 2 inches below the axilla. The width of two fingers is often used to approximate this distance. The distal end of the crutch should come to a point 2 inches lateral and 6 inches anterior to the foot. A general estimate of crutch height can be obtained prior to standing by subtracting 16 inches from the patient's height. With the shoulders relaxed, the handpiece should be adjusted to provide 20 to 30 degrees of elbow flexion.

Supine. From this position the measurement is taken from the anterior axillary fold to a surface point (mat or treatment table) 6 to 8 inches (5 to 7.5 cm) from the lateral border of the heel.

Forearm crutches. Standing is the position of choice for measuring forearm crutches. From a standing position in the parallel bars, the distal end of the crutch should be positioned at a point 2 inches lateral and 6 inches anterior to the foot. With the shoulders relaxed the height should then be adjusted to provide 20 to 30 degrees of elbow flexion. The forearm cuff is adjusted separately. Cuff placement should be on the proximal third of the forearm, approximately 1 to 1.5 inches below the elbow.

Gait Patterns for Use of Crutches

Gait patterns are selected on the basis of the patient's balance, coordination, muscle function, and weight-bearing status. The gait patterns differ significantly in their energy requirements, BOS, and the speed with which they can be executed.

Prior to initiating instruction in gait patterns, several important points should be emphasized to the patient:

1. During crutch use, body weight should always be *borne on the hands* and not on the axillary bar. This will prevent pressure on both the vascular and nervous structures located in the axillary region.
2. Balance will be optimal by always maintaining a wide (tripod) BOS. Even when in a resting stance, the patient should be instructed to keep the crutches at least 4 inches (10 cm) to the front and to the side of each foot. The foot should not be allowed to achieve parallel alignment with the crutches. This will jeopardize anterior-posterior stability by decreasing the BOS.

3. When using standard crutches, the axillary bars should be held close to the chest wall to provide improved lateral stability.

4. The patient should also be cautioned about the importance of holding the head up and maintaining good postural alignment during ambulation.

5. Turning should be accomplished by stepping in a small circle rather than pivoting.

Three-point gait. In this type of gait three points of support contact the floor. It is used when a non-weight-bearing status is required on one lower extremity. Body weight is borne on the crutches instead of on the affected lower extremity. The sequence of this gait pattern is illustrated in Figure 14–16.

Partial-weight-bearing gait. This gait is a modification of the three-point pattern. During forward progres-

sion of the involved extremity, weight is borne partially on both crutches *and* on the affected extremity (Fig. 14–17). During instruction in the partial-weight-bearing gait, emphasis should be placed on use of a normal heel-toe progression on the affected extremity. Often the term *partial-weight-bearing* is interpreted by the patient as meaning that only the toes or ball of the foot should contact the floor. Use of this positioning over a period of days or weeks will lead to heel cord tightness. Limb load monitors are often a useful adjunct to partial-weight-bearing gait training and are described later in this chapter. These devices provide auditory feedback to the patient regarding the amount of weight borne on an extremity.

Four-point gait. This pattern provides a slow, stable gait as three points of floor contact are maintained. Weight is borne on both lower extremities and typically is used with bilateral involvement due to poor balance, incoordination, or muscle weakness. In this gait pattern one crutch is advanced and then the opposite lower extremity is advanced. For example, the left crutch is moved forward, then the right lower extremity, followed by the right crutch and then the left lower extremity (Fig. 14–18).

Two-point gait. This gait pattern is similar to the four-point gait. However, it is less stable because only

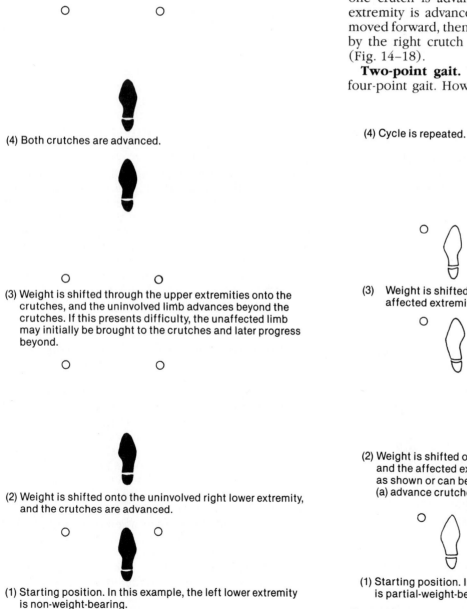

(5) Cycle is repeated.

(4) Both crutches are advanced.

(3) Weight is shifted through the upper extremities onto the crutches, and the uninvolved limb advances beyond the crutches. If this presents difficulty, the unaffected limb may initially be brought to the crutches and later progress beyond.

(2) Weight is shifted onto the uninvolved right lower extremity, and the crutches are advanced.

(1) Starting position. In this example, the left lower extremity is non-weight-bearing.

Figure 14–16. Three-point gait pattern.

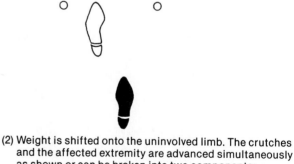

(4) Cycle is repeated.

(3) Weight is shifted onto the crutches and partially to the affected extremity, and the unaffected limb advances.

(2) Weight is shifted onto the uninvolved limb. The crutches and the affected extremity are advanced simultaneously as shown or can be broken into two components: (a) advance crutches, (b) advance affected extremity.

(1) Starting position. In this example, the left lower extremity is partial-weight-bearing.

Figure 14–17. Partial-weight-bearing gait; modification of the three-point gait pattern.

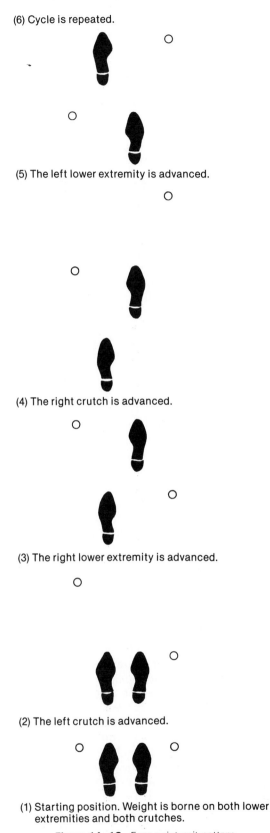

(6) Cycle is repeated.

(5) The left lower extremity is advanced.

(4) The right crutch is advanced.

(3) The right lower extremity is advanced.

(2) The left crutch is advanced.

(1) Starting position. Weight is borne on both lower extremities and both crutches.

Figure 14–18. Four-point gait pattern.

two points of floor contact are maintained. Thus, use of this gait requires better balance. The two-point pattern more closely simulates normal gait, inasmuch as the opposite lower and upper extremity move together (Fig. 14–19).

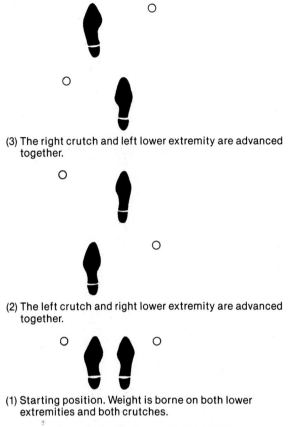

(4) Cycle is repeated.

(3) The right crutch and left lower extremity are advanced together.

(2) The left crutch and right lower extremity are advanced together.

(1) Starting position. Weight is borne on both lower extremities and both crutches.

Figure 14–19. Two-point gait pattern.

Two additional, less commonly used crutch gaits are the *swing-to* and *swing-through* patterns. These gaits are often used when there is bilateral lower extremity involvement, such as in spinal cord injuries. The swing-to gait involves forward movement of both crutches simultaneously, and the lower extremities "swing to" the crutches. In the swing-through gait the crutches are moved forward together, but the lower extremities are swung beyond the crutches. Both these crutch patterns are discussed in greater detail in Chapter 26 (Traumatic Spinal Cord Injury).

WALKERS

Walkers are used to improve balance and to relieve weight bearing either fully or partially on a lower extremity. Of the three categories of ambulatory assistive devices, walkers afford the greatest stability. They *provide a wide BOS, improve anterior and lateral stability and allow the upper extremities to transfer body weight to the floor.*

Walkers are typically made of tubular aluminum with molded vinyl handgrips and rubber tips. They are adjustable in adult sizes from approximately 32 to 37 inches (81 to 92 cm), with children's, youth, and tall sizes available. Several modifications to the standard design are available and are described below.

1. A folding mechanism. Folding walkers are particularly useful for patients who travel. These walkers can be easily collapsed to fit in an automobile or other storage space.

2. Handgrips. Enlarged and molded handgrips are available, and may be useful for some patients with arthritis.
3. Platform attachments. This adaptation is used when weight bearing is contraindicated through the wrist and hand (described in crutch section).
4. Reciprocal walkers. These walkers are designed to allow unilateral forward progression of one side of the walker. A disadvantage of this design is that some inherent stability of the walker is lost. However, they are useful for patients incapable of lifting the walker with both hands and moving it forward.
5. Casters. This adaptation should be used very judiciously because the stability of the walker will be reduced. Walkers with front wheels (sometimes called ''rolling'' walkers), however, may allow functional ambulation for patients who are unable to lift and to move a conventional walker. Pressure brakes should always be used with casters.
6. Stair-climbing walkers. Walkers designed for use on stairs are commercially available. Regardless of design, walkers tend to be extremely unsafe on stairs and should be avoided.

Advantages. Walkers provide four points of floor contact with a side BOS. They provide a high level of stability. They also provide a sense of security for patients fearful of ambulation. They are relatively lightweight and easily adjusted.

Disadvantages. Walkers tend to be cumbersome, are awkward in confined areas, and are difficult to maneuver through doorways and into cars. They eliminate normal arm swing and cannot be used safely on stairs.

Measuring Walkers

The height of a walker is measured in the same way as that of a cane. The walker should come to approximately the greater trochanter and allow for 20 to 30 degrees of elbow flexion.

Gait Patterns for Use of Walkers

Prior to initiating instruction in gait patterns, several points related to use of the walker should be emphasized with the patient:
1. The walker should be picked up and placed down on *all four legs simultaneously* to achieve maximum stability. Rocking from the back to front legs or sliding the walker forward should be avoided because it decreases the effectiveness and safety of the assistive device.
2. The patient should be encouraged to hold the head up and to maintain good postural alignment.
3. The patient should be cautioned not to step too close to the front crossbar. This will decrease the overall BOS and may cause the patient to fall backward.

There are three types of gait patterns used with walkers. These are the full, partial, and non-weight-bearing gaits. The sequence for each pattern follows.

Full-weight-bearing
1. The walker is picked up and moved forward about an arm's length.

2. The first lower extremity is moved forward.
3. The second lower extremity is moved forward past the first.
4. The cycle is repeated.

Partial-weight-bearing
1. The walker is picked up and moved forward about an arm's length.
2. The involved lower extremity is moved forward, and body weight is transferred partially onto this limb and partially through the upper extremities to the walker.
3. The uninvolved lower extremity is moved forward past the involved limb.
4. The cycle is repeated.

Non-weight-bearing
1. The walker is picked up and moved forward about an arm's length.
2. Weight is then transferred through the upper extremities to the walker. The involved limb is held anterior to the patient's body but does not make contact with the floor.
3. The uninvolved limb is moved forward.
4. The cycle is repeated.

USE OF ASSISTIVE DEVICES ON LEVEL SURFACES AND STAIRS

Level Surfaces

Gait-training activities on indoor surfaces are begun once the patient has achieved appropriate skill and balance in parallel bar activities (including moving to and from standing and sitting positions, turning, and use of the selected gait pattern). Use of the parallel bars often continues concurrently with initial gait training on indoor surfaces. At this point in the progression, continued use of the parallel bars typically emphasizes advanced activities and/or work on specific deviations.

Several important preparatory activities should precede ambulation on level surfaces with the assistive device. These activities may be completed in the parallel bars for added security. However, if the width of the bars is not adjustable, the BOS of the assistive device may make movement within the bars difficult and unsafe. An alternative is to move the patient outside but next to the parallel bars or near a treatment table or wall. These preparatory activities include
1. Instruction in assuming the standing and seated positions with use of the assistive device. These techniques are outlined in Table 14–4 for each category of assistive device.
2. Standing balance activities with the assistive device (similar to those using the parallel bars, described earlier).
3. Instruction in use of assistive device (with selected gait pattern) for forward progression and turning.
As mentioned earlier, demonstrating these activities by assuming the role of the patient during verbal explanations is an effective teaching approach. Following the

Table 14-4 BASIC TECHNIQUES FOR ASSUMING STANDING AND SEATED POSITIONS WITH ASSISTIVE DEVICES

I. CANE
   A. *Coming to standing*
      1. Patient moves forward in chair.
      2. Cane is positioned on uninvolved side (broad-based cane) or leaned against armrest (standard cane).
      3. Patient leans forward and pushes down with both hands on armrests, comes to a standing position, and then grasps cane. With use of a standard cane, the cane may be grasped loosely with fingers prior to standing and the base of the hand used for pushing down on armrests.
   B. *Return to sitting*
      1. As the patient approaches the chair, the patient turns in a small circle toward the uninvolved side.
      2. The patient backs up until the chair can be felt against the patient's legs.
      3. The patient then reaches for the armrest with the free hand, releases the cane (broad-based), and reaches for the opposite armrest. A standard cane is leaned against the chair as the patient grasps the armrest.

II. CRUTCHES
   A. *Coming to standing*
      1. The patient moves forward in the chair.
      2. Crutches are placed together in a vertical position on the *affected* side.
      3. One hand is placed on the handpieces of the crutches; one on the armrest of the chair.
      4. The patient leans forward and pushes to a standing position.
      5. Once balance is gained, one crutch is cautiously placed under the axilla on the unaffected side.
      6. The second crutch is then carefully placed under the axilla on the affected side.
      7. A tripod stance is assumed.
   B. *Return to sitting*
      1. As the patient approaches the chair, the patient turns in a small circle toward the uninvolved side.
      2. The patient backs up until the chair can be felt against the patient's legs.
      3. Both crutches are placed in a vertical position (out from under axilla) on the *affected* side.
      4. One hand is placed on the handpieces of the crutches; one on the armrest of the chair.
      5. The patient lowers to the chair in a controlled manner.
      [*Note:* See Chapter 26, Traumatic Spinal Cord Injury for alternative methods using bilateral knee ankle orthoses.]

III. WALKER
   A. *Coming to standing*
      1. The patient moves forward in the chair.
      2. The walker is positioned directly in front of the chair.
      3. The patient leans forward and pushes down on armrests to come to standing.
      4. Once in a standing position, the patient reaches for the walker, one hand at a time.
   B. *Return to sitting*
      1. As the patient approaches the chair, the patient turns in a small circle toward the stronger side.
      2. The patient backs up until the chair can be felt against the patient's legs.
      3. The patient then reaches for one armrest at a time.
      4. The patient lowers to the chair in a controlled manner.

demonstration, verbal cueing and explanations can be used again to guide performance of the activity.

Following these preliminary instructions, gait training using the assistive device can be begun on level surfaces. The following guarding technique (Fig. 14–20) should be used.

1. The therapist stands posterior and lateral to the patient's weaker side.
2. A wide BOS should be maintained with the therapist's leading lower extremity following the assistive device. The therapist's opposite lower extremity should be externally rotated and follow the patient's weaker lower extremity.
3. One of the therapist's hands is placed posteriorly on the guarding belt and the other anterior to, but *not touching*, the patient's shoulder on the weaker side.

Should the patient's balance be lost during gait training, the hand guarding at the shoulder should make contact. Frequently the support provided by the therapist's hands at the shoulder and on the guarding belt will be enough to allow the patient to regain balance. If the balance loss is severe, the therapist should move in toward the patient so that the body and guarding hands can be used to provide stabilization. The patient should be allowed to regain balance while "leaning" against the therapist. If balance is not recovered and it is apparent the patient is going to fall, further attempts should not be made to hold the patient up because this is likely to result in injury to the patient and/or the therapist. In this situation the therapist should continue to brace the patient against the body and move with the patient to a sitting position to break the fall and to protect the head. It is also important to talk to the patient ("Help me lower you to the floor") so that the patient does not continue to struggle to regain balance.

Gait-training activities on level surfaces should include instruction and practice in passage through doorways, elevators, and over thresholds. When using crutches, doorways are most easily approached from a diagonal. A hand must be freed to open the door and one crutch must be placed in a position to hold it open. The patient then gradually proceeds through the doorway, using the crutch to open the door wider if necessary.

Because many patients using a walker or cane may have balance problems, careful assessment will determine the safest methods for passage through doorways. A patient using a walker with sufficient balance may be able to use a technique similar to that described above.

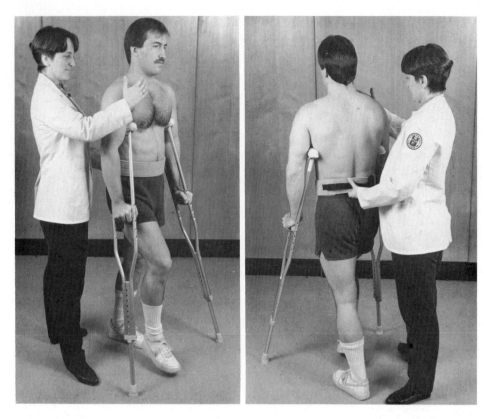

Figure 14–20. Anterior (*left*) and posterior (*right*) views of guarding technique for level surfaces, demonstrated with use of crutches. The same positioning is used with canes and walkers.

Stair Climbing

The next activity in the gait-training progression is stair climbing. Ideally, firsthand information from a home visit will provide information about the type and number of stairs the patient will be required to use. However, careful questioning of the patient and/or family members generally will provide sufficient information on which to plan. The information obtained should include the height and number of stairs, presence and stability of railings, and condition and type of floor covering or pavement leading to and on the stairs.

Several general guidelines should be relayed to the patient during instruction in stair climbing. First, if a railing is available it should always be used. This is true even if it requires placing an assistive device in the hand in which it is not normally used. For stair climbing with axillary crutches using a railing, both crutches are placed together under one arm. Second, the patient should be cautioned that the stronger lower extremity always leads going up the stairs, and the weaker or involved limb always leads coming down ("up with the good and down with the bad").

The progressions of stair-climbing techniques are presented in Table 14–5. The following guarding technique should be used by the therapist during stair climbing.

ASCENDING STAIRS (Fig. 14–21)
1. The therapist is positioned posterior and lateral on the affected side *behind* the patient.
2. A wide BOS should be maintained with each foot on a different stair.
3. A step should be taken only when the patient is *not* moving.
4. One hand is placed posteriorly on the guarding belt and one is anterior to, *but not touching,* the shoulder on the weaker side.

DESCENDING STAIRS (Fig. 14–22)
1. The therapist is positioned anterior and lateral on the affected side *in front* of the patient.
2. A wide BOS should be maintained with each foot on a different stair.
3. A step should be taken only when the patient is *not* moving.
4. One hand is placed anteriorly on the guarding belt and one is anterior to, *but not touching,* the shoulder on the weaker side.

Should the patient's balance be lost during stair climbing, the following procedure should be followed: First, contact should be made with the hand guarding at the shoulder. Next, the therapist should move toward the patient to help brace the patient (the patient should never be pulled toward the therapist on stairs) or leaned toward the wall of the stairwell (if available). Finally, if needed, the therapist can move with the patient to sit the patient down on the stairs. Remember to inform the patient of your intentions ("I'm going to sit you down").

Curbs and Ramps

The technique for climbing curbs is essentially the same as that of climbing a single stair (see Table 14–5). A useful lead-up activity to curb climbing is provided by a series of small, free-standing, wooden platforms with nonslip coverings. These can be fabricated easily in increments of height. For additional security they can be

Table 14–5 STAIR-CLIMBING TECHNIQUES*

I. CANE
   A. *Ascending*
      1. The unaffected lower extremity leads up.
      2. The cane and affected lower extremity follow.
   B. *Descending*
      1. The affected lower extremity and cane lead down.
      2. The unaffected lower extremity follows.

II. CRUTCHES: THREE-POINT GAIT (non-weight-bearing gait)
   A. *Ascending*
      1. The patient is positioned close to the foot of the stairs. The involved lower extremity is held back to prevent "catching" on the lip of the stairs.
      2. The patient pushes down firmly on both handpieces of the crutches and leads up with the unaffected lower extremity.
      3. The crutches are brought up to the stair that the unaffected lower extremity is now on.
   B. *Descending*
      1. The patient stands close to the edge of the stair so that the toes protrude slightly over the top. The involved lower extremity is held forward over the lower stair.
      2. Both crutches are moved down *together* to the *front* half of the next step.
      3. The patient pushes down firmly on both handpieces and lowers the unaffected lower extremity to the step that the crutches are now on.

III. CRUTCHES: PARTIAL-WEIGHT-BEARING GAIT
   A. *Ascending*
      1. The patient is positioned close to the foot of the stairs.
      2. The patient pushes down on both handpieces of the crutches and distributes weight partially on the crutches and partially on the affected lower extremity while the unaffected lower extremity leads up.
      3. The involved lower extremity and crutches are then brought up together.
   B. *Descending*
      1. The patient stands close to the edge of the stair so that the toes protrude slightly over top of the stair.
      2. Both crutches are moved down *together* to the *front* half of the next step. The affected lower extremity is then lowered (depending on patient skill, these may be combined). *Note:* When crutches are not in floor contact, greater weight must be shifted to the uninvolved lower extremity to maintain a partial-weight-bearing status.
      3. The uninvolved lower extremity is lowered to the step the crutches are now on.

IV. CRUTCHES: TWO- AND FOUR-POINT GAIT
   A. *Ascending*
      1. The patient is positioned close to the foot of the stairs.
      2. The right lower extremity is moved up and then the left lower extremity.
      3. The right crutch is moved up and then the left crutch is moved up (patients with adequate balance may find it easier to move the crutches up together).
   B. *Descending*
      1. The patient stands close to the edge of the stair.
      2. The right crutch is moved down and then the left (may be combined).
      3. The right lower extremity is moved down and then the left.

*The sequences presented here describe stair-climbing techniques without the use of a railing. When a secure railing is available, the patient should be instructed to use it always.

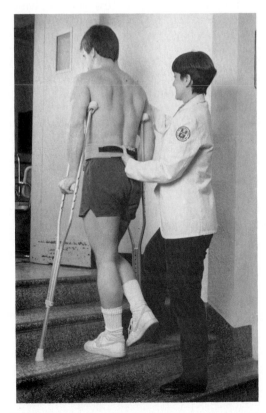

Figure 14–21. Guarding technique for ascending stairs.

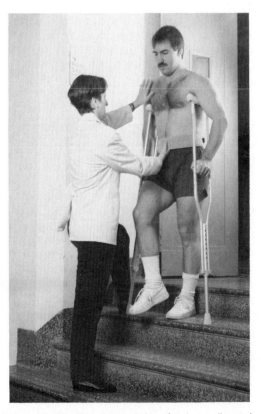

Figure 14–22. Guarding technique for descending stairs.

placed next to or within the parallel bars, and a progression can be made from a 3- or 4-inch increment to a 7-inch curb height.

Ramps can be negotiated in several ways. If the incline is very gradual, it may be sufficient simply to instruct the patient to use smaller steps. However, for steeper inclines the patient should be instructed to use smaller steps and to traverse the ramp (use a diagonal, zigzag pattern) for both ascending and descending.

Outdoor Surfaces

Activities on outdoor surfaces are among the final components of a gait-training progression. They must be specifically assessed to determine their appropriateness for an individual patient. Basic outdoor activities include

1. Exit and entrance through outside doors and thresholds.
2. Gait training on outdoor, uneven surfaces.
3. Curbs, ramps, and stair climbing.
4. Crossing the street in the time allotted by a traffic light.
5. Entering and exiting public or private transportation.

ADJUNCT TRAINING DEVICES

Limb Load Monitors

A limb load monitor is a form of biofeedback that has gained increased clinical use as an adjunct intervention during gait training. The limb load monitor incorporates a strain gauge attached to the sole or heel of the shoe. When a force or pressure is applied, the strain gauge is deformed and an auditory signal provides feedback to the wearer. As pressure increases, the signal becomes louder or more rapid. This feedback provides information about the amount of weight bearing on a limb.[16,17] Limb load monitors can also be used to reinforce the correctness or timing of a movement. For example, an audible noise or buzzer sounding when the heel makes contact with the floor can provide immediate feedback on foot placement.[18] Similar devices can also be attached to a cane (often referred to as a "biofeedback cane"). The principle of operation is the same and incorporates a strain gauge. Auditory signals provide the patient with information on placement as well as pressure applied to the cane. Biofeedback is discussed in detail in Chapter 32.

Orthotics

A wide variety of orthotic devices are incorporated within gait-training programs to improve efficiency and safety, to diminish or eliminate gait deviations, and to decrease energy expenditure. These devices span a wide spectrum of functions from a relatively simple Swedish knee cage designed to control recurvatum to the more specialized reciprocating gait orthosis. This later device provides important advantages during early gait training for patients with bilateral lower extremity involvement. As the patient shifts weight onto one leg, the opposite leg is advanced forward via cable attachments. During this early training, the parallel bars or a walker is typically used. The reader is referred to Chapter 30 for a thorough discussion of orthotic applications.

SUMMARY

This chapter presented a general framework of preambulation exercises and gait-training activities. Each component should be considered during treatment planning. Through a process of careful assessment, the appropriate elements of the mat progression, specific treatment techniques, and segments of the upright progression can be selected for an individual patient. Additional factors that will influence treatment planning include the patient's diagnosis, medical history, weight-bearing status, and input from the patient regarding ambulatory goals.

QUESTIONS FOR REVIEW

1. Identify the goals of a preambulation exercise program.
2. Outline a general parallel bar progression that would be appropriate for a patient preparing to use a partial-weight-bearing crutch gait.
3. Contrast and compare the advantages and disadvantages of each category of ambulatory assistive device: canes, crutches, and walkers.
4. Explain the method used for measuring a cane, crutches, and a walker.

5. Describe the sequence for instructing a patient to rise from and return to a sitting position with a cane, crutches, and a walker.
6. Describe therapist positioning and hand placement for guarding the patient on level surfaces and stairs.
7. Describe the sequence for the following crutch gaits: four-point, two-point, three-point, and partial-weight-bearing.

REFERENCES

1. Voss, DE, Ionta, MK, and Myers, BJ: Proprioceptive Neuromuscular Facilitation: Patterns and Techniques, ed 3. Harper & Row, Philadelphia, 1985.

2. Sullivan, PE, Markos, PD, and Minor, MAD: An Integrated Approach to Therapeutic Exercise: Theory and Clinical Application. Reston, Reston, VA, 1982.

3. Voss, DE: Proprioceptive neuromuscular facilitation (NUSTEP Proceedings). Am J Phys Med 46:838, 1967.
4. Myers, BJ: The proprioceptive neuromuscular facilitation (PNF) approach. In Trombly, CA (ed): Occupational Therapy for Physical Dysfunction, ed 3. Williams & Wilkins, Baltimore, 1989, p 135.
5. Stockmeyer, SA: An interpretation of the approach of Rood to the treatment of neuromuscular dysfunction (NUSTEP Proceedings). Am J Phys Med 46:900, 1967.
6. Trombly, CA: Rood approach. In Trombly, CA (ed): Occupational Therapy for Physical Dysfunction, ed 2. Williams & Wilkins, Baltimore, 1989, p. 97.
7. Hollis, M: Practical Exercise Therapy. Blackwell Scientific, Boston, 1981.
8. Ryerson, SD: Hemiplegia resulting from vascular insult or disease. In Umphred, DA (ed): Neurological Rehabilitation, ed 2. CV Mosby, St Louis, 1990, p 619.
9. Smidt, GL and Mommens, MA: System of reporting and comparing influences of ambulatory aids on gait. Phys Ther 60:551, 1980.
10. Jebsen, RH: Use and abuse of ambulatory aids. JAMA 199:63, 1967.
11. Norkin, CC and Levangie, PK: Joint Structure and Function: A Comprehensive Analysis, ed 2. FA Davis, Philadelphia, 1992.
12. Elson, RA and Charnley, J: The direction of the resultant force in total prosthetic replacement of the hip joint. Med Biol Eng 6:19, 1968.
13. Ely, DD and Smidt, GL: Effect of cane on variables of gait for patients with hip disorders. Phys Ther 57:507, 1977.
14. Blount, WP: Don't throw away the cane. J Bone Joint Surg [Am] 38A:695, 1956.
15. Hinton, CA and Cullen, KE: Energy expenditure during ambulation with ortho crutches and axillary crutches. Phys Ther 62:813, 1982.
16. Trombly, CA: Biofeedback as an adjunct to therapy. In Trombly, CA (ed): Occupational Therapy for Physical Dysfunction, ed 2. Williams & Wilkins, Baltimore, 1989, p 316.
17. Gapsis, JJ, et al: Limb load monitor: evaluation of a sensory feedback device for controlled weight bearing. Arch Phys Med Rehabil 63:38, 1982.
18. Rinehart, MA: Strategies for improving motor performance. In Rosenthal, M, et al: Rehabilitation of the Adult and Child with Traumatic Brain Injury, ed 2. FA Davis, Philadelphia, 1990, p 331.

SUPPLEMENTAL READINGS

Barnes, B: Ambulation outcomes after hip fracture. Phys Ther 64:317, 1984.
Baruch, IM and Mossberg, KA: Heart-rate response of elderly women to nonweight-bearing ambulation with a walker. Phys Ther 63:1782, 1983.
Basmajian, JV: Crutch and care exercise and use. In Basmajian, JV and Wolf, SL (eds): Therapeutic Exercise, ed 5. Williams & Wilkins, Baltimore, 1990, p 125.
Blanke, DJ and Hageman, PA: Comparison of gait of young men and elderly men. Phys Ther 69:144, 1989.
Bohannon, RW and Gibson, DF: Effectiveness of a rolling board treatment for improving gait. Phys Ther 66:349, 1986.
Brown, M, et al: Walking efficiency before and after total hip replacement. Phys Ther 60:1259, 1980.
Fillyaw, M: Modified walker for patients with polyarticular rheumatoid arthritis (suggestion from the field). Phys Ther 64:205, 1984.
Gussoni, M, et al: Energy cost of walking with hip impairment. Phys Ther 70:295, 1990.
Hinmann, JE, et al: Age-related changes in speed of walking. Med Sci Sports Exerc 20:161, 1988.
Kathrins, BP and O'Sullivan, S: Cardiovascular responses during nonweight-bearing and touchdown ambulation. Phys Ther 64:14, 1984.
Lerner-Frankiel, M, et al: Functional community ambulation: What are the criteria? Clin Manage Phys Ther 6:12, 1986.
McFayden, BJ and Winter, DA: An integrated biomechanical analysis of normal stair ascent and descent. J Biomech 21:733, 1988.
Nielsen, DH, et al: Clinical determination of energy cost and walking velocity via stopwatch or speedometer cane and conversion graphs. Phys Ther 62:591, 1982.
Opara, CU, Levangie, PK, and Nelson, DL: Effects of selected assistive devices on normal distance gait characteristics. Phys Ther 65:1188, 1985.
Palmer, ML and Toms, JE: Manual for Functional Training, ed 3. FA Davis, Philadelphia, 1992.
Patterson, R and Fisher, SV: Cardiovascular stress of crutch walking. Arch Phys Med Rehabil 62:257, 1981.
Reisman, M, et al: Elbow movement and forces at the hands during swing-through axillary crutch gait. Phys Ther 65:601, 1985.
Skinner, SR, et al: Functional demands on the stance limb in walking. Orthopedics 8:355, 1985.
Soderberg, GL: Gait and gait retraining. In Basmajian, JV and Wolf, SL (eds): Therapeutic Exercise, ed 5. Williams & Wilkins. Baltimore, 1990, p 139.
Sullivan, PE and Markos, PD: Clinical Procedures in Therapeutic Exercise. Appleton & Lange, Norwalk, CT, 1987.
Winter, DA, et al: Biomechanical walking pattern changes in the fit and healthy elderly. Phys Ther 70:340, 1990.

GLOSSARY

Counterrotation (in rolling): Simultaneous movement of the upper and lower segments of the trunk in opposite directions.

Developmental sequence: An established pattern of developmental activities by which a child acquires the control needed for functional movement.

Elevation activities: A general term used in gait training to describe an ambulatory activity requiring movement from one level surface to another (e.g., negotiating curbs, climbing stairs or ramps).

Four-point gait: One crutch is moved forward, the opposite lower extremity is advanced, the other crutch is moved forward and opposite lower extremity advanced; slow, stable gait pattern.

Log rolling: Rolling in which movement of the entire trunk rotates as a unit around the longitudinal axis of the body.

Long sitting: Sitting with knees extended on a supporting surface.

Lordosis (lordotic): Abnormally increased anterior curvature of the lumbar spine.

Orthostatic (postural) hypotension: A lower than normal drop in blood pressure as a result of movement to a standing position; may be severe after prolonged bed rest or confinement to a sitting position.

Partial-weight-bearing (PWB) gait: A modification of the three-point gait pattern; during stance phase on the affected extremity, weight is borne partially on the affected extremity and partially on the crutches; the crutches and affected lower extremity are advanced together, the uninvolved lower extremity steps past the crutches; a partial-weight-bearing gait may also be achieved with a walker.

Quadruped: All-fours position; weight bearing on hands and knees.

Segmental rolling: Rolling in which the upper or lower segment of the trunk moves independently while the opposite segment is stable.

Short sitting: Sitting with knees flexed over a supporting surface such as a mat or bed.

Swing-through gait: Both crutches are moved forward together, both lower extremities then swing beyond the crutches; typically used with severe involvement or paralysis of both lower extremities.

Swing-to gait: Both crutches are moved forward together, both lower extremities then swing to the crutches; typically used with severe involvement or paralysis of both lower extremities.

Three-point gait: A non-weight-bearing (NWB) gait; weight is borne on the crutches instead of on the affected lower extremity; both crutches are advanced and the unaffected lower extremity steps past the crutches.

Two-point gait: One lower extremity and the opposite crutch are advanced together; this is repeated with the other crutch and lower extremity.

Chronic Pulmonary Dysfunction*

Julie Ann Starr

OBJECTIVES

1. Define the disease processes (including definition, etiology, pathophysiology, clinical presentation, and clinical course) of chronic obstructive pulmonary disease, asthma, cystic fibrosis, and restrictive lung disease.
2. Describe assessment procedures (including patient interview, vital signs, observation, inspection, palpation, auscultation, and laboratory tests) for a patient with pulmonary disease.
3. Identify the potential benefits and goals of pulmonary rehabilitation.
4. Describe the rehabilitative management of a patient with chronic pulmonary dysfunction.
5. Value the therapist's role in the management of a patient with chronic pulmonary dysfunction.

Thirty years ago, patients with chronic pulmonary disease were given a standard prescription for rest and avoidance of exercise.[1] Well into the 1960s, the stress imposed by exercise was considered deleterious to people with pulmonary disorders.[2] They were treated as invalids, sometimes being referred to as respiratory cripples.[3] A 1964 study by Pierce and coworkers[2] provided the impetus to change direction in the treatment of pulmonary dysfunction. The authors documented exercise training effects in their subjects with chronic obstructive pulmonary disease (COPD). These training effects included decreases in exercising heart rate, respiratory rate, minute ventilation, oxygen consumption, and carbon dioxide production at similar exercise intensities. They also found an increase in exercise tolerance. Reconditioning of patients with chronic obstructive pulmonary disease (COPD) was found to be possible. Many researchers have since confirmed the positive effects of exercise training on individuals with pulmonary disease.[4-10]

Chronic obstructive pulmonary disease and asthma are the most common chronic lung diseases for which pulmonary rehabilitation is rendered. Advances in medical management of cystic fibrosis have resulted in a longer survival rate, but with an increased pulmonary

dysfunction; these patients thus become candidates for pulmonary rehabilitation. Patients with restrictive pulmonary disease have generally been excluded from pulmonary rehabilitation programs owing to their exercise intolerance. Recent information provides support for the use of pulmonary rehabilitation with this patient population.[11]

In this chapter, chronic pulmonary diseases (COPD, asthma, cystic fibrosis, and restrictive lung disease) will be discussed, as well as the physical therapy assessment and treatment of patients with chronic pulmonary disease. A brief review of ventilation and respiration are warranted for a better understanding of the disease pathologies, and of the physical therapy assessment that follow. The suggested reading at the end of this chapter contains references for a more in-depth and thorough review of respiratory physiology.

RESPIRATORY PHYSIOLOGY

Ventilation

Air is inspired through the nose or mouth, through all of the conducting airways until it reaches the distal respiratory unit, which contains the respiratory bronchiole, alveolar ducts, alveolar sacs, and the alveoli (Fig. 15–1). The act of moving air in and out of the lungs is termed **ventilation.** The terminology used to identify the amount of air involved in ventilation is described in the following section.

---

*Parts of this chapter appear in Brannon, F, et al: Cardiopulmonary Rehabilitation: Basic Theory and Application, ed 2. FA Davis, Philadelphia, 1992, and Lesson 8 and Lesson 10, In Touch Series, American Physical Therapy Association, 1991. Used here with permission of the publishers.

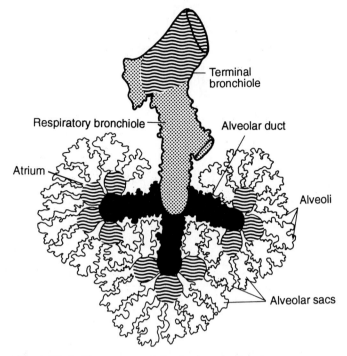

Figure 15–1. The anatomy of the distal conducting airway, the terminal bronchiole and the respiratory unit, the respiratory bronchiole, alveolar ducts, alveolar sacs, and alveoli. (From Brannon, FJ, Foley, MW, Starr, JA, Black, MG: Cardiopulmonary Rehabilitation: Basic Theory and Application, ed 2, FA Davis, Philadelphia, 1993, p 43, with permission.)

Lung Volumes and Capacities

At full inspiration, the lungs contain their maximum amount of gas. This volume of air is called **total lung capacity** (TLC), which can be divided into four separate volumes of air: (1) tidal volume, (2) inspiratory reserve volume, (3) expiratory reserve volume, and (4) residual volume. Combinations of two or more of these lung volumes are termed capacities. Figure 15–2 illustrates the relationship of lung volumes and capacities.

TIDAL VOLUME

The amount of air inspired and expired during normal resting ventilation is termed **tidal volume** (TV). As this tidal volume of air enters the respiratory system, it travels through the conducting airways to reach the respiratory units. Tidal volume is about 500 mL/breath for a young, healthy, white male. The amount of inspired air that actually reaches the distal respiratory unit and takes part in gas exchange is about 350 mL of the 500 mL total. The remaining 150 mL of the inhaled tidal breath remains in the conducting airways and does not take part in gas exchange.

INSPIRATORY RESERVE VOLUME

When only a tidal breath occupies the lungs, there is "room" for additional air that can be further inhaled. This volume in excess of that used in tidal breathing is the **inspiratory reserve volume** (IRV). Aptly named, it is the volume of air that can be inspired when needed, but is usually kept in reserve.

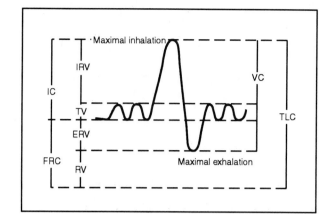

Figure 15–2. Lung volumes and capacities. IRV = inspiratory reserve volume; TV = tidal volume; ERV = expiratory reserve volume; RV = residual volume; IC = inspiratory capacity; FRC = functional residual capacity; VC = vital capacity; TLC = total lung capacity.

EXPIRATORY RESERVE VOLUME

There is a quantity of air that can potentially be exhaled beyond the end of a tidal exhalation. Though it is kept in reserve, the volume of air that can be exhaled in excess of tidal breathing is called the **expiratory reserve volume** (ERV).

RESIDUAL VOLUME

The lungs are not completely emptied of air after maximally exhaling the expiratory reserve volume. The volume of air remaining within the lungs when ERV has been exhaled is called the **residual volume** (RV).

INSPIRATORY CAPACITY

The sum of the tidal volume plus the inspiratory reserve volume is known as the **inspiratory capacity** (IC). This refers to the volume of air that can be inspired beginning from a tidal exhalation.

FUNCTIONAL RESIDUAL CAPACITY

The combination of residual volume and expiratory reserve volume is the **functional residual capacity** (FRC). Functional residual capacity is the volume of air that remains in the lungs at the end of a tidal exhalation.

VITAL CAPACITY

The sum of inspiratory reserve volume, tidal volume, and expiratory reserve volume is called the **vital capacity** (VC). It is the total volume of air within the lungs that is under volitional control. The common method of measuring vital capacity is to achieve maximal inspiration, then forcibly exhale all of the air as hard and as fast as possible until ERV has been exhausted. Because this is a forced expiratory maneuver, it is termed the forced vital capacity or FVC.

Flow Rates and Mechanics

Flow rate measures the volume of gas moved in a period of time. Expiratory flow rates, therefore, are measurements of exhaled gas volume divided by the amount of time required for the volume to be exhaled. Flow rates reflect the ease with which the lungs can be ventilated and are related to the elasticity of the lung parenchyma.[12] An important air flow measurement is the volume of air that can be forcefully exhaled during the first second of a forced vital capacity maneuver. This is called the **forced expiratory volume** in one second, or **FEV_1**. In healthy individuals, FEV_1 is between 75 and 85 percent of the total FVC ($FEV_1/FVC = 75-85\%$).[12] Inspiratory flow rates can also be determined by measuring the amount of air inspired and the amount of time necessary for the inhalation.

Lung volumes, capacities, and flow rates are dependent upon height, age, gender, and race. Any alteration in the properties of the lungs or chest wall will change the lung volumes, capacities, or flow rates.

Respiration

Respiration is a term used to describe the gas exchange within the body. This should not be confused with ventilation, which describes only the movement of air. External respiration is the exchange of gas that occurs at the alveolar capillary membrane between atmospheric air and the pulmonary capillaries. Internal respiration takes place at the tissue capillary level between the tissues and the surrounding capillaries. The following discussion follows the course of gas exchange, specifically that of oxygen and carbon dioxide, during both external and internal respiration.

For external respiration to take place, there must first be an inhalation of air from the environment, through the conducting airways, and into the alveoli. Oxygen diffuses through the alveolar wall, through the interstitial space, and through the pulmonary capillary wall. Most of the oxygen (98.5%) then travels through the blood plasma into the red blood cell where it occupies one of the gas-carrying sites of hemoglobin.[13] A small portion of dissolved oxygen (1.5%) is carried in the plasma.

The oxygenated blood returns to the left side of the heart via the pulmonary veins; from there it travels through the aorta, and then through a network of connecting arteries, arterioles, and capillaries, until its destination, the tissue, is reached. Internal respiration takes place as the arterial blood reaches the tissue level. Oxygen now diffuses from the gas-carrying sites of hemoglobin, out of the red blood cell, out of the capillary, through the cell membranes, and into the mitochondria of the working cells. Again, this process occurs through diffusion.

Carbon dioxide (CO_2), which is produced at the tissue level as a by-product of metabolism, diffuses out of the working cells and into the capillaries. Carbon dioxide is transported through the venous system into the right side of the heart. Once the carbon dioxide makes its way to the pulmonary capillary, it diffuses out through the capillary membrane, through the interstitial space, and into the alveoli, where it is finally exhaled into the atmosphere.

When the cycle of external and internal respiration has occurred, oxygen has been provided to the body tissues and carbon dioxide has been removed. Of course, this system is dependent upon an intact cardiovascular system to pump the blood through the lungs, deliver it to the working cells, and then return it back to the lungs, all in a timely fashion.

CHRONIC LUNG DISEASES

Chronic Obstructive Pulmonary Disease

Chronic obstructive pulmonary disease is the most common chronic pulmonary disorder and its prevalence is increasing. It has been estimated that over 18.5 million Americans are afflicted with this disease,[14] which is the leading cause of chronic disability in the United States.[15]

Chronic obstructive pulmonary disease is a disorder characterized by abnormal values of expiratory air flow that do not change markedly over periods of several months of observation.[16] The pulmonary impairments that comprise COPD are peripheral airways disease, chronic bronchitis, and emphysema.

According to the American Thoracic Society, **peripheral airways disease** results in abnormalities in the terminal and respiratory bronchioles (Fig. 15–1). These changes include inflammation, fibrosis, and narrowing of these airways.[16,17] **Chronic bronchitis** is defined as chronic cough and expectoration, when other specific causes of cough can be excluded,[16] which persists for at least a 3-month period for at least 2 consecutive years.[18] **Emphysema** is defined as abnormal enlargement of the distal respiratory unit accompanied by destructive changes of the alveolar walls without obvious fibrosis.[16] Overdistension of the air spaces without destruction of the alveolar walls, as normally seen in aging, is not included in the definition of emphysema. Since peripheral airways disease, chronic bronchitis, and emphysema can coexist, and their clinical signs and symptoms overlap, the term COPD is useful in the clinical setting to describe the various combinations of these disorders.

ETIOLOGY OF CHRONIC OBSTRUCTIVE PULMONARY DISEASE

Chronic inflammation caused by the irritation of inhaled cigarette smoke is the major causal agent in the development of COPD. There is a direct relationship between the amount and duration of cigarette smoking and the severity of the lung disease although significant individual variation does exist.[14] The etiologic role of other factors, such as agents inhaled from occupational exposure without the effects of smoking, appears to be relatively insignificant.[14,19]

PATHOPHYSIOLOGY OF CHRONIC OBSTRUCTIVE PULMONARY DISEASE

The pathophysiology of COPD is characterized by a number of individual components that contribute to the disease process. Chronic inflammation from inhaling pollutants causes glands and goblet cells within the bronchial walls to hypertrophy. Excessive secretions are then produced, which either partially or completely obstruct the airway. As air enters the lungs, the airways are pulled open, increasing the diameter of the lumen. As the air exits, airways decrease in size. When excessive secretions are present in an airway, air can be inspired around the secretions. During exhalation, however, only some of the air escapes before the airway closes down around the secretions, trapping air distal to the obstruction. Partial obstruction of an airway by mucus accounts for the **hyperinflation** seen in these patients. Complete obstruction of the airways will result in absorption **atelectasis.**

Decreases in ciliary function and alterations in physiochemical characteristics of bronchial secretions also impair airway clearance and contribute to airway obstruction.[19] Stagnant bronchial secretions predispose the patient to recurrent respiratory tract infections.

Damaged and inflamed mucosa shows an increased sensitivity of the irritant receptors within the bronchial walls, which in turn cause bronchial **hyperreactivity.**

Destruction of pulmonary tissue results in loss of the normal elastic recoil properties of the lungs. During expiration, some airways collapse from a lack of support by the surrounding elastic parenchyma.[19] Premature airways collapse also causes hyperinflation or air trapping and reduced expiratory flow rates.

In the advanced stages of the disease, destruction of the alveolar capillary membrane may be present. Ventilation of the alveoli and **perfusion** of the capillary are no longer matched. This results in **hypoxemia,** a condition in which a decreased amount of oxygen is carried by the blood to the tissues. As the disease progresses, and more areas of the lung become involved, hypoxemia will worsen and **hypercapnia,** a condition in which there is an increased amount of carbon dioxide within the arterial blood, will develop. Increased pulmonary vascular resistance secondary to capillary destruction and reflex vasoconstriction in the presence of hypoxemia and hypercapnia results in right ventricular hypertrophy, or **cor pulmonale.** Polycythemia, an increase in the amount of circulating red blood cells, is another complication of advanced COPD.[20]

CLINICAL PRESENTATION OF CHRONIC OBSTRUCTIVE PULMONARY DISEASE

Patients with COPD will present with symptoms of chronic cough, expectoration, and exertional dyspnea. The intensity of each symptom varies according to the patient's unique combination of individual diseases (peripheral airway disease, chronic bronchitis, emphysema) which contribute to the clinical diagnosis of COPD.

Cough and expectoration appear slowly and insidiously. Dyspnea is first evidenced during exertion. As the disease progresses, symptoms worsen. Respiratory infections are common. Dyspnea occurs at lower activity levels. Severely involved patients may appear dyspneic even at rest.

On physical examination, the thorax appears enlarged owing to loss of lung elastic recoil. The anteroposterior diameter of the chest increases and a dorsal kyphosis is noted. These anatomic changes give the patient a "barrel chest" appearance. As a result of lung hyperinflation, breath sounds and heart sounds are usually distant and somewhat difficult to hear. Increased secretions that partially obstruct the bronchi may result in expiratory **wheezing. Crackles** may also be present. Hypertrophy of accessory muscle of ventilation, pursed-lip breathing, **cyanosis,** and **digital clubbing** may all be present in the advanced stages of COPD. (See the section on pulmonary assessment for clarification of terms.)

A significant and progressive increase in airway obstruction is reflected in decreases in expiratory flow rates, especially FEV_1. Pulmonary function studies reveal that these changes do not show a major reversibility in response to pharmacologic agents. Inspiratory flow rates may also be reduced as a result of increased secretions in the airways. There is an increase in residual volume, which may be several times the normal value due to air trapping.[18] As a result, functional residual capacity is also increased. Figure 15–3 shows the changes in lung volumes and capacities that occur in obstructive pulmonary disease.

Arterial blood gas analyses may reflect hypoxemia in

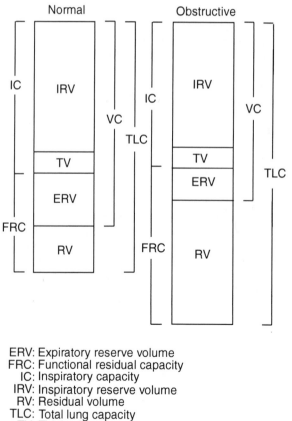

ERV: Expiratory reserve volume
FRC: Functional residual capacity
  IC: Inspiratory capacity
 IRV: Inspiratory reserve volume
  RV: Residual volume
 TLC: Total lung capacity
  TV: Tidal volume

Figure 15–3. Lung volumes of a healthy pulmonary system compared with the lung volumes found in obstructive disease. (From Rothstein, J, Roy, S, and Wolf, S: The Rehabilitation Specialist's Handbook, FA Davis, Philadelphia, 1991, p 604, with permission.)

the early stages of COPD. Hypercapnia appears as the disease progresses.

With disease progression, chest radiographs show several characteristic findings. These include depressed and flattened hemidiaphragms; alteration in pulmonary vascular markings; hyperinflation of the thorax, evidenced by an increased anteroposterior diameter of the chest; and an increased retrosternal airspace, **hyperlucency,** elongation of the heart, and right ventricular hypertrophy.

COURSE AND PROGNOSIS OF CHRONIC OBSTRUCTIVE PULMONARY DISEASE

The clinical course of COPD can run for 30 years or more.[19,20] Several researchers suggest peripheral airways disease may actually be a precursor to the development of COPD.[16,17,21] Early detection of peripheral airway abnormalities may allow for a timely alteration in the patient's personal life-style and environment. Such intervention may halt or even reverse the progression of the peripheral airways disease and prevent development of COPD.[22]

In some, but not all, patients with peripheral airways disease, progression of lung disease will continue. Patients may develop the symptoms of chronic bronchitis, chronic cough, and expectoration. Some patients may demonstrate these findings for many years before developing signs or symptoms of emphysema. The progression to emphysema is evidenced by an increase in the severity of airway obstruction, deterioration of pulmonary function test values, and more frequent respiratory tract infections.[23]

Expiratory flow rates measured during stable periods are good indicators of the progression of COPD. There is also a good correlation between the severity of airway obstruction, as judged by FEV_1, and mortality rates. The rate of decrease in FEV_1 was found to be approximately 54 ml/year in a cross-sectional study.[24] Smoking cessation has been shown to delay this decline in function.[25] With an FEV_1 below 750 mL/second, few patients survive 5 years.[19]

Asthma

Asthma is a clinical syndrome characterized by increased reactivity of the tracheobronchial tree in the presence of various stimuli.[16] The most remarkable feature of asthma is the episodic attacks of wheezing and dyspnea. These attacks improve either spontaneously or with medical therapy and are interspersed with intervals that are symptom-free.

ETIOLOGY OF ASTHMA

Asthma is a common respiratory disease of uncertain etiology that may begin at any age. Although the exact mechanism of airway hyperreactivity is unknown, genetic predisposition,[26] environmental contributions,[27] autonomic nervous system imbalance, and mucosal epithelial damage[19] have been implicated in the development of asthma. The airways of asthmatics are hypersensitive to a variety of factors including allergens, respiratory tract infections, respiratory irritants, cold air, emotional stresses, exercise, and chemical substances. Any or all of these may precipitate or aggravate the symptoms of asthma.

PATHOPHYSIOLOGY OF ASTHMA

The major physiologic manifestation of asthma is widespread narrowing of the airways. The airway narrowing occurs as a result of **bronchospasm,** inflammation of the bronchial mucosa, and increased bronchial secretions. The narrowed airways increase the resistance to airflow and cause air trapping, leading to hyperinflation. These narrowed airways provide an abnormal distribution of ventilation to the alveoli.

CLINICAL PRESENTATION OF ASTHMA

The clinical symptom of asthma is airway narrowing with varying degrees of dyspnea and wheezing. During an acute exacerbation, the chest is usually held in an expanded position, indicating that hyperinflation of the lungs has occurred. Accessory muscles of ventilation are used for breathing and expiratory wheezes can be heard over the entire chest. Sometimes, crackles can be heard as well. With severe airway obstruction, breath sounds may markedly decrease due to poor air movement; wheezing may occur on inspiration as well as expiration; and intercostal, supraclavicular, and substernal **retractions** may be present on inspiration.[19]

Chest radiographs taken during an asthmatic exacerbation usually indicate hyperinflation, as evidenced by an increase in the anteroposterior diameter of the chest and hyperlucency of the lung fields. Less commonly, chest radiographs may reveal areas of atelectasis, or infiltrates from the bronchial obstruction. Normal chest radiographs can be seen between asthma exacerbations.

The most consistent change during an exacerbation of asthma is decreased expiratory flow rates (FEV_1). Residual volume and functional residual capacity are increased because of air trapping, at the expense of vital capacity and inspiratory reserve volume, which are reduced. The reversibility of these pulmonary function test abnormalities is characteristic of asthma. During remission, the patient with asthma may have normal or near-normal values.

The most common arterial blood gas finding during an asthmatic exacerbation is mild to moderate hypoxemia. Usually some degree of **hypocapnia** is present secondary to hyperventilation. With severe attacks, hypoxemia may be more pronounced and with further clinical deterioration, hypercapnia occurs, indicating the patient is exhausted and respiratory failure is imminent.[19,28,29]

CLINICAL COURSE AND PROGNOSIS OF ASTHMA

By the time adulthood is reached, 33 percent of asthmatic children do not have symptoms of asthma.[19] When the onset of symptoms begins later in life, the clinical course is usually more progressive. Pulmonary function tests during periods of remission become less normal;

yet asthma, without other concomitant complicating disease, has a relatively low mortality rate.[27]

Cystic Fibrosis

Cystic fibrosis (CF) is a disease characterized by an exocrine gland dysfunction that results in abnormally viscid secretions. Cystic fibrosis affects many organ systems. Viscous secretions obstruct the airways and pancreatic ducts; obstruction of the former causes chronic pulmonary disease, and of the latter results in malabsorption of food and nutritional compromise.

ETIOLOGY OF CYSTIC FIBROSIS

Cystic fibrosis is a hereditary disease transmitted as an autosomal recessive (Mendelian) trait.[30] The incidence in white children is approximately 1 in 2000 live births. Although less common in the black population, 2.25 percent of all CF patients identified by the Cystic Fibrosis Foundation in 1979 were black.[31] Cystic fibrosis is rare in the Asian population.[31]

PATHOPHYSIOLOGY OF CYSTIC FIBROSIS

Chronic pulmonary disease in CF is related to the abnormally viscous mucus secreted by the tracheobronchial tree. The function of the mucociliary transport is impaired by the altered secretions and results in airway obstruction, recurrent infection, and hyperinflation. Partial or complete obstruction of the airways reduces ventilation to the alveolar units. Ventilation and perfusion within the lungs are uneven. Fibrotic changes are also found in the lung parenchyma.

CLINICAL PRESENTATION OF CYSTIC FIBROSIS

The diagnosis of cystic fibrosis may be suspected in patients who present with a positive family history of the disease, with recurrent respiratory infections from *Staphylococcus aureus* and *Pseudomonas aeruginosa,* or with a diagnosis of malnutrition and/or failure to thrive. A chloride concentration of 60 meq/l (milliequivalents per liter) found in the sweat of children is a positive test for the diagnosis of cystic fibrosis.

Pulmonary function studies show obstructive impairments: decreased FEV_1, decreased FVC, increased residual volume, and increased functional residual capacity. The abnormal ventilation-perfusion relationship within the lungs results in hypoxemia and hypercapnia, as shown by arterial blood gas analysis. As the disease progresses, destruction of the alveolar capillary network causes pulmonary hypertension and cor pulmonale.

In advanced disease, chest radiographs show diffuse hyperinflation, increased lung marking, and atelectasis.

COURSE AND PROGNOSIS OF CYSTIC FIBROSIS

Life expectancy continues to increase owing to advances in early diagnosis and improved medical management. Though some patients still die in infancy and early childhood, the majority of patients currently survive into adulthood.[32] Treatment of the pulmonary dysfunction caused by cystic fibrosis centers around removal of the abnormal secretions and prompt treatment of pulmonary infections. In 90 percent of cases, pulmonary involvement is the cause of death.[30]

Gastrointestinal dysfunctions from cystic fibrosis can be aided by proper diet, vitamin supplements, and replacement of pancreatic enzymes.

Restrictive Lung Disease

Restrictive lung disease is actually a group of diseases with differing etiologies. What these disorders have in common is a difficulty in expanding the lungs and a reduction in lung volume. This restriction can come from diseases of the alveolar parenchyma and/or the pleura that result in fibrosis of the alveoli, interstitial lung parenchyma, and pleura. The restriction can also be caused by changes in the chest wall or in the neuromuscular apparatus.[33] For the purpose of this discussion, those diseases most likely to be encountered in a pulmonary rehabilitation setting will be presented (i.e., restrictive diseases of the lung parenchyma and pleura).

ETIOLOGY OF RESTRICTIVE LUNG DISEASE

This group of disorders has a variety of causes. Numerous agents, such as radiation therapy, inorganic dust, inhalation of noxious gases, oxygen toxicity, asbestos exposure, and tuberculosis can cause damage to the pulmonary parenchyma and pleura and result in restrictive pulmonary disease.

PATHOPHYSIOLOGY OF RESTRICTIVE LUNG DISEASE

The particular changes occurring within the lungs depends upon the etiologic factors of restrictive disease. Parenchymal changes often begin with chronic inflammation and a thickening of the alveoli and interstitium. As the disease progresses, distal air spaces became fibrosed making them more resistant to expansion (i.e., less distensible). Consequently, lung volumes are reduced. A reduced pulmonary vascular bed eventually leads to hypoxemia and cor pulmonale.

In pleural diseases, thickened plaques of collagen fibers cause fibrosis, which may be found in various locations. In asbestos exposure, for example, the plaques are found on the parietal pleura. The mechanism responsible for plaque development is not completely clear. There may also be parenchymal alterations that accompany pleural diseases. These changes may be due to injury, or to inflammatory reactions that lead to fibrosis.

CLINICAL PRESENTATION OF RESTRICTIVE LUNG DISEASE

Dyspnea is the classic symptom of restrictive lung diseases. A nonproductive cough is often encountered; weakness and early fatigue are also common.

Signs of restrictive lung disease include rapid, shallow

breathing; limited chest expansion; crackles, especially over the lower lung fields; digital clubbing; and cyanosis.

In the early stages of parenchymal restrictive disease, the chest radiograph reveals fine interstitial markings, which look like ground glass. In long-standing fibrosis there is radiographic evidence of diffuse infiltrates, and the appearance of the lung has been likened to that of a honeycomb. Reduction in lung volumes can be seen serially on the chest radiograph. Radiographic evidence of pleural thickening can also be seen, especially on oblique films.

Pulmonary function tests reveal a reduction in vital capacity, functional residual capacity, and total lung capacity. Residual volume may be normal or near normal and expiratory flow rates remain normal. Figure 15–4 shows the changes in lung volumes and capacities that occur in restrictive pulmonary disease.

Arterial blood studies show varying degrees of hypoxemia and hypocapnia. Hypoxemia at rest is usually exacerbated by exercise. Exercise may significantly lower oxygenation, even for patients with normal oxygenation at rest.

COURSE AND PROGNOSIS OF RESTRICTIVE LUNG DISEASE

Restrictive pulmonary disease may have a slow onset but is chronic and progressive in nature. Survival

depends on the type of restrictive disease, the etiologic factor, and the treatment. Chest radiographs are insensitive indicators of the extent of the disease.[34] Hypercapnia is an ominous sign, indicating the terminal stage of pulmonary fibrosis.

MEDICAL MANAGEMENT OF PULMONARY DISEASE

Pharmacologic agents provide the foundation for the medical management of pulmonary disease. These drugs can affect exercise performance, heart rate, and blood pressure, both at rest and with exercise. It is important to know the medications used in pulmonary care and their effects on the pulmonary system.

Broad classifications of drugs often used in the care of patients with pulmonary disease are found in Table 15–1. It is not unusual for patients to be on a combination of drugs for the management of their pulmonary disease.

Bronchodilators, such as those classified as sympathomimetics, methylxanthines, and parasympatholytics, are commonly prescribed drugs for patients with pulmonary disease. Bronchodilators are used to reduce airway obstruction and resistance to airflow by increasing the size of the airway lumen. It is advisable for patients to use their prescribed inhaled bronchodilators prior to the onset of activity to enhance exercise performance.

Although the mechanisms of each of these drugs is different, all can increase resting heart rate. Employing the Karvonen formula for exercise intensity, the elevated resting heart rate is acknowledged and a more appropriate target heart rate is calculated. The use of the rate of perceived shortness of breath may also be used as an accurate indicator of exercise intensity.

Anti-inflammatory drugs, such as corticosteriods, are also used in the treatment of chronic pulmonary disease. Steroids reduce inflammation of the tracheobronchial mucosa, which aid in bronchodilation, and suppression of the immune response. Steroids have many negative side effects such as muscle wasting, increase in blood pressure, tachycardia, osteoporosis, and increased susceptibility to and masking of infection. The mode of exercise deserves special consideration in patients on long-term steroid therapy. Low impact or lower intensity of exercise (with careful patient monitoring) may be warranted.

Cromolyn sodium (Intal) has the ability to prevent the inflammatory response. Because of its action, Intal is a prophylactic drug, not one to be called upon in an acute situation. Its preventative capacity makes it useful in maintainance therapy.

Pulmonary infections can be devastating to the patient and cause major setbacks in pulmonary rehabilitation efforts. To treat these infections, antibiotics are administered. Antibiotics may be divided into five basic categories: penicillins, cephalosporins, aminoglycosides, tetracyclines, and erythromycins. The action of these drugs is either bacteriostatic or bactericidal. Organisms can be sensitive to some antibiotics while resistant to

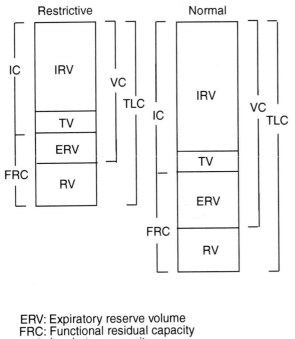

ERV: Expiratory reserve volume
FRC: Functional residual capacity
IC: Inspiratory capacity
IRV: Inspiratory reserve volume
RV: Residual volume
TLC: Total lung capacity
TV: Tidal volume

Figure 15–4. Lung volumes of a healthy pulmonary system compared with the lung volumes found in restrictive disease. (From Rothstein, J, Roy, S, and Wolf, S: The Rehabilitation Specialist's Handbook, FA Davis, Philadelphia, 1991, p 604, with permission.)

Table 15-1   PULMONARY DRUGS*

Use	Side Effects	Drug Names	Routes of Administration
I. Sympathomimetics			
Smooth muscle relaxation Bronchodilation	Tachycardia Palpitations GI distress Nervousness Tremor Headache Dizziness	Isoproterenol Epinephrine (Ephedrine) Isoetharine (Bronkosol) Metaproterenol (Alupent) Terbutaline (Brethine) Albuterol (Proventil, Ventolin)	Inhaled PO IM IV
II. Methylxanthines			
Smooth muscle relaxation Bronchodilation	Tachycardia Arrhythmias GI distress Nervousness Headache Dizziness	Aminophylline (Aminodur) Theophylline (Elixophyllin) (Slo-phyllin, Theodur) (Fleet Theophyllin) Oxtriphyllin (Choladril)	Inhaled PO IV PR
III. Parasympatholytic			
Blocks smooth muscle constriction Maintains bronchodilation	Tachycardia Palpitations Drying of tracheal secretions Throat irritation Photophobia Urinary retention Constipation	Ipratropium bromide (Atrovent) Atropine Sulfate	Inhaled IM IV Subcutaneous
IV. Corticosteroids			
Reduces mucosal edema Reduces inflammation Reduces immune response	Increased BP Sodium retention—edema Muscle wasting Osteoporosis GI irritation Atherosclerosis Hypercholesteremia Increased susceptibility to infections	Prednisone Hydrocortisone (Cortisol) Triamcinolone acetonide (Azmacort) Beclamethasone (Vanceril, Beclovent)	Inhaled PO IM IV
V. Cromolyn Sodium			
Inhibits antigen-antibody response	Throat irritation Cough Bronchospasm	Intal Fivent	Inhaled

*Generic drugs are known by other proprietary names in addition to those given above.
GI = gastrointestinal; IM = intramuscular; IV = intravenous; PO = oral; PR = parenteral.

others. A culture and sensitivity test by the bacteriology lab will uncover which bacteria are present in the sputum, and which antibiotics are most likely to be effective in clearing the infection.

REHABILITATION FOR THE PATIENT WITH PULMONARY DISEASE

Chronic pulmonary disease and its associated dysfunction have a slow onset, and a progressive course. Activities that result in the uncomfortable sensation of dyspnea are avoided by the person with pulmonary dysfunction. Family and friends often discourage these patients from exerting themselves for fear of untoward effects.[35] A slow but steady decrease in these patients' activities will soon follow. It is not uncommon for someone with pulmonary disease to have lost many func-

tional abilities before ever seeking medical help. The goal of pulmonary rehabilitation is to interrupt this downward spiraling of physical ability.[36]

Treatment Goals

- To provide ongoing secretion removal to optimize respiration.
- To initiate exercise training to improve the present level of function.
- To promote self-management of pulmonary disease.
- To provide patient and family education.

Pulmonary Assessment

The assessment of a patient's pulmonary status has several purposes: (1) to evaluate the appropriateness of the patient's participation in a pulmonary rehabilitation program, (2) to determine the therapeutic measures most appropriate for the participant's treatment program, (3) to monitor the participant's physiologic response to exercise, and (4) to have the participant's treatment program progress appropriately over a period of time.

Patient Interview

A patient interview should begin with the "chief complaint," the patient's perception of why pulmonary rehabilitation is being sought. Commonly, the chief complaint will center on a loss of function. A medical history contains pertinent pulmonary symptoms specific to that patient: cough, sputum production, wheezing, and shortness of breath. Occupational, social, medication, and family histories should also be recorded.

Physical Examination

VITAL SIGNS

Temperature, blood pressure, heart rate, and respiratory rate should be evaluated and recorded (see Chapter 4). An individual's height should be measured because there is a direct relationship between height and lung volumes. A stadiometer is recommended for this measurement. Weight should be measured on a standard balance scale and each evaluation of weight should be performed on the same scale.

OBSERVATION, INSPECTION, AND PALPATION

By observing the neck and shoulders of a patient with pulmonary disease, the use of the accessory muscles of ventilation can be observed. A normal configuration of the thorax reveals a ratio of anteroposterior (A-P) to lateral diameter of 2:1. Emphysema causes destruction of the lung parenchyma, which results in an increase in the A-P diameter and a reduction of this ratio (1:1). During inhalation and exhalation both sides of the thorax should move symmetrically.

Cyanosis is a bluish discoloration of the skin that can be observed periorally, periorbitally, and in nail beds; it indicates hypoxemia.[37] In digital clubbing of the fingers and toes, another indicator of hypoxemia, there is an increase in the angle created by the distal phalynx and the point where the nail exits from the digit.[37] The tip of the distal phalynx becomes bulbous.

AUSCULTATION OF THE LUNGS

Auscultation involves listening over the chest wall to the airways as gas enters and exits the lungs. To perform auscultation of the lungs, a stethoscope is placed firmly on the patient's thorax over the lung tissue. The patient is asked to inspire fully through an open mouth; then to exhale quietly.[38] Inhalation and the beginning of exhalation normally produce a soft rustling sound. The end of exhalation is silent. This characteristic of a normal breath sound is termed **vesicular.** When a louder, more hollow and echoing sound occupies a larger portion of

the ventilatory cycle, the breath sounds are referred to as **bronchial.** When the breath sounds are very quiet and barely audible, they are termed **decreased.** These three terms, vesicular, bronchial, and decreased, allow the listener to describe the intensity of the breath sound.[39]

In addition to the normal and abnormal intensity of the breath sound, there may be additional sounds and vibrations heard during auscultation. These are called **adventitious breath sounds.** These sounds are superimposed upon the already-described intensity of the breath sound. According to the American College of Chest Physicians and the American Thoracic Society, there are two types of adventitious sounds: crackles and wheezes.[40] Crackles, historically termed rales, are thought to occur when previously closed small airways and alveoli are rapidly reopened.[41] Wheezes are more musical in nature. A decrease in the size of the lumen of the airway will create a wheezing sound, much as stretching the neck of an inflated balloon narrows the passageway through which air must escape and produces a whistling sound.

LABORATORY TESTS

Various laboratory studies may be performed to evaluate patients with pulmonary disease. These include chest radiographs, pulmonary function tests (PFTs), graded exercise tests (GXT), arterial blood gas analysis (ABG), oxygen saturation measurements (SaO$_2$), and electrocardiograms.

Exercise Testing in Patients with Pulmonary Disease

A determination of functional capacity is part of the assessment of a patient with pulmonary disease. A **graded exercise test** can provide the objective information to (1) document a patient's symptomatology and physical impairment, (2) prescribe safe exercise, (3) document changes in oxygenation during exercise and evaluate the need for supplemental oxygen, and (4) evaluate any changes in pulmonary function during exercise intervention.

EXERCISE TESTING PROTOCOLS

A graded (gradually increasing intensity) exercise test should stress the patient with pulmonary dysfunction to the point of limitation, while vital signs are monitored to ensure safety. Arterial blood gas analysis measured during exercise provides the best method for determining arterial oxygenation and the adequacy of alveolar ventilation. The ECG, continuously recorded during exercise, records the exercise heart rate and electrical activity of the cardiac conduction system. Blood pressure measurements, recorded at 2-minute intervals during exercise, and during recovery from the test, provide information on the hemodynamic status of the patient.

There are a number of test protocols available to assess the functional abilities of patients with pulmonary disease. These protocols are outlined in Table 15–2.[42–48] Procedures and equipment requirements for measuring

Table 15–2 PROTOCOLS USED FOR EXERCISE TESTING THE PATIENT WITH PULMONARY DISEASE

Mode	Author	Protocol
Walk test	Cooper[41]	Ambulate as far as possible in 12 minutes
	Guyatt, et al.[42]	Ambulate as far as possible in 6 minutes
Cycle test	Jones[43]	Begin with 100 kpm (17 W), increase 100 kpm
	Jones and Campbell[44]	Begin with 25 W, increase 15 W/min
	Berman and Sutton[45]	Begin with 100 kpm, increase 100 kpm every min or 50 kg/min every min when FEV_1 less than 1 L/sec
	Massachusetts Respiratory Hospital	Begin at 25 W, 10 W every 20 sec or 5 W every 20 sec when FEV_1 less than 1 L/sec
Treadmill tests	Naughton[46]	2 mph constant 0 grade 3.5% grade every 3 min
	Balke[47]	3.3 mph constant 0 grade 3.5% grade every 2 min
	Massachusetts Respiratory Hospital	1.5 mph constant 0 grade 4% grade every 2 min 2% grade every 2 min if FEV_1 is less than 1 L/sec

From Brannon, F, et al: Cardiac Rehabilitation: Basic Theory and Application, FA Davis, 1992, p 269, with permission.

functional ability range from the very simple 12-minute walk test to more sophisticated treadmill and cycle protocols. (Refer to the section on exercise protocols in Chapter 16, Coronary Artery Disease, for more information on exercise protocols.)

TEST TERMINATION

The symptom-limited graded exercise test requires the patient to continue the exercise protocol until symptoms dictate cessation. Criteria for stopping a pulmonary exercise test are listed in Table 15–3.[49–51]

INTERPRETATION OF GRADED EXERCISE TEST RESULTS

Functional capacity assessed by a GXT allows for appropriate vocational counseling assessment and provides the documentation necessary for addressing disability.[52]

The need for supplemental oxygen is indicated if a patient becomes hypoxemic during the exercise test session. A decrease in the arterial partial pressure of oxygen (PaO_2) of greater than 20 mmHg, or a PaO_2 of less than 55 mmHg, are indications of a need for oxygen supplementation.[53] (The normal value for PaO_2 is 95 to 100 mmHg.)

Pulmonary function tests performed prior to and following an exercise test document the effects of exercise on lung function. A reduction of 10 percent in FEV_1 is an indication to provide bronchodilator therapy.[54]

Finally, a prescription for exercise that will safely promote cardiopulmonary fitness can be developed based on the GXT. This is the topic for the next section.

Table 15–3 GRADED EXERCISE TEST TERMINATION CRITERIA

1. Maximal shortness of breath
2. A fall in PaO_2 of greater than 20 mmHg or a PaO_2 less than 55 mmHg
3. A rise in $PaCO_2$ of greater than 10 mmHg or greater than 65 mmHg
4. Cardiac ischemia or arrhythmias
5. Symptoms of fatigue
6. Increase in diastolic blood pressure readings of 20 mmHg, systolic hypertension greater than 250 mmHg, decrease in blood pressure with increasing workloads
7. Leg pain
8. Total fatigue
9. Signs of insufficient cardiac output
10. Reaching a ventilatory maximum

From Brannon, F, et al: Cardiopulmonary Rehabilitation: Basic Theory and Application, FA Davis, 1992, p 270, with permission.

Exercise Prescription

Exercise prescription incorporates four variables that together provide an individually tailored exercise formula designed to produce an increase in functional capacity. These variables are mode, intensity, duration, and frequency.

MODE

Any type of sustained **aerobic exercise** that generally involves large muscle groups is appropriate for pulmonary rehabilitation. Such activities might include walking, jogging, rowing, cycling, swimming, and arm ergometry. Many programs utilize a circuit type of approach to train different muscle groups and to maintain the participant's interest.

INTENSITY

Three techniques are commonly used to prescribe and monitor exercise intensity. They are heart rate, a rating of perceived exertion (RPE), and metabolic energy expenditure (VO_2 or METs).[55–62]

Heart Rate

There are several methods for establishing a target heart rate range (THRR) and a target heart rate (THR). The THRR defines safety guidelines for exercise intensity during the treatment session. The THR for a specific patient defines the most appropriate HR within the prescribed THRR to ensure cardiorespiratory endurance training.

The most commonly used method to determine the THRR and the THR is the heart rate reserve method or Karvonen formula.[58] The heart rate reserve is the difference between the resting heart rate in the seated position and the maximal achieved heart rate on a GXT. To calculate the THRR for a patient, percentages of the heart rate reserve are added to the resting heart rate. The equation for determining the THRR is

(Maximal heart rate − resting heart rate)
(40% to 85%) + resting heart rate = THRR

For example, on a GXT, the maximal heart rate achieved was 165 beats per minute. Resting heart rate was 85 beats per minute. Therefore, heart rate reserve is calculated as $165 - 85 = 80$; 40% of 80 + resting heart rate = 117; 85% of 80 + resting heart rate = 153. Thus, for this patient, a THRR of 117–153 has been calculated.

Determining the appropriate THR requires careful consideration of individual abilities and disabilities. For pulmonary patients with mild to moderate impairment, the THR should be calculated using a minimum of 50 percent and a maximum of 60 percent to 70 percent of the heart rate reserve.[63] Patients with moderate to severe pulmonary impairment will reach their ventilatory maximum before their cardiovascular maximum is approached. For these patients, exercise intensities that approach their maximum ventilatory limits or the upper end of the THRR can be used.[10,64]

Rate of Perceived Shortness of Breath

Pulmonary patients can use a scale similar to the Borg scale of perceived exertion by rating their perceived shortness of breath. (See Chapter 16, Coronary Artery Disease, for more information about the Borg scale of perceived exertion.) Because pulmonary patients often have poor ventilatory reserves but adequate heart rate reserves, the use of a scale of perceived shortness of breath becomes a useful tool for monitoring exercise intensity by subjective means (Table 15–4). Ratings between four and six, mildly short of breath to moderately short of breath, define the range within which pulmonary patients generally work.

Exercise by Metabolic Equivalents

A GXT reports a functional capacity in terms of VO_2 or maximum METs attained during exercise. One **metabolic equivalent (MET)** equals 3.5 mL of oxygen used per kilogram of body weight. An activity can be categorized according to the **oxygen consumption** required to perform that activity or in other words, the number of METs required to perform that activity. Exercise intensity can be prescribed using 40 percent to 85 percent of the maximum METs achieved on a GXT. There are some difficulties using METs to prescribe exercise intensity for patients with pulmonary disease. Often, a normative table is used to prescribe exercise; but pulmonary patients do not respond to exercise in a normative fashion. The participant has an individual oxygen consumption for each activity, and this may vary considerably from the normative chart. Day-to-day variations in environmental conditions, patients' abilities, stress level, and performance of the activity may change the metabolic cost of an activity. The difference between the actual oxygen expenditure and predicted norms makes prescribing exercise intensity by METs somewhat imprecise.

For the pulmonary patient, exercise intensity should be based on symptoms of shortness of breath and fatigue more than strict HR or fixed work levels.[65,66] Usually clinicians prefer to prescribe exercise by utilizing a combination of prescription by HR and the rate of perceived exertion or shortness of breath. It should be emphasized that exercise intensity should be prescribed within a "range" as a patient can demonstrate HR fluctuations of up to 10 percent during a single exercise session.

DURATION

Exercising within the target heart rate for at least 20 minutes is recommended. The duration of the training session varies according to patient tolerance, with some participants not being able to maintain the exercise intensity prescribed for the full 20 minutes. Frequent rest periods can be interspersed with exercise to accomplish a total of 20 minutes of exercise.

FREQUENCY

The frequency of exercise refers to the number of sessions performed on a weekly basis during the exercise training period. The frequency of exercise is often dependent on the intensity that can be achieved and the duration it can be maintained. If 20 minutes of aerobic exercise can be accomplished within the THR, then three to five evenly spaced workouts per week are recommended. More frequent exercise sessions are recommended for patients with lower functional abilities. One to two daily sessions are advisable for patients with very low functional work capacities.

Table 15–4 SUBJECTIVE DEFINITIONS FOR A TEN-POINT PERCEIVED SHORTNESS OF BREATH SCALE

Score	Activity	Perceived Shortness of Breath
1	Rest	Not short of breath
2	Minimal activity	Minimally short of breath
3	Very light activity	Slightly short of breath
4	Light activity	Mildly short of breath
5	Somewhat hard activity	Mildly to moderately short of breath
6	Hard activity	Moderately short of breath
7		Moderately to severely short of breath
8	Very hard activity	Severely short of breath
9		Breathing is not in control
10	Very, very hard activity	Maximally short of breath

Adapted from Pulmonary Rehabilitation Program, Massachusetts Respiratory Hospital, Braintree, MA.

Pulmonary Rehabilitation Session

The pulmonary rehabilitation session includes the following components: check-in period, warm-up, aerobic exercise, cool-down, and education.

The check-in period is a time to take vital signs, including heart rate, respiratory rate, blood pressure, auscultation of the lungs, and weight. It is also the time to discuss with patients their medication schedule, any problems they have encountered, and any changes that need to be noted and addressed by a member of the pulmonary rehabilitation team. If the patient was found to have a decrease in FEV, of 10 percent or more on their GXT, a prescribed inhaler should be used at this time. If a patient was found to have a decrease in oxygenation with exercise, the supplemental oxygen should be readied at this time.

Prior to the aerobic period of exercise, the participant performs stretching exercises to prevent musculoskeletal injuries. Stretching exercises should be performed during exhalation to prevent a Valsalva maneuver, which would worsen a participant's pulmonary capabilities. Patients often use accessory muscles of ventilation during the exercise program; therefore, the neck should be incorporated into the stretching program. It is also a time to slowly increase the HR and BP to ready the cardiovascular system for aerobic exercise. This is usually accomplished by performing the same mode of exercise that will be used in the aerobic portion of the program but with a lower intensity, with an emphasis on controlled breathing. For example, cycling with no resistance could be used as a warm-up activity for a patient with a biking program. The warm-up portion of the program lasts about 10 to 15 minutes.

The aerobic portion of the rehabilitation session consists of aerobic exercise of the appropriate mode, intensity, and duration to maintain the THR chosen in the exercise prescription. This portion of the program lasts from at least 20 minutes up to 60 minutes. The participant can be monitored by using a rating of perceived shortness of breath, heart rate, respiratory rate, and oximetry (which noninvasively monitors oxygenation within the blood).

The aerobic training period should be followed immediately by a cool-down period. This consists of 5 to 15 minutes of low-level aerobic activities that slowly return the cardiovascular system to near pre-exercise levels. Again, there is an emphasis on controlled breathing. Finally, stretching exercises are repeated to maintain joint and muscle integrity and to prevent injury.

The concept of self-management is promoted in the educational sessions of a pulmonary rehabilitation program. The patient's assumption of responsibility for his or her own wellness and independence must be fostered. By using both individual and group processes for education, the benefits of both types of interaction can be attained. Participants are given individual one-on-one time to identify their own needs and to address issues that are particular to themselves. Benefits from group discussions include support from peers regarding the patient's feelings or needs, learning from others' experiences and questions, and the socialization only a group can provide. Key components of an education program can be found in Table 15–5.

Exercise Progression

Modifications in the duration and intensity of the exercise session should be made as an individual physiologically adapts to exercise. Exercise progression is appropriate when the individual perceives the intensity of the exercise session to be easier or when the same exercise intensity is performed with a lesser degree of shortness of breath and lower HR.

The duration of exercise should be increased by extending the amount of time spent in continuous aer-

Table 15–5 EDUCATION SESSION TOPICS

Anatomy and physiology of respiratory disease
Pulmonary hygiene techniques
Effects of exercise
Nutrition and pulmonary disease
Energy-saving techniques
Stress management and relaxation
Smoking and environmental factors
Medications and oxygen therapy
Psychosocial aspects of COPD
Diagnostic techniques
General management of COPD
Community services

Adapted from Pulmonary Rehabilitation Program, Massachusetts Respiratory Hospital, Braintree, MA.
COPD = chronic obstructive pulmonary disease.

obic activity and decreasing the amount of time spent in rest periods. The goal of duration progression would be a continuous 20 minutes of aerobic activity without the need for a rest. When at least 20 minutes of activity can be accomplished, then an increase in exercise intensity can be proposed.

A patient's age, functional ability, symptoms, and severity of disease must be considered prior to any change in the exercise prescription. It is advisable, when considerable change in a participant's ability has occurred, to perform a new GXT. The new exercise prescription will allow for a safe and comfortable progression of exercise under controlled guidance.

Program Duration

Improved exercise tolerance can be initiated on an inpatient hospital admission, or as an outpatient. Because of the limited length of stays in many hospital admissions, most increases in functional capacity occur as an outpatient. Generally, conditioning exercises are conducted three times per week over a course of 6 to 8 weeks. At the end of the rehabilitation program, patients are reevaluated. A second exercise test is performed to assess the exercise prescription for continuation of care.

An unfortunate reality is that patients with pulmonary dysfunction often have respiratory setbacks from exacerbations of their disease. Continued contact and encouragement in the form of periodic evaluation is essential to maintain the new level of physical activity. However, reimbursement for such care is difficult to obtain.[67] Patients are encouraged to join community-based groups that facilitate compliance with their medical and exercise regimens (e.g., the Better Breathing Club, sponsored by the American Lung Association).

Home Exercise Programs

A home exercise program usually begins while the participant is still enrolled in an outpatient pulmonary rehabilitation program. When the staff deems it feasible (based on exercise and lab data), the participant can be assigned exercise activities to be done at home. The patient returns to the outpatient clinic with an exercise log containing the heart rate, RPEs, exercise parameters, and any problems that may have occurred during the home program. The staff analyzes this data and adjusts the home program if necessary. Progression of the patient to a home program is an important goal of the rehabilitation program.

Multispecialty Approach

A diversity of health professionals are essential to meet the medical, physical, social, and psychologic needs of the patient with pulmonary disease. The team may include nurses, physicians, physical therapists, occupational therapists, nutritionists, respiratory therapists, exercise physiologists, sex therapists, psychiatrists, psychologists, social workers, recreational therapists, clergy, and most importantly, the patient and the patient's family.

Additional Components of Pulmonary Rehabilitation

Although aerobic exercise training is integral to pulmonary rehabilitation, patients may require added services and information to optimize their exercise capability and to improve quality of life. The following section covers other essential elements of a pulmonary rehabilitation program; secretion removal techniques, ventilatory muscle training and breathing reeducation, pacing, and smoking cessation.

SECRETION REMOVAL TECHNIQUES

Secretion retention can interfere with ventilation and the diffusion of oxygen and carbon dioxide. An assessment of the pulmonary system will identify the areas of secretion retention. An individualized program of secretion removal techniques directed to the areas of involvement can optimize ventilation and therefore gas exchange capabilities. Patients with secretion retention may improve their performance on an exercise regimen if the proper secretion removal techniques are provided prior to the exercise session.

Postural Drainage

Positioning a patient so that the bronchus of the involved lung segment is perpendicular to the ground is the basis for **postural drainage**. Using gravity, these positions assist the mucociliary transport system in removing excessive secretions from the tracheobronchial tree. Standard postural drainage positions are presented in Figure 15–5.

Although these postural drainage positions are optimal for gravity drainage of specific lung segments, they may not be realistic for some patients. The standard position for postural drainage could make a patient's respiratory status, or a concomitant problem, worse. Modification of these standard positions may prevent any untoward effects and still enhance secretion removal. Table 15–6 lists precautions that should be considered prior to instituting postural drainage with patients enrolled in an outpatient pulmonary rehabilitation program. These are not absolute contraindications, rather relative precautions. The list is not meant to be all-inclusive; however, it does provide the reader with a range of dysfunction that should be considered prior to instituting postural drainage.

Percussion

Percussion is a force rhythmically applied with the therapist's cupped hands to the patient's chest wall. The percussion technique is applied to a specific area on the thorax that corresponds to an underlying involved lung segment. The technique is typically administered for from 2 to 5 minutes over each involved lung segment. Percussion is thought to release the pulmonary secretions from the wall of the airways and into the lumen of the airway.[68] Unfortunately, this process seems to be nondirectional. That is, the secretions may be moved closer to the glottis or deeper into the pulmonary parenchyma. By coupling percussion with the appropriate postural drainage position for a specific lung segment, the probability of secretion removal is enhanced.[69-71] Since percussion is a force directed to the thorax, there are conditions that need to be evaluated prior to its use. These precautions are outlined in Table 15–7. The list is again by no means all-inclusive. It does provide some general guidelines that deserve consideration when percussion is part of the therapeutic regimen. It should be noted also that some modification of this technique can be made in order to enhance patient tolerance.

Shaking

Following a deep inhalation, a bouncing maneuver is applied to the rib cage throughout the expiratory phase of breathing. This **shaking** is applied to a specific area on the thorax that corresponds to the underlying involved lung segment. Five to seven trials of shaking are appropriate in order to hasten the removal of secretions via the mucociliary transport system and prevent possible hyperventilation. Shaking is commonly used following percussion in the appropriate postural drainage position.[35,72] Because this technique consists of a force applied to the thorax, the same considerations are needed as in the application of percussion.

Airway Clearance

Once the secretions have been mobilized with postural drainage, percussion, and shaking or vibration, the task of removing the secretions from the airways is undertaken. Coughing is the most common and easiest means of clearing the airway. Huffing is another method of airway clearance that is useful for patients with COPD. High intrathoracic pressures, such as those generated during coughing, can force the closing of small airways in some patients. By trapping air behind the closed airway, the forced expulsion of air during a cough becomes ineffective in clearing secretions. A huff uses many of the same steps of coughing, without creating the high intrathoracic pressures. The patient is asked to take a deep breath and rapidly contract the abdominal muscles and forcefully saying "HA HA HA."

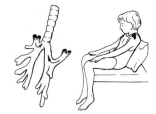

UPPER LOBES Apical Segments

Bed or drainage table flat.

Patient leans back on pillow at 30° angle against therapist.

Therapist claps with markedly cupped hand over area between clavicle and top of scapula on each side.

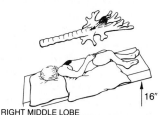

UPPER LOBES Posterior Segments

Bed or drainage table flat.

Patient leans over folder pillow at 30° angle.

Therapist stands behind and claps over upper back on both sides.

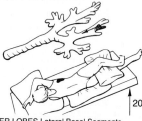

RIGHT MIDDLE LOBE

Foot of table or bed elevated 16 inches.

Patient lies head down on left side and rotates ¼ turn backward. Pillow may be placed behind from shoulder to hip. Knees should be flexed.

Therapist claps over right nipple area. In females with breast development or tenderness, use cupped hand with heel of hand under armpit and fingers extending forward beneath the breast.

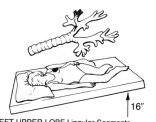

LEFT UPPER LOBE Lingular Segments

Foot of table or bed elevated 16 inches.

Patient lies head down on right side and rotates ¼ turn backward. Pillow may be placed behind from shoulder to hip. Knees should be flexed.

Therapist claps with moderately cupped hand over left nipple area. In females with breast development or tenderness, use cupped hand with heel of hand under armpit and fingers extending forward beneath the breast.

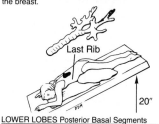

LOWER LOBES Lateral Basal Segments

Foot of table or bed elevated 20 inches.

Patient lies on abdomen, head down, then rotates ¼ turn upward. Upper leg is flexed over a pillow for support.

Therapist claps over uppermost portion of lower ribs. (Position shown is for drainage of right lateral basal segment. To drain the left lateral basal segment, patient should lie on his right side in the same posture).

LOWER LOBES Posterior Basal Segments

Foot of table or bed elevated 20 inches.

Patient lies on abdomen, head down, with pillow under hips. Therapist claps over lower ribs close to spine on each side.

Figure 15–5. Positions used for postural drainage. (From Rothstein, J, Roy, S, and Wolf, S: The Rehabilitation Specialists Handbook, FA Davis, Philadelphia, 1991, pp 624–625, with permission.)

This allows a forced expiration through a stabilized open airway and makes secretion removal more effective.[73]

VENTILATORY MUSCLE TRAINING AND BREATHING RE-EDUCATION

The inability to sufficiently increase ventilation is often the limiting factor in functional activities and exercise tolerance of patients with pulmonary dysfunction. Optimizing the ventilatory function can decrease the work of breathing and improve the ability to perform work. Ventilatory muscle training has been utilized to improve the strength and endurance of the muscles of ventilation, thus increasing the efficiency of breathing. Breathing reeducation teaches a more efficient pattern of ventilation, which decreases the work of breathing.

There are specific devices, inspiratory muscle trainers (IMTs), which load the inspiratory muscles via graded aperture openings. The patient breathes in through this narrowed opening, which loads the inspiratory muscles and thereby trains the muscles of inspiration.[74] By changing the size of the aperture opening, training programs for both strength and endurance of the inspiratory muscles can be formulated.

Teaching a more efficient pattern of breathing, although not a physiologic training technique, can alter the work of breathing. Encouraging the use of the diaphragm, the principle and most efficient muscle of inspiration, can decrease the oxygen cost of breathing. Decreasing the use of accessory muscles also decreases the work of breathing. Biofeedback can emphasize the proper use of the diaphragm and inhibit the use of accessory muscles during the ventilatory cycle.

Pursed-lip breathing, when used by patients with COPD, has been shown to decrease respiratory rate and increase tidal volume.[75] Pursed-lip breathing may delay

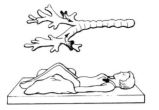

UPPER LOBES Anterior Segments

Bed or drainage table flat.

Patient lies on back with pillow under knees.

Therapist claps between clavicle and nipple on each side.

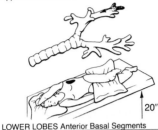

LOWER LOBES Anterior Basal Segments

Foot of table or bed elevated 20 inches.

Patient lies on side, head down, pillow under knees.

Therapist claps with slightly cupped hand over lower ribs. (Position shown is for drainage of <u>left</u> anterior basal segment. To drain the right anterior basal segment, patient should lie on his left side in same posture).

LOWER LOBES Superior Segments

Bed or table flat.

Patient lies on abdomen with two pillows under hips.

Therapist claps over middle of back at tip of scapula on either side of spine.

Figure 15–5. Continued.

or prevent airway collapse, allowing for better gas exchange.[76]

PACING

Pacing referes to the performance of an activity within the limits or boundaries of that patient's breathing capacity. Oftentimes, this means the activity needs

Table 15–6 PRECAUTIONS FOR POSTURAL DRAINAGE

Precautions for the use of the *Trendelenberg* position
  Circulatory: pulmonary edema, congestive heart failure, hypertension
  Abdominal: obesity, abdominal distention, hiatal hernia, nausea, recent food consumption
  Shortness of breath made worse with the Trendelenberg position
Precautions for the use of the sidelying position
  Vascular: axillofemoral bypass graft
  Musculoskeletal: arthritis, recent rib fracture, shoulder bursitis, or tendonitis, any conditioning that would make appropriate postural drainage positioning uncomfortable

Table 15–7 PRECAUTIONS FOR THE USE OF PERCUSSION AND SHAKING

Circulatory: **hemoptysis,** coagulation disorders (increased partial thromboplastin time (PTT) or prothrombin time (PT), platelet count below 50,000
Musculoskeletal: fractured ribs, flail chest, degenerative bone disease

to be broken down into component parts in such a fashion that the activity is performed at a rate that does not exceed breathing limitations. By breaking activities down into component parts, interspersing rest periods between each component, the total activity is completed without dyspnea and fatigue.

The goal of pacing is to safely complete an activity without dyspnea. Pacing can and should be part of every activity that would otherwise cause dyspnea. Pacing refers to daily tasks such as activities of daily living (ADLs), ambulation, stair climbing, and so forth. It is not a technique used during the aerobic portion of a pulmonary rehabilitation program. During exercise, some shortness of breath should and will occur.

SMOKING CESSATION

Smoking is the leading cause of the development of COPD, as well as a contributing cause to many other disease processes; therefore, a special focus on the effects of smoking and smoking cessation should be included in pulmonary rehabilitation programs. According to the 1987 position statement of the American Thoracic Society, smoking cessation should be of highest priority in the comprehensive care of patients with COPD.[16]

There are many types of smoking cessation programs, such as behavior modification, cold turkey, diversion therapy, aversion therapy, nicotine gum, or nicotine patch.[77–81] No one single method of smoking cessation can claim a higher success rate over another in the long run. A comprehensive treatment approach incorporating many different smoking cessation strategies has a higher abstention rate than any single specific technique.[82,83] It is the role of the clinician to guide the patient in his or her efforts to quit smoking, not necessarily to provide this service. The regional offices of the American Lung Association and the American Cancer Society are good resources for local smoking cessation centers.

SUMMARY

Pulmonary rehabilitation programs have become well established in recent years. Components of these programs typically include exercise training, respiratory care instruction, education, and psychosocial support.[84] The slow and steady decreases in a person's activity secondary to increases in pulmonary discomfort can be interrupted by pulmonary rehabilitation. Increases in exercise tolerance have been documented and maintained in follow-up studies.[42,85,86] Increases in functional abilities can make the difference between a life-style of independence and one of dependence. Haas and Cardon[87] reported that for patients who did not receive pulmonary rehabilitation the percentage who were admitted to nursing homes and were not able to provide their own self-care was greater than for patients who did receive pulmonary rehabilitation. A reduction in the number of hospitalizations or hospital days by patients following pulmonary rehabilitation has been reported.[51,65,88-90] Decreases in symptoms and increases in the quality of life for patients who have participated in pulmonary rehabilitation programs have also been reported.[9,42,65,91,92] Physical therapists have the important role of assessing patients, determining their potential, and through exercise prescription and exercise programs, ensuring that rehabilitation goals are realized.

QUESTIONS FOR REVIEW

1. How does the clinical presentation of obstructive disease differ from the clinical presentation of restrictive disease?

2. Explain how increased secretions within the tracheobronchial tree in chronic bronchitis lead to emphysema.

3. What would be the expected breath sounds of a patient with emphysema? With asthma during an exacerbation? (Remember to describe intensity as well as adventitious sounds.)

4. What is the best evaluative test to assess the extent of pulmonary disease?

5. What are the pulmonary end points to a symptom-limited graded exercise test?

6. How does exercise prescription differ for a patient with mild pulmonary disease and the patient with severe pulmonary disease?

7. How do you know when to progress a patient's exercise program? What is the nature of that progression? When is another exercise test warranted?

8. How would you explain stair climbing that utilizes the principles of pacing to a patient with pulmonary disease? How would you combat the patient's assumption that it would take longer to climb stairs with pacing than without?

9. Design a secretion removal treatment plan for a patient with cystic fibrosis that can be carried out by his or her family prior to coming to pulmonary rehabilitation.

10. What evidence is presented in the current literature regarding the benefits of pulmonary rehabilitation?

REFERENCES

1. Hughes, R and Davison R: Limitation of exercise reconditioning in COLD. Chest 83:241, 1983.
2. Pierce, A, et al: Responses to exercise training in patients with emphysema. Arch Intern Med 114:28, 1964.
3. Hale, T, Cumming, G, and Spriggs, J: The effects of physical training in chronic obstructive pulmonary disease. Bull Eur Physiopath Resp 14:593, 1978.
4. Miller, W: Rehabilitation of patients with chronic obstructive pulmonary disease. Med Clin North Am 51:349, 1967.
5. Paez, P, et al: The physiological basis of training patients with emphysema. Am Rev Resp Dis 95:944, 1967.
6. Bass, H, Whitcomb, J, and Forman, R: Exercise training: therapy for patients with chronic obstructive pulmonary disease. Chest 57:116, 1970.
7. Vyas, M, et al: Response to exercise in patients with chronic airway obstruction, I. Effects of exercise training. Am Rev Respir Dis 103:390, 1971.
8. Woolf, C: A rehabilitation program for improving exercise tolerance in patients with chronic lung disease. Can Med Assoc J 106:1289, 1972.
9. Bebout, D, et al: Clinical and physiological outcomes of a university hospital pulmonary rehabilitation program. Respiratory Care 28:1468, 1983.
10. Carter, R, et al: Exercise conditioning in the rehabilitation of patients with chronic obstructive pulmonary disease. Arch Phys Med Rehabil 69:118, 1988.
11. Foster, S and Thomas, H: Pulmonary rehabilitation in lung disease other than chronic obstructive pulmonary disease. Am Rev Respir Dis 141:601, 1990.
12. West, J: Respiratory Physiology: The Essentials. Williams & Wilkins, Baltimore, 1979.
13. Martin, D and Youtsey, J: Respiratory Anatomy and Physiology. CV Mosby, St Louis, 1988.
14. Hammon, W: Pathophysiology of chronic pulmonary disease. In Frownfelter, D (ed): Chest Physical Therapy and Pulmonary Rehabilitation: An Interdisciplinary Approach, ed 2. Year Book Medical Publishers, Chicago, 1987, p 91.
15. Feinleib, M, et al: Trends in COPD morbidity and mortality in the United States. Am Rev Resp Dis 140:S9, 1989.
16. American Thoracic Society. Standards for the diagnosis and care of patients with chronic obstructive pulmonary disease (COPD) and asthma, 1987. Am Rev Respir Dis 136:225, 1987.
17. Thurlbeck, ZW: Chronic airflow obstruction in lung disease. In Major Problems in Pathology, vol 5. WB Saunders, Philadelphia, 1976.
18. Morris, J (Chairman): Chronic obstructive pulmonary disease. American Lung Association Publication, New York, 1981.
19. Farzan, S: A concise handbook of respiratory diseases, ed 2. Reston, Reston, VA, 1985.
20. Sheldon, J: Boyd's Introduction to the Study of Disease, ed 10. Lea & Febiger, Philadelphia, 1988.
21. Wright, J, et al: The detection of small airways disease. Am Rev Respir Dis 129:989, 1984.
22. Cosio, M, et al: The relationship between structural changes in small airways and pulmonary function tests. N Engl J Med 298:1277, 1977.
23. Bates, D: The fate of the chronic bronchitic: A report of the 10-year follow-up in the Canadian department of veteran's affairs coordinated study of chronic bronchitis. Am Rev Respir Dis 108:1043, 1973.
24. Travers, G, Cline, M, and Burrows, B: Predictors of mortality in chronic obstructive pulmonary disease. Am Rev Respir Dis 119:902, 1979.
25. Nemeny, B, et al: Changes in lung function after smoking cessation: an assessment from a cross sectional survery. Am Rev Respir Dis 125:122, 1982.
26. Sibbald, B, et al: Genetic factors in childhood asthma. Thorax 35:671, 1980.
27. Burney, P: Prevalence and mortality from asthma. In Vermeiere, P, Demedts, M, and Yernault, J (ed): Progress in Asthma and COPD. Elsevier Science Publishing Co., Amsterdam, 1989.
28. Berte, J: Critical Care, the Lungs, ed 2. Appleton-Century-Crofts, Norwalk, CT, 1986.
29. Burki, N: Pulmonary Diseases. Medical Examination, Garden City, NY, 1982.
30. Wood, R, Boat, T, and Doershuk, C: State of the art: cystic fibrosis. Am Rev Respir Dis 113:833, 1976.

31. Tecklin, J: Pediatric Physical Therapy. JB Lippincott, Philadelphia, 1989.
32. Murphy, S: Cystic fibrosis in adults: diagnosis and management. Clin Chest Med 8:695, 1987.
33. West, J: Pulmonary Pathophysiology—the Essentials. Williams & Wilkins, Baltimore, 1977.
34. Williams, M: Essentials of pulmonary medicine. WB Saunders, Philadelphia, 1982.
35. Moser, K, Archibald, C, and Hansen, P: Better Living and Breathing, A Manual for Patients, ed 2. CV Mosby, St. Louis, 1980, p 46.
36. Frownfelter, D: Pulmonary rehabilitation. In Frownfelter D: Chest physical therapy and pulmonary rehabilitation. Year Book Medical, Chicago, 1987, p 295.
37. Bell, C, et al: Home Care and Rehabilitation in Respiratory Medicine. JB Lippincott, Philadelphia, 1984.
38. Traver, G: Assessment of the thorax and lungs. Am J Nurs 73:466, 1973.
39. Murphy, R: Auscultation of the lung: past lessons, future possibilities. Thorax 36:99, 1981.
40. Pulmonary terms and symbols: a report of the ACCP-ATS joint committee on pulmonary nomenclature. Chest 67:583, 1975.
41. Forgacs, P: Crackles and wheezes. Lancet 2:203, 1967.
42. Cooper, K: A means of assessing maximal oxygen intake: correlation between field and treadmill walking. JAMA 203:201, 1968.
43. Guyatt, G, Berman, L, and Townsend, M: Long-term outcome after respiratory rehabilitation. Can Med Assoc J 137:1089, 1987.
44. Jones, N: Exercise testing in pulmonary evaluation: rationale, methods and the normal respiratory response to exercise. N Engl J Med 293:541, 1975.
45. Carter, R, et al: Exercise gas exchange in patients with moderate severe to severe chronic obstructive pulmonary disease. J Cardiopulmonary Rehabil 9:243, 1989.
46. Berman, L and Sutton, J: Exercise for the pulmonary patient. J Cardiopulmonary Rehabil 6:55, 1986.
47. Naughton, J, Balke, B, and Poarch, R: Modified work capacity studies in individuals with and without coronary artery disease. J Sports Med 4:208, 1964.
48. Balke, B and Ware, R: An experimental study of physical fitness of air force personnel. US Armed Forces Med J 10:675, 1959.
49. American Thoracic Society: Evaluation of impairment secondary to respiratory disease. Am Rev Resp Dis 126:945, 1982.
50. Weber, K and Janicki, J: Cardiopulmonary exercise testing. WB Saunders, Philadelphia, 1986.
51. Zadai, C: Rehabilitation of the patient with chronic obstructive pulmonary disease. In Irwin, S and Tecklin, J (eds): Cardiopulmonary Physical Therapy. CV Mosby, St. Louis, 1985.
52. Hodgkins, J, Zorn, E, and Connors, G: Pulmonary rehabilitation; guidelines to success. Butterworth, Boston, 1984.
53. Wilson, P, Bell, C, and Norton, A: Rehabilitation of the heart and lungs. Beckman Instruments, Fullerton, CA, 1980.
54. O'Ryan, J and Burns, D: Pulmonary rehabilitation from hospital to home. Yearbook Medical, Chicago, 1984.
55. American College of Sports Medicine. Guidelines for exercise testing and prescription, ed 4. Lea & Febiger, Philadelphia, 1991.
56. American Heart Association Medical/Scientific Statement: Special report—exercise standards—a statement for health professionals. The American Heart Association. Circulation 82:2286, 1990.
57. American College of Sports Medicine 1990: Position stand: the recommended quantity and quality of exercise for developing and maintaining cardiorespiratory and muscular fitness in healthy adults. Med Sci Sports Exerc 22:265, 1990.
58. Karvonen, M, Kentala, K, and Mustala, O: The effects of training on heart rate: a longitudinal study. Ann Med Exp Biol Fenn 35:307, 1957.
59. Davis, J and Convertino, V: A comparison of heart rate methods for predicting endurance training intensity. Med Sci Sports 7:295, 1975.
60. Pollock, ML and Wilmore, JH (eds): Exercise in Health and Disease Evaluation and Prescription for Prevention and Rehabilitation, ed 2. WB Saunders, Philadelphia, 1990.
61. Borg, G: Psychophysical bases of perceived exertion. Med Sci Sports Exerc 14:377, 1982.
62. Noble, B: Clinical applications of perceived exertion. Med Sci Sports Exerc 14:406, 1982.
63. Hodgkins, J: Prognosis in chronic obstructive pulmonary disease. Clin Chest Med 11:555, 1990.
64. Reis, A: Endurance exercise training at maximal targets in patients with chronic obstructive pulmonary disease. J Cardiopulmonary Rehabil 7:594, 1987.
65. Ries, A: Position paper of the American Association of Cardiovascular and Pulmonary Rehabilitation: scientific basis of pulmonary rehabilitation. J Cardiopulmonary Rehabil 10:418, 1990.
66. Belman, M: Exercise in chronic obstructive pulmonary disease. Clin Chest Med 7:585, 1986.
67. Elkousy, N, et al: Outpatient pulmonary rehabilitation: a medicare fiscal intermediary's viewpoint. J Cardiopulmonary Rehabil 11:492, 1988.
68. Kigin, C: Advances in chest physical therapy. In Current Advances in Respiratory Care, American College of Chest Physicians, Parkridge, IL, 1984.
69. Chopra, S, et al: Effects of hydration and physical therapy on tracheal transport velocity. Am Rev Resp Dis 115:1009, 1977.
70. Denton, R: Bronchial secretions in cystic fibrosis. Am Rev Resp Dis 86:41, 1962.
71. Mazzocco, M, et al: Physiologic effects of chest percussion and postural drainage in patients with bronchiectasis. Chest 88:360, 1985.
72. Zack, M and Oberwaldner, B: Chest physiotherapy—the mechanical approach to antiinfective therapy in cystic fibrosis. Infection 15:381, 1987.
73. Hietpas, B, Roth, R, and Jensen, W: Huff coughing and airway patency. Resp Care 24:710, 1979.
74. Sonne, L and David, J: Increased exercise performance in patients with severe COPD following inspiratory resistive training. Chest 81:436, 1982.
75. Thoman, R, Stoker, G, and Ross, J: The efficacy of pursed-lips breathing in patients with chronic obstructive pulmonary disease. Am Rev Respir Dis 93:100, 1966.
76. Kigin, C: Breathing exercises for the medical patient: the art and the science. Phys Ther 70:700, 1990.
77. Harris, M and Rothberg, C: A self-control approach to reducing smoking. Psychol Rep 31:165, 1972.
78. Horn, D and Waingrow, S: Some dimensions of a model for smoking behavior change. Am J Public Health 56(Suppl 12):21, 1966.
79. Relinger, J, et al: Utilization of adverse rapid smoking in groups: efficacy of treatment and maintenance procedures. J Consult Clin Psychol 45:245, 1977.
80. Russell, M, Raw, M, and Jarvis, M: Clinical use of nicotine chewing gum. BMJ 280:1599, 1980.
81. Guilford, J: Group treatment versus individual initiative in the cessation of smoking. J Appl Psychol 56:162, 1972.
82. Peters, J and Lim, V: Smoking cessation techniques. In Hodgkins, J, Zorn, E, and Connors, G (eds): Pulmonary Rehabilitation: Guidelines to Success. Butterworth, Boston, 1984.
83. Lando, J: Successful treatment of smokers with a broad spectrum behavior approach. J Consult Clin Psychol 45:361, 1977.
84. Eakin E, et al: Clinical trial of rehabilitation in chronic obstructive pulmonary disease: compliance as a mediator of change in exercise endurance. J Cardiopulmonary Rehabil 12:105, 1992.
85. Swerts, M, et al: Exercise training as a mediator of increased exercise performance in patients with chronic obstructive pulmonary disease. J Cardiopulmonary Rehabil 12:188, 1992.
86. Tydeman, D, et al: An investigation into the effects of exercise tolerance training on patients with chronic airways obstruction. Physiotherapy 70:261, 1984.
87. Haas, A and Cardon, H: Rehabilitation in chronic obstructive pulmonary disease: a 5 year study of 252 male patients. Med Clin North Am 53:593, 1969.
88. Lertzman, M and Cherniack, R: Rehabilitation of patients with chronic obstructive pulmonary disease. Am Rev Respir Dis 114:1145, 1976.
89. Hudson, L, Tyler, M, and Petty, T: Hospitalization needs during an outpatient rehabilitation program for severe chronic airway obstruction. Chest 70:606, 1976.
90. Jensen, P: Risk, protective factors, and supportive interventions in chronic airway obstruction. Arch Gen Psychiatry 40:1203, 1983.
91. Petty, T, et al: A comprehensive care program for chronic airway obstruction: methods and preliminary evaluation of symptomatic and functional improvement. Ann Intern Med 70:1109, 1969.
92. Mall, R and Medeiros, M: Objective evaluation of results of a pulmonary rehabilitation program in a community hospital. Chest 94:1156, 1988.

SUPPLEMENTAL READINGS

American College of Sports Medicine. Guidelines for Exercise Testing and Prescription, ed 4. Lea & Febiger, Philadelphia, 1991.

American Thoracic Society: Standards for the diagnosis and care of patients with chronic obstructive pulmonary disease (COPD) and asthma. Am Rev Respir Dis 136:225, 1987.

Brannon, F, Foley, M, and Starr, J: Cardiopulmonary Rehabilitation: Basic Theory and Application. FA Davis, Philadelphia, 1992.

Farzan, S: A Concise Handbook of Respiratory Diseases, ed 2. Reston, Reston, VA, 1985.

Frownfelter, D: Chest Physical Therapy and Pulmonary Rehabilitation: An Interdisciplinary Approach, ed 2. Year Book Medical, Chicago, 1987.

Harper, R: A Guide to Respiratory Care. JB Lippincott, Philadelphia, 1981.

Hodgkins, J, Zorn, E, and Connors, G: Pulmonary Rehabilitation: Guidelines to Success. Butterworth, Boston, 1984.

Irwin, S and Tecklin, J (eds): Cardiopulmonary Physical Therapy, ed 2. CV Mosby, St Louis, 1989.

Lehnert, B and Schachter, EN: The Pharmacology of Respiratory Care. CV Mosby, St Louis, 1980.

Martin, D and Youtsey, J: Respiratory Anatomy and Physiology. CV Mosby, St Louis, 1988.

O'Ryan, J and Burns, D: Pulmonary Rehabilitation from Hospital to Home. Year Book Medical, Chicago, 1984.

Ries, A: Position paper of the American Association of Cardiovascular and Pulmonary Rehabilitation: Scientific basis of pulmonary rehabilitation. J Cardiopulmonary Rehabil 10:418, 1990.

GLOSSARY

Adventitious breath sounds: Crackles or wheezes; heard, during auscultation, in addition to the overall quality of the breath sound.

Aerobic exercise: Any sustained exercise where the required energy is supplied by the available oxygen within the system.

Asthma: A clinical syndrome characterized by increased reactivity of the tracheobronchial tree to various stimuli.

Atelectasis: Alveolar collapse involving part or all of the lung due to the complete absorption of gas or the inability of the alveoli to expand.

Auscultation: Listening through the chest wall to air movement by means of a stethoscope.

Bronchial breath sounds: A hollow or echoing breath sound that occupies more of the ventilatory cycle than normal.

Bronchospasm: Contraction of the smooth muscle within the walls of the airways to cause narrowing of the lumen.

Chronic bronchitis: A clinical syndrome characterized by persistent cough and expectoration for at least a 3-month period for at least 2 consecutive years.

Cor pulmonale: Right ventricular enlargement from a primary pulmonary cause.

Crackles: An adventitious sound heard during lung auscultation and related to the opening of previously closed small airways and alveoli.

Cyanosis: A bluish coloration of the skin in response to hypoxemia.

Cystic fibrosis: A genetic disorder characterized by an exocrine gland dysfunction that results in abnormally viscid secretions.

Decreased breath sounds: Diminished or distant sounds heard during lung auscultation.

Digital clubbing: A sign of hypoxemia in which the tip of the distal phalynx (finger or toe) becomes bulbous and the nail of that digit exits at an increased angle.

Emphysema: An abnormal enlargement of the distal respiratory unit that is accompanied by destructive changes of the alveolar walls without obvious fibrosis.

Exercise prescription: An individualized exercise program specifying mode, intensity, frequency, and duration.

Expiratory reserve volume: The volume of air that can be exhaled following a normal resting exhalation.

Flail chest: Two or more ribs broken in two or more places.

Forced expiratory volume (FEV): The volume of air forcibly exhaled during the first second of a forced vital capacity maneuver.

Functional residual capacity (FRC): The amount of air remaining in the lung after a normal resting exhalation. Expiratory reserve volume plus the residual volume equals functional residual capacity.

Graded exercise test (GXT): The observation and recording of an individual's cardiopulmonary responses during gradually increasing exercise challenges to determine the body's capacity to adapt to physical work. Tests may be maximal or submaximal.

Hemoptysis: The presence of blood in the sputum.

Hypercapnia: An increase in the amount of carbon dioxide within the arterial blood.

Hyperinflation: An abnormal increase in the amount of air within the lung tissue.

Hyperlucency: An increase in the penetration of x-rays seen on a good quality chest radiograph; it indicates hyperinflation of the chest.

Hyperreactivity: An increase in the sensitivity of the airway walls to stimuli.

Hypocapnea: A decrease in the amount of carbon dioxide within the arterial blood.

Hypoventilation: An increase in the amount of carbon dioxide within the arterial blood due to a decrease in alveolar ventilation.

Hypoxemia: A decrease in the amount of oxygen within the arterial blood.

Inspiratory capacity: The total amount of air that can be inspired after a tidal exhalation. Inspiratory reserve volume plus residual volume equals inspiratory capacity.

Inspiratory reserve volume: The amount of air that can be inspired after a tidal inspiration.

Metabolic equivalent (MET): A rating of energy expenditure for a given activity based on oxygen consumption. One MET equals 3.5 ml of oxygen used per kilogram of body weight per minute.

Oxygen consumption (VO_2): The volume of oxygen that is used by the tissues in 1 minute.

Pacing: The breaking down of an activity of daily living (ADL) into manageable components, with interspersed rest periods between each component such that the ADL can be completed without any occurrence of dyspnea.

Percussion: A force rhythmically applied with the therapist's cupped hands to the patient's thorax and thought to release secretions from the wall of the airways.

Perfusion (pulmonary): Blood flow through the pulmonary vascular bed.

Peripheral airways disease: Inflammation, fibrosis, and narrowing of the terminal and respiratory bronchioles.

Postural drainage: Positioning a patient such that the bronchus is perpendicular to the ground and the mucociliary transport of secretions is facilitated.

Rate of perceived shortness of breath: A subjective assessment of shortness of breath as it relates to exercise intensity.

Residual volume: The amount of air that remains in the lungs at the end of a full exhalation.

Respiration: The exchange of gas within the body. External respiration is the exchange of gas between the alveoli and the pulmonary capillaries. Internal respiration is the exchange of gas between the capillaries and the working cells of the body.

Restrictive lung disease: A group of pulmonary disorders characterized by difficulty in expanding the lungs and a reduction in total lung volume.

Retractions: The inward movement of the intercostal spaces during inspiration, usually during respiratory distress.

Shaking: A bouncing maneuver applied to the rib cage throughout the expiratory phase of breathing by the hands of the therapist. It is thought to assist the mucociliary transport system.

Tidal volume: The amount of air that is inspired or expired during normal resting ventilation.

Total lung capacity: The volume of air that is within the lungs at full inspiration.

Trendelenberg position: An inclined bed position such that the head of the bed is lower than the foot.

Ventilation: The act of moving air in and out of the lungs.

Vesicular breath sounds: The normal intensity of a breath sound heard during auscultation of the lungs.

Vital capacity: The greatest volume of air that can be exhaled from a full inspiration, or the greatest volume of air that can be inhaled from a full exhalation.

Wheeze: A musical adventitious sound heard during lung auscultation when expired air is forced through a narrowed airway.

CHAPTER 16

Coronary Artery Disease

Susan B. O'Sullivan

OBJECTIVES

1. Define terms associated with the pathology and management of coronary artery disease.
2. Describe the etiology, pathophysiology, symptomatology, and sequela of coronary artery disease.
3. Describe diagnostic and evaluative procedures commonly associated with coronary artery disease.
4. Describe the rehabilitative management of the patient with coronary artery disease.
5. Evaluate the therapist's role in the management of patients with coronary artery disease.

Cardiovascular disease is the leading cause of death in the United States today, accounting for nearly 1 million deaths each year (43% of all deaths). An estimated 70 million Americans have one or more forms of heart and blood vessel disease.[1] This high incidence is seen primarily in Western industrialized societies and can be regarded as a manifestation of civilization and progress.[2] However, this picture appears to be changing. The American Heart Association reports an absolute decline in deaths from cardiovascular disease in recent years.[3,4] Despite this downward trend, these diseases remain the leading cause of death and morbidity in the United States. Their effect can be measured both in terms of the disabilities produced and the economic burden placed on the patient, family, and community as a result of health care costs and loss of income.

EPIDEMIOLOGY OF CARDIOVASCULAR DISEASES

Epidemiologic studies reveal that certain risk factors are associated with the development of cardiovascular disease. Studies such as the Framingham Study in Framingham, Massachusetts, have helped to identify a variety of factors that increase a person's risk of developing cardiovascular disease. Major risk factors identified that can be modified through life-style changes and include high blood pressure, high blood **cholesterol,** cigarette smoking, and physical inactivity. Other contributing and potentially modifiable risk factors include diabetes mellitus, obesity, and stress. Risk factors that cannot be changed included heredity, male sex, and increasing age. These risk factors permit the likelihood of developing cardiovascular disease to be predicted before the actual symptoms appear. The more risk factors an indi-

vidual presents or the greater the problem with any single risk factor, the greater is the overall risk of cardiovascular disease. It is important to note that the effect of two or more risk factors is not additive in nature but rather that the risk multiplies with each additional factor.[4] In an effort to reduce the risk of developing cardiovascular disease, the American Heart Association recommends screening for risk factors and the routine application of preventive measures.[5] As individuals continue to modify their life-style and maintain an interest in their personal health, the incidence of coronary heart disease may continue to decrease.

CLINICAL MANIFESTATIONS OF CARDIOVASCULAR DISEASES

Arteriosclerosis, commonly called hardening of the arteries, includes a variety of conditions that cause the artery walls to thicken and lose elasticity. The resulting symptoms vary according to the type of vessel involved, and the site and extent of disease within the vessel. Arteriosclerosis, which affects the innermost layer of the vessels, is called type I or intimal arteriosclerosis. Progressive hardening of the arteries occurs normally in most individuals as they grow older. When the intimal lesion exceeds the thickness of the media or middle layer the vessel is considered atherosclerotic. **Atherosclerosis** is defined as a form of arteriosclerosis in which the inner layers are made thick and irregular by deposits of a fatty substance, cholesterol; cellular waste products; calcium; and fibrin. The internal channel of arteries becomes partially or totally blocked, and blood supply is reduced. Atherosclerosis is seen in large and medium-sized vessels. Type II or medial sclerosis affects the middle layer of the vessel and results in calcification and hypertrophy.

Individuals with this type of arteriosclerosis develop pipestem or rigid arteries, typically in medium-sized vessels such as the brachial artery. Blood flow is not usually reduced. Type III or arteriolar sclerosis affects small blood vessels, with characteristic changes in both the media and intima. Blood flow is reduced and hypertension results.[6,7]

The pathogenic process of atherosclerosis is thought to begin with an initial injury to the endothelial cells and sublying intima. Damage may be caused by physical abrasion by blood substances, or by arterial blood pressures pulsating on the vessel wall. Following the initial injury, endothelial cells swell and platelets adhere to the vessel wall, causing proliferation of smooth muscle cells and the binding of lipid substances. In the later stages of atherosclerosis these fatty streaks develop into mature atheromatous plaques stimulated by a platelet-derived growth factor that causes continued proliferation of fibroblasts and smooth muscle cells. As this process continues, progressive narrowing of the vessel results. The protrusion of rough plaques into the circulating blood causes blood clots to develop. The end result is often the formation of a **thrombosis** (a blood clot within a vessel) or an **embolus** (a blood clot that forms in the blood vessels in one part of the body and travels to another). Rupture of the degenerated area is also possible.[6-8]

Clinical manifestations of coronary artery disease (CAD) include ischemia, infarction, sudden death, and heart failure. **Ischemia** is a temporary oxygen deficiency of the tissues. **Angina pectoris** is an example of an ischemic condition in which the heart muscle receives an insufficient oxygen and blood supply, with resultant pain in the chest. Ischemic symptoms are reversible events but may herald more serious cardiovascular pathology. **Myocardial infarction** or cell death occurs when the blood supply is severely reduced (an occlusion of greater than 75% of the supplying artery) or stopped. Infarction is an irreversible injury. **Aneurysm** is a dilation or saclike bulging of a vessel or wall. These weakened areas may rupture, often in hypertensive patients, and cause sudden death.

The leading cause of sudden death in individuals with cardiovascular disease is electrical complication caused by **arrhythmias.** An arrhythmia (dysrhythmia) is the loss of, or an irregularity in, normal heart rhythm. **Heart failure** is the mechanical failure of the heart to maintain adequate circulation of the blood. Heart failure after infarction results from the heart's inability to pump out all the blood it receives.[4,9]

Typically, the patient with myocardial infarction presents with atherosclerotic involvement of two or three coronary arteries in which 75 percent or more of the lumen of the vessel is restricted. The overt signs of disease normally do not occur until the obstruction is relatively severe and the disease is in its chronic stage. It has also been estimated that 25 percent of patients with coronary artery disease present with sudden death as their first and only symptom.[10] The long-term prognosis for the survivors of coronary artery disease depends upon the extent and location of the existing disease.

Determinants of Coronary Artery Disease

The clinical manifestations of coronary artery disease (CAD) represent an imbalance between the oxygen demands of the heart and the available oxygen supply. Several factors determine the myocardial oxygen demands (MVO_2). The major determinants include **heart rate,** contractility of the myocardium and intramyocardial tension, which is the product of ventricular pressure and volume (Fig. 16–1).[11]

Oxygen supply to the heart is determined by coronary blood flow and the oxygen content of arterial blood. Blood is delivered to the myocardium by the right and left coronary arteries, which come directly off the aorta and branch into a vascular network that supplies the heart (Fig. 16–2). Familiarity with coronary circulation will improve the reader's understanding of the clinical relevance of an occlusion, since the location will determine to a large degree any residual functional abnormalities.

The right coronary artery (RCA) originates from the aorta and runs inferior in the atrioventricular sulcus. It supplies the right atrium and most of the right ventricle. It commonly gives off a branch to the left ventricle, supplying portions of the posterior and inferior walls. It also supplies the conduction system of the heart (SA node, AV node, and bundle of His) and the interventricular septum.

The left coronary artery (LCA) also originates from the aorta and bifurcates into two branches, the left anterior descending artery and the circumflex branch. The left anterior descending artery supplies the anterior, superior, and lateral walls of the left ventricle and portions of the interventricular septum. It may also give off branches to the right ventricle. The left circumflex artery supplies the lateral and inferior walls of the left ventricle and portions of the left atrium. It may also supply portions of the posterior wall.

While these patterns represent those commonly found in coronary circulation, it is important to note that the

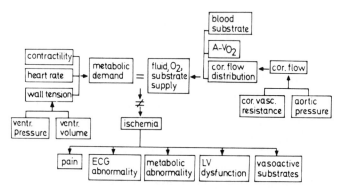

Figure 16–1. The oxygen supply-demand relationships for patients with ischemic heart disease. Supply and delivery are influenced by multiple factors. When contractility, wall tension, heart rate, or other parameters in the left side of the diagram are increased, there must be a corresponding increase in delivery. If there is no increase in delivery, ischemia may result. (From Ellestad, M: Stress Testing Principles and Practice, ed 2, FA Davis, Philadelphia, 1980, p 24, with permission.)

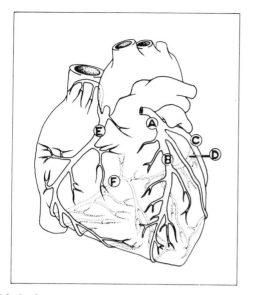

Figure 16–2. Coronary circulation. (A) Left main coronary artery, (B) left anterior descending coronary artery, (C) left circumflex coronary artery, (D) posterior circumflex coronary artery, (E) right coronary artery, and (F) Posterior descending artery.

distribution of blood supply is variable from individual to individual. Since the left ventricle is the major pumping station for the body, the left coronary system, which supplies up to 70 percent of the left ventricular mass, becomes the most significant branch in terms of myocardial injury and residual functional work capacity. The most common site of severe narrowing and infarction in the LCA is within the first 2 cm of the origin of the left anterior descending and left circumflex arteries; in the RCA, narrowing and infarction occur more frequently in the distal third of the artery.[8]

Myocardial metabolism is essentially aerobic and requires a very high rate of oxygen extraction from the blood, as well as a continuous flow of blood through the myocardium. With exercise at any level very little additional oxygen extraction can occur. Therefore the increased demands of the myocardium must be met by increasing the total volume of coronary blood flow. At rest, most of the left ventricular coronary flow occurs during diastole. Thus, diastolic pressure and duration are important determinants of coronary blood flow. **Tachycardia** (heart rate greater than 100 beats/min) reduces diastolic time and may significantly reduce blood flow, causing ischemia in patients with coronary artery disease;[12] therefore, regulation of heart rate is essential if the symptoms of ischemia (angina, left ventricular dysfunction, or electrical instability) are to be prevented. Myocardial performance with increasing intensities of exercise may be altered in coronary artery disease. **Stroke volume** may decrease instead increasing as anticipated, and this decrease may cause exercise-induced hypotension. This is termed inotropic incompetence. Heart rate may not increase linearly with increasing workload intensity, as expected, or it may decrease. This response has been termed chronotropic incompetence. Both inotropic and chronotropic incompetence are markers of a poor prognosis.[13]

The autonomic nervous system also influences the heart and blood vessels through both direct neural and indirect neurohumoral effects. Sympathetic fibers increase the overall activity of the heart, increasing both the rate and force of contraction and myocardial metabolism. Parasympathetic stimulation produces the opposite effect, decreasing the overall activity and metabolism of the heart. Sympathetic stimulation constricts coronary as well as most other arteries, causing increased flow resistance and elevating pressures. Parasympathetic stimulation has almost no effects on blood vessels, although pressures generally fall due to decreased pumping action of the heart. Indirectly the sympathetic nervous system regulates coronary vascular resistance by stimulating the adrenal cortex to secrete **catecholamines,** norepinephrine and epinephrine, into the circulating bloodstream. This hormonal release causes similar but more long-lasting and potent effects than direct sympathetic stimulation. Blood vessels vasoconstrict and heart activity is increased. Control of these responses is exerted by the central nervous system in the vasomotor center located in the brainstem. Arterial pressure is regulated by the vasomotor center through the baroreceptor reflex. This reflex is activated by pressure or stretch receptors located in the walls of large systemic arteries, especially in the internal carotid arteries and the aortic arch. Chemoreceptors located in the carotid and aortic bodies react to changes in arterial oxygen concentration and, through brainstem activation, exert a controlling influence on blood pressure as well as respiration. Stimulation of the motor cortex, hypothalamus, or other higher nervous centers can excite or inhibit the vasomotor center in response to exertion, or emotional or alarm patterns. Catecholamine levels elevated by stress or cigarette smoking can contribute to the pathogenesis of hypertension, endothelial damage, and atherosclerosis.[6,10]

The Patient with Angina

Angina pectoris is pain secondary to temporary, localized ischemia. It is substernal in location, although some patients experience radiation into the left shoulder and arm. Patients complain of retrosternal burning, numbness, or discomfort. Onset may be gradual or sudden. Other symptoms, such as dyspnea, indigestion, dizziness, syncope, and anxiety, may also be noted during the attack. Classic angina is precipitated by physical exertion. Distress may be brought on sooner by less activity in hot or cold temperatures, after eating, or during periods of emotional stress. The ischemia that results from the inadequate coronary blood flow causes depressed left ventricular function, which is evidenced by changes in the **electrocardiogram (ECG)**, chiefly by **ST segment depression.** Angina is a reversible symptom and can be relieved by rest or removal of the precipitating cause. It can also be managed with drugs, for example, nitroglycerin. The term **stable angina** is used to refer to pain that has been present for some time, is brought on by exertion, and is relieved by rest and nitroglycerin. **Unstable angina** (also termed preinfarction angina) is characterized by a change in the quality, frequency, intensity, duration, or timing of pain. Thus pain may occur at rest, without any obvious precipitating factor, with minimal effort, or for prolonged periods. A crescendo effect may also be evident, with increasing difficulty in controlling the pain. Patients with unstable angina are at risk for myocardial infarction or sudden death.[9,14]

Clinically, angina is evaluated by determining the angina threshold, defined as the level of physical activity that usually precipitates the signs of cardiac dysfunction (pain) and electrical instability. Patients with angina typically develop symptoms at a consistent level of their rate-pressure product (heart rate × systolic blood pressure). This information may be obtained from a personal history or by observing the patient's performance on a graded exercise test, which is a measured exercise challenge designed to determine an individual's functional capacity during a physical stress. Angina may also be investigated with radionuclide imaging (e.g., thallium scan), magnetic resonance imaging (MRI), or coronary angiography (injection of radiopaque dye and x-ray). These tests allow for improved determination of the exact location and extent of coronary artery disease and appropriate therapeutic intervention.[4,9]

The Postsurgical Patient

In cases of severe, disabling CAD, balloon **angioplasty** (percutaneous transluminal coronary angioplasty or PTCA) or **coronary artery bypass graft** (CABG) may be recommended to achieve revascularization of the myocardium. Balloon angioplasty involves the threading of a balloon-tipped catheter into the coronary arteries to the point of the blockage. Inflation of the balloon tip compresses the atherosclerotic plaque, widening the diameter of the blood vessel. The balloon tip is then deflated and the catheter withdrawn. About 25 percent of people who have this procedure experience renarrowing of the artery, usually within the first 6 months.[4] A CABG procedure involves bypassing one or more obstructed arteries, either by the anastomosing of a vein graft from the aorta to the coronary artery at a point distal to the obstruction, or by patch grafting to widen the obstructed artery. Postsurgical patients who may be candidates for a rehabilitation program include those with pacemaker implantation, valve replacement, or cardiac transplant.

The Patient with Myocardial Infarction

Myocardial infarction (MI) is the death of myocardial tissue secondary to prolonged ischemia. It is the result of thrombus formation with complete occlusion or severe stenosis (greater than 75%) of a coronary artery. It is often associated with one or more of the following symptoms: uncomfortable pressure, fullness, squeezing or pain in the center of the chest, lasting more than a few minutes; radiating pain to the shoulders, neck, or jaw; chest discomfort with lightheadedness, fainting, sweating, nausea, or shortness of breath.[4] The functional damage that results is permanent, and the prognosis depends upon the artery involved, the amount of cardiac muscle tissue involved, and the patency and adequacy of the remaining circulation. Infarction places an increased load on healthy myocardial tissue, which may then become abnormal with time. Metabolic and electrical abnormalities are caused by the necrosis and natural healing process.[9,10]

Vital signs are typically altered. Temperature elevation is common during the initial few days following MI. Heart rates may be abnormally slow (bradycardia) or fast (tachycardia). **Dyspnea** is a common finding and is associated with left ventricular dysfunction, as is a hypotensive systolic pressure. Auscultation of the heart may reveal abnormal heart sounds (e.g., extra S3 and S4 heart sounds). Normally only S1 (mitral and tricuspid valve closure) and S2 (pulmonic and aortic valve closure) sounds are heard. An S3 sound is indicative of ventricular filling, which is associated with large infarctions and poor ventricular compliance. An S4 sound is indicative of decreased ventricular compliance during atrial systole. Heart murmurs may also be present.[14]

Laboratory tests usually reveal an elevation in the white blood cell count, and **serum enzyme** levels. Serum enzymes are the most powerful diagnostic tool of the three. Many times these are termed cardiac enzymes, although they are released in instances of cell death other than myocardial infarction. These enzymes include serum glutamic-oxaloacetic transaminase (SGOT), also known as aspartate aminotransferase (AST), lactate dehydrogenase (LDH), and creatine phosphokinase (CPK). Figure 16–3 indicates the characteristic levels of elevation and the time frame in which they remain elevated following myocardial infarction. Separation of CPK into isoenzymes by electrophoresis

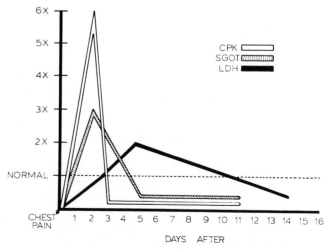

Figure 16–3. Cardiac enzyme elevation following myocardial infarction. Creatine phosphokinase and SGOT characteristically begin to rise early and reach peak activity 24 hours after onset; activity returns to normal by the 3rd to 5th days. SLDH begins to rise 12 to 24 hours following infarction and reaches peak activity by day 3. Activity may remain elevated as long as 10 days after onset. SGOT = serum glutamic-oxaloacetic transaminase.

or radioimmunoassay has revealed a specific isoenzyme released in cardiac muscle necrosis, known as MB-CPK. It appears within 4 hours of infarction and peaks by 36 hours.[7,15] Serum lipids (total cholesterol, LDL levels) are also typically elevated in CAD.

The electrocardiographic changes resulting from acute myocardial infarction remain one of the most reliable cues in diagnosing infarction. These changes may appear as early as 30 minutes or, rarely, as late as 2 weeks following the insult. Characteristically, the center zone of infarcted tissue cannot depolarize or repolarize and becomes a "functional hole" in the normal conduction of the myocardium. Pathologic Q waves become apparent in the ECG (if the height of the Q wave is greater than one-quarter of the size of the R wave it is considered indicative of myocardial infarction). The muscle tissue that surrounds the infarcted area is called the zone of injury and causes elevation of the ST segment on the electrocardiogram. Adjacent to this area is an area of ischemic tissue that causes the T wave to invert (Figs. 16–4 and 16–5). During the recovery process, the ST segment often returns to normal within a few days, and the T wave returns to normal within a few months; however, the abnormal Q wave usually remains. The electrocardiogram can be used to localize the site of the infarct by studying the appearance of the Q waves in the 12 different leads. Since each lead picks up an electrical signal from a slightly different angle it is possible to locate the infarcted area within certain limits. These changes are summarized in Table 16–1.[16-18]

Imaging may reveal abnormal wall movements, valvular function, and **ejection fractions**. Additional testing may also include radionuclide imaging studies. A thallium scan may reveal "cold spots" suggestive of ischemia or old infarction. "Hot spots" indicate acute infarction. Positron emission tomography (PET scans) can also identify ischemia and infarcted areas. Cardiac **catheterization** and coronary arteriography can be used to visualize the coronary arteries and stenotic areas prior to surgery.[14]

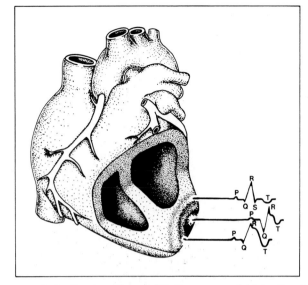

Figure 16–5. Electrocardiogram following myocardial infarction. The inner zone represents the zone of infarction, which causes a large Q wave to appear on the electrocardiogram. The middle zone represents the zone of injury, which causes elevation of the ST segment on the electrocardiogram. The outer zone represents the zone of ischemia, which causes the T wave to invert on the electrocardiogram.

CARDIAC COMPLICATIONS

Following an MI, patients may develop any number of complications. Electrical instability is the most common, and predisposes the patient to dysrhythmias.

Cardiogenic shock is seen in acute MI when there is a loss of more than 40 percent of ventricular muscle (pump failure). It results in a severe reduction of cardiac output and **blood pressure** and contributes to reduced coronary flow, additional myocardial ischemia and

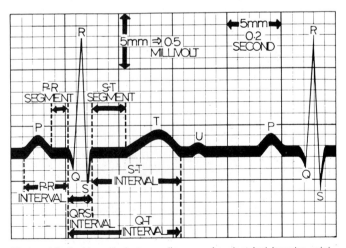

Figure 16–4. Normal electrocardiogram. An electrical impulse originates from the SA node and spreads across the atria, depolarizing them and yielding a P wave. At the atrioventricular node there is a brief 1/10 second pause followed by depolarization of the ventricles, yielding a QRS complex. The T wave represents ventricular repolarization.

Table 16–1 ELECTROCARDIOGRAPHIC CHANGES FOLLOWING MYOCARDIAL INFARCTION

A. Sequential phases in infarction	
1. Acute	ST elevation (earliest change)
	Tall, hyperacute T waves
	New Q or QS wave
2. Evolving	Deep T wave inversions may persist; usually returns to normal (months)
	ST elevation returns to baseline (days)
	Q or QS waves may decrease in size, rarely disappear
B. Infarction type	
1. Subendocardial intramural	ST-T changes: ST depression or T wave inversion
	Without QRS changes
2. Transmural	Abnormal Q or QS waves in leads overlying the infarct
	ST-T changes
C. Infarction site*	
1. Anterior infarction:	Q or QS in V1 to V4
2. Lateral infarction:	Q or QS in lead I, aV1
3. Inferior infarction:	Q or QS in leads II, III, aVf
4. Posterior infarction:	Large R waves in V1–V3
	ST depression V1, V2, or V3

Adapted from Goldberger and Goldberger,[16] and Conover.[17]

*Standard 12-lead electrocardiogram: leads I to III, aVr, aV1, and aVf are limb leads; V1 to V6 are chest leads.

Table 16–2 DECONDITIONING EFFECTS OF PROLONGED BEDREST

A decrease in physical work capacity
An increase in the heart rate response to effort
A decrease in adaptability to change in posture, which is manifest primarily as orthostatic hypotension
A decrease in the circulation blood volume (with plasma volume) decreasing to a greater extent than red cell mass)
A decrease in lung volume and vital capacity
A decrease in serum protein concentration
A negative nitrogen and calcium balance
A decrease in the contractile strength of the body musculature

From Wenger, N: *Coronary Care: Rehabilitation after Myocardial Infarction.* American Heart Association, New York, 1973. By permission of the American Heart Association.

necrosis (extension of infarct). The mortality rate for patients developing cardiogenic shock is very high, about 80 percent. Heart failure results when cardiac output fails to meet metabolic demands of the body. It may result from a number of other causes in addition to acute MI (e.g., hypertension, valvular disease, congenital heart disease, cardiomyopathy). Cardiac failure is characterized by a reduction in cardiac output and an elevation of ventricular and diastolic filling pressure. Initially failure may affect one ventricle or the other but eventually both are affected. Failure of the left ventricle results in **pulmonary edema.** This condition can be life-threatening and results from increased pulmonary venous pressures. The term **congestive heart failure** indicates circulatory congestion resulting from heart failure, and is manifested by retention of fluid and the formation of edema. **Cardiomegaly,** an enlargement of the heart, may result from dilatation and/or hypertrophy. It is seen on radiographs in patients with long-standing angina or with recurrent infarctions. **Ventricular aneurysm** or rupture of the ventricular wall may occur secondary to the liquefaction stage of necrosis of the myocardium. Ischemic injury to the papillary muscles may result in **mitral insufficiency** (mitral valve regurgitation and heart murmurs). Thromboemboli in peripheral (thrombophlebitis) or pulmonary veins may result from prolonged bed rest and inactivity.[9,19]

Contraindications for entry into inpatient and outpatient exercise programs are presented in Table 16–2. Rehabilitation may be possible for some of these patients as their complications resolve and their condition stabilizes. Patients without complications can be referred for rehabilitation programming almost immediately.

MEDICAL MANAGEMENT

The patient recovering from MI or cardiac surgery is usually admitted to the coronary care unit (CCU) with a period of complete bed rest, followed by modified bed rest for the rest of the hospital stay. The patient is typically transferred from the CCU to a step-down hospital unit (e.g., progressive care, cardiac rehabilitation unit) for the remainder of the hospitalization. Since electrical

complications may be numerous and these represent the leading cause of sudden death, continuous electrocardiographic monitoring is instituted immediately. This continues for the first few days of hospitalization, after which modified monitoring or radiotelemetry (ambulatory monitoring) may be used during the remainder of the hospitalization.

Pharmacology

Cardiovascular pharmacologic agents are critical elements in the medical management of patients with CAD. There is a wide spectrum of medications available, with new drugs being developed all the time. Patients may be given any of a number of agents, including **antiarrhythmic** agents, antihypertensive agents, nitrites and nitroglycerin drugs, **beta-blockers, calcium channel blockers, digitalis,** diuretics, vasodilators, hyperlipidemic agents, bronchodilators, and peripheral vasodilators. It is beyond the scope of this text to address this complex topic. For further study, the reader is referred to excellent texts by Ciccone[20] and Malone.[21] Therapists working with patients having CAD must be familiar with these medications, including the indications, side effects, and associated hemodynamic responses at rest and with exercise. The effects of some of the more widely used cardiac drugs on heart rate, blood pressure, ECG findings, and exercise are effectively discussed in *Guidelines for Exercise Testing and Prescription* by the American College of Sports Medicine.[22]

REHABILITATIVE PROGRAMMING FOR THE PATIENT WITH CORONARY ARTERY DISEASE

Cardiac rehabilitation is a multiphasic program designed to assist the patient with CAD in returning to a full and productive life. A multidisciplinary team typically consists of physician, nurse, physical and occupational therapists, nutritionist, psychologist, social worker, and vocational counselor who provide the rehabilitation components: exercise therapy, psychologic counseling, vocational counseling, and behavioral intervention. Risk factor modification focuses on dietary change, smoking cessation, and stress management. Continuing medical surveillance is provided to ensure the safety of the patient. Cardiac rehabilitation is divided into three phases: inpatient (phase I), outpatient (phase II), and community programs (phase III).

Inpatient Cardiac Rehabilitation (Phase I)

GOALS
1. Initiate early physical activity to
   a. Return to activities of daily living (ADLs).
   b. Offset the deleterious effects of bed rest.

c. Help allay anxiety and depression.

d. Provide medical surveillance.

2. Initiate patient and family education

a. Outline the course of cardiac rehabilitation and plan for resumption of life at home.

b. Promote risk factor reduction.

Cardiac patients vary widely in their severity of disease. Goals therefore need to be individualized, realistic, and consistent, within the limitations imposed by the disease. Some patients will be quite limited in their exercise capacity and ADLs, while other patients will be able to engage in the full spectrum of rehabilitation programming.

ASSESSMENT

Chart Review

The first part of an assessment is a thorough review of the patient's chart. Items important to note include

1. Medical problems, past medical history, physician's exam

2. Medications

3. Laboratory studies

a. Blood tests

b. Cardiac enzymes

c. Cholesterol, triglycerides

4. Diagnostic studies

a. Chest radiograph

b. Cardiograms (resting, exercise, vector, echo ECGs)

c. Catheterization data

d. Radionuclide studies

e. Surgical report

5. Nursing notes, reports from other members of the cardiac rehabilitation team and consultants

Reviewing the chart daily will reveal any changes in the patient's cardiac status from day to day. Changes in enzyme levels, ECG patterns, or other diagnostic data may herald the emergence of complications or an extension of infarction. Cardiac patients may also have numerous other medical problems, such as diabetes, chronic lung disease, and so forth. The medical management and response to treatment of these other conditions will greatly influence clinical decision making and cardiac recovery.[23]

Patient Interview

The therapist should next interview the patient. An assessment of overall cognition (e.g., orientation, memory, learning needs, comprehension) should be obtained. Questions can be posed to elicit information about the patient's response to health and illness, insight, coping style, support system, knowledge of heart disease, risk-factor profile, and personal goals. The therapist will want to pay special attention to prior lifestyle, exercise, and recreational interests and habits. Vocational information should be obtained concerning the type of work, average number of hours per week, attitude toward job, and work-related pressures. The patient should be questioned about pain. Anginal pain should be investigated for precipitating factors, duration, frequency, methods used to relieve pain, and limitations in daily activity. The intense pain in infarction is usually time-limited, and generally lasts from hours to

the first few days. Chest wall pain following bypass surgery is generally sharp and is influenced by respiratory movements.

It is important to note that not all the information from the interview process can be secured in a single session, but rather is obtained from a series of sessions with the patient. As the patient begins to feel better and less anxious, he or she will be able to communicate more readily, and a total picture of present functional level, previous life-style and the information necessary for effective rehabilitation programming will begin to emerge. The interview also serves a second very important function of establishing rapport and trust between patient and therapist. This creates an environment for mutual goal setting and can ensure improved compliance in the overall rehabilitation program. The interview session can also be used to initiate early patient education. It is often helpful to the patient at this point if the total cardiac rehabilitation program is outlined, so that he or she has a clear understanding of the convalescent period and the plan for resumption of normal activities. Interviews with family members should also be scheduled as needed.

Physical Examination

Vital signs (e.g., temperature, heart rate, blood pressure, respiratory rate) should be obtained. Some temperature elevation during the first few days following MI is normal, whereas persistent fever may be indicative of more serious complications (infection or dehydration). Increased temperatures have the added significance of increasing the metabolic rate of the tissues and therefore the demand on the heart. A fall in temperature (hypothermia) may result with the fall in blood flow seen in shock or heart failure.

Overall pulse may be hypokinetic or weak due to low cardiac output. **Tachycardia** (heart rates >100 beats/min) can be seen in patients with CAD, fever, anxiety, and in individuals who are significantly deconditioned. **Bradycardia** (heart rates <60 beats/min) may be related to cardiac medications (e.g., beta-blockers such as propanolol), vagal stimuli, or MI. An irregular pulse is usually indicative of dysrhythmias. The influence of exercise and activity on heart rate will be routinely assessed to gauge the patient's progress during cardiac rehabilitation. Blood pressures (BP) should be obtained. Increased BP may be related to inadequate cardiac output associated with stress, pain, hypoxia, drugs, or CAD. Decreased BP may be related to bed rest, drugs, dysrhythmias, shock, or MI. The influence of position (supine or upright standing) and exercise on BP will be closely examined throughout the course of rehabilitation.

Respiratory rate should be obtained. **Dyspnea** (shortness of breath) is a common finding with left ventricular dysfunction. Patients may experience **orthopnea,** the ability to breathe without discomfort only in an upright position. Exertional dyspnea may be related to CAD and/or overall levels of deconditioning. Dyspnea may also occur as a reaction to anginal pain. Inspection of the thorax can reveal the shape, size, and wall movement (respiratory patterns), as well as localized areas of pain.

Auscultation of the chest using a stethoscope can reveal decreased or absent breath sounds in the various lung fields and the presence of adventitious sounds (crackles or wheezes). Patients with congestive heart failure typically present with crackles. Auscultation of the heart can be used to determine apical pulse and heart sounds (normal first and second heart sounds, as opposed to extra heart sounds, **gallop rhythm,** or murmurs).

The patient's skin color should be inspected. Potential changes associated with decreased cardiac output include cyanosis, a bluish color of the skin and nailbeds, or pallor, the absence of a pink rosy color. Check also for the presence of **diaphoresis** (excess sweating). Examination of the extremities can reveal information about peripheral pulses and edema. Items such as range of motion, muscle strength, sensation, balance, coordination, and gait can be examined as the patient's medical condition and tolerance permit. Patients can be expected to exhibit generalized fatigue associated with decreased cardiac output, drugs, and/or electrolyte imbalance.[14,24]

EXERCISE

One of the primary goals of inpatient exercise is to alleviate the harmful effects of prolonged bed rest and deconditioning. These have been clearly delineated by the studies of Salten and coworkers[25] and are summarized in Table 16–2. The psychologic complications following myocardial infarction have been reported by a number of investigators, notably Hackett and Cassem.[26–28] They have identified anxiety (threat of death) and depression (threat of invalidism) as the two most common psychologic symptoms following an acute coronary event. These symptoms are best counteracted by early, supervised physical activity, which allows the patient to regain control of his or her life and become independent in self-care and in some activities of daily living prior to discharge. The patient is thus reassured that he or she can perform these activities safely at home without fear of "overdoing it" and risking reinfarction and death. A supportive, calm, and reassuring attitude will go a long way in assisting in the patient's psychologic recovery.

The initial **exercise prescription** is dependent upon the patient's individual status and level of recovery. The physician approves entry of the patient into cardiac rehabilitation and determines the level of activity and progressions (see Table 16–3). Careful monitoring is necessary to ensure that the level of intensity of exercise is appropriate for the patient. Patients who demonstrate signs and symptoms inappropriate to exercise therapy exhibit (1) increased HR above the prescribed limit; (2) marked change in BP with exercise; (3) significant exertional dyspnea; (4) myocardial ischemia, angina, or significant dysrhythmias; (5) incisional pain; or (6) excessive fatigue. If any of these are present, further diagnostic evaluation and changes in the exercise prescription are indicated. Criteria for termination of an inpatient exercise session are generally more conservative than for the other phases of rehabilitation (Table 16–4).[22]

Table 16–3 CONTRAINDICATIONS FOR ENTRY INTO INPATIENT AND OUTPATIENT EXERCISE PROGRAMS

1. Unstable angina
2. Resting systolic blood pressure >200 mmHg or resting diastolic blood pressure >100 mmHg
3. Orthostatic blood pressure drop of ≥20 mmHg
4. Moderate to severe aortic stenosis
5. Acute systemic illness or fever
6. Uncontrolled atrial or ventricular dysrhythmias
7. Uncontrolled sinus tachycardia (>120 beats·min^{-1})
8. Uncontrolled congestive heart failure
9. 3° A-V heart block
10. Active pericarditis or myocarditis
11. Recent embolism
12. Thrombophlebitis
13. Resting ST displacement (>3 mm)
14. Uncontrolled diabetes
15. Orthopedic problems that would prohibit exercise

From American College of Sports Medicine: Guidelines for Exercise Testing and Training, ed. 4 Lea & Febiger, Philadelphia, 1991, p 126, with permission.

Specific program components are selected on the basis of low intensity, gradually increasing metabolic cost, safety, and dynamic nature. Activities are described in **METs**, or **metabolic equivalents,** which measure the energy requirement for basal homeostasis while the subject is awake and in a sitting position. A MET is approximately 3.5 to 4.0 ml of oxygen per kilogram of body weight per minute. Most inpatient programs begin with activities of around 2 to 3 METs and progress to 3 to 5 METs at the time of discharge. Metabolic equivalent (MET) activity charts are readily available (Table 16–5).

Initial activities include self-care, resumption of upright sitting, and selected arm and leg exercises designed to improve flexibility and muscle tone. Supervised ambulation is generally begun 3 to 5 days after the event. Specific exercise progressions within a program generally include

1. Passive to active to resistive exercise.

Table 16–4 CRITERIA FOR TERMINATION OF AN INPATIENT EXERCISE SESSION

1. Fatigue
2. Failure of monitoring equipment
3. Light-headedness, confusion, ataxia, pallor, cyanosis, dyspnea, nausea, or any peripheral circulatory insufficiency
4. Onset of angina with exercise
5. Symptomatic supraventricular tachycardia
6. ST displacement (3 mm) horizontal or downsloping from rest
7. Ventricular tachycardia (3 or more consecutive PVCs)
8. Exercise-induced left bundle branch block
9. Onset of 2° and/or 3° A-V block
10. R on T PVCs (one)
11. Frequent multifocal PVCs (30% of the complexes)
12. Exercise hypotension (>20 mm Hg drop in systolic blood pressure during exercise)
13. Excessive blood pressure rise: systolic ≥220 mm Hg or diastolic ≥110 mm Hg
14. Inappropriate brachycardia (drop in heart rate greater than 10 bpm) with increase or no change in work load

From American College of Sports Medicine, ed. 4 Lea & Febiger, Philadelphia, 1991, p 127, with permission.

Table 16–5 METABOLIC EQUIVALENT (MET) ACTIVITY CHART

Intensity (70-kg Person)	Endurance Promoting	Occupational	Recreational
1½–2 METs 4–7 mL/kg/min 2–2½ kcal/min	Too low in energy level	Desk work, driving auto, electric calculating machine operation, light housework, polishing furniture, washing clothes	Standing, strolling (1 mph), flying, motorcycling, playing cards, sewing, knitting
2–3 METs 7–11 mL/kg/min 2½–4 kcal/min	Too low in energy level unless capacity is very low	Auto repair, radio and television repair, janitorial work, bartending, riding lawn mower, light woodworking	Level walking (2 mph), level bicycling (5 mph), billiards, bowling, skeet shooting, shuffleboard, powerboat driving, golfing with power cart, canoeing, horseback riding at a walk
3–4 METs 11–14 mL/kg/min 4–5 kcal/min	Yes, if continuous and if target heart rate is reached	Brick laying, plastering, wheelbarrow (100-lb load), machine assembly, welding (moderate load), cleaning windows, mopping floors, vacuuming, pushing light power mower	Walking (3 mph), bicycling (6 mph), horseshoe pitching, volleyball (6-person, noncompetitive), golfing (pulling bag cart), archery, sailing (handling small boat), fly fishing (standing in waders), horseback riding (trotting), badminton (social doubles)
4–5 METs 14–18 mL/kg/min	Recreational activities promote endurance; occupational activities must be continuous, lasting longer than 2 minutes	Painting, masonry, paperhanging, light carpentry, scrubbing floors, raking leaves, hoeing	Walking (3½ mph), bicycling (8 mph), table tennis, golfing (carrying clubs), dancing (foxtrot), badminton (singles), tennis (doubles), many calisthenics, ballet
5–6 METs 18–21 mL/kg/min	Yes	Digging garden, shoveling light earth	Walking (4 mph), bicycling (10 mph), canoeing (4 mph), horseback riding (posting to trotting), stream fishing (walking in light current in waders), ice or roller skating (9 mph)
6–7 METs 21–25 mL/kg/min 7–8 kcal/min	Yes	Shoveling 10 times/min (4½ kg or 10 lb), splitting wood, snow shoveling, hand lawn mowing	Walking (5 mph), bicycling (11 mph), competitive badminton, tennis (singles), folk and square dancing, light downhill skiing, ski touring (2½ mph), water skiing, swimming (20 yards/min)
7–8 METs 25–28 mL/kg/min 8–10 kcal/min	Yes	Digging ditches, carrying 36 kg or 80 lb, sawing hardwood	Jogging (5 mph), bicycling (12 mph), horseback riding (gallop), vigorous downhill skiing, basketball, mountain climbing, ice hockey, canoeing (5 mph), touch football, paddleball
8–9 METs 28–32 mL/kg/min 10–11 kcal/min	Yes	Shoveling 10 times/min (5½ kg or 14 lb)	Running (5½ mph), bicycling (13 mph), ski touring (4 mph), squash (social), handball (social), fencing, basketball (vigorous), swimming (30 yards/min), rope skipping
10+ METs 32+ mL/kg/min 11+ kcal/min	Yes	Shoveling 10 times/min (7½ kg or 16 lb)	Running (6 mph = 10 METs, 7 mph = 11½ METs, 8 mph = 13½ METs, 9 mph = 15 METs, 10 mph = 17 METs), ski touring (5+ mph), handball (competitive), squash (competitive), swimming (greater than 40 yards/min)

From Fox, SM, Naughton, JP, Gorman, PA: Physical activity and cardiovascular health: 3. The exercise prescription: frequency and type of activity. Mod Con Cardiovasc Dis 41:26–27, 1972, with permission.

2. Distal to intermediate to proximal joint exercises.
3. Extremity to trunk exercises.
4. Lying to sitting to standing exercises.
5. Progressive increases in ambulation distances and progression to stair climbing (down) and stair climbing (up).

The metabolic cost of these activities can be increased by

1. Altering the specific type of activity.
2. Increasing the time (duration) spent on the activity.
3. Altering the position of the body.

Initially patients are seen 2 to 4 times daily for 5 to 10 minutes each. As tolerance improves, the duration can be lengthened to 20 to 30 minutes, while the frequency is decreased to 1 to 2 times daily. The sessions are brief but as the patient improves, a pattern of warm-up, endurance aerobic activity, and cool-down segments should be instituted.

One of the earliest inpatient rehabilitation programs is the seven-step myocardial infarction program developed by Nanette Wenger, M.D., Charles Gilbert, M.D., and Mary Skorapa, M.D. at Grady Hospital in Atlanta (Table 16–6). The program has three parallel levels of activity: supervised exercise, CCU/ward activity, and educational/recreational activity. The program itself is not varied from patient to patient, although the time spent at each step may vary, depending upon the patient's responses. This protocol has served as the model for most inpatient cardiac rehabilitation programs.[29]

In comparison with patients recovering from MI, postsurgical patients generally begin rehabilitation sooner, often ambulating on the first treatment day. Activity progression is also faster and patients work at a slightly higher intensity. While chest tubes may still be in place early on, these should not prevent the patient from par-

Table 16–6 INPATIENT REHABILITATION: 7-STEP MYOCARDIAL INFARCTION PROGRAM

Step	Date	M.D. Initials	Nurse/PT Notes	Supervised Exercise	CCU/Ward Activity	Educational-Recreational Activity
				CCU		
1	—			Active and passive ROM all extremities, in bed Teach patient ankle plantar and dorsiflexion—repeat hourly when awake	Partial self-care Feed self Dangle legs on side of bed Use bedside commode Sit in chair 15 min 1–2 times/day	Orientation to CCU Personal emergencies, social service aid as needed
2	—			Active ROM all extremities, sitting on side of bed	Sit in chair 15–30 min 2–3 times/day Complete self-care in bed	Orientation to rehabilitation team, program Smoking cessation Educational literature if requested Planning transfer from CCU
				Ward		
3	—			Warm-up exercises, 2 METs: Stretching Calisthenics Walk 50 ft and back at slow pace	Sit in chair ad lib Go to ward class in wheelchair Walk in room	Normal cardiac anatomy and function Development of atherosclerosis What happens with myocardial infarction 1–2 METs craft activity
4	—			ROM and calisthenics, 2.5 METs Walk length of hall (75 ft) and back, average pace Teach pulse counting	Out of bed as tolerated Walk to bathroom Walk to ward class, with supervision	Coronary risk factors and their control
5	—			ROM and calisthenics, 3 METs Check pulse counting Practice walking few stairsteps Walk 300 ft bid	Walk to waiting room or telephone Walk in ward corridor prn	Diet Energy conservation Work simplification techniques (as needed) 2–3 METs craft activity
6	—			Continue above activities Walk down flight of steps (return by elevator) Walk 500 ft bid Instruct in home exercise	Tepid shower or tub bath, with supervision To occupational therapy, cardiac clinic teaching room, with supervision	Heart attack management: Medications Exercise Surgery Response to symptoms Family, community adjustments on return home Craft activity prn
7	—			Continue above activities Walk up flight of steps Walk 500 ft bid Continue home exercise instruction; present information regarding outpatient exercise program	Continue all previous ward activities	Discharge planning: Medications, diet, activity Return appointments Scheduled tests Return to work Community resources Educational literature Medication cards Craft activity prn

From Wenger, N: Rehabilitation of the patient with symptomatic atherosclerotic coronary disease. In Hurst, JW (ed): The Heart, ed 5. McGraw-Hill, New York, 1982, p 1151, with permission.

ticipating in exercise. Following surgery, greater emphasis is placed on upper extremity range of motion (ROM) exercises to counteract shoulder and chest wall pain and reduced motion. Lateral stretching of the chest that pulls on the incision site should be avoided. Incisional pain and edema and pain and numbness in the leg where the saphenous vein graft was removed are problems that may be expected during early recovery. Table 16–7 presents an inpatient cardiac rehabilitation program for patients after coronary artery bypass surgery.[30,31]

Although cardiac rehabilitation protocols may vary

Table 16–7 INPATIENT REHABILITATION PROGRAM GUIDELINES AFTER OPEN HEART SURGERY

Step/Date	Cardiac Rehab/Physical Therapy	Ward Activity*	Patient Education
1 1.5 METs —/—/—	*AM WARD TX:* SITTING with feet supported: Active-assistive to active ROM to major muscle groups; active ankle exercises; active scapular elevation/depression, retraction/protraction, 3–5 reps; deep breathing. Monitored ambulation of 100 ft as tolerated. *PM WARD TX:* SITTING with feet supported: Active ROM to major muscle groups, 5 reps; deep breathing. Monitored ambulation 100–200 ft with assistance as tolerated.	1. Begin sitting in chair (when stable) several times/day for 10–30 min. 2. May ambulate 100–200 ft with assistance, once or twice daily.	Orient to CVICU. Reinforce purpose of physical therapy and deep breathing exercises. Orient to exercise component of rehabilitation program. Answer patient and family questions regarding progress.
2 1.5 METs —/—/—	*WARD TX:* SITTING: Repeat exercises from step 1 and increase repetitions to 5–10; deep breathing bid. Monitored ambulation of 200 ft with assistance as tolerated (stress correct posture) bid.	Continue activities from step 1.	Continue above.
3 1.5–2 METs —/—/—	*WARD TX:* STANDING: Begin active upper extremity and trunk exercises bilaterally without resistance (shoulder: flexion, abduction, internal/external rotation, hyperextension, circumduction backwards; elbow flexion; trunk; lateral flexion; rotation), knee extension (if appropriate); ankle exercises; 5–10 reps; bid. Monitored ambulation of 300 ft bid.	Increase ambulation to 300 ft or approximately 3 corridor lengths at slow pace with assistance, bid.	Begin pulse-taking instruction when appropriate and explain RPE scale. Answer questions of patient and family. Reorient patient and family to ICCU. Encourage family attendance at group classes.
4 1.5–2 METs —/—/—	*WARD TX:* STANDING: Active exercises from step 3, 10–15 reps; bid. Monitored ambulation of 424 ft bid.	Increase ambulation to 1 lap† (424 ft or once around square) at slow pace with assistance bid.	
5 1.2–2.5 METs —/—/—	*WARD TX:* STANDING: Active exercises from step 3, 15 reps; once daily. Monitored ambulation for 5–10 min (424–848 ft) as tolerated. *EXERCISE CENTER:* Walk to inpatient exercise center (IEC) for monitored ROM/strengthening exercises from step 3, 15 reps; leg stretching (posterior thigh muscles, gastrocnemius), 10 reps; treadmill and/or bicycle 5–10 min (refer to treadmill/bicycle protocol) with physician approval.	1. Increase ambulation up to 3 laps (up to 1320 ft) daily as tolerated. 2. Begin participating in daily ADL and personal care as tolerated. 3. Encourage chair sitting with legs elevated.	Orient to IEC. Continue instruction in pulse-taking and use of RPE scale. Explain value of exercise. Present T-shirt and activity log.
6 1.5–2.5 METs —/—/—	*WARD TX:* STANDING: Active exercises from step 3 with 1-lb weight each upper extremity, 15 reps; once daily. Monitored ambulation for 10–15 min (up to 1980 ft) if appropriate. *EXERCISE CENTER:* Walk to IEC for monitored ROM/strengthening exercises from step 5 with 1-lb weight each upper extremity, 15 reps; leg stretching, 10 reps; treadmill and/or bicycle 15–20 min; and stair-climbing (6–12 stairs) with assistance.	1. Increase ambulation up to 5 laps (up to 1980 ft) daily. 2. Encourage independence in ADL. 3. Encourage chair sitting with legs elevated.	Give discharge booklet and general discharge instructions to patient and family. Encourage group class attendance. Individual instruction by physical therapist, nutritionist, pharmacist.
7 2–3 METs —/—/—	*WARD TX:* STANDING: Active exercises from step 3 with 1-lb weight each upper extremity, 15 reps; once daily. Monitored ambulation for 15–20 min (up to 3300 ft) if appropriate. *EXERCISE CENTER:* Walk to IEC for monitored ROM/strengthening exercises from step 5 with 1-lb weight each upper extremity, 15 reps; leg stretching, 10 reps; treadmill and/or bicycle 20–30 min; and stair-climbing (up to 14 stairs) with assistance.	1. Continue activities from step 6. 2. Increase ambulation up to 8 laps (up to 3300 ft) daily.	Discuss referral to phase 2 program if appropriate.

Table 16–7 INPATIENT REHABILITATION PROGRAM GUIDELINES AFTER OPEN HEART SURGERY *(Continued)*

Step/Date	Cardiac Rehab/Physical Therapy	Ward Activity*	Patient Education
8 2–3 METs —/—/—	*WARD TX:* STANDING: Exercises from step 3 with 2-lb weight each upper extremity, 15 reps; once daily. Monitored ambulation if appropriate. *EXERCISE CENTER:* Walk to IEC for monitored ROM/strengthening exercises from step 5 with 2-lb weight each upper extremity, 15 reps; leg stretching, 10 reps; treadmill and/or bicycle 20–30 min; and stair-climbing (up to 16 stairs).	1. Continue activities from step 7. 2. Increase ambulation up to 9 laps (up to 3746 ft) daily.	Reinforce prior teaching. Explain predischarge graded exercise test (PDGXT) and upper limit heart rate. Continue with possible referral to phase 2.
9 2–3 METs —/—/—	*WARD TX:* STANDING: Exercises from step 3 with 2-lb weight each upper extremity, 15 reps; once daily. Monitored ambulation if appropriate. *EXERCISE CENTER:* Walk to IEC for monitored ROM/strengthening exercises from step 5 with 2-lb weight each upper extremity, 15 reps; leg stretching, 10 reps; treadmill and/or bicycle 20–30 min; and stair-climbing (up to 18 stairs).	1. Continue activities from step 8. 2. Increase ambulation up to 12 laps (up to 5060 ft) daily.	Give final discharge instructions. Complete referral to phase 2.
10 2–3 MET —/—/—	*WARD TX:* STANDING: Exercises from step 3 with 3-lb weight each upper extremity, 15 reps; once daily. Monitored ambulation if appropriate. *EXERCISE CENTER:* Walk to IEC for monitored ROM/strengthening exercises from step 5 with 3-lb weight each upper extremity, 15 reps; leg stretching, 10 reps; treadmill and/or bicycle 20–30 min; and stair-climbing (up to 24 stairs). A predischarge graded exercise test (PDGXT) is recommended at this time.	1. Continue activities from step 9. 2. Increase ambulation up to 14 laps (up to 5940 ft) daily.	

From Pollack, M: Exercise regimens after myocardial revascularization surgery: rationale and results. In Wenger, N (ed): Exercise and the Heart, ed 2, FA Davis, Philadelphia, 1985, pp 163–165, with permission.

*Ward activity = activities performed alone, with family, or primary nurse.

†Lap = distance of approximately 424 feet or once around square.

Heart rates, blood pressures, and comments are recorded on inpatient data record or exercise log.

from one institution to another, the roles of the physical therapist in overseeing the exercise portion of the rehabilitation program remain fairly constant. These include (1) evaluating the physiologic responses to exercise and activity, (2) supervising the exercises and ambulation, (3) accurately charting and recording the patient's progress and responses, (4) assisting in patient and family education, and (5) preparing the patient for discharge and the remaining phases of the cardiac rehab program.

Monitoring Exercise Responses

Heart rate. Heart rate is recorded before, during, and after each exercise or exercise session. Because heart rate normally increases in a linear manner as work loads increase, it provides a simple, easily measurable index of myocardial oxygen consumption and myocardial work. Heart rates can be determined by palpating pulse with a light but firm pressure. Two sites are available: the radial pulse, which is the most commonly used, and the carotid pulse. Caution must be used when taking the carotid pulse since too much pressure on the carotid sinus can slow the pulse rate and result in a false reading or other, more dangerous, consequences. Press gently on either side of the Adam's apple and be sure to press

only one carotid artery at a time. The first pulse is counted as zero and the count is maintained for 30 to 60 seconds. During exercise, a short-duration count (10 seconds) may be used and the number can be multiplied to calculate a minute rate. The heart rate should be taken immediately after exercise as heart rate will fall rapidly as recovery progresses.

Heart rates at rest and during exercise are limited by certain drugs, notably beta-adrenergic blocking agents, and some antihypertension drugs. In these cases, heart rate is low at rest and rises very little with exercise. Certain patients with severe myocardial dysfunction may also be limited in their heart rate response, demonstrating chronotropic incompetence.[22] The use of heart rate in monitoring performance is therefore limited, and other physiologic parameters assume greater importance.

Most of the activities in phase 1 programs are of such low intensity that the heart rate rises very little. Heart rates are generally restricted to standing resting heart rates plus 10 to 20 beats/min. Activity should be terminated if the heart rate exceeds these or other predetermined end points, or if it fails to increase or decreases as the work load increases. Anxious patients may experience a small anticipatory rise in heart rate before exercise is started but this should level off once exercise begins.

Blood pressure. Blood pressures are routinely taken before, during, and after exercise. Pressure taken and recorded during an activity provides the most clinically useful information, since the **rate-pressure product** (heart rate × systolic blood pressure) is a commonly accepted index of myocardial oxygen consumption.[32,33] When blood pressures are being recorded during activity, the therapist should instruct the patient to continue exercising (e.g., walk in place). The patient's arm should be held in extension and elevation to about heart height, with the stethoscope placed directly over the brachial artery in the antecubital fossa. It is important to take postexercise blood pressures immediately after the activity, within the first 15 seconds since pressures usually fall rapidly once an activity is stopped. A linear increase in systolic pressure is expected with increasing levels of work. Diastolic pressures generally change very little from rest to maximum work load in healthy individuals. Abnormal blood pressure responses to increased intensity of work and contraindications to continuing exercise include (1) a failure of the systolic pressure to rise as exercise progresses, (2) a hypertensive blood pressure response (greater than 200 mmHg systolic pressure or greater than 110 mmHg diastolic pressure), or (3) a progressive fall in systolic pressure of 10 to 15 mmHg. The latter is a serious sign and may herald the development of shock.[22]

Electrocardiograms. The therapist working with a cardiac patient will need to acquire a working knowledge of the electrocardiogram and its interpretation. When assessing cardiac function it is important to assess the ECG at rest, during exercise, and following exercise during the recovery period. The patient is monitored continuously, at first via bedside hookup to the ECG. As the patient progresses through the program, radiotelemetry of the ECG may be employed, especially during new or stressful activities or with high-risk patients. A thorough understanding of ECG interpretation is beyond the scope of this chapter. The reader is referred to excellent texts by Dubin[34] and Goldberger and Goldberger.[16] Basic competence for the therapist working in cardiac rehabilitation includes the ability to recognize rate disturbances, ventricular dysrhythmias, and changes in the ST segment. Rate can be calculated on the ECG by counting the number of intervals between QRS complexes in a 6-second strip and multiplying by 10. Rhythm and ST changes can be determined from a comparison with the normal shape of the ECG complex (Fig. 16–4).

Ventricular dysrhythmias are closely correlated to coronary artery disease and sudden death. These include certain types of **premature ventricular contractions** (PVCs), ventricular tachycardia, and ventricular **fibrillation.** A PVC originates from an **ectopic pacemaker** located in the ventricular myocardium outside the normal nervous conduction system. The ectopic beat occurs very early in the cycle, and is followed by a long (compensatory) pause. It is also characterized by the absence of a P wave and by a slow conduction time, which pro-

duces a very wide QRS complex. While PVCs may occasionally occur at rest and during exercise in the normal individual, they become a concern in the patient with coronary artery disease. Serious PVCs include those of high frequency (greater than five per minute), sequential (two or more consecutive discharges), multifocal (originating from more than one ectopic focus) (Fig. 16–6), or R on T phenomena (a PVC occurring so early it falls on the T wave of the previous beat). *Ventricular tachycardia* is a run of more than four PVCs in rapid succession, all originating from the same focus. It characteristically produces a rapid ventricular rate (150 to 200 beats/min), which seriously impairs cardiac output and heart function (Fig. 16–7). In *ventricular fibrillation,* the heart rate is so rapid (greater than 300 beats/min) that the ventricles cannot fill, and cardiac output is at a standstill. The chaotic twitching of the ventricles produces a totally irregular appearance on the ECG (Fig. 16–8) and complete cardiac arrest.[16,17,34]

Examination of the changes in the ST segment may reveal persistent ischemia in the myocardium, an increased likelihood of serious arrhythmias, and serious functional impairment. Normally the ST segment is isoelectric or falls on the baseline. The baseline or reference line is determined by drawing a line from one PQ junction to the next PQ junction. The J point is defined as the point at which the ST segment changes its slope. The magnitude of ischemic deviation (depression or elevation) is determined by measuring the distance between the J point and the baseline (Fig. 16–9). An abnormal response is a horizontal ST or downsloping ST segment depression of 0.10 mV or more for 80 milliseconds. Downsloping ST segment depression is considered more serious than horizontal.[35] The amount and type of ischemic deviation will vary, depending upon the severity of the underlying coronary artery disease and on the level of exertion. In some patients, the ST

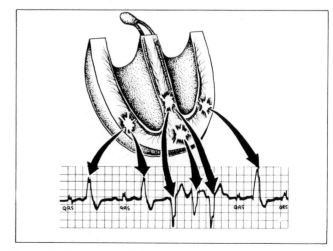

Figure 16–6. Multifocal PVCs. Multifocal PVCs originate from multiple ventricular ectopic foci or pacemakers. Each focus produces its own distinct PVC every time it fires. Like all other PVCs, it occurs early in the cardiac cycle and is followed by a compensatory pause. It is characterized by the absence of a P wave and a wide, bizarre looking QRS complex that results from its slow ventricular conduction. PVC = premature ventricular contraction.

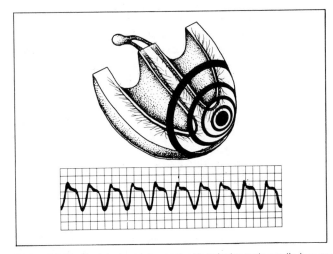

Figure 16–7. Ventricular tachycardia. Ventricular tachycardia is a run of more than four PVCs. It results from a single ventricular ectopic focus and produces a rate of 150 to 200 beats per minute. Heart function is seriously impaired. PVC = premature ventricular contraction.

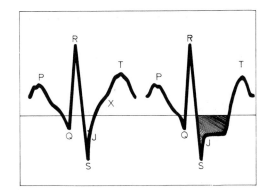

Figure 16–9. ST segment depression. Changes in the ST segment are determined by measuring the amount of deflection of the J point from the isoelectric line. This line is considered to be the baseline and is determined by a line that connects successive points at the PQ junction. This diagram illustrates ST segment depression of about 2 mm.

segment is flat at rest but becomes depressed as the level of physical exertion increases. For other patients, ST segment depression is apparent at rest or during the postexercise recovery period.[11,22]

Because almost every known type of cardiac dysrhythmia may be induced by exercise, the therapist will need to develop additional competencies in ECG interpretation. Less serious dysrhythmias include the atrial dysrhythmias: premature atrial contractions (PACs), paroxysmal atrial tachycardia (PAT), atrial fibrillation, and atrial flutter. Conduction defects represent a failure in the electrical conduction system and can be life-threatening (e.g., third-degree **heart blocks**).

SIGNS AND SYMPTOMS OF EXERTIONAL INTOLERANCE

The therapist must be constantly on the lookout for ischemic manifestations that may herald an intolerance to the level of physical activity prescribed. The signs and

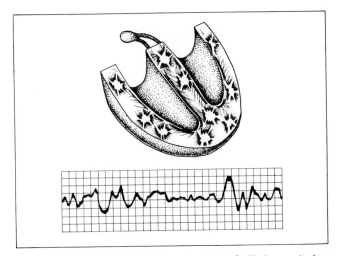

Figure 16–8. Ventricular fibrillation. Ventricular fibrillation results from many ventricular ectopic foci and produces an irregular or chaotic twitching of the ventricles. There is no effective cardiac output (cardiac arrest).

symptoms of excessive effort include (1) persistent dyspnea; (2) dizziness or confusion; (3) anginal pain; (4) severe leg claudication; (5) excessive fatigue; (6) pallor, cold sweat; (7) ataxia; or (8) pulmonary rales.[22] Table 16–8 presents scales that are used to grade angina and dyspnea. Responses that may be delayed for as long as several hours include (1) prolonged fatigue, (2) insomnia, and (3) sudden weight gain due to fluid retention. If the cardiac patient exhibits any of these symptoms, the exercise session should be terminated immediately and the intensity reduced in subsequent sessions. The information should be reported to the physician and recorded in the medical record.[22,35]

Subjective rating of the intensity of exertion has been used to quantify effort during exercise. The original **Ratings of Perceived Exertion** scale (RPE) developed by Borg has been used extensively. It consists of numbers ranging from 6 to 20, which patients use to rate their perceptions of how hard they are working. Descriptive words accompany the numbers such as hard, or very hard. A more recent version, also by Borg, is the 10-point scale (Table 16–9).[36] Both local symptoms (muscle aches, cramps, pain, or fatigue) and central symptoms (feelings of being tired or breathless) contribute to the overall feelings of work performance. High correlations

Table 16–8 ANGINA AND DYSPNEA SCALES

Angina Scale	Characteristics
1+	Light, barely noticeable
2+	Moderate, bothersome
3+	Severe, very uncomfortable
4+	Most severe pain ever experienced

Dyspnea Scale	Characteristics
+1	Mild, noticeable to patient but not observer
+2	Mild, some difficulty, noticeable to observer
+3	Moderate difficulty, but can continue
+4	Severe difficulty, patient cannot continue

From American College of Sports Medicine, Guidelines for Exercise Testing and Prescription, ed. 4. Lea & Febiger, Philadelphia, 1991, p 73, with permission.

Table 16–9 BORG'S ORIGINAL RATE OF PERCEIVED EXERTION SCALE AND REVISED SCALE

Rate of Perceived Exertion	Scale	New Rating Scale
6	0	Nothing at all
7 Very, very light	0.5	Very, very weak
8	1	Very weak
9 Very light	2	Weak
10	3	Moderate
11 Fairly light	4	Somewhat strong
12	5	Strong
13 Somewhat hard	6	
14	7	Very strong
15 Hard	8	
16	9	
17 Very hard	10	Very, very strong
18		Maximal
19 Very, very hard		

Borg, GV: Psychophysical bases of perceived exertion. Med Sci Sports Exerc 14:377–387, 1982, with permission.

of RPE ratings with HR and aerobic power (VO_2) have been found in normal individuals and in patients with cardiac disease. This type of rating is particularly useful when HR proves to be an impractical measure (e.g., for patients on beta-blockers or calcium channel blocking medications).[37-39]

The use of multiple factors (including HR, BP, ECG changes, signs and symptoms, and RPE) appears to provide the safest way to determine exercise tolerance levels. Reliance on any one measure while ignoring others is neither safe nor appropriate. Table 16–10 presents patient characteristics associated with increased risk for cardiac events during exercise programs.

Supervision of Exercise Programs

Phase 1 programs are designed to provide a safe progression of activities during the patient's early convales-

Table 16–10 PATIENT CHARACTERISTICS ASSOCIATED WITH AN INCREASED RISK FOR CARDIAC EVENTS DURING EXERCISE

Clinical Status
  Multiple myocardial infarctions
  Poor left ventricular function (ejection fraction <40% at rest)
  History of chronic congestive heart failure
  Rest or unstable angina pectoris
  Complex dysrhythmias
  Left main coronary artery or three-vessel atherosclerosis on angiography
Exercise Test Response
  Low exercise tolerance (<4 METs)
  Low peak heart rate off drugs (<120 beats/min)
  Severe ischemia (ST >2 mm)
  Angina pectoris at low heart rate or work load
  Inappropriate systolic blood pressure response (decrease with increasing work loads)
  Complex cardiac dysrhythmias, especially in patients with poor left ventricular function
Exercise Training Participation
  Exercises above prescribed limits

From American College of Sports Medicine, Guidelines for Exercise Testing and Prescription, ed. 4. Lea & Febiger, Philadelphia, 1991, p 124, with permission.

cence. Although the exercises included are generally simple, it is important to make sure that the patient performs each exercise correctly. Any alteration in how the exercise is done may change the predicted metabolic cost of the activity and produce unexpected and/or undesired cardiovascular responses. Specific problems that might affect performance include (1) orthopedic problems (restricted ROM, specific muscle weakness, postural deviations), (2) chronic respiratory problems, and (3) neurologic impairments. The dynamic nature of activity and rhythmic breathing should be stressed in order to avoid the dangers of breath holding isometric exercise, and **Valsalva maneuver.** The latter involves breath holding and forcible exhalation with the glottis, nose, and mouth closed. It results in increased intrathoracic-intraabdominal pressures that impair venous return and decrease cardiac output. Isometric exercise greater than 20 percent of maximum voluntary contraction results in an increased pressure load on the heart, as evidenced by increased peripheral vascular resistance and sudden increases in both systolic and diastolic blood pressures. The patient with an ischemic left ventricle does not tolerate these changes well and is vulnerable to dangerous arrhythmias and angina.[12]

Exercise sessions should be coordinated with other hospital activities (meals, occupational therapy, medical rounds, and so forth) to ensure that adequate rest periods are provided. Exercise should be scheduled at least 1 hour after meals and should be avoided during periods of acute emotional stress. The patient should be made aware of the importance of gradual warm-ups and cooldowns along with the aerobic activity, and of balancing activity with rest so that he or she will be able to continue this pattern after discharge.

Accurate Recording and Charting

Daily charting typically includes date, time, activity, level of intensity (heart rate prescription), and duration. The patient's responses to the session are recorded, including pre- and postexercise HRs and BPs and, if monitoring is used, an exercise-obtained rhythm strip. The number of episodes and rate (number per minute) of dysrhythmias and/or angina should be charted along with the trigger (if known) and the response to intervention. Medication changes and complicating problems (e.g., orthopedic, neurologic) should also be noted. Finally, the therapist should record any significant observations concerning the patient's emotional and psychologic state, concerns, cooperation, and adherence to program regulations. Programs that use a protocol sheet generally allow the physician to initial approval for the level of activities that are to be performed.[40]

PATIENT AND FAMILY EDUCATION

Each member of the cardiac rehabilitation team contributes to the total patient and family education program. The goals of the educational program are to (1): improve understanding of coronary disease and its management, (2) modify risk factors, (3) alleviate fears and anxieties, so that the patient can assume some responsibility for health care, (4) teach general activity guidelines, energy conservation, self-monitoring techniques, and (5) teach cardiopulmonary resuscitation (CPR) to a family member. The program may utilize informal teaching and formalized group classes. Aspects of the program with which the physical therapist will most likely be involved include instruction about physical activity and monitoring procedures. Educational plans should reflect individual learning styles, specific needs, and the educational level of patients and family members. A variety of educational methodologies and materials (audiovisual and written) and a clear method of evaluation are sound patient education practices. Lifestyle changes and long-term compliance in exercise are difficult for patients to achieve and require a consistent educational approach from all team members, as well as family support.

DISCHARGE PLANNING

The therapist should review with the patient the home exercise program, general activity guidelines and restrictions for exercising at home, monitoring procedures, and warning signs of exertional intolerance. Knowledge of the person's activity, work, and leisure activities is necessary to tailor specific prescriptive elements. Sample discharge instructions and suggestions for exercising at home are provided in Tables 16–11 and 16–12.

Prior to discharge, a thallium scan or a low-level, symptom-limited **graded exercise testing (GXT)** may be performed. These procedures have been demonstrated to be safe and effective in providing objective information on the patient's functional capacity and in prescribing exercise during phase 2 rehabilitation. It also helps to reassure the patient about going home and may help evaluate the patient's readiness to return to work.[41] A more detailed description of graded exercise testing follows.

Prior to discharge the patient should also visit the facility's outpatient program. Referral forms should be completed and an appointment time scheduled to begin phase II programming. Continued access to rehabilitation staff is important to allay fears and answer any questions that may come up.[22]

Outpatient or Home Exercise Programs (Phase II)

Phase II rehabilitation includes the early at-home period following hospitalization, through the recuperative period, typically up to 8 to 12 weeks after discharge. Patients may participate in a hospital-based outpatient program, a home exercise program, or a combination of these. Since patients with recent MI and/or coronary artery bypass surgery remain at risk for dysrhythmias, continued medical surveillance at a hospital or other facility is advisable. Staff trained in ECG monitoring, emergency care, and supervision of exercise programs provide an important safety net. If home or community-based programs are utilized, regular check-ups, including monitored exercise performance at an outpatient program, are advisable.[22]

Table 16–11 CARDIAC REHABILITATION CENTER DISCHARGE INSTRUCTIONS

Name ————————————— Date ————

Congratulations on your improvement and going home! Continued moderate exercise and attention to healthful living habits will facilitate your return to normal health. The following will assist you in this program. *Keep a record of your responses to exercise (attached)* and *take it with you* each time you visit your personal doctor and the cardiac rehabilitation center.

HOME EXERCISE PROGRAM

Top heart rate ——————— beats/min
Lying
 1. Move legs outward
 2. Straight arm raise
 3. Knee to chest
Sitting
 4. Toe touch
 5. Move legs outward
 6. Move arms outward
 7. Move arms forward and backward with arms elevated
Standing
 8. Arm circles
 9. Side trunk bends
10. Rocking on toes
11. Slight knee bends
12. Trunk circles
Each exercise should be repeated ——————— times in a row,
                                 ——————— times a day

INSTRUCTIONS FOR WALKING

An exercise program for you began in the hospital and should be continued at home. Walking is excellent exercise. The following is a guide to be used *with the precautions* outlined for you by your physician.
A. Warm up by doing the stretching exercises (as noted above) and walk at a slow pace for ——————— minutes.
B. After checking your warm-up pulse rate, resume walking at a faster pace for ——————— minutes at your prescribed heart rate of ———————. Check your pulse intermittently to see that it is not too fast or too slow.
C. Cool off by walking at a slow pace for ——————— minutes.
Your intervals are ———————————————
Your prescribed target heart rate is ———————————
If you have any questions ask the exercise therapist in charge of your cardiac rehabilitation program or call at ———————————.

From Guidelines for Cardiac Rehabilitation Centers, American Heart Association, Greater Los Angeles Affiliate, 1982. By permission of the American Heart Association.

GOALS
 1. Improve functional capacity.
 2. Progress toward full resumption of habitual and occupational activities.
 3. Promote positive life-style changes

THE OUTPATIENT PROGRAM

Outpatient cardiac rehabilitation programs generally are administered 3 or 4 times per week. Durations range from as low as 10 to 15 minutes initially, to 30 to 60 minutes a week as levels of fitness improve. Programs may offer a single mode of training (e.g., walking program) or may offer several different modes of exercise. With the latter option, circuit training may be utilized, for example, the patient spends a prescribed amount of time at one exercise station before moving on to the

Table 16–12 SUGGESTIONS FOR EXERCISING AT HOME

Walk daily. Always include an adequate warm-up and cool-down period in each exercise session. Choose a comfortable pace.

Rest ½ to 1 hour twice a day for the first few weeks at home. Sleep 6 to 8 hours every night.

Space exercise and activity periods evenly with adequate rest periods.

Wait at least 1 hour after meals before exercising.

Avoid extremes in weather: In the winter, exercise during the warmer parts of the day; in the summer, exercise in the early morning or evening.

Avoid bursts of speed, strenuous steps or hills, and strong winds while walking.

Avoid vigorous arm and shoulder activities, especially overhead arm activity (arm activity requires more energy than leg activity).

Avoid lifting heavy weights or objects (isometric exercise).

Avoid situations and people who make you anxious or angry. Don't exercise when you feel tense. Instead, practice relaxation techniques.

If you feel tired or have chest pain, dizziness, or shortness of breath—no matter what you are doing—stop and rest.

Do not exceed your target heart rate.

Take your medications as ordered. If you need to take nitroglycerin before or during exercise, remember to do so. Any change (either increase or decrease) in certain medications may affect your exercise performance.

Don't exercise if you have an acute illness.

Adopt a pace of daily activity that is not rushed. Plan your day so that you can get everything done without being tense or hurried.

Conserve your energy whenever possible: Adapt your living situation for maximum convenience. Eliminate unnecessary tasks; plan your day in advance.

Pay attention to warning signs: Call your physician or therapist if you have any of the following:

Pain or chest discomfort that does not go away with medication or with 15 minutes of rest

Marked shortness of breath

Dizziness

Excess fatigue

Unusual palpitations

Overly slow or very fast heart rate that does not return to normal after a short rest period

Report to your physician immediately any signs that may be indicative of developing congestive heart failure, including

Swelling of your feet and ankles

Sudden weight gain of 2 to 3 pounds when you know you have not been overeating

Sleeping on two to three pillows at night so that you can breathe better

Adapted from Cardiac Rehabilitation Committee;[26] Cardiac Clinic–Grady Memorial Hospital;[54] and North Carolina Myocardial Infarction Rehabilitation Program.[56]

next (e.g., treadmill, cycle **ergometer,** arm ergometer, weights). Rotation through the various stations generally alternates body areas (i.e., arm crank to cycle to wall pulleys to treadmill). Programs may utilize **interval training,** in which a work interval is followed by a rest interval, or a continuous training mode. The advantage of interval training over continuous training is that it allows the individual to work at a higher intensity and perform more work during exercise. Circuit-interval training represents a combination of the two approaches and is a common approach in cardiac rehabilitation.[22]

Cardiovascular adaptation to work during the training session is monitored by a number of factors, including HR, BP, rhythm disturbances, perceived exertion, and signs of exertional intolerance (all previously discussed). Graduated telemetry monitoring is common.

This consists of continuous radiotelemetry during the initial training sessions and progresses to intermittent monitoring. Periodic spot checks of rhythm with defibrillator paddles may also be used. Patients with significant cardiovascular problems (e.g., severely depressed left ventricular function, or ventricular dysrhythmias at rest or increasing with exercise) may remain on continuous monitoring as a safety precaution. Pulse, pressure, and RPE monitoring are routinely taken at prescribed intervals during the training session. As training progresses, the level of monitoring decreases and the patient's responsibility in self-monitoring increases. Patients learn how to maintain their activity levels within the designated safe range of the exercise prescription. One suggested exit point from a phase II program is the attainment of a 9-MET capacity.[42] A 5-MET capacity is considered the minimum, safe level needed to meet essential ADLs.[22]

Phase II programs have a strong component of patient education. Patients continue to develop an understanding of the basic pathophysiology of their disease, the goals and rationale for exercise, self-monitoring, drugs, risk factors, and life-style modification. The presence of a supportive staff and peer group can greatly assist in the overall process of psychosocial adjustment. Many individuals receive significant benefits from the camaraderie and companionship of the group. Program compliance is an important issue. Since individuals become motivated when they perceive themselves to be in control of their own behavior, mutual goal setting is a key element. The patient must (1) perceive the beneficial effects of exercise and risk factor modification on his or her lifestyle and disease processes, (2) be held accountable for meeting goals, and (3) be provided with frequent feedback about successes or failures. Therapists need to be effective role models for optimal health and fitness, and to be flexible in selecting and scheduling activities that the patient wants to do.[43–45]

THE HOME PROGRAM

Some patients with low-risk cardiac involvement may be candidates for exercise in a home program. During the first 2 weeks the patient is advised to continue exercising at the same level at which he or she was performing at the time of discharge (Table 16–10). This includes a daily period of aerobic exercise (e.g., biking, walking). For the patient who remains asymptomatic, the exercise duration and frequency can be gradually increased. Patients exercising at home should be skilled in self-monitoring techniques and diligent in keeping follow-up clinic appointments at a rehab facility. Transtelephonic ECG monitoring is an additional safety measure. Family members should be trained in CPR. Table 16–12 includes sample home exercise instructions.

Some patients may benefit from a combination approach, in which exercise is supervised in the clinic once a week and the patient exercises at home twice a week. Effects of aerobic training at home are comparable to a purely hospital-supervised program. Additional benefits in reducing anxiety may also be evident for the patient engaged in a walking program.[46]

GRADED EXERCISE TESTING

Graded exercise testing is the observation and recording of the patient's cardiovascular responses during a measured exercise stress. The goals of testing are (1) to observe the electrocardiographic changes representative of myocardial ischemia and coronary artery disease during known work loads, and (2) to determine the functional aerobic capacity of the individual. Thus it can be used for diagnostic and prognostic evaluation, as a basis for exercise prescription, and to evaluate the effects of medical and rehabilitative intervention. The two major modes of exercise testing utilize devices (treadmill or bicycle ergometer) that allow for precise calibration and increase of work load (Fig. 16–10). The test begins with a low-level work load and gradually increases to the point of cardiovascular limitation (multistage testing). Stages are usually 2 to 3 minutes in duration, and allow the patient to reach **steady state** (a work situation in which oxygen uptake equals the oxygen requirement of the tissues). Steady state work can be detected during exercise by observing the heart rate response, which levels off to a constant rate (usually within three to four beats of the previous heart rate). Work load increases at each stage may range from as low as 0.5 MET for patients with significant disease to 1 to 3 METs for apparently healthy individuals. Heart rate, blood pressure, ratings of perceived exertion, and signs and symptoms of exertional intolerance are closed monitored throughout the test and during recovery. Various testing protocols have been developed; some are continuous (using a progressive increase in workload), while others are intermittent (alternating work with rest periods). Tests can also be submaximal (stopped at a predetermined end point or when exertional symptoms develop) or maximal (allowing the patient to reach maximum heart rate). The reader is referred to Ellestad's *Stress Testing*[11] and the American College of Sports Medicine's *Guidelines for Exercise Testing and Prescription*[22] for further study.

Patients with moderate or low risk can be given a symptom-limited exercise test. Information gained from the test about peak exercise intensity, peak heart rate, ability to increase systolic blood pressure, angina threshold, ST segment depression, and ventricular dysrhythmias is then used to determine a safe exercise prescription. Certain patients who are at high risk are not suitable candidates for exercise testing (Table 16–13). These patients may be tested after their medical condi-

Oxygen Requirements for Step, Treadmill, and Bicycle Ergometer

Functional Class	METS	O$_2$ Requirements ml O$_2$/kg/min	Step Test — Nagle Balke Naughton (2 min stages, 30 steps min)	Treadmill — Bruce (3 min stages) mph	Bruce %gr	Treadmill — Kattus (3 min stages) mph	Kattus %gr	Treadmill — Balke %grade at ¾ mph	Treadmill — Balke %grade at 3 mph	Bicycle Ergometer (For 70 kg body weight) kgm/min
Normal and I	16	56.0	Step height increased 4 cm q 2 min					26		
	15	52.5						24		
	14	49.0				4	22	22		
	13	45.5	Height (cm)	4.2	16			20		1500
	12	42.0	40			4	18	18	22.5	1350
	11	38.5	36					16	20.0	1200
	10	35.0	32			4	14	14	17.5	1050
	9	31.5	28	3.4	14			12	15.0	900
	8	28.0	24			4	10	10	12.5	
	7	24.5	20	2.5	12	3	10	8	10.0	750
II	6	21.0	16					6	7.5	600
	5	17.5	12	1.7	10	2	10	4	5.0	450
III	4	14.0	8					2	2.5	300
	3	10.5	4						0.0	
	2	7.0								150
IV	1	3.5								

Figure 16–10. Oxygen requirements for step, treadmill, and bicycle ergometer. Oxygen requirements increase with work loads from bottom of chart to top in various exercise tests of the step, treadmill, and bicycle ergometer types. (From American Heart Association: The Exercise Standards Book, 1979, p 11, with permission.)

Table 16–13 CONTRAINDICATIONS TO EXERCISE TESTING

Absolute Contraindications

1. A recent significant change in the resting ECG suggesting infarction or other acute cardiac events
2. Recent complicated myocardial infarction
3. Unstable angina
4. Uncontrolled ventricular dysrhythmia
5. Uncontrolled atrial dysrhythmia that compromises cardiac function
6. 3° A-V block
7. Acute congestive heart failure
8. Severe aortic stenosis
9. Suspected or known dissecting aneurysm
10. Active or suspected myocarditis or pericarditis
11. Thrombophlebitis or intracardiac thrombi
12. Recent systemic or pulmonary embolus
13. Acute infection
14. Significant emotional distress (psychosis)

Relative Contraindications

1. Resting diastolic blood pressure > 120 mmHg or resting systolic blood pressure > 200 mmHg
2. Moderate valvular heart disease
3. Known electrolyte abnormalities (hypokalemia, hypomagnesemia)
4. Fixed-rate pacemaker (rarely used)
5. Frequent or complex ventricular ectopy
6. Ventricular aneurysm
7. Cardiomyopathy, including hypertrophic cardiomyopathy
8. Uncontrolled metabolic disease (e.g., diabetes, thyrotoxicosis, or myxedema)
9. Chronic infectious disease (e.g., mononucleosis, hepatitis, AIDS)
10. Neuromuscular, musculoskeletal, or rheumatoid disorders that are exacerbated by exercise
11. Advanced or complicated pregnancy

From American College of Sports Medicine. Guidelines for Exercise Testing and Prescription, ed. 4. Lea & Febiger, Philadelphia, 1991, p 59, with permission.

tions are stabilized. A third group of patients who exhibit relative contraindications may be tested at the discretion of the physician, after additional evaluation. Exercise tests may be given early (phase I, postinfarction predischarge GXT). Most patients have a GXT 4 to 6 weeks postevent; this is then repeated periodically during cardiac rehabilitation and recovery.[22,35]

THE EXERCISE PRESCRIPTION
Type

Conditioning exercises. Conditioning exercises use large muscle groups performing sustained, rhythmic, **aerobic exercise.** Commonly used activities include walking, jogging, running, swimming, rowing, and stationary bicycling or any combination thereof. Some activities are fairly easy to prescribe because the velocity is maintained and the metabolic cost of the activity is fairly constant (e.g., walking, jogging, or cycling). Conditioning activities in which the metabolic cost varies considerably from patient to patient depending upon the patient's overall skill or because of the intermittent intensity of the activity may not be as suitable for the patient with CAD, particularly in the early phases of the program. Examples of skill-dependent activities include swimming or cross-country skiing, while endurance games are examples of activities that are highly variable in intensity. They can be incorporated gradually into a training program as the patient's functional work capacity improves and his or her exercise tolerance becomes better known.[12,22,35]

Warm-up and cool-down exercises are aerobic activities that gradually increase or decrease the intensity of exercise to allow for gradual circulatory adjustment and to help reduce the incidence of arrhythmias. They also help to minimize oxygen deficit and lactic acid accumulation and modify muscle temperature gradually. Cool-down exercises are particularly important in helping to prevent venous pooling, orthostatic hypotension, and/or nausea. Flexibility exercises designed to limber up muscles and promote adequate ROM in all joints are also included during these time periods. Stretching of major muscle groups including the trunk should be performed. The stretches should be done slowly, sustained for 10 to 30 seconds, and repeated three to five times. A period of active warm-up is advised before vigorous stretching to reduce the risk of injury.[22,35]

The principle of specificity of training is important to consider when trying to improve the patient's functional work capacity for a particular task or type of work. The training effect is specific to the skeletal muscles that are used. Thus, if the therapist is training a patient with paraplegia and a cardiac disability and the objective is to improve cardiovascular endurance in propelling a wheelchair, sustained arm work must be used to produce the training effect. Similarly, patients returning to occupations requiring substantial amounts of arm work should also undergo an arm training regimen. Arm ergometers, rowing machines, or wall pulleys may be used for the dynamic activity. If arm exercises are used it is important to consider that oxygen uptake, heart rate, and systolic blood pressure are significantly greater during arm exercise than during leg exercise at the same submaximal work load. The anginal threshold is also reached at a lower work load. The exercise prescription should be based upon the results of an arm GXT, and the resistance needs to be kept low to avoid a pressure response produced by the isometric component that typically characterizes arm work.[47]

Strength training. Exercises to improve upper body muscle strength and endurance may be included to ensure that the demands of normal ADLs or occupational tasks are met. Moderate work loads (30% to 40% of the maximal voluntary contraction) have been used safely in cardiac rehabilitation programs as early as 6 weeks into phase II to supplement aerobic exercise without adverse effects on cardiac ischemia. Peak heart rates and peak blood pressures were found to be similar to those accompanying aerobic exercise, while significant increases in strength were noted.[48-50] Higher levels of resistance training have also been reported.[51] Individuals selected for these programs were clinically stable and were participating in an ongoing aerobic training program. Strength conditioning is commonly performed using circuit training and a combination of free weights, weight machines, and graded calisthenics. The dynamic, low to moderate resistance, high-repetition, isotonic routines are ideally performed two to three times a week. Exercises should be monitored closely and the patient instructed to breathe rhythmically throughout, without breath-holding. Since the BP response is related to the percentage of maximal voluntary contraction, any increase in strength will result in a lower blood pressure response to any given submaximal work load. Thus the individual will be able to perform strength tasks with less strain on the heart following such training. High resistance and anerobic exercise should be avoided with high-risk, symptomatic patients with CAD, as they dramatically increase BP and the work of the heart.[12,22,35]

Relaxation training. Relaxation training is an effective adjunct to exercise training. These exercises are designed to relieve either generalized or specific muscle tension. Slow breathing patterns are typically part of the training and may be important in promoting parasympathetic activity and counteracting sympathetic reactivity. One frequently used method is Jacobson's progressive relaxation,[52] which consists of systematically learning to tense and then actively relax various muscle groups in the body. The patient is instructed to consciously be aware of the different feelings associated with tension and relaxation. Benson's relaxation response,[53] transcendental meditation, yoga, and biofeedback have also been used successfully in cardiac programs to help patients relax. Relaxation is typically practiced following exercise, first in supine and then in more upright postures (sitting, standing). The patient is instructed to also practice at home or at work during stressful periods. Relaxation training may also be incorporated into the aerobic training session either as part of the warm-up or more commonly the cool-down session. Results of relaxation training include bradycardia at rest and at all levels of effort. Ischemic changes (ST abnormalities) and cardiac events have also been found to decrease.[54-57] Successful stress management coupled with permanent life-style modification can significantly reduce risk factors in coronary disease.

Intensity

Exercise intensity is typically prescribed as a percentage of functional capacity and is based on the results of the GXT. An adequate training intensity falls between 40 and 85 percent of the patient's functional capacity. Patients with a low functional capacity may begin training at 40 to 60 percent capacity and progress to training rates of 60 to 70 percent of functional capacity (a training intensity used with healthy adults). Lower initial intensities may also be considered with sedentary individuals who do not exercise regularly, or individuals with other medical conditions (e.g., orthopedic limitations, obesity). The American College of Sports Medicine[22] identifies three techniques that can be used to prescribe and monitor exercise intensity: heart rate, RPE, and MET values of physical activities.

Exercise prescription by heart rate. Exercise can be prescribed by heart rate because a relatively linear relationship exists between work intensity, oxygen consumption (VO_2), and heart rate. Three different methods utilizing HR are available. First, the prescription can be determined based on a fixed percentage of the patient's maximum heart rate (HR_{max}), the highest heart rate safely achieved during the GXT. The HR_{max} is then multiplied by the conditioning intensity to determine target heart rate (70–85% of HR_{max} closely corresponds to 60–80% of functional capacity or VO_2 max). A second method is used in situations where a maximal GXT is not possible. The HR_{max} is then estimated from a line plotting the relationship between heart rates and VO_2 at submaximal work loads. Target heart rate can also be determined by the heart rate range or reserve method (Karvonen method). This is an attempt to approximate heart rate and VO_2 max more closely. The conditioning intensity (60–80%) is applied to the difference between HR_{max} and resting heart rate, using the following formula:

$$60\% \text{ to } 80\% \ (HR_{max} - \text{ resting heart rate}) + \text{ resting heart rate} = \text{target heart rate}$$

For patients who have not been tested using GXT, maximum heart rate is generally estimated to be 220 minus the patient's age. For upper extremity work, an estimate of 220 minus the patient's age minus 11 is used. Because there is greater risk of cardiac complications such as arrhythmias and cardiac arrest with higher HRs, the intensity should not exceed 85 percent of maximum heart rate in supervised programs and 75 percent in unsupervised training.[12,22,35]

Training regimens may be continuous or discontinuous. If discontinuous work is used, the heart rate may fall either 10 percent higher or lower than the target heart rate, as long as the duration of each averages out to the prescribed target level. The intensity of the work load should be decreased if the heart rate rises consistently more than 4 bpm above the target heart rate. The work load should be increased if the heart rate falls below the target in three consecutive work loads.[22]

It is important to remember that alterations in the relationship between HR and exercise intensity may occur as a result of environmental conditions, psychologic stimuli, or disease. Heart rate cannot be safely used to prescribe safe work loads in the following situations

1. Isometric exercise
2. Valsalva maneuver
3. Heavy arm work
4. Environmental extremes
5. Beta blockade medications
6. Pacemaker

Exercise prescription by perceived exertion. Borg's RPE scale is useful in evaluating a subject's perceived response to exercise intensity during all phases of cardiac rehabilitation (Table 16–9). Using the original scale, RPE values less than 12 (light) approximate 40 to 50 percent of maximum capacity; 12 to 13 (somewhat hard), approximate 60 to 70 percent of maximum capacity; and 14 to 16 (hard) approximate 75 to 95 percent of maximum capacity.[35] Thus patients need to learn to utilize ratings between 12 (somewhat hard) and 16 (hard) to pace the intensity of their work. Using the 10-point scale, this would correspond to values between 4 and 6. The combination of HR and RPE provides an effective strategy to teach patients to regulate the intensity of their work. As patients become more secure in their own self-monitoring and in the accuracy of their perceptions of work intensity, HR monitoring can decrease and RPE can assume an increased role.[22]

Exercise prescription by METs. Exercise intensity is

also prescribed in METs, determined as a percentage of the **physical work capacity (VO₂ max)** obtained from the graded exercise test. Forty to 85 percent of VO_{2max} is adequate to achieve a training effect. Activities are selected that are known to fall within that rate of energy expenditure (Table 16–6). However, problems can arise from using only METs to prescribe intensity of work. Very often discontinuous work must be used to achieve an average exercise intensity. For example, to jog at 7 METs a patient would have to walk part of the time at 5 METs and run part of the time at 10 METs. The high-intensity period may present hazards for some patients initially. Exercise intensity should therefore be maintained near the lower intensity range until the patient's responses to exercise are well known. Differences in overall skill or changes in speed or intensity can alter the known metabolic cost of an activity. Environmental conditions such as heat, cold, high humidity, altitude, wind; changes in terrain or running surface, such as hills; or clothing can also alter the known metabolic cost of an activity. Finally, the stress of competition (type A behaviors or high emotions) can increase the known metabolic cost of an activity. Most clinicians overcome these difficulties by prescribing exercise intensity using a combination approach (e.g., heart rate, RPE, and METs). As training progresses the work load in METs will increase in order to maintain the same target heart rate or RPE.[22,35]

Duration

The duration of the training session varies according to patient tolerance, ranging from 15 to 60 minutes. Ideally the patient exercises at moderate intensities and for a moderate duration with warm-up and cool-down periods of 10 minutes each and a minimum of 20 to 30 minutes at target training intensity. Because duration varies inversely with intensity, the duration must be longer with lower training intensities. Excessively long workouts do not yield significant additional training benefits and only increase the likelihood of orthopedic complications and poor compliance, as well as other ramifications of overtraining. As training progresses, the duration is increased first, then the intensity. Following a layoff period, both intensity and duration should be decreased. The length of the warm-up and cool-down periods should never be decreased in patients with cardiac involvement.[22,35]

Frequency

The frequency of activity is dependent upon its intensity and duration. Three to five evenly spaced workouts per week is recommended for individuals with functional capacities above 5 METs, exercising at moderate intensities and for moderate duration. One or two daily sessions are advisable for patients with functional work capacities between 3 and 5 METs, while for individuals with capacities less than 3 METs, sessions of 5 minutes duration several times daily are recommended.[22]

Rate of Progression

Modifications in the exercise prescription occur as an individual demonstrates physiologic adaptations to

exercise. Changes in the exercise prescription are warranted when the individual's perception of exercise intensity changes (e.g., exercise is perceived as easier), when the HR is lower for a given exercise intensity, or when symptoms of ischemia (e.g., angina) do not appear at the usual exercise intensity. A number of factors must be taken into consideration including age, health status, functional capacity, preferences, and personal goals and needs. Individuals who are symptomatic, sedentary, or elderly will require more time in adapting to a conditioning stimulus. Progression therefore is more gradual. A repeat GXT may be indicated to modify the exercise prescription at certain points in the program. Any significant change in the level of activity should be accompanied by an increase in the level of monitoring to ensure safety. Reasons for temporarily reducing or deferring physical activity are presented in Table 16–14.

Medications can affect responses to exercise and require alterations in the exercise prescription. The clinican will need to acquire a good working knowledge of cardiac medications and their effect on exercise performance. Some general considerations are addressed here; the reader is referred for additional study to more comprehensive references.[20-22] Prophylactic use of nitrates prior to participation in exercise programs may be helpful in preventing symptoms and increasing exercise capacity in patients who develop angina during exercise. They do not diminish the training effect, and the need for nitrates may actually be reduced or eliminated as training progresses. Nitrates and calcium channel blockers produce peripheral vasodilation that can lead to hypotension. Thus patients on these medications are more susceptible to hypotension (due to, for example, sudden changes in posture or heat stress. Patients on beta-blockers will have lower resting and exercise heart rates and blood pressures. This blunted exercise response means that exercise work loads may be lower and should be adjusted carefully. Rating of perceived

---

Table 16–14 REASONS FOR TEMPORARILY REDUCING OR DEFERRING PHYSICAL ACTIVITY

Intercurrent illness—febrile, injury, gastrointestinal
Progression of cardiac disease
Orthopedic problem
Emotional turmoil
Severe sunburn
Alcoholic hangover
Cerebral dysfunction—dizziness, vertigo
Sodium retention—edema, weight gain
Dehydration
Environmental factors
    Weather—excessive heat or cold, humidity or wind
    Air pollution—smog, CO
Overindulgence
    Large, heavy meal within 2 hours
    Coffee, tea, coke (xanthines and other stimulating beverages)
Drugs—decongestants, bronchodilators, atropine, weight reducers
    (anorectics)

From American Heart Association, Committee on Exercise: Exercise Training and Training of Individuals with Heart Disease or at High Risk for Its Development: A Handbook for Physicians. American Heart Association, New York, 1975, with permission.

exertion and exertional signs are better measures of response to exercise intensity than target HR alone. Antiarrhythmic drugs may produce cardiotoxic side effects. Increased arrhythmias may occur, or other side effects such as faintness or dizziness. Clinicians need to be alert to any change in the effect of medications and exercise performance; these changes should be reported promptly to the physician.

Community Exercise Programs (Phase III)

Patients entering community exercise programs include individuals who participated in phase I and II programs (typically 6 to 12 weeks after discharge), and individuals with no prior involvement in an organized program. Patients may exhibit a variety of cardiorespiratory impairments or be at high risk for their development. Before beginning the program, a history, medical evaluation, and GXT are required. Admission criteria vary, and generally include clinically stable or decreasing angina, medically controlled arrhythmias during exercise, knowledge of symptoms, and the ability to self-regulate exercise. In addition, a minimum functional capacity of 5 METs is a suggested requirement.[22]

GOALS

1. Maintain function
2. Promote life-long commitment to physical fitness and personal health management

The phase III program provides a place where individuals may exercise regularly and safely under the direction of an exercise specialist (e.g., American College of Sports Medicine [ACSM] certified exercise physiologist, or less commonly a physical therapist). These individuals are knowledgeable in exercise prescription, exercise monitoring, and emergency procedures. Participation in phase III programs may last for several months or indefinitely. Individuals are expected to progress from supervision to self-regulation of their exercise programs. Regular medical follow-up and periodic GXT (e.g., every 3 or 6 months, or annually) are required. Exercise prescription methods are the same as for phase II. Individuals generally work at a level of 50 to 85 percent of functional capacity, three to four sessions per week. Sessions may be 45 minutes or more. Because dropout rates can be quite high (approaching 50%), phase III programs focus on addressing the specific concerns of compliance with exercise and behavioral life-style intervention goals using specific motivational techniques (e.g., rewards, ceremonies, recreational activities). A follow-up mechanism should be part of any discharge plan from community programs.[22]

Chronic Ventricular Failure

Patients with congestive heart failure (CHF) or cardiomyopathy are often incapacitated as a result of significant ventricular dysfunction and decreased cardiac output. Performance is also limited by increased pulmonary pressures and impairments in peripheral muscle function associated with chronic inactivity, and changes in vasomotor capacity. These patients exhibit low functional work capacities: patients with mild or moderate chronic heart failure are generally limited to activities of 3 to 4 METs (class II or III, Table 16–15); patients with severe chronic heart failure often have symptoms of ischemia or dyspnea at rest and during ADLs despite the use of cardiac medications (class IV). Even modest gains in functional capacity (1–2 METs) can significantly improve a patient's abilities in daily activities and therefore affect overall quality of life. Changes as a result of graduated exercise training in patients with chronic heart failure include improved VO_2max, decreased heart rate at rest, and decreased heart rate and blood pressure in response to submaximal exercise loads. Left ventricular performance (e.g., ejection fractions, volume, wedge pressures) remain basically unchanged. Thus improvements in overall functional capacity are due largely to the enhancement of peripheral mechanisms.[58-62]

Patients with CHF who are medically stable can safely participate in low to moderate exercise training programs. Unstable patients who demonstrate uncompensated failure (e.g., fulminant pulmonary edema with exercise), are not considered safe candidates.[35] Evaluation by exercise testing or radiotelemetry during physical activity can be used to evaluate work capacity and monitor exercise performance. Limiting symptoms of shortness of breath and fatigue are important and must be considered in the exercise prescription in addition to aerobic capacity. Exercise is excessive if patients become symptomatic or experience excessive fatigue (e.g., lasting for several hours). Rating of perceived exertion is also an important monitoring technique because heart rate responses may be abnormal. Monitoring of ECG and blood pressure is critical because exercise may induce dysrhythmias and hypotension both during and after exercise. Pharmacologic management with digitalis and diuretic therapy may result in an electrolyte imbalance (hypokalemia, hypomagnesemia). This in turn can produce potentially lethal ventricular dysrhythmias. In addition, patients on digitalis may demonstrate ST depression on the ECG (a false positive), making interpretation unreliable.[22]

Exercise protocols allow for very low initial work loads and more gradual increments in exercise intensity. An interval training regime with frequent rest periods is necessary. Other aspects or programming are similar (e.g., the use of a warm-up period, a dynamic exercise period, and a cool-down). An example of such a program is included in Table 16–16. Close supervision is necessary throughout the session. The therapist should be supportive and instructive. These patients are in need of physiologic counseling: how to keep activity within the limits of exercise tolerance, methods of energy conservation, balancing rest with activity. Exercise that exceeds the patient's tolerance can overload the heart and result in acute failure. Patient education is often complicated by the signs of memory loss and irritability that accompany decreased cerebral blood flow. These patients may be anxious or depressed and can be difficult to motivate. The therapist can have a major role in

Table 16–15 FUNCTIONAL AND THERAPEUTIC CLASSIFICATIONS OF PATIENTS WITH DISEASES OF THE HEART

Functional	Continuous-Intermittent Permissible Work Loads	Maximal
Class I	4.0–6.0 cal./min. Patients with cardiac disease but without resulting limitations of physical activity. Ordinary physical activity does not cause undue fatigue, palpitation, dyspnea, or anginal pain.	6.5 METs
Class II	3.0–4.0 cal./min. Patients with cardiac disease resulting in slight limitation of physical activity. They are comfortable at rest. Ordinary physical activity results in fatigue, palpitation, dyspnea, or anginal pain.	4.5 METs
Class III	2.0–3.0 cal./min. Patients with cardiac disease resulting in marked limitation of physical activity. They are comfortable at rest. Less than ordinary physical activity causes fatigue, palpitation, dyspnea, or anginal pain.	3.0 METs
Class IV	1.0–2.0 cal./min. Patients with cardiac disease resulting in inability to carry on any physical activity without discomfort. Symptoms of cardiac insufficiency or of the anginal syndrome may be present even at rest. If any physical activity is undertaken, discomfort is increased.	1.5 METs
Therapeutic		
Class A	Patients with cardiac disease whose physical activity need not be restricted in any way.	
Class B	Patients with cardiac disease whose ordinary physical activity need not be restricted but who should be advised against severe or competitive efforts.	
Class C	Patients with cardiac disease whose ordinary physical activity should be moderately restricted, and whose more strenuous efforts should be discontinued.	
Class D	Patients with cardiac disease whose ordinary physical activity should be markedly restricted.	
Class E	Patients with cardiac disease who should be at complete rest or confined to bed or chair.	

Reprinted by permission of the American Heart Association, New York.

assisting the patient in overcoming these feelings through physical activity and in facilitating the patient's adjustment to chronic and even terminal disability. Additional rehabilitation goals for chronic heart patients include (1) maintenance of pulmonary hygiene, adequate respiratory ventilation, and good breathing and coughing patterns, (2) prevention of venous stasis and thromboembolism associated with prolonged bedrest, (3) prevention of decubitus ulcers associated with prolonged bedrest, and (4) control of anxiety and tension.

Efficacy of Cardiac Rehabilitation

The benefits of exercise training in patients with coronary artery disease include improved functional capacity, and decreased heart rate and blood pressure, two major determinants of myocardial oxygen demand. Thus training allows individuals to better meet the circulatory demands of activities of daily living and exercise. These and other changes in functional capacity are similar to those reported for healthy individuals and are summarized in Table 16–17.[64-68] Although most patients recovering from MI can be expected to improve spontaneously, individuals involved in an exercise group achieve significantly greater functional capacities (approximately 20–25% greater) than those with no specific intervention. Those patients with marked limitations in maximum work capacity (less than 7 METs) may attain the greatest benefit from exercise training programs.[42]

Improved quality of life, self-image, self-efficacy, and reduced anxiety and depression are frequently cited benefits for individuals participating in cardiac rehabilitation programs.[57,69,70] However, there are few randomized and controlled studies, and results cannot be deemed conclusive.[42] Risk factor modification based on health education components (e.g., teaching, counseling) are important outcomes of cardiac rehabilitation programs. Expected changes that contribute to improving cardiovascular outcome include dietary changes, cessation of smoking, and stress reduction. Exercise also aids in risk factor modification, producing weight reduction, increased lean body mass, lowered serum triglycerides, increased high-density lipoproteins, decreased platelet adhesiveness and altered adrenergic responses to stress.[71]

Numerous intervention studies have shown a trend toward reduced mortality in individuals enrolled in cardiac rehabilitation programs compared to usual care. In a review of randomized trials of rehabilitation with exercise after myocardial infarction, O'Conner et al.[71] report that exercise reduced risk of death by 20 percent and that the reduction persists for at least 3 years after infarction. However, methodologic problems have plagued many of these studies, and the data is by no means conclusive.[72]

The amount of improvement in individual patients will vary considerably depending on age, the location and degree of cardiac damage and related symptomatology, overall health, risk factors, functional work capacity, magnitude of the training stimulus, and psychosocial status. Some patients will be extremely limited in their ability to participate fully in these programs and may in fact be unable to increase their physical work capacity at all. The psychologic benefits of participating in such programs must be weighed carefully when considering referral or discharge.

Cardiac rehabilitation programs appear to be safe. Van Camp and Peterson[73] investigated the cardiac risks of

Table 16–16 SUGGESTED INTERDISCIPLINARY STAGES FOR PATIENTS WITH CARDIOPULMONARY HISTORY AND/OR PRECAUTIONS

Stage/MET Level*	ADL and Mobility	Exercise	Recreation
Stage I (1.0–1.4 METs)	*Sitting:* Self-feeding, wash hands and face, bed mobility.† Transfers Progressively increase sitting tolerance	*Supine:* (A) or (AA) exercise to all extremities (10–15 times per extremity) *Sitting:* (A) or (AA) exercise to *only* neck and LEs Include deep breathing exercise	Reading, radio, table games, (noncompetitive), light handwork
Stage II (1.4–2.0 METs)	*Sitting:* Self-bathing, shaving, grooming, and dressing in hospital Unlimited sitting *Ambulation:* At slow pace, in room as tolerated	*Sitting:* (A) exercise to all extremities, progressively increasing the number of repetitions† NO ISOMETRICS	*Sitting:* Crafts (e.g., painting, knitting, sewing, mosaics, embroidery) NO ISOMETRICS

Stage III
 	
(2.0–3.0 METs)
	Sitting: Showering in warm water, homemaking tasks with brief standing periods to transfer light items, ironing
	Standing: May progress to grooming self.
	Ambulation: May begin slow paced ambulation outside room on levels, for short distances
		Sitting: W/C mobility limited distances
		Standing: (A) exercise to all extremities and trunk progressively increasing the number of repetitions†
		May include:
		  1. Balance exercises
		  2. Light mat activities without resistance
		Ambulation: Begin progressive ambulation program at 0% grade and comfortable pace
			Sitting: Card playing, crafts, piano, machine sewing, typing†

Stage IV
 	
(3.0–3.5 METs)
	Standing: Total washing, dressing, shaving, grooming, showering in warm water; kitchen/homemaking activities while practicing energy conservation (e.g., light vacuuming, dusting and sweeping, washing light clothes)
	Ambulation: unlimited distance walking at 0% grade, inside and/or outside†
		Standing: Continue all previous exercise, progressively increasing
		  1. Number of repetitions
		  2. Speed of repetitions
		May include additional exercises to increase work load up to 3.5 METs, balance and mat activities with mild resistance
		Ambulation: Unlimited on level surfaces inside and/or outside† progressively increasing speed and/or duration for periods up to 15–20 minutes or until target heart rate is reached†
		Stairs: May begin slow stair climbing to patient's tolerance up to two flights
		Treadmill: 1 mph at 1% grade, progressing to 1.5 mph at 2% grade*
		Cycling: Up to 5.0 mph without resistance
			Candlepin bowling
			Canoeing—slow rhythm, pace
			Golf putting
			Light gardening: weeding and planting
			Driving†

Stage V
 	
(3.5–4.0 METs)
	Standing: Washing dishes, washing clothes, ironing, hanging light clothes, and making beds	*Standing:* Continue exercises as in stage IV, progressively increasing
		  1. Number of repetitions
		  2. Speed of repetitions
		May Add additional exercises to increase work load up to 4.0 METs
		Ambulation: As in stage IV, increasing speed up to 2.5 mph on level surfaces†
		Stairs: As in stage IV and progressively increasing, if increasing to patient's tolerance
		Treadmill: 1.5 mph at 2% grade, progressing to 1.5 mph at 4% grade up to 2.5 mph at 0% grade†
		Cycling: Up to 8 mph without resistance†
		May use up to 7–10 lbs† of weight for UE and LE exercise in sitting
			Swimming (slowly)
			Light carpentry
			Golfing (using power cart)
			Light home repairs

Stage VI (4.0–5.0 METs)	*Standing:* Showering in hot water, hanging and/or wringing clothes, mopping, stripping and making beds, raking	*Standing:* As in stage V *Ambulation:* As in stage V—increasing speed to 3.5 mph on level surfaces† *Stairs:* As in stage V *Treadmill:* 1.5 mph at 4–6% grade, progressing to 3.5 mph at 0% grade† *Cycling:* Up to 10 mph without resistance May use up to 10–15 lbs of weight in UE and LE exercises in sitting	Swimming (no advanced strokes) Slow dancing Ice or roller skating (slowly) Volleyball Badminton Table tennis (noncompetitive) Light calisthenics

From Spaulding Rehabilitation Hospital, Boston, MA, 1987, with permission.

*Activity stages may need to be modified if the patient has other physical disabilities. A trendscriber evaluation is suggested when a patient is ready to progress to a higher level of activity.

†Please refer to physician's guidelines.

Table 16–17 POSSIBLE EFFECTS OF PHYSICAL TRAINING

Decreased heart rate at rest and during exercise
Increased rate of heart rate recovery after exercise
Increased stroke volume (blood volume pumped per heart beat)
Myocardial hypertrophy (increased size of heart muscle)
Increased myocardial oxygen supply
Increased myocardial contractility (strength of muscle contraction)
Decreased blood pressure at rest and during exercise
Increased angina threshold secondary to decreased myocardial
 oxygen consumption (decreased rate-pressure product)
Decreased serum lipoproteins (cholesterol, triglycerides)
Improved respiratory capacity during exercise (increased diffusion of
 respiratory gases, reduced residual volume, increased blood
 supply)
Improved functional capacity of the exercising muscles (increased
 skeletal muscle blood flow, improved muscle strength, increased
 metabolic and enzymatic function of muscle cells)
Reduced body fat, increased lean body weight (muscle mass)
Increased glucose tolerance
Improved blood fibrinolytic activity and coagulability
Improved self-confidence and sense of well-being; reduced strain and
 nervous tension

Adapted from Amsterdam, EA, Wilmore, JH, and DeMaria, AN (eds): Exercise in Cardiovascular Health and Disease. Yorke Medical Books, New York, 1977, and from Astrand and Rodah.[64]

51,303 patients who exercised in 167 randomly selected outpatient programs for a total of 2,351,916 patient-hours. The number of cardiac arrests was 21, with 3 fatalities. The rate of arrests was determined to be 8.9 per million patient-hours of exercise. Eight nonfatal myocardial infarctions were reported with an overall rate of 3.4 nonfatal infarctions per million patient-hours. No differences that could be ascribed to size or extent of monitoring were reported in these programs; patient entry criteria were not investigated.

SUMMARY

Cardiac rehabilitation as a therapeutic measure for restoring functional capacity to patients with heart disease has progressed rapidly during the last 25 years. Programs have become more sophisticated and more individualized. Multilevel care from the acute facility to rehabilitation and community centers is available. Rehabilitation personnel have become more skilled and experienced in dealing with problems associated with cardiac disease. Research has revealed that the exercise capacity of these patients can be improved and that these programs are safe. It has also shown that these programs can significantly reduce the length of hospitalization and improve the overall functional status of the patient at discharge. Evidence of the role of exercise in preventing myocardial infarction or the recurrence of other coronary events is accumulating. Physical therapists have an important role in monitoring and prescribing safe exercise programs for patients with a variety of cardiovascular diseases. The expert skills and experience of the therapist can be utilized in the acute care setting, outpatient programs, community-based programs, or in the rehabilitation setting.

QUESTIONS FOR REVIEW

1. What are the clinical manifestations of coronary artery disease? How do they differ in their pathophysiology, evaluation, and medical management?

2. What are the critical ECG changes that herald exertional intolerance? What are the other signs and symptoms of exertional intolerance?

3. Identify and describe three life-threatening arrhythmias.

4. How do the exercise programs in phase I, phase II, and phase III differ? Do the goals differ?

5. How can exercises be modified to increase the exercise challenge for the patient with cardiac disease? In supervising exercises, what considerations are important to keep in mind?

6. Define graded exercise test. What are the clinical end points of such testing? What is the difference between predischarge testing and the testing typically done for entrance into phase III programs?

7. Name three motivational strategies to insure life-long commitment to exercise. Name three effective patient education strategies.

8. What are the common psychologic reactions to infarction? How can they best be handled?

9. What are the major elements of the exercise prescription? What factors make up each of these elements?

10. How can a patient safely progress through an exercise program? What factors are important in determining if a change is needed in the exercise prescription?

11. What evidence is present in the research literature about the effectiveness of cardiac rehabilitation programs?

12. How are programs modified for the complicated cardiac patient with pronounced left ventricular dysfunction? What are some of the additional problems this patient faces?

REFERENCES

1. American Heart Association: Fact Sheet on Heart Attack, Stroke and Risk Factors. American Heart Association, Dallas, 1993.
2. Borhani, N: Epidemiology of coronary disease. In Amsterdam, EA, Wilmore, JH, and DeMaria, A (eds): Exercise in Cardiovascular Health and Disease. Yorke Medical Books, New York, 1977.
3. Kannel, W: Downward trend in cardiovascular mortality. JAMA 247:887, 1982.
4. American Heart Association: Heart and Stroke Facts. American Heart Association, Dallas, 1992.
5. American Heart Association: Coronary Risk Factor Statement for the American Public. American Heart Association, Dallas, 1987.
6. Guyton, A: Textbook of Medical Physiology, ed 7. WB Saunders, Philadelphia, 1986.
7. Roberts, WC: The coronary arteries in ischemic heart disease: fact and fancies. Triangle 16:77, 1977.
8. Sheldon, H: Boyd's Introduction to the Study of Disease, ed 9. Lea & Febiger, Philadelphia, 1984.

9. Harvey, AM, et al: The Principles and Practice of Medicine, ed 26. Appleton & Lange, Norwalk, CT, 1988.
10. Davies, M and Nelson, W: Understanding Cardiology. Butterworth, Boston, 1978.
11. Ellestad, M: Stress Testing: Principles and Practice, ed 3. FA Davis, Philadelphia, 1986.
12. Wenger, N (ed): Exercise and the Heart, ed 2. FA Davis, Philadelphia, 1985.
13. Wenger, ND: Coronary Care: Rehabilitation of the Patient with Symptomatic Coronary Atherosclerotic Heart Disease. American Heart Association, Dallas, 1981.
14. Stillwell, S and Randall, E: Pocket Guide to Cardiovascular Care. CV Mosby, St Louis, 1990.
15. Galen, RS: The enzyme diagnosis of myocardial infarction. Prog Hum Pathol 6:141, 1975.
16. Goldberger, A and Goldberger, E: Clinical Electrocardiography—A Simplified Approach, ed 2. CV Mosby, St. Louis, 1981.
17. Conover, MB: Understanding Electrocardiography—Physiological and Interpretive Concepts, ed 3. CV Mosby, St. Louis, 1980.
18. Brannon, F, Geyer, M, and Foley, M: Cardiac Rehabilitation. FA Davis, Philadelphia, 1988.
19. Andreoli, KG, Fowkes, VK, Zipes, DP, and Wallace, AG: Comprehensive Cardiac Care—A Text for Nurses, Physicians, and Other Health Practitioners, ed 5. CV Mosby, St. Louis, 1987.
20. Ciccone, C: Pharmacology in Rehabilitation. FA Davis, Philadelphia, 1990.
21. Malone, T: Physical and Occupation Therapy: Drug Implications for Practice. JB Lippincott, Philadelphia, 1989.
22. American College of Sports Medicine: Guidelines for Exercise Testing and Prescription, ed 4. Lea & Febiger, Philadelphia, 1991.
23. Schoneberger, M, Schoneberger, B, and Lunsford, B: Chart review and physical assessment prior to exercise. In Amundsen, L (ed): Cardiac Rehabilitation. Churchill Livingstone, New York, 1981.
24. Irwin, S and Blessey, R: Patient Evaluation. In Irwin, S and Tecklin, J (eds): Cardiopulmonary Physical Therapy. CV Mosby, St. Louis, 1985.
25. Salten, B, Blomquist, G, Mitchell, J, Johnson, R, Widenthal, K, and Chapman, C: Response to submaximal and maximal exercise after bedrest and training. Circulation 38:7, 1968.
26. Cassen, NH and Hackett, TO: Psychological rehabilitation of myocardial infarction patients in the acute phase. Heart Lung 2:382, 1973.
27. Hackett, T and Cassen, N: Coronary Care: Patient Psychology. American Heart Association, New York, 1975.
28. Hackett, T and Cassem, N: Psychologic aspects of rehabilitation after myocardial infarction and coronary artery bypass surgery. In Wenger, N and Hellerstein, H (eds): Rehabilitation of the Coronary Patient, ed 2. John Wiley & Sons, New York, 1984.
29. Wenger, N: Early ambulation physical activity: myocardial infarction and coronary artery bypass surgery. Heart Lung 13:14, 1984.
30. Pollock, M: Exercise regimes after myocardial revascularization surgery: rationale and results. In Wenger, N (ed): Exercise and the Heart, ed 2. FA Davis, Philadelphia, 1985.
31. Johnson, D: The rehabilitative approach to patients undergoing coronary bypass surgery. In Wenger, N and Hellerstein, H (eds): Rehabilitation of the Coronary Patient, ed 2. John Wiley & Sons, New York, 1984.
32. Kitamura, K, et al: Hemodynamic correlates of myocardial oxygen consumption during upright exercise. J Appl Physiol 32:516, 1972
33. Baller, D, et al: Comparison of myocardial oxygen consumption indices in man. Clin Cardiol 3:116, 1980.
34. Dublin, D: Rapid Interpretation of EKGs. Cover, Tampa, FL, 1974.
35. American Heart Association: Exercise Standards—A Statement for Health Professionals. American Heart Association, Dallas, 1991.
36. Borg, G: Psychophysical bases of perceived exertion. Med Sci Sports Exerc 14:377, 1982.
37. O'Sullivan, S: Perceived exertion—a review. Phys Ther 64:343, 1984.
38. Noble, B: Clinical applications of perceived exertion. Med Sci Sports Exer 14:406, 1982.
39. Guttmann, MC, et al: Perceived exertion-heart rate relationship during exercise testing and training in cardiac patients. J Cardiac Rehabil 1:52, 1981.
40. American Association of Cardiovascular and Pulmonary Rehabili-tation: Guidelines for Cardiac Rehabilitation Programs. Human Kinetics, Champaign, IL, 1991.
41. Johnston, B: Exercise testing for patients after myocardial infarction and coronary bypass surgery: emphasis on predischarge phase. Heart Lung 13:18, 1984.
42. Greenland, P and Chu, J: Efficacy of cardiac rehabilitation services. Ann Intern Med 15:650, 1988.
43. Williams, M: Motivating the patient for long-term commitment. In Fardy, P, Bennet, J, Reitz, N, and Williams, M (eds): Cardiac Rehabilitation—Implications for the Nurse and Other Health Professionals. CV Mosby, St. Louis, 1980.
44. Serfass, R and Gerberich, S: Exercise for optimal health: strategies and motivational considerations. In Forum: Exercise and Health. Academic Press, New York, 1984.
45. Carmody, T, et al: Physical exercise rehabilitation: long-term drop-out rate in cardiac patients. J Behav Med 3:163, 1980.
46. Kugler, J, et al: Hospital supervised vs home exercise in cardiac rehabilitation: effects on aerobic fitness, anxiety, and depression. Arch Phys Med Rehabil 71:322, 1990.
47. Fardy, PS, Web, D, and Hellerstein, HK: Benefits of Arm Exercise in Cardiac Rehabilitation. Physician and Sports Medicine 5:31, 1977.
48. Sparling, P, et al: Strength training in a cardiac rehabilitation program: a six-month follow-up. Arch Phys Med Rehabil 71:148, 1990.
49. Butler, R, Palmer, G, and Rogers, F: Circuit weight training in early cardiac rehabilitation. JAOA 92:77, 1992.
50. Keleman, M, et al: Circuit weight training in cardiac patients. J Am Coll Cardiol 7:38, 1986.
51. Faigenbaum, A, et al: Physiologic and symptomatic responses of cardiac patients to resistance exercise. Arch Phys Med Rehabil 71:395, 1990.
52. Jacobson, E: Progressive Relaxation. University of Chicago Press, Chicago, 1938.
53. Benson, H: The Relaxation Response. Avon, New York, 1975.
54. Van Dixhoorn, J, et al: Physical training and relaxation therapy in cardiac rehabilitation assessed through a composite criterion for training outcome. Am Heart J 118:545, 1989.
55. Van Dixhoorn, J, et al: Cardiac events after myocardial infarction: possible effects of relaxation therapy. Eur Heart J 8:1210, 1987.
56. Hayward, C, Piscopo, J, and Santos, A: Physiologic effects of Benson's relaxation response during submaximal aerobic exercise in coronary artery disease patients. J Cardiopulmon Rehabil 7:534, 1987.
57. Bohachick, P: Progressive relaxation training in cardiac rehabilitation: effect on psychologic variables. Nurs Res 33:283, 1984.
58. Thompson, PD: The benefits and risks of exercise training in patients with chronic coronary artery disease. JAMA 259:1537, 1988.
59. Folta, A, and Metzger, B: Exercise and functional capacity after myocardial infarction. Image 21:215, 1989.
60. Sullivan, M, Higginbotham, M, and Cobb, F: Increased exercise ventilation in patients with chronic heart failure: intact ventilatory control despite hemodynamic and pulmonary abnormalities. Circulation 77:552, 1988.
61. Dubach, P, and Froelicher, V: Cardiac rehabilitation for heart failure patients. Cardiology 76:368, 1989.
62. Shabetai, R: Beneficial effects of exercise training in compensated heart failure. Circulation 78:775, 1988.
63. Conn, E, Williams, R, and Wallace, A: Exercise responses before and after physical conditioning in patients with severely depressed left ventricular function. Am J Cardiol 49:296, 1982.
64. Astrand, P and Rodahl, K: Textbook of Work Physiology, ed 3. McGraw-Hill, New York, 1986.
65. Rigotti, N, Thomas, G, and Leaf, A: Exercise and coronary heart disease. Annu Rev Med 34:391, 1983.
66. Fletcher, G: Long-term exercise in coronary artery disease and other chronic disease states. Heart Lung 13:28, 1984.
67. Eichner, E: Exercise and heart disease—epidemiology of the "exercise hypothesis". Am J Med 75:1008, 1983.
68. Van Dixhoorn, J, Duivenvoorden, H, and Pool, J: Success or failure of exercise training after myocardial infarction: Is the outcome predictable? J Am Coll Cardiol 15:974, 1990.
69. Roviaro, S, Holmes, D, and Holmsten, R: Influence of a cardiac rehabilitation program on the cardiovascular, psychological, and social functioning of cardiac patients. J Behav Med 7:61, 1984.

70. Gulanick, M: Is phase 2 cardiac rehabilitation necessary for early recovery of patients with cardiac disease? A randomized, controlled study. Heart Lung 20:9, 1991.

71. O'Conner, G, et al: An overview of randomized trials of rehabilitation with exercise after myocardial infarction. Circulation 80:234, 1989.

72. Dafoe, W: The challenge of cardiac rehabilitation. In Eisenberg, M, and Grzesiak, R (eds): Advances in Clinical Rehabilitation, vol 3. Springer, New York, 1990, p 97.

73. Van Camp, S, and Peterson, R: Cardiovascular complications of outpatient cardiac rehabilitation programs. JAMA 256:1160, 1986.

SUPPLEMENTAL READINGS

American Association of Cardiovascular and Pulmonary Rehabilitation: Guidelines for Cardiac Rehabilitation Programs. Human Kinetics, Champaign, IL, 1991.

American College of Sports Medicine: Guidelines for Exercise Testing and Prescription, ed 4. Lea & Febiger, Philadelphia, 1991.

American College of Sports Medicine: Resource Manual for Guidelines for Exercise Testing and Prescription. Lea & Febiger, Philadelphia, 1988.

American Heart Association: Exercise standards: A statement for health professionals from the American Heart Association. Circulation 82:2286, 1990.

Brannon, F, Geyer, M, and Foley, M: Cardiac Rehabilitation. FA Davis, Philadelphia, 1988.

Ellestad, M: Stress Testing: Principles and Practice, ed 3. FA Davis, Philadelphia, 1986.

Fardy, P, Yankowitz, F, and Wilson, P: Cardiac Rehabilitation: Adult Fitness and Exercise Testing, ed 2. Lea & Febiger, Philadelphia, 1988.

Froelicher, V: Exercise and the Heart, ed 2. Year Book Medical, Chicago, 1987.

Gordon, N, and Gibbons, L: The Cooper Clinic Cardiac Rehabilitation Program. Simon & Schuster, New York, 1990.

Pollack, M, and Wilmore, J: Exercise in Health and Disease, ed 2. WB Saunders, Philadelphia, 1990.

Wenger, N and Hellerstein, H: Rehabilitation of the Coronary Patient, ed 2. John Wiley & Sons, New York, 1984.

Wenger, N: Exercise and the Heart, ed 2. FA Davis, Philadelphia, 1985.

Wilson, P, Fardy, P, and Froelicher, V: Cardiac Rehabilitation, Adult Fitness, and Exercise Testing, ed 2. Lea & Febiger, Philadelphia, 1988.

GLOSSARY

Aerobic exercise: Exercise during which the energy needed is supplied by the oxygen inspired.

Age-predicted maximal heart rate: The highest heart rate attained during maximal exercise; generally considered 220 minus an individual's age in years.

Anaerobic exercise: Exercise during which the energy needed is provided without utilization of inspired oxygen. This type of exercise is limited to short bursts of vigorous activity.

Aneurysm: A localized abnormal dilatation of a blood vessel or ventricle.

Angina pectoris: A condition in which the heart muscle receives an insufficient blood supply, with ensuing pain in the chest and often in the left arm and shoulder. Commonly results from activity or emotion in patients with atherosclerosis.

Stable: Classic angina brought on by effort or exertion.

Unstable: Preinfarction angina characterized by a change in the quality, frequency, intensity, duration or timing of pain; crescendo pain that is difficult to control.

Angiocardiography: Radiographic examination of the heart and blood vessels which follows the course of an opaque fluid injected into the bloodstream.

Antiarrhythmics: Agents which are used to treat cardiac arrhythmias. Commonly used drugs include lidocaine, quinidine, procainamide, disopyramide (Norpace), Phenytoin (Dilantin), and so on.

Arrhythmia or dysrhythmia: A loss of or an irregularity in normal heart rhythm.

Arteriosclerosis: Commonly called hardening of the arteries; includes a variety of conditions that cause the artery walls to thicken and lose elasticity.

Atherosclerosis: A form of arteriosclerosis. The inner layers of artery walls are made thick and irregular by deposits of a fatty substance. The internal channel of the arteries becomes narrowed and blood supply is reduced.

Beta-adrenergic blocking agent (beta-blockers): A substance which interferes with the transmission of stimuli through pathways that normally allow sympathetic nervous stimuli to be effective. These drugs decrease heart rate, blood pressure, contractility, and stroke volume, and result in decreased myocardial oxygen demands and decreased angina pectoris. Commonly used drugs include propranolol, metoprolol, nadolol, atenolol, and timolol.

Blood pressure: The pressure exerted by the blood on the wall of any vessel. Systolic pressure reflects the resultant pressure during ventricular contraction; diastolic pressure reflects the resultant pressure when the ventricles are relaxed; normally 120/80 mmHg.

Bradycardia: An abnormally slow heart rate (generally below 60 bpm).

Calcium channel blocking agent (calcium channel blocker): A substance that inhibits the flow of calcium ions across membranes in smooth muscle. These drugs cause vasodilation and relieve angina pain and coronary artery spasm. Commonly used drugs include verapamil, nifedipine, and diltiazem.

Cardiogenic shock: Failure to maintain blood supply to the circulatory system and tissues because of inadequate cardiac output.

Cardiomegaly: Hypertrophy of the heart.

Catecholamines: Circulating compounds (epinephrine and norepinephrine) that are secreted by the sympathetic nervous system and the adrenal medulla; they act to increase cardiac rate, contractility, automaticity, and excitability.

Catheterization: The process of examining the heart by introducing a thin tube (catheter) into a vein or artery and passing it into the heart.

Cholesterol: A fatlike substance found in various tissues. Elevated blood levels are associated with increased risk of coronary atherosclerosis when transported by low-density lipoproteins. Cholesterol transported by high-density lipoproteins is inversely associated with coronary risk.

Coronary artery bypass graft (CABG): Surgery to improve the blood supply to the heart muscle when narrowed coronary arteries reduce flow of the oxygen-containing blood vital to the pumping heart.

Diaphoresis: Profuse sweating.

Digitalis: A drug that strengthens the contraction of the heart muscle, slows the rate of contraction of the heart, and promotes the elimination of fluid from body tissues.

Dyspnea: Air hunger resulting in labored or difficult breathing, sometimes accompanied by pain; normal when due to vigorous work or athletic activity.

Ectopic pacemaker: An electrical impulse that originates from a pacemaker other than the normal conducting system; can occur in the atria, the A-V node, or in either ventricle when normal pacing fails.

Ejection fraction (EF): The difference between left ventricular end diastolic volume and left ventricular end systolic volume.

Electrocardiogram (ECG or EKG): A record of the electrical activity of the heart; shows certain waves called P, Q, R, S, and T waves; sometimes a U wave.

Embolus: A blood clot that forms in blood vessels in one part of the body and travels to another.

Ergometer: A calibrated instrument used to accurately determine work load during an exercise challenge; commonly a treadmill or stationary bicycle.

Exercise prescription: An individualized exercise program involving frequency, intensity, time (duration), and type (FITT).

Fibrillation: Uncoordinated contractions of the heart muscle occurring when individual muscle fibers take up independent irregular contractions. It may be atrial or ventricular in origin.

Gallop rhythm: An abnormal third or fourth heart sound in a tachycardia of 100 or more beats per minute.

Graded exercise test (GXT, stress test): The observation and recording of an individual's cardiovascular responses during a measured exercise challenge in order to determine capacity to adapt to physical stress. Tests may be maximal (maximal oxygen uptake) or submaximal (a predetermined end point or when symptoms of exertional intolerance develop).

Heart block: Interference with conduction of electrical impulses from the atria to the ventricles; can be partial or complete. This can result in dissociation of the rhythms and contractions of the atria and the ventricles.

Heart failure: Cessation of heartbeat; a syndrome or clinical condition resulting from failure of the heart to maintain adequate circulation of blood. May result in failure of the right or left ventricle or both.

Heart failure, congestive: Condition characterized by weakness, breathlessness, abdominal discomfort, edema in the lower portions of the body, resulting from venous stasis and reduced outflow of blood from the left side of the heart.

Heart rate: The number of ventricular beats per minute; normally 70 beats/min.

Imaging (cardiac or myocardial): The production of a picture, image, or shadow that represents the object being investigated. Noninvasive cardiac techniques including radionuclide cineangiography, myocardial perfusion scintigraphy, nuclear magnetic resonance imaging, echocardiography, and so on.

Interval training: A method of organizing an exercise routine into periods of activity with warm-up, peak, and cool-down periods.

Ischemia: Local and temporary deficiency of blood supply due to obstruction of the circulation to a part.

Isometric exercise: Contraction of a muscle that is not accompanied by movement of joints that would normally be moved by that muscle's action.

MET (metabolic equivalent): The rate of energy expenditure requiring an oxygen consumption of 3.5 ml of oxygen per kilogram of body weight per minute (3.5 ml/kg/min). This unit corresponds to the basal metabolic rate while sitting.

Mitral insufficiency (regurgitation): Back flow of blood from the left ventricle into the left atrium due to failure of the valve to close completely.

Myocardial infarction: Condition caused by occlusion of one or more of the coronary arteries, resulting in necrosis following cessation of blood supply. Symptoms include prolonged heavy pressure or squeezing pain in the center of chest behind the sternum. The pain may spread to shoulder, neck, arm, hand, back, teeth, or to the jaw. These symptoms may be accompanied by nausea and vomiting, sweating, and shortness of breath.

Orthopnea: Respiratory condition in which there is discomfort in breathing but erect sitting or standing position.

Physical work capacity (PWC, VO₂max, or maximal aerobic power): Physiologic maximal work performance defined as that level of performance beyond which the oxygen uptake fails to increase further with increasing work.

Premature ventricular contraction (PVC) or premature atrial contraction (PAC). A disorder of rhythm and contraction caused by abnormal ectopic foci in the ventricle (PVC) or in the atria (PAC) and which causes impulses to be discharged earlier or more frequently than those from the SA node.

Pulmonary edema: Accumulation of fluid in the lungs due to left-sided failure of the heart, i.e., more blood is supplied to the pulmonary circulation than is removed.

Rate pressure product (RPP): An index of myocardial oxygen consumption determined by the product of heart rate and mean systolic blood pressure.

Ratings of perceived exertion (RPE or Borg scale): A subjective assessment of the intensity of work.

Serum enzymes (cardiac enzymes): Enzymes such as creatine phosphokinase (CPK), lactate dehydrogenase (LDH), and serum glutamic-oxaloacetic transminase (SGOT) that are released into the circulation from myocardial muscle when cell death takes place.

ST segment depression: A depression of the ST segment on the ECG that occurs in the presence of myocardial ischemia. Greater than 1 mm horizontal or downsloping, or 1.5 mm upsloping depression, is considered significant.

Steady state: A balanced physiologic state in which the oxygen uptake equals the oxygen consumption during work. It can be recognized during exercise by leveling off of the heart rate to a constant level.

Stroke volume: The amount of blood ejected by the left ventricle at each beat.

Tachycardia: A heart rate of greater than 100 beats/min. It may be initiated normally by the SA node (sinus) or by an abnormal ectopic foci in the atria (atrial), AV node (nodal) or ventricles (ventricular).

The term paroxysmal indicates a tachycardia that begins and ends suddenly.

Thrombosis: The formation, development, or existence of a blood clot (thrombus) inside a blood vessel or cavity of the heart.

Valsalva maneuver: Attempt to forcibly exhale with the glottis, nose, and mouth closed. It causes increased intrathoracic pressure, slowing of the pulse, decreased return of blood to the heart, and increased venous pressure, and increases the likelihood of dangerous arrhythmias in cardiac patients.

Vasodilators: Drugs which causes dilation of blood vessels; often used in the treatment of angina pectoris. Commonly used drugs include nitroglycerin and isosorbide dinitrate.

Ventricular aneurysm: Localized dilation or bulging of the ventricular wall of the heart.

Stroke

Susan B. O'Sullivan

OBJECTIVES

1. Define terms associated with the pathology and management of stroke.
2. Describe the etiology, pathophysiology, symptomatology, and sequelae of stroke.
3. Identify and describe the diagnostic and assessment procedures used to evaluate stroke.
4. Identify and describe strategies for effective rehabilitative management during the acute and postacute phases.
5. Value the role of the physical therapist in assisting recovery from stroke.

Stroke, or cerebrovascular accident (CVA), is defined as sudden, focal neurologic deficit resulting from ischemic or hemorrhagic lesions in the brain. Clinically, a variety of deficits are possible, including impairments of sensory, motor, mental, perceptual, and language functions. Motor deficits are characterized by paralysis (**hemiplegia**) or weakness (**hemiparesis**) on the side of the body opposite the site of the lesion. The term hemiplegia is often used generically to refer to the wide variety of problems that result from stroke. The location and extent of the lesion and the amount of collateral blood flow determine the severity of neurologic deficits in an individual patient. Strokes may be categorized by etiologic categories (thrombosis, embolus, or hemorrhage), management categories (transient ischemic attack, minor stroke, major stroke, deteriorating stroke, young stroke), and anatomic categories (specific vascular territory).

EPIDEMIOLOGY

Stroke is the third leading cause of death and the most common cause of adult disability in the United States. It affects approximately 500,000 new victims each year with the estimated number of stroke survivors close to 3 million. Roughly 30 percent die during the acute phase, and of the survivors 30 to 40 percent will have severe disability. The incidence of stroke increases dramatically with age, occurring in about 1 percent of the population aged 65 to 74. Only an estimated 20 percent of strokes occur in individuals under the age of 65. Men have a 30 percent greater incidence of stroke than women. The incidence of stroke and hypertension is also more than 60 percent higher in African-Americans than in whites. Epidemiologic studies have revealed a steady decline in the incidence of stroke in the last 30 years and especially in the last decade. Similar downward trends have also been noted in the incidence of cardiovascular disease. Better diagnosis and treatment, and control of stroke risk factors, especially hypertensive therapy, have been implicated in contributing to the rates of decline.[1-3]

ETIOLOGIC CATEGORIES

A number of mechanisms may result in vascular insufficiency and stroke. The most common causes include (1) thrombus, (2) embolism, and (3) hemorrhage secondary to aneurysm or trauma.

Atherosclerosis is a major contributory factor in occlusive vascular disease and is characterized by plaque formation and progressive narrowing of the vessel. The principal sequelae of this process are stenosis, ulceration of the atherosclerotic lesions, and thrombosis. **Cerebral thrombosis** refers to the formation or development of a blood clot or thrombus within the cerebral arteries or their branches. Thrombi result from platelet adhesion and aggregation, coagulation of fibrin, and decreased fibrinolysis. It should be noted that lesions of extracranial vessels (carotid or vertebral arteries) can also produce symptoms of stroke. Thrombi lead to ischemia, or occlusion of an artery with resulting infarction or tissue death (atherothrombotic brain infarction or ABI). Thrombi can also become dislodged and travel to another site in the form of an artery to artery embolus.

Cerebral emboli (CE) are traveling bits of matter such as thrombi, tissue, fat, air, bacteria or other foreign bodies that are released into the bloodstream and travel to the cerebral arteries where they produce occlusion and infarction. They are commonly associated with cardiovascular disease (valvular disease, myocardial infarc-

tion, arrhythmias, congenital heart disease) or systemic disorders that produce septic, fat, or air emboli.

Hemorrhage occurs from abnormal bleeding due to rupture of a blood vessel. Tissue death results from both ischemic and mechanical injury. Restriction of distal blood flow and the increased pressure resulting from the enlarging clot are underlying factors. **Intracerebral hemorrhage (IH)** is caused by rupture of one of the cerebral vessels with subsequent bleeding into the brain. **Subarachnoid hemorrhage (SH)** occurs from bleeding into the subarachnoid space and may be spontaneous (rupture of a **berry aneurysm,** bleeding from an **arteriovenous malformation** or **AVM**) or secondary to trauma. *Hypertension* (HTN) is a precipitating factor, and the affected vessel is often weakened by atherosclerosis. With massive cerebral bleeding, death can occur within hours, since intracranial pressure increases rapidly and adjacent cortical tissue may be displaced or compressed.[4,5]

Atherothrombotic brain infarction is the most common type of stroke, accounting for 57% of all strokes. Cerebral embolus accounts for 16% of strokes, while subarachnoid hemorrhage and intracerebral hemorrhage account for 10% and 4% respectively.[6]

Risk Factors

Cardiovascular diseases affecting the brain and heart share a number of common risk factors important to the development of atherosclerosis. Major risk factors for stroke are high blood pressure, heart disease, and diabetes. In ABI patients, 70 percent have hypertension, 30 percent coronary heart disease, 15 percent congestive heart disease, 30 percent peripheral arterial disease, and 15 percent diabetes. This coexistence of vascular problems increases significantly with the age of the patient. Patients with marked elevations of hematocrits are at an increased risk of occlusive stroke due to a generalized reduction of cerebral blood flow. Cardiac disorders, such as rheumatic heart valvular disease, endocarditis, arrhythmias (particularly atrial fibrillation), or cardiac surgery significantly increase the risk of embolic stroke. Cigarette smoking is another important risk factor for stroke, as are transient ischemic attacks (TIAs). While only 10 percent of strokes are preceded by TIAs, about 36 percent of individuals who experience one or more TIAs will go on to develop a stroke within 5 years. Secondary risk factors associated with increased risk of heart disease and stroke include physical inactivity, obesity, excessive alcohol consumption, and elevated blood cholesterol and lipids. As with the cardiac risk profile, the more risk factors present or the greater the degree of abnormality of any one factor, the greater the risk of stroke. A history of prior stroke also increases the risk of additional strokes.[1,4,7]

Pathophysiology

Interruption of blood flow for only a few minutes sets in motion a series of pathoneurologic events. Complete cerebral circulatory arrest results in irreversible cellular damage with a core area of focal infarction. The area surrounding the core is termed the ischemic prenumbra and consists of viable but metabolically lethargic cells. The ischemia triggers a number of damaging and potentially reversible events including the release of cascades of chemicals. The release of excess glutamate, an excitatory neurotransmitter, causes changes in calcium ion distribution with the activation of destructive enzymes. The overall effect is one of additional neuronal death, generally within hours, and extension of infarction into the prenumbra area. Research efforts are currently directed to development of drugs that might reverse the metabolic changes of the ischemic brain.[8]

Cerebral edema, an accumulation of fluids, begins within hours of the insult and reaches a maximum by about 4 days. It is the result of tissue necrosis and widespread rupture of cell membranes. The swelling then gradually subsides, generally disappearing by 3 weeks. Significant edema can elevate intracranial pressures and produce contralateral and caudal shifts of brain structures. It is the commonest cause of death in acute stroke and a common finding with large infarcts involving the middle cerebral artery.[9]

MANAGEMENT CATEGORIES

A **transient ischemic attack** refers to the temporary interruption of blood supply to the brain. Symptoms of focal neurologic deficit may last for only a few minutes or for several hours, but do not last over 24 hours. After the attack is over there is no evidence of residual brain damage or permanent neurologic dysfunction. Transient ischemic attacks may result from a number of different etiologic factors including occlusive attacks, emboli, reduced cerebral perfusion (arrhythmias, decreased cardiac output, hypotension, overmedication with antihypertensive medications, **subclavian steal syndrome**) or cerebrovascular spasm. Its major clinical significance is as a precursor to both cerebral infarction and myocardial infarction.[5]

Patients are classified as having a **major stroke** in the presence of stable, usually severe, deficits. The term **deteriorating stroke** is used to refer to the patient whose neurologic status is deteriorating after admission to the hospital. This change in status may be due to cerebral or systemic causes (e.g., cerebral edema, progressing thrombosis). The category of **young stroke** is used to refer to stroke affecting persons below the age of 45. Younger individuals have the potential for better recovery.[9]

ANATOMIC CATEGORIES

Cerebral blood flow varies with the patency of the vessels. Progressive narrowing secondary to atherosclerosis decreases blood flow. As in coronary heart disease, symptomatic changes generally result from a restriction of flow greater than 80 percent. The symptomatology of stroke is dependent upon a number of factors including

(1) the location of the ischemic process, (2) the size of the ischemic area, (3) the nature and functions of the structures involved, and (4) the availability of collateral blood flow. Symptomatology may also depend upon the rapidity of the occlusion of a blood vessel since slow occlusions may allow collateral vessels to take over while sudden events do not.[10]

Cerebral Blood Flow

Knowledge of cerebral vascular anatomy is essential to understand the symptomatology, diagnosis, and management of stroke. A brief review is therefore helpful. Extracranial blood supply to the brain is provided by right and left internal carotid arteries and by the right and left vertebral arteries. The internal carotid artery begins at the bifurcation of the common carotid artery and ascends in the deep portions of the neck to the carotid canal. It turns rostromedially and ascends into

the cranial cavity. There it pierces the dura mater and gives off the ophthalmic and anterior choroidal arteries before bifurcating into the middle and anterior cerebral arteries. The anterior communicating artery communicates with the anterior cerebral arteries of either side, giving rise to the rostral portion of the *circle of Willis* (Fig. 17–1). The vertebral artery is a branch of the subclavian artery; it enters the vertebral foramen of the sixth cervical vertebra and travels through the foramina of the transverse processes of the upper six cervical vertebra to the foramen magnum and into the brain. There it travels in the posterior cranial fossa ventrally and medially and unites with the vertebral artery from the other side to form the basiliar artery at the upper border of the medulla. The cerebellum is supplied by three pairs of cerebellar arteries that arise from the vertebrobasiliar system. At the upper border of the pons, the basiliar artery bifurcates to form the posterior cerebral arteries and the posterior portion of the circle of Willis. Posterior communicating arteries connect the posterior cerebral

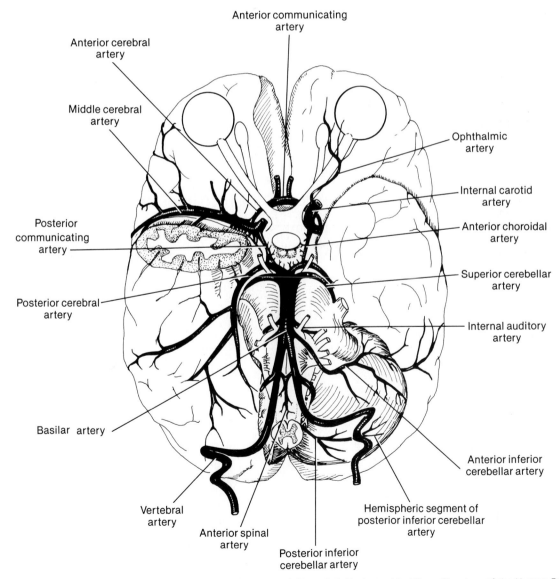

Figure 17–1. Cerebral circulation: Circle of Willis. (From DeArmond, S, et al: A Photographic Atlas—Structure of the Human Brain, ed 2, Oxford University Press, New York, 1976, p 171, with permission.)

arteries with the internal carotid arteries and complete the circle of Willis.

Determinants of Cerebral Blood Flow

Cerebral blood flow (CBF) is controlled by a number of **autoregulatory mechanism,** which modulate a constant rate of blood flow through the brain. These mechanisms provide homeostatic balance, counteracting fluctuations in systolic blood pressure while maintaining a normal flow of 50 to 60 ml per 100 grams of brain tissue per minute. The brain has high oxygen demands and requires a continuous, rich perfusion of blood. Cerebral flow represents approximately 17 percent of available cardiac output.

Chemical regulation of CBF occurs in response to changes in blood concentrations of carbon dioxide or oxygen. Vasodilation and increased CBF are produced in response to an increase in $PaCO_2$ or a decrease in PaO_2, while vasoconstriction and decreased CBF are produced by the opposite stimuli. Blood flow is also altered by changes in the blood pH. A fall in pH (increased acidity) produces vasodilation, while a rise in pH (increased alkalinity) produces a decrease in blood flow. Neurogenic regulation alters blood flow by vasodilating vessels in direct proportion to local function of brain tissue. Released metabolites probably act directly on the smooth muscle in local vessel walls. Changes in blood viscosity or intracranial pressures may also influence CBF.[9] Changes in blood pressure produce minor alterations of CBF. As pressure rises, the artery is stretched, resulting in contraction of smooth muscle in the vessel wall. Thus, the patency of the vessel is decreased, with a consequent decrease in CBF. As pressure falls, contraction lessens and CBF increases. Following stroke, autoregulatory mechanisms may be impaired.[11]

Vascular Syndromes

Stroke produces focal signs specific to the artery involved. These findings are summarized in Table 17–1.

Interruption of blood flow by atherosclerotic plaques occurs at certain sites of predilection. These generally include bifurcations, constrictions, dilation, or angulations of arteries. The most common sites for lesions to occur are at the origin of the common carotid artery, in the internal carotid artery at the level of the carotid sinus or at its transition into the middle cerebral artery, at the main bifurcation of the middle cerebral artery, and at the junction of the vertebral arteries with the basiliar artery[5] (Fig. 17–2).

ANTERIOR CEREBRAL ARTERY STROKE

The anterior cerebral artery (ACA) is the first and smaller of two terminal branches of the internal carotid artery. It supplies the medial aspect of the cerebral hemisphere (frontal and parietal lobes) and subcortical structures, including the anterior internal capsule, inferior caudate nucleus, anterior fornix, and anterior four-fifths of the corpus callosum. Since the anterior communicating artery allows perfusion of the proximal

Table 17–1 SYNDROMES RESULTING FROM OCCLUSION OF CEREBRAL ARTERIES

Artery	Structures Supplied	Coma	Diplopia	Homonymous Hemianopsia	Mental Confusion	Aphasia (If Dominant Side Involved)	Contralateral Hemiplegia	Contralateral Sensory Loss	Pseudo-Bulbar Palsy	Flaccid Quadriplegia	Thalamic Syndrome
Carotid Internal	Subcortical structures: ophthalmic a.: eye, orbital structures choroidal a.: choroid plexus, int. capsule Cortex: anterior cerebral a., middle cerebral a., posterior communicating a.	X		X	X	X	X	X			
Anterior Cerebral	Cortex: medial aspect of frontal and parietal lobes Subcortical structures: anterior limb of the internal capsule, caudate nucleus, putamen, corpus callosum				X	X	X Mostly lower extremity involvement	X Mostly lower extremity involvement			
Middle Cerebral	Cortex: lateral aspect of frontal, temporal, parietal, and occipital lobes Subcortical structures: head of caudate nucleus, putamen, external capsule, claustrum and anterior internal capsule	X		X		X	X Mostly upper extremity involvement	X Mostly upper extremity involvement			
Posterior Cerebral	Cortex: medial aspect of occipital lobe, medial and inferior aspect of temporal lobe, corpus callosum Subcortical structures: posterior diencephalon, thalamus, midbrain			X		X	X May be transient	X			X
Vertebro-Basilar	Brainstem: medulla, pons, midbrain cerebellum, labyrinths	X	X				X		X	X Locked-in syndrome	

X indicates the presence of clinical sign.
a = artery; int = internal.

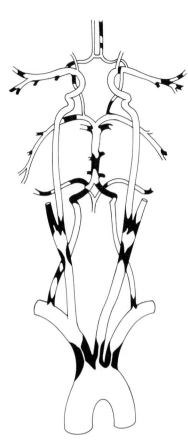

Figure 17–2. Preferred sites for atherosclerotic plaque. (From American Heart Association, Diagnosis and Management of Stroke, 1979, p 4, with permission.)

anterior cerebral artery from either side, occlusion proximal to this point results in minimal deficit. More distal lesions produce deficits of contralateral hemiparesis and cortical sensory loss with greater involvement of the lower extremity than upper extremity. Involuntary grasp reflex in the affected upper extremity and incontinence are common. Extensive frontal lobe infarction produces significant memory and behavioral impairments. Right-hemisphere damage to the frontal lobe may cause **unilateral neglect.** Damage to the supplementary motor area of the dominant hemisphere may produce **aphasia.** Impaired function of the corpus callosum may lead to hemispheric disconnection, characterized by **apraxia** and **agraphia.**

MIDDLE CEREBRAL ARTERY STROKE

The middle cerebral artery (MCA) is the most common site of stroke. The middle cerebral artery is the second of the two main branches of the internal carotid artery and supplies the lateral aspect of the cerebral hemisphere (frontal, temporal, and parietal lobes) and subcortical structures, including the internal capsule (posterior portion), corona radiata, globus pallidus (outer part), most of the caudate nucleus, and the putamen. Superficial MCA occlusion results in contralateral hemiparesis or hemiplegia and sensory deficit of the face, arm, and leg, with the face and arm more involved than the leg. **Homonymous hemianopsia** (visual field defect) and loss of conjugate gaze to the opposite side

also results. Deep MCA syndrome results in a pure motor hemiplegia without sensory or visual deficits. Infarction secondary to proximal MCA occlusion often produces significant cerebral edema with increased intracranial pressures and may lead to brain herniation, coma, or death.

Lesions of the parietooccipital cortex of the dominant hemisphere (usually the left hemisphere for most individuals) can produce aphasia. Lesions of the right parietal lobe of the nondominant hemisphere (usually the right hemisphere for most individuals) can produce unilateral neglect, **anosognosia** (unawareness of the hemiplegia), apraxia, and spatial disorganization.

INTERNAL CAROTID ARTERY STROKE

Complete occlusion of the internal carotid artery produces massive infarction in both middle cerebral and anterior cerebral arterial territories. Extensive cerebral edema occurs and often leads to coma and death. Incomplete occlusions can produce a mixture of middle cerebral or anterior artery symptoms.

POSTERIOR CEREBRAL ARTERY STROKE

The two posterior cerebral arteries (PCAs) arise as terminal branches of the basiliar artery and each supplies the corresponding occipital lobe and medial and inferior temporal lobe. It also supplies the upper brainstem, midbrain, and posterior diencephalon, including most of the thalamus. Occlusion of thalamic branches may produce hemianesthesia (contralateral sensory loss) or, some months later, **thalamic sensory syndrome** (a persistent and unpleasant hemibody sensation). Occipital infarction may cause homonymous hemianopsia, visual **agnosia, prosopagnosia** (inability to recognize faces) or, if bilateral, cortical blindness. Temporal lobe ischemia may result in an amnesic syndrome with memory loss. Involvement of subthalamic branches may involve the adjacent midbrain and produce a wide variety of deficits (e.g., ocular signs such as skew deviation, athetoid posturing, postural tremor, hemiballismus). Contralateral hemiplegia occurs with involvement of the cerebral peduncle.

VERTEBROBASILIAR ARTERY STROKE

The basiliar artery originates from the two vertebral arteries at the inferior border of the pons and terminates at the upper border of the pons in the two posterior arteries. Branches supply the pons, inner ear, and cerebellum. Complete occlusion of the basiliar artery is often fatal. Patients experience progressive occipital headache, diplopia, progressive hemi- or quadriplegia, bulbar paralysis, and coma. **Locked-in syndrome (LIS)** results from ventral pontine lesions and is defined as quadriplegia and anarthria with preserved consciousness. Thus the patient cannot move or speak but remains alert and oriented. Only one voluntary movement, vertical gaze, remains. Communication can be established via vertical eye movements. Mortality rates are high (59%), and those patients that do survive are usually left with severe impairments associated with brainstem dysfunction.[12,13]

Occlusions of the vertebrobasilar system can produce a variety of symptoms with both ipsilateral and contralateral signs, since some of the tracts in the brain stem will have crossed and others will not. Cerebellar and cranial nerve abnormalities also occur. Symptoms can include visual loss, homonymous hemianopsia, diplopia, facial numbness or weakness, tinnitus, dysarthria, or dysphagia. Hemiparesis of one or more limbs can occur with corticospinal tract involvement. Sensory loss and paresthesias of the face, and upper or lower limbs may occur with ischemia of the lemniscal system. Pain and temperature sensations may be lost on the opposite side with spinothalamic tract involvement. Altered consciousness may result from ischemia of the reticular activating system. **Drop attacks** (sudden loss of tone in the lower limbs) may result from ischemia of the medullary pyramids. Branch occlusions (cerebellar occlusions) result in ataxia, nystagmus, vertigo, nausea, or vomiting. Occulsion of the inferior cerebellar artery produces lateral medullary syndrome. **Horner's syndrome** and decreased sweating can result from descending sympathetic tract involvement.[14]

DIAGNOSIS

History and Examination

An accurate history profiling the timing of neurologic events is obtained from the patient—or from family members in the case of the unconscious or noncommunicative patient. Of particular importance are the pattern of onset and the course of initial neurologic symptoms. An abupt onset with rapid coma is suggestive of cerebral hemorrhage or brainstem stroke. Severe headache typically precedes loss of consciousness. An embolus also occurs rapidly with no warning and is frequently associated with heart disease and/or heart complications. A more progressive and uneven onset is typical with thrombosis. The physician also investigates the patient's past history including episodes of TIAs or head trauma, presence of major or minor risk factors, medications, and pertinent family history. Any recent alterations in patient function (either transient or permanent) are thoroughly investigated.

The physical examination of the patient includes an investigation of vital signs (heart rate, respiratory rate, blood pressure) and signs of cardiac decompensation. The neurologic exam stresses function of the cerebral hemispheres, cerebellum, cranial nerves, eyes, and sensorimotor system. The presenting symptoms will help to determine the location of the lesion, while comparison of both sides of the body will reveal the side of the lesion. Bilateral signs are suggestive of brainstem lesions or massive cerebral involvement.

Neurovascular tests are also performed. These include
1. Neck flexion. Meningeal irritation secondary to SH will produce resistance or pain with neck flexion.
2. Palpation of arteries. Both superficial and deep arteries are palpated including temporal, facial, carotid, subclavian, brachial, radial, abdominal aorta, and lower extremity arteries.
3. Ascultation of heart and blood vessels. Abnormal heart sounds, murmurs, or bruits may be present and indicate increased flow turbulence and stenosis in a vessel.
4. Ophthalmic pressures. Abnormal pressures in the opthalmic artery may indicate problems in the internal carotid artery.

Diagnostic Tests

There are a number of routine tests that are performed. Laboratory tests assess the general state of systemic circulation and body function. Electrocardiograms (ECGs) and chest radiographs assess heart and lung function. Computerized tomography (CT) scans, magnetic resonance images (MRIs), and angiography focus more specifically on alterations in brain structure. Diagnostic tests generally include
1. Urinalysis (detects infection, diabetes, renal failure, or dehydration).
2. Complete blood count (CBC); prothrombin time.
3. Erythrocyte sedimentation rate.
4. Blood sugar.
5. Serologic tests for syphilis.
6. Blood chemistry profile: serum electrolytes, serum cardiac enzyme levels. (Elevation of the creatinine phosphokinase isozyme CPK-MB is indicative of coincidental cardiac infarction.)
7. Blood cholesterol and lipid profile.
8. Radiograph of the chest (heart size, lungs).
9. ECG (arrhythmias, alterations in wave formation). Stroke patients may have coincidental heart disease, or stroke may cause ECG abnormalities, typically T-wave inversion, prolonged QT interval, and ST inversion.
10. Computerized tomography scan. In the acute phase, the CT scans may be negative or may reveal signs of edema and displacement of brain structures. They can distinguish hemorrhagic stroke from ischemic stroke. Later CT scans, ideally taken several days after the initial stroke, typically delineate infarction by showing areas of decreased density. The CT scan also distinguishes between causative factors (infarction versus hemorrhage) and detects nonvascular causes of stroke (tumor). These findings have allowed more precise localization of lesions and have revolutionized the diagnosis of stroke. It is important to remember that the extent of CT lesion does not necessarily correlate with clinical signs or changes in function (Fig. 17–3).
11. Magnetic resonance imaging. Greater resolution of cerebral gray and white matter is obtained with MRI than with a CT scan. Magnetic resonance imaging also allows detection of cerebral infarction much earlier, within 2 to 6 hours after stroke.
12. Positron emission tomography (PET). The use of PET allows imaging of regional blood flow and localized cerebral metabolism. Early use of PET

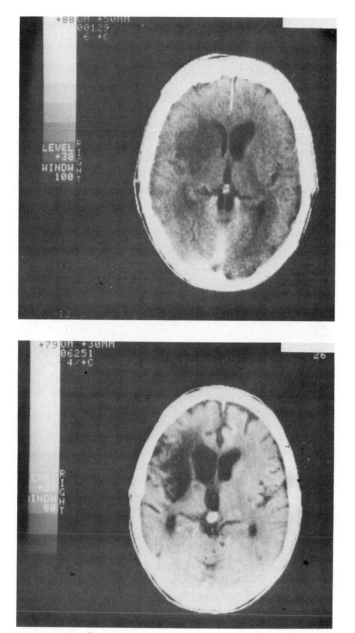

Figure 17–3. Computed tomography scan of a patient with infarction of the middle cerebral artery territory. (From Hachinski, V, and Norris, JW: The Acute Stroke, FA Davis, Philadelphia, 1985, p 194, with permission.)

scanning may help determine lesion location. Scanning may also help to determine areas of tissue where ischemia is reversible. The high cost and limited accessibility of this diagnostic tool limit its use.

13. Cerebral angiography. Cerebral angiography involves the injection of radiopaque dye in blood vessels with subsequent radiography. It may be used if CT scans or MRIs are unavailable or in selected cases in which surgery is considered (stenosis, arteriovenous malformations). The risks of angiography are relatively high; death or stroke occurs in 1 to 2 percent of cases, with minor complications in 5 to 6 percent of cases.[4,5,9]

CLINICAL MANIFESTATIONS

Signs and Symptoms

SENSATION

Sensation is frequently impaired but rarely absent on the hemiplegic side. The type and extent of deficit is related to the location and extent of the vascular lesion. Specific, localized areas of dysfunction are common with cortical lesions, while diffuse involvement throughout the whole side suggests deeper lesions involving the thalamus and adjacent structures. Symptoms of crossed anesthesia (ipsilateral facial impairments with contralateral trunk and limb deficits) typify brainstem lesions. Proprioceptive losses are common. In one study 44 percent of patients with stroke demonstrated significant proprioceptive loss; associated impairments were noted in motor power, postural function, and overall level of disability.[15] Loss of superficial touch, and pain and temperature sensation is also common and contributes to overall perceptual dysfunction and risk of self-injury. Patients may experience impairments in any of the combined sensations such as two-point discrimination or stereognosis. *Homonymous hemianopsia,* a visual field defect, is common in hemiplegia. The patient experiences blindness of the nasal half of one eye and temporal half of the other eye. The term right or left is used to designate the side of the visual defect and corresponds to the hemiplegic side. Field defects contribute to the patient's overall lack of awareness of the hemiplegic side. Patients may also experience impairments in depth perception that are concomitant with other problems in spatial relationships (see Chapter 28). **Forced gaze deviation** occurs due to the involvement of muscles controlling eye movements. Unopposed action of eye muscles causes the eyes to deviate in the direction of the intact musculature. Patients with hemispheric lesions may look away from the hemiplegic side, while patients with brainstem lesions may look toward the hemiplegic side.[10]

MOTOR FUNCTION
Sequential Recovery Stages

During the early stages of stroke, flaccidity with no voluntary movement is common. Usually this is replaced by the development of spasticity, hyperreflexia, and mass patterns of movement, termed **synergies.** Muscles involved in synergy patterns are often so strongly linked together that isolated movements outside the mass synergistic patterns are not possible. As recovery progresses, spasticity and synergies begin to decline and advanced movement patterns become possible. This general pattern of recovery was described in detail by Twitchell[16] and Brunnstrom[17,18] who elaborated the process into six distinct stages (Table 17–2). Bobath collapsed the sequence into three main recovery stages: (1) the initial flaccid stage, (2) the stage of spasticity, and (3) the stage of relative recovery.[19] Additional investigators have confirmed this pattern of motor recovery following stroke.[20–22] Several important points merit consideration. Motor recovery occurs in a relatively predictable

Table 17-2 SEQUENTIAL RECOVERY STAGES IN HEMIPLEGIA

STAGE 1 Recovery from hemiplegia occurs in a stereotyped sequence of events that begins with a period of *flaccidity* immediately following the acute episode. *No movement of the limbs* can be elicited.

STAGE 2 As recovery begins, the basic limb synergies or some of their components may appear as associated reactions, or *minimal voluntary movement* responses may be present. At this time, *spasticity* begins to develop.

STAGE 3 Thereafter, the patient gains *voluntary control of the movement synergies*, although full range of all synergy components does not necessarily develop. *Spasticity* has further increased and may become *severe*.

STAGE 4 Some *movement combinations that do not follow the paths of either synergy* are mastered, first with difficulty, then with more ease, and *spasticity begins to decline*.

STAGE 5 If progress continues, *more difficult movement combinations* are learned as the basic limb synergies lose their dominance over motor acts.

STAGE 6 With the *disappearance of spasticity*, individual joint movements become possible and *coordination* approaches normal. From here on, as the last recovery step, normal motor function is restored, but this last stage is not achieved by all, for the recovery process can plateau at any stage.

From Brunnstrom, S: Movement Therapy in Hemiplegia. Harper & Row, New York, 1970, with permission.

pattern. The recovery stages are viewed as sequential, although variability in the clinical picture at each stage is possible. Not all patients recover fully. Patients may plateau at any stage, depending upon the severity of their involvement and their capacity for adaptation. Finally, recovery rates differ among patients.

Alterations in Tone

A critical concept in the management of the patient with stroke is the ability to recognize tonal changes and synergy movement patterns as separate and distinct clinical findings and to understand the relationship between the two. *Flaccidity* is usually present immediately after the stroke and is generally short-lived, lasting hours, days, or weeks. *Spasticity* emerges in about 90 percent of cases and tends to occur in predictable muscle groups, commonly the antigravity muscles. The effects of spasticity include restricted movement and static posturing of the limbs. In the upper extremity, spasticity is frequently strong in scapular retractors; shoulder adductors, depressors, and internal rotators; elbow flexors and forearm pronators; and wrist and finger flexors. In the neck and trunk, spasticity may cause slumping (increased side-flexion) to the hemiplegic side. In the lower extremity, spasticity is often found in the pelvic retractors; hip adductors and internal rotators; hip and knee extensors; plantar flexors and supinators; and toe flexors.[19]

The automatic adjustment of muscle tension that occurs normally in preparation for and during a movement task, termed automatic postural tone, may also be impaired.[23] Thus patients with stroke may lack the ability to stabilize proximal joints and trunk appropriately, with resulting malalignment of body segments and, in long-standing cases, fixed musculoskeletal impairments. Loss of automaticity is particularly problematic since patients

would be required to exert conscious control over aspects of movement not normally under cortical control.

Synergy Patterns

Synergy patterns of the extremities are stereotyped, primitive movement patterns associated with the presence of spasticity. They may be elicited either reflexly, as associated reactions, or as voluntary movement patterns. There are two basic synergies of each extremity: a flexion synergy and an extension synergy (presented in Table 17-3). An inspection of the synergy components reveals that certain muscles not usually involved in either synergy including the (1) latisimus dorsi, (2) teres major, (3) serratus anterior, (4) finger extensors, and (5) ankle evertors. These muscles, therefore, are generally difficult to rehabilitate and represent important functional limitations for many patients in their activities and in gait. Loss of isolated movement patterns also has important functional implications.[18,24]

Reflexes

Reflexes are altered and vary according to the stage of recovery. Initially, stroke results in hypotonia and areflexia. During the middle stages of recovery when spasticity and synergies are strong, hyperreflexia emerges. Stretch reflexes become hyperactive and patients typically demonstrate clonus and the clasp-knife reflex. Cutaneous reflexes (positive Babinski) may be present. Primitive or tonic reflex patterns may appear in a readily identifiable form. Thus, movement of the head frequently elicits an obligatory change in resting tone or movement of the extremities. Flexion of the neck results in flexion of the arms and extension of the legs; extension of the neck produces the opposite responses (**symmetric tonic neck reflex—STNR**). Head rotation to the left causes extension of the left arm and leg (jaw limbs) with flexion of the right arm and leg (skull limbs); head rotation to the right causes the reverse pattern (**asymmetric tonic neck reflex—ATNR**). Supine positioning produces an increase in extensor tone, while prone positioning increases flexor tone (**sym-**

Table 17-3 SYNERGY PATTERNS OF THE EXTREMITIES

	Flexion Synergy Components	**Extension Synergy Components**
Upper Extremity	Scapular retraction/ elevation or hyperextension	Scapular protraction
	Shoulder abduction, external rotation	Shoulder adduction,* internal rotation
	Elbow flexion*	Elbow extension
	Forearm supination	Forearm pronation*
	Wrist and finger flexion	Wrist and finger flexion
Lower Extremity	Hip flexion,* abduction, external rotation	Hip extension, adduction,* internal rotation
	Knee flexion	Knee extension*
	Ankle dorsiflexion inversion	Ankle plantarflexion,* inversion
	Toe dorsiflexion	Toe plantarflexion

*Generally the strongest components.

metric tonic labyrinthine reflex—STLR). Rotation of the upper trunk with respect to the pelvis may also influence movement of the extremities. Rotation toward the hemiplegic side results in flexion of the hemiplegic upper extremity and extension of hemiplegic lower extremity. Rotation toward the uninvolved side produces the opposite responses (tonic lumbar reflex—TLR). Finally, pressure on the bottom of the hemiplegic foot may produce a strong co-contraction response of lower extremity extensors and flexors, resulting in a rigidly extended and fixed limb (positive supporting reaction).[18,19,25]

Associated reactions are also commonly present. These consist of abnormal, automatic responses of the involved limb resulting from action occurring in some other part of the body, either by voluntary or reflex stimulation (e.g., yawning, sneezing, coughing, stretching). They are easier to elicit in the presence of spasticity and frequently interact with tonic reflexes. Generally, although this is not true in every case, associated reactions elicit the same direction of movement in the contralateral upper extremity (i.e., flexion evokes flexion), while in the lower extremity opposite movements are elicited (i.e., flexion of one lower extremity evokes extension of the other). Specific associated reactions have also been identified. Elevation of the hemiplegic arm above the horizontal may elicit an extension and abduction response of the fingers (Sougues' phenomenon). Resistance to abduction or adduction produces a similar response in the opposite limb (adduction elicits adduction) in both the upper and lower extremities (Raimiste's phenomenon). Homolateral limb synkinesis is the term used to describe the mutual dependency that exists between hemiplegic limbs (flexion of the arm elicits flexion of the leg on the hemiplegic side).[19,21,24,26]

Higher level balance reactions (righting, equilibrium, protective extension reactions) are frequently impaired or absent. Patients may be unable to maintain their head in its normal upright alignment (face vertical with the mouth in a horizontal position) in response to a change in body position or movement. Impaired righting reactions (RR) are also evident when rotation of either the head or trunk within the body axis fails to produce a log rolling (trunk moving as one unit) or segmental rolling (head, upper trunk, then lower trunk) pattern. Lack of equilibrium reactions (ER) may cause the patient to lose balance and fall in response to a change of the center of mass (COM) over the base of support (BOS). Protective extension (PE) of either hemiplegic limb in response to falling is also commonly impaired or absent.

Paresis

Paresis or weakness is a common finding. Patients with spastic hemiparesis are unable to generate normal levels of force necessary for initiating and controlling movement or for maintaining posture. Specific changes occur in both the motor neuron and muscle. The number of functioning agonist motor units is decreased, by as much as 50 percent at 6 months in some patients with stroke.[27] The recruitment order of motor units may be altered and firing rates decreased. Thus patients have increased difficulties trying to maintain a constant level of force production. Denervation potentials are common, the result of denervation changes in the corticospinal tracts. Changes in muscle include atrophy of muscle fibers with a greater loss of fast-twitch fibers. Contraction time is increased with increased fatigability noted in paretic muscles. Patients consistently report that increased effort produces less than maximum muscular force.[28]

Active restraint arising from antagonist muscles can influence agonist strength. Bobath[19] has suggested that spasticity of antagonist muscles is a major factor in the agonist weakness. Bohannon et al.[29] challenge this conclusion. These investigators demonstrated a correlation between paresis and spasticity in agonist muscles but not with antagonist spasticity. Inappropriate co-activation of agonist-antagonist muscles is another form of active restraint and may be more of a factor than spasticity, especially in rapid and reciprocal contractions.[30,31] Passive restraint secondary to abnormal mechanical changes in the soft tissues can also affect agonist strength.

Not all muscle groups are affected equally. The amount of paresis experienced by the patient may also vary according to specific situational contexts. Thus a patient may appear stronger in some functional tasks than in others. Paresis on the "supposedly normal" unaffected side has also been reported.[32,33]

Incoordination

Incoordination can result from cerebellar or basal ganglia involvement, from proprioceptive losses, or from motor weakness. Ataxia of the extremities or trunk is common in patients with cerebellar lesions. Reciprocal interaction with graded control of agonist-antagonists muscle pairs and synergistic activation may be impaired. The stretch reflex responses that allow automatic adaption of muscles to changes to posture and movement are commonly abnormal.[10,21]

Motor Programming Deficits

Hemispheric differences have been reported in the area of movement control. The left hemisphere has a primary role in the sequencing of movements. Thus patients with left CVA (right hemiplegia) have increased difficulty initiating and performing sequences of movements, and may take longer to learn a task. They also demonstrate slower movements overall, with more positioning errors. The right hemisphere, on the other hand, may have an increased role in sustaining a movement or posture. Thus patients with right CVA (left hemiplegia) characteristically demonstrate motor impersistence (inability to sustain a movement or posture).[34,35]

Patients with left hemisphere lesions are also more likely to present with apraxia. Apraxia is defined as an inability to perform purposive movements although there is no sensory or motor impairment. Problems exist in performing previously learned movements, gestures, and sequences of movements. Two categories of apraxia are (1) ideomotor, where movement is not possible upon command but may occur automatically, and (2) ideational, where purposeful movement is not possible, either automatically or on command.

Thus patients with left hemisphere damage are more likely to present with motor programming deficits than are patients with right hemisphere damage. In a study of motor programming differences, Light and coworkers[36] found support for these conclusions and in addition noted deficits in motor programming in both involved and "uninvolved" arms of patients with left CVA.

FUNCTIONAL ABILITIES

Functional mobility skills following stroke are typically impaired or absent and vary considerably from patient to patient. In general, rolling, sitting up, transfers, standing up, and walking pose significant problems for the moderately to severely involved patient with acute stroke. Basic ADL skills such as feeding and dressing are also compromised. The ability to perform functional tasks is influenced by a number of factors. Motor and perceptual impairments have the greatest impact on functional performance, but other limiting factors include disorientation, communication disorders, sensory loss, and decreased cardiorespiratory endurance.[37,38]

SPEECH AND LANGUAGE DISORDERS

Patients with lesions involving the parietooccipital cortex of the dominant hemisphere (typically the left hemisphere) demonstrate speech and language impairments. *Aphasia* is the general term used to describe an acquired communication disorder caused by brain damage and characterized by an impairment of language comprehension, formulation, and use. Aphasia has been estimated to occur in up to 40 percent of all stroke patients.[39] There are many different types of aphasias; major classification categories are fluent, nonfluent, and global. In **fluent aphasia,** speech flows smoothly, with a variety of grammatical constructions and preserved melody of speech. Auditory comprehension is impaired. In **nonfluent aphasia** the flow of speech is slow and hesitant, vocabulary is limited, and syntax is impaired. Articulation may be labored. Comprehension is good. *Global aphasia* is a severe aphasia characterized by marked impairments of the production and comprehension of language. It is often an indication of extensive brain damage. (See Chapter 29 on neurogenic disorders of speech and language for a complete discussion of this topic.)

Patients with stroke may also present with **dysarthria.** This term refers to a category of motor speech disorders caused by impairment in parts of the central or peripheral nervous system that mediate speech production. Respiration, articulation, phonation, resonance, and/or prosody may be affected. Volitional and automatic actions, for example, chewing and swallowing (dysphagia), and movement of the jaw and tongue, may also be impaired. In patients with stroke, dysarthria can accompany aphasia, complicating the course of rehabilitation.

PERCEPTUAL DEFICITS

Lesions of the parietal lobe of the nondominant hemisphere (typically the right hemisphere) can produce perceptual deficits. These may include visuospatial dis-

tortions, disturbances in body image, and unilateral neglect. Patients with visuospatial impairments may not be able to judge distance, size, position, rate of movement, form, or the relation of parts to the whole. Thus the patient may consistently bump the wheelchair into the door frame and is unable to get through the doorway. With **topographical disorientation,** the patient consistently gets lost going from one place to another. Patients may also experience difficulties in distinguishing figure-ground relationships. The brakes on a wheelchair may be indistinguishable from the rest of the parts of the wheelchair. Problems in the perception of verticality, especially in dimly lit areas, may also occur. This may be manifested by a patient who is constantly leaning over to one side. **Body scheme** (a postural model of the body and the relationship of its parts) and **body image** (a visual and mental image of one's body that includes feelings about one's body) may be distorted. Patients with unilateral neglect are generally unaware of what happens on the hemiplegic side. A severe form (anosognosia) includes frank denial of the presence or severity of one's disability. Sensory losses and hemianopsia frequently contribute to this perceptual problem.[40] The reader is referred to Chapter 28 on perceptual deficits for a more complete discussion of these deficits.

COGNITIVE AND BEHAVIORAL CHANGES

Patients with stroke differ widely in their approach to processing information and in their behavioral styles. Those with left hemisphere damage (right hemiplegia) demonstrate difficulties in processing information in a sequential, linear manner. They are frequently described as negative, anxious, and depressed. They are likely to be slower, more cautious, uncertain, and insecure. This makes them more hesitant when performing tasks and increases the need for more frequent feedback and support. They tend, however, to be realistic in their appraisal of their existing problems.

Patients with right hemisphere damage (left hemiplegia), on the other hand, demonstrate difficulty in grasping the whole idea or the overall organization of a pattern or activity. These patients are frequently described as indifferent, quick and impulsive, and euphoric. They tend to overestimate their abilities while minimizing or denying their problems. Safety is therefore a far greater issue with left hemiplegia, where poor judgment is common. These patients also require a great deal of feedback when learning a new task. The feedback should be focused on slowing down the activity, checking each component part, and relating it to the whole task. The patient with left hemiplegia frequently cannot attend to visuospatial cues effectively, especially in a cluttered or crowded environment.[34,41,42] Table 17-4 summarizes behaviors attributed to the left and right hemispheres.

Cognitive deficits may exist across a wide area of function. Deficits in orientation, attention, information processing speed, conceptual abilities, executive functioning, memory, and learning can occur. They may be primary impairments resulting from the stroke, or premorbid changes associated with pathologic aging. The patient with stroke typically has a short retention span,

Table 17–4 BEHAVIORS ATTRIBUTED TO THE LEFT AND RIGHT HEMISPHERES

Behavior	Left Hemisphere	Right Hemisphere
Cognitive style	Processing information in a sequential, linear manner Observing and analyzing details	Processing information in a simultaneous, holistic, or gestalt manner Grasping overall organization or pattern
Perception/cognition	Processing and producing language	Processing nonverbal stimuli (environmental sounds, speech intonation, complex shapes, and designs) Visual-spatial perception Drawing inferences, synthesizing information
Academic skills	Reading: sound-symbol relationships, word recognition, reading comprehension Performing mathematical calculations	Mathematical reasoning and judgment Alignment of numerals in calculations
Motor	Sequencing movements Performing movements and gestures to command	Sustaining a movement or posture
Emotions	Expression of positive emotions	Expression of negative emotions Perception of emotion

remembering only the first few bits of information in a series of commands. Immediate and short-term memory are often impaired, while long-term memory remains intact. Thus the patient cannot remember the instructions for a new task given only 30 seconds ago but can remember things done 30 years ago. The patient may also have difficulties in generalizing information. Thus information learned in one setting cannot be transposed to other situations.[43]

The patient with stroke may demonstrate an emotional dysregulation syndrome termed **emotional lability.** It is characterized by pathologic laughing and weeping in which the patient changes quickly from laughing to crying with only slight provocation. Such a patient is typically unable to inhibit the expression of spontaneous emotions. Frequent crying may also accompany depression.[44,45]

Sensory losses coupled with an unfamiliar hospital environment and inactivity following acute stroke can lead to symptoms of sensory deprivation such as irritability, confusion, restlessness, and sometimes psychosis, delusions, or hallucinations. Nighttime may be particularly problematic. Positioning the bed with the affected side toward the door limits social interaction and may increase the patient's disorientation. Some patients with diminished capacity are equally unable to deal with a sensory overload, produced by too much stimulation. Altered arousal levels are implicated.

Dementia can result from multiple infarcts of the brain, termed *multiinfarct dementia*. It is characterized by a generalized decline in higher brain functions and typified by faulty judgments, impaired consciousness, poor memory, diminished communication, and behavioral or mood alterations. These changes are often associated with episodes of cerebral ischemia, focal neurologic signs, and hypertension. The patient may fluctuate between periods of impaired function and periods of improved or normal function.[43]

Epileptic seizures occur in a small percentage of stroke patients and are slightly more common in occlusive carotid disease (17%) than in MCA disease (11%).

Seizures also occur at the onset of cerebral hemorrhage in about 15% of the cases. They tend to be of the partial motor type and in some patients may occur as the initial presenting symptom.[46]

BLADDER AND BOWEL DYSFUNCTION

Urinary incontinence may require the temporary use of an indwelling catheter. Generally this problem improves quickly. Early removal of a catheter is desirable to prevent the development of infection. Patients are frequently impacted and may require stool softeners and low residue diets to resolve this problem.

OROFACIAL DYSFUNCTION

Swallowing dysfunction, **dysphagia,** is a common complication after stroke. It occurs in lesions affecting the medullary brainstem (cranial nerves IX and X) as well as in acute hemispheric lesions. In patients referred for detailed evaluation of dysphagia, the most frequent problem seen is delayed triggering of the swallowing reflex (86% of patients) followed by reduced pharyngeal peristalsis (58% of patients) and reduced lingual control (50% of patients). Poor jaw and lip closure, altered sensation, impaired head control, and poor sitting balance also contribute to the patient's swallowing difficulties. Most demonstrate multiple problems that result in drooling, difficulty ingesting food, aspiration, dysarthria, and asymmetry of the muscles of facial expression. Decreased nutritional intake may require the temporary use of a nasogastric tube for feeding. These problems have tremendous social implications, for the patient frequently feels humiliated and frustrated by their presence.[47]

Secondary Impairments

PSYCHOLOGIC PROBLEMS

The patient who has had a stroke is often frustrated by changes in the ability to sense, move, communicate, think, or act as he or she did before. Common psychologic reactions include anxiety, depression, or denial. Additionally, the patient's behavior may be influenced by cognitive deficits that leave him or her irritable, inflexible, hypercritical, impatient, impulsive, apathetic, or overdependent on others. These behaviors along with a poor social perception of one's self and environment may lead to increasing isolation and stress. Depression is extremely common, occurring in about one-third of the cases. Most patients remain significantly depressed for many months, with an average time of 7 to 8 months. The period from 6 months to 2 years after a CVA is the most likely time for depression to occur. Depression occurs in both mildly and severely involved patients and thus is not significantly related to the degree of impairment. Patients with lesions of the left hemisphere may experience more frequent and more severe depression than patients with right hemisphere or brainstem strokes.[37,38] These findings suggest that post-stroke depression may not be simply a result of psychologic reaction to disability but rather a primary impairment directly related to the CVA.[43–48]

DECREASING RANGE OF MOVEMENT, CONTRACTURE, AND DEFORMITY

Decreasing range of movement (ROM), contracture, and deformity may result from loss of voluntary movement and immobilization. Flexibility of connective tissue is lost and muscles experience disuse atrophy. As contractures progress, edema and pain may develop and further restrict attempts to gain motion. In the upper extremity, limitations in shoulder motions are common. Patients also frequently develop contractures of the elbow, wrist and finger flexors, and forearm pronators. In the lower extremity plantarflexion contractures are common. Alterations in alignment coupled with decreased efficiency of muscles may lead to increased energy expenditure, altered patterns of movement, and excessive effort.

DEEP VENOUS THROMBOSIS

Deep venous thrombosis (DVT) and pulmonary embolism are potential complications for all immobilized patients. Common symptoms of DVT include calf pain or tenderness, swelling, and discoloration of the leg. About 50 percent of the cases do not present with clinically detectable symptoms and can be identified by phlebography or other noninvasive techniques. Anticoagulants and antiplatelet agents are the primary medical treatments, along with bed rest and elevation of the affected limb.

PAIN

Patients with lesions affecting the thalamus (posterolateral ventral nuclei) may initially experience a contralateral sensory loss. After several weeks or months this may be replaced by a severe burning pain generalized on the hemiplegic side (*thalamic syndrome*). Pain is increased by stimuli or contact with that side. Thalamic syndrome is extremely debilitating and the patient generally has a poor functional outcome.

Pain may also result from muscle imbalances, improper movement patterns, musculoskeletal strain,

and poor alignment. For example, knee pain is a common finding with prolonged or severe hyperextension during gait. The sequelae of pain are reduced function, impaired concentration, depression, and decreased rehabilitation potential.

SHOULDER DYSFUNCTION
Shoulder Subluxation and Pain

Shoulder pain is extremely common following stroke, occurring in 70 to 84 percent of patients.[49] Pain is typically present with movement and, in more severe cases, at rest. Several causes of shoulder pain have been widely proposed. In the flaccid stage, proprioceptive impairment, lack of tone, and muscle paralysis reduce the support and normal seating action of the rotator cuff muscles, particulary the supraspinatus. The ligaments and capsule thus become the shoulder's sole support. The normal orientation of the glenoid fossa is upward, outward, and forward, so that it keeps the superior capsule taut and stabilizes the humerus mechanically. Any abduction or forward flexion of the humerus, or scapular depression and downward rotation, reduces this stabilization and causes the humerus to sublux. Initially the subluxation is not painful, but mechanical stresses resulting from traction and gravitational forces produce persistent malalignment. Glenohumeral friction-compression stresses also occur between the humeral head and superior soft tissues during flexion or abduction movements in the absence of normal simultaneous rotation of the arm and normal scapulohumeral rhythm. In the spastic stage, abnormal muscle tone contributes to poor scapular position (depression, retraction, and downward rotation) and contributes to subluxation and restricted movement. Secondary tightness in ligaments, tendons, and joint capsule quickly develops. Adhesive capsulitis is a common finding. Poor handling and positioning of the hemiplegic arm have also been implicated in producing joint microtrauma and pain. Activities that traumatize the shoulder include passive range of motion (PROM) without adequate mobilization of the scapula, pulling on the arm during a transfer, or using reciprocal pulleys.[49,50]

Pain develops in a typical pattern. Patients at first report sharp end-range pain with movement and can easily pinpoint the location of the pain. If the causative factors are not addressed, pain increases to include pain on all movement, particularly with shoulder flexion and abduction. Increasing pain may also be experienced in certain positions, for example, lying in bed at night. Eventually the patient complains of intense pain and does not tolerate any movement of the arm. At this point the pain is diffuse and not easily localized. Pain may extend into the arm and hand.[51]

Reflex sympathetic dystrophy (RSD or shoulder-hand syndrome) also occurs in approximately 12 to 25 percent of the cases.[52] The patient experiences swelling and tenderness of the hand and fingers along with shoulder pain. Sympathetic vasomotor changes are evident and include warm, red, and glossy skin. Trophic changes of the fingernails develop (i.e., the nails appear white, opaque). The patient experiences increasing pain with movement and further immobilization leads to increased stiffness, contracture, and atrophy of muscle. In the late stages the skin is typically cool, cyanotic, and damp. Fibrous and articular changes progress. The hand typically becomes contracted in metacarpophalangeal (MP) extension and interphalangeal (IP) flexion, similar to the "intrinsic minus hand." There is marked atrophy of thenar and hypothenar muscles with flattening of the hand. Osteoporotic changes become evident on radiographs. Early diagnosis and treatment are critical in preventing or minimizing the late changes of RSD. Because of close daily contact with the patient, the therapist is frequently one of the first to recognize and report early signs and symptoms. Radionuclide bone scans (scintigraphy) can be used to reliably confirm early symptoms of RSD.

DECONDITIONING

Patients who suffer a stroke as a result of cardiac disease may demonstrate impaired cardiac output, cardiac decompensation, and serious rhythm disorders. If these problems persist, they can directly alter cerebral perfusion and produce additional focal signs (e.g., mental confusion). Cardiac limitations in exercise tolerance may restrict the patient's rehabilitation potential and require diligent monitoring and careful exercise prescription by the physical therapist. Deconditioning is a common finding in older adults with limited activity levels and may have been present prior to the stroke. Age-related changes in the cardiorespiratory systems (reduced cardiac output, decreased maximal oxygen uptake, decreased resiratory capacity) and musculoskeletal systems (decreased muscle mass, strength, lean body mass) all affect activity tolerance and endurance levels. Prolonged bed rest during the acute stroke phase further diminishes rehabilitation potential, decreases energy reserves, and increases activity intolerance. Activity intolerance may also be related to depression, a common finding in stroke.[53]

RECOVERY FROM STROKE

Mortality for initial strokes varies considerably with an overall rate ranging from 22 to 37 percent at 3 weeks to 1 month, 25 to 50 percent at 1 year, and 68 to 72 percent at 5 years.[54] At 10 years only 35 percent of patients are still alive.[6] The type of stroke is significant in determining survival. Patients with intracerebral hemorrhage account for the largest number of deaths following an acute episode (59 to 72% at 3 months) followed by subarachnoid hemorrhage (43% at 3 months) and thromboembolic stroke (30% at 3 months). Survival rates are dramatically lessened by a number of medical conditions and comorbidities, including age, hypertension, heart disease, and diabetes. Loss of consciousness at stroke onset, lesion size, persistent severe hemiplegia, multiple neurologic deficits, and history of previous stroke are also important predictors of mortality. Most patients suffer recurrent episodes of stroke, usually of the same type, and these are influenced by the same risk factors influencing survival.[55]

Recovery from stroke is fastest in the first few weeks after onset, with most measurable neurologic recovery (perhaps 90%) occurring in the first 3 months. Patients may continue to make functional gains for longer periods, up to 6 months or a year after insult. A few patients may demonstrate remarkable and unexpected recovery with improvements occurring over a period of years. Rates of improvement will vary across management categories: patients suffering minor stroke may rapidly recover with few or no residual deficits, while patients with severe stroke may demonstrate limited recovery. An important finding is that recovery has been demonstrated even in patients with extensive central nervous system (CNS) damage and advanced age.[21,22,56-58]

Early recovery is generally thought to be the result of resolution of local vascular and metabolic factors. Thus the reduction of edema, absorption of damaged tissue, and improved local circulation allows intact neurons that were previously inhibited to regain function. Central nervous system plasticity is thought to account for continuing recovery. In the presence of cell death, functional reorganization of the CNS (function-induced plasticity) may occur. A number of different mechanisms have been identified, including collateral sprouting and unmasking. Sprouting involves synaptic reclamation of a denervated region by nearby intact neurons. Unmasking refers to the release (uncovering) of previously inactive neurons, which then take over function of the damaged neurons. These processes are thought to occur both locally and at brain areas remote from the lesion. The redevelopment of adequate CNS inhibitory mechanisms may underlie the emergence of selective movement control and inhibition mass movements and pathologic reflexes. Results from animal studies also suggest that environment plays an important part in recovery. Brain-injured rats raised in "enriched conditions" did considerably better than rats raised in "impoverished conditions."[56-58]

MEDICAL MANAGEMENT

Medical management includes the identification and control of stroke risk factors. Primary prevention strategies may include

1. Regulation of blood pressure.
2. Dietary adjustments: reduced intake of saturated fats, and control of hypercholesterolemia, and sodium and potassium intakes.
3. Cessation of smoking.
4. Platelet-inhibiting therapy (aspirin)—use of platelet antiaggregants, or anticoagulants.
5. Control of associated diseases (e.g., diabetes, heart disease).
6. Surgery (carotid or vertebrobasilar endarterectomy, angioplasty).

Medical management of acute cerebral infarction and progressing stroke generally includes strategies to

1. Restore fluid and electrolyte balance.
2. Maintain adequate airway and pulmonary function. Patients in the acute stage may require suctioning

but rarely require intubation or assisted ventilation. Oxygen therapy (nasal mask or catheter oxygen therapy) may improve clinical signs of hypoxia but is not normally indicated.

3. Maintain sufficient cardiac output. If the causes of stroke are cardiac in origin, medical management focuses on control of arrhythmias and cardiac decompensation.

4. Prevent hypoxia and control blood pressure. Hypotension is managed with volume expanders. Hypertension agents may be used but have the added risk of inducing hypotension and decreasing cerebral perfusion.

5. Prevent hypoglycemia or hyperglycemia.

6. Control seizures and infections.

7. Control intracranial pressure and uncal herniation using antiedema agents. Ventriculostomy may be indicated to monitor and drain cerebrospinal fluid (CSF).[59,60]

Additional strategies currently under intense investigation include

1. Administration of clot-dissolving enzymes (fibrinolysins such as tissue plasminogen activator [tPA] or streptokinase), with rapid referral to neurologic services.

2. Strategies aimed at increasing cerebral perfusion (hemodilution) and interrupting the cytotoxic chain of events (e.g., glutamate receptor blockers, calcium channel blockers, barbiturates, or naloxone).[8,60]

Neurosurgery may be indicated in cases where intracranial bleeding or compression cause elevated intracranial pressures, since death may result from brain herniation and brainstem compression. Generally superficial or lobar lesions (subdural hematoma, aneurysm, subarachnoid hemorrhage, and arteriovenous malformation) are more amenable to neurosurgery than large, deep lesions.[59]

REHABILITATIVE MANAGEMENT

General Considerations

Rehabilitation begun early in the acute stage optimizes the patient's potential for functional recovery. Early mobilization prevents or minimizes the harmful effects of deconditioning and the potential for secondary impairments. Functional reorganization is promoted through use of the affected side. Maladaptive patterns of movement and poor habits may be prevented. Mental deterioration can be reduced through the development of a positive outlook and an early, organized plan of care that stresses resumption of normal, everyday activities. In the acute care setting, patients may be referred for rehabilitation services or may be admitted to a specific stroke rehabilitation unit. Both groups have consistently demonstrated significantly improved functional outcomes when compared to patients not receiving those services.[61-65]

Patients with moderate or severe residual deficits gen-

erally require intensive inpatient rehabilitation services to assist functional recovery. Optimal timing of rehabilitation based upon individual patient readiness is also an important consideration. A number of factors appear to be related to rehabilitation readiness, including the side of the lesion. There is some evidence to suggest that patients with right hemiplegia may respond more favorably to earlier comprehensive rehabilitation efforts. Patients with left hemiplegia who suffer more cognitive-perceptual deficits and generally have longer rehabilitation stays may benefit from the additional preadmission time to allow for cognitive and perceptual-motor reorganization. Equally important factors that might influence the timing of rehabilitation efforts include medical stability, motivation, patient endurance, stage of recovery, and ability to learn. In an era of time-limited payment for comprehensive rehabilitation services, selecting the optimal time for rehabilitation training may prevent unnecessary patient failures and improve long-term functional outcomes.[66,67]

Comprehensive services for the patient with stroke can best be provided by a team of rehabilitation specialists including the physician, nurse, physical therapist, occupational therapist, speech pathologist, and medical social worker. Additional disciplines may also include a neuropsychologist, audiologist, dietician, or opthalmologist. One of the critical aspects of communication with team members is the development of an integrated plan of care with collaborative goals, and treatments that are mutually reinforced in all therapies.[68]

Assessment

The physical therapy assessment will be determined by each patient's unique needs and problems. Comprehensive assessment of the patient with neurologic impairments may include any of a number of assessments (Table 17–5). (See earlier chapters for a more complete discussion of these assessments.)

MENTAL STATUS

It is important to assess cognitive function first since it may affect the results of other assessments. An evaluation of level of consciousness, memory (immediate recall, short- and long-term), orientation (to person, place, time), ability to follow instructions (one-, two-, and three-level commands), higher cortical functions (calculation ability, abstract reasoning), and attention span should be included, as well as an investigation of behavioral and emotional responses. Learning deficits, including retention and generalization deficits, can significantly impede rehabilitation efforts and should be identified early.

COMMUNICATION ABILITY

Because communication deficits may also severely limit the validity of other assessments, patient comprehension should be fully ascertained before proceeding with these evaluations. Close collaboration with the speech pathologist will be important in making an accurate determination of the patient's communication defi-

Table 17–5 ASSESSMENT BATTERY FOR NEUROLOGICALLY IMPAIRED PATIENTS

Demographic information
History
Patient's chief complaint
Mental status
Communication ability
Sensation
Perception
Joint mobility
   Range of motion (ROM)
   Joint play
   Soft tissue compliance
Skin condition
Edema
Motor control
   Muscle tone
   Reflexes/reactions
   Strength
   Voluntary movement patterns
   Motor planning ability
   Coordination
   Balance
Functional mobility skills
   Bed mobility
   Transfers
   Wheelchair mobility
   Gait
Endurance/cardiorespiratory status
Discharge planning
   Environmental assessment
   Equipment needs

cits. Impairments in receptive language (word recognition, auditory comprehension, reading comprehension) and/or expressive language function (word finding, fluency, writing, spelling) should be noted. It is not uncommon for staff to overestimate the patient's abilities to understand speech. A quick assessment to check an individual's level of understanding can be performed by saying one thing to the patient and gesturing another (e.g., "It's hot in here" and putting on a sweater). The functional deficits of dysarthria and dysphagia should be carefully examined. Alternate forms of communication (gestures, movements, pantomime) should be well established before additional testing begins.

SENSATION

A sensory examination should include superficial, proprioceptive, and combined sensations. Deficits may be apparent in one sensory modality and not in others. Differences can also be expected between the hemiplegic extremities. Comparisons with the intact side can be made, but the therapist should be cognizant that deficits may exist in the supposedly "normal" extremities secondary to effects of comorbid conditions or aging. The visual system should be carefully investigated, including tests for acuity, peripheral vision, depth perception, and hemianopsia. Hearing status should be determined.

PERCEPTION

Significant information on sensory and perceptual deficits will be provided by close collaboration with the occupational therapist. Many tests and formalized test batteries have been developed to assess body scheme,

body image, spatial relations, agnosia, and apraxia. These are discussed fully in Chapter 28. Since the patient with left hemiplegia may behave in ways which tend to minimize his disabilities, it is easy for staff to overestimate the patient's perceptual abilities. The use of gestures or visual cues may decrease this patient's ability to perform, whereas verbal cues (either the therapist's or the patient's) may permit success. Carefully structuring the environment (minimizing clutter and activity, using clear reference points, a well-lit room) will also improve patient performance.[40]

JOINT MOBILITY

An assessment of joint mobility should include an evaluation of range of motion (ROM), joint play, and soft-tissue compliance. Problems with spasticity may result in inconsistent ROM findings, since alterations in tone may exist from one testing session to the next. Thus tonal abnormalities should be noted at the time of examination. Active ROM tests may be invalid since synergy dominance may influence performance and preclude movement in standard AROM tests. Fixed contracture and developing deformity should be carefully documented.

MOTOR CONTROL

The patient with stroke typically exhibits a number of deficits in motor control. An evaluation of tone, reflexes (primitive, tonic reflexes), and higher-level postural reactions is necessary. Voluntary movement patterns should be examined for synergy dominance and selective movement control (in synergy or out of synergy). Those movements with selective control should be examined closely for coordination and timing deficits. Strength should be examined.[69] In the early recovery stages, traditional manual muscle tests may be invalid in the presence of significant problems of spasticity, reflex, and synergy dominance. An estimation of strength can alternately be made from observation of performance during functional tasks. An assessment of the strength of key muscles for upper extremity function (shoulder and elbow flexion, prehension) and lower extremity function (hip flexion, knee extension, ankle dorsiflexion) has been weighted to yield a Motoricity Index score. This index can be rapidly administered and has proved to be reliable in assessing motor impairment after stroke.[70,71] The examination should also include an investigation of motor planning abilities,[36] postural control and balance.[72,73]

Specific hemiplegic assessment tools are available. Brunnstrom and Bobath developed methods that have been widely utilized or adapted. The Brunnstrom assessment[18] is based upon sequential recovery stages, and carefully plots the emergence, dominance, and variation of the motion synergies. Both synergy and isolated movements are assessed in terms of the active ROM completed. Gross sensory changes and tone alterations (flaccidity or spasticity) associated with specific stages of recovery are also determined. Late-stage control is assessed by timed tasks in which the patient is asked to complete test items as quickly as possible. This test also presents a qualitative analysis of hand function and lower extremity control in sitting, standing, and walking.

Fugl-Meyer and coworkers[74,75] expanded on the work of Brunnstrom to develop the Fugl-Meyer Assessment of Physical Performance (FMA). They used many of the Brunnstrom test items organized into five sequential recovery stages. Their test improvements consisted of the development of a three-point ordinal scale with grades ranging from 0 (item cannot be performed) to 2 (item can be fully performed). Specific subtests (upper extremity function, lower extremity function, balance, sensation, and joint motion and/or joint pain) with subtest scores are available (e.g., upper extremity maximum score is 66 while the lower extremity maximum score is 34). The cumulative test score for all components is 226. The validity and high reliability ($r = .99$) of this instrument have been established. Quantifiable outcome data allow this instrument to be used for research purposes.[76]

The Bobath assessment[19] is based upon a qualitative assessment of postural and movement patterns in early, middle, or late recovery stages. Tonal abnormalities (flaccidity or spasticity) are assessed during both passive and active movements. The therapist may place the limbs in various positions and observe the patient's responses during attempts to hold the position (placing and holding). Tests for active movements are divided into two groups: advanced movement combinations (out of synergy movements) progressing from easiest to most difficult, and tests for balance and/or automatic postural responses. Individual assessment items can also be used as a basis for treatment using this approach since they represent an advanced recovery progression. Since the central state and general function of patients may vary considerably from one treatment session to the next, frequent (daily) reassessments are recommended. A modification of the Bobath evaluation to improve quantification of performance and correlations with other hemiplegic assessments has been reported in the literature.[77-79]

The Motor Assessment Scale (MAS) was developed by Carr and Shephard[80] to measure functional capabilities of the patient with stroke. This scale uses eight items of motor function, including movement transitions (supine to sidelying, supine to sit, sit to stand), balanced sitting, walking, upper-arm function, hand function and advanced hand function. The ninth item evaluates general tonus. Each item is scored on a seven-point scale (0 to 6). The scale has been shown to be highly reliable ($r = .87-1.0$) with high concurrent validity (correlated with the Fugl-Meyer assessment).[81]

GAIT

Gait is usually altered following a stroke, due to a number of factors, including impairments in sensation and perception, and motor control. Some of the more common problems in hemiplegic gait and their possible causes are summarized in Table 17-6. Assessment of gait may be done using a subjective rating system and/or objective measures (see Chapter 10). Individual rating systems may bias the examiner to identify problems in specific areas. For example, the Brunnstrom form assesses independence from synergies, based on a nor-

Table 17-6 GAIT PROBLEMS COMMONLY SEEN FOLLOWING STROKE

Stance Phase

Trunk/pelvis
  Unawareness of affected side: poor proprioception
  Forward trunk:
    Weak hip extension
    Flexion contracture
Hip
  Poor hip position (typically adduction or flexion): poor proprioception
  Trendelenburg limp: weak abductors
  Scissoring: spastic adductors
Knee
  Flexion during forward progression
    Flexion contracture combined with weak knee extensors and/or poor proprioception
    Ankle dorsiflexion range past neutral, combined with weak hip and knee extension or poor proprioception at knee and ankle
    Weakness in extension pattern or in selective motion of hip and knee extensors and plantarflexors
    Slow contraction of knee extensors/knee remains flexed 20° to 30° during forward progression
  Hyperextension during forward progression
    Plantarflexion contracture past 90 degrees
    Impaired proprioception: knee wobbles or snaps back into recurvatum
    Severe spasticity in quadriceps
    Weak knee extensors: compensatory locking of knee in hyperextension
Ankle/foot
  Equinus gait (heel does not touch the ground); spasticity or contractures of gastroc-soleus
  Varus foot (patient bears weight on the lateral surface of the foot): hyperactive or spastic anterior tibialis, post tibialis, toe flexors, and soleus
  Unequal step lengths: hammer toes caused by spastic toe flexors prevent the patient from stepping forward onto the opposite foot because of pain/weight bearing on flexed toes
  Lack of dorsiflexion range on the affected side (approximately 10 degrees is needed)

Swing Phase

Trunk/pelvis
  Insufficient forward pelvic rotation (pelvic retraction): weak abdominal muscles
  Inclination to sound side for foot clearance: weakness of flexor muscles
Hip
  Inadequate flexion
  Weak hip flexors, poor proprioception, spastic quadriceps, abdominal weakness (hip hikers), hip abductor weakness of opposite side
  Abnormal substitutions include circumduction, external rotation/adduction, backward leaning of trunk/dragging toes; momentum/uncontrolled swing
  Exaggerated hip flexion: strong flexor synergy
Knee
  Inadequate knee flexion
  Inadequate hip flexion and poor foot clearance; spastic quadriceps
  Exaggerated but delayed knee flexion: strong flexor synergy
  Inadequate knee extension at weight acceptance: spastic hamstrings or sustained total flexor pattern
  Weak knee extensors or poor proprioception
Ankle/foot
  Persistent equinus and/or equinovarus: plantarflexor contracture or spasticity; weak dorsiflexors, delayed contraction of dorsiflexors/toes drag during midswing
  Varus: spastic anterior tibialis, weak peroneals, and toe extensors
  Equinovarus: spasticity of post tibialis and/or gastroc-soleus
  Exaggerated dorsiflexion: strong flexor synergy pattern

From educational materials used at Rancho Los Amigos Medical Center, Downey, CA, and Spaulding Rehabilitation Hospital, Boston, MA.

mal recovery sequence; the Bobath assessment stresses qualitative control and balance reactions; while the Barthel index stresses functional independence and endurance. The accuracy of rating scales for observational gait analysis is highly dependent upon the skill of the examiner and the consistency and endurance of the patient; these latter may be limited following a stroke. Subjective systems can be improved by the addition of videotaping, which allows the permanent recording of gait patterns. The therapist can then replay the tape and reexamine gait deficits without tiring the patient. Depending upon the complexity of the equipment, the speeds can also be adjusted and the action stopped at a point where further investigation is warranted.[82,83] Objective systems (walkways, foot switches, grid systems) have also been used to accurately assess temporal gait factors in neurologic patients.[84] Data obtained from both types of assessments can provide meaningful insight into the type and degree of gait deviations seen with hemiplegia, as well as the specific cause of the problem.

FUNCTIONAL ASSESSMENT

At varying stages of recovery, functional mobility skills (bed mobility, movement transitions, transfers, locomotion, stairs), basic ADL skills (feeding, hygiene, dressing), and instrumental ADL skills (communication, home chores) should be carefully assessed (see Chapter 11). Functional testing frequently serves to evaluate outcomes of stroke rehabilitation and determine long-term placement. The Barthel index is one of the more reliable and widely used scales to measure stroke outcomes.[85-88] Granger et al.[89] reported that a score of 60 (out of a possible 100) was pivotal in determining the attainment of assisted independence. Patients with stroke having scores below this level demonstrated marked dependence, while scores below 40 demonstrated severe dependence. These patients typically had longer rehabilitation stays and were less likely to have successful outcomes, for example, discharge to home. Outcome studies using other functional scales (e.g., the Functional Independence Measure or FIM) are also available.[90,91]

Acute Stroke Rehabilitation

Rehabilitation during the acute stage can begin as soon as the patient is medically stabilized, typically within 72 hours. Goals of physical therapy during the early rehabilitation might include

1. Maintain ROM and prevent deformity.
2. Promote awareness, active movement, and use of the hemiplegic side.
3. Improve trunk control, symmetry, and balance.
4. Improve functional mobility.
5. Initiate self-care activities.
6. Improve respiratory and oromotor function.
7. Monitor changes associated with recovery.

POSITIONING

Positioning of the patient is one of the first considerations during early rehabilitation. The room should be arranged to maximize patient awareness of the hemiplegic side. A bed positioned with the hemiplegic side towards the main part of the room, door and source of interaction (nursing, family, TV) will stimulate the patient to turn toward and engage the affected side. The resulting sensory stimulation to the stroke side counteracts the effects of the stroke and promotes intergration and symmetry of the two sides of the body. However, this may be contraindicated in cases of unilateral neglect or anosognosia since the arrangement may contribute to sensory deprivation and withdrawal.

Consideration is also given to the position of the patient in bed. Early on, the patient is likely to spend significant time in bed. An effective positioning program seeks to prevent undesirable postures, which can lead to contractures or decubitus ulcers. Since most stroke patients will become spastic, a positioning program also aims to position the patient out of tone-dependent and reflex-dependent postures. Patients are generally placed on a positioning schedule with turning every 2 to 3 hours. Assumption of upright postures (sitting and standing) is promoted as soon as possible.

The following postures are commonly assumed and should be *avoided*:[19,51]

1. Lateral side flexion of the head and trunk toward the affected side with head rotation toward the unaffected side.
2. Depression and retraction of the scapula, internal rotation and adduction of the arm, elbow flexion and forearm pronation, wrist and finger flexion.
3. Retraction and elevation of the hip, with hip and knee extension and hip adduction; or hip and knee flexion with hip abduction. Ankle plantarflexion is common to both.

The supine position should be balanced with other positions since there is a high risk of pressure sore development in the sacral area, heel, and lateral malleolus if the leg is externally rotated. It also maximizes reflex effects. Thus extensor tone associated with the tonic labyrinthine reflex and tonal responses associated with head positions of the tonic neck reflexes (ATNR, STNR) may be promoted. A footboard should be avoided since abnormal extensor responses of the foot and leg may be stimulated with a contact stimulus to the ball of the foot (positive support reaction). Similarly, objects should not be placed in the hand since the grasp reflex may be stimulated, increasing flexor spasticity. Attention should also be directed to the hemiplegic shoulder. Correct positioning protects the shoulder from downward displacement by controlling the scapula position in slight protraction and upward rotation. Gentle approximation forces through the shoulder joint can also assist in preventing shoulder subluxation.

Common positions that should be *promoted* include:[19,51]

1. Lying in the supine position. The head and trunk should be positioned in midline or flexed slightly toward the sound side to elongate muscles on the hemiplegic side. A small pillow or towel under the scapula will assist in scapula protraction. The arm can rest on a supporting pillow, extended and in abduction, with wrist and finger extension. The pel-

vis is also protracted (on a small pillow or towel roll) with the leg in a neutral position relative to rotation. The affected knee is positioned with a small towel roll to prevent hyperextension (Fig. 17–4).

2. Lying on the sound side. When the patient is lying on the unaffected side, the trunk should be straight. A small pillow under the rib cage can be used to elongate the hemiplegic side. The affected shoulder is protracted with the arm well forward on a supporting pillow, with the elbow extended and the forearm in neutral or supinated. The pelvis is protracted and the affected leg flexed at the knee with the hip extended, in neutral rotation and supported by a pillow. (Fig. 17–5)

3. Lying on the affected side. When the patient is lying on the affected side, the trunk should be straight. The affected shoulder underneath is positioned well forward with the elbow extended and forearm supinated. The affected leg is positioned in hip extension with knee flexion. An alternate position has slight hip and knee flexion with pelvic protraction. The unaffected leg is positioned in flexion on a supporting pillow (Fig. 17–6).

4. Sitting (in bed or in a wheelchair). The patient should sit upright with trunk and head in midline alignment. Symmetrical weight bearing on both buttocks should be encouraged. The legs should be in neutral with respect to rotation. When sitting in bed, pillows may be needed to bring the trunk to the upright position. When sitting in a chair, the hips and knees should be positioned in 90 degrees of flexion, with weight bearing on the posterior thighs and with the feet flat. In bed, the arm can be supported on a pillow or adjustable table, while in a wheelchair an arm board or lap board can be used. The scapula should again be slightly protracted with wrist and fingers extended in a functional open position.

RANGE OF MOTION AND PREVENTION OF LIMB TRAUMA

Range of motion exercises during early recovery serve to maintain normal range in flaccid, nonfunctional limbs and to maintain mobility of the joint capsule. In the upper extremity, correct ROM techniques should

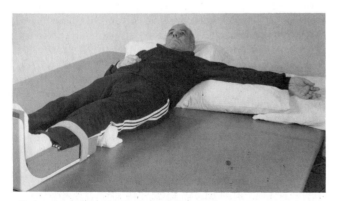

Figure 17–4. Positioning for the acute stroke patient: lying supine.

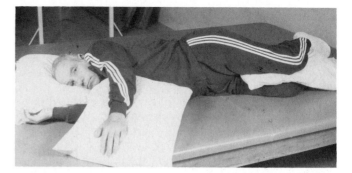

Figure 17–5. Positioning for the acute stroke patient: on the unaffected side.

include careful attention to external rotation of the arm, with scapular mobilization and upward rotation during shoulder elevation activities (Fig. 17–7). If these motions are not performed, the patient is likely to experience shoulder impingement, rotator cuff injury, and pain. The use of overhead pulleys for self-ROM is generally contraindicated for the above reasons.[92] Full ROM should be performed in all shoulder motions. Inadequate ranging can lead to the development of adhesive capsulitis and/or shoulder-hand syndrome.[93] Tightness and swelling of the wrist and finger flexors may develop. Daily range of motion, elevation, massage, icing, or compression wrapping may improve the status of the hand. Splinting in a functional position can also be considered. Either dorsal or volar resting pan splints that incorporate the forearm, wrist, and hand are commonly used.

During position changes, care must be taken not to pull on the arm or let it hang unsupported, since the risk of a traction injury would be increased. A hemisling with pads beneath the elbow and wrist and/or hand may be used to support the arm and prevent subluxation. While such slings are effective in mechanically supporting the shoulder during activity, they have the negative feature of positioning the arm close to the body in adduction and internal rotation. With prolonged use, contractures and increased flexor tone may develop. Slings may also impair trunk mobility, balance reactions, and positive body image. An alternate approach to the traditional sling is a humeral cuff maintained by a figure-eight harness (Bobath sling). This device supports the upper arm and shoulder with a cuff while avoiding the internally rotated, flexed arm (Fig. 17–8). Careful monitoring of circulation is necessary when using this type of sling. A

Figure 17–6. Positioning for the acute stroke patient: on the affected side.

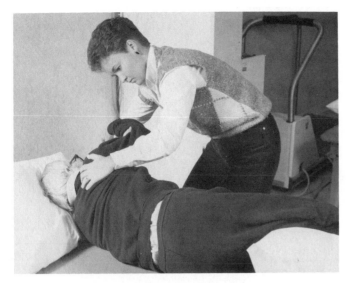

Figure 17–7. Range of motion exercises for the affected upper extremity. The therapist carefully mobilizes the scapula during arm elevation.

padded arm trough attached to the arm of a wheelchair is a third type of device commonly used. The support height and arm position are adjusted to control for subluxation. In a study comparing the effectiveness of three different devices, the hemisling and arm trough proved more effective than the Bobath sling in controlling subluxation.[94]

As spasticity emerges, the use of a sling is generally contraindicated. Care must be taken to mobilize the arm and prevent prolonged posturing, especially in internal rotation and adduction with pronation, wrist, and finger flexion. Full range of motion in shoulder elevation activities (stressing elongation of the pectoralis major and latissimus dorsi with scapular rotation) should be maintained. Exercise procedures should concentrate on the action of the serratus anterior, emphasizing scapula

Figure 17–8. Sitting, with extended arm support. The patient is wearing a Bobath arm sling with humeral cuff to prevent subluxation of the shoulder. The therapist assists in stabilizing the elbow and fingers in extension.

upward rotation. This can be accomplished in a number of postures (supine, sidelying, or sitting) using the techniques of placing and holding, or modified hold-relax active movement (HRA) with the arm externally rotated and extended, and an open hand. Weight bearing on the affected arm with joint approximation will also improve the stabilizing responses of the shoulder muscles and decrease spasticity. This can be accomplished by using an on-elbow posture (sidelying on elbow or sitting with elbow weight bearing on a padded stool), or sitting with weight bearing on an extended arm. Finger abduction splints or finger spreaders may be utilized, in cases where spasticity predominates, to reduce flexor tone and maintain range in the fingers.

Since most patients regain some use of their lower extremities early in recovery, range of motion techniques should focus on specific areas of deficit. For many patients the foot and ankle control remains limited and tone quickly progresses from initial flaccidity to spasticity, typically in the plantar flexors. Techniques designed to elongate plantar flexors through slow, maintained stretch and to activate weak dorsiflexors, thereby reciprocally inhibiting plantar flexors, may prove more successful than straight passive ROM. Thus weight bearing and rocking in modified plantigrade or prolonged static positioning using adaptive equipment (i.e., tilt table with toe wedges) can gain motion while inhibiting spastic plantar flexors. Johnstone[95] suggests using orally inflated pressure splints to maintain limbs in antispasm positions and to promote sensory reeducation.

FUNCTIONAL MOBILITY ACTIVITIES

The loss of sensory and motor function on one side will present a tremendous challenge for the patient struggling to adjust, relearn movement on the affected side, and integrate his or her movements using both sides of the body. Initial treatment strategies should focus on using both sides of the body rather than just the sound side (a compensatory training approach). Guided and active assisted movements provide a good early base for learning. The patient should be given only as much assistance as needed and should be encouraged to actively participate in movement as soon and as much as possible. Too much assistance on the part of the therapist can foster dependency and impede motor learning.

Early activities should focus on rolling, sitting up, bridging, sitting, standing, and transfers. Rolling and sitting up should be encouraged in both directions, onto the sound side to promote early independence and onto the affected side to encourage functional reintegration of the hemiplegic side. Extremity movement patterns can facilitate improved rolling through momentum and the fostering of segmental trunk rotation patterns. With both hands clasped together in a prayer position, the patient can actively assist flexion and upper trunk rotation onto a sidelying on elbow posture. In addition to promoting early weight bearing on the hemiplegic shoulder and hip, this posture also elongates the lateral trunk flexors, which may be spastic. The patient can then be assisted in moving the legs over the edge of the bed and pushing up to full sitting position using both arms. The lower extremity (LE) can assist in rolling by pushing off from a flexed and adducted, hooklying position (Fig. 17–9). This encourages an important advanced limb pattern needed for gait—hip extension with knee flexion—and also facilitates early weight bearing in the supine position. An alternate method involves using a proprioceptive neuromuscular facilitation (PNF) chop pattern, which also encourages upper trunk rotation and flexion with upper extremity (UE) diagonal movement. The patient can be taught to use the leg to assist in rolling by pulling the hip and knee up and across the body in a LE D1 flexion pattern (flexion, adduction, external rotation).

Bridging activities develop control in important functional tasks, including the use of a bedpan and initial bed mobility. They also develop pelvic control, advanced limb control (hip extension with knee flexion, foot eversion), and early LE weight bearing (Fig. 17–10). Bridging activities should include assisted and independent assumption of the posture, holding in the posture, and moving in the posture (weight-shifting side-to-side, bridge, and place activities). If the affected lower extremity is unable to hold in a hooklying position, the therapist will need to assist by stabilizing the foot during the bridge activity.

Early upright activities should focus on the development of control in both sitting and standing. A progression that can be utilized includes first holding in the posture (stability), moving in the posture (controlled mobility), and finally challenges to dynamic balance. In sitting, the therapist can aid the patient in initially maintaining the posture by ensuring proper pelvic alignment (particularly pelvic anteroposterior alignment, so that the patient's foot is flat on the support surface) and by having the patient use extended arms for support. It is important to use the affected arm for support rather than leave it hanging. Gentle resistance can be applied to assist in holding, using techniques of alternating isometrics and rhythmic stabilization. Gentle rocking movements should incorporate moving forward, back-

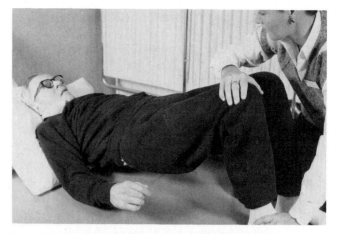

Figure 17–10. Early mobility activities: bridging. The patient combines hip extension with knee flexion. The therapist assists in stabilizing the affected leg in flexion.

ward, side-to-side, and in rotatory directions. Manual contacts in the direction of the movement combined with gentle resistance (slow reversals, slow reversal hold) can provide important early learning cues. Upper extremity activities that encourage shoulder range of motion (arms cradled position, prayer position hands to floor, chop or lift patterns) can also be added. Modified plantigrade is an ideal early standing posture in which to develop control. The affected arm is extended and weight bearing (out of synergy), while the affected leg is holding (also out of synergy). In addition the posture has a wide base of support and is very stable. Progression to upright standing activities in the parallel bars can then occur, first with arm support, and then without arm support.

During early transfers, the patient may be more or less a passive participant. Adjusting the hospital bed to the height of the chair or wheelchair will help to ease the transfer. Staff often emphasize the sound side by placing the chair to that side and having the patient stand and pivot a quarter turn on the unaffected leg before sitting down. While this technique promotes early and safe independence in transfers, it neglects the affected side and may make subsequent training more difficult. The patient should be taught to transfer to both sides early on. Transferring to the hemiplegic side may be more difficult at first but will assist in overall reeducation and reintegration of the two sides of the body (Fig. 17–11). When transferring, the patient's affected arm can be stabilized in extension and external rotation against the therapist's body. Alternately, the patient's arms (hands in prayer position) can be placed to one side on the therapist's shoulders. The therapist can then assist in the forward weight shift by using manual contacts, either at the upper trunk or pelvis. The affected leg may be stabilized by the therapist's knee exerting a counterforce on the patient's as needed.

RESPIRATORY AND/OR OROMOTOR ACTIVITIES

Goals of early training include normalizing respiratory, facial, swallowing, and chewing functions. Patients on prolonged bed rest with marked deconditioning,

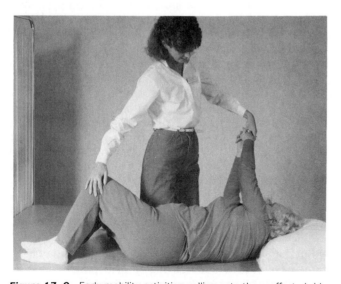

Figure 17–9. Early mobility activities: rolling onto the unaffected side. The patient pushes off with her affected left extremity and brings her hip forward. The therapist assists the movement and the inhibitory pattern (prayer position) of the upper extremities.

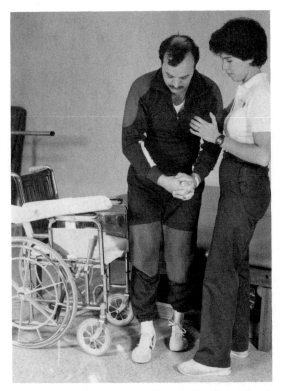

Figure 17–11. Transferring to the affected side. The patient learns to control standing up and pivoting with the affected leg leading. The therapist assists in balance.

marked paralysis, or dysarthria may experience impaired or shallow breathing patterns. Improved chest expansion can be achieved by effective use of manual contacts, resistance, and stretch to various chest wall segments. Diaphragmatic, basal, and lateral costal expansion should be stressed. A prespeech activity consists of having the patient maintain a vocal expression (e.g., "ah") during the entire expiratory phase, since poor breath control often contributes to soft or vacillating production of sounds. Respiratory activities should be combined with other movement patterns whenever possible (e.g., inspiration with PNF reverse chop pattern and expiration with chop). During any sustained activity (isometric holding), breath control should be emphasized; the Valsalva maneuver should always be avoided. This is especially important in stroke patients with documented concomitant cardiovascular problems.

Facial movements should be encouraged and facilitated whenever necessary. This may include the use of stretch, resistance, or quick ice to stimulate the desired function. Emphasis should be placed on the affected muscles in order to regain a balance of function. The use of a mirror may be helpful in treatment, providing the patient does not have visuospatial dysfunction.

The goals of oromotor retraining are (1) to improve strength, coordination, and range of oral musculature, (2) to promote normal feeding through graduated resumption of activities, and (3) to promote volitional control through effective verbal coaching. A key element is the attainment of an upright sitting posture with hips well back, symmetrical weight bearing, and feet flat on the floor. The head should be erect and in its normal

position rather than extended or tipped back. This reduces the chances of aspiration or choking and promotes normal swallowing through appropriate alignment of the necessary structures. If the patient lacks adequate head control, the head should be supported either manually or with supports. Food should be positioned at an appropriate height and distance from the patient and in the patient's visual field. Adapted utensils, plateguards, and nonslip mats can be used to assist in the transfer of food to the mouth. Food should be at first semimoist (e.g., pureed food, pasta, boiled chicken) progressing to foods rich in taste, smell, and texture, qualities which assist in facilitating the swallowing reflex. Sensation, reflex activity (gag), and breath control are essential to normal swallowing. Patients can be assisted with jaw closure, lip closure, and tongue control as necessary. Facilitation techniques (quick ice, quick stretch, resistance) can be used to stimulate the muscles responsible for jaw opening and closing. Jaw movements can be stimulated by vibrating or pressing above the upper lip for closure and under the lower lip for opening. Jaw closure can also be assisted when necessary during feeding by holding the jaw firmly closed using a jaw control technique (e.g., thumb on jaw line, index finger between lower lip and chin, and middle finger under chin applying firm pressure). Tongue movements can be resisted manually (using a sterile gauze or glove to cover finger) or with a moist tongue depressor. Firm pressure to the anterior third of the tongue can be used to stimulate the posterior elevation of the tongue necessary for swallowing. Sucking control and saliva production can be stimulated using small amounts of ice water or an ice cube. The therapist can also apply deep pressure on the neck above the thyroid notch to stimulate sucking. Resisted sucking can be promoted using a straw and very thick liquids (slushes, shakes), or by holding the open end of the straw against the finger. As sucking control proceeds, thinner liquids can be substituted. Patients with a hypoactive gag reflex may be stimulated briefly with a cotton swab to develop this response. An additional consideration for successful feeding includes management of the environment (pleasant, free from distraction, devoid of unpleasant sights and smells). The patient's full attention should be directed to the task at hand by using appropriate and consistent verbal cues.[95,96]

Postacute Rehabilitation

Many goals and treatment activities begun during early recovery are continued throughout the course of the patient's rehabilitation. Some are modified to appropriately challenge the patient and propel him or her to optimal recovery. During the middle and late stages of recovery, the patient is out of bed and involved in a variety of activities and therapies. It is important to monitor cardiorespiratory endurance carefully and avoid overtiring the patient. Physical therapy goals typically include

1. Prevent or minimize secondary complications.
2. Compensate for sensory and perceptual loss.
3. Promote selective movement control and normalization of postural tone.

4. Improve postural control and balance.
5. Develop independent functional mobility skills.
6. Develop independent ADLs.
7. Develop functional cardiorespiratory endurance.
8. Encourage socialization and motivation.

MOTOR CONTROL TRAINING
General Considerations

Training should focus on improving motor control by stressing selective (out-of-synergy) movement patterns. Movement combinations that allow success in functional tasks (e.g., feeding, dressing, gait) should be emphasized. Patients frequently respond to movement commands with gross or mass patterns of movement and excessive effort. The linking together of the proper components and the refinement of isolated control requires a great deal of mental concentration and volitional control. Inhibition of unwanted activity and excessive effort is crucial to the patient's success. Movements that are performed too quickly or too strongly will be ineffective in producing the control needed. Initially the therapist should select postures that assist the desired motion and/or reduce tone and reflex interference. As control develops, postures can be changed to more difficult ones that challenge developing control. Resistance to movement should be minimal. Often the resistance of gravity acting on the body, or slight manual resistance, is enough to initiate or facilitate the correct muscular responses. Normal function implies a tremendous variability in movement performance. Muscles need to be activated in a variety of patterns and contexts. Eccentric contractions are generally easier to perform than concentric (more tension can be generated with less metabolic cost). Isometric contractions (holding in mid or shortened ranges) are also important since increased recruitment of static gamma motoneurons occurs, thus providing additional facilitation for weak or hypotonic muscles. The clinician should stress holding or eccentric contractions before concentric ones. Weak muscles (antagonistic to strong spastic muscles) should be activated first in unidirectional patterns, and then challenged by activities that stress slow reciprocal movements. This emphasis on balanced interaction of both agonists and antagonists is crucial for normal coordination and effective function.

If the patient is hypotonic and/or unable to initiate movement, effective strategies may include direct facilitation of movement using a variety of different stimuli. Extereoceptive, proprioceptive, and reflex stimulation techniques can be utilized. Some disagreement exists, however, over the type of movements that ought to be stimulated. Brunnstrom[18] advocated the use of synergistic patterns in early recovery for those patients unable to move at all. These patterns are viewed as part of recovery and used to bridge the gap between flaccidity and early movement. Once voluntary movement is achieved, synergistic patterns are then modified to selective (out-of-synergy) patterns. The use of synergistic patterns is therefore limited to a small number of patients who demonstrate no voluntary return of movement. Patients who have voluntary control (stage 2 recovery or beyond—see Table 17–2) would be inappropriate candidates for this type of training.

Still others, adhering to the neurodevelopmental treatment (NDT) philosophy developed by Bobath believe that emphasis on synergistic movements can lead to an increase in spasticity, poor control of selective movement patterns and widespread abnormal reflex activity. In NDT the patient learns to control tone and movement through the use of reflex inhibiting patterns that promote "normal" selective movements (out-of-synergy) during functional activities. Automatic reactions (righting, equilibrium, protective extension) are facilitated through the use of postural and sensory stimulation.[19,51]

Coordinated movement can also be promoted using PNF movement patterns. For example, the therapist might select D1 extension with the knee flexing if the patient were experiencing incomplete knee flexion with hip extension at toe-off. Appropriate PNF techniques might include slow reversals, timing for emphasis with repeated contractions if components are deficient, or hold-relax active movement if initiation of movement is difficult. The technique of agonistic reversals is effective in developing the eccentric control necessary for normal function. Thus activities of bridging, stand to sit, or kneeling to heel-sitting might be practiced using an AR technique.[98]

Efficacy of Physical Therapy Methods

Attempts have been made to validate the rehabilitation approaches through controlled research trials. Studies attempting to delineate differences between traditional exercise approaches (ROM, compensatory functional training) and neuromuscular facilitation approaches (Bobath, Brunnstrom) have failed to show significant advantages in one approach over another.[88,99–101] Wagenaar et al.[102] compared the effectiveness of two neurologic approaches, Brunnstrom and NDT, using functional recovery measures (Barthel index and Action Research Arm test). They found no significant difference between these methods in influencing functional recovery, with the exception of one patient whose speed of walking benefited from the Brunnstrom approach. Basmajian et al.[103] compared electromyographic (EMG) biofeedback therapy and Bobath therapy on upper extremity function and also failed to find a difference in outcome between these two therapies. As in the previous studies, improvements were noted in both groups. Important conclusions to be drawn from these studies are (1) collectively they provide consistent evidence for the beneficial effects of physical therapy, and (2) there is as yet no one optimal therapy for patients with stroke.[104] It should be pointed out that these studies were subject to numerous confounding variables, including small sample size, heterogeneity of the stroke population, overlaps of treatments, and late rehabilitation starts. Since patients with stroke present with variable symptoms, rigid adherence to any one approach may yield unsatisfactory results. Most therapists take an eclectic approach, selecting procedures from the different approaches that have the greatest chance of success. Choice of therapeutic techniques may also be dependent on other factors, including ease of delivering care, cost-effectiveness, and length of stay.

Tone Reduction

Patients who demonstrate the strong spasticity typically seen during the middle phases of recovery may benefit from a number of techniques designed to modify or reduce tone. These include positioning out of reflex-dependent postures, reflex-inhibiting patterns that encourage movement of the weak and hypotonic antagonists, and avoiding excess effort and heavy resistance. Rhythmic rotation of limbs with slow, steady passive movement out of the spastic pattern may also serve to decrease tone, while providing ROM to the spastic limb.[19,51] A reduction in truncal tone can be promoted through techniques of rhythmic initiation or slow reversals combined with upper and lower trunk rotation (Fig. 17–12). Postures of sidelying, sitting, or hooklying are frequently used. Proprioceptive neuromuscular facilitation extremity or trunk patterns (chopping or lifting) that emphasize diagonal and rotational movements combined with techniques designed to reduce tone (e.g., rhythmic initiation) may also be helpful.[98] Local facilitation techniques (muscle tapping, vibration) may prove successful in stimulating weak antagonists and reducing spasticity in some patients. However, as Bobath points out,[19] reciprocal relationships are not always normal, particularly in the presence of strong spasticity, so that these techniques may be ineffective, serving to increase rather than decrease tone in the spastic muscles. Exercise procedures that take advantage of prolonged pressure on long tendons and the resultant inhibition are also effective in reducing tone. A common exercise for hemiplegics involves weight bearing on an extended, abducted, and externally rotated arm with the wrist and fingers extended (Fig. 17–13). Slow rocking movements add to the inhibitory effect on the spastic wrist and finger flexors. Spasticity in the quadriceps can be similarly inhibited through weight bearing in kneeling or quadruped positions. Orally inflatable pressure splints have also been used effectively to assist in the maintenance of inhibiting patterns by providing prolonged stretch and inhibition to spastic muscles. They also aid in providing stability and allow early weight bearing on a limb during training activities.[95,105]

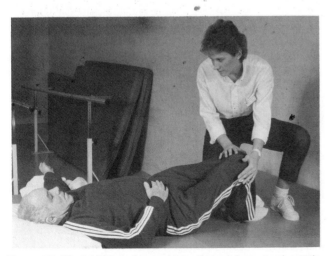

Figure 17–12. Inhibition of truncal tone through lower trunk rotation. The therapist uses the technique of rhythmic initiation to increase mobility.

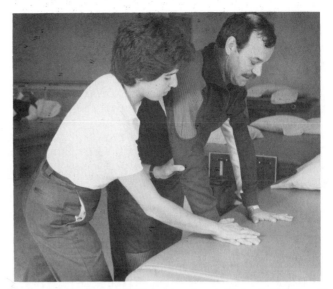

Figure 17–13. Early weight bearing in modified plantigrade with extended arms. The therapist assists elbow and finger extension.

Techniques that produce a generalized reduction in tone by decreasing CNS arousal mechanisms include slow stroking down the posterior primary rami, and soothing verbal commands. Gentle rocking (sidelying rolling, rocking chair) works through the vestibular system to also produce a generalized reduction in tone.

Prolonged icing using ice wraps, ice packs, or ice massage may decrease spasticity by slowing conduction in nerves and muscles and decreasing muscle spindle activity. Once tone is reduced, the therapist should emphasize active movement out of the positions of spasticity. This can prolong the inhibitory effects and produce less restrictive movements.

Compensation for Sensory Loss

Patients who have significant sensory loss may demonstrate impaired or absent spontaneous movement because of the lack of feedback signals before and during movement. The more the patient can be made to use the affected side, the greater the chance of increased sensory awareness and function. Conversely, the patient who refuses to use the hemiplegic side contributes to the problem of persistent lack of sensorimotor experience. Without attention during treatment, this learned nonuse phenomenon can contribute to further deterioration.[106] Treatment should therefore involve the patient using the hemiplegic side in volitional motor tasks. The presentation of repeated sensory stimuli will maximize use of residual sensory function and CNS reorganization. Stretch, stroking, superficial and deep pressure, and weight bearing with approximation can all be used during therapy to increase sensory input. Training should also focus on localization of touch. Electrical stimulation has been used to assist in activation and localization of sensorimotor responses.[107] The selection of inputs should be directly related to the functional task at hand and provided to those surfaces directly used in the task (e.g., stroking with different textured objects over the hand). Stimulation should be of sufficient intensity to engage the system but not to produce adverse effects.

The patient's attention should be focused directly on the task at hand. Patient involvement in the selection of important functional tasks, and provision of immediate rewards and reinforcement, can also be used to assist learning.[108]

Johnstone[95] suggests that inflatable pressure splints can be used during treatment to provide additional sensory stimulation to deep pressure, muscle, and joint senses. In more severe cases, she suggests a program of intermittent pressure therapy to stimulate movement within the tissues and overcome problems of sensory accommodation.

A safety education program for awareness of sensory deficits and care of anesthetic limbs should also be instituted. This is particularly important for preventing upper limb trauma during transfer and wheelchair activities. Training for those patients with hemianopsia and unilateral neglect traditionally includes emphasis on scanning the visual environment on the affected side.

Postural Control and Balance

Activities begun during early training that focus on upright static control and balance should be continued and extended. Sit-to-stand transitions should be practiced, with an emphasis on symmetrical weight bearing and controlled responses of the hemiplegic side (Fig. 17–14). Trunk rotation can be increased by having the patient stand up and shift the pelvis to one side or the other before sitting down. By using a platform mat for this activity, the patient can move all the way around the mat first in one direction, then in the other. Arms should be clasped and held straight ahead during this activity. Modified plantigrade is an ideal posture to focus on symmetrical standing. Progression can then occur to supported standing in the parallel bars and to free standing.

Once initial control is achieved, the patient is ready to practice more dynamic balance activities. The therapist should have the patient explore his or her limits of stability (LOS) through low-frequency sway. Thus the

patient learns how far in any one direction he or she can move while maintaining upright stability. Patients with stroke typically demonstrate reduced voluntary sway, with more weight being directed on the sound side than on the affected side. The therapist will therefore need to stress symmetrical postures, as well as activities that overcompensate, shifting the weight more onto the affected extremities. Gentle perturbations can be used to displace the patient's center of mass (COM) and stimulate postural adjustments. The therapist can also have the patient sit or stand on a moveable support surface, thereby stimulating adjustments through displacement of the base of support (BOS). For example, a gymnastic ball or equilibrium board can be used (Fig. 17–15). The patient learns to actively control posture while the device is moved, or while the patient actively moves the device. Anticipatory postural adjustments can be challenged by having the patient perform voluntary movements that have a destabilizing effect. For example, the therapist can utilize static-dynamic activities of PNF chopping or lifting patterns or cone stacking activities (Fig. 17–16). Dynamic tasks such as catching or kicking a ball challenge balance and include the added challenge of anticipatory timing. These tasks also redirect the patient's attention to a task at hand rather than on balance itself, thus testing the automaticity of postural responses.[109,110]

Postural reactions are organized into a limited number of motor strategies or synergies (see Chapter 13). Patients with stroke typically exhibit delayed, varied, or absent responses. Latency, amplitude, and timing of muscle activity are all characteristically disturbed.[110] It is therefore important to proceed slowly in training and to select challenges appropriate for the patient's level of control. The patient's attention should be directed to the appropriate muscle activity and strategies needed to maintain balance. Postural biofeedback (center-of-pressure biofeedback) provided from standing on a force plate system has been effective in improving balance responses in patients.[111–114] There are a number of different balance devices currently on the market (e.g., Balance Master) that can be utilized in training. Finally,

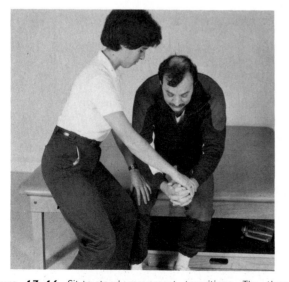

Figure 17–14. Sit-to-stand movement transitions. The therapist assists the patient in straightening his knee while he brings his center of gravity forward.

Figure 17–15. Balance training in supported standing using a large gymnastic ball. One therapist stimulates medio-lateral balance reactions while the other therapist supports and assists the patient.

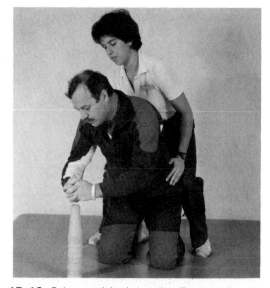

Figure 17–16. Balance training in kneeling. The therapist uses protective guarding at the hips while the patient reaches over and touches the stacked cones.

safety education on the prevention of falls is a critical factor in ensuring maintenance of the patient's hard-won functional independence.

Upper Extremity Control

Initial mobility of the upper extremity can be achieved by focusing first on scapular motions. Since the typical spastic pattern is one of retraction and fixation, protraction with external rotation should be emphasized. This is typically performed in a sidelying or supine position, where the patient's arm is supported in shoulder elevation with elbow extension. The arm is mobilized forward and the patient is asked to hold this position. If holding is successful, then eccentric and reciprocal movements are attempted (using techniques of hold-after positioning, push-pull, modified hold-relax active movement, or slow reversals). Once initial control is achieved, the posture can be altered to a more challenging one (e.g., sitting) and more active control of shoulder and elbow components can be added through an increasing range (e.g., D1 thrust pattern; arm raising to forward or side horizontal, arm overhead). The patient should be taught to mobilize the affected arm using hands clasped together (prayer position).

Movements that should be stressed include hand to mouth and hand to opposite shoulder, since these have important functional implications in feeding and dressing. Elbow extension movements combined with shoulder abduction or flexion should also be stressed to counteract the effects of the dominant flexion synergy. This can be achieved through extension (weight-bearing) activities performed in sitting, modified plantigrade (Fig. 17–13), or standing positions. The quadruped posture provides the greatest challenge for upper extremity weight bearing but may be too difficult for some stroke patients. An alternate posture would be sitting, weight bearing on an extended arm on a stool in front, or modified plantigrade. Control should progress from initial

holding in the posture to controlled mobility using rocking movements.

Training of hand function should emphasize forearm, wrist, and finger movements independent of shoulder and elbow motions. Excessive shoulder adduction, elbow flexion, pronation, and finger flexion are the typical spastic patterns that must be counteracted. Voluntary release is generally much more difficult to achieve than voluntary grasp, and inhibitory techniques may be necessary before extension movements are successful. Prehension patterns should be practiced and manipulation of common objects (pencil, fork, toothbrush) attempted. The therapist needs to observe these movements carefully and to assist the patient in eliminating those aspects of performance that interfere with effective control.

Lower Extremity Control

Training of the lower extremity essentially prepares the patient for ambulation. Pregait mat activities should concentrate on working muscles in the appropriate combinations needed for gait. For example, hip and knee extensors need to be activated with abductors and dorsiflexors for early stance. Strong synergy combinations also need to be broken up (e.g., hip and knee extension). A variety of activities can be used, including bridging, supine knee flexion with hip extension over the side of the mat, or standing modified plantigrade with knee flexion. Hip adduction should be stressed during flexion movements of the hip and knee, while abduction should be stressed during extension movements (e.g., supine, PNF D1 lower extremity diagonal; sitting, crossing and uncrossing the hemiplegic leg). Pelvic control is important and can be promoted through lower trunk rotation activities that emphasize forward pelvic rotation (protraction) in a number of postures (e.g., sidelying; supine, modified hooklying with the hemiplegic leg pushing off; kneeling; or standing).

An effective progression increases the challenge to the patient gradually by modifying postures until synergy influence is completely lacking (e.g., hip abduction can be performed first in hooklying, then supine, sidelying, modified plantigrade, and standing positions). Contraction patterns should also be varied. Thus, dorsiflexors can be first activated in a sitting posture by using first a holding contraction, then an eccentric letting go, and finally a shortening contraction. This simulates the functional expectations of the normal gait cycle as the foot goes from swing phase through stance.

Voluntary control of eversion is often difficult to achieve since these muscles do not function in either synergy. The application of stretch and resistance to these muscles during a pattern that activates dorsiflexors may be effective in initiating a response. Postural challenges may also elicit these muscles automatically, even though voluntary control is lacking. Control of knee function is also problematic. Reciprocal action (smooth reversals of flexion and extension movements) should be stressed early, beginning first in sitting, then in supine-hooklying, prone, modified plantigrade, or supported standing positions (Fig. 17–17), and progressing to standing and walking. Dissociation of arm movements

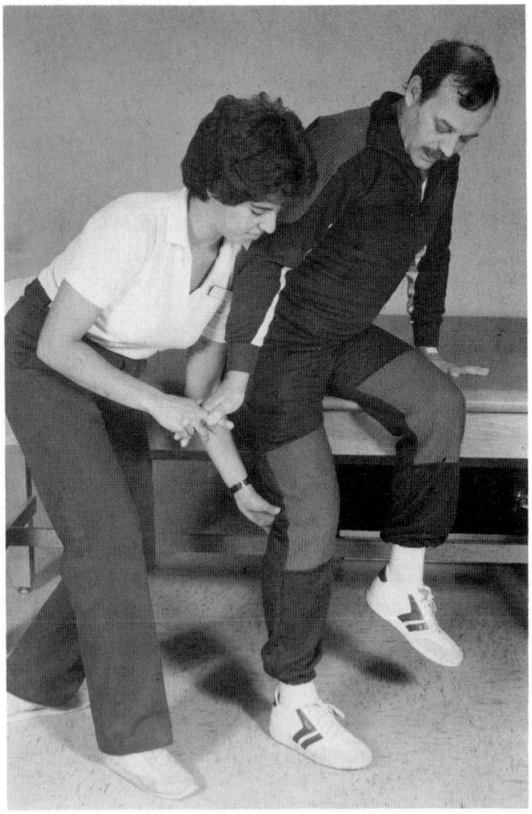

Figure 17–17. Early weight bearing on the affected leg. The therapist assists controlled, small range flexion, and extension movements of the knee. The affected arm is maintained in an inhibitory pattern.

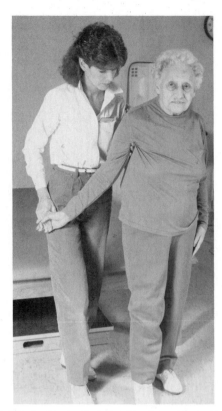

Figure 17–18. Assisted ambulation. The therapist provides support on the patient's affected side. The arm is maintained in elevation, extension and abduction to inhibit the typical flexed and adducted arm posture.

during lower extremity training is also an important consideration and may be achieved through the use of pre-positioning and voluntary control (e.g., having the patient hold clasped hands together overhead in a "prayer position" during a lower extremity activity).

Gait Training

Walking is usually initiated early on, before selective movement and balance control are achieved. It can be used to motivate patients and minimize deconditioning but increases the risk of developing persistent and faulty habits. While ambulation aids such as quad canes assist early mobilization, they can also distort balance, promoting an excessive weight shift onto the unaffected side. Gait training should focus on the attainment of control in the selective movements necessary for gait with appropriate timing. Specific movement deficiencies should be identified and corrected. Initially this may require focusing on the specific muscle actions or combinations in other less demanding postures and then practicing them in an upright position (e.g., lower trunk rotation is practiced first sidelying, then kneeling, plantigrade, and finally standing and walking). Performance is context specific. The therapist cannot assume carryover from practice in one position to another. Persistent posturing of the upper extremity in flexion and adduction during gait can be controlled through positioning the hemiplegic arm in extension and abduction with the hand open (Fig. 17–18).

Advanced gait training should continue to emphasize selective movement control and normal timing. Gait can be practiced forwards, backwards, sidewards, and in a crossed pattern (braiding). Elevation activities (stair climbing, step over step; over and around obstacles) and community activities (on different terrains) should also be practiced. Timing can be improved through the use of resisted progression technique, stimulating music, or a treadmill. At this point in recovery the patient should be able to monitor his or her own performance and recognize and initiate corrective actions. The patient should be able to vary the speed of walking and maintain performance while cognitively engaged in other activities such as carrying on a conversation. The patient should also feel confident walking in all types of situations likely to be encountered in daily life.

An orthosis may be required when persistent problems prevent safe ambulation. Prescription will depend upon the unique problems each patient presents. The pattern of mediolateral instability and weakness at the ankle and knee, and the extent and severity of spasticity and sensory deficits of the limb are the major factors to be considered when prescribing an orthosis. Temporary devices (e.g., dorsiflexion assists) may be used during the early stages while recovery is proceeding, to allow the patient to practice standing and early walking. Permanent devices are prescribed once the patient's status is relatively stable. Extensive bracing using a knee-ankle-foot orthosis (KAFO) is rarely indicated or successful. An ankle-foot orthosis (AFO) is commonly pre-

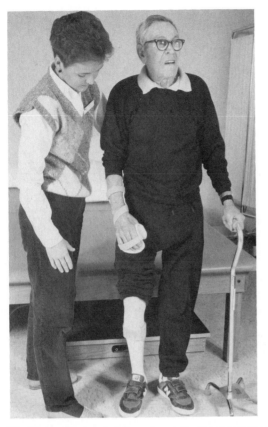

Figure 17–19. Assisted ambulation using a plastic ankle-foot orthosis and quad cane.

scribed to control deficient knee and ankle and/or foot function. These may include a molded AFO (polypropylene AFO, plastic spiral AFO, plastic solid ankle AFO; Fig. 17–19), or conventional double upright/dual channel AFO. In this latter device a posterior stop can be added to limit plantarflexion while a spring assist can be added to assist dorsiflexion. An air-stirrup ankle brace can be used to provide mediolateral stability at the subtalar joint while allowing dorsiflexion and plantar flexion.[115] Knee problems in hemiplegia can usually be controlled by adjusting the position of the ankle. An ankle set in 5 degrees dorsiflexion limits knee hyperextension, while an ankle set in 5 degrees plantarflexion stabilizes the knee during midstance.[116] A patient with mild knee hyperextension without foot and/or ankle instability may benefit from the application of a Swedish Knee Cage to protect the knee. (See Chapter 30 for a more complete description of these devices.) The therapist must frequently reassess the patient's motor function and the need for an orthosis, since continuing recovery may warrant a prescriptive change or discontinuing the use of a device.

FUNCTIONAL TRAINING

Functional mobility training begun during the acute phase should be continued and extended. A variety of activities and postures can be utilized. Additional postures such as prone on elbows, sidesitting, kneeling, half-kneeling can be utilized, although they may not be appropriate for all older clients. Patients should also be instructed in strategies for getting down to and up from the floor. Therapists need to provide an adequate amount of support, while allowing the patient to relearn control through active processing of movement. Varying the contexts (changing the environment) is important in ensuring adaptability and generalizability of responses.

Training in activities of daily living is usually directed by the occupational therapist. Continuity between therapies is important to ensure that activities are being done consistently and in the most efficient manner. The reference for all training should be the patient's home environment and normal daily activity. Energy conservation techniques should be incorporated into the patient's daily plan.

MOTOR LEARNING STRATEGIES

Recovery from stroke is based on the brain's capacity for reorganization and adaptation. An effective rehabilitation plan capitalizes on this potential and encourages movement patterns closely linked to normal performance. Function should be stressed at all times, and the function should be meaningful and important to the patient. Optimal motor learning can be ensured through attention to a number of factors. Demonstrate the desired task at the ideal performance speed. Manually guide the patient through the desired movement to assist in his or her understanding of the task and its components. Encourage early active participation of the affected side. Practicing the movements on the unaffected side first can yield important transfer effects to the affected side. Simultaneous practice of similiar movements on both sides (bilateral activities) can also improve learning, while promoting integration of both sides of the body. Visualization of the movement components (mental practice) can help some patients in initially organizing the movement. During early learning visual guidance is extremely important. This can be facilitated by having the patient watch the movement. If the patient needs glasses, make sure they are worn during therapy. Use of a mirror can be an effective technique for some patients to improve visual feedback, especially during postural activities.

During later learning, proprioception becomes important for movement refinement. This can be encouraged by early and carefully reinforced weight bearing (approximation) on the affected side in upright activities. Additional proprioceptive inputs (manual contacts, tapping, stretch, tracking resistance, antigravity postures, or vibration) can be used to improve movement feedback and stimulate the necessary components. The patient should be encouraged to "feel the movement" and learn to recognize correct movement responses from incorrect ones. Assist the patient in learning to eliminate the unnecessary movement components. Extereoceptive inputs (light rubbing, brushing, ice application) may provide additional sources of information, particularly where distortions of proprioception exist. However, great care must be taken to avoid sensory bombardment or feedback dependence. To do this requires careful assessment during each treatment session. Pain and fatigue (either mental or physical) should be avoided, since each will be associated with a decrease in motor performance. Careful attention to the learning environment will also yield important therapeutic gains. Reduce distractions and provide a consistent and comfortable place in which the patient can exercise. Provide clear, simple verbal instructions; do not overload the patient with excessive or wordy commands. Monitor performance carefully and give accurate feedback. Reinforce correct performance and intervene when movement errors become consistent. Organize the patient's schedule so that practice sessions are relatively short and the patient has adequate rest. Coordinate staff efforts to ensure that the patient is being asked to perform the task consistently with the same performance expectations. Progress and challenge the patient with a new task as soon as the previous one has been mastered. Encourage the patient to be self-suffi-cient and to develop self-assessment skills, goals, and problem-solving skills. Begin and end treatment ses-sions on a positive note, ensuring the patient has success in treatment and continuing motivation. Finally, com-municate, support, and encourage the patient; recovery from stroke is an extremely stressful experience and will challenge the abilities of both patient and thera-pist.[117–119]

BIOFEEDBACK

Electromyographic biofeedback (EMG-BFB) may be used to improve motor function in patients with hemi-plegia. This technique allows patients to alter motor unit activity based upon audio and visual feedback informa-tion. Thus firing frequency can be decreased in spastic muscles, or increased, along with recruitment of addi-tional motor units, in weak, hypoactive muscles. (See Chapter 32 for a more complete description of this topic.) Patients in the chronic stage (typically defined as 1 year post-stroke) or patients in late recovery for whom spontaneous recovery is more or less complete (4 to 6 months post-stroke) have consistently demonstrated positive results that may be attributed to biofeedback therapy. Benefits include improvements in ROM, motor control, function, and relaxation. Most studies indicate that its greatest effectiveness is achieved when it is used as an adjunct to regular therapy in a combined approach.[120–122] Following an initial training period, EMG-BFG can also be self-administered, allowing patients to practice on their own.

Successful biofeedback applications in the trunk and lower extremity have focused on improving posture and balanced control of ankle and knee muscles. Programs typically begin training in the more dependent postures (e.g., sitting) and gradually progress to more upright postures. Dynamic control using feedback during gait has also been utilized. Electromyography or electrogo-niometric information can improve control of the limb and eliminate problematic gait deviations such as genu recurvatum or limited dorsiflexion in swing.[122,123] Limb load devices that give feedback about the amount of loading or weight bearing on the hemiplegic limb have also been effective in improving gait. Patients receiving this training demonstrate more normal weight bearing and stance times on their affected limb and increased

swing times on their unaffected limb.[124] Upper extremity applications in stroke rehabilitation have largely focused on relaxing the spasticity of muscles such as pectoralis major, biceps, or wrist and finger flexors. Significant improvements in initiating voluntary finger extension have also been reported following upper extremity bio-feedback training.[125–127]

ELECTRICAL STIMULATION

Neuromuscular electrical stimulation (NMES) may be used with patients recovering from stroke to facilitate voluntary motor control, to temporarily reduce spasti-city, and/or to substitute for an orthosis.[122,128] Neuromus-cular electrical stimulation has been shown to increase the ability of muscle to exert force, by preferentially acti-vating the fast-contracting motor units.[129] Effective treat-ment results in stroke rehabilitation have been reported using NMES to improve dorsiflexor function,[130,131] wrist extension function,[132,133] and spasticity reduction associ-ated with antagonist muscle activation.[134] The term func-tional electrical stimulation (FES) refers to the regular use of ES in functional tasks. Functional electrical stim-ulation to the posterior deltoid and supraspinatus mus-cles has been used in patients with stroke to reestablish glenohumeral alignment and reduce subluxation.[135] It has also been used to assist dorsiflexor function in place of an AFO or as an adjunct. Patterned FES, in which a multichannel program was developed from individual profiles of EMG and anthropometric measurements yielded significant improvement in active ROM of para-lyzed limbs. Since this group of patients had limbs that had been paralyzed for more than 6 months, the results suggest a significant CNS learning effect from FES.[136]

ISOKINETICS

Isokinetic training may be used to improve the timing of reciprocal movements of the lower extremities required for gait. The therapist should initially preset movements to utilize slower speeds and gradually prog-ress to more rapid speeds as control improves. If consis-tency in maintaining a steady rhythm is problematic, a metronome can be used to pace the activity. With some types of equipment, the patient's position can be modi-fied to approach a more upright standing position. A rate of movement approaching 1 cycle per second, which is within normal parameters for heel-strike to heel-strike, should be the desired end point of treatment.[137]

EXERCISE CONDITIONING

Patients with stroke demonstrate decreased levels of physical conditioning following periods of prolonged immobility and reduced activity. The energy costs to complete many of the functional tasks in their daily lives are higher than normal owing to the abnormal ways in which they perform these activities.[138–141] Many patients also demonstrate concomitant cardiovascular disease and may be recovering from acute cardiac events at the same time.[142] These patients can benefit from an orga-nized exercise program to improve cardiovascular fit-ness as part of their rehabilitation. The geriatric survivor with compromised cardiovascular function can benefit from an ambulation program regulated by signs and symptoms of activity intolerance.[53] Other stroke survivors should be able to engage in a more traditional exercise conditioning program.

To ensure patient safety, patients should receive a thorough evaluation before starting a program.[143] Adequate supervision, monitoring, and safety education about warning signs for impending stroke and heart attack are also important considerations.[144] Considerations for prescription should be based upon individual abilities and the interests of the patient. The components of an exercise program should include type of exercise, frequency, intensity, and duration (see Chapter 16). Warm-up and cool-down sessions should include stretching and strengthening elements as well as aerobic elements of increasing or decreasing intensity. Typical aerobic elements include cycle ergometry (arm, leg), walking and/or stair climbing. A frequency of 3 to 5 days a week with an intensity of 60 to 85 percent of the age-predicted maximal heart rate (HRmax), 50 to 80 percent of maximal oxygen consumption (VO$_2$max), or RPE (ratings of perceived exertion) value of 12 to 13 should provide an adequate training stimulus. The duration will vary (e.g., from 15 to 60 min) depending upon the frequency and intensity of the activity.[145-147] The use of a training log or exercise diary is an excellent way to keep track of prescriptive elements, objective measurements (heart rate, RPE, blood pressure), and subjective reactions (perceived enjoyment).[144]

Conditioning programs for patients with stroke can yield significant improvements in physical fitness, functional status, psychologic outlook, and self-esteem.[148,149] Regular exercise may also have the additional benefit of reducing risk from recurrent stroke.[147] Finally, patients who participate in a regular conditioning program may be more successful in adopting continuing, lifelong exercise habits and in moving beyond the disability of stroke.[144]

Patient and Family Education

Stroke represents a major health crisis for many patients and their families. Ignorance about the cause of the illness or the recovery process and misconceptions concerning the rehabilitation program and potential outcome can negatively influence coping responses. Frequently the problems seem unmanageable and overwhelming for the family, especially when faced with alterations in the patient's behavior, cognition, and emotion. Patients may feel depressed, isolated, irritable, or demanding. Families often demonstrate reactions that include initial relief and hope for full recovery, followed by feelings of entrapment, depression, anger, or guilt when complete recovery does not occur. These changes and feelings can strain even the best of relationships.[44] Psychologic, sexual, leisure and vocational counseling can assist in improving the overall quality of life and should be implemented as needed. Therapists can often have a dramatic influence on this situation because of the high frequency of contact and the often close rela-

tionships that develop with patients and their families. There are a number of important guidelines to follow when planning interactions and educational sessions with patients and their families:

1. Give accurate, factual information; counsel family members about the patient's capabilities and limitations; *avoid* predictions that categorically define expected function or future recovery.
2. Structure interventions carefully, giving only as much information as the patient or family needs or can assimilate; be consistent and repeat information.
3. Provide a forum for open discussion and communication.
4. Be supportive, sensitive, and maintain a hopeful manner.
5. Assist patients and families in confronting alternatives and developing problem-solving abilities.
6. Motivate and provide positive reinforcement in therapy; enhance patient satisfaction and self-esteem.
7. Refer to support and self-help groups such as the American Heart Association Stroke Clubs.[44,150]

Discharge Planning

Family members should regularly participate in therapy sessions to learn proper exercise techniques and exercises designed to support the patient's independence. Home visits should be made prior to discharge to evaluate the home's physical structure and accessibility. Potential problems can be identified and corrective measures initiated. Home adaptions, assistive devices, and supportive services should be in place before the patient is discharged home. Several trial stays may be helpful in smoothing the transition from rehabilitation center to home. Patients with residual stroke deficits who will be receiving outpatient or home therapy should be given all the necessary information concerning these services. Long-term follow-up at regularly scheduled intervals should be initiated in order to maintain patients at their highest possible level.

Stroke Rehabilitation Outcomes

Rehabilitation programs for patients with stroke have been shown to improve functional outcomes and allow patients to regain independence.[104,151,152] Between 75 and 85 percent of patients are discharged home, and of these 80 percent are independent in ambulation, and 66 percent can ambulate with assistive devices. Between 50 and 66 percent are independent in ADLs and only 17 percent require assistance in bowel and bladder care.[153] Health care costs are also minimized when compared to long-term placement in nursing homes.[154,155]

Stroke outcome studies have yielded inconsistent results. Some patients demonstrate spontaneously good recovery without the benefits of rehabilitation, while other patients demonstrate poor recovery of function regardless of rehabilitation efforts. Current recommendations from the World Health Organization suggest that rehabilitation efforts should be directed toward the middle band of patients who can make satisfactory recovery only through intensive rehabilitation.[60] Major difficulties in stroke outcome studies appear to be the lack of uniform criteria in the selection of patients for rehabilitation, as well as differences in duration, type, and onset of rehabilitation programming.[90,103,156–157]

Patients who generally do poorly in rehabilitation demonstrate (1) decreased alertness, inattention, poor memory, and an inability to learn new tasks or follow simple commands, (2) severe neglect or anosognosia, (3) significant medical problems, particularly cardiovascular or degenerative joint disease, (4) serious language disturbances, and (5) less well defined social and economic problems.[158–160]

Most patients are able to maintain their independent living status following discharge. The severity of physical disability, age, and persistent psychologic and/or emotional problems (depression, irritability) are the primary factors that determine continuing success in independent living and quality of life. Other key factors identified include marital status (the presence of a helpful, caring spouse), elimination of home barriers, and transportation.[161,162]

SUMMARY

Stroke can result from a number of different vascular events that interrupt cerebral circulation and impair brain function. These include cerebral thrombosis, emboli, or hemorrhage. The location and size of the ischemic process, the nature and functions of the structures involved, and the availability of collateral blood flow all influence the symptomatology that evolves. For many patients, stroke represents a major cause of disability, with diffuse problems affecting widespread areas of function. From a practical standpoint, patients with stroke present a tremendous challenge for clinicians. Effective rehabilitation should take advantage of spontaneous recovery. Rehabilitation also seeks to prevent or lessen secondary impairments and provide an effective environment for the relearning of functional skills.

QUESTIONS FOR REVIEW

1. Differentiate between occlusive lesions in each of the major cerebral arteries in terms of the symptoms produced. What are the hemispheric differences?

2. What are the major causes of stroke? Define and explain each.

3. What diagnostic measures are used to confirm stroke?

4. Describe the normal recovery process in stroke. What are the typical stages?

5. What are the major sensory, motor, language, perceptual and mental deficits produced with stroke?

6. Describe the dynamics and causative factors of shoulder dysfunction in hemiplegia. How should this knowledge influence your evaluation and treatment?

7. Differentiate between common hemiplegic assessments including those of Brunnstrom and Bobath.

8. What are the key strategies in positioning the patient with stroke during the acute stage?

9. Identify critical motor learning strategies for treating the patient with stroke.

10. List four activities that could be used in the acute phase of rehabilitation to mobilize the patient.

11. Oromotor training should focus upon key functions. What are they?

12. Describe three strategies to reduce muscle tone.

13. What is the principal focus of motor control training during the active (postacute) phase of rehabilitation?

14. How can timing deficits in ambulation be overcome? Identify two strategies.

15. Identify and describe common orthotic devices used in stroke rehabilitation. What are the major indications and contraindications for each?

16. List the possible uses of EMG-BFB and NMES in the rehabilitation of patients with stroke.

17. What factors should be considered when teaching the patient and his or her family about stroke and stroke rehabilitation?

18. What are the major factors affecting stroke outcome?

REFERENCES

1. American Heart Association: Heart and Stroke Facts. American Heart Association, Dallas, 1992.
2. Kurtzke, J: Epidemiology of cerebrovascular disease. In Office of Scientific Health Reports, NINCDS, NIH: The National Survey of Stroke, Stroke 12(Suppl):1, 1981.
3. Kannel, W and Wolf, P: Epidemiology of cerebrovascular disease. In Russell, R (ed): Vascular Diseases of the Central Nervous System, ed 2. Churchill Livingstone, Edinburgh, 1983.
4. Wade, E, et al: Stroke: A Critical Approach to Diagnosis, Treatment, and Management. Year Book Medical, Chicago, 1985.
5. Russell, R: Vascular Disease of the Central Nervous System, ed 2. Churchill Livingstone, Edinburgh, 1983.
6. Sacco, R, et al: Survival and recurrence following stroke—the Framingham study. Stroke 13:290, 1982.
7. American Heart Association: Fact Sheet on Heart Attack, Stroke and Risk Factors. American Heart Association, Dallas, 1993.
8. Zivin, J and Choi, D: Stroke therapy. Scientific American July:56, 1991.
9. Hachinski, V and Norris, J: The Acute Stroke. FA Davis, Philadelphia, 1985.
10. Haerer, A: Clinical manifestations of occlusive cerebrovascular disease. In Smith, R (ed): Stroke and the Extracranial Vessels. Raven Press, New York, 1984.
11. Fieschi, C and Lenzi, G: Cerebral blood flow and metabolism in stroke patients. In Russell, R (ed): Vascular Diseases of the Central Nervous System, ed 2. Churchill Livingstone, Edinburgh, 1983.
12. Haig, A, Katz, R, and Sahgal, V: Locked-in syndrome: review. Curr Concepts Rehabil Med 2:12, 1986.
13. Haig, A, Katz, R, and Sahgal, V: Mortality and complications of the locked-in syndrome. Arch Phys Med Rehabil 68:24, 1987.

14. Toole, J: Cerebrovascular Disorders, ed 3. Raven Press, New York, 1984.
15. Smith, D, Akhtar, A, and Garraway, M. Proprioception and spatial neglect after stroke. Age Ageing 12:63, 1983.
16. Twitchell, T: The restoration of motor function following hemiplegia in man. Brain 47:443, 1951.
17. Brunnstrom, S: Motor testing procedures in hemiplegia based on recovery stages. J Am Phys Ther Assoc 46:357, 1966.
18. Brunnstrom, S: Movement Therapy in Hemiplegia. Harper & Row, New York, 1970.
19. Bobath, B: Adult Hemiplegia: Evaluation and Treatment, ed 2. Wm Heinemann Medical Books, London, 1978.
20. Fugl-Meyer, A, et al: The post stroke hemiplegic patient, I. A method for evaluation of physical performance. Scand J Rehabil Med 7:13, 1976.
21. Gray, C, et al: Motor recovery following acute stroke. Age and Ageing 19:179, 1990.
22. Wade, D, Wood, V, and Hewer, R: Recovery after stroke—the first 3 months. J Neurol Neurosurg Psychiatry 48:7, 1985.
23. Schenkman, M and Butler, R: Automatic postural tone in posture, movement, and function. Forum on physical therapy issues related to cerebrovascular accident. American Physical Therapy Association, Alexandria, VA, 1992.
24. Michels, E: Synergies in hemiplegia. Clin Management 1:9, 1981.
25. Bobath, B: Abnormal Postural Reflex Activity Caused by Brain Lesions, ed 3. Wm Heinemann Medical Books, London, 1985.
26. Mulley, G: Associated reactions in the hemiplegic arm. Scand J Rehabil Med 14:17, 1982.
27. McComas, A, et al: Functional changes in motorneurons of hemiparetic patients. J Neurol Neurosurg Psychiatry 36:183, 1973.
28. Bourbonnais, D and Vanden Noven, S: Weakness in patients with hemiparesis. Am J Occup Ther 43:313, 1989.
29. Bohannon, R and Smith, M: Relationship between static muscle strength deficits and spasticity in stroke patients with hemiparesis. Phys Ther 67:1068, 1987.
30. Knutsson, E and Martensson, A: Dynamic motor capacity in spastic paresis and its relation to prime mover dysfunction, spastic reflexes, and antagonist co-activation. Scand J Rehabil Med 12:93, 1980.
31. Mizrahi, E and Angel, R: Impairment of voluntary movement by spasticity. Ann Neurol 5:594, 1979.
32. Watkins, M, Harris, B, and Kozlowski, B: Isokinetic testing in patients with hemiparesis: a pilot study. Phys Ther 64:184, 1984.
33. Sjostrom, M, et al: Post stroke hemiplegia, crural muscle strength and structure. Scand J Rehabil Med &: 53, 1980.
34. Murray, E: Hemispheric specialization. In Fisher, A, Murray, E, and Bundy, A (eds): Sensory Integration Theory and Practice. FA Davis, Philadelphia, 1991.
35. Kimura, D: Acquisition of a motor skill after left-hemisphere damage. Brain 100:527, 1977.
36. Light, K, Purser, J, and Guiliani, C: Motor programming deficits of patients with left versus right CVA's. Forum on Physical Therapy Issues Related to Cerebrovascular Accident. American Physical Therapy Association, Alexandria, VA, 1992.
37. Mills, V and DiGenio, M: Functional differences in patients with left or right cerebrovascular accidents. Phys Ther 63:481, 1983.
38. Bernspang, B, et al: Motor and perceptual impairments in acute stroke: effects on self-care ability. Stroke 18:1081, 1987.
39. Boller, F: Strokes and behavior: disorders of higher cortical functions following cerebral disease. Disorders of language and related functions. Stroke 12:532, 1981.
40. Siev, E, Freishtat, B, and Zoltan, B: Perceptual and Cognitive Dysfunction in the Adult Stroke Patient. Slack, Thorofare, NJ, 1986.
41. Diller, L: Perceptual and intellectual problems in hemiplegia: implications for rehabilitation. Med Clin North Amer 53:575, 1969.
42. American Heart Association: How Stroke Affects Behavior. American Heart Association, Dallas, 1991.
43. Pearce, J: Dementia in cerebral arterial disease. In Russell, R (ed): Vascular Disease of the Central Nervous System, ed 2. Churchill Livingstone, Edinburgh, 1983.
44. Binder, L: Emotional problems after stroke. Stroke 15:174, 1984.
45. Robinson, R and Szetela, B: Mood change following left hemispheric brain injury. Ann Neurol 9:447, 1981.
46. Cocito, L, Fafale, E, and Reni, L: Epileptic seizures in cerebral arterial occlusive disease. Stroke 13:189, 1982.
47. Veis, S and Logemann, J: Swallowing disorders in persons with cerebrovascular accident. Arch Phys Med Rehabil 66:372, 1985.
48. Robinson, R and Price, T: Post-stroke depressive disorders: a follow-up study of 103 patients. Stroke 13:635, 1982.
49. Bruton, J: Shoulder pain in stroke—patients with hemiplegia or hemiparesis following cerebrovascular accident. Physiotherapy 71:2, 1985.
50. Calliet, R: The Shoulder in Hemiplegia. FA Davis, Philadelphia, 1980.
51. Davies, P: Steps to Follow. Springer-Verlag, New York, 1985.
52. Tepperman, P, et al: Reflex sympathetic dystrophy in hemiplegia. Arch Phys Med Rehabil 65:442, 1984.
53. Mol, V and Baker, C: Activity intolerance in the geriatric stroke patient. Rehabil Nursing 16:337, 1991.
54. Johnston, M, et al: Prediction of outcomes following rehabilitation of stroke patients. Neurorehabilitation 2:72, 1992.
55. Solzi, J, Ring, H, Najenson, T, and Luz, Y: Hemiplegics after a first stroke: late survival and risk factors. Stroke 14:703, 1983.
56. Finger, S and Stein, D: Brain Damage and Recovery. Academic Press, New York, 1982.
57. Dombovy, M and Bach-y-Rita, P: Clinical observations on recovery from stroke. Adv Neurol 47:265, 1988.
58. Bach-y-Rita, P (ed): Recovery of Function: Theoretical Considerations for Brain Injury Rehabilitation. University Park Press, Baltimore, 1980.
59. Grotta, J: Current medical and surgical therapy for cerebrovascular disease. N Engl J Med 317:1505, 1987.
60. World Health Organization: Stroke—1989: recommendations of stroke prevention, diagnosis, and therapy. Stroke 20:1407, 1989.
61. Strand, T, et al: A non-intensive stroke unit reduces functional disability and the need for long-term hospitalization. Stroke 16:29, 1985.
62. McCann, B and Culbertson, R: Comparisons of two systems for stroke rehabilitation in a general hospital. J Am Geriatr Soc 24:211, 1976.
63. Hamrin, E: Early activation in stroke: does it make a difference? Scand J Rehabil Med 14:101, 1982.
64. Garraway, M: Stroke rehabilitation units: concepts, evaluation, and unresolved issues. Stroke 16:178, 1985.
65. Hayes, S and Carroll, S: Early intervention care in the acute stroke patient. Arch Phys Med Rehabil 67:319, 1986.
66. Johnston, M and Keister, M: Early rehabilitation for stroke patients: a new look. Arch Phys Med Rehabil 65:437, 1984.
67. Novack, T, Satterfield, W, and Connor, M: Stroke onset and rehabilitation: time lag as a factor in treatment outcome. Arch Phys Med Rehabil 65:316, 1984.
68. Feigenson, J and McCarthy, M: Guidelines for establishing a stroke rehabilitation unit. N Y State J Med 34:1430, 1977.
69. Bohannon, R: Measurement and treatment of paresis in the geriatric patient. Top Geriatr Rehabil 7:15, 1991.
70. Collin, C and Wade, D: Assessing motor impairment after stroke: a pilot reliability study. J Neurol Neurosurg Psychiatry 53:576, 1990.
71. Collen, C, Wade, D, and Bradshaw C: Mobility after stroke: reliability of measurements of impairment and disability. Int Disabil Stud 12:6, 1990.
72. Badke, M and DiFabio, R: Balance deficits in patients with hemiplegia: considerations for assessment and treatment. Balance: Proceedings of the APTA Forum. American Physical Therapy Association, Alexandria, VA, 1990.
73. Badke, M and Duncan, P: Patterns of rapid motor responses during postural adjustments when standing in healthy subjects and hemiplegic patients. Phys Ther 63:13, 1983.
74. Fugl-Meyer, A: Post-stroke hemiplegia assessment of physical properties. Scand J Rehabil Med 7:85, 1980.
75. Fugl-Meyer, A: The post-stroke hemiplegic patient, I. A method for evaluation of physical performance. Scand J Rehabil Med 7:13, 1975.
76. Duncan, P, Priopst, M, and Nelson, S: Reliability of the Fugl-Meyer Assessment of Sensorimotor Recovery following cerebrovascular accident. Phys Ther 63:1606, 1983.
77. Guarna, R, et al: An evaluation of the hemiplegic subject based on the Bobath approach, I. The model. Scand J Rehabil Med 20:1, 1988.
78. Corriveau, H, et al: An evaluation of the hemiplegic subject based

on the Bobath approach, II. The evaluation protocol. Scand J Rehabil Med 20:5, 1988.

79. Arsenault, A, et al: An evaluation of the hemiplegic subject based on the Bobath approach, III. A validation study. Scand J Rehabil Med 20:13, 1988.

80. Carr, J, Shephard, R, Nordholm, L, and Lynne, D: Investigation of a new motor assessment scale for stroke patients. Phys Ther 65:175, 1985.

81. Pool, J and Whitney, S: Motor Assessment Scale for stroke patients: concurrent validity and interrater reliability. Arch Phys Med Rehabil 69:195, 1988.

82. Turnbull, G and Wall, J: The development of a system for the clinical assessment of gait following a stroke. Physiotherapy 71:294, 1985.

83. Pink, M: High speed video application in physical therapy. Clinical Management 5:14, 1985.

84. Holden, M, et al: Clinical gait assessment in the neurologically impaired: reliability and meaningfulness. Phys Ther 64:35, 1984.

85. Mahoney, F and Barthel, D: Functional evaluation: Barthel Index. Md State Med J 14:61, 1965.

86. Delong, G and Branch, L: Predicting the stroke patient's ability to live independently. Stroke 13:648, 1982.

87. Wade, D, Silbeck, C, and Hewer, R: Predicting Barthel ADL score at 6 months after an acute stroke. Arch Phys Med Rehabil 64:24, 1983.

88. Logigian, M, Samuels, M, and Falconer, J: Clinical exercise trial for stroke patients. Arch Phys Med Rehabil 64:364, 1983

89. Granger, C, et al: Stroke rehabilitation: analysis of repeated Barthel Index measures. Arch Phys Med Rehabil 60:14, 1979.

90. Johnston, M, et al: Prediction of outcomes following rehabilitation of stroke patients. Neurol Rehabil 2:72, 1992.

91. Hall, K: Overview of functional assessment scales in brain injury rehabilitation. Neurol Rehabil 2:98, 1992.

92. Kumar, R, et al: Shoulder pain in hemiplegia: the role of exercise. Am J Phys Med Rehabil 69:205, 1990.

93. Bohannon, R, et al: Shoulder pain in hemiplegia: statistical relationship with five variables. Arch Phys Med Rehabil 67:514, 1986.

94. Brooke, M, et al: Shoulder subluxation in hemiplegia: effects of three different supports. Arch Phys Med Rehabil 72:582, 1991.

95. Johnstone, M: Therapy for Stroke. Churchill Livingstone, New York, 1991.

96. Zimmerman, J and Oder, L: Swallowing dysfunction in the acutely ill patient. Phys Ther 61:1755, 1981.

97. Carr, E: Assessment and treatment of feeding difficulties after stroke. Top Geriatr Rehabil 7:35, 1991.

98. Voss, D, Ionta, M, and Myers, B: Proprioceptive Neuromuscular Facilitation, ed 3. Harper & Row, Philadelphia, 1985.

99. Stern, P, et al: Factors influencing stroke rehabilitation. Stroke 2:213, 1971.

100. Lord, J and Hall, K: Neuromuscular reeducation versus traditional programs for stroke rehabilitation. Arch Phys Med Rehabil 67:88, 1986.

101. Dickstein, R, et al: Stroke rehabilitation: three exercise therapy approaches. Phys Ther 66:1233, 1986.

102. Wagenaar, R, et al: The functional recovery of stroke: a comparison between neuro-developmental treatment and the Brunnstrom method. Scand J Rehabil Med 22:1, 1990.

103. Basmajian, J, et al: Stroke treatment: comparison of integrated behavioral physical therapy vs traditional physical therapy programs. Arch Phys Med Rehabil 68:267, 1987.

104. Ernst, E: A review of stroke rehabilitation and physiotherapy. Stroke 21:1082, 1990.

105. Johnstone, M: Restoration of Motor Function in the Stroke Patient, ed 3. Churchill Livingstone, New York, 1987.

106. Taub, E: Somatosensory deafferentation research with monkeys: implications for rehabilitation medicine. In Ince, L (ed): Behavioral Psychology in Rehabilitation Medicine: Clinical Applications. Williams & Wilkins, Baltimore, 1980, pp 371–401.

107. Dannenbaum, R and Dykes, R: Sensory loss in the hand after sensory stroke: therapeutic rationale. Arch Phys Med Rehabil 69:833, 1988.

108. Weinberg, J, et al: Training sensory awareness and spatial organization in people with right brain damage. Arch Phys Med Rehabil 60:491, 1979.

109. Hocherman, S and Dickstein, R: Postural rehabilitation in geriatric stroke patients. Top Geriatr Rehabil 7:60, 1991.

110. Badke, M and DiFabio, R: Balance deficits in patients with hemi-

plegia: considerations for assessment and treatment. In Duncan, P (ed): Balance: Proceedings of an APTA Forum. APTA, Alexandria, VA, 1990.

111. Hochemann, S, Dickstein, R, and Pillar, T: Platform training and postural stability in hemiplegia. Arch Phys Med Rehabil 65:588, 1984.

112. Shumway-Cook, A, Anson, D, and Haller, S: Postural sway biofeedback: its effect on reestablishing stance stability in hemiplegic patients. Arch Phys Med Rehabil 69:395, 1988.

113. Winstein, C, et al: Standing balance training: effect on balance and locomotion in hemiparetic adults. Arch Phys Med Rehabil 70:755, 1989.

114. Winstein, C: Balance retraining: Does it transfer? In Duncan, P (ed): Balance: Proceedings of an APTA forum. APTA, Alexandria, VA, 1990.

115. Burdett, R, et al: Gait comparison of subjects with hemiplegia walking unbraced, with ankle-foot orthosis, and with air-stirrup brace. Phys Ther 68:1197, 1988.

116. Lehmann, J, Ko, M, and DeLateur, B: Knee moments: origin in normal ambulation and their modification by double-stopped ankle-foot orthoses. Arch Phys Med Rehabil 63:345, 1982.

117. Schmidt, R: Motor Control and Learning. Human Kinetics, Champaign, IL, 1982.

118. Magill, R: Motor Learning Concepts and Applications, ed 4. Brown & Benchmark, Dubuque, IA, 1993.

119. Carr, J and Shepherd, R: A Motor Relearning Programme for Stroke, ed 2. Aspen, Rockville, MD, 1987.

120. Wolf, S and Binder-Macleod, S: Electromyographic biofeedback applications to the hemiplegic patient—changes in lower extremity neuromuscular and functional status. Phys Ther 63:1404, 1983.

121. Wolf, S: Electromyographic biofeedback applications to stroke patients—a critical review. Phys Ther 63:1448, 1983.

122. Cozean, C, Pease, W, and Hubbell, S: Biofeedback and functional electric stimulation in stroke rehabilitation. Arch Phys Med Rehabil 69:401, 1988.

123. Hogue, R and McCandless, S: Genu recurvatum: auditory biofeedback treatment for adult patients with stroke or head injuries. Arch Phys Med Rehabil 64:368, 1983.

124. Binder, S, Moll, C, and Wolf, S: Evaluation of electromyographic biofeedback as an adjunct to therapeutic exercise in treating the lower extremities of hemiplegic patients. Phys Ther 61:886, 1981.

125. Prevo, A, Visser, S, and Vogelaar, T: Effect of EMG feedback on paretic muscles and abnormal co-contraction in the hemiplegic arm, compared with conventional physical therapy. Scand J Rehabil Med 14:121, 1982.

126. Basmajian, J, Gowland, C, and Brandstater, M: EMG feedback treatment of upper limb in hemiplegic stroke patients: a pilot study. Arch Phys Med Rehabil 63:613, 1982.

127. Wolf, S and Binder-Macleod, S: Electromyographic biofeedback applications to the hemiplegic patient—changes in upper extremity neuromuscular and functional status. Phys Ther 63:1393, 1983.

128. Baker, L: Clinical uses of neuromuscular electrical stimulation. In Nelson, R and Currier, D (eds): Clinical Electrotherapy. Appleton & Lange, Norwalk, CT, 1987, p 115.

129. Trimble, M, and Enoka, R: Mechanisms underlying the training effects associated with neuromuscular electrical stimulation. Phys Ther 71:273, 1991.

130. Cranstam, B, Larsson, L, and Prevec, T: Improvement of gait following functional electrical stimulation. Scand J Rehabil Med 9:7, 1977.

131. Merlitte, R, Galante, A, and Furlan, I: Clinical experience of electronic peroneal stimulators in 50 hemiparetic patients. Scand J Rehabil Med 11:111, 1979.

132. Bowman, B, Baker, L, and Waters, R: Positional feedback and electrical stimulation: an automated treatment for the hemiplegic wrist. Arch Phys Med Rehabil 60:497, 1979.

133. Packman-Braun, R: Relationship between functional electrical stimulation duty cycle and fatigue in wrist extensor muscles of patients with hemiparesis. Phys Ther 68:51, 1988.

134. Levine, M, Knott, M, and Kabat, H: Relaxation of spasticity by electrical stimulation of antagonist muscles. Arch Phys Med 33:668, 1952.

135. Baker, L and Parker, K: Neuromuscular electrical stimulation of the muscles surrounding the shoulder. Phys Ther 66:1930, 1986.

136. Smith, L: Restoration of volitional limb movement of hemiplegics

following patterned functional electrical stimulation. Percept Mot Skills 71:851, 1990.

137. Nelson, A: Strategies for improving motor control. In Rosenthal, M, Griffith, E, Bond, M, and Miller, J (eds): Rehabilitation of the Head Injured Adult. FA Davis, Philadelphia, 1983.

138. Corcoran, P, et al: Effects of plastic and metal braces on speed and energy cost of hemiparetic ambulation. Arch Phys Med Rehabil 51:69, 1970.

139. Hirschberg, G and Ralston, H: Energy cost of stairclimbing in normal and hemiplegic subjects. Am J Phys Med 44:165, 1965.

140. Bard, G: Energy expenditure of hemiplegic subjects during walking. Arch Phys Med Rehabil 44:368, 1963.

141. Roth, E, Mueller, K, and Green, D: Cardiovascular response to physical therapy in stroke rehabilitation. Neurorehabilitation 2:7, 1992.

142. Roth, E, Mueller, K, and Green, D: Stroke rehabilitation outcome: impact of coronary artery disease. Stroke 19:41, 1988.

143. King, M, et al: Adaptive exercise testing for patients with hemiparesis. J Cardiopulmon Rehabil 9:237, 1989.

144. Gordon, N: Stroke: Your Complete Exercise Guide. Human Kinetics, Champaign, IL, 1993.

145. American College of Sports Medicine: Guidelines for Exercise Testing and Prescription. Lea & Febiger, Philadelphia, 1991.

146. Monga, T, et al: Cardiovascular response to acute exercise in patients with cerebrovascular accidents. Arch Phys Med Rehabil 69:937, 1988.

147. American Association of Cardiovascular and Pulmonary Rehabilitation: Guidelines for Cardiac Rehabilitation Programs. Human Kinetics, Champaign, IL, 1991.

148. Brinkmann, J and Hoskins, T: Physical conditioning and altered self-concept in rehabilitated hemiplegic patients. Phys Ther 59:859, 1979.

149. Tangeman, P, Banaitis, D, and Williams, A: Rehabilitation of

150. Mulhall, D: Stroke: a problem for patient and family. Physiotherapy 67:195, 1981.

151. Davidoff, G, et al: Acute stroke patients: long-term effects of rehabilitation and maintenance of gains. Arch Phys Med Rehabil 72:869, 1991.

152. Tangeman, P, Banaitis, D, and Williams, A: Rehabilitation of chronic stroke patients: changes in functional performance. Arch Phys Med Rehabil 71:876, 1990.

153. Czyrny, J, Hamilton, B, and Gresham, G: Rehabilitation of the stroke patient. In Eisenberg, M and Grzesiak, R (eds): Advances in Clinical Rehabilitation, vol 3. Springer, New York, 1990.

154. Feigenson, J: Stroke rehabilitation: outcome studies and guidelines for alternative levels of care. Stroke 12:372, 1981.

155. Johnston, M and Keith, R: Cost-benefits of medical rehabilitation: review and critique. Arch Phys Med Rehabil 64:147, 1983.

156. Lind, K: A synthesis of studies on stroke rehabilitation. Chronic Dis 35:133, 1982.

157. Dombovy, M, Sandok, B, and Basford, J: Rehabilitation for stroke: a review. Stroke 17:363, 1986.

158. Dove, H, Schneider, K, and Wallace, J: Evaluating and predicting outcome of acute cerebral vascular accident. Stroke 15:858, 1984.

159. Lundgren, J, et al: Site of brain lesion and functional capacity in rehabilitated hemiplegics. Scand J Rehabil Med 14:141, 1982.

160. Wade, D, Hewer, R, and Wood, V: Stroke: influence of patient's sex and side of weakness on outcome. Arch Phys Med Rehabil 65:513, 1984.

161. DeJong, G and Branch, L: Predicting the stroke patient's ability to live independently. Stroke 13:648, 1982.

162. Ahlsio, B, Britton, M, Murray, V, and Theorell, T: Disablement and quality of life after stroke. Stroke 15:886, 1984.

SUPPLEMENTAL READINGS

Charness, A: Stroke/Head Injury—A Guide to Functional Outcomes in Physical Therapy Management. Aspen Publishers, Rockville, MD, 1986.

Carr, J and Shephard, R: A Motor Relearning Programme for Stroke, ed 2. Aspen Publishers, Rockville, MD, 1988.

Davies, P: Steps to Follow—A Guide to the Treatment of Adult Hemiplegia. Springer-Verlag, New York, 1985.

Davies, P: Right in the Middle—Selective Trunk Activity in the Treatment of Adult Hemiplegia. Springer-Verlag, New York, 1990.

Duncan, P and Badke, M: Stroke Rehabilitation: The Recovery of Motor Control. Year Book Medical Publishers, Chicago, 1987.

Johnston, M: Therapy for Stroke. Churchill Livingstone, New York, 1991.

Sawner, K and LaVigne, J: Brunnstrom's Movement Therapy in Hemiplegia, ed 2. JB Lippincott, Philadelphia, 1992.

Siev, E, Freishtat, B, and Zoltan, B: Perceptual and Cognitive Dysfunction in the Adult Stroke Patient. Slack, Thorofare, NJ, 1986.

GLOSSARY

Agnosia: The inability to recognize familiar objects with one sensory modality, while retaining the ability to recognize the same object with other sensory modalities.

Agraphia: Loss of the ability to write.

Anosognosia: A perceptual disability that includes denial, neglect, and lack of awareness of the presence or severity of one's problems.

Aphasia: Communication disorder caused by brain damage and characterized by an impairment of language comprehension, formulation, and use.

    Fluent aphasia: A type of aphasia in which speech flows smoothly, with a variety of grammatical constructions and preserved melody of speech; paraphasias and circumlocutions may be present. Auditory comprehension may be impaired (e.g., Wernicke's aphasia).

    Global aphasia: A severe aphasia characterized by marked impairments of the production and comprehension of language.

    Nonfluent aphasia: A type of aphasia in which the flow of speech is slow and hesitant, vocabulary is limited, and syntax is impaired. Articulation may be labored (e.g., Broca's aphasia).

Apraxia: A disorder of voluntary learned movement, characterized by an inability to perform purposeful movements and cannot be accounted for by inadequate strength, loss of coordination, impaired sensation, attentional deficits, or lack of comprehension.

Arteriovenous malformation (AVM): An abnormality in embryonal development leading to a skein of tangled arteries and veins, usually without an intervening capillary bed. It commonly occurs along the distribution of the middle cerebral artery and its rupture produces cerebral hemorrhage.

Associated reactions: Automatic responses of the limbs as a result of action occurring in some other part of the body, either by voluntary or reflex stimulation. In hemiplegia, these reactions are stereotyped and abnormal.

Asymmetric tonic neck reflex (ATNR): Head rotation to the left causes extension of the left arm and leg (skull limbs) with flexion of the right arm and leg (jaw limbs); head rotation to the right causes the reverse pattern.

Ataxia: A general term used to describe uncoordinated movement; may influence gait, posture, and patterns of movements.

Atherosclerosis: Thickening of the walls of the arteries with loss of elasticity and contractility.

Autoregulatory mechanisms (cerebral): Mechanisms that modulate a constant rate of blood flow through the brain.

Berry aneurysm: Small saccular congenital aneurysm of a cerebral vessel; communicates with the vessel by a small opening.

Body image disorder: A disturbed perception in the visual and mental image of one's body, including the feelings about one's body, especially in relation to health and disease.

Body scheme disorder: A disturbed perception in the postural model of one's body, including the relationship of the body parts to each other and the relationship of the body to the environment.

Cerebral embolus: A blood clot that forms in the blood vessels in one part of the body and travels to cerebral vessels.

Cerebral hemorrhage: Escape of blood into tissues of the brain.

Cerebral thrombosis: Formation of a blood clot in a blood vessel leading to the brain.

Dementia: Irrecoverable deteriorative mental state characterized by absence of or reduction in intellectual faculties; associated with organic brain disease. Multiinfarct dementia is the result of multiple small strokes.

Drop attack: Sudden loss of tone in the lower limbs; associated with ischemia of the medullary pyramids.

Dysarthria: Term for a category of motor speech difficulties caused by impairment in the parts of the central or peripheral nervous system that mediate speech production.

Dysphagia: Inability to swallow or difficulty in swallowing.

Emotional lability: Unstable or changeable emotional state.

Flaccidity: Defective or absent muscle tone.

Forced gaze deviation: Deviation of the eyes secondary to unopposed action of eye muscles. In stroke, eyes may deviate in the direction of the intact muscles.

Hemiparesis: Partial or incomplete paralysis affecting one half of the body.

Hemiplegia: Paralysis of one half of the body.

Homonymous hemianopsia: Inability to see half the field of vision of one or both eyes.

Horner's syndrome: Contraction of the pupil, partial ptosis of the eyelid, enophthalmos, and sometimes loss of sweating over the affected side of the face; due to paralysis of the cervical sympathetic nerve trunk.

Intracerebral hemorrhage (IH): Rupture of one of the cerebral vessels with subsequent bleeding into the brain.

Locked-in syndrome (LIS): Quadriplegia and anarthria with preserved consciousness; secondary to a ventral pontine lesion.

Perseveration: Continued repetition of a meaningless word or movement.

Prosopagnosia: An inability to recognize faces or other visually ambiguous stimuli as being familiar and distinct from one another.

Raimiste's phenomenon: An associated reaction in which abduction or adduction of the normal limb produces a similar response in the affected limb.

Reflex sympathetic dystrophy (RSD, shoulder-hand syndrome): Sympathetic vasomotor symptoms secondary to prolonged immobility of the shoulder or hand.

Spasticity: Increased tone or contraction of muscle causing stiff, awkward movements; the result of an upper motor lesion.

Stroke: Sudden, focal neurologic deficit resulting from ischemic or hemorrhagic lesions in the brain.

    Deteriorating stroke: Neurologic status is deteriorating after admission to the hospital.

    Major stroke: Stable, usually severe deficit.

    Young stroke: Affecting persons below the age of 45.

Subarachnoid hemorrhage (SH): Rupture of one of the cerebral vessels with subsequent bleeding into the subarachnoid space.

Subclavian steal syndrome: Shunting of blood, which was destined for the brain, away from the cerebral circulation. This occurs when the subclavian artery is occluded. Blood then flows from the opposite vertebral artery across to and down the vertebral artery on the side of the occlusion.

Symmetric tonic labyrinthine reflex (STLR): A response to positioning in which the supine position produces an increase in extensor tone and the prone position increases flexor tone.

Symmetric tonic neck reflex (STNR): A response to flexion of the neck that results in flexion of the arms and extension of the legs; extension of the neck produces the opposite responses.

Synergies (mass): Stereotyped, primitive movement patterns associated with the presence of spasticity.

Thalamic sensory syndrome (thalamic pain): Continuous, unpleasant sensation on the hemiplegic side.

Tonic lumbar reflex (TLR): Rotation of the upper trunk toward the affected side produces flexion of the upper limb and extension of the lower limb. Rotation towards the sound side produces the opposite response.

Topographical disorientation: Difficulty in understanding and remembering the relationship of one place to another.

Transient ischemic attack (TIA): Temporary interference with blood supply to the brain. Symptoms of neurologic deficit may last for only a few minutes or for several hours. After the attack no evidence of residual brain damage or neurologic damage remains.

Unilateral neglect: The inability to register and to integrate stimuli and perceptions from one side of the environment (usually the left). As a result, the patient ignores stimuli occurring in that side of personal space.

Peripheral Vascular Disease

Joseph M. McCulloch

OBJECTIVES

1. Define terms pertinent to the study of peripheral vascular disease.
2. Plan for the examination of a patient who presents with symptoms related to the peripheral vascular system.
3. Describe the epidemiologic and pathophysiologic factors that contribute to peripheral vascular disease.
4. Explain why diabetes is considered as a peripheral vascular disease.
5. Identify the role of the physical therapist in the rehabilitative management of patients with peripheral vascular disease.

When one thinks about peripheral vascular disease, the clinical picture of a patient with arterial insufficiency, cramping and **gangrene,** frequently comes to mind. Involvement of the arterial system is certainly a major component in peripheral vascular disease. However, one must also give serious consideration to the clinical presentation and treatment resulting from involvement of the venous and lymphatic systems. In a general sense, peripheral vascular disease can be thought of as any of a number of conditions that may affect the circulatory system external to the heart. Because peripheral vascular disease encompasses such a diverse group of conditions, it is difficult, if not impossible, to discuss their etiologies in a global sense. An evaluation of the etiologic factors related to each specific subsystem is more appropriate. It should be brought to the reader's attention early on that environment and life-style are major factors in the development of many of the diseases to be discussed. Nicotine and high cholesterol diets are probably the most frequently reported factors.

ANATOMIC CONSIDERATIONS

Considering the cardinal principle of the circulatory system put forth by John Hunter over a century ago, it becomes quite understandable why the system is laid out in the manner that it is. Hunter stated that "To maintain a circulation sufficient for the part and no more" is the primary function of the circulatory system.[1] When examined in a simplistic manner it is apparent that pathologic conditions of the circulatory system basically result in problems with supplying nutrients and removing waste products.

Arterial System

Blood enters the peripheral arterial system from the left ventricle after having been oxygenated in the lungs. Structurally, arteries are divided into three layers or tunics: the tunica intima, tunica media, and tunica adventicia, which course from within the artery to the outside (Fig. 18–1). These layers are composed of varying amounts of muscle cells, connective tissue, and other differentiated and undifferentiated cells; the exact makeup of the layers depends on the specific location and function of the artery. Arteries with a highly elastic makeup are found closer to the heart while the more muscular ones reside peripherally.[2] The arterial system appears to function without the assistance of valves, with the exception of those in the heart. The geometric layout of the system greatly influences blood flow and, as will be discussed later, plays a major role in pathology. As the larger arteries course through the body, they continually bifurcate or branch, resulting in successively smaller arterial subunits until they reach the capillary beds, where gaseous exchange occurs.

Venous System

Although the walls of veins, like arteries, can be divided into three layers, the layers tend to be less distinct and, for this reason, are seldom discussed. The

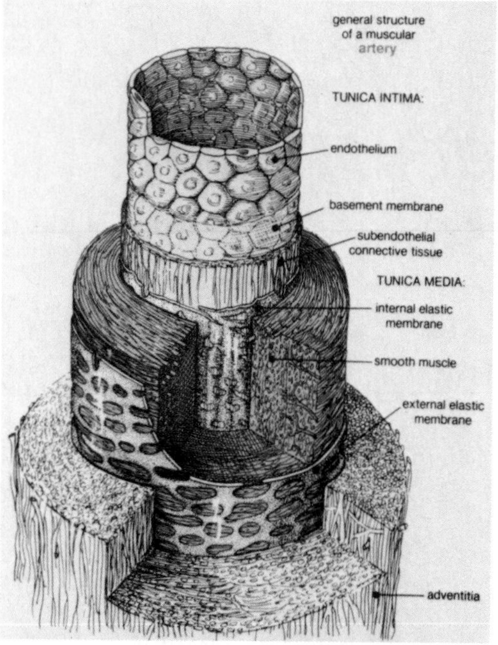

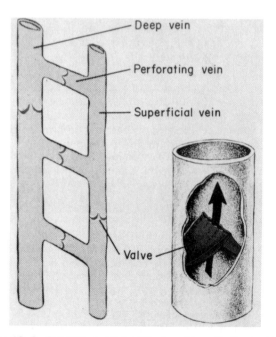

general structure
of a muscular
artery

TUNICA INTIMA:

endothelium

basement membrane

subendothelial
connective tissue

TUNICA MEDIA:

internal elastic
membrane

smooth muscle

external elastic
membrane

adventitia

Figure 18–1. Structure of the arterial walls. (From Melloni's Illustrated Medical Dictionary, ed 2, with permission.)

venous walls, however, are thinner than their arterial counterparts and therefore more transparent.[2] The innermost layer or tunic forms periodic folds along its course. These folds make up the venous valves, which provide the functional foundation of the system[3] (Fig. 18–2). Although delicate in appearance and structure, the valves or cusps can withstand rather strong forces without failure.

Poorly oxygenated blood, leaving the capillary bed, enters the venous system through the venules. The venules in turn empty into the collecting veins and finally

Deep vein

Perforating vein

Superficial vein

Valve

Figure 18–2. The venous valves of the legs. (From Textbook of Medical Physiology, ed 7. WB Saunders, Philadelphia, with permission.)

into the superior and inferior vena cavae. Veins course in company with arteries and have a similar branching pattern. At several places in the body, including below the elbows and knees, paired veins are found. These veins are located one on each side of the artery and are joined along their course by short **anastomotic** bridges.[3]

Because most venous problems seen by physical therapists occur in the lower extremities, a few moments will be spent discussing the functional layout of the leg veins. Each leg has three basic sets of veins termed *subcutaneous or superficial, deep or intramuscular,* and *perforating or communicating.* The superficial veins have rather thick and muscular walls and occur in groups of two in each extremity. The perforating veins serve the function of connecting the superficial and deep systems. Both the perforating and deep veins are thin-walled and less muscular. The deep veins course along with their corresponding arteries, as mentioned previously. The lower extremity is served by two major venous vessels, the great and small saphenous veins.[4]

Skeletal muscles contain very large, thin-walled veins, which are frequently referred to as sinusoids. These collecting reservoirs are an important part of the calf muscle pump mechanism which will be discussed later.[5]

Lymphatic System

The lymphatic system is comprised of three major components: the *capillaries and peripheral plexuses,* the *collecting vessels,* and the *lymph nodes.* The *lymphatic capillaries* are the most peripheral structures in the system and anastomose to form what are termed peripheral plexuses. These plexuses, consisting solely of a layer of endothelial cells, lie in direct contact with the tissues and give rise to short channels that lead to the collecting ducts.

Three types of *collecting ducts* exist. The main differences in the ducts are the number of muscular layers present. They range in complexity from those with a single muscular layer, to those with two, and finally three layers of muscle. The second type, with two muscular layers, is most common.[6] The walls of all of these vessels are only 0.5 to 1 mm in diameter. These vessels are more plentiful than veins, and tend to accompany the veins as they course through the body.[2,4] Their thin walls make them more delicate than arteries and veins and therefore more susceptible to trauma. Any injury significant enough to affect venous return most likely inflicts damage to the lymphatics. The ramifications for edema become apparent.

Lymph Nodes

Lymph nodes range in size from several millimeters to greater than 1 cm and consist of small accumulations of lymphocytes housed in an encapsulated network of connective tissue.[2,6] The nodes serve two basic purposes. The first is that of a filtering and phagocytosis system whereby the nodes work to rid the body of unwanted substances that have been deposited into their dense network. The second function of the node is the production of lymphocytes. After being cleansed of unwanted particulate matter by the lymph nodes, almost all lymph, with its newly acquired lymphocytes, proceeds through the thoracic duct into the systemic circulation.

The lymphatic and venous systems work in harmony to absorb the arterial capillary filtrate. It is estimated that approximately 10 percent of this filtrate, and almost all protein molecules, are handled via the lymphatic system.[4] The roles of the venous and lymphatic systems in edema production and control will be discussed later.

PATHOPHYSIOLOGIC CONSIDERATIONS

As previously mentioned, most forms of peripheral vascular disease encountered in physical therapy practice occur in the lower extremities. Because older individuals are more commonly affected by these disorders, other complicating conditions may be encountered such as diabetes, stroke, and heart failure. Table 18–1 provides a brief classification of the more common conditions encountered by the physical therapist. Each will be discussed briefly.

Arterial Dysfunction

By far the most common form of chronic occlusive vascular disease affecting the lower extremities is **arteriosclerosis obliterans.** Arteriosclerosis obliterans is known by various names such as chronic occlusive arterial disease, obliterative arteriosclerosis, and atherosclerotic occlusive disease. It is a peripheral manifestation of the generalized disease, **atherosclerosis.**[7] Approximately 95 percent of all cases of chronic occlusive arterial disease are of this type.[8] Since it is a slowly devel-

Table 18–1 COMMON PERIPHERAL VASCULAR DISEASES

Arterial Disease
  Chronic
    Arteriosclerosis obliterans
    Thromboangitis obliterans
    Diabetic angiopathy
  Acute
    Arterial thrombosis
    Embolic occlusion
    Vasospastic disease
Venous Disease
  Chronic
    Varicose veins
    Chronic venous insufficiency
  Acute
    Venous thrombosis
Lymphatic Disease
  Primary (congenital) lymphedema
  Secondary (acquired) lymphedema

oping, degenerative process, its manifestations occur insidiously. Ross[9] theorizes that the disease begins with monocyte adherence to the endothelial wall following some form of physical damage such as trauma, hypertension, or a biochemical process. A fatty streak begins to develop and subsequently results in the production of an atheromatous plaque in the intima of the artery. As the plaque increases in size the lumen is narrowed and linear flow of blood is impaired.

One of the earliest presenting symptoms in this disease is **intermittent claudication.** As the disease progresses, arterial flow may become impaired to the point that pain is present even at rest. The clinical evaluation of a patient with this pathology reveals diminished or absent pedal pulses and positive signs of rubor of dependency, which will be discussed later. As the process becomes more pronounced, **trophic changes** begin to occur and the foot becomes colder to the touch. In late stages of the disease, ulcerations may develop as a result of tissue **ischemia.** This occurs even more frequently in persons whose disease is complicated by diabetes.[7]

Thromboangiitis obliterans (Buerger's disease), is the second most common form of chronic occlusive arterial disease.[7] The disease process is similar to that of arteriosclerosis obliterans but is unique in that it tends to occur predominantly in young, male smokers. Beurger's disease is first manifested in the distal aspects of the extremities and progresses proximally. It has been demonstrated that cessation of smoking arrests the disease.[10] The pathology responsible for the clinical symptoms of decreased tissue temperature (cold distal extremities) and eventual tissue necrosis, is an inflammatory process in the veins and arteries that appears to be directly related to tobacco use. Nicotine is also a very potent vasoconstrictor and is responsible for the more immediate decrease in skin temperature seen in smokers.

Physical therapists are less likely to be involved in the treatment of individuals with acute arterial disease than those with more chronic problems. Nevertheless, it is important that these diseases and their signs and symptoms be recognized, should they occur during therapy for some other problem. The sudden loss of blood flow to an extremity, regardless of cause, is an emergency that requires immediate attention. The most common forms of acute arterial occlusion are arterial thrombosis, embolism, and vasospastic disease. Any of these conditions can result in the classic signs and symptoms of pain, pallor, loss of pulses, paresthesia, and paralysis.[11]

Arterial embolism is probably the most frequently encountered form of acute arterial disease. Emboli can arise from any of numerous sites and be composed of various substances. Probably, one of the most frequently occurring types results from the dislodging of a preexisting thrombus in the heart. The thrombus then migrates to a peripheral arterial vessel.

Arterial thrombi occur less frequently than emboli and usually occur in the area of a previously existing atherosclerotic lesion. In the normal individual, blood flows through the arteries in a laminar or streamline manner. When the arterial lumen narrows in the presence of an atherosclerotic lesion, the blood flow becomes turbulent. This swirling motion of the blood slows its passage through the area and permits platelets to collect. The platelet aggregate, together with significant amounts of fibrin, leads to the development of the thrombus. The severity of the problems that ensue is related to the location and size of the thrombus. Severe ischemia is usually the result of thrombi development at the aortic **bifurcation** while thrombi in other areas, well served by collateral flow, may manifest only minor problems.

Vasospastic disease in the extremities, while including such processes as **livedo reticularis** and **acrocyanosis,** is most frequently referred to as **Raynaud's phenomenon.** Vasospastic disorders are characterized by changes in skin color and temperature. This is in contrast to the findings of intermittent claudication and tissue necrosis seen in other arterial disorders. The arterial spasm that occurs appears to be localized to the small arteries and **arterioles.**[12]

Raynaud's phenomenon can be precipitated by exposure to cold or by emotional stress. The phenomenon is manifested by changes in skin color of the digits. The color changes range from **pallor** to **cyanosis** and **rubor.** Pain and numbness tend to occur with the pallor and cyanosis. The condition can occur secondarily with such conditions as **scleroderma, thoracic outlet syndrome,** and occlusive arterial disease.

Diabetes Mellitus

Diabetes mellitus is a major risk factor in peripheral vascular disease. Fifty percent of all nontraumatic amputations are attributed to diabetes.[13] Diabetes presents with both metabolic and vascular components, which are likely strongly interrelated. Metabolically, there is an inappropriate elevation in the blood glucose level, which is associated with a disturbed lipid and protein metabolism. The vascular dysfunction involves an accelerated version of the previously discussed atherosclerotic process.[14] Microangiopathy and neuropathy appear to be major problems associated with this disease. It is not clear however whether the peripheral neuropathies are a result of the atherosclerotic changes in the microcirculation or are directly the result of a metabolic alteration of neuronal tissue.[15] Regardless of the cause, the alteration in cutaneous sensation becomes a major problem as patients tend to develop neurotrophic ulcers due to an inability to perceive pressure on body parts, particularly the feet.

Venous Dysfunction

Chronic venous insufficiency is probably one of the most frequently seen vascular problems in the physical therapy clinic. This is due both to its high incidence— 12 percent of the adult population—and the success of therapy.[16] Venous insufficiency, previously termed venous stasis, is usually manifested by dilated veins, leg pain, edema, and cutaneous changes such as **stasis dermatitis.**[17] Venous insufficiency can be the result of a singular cause such as venous occlusion, a valvular defect, or problems in the calf muscle pump mechanism. It can likewise be due to any combination of these situations. Regardless of the initial cause, the end result is often a high ambulatory pressure in the venous system which leads to capillary dilatation and a subsequent dermal ulceration.[18]

Many patients however may manifest only superficial varicose veins, without an ulceration occurring. In such individuals it is likely that the venous system is able to adequately compensate for the dysfunctional components. The varicosities that occur may be hereditary or acquired. Acquired or secondary varicosities result from proximal obstruction to venous return, as seen with pregnancy or a pelvic mass. The increased pressure placed on the venous system leads to valve failure and the tortuous appearance noted in the more superficial veins.

Acute venous thrombosis, like arterial thrombosis, is not a condition treated by the physical therapist. An understanding of the clinical features of this process will be of importance to the therapist, should they appear during the treatment of some other condition. Acute venous thrombosis results in what has been described as a bursting type of pain, resulting from obstruction to venous outflow.[19] The several types of patients predisposed to development of acute venous thrombosis are dehydrated elderly individuals on bed rest, individuals who apply elastic wraps inappropriately after a musculoskeletal injury, and patients on estrogen therapy.

Lymphatic Dysfunction

Lymphedema is manifested by an excessive accumulation of tissue fluid due to disruption of the lymph channels. Lymphedema can be classified as primary or secondary, depending on whether it is congenital or acquired. Persons with congenital lymphedema have a faulty lymphatic system due to a complete failure of lymph vessels to develop (**agenesis**) or poorly developed vessels (**aplasia**).[20] Secondary lymphedema results from the same situations that lead to secondary varicosities (e.g., pelvic masses or other space occupying lesions).

The Subjective Examination

Examination of the vascular patient should be initiated by taking a complete history. In addition to ascertaining the patient's reasons for seeking medical attention, other baseline information should be obtained. This includes the patient's age, sex, race, height, weight, and occupation.

The patient should be asked to describe, in detail, the problems that led to or coincided with the current problem. It is important to ascertain how the body responds to such factors as cold, heat, position, and minor or severe trauma. Any past history of varicosities, pulmonary emboli, or other systemic conditions affecting limb circulation (diabetes, hypertension, atrial fibrillation, congestive heart failure, or myocardial infarction) should be noted.

Other questions should focus on social habits, especially tobacco use. The type, frequency, and duration of smoking should be noted. Detailed information should be obtained on any previous surgical procedures that may have involved the vascular system (e.g., **sympathectomy, vascular prosthesis, endarterectomy,** amputation).

Next the patient should describe the current problems being experienced. Careful documentation should be made of episodes of intermittent claudication, rest pain, swelling, numbness, and tingling.

Objective Examination

TROPHIC CHANGES AND PIGMENTATION

The patient's skin should be examined, making sure to note any evidence of abnormal pigmentation, dermatitis, ulceration, and effects of position on skin color. Skin color is produced primarily by blood in the superficial **venules.** The skin will take on a chalky white appearance if the arterial flow is absent or decreased. When partial but inadequate arterial flow is present, the skin may be either red or cyanotic, depending on temperature and oxygenation.

Loss of hair over the digits, combined with dry skin and thickened nails, indicates poor vascular nutrition. This situation is one quite likely to lead to tissue breakdown.

Discoloration of the tissues, if present, will frequently be brownish in nature. Brownish pigmentation can be a sign of venous involvement, in which case it is usually caused by **hemosiderin,** a pigment released from lysed red cells. The pigment stains the tissues permanently and thus serves as an indicator of previous venous problems. If varicosities are present, an attempt should be made to determine whether they are primary or secondary in nature.

TEMPERATURE

Gross variations in skin temperature can be noted by palpation. If a discrepancy appears to exist, objective clinical measurements should be made with a **thermistor** or **radiometer.** Thermistors (Fig. 18–3) are essentially electronic thermometers that measure temperature via a probe placed directly on the skin. Radiometers (Fig. 18–4), on the other hand, measure the infrared radiations emitted by the body. While radiometers provide a quick means of scanning the area to assess temperature changes, their higher costs often make them less practical.

PULSES

The quality and presence of pulses should be determined for every patient with vascular disease. While the radial and carotid pulses are most frequently evaluated,

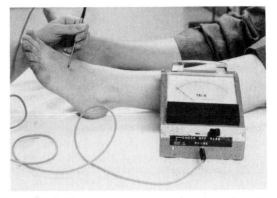

Figure 18–3. Temperature measurement using a thermistor.

the therapist must be able to locate and assess all palpable pulses, including the temporal, external carotid, brachial, radial, ulnar, abdominal, common iliac, femoral, popliteal, dorsalis pedis, and posterior tibial. Pulses can be graded as 2+ = normal, 1+ = diminished, and 0 = absent. Variations in patient size can frequently make palpation of pulses difficult. In these instances, the use of sensitive equipment, such as Doppler ultrasound, may be necessary. The Doppler unit will be discussed later in this chapter.

AUSCULTATION

As was mentioned previously, blood flow is usually laminar in nature. If you were to listen with a stethoscope over an artery while blood is flowing in this direct fashion, you would not be able to detect any signs of blood flow. When the motion becomes turbulent, as occurs in the presence of any situation that narrows the arterial lumen, a swishing sound will be detected. This sound is known as a **bruit** and is very similar to the sound heard through a stethoscope when taking a blood pressure measurement. All large arteries in the neck, abdomen, and limbs should be examined for bruits. If one is noted that has not been brought to the attention of a physician, the physician should be notified. It is also advisable to listen over large scars for possible **arteriovenous fistulas,** which result when blood is improperly shunted between the arterial and venous systems.

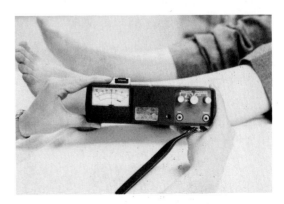

Figure 18–4. Temperature measurement using a radiometer.

BLOOD PRESSURE

Routine blood pressure measurements should be taken prior to the initiation of any therapy. The patient should be placed in either the sitting or supine position and the pressure determined in both upper extremities. A properly fitting cuff should be placed around the upper arm, with the lower edge of the cuff approximately 1 in above the elbow. Cuffs that are too wide will produce readings that are too low, while those that are too large will produce an artificially high reading. To assure a proper fitting cuff on an adult, the therapist should measure the circumference of the limb and then select a cuff that is as wide as one-third to one-half of the limb circumference. The length of the bladder in the cuff should be approximately 80 percent of the limb circumference. In children, the cuff width should be such that it covers approximately two thirds of the upper arm.

The suggested method for recording blood pressure measurements for vascular patients is to use three recording intervals.[21] This helps to avoid confusion since there is often a discrepancy in what individuals record as the diastolic reading. Some examiners record the muffling of the sound, while others record the disappearance. Using all three recording points, as listed below, will help to avoid this confusion.
1. First audible sound (systolic)
2. Muffling of sound (diastolic)
3. Disappearance of sound (diastolic)

EDEMA

There are four main causes of edema:
1. Increased capillary permeability
2. Decreased osmotic pressure of plasma proteins
3. Increased pressure in venules and capillaries
4. Obstruction to lymphatic flow

Edema, if not corrected, can lead to tissue necrosis. It is therefore extremely important that objective measurements be made in order to judge whether extremities are increasing or decreasing in size. Several methods exist for monitoring girth and volume. Girth measurements are usually made with the patient supine. Using a skin pencil, the therapist locates a bony landmark and then makes marks 10 cm above and below this point. The circumference is measured at each marking (Fig. 18-5).

Volumetric measurement is a more accurate, yet more

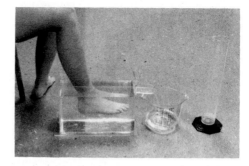

Figure 18-6. Volumetric measurement of the foot.

time consuming, means of assessing limb size. It is particularly valuable when measuring irregular surfaces such as the feet, where use of a tape measure is unreliable. To perform a volumetric measurement, one needs a volumeter. The volumeter (Fig. 18-6) is a specially designed tank with an overflow spout. A graduated cylinder is also required. The patient is positioned so that the extremity to be evaluated can be lowered into the volumeter. The volumeter should have previously been filled to overflowing and allowed to sit until all dripping from the spout has ceased. As the extremity is placed into the container, all displaced water is collected and measured. The amount of water (in milliliters) is recorded. Since the volume water occupies can vary at different temperatures, it is suggested that some attention be paid to assuring that the same temperature water is used with each subsequent measurement. This factor is of greater importance when these measurements are being made in a research setting.

Tests of Peripheral Venous Circulation

Many tests that will be performed on the arterial system require that a normally functioning venous system be present. For this reason, venous tests should be performed prior to the arterial tests.

PERCUSSION TEST

This test is designed to assess the competence of the greater saphenous vein. The test is performed by having the patient stand so that any varicosities present will fill with blood. A segment of the vein below the knee is palpated while simultaneously percussing the vein above the knee. Detecting a fluid wave under the palpating finger indicates that the valves are incompetent and a continuous column of blood is present. If the valves were competent, they would function as baffles that would dampen the fluid wave making it nonpalpable.

TEST FOR DEEP VEIN THROMBOPHLEBITIS

To check for deep vein thrombophlebitis, the therapist should squeeze the gastrocnemius while forcefully dorsiflexing the patient's ankle. In acute thrombophlebitis, this maneuver causes a great deal of pain. This is

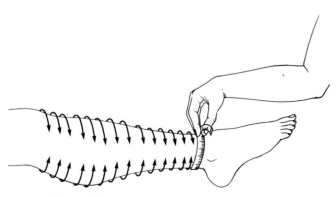

Figure 18-5. Circumferential measurement of girth.

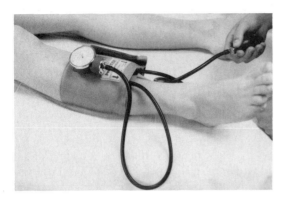

Figure 18–7. Cuff test for assessing acute thrombophlebitis.

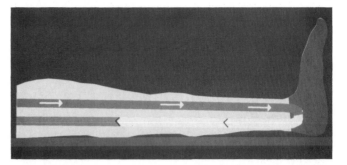

Figure 18–8. Schematic representation of rubor of dependency.

reported as a positive *Homan's sign.* Often patients have a minimally positive Homan's sign. In such situations, the examiner can use a blood pressure cuff to aid in objectifying the test. The cuff is applied around the calf and inflated. Patients in acute distress will not be able to tolerate pressures greater than 40 mmHg. If pathology is not present quite high pressures can be tolerated (Fig. 18–7). It should be emphasized that the cuff should not be inflated any further once any discomfort is reported.

Tests of Peripheral Arterial Circulation

RUBOR OF DEPENDENCY

This test is used to assess the adequacy of arterial circulation by evaluating the skin color changes that occur with elevation and lowering of the extremity. The test is performed by placing the patient supine and noting the color of the soles of the feet. With normal circulation, the soles should be pinkish in appearance. The legs are then elevated to about 45 degrees. This may result in a slight blanching of the extremities. If a quick loss of color occurs resulting in a dead, grayish-white appearance, one can suspect arterial involvement. After returning the legs to a dependent position, individuals with proper arterial circulation will display a quick pink flush in the feet. If the arterial circulation is impaired, the color change may take more than 30 seconds to occur and will be a very bright red (Fig. 18–8). This occurs due to the fact that arterial flow is insufficient and cannot overcome gravity when the legs are elevated. Since venous blood leaves the leg, the next blood into the leg, once it is returned to the examining table, is pure arterial blood. In addition, arterial vasodilation has likely occurred during the ischemic period. As the blood flows into the capillaries, a hyperemia is noted.

VENOUS FILLING TIME

This test measures the time necessary for the superficial veins to refill after emptying. The test is only of use in persons with a normal venous system since any valvular problems could permit retrograde venous flow and not give a good picture of filling via the normal arterial pathway. The patient is placed supine for this test also, and the legs are elevated and milked of venous blood.

After this has been accomplished, the patient hangs the legs over the edge of the table. The time necessary for the veins to refill is noted. A time greater than 10 to 15 seconds indicates arterial insufficiency. The therapist should not be confused by the name of this test. Though it is termed venous filling time, it is a measure of arterial flow through the capillaries into the veins.

CLAUDICATION TIME

Intermittent claudication is a fairly subjective, yet valuable source of information when assessing a patient's response to therapy. One means of objectifying this information is to have the patient walk at 1 mile per hour on a treadmill set at level grade. The period of time walked, before claudication prevents further activity, is recorded. Since the environment is controlled, the same test can be repeated at future times to assess functional improvement.

Other Special Tests

DOPPLER ULTRASOUND

Doppler ultrasound provides a noninvasive means for the therapist to assess arterial flow (Fig. 18–9). Explained simply, the Doppler unit is a transcutaneous detector of blood flow within a vessel. As the name implies, the unit uses the Doppler principle to determine flow. Working in a manner similar to a clinical ultrasound unit, the Doppler unit transmits a 5- to 10-MHz signal into a blood vessel. If blood cells are moving through the vessel, the sound waves are reflected back to the Doppler unit at an altered frequency. This frequency shift is presented to the examiner via an audible

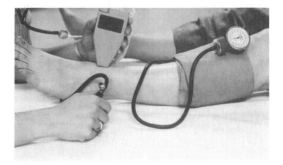

Figure 18–9. Doppler examination of the lower extremity.

signal. Because of its sensitivity, the Doppler unit is useful in locating nonpalpable pulses.

Not only is the Doppler unit useful in detecting pulses, but the device is of great benefit in measuring systolic blood pressure in the extremities. One test that is frequently performed on patients with vascular disease is the ankle/brachial index (ABI). Although one cannot be taught how to perform the test in this text, the following serves as a brief overview of the process. Those wishing a more extensive explanation of the procedure are referred to the chapter on Doppler ultrasound by MacKinnon.[22]

To obtain an ABI, a blood pressure cuff is placed around the leg at the ankle level and inflated until blood flow ceases. As the cuff is released, the examiner listens over the dorsalis pedis or posterior tibial artery. When a signal is detected, the reading in millimeters of mercury (mmHg) is noted. The process is repeated by placing the cuff around the arm at about the midbiceps level and the cuff is again inflated until all flow ceases. As the cuff is slowly deflated, the examiner listens over the radial artery at the wrist. When a signal is detected, the pressure is again noted. To obtain the ABI, the examiner simply divides the lower extremity measurement by the upper extremity measurement.

Because the Doppler method is very sensitive, it can measure a systolic pressure sooner than it can be detected audibly with a stethoscope. The measurements obtained with a Doppler exam are recorded as an index comparing upper and lower extremity measurements. This means therefore that if the systolic pressure obtained in the lower extremity is divided by that obtained in the upper extremity, a value greater than or equal to 1.0 should be noted. This value is termed the *Doppler Index* or *ABI*. Persons with indices of about 0.75 have arterial involvement but may not yet be symptomatic. If the ABI is 0.5 or less, the patient will usually have significant symptomatology.

AIR PLETHYSMOGRAPHY

A relatively new addition in noninvasive vascular technology is the air plethysmograph (APG). The APG utilizes an air-filled bladder to quantitate venous function and provide the examiner with practical information about the peripheral venous system. The APG-1000* is a calibrated pneumatic plethysmograph and chart recorder that objectively measures volume. The unit consists of a polyurethane cuff that fits around the calf and is then connected to a pressure transducer and microprocessor. The cuff is inflated to a pressure of 6 mmHg, termed the bias pressure. This pressure serves to lightly secure the cuff to the calf, ensuring contact and preventing cuff movement during standing tests. Prior to testing, the cuff is calibrated by infusing 100 ml of air from a syringe. Once calibration is complete, several tests can then be performed. The first test examines patency of the venous system. An occlusion cuff is placed around the proximal thigh and inflated to a pressure of 80 mmHg. This pressure occludes venous return yet still permits arterial inflow. As the calf fills with

blood, the chart recorder registers the increasing volume of the extremity. Once a plateau is reached, the occlusion cuff is rapidly deflated and the time necessary for limb volume to return to baseline is noted. Normally, at least 40 percent of the venous volume should leave the extremity in the first second. Anything below this level indicates some type of proximal obstruction in the venous system.

Following occlusion testing, the venous volume is allowed to once again equilibrate. The patient is then assisted to the standing position and a measurement is made to determine how quickly the calf refills with blood. A very rapid refilling is indicative of venous reflux. Normally the calf should not fill any faster than 2 ml/s. The patient next rises onto the toes as a measurement of calf muscle ejection volume is made (Fig. 18–10). Normally more than 60 percent of the calf venous volume is ejected with a single calf muscle contraction. Once the ejection fraction is computed the patient next performs 10 successive toe rises at a rate of about one per second. The amount of venous blood remaining in the system after this maneuver is termed the residual volume and correlates directly with ambulatory venous pressure.

The APG is a simple device to use and shows great promise as a tool to assist in the evaluation of various forms of treatment. For instance, calf ejection fractions can be performed with and without compression stockings to evaluate whether or not the stockings are truly assisting venous return.

ADJUNCTIVE TESTING

Numerous other diagnostic studies, performed by physicians and other health personnel, can provide

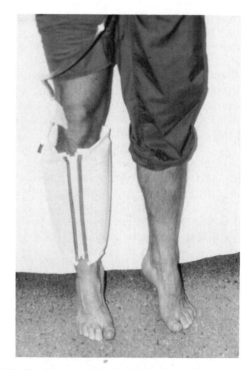

Figure 18–10. Measurement of calf ejection volume by means of air plethysmography.

*ACI Medical, 9249 Glenoaks Blvd., Sun Valley, CA 91352.

information valuable to the therapist in establishing a treatment program. The therapist should become familiar with the results of some of these tests such as venography, arteriography, lymphangiography, strain-gauge plethysmography, and duplex scanning.

TREATMENT

Acute Arterial Disease

The treatment of acute arterial disease usually requires medical and/or surgical intervention. Administration of heparin is usually begun in order to prevent further thrombus formation. Once a patient is stabilized medically, the usual treatment of choice is a thromboembolectomy.

Postoperative care by the physical therapist centers on preventing pressure, monitoring pulse and temperature, and enhancing venous return. The patient should be checked to assure there is no binding clothing to impede blood flow. A turning schedule should be instituted making sure that the surgical site is always visible. The patient should never be positioned in such a way that pressure is applied to the surgical area.

Patients with arterial disease run the risk of recurrence of emboli during recovery. Because of this, pulses and skin temperature should be monitored and recorded. A Doppler unit is useful in detecting poorly palpable pulses, but a blood pressure cuff is not utilized unless the surgeon specifically wishes to obtain a systolic pressure reading. Any significant changes in pulse character or skin temperature should be reported immediately.

Venous insufficiency in the calf can pose problems postoperatively. The physical therapist should use conservative measures such as gentle massage and passive dorsiflexion of the ankles to assist venous return. The lower extremities should not be elevated, however, as the compromised arterial system may be unable to provide proper tissue perfusion against gravity.

Chronic Arterial Disease

The primary goals of treatment for patients with chronic arterial disease are to improve circulation, and to instruct the patient in home management. While the exact mechanism is not clearly understood, there is general agreement in the literature that exercise leads to reduction of claudication.[23-26] The reported studies involved exercise regimens ranging from 8 weeks to 6 months in duration and included both walking and bicycling programs. In 1924, Buerger[27] developed an exercise program aimed at enhancing the formation of collateral circulation. His program consisted of a systematic series of exercises in which the legs were alternately raised and then placed in a dependent position, for varying periods of time. The exercises were performed several times per session and then several times throughout the day. Beurger's exercises have been advocated for years in the treatment of chronic arterial insufficiency, in spite of the fact that they were proved ineffective as far

Table 18–2 GENERAL INSTRUCTIONS FOR PATIENTS WITH PERIPHERAL VASCULAR DISEASE AND PRINCIPLES OF FOOT CARE

1. Feet should be washed each night with a mild soap and warm water.
2. While the feet are still wet, apply a liberal amount of petrolatum jelly and then pat off remaining water.
3. Wear clean socks daily. White socks are preferable as the dyes in some color socks may be irritating.
4. Shoes should be loose fitting and preferably custom fitted.
5. Cut toenails straight across or have your therapist or physician cut them for you.
6. Do not cut corns or calluses—see therapist or physician.
7. Be careful not to impede blood flow in the extremities. Do not wear tight or constricting clothing.
8. Do not put medications or ointments on your feet unless they have been medically prescribed.
9. Do not use tobacco in any form.

back as 1953.[28] This author does not feel they have any clinically significant use.

Home programs for patients can include walking and or bicycling protocols, in addition to a generalized aerobic workout. Such programs can, and should, be very simple in design. The primary purpose of the programs is to increase walking or cycling times and, in so doing, to "stress" the circulatory system. It is the intent of the exercises to make demands on the circulatory system in hopes that collateral sprouting will be encouraged. Patients should be requested to keep a log of their exercise time and distance and to try and improve on each every day. Patients with complicating neurologic involvement, resulting in insensitivity in the feet, should be instructed in techniques of inspection and proper foot care. A set of general instructions for patients with peripheral vascular disease is found in Table 18–2.

Acute Venous Disease

Physical therapists are not frequently involved in the treatment of acute venous disease. Since thrombophlebitis is a potentially fatal disease, patients are usually placed on bed rest and anticoagulant therapy. On occasion, the physical therapist will be requested to provide moist heat to the extremities. As the patient's condition improves, the therapist may play a role in reinstituting exercise and ambulation.

Chronic Venous Disease

The goals of treatment for patients with chronic venous disease are to decrease edema, prevent and/or heal ulcerations, and provide patient education. Physical therapy has a great deal to offer the patient with chronic venous insufficiency. Proper intervention can delay, and often prevent, the need for surgery.

Edema secondary to venous insufficiency can be effectively treated by use of an intermittent compression pump and custom-fitted stockings (Figs. 18–11 and 18–12). The compression pump and stockings serve the purpose of providing an external force to assist in the

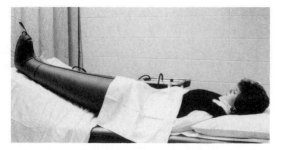

Figure 18–11. Patient receiving treatment with Jobst intermittent compression pump.

removal of edema from tissues. Pumping should always precede the fitting of the patient for custom-fabricated stockings. These stockings are only of value once the edema has been removed. Patients who are fitted prematurely tend to continue to remain edematous and may eventually develop a venous ulceration.

During the stages where the patient is still receiving treatment on the intermittent compression pump and stockings have not been fitted, the girth reductions gained by therapy can be maintained by use of tubular elastic gauze, such as Tubigrip.* Tubular gauze comes in various sizes and can be sized to provide a better fit than can be obtained by many prefabricated support garments. Once girth measurements stabilize, the patient can then be fitted with a custom-made elastic garment such as the Jobst† stocking. To avoid a relapse of edema, stockings should be reordered well in advance of needing replacement.

In any situation where one is considering the use of compression therapy, care should be taken to assure the patient does not have acute thrombophlebitis or arterial insufficiency. In thrombophlebitis there is the risk of causing an embolism, while in arterial insufficiency the concern is further impeding arterial flow in an already compromised area.

Exercise programs are of great benefit to patients with chronic venous disease. However, the patient should be carefully instructed to elevate the extremities after exercise, until the heart rate returns to normal. The increased blood flow caused by exercise could other-

wise lead to an increased volume of venous blood in the dependent extremities.

The more information the patient has about the disease process, the more likely he or she is to follow a treatment protocol. Proper patient education should include information about foot care, as mentioned previously.

Venous insufficiency ulcerations are unfortunately an inevitability in many patients. Should these develop, local wound care and pressure dressings are indicated. Care should be taken to avoid the overzealous use of whirlpool therapy. Venous wounds are usually very moist. Further hydration is seldom necessary. Instead, what is indicated is cleansing. This can be accomplished by use of a basin of tap water or saline. Placing the extremity into a warm whirlpool for twenty minutes, in a dependent position, only invites more swelling. Intermittent compression therapy has a role in ulcer treatment, since it is only after edema is removed that healing will occur.[29] The extremity should be placed in a plastic bag to prevent the compression sleeve from becoming soiled. The Unna boot* (Fig. 18–13) is an excellent device to apply between treatment sessions. The Unna boot consists of a wide mesh cotton gauze that has been impregnated with zinc oxide, calamine, and gelatin. The "boot" is applied in a manner similar to an elastic bandage. Once the bandage sets, it forms a semirigid dressing and since it does not give like an elastic bandage, it does not permit swelling to recur. The zinc oxide and calamine have also been advocated for the treatment of venous ulcerations. At one time, it was felt that topically applied zinc would facilitate wound healing. This is not the case, unless the person is zinc deficient. In such cases, orally administered zinc would be most desirable. The calamine functions as a drying agent.

Wound care becomes a major factor to consider in the treatment of many patients with venous insufficiency. While it is beyond the scope of this chapter to discuss all of the factors that must be considered in wound man-

---

*Miles Pharmaceutical, 1127 Myrtle St., Elkhart, IN.

---

*Seton, Tubiton House, Oldham OL13HS, England.
†Jobst, Toledo, OH.

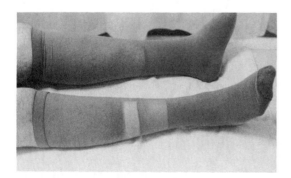

Figure 18–12. Patient wearing custom fitted support stockings.

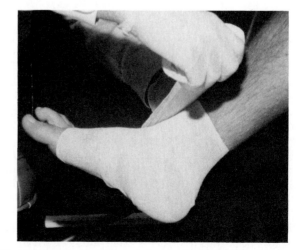

Figure 18–13. Unna's boot being applied to the lower extremity.

agement, several warrant mention. Numerous synthetic dressings are available on the market today. In selecting any dressing, the therapist must be ever mindful of the objectives of treatment and assure that the dressing selected is appropriate for the present state of the wound. In situations where very moist wounds are present, exudate absorbers such as hydrocolloid and alginate dressings might be appropriate. In cases where the wound is very dry, premoistened alginate dressings or hydrogels might prove beneficial. There is little use in this day and age for the traditional wet-to-dry gauze dressing. If cotton gauze dressings are used they would more than likely provide a better wound environment if used wet to wet and not permitted to completely dry. The reader is referred to the text *Wound Healing: Alternatives in Management*[30] for a more thorough discussion of wound management.

Lymphatic Disease

Because the lymphatic system works in synergy with the venous system, the techniques mentioned previously are appropriate in treating edema secondary to lymphatic dysfunction. The goals of therapy are the same: to decrease swelling and provide patient education. The therapist should be aware, however, that lymphedema is due often to carcinoma or other serious pathology. Any treatment technique utilized should be selected with consideration to possible adverse secondary effects.

SUMMARY

This chapter has attempted to provide the student and practicing clinician with an overview of the more commonly encountered peripheral vascular diseases. The means by which they are evaluated and suggested mechanisms of management have also been discussed. The author's main purpose has been to provide the reader with an understanding of the importance of examining the peripheral vascular system of any patient whose symptoms indicate vascular involvement, regardless of the current diagnosis. Many of the vascular problems encountered in practice can be helped by treatment, and more serious problems avoided, if treatment is initiated early.

QUESTIONS FOR REVIEW

1. Compare and contrast the presenting clinical symptoms of patients with the three majors types of peripheral vascular disease.

2. Discuss the relationships that exist between smoking and the development of peripheral vascular disease.

3. When evaluating a patient with arterial insufficiency, which evaluative tests would be unreliable if a concurrent venous insufficiency is present?

4. In the evaluation of a patient with peripheral vascular disease, what signs and symptoms would indicate to a physical therapist the need to refer a patient for further medical evaluation?

5. Explain how diabetes results in the loss of sensation in the feet and what the physical therapist must consider in developing a treatment program for a patient with diabetes.

6. Having evaluated a patient who presents with a classical picture of venous insufficiency, discuss short-term and long-term goals and available therapeutic intervention.

7. Explain how persistent edema prevents the resolution of a venous ulcer.

REFERENCES

1. Palmer, JF: The Works of John Hunter, FRS, vol 3. Longman Group, London, 1835.
2. Stehbens, WE: Hemodynamics and the Blood Vessel Wall. Charles C Thomas, Springfield, IL, 1979, p 17.
3. Basmajian, JV: Grant's Method of Anatomy, ed 10. Williams & Wilkins, Baltimore, 1980, p 29.
4. Sabiston, DC (ed): Davis-Christopher Textbook of Surgery, ed 11. WB Saunders, Philadelphia, 1977, pp 1794–1840.
5. Sumner, DS: Applied physiology of venous problems. In Bergan, JJ and Yao, JST (eds): Surgery of the Veins. Grune and Stratton, Orlando, FL, 1995, pp 3–31.
6. Battezzati, M and Donini, I: The Lymphatic System. John Wiley & Sons, New York, 1972, p 38.
7. deWolfe, VG: Chronic occlusive arterial disease of the lower extremities. In Spittell, JA (ed): Clinical Vascular Disease. FA Davis, Philadelphia, 1983, pp 15–16.
8. Fairbain, JF, Joyce, JW, and Pairolero, PC: Acute arterial occlusion of the extremities. In Juergens, JL, Spittell, JA, and Fairbairn, JF (eds): Peripheral Vascular Disease. WB Saunders, Philadelphia, 1980, pp 381–401.
9. Ross, R: The pathogenesis of atherosclerosis—an update. N Engl J Med 314:488, 1986.
10. Correlli, F: Buerger's disease: cigarette smoker disease may always be cured by medical therapy. J Cardiovasc Surg (Torino) 14:28, 1973.
11. Hollier, LH: Acute arterial occlusion. In Spittell, JA (ed): Clinical Vascular Disease. FA Davis, Philadelphia, 1983, pp 49–58.
12. Spittell, JA: Clinical Vascular Disease. FA Davis, Philadelphia, 1983, pp 75–88.
13. Colwell, JA: Pathophysiology of vascular disease in diabetes: effects of gliclazide. Am J Med 90(Suppl):6a–50s, 1991.
14. Steinke, J and Soeldner, JS: Diabetes mellitus. In Thorn, GW, et al (eds): Harrison's Principles of Internal Medicine. McGraw-Hill, New York, 1977, pp 563–564.
15. Pfeifer, MA and Greene, DA: Diabetic Neuropathy Current Concepts. Upjohn, Kalamazoo, MI, 1985, pp 13–17.
16. Coon, WW, Willis, PW, and Keller, JB: Venous thromboembolism and other venous disease in the Tecumseh community health study. Circulation 48:839, 1973.
17. O'Connell, TF and Shepard, AD: Chronic venous insufficiency. In Jarrett, F and Hirsch, J (eds): Vascular Surgery of the Lower Extremity. CV Mosby, St. Louis, 1985, p 5.
18. Browse, NL: The pathogenesis of venous ulceration: a hypothesis. J Vasc Surg 7:468, 1988.
19. Hume, M: Acute venous thrombosis. In Spittell, JA (ed): Clinical Vascular Disease. FA Davis, Philadelphia, 1983, pp 121–132.

20. Kinmouth, JB, Taylor, GW, and Tracy, GD: Primary lymphoedema: clinical and lymphangiographic studies of a series of 107 patients in which lower limbs were affected. Br J Surg 45:1, 1957.
21. DeGowin, EL and DeGowin, RL: Bedside Diagnostic Examination, ed 5. Macmillan, New York, 1987, p 399.
22. MacKinnon, JL: Doppler ultrasound assessment in peripheral vascular disease. In Kloth, LC, McCulloch, JM, and Feedar, JA (eds): Wound Healing: Alternatives in Management. FA Davis, Philadelphia, 1990, pp 119–132.
23. Ruell, PA, Imperial, ES, Bonar, FJ, Thursby, PF, and Gass, GC: Intermittent claudication: the effect of physical training on walking tolerance and venous lactate concentration. Eur J Appl Physiol 52:420, 1984.
24. Jonason, T, Jonzon, B, Ringqvist, I, and Oman-Rydberg, A: Effect of physical training on different categories of patients with intermittent claudication. Acta Med Scand 206:253, 1979.
25. Sorlie, D and Myhre, K: Effects of physical training in intermittent claudication. Scand J Clin Lab Invest 38:217, 1978.
26. Ekroth, R, Dahllof, A, Gundevall, JH, and Schersten, T: Physical training of patients with intermittent claudication: indications, methods and results. Surgery 84:640, 1978.
27. Buerger, L: The Circulatory Disturbances of the Extremities. WB Saunders, Philadelphia, 1924.
28. Wisham, LH, Abramson, AS, and Ebel, A: Value of exercise in peripheral arterial disease. JAMA 153:10, 1953.
29. McCulloch, JM: Intermittent compression for treatment of a chronic stasis ulceration. Phys Ther 61:1452, 1981.
30. Kloth, LC, McCulloch, JM, and Feedar, JC (eds): Wound Healing: Alternatives in Management. FA Davis, Philadelphia, 1990.

SUPPLEMENTAL READINGS

Ellis, H: Varicose Veins: How They are Treated and What You Can Do to Help. Arco, New York, 1982.
Barker, WF: Peripheral Arterial Disease, ed 2. WB Saunders, Philadelphia, 1975.
Holling, HE: Peripheral Vascular Diseases: Diagnosis and Management. JB Lippincott, Philadelphia, 1972.

Kappert, A and Winsor, T: Diagnosis of Peripheral Vascular Disease. FA Davis, Philadelphia, 1972.
Spittell, JA: Contemporary issues in peripheral vascular disease. Cardiovasc Clin 22:3, 1992.

GLOSSARY

Acrocyanosis: Cyanosis of the extremities due to a vasomotor disturbance. It is seen in catatonia or hysteria.

Agenesis: The failure of an organ or part of an organ to develop or grow.

Anastomotic: Pertaining to the natural communication between two vessels.

Aplasia: The failure of an organ or tissue to develop normally.

Arteriole: The smallest subunit of the arterial system.

Arteriosclerosis: A condition whereby there is hardening of the walls of arteries. This may involve the intima and media.

Arteriovenous fistula: An abnormal connection between the arterial and venous systems.

Atherosclerosis: A form of arteriosclerosis in which yellowish plaques (atheromas) form within the vessel walls. The plaques consist of lipids, and other blood-borne substances.

Bifurcation: A point of branching or forking of a vessel.

Bruit: An adventitious sound, heard in a blood vessel during auscultation, that is caused by the turbulent flow of blood.

Capillary: A small blood vessel that connects arterioles to venules.

Cyanosis: A slightly bluish-gray or purple discoloration of the skin caused by a decreased hemoglobin content in the blood.

Endarterectomy: An excision or removal of the thickened, atheromatous intimal layer of an artery.

Fistula: An abnormal connection between two areas.

Gangrene: Tissue death or necrosis; usually due to impaired or absent blood supply.

Hemosiderin: A pigment released from hemoglobin due to red cell lysis.

Intermittent claudication: A severe pain in the lower extremity that occurs with activity but subsides with rest. It is the result of inadequate arterial blood supply to the exercising muscles.

Ischemia: A restriction in blood supply to a body part; usually local and temporary in nature.

Livedo reticularis: A semipermanent bluish discoloration of the skin that is aggravated by exposure to cold.

Pallor: Paleness or absence of coloration in the skin.

Radiometer: A temperature-measuring device designed to measure infrared radiation.

Raynaud's phenomenon: A process initiated by exposure to cold or emotional disturbance. It results in intermittent episodes of pallor followed by cyanosis, then redness of the digits, before a return to normal.

Rubor: Redness of the skin caused by inflammation.

Scleroderma: A chronic disease of unknown etiology that causes a sclerosis or hardening of the skin and other internal organs.

Stasis dermatitis: An inflammatory condition of the skin caused by pooling of venous blood.

Sympathectomy: A partial excision of the sympathetic portion of the autonomic nervous system.

Thermistor: A temperature-measuring device designed to gauge the contact temperature of the skin.

Thoracic outlet syndrome: A condition caused by compression of the brachial plexus nerve trunks, with or without vascular compromise.

Trophic changes: Observable alterations of the skin and digits due to poor arterial nutrition.

Vascular prosthesis: Any artificial component placed into the vascular system to perform a function previously performed by a unit of the system. An example is an artificial heart valve.

Venule: The smallest subunit of the venous system.

APPENDIX A STANDARD VASCULAR EXAMINATION WORKSHEET

Patient's Name _____ Age _____
Occupation _____ Sex _____

Problem:

History and Subjective Exam
When did the problem begin? _____
How did it begin (onset)? _____
  Was it sudden? Gradual? _____
  Was there an associated injury (mechanism)? _____
  Was it spontaneous (nontraumatic)? _____
  What was first noticed? _____
  Were there predisposing factors? _____
How has the problem progressed since onset? _____
  Is it better or worse? _____
What relevant family history exists? _____
What relevant personal history exists? _____
Has the patient been treated for this problem previously? _____
  If yes, what has the treatment been? _____
  What was the response to treatment? _____
What are the present symptoms? (area, depth, intensity, type) _____
  Are there associated paresthesias? Anesthesias? _____
How do the symptoms behave? _____
  Are they constant? _____
  Do they vary in intensity? _____
  When are they present? _____
  What brings them on? _____
  What makes them increase? _____
  What relieves them? _____
  How long do they last? _____
What is the patient's state of health? _____
Have any diagnostic studies been performed? _____
  If yes, what were the results? _____
Has the patient noticed any color changes in the extremities? _____
How is the condition affected by rest? Activity? _____
What medications is the patient currently taking? _____

Objective Examination
General observations
  Gait _____
  How does the person move? _____
  Overall appearance? _____
  Weight? _____
Range of motion of affected areas: _____
Palpation
  Skin temperature? _____
  Pulses? _____
  Sensory exam? _____
Clinical measurements
  Temperature (oral)? _____
  Blood pressure (supine/sitting)? _____
  Deep tendon reflexes? _____
  Auscultation for bruits? _____
  Test for rubor of dependency? _____
  Venous filling time? _____
  Percussion test? _____
  Cuff test for deep vein thrombophlebitis?
  Claudication time? _____
  Doppler measurements? _____
  Air plethysmography? _____
  Other tests? _____

Assessment
Do the objective findings correlate with the subjective complaints? Is the nature of this problem such that physical therapist should not be treating this patient? Are findings consistent with diagnosis for which the patient was referred?

Plan
What are your short-term and long-term goals for this patient?
What treatment measures do you wish to use to achieve these goals?
What will be the frequency of treatment?
What home program might this patient need?

Assessment and Treatment of Individuals Following Lower Extremity Amputation

Bella J. May

OBJECTIVES

1. Identify major etiologic factors leading to amputation surgery.
2. Describe the major concepts involved in amputation surgery.
3. Describe the major methods of postoperative management.
4. Develop an evaluation plan for a lower extremity amputee.
5. Properly position a lower extremity amputee postoperatively.
6. Describe and demonstrate a method of proper residual limb bandaging.
7. Develop an exercise program for a lower extremity amputee.
8. Be aware of the psychologic impact of lower extremity amputation.

As you enter the physical therapy department this Monday morning, you note several new referrals coming out of the computer printer. You reflect that it is almost a year since you graduated from physical therapy school. The time has gone by so fast and you have learned so much. You are pleased you took this position in a large regional hospital as you have had the opportunity to rotate through various services. You are currently working with general medical and surgical patients including those who have had vascular surgery.

You reach for the printout of new referrals and see one for Ms. Edna Sampson, a 72-year-old woman with diabetes and atherosclerosis. You treated her several months ago for an ulcer on the plantar surface of her right first metatarsal and know she had some problems with diabetic control. Ms. Sampson had a right below-knee amputation Saturday afternoon and is now referred for therapy. You are a little sad. Ms. Sampson is a widow and lives alone although she has three grown children and six grandchildren in town. You remember how she talked about her garden and her other activities and wonder what her prognosis will be for rehabilitation.

The major cause of lower extremity amputation today continues to be **peripheral vascular disease** (PVD), particularly when associated with smoking and diabetes.[1-3] Despite major improvements in noninvasive diagnosis, revascularization, and wound-healing techniques, it has been reported that 2 to 5 percent of individuals with PVD without diabetes, and 6 to 25 percent of those with PVD and diabetes, come to amputation.[4-8] Perioperative mortality has been variously reported as between 7 and 13 percent and is usually associated with other medical problems such as cardiac disease and strokes.[8-10]

The second leading cause of amputation is trauma, usually from motor vehicle accidents or gunshots. Individuals with traumatic amputations are usually young adults and more frequently men.[11-12] Improved imaging techniques, more effective chemotherapy, and better limb salvage procedures have reduced the incidence of amputation from osteogenic sarcoma. Tumor resection followed by limb reconstruction frequently provides as functional an extremity as a prosthesis and does not appear to affect 5-year survival rates, which have increased from about 20 percent in the 1970s to 60 to 70 percent in the 1980s.[13-17] Regardless of the cause of amputation, physical therapists have a major role in the rehabilitation program, and early onset of appropriate treatment influences the eventual level of rehabilitation.

LEVELS OF AMPUTATION

Traditionally, levels of amputation have been identified by anatomical considerations such as above-knee and below-knee. In 1974, the Task Force on Standardization of Prosthetic-Orthotic Terminology developed an international classification system to define amputation levels. Table 19–1 depicts the major terms in common use today.

Traumatic amputations may be performed at any level; the surgeon tries to maintain the greatest bone length and save all possible joints. A variety of surgical techniques may be necessary to create a functional residual limb. Guillotine amputations may precede secondary closure with skin flaps; occasionally, free tissue flaps may be used to cover deformities. Amputations for vascular diseases are generally performed at partial foot, below-knee, or above-knee levels. The lower extremity vascular supply militates against effective residual limb healing at the Syme's level in most instances.

Clients with unilateral below-knee amputations, regardless of age, are quite likely to become functional prosthetic users; many individuals with bilateral below-knee amputations can be successfully rehabilitated. Elderly people with unilateral above-knee amputations have more difficulty becoming prosthetically independent, and most clients with bilateral above-knee amputations do not become functional prosthetic users.[17–22] Generally, hip disarticulation, hemipelvectomies, and hemicorporectomies are performed either for tumors or for severe trauma and represent a small percentage of the amputee population.

> As you prepare to go see Ms. Sampson, you mentally review what you know about amputation surgery and the healing process. You are pleased that her amputation was at a below-knee level but are concerned about the potential for primary healing. You think about the effects of surgery and the factors that will influence healing.

Table 19–1 LEVELS OF AMPUTATION

Partial toe	Excision of any part of one or more toes
Toe disarticulation	Disarticulation at the metatarsal phalangeal joint
Partial foot/ray resection	Resection of the 3rd, 4th, 5th metatarsals and digits
Transmetatarsal	Amputation through the midsection of all metatarsals
Syme's	Ankle disarticulation with attachment of heel pad to distal end of tibia; may include removal of malleoli and distal tibial/fibular flares
Long below-knee (transtibial)	More than 50% of tibial length
Below-knee (transtibial)	Between 20 and 50% of tibial length
Short below-knee (transtibial)	Less than 20% of tibial length
Knee disarticulation	Amputation through the knee joint; femur intact
Long above knee (transfemoral)	More than 60% of femoral length
Above knee (transfemoral)	Between 35 and 60% of femoral length
Short above knee (transfemoral)	Less than 35% of femoral length
Hip disarticulation	Amputation through hip joint; pelvis intact
Hemipelvectomy	Resection of lower half of the pelvis
Hemicorporectomy	Amputation of both lower limbs and pelvis below L-4, L-5 level

Surgical Process

The specific type of amputation surgery is at the discretion of the surgeon and is often determined by the status of the extremity at the time of amputation. The surgeon must remove the part of the limb that must be eliminated, and allow for primary or secondary wound healing, as well as construct a residual limb for optimum prosthetic fitting and function. Numerous factors affect the decision on the level of amputation. Conservation of residual limb length is important as is uncomplicated wound healing. Surgical techniques vary with the level and cause of amputation and a description of each type of surgical procedure is beyond the scope of this book. However, the physical therapist needs to understand some of the basic principles of amputation surgery.

Skin flaps are as broad as possible and the scar should be pliable, painless, and nonadherent. For most above-knee and non-dysvascular below-knee amputations, equal-length anterior and posterior flaps are used, placing the scar at the distal end of the bone (Figs. 19–1 and 19–2) Long posterior flaps are used in **dysvascular** below-knee amputations, as the posterior tissues have a better blood supply than anterior skin. This places the scar anteriorly over the distal end of the tibia; care must be taken to ensure that the scar does not become adherent to the bone (Fig. 19–3A and B). Stabilization of major muscles allows for maximum retention of function. Muscle stabilization may be achieved by myofascial closure, myoplasty, myodesis, or **tenodesis.** In most below-knee and above-knee amputations, a combination of **myoplasty** (muscle-to-muscle closure) and myofascial closure is used to ensure that the muscles are properly stabilized and do not slide over the end of the bone. In some centers, **myodesis** (muscle attached to periosteum or bone) is employed, particularly in below-knee amputations. Whatever the technique, muscle stabilization under some tension is desirable at all levels where muscles must be transected.

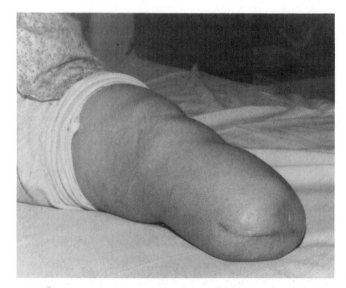

Figure 19–1. Below-knee residual limb with incision from equal length flaps.

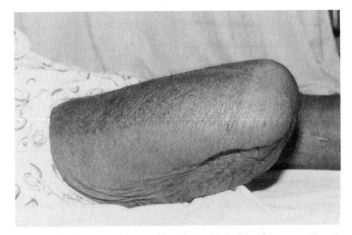

Figure 19–2. Above-knee residual limb with incision from equal length flaps.

Severed peripheral nerves form **neuromas** in the residual limb. The neuroma must be well surrounded by soft tissue so as not to cause pain and interfere with prosthetic wear. Surgeons identify the major nerves, pull them down under some tension, then cut them cleanly and sharply and allow them to retract into the soft tissue of the residual limb. Neuromas that form close to scar tissue or bone generally cause pain and may require later resection or revision.

Hemostasis is achieved by ligating major veins and arteries; **cauterization** is used only for small bleeders. Care is taken not to compromise circulation to distal tissues, particularly the skin flaps, which are important to uncomplicated wound healing.

Bones are sectioned at a length that allows wound closure without excessive redundant tissue at the end of the residual limb, and without placing the incision under great tension. Sharp bone ends are smoothed and rounded; in the below-knee amputations, the anterior portion of the distal tibia is **beveled** to reduce the pressure between the end of the bone and the prosthetic

socket. Care is taken to ensure that the bone is physiologically prepared for the pressures of prosthetic wear. The closure follows the principles of good surgical practice in that tissue layers are approximated under normal physiologic tension. Drainage tubes may be inserted as necessary.

In a traumatic amputation, the surgeon attempts to save as much bone length and viable skin as possible, and to preserve proximal joints while providing for appropriate healing of tissues without secondary complications such as infection. In potentially "dirty" amputations, the incision may be left open with the proximal joint immobilized in a functional position for 5 to 9 days to prevent invasive infection. Secondary closure also allows the surgeon to shape the residual limb appropriately for prosthetic rehabilitation.

Amputation for vascular disease is generally considered an elective procedure; the surgeon determines the level of amputation by evaluating tissue viability through a variety of measures. Segmental limb blood pressures can be determined by Doppler systolic blood pressure measurement, transcutaneous oxygen measurement, determination of skin blood flow by radioisotope techniques, or by plethysmography. Doppler systolic blood pressure measures have been reported to be quite accurate in predicting viable level of amputation but have not been as accurate in predicting amputations that do not heal.[20,21,23] Improvements in noninvasive assessment techniques have greatly reduced the use of arteriography to determine amputation level.

Healing Process

The surgeon's goal is to amputate at the lowest possible level compatible with healing. There are a number of factors that may affect healing. Postoperative infection, whether from external or internal sources is a major concern. Individuals with contaminated wounds, from injury, infected foot ulcers, or other causes are at

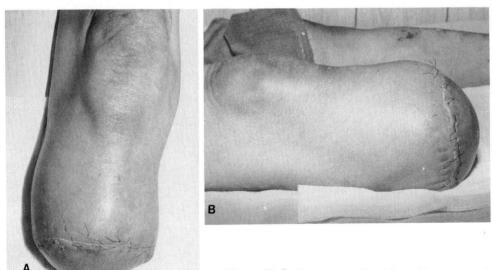

Figure 19–3. Below-knee residual limb with anterior incision from a long posterior flap.

greater risk. Research indicates that smoking is a major deterrent to wound healing, with one study reporting that cigarette smokers had a 2:5 higher rate of infection and reamputation than nonsmokers.[24] There is some indication that failed attempts at limb revascularization may negatively influence healing at below-knee levels[5,25–28] Other factors influencing wound healing are the severity of the vascular problems, diabetes, renal disease, and other physiologic problems such as cardiac disease.[5,25–28]

REHABILITATION GOALS

What will be the most appropriate goals for Ms. Sampson at this time, you ask yourself. You wish you had seen her just before the amputation so you could have begun preparing her for the rehabilitation program. You know you will have only a few days before she is discharged home and you need to develop a functional goal as soon as possible. You also wonder if a home health referral will be possible after she leaves the hospital.

The earlier the onset of rehabilitation, the greater the potential for success. The longer the delay, the more likely the development of complications such as joint contractures, general debilitation, and a depressed psychologic state. The postoperative program can be arbitrarily divided into two phases, the preprosthetic phase, which is the time between surgery and fitting with a definitive prosthesis, or until a decision is made not to fit the client; and the prosthetic phase, which starts with delivery of a permanent replacement limb. The long-term goal of the total rehabilitation program is to help the client regain the presurgical level of function. For some, it will mean return to gainful employment with an active recreational life. For others, it will mean independence in the home and community. For still others, it may mean living in the sheltered environment of a retirement center or nursing home. If the amputation resulted from long-standing chronic disease, the goal may be to help the person function at a higher level than immediately before surgery. The major goals of the preprosthetic period are to

1. Promote as high a level of independent function as possible prior to prosthetic fitting.
2. Guide the development of the necessary physical and emotional level for eventual prosthetic rehabilitation.

If the cause of amputation was peripheral vascular disease, a third general goal would be to teach the individual proper care of the remaining lower extremity and an understanding of the disease process.

The major goals of the preprosthetic program generally are to

1. Reduce (prevent) postoperative edema and promote healing of the residual limb.
2. Prevent contractures and other complications.
3. Maintain or regain strength in the affected lower extremity.
4. Maintain or increase strength in the remaining extremities.

5. Assist with adjustment to the loss of a body part.
6. Regain independence in mobility and self-care.
7. Learn proper care of the other extremity.

Specific short-term goals for Ms. Sampson might include

1. Achieve independence in bed mobility and basic transfers.
2. Achieve supervised or independent mobility with crutches or walker.
3. Demonstrate a knowledge of proper residual limb positioning, bandaging, and care.
4. Demonstrate a knowledge of basic residual limb exercises.

The success of the rehabilitation program is determined to some extent by the individual's psychologic-physiologic status and the physical characteristics of the residual limb. The longer the residual limb, the better the potential for successful prosthetic ambulation, regardless of the level of amputation. A well-healed, cylindrical limb with a nonadherent scar is easier to fit than one that is conical or has redundant tissue distally or laterally. The vascular status of the remaining extremity will affect the rehabilitation program as will the physiologic age of the individual. The presence of conditions such as diabetes, cardiovascular disease, visual impairment, limitation of joint motion, and muscle weakness may affect the eventual level of function. In the final analysis, a cooperative client who takes an active part in the rehabilitation program is necessary for achievement of rehabilitation goals. If the client is noncompliant, it behooves the therapist to try to understand what is driving the client's motivation and to make sure the client understands the relationship between the preprosthetic program and eventual prosthetic rehabilitation.

THE CLINIC TEAM

The majority of amputations today are performed by vascular surgeons who may or may not be knowledgeable about prosthetic rehabilitation. Referral to an amputee clinic or to physical therapy may be delayed for many weeks as the surgeon waits until the residual limb heals completely and the postoperative edema has been absorbed. Such delays are undesirable and may limit the eventual level of rehabilitation. Ideally, the clinic team should become involved before surgery, or at least immediately after. Unfortunately, many amputations are performed in hospitals without the services of an amputee clinic or a well-trained team that can develop and supervise the program. The physical therapist may be the only person with competence in prosthetic rehabilitation. Close contact with the vascular surgeons in one's facility may serve to increase the likelihood of early referrals.

Members

The amputee clinic team plans and implements comprehensive rehabilitation programs designed to meet the physical, psychologic, and economic needs of the

Table 19–2 AMPUTEE CLINIC TEAM FUNCTIONS

Physician	Clinic chief; coordinates team decision making; supervises client's general medical condition; orders appliances.
Physical therapist	Evaluates and treats clients through preprosthetic and prosthetic phases; makes recommendations for prosthetic components and whether or not to fit the client. May be clinic coordinator.
Prosthetist	Fabricates and modifies prosthesis; recommends prosthetic components; shares data on new prosthetic developments.
Occupational therapist	Assesses and treats patients with upper extremity amputations; makes recommendation for components.
Social worker	Financial counselor and coordinator; liaison with third party payers and community agencies; helps family cope with social and financial problems.
Dietician	Consultant for diabetic clients or those needing dietary guidance.
Vocational counselor	Assesses client's employment potential; helps with education, training, and placement.

patient with an amputation. Most amputee clinic teams are located in rehabilitation facilities or university health centers. The team generally includes a physician, physical therapist, occupational therapist, prosthetist, social worker, and vocational counselor. Other health professionals who often contribute to the team are the nurse, dietitian, psychologist, and, possibly, administrative coordinator. Table 19–2 outlines the major functions of team members. Clinic frequency is dictated by the caseload; clients are seen regularly and decisions are made using input from all team members. A screening clinic held by the physical and occupational therapists prior to the actual amputee clinic allows for the careful evaluation of each person to be seen and improves the effectiveness of the clinic function.[29] In centers without an amputee clinic, close communication between the client, surgeon, and physical therapists, with the later addition of the prosthetist, is important to ensure an optimum level of decision making.

POSTOPERATIVE DRESSINGS

Reading the chart before going to see Ms. Sampson, you note that the surgeon did not use a rigid postoperative dressing but rather applied a soft dressing covered with an elastic wrap. This information raises your concerns about edema control. Scanning the chart, you note that the surgery went well, that Ms. Sampson is afebrile, that vital signs are within normal limits, that she is not spilling sugar and that she is voiding appropriately. The incision is reported to look clean and the drain is to be removed tomorrow morning. The nursing staff had her out of bed yesterday twice. You also check Ms. Sampson's medications, finding that she is on medication for diabetes, hypertension, and pain as needed. She had pain medication about an hour ago.

Surgeons have several options regarding the postoperative dressing including (1) immediate postoperative fitting or rigid dressing, (2) semirigid dressing, (3) controlled environment, or (4) soft dressing. It is important

for some sort of edema control to be used, as excessive edema in the residual limb can compromise healing and cause pain.

Rigid Dressings

In the early 1960s, orthopedic surgeons in the United States started experimenting with a technique developed in Europe that consisted of fitting the residual limb with a plaster of Paris socket in the configuration of the definitive prosthesis. An attachment incorporated at the distal end of the dressing allows the later addition of a prosthetic foot and pylon to allow limited weight-bearing ambulation within a few days or a week of surgery.[30-32] Use of immediate postoperative rigid dressings varies greatly and they are more prevalent in some areas of the country than others. Generally, orthopedic surgeons use the technique more than vascular surgeons. The advantages of the technique are

1. It greatly limits the development of postoperative edema in the residual limb, thereby reducing postoperative pain and enhancing wound healing.
2. It allows for earlier ambulation with the attachment of a pylon and foot.
3. It allows for earlier fitting of the definitive prosthesis by reducing the length of time needed for shrinking the residual limb.
4. It is configured to each individual residual limb.

The major disadvantages are

1. It requires careful application by individuals knowledgeable about prosthetic principles.
2. It requires close supervision during the healing stage.
3. It does not allow for daily wound inspection and dressing changes.

Semirigid Dressings

There are a number of semirigid dressings that have been reported in the literature, and which may or may not be used in a particular center. All provide better control of edema than the soft dressing but each has some disadvantage that limits its use. The **Unna paste dressing,** a compound of zinc oxide, gelatin, glycerin, and calamine, may be applied in the operating room. Its major disadvantage is that it may loosen easily and is not as rigid as the plaster of Paris dressing. Little[33,34] first reported the use of an air splint to control postoperative edema as well as to aid in early ambulation (Fig. 19–4). The air splint is a plastic double-wall bag that is pumped to the desired level of rigidity. It has a zipper and encases the entire extremity, which is covered with an appropriate postsurgical dressing. While an air splint allows visual wound inspection, the constant pressure does not intimately conform to the shape of the residual limb. The environment of the plastic is hot and humid, requiring frequent cleaning. The Controlled Environment Treatment (CET) was developed at the National Biomechanical Research and Development Unit of Roehampton, England and has been used in some centers in

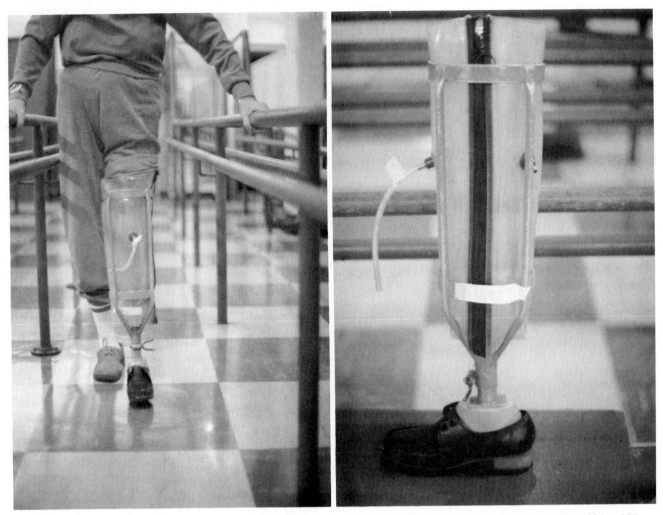

Figure 19–4. Air splint. (From Sanders, GT: Lower Limb Amputations: A Guide to Rehabilitation. FA Davis, Philadelphia, 1986, p 363, with permission.)

the United States.[35,36] The CET is composed of a console that controls pressure, temperature, and humidity, and sterilizes the air in the unit; and a polyvinyl transparent bag that encases the residual limb. The bag's flexibility allows active exercises of the involved extremity as well as standing at bedside, but the hose and machine limit bed mobility and ambulation.

Soft Dressings

The soft dressing is the oldest method of postsurgical management of the residual limb. Currently there are two forms of soft dressings: the elastic wrap and the elastic **shrinker.** The major advantages are that they are

1. Relatively inexpensive.
2. Lightweight and readily available.
3. Easily laundered.

The major disadvantages are that

1. There is relatively poor control of edema.
2. The elastic wrap requires skill in proper application.
3. The elastic wrap needs frequent reapplication.
4. Either the wrap or the shrinker can slip and form a tourniquet.

5. New shrinkers must be purchased as the residual limb gets markedly smaller.

ELASTIC WRAP

The elastic wrap may be applied over the postsurgical dressing if care is taken to ensure proper compression. A dressing is applied to the incision, followed by some form of gauze pad, then the compression wrap. The soft dressing is indicated in cases of local infection but is not the treatment of choice for the majority of individuals. The person or a family member should learn to apply the wrap as soon as possible after wound care is no longer necessary. Many elderly patients with above-knee amputations do not have the necessary balance and coordination to wrap effectively.

Some surgeons prefer delaying elastic wrap until the incision has healed and the sutures have been removed. Leaving the residual limb without any pressure wrap allows full development of postoperative edema, which may be quite uncomfortable and which may interfere with the circulation in the many small vessels in the skin and soft tissue, thereby potentially compromising healing. The therapist can discuss the benefits of early wrapping if no other form of rigid dressing is used.

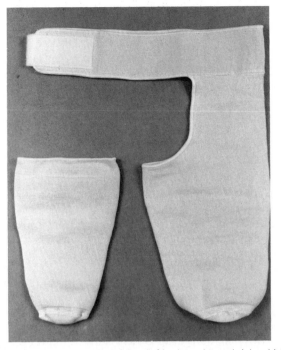

Figure 19–5. Below-knee shrinker (left), above-knee shrinker (right).

One of the major drawbacks of the elastic wrap is that it needs frequent rewrapping. Movement of the residual limb against the bedclothes, bending and extending the proximal joints, and general body movements will cause slippage and changes in pressure. Covering the finished wrap with a stockinet helps reduce some of the wrinkling. However, careful and frequent rewrapping is the only effective way to prevent complications. Nursing staff, family members, and the client, as well as the therapy staff, need to assume responsibility for frequent inspection and rewrapping of the residual limb. Residual limb wrapping is described in detail later in this chapter.

SHRINKERS

Shrinkers are socklike garments knitted of heavy rubber-reinforced cotton; they are conical in shape and come in a variety of sizes (Fig. 19–5) Shrinkers come in different sizes so it is not economical to purchase a shrinker while the residual limb is still covered with gauze dressings. Elastic wrap and shrinkers will be discussed in greater detail later in this chapter.

ASSESSMENT

As you enter Ms. Sampson's room you find her lying in bed, alert and awake. An incentive spirometer is on the bedside table. Ms. Sampson looks tired and you realize you will not be able to gather all the information you need during this one visit. You think through the data that must be collected and begin to set priorities, deciding what needs to be done today and what can be put off for another time. Since Ms. Sampson will probably not be in the hospital long, information regarding the status of the residual limb, her postsurgical cardiopulmonary and gen-

eral physiologic function, her ability to be mobile, the condition of the remaining lower extremity, and her feelings about the amputation may be the most important data to obtain.

Careful assessment of each individual is an integral part of the management following an amputation. Assessment data are obtained continuously throughout this period, as the incision heals and the person's tolerance improves. Table 19–3 outlines the typical data needed during a preprosthetic assessment. The availability of some of this data will depend in part on the treatment of the residual limb by the surgeon.

Range of Motion

Gross range of motion estimations are adequate for assessment of the uninvolved extremity but specific goniometric measurements are necessary for the amputated side. Hip flexion and extension, and abduction and adduction measurements are taken early in the postoperative phase after below-knee amputation. Measurement of knee flexion and extension are taken, if the dressing allows, after some incisional healing has occurred. Hip flexion and extension, and abduction and adduction range of motion measurements are taken several days after surgery, when the dressing allows, following above-knee amputation. Measurement of internal and external hip rotation is difficult to obtain and unnecessary if no gross abnormality or pathology is evident. Joint range of motion is monitored throughout the preprosthetic period.

Muscle Strength

Gross manual muscle testing of the upper extremities and uninvolved lower extremity is performed early in the postoperative period. Manual muscle testing of the involved lower extremity must usually wait until most healing has occurred. With a below-knee amputation, good strength in the hip extensors and abductors, as well as the knee extensors and flexors, is needed for satisfactory prosthetic ambulation. The client with an above-knee amputation uses the hip extensors and abductors to a great extent. The strength of these muscles should be monitored throughout the preprosthetic program.

Residual Limb

Circumferential measurements of the residual limb are taken as soon as the dressing will allow, then regularly throughout the preprosthetic period. Measurements are made at regular intervals over the length of the residual limb. Circumferential measurements of the below-knee or Syme residual limb are started at the medial tibial plateau and taken every 5 to 8 cm (1.97 to 3.15 inches), depending on the length of the limb. Length is measured from the medial tibial plateau to the end of the bone.

Circumferential measurements of the above-knee or

Table 19–3 PREPROSTHETIC ASSESSMENT GUIDE

General medical information	1. Cause of amputation (e.g., disease, tumor, trauma, congenital)
	2. Associated diseases/symptoms (e.g., neuropathy, visual disturbances, cardiopulmonary disease, renal failure, congenital anomalies)
	3. Current physiologic state (e.g., postsurgical cardiopulmonary status, vital signs, duration of time out of bed, pain)
	4. Medications
Skin	1. Scar (e.g., healed, adherent, invaginated, flat)
	2. Other lesions (e.g., size, shape, open, scar tissue)
	3. Moisture (e.g., moist, dry, scaly)
	4. Sensation (e.g., absent, diminished, hyperesthesia)
	5. Grafts (e.g., location, type, healing)
	6. Dermatologic lesions (e.g., psoriasis, eczema, cysts)
Residual limb length	1. Bone length (below-knee, limbs measured from medial tibial plateau; above-knee, limbs measured from ischial tuberosity or greater trochanter)
	2. Soft tissue length (note redundant tissue)
Residual limb shape	1. Cylindrical, conical, bulbous end, etc.
	2. Abnormalities (e.g., "dog ears", adductor roll)
Vascularity (both limbs if amputation cause is vascular)	1. Pulses (e.g., femoral, popliteal, dorsalis, pedis, posterior tibial)
	2. Color (e.g., red, cyanotic)
	3. Temperature
	4. Edema (circumference measurement, water displacement measurement, caliper measures)
	5. Pain (type, location, duration)
	6. Trophic changes
Range of motion (ROM)	1. Residual limb (specific for remaining joints)
	2. Other lower extremity (gross for major joints)
Muscle strength	1. Residual limb (specific for major muscle groups)
	2. Other extremities (gross for necessary function)
Neurologic	1. Pain (phantom—differentiate sensation or pain, neuroma, incisional, from other causes)
	2. Neuropathy
	3. Cognitive status (e.g., alert, oriented, confused)
	4. Emotional status (e.g., acceptance, body image)
Functional status	1. Transfers (e.g., bed to chair, to toilet, to car)
	2. Mobility (e.g., ancillary support, supervision)
	3. Home/family situation (e.g., caregiver, architectural barriers, hazards)
	4. Activities of daily living (e.g., bathing, dressing)
	5. Instrumental activities of daily living (e.g., cooking, cleaning)
Other	1. Preamputation status (e.g., work, activity level, degree of independence, life-style)
	2. Prosthetic goals (e.g., desire for prosthesis, anticipated activity level and life-style)
	3. Financial (e.g., available payment for prosthesis)
	4. Prior prosthesis (if bilateral)

through-knee residual limb are started at the ischial tuberosity or the greater trochanter, whichever is most palpable, and taken every 8 to 10 cm (3.15 to 3.94 inches). Length is measured from the ischial tuberosity or the greater trochanter to the end of the bone. If there is considerable excess tissue distal to the end of the bone, then length measurements are taken to both the end of the bone and the incision line. For accuracy of repeat measurements, exact landmarks are carefully noted. If the ischial tuberosity is used in above-knee measurements, hip joint position is noted as well. Other information gathered about the residual limb includes its shape (conical, bulbous, redundant tissue), skin condition, and joint proprioception.

The Phantom Limb

The majority of individuals will encounter a **phantom limb** following an amputation. In its simplest form, the phantom is the sensation of the limb that is no longer there. The phantom, which usually occurs initially immediately after surgery, is often described as a tingling, pressure sensation, sometimes a numbness. The distal part of the extremity is most frequently felt although, on occasion, the person will feel the whole extremity. The sensation is responsive to external stimuli such as bandaging or rigid dressing; it may dissipate over time or the person may have the sensation throughout life. Phantom sensation may be painless and usually does not interfere with prosthetic rehabilitation. It is important for the client to understand that the feeling is quite normal.

Phantom pain, on the other hand, is usually characterized as either a cramping or squeezing sensation, a shooting or a burning pain. Some clients report all three. The pain may be localized or diffuse; it may be continuous or intermittent, and triggered by some external stimuli. It may diminish over time or may become a permanent and often disabling condition. In the first 6 months following surgery, phantom pain has been found to be related to preoperative limb pain in location and intensity. However, that relationship does not last, and preoperative pain is not believed to be related to long-term phantom pain.[37] There is little agreement about the cause or treatment of either phantom sensation or pain and the literature is replete with studies of the phenomena.[38-42] Melzack[43] suggested that at least 70 percent of patients with amputation suffer with phantom pain. He indicated that clients view the phantom as part of themselves regardless of where it is felt in relation to the body. Melzack suggests that phantom sensation and pain originate in the cerebrum.

> I postulate that the brain contains a neuromatrix, or network of neurons, that, in addition to responding to sensory stimulation, continuously generates a characteristic pattern of impulses indicating that the body is intact and unequivocally one's own. [p 123]

He refutes the general belief that phantom sensation and pain occur only with acquired amputations after the age of 5 or 6, indicating that all individuals who are missing a limb from whatever cause, as well as individuals who lose the use of their limbs through spinal cord injury, feel the missing limbs. Melzack believes that the brain not only responds to stimuli but can generate perceptual experiences without external stimuli. "We do not need a body to feel a body" (p 126). While management of phantom pain continues to be problematic, Melzack states:

> ... phantom limbs are a mystery only if we assume the body sends sensory messages to a passively receiving brain. Phantoms become comprehensible once we recognize that the brain generates the experience of the body. Sensory inputs merely modulate that experience; they do not directly cause it. [p 126]

The residual limb should be carefully examined to differentiate phantom pain from any other condition such as a neuroma. Sometimes, wearing a prosthesis will ease the phantom pain. Noninvasive treatments such as ultrasound, icing, transcutaneous electrical nerve stimulation (TENS), or hand massage have been used with varying success. Mild nonnarcotic analgesics have been of limited value with some individuals and no particular narcotic analgesic has proven effective. On occasion, in the presence of trigger points, injection with steroids or local anesthetic has reduced the pain temporarily. A variety of surgical procedures such as chordotomies, *rhizotomies,* and peripheral *neurectomies* have been tried with limited success. In some instances, hypnosis has been useful in carefully selected clients. The treatment of phantom pain can be very frustrating for the clinic team and the client.[38-43]

Other Data

The vascular status of the uninvolved lower extremity is determined and its condition noted. Data gathered includes condition of the skin, presence of pulses, sensation, temperature, edema, pain on exercise or at rest, presence of wounds, ulceration, or other abnormalities.

Activities of daily living including transfer and ambulatory status are evaluated and documented. Information on the client's home situation, including any constraints or special needs, are valuable in establishing an individually relevant treatment program. Data regarding presurgical activity level and the person's own long-range goals are obtained through interview.

The person's apparent emotional status and degree of adjustment are noted. Exploration of the client's suitability and desire for a prosthesis is begun and continues throughout the preprosthetic period. Any other problems that may affect the rehabilitation program and goals are assessed and documented.

EMOTIONAL ADJUSTMENT

As you perform the initial assessment of Ms. Sampson and talk with her about the amputation, you realize that she is quite depressed. While losing the limb did not come as a shock since she had been struggling with a foot ulcer that would not heal, she verbalizes concern about her ability to return to her own home. She keeps saying "I don't want to go to one of those places."

Initial reaction to the loss of a limb is usually grief and depression. If the amputation was traumatic, the immediate reaction may include disbelief. The person may experience insomnia, restlessness, and have difficulty concentrating. Some individuals may actually mourn the possible loss of a job or the ability to participate in a favorite sport or other activities rather than the lost limb per se. In the early stages, the individual's grief may alternate with feelings of hopelessness, despondency, bitterness, and anger. Socially the client may feel lonely, isolated, and the object of pity. Concerns about the future, about body image and function, about the responses of family and friends, and about employment all affect the individual's reactions.

Long-term adjustment depends to a great extent on the individual's basic personality structure, sense of accomplishment, and place in the family, community, and world. In general, many patients with amputation make a satisfactory adjustment to the loss and are reintegrated into a full and active life. In achieving final acceptance, the individual may go through a number of stages including denial, anger, euphoria, and social withdrawal.

Some individuals may try to avoid distressing thoughts of the lost limb through conscious self-control or by avoiding situations or people that remind them of the lost limb. Some may display temper tantrums or irrational resentment. Some may revert to childlike states of helplessness and dependence.

Many individuals are not fully aware of the consequences of amputation and may fear other physical limitations as a result of the surgery. Fear of impotence or sterility may lead some men to make grandiose statements or display reckless behavior to mask the fear. Thorough explanations of the amputation process and its implications by the surgeon or other health worker may alleviate many of these fears.

Generally people who have had an amputation may dream of themselves as not being amputated. This image may be so vivid that they fall as they get up at night and attempt to walk to the bathroom without a prosthesis or crutches. Individuals who have lost their leg through injury may dream about the battle or accident in which they were injured. Such reenacts may lead to insomnia, trembling fits, speech impediments, and difficulty with concentration. In general, individuals with congenital amputations or amputations acquired before the age of 5 do not have some of the problems mentioned above, since their amputation is a part of their developed self-image.

Psychologic Support

The client needs to receive reassurance and understanding from the entire rehabilitation team. The staff should create an open and receptive environment and be willing to listen. The patient should know what to expect during the entire process. The steps of rehabilitation and the expectations should be carefully explained by the surgeon and therapists. Audiovisual media, such as films or slides, may be helpful in orienting the patient.

Others with amputations who have made satisfactory adjustments in their lives and have successfully completed rehabilitation may provide support and encouragement to the new client in private or group sessions. Professionals skilled in group dynamics should be present, especially for medical or technical advice regarding such issues as diabetes, medications, or peripheral vascular disease. Family and friends are often invited to attend. The atmosphere should be nonthreatening so clients can express their feelings and frustrations.

Clients have various attitudes toward the prosthesis. Some are particularly concerned about its appearance, hoping that it will conceal their disability and give the illusion of an intact body. Others claim to be concerned primarily with the restoration of function. When the artificial limb is fitted, the client must face the fact that the natural limb has been lost irrevocably. If individuals with amputations have been told that the prosthesis will replace their own limb then they may have unrealistic expectations that the appearance and function will be as good as in the nonamputated extremity. Realistic adjustment will be necessary as the person learns to use the artificial substitute. Good predictors for adjustment to the prosthesis are motivation to master the prosthesis and return to an active life-style.

The Elderly

The elderly individual with a lower extremity amputation is usually not content to sit in a wheelchair or limp with a walker, but seeks effective rehabilitation services and a meaningful life-style. The immediate reaction to amputation is no different than that of any other individual except that the amputation will usually not come as a surprise. The reaction may depend in part on the severity of preoperative pain and the extent of attempts to save the limb. Individuals who have suffered considerable pain may be grateful that the pain has ended. Clients who underwent extensive medical and surgical procedures to save the limb may have a sense of failure that the efforts were not successful. In general, the reactions of an elderly person will be similar to that of any other adult individual with an amputation. Some may feel a sense of hopelessness or despair, and have a preoccupation with impending death. Some may experience insomnia, anorexia, or withdrawal. Some elderly individuals may experience a loss of self-esteem and be afraid of becoming dependent. In some instances, the person may express that they have nothing to live for and desire death. Occasionally suicide may be attempted. The elderly person seldom uses denial since the functional and anatomical deficit is obvious. Elderly individuals are more likely to dream that the amputation has taken place than younger individuals. The elderly person may view the amputation as presaging death because the rest of the body is vulnerable.

If preoperative attitudes are unrealistically hopeful then postoperative disturbances may be more severe. The elderly person should not be led to expect a total cure. Learning to use an artificial limb may be slow and difficult, but the client may not express discouragement in front of the optimism of others. Sharing and support from other elderly individuals can be quite helpful, as can a realistic attitude by rehabilitation team members.

Complete rehabilitation includes not only preparation of the individual physically and psychologically for the community, but preparation of the community for the patient. Public education media can be used to inform people of the potentials of individuals with amputation in society and employment. As with other physically challenged individuals, those with amputations need to be accepted and integrated into the community because of their abilities and not their disabilities.

TREATMENT PROGRAM

If Ms. Sampson is to return to her own home, she will need to be ambulatory and be able to take care of her residual limb. If she goes to her own home rather than a rehabilitation center, she will need some homemaking help as well as home health care for continued nursing and physical therapy. On the other hand, transfer to a rehabilitation center might help her reach a level of independence adequate to be able to function at home with minimal support until she can be fitted with a prosthesis. You decide to discuss this further with the physician and social worker. In the meantime, you realize that your treatment program will need to focus on functional mobility, residual limb care, and the care of the other leg.

Residual Limb Care

Individuals not fitted with a rigid dressing or a temporary prosthesis use elastic wrap or shrinkers to reduce the size of the residual limb. The client or a member of the family applies the bandage, which is worn 24 hours a day, except when bathing.

Removable rigid dressing for use with below-knee amputations are available and may be an important alternative to the elastic wrap. Regretfully, there are fewer alternatives for the above-knee amputation; rigid dressings and inexpensive temporary prostheses are more difficult to fabricate, and elastic wraps or shrinkers are only minimally effective. It may be advisable to fit the above-knee amputation with a definitive prosthesis early, then adjust for shrinkage by using additional socks or a liner.

Edema in the residual limb is often difficult to control owing to complications of diabetes, cardiovascular disease, or hypertension. Therapeutically, an intermittent compression unit can be used to reduce edema on a temporary basis. Above-knee and below-knee sleeves are commercially available.

Proper hygiene and skin care are important. Once the incision is healed and the sutures removed, the person can bathe normally. The residual limb is treated as any other part of the body; it is kept clean and dry. Individuals with dry skin may use a good skin lotion. Care must be taken to avoid abrasions, cuts, and other skin problems. Friction massage, in which layers of skin, subcutaneous tissue, and muscle are moved over the respective underlying tissue, can be used to prevent or mobilize adherent scar tissue. The massage is done gently, after the wound is healed and no infection is present. Clients can learn to properly perform a gentle friction massage to mobilize the scar tissue and help decrease hypersensitivity of the residual limb to touch and pressure. Early handling of the residual limb by the client is an aid to acceptance and is encouraged, particularly for individuals who may be repulsed by the limb.

The client is taught to inspect the residual limb with a mirror each night to make sure there are no sores or impending problems, especially in areas not readily visible. If the person has diminished sensation, careful inspection is particularly important. Since the residual limb tends to become a bit edematous after bathing, as a reaction to the warm water, nightly bathing is recommended, particularly once a prosthesis has been fitted. The elastic bandage, shrinker, or removable rigid dressing is reapplied after bathing. If the person has been fitted with a temporary prosthesis, the residual limb is wrapped at night and any time the prosthesis is not worn. Sometimes, individuals fitted in surgery with a rigid dressing then transferred immediately into a temporary prosthesis do not know how to bandage, and encounter difficulties with edema after they remove the prosthesis at night. Learning proper bandaging is part of the therapy program for all individuals with amputation since most people need to wrap the limb at one time or another.

Clients have been known to apply a variety of "home and folk remedies" to the residual limb. Historically, it was believed that the skin had to be toughened for prosthetic wear by beating it with a towel-wrapped bottle. Various ointments and lotions have been applied, residual limbs have been immersed in substances such as vinegar, salt water, and gasoline to harden the skin. While the skin does need to adjust to the pressures of wearing an artificial limb, there is no evidence to indicate that "toughening" techniques are beneficial. Such methods may actually be deleterious, as research indicates that soft, pliable skin is better able to cope with stress than tough, dry skin. Client education on proper skin care can reduce the use of home remedies.

The skin of the residual limb may be affected by a variety of dermatologic problems such as eczema, psoriasis, or radiation burns. Some of these conditions may mitigate against fitting or wrapping. Treatment may include ultraviolet irradiation, whirlpool, reflex heating, hyperbaric oxygen, or medication. Care must be taken in using ultraviolet or heat with the dysvascular patient. The whirlpool may not be the treatment of choice since it increases circulation and edema in the part under treatment. The advantages of the whirlpool as a cleansing agent for skin problems, infected wounds, or incidence of delayed healing must be balanced against its disadvantages before effectiveness can be determined for any individual person.

Residual Limb Wrapping

There are many methods of wrapping the residual limb and most therapists will adapt a method to their own needs. Clients tend to wrap their own residual limb in a circular manner, often creating a tourniquet that may compromise healing and foster the development of a bulbous end. While the below-knee residual limb can be effectively wrapped in a sitting position, it is difficult to properly wrap and anchor the above-knee limb while sitting. Elderly clients often cannot balance themselves

in the standing position while wrapping. An effective bandage will be smooth and wrinkle free, will emphasize angular turns, will provide pressure distally, and will encourage proximal joint extension. The ends of bandages should be fastened with tape, safety pins, or Velcro rather than clips, which can cut the skin and do not anchor well. A system of wrapping that uses mostly angular or figure-eight turns was developed specifically to meet the needs of the elderly and has been in use for the past 30 years.[44] Figures 19–6 and 19–7 illustrate the techniques.

THE BELOW-KNEE BANDAGE

Two 4-in elastic bandages will usually be enough to wrap most below-knee residual limbs. Very large residual limbs may require three bandages. The below-knee bandages should not be sewn together so that the weave of each bandage can be set at an angle to each other to provide more support. While an elastic wrap does not provide as much pressure as a rigid dressing, it must help deter the development of postsurgical edema as much as possible; therefore, a firm, even pressure against all soft tissues is desirable. If the incision is placed anteriorly, then an attempt should be made to

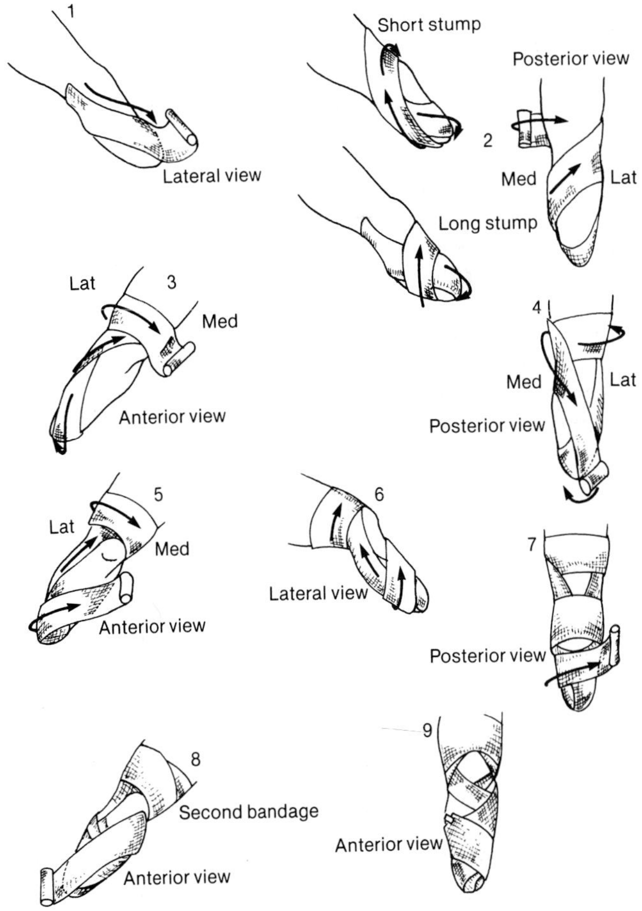

Figure 19–6. Below-knee residual limb wrapping. (From Sanders, GT: Lower Limb Amputations: A Guide to Rehabilitation. FA Davis, 1986, p 365, with permission.)

Figure 19–7. Above-knee residual limb wrapping. (From Sanders, GT: Lower Limb Amputations: A Guide to Rehabilitation. FA Davis, Philadelphia, 1986, p 366, with permission.)

bring the bandages from posterior to anterior over the distal end.

The first bandage is started at either the medial or lateral tibial condyle and brought diagonally over the anterior surface of the limb to the distal end. One edge of the bandage should just cover the midline of the incision in an anterior-posterior plane. The bandage is continued diagonally over the posterior surface, then back over the beginning turn as an anchor. At this point, there is a choice; the bandage may be brought directly over the beginning point as indicated in step 2, or it may be brought across the front of the residual limb in an "X" design. The latter is particularly useful with long residual limbs, and aids in bandage suspension. An anchoring turn over the distal thigh is made, making sure that the wrap is clear of the patella and is not tight around the distal thigh.

After a single anchoring turn above the knee, the bandage is brought back around the opposite tibial condyle and down to the distal end of the limb. One edge of the bandage should overlap the midline of the incision and the other wrap by at least ½ inch to ensure adequate distal end support. The figure-eight pattern is continued as depicted in steps 4 through 7 until the bandage is used up. Care should be taken to completely cover the residual limb with a firm and even pressure. Semicircular turns are made posteriorly to align the bandage to cross the anterior surface in an angular line. This maneuver provides greater pressure on the posterior soft tissue while distributing pressure anteriorly where the bone is close to the skin. Each turn should partially overlap other turns so the whole residual limb is well covered. The pattern is usually from proximal to distal, and back to proximal, starting at the tibial condyles and covering both condyles as well as the patellar tendon. Usually, the patella is left free to aid in knee motion, although with extremely short residual limbs, it may be necessary to cover it for better suspension.

The second bandage is wrapped like the first, except

that it is started at the opposite tibial condyle from the first bandage (step 8). Bringing the weave of each bandage in opposite directions exerts a more even pressure. With both bandages, an effort is made to bring the angular turns across each other rather than in the same direction.

THE ABOVE-KNEE BANDAGE

For most residual limbs, two 6-inch and one 4-inch bandages will adequately cover the limb. The two 6-inch bandages can be sewn together end-to-end, taking care not to create a heavy seam; the 4-inch bandage is used by itself. The client is depicted sidelying in Figure 19–7, which allows a family member or therapist easy access to the residual limb. The client with good balance on the remaining limb can bandage himself or herself in the standing position, but it is difficult for the client to self-bandage correctly in the sitting position.

The 6-inch bandages are used first. The first bandage is started in the groin and brought diagonally over the anterior surface to the distal lateral corner, around the end of the residual limb, and diagonally up the posterior side to the iliac crest and around the hips in a spica. The bandage is started medially so that the hip wrap will encourage extension. After the turn around the hips, the bandage is wrapped around the proximal portion of the residual limb high in the groin, then back around the hips. Although this is a proximal circular turn, it does not create a tourniquet as long as it is continued around the hips. Going around the medial portion of the residual limb high in the groin ensures coverage of the soft tissue in the adductor area, and reduces the possibility of an adductor roll, a complication that can seriously interfere with comfortable prosthetic wear. In most instances, the first bandage ends in the second spica and is anchored with tape or pin.

The second 6-inch bandage is wrapped like the first, but is started a bit more laterally. Any areas not covered with the first bandage must be covered at this time. The second bandage is also anchored in a hip spica after the first figure-eight and after the second turn high in the groin. While more of the first two bandages are used to cover the proximal residual limb, care must be taken that no tourniquet is created. Bringing the bandage directly from the proximal medial area into a hip spica helps keep the adductor tissue covered and prevents rolling of the bandage to some degree.

The 4-inch bandage is used to exert the greatest amount of pressure over mid and distal areas of the residual limb. It is usually not necessary to anchor this bandage around the hips, as friction with the already applied bandages and good figure-eight turns provide adequate suspension. The 4-inch bandage is generally started laterally to bring the weave across the weave of previous bandages. The most effective wrap consists of regular figure-eight turns in varied patterns to cover all the residual limb.

Bandages are applied with firm pressure from the outset. Elastic bandages can be wrapped directly over a soft postsurgical dressing so that bandaging can begin immediately after surgery. The elastic wrap controls edema more effectively if minimal gauze coverage is used over the residual limb. Several gauze pads placed just over the incision usually give adequate protection without compromising the effect of the wrap. Care must be taken to avoid any wrinkles or folds, which can cause excessive skin pressure, particularly over a soft dressing.

SHRINKERS

The below-knee shrinker is rolled over the residual limb to midthigh and is designed to be self-suspending. Individuals with heavy thighs may need additional suspension with garters or a waist belt. Currently available above-knee shrinkers incorporate a hip spica that provides good suspension except with obese individuals. Care must be taken that the client understands the importance of proper suspension as any rolling of the edges or slipping of the shrinker can create a tourniquet around the proximal part of the residual limb. Shrinkers are easier to apply than elastic bandages and may be a better alternative, particularly for the above-knee residual limb. Shrinkers are more expensive to use than elastic wrap; the initial cost is greater, then new shrinkers of smaller sizes must be purchased as the limb volume decreases. However, shrinkers are a viable option for individuals who are not able to properly wrap the residual limb.

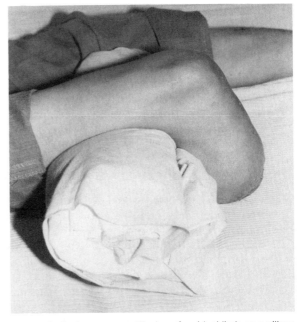

Figure 19–8. Improper positioning of residual limb on a pillow.

Positioning

One of the major goals of the early postoperative program is to prevent secondary complications such as contractures of adjacent joints. Contractures can develop as a result of muscle imbalance or fascial tightness, from a protective withdrawal reflex into hip and knee flexion, from loss of plantar stimulation in extension, or as a result of faulty positioning such as prolonged sitting. The client should understand the importance of proper positioning and regular exercises in preparing for eventual prosthetic fit and ambulation.

With the below-knee amputation, full range of motion in the hips and knee, particularly in extension, is needed. While sitting, the client can keep the knee extended by using a posterior splint or a board attached to the wheelchair. The client with an above-knee amputation needs full range of motion in the hip, particularly in extension and adduction. Prolonged sitting is to be avoided, especially for individuals who have difficulty walking on crutches. Some time each day should be spent in the prone position. Elevation of the residual limb on a pillow following either above-knee or below-knee amputation can lead to the development of hip flexion contractures and should be avoided (Figs. 19–8 and 19–9). The early postoperative period is critical in establishing positive patterns of activity that will aid the client throughout the rehabilitative period. Taking the time to teach the client to assume responsibility for his or her own care can reap later benefits.

Contractures

Some individuals will present with hip or knee flexion contractures. Mild contractures may respond to manual mobilization and active exercises, but it is almost impossible to reduce moderate to severe contractures by manual stretching, especially hip flexion contractures. There are some who advocate holding the extremity in a stretched position with weights for a considerable length of time. There is little evidence that this traditional approach is successful. Active stretching techniques are more effective than passive stretching; hold-contract and resisted motion of antagonist muscles may increase range of motion, particularly of the knee. One of the more effective ways of reducing a knee flexion contracture is to fit the client with a patellar tendon-bearing (PTB) prosthesis aligned in a manner that places the hamstrings on stretch with each step. Such prosthetic alignment provides an active stretch that is quite effective. Hip flexion contractures are more frequently found in above-knee amputations. It is difficult to walk out a hip flexion contracture with the above-knee prosthesis. In some instances, depending on the severity of the contracture and the length of the residual limb, the contracture can be accommodated in the alignment of the prosthesis. A hip or knee flexion contracture

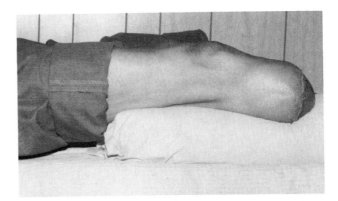

Figure 19–9. Improper positioning of residual limb over a pillow.

of less than 15 degrees is not usually a problem. Prevention, however, continues to be the best treatment for contractures.

Exercises

The exercise program is individually designed and includes strengthening, balance, and coordination activities. The postsurgical dressing, degree of postoperative pain, and healing of the incision will determine when resistive exercises for the involved extremity can be started. The postoperative exercise program can take many forms, and a home program is desirable. The hip extensors and abductors, and knee extensors and flexors are particularly important for prosthetic ambulation. Figures 19–10 and 19–11 depict a series of exercises particularly well designed to strengthen key muscles around the hip and knee. These exercises can be adapted for a home program since they are simple to perform and require no special equipment.

A general strengthening program that includes the trunk and all extremities is often indicated, particularly for the elderly person who may have been quite sedentary prior to surgery. Proprioceptive neuromuscular exercise routines are also beneficial in amputee rehabilitation programs. The exercise program needs to be individually developed and needs to emphasize those muscles that are most active in prosthetic function. Isometric exercises as depicted in Figures 19–10D and 19–11A may be contraindicated for individuals with cardiac disease or hypertension. Both exercises can be modified by having the client actually lift the buttocks off the treatment table in a modified bridging exercise.

The younger, more active patient with traumatic amputation does not usually lose a great deal of muscle strength. Many elderly individuals, however, are relatively sedentary after surgery and need encouragement to develop good strength, coordination, and cardiopulmonary endurance for later ambulation.

Ideally, the exercise program should be sequenced for progressive motor control, increasing coordination, and function. The client should progress from bed to mat activities using exercises that emphasize coordi-

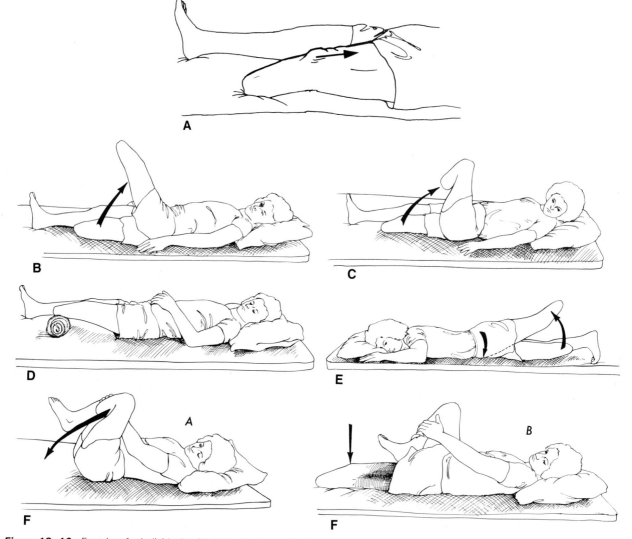

Figure 19–10. Exercises for individuals with below-knee amputations to maintain or increase muscle strength and flexibility. (Used with permission of the Physical Therapy Department at the Rehabilitation Institute of Chicago.)

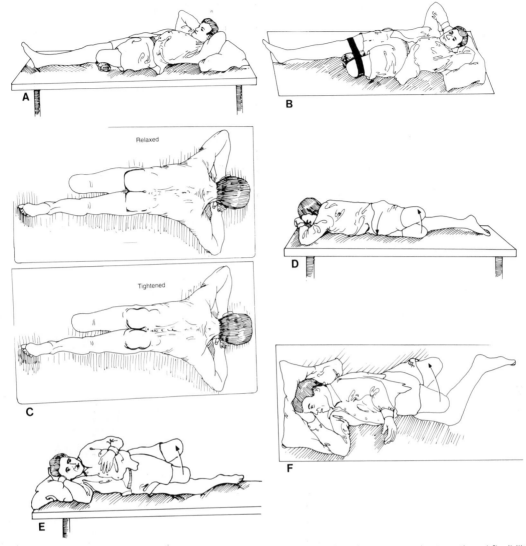

Relaxed

Tightened

Figure 19–11. Exercises for individuals with above-knee amputations to maintain or increase muscle strength and flexibility. (Adapted from the Physical Therapy Department at the Rehabilitation Institute of Chicago.)

nated functional mobility. The client's postoperative status will be determined to a great extent by the preoperative activity level, length of time of disability, and other medical problems, as well as the effects of the surgery itself. Since many clients are discharged from the hospital as early as a week after surgery, referral to a rehabilitation center or home health agency is important to provide the necessary continuity of care.

Early mobility is important to total physiologic recovery. The client needs to resume independent activities as soon as possible. Movement transitions (supine-to-sit, sit-to-stand) are preliminary to ambulation activities. Care must be taken during early bed and transfer movements to protect the residual limb from any trauma. The client must be advised not to push on or slide the residual limb against the bed or chair. The client also needs to be cautioned against spending too much time in any one position to prevent the development of joint contractures or skin breakdowns.

Most individuals with unilateral amputations have little difficulty adjusting to the change in balance point that results from the loss of a limb. Sitting and standing balance activities are a useful part of the early postsurgical program. Upper extremity strengthening exercises with weights or elastic bands are important in preparation for crutch walking. Shoulder depression and elbow extension are particularly necessary to improve the ability to lift the body in ambulation. Individuals with bilateral amputations who have one healed residual limb will often use that limb as a prop for bed activities and transfers. Often a debilitated person with bilateral amputations (one new amputation and one old amputation) who is unable to lift the body with the arms will be able to transfer when allowed to use the old prosthesis fitted to the original residual limb to push on.

Mobility

Walking is an excellent exercise and necessary for independence in daily life. Gait training can start early in the postoperative phase, and the patient with a unilateral lower extremity amputation can become quite independent using a swing-through gait on crutches. Many elderly individuals have difficulty learning to walk on crutches. Some are afraid, some lack the necessary balance and coordination, and others lack endurance. Some studies have indicated that walking with crutches without a prosthesis requires a greater expenditure of energy than walking with a prosthesis.

Independence in crutch walking is a goal worthy of considerable therapy time. The individual who can ambulate with crutches will develop a greater degree of general fitness than the person who spends most of the time in a wheelchair. Crutch walking is good preparation for prosthetic ambulation and the person who can learn to use crutches will not have difficulty learning to use a prosthesis. However, the individual who cannot learn to walk with crutches independently may still become a very functional prosthetic user. It may take considerable time for an elderly person to learn to use crutches, but the benefits are worth the efforts. Even if the individual can only use crutches in the sheltered environment of the home, such ambulation should be encouraged.

There are advantages and disadvantages to using a walker for support during the preprosthetic period. Certainly, walking with a walker is physiologically and psychologically more beneficial than sitting in a wheelchair, but a walker should be used only if the person cannot learn to walk with crutches. A walker is sturdier than crutches but cannot be used on stairs and curbs. It is sometimes difficult for the person who has used a walker during the preprosthetic period to switch to one crutch or cane when fitted with a prosthesis. In addition the gait pattern used with a walker is not appropriate with a prosthesis. All clients need to learn some form of mobility without a prosthesis for use at night or when the prosthesis is not worn for some reason.

Temporary Prostheses

Many patients are not fitted with any type of prosthetic appliance until the residual limb is free from edema and much of the soft tissue has shrunk, a process which can take many months of conscientious limb wrapping and exercises. During this period, the client is limited to a wheelchair or to ambulation with crutches or a walker. Most individuals cannot return to work or fully participate in activities of daily living while waiting for the residual limb to mature. Once fitted with a definitive prosthesis, the residual limb continues to change in size and a second prosthesis is often required within the first year. Early fitting with a temporary prosthesis can greatly enhance the postsurgical rehabilitation program. A temporary prosthesis includes a socket designed and constructed according to regular prosthetic principles and attached to some form of pylon, a foot, and some type of suspension. Figures 19–12 and 19–13 depict two different temporary below-knee prostheses, both suspended by a sleeve. Figure 19–13 shows the socket itself with the sleeve removed. (See Chapter 20 for more detail on prosthetic components.)

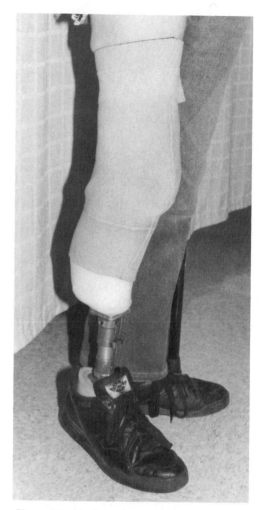

Figure 19–12. Below-knee temporary prosthesis.

A temporary prosthesis can be fitted as soon as the wound has healed. There are many advantages to using a temporary prosthesis:

1. It shrinks the residual limb more effectively than the elastic wrap.
2. It allows early bipedal ambulation.
3. Many elderly people can walk safely with a temporary prosthesis and crutches who otherwise would not be ambulatory during the preprosthetic period.
4. Some individuals can return to work.
5. It provides a means of evaluating the rehabilitation potential of individuals with a questionable prognosis.
6. It is a positive motivating factor in that it provides a replacement for the missing part of the body.
7. It reduces the need for a complex exercise program since many people can return to full active daily life.
8. It can be used by individuals who may have difficulty obtaining payment for a definitive prosthesis.

The below-knee temporary socket may be simply constructed of plaster of Paris or it may be prosthetically fabricated from plastic materials. In all instances the socket design should follow regular prosthetic principles and should incorporate the use of a regular prosthetic foot

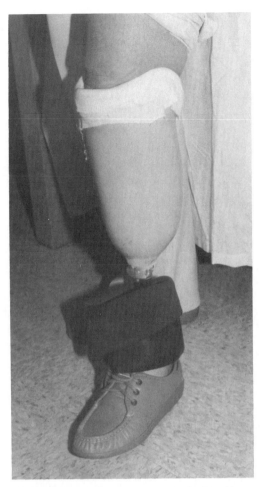

Figure 19–13. Below-knee temporary prosthesis with suspension sleeve lowered to show socket.

attached to the socket with an aluminum pipe for proper gait pattern and weight distribution. A crutch tip, frequently used in the early days, does not adequately distribute the forces transmitted from the floor to the end of the residual limb and is now contraindicated, particularly for the dysvascular person. Many temporary sockets today are made of lightweight thermoplastic materials that can be formed over a positive cast of the residual limb; some are constructed of a fiberglass material that can be formed directly over the residual limb. The prosthesis is usually suspended by a supracondylar cuff to which a waist belt can be added if necessary. The prosthesis is worn with a wool sock of appropriate thickness; when the residual limb has shrunk so that three heavy wool socks are needed to maintain socket fit, a new socket needs to be constructed. The socket can be fabricated by a therapist, prosthetist, physician, or any individual who understands the application of prosthetic principles and socket design. Prosthetic components such as feet of various sizes, suspension straps, knee joints, and pylons are now generally available.

It is easier to fabricate a below-knee socket but the use of a temporary prosthesis is very important in the rehabilitation of the above-knee amputation.[45] The temporary prosthesis for an above-knee amputation should incorporate the regular socket, articulated knee joint, foot, and pylon. Suspension may be with Silesian bandage or pelvic band.

EDUCATING THE CLIENT

As you work with Ms. Sampson, you are glad that you started teaching her about PVD and the care of her legs when you were initially treating her. If she is to return home from the hospital, she needs to learn and understand enough to be a partner in the rehabilitation process rather than a passive recipient of information. You know that teaching is not telling and that you have to devise ways to actively involve Ms. Sampson in learning important concepts and activities. From experience you have learned that the better clients understand the care of their own bodies, the greater the compliance with home programs.

Client education is an integral and ongoing part of the rehabilitation program. Information on the care of the residual limb, proper care of the uninvolved extremity, positioning, exercises, and diet, if the client is a diabetic, is necessary for the client to be a full participant in the rehabilitation program.

Many individuals with vascular disease who lose one leg will be concerned about the other leg and receptive to learning proper care. An understanding of the physiologic and functional implications of PVD helps the individual assume responsibility for the care of the unamputated extremity. A client education program must be individually designed to be relevant and may include

1. A discussion of the disease process and the physiologic effects of the symptoms experienced.
2. Information on the benefits of exercises, lower extremity cleanliness, proper foot care, and proper shoe fitting.
3. Methods of edema control.
4. The use of exercise to improve circulatory status.

Edema, pain, and changes in skin color or temperature may indicate impending problems. If the person is ambulatory on the remaining extremity, these symptoms may indicate too much stress; if the person spends considerable time sitting with the leg in a dependent position, it may be necessary to elevate the extremity. Intermittent claudication (cramping of the calf) during activity is an indication of a need to stop, at least temporarily. The collateral circulation of the remaining extremity is developed slowly through a progressive program of exercises and ambulation. It is important to remember that too little activity may be as harmful as too much.

Care must be taken not to overwhelm the client with too much information at one time, as information overload results in noncompliance. It is more effective to prioritize the information and ask the person to remember one new thing each session rather than try to teach a complex program at one time. It is also important for the program to be tailored to the individual's life-style. Involving the client in establishing priority and timing enhances compliance. Compliance is also increased if the program meets the person's own goals. The same approach can be used for the home exercise program. Once the client is discharged, either weekly clinic visits or home health supervision throughout the preprosthetic phase provide a check on home activities, on the condition of the residual limb, and support to the client and family.

BILATERAL AMPUTATION

The preprosthetic program for the person with bilateral lower extremity amputations is similar to the program developed for someone with a unilateral amputation except, possibly, ambulation. If the individual was fitted and ambulatory after unilateral amputation, the prosthesis is useful for transfer activities and limited ambulation in parallel bars. Occasionally, the individual may be able to use the prosthesis with external support to get around the house more easily, particularly for bathroom activities. Fitting with a temporary prosthesis, as previously mentioned, is advisable, particularly if the amputations are at below-knee levels. The higher the initial level of amputation, the more difficult ambulation becomes.

All individuals with bilateral amputations need a wheelchair on a permanent basis. The chair should be as narrow as possible with removable desk arms and removable leg rests. Amputee wheelchairs with offset rear wheels and no leg rests are not recommended unless the therapist is sure that the person will never be fitted with prostheses, even cosmetically. It is easier to add antitipping devices to the rear of the wheelchair or to attach small weights to the front uprights for use when the foot rests are removed.

The preprosthetic program includes mat activities designed to help the person regain a sense of body position and balance, upper extremity and residual limb strengthening exercises, wheelchair transfers, and regular range of motion exercises. With bilateral amputations, individuals spend considerable time sitting and are therefore more prone to develop flexion contractures, particularly around the hip joint. The client should be encouraged to sleep prone if possible, or at least spend some time in the prone position each day. The therapy program also emphasizes range of motion of the residual limb. Some people move about their homes on their knees, the ends of the residual limbs, or the buttocks. The knee pads made of heavy rubber and used by field workers are effective protectors for the residual limbs. Protectors can also be fabricated of foam or felt.

Temporary prostheses are of great value in the rehabilitation of patients with bilateral below-knee amputations. Temporary prostheses are used to evaluate ambulation potential and as an aid to balance and transfer activities. If the individual was initially fitted as a unilateral amputee, the temporary prosthesis will allow some resumption of ambulation. The ambulatory potential of the patient with bilateral above-knee amputations is uncertain, particularly among the elderly.

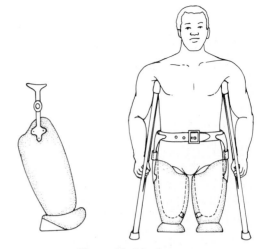

Figure 19–14. Stubbies.

The person with bilateral above-knee amputations can be fitted with shortened prosthesis called "**stubbies**" (Fig. 19–14). Stubby prostheses have regular sockets, no articulated knee joints or shank, and modified rocker bottoms turned backward to prevent the individual from falling backward. Since the client's center of gravity is much lower to the ground and the prostheses are non-articulated, they are relatively easy to use. Stubbies allow the individual with bilateral above-knee amputations to acquire erect balance and participate in ambulatory activities quickly and with only moderate expenditures of energy. Their acceptance by clients, however, is quite variable; some like to use them for activities of daily living in the home but rely on a wheelchair outside the home. Although prescribed rather rarely, they are most effective for individuals with short residual limbs or those who will not be able to ambulate with regular prostheses. Temporary prostheses of different heights can be used to determine the ambulatory potential of the client with bilateral amputation but care must be taken to ensure that the temporary limbs are constructed well enough to tolerate the stresses generated in walking.

NONPROSTHETIC MANAGEMENT

The preprosthetic period is designed to determine the individual's suitability for prosthetic replacement. Not all people with amputations are candidates for a prosthesis, regardless of personal desire. The cost of the prosthesis and the energy demands of prosthetic training require that the clinic team use some judgment in selecting individuals for fitting.

There is no general rule that can safely be applied to all clients in making the decision to fit or not to fit. The client is part of the decision-making process but the fact that the individual wants a prosthesis is not enough. Many people are not aware of the physiologic demands of prosthetic ambulation, particularly at above-knee levels. The development of lightweight prostheses, safety knees, hydraulic mechanisms, and energy-conserving feet have made it possible to successfully fit many more individuals than in the past; however, some consideration to nonfitting is necessary.

Below-Knee Levels

Most individuals amputated at any below-knee level can be successfully fitted with a prosthesis. Flexion contractures, scars, poorly shaped residual limbs, and adherent skin are not necessarily contraindications for fitting, even though such problems create difficulty with socket fit. Circulatory problems in the nonamputated extremity, unless so severe as to preclude any ambulation, are indications for fitting at the earliest possible time, since bipedal ambulation reduces stress on the remaining extremity. Additionally, the individual who has learned to ambulate with one prosthesis is more likely to be able to ambulate with two. That is, it is easier to learn to use bilateral prostheses if a person has previously learned to use a single prosthesis. There are few contraindications to fitting someone who has a below-knee amputation other than contraindications to ambulation itself. Individuals who were not ambulatory prior to surgery for reasons other than the problems leading to the amputation, will probably not be ambulatory with an amputation. However, individuals who were nonambulatory and debilitated because of infection, loss of diabetic control, and ulcers will probably regain the necessary strength and coordination for ambulation after the diseased limb has been removed. Generally, individuals requiring nursing or custodial care will not be able to use a prosthesis; often equipment sent to a nursing home becomes lost, and fitting such individuals may be a waste of limited resources.

Above-Knee Levels

Many clients with unilateral above-knee amputations can become relatively functional prosthetic users with or without external support. The physiologic demands of walking with an above-knee prosthesis are considerably higher than walking with a below-knee prosthesis and not all individuals have the necessary balance, strength, and energy reserves.[46] Severe hip flexion contractures, weakness or paralysis of hip musculature, and poor balance and coordination may mitigate against successful ambulation. The person's level of activity and participation in the preprosthetic program helps in determining potential for prosthetic ambulation. A temporary prosthesis is a good assessment tool.

Most individuals amputated at hip levels are younger and learn to use a prosthesis relatively easily. While early fitting is physically and psychologically beneficial, active involvement in chemotherapy or radiation therapy will delay fitting. Radiation therapy often burns the skin, making fitting impossible until the skin has healed. Clients undergoing chemotherapy are often ill, lose weight, and usually do not have the energy to participate in a prosthetic training program. The preprosthetic program is individually adjusted and modified until the chemotherapy is complete. If the person has lost considerable weight, fitting may have to be delayed since it is difficult to adjust a prosthesis for increases in weight.

Bilateral Amputations

Fitting or not fitting a patient with bilateral amputations is a difficult decision. Young, agile individuals are generally good candidates for prosthetic fitting. Most bilateral below-knee amputees can become quite functional with prostheses. Most bilateral above-knee clients have considerable difficulty learning to use two prostheses. Clients with one above-knee and one below-knee amputation generally can learn to use two prostheses if the first amputation was at the above-knee level, and if the person successfully used an above-knee prosthesis before losing the other leg.

The person who has lost both lower extremities needs more strength, better coordination, better balance and greater cardiorespiratory reserves than the person who has lost one lower extremity. The decision to fit or not to fit is made after careful individual evaluation of the person's total potential and needs.

The Therapy Program

Individuals who are not fitted with a prosthesis need to become as independent as possible in a wheelchair. The therapy program includes all transfer and activities of daily living and education in the proper care of the residual limb. Wrapping the residual limb is no longer necessary unless the person is more comfortable with the limb covered. The program emphasizes sitting balance, moving safely in and out of the wheelchair, and other activities to support as independent a life-style as the person's physical and psychologic condition allows.

SUMMARY

Most individuals with lower extremity amputations can be helped to return to a full and useful life following the loss of a limb. A program of postoperative care that includes consideration of physical and emotional needs will enable most clients to become functional prosthetic users. Many prosthetic problems can be avoided by properly preparing the individual for prosthetic wear. In this chapter concepts related to the postoperative management of the individual with a lower extremity amputation have been presented. Through a process of careful assessment and open communication, a comprehensive program designed to meet the needs of an individual client can be achieved. The individuality of each person presenting for treatment is one of the challenges of physical therapy practice.

QUESTIONS FOR REVIEW

1. Discuss the advantages and disadvantages of the following methods of postsurgical residual limb management:
   a. Rigid dressing
   b. CET
   c. Air splint
   d. Soft dressing

2. Discuss the proper method of wrapping the below-knee and the above-knee residual limb.

3. A 72-year-old man with a history of diabetes, cardiovascular disease, and peripheral vascular disease has been referred for physical therapy 24 hours after right below-knee amputation for gangrene. What are the eval-uation data that are needed to plan an appropriate treatment program? Which are the most critical to obtain on the first visit?

4. Design an exercise program for an 82-year-old patient with a left above-knee amputation who is referred 2 weeks after amputation surgery.

5. Discuss the advantages and disadvantages of teaching an elderly patient with a unilateral amputation to walk with crutches versus walking with a walker.

6. Which preprosthetic activities are more important with bilateral amputations than unilateral amputations? How might you teach these activities?

REFERENCES

1. Levy, LA: Smoking and peripheral vascular disease. Clin Podiatr Med Surg 9:165, 1992.
2. Ritz, G, Friedman, S, and Osbourne, A: Diabetes and peripheral vascular disease. Clin Podiatr Med Surg 9:125, 1992.
3. Malone, JM and Goldstone, J: Lower extremity amputation. In Moore, WS (ed): Vascular Surgery: A Comprehensive Review. Grune & Stratton, New York, 1984.
4. Yeager, RA, Moneta, GL, Taylor, LM Jr, et al: Surgical management of severe acute lower extremity ischemia. J Vasc Surg 15:385, 1992.
5. Taylor, LM, Jamre, D, Dalman, RL, and Porter, JM: Limb salvage vs amputation for critical ischemia. Arch Surg 126:1251, 1991.
6. McIntyre, KE Jr: The diabetic foot and management of infectious gangrene. In Moore, WS and Malone, JHM (eds): Lower Extremity Amputation. WB Saunders, Philadelphia, 1989.
7. Moss, SE, Klein, R, and Klein, BE: The prevalence and incidence of lower extremity amputation in a diabetic population. Arch Intern Med 152:610, 1992.
8. Knighton, DR, Fylling, CP, Fiegel, VD, and Cerra, F: Amputation prevention in an independently reviewed at-risk diabetic population using a comprehensive wound care protocol. Am J Surg 160:466, 1990.
9. Krajewski, LP and Olin, JW: Atherosclerosis of the aorta and lower extremities arteries. In Young, JR, Graor, RA, Olin, JW, and Bartholomew, JR: Peripheral Vascular Diseases. Mosby Year Book, St Louis, 1991.
10. Harris, KA, van Schie, L, Carroll, SE, Deathe, A, Maryniak, O, Meads, GE, and Sweeney, JF: Rehabilitation potential of elderly patients with major amputations. J Cardiovasc Surg (Torino) 32:463, 1991.
11. Glattly, HW: A statistical study of 12,000 new amputees. South Med J 57:1373, 1964.
12. Kay, HW and Newman, JD: Relative incidence of new amputations: statistical comparisons of 6,000 new amputees. Orth-Pros 29:3, 1975.
13. Lane, JM, Kroll, MA, and Rossbach, P: New advances and concepts in amputee management after treatment for bone and soft-tissue sarcomas. Clin Orthop 256:22, 1990
14. Link, MP, Goorin, AM, Horowitz, M, Meyer, WH, Belasco, J, Baker, A, Ayala, A, and Shuster, J: Adjuvant chemotherapy of high-grade osteosarcoma of the extremity. Clin Orthop 270:8, 1991.
15. Simon, M: Limb salvage for osteosarcoma in the 1980s. Clin Orthop 270:264, 1990.
16. Springfield, DS: Introduction to limb-salvage surgery for sarcomas. Orthop Clin North Am 22:1, 1991.
17. Yaw, KM and Wurtz, LD: Resection and reconstruction for bone tumors in the proximal tibia. Orthop Clin North Am 22:133, 1991.
18. Waters, RL, et al: Energy cost of walking of amputees: The influence of level of amputation. J Bone Joint Surg 58A:42, 1976.
19. Steinberg, FU, et al: Prosthetic rehabilitation of geriatric amputee patients: a follow-up study. Arch Phys Med Rehabil 66:742, 1985.
20. Malone, JM and Lalka, SG: Amputation level selection by Doppler assessment in Moore, WS (ed): Vascular Surgery: A Comprehensive Review. Grune & Stratton, New York, 1984.
21. Michaels, JA: The selection of amputation level: an approach using decision analysis. Eur J Vasc Surg 5:451, 1991.
22. Sarin, S, Shami, S, Shields, DA, Scurry, JH, and Smith, PD: Selection of amputation levels: a review. Eur J Vasc Surg 5:611, 1991.
23. Spence, VA, et al: Assessment of tissue viability in relation to selection of amputation level. Prosthet Int 8:67, 1984.
24. Lind, J, Kramhhaft, M, and Badtker, S: The influence of smoking on complications after primary amputations of the lower extremity. Clin Orthop 267:211, 1991.
25. Evans, WE, Hayes, JP, and Vermillion, BO: Effect of a failed distal reconstruction on the level of amputation. Am J Surg 160:217, 1990.
26. Tsang, GMK, Crowson, MC, Hickey, NC, and Simms, MH: Failed femorocrural reconstruction does not prejudice amputation level. Br J Surg 78:1479, 1991.
27. Ljungman, C, Adami, HO, Bergqvist, D, Sparen, P, and Bergstrom, R: Risk factors for early lower limb loss after embolectomy for acute arterial occlusion: a population-based case-control study. Br J Surg 78:1482, 1991.
28. Malone, JM: Complications of lower extremity amputation. In Moore, WS (ed): Vascular Surgery: A Comprehensive Review. Grune & Stratton, New York, 1984.
29. May, BJ: A statewide amputee rehabilitation programme. Prosthet Orthot Int 2:24, 1978.
30. Burgess, EM: Amputations of the lower extremities. In Nickel, VL (ed): Orthopedic Rehabilitation. Churchill-Livingstone, New York, 1982, p 377.
31. Sarmiento, A, May, BJ, Sinclair, WF, et al: Lower-extremity amputation: the impact of immediate post surgical prosthetic fitting. Clin Orthop 68:22, 1967.
32. Harrington, IJ, Lexier, R, Woods, J, McPolin, MF, and James, GF: A plaster-pylon technique for below-knee amputation. J Bone Joint Surg [Br] 73:76, 1991.
33. Little, JM: A pneumatic weight bearing prosthesis for below-knee amputees. Lancet 1:271, 1971.
34. Little, JM: The use of air splints as immediate prosthesis after below-knee amputation for vascular insufficiency. Med J Aust 2:870, 1970.
35. Burgess, EM: Wound healing after amputation: effect of controlled environment treatment, a preliminary study. J Bone Joint Surg Am 60A:245, 1978.
36. Kegel, B: Controlled environment treatment (CET) for patients with below-knee amputations. Phys Ther 56:1366, 1976.
37. Jensen, TS, Krebs, B, Nielsen, J, and Rasmussen, P: Immediate and long-term phantom limb pain in amputees: incidence, clinical characteristics and relationship to pre-amputation limb pain. Pain 21:267, 1985.
38. Iacono, RP, Linford, J, and Sandyk, R: Pain management after lower extremity amputation. Neurosurgery 20:496, 1987.
39. Fisher, A and Meller, Y: Continuous postoperative regional analgesia by nerve sheath block for amputation surgery—a pilot study. Anesth Analg 72:300, 1991.
40. Malawer, MM, Buch, R, Khurana, JS, Garvey, T, and Rice, L: Post-

operative infusional continuous regional analgesia. Clin Orthop 266:227, 1991.

41. Mouratoglou, VM: Amputees and phantom limb pain: a literature review. Physiotherapy Practice 2:177, 1986.
42. Sherman, RA, Ernst, JL, Barja, RH, and Bruno, GM: Phantom pain: a lesson in the necessity for careful clinical research on chronic pain problems. Rehabil Res Dev 25:7, 1988.
43. Melzack, R: Phantom limbs. Scientific American 266:120, 1992.
44. May, BJ: Stump bandaging of the lower extremity amputee. Phys Ther 44:808, 1964.
45. Parry, M and Morrison, JD: Use of the Femurett adjustable prosthesis in the assessment and walking training of new above-knee amputees. Prosthet Orthot Int 13:36, 1989.
46. Perry, J: Gait Analysis: Normal and Pathological Function. Slack, Thorofare, NJ, 1992.

SUPPLEMENTAL READINGS

Burgess, EM, Romano, RL, and Zettle, JH: The management of lower extremity amputations. Veterans Administration Report 10-6, U.S. Government Printing Service, New York, 1969.

Burgess, EM and Pedeganza, LR: Controlled environment treatment for limb surgery and trauma. Bull Prosthet Res Dev 10–28:16, 1977.

Burgess, EM: Post operative management. In Atlas of Limb Prosthetics. CV Mosby, St. Louis, 1981.

Ghiulamila, RI: Semirigid dressing for post operative fitting of below knee prosthesis. Arch Phys Med Rehabil 53:186, 1972.

Manella, KJ: Comparing the effectiveness of elastic bandages and shrinker socks for lower extremity amputees. Phys Ther 61:334, 1981.

May, BJ: Residual Limb Bandaging, a videotape. Division of Biomedical Communications, Medical College of Georgia, Augusta, GA, 1981.

Mench, G and Ellis, P: Physical Therapy Management of Lower Extremity Amputations. Aspen, Rockville, MD, 1986.

Redhead, RG and Snowdon, C: A new approach to the management of wounds of the extremities: controlled environment treatment and its derivatives. Prosthet Orthop Int 2:148, 1978.

Schnell, MD and Bunch, WH: Management of pain in the amputee. In Atlas of Limb Prosthetics. CV Mosby, St Louis, 1981.

Troup, IM: Controlled environment treatment (CET). Prosthet Orthop Int 4:15, 1980.

Wu, Y, Keagy, RD, Krick, HJ, et al: An innovative removable rigid dressing technique for below-the-knee amputations. J Bone Joint Surg 61:724, 1979.

GLOSSARY

Beveling (of bone): The process of smoothing the cut ends of bone to prevent rough edges that could cause skin irritations from pressure against the prosthetic socket.

Cauterization: Destruction of tissue by use of a caustic agent such as heat, cold, electricity, or corrosive chemicals.

Dysvascular: Decreased peripheral vascular circulation; usually applied to arterial diseases.

Hemostasis: Arrest of bleeding.

Immediate postoperative prosthesis: Application of a temporary prosthesis immediately following amputation; usually consists of a plaster of Paris socket, pylon, and foot.

Myodesis: Method of muscle stabilization following amputation in which the cut muscle is sutured to periosteum or bone.

Myofascial closure: Method of muscle stabilization following amputation in which muscle is sutured to fascia; often used in combination with myoplasty.

Myoplasty: Method of muscle stabilization following amputation in which muscle is sutured to muscle; the cut flexor and extensor muscles are surgically attached; often used in combination with myofascial closure.

Neurectomy: Partial or total excision or resection of a nerve.

Neuroma: Collection of nerve cells that develops following transection of a nerve.

Peripheral vascular disease (PVD): A general term used to describe any disorder that interferes with arterial or venous blood flow of the extremities.

Phantom limb: The sensation that a part of the body that has become desensitized or has been amputated is still there.

Phantom pain: Pain originating from the desensitized or amputated body part.

Rhizotomy: Division or severance of a nerve root.

Shrinker: Commercially made socklike garment of heavy rubber-reinforced cotton, and designed to fit a residual limb.

Stubbies: Short above-the-knee prosthetic sockets set on modified rocker feet and used to help individuals with bilateral above-knee amputations move around outside of a wheelchair.

Tenodesis: Surgical attachment of a tendon to a bone.

Unna paste dressing: A semirigid dressing, consisting of gauze impregnated with zinc oxide, gelatin, glycerin, and calamine, that is wrapped on the foot and lower limb and used in the management primarily of venous ulcers and occasionally with arterial foot ulcers.

CHAPTER 20

Prosthetic Assessment and Management

Joan E. Edelstein

OBJECTIVES

1. Relate various levels of amputation to prosthetic restoration.
2. Describe the major components of below-knee and above-knee prostheses, including advantages and disadvantages of alternative components and materials.
3. Describe the distinctive features of partial foot, Syme's, and knee and hip disarticulation prostheses.
4. Outline the maintenance program for each prosthetic component.
5. Identify the principal features of below-knee and above-knee prosthetic assessment.
6. Recognize the physical therapist's role in management of individuals with lower-limb amputation.

A *prosthesis* is a replacement of a body part. A *prosthetist* is a health care professional who designs, fabricates, and fits prostheses. In the broadest sense, prostheses include dentures, wigs, and plastic heart valves. The physical therapist, however, is concerned primarily with limb prostheses (i.e., artificial legs and arms) and the management of individuals with lower- and upper-limb amputation.

Lower-limb amputation is much more prevalent than loss of the upper limb. The major causes of amputation are peripheral vascular disease, trauma, malignancy, and congenital deficiency. Vascular disease accounts for most leg amputations in individuals older than 50.[1] Trauma is responsible for the majority of amputations in younger adults and adolescents. Trauma and vascular disease are more common among men. Bone and soft tissue tumors are sometimes treated by removal of the limb, and adolescence is the period of peak incidence. *Congenital deficiency* refers to absence or abnormality of a limb evident at birth.

This chapter focuses on the lower limb because more individuals have lost a portion of the leg, as compared with the arm, and because the physical therapist is expected to assume a major role in management of the patient with lower-limb amputation. Prostheses will be described, together with a program for training patients in their use.

LOWER-LIMB PROSTHETIC DEVICES

The concept of replacing a missing limb is very old. Prostheses, such as a forked stick forming a peg leg to support a below-knee amputation limb, were known in antiquity. Today, most individuals with lower-limb amputation are provided with a prosthesis. Function with one leg is very different from maneuvering with two legs; in contrast, most daily activities and vocational tasks are performed with a single upper limb.

The principal lower-limb prostheses are partial foot, Syme's, below-knee, and above-knee, as well as knee and hip disarticulation. The physical therapist should be familiar with their characteristics and their maintenance.

Partial Foot Prostheses

The purposes of partial foot prostheses are (1) to restore, as much as possible, foot function, particularly in walking, and (2) to simulate the shape of the missing foot segment. The patient who has lost one or more toes may simply pad the toe section of the shoe to improve the appearance of the upper portion of the shoe. Standing will not be affected, assuming the metatarsal heads remain. Late stance will be less forceful, particularly if the phalanges of the great toe are absent. An arch support helps to maintain alignment of the amputated foot.

Transmetatarsal amputation disturbs foot appearance more noticeably. A prosthesis prevents the shoe from developing an unnatural crease in the forefoot area. The patient bears most weight on the heel and reduces the amount of time spent on the affected foot during walking. A particularly useful prosthesis consists of a plastic socket for the remainder of the foot. The socket is affixed to a rigid plate that extends the full length of the inner sole of the shoe. The plate has a cosmetic toe filler. The socket protects the amputated ends of the metatarsals, while the rigid plate restores foot length so that the person can spend more time during the stance phase of gait on the affected side than would otherwise be the case. To aid late stance, the bottom of the prosthesis or the sole of the shoe may have a convex, rocker bar.

Amputation or disarticulation through the tarsals poses the additional problem of retaining the small foot segment in the shoe during swing phase. Foot length is apt to be diminished further by an equinus deformity of the amputation limb, resulting from unbalanced contraction of the triceps surae. Consequently, the prosthesis described for the transmetatarsal amputation may be augmented with a plastic calf shell, which is strapped around the leg.

Below-Knee Prostheses

The below-knee (**transtibial**) level refers to an amputation in which the tibia and fibula are transected. The patient retains the anatomic knee and its motor and sensory functions. This is the predominant site of amputation, particularly for individuals with vascular disease. From a functional and prosthetic viewpoint, the **Syme's amputation** is similar; amputation is just above the malleoli, with all foot bones removed and the calcaneal fat pad retained. The amputation limb is longer than in the below-knee amputation, improving prosthetic control; in addition, the individual with a Syme's amputation may be able to tolerate significant weight through the end of the limb. Prostheses for both the Syme's and below-knee levels include a foot-ankle assembly and socket; the below-knee prosthesis also has a shank and a suspension component.

FOOT-ANKLE ASSEMBLY

The prosthetic foot serves to restore the general contour of the patient's foot, absorbs shock at heel contact, plantarflexes in early stance, and simulates metatarsophalangeal hyperextension (toe-break action) in the latter part of stance phase (Fig. 20–1). Many foot-ankle assemblies also provide slight motion in the frontal and transverse planes.[2]

Nonarticulated Feet

Most feet prescribed in the United States are nonarticulated, presenting a one-piece external appearance, without a cleft between the foot and lower portion of the shank. As compared with articulated feet, nonarticulated components are lighter in weight, more durable, and more attractive; some versions are made to suit high-heeled shoes.

SACH foot. The **solid ankle cushion heel (SACH)** assembly predominates in current practice. It consists of a wood **keel,** which terminates at a point corresponding to the metatarsophalangeal joints. The rigid section is covered by rubber; the posterior portion is resilient, to absorb shock and to permit plantarflexion in early stance. Anteriorly, the junction of the keel and rubber toe allows the foot to hyperextend at late stance. The SACH foot is manufactured in a wide range of sizes to accommodate infants, adolescents, and adults, and with

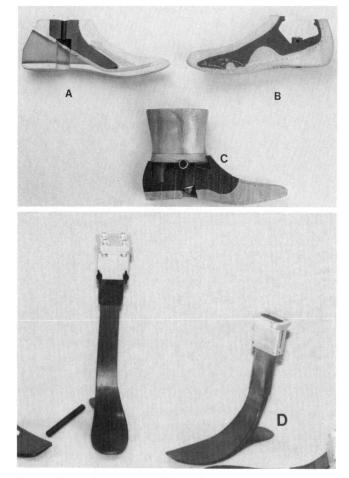

Figure 20–1. Cross-section of foot-ankle assemblies: (A) SACH, (B) SAFE, (C) single-axis, (D) Springlite with adjustment rod.

heel cushions of varying degrees of compressibility for those who strike the foot with different amounts of force, as well as in several plantarflexion angles to fit shoes with diverse heel heights. The heel cushion allows a very small amount of mediolateral and transverse motion.

Other nonarticulated feet. A version of the SACH foot is the **stationary attachment flexible endoskeleton (SAFE) foot.**[3] It has a rigid ankle block joined to the posterior portion of the keel at a 45-degree angle, which is comparable to that of the anatomic subtalar joint. The junction permits the *SAFE foot* wearer to maintain contact with moderately uneven terrain, because of the greater range of mediolateral motion permitted in the rear-foot. The *SAFE foot,* however, is somewhat heavier, more expensive, and less durable than the SACH foot. The *Seattle foot* incorporates a slightly flexible plastic keel, which bends somewhat at heel contact, storing energy.[4] At late stance, the keel recoils as the wearer unloads the foot, releasing energy for a springy termination to stance. Both the *Flex-Foot* and the *Springlite foot* include a long band of carbon fiber material, which extends from the toe to the proximal shank, as well as a posterior heel section. The long band acts as a leaf spring, enabling the foot to store considerable energy in early and mid stance, and then to release energy at the end of stance phase.[5,6] Active wearers, such as those who play basketball or run, utilize the energy-storing and energy-releasing capacity of these feet.[7] They are, however, more expensive than alternative assemblies.

Articulated Feet

These components are manufactured with separate foot and lower shank sections, joined by a metal bolt or cable. The ease of foot motion is controlled by the use of rubber. In the rear is a resilient bumper to absorb shock and to control plantarflexion excursion; it is easy for the prosthetist to substitute a firmer or softer bumper, depending on the patient. A heavy or very active client requires a firm bumper, while a frail individual needs a bumper that is soft enough to permit the foot to plantarflex with minimal loading. At early stance, slight loading of the heel causes the foot to plantarflex, to ensure that the wearer achieves the stable foot-flat position. Anterior to the ankle bolt is firmer rubber, the dorsiflexion stop, which resists dorsiflexion as the wearer moves forward over the foot. Articulated feet are subject to eventual loosening, which may be signalled by a squeaking noise.

Single-axis feet. The most common example of an articulated foot is the **single-axis foot.** It permits plantarflexion and dorsiflexion, as well as toe-break action, but does not allow mediolateral or transverse motion. Some people prefer this simplicity of control.

Multiple-axis feet. These components move slightly in all planes to aid the wearer in maintaining maximum contact with the walking surface, even if the surface slopes or presents slight irregularities. **Multiple-axis** feet are heavier and less durable than single-axis or non-articulated feet.

The clinician can select from a wide array of foot-ankle assemblies, in addition to the representative components described here.

Rotators

A rotator is a component placed above the prosthetic foot to absorb shock in the transverse plane. This action protects the user from chafing, which would otherwise occur if the socket were permitted to rotate against the skin. Rotators are most often used with single-axis feet and by very active individuals with above-knee amputations.[8]

SHANK

Adjacent to the foot-ankle assembly (or rotator) in a below-knee prosthesis is the shank. It restores leg length and shape, and transmits the wearer's body weight from the socket to the foot. Two types of shank are used: **exoskeletal** and **endoskeletal.** The Syme's prosthesis does not have a shank because the socket encasing the amputation limb extends to the foot-ankle assembly.

Exoskeletal Shank

The *exoskeletal shank* (Fig. 20–2) is usually made of wood. It presents a rigid exterior, shaped to stimulate the contour of the leg. The shank is finished with plastic

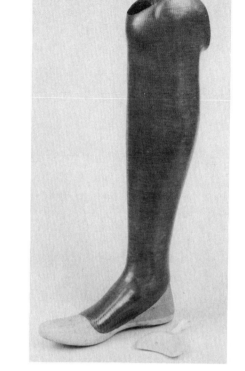

Figure 20–2. Below-knee prosthesis with SACH foot, exoskeletal shank, patellar-tendon-bearing socket, and supracondylar wedge suspension.

tinted to match the wearer's skin color; some individuals opt for a multicolored or patterned shank. The exoskeletal shank, sometimes called **crustacean,** is very durable and, with the plastic finish, impervious to liquids and most abrasives.

Endoskeletal Shank

In contrast, the *endoskeletal shank* (Fig. 20–3) consists of a central aluminum or rigid plastic pylon covered with foam rubber and a sturdy stocking or similar finish. The endoskeletal, or **modular,** shank presents a more lifelike appearance than does the shiny exoskeletal shank. In addition, the pylon has a mechanism that permits making slight adjustment of the angulation of the prosthesis; this may contribute to the comfort and ease of walking. A few prosthetic foot-ankle assemblies, such as the Flex-Foot, incorporate an endoskeletal shank.

SOCKET

The amputated limb fits into a receptacle called the *socket* (Fig. 20–4). Although the original name for the modern below-knee socket was the patellar-tendon-bearing (**PTB**) socket,[9] the socket is designed to contact all portions of the amputated limb for maximum distribution of load, as well as to assist venous blood circulation and to provide tactile feedback. A more accurate name is *total contact.* Sockets are custom-molded of plastic, which is shaped over a model of the amputated limb. The prosthetist alters the model to improve comfort. Socket fabrication may be achieved by hand or by **computer-aided design/computer-aided manufac-**

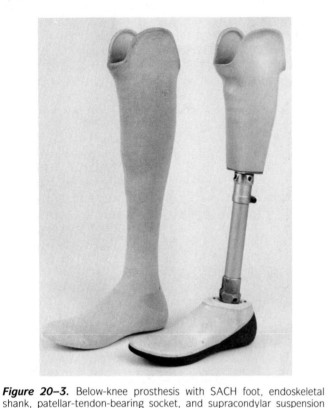

Figure 20–3. Below-knee prosthesis with SACH foot, endoskeletal shank, patellar-tendon-bearing socket, and supracondylar suspension with and without foam rubber covering.

ture (**CAD-CAM**) involving an electronic sensor, which transmits a detailed map of the patient's limb to a computerized program consisting of socket shape variations. The prosthetist selects the most appropriate shape, which is transmitted to an electronic carver that creates the model over which the plastic is shaped. Whether the model is made by hand or by computer, it provides **reliefs** in the socket; these are concavities in the socket over areas contacting sensitive structures, such as bony prominences; reliefs are located over the fibular head, tibial crest, tibial condyles, and anterodistal tibia. The posterior brim is trimmed to provide adequate room for the medial and lateral hamstring tendons, so that the patient is comfortable when sitting. **Build-ups** are convexities in the socket over areas contacting pressure-tolerant tissues, such as the belly of the gastrocnemius; the patellar ligament; proximomedial tibia, corresponding to the pes anserinus; and the tibial and fibular shafts.

When viewed from above, the socket resembles a triangle, the apex of which is formed by the relief for the tibial tubercle and crest, and the base angles of which are the hamstring reliefs. The anterior wall terminates at the midpatella, or above. The medial and lateral walls extend at least to the femoral epicondyles. The posterior wall lies across the popliteal fossa.

The socket is aligned on the shank in slight flexion to enhance loading on the patellar ligament, as well as to prevent genu recurvatum and resist the tendency of the

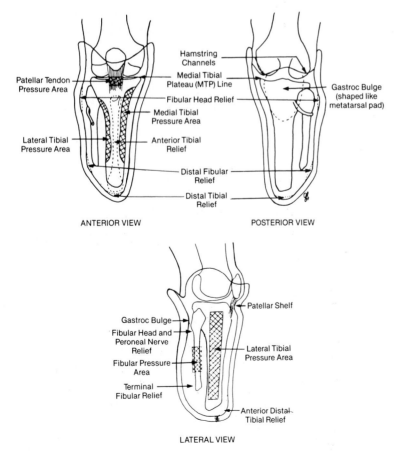

Figure 20–4. Patellar-tendon-bearing socket. (From Sanders, GT: *Lower Limb Amputations: A Guide to Rehabilitation.* FA Davis, Philadelphia, 1986, p 176, with permission.)

amputation limb to slide down the socket. Flexion also facilitates contraction of the quadriceps muscle. The socket is also aligned with a slight lateral tilt to reduce loading on the fibular head.

Lined Socket

The below-knee prosthetic socket generally includes a resilient **polyethylene** foam liner. In addition to cushioning the amputation limb, the removable liner facilitates alteration of socket size; the prosthetist can add material to the outside of the liner, reducing the volume of the socket while preserving smooth interior contours. The liner, however, adds to the bulk of the prosthesis and is a heat insulator, which the wearer may find uncomfortable in the summer. The Syme's prosthesis has a liner that assists entry of the bulbous distal end of the amputation limb, enabling the wearer to don the prosthesis easily.

Unlined Socket

Although the unlined socket is sometimes referred to as a hard socket, that term is a misnomer, for the wearer has a soft interface provided by socks or a sheath worn with the unlined socket. Occasionally a resilient pad is placed in the bottom of the unlined socket to cushion the distal end of the amputation limb. The unlined socket is more satisfactory for the individual whose limb has stabilized in volume, because the socket shape is more difficult to alter than it is in the lined socket.

Syme's Socket

Because the client with a Syme's amputation can usually bear significant weight through the distal end of the amputation limb, the Syme's socket (Fig. 20–5) does not need to provide proximal loading. The socket trimlines are slightly lower, and the frontal and sagittal plane alignment less tilted, as compared with a below-knee socket. Relief for the tibial crest remains an important feature of the socket. If the distal end of the Syme's limb is markedly bulbous, the lower part of the medial wall can be made removable; the patient dons the socket, then fastens the wall section in place.

SUSPENSION

During the swing phase of walking, or whenever the wearer is not standing on the prosthesis, such as when climbing stairs or jumping, the prosthesis requires some form of suspension.[10]

Cuff Variants

The modern below-knee prosthesis originated with a supracondylar *cuff,* (Fig. 20-6) which is still widely used. The cuff, a leather strap encircling the thigh immediately above the femoral epicondyles, permits the user to adjust the snugness of suspension easily. Some individuals, however, object to the profile of the distal thigh created by the cuff. Others who have severely arthritic hands or limited vision have difficulty engaging the buckle or pressure loop closure on the cuff.

The cuff may be augmented by a **fork strap** and *waist belt.* The elastic fork strap extends from the outside of the anterior portion of the socket to the waist belt. The fork strap and waist belt may be indicated for individuals

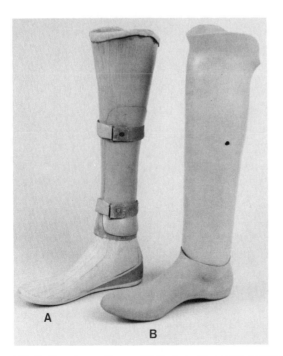

Figure 20–5. Syme's prostheses. (A) Socket with medial opening, (B) socket with continuous walls and flexible liner.

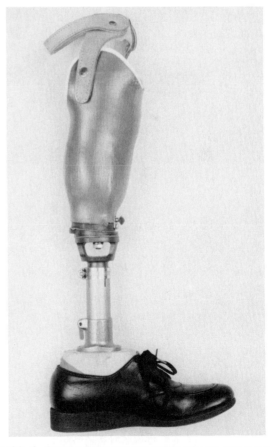

Figure 20–6. Below-knee temporary prosthesis with cuff suspension. Socket is mounted on an adjustable pylon shank with SACH foot.

who climb ladders or engage in other activities during which the prosthesis is unsupported by the ground for long periods. An alternate to the cuff is a rubber *sleeve,* a tubular component that covers the proximal socket and the distal thigh. The sleeve provides excellent suspension and a streamlined silhouette when the wearer sits. Donning the sleeve, however, requires two strong hands and a thigh that does not have excessive subcutaneous tissue.

Distal Attachment

Very secure suspension is achieved with the use of a silicone sheath and special hardware. The sheath clings to the patient's skin during the swing and stance phases of walking. At the end of the sheath is a small fixture. The user inserts a rod that passes through the shank just below the socket, continues through the fixture on the sheath, and terminates at the other side of the shank. During the swing phase, the rod prevents the prosthesis from slipping away from the sheath.

Brim Variants

The prosthesis may be suspended by its socket walls extended proximally.

Supracondylar suspension. With **supracondylar (SC)** suspension (Fig. 20–7), the medial and lateral walls extend above the femoral epicondyles. The medial wall has a plastic wedge, which the client removes to don the prosthesis; the wedge is then placed between the socket and the medial epicondyle to retain the pros-

thesis on the limb. Alternatively, the wedge can be incorporated in a liner; for donning, the patient applies the liner, then inserts the amputation limb, with liner, into the socket. Supracondylar suspension increases mediolateral stability of the prosthesis, presents a pleasing contour at the knee, and eliminates the need to engage a buckle or pressure loop on a cuff. It is more difficult to fabricate, hence more expensive, and not readily adjustable.

Supracondylar/suprapatellar suspension. Presenting a contour of medial and lateral walls similar to the supracondylar suspension, the **supracondylar/suprapatellar (SC/SP)** suspension (Fig. 20–8) also features an anterior wall, which terminates above the patella. The short amputation limb is accommodated by SC/SP suspension. The high anterior wall may interfere with kneeling and presents a conspicuous appearance when the wearer sits.

Thigh Corset

Some individuals with very sensitive skin on the amputation limb may benefit from thigh corset suspension (Fig. 20–9). Metal hinges attach distally to the medial and lateral aspects of the socket and proximally to a leather corset. Corset heights vary and may reach the ischial tuberosity for maximum weight relief on the amputated limb. The hinges increase frontal plane stability, and the corset leather increases area for load dis-

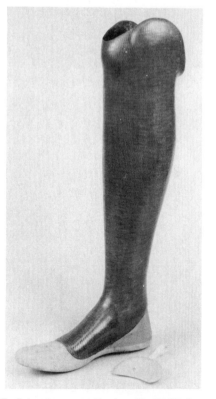

Figure 20–7. Below-knee prosthesis with SACH foot, exoskeletal shank, patellar-tendon-bearing socket, and supracondylar wedge suspension.

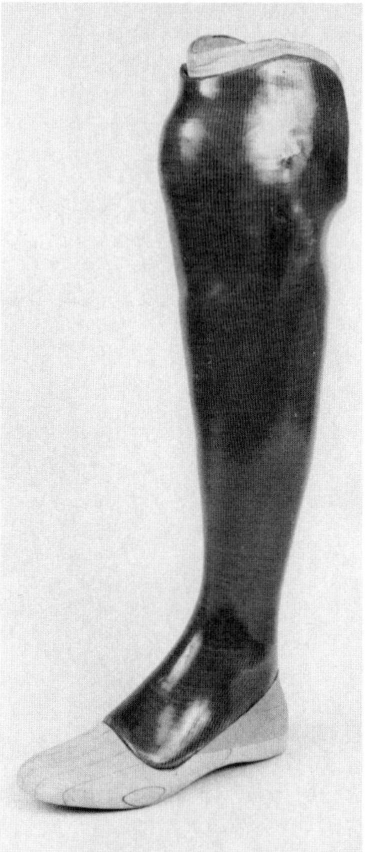

Figure 20–8. Below-knee prosthesis with supracondylar/suprapatellar suspension.

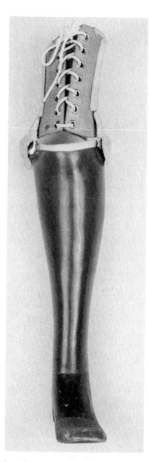

Figure 20–9. Below-knee prosthesis with thigh corset suspension.

tribution. The resulting prosthesis, however, is heavier and apt to foster **piston action** because the hinges have a single pivot joint that does not articulate colinearly with the anatomic knee. Prolonged use of a thigh corset causes pressure atrophy of the thigh. A corset suspension is more difficult to don because the wearer must fasten laces or series of pressure-loop straps.

Syme's suspension. The Syme's prosthesis is generally suspended by the contour of its brims and socket walls, without a cuff or other suspension mechanism.

Above-Knee Prostheses

Individuals with amputation between the femoral epicondyles and greater trochanter are fitted with above-knee (**transfemoral**) prostheses. Those whose limbs include the distal part of the femur can wear a knee disarticulation prosthesis, which differs from the above-knee prosthesis in the type of knee unit and socket. If the amputation is proximal to the trochanter, the patient cannot retain or control an above-knee prosthesis and is therefore a candidate for a hip disarticulation prosthesis. The above-knee prosthesis consists of (1) foot-ankle assembly, (2) shank, (3) knee unit, (4) socket, and (5) suspension device.

The SACH foot is most commonly used for above-knee prostheses. Because the single-axis foot reaches

the foot-flat position with minimal application of load, it is somewhat more frequently prescribed for above-knee than for below-knee prostheses. Any of the newer feet, such as the Seattle and Flex-Foot, can be incorporated in an above-knee prosthesis. As compared with wearers of below-knee prostheses, most people who use above-knee prostheses do not load the prosthesis as vigorously. Consequently, less energy can be stored and released in a prosthetic foot.

Either the sturdy exoskeletal shank or the endoskeletal shank may be used. The latter creates a pleasing appearance, particularly in the knee area, and is adjustable; in addition, it is lighter in weight than an exoskeletal shank. Problems of durability remain, particularly at the knee, where constant bending of the joint accelerates deterioration of the rubber cover.

KNEE UNIT

The prosthetic knee enables the user to bend the knee when sitting or kneeling and, in most instances, also permits knee flexion during the latter portion of the stance phase and throughout the swing phase of walking. Commercial knee units may be described according to four features: (1) **axis,** (2) **friction mechanism,** (3) **extension aid,** and (4) **mechanical stabilizer.** Many combinations of features are available; not every knee unit has all four components.[11]

Axis System

The thigh piece can be connected to the shank either by a simple **single-axis hinge** (Fig. 20–10), the usual arrangement, or by **polycentric linkage** (Fig. 20–11).

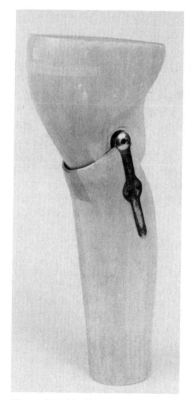

Figure 20–10. Single-axis knee unit.

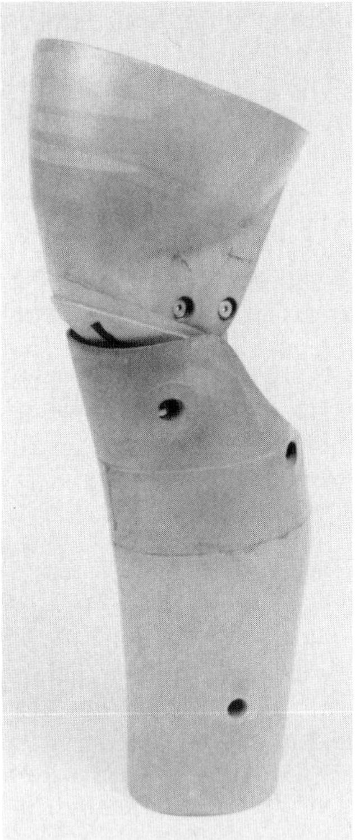

Figure 20–11. Polycentric knee unit.

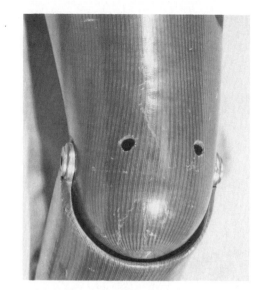

Figure 20–12. Single-axis, constant friction knee unit. Note the two screws that permit adjusting the friction.

Polycentric systems provide greater stability to the knee, inasmuch as the momentary center of knee rotation is posterior to the wearer's weight line during most of stance phase; this style is less common because of its greater complexity and because other means are available to stabilize the knee.

Friction Mechanism

In the simplest sense, the leg of the above-knee prosthesis is a pendulum swinging about the knee. For the elderly individual who walks slowly for short distances, a basic pendulum is adequate. For more energetic walkers, however, adjustable friction mechanisms that modify the pendular action of the knee are desirable to reduce the asymmetry between the motions of the sound and prosthetic legs. If the knee does not have sufficient friction to retard its natural pendular action, the individual who walks rapidly experiences *high heel rise* at the beginning of swing phase and *terminal impact* of the knee (abrupt, often noisy, extension) at the end of swing phase.

Friction mechanisms change the knee swing by modifying the speed of knee motion during various parts of swing phase and by affecting knee swing according to walking speed.

Time. The most popular knee unit has **constant friction** (Fig. 20–12), generally including a clamp that grasps the knee bolt. Throughout a given swing phase, the amount of friction is unvarying. It is easy to loosen or to tighten the clamp to change the ease of knee motion.

A more sophisticated device applies **variable friction,** in which the amount of friction changes during a given swing phase. At early swing, high friction is applied to retard heel rise; during midswing, friction diminishes to permit the knee to swing easily; at late swing, friction increases to dampen impact.

Medium. The medium through which friction is applied influences performance. The usual medium is **sliding friction,** such as when a clamp slides about the knee bolt. This method is simple, but it does not accommodate automatically to changes in walking speed. A more complex approach uses fluid, either oil (**hydraulic friction**)[12] (Fig. 20–13), or air (**pneumatic friction**). Unlike sliding friction, fluid friction varies directly with velocity. Thus with a hydraulic or pneumatic unit, if the wearer suddenly walks faster, the knee increases friction instantly, to prevent high heel rise and terminal impact. Consequently, the movements of the prosthetic and sound limbs are more symmetrical than would be the case with sliding friction.[13] Oil or air is contained in a cylinder in the knee unit. A piston descends in the cylinder during early swing, causing the knee to flex. The speed of piston descent depends on the type of fluid and the walking speed. Later, the piston ascends, extending the knee.

Hydraulic units provide more friction than do pneumatic devices. Both types are more expensive than the simpler sliding friction designs.

Various combinations of friction designs are manufactured, such as constant sliding friction, variable sliding friction, and variable fluid friction.

Extension Aid

Many knee units have a mechanism to assist knee extension during the latter part of swing phase. The simplest type is an external aid, consisting of elastic webbing located in front of the knee axis. The elastic stretches when the knee flexes in early swing and recoils to extend the knee in late swing. Webbing tension is easily adjusted, but tends to pull the knee into extension when the wearer sits. The internal extension aid is an elastic strap or coiled spring within the knee unit. It

Figure 20–13. Mauch Swing 'N Stance single-axis, hydraulic knee unit, which provides both brake and lock options depending on the position of the "U" shaped fixture at the back of the unit. The unit is attached to half a thigh-shank component to expose the knee bolt.

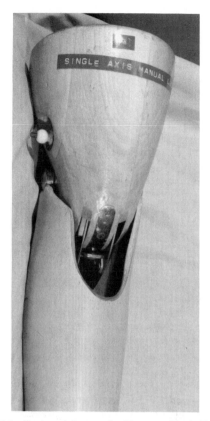

Figure 20–14. Single-axis knee unit with manual lock. Note the white knob that the wearer uses to disengage the lock.

functions identically to the external aid during walking, but, unlike the external aid, the internal type keeps the knee flexed when the individual sits. Acute knee flexion causes the strap or spring to pass behind the knee axis, maintaining the flexed attitude.

Stabilizers

Most knee units do not have a special device to increase stability. The patient controls knee action by hip motion, aided by the alignment of the knee in relation to other components of the prosthesis. The prosthetic knee joint is usually aligned posterior to a line extending from the trochanter to the ankle. Elderly or debilitated patients may benefit from additional mechanical security.

Manual lock. The simplest mechanical stabilizer is a manual lock (Fig. 20–14), in which a pin lodges in a receptacle and is released only when the wearer manipulates an unlocking lever. When engaged, the manual lock prevents knee flexion. The user is secure not only during early stance, but through the rest of the gait cycle when knee flexion would be desirable. To compensate for difficulty in advancing the locked prosthesis, the shank should be shortened approximately 1 cm (½ in). Another problem inherent with the manual lock is the need to disengage it when the wearer sits.

Friction brake. A more elaborate stabilizing system, the **friction brake** (Fig. 20–15) provides very high friction during early stance, resisting any tendency of the knee to flex. One design, incorporated in a sliding fric-

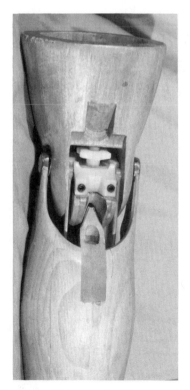

Figure 20–15. Single-axis knee unit with constant friction, internal spring extension aid, and brake.

tion unit, involves the mating of a wedge and groove upon loading, assuming the knee is flexed less than 25 degrees. Another version of friction brake is found in several hydraulic units; during early stance additional fluid resistance markedly retards piston descent and thus maintains the knee stable.

From midstance through heel contact, friction brakes do not interfere with knee motion. In addition, they do not impede the patient who transfers from standing to sitting. Such devices add to the cost of the prosthesis and, if improperly used, may not protect the patient from falling.

SOCKET

As is the case with all prosthetic sockets, the above-knee socket should be a *total contact* device to distribute load over the maximum area, thereby reducing pressure. Total contact fitting also provides counterpressure to assist venous return and prevent distal edema, and it enhances sensory feedback to foster better control of the prosthesis.

Most above-knee sockets are made of a combination of plastics. A *flexible socket* (Fig. 20–16) of thin polyethylene thermoplastic, encompasses the entire amputation limb.[14] The plastic can be spot-heated to facilitate alteration of socket fit. It adheres to the skin better than does rigid plastic, thereby improving suspension; it also dissipates body heat more effectively and affords the wearer sensory input from external objects, such as chairs. The socket is encased in a rigid frame so that the wearer may transmit weight through the distal components of the prosthesis to the ground.

Above-knee sockets are designed to emphasize loading on pressure-tolerant structures, such as the ischial tuberosity, gluteal musculature, sides of the thigh, and, to a lesser extent, distal end of the amputation limb. The socket must avoid pressure on the pubic symphysis and perineum.

Quadrilateral socket. The traditional above-knee socket is quadrilateral in shape when viewed from above (Fig. 20–17). The socket features a horizontal posterior shelf for the ischial tuberosity and gluteal musculature, a medial brim at the same level as the posterior shelf, an anterior wall 6 to 8 cm (2½ to 3 in) higher to apply a posteriorly directed force to the thigh to retain the tuberosity on its shelf, and a lateral wall the same height as the anterior wall to aid in mediolateral stabilization. Concave reliefs are (1) anteromedial for the pressure-sensitive adductor longus tendon, (2) posteromedial for the sensitive hamstring tendons and sciatic nerve, (3) posterolateral to permit the gluteus maximus to contract and to bulge without being crowded, and (4) anterolateral to allow adequate room for the rectus femoris. The anterior wall has a convexity, *Scarpa's bulge,* to maximize pressure distribution in the vicinity of the femoral triangle. The lateral wall may have reliefs for the greater trochanter and the distal end of the femur.

Ischial containment socket. A newer design (Fig. 20–18) is sometimes called *CAT-CAM* (contoured adducted trochanter-controlled alignment method) or *narrow M-L* (medio-lateral).[15,16] Its walls cover the ischial tuberosity and part of the ischiopubic ramus to augment socket stability. The mediolateral width of the socket is narrower than that of the quadrilateral socket to increase frontal plane stability and minimize bulk between the legs. The anterior wall is lower than in the quadrilateral socket, while the lateral wall covers the greater trochanter. Weight bearing occurs on the sides and bottom of the amputation limb.

Both the quadrilateral and the ischial containment

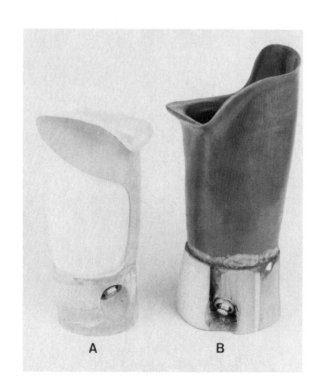

Figure 20–16. Quadrilateral total suction sockets: (A) flexible socket in rigid frame, (B) rigid polyester laminate socket.

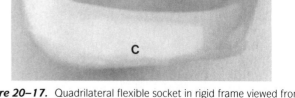

Figure 20–17. Quadrilateral flexible socket in rigid frame viewed from above: (A) anterior wall, (B) medial wall, (C) posterior wall, (D) lateral wall.

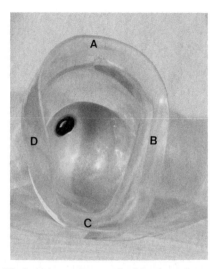

Figure 20–18. Ischial containment flexible above-knee socket. Note the relatively narrow mediolateral dimension. (*A*) Anterior brim, (*B*) medial brim, (*C*) posterior brim, (*D*) lateral brim.

socket can be made of a combination of flexible and rigid plastic, or entirely of rigid material.

Fit and alignment. Regardless of socket shape and materials, the socket should fit snugly to minimize the risk of chafing and to maximize the wearer's control of the prosthesis. Slight socket flexion is desirable for several reasons: (1) to facilitate contraction of the hip extensors, (2) to reduce lumbar lordosis, and (3) to provide a zone through which the thigh may be extended in order to permit the wearer to take steps of approximately equal length. For wearers of quadrilateral sockets, socket flexion also enhances positioning the ischial tuberosity on the posterior brim.

SUSPENSION

Three means are used to suspend the above-knee prosthesis: (1) total suction, (2) partial suction, and (3) no suction.

Suction Suspension

Suction refers to the pressure difference inside and outside the socket. With suction suspension, internal socket pressure is less than external pressure; consequently, atmospheric pressure causes the socket to remain on the thigh. The socket brim must fit snugly, and a one-way air release *valve* is located at the bottom of the socket.

Total suction. Maximum control of the prosthesis without any encumbering auxiliary suspension, can be achieved only if the socket fits very snugly to give total suction (Fig. 20–19); if the patient experiences changes in amputation limb volume, suction will be lost.

Partial suction. A socket that is slightly loose may enable partial suction suspension. The patient wears a sock. Because socket fit is looser, an auxiliary suspension aid is needed, either a fabric *Silesian bandage* (Fig. 20–20), or a rigid plastic or metal *hip joint and pelvic band* (Fig. 20–21). These aids encircle the pelvis. The Silesian bandage also controls the transverse plane orientation of the prosthesis on the thigh, while the hip joint restricts transverse and frontal motion at the hip. The pelvic band adds weight to the prosthesis and may impose uncomfortable pressure against the torso when the wearer sits.

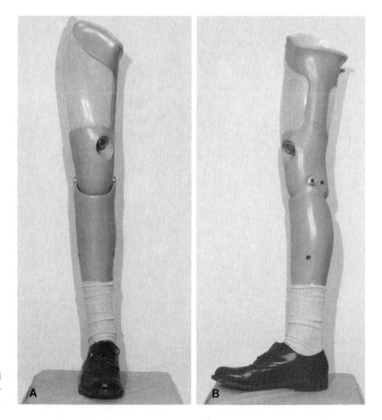

Figure 20–19. Above-knee prosthesis with SACH foot, exoskeletal shank, single-axis constant friction knee unit, and quadrilateral flexible socket with suction suspension. (*A*) Anterior view, (*B*) medial view.

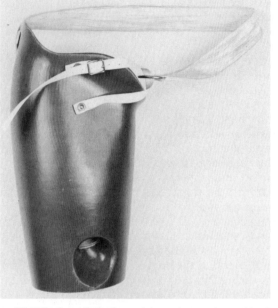

Figure 20–20. Quadrilateral partial suction socket with Silesian bandage.

No Suction

If the socket has a distal hole, but no valve, then pressure is the same as that outside (i.e., there is no difference in pressure). The client wears one or more socks and requires a pelvic band. The relatively loose socket makes donning easy but hinders control of the prosthesis and sitting comfort.

Disarticulation Prostheses

Individuals with knee or hip disarticulation wear prostheses that include the same distal components as prostheses for lower levels. Any prosthetic foot can be used and either an endoskeletal or exoskeletal shank. The major distinction, therefore, is in the proximal portion of the prostheses.

KNEE DISARTICULATION PROSTHESES

When amputation is at or distal to the femoral epicondyles, the patient should have excellent prosthetic control because (1) thigh leverage is at a maximum, (2) most of the body weight can be borne through the distal end of the femur, and (3) the broad epicondyles provide rotational stability. The problem presented by knee disarticulation is primarily cosmetic; when the individual sits, the thigh on the amputated side may protrude slightly. The knee disarticulation prosthesis (Fig. 20–22) has a streamlined knee that minimizes protrusion, as well as a specially designed socket.

Socket

Two types of socket are in current use. Both are made of plastic and usually terminate below the ischial tuberosity. Generally, no additional suspension aids are needed. One version features an anterior opening to

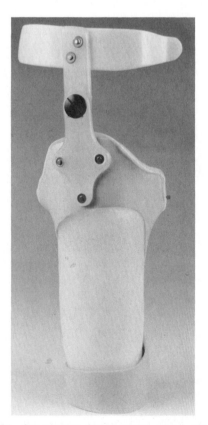

Figure 20–21. Quadrilateral partial suction socket with rigid plastic pelvic band attachment.

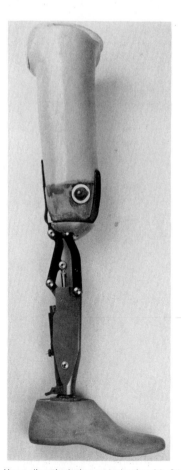

Figure 20–22. Knee disarticulation prosthesis with SACH foot, endoskeletal shank, polycentric hydraulic friction knee unit, and quadrilateral socket with suction suspension.

accommodate a bulbous amputation limb. After the limb is inserted the wearer closes the socket with lacing or pressure-loop tapes. The other design has no anterior opening and is suitable for limbs that are not bulbous.

Knee Unit

Several units are specially manufactured for knee disarticulation. All have a thin proximal attachment plate to minimize added thigh length. One may choose among hydraulic, pneumatic, and sliding friction units, with or without polycentric linkage. Even with a special knee unit, the thigh will be slightly longer. Consequently, the shank is shortened equivalently, so that when the person stands, the pelvis is level. When the individual sits, the thigh on the prosthetic side will project slightly.

HIP DISARTICULATION PROSTHESES

A hip disarticulation prosthesis (Fig. 20–23) is fitted to a person with amputation above the greater trochanter (*very short above-knee*), removal of the femoral head from the acetabulum (*hip disarticulation*), or removal of the femur and some portion of the pelvis (*hemipelvectomy*). Prostheses for proximal levels share common hip, knee, and foot assemblies and alignment, but differ with regard to socket design. The endoskeletal thigh and shank predominate because they afford appreciable weight saving in these massive prostheses.

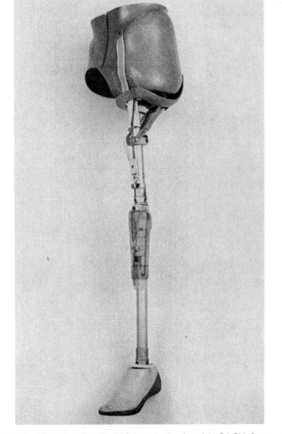

Figure 20–23. Hip disarticulation prosthesis with SACH foot, endoskeletal shank, single axis knee with extension aid, single axis hip with extension aid, and rigid socket.

Socket

The basic socket is plastic molded to provide weight bearing on the ipsilateral ischial tuberosity and both iliac crests. The person with a hemipelvectomy who does not retain the ipsilateral tuberosity or crest has a socket with a higher proximal trimline, sometimes encompassing the lower thorax. This individual supports weight on the remainder of the pelvis, on the abdomen, and perhaps on the lower ribs.

Hip Unit

Various joints provide hip flexion. They have an extension aid to bias the prosthesis toward the stable neutral position. Positioning the mechanical hip anterior to a point corresponding to the anatomic hip also contributes to hip stability. The joint is below the normal hip, so that with sitting, the prosthetic thigh will not protrude unattractively.

Stability

Several attributes combine to make the hip disarticulation prosthesis very stable, namely, the hip extension aid, anterior placement of the hip joint, posterior placement of the knee unit, and a knee extension aid. The prosthesis may be shortened slightly, primarily to aid clearance during swing phase, but also to encourage the wearer to apply maximum weight to the prosthesis and to increase stability.

Socks and Sheaths

All individuals with lower-limb amputations, except those wearing above-knee prostheses suspended by total suction or those using a sheath, require a supply of clean socks of appropriate material, size, and shape. It is expeditious to include an order of at least a dozen socks at the time the prosthesis is ordered, so that third party payment may cover this relatively inexpensive but important accessory.

Fabric socks are woven in various thicknesses, referred to as *ply,* designating the number of threads knitted together. *Cotton* socks absorb perspiration readily and are the least allergenic; they are made in two-, three-, and five-ply, the last being the thickest. *Wool* socks provide good cushioning, woven in three- five, and six-ply; they are expensive and must be laundered carefully. *Orlon/Lycra* socks are manufactured in two- and three-ply thickness. They can be washed easily without shrinking. This synthetic fabric combination affords considerable resilience, but does not absorb much perspiration.

A *nylon sheath* creates a smooth surface over the skin, thereby reducing the risk of chafing, especially in hot weather and among those with much scarring. Some below-knee prosthesis wearers are able to use a woman's knee-high nylon stocking if the amputation limb is slender. Because nylon does not absorb perspiration, liquid passes through the weave to be absorbed by an outer sock of cotton, wool, or Orlon/Lycra.

Silicone, urethane, and other synthetic sheaths provide excellent shock absorption and abrasion resistance; they also can aid in suspending the socket on the patient's limb, and are designed to be worn next to the skin. They are, however, more expensive than fabric socks or sheaths.

Regardless of material, the shape of the sock or sheath is important for comfort. An interface of proper size fits smoothly without wrinkling or undue stretching. The sock or sheath should be long enough to terminate above the most proximal part of the socket or thigh corset.

It is common practice to add more socks as the amputated limb shrinks. Nevertheless, when the patient requires a total of 15 ply of socks to achieve snug fit, the socket should be altered or replaced by the prosthetist. Excessive sock padding distorts the weight-bearing characteristics of the socket, losing the effect of strategically placed build-ups and reliefs.

Prosthetic Maintenance

Optimal function depends on proper care of socks or sheaths, prosthesis, amputation limb, and intact limb, as well as general health maintenance. Guidelines for personal hygiene are presented in the preceding chapter. In addition to ensuring cleanliness, the individual should wear a well-fitting sock and shoe on the sound foot, the mate to the shoe on the prosthesis. Both shoes should be in excellent condition.

As with any appliance, the prosthesis benefits from simple regular maintenance, which generally avoids costly, time-consuming repairs. Printed instructions pertaining to prosthesis and socks or sheath are helpful for patient education.

SOCKET AND SUSPENSION

Plastic sockets should be washed with a cloth dampened in warm water that has a very small amount of mild soap dissolved in it. The socket is then wiped with a damp, soap-free cloth and dried with a fresh towel. In warm climates, the socket should be washed every evening so that it will be completely dry when the patient dresses the following morning.

The above-knee suction valve should be brushed daily to remove talcum and lint which might clog the tiny aperture. The valve should be inserted and removed only with one's fingers, for tools are apt to damage the internal mechanism or outer threads.

Leather corsets should be kept dry. Use of saddle soap will keep leather clean. If the patient is incontinent, the thigh corset should be made of flexible polyester laminate or polypropylene, which is impervious to urine.

Socket liners made of polyethylene foam can be washed by hand in tepid water with mild soap, rinsed, and air-dried overnight. They should not be subjected to direct sunlight when removed from the prosthesis.

KNEE UNIT

Sliding friction mechanisms tend to loosen with walking and thus require periodic tightening to retain the original adjustment. The frequency of tightening depends on how much the wearer walks. Most units have a pair of screws in front or in the rear of the knee

unit that can be turned clockwise with an Allen wrench or common screwdriver. After turning each screw a quarter turn, the client should walk for at least 5 minutes to ascertain the effectiveness of the adjustment.

Squeaking at the knee or articulated ankle indicates the need for oil.

The rubber or felt extension bumper in the knee unit will erode after prolonged vigorous use, and the wearer will then notice that the knee begins to hyperextend. The bumper, visible when the knee is flexed, must be replaced by the prosthetist.

The external kick strap extension aid gradually loses its elasticity. The user will then experience high heel rise in early swing and slow knee extension at the end of swing phase. The simplest approach is to tighten the strap through its buckle. Eventually, the prosthetist will need to replace the elastic webbing. Internal elastic extension aids are not subject to rubbing from the trouser leg or skirt and thus do not lose elasticity as readily. Steel spring internal aids retain their effectiveness for the life of the prosthesis.

Pneumatic and hydraulic units must be protected against tears of the rubber shield protecting the piston. The piston must not be scratched, for this would allow air and debris to enter the cylinder. Air bubbles in the unit will cause a spongy feeling, and possibly noise, with walking. At night, the prosthesis should be stored upright, with the knee extended to exclude air from the cylinder.

FOOT-ANKLE ASSEMBLY

One should avoid getting the prosthetic foot wet, especially if the foot is an articulated model. If this happens, the shoe and sock should be removed to allow the foot to dry completely, away from direct heat. The wearer should also avoid stepping into sand and similar materials that might enter the cleft between the foot and shank section and restrict the excursion of the foot. The prosthetist would have to disassemble the foot to clean it.

The client should inspect the foot periodically to spot cracking at the toe-break or tip of the keel; such a crack will curl the toes and prevent smooth transition during late stance. A deteriorated heel cushion or plantar bumper will cause one to appear to be walking in a hole.

Although most feet are now molded to simulate toes, the patient should not walk barefooted because the sole of the prosthetic foot is not intended to resist much abrasion.

Socks wear much more quickly on the prosthetic side, because the hard foot assembly and shank rub against the fabric. Stair risers also scuff the sock. Some people find that wearing two socks helps cushion the outer one against premature formation of holes.

The individual must be instructed regarding wearing shoes of the same heel height as was the case when the prosthesis was aligned. Too low a heel interrupts late stance; an unduly high heel makes the knee less stable. If the prosthesis has the usual foot designed for low-heeled shoes, and the wearer wishes to wear flat-heeled shoes, a 1 cm (½ in) shim should be placed inside both shoes at the heel. High-heeled shoes require that the foot be changed, either by unbolting it and replacing it with a foot with an appropriate plantarflexion angle, or by adjusting a heel-height screw found in certain models of feet. Boots and other footwear with stiff upper sections restrict the action of any foot assembly that is designed to provide substantial dorsiflexion and plantarflexion.

Removing the shoe is easier if the prosthesis is not worn. With the shoe unlaced completely, one grasps the counter, then pushes the heel of the shoe off the back of the foot. Finally, pull the shoe upward off the forefoot. The shoe should be put on the prosthetic foot with the aid of a shoehorn.

EXTERIOR FINISH

The usual finish of exoskeletal shanks is polyester laminate, which is impervious to most liquids. It needs only to be wiped periodically with a cloth dampened with dilute detergent to remove surface soil. Marks can be scoured gently with kitchen cleanser; excessive abrasion will dull the finish.

The soft foam cover of the endoskeletal prosthesis requires reasonable caution against exposure to direct heat, penetrating objects, and solvents. The outer covering will need replacement whenever it becomes unacceptably soiled or torn. The above-knee version tends to deteriorate at the knee, especially if the wearer kneels a great deal.

PHYSICAL THERAPY MANAGEMENT

Physical therapists participate in the management of patients with amputation at several key stages: (1) preoperative, (2) postoperative-preprosthetic, (3) prosthetic prescription, (4) prosthetic assessment, and (5) prosthetic training.

The first two stages are described in the preceding chapter. The following discussion emphasizes the responsibilities of the physical therapist with regard to the patient and prosthesis. Ideally, the therapist works as a member of a **clinic team,** together with the physician and prosthetist. Others, such as a social worker, vocational counselor, and psychologist, may participate in the team on a regular basis or as needed. The clinic team provides the best environment for exchange of information and viewpoints regarding the patient and fosters efficient treatment. The team meets to formulate the prospective prescription, to assess the newly delivered prosthesis, and to reassess the patient and prosthesis upon completion of prosthetic training. The therapist, therefore, has an integral part to play in these critical points in rehabilitation, as well as conducting prosthetic training. If a formal clinic team is not established in the therapist's work setting, then one must coordinate the recommendations of the physician and prosthetist.

With either administrative situation, the physical therapist:

1. Performs preprescription assessment
2. Contributes to prosthetic prescription
3. Assesses the prosthesis
4. Facilitates prosthetic acceptance
5. Trains the patient to don, use, and maintain the prosthesis

Preprescription Assessment

Successful prosthetic rehabilitation depends on matching the individual's physical and psychosocial characteristics to a prosthesis composed of carefully selected components.

PHYSICAL EXAMINATION

The physical therapist should measure and record the patient's physical attributes, such as active and passive range of motion of all lower-limb joints on both lower extremities. Knee and hip flexion contractures compromise prosthetic alignment and appearance. A knee lock may be needed in an above-knee prosthesis, and an alternative socket design for a below-knee prosthesis. Severe contractures preclude fitting with conventional components, or may contraindicate provision of any prosthesis. The deleterious effects of contractures are especially serious with bilateral amputations.

Amputation limb length is measured. The individual with a short below-knee amputation may require SC/SP suspension. Every attempt should be made to fit the patient with a short above-knee amputation with suction or partial suction suspension to retain the prosthesis on the thigh.

Muscle strength of all limbs and trunk should be evaluated. Frequently, the elderly patient with vascular disease experiences reduced physical activity as leg pains and foot ulceration develop. Such an individual may present marked debility, which would interfere with prosthetic use or necessitate use of a locking-knee unit.

The therapist should inspect the skin, noting any lesions. The patient may require a nylon or silicone sheath to provide a smooth interface between socket and skin to avoid irritating tender or grafted skin.

Sensory function is another factor requiring assessment. For example, an individual with impaired proprioception at the knee will need extra prosthetic stability in the form of higher medial and lateral walls, or side joints attached to a thigh corset, on the below-knee prosthesis. Blindness does not preclude fitting but poses problems with regard to selecting components that are easy to don, as well as altering the training program. If the patient complains of a neuroma, the problem must be addressed surgically or conservatively before fitting can proceed.

Physical therapists assess the ability of patients to learn and retain new information, as well as short- and long-term memory. If the individual displays significant changes associated with organic brain syndrome, then prosthetic fitting is contraindicated.

Other neurologic changes, such as cerebrovascular accident, complicate fitting and training. Ipsilateral hemiplegia is not as detrimental to prosthetic rehabilitation as contralateral paralysis. In both instances, the prosthesis should be designed for maximum stability.

The circulatory status of the amputation and sound

limbs requires scrutiny. Sequential measurements of amputation limb circumference, as well as palpation, will indicate whether the patient has edema. Measures should be instituted to stabilize limb volume so that the patient can retain the fit of the prosthetic socket. The dysvascular patient may benefit from prosthetic fitting, which transfers some stress from the contralateral limb. In addition, should the person come to bilateral amputation, previous experience with donning and controlling a unilateral prosthesis is invaluable in adjusting to a pair of prostheses.

Prosthetic prescription also hinges on the patient's cardiopulmonary condition. The clinic team must formulate a realistic goal based on the individual's physical capacity, particularly as related to exercise tolerance and endurance. The person who is not expected to walk rapidly is an unlikely candidate for an energy-storing/releasing foot or a fluid-controlled knee unit. Nevertheless, a fluid-controlled knee unit that incorporates a braking mechanism is appropriate for selected feeble patients. Severe cardiac disease contraindicates prosthetic fitting.

Obesity is another factor to be considered in the preprescription assessment. The obese individual is more apt to fluctuate in body weight, necessitating provision of socket liners and several socks to compensate for changing limb circumference. Similarly, those who have renal disease, especially if requiring dialysis, experience volume changes that need prosthetic accommodation.

Arthritis affects prosthesis prescription. Diminished lower-limb mobility or deformity compromises prosthetic alignment. Patients with hip or knee arthroplasty, however, function quite well in the prosthesis. Hand and wrist stiffness and malalignment affect the mode of donning; a laced corset should be avoided. Canes and crutches may require modification.

One of the most useful assessment procedures involves observing the patient's ability to transfer from bed to wheelchair. To accomplish this maneuver, the individual must have reasonable strength, balance, and coordination, as well as adequate comprehension.

PSYCHOSOCIAL ASSESSMENT

The physical therapist ordinarily treats the patient more frequently than any other member of the clinic team and so is more likely to be attuned to the individual's attitudes. The patient and family who are excessively fearful will be served best by prosthetic rehabilitation beginning with a **temporary prosthesis.** Motivation is a cardinal determinant of prosthetic outcome. Again, strong motivation demonstrated through use of a temporary prosthesis and compliance with other elements of the rehabilitation program are reliable predictors of prosthetic success. One should guard against unrealistic expectations. Involving the patient and family in group situations with other persons with amputation, in the physical therapy department and in social environments, fosters constructive attitudes.

The therapist should also weigh the likelihood that the individual will be able to care for complex mechanisms and have the financial resources to obtain pros-

thetic servicing, especially of components, such as the foam rubber covering of the endoskeletal shank, that are less durable.

Prosthetic Prescription

Because no prosthetic component is ideal for all clients, it is necessary to select components that are most apt to meet the individual's needs. Alternatives for every element of the prosthesis have advantages and disadvantages. The task of the physical therapist, in conjunction with other team members, is to judge the relative merits of various feet, shanks, and other components in light of objective and subjective information pertaining to the prosthetic candidate.

Some people can be expected to function best with a sophisticated prosthesis that enhances the wearer's ability to engage in vigorous walking and athletics. Others are best served by a simple, inexpensive device. The most accurate predictor of future function is the patient's performance with a previous prosthesis. For the wearer who seeks a replacement prosthesis, the clinic team should consider the extent of use of the previous limb, together with any changes in the patient's physique and life-style. For example, if the person fitted with one prosthesis now returns with bilateral amputation, never having used the original prosthesis, that patient is a very poor candidate for bilateral prosthetic fitting. In contrast, another person who had been fitted with a simple above-knee prosthesis expresses the wish to participate in sports. By demonstrating good use of the original prosthesis, that individual is likely to derive considerable benefit from a new prosthesis with a fluid-controlled knee unit and an energy-storing/releasing foot.

Prescription for the new patient is more difficult. Depending on the interval between amputation surgery and prescription, the amputation limb may not have stabilized in volume; the patient may not have achieved the maximum benefit from the preprosthetic program. The best criterion for prosthetic prescription in such an instance is performance with a *temporary (provisional) prosthesis.* This appliance includes a well-fitting socket, suitable suspension, pylon, and foot; and, with the above-knee model, it usually has a knee unit. The temporary prosthesis also serves for preliminary gait and activities training. The major difference between the temporary and *definitive (permanent) prosthesis* is appearance. The temporary socket is designed for easy alteration to accommodate change in amputation limb volume. Ordinarily, little attention is paid to the color and shape of the temporary prosthesis.

BELOW-KNEE TEMPORARY PROSTHESIS

Most below-knee temporary prostheses have a plaster socket molded to the amputated limb. Plaster is inexpensive, readily available, and easy to use. The resulting socket, however, is rather heavy and bulky. Alternatively, sockets can be made of thermoplastic material which becomes malleable at temperatures low enough to permit forming directly on the patient. One can also obtain mass-produced adjustable sockets; it is necessary to pad the socket bottom so that the amputation limb does not develop distal edema. Suspension is usually by a cuff or thigh corset. The pylon can be an aluminum component manufactured for this purpose; such a pylon has a proximal fixture permitting small changes in prosthetic alignment. A simpler pylon can be made with polyvinylchloride piping, such as used for plumbing. The pipe is lightweight and can be spot-heated to enable slight alteration in alignment. A SACH foot is customary on temporary prostheses.

ABOVE-KNEE TEMPORARY PROSTHESIS

The easiest approach is to use a prefabricated polypropylene socket (Fig. 20–24), which is manufactured in several sizes and has straps for circumferential adjustment. The socket can be suspended with a Silesian bandage or pelvic band, and is mounted on a knee unit, which may include a manual lock. Alternatively, a custom-fabricated socket of plaster or low-temperature thermoplastic can be used. Some individuals with bilateral above-knee amputations use a pair of *stubbies*. These are nonarticulated prostheses; the sockets are mounted on short platforms, drastically reducing the wearer's height in order to increase balance stability.

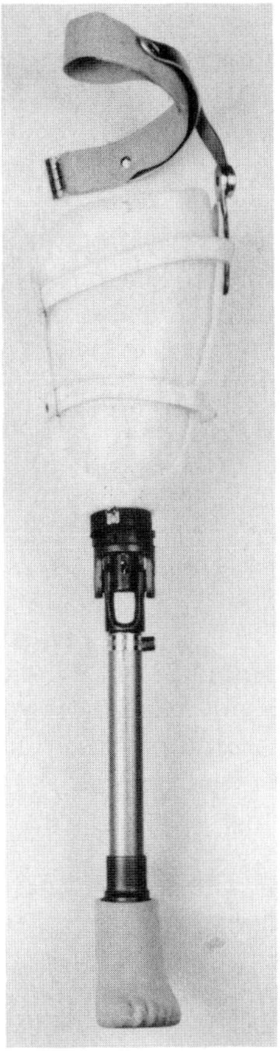

Figure 20–24. Above-knee temporary prosthesis with adjustable polypropylene socket, pelvic band, and adjustable pylon shank with SACH foot.

The platforms each have a rearward projection to protect the patient from a backward fall.

Prosthetic Assessment

The prosthesis should be assessed before the patient engages in prosthetic training and should be reassessed at the conclusion of training. The procedure is intended to determine the adequacy of prosthetic fit and function, as well as the wearer's opinion of appearance and overall satisfaction.

In many institutions, the physical therapist assesses the prosthesis and presents a summary of findings to the clinic team. The team makes the final determination regarding the acceptability of the prosthesis. At initial evaluation, the team has three options: (1) pass, (2) provisional pass, and (3) fail. Pass indicates that no changes are needed in the prosthesis and the patient can proceed to training. Provisional pass signals that one or more minor problems require correction, none of which would interfere with training. Failure is the team's judgment that the prosthesis has a major fault that should be corrected to the team's satisfaction prior to commencement of prosthetic training. For example, poor finishing of the prosthetic foot merits a provisional pass, whereas a socket that abrades the amputated limb should be graded as fail.

If the therapist intends to train a patient who is not managed by a formal clinic team, it is especially critical that one evaluate the prosthesis prior to initiating training to discover any problems that would negate the future program.

At the final evaluation, two ratings are available: pass indicates that no problems exist and the patient uses the prosthesis in a manner commensurate with that individual's physical capacity; fail means that major or minor problems remain.

No special materials are needed to assess the prosthesis, except for a checklist and a straight chair. For final evaluation, stairs and a ramp are needed. Appendices A and B contain the checklists referred to in the following sections.

BELOW-KNEE EVALUATION

Most items on the checklist in Appendix A are self-explanatory. Each contributes to forming an accurate judgment of the adequacy of the prosthesis.

Static Assessment

The prosthesis is assessed while the wearer stands and sits. In addition, the amputation limb and details of the prosthesis are examined. The prosthesis should be compared with the prescription. Departures from the original specifications must be approved by the individual who authorized the prescription.

The new wearer should stand in the parallel bars or other secure environment, attempting to bear equal weight on both feet. The therapist should solicit subjective comments about comfort. Estimates of anteroposterior and mediolateral alignment are aided by slipping a sheet of paper under various parts of the shoe. Ideally, the patient should stand with both heels and soles flat on the floor. Malalignment, indicated by excessive bearing on one portion of the shoe, may be confirmed by subsequent analysis of gait.

Most prostheses are constructed so that when the individual stands, the pelvis is level. If the pelvis tilts, the therapist should place lifts under the foot on the shorter side to restore a level pelvis. If the total lift measures 1 cm (½ in) or less, no attention is needed. For greater discrepancy, one should seek causative factors. An amputation limb that sinks too far into the socket will make the prosthetic side appear short, and the wearer will probably complain of discomfort.

Piston action refers to vertical motion of the socket when the patient elevates the pelvis. It is evident during gait as an up-and-down movement of the socket on the limb. Socket slippage is caused by looseness or inadequate suspension, or both. Socket walls should fit snugly, as should the thigh corset if it is part of the prosthesis.

Comfortable sitting is a primary need for all people. The posterior brim should not impinge into the popliteal fossa, and hamstring reliefs should be adequate, especially on the medial side, where the semitendinosus and semimembranosus insert relatively distally. Placement of the tabs of the cuff or the joints of the corset also influences sitting comfort.

Dynamic Assessment

Appraisal of the gait pattern and performance of other ambulatory activities is important. The new wearer will have had brief experience walking in the prosthesis during the course of fabrication. While a smooth gait is unlikely on the day of initial evaluation, gross departure from the usual gait exhibited by others with below-knee prostheses should be noted and causes sought. Below-knee analysis focuses on action of the knee during stance phase. Both knees should flex in a controlled manner during early and late stance phase. Excessive flexion indicates that the socket is aligned too far anterior in relation to the foot, or is excessively flexed; this deviation may cause the patient to fall. If the knee flexes too much only during early stance, the cause may be a heel cushion that is too firm for that wearer. Conversely, insufficient knee flexion results from posterior displacement of the socket or inadequate socket tilting. When viewed in the frontal plane, the socket brim should maintain reasonable contact with the leg; excessive lateral thrust of the prosthetic brim suggests that the prosthetic foot has been positioned too far medially. Table 20-1 summarizes the prosthetic and anatomic causes of gait deviations.[17]

At the initial assessment, performance on stairs and inclines may be omitted because the patient has not had training in these activities.

Assessment with the Prosthesis off the Patient

After conducting the dynamic assessment, the therapist should examine the amputation limb for signs of proper loading. The posterior wall should be at the same level as the build-up for the patellar ligament when the

Table 20-1 BELOW-KNEE PROSTHETIC GAIT ANALYSIS

Deviation	Prosthetic Causes	Anatomic Causes
EARY STANCE		
1. Excessive knee flexion	High shoe heel Insufficient plantarflexion Stiff heel cushion Socket too far anterior Socket excessively flexed Cuff tabs too posterior	Flexion contracture Weak quadriceps
2. Insufficient knee flexion	Low shoe heel Excessive plantarflexion Soft heel cushion Socket too far posterior Socket insufficiently flexed	Extensor hyperreflexia Weak quadriceps Anterodistal pain Arthritis
MID STANCE		
1. Excessive lateral thrust	Excessive foot inset	
2. Medial thrust	Foot outset	
LATE STANCE		
1. Early knee flexion: drop off	High shoe heel Insufficient plantarflexion Keel too short Dorsiflexion stop too soft Socket too far anterior Socket excessively flexed Cuff tabs too posterior	Flexion contracture
2. Delayed knee flexion: walking uphill	Low shoe heel Excessive plantarflexion Keel too long Dorsiflexion stop too stiff Socket too far posterior Socket insufficiently flexed	Extensor hyperreflexia

patient stands. Because one cannot ascertain this relationship when the prosthesis is being worn, a substitute check is performed. Stand the prosthesis on a table; place the end of a long pencil or ruler on the anterior socket bulge and rest the ruler on the posterior brim. In a well-constructed prosthesis, the ruler will slant upward toward the rear, indicating that when the individual stands in the prosthesis and compresses the heel cushion, the wall will be at the proper height.

Any straps or cuff should provide reasonable adjustability. Construction is a guide to future durability, as well as contributing to acceptable appearance of the prosthesis.

ABOVE-KNEE EVALUATION

A similar checklist is used to assess the above-knee prosthesis (Appendix B). It is most important to recognize that seldom is one item of major significance. The therapist and entire team should look for patterns that might herald future difficulty. For example, malalignment detected in static analysis should be confirmed during gait.

Static Assessment

The client who has a flesh roll above the socket either did not don the socket properly or has a thigh that is larger than that for which the socket was made. Perineal pressure results from sharpness of the medial brim or insufficiency of the adductor longus relief in a quadrilateral socket.

The knee unit should be stable enough to withstand a blow delivered by the therapist to the posterior aspect of the unit. Stability is influenced by the alignment of the knee in relation to the hip and prosthetic ankle. The farther posterior the knee bolt, the more stable will be the knee. Polycentric linkage and mechanical stabilizers also contribute to stability.

If the socket is opaque, the only way to judge its snugness is by palpating tissue protruding through the valve hole when the valve is removed.

The checklist is designed to aid the clinician in assessing the fit of the socket, regardless of shape or material. If the prosthesis has a quadrilateral socket, proper location of the adductor longus tendon and ischial tuberosity ensures that the patient has donned the socket correctly. A horizontal posterior brim allows weight to be borne on the gluteal musculature as well as the ischial tuberosity.

The ischial containment socket is intended to cover the ischial tuberosity, yet allow the client to move the hip in all directions comfortably, without socket gapping.

The lateral attachment of the Silesian bandage should be superior and posterior to the greater trochanter for best control of prosthetic rotation. Anteriorly, the attachment should be at the level of the ischial seat, or slightly below, to aid in adducting the prosthesis.

The pelvic joint and band should fit the torso snugly for optimum control of the prosthesis and to minimize bulkiness.

The patient should be able to sit comfortably with the prosthesis. Posterior discomfort may indicate inadequate hamstring relief, or a sharp or thick posterior brim.

Dynamic Assessment

Gait analysis gives the clinic team members the opportunity to assess the adequacy of socket fit, and of prosthesis alignment and adjustment. The patient also influences the walking pattern by the timing and force of muscular contraction and the presence or absence of contractures. The goal of walking with an above-knee prosthesis is a comfortable, safe, efficient gait, rather than duplicating the gait of someone wearing a below-knee prosthesis or who does not have amputation. Table 20–2 summarizes above-knee prosthetic gait deviations.[18,19]

Deviations best viewed from behind. Many indi-

Table 20–2 ABOVE-KNEE PROSTHETIC GAIT ANALYSIS

Deviation	Prosthetic Causes	Anatomic Causes
LATERAL DISPLACEMENTS		
1. Abduction: stance	Long prosthesis	Abduction contracture
	Abducted hip joint	Weak abductors
	Inadequate lateral wall adduction	Laterodistal pain
	Sharp or high medial wall	Adductor redundancy
		Instability
2. Circumduction: swing	Long prosthesis	Abduction contracture
	Locked knee unit	Poor knee control
	Loose friction	
	Inadequate suspension	
	Small socket	
	Loose socket	
	Foot plantarflexed	
TRUNK SHIFTS		
1. Lateral bend: stance	Short prosthesis	Abduction contracture
	Inadequate lateral wall adduction	Weak abductors
	Sharp or high medial wall	Hip pain
		Instability
		Short amputation limb
2. Forward flexion: stance	Unstable knee unit	Instability
	Short walker or crutches	
3. Lordosis: stance	Inadequate socket flexion	Hip flexion: contracture
		Weak extensors
ROTATIONS		
1. Medial (lateral) whip: heel off	Faulty socket contour	With sliding friction unit; fast pace
	Knee bolt externally (internally) rotated	
	Foot malrotated	
	Prosthesis donned in malrotation	
2. Foot rotation at heel contact	Stiff heel cushion	
	Malrotated foot	
EXCESSIVE KNEE MOTION		
1. High heel rise: early swing	Inadequate friction	
	Slack extension aid	
2. Terminal impact: late swing	Inadequate friction	Forceful hip flexion
	Taut extension aid	
REDUCED KNEE MOTION		
1. Vault: swing	See above: circumduction	With sliding friction unit; fast pace
2. Hip hike: swing	See above: circumduction	
UNEVEN STEP LENGTH	Uncomfortable socket	Hip flexion contracture
	Insufficient socket flexion	Instability

viduals with above-knee amputation abduct the prosthesis to improve frontal plane balance. Hip abduction contracture predisposes to this deviation, which is seen in stance phase. Inadequate socket adduction, socket looseness, or medial discomfort causes the fault. *Circumduction* is a displacement exhibited in swing phase if the prosthesis is too long or if the patient is reluctant to allow the knee to bend. Socket looseness also may result in circumduction. The patient may shift the trunk excessively. Lateral trunk bending toward the prosthetic side during stance phase generally accompanies abducted gait. It should be noted, however, that all individuals with above-knee amputation have an incomplete abductor mechanism, and tend to compensate by bending toward the prosthetic side. Although the hip joint and gluteus medius are usually in good condition, lack of skeletal continuity to the ground compromises the effectiveness of abductor contraction. If the prosthesis is too long, the patient is apt to abduct; if it is too short, one will see lateral bending without abduction.

Whips refer to rotation of the heel at late stance. If the socket does not fit well, contraction with bulging of the thigh musculature will cause the prosthesis to rotate abruptly as it is being unloaded at the end of stance phase. Less likely, malrotation of the knee unit or foot-ankle assembly may contribute to whipping. Rotation of the foot on heel contact is a much more serious deviation. It indicates inadequate compression of the heel cushion or plantar bumper and can result in a fall.

Deviations best viewed from the side. Forward trunk shifting in stance phase is a compensation that some patients use to cope with knee instability. If the walker or crutches are too short, the individual will lean forward. Lumbar lordosis results from inadequate socket flexion and is aggravated by a hip flexion contracture.

Improper adjustment of the knee unit gives rise to uneven heel rise and terminal swing impact. If both deviations are present, the probable cause is insufficient friction. If the knee exhibits impact without undue heel rise, it is more likely that the extension aid is too tight.

To compensate for reduced knee motion, the vigorous walker may *vault,* excessively plantarflexing the sound ankle to afford extra room to clear the prosthesis during prosthetic swing phase. A less strenuous compensation for actual or functional prosthesis length is *hip hiking,* when the patient elevates the pelvis on the prosthetic side.

Step lengths will be unequal if the patient has a hip flexion contracture or inadequate balance; a longer step is taken with the prosthesis. The longer prosthetic step gives the person more time on the sound limb. A flexion contracture prevents the sound limb from passing the prosthetic side during swing phase on the sound side.

Assessment with the Prosthesis off the Patient

Following the static assessment, the therapist should examine the prosthesis and amputation limb as indicated on the checklist. A resilient back pad enables the patient to sit quietly without undue trouser or skirt abrasion. The pad is unnecessary with a flexible socket.

Facilitating Prosthetic Acceptance

Amputation generally is regarded as a grievous occurrence, with its visibility a constant reminder of the individual's abnormality. The physical therapist can assist the patient and family to accept the reality of amputation and the prosthesis by verbal and nonverbal communication. One's calm respect for the patient as a worthy human being, regardless of limb condition, should set a model for the attitudes of others. Clinic team management accords not only the benefits of better prosthetic provision but also brings the individual in contact with clinicians who convey experience and confidence in dealing with problems that the person may have considered unique.

As soon as possible, the hospitalized patient should be treated in the physical therapy department, rather than on the ward. The bustle of the department should help dispel despondency. Although postoperative mourning is expected, prolonged depression is not constructive. Peer support groups are often very effective in aiding acceptance of the prosthesis and in learning special procedures for accomplishing activities. Observation and eventual participation in sports programs for the physically challenged is another way people learn to cope and gain the most from rehabilitation.

The physical therapist, by virtue of close daily contact with the patient, is also in a position to recommend to the clinic those who might profit from psychologic counseling and psychiatric services.

Prosthetic Training

Learning to use a prosthesis effectively involves being able to don it correctly, to develop good balance and coordination, to walk in a safe and reasonably symmetrical manner, and to perform other ambulatory and self-care activities. Treatment goals depend on the patient's physical status, preprosthetic experience, and quality of prosthesis. Using the prosthesis only to assist in transferring from the wheelchair to the toilet may be an appropriate goal for an elderly, multidisabled person, whereas the program for the youngster with traumatic amputation might extend to a full range of sports.

DONNING

Correct application of the prosthesis and frequent inspection of the amputation limb are very important, especially for the beginner and those with poor circulation. Patients with partial foot, Syme's, and below-knee amputations can don the prosthesis while seated, after having applied the correct number and sequence of socks or sheath. Then, in most instances, the individual simply inserts the amputation limb into the socket. With SC/SP suspension, one applies the liner to the amputation limb, then inserts the limb and liner into the socket. The initial entry into the socket with corset suspension may be made while sitting; however, final tightening of laces or straps should be done in the standing position to ensure that the limb is lodged suitably in the socket.

Those with above-knee amputation also can begin the donning process while seated. Total suction wearers may use either a pulling or pushing method. To pull oneself into the socket, the patient applies a light dusting of talcum powder to the thigh to reduce friction. Then one applies a pulling sock, a tubular cotton stockinette approximately 76 cm (30 in) long, or a roll of elastic bandage wound around the thigh, or a nylon stocking. Whatever the donning aid, it should be placed high in the groin to pull in proximal tissues. After placing the sock-encased thigh into the socket, one draws the distal end of the aid through the valve hole. Although it is possible to complete the donning process while seated, most people prefer to stand while pulling the sock or other aid out through the valve hole. By leaning forward, the body's weight line will prevent the prosthetic knee from flexing inadvertently. The patient alternately flexes and extends the sound hip and knee while tugging downward on the donning aid until it slips from the prosthesis. Finally, one inserts the valve.

To push into the socket, one should coat the thigh with a lubricating lotion, push it into the socket, then install the valve. Patients who use partial suction apply a sock, making certain the proximal margin of the sock extends to the inguinal ligament. The patient then introduces the amputation limb into the socket, taking care that the thigh is correctly oriented; pulls the distal end of the sock down through the valve hole enough to ensure that the skin is smooth; tucks the sock back into the socket; and inserts the valve. Finally, one secures the pelvic band or Silesian bandage. If suction is not used, donning is similar to the method used with partial suction, except there is no valve.

BALANCE AND COORDINATION

Exercises are similar for all patients with lower-limb amputations, although the individual with an above-knee or hip disarticulation prosthesis may be expected to encounter more difficulty controlling the mechanical knee as compared with those who need only deal with two anatomic knees. All must learn to bear weight on the amputated side. A graduated program for increasing prosthetic tolerance minimizes the danger of skin abrasion, particularly if the amputation limb presents skin grafts, poor circulation, or diminished sensation. Exercise and rest should be alternated, with cardiopulmonary monitoring a routine part of the program, especially for high-risk individuals.[20]

Some clinicians eschew parallel bars because the fearful patient pulls on them, which will be fruitless when progressing to a cane. When bars are used, the therapist should encourage the patient to rest the open hand on the bar for support, rather than to use viselike grip. A plinth or sturdy table offers the dual advantages of providing good support on only one side, ordinarily the contralateral side, and unidirectional control, because the patient can only push, never pull, for balance.

Static erect balance reintroduces the novice to bipedal posture. The patient should strive for level pelvis and shoulders, vertical trunk without excessive lordosis, and equal weight bearing. The therapist should guard and assist the patient. Standing near the prosthesis encourages the patient to shift onto it. To suggest symmetrical performance, refer to the limbs as "right" and "left," or "sound" and "prosthetic," rather than discouraging the patient with "good" and "bad." The client must learn to exploit proximal sensory receptors to maintain balance and to perceive the position of the prosthesis without looking at the floor. Some patients respond well to use of a mirror for visual feedback.

Dynamic exercises improve mediolateral, sagittal, and rotary control. The patient learns that hip flexion causes the knee to bend, and hip extension stabilizes the knee during stance phase. Placing the sound foot ahead of the prosthesis makes the prosthetic knee more stable. Patients should be instructed in weight shifting in both symmetrical and stride positions and in stepping movements. Stepping on a low stool with the sound leg obliges the patient to shift weight onto the prosthesis and increases stance phase duration on the prosthesis.[21] Symmetrical performance is fostered by having all exercises performed rhythmically with both the right and left legs.

GAIT TRAINING

Walking is a natural progression from dynamic balance exercises, as the patient takes successive steps. Some patients respond well to viewing themselves on videotape;[22] the cassettes also form a valuable record of performance and progress. Videotapes are useful reinforcements of instruction for the patient who has a home rehabilitation program. Rhythmic counting and walking in time with music in 2/4 time are other ways of improving gait symmetry and speed.

A cane or pair of forearm crutches are appropriate aids for the client who is unable to achieve a safe gait without undue fatigue. Sometimes the cane is used only outdoors to aid in negotiating curbs and other ground irregularities and to signal oncoming traffic. Ordinarily the cane is used on the contralateral side to enhance frontal plane balance. If bilateral assistance is required, a pair of forearm crutches is preferable to two canes. The crutches remain clasped around the forearms when the user opens a door. Axillary crutches tempt the patient to lean on the axillary bars, risking impingement of the radial nerves; they are inconvenient when one climbs stairs. A walker often encourages the user to lean too far forward.

FUNCTIONAL ACTIVITIES

The prosthesis wearer who is learning to walk also should gain experience in performing other skills. Activities, such as transferring to various chairs, vary the program and, for some patients, may be more important than long-distance ambulation. The training program for vigorous individuals includes stair climbing, negotiating ramps, retrieving objects from the floor, kneeling, sitting on the floor, running, driving a car, and engaging in sports. The fundamental difference between these activities and walking is the way each leg is used. Walking implies symmetrical usage, but the other activities are done asymmetrically, with greater reliance on the strength, agility, and sensory control of the sound limb.

Generally the patient should have the opportunity to analyze a new situation, rather than depend on directions from the therapist. Most tasks can be accomplished safely in several ways. The learner profits from observing other prosthesis wearers as well as from professional instruction.

Transfers

Rising from different chairs, the toilet, and car are primary skills even for people who are elderly or debilitated. Most patients enter the physical therapy department in a wheelchair. Initially, the patient can park the chair at the parallel bars or at a plinth. After locking the wheelchair and raising the footrests, the patient should sit forward and transfer weight to the intact leg, then push down on the chair armrests. The individual will find that placing the sound foot close to the chair enables rising by extending the knee and hip on the sound side.

Sitting is accomplished by placing the sound foot close to the chair and lowering oneself by controlled hip and knee flexion on the sound side.

For both standing and sitting, the beginner should have the advantage of a chair with armrests that enable use of the hands to control and to assist trunk movement. Later the person should practice sitting in deep upholstered sofas and low chairs, as well as benches, the toilet, and other seats that do not have armrests. Transfer into an automobile should be an integral part of the training regimen; otherwise, the patient faces a gloomy future, confined to home or dependent on special transportation systems. To enter the right, passenger, side, the prosthetic wearer faces toward the front of the car. The person with a right prosthesis puts the right hand on the door post and the left hand on the back of the front seat, then swings the left leg into the car, slides onto the car seat, and finally places the prosthesis in the car. The individual with a left prosthesis may find that sitting sideways with both feet out the car door is easiest. One then pivots on the seat while swinging the prosthesis into the car, then puts the intact right foot inside the car.

Climbing

Patients with Syme's and below-knee amputations generally ascend and descend stairs and inclines with steps of equal length in step-over-step progression. Those with unilateral above-knee amputation, in contrast, ascend by leading with the sound foot and learn to descend by first placing the prosthesis on the lower step. A few with above-knee amputation subsequently learn to control prosthetic knee flexion in order to descend step-over-step.

Curbs present a slightly different problem, for there is no handrail. The techniques are basically the same, however. If the stairs, ramp, or curb are too steep, the individual may climb diagonally, or sidestep with the prosthesis kept on the downhill side.

FINAL EVALUATION AND FOLLOW-UP CARE

Economic strictures may compel the therapist to conclude the training program after the patient is able to walk and to negotiate basic transfers and climbing activities. Prior to discharge, the patient and prosthesis should be reassessed to make certain that socket fit, prosthetic appearance, and function are acceptable. The checklist used for initial evaluation can be used.

The new prosthesis wearer should return to the training site at regular intervals so that the clinic team may assess socket fit. Most will require major socket revision or replacement during the first year to accommodate shrinkage. Follow-up visits are good opportunities to augment training and to encourage the individual to engage in the widest possible range of activities.

Functional Capacities

Functional capacities refer to the individual's ability to walk, to transfer from chairs, to climb stairs, and to perform other ambulatory activities, including recreational endeavors. A primary responsibility of the clinic team is to predict the probable function of the person with a new amputation, in order to determine whether the individual would benefit from a prosthesis, and what degree of activity is likely.[23,24] Because many with lower-limb amputation are elderly with several medical problems, the need for accurate forecasting and ongoing monitoring is especially critical.

Walking with a prosthesis increases energy cost.[25] Compared with those people with two sound limbs, the individual with a unilateral below-knee prosthesis requires slightly more oxygen when walking at a comfortable speed; the person wearing an above-knee prosthesis consumes nearly 50 percent more oxygen than normal.[26] The prosthesis wearer chooses a comfortable pace, because at a speed that is natural for the individual, the energy cost per minute is similar to that of the person who does not require a prosthesis, although speed is slower. The lower the amputation level, the less the metabolic disadvantage. Among persons with below-knee amputations older than 40, those with long amputation limbs average minimal increase in energy, but persons with shorter limbs work harder. Those with bilateral below-knee amputations expend less energy than those with unilateral above-knee amputation. Individuals whose amputation was traumatic perform more efficiently than those whose amputation was caused by vascular disease, at every amputation level.[27-29] People who sustained trauma walk faster and use less oxygen than their dysvascular counterparts.

The metabolic toll results in part from the socket, which surrounds semifluid tissue, giving imperfect anchorage. The resulting pseudoarthrosis is more difficult to control than is an intact limb. The foot-ankle assembly transmits no plantar tactile or proprioceptive sensation, does not move through as large an excursion as the normal foot, and does not initiate the dynamic propulsion characteristic of normal gait. The above-knee prosthesis also incorporates a knee unit that provides no proprioception to the wearer. The problem is aggravated by the fact that a prosthesis is operated by remotely located muscles that contract longer and more forcefully than in normal gait. With above-knee amputation, for example, the prosthetic foot is placed by hip motion. The resulting alteration of motion is reflected in asymmetry of timing, further disturbing gait smoothness. Individuals with prostheses walk with greater vertical movement, inasmuch as the knee, whether prosthetic for the above-knee prosthesis wearer or anatomic in the below-knee wearer, does not flex as much as the contralateral knee during stance phase.

For many with amputation, function is not limited to walking. They participate in a wide array of sports, most of which require little or no prosthetic modification, for example, bowling, tennis, golf, and baseball. Sometimes minor adaptations are helpful; for example, bicycle toe clips enable the individual to lift the pedal as well as to push it. Other activities, such as swimming, are generally performed without a prosthesis. Ski programs are conducted at many resorts; most with unilateral amputation ski "three track"; that is, without a prosthesis but with small rudders on both ski poles. Acquainting the client with recreational clubs and with simple techniques for engaging in sports is a superb way of enhancing the person's functional capacity.

SUMMARY

This chapter has focused on management of people with lower-limb amputation. Characteristics and function of the principal lower-limb prostheses and prosthetic components have been discussed. In addition, the responsibilities of the physical therapist in prosthetic management have been emphasized.

Successful prosthetic rehabilitation depends on close collaboration among the patient, physical therapist, physician, prosthetist, and other team members. This will provide an environment for information exchange and will foster coordinated treatment. The result will be an optimum match between the patient's physical and psychosocial characteristics and a prosthesis capable of fulfilling its intended purposes.

QUESTIONS FOR REVIEW

1. What are the principal causes of amputation in the elderly? In the young?

2. Describe appropriate prostheses for individuals with various partial foot amputations.

3. Distinguish between the Syme's and the below-knee amputation limbs and prostheses.

4. What prosthetic feet are especially suitable for geriatric patients? Why?

5. Name the reliefs and build-ups in the below-knee socket.

6. Contrast the modes of suspension for the below-knee prosthesis. Which suspension is indicated for an individual with a short amputation limb?

7. Classify knee units according to friction mechanisms.

8. Compare the quadrilateral and the ischial containment above-knee sockets.

9. Describe the modes of suspension of an above-knee prosthesis. In which type(s) does the client wear a sock?

10. How is the wearer of a hip disarticulation prosthesis prevented from inadvertently flexing the hip and knee?

11. Outline a maintenance program for an above-knee prosthesis with hydraulic knee unit and endoskeletal shank.

12. What factors should be assessed prior to formulating a prosthetic prescription?

13. How can the physical therapist assess and improve the patient's psychologic status?

14. What features of the below-knee prosthesis are considered in static assessment? In dynamic assessment?

15. Delineate the training program for a patient with a new above-knee prosthesis.

REFERENCES

1. Stern, PH: The epidemiology of amputations. Phys Med Rehabil Clin North Am 2:253, 1991.
2. Edelstein, JE: Prosthetic feet: state of the art. Phys Ther 68:1874, 1986.
3. Campbell, JW and Childs, CW: The SAFE foot. Orthot Prosthet 34:3, 1980.
4. Burgess, E, et al: The Seattle prosthetic foot: a design for active sports. Orthot Prosthet 37:25, 1983.
5. Barth, DG, Schumacher, L, and Thomas, SS: Gait analysis and energy cost of below-knee amputees wearing six different prosthetic feet. J Prosthet Orthot 4:63, 1992.
6. Menard, MR, et al: Comparative biomechanical analysis of energy-storing prosthetic feet. Arch Phys Med Rehabil 73:451, 1992.
7. Torburn, L, et al: Below-knee amputee gait with dynamic elastic response prosthetic feet: a pilot study. J Rehabil Res Dev 27:369, 1990.
8. Racette, W and Breakey, JW: Clinical experience and functional considerations of axial rotators for the amputee. Orthot Prosthet 31:29, 1977.
9. Radcliffe, C: The biomechanics of below-knee prostheses in normal, level bipedal walking. Artif Limbs 6:16, 1962.
10. Veterans Administration: Variants of the PTB (patellar-tendon-bearing) below-knee prosthesis. Bull Prosthet Res 10–13:120, 1970.
11. Veterans Administration: Selection and application of knee mechanisms. Bull Prosthet Res 10–18:90, 1972.
12. Erback, JR: Hydraulic prostheses for above-knee amputees. J Am Phys Ther Assoc 43:105, 1963.
13. Murray, MP, et al: Gait patterns in above-knee amputee patients: hydraulic swing control vs constant friction knee components. Arch Phys Med Rehabil 64:339, 1983.
14. Kristinsson, O: Flexible above-knee socket made from a low density polyethylene suspended by a weight transmitting frame. Orthot Prosthet 37:25, 1983.

15. Pritham, CH: Biomechanics and shape of the above-knee socket considered in light of the ischial containment concept. Prosthet Orthot Int 14:9, 1990.

16. Gottschalk, FA, et al: Does socket configuration influence the position of the femur in above-knee amputation? J Prosthet Orthot 2:94, 1989.

17. Breakey, J: Gait of unilateral below-knee amputees. Orthot Prosthet 30:17, 1976.

18. Zuniga, EN, et al: Gait patterns in above-knee amputees. Arch Phys Med Rehabil 53:373, 1972.

19. Edelstein, JE: Prosthetic and orthotic gait. In Smidt, GL (ed): Gait in Rehabilitation. Churchill Livingstone, New York, 1990.

20. Adler, JC, et al: Treadmill training program for a bilateral below-knee amputee with cardiopulmonary disease. Arch Phys Med Rehabil 68:858, 1987.

21. Gailey, RS and McKenzie, A: Prosthetic Gait Training Program for Lower Extremity Amputees. University of Miami School of Medicine, Miami, 1989.

22. Netz, P, Wersen, K, and Wetterberg, M: Videotape recording: a complementary aid for the walking training of lower limb amputees. Prosthet Orthot Int 5:147, 1981.

23. Muecke, L, et al: Functional screening of lower-limb amputees: a role in predicting rehabilitation outcome? Arch Phys Med Rehabil 73:851, 1992.

24. Nissen, SJ and Newman, WP: Factors influencing reintegration to normal living after amputation. Arch Phys Med Rehabil 73:548, 1992.

25. Huang, C, et al: Amputation: energy cost of ambulation. Arch Phys Med Rehabil 60:18, 1979.

26. Gonzales, EG, Corcoran, PJ, and Reyes, RL: Energy expenditure in below-knee amputees: correlation with stump length. Arch Phys Med Rehabil 55:111, 1974.

27. Waters, RL and Perry, J: Energy expenditure of amputee gait. In Moore, WS and Malone, JM (eds): Lower Extremity Amputation. WB Saunders, Philadelphia, 1989.

28. Medhat, A, Huber, PM, and Medhat, MA: Factors that influence the level of activities in persons with lower extremity amputation. Rehabil Nurs 15:13–18, 1990.

29. Siriwardena, G and Bertrand, P: Factors influencing rehabilitation of arteriosclerotic lower limb amputees. J Rehabil Res Dev 28:35, 1991.

SUPPLEMENTAL READING

Banerjee, SN (ed): Rehabilitation Management of Amputees. Williams & Wilkins, Baltimore, 1982.

Bowker, JH and Michael, JW (eds): Atlas of Limb Prosthetics, ed 2. CV Mosby, St Louis, 1992.

Burgess, EM and Rappoport, A: Physical Fitness: A Guide for Individuals with Lower Limb Loss. Department of Veterans Affairs, Washington, DC, 1992.

Culham, EG, Peat, M, and Newell, E: Below-knee amputation: a comparison of the effect of the SACH foot and single axis foot on electromyographic patterns during locomotion. Prosthet Orthot Int 10:15, 1986.

Czerniecki, JM, Gitter, AG, and Munro, C: Joint moment and muscle power output characteristics of below knee amputees during running: the influence of energy storing prosthetic feet. J Biomechanics 20:529, 1991.

Davidoff, GN, et al: Exercise testing and training of persons with dysvascular amputation: safety and efficacy of arm ergometry. Arch Phys Med Rehabil 73:334, 1992.

Engstrom, B and Van de Van, C: Physiotherapy for Amputees: The Roehampton Approach. Churchill Livingstone, New York, 1985.

Ham, R and Cotton, L: Limb Amputation: From Aetiology to Rehabilitation. Chapman & Hall, London, 1991.

Karacoloff, LA, Hammersley, CS, and Schneider, FJ: Lower Extremity Amputation: A Guide to Functional Outcomes in Physical Therapy Management, ed 2. Aspen, Gaithersburg, MD, 1992.

Kawamura, I and Kawamura, J: Some biomechanical evaluations of the

ISNY flexible above-knee system with quadrilateral socket. Orthot Prosthet 40:17, 1986.

Kegel, B: Sports for the Leg Amputee. Medic, Redmond, WA, 1986.

Kostuik, JP: Amputation Surgery and Rehabilitation. Churchill Livingstone, New York, 1981.

Mensch, G and Ellis, PM: Physical Therapy Management of Lower Extremity Amputations. Aspen, Gaithersburg, MD, 1986.

Moore, TJ, et al: Prosthetic usage following major lower extremity amputation. Clin Orthop 238:219, 1989.

Moore, WS and Malone, JM (eds): Lower Extremity Amputation. WB Saunders, Philadelphia, 1989.

Murdoch, G and Donovan, RG (eds): Amputation Surgery and Lower Limb Prosthetics. Blackwell, Oxford, 1988.

Narang, IC, et al: Functional capabilities of lower limb amputees. Prosthet Orthot Int 8:43, 1984.

Novotny, MP: Psychosocial issues affecting rehabilitation. Phys Med Rehabil Clin North Am 2:273, 1991.

Palmer, ML and Toms, JE: Manual for Functional Training, ed 3. FA Davis, Philadelphia, 1992.

Rubin, G, Fischer, E, and Dixon, M: Prescription of above-knee and below-knee prostheses. Prosthet Orthot Int 10:117, 1986.

Sanders, GT: Lower Limb Amputations: A Guide to Rehabilitation. FA Davis, Philadelphia, 1986.

Schuch, CM: Report from international workshop on above-knee fitting and alignment techniques. Clin Prosthet Orthot 12:81, 1988.

GLOSSARY

Alignment: Position of one component relative to another; alignment refers to both angular and linear positions

Axis (prosthetic): Component of the prosthetic knee unit; creates the connection between the thigh piece (socket) and shank; may be either a single-axis hinge or polycentric linkage.

Build-up: Convexity within a socket to increase loading on pressure-tolerant tissues.

Clinic team: Group of health care professions that conducts prosthetic (and/or orthotic) rehabilitation. The basic team consists of a physician who serves as chief, physical (and/or occupational) therapist, and prosthetist (and/or orthotist). Others may participate on a regular or specific basis, such as social worker, vocational counselor, psychologist.

Computer-aided design/computer-aided manufacture (CAD-CAM): Prosthetic construction that involves electronic mapping of the amputation limb, relating the limb shape to socket designs, and automatic carving of a positive model over which plastic is molded to create the socket.

Endoskeletal (modular, pylon): Prosthetic shank in which the support consists of a rigid pipe usually covered with resilient material to simulate the contour of the contralateral leg. **Modular** refers to the ease of interchanging foot and knee units. **Pylon** is the pipe itself, although "pylon" is also used to signify a temporary prosthesis.

Exoskeletal (crustacean): Prosthetic shank in which the support consists of rigid material at the periphery, usually covered with a thin layer of polyester laminate. **Crustacean** refers to the placement of the supporting structure externally, as is the case with animals such as the lobster.

Extension aid: Mechanism designed to assist prosthetic

knee extension during the latter part of swing phase; may consist of elastic webbing placed externally across the knee unit, or an elastic strap or metal spring within the knee unit.

Fork strap: Prosthetic suspension and knee extension aid; consists of a fork-shaped elastic strap extending from the anterior portion of the below-knee prosthetic shank to a waist belt.

Friction brake: Device in a prosthetic knee unit that resists knee flexion during early stance phase, commonly a spring-loaded wedge that is forced into a groove upon transfer of body weight to the prosthesis.

Friction mechanism: Device which permits adjusting the resistance to swing of the prosthetic knee unit.

Constant friction: Mechanism that applies uniform resistance throughout swing phase; may be incorporated in sliding or hydraulic friction mechanisms.

Variable friction: Mechanism that applies greater friction at early and late swing; may be incorporated in sliding, hydraulic, or pneumatic friction mechanisms.

Sliding friction: Mechanism consisting of solid structures that resist motion by moving against each other, such as a clamp on the knee bolt.

Fluid friction: Mechanism consisting of a cylinder (**hydraulic,** oil-filled; or **pneumatic,** air-filled) in which a piston connected to the knee hinge moves up and down. Fluid friction knee units automatically compensate for changes in walking speed, increasing friction when the wearer walks faster.

Ischial containment socket: Above-knee socket that covers the ischial tuberosity and is relatively narrow in width.

Keel: Rigid longitudinal portion of a prosthetic foot terminating distally at a point corresponding to the metatarsophalangeal joints.

Mechanical stabilizer: A device that increases stability of the prosthetic knee unit, such as a manual lock or friction brake.

Multiple axis: A mechanism in an articulated prosthetic foot that permits sagittal, frontal, and transverse plane motion.

Patellar-tendon-bearing (PTB): Refers to the modern total-contact below-knee socket that places moderate load on the patellar ligament (tendon).

Piston action: Vertical motion of the prosthetic socket on the amputation limb; evident during gait as an up-and-down movement of the prosthesis. Pistoning is caused by looseness of the socket or inadequate suspension, or both.

Polycentric linkage: Mechanism in a knee unit that permits the momentary axis of knee flexion to change through the arc of motion; a common design is the four-bar linkage, consisting of two pairs of two bars of unequal length, pivoting on both ends, on the medial and lateral sides of the knee unit. Polycentric linkage increases knee stability.

Polyester laminate: Thermosetting plastic used for rigid prosthetic sockets and for finishing the exterior of exoskeletal shanks. Polyester resin saturates layers of fabric, producing a hard, durable material.

Polyethylene: Thermoplastic material used for flexible sockets; the plastic becomes malleable when heated, permitting its contour to be changed.

Relief: Concavity within a socket to decrease loading on pressure-sensitive tissue.

Single-axis: Prosthetic articulation that permits motion only in the sagittal plane about a fixed bolt.

Single-axis foot: Prosthetic foot that provides plantarflexion and dorsiflexion at a point corresponding to the anatomic ankle.

Single-axis knee: Prosthetic unit that permits flexion and extension at a point corresponding to the epicondylar level.

Solid ankle cushion heel (SACH) foot: Prosthetic foot in which the posterosuperior portion of the keel is attached to the shank, without a definite ankle joint, and a posteroinferior compressible wedge permits plantarflexion during early stance. The distal end of the keel permits hyperextension of the foot during late stance.

Stationary attachment flexible endoskeleton (SAFE) foot: Prosthetic foot that has a rigid ankle block attached to the shank, without a definite ankle joint; the anterior portion of the block terminates at a 45-degree angle, abutting a somewhat more flexible keel, to permit inversion and eversion. The distal end of the keel permits hyperextension of the foot during late stance. The posteroinferior surface has compressible material to permit plantarflexion during early stance.

Suction: Mode of prosthetic suspension in which an airtight socket is held on the amputation limb by atmospheric pressure. (Pressure is greater on the outside than on the inside of the socket.) Commonly, suction suspension is used on above-knee prostheses, in which the snug socket has an air-release valve.

Supracondylar (SC) suspension: Mode of below-knee prosthetic suspension in which the socket is held on the amputation limb by snug contact immediately above the femoral epicondyles; a plastic wedge is inserted between the medial epicondyle and the proximomedial socket wall.

Supracondylar/suprapatellar (SC/SP) suspension: Mode of below-knee prosthetic suspension in which the socket is held on the amputation limb by supracondylar suspension augmented by a high anterior socket margin that terminates immediately above the patella.

Syme's amputation: Amputation at the supramalleolar level, in which all foot bones are removed and the calcaneal fat pad is attached to the anterior skin flap to cushion the distal end of the limb.

Temporary (provisional) prosthesis: Device consisting of a socket designed to accept full weight bearing, attached to a pylon and foot. Unlike a definitive (permanent) prosthesis, the temporary one may not be cosmetically finished. For the above-knee prosthesis, the pylon usually is surmounted by a knee unit.

Transfemoral: Above-knee

Transtibial: Below-knee

APPENDIX A   BELOW-KNEE PROSTHETIC EVALUATION

1. Is the prosthesis as prescribed?
2. Can the client don the prosthesis easily?

Standing

3. Is the client comfortable when standing with the heel midlines 15 cm (6 in) apart?
4. Is the anteroposterior alignment satisfactory?
5. Is the mediolateral alignment satisfactory?
6. Do the contours and color of the prosthesis match the opposite limb?
7. Is the prosthesis the correct length?
8. Is piston action minimal?
9. Does the socket contact the amputation limb without pinching or gapping?

Suspension

10. Does the suspension component fit the amputation limb properly?
11. Does the cuff, fork strap, or thigh corset have adequate provision for adjustment?

Sitting

12. Can the client sit comfortably with hips and knees flexed 90 degrees?

Walking

13. Is the client's performance in level walking satisfactory?
14. Is the client's performance on stairs and ramps satisfactory?
15. Can the client kneel satisfactorily?
16. Does the suspension function properly?
17. Does the prosthesis operate quietly?
18. Does the client consider the prosthesis satisfactory as to comfort, function, and appearance?

Prosthesis Off the Client

19. Is the skin free of abrasions or other discolorations attributable to this prosthesis?
20. Is the socket interior smooth?
21. Is the posterior wall of the socket of adequate height?
22. Is the construction satisfactory?
23. Do all components function satisfactorily?

APPENDIX B   ABOVE-KNEE PROSTHETIC EVALUATION

1. Is the prosthesis as prescribed?
2. Can the client don the prosthesis easily?

Standing

3. Is the client comfortable when standing with the heel midlines 15 cm (6 in) apart?
4. Is any flesh roll above the socket minimal?
5. Is the client free from vertical pressure in the perineum?
6. Do the contours and color of the prosthesis match the opposite limb?
7. Is the prosthesis the correct length?
8. Is the knee stable?
9. When the socket valve is removed, is the distal tissue firm?

Quadrilateral Socket

10. Does the ischial tuberosity rest on the posterior brim?
11. Is the posterior brim approximately parallel to the floor?
12. Is the adductor longus tendon located in the anteromedial corner?

Ischial Containment Socket

13. Does the posteromedial corner of the socket cover the ischial tuberosity?
14. Can the client hyperextend the hip on the amputated side comfortably?
15. Can the client flex the hip 90 degrees comfortably, without socket gapping?
16. Can the client abduct the hip on the amputated side comfortably, without socket gapping?

Suspension

17. Does the Silesian bandage control prosthetic rotation and adduction adequately?
18. Does the pelvic band conform to the torso?

Sitting

19. Can the client sit comfortably with hips and knees flexed 90 degrees?
20. Does the socket remain securely on the thigh, without gapping or rotating?
21. Are both thighs approximately the same length and height from the floor?
22. Can the client lean forward to touch the shoes?

Walking

23. Is the client's performance in level walking satisfactory?
24. Is the client's performance on stairs and ramps satisfactory?
25. Does the suspension function properly?
26. Does the prosthesis operate quietly?
27. Does the client consider the prosthesis satisfactory as to comfort, function, and appearance?

Prosthesis Off the Client

28. Is the skin free of abrasions or other discolorations attributable to this prosthesis?
29. Is the socket interior smooth?
30. With the prosthesis fully flexed on a table, can the thigh piece be brought to at least the vertical position?
31. If the socket is totally rigid, is a back pad attached?
32. Is the construction satisfactory?
33. Do all components function satisfactorily?

Andrew A. Guccione

OBJECTIVES

1. Describe the epidemiology, pathology, pathogenesis, disease course, and common clinical manifestations of arthritis.
2. Identify the medical diagnostic procedures commonly used in the evaluation of arthritis, including laboratory tests and radiography.
3. Describe the medical management of the individual with arthritis.
4. Differentiate between rheumatoid and osteoarthritis.
5. Explain the procedures commonly used in assessing the individual with rheumatoid or osteoarthritis.
6. Discuss the rehabilitation management of the individual with arthritis.
7. Describe responses to psychosocial factors associated with arthritis that affect achievement of rehabilitation goals.
8. Explain the importance of a team approach for the individual with arthritis.

The terms *arthritis* and *rheumatism* are generic references to an array of over 100 diseases that are divided into 10 classification categories. Two major forms of arthritis will be considered in this chapter. **Rheumatoid arthritis (RA),** a systemic inflammatory disease, will be presented in detail; **osteoarthritis (OA),** a localized process that has been known in the past as degenerative joint disease (DJD), will also be discussed. Taken together, these two forms of arthritis account for most of the cases of arthritis that a physical therapist is likely to encounter in clinical practice.

Rheumatoid arthritis is a major subclassification within the category of diffuse connective tissue diseases that also includes juvenile arthritis, **systemic lupus erythematosus,** progressive systemic sclerosis or scleroderma, polymyositis, and dermatomyositis. The first clinical description of the disease is attributed to Landré-Beauvais in 1800, although the analysis of pictorial art of the late Renaissance has provided some evidence for the existence of RA in earlier times. Early descriptive comparisons of patient symptomatology were complicated by the lack of uniform agreement about the distinguishing characteristics of the disease, a difficulty that persists even today, given the wide spectrum of clinical presentations associated with this disease. Although the term "rheumatoid arthritis" was first used by Garrod in 1858, it was not accepted by the American Rheumatism Association (ARA) as the official terminology until 1941. The American College of Rheumatology (ACR), formerly the ARA, has revised the diagnostic terminology and criteria for rheumatoid arthritis

several times in the last 35 years and continues to monitor them for accuracy and validity.[1]

CLASSIFICATION CRITERIA

Clinically, the differential diagnosis of RA is predicated by the patient's signs and symptoms and the careful exclusion of other disorders. When conducting epidemiologic and other kinds of research studies, it is often necessary to identify homogeneous groups of individuals with relatively similar signs and symptoms of RA, given the wide spectrum of clinical presentations seen in this disease. Although other sets of criteria exist for this purpose, the ACR classification criteria are most often used to determine whether an individual's clinical presentation should be counted as a case of RA. Previously, the criteria allowed four classifications of RA: classical, definite, probable, and possible. The latter two designations were problematic as many patients with probable or possible RA often were discovered to have another disease when reexamined at a later time. Therefore, new criteria were tested and established in 1987. There are based on a combination of signs, symptoms, and laboratory findings that have persisted for a specified period of time (Table 21–1).[2] A diagnosis of RA is now established upon the presentation of four of the seven listed criteria. The joint signs and symptoms described in criteria 1 through 4 must have lasted for at least 6 weeks.[1,2]

Table 21–1 THE 1987 REVISED CRITERIA FOR THE CLASSIFICATION OF RHEUMATOID ARTHRITIS*

Criterion	Definition
1. Morning stiffness	Morning stiffness in and around the joints, lasting at least one hour before maximal improvement
2. Arthritis of three or more joint areas	At least three joint areas simultaneously have had soft tissue swelling or fluid (not bony overgrowth alone) observed by a physician. The 14 possible areas are right or left PIP, MCP, wrist, elbow, knee, ankle, and MTP joints.
3. Arthritis of hand joints	At least one area swollen (as defined above) in a wrist, MCP, or PIP joint
4. Symmetric arthritis	Simultaneous involvement of the same joint areas (as defined in 2) on both sides of the body (bilateral involvement of PIPs, MCPs, or MTPs is acceptable without absolute symmetry)
5. Rheumatoid nodules	Subcutaneous nodules, over bony prominences, or extensor surfaces, or in juxtaarticular regions, observed by a physician
6. Serum rheumatoid factor	Demonstration of abnormal amounts of serum rheumatoid factor by any method for which the result has been positive in <5% of normal control subjects
7. Radiographic changes	Radiographic changes typical of rheumatoid arthritis on posteroanterior hand and wrist radiographs, which must include erosions or unequivocal bony decalcification localized in or most marked adjacent to the involved joints (osteoarthritis changes alone do not qualify)

From Arnett,[2] p 319, with permission.

*For classification purposes, a patient shall be said to have rheumatoid arthritis if he or she has satisfied at least four of these seven criteria. Criteria 1 through 4 must have been present for at least 6 weeks. Patients with two clinical diagnoses are not excluded. Designation as classic, definite, or probable rheumatoid arthritis is *not* to be made.

EPIDEMIOLOGY

The calculation of prevalence rates can be complicated by the type of RA a person had at the time the epidemiologic survey was conducted, as well as the criteria used. When the prevalence of RA in Sudbury, Massachusetts, was studied using both the 1958 ARA criteria and the more stringent New York criteria, remarkable differences at follow-up were reported; this emphasized the difficulty with prevalence studies that used less stringent inclusion criteria, such as those that had been previously accepted for probable and possible RA.[3] It has been estimated that in 1988 there were 4 to 6 million cases of RA, with 100,000 to 200,000 new cases of RA that year.[4] Rheumatoid arthritis affects women two to three times more often than men in the typical years of onset between the ages of 20 to 60. Men and women over the age of 65 appear to be affected at the same rate. There is a general increase in prevalence for both sexes as age increases. Although RA is found around the world, there are some differences in the prevalence of RA in certain subpopulations, a fact that suggests a possible role for genetic or environmental factors in the etiology of the disease. For example, black Americans may have a lower prevalence of RA than whites, whereas several Native American groups demonstrate higher prevalence rates. There also is a lower prevalence of RA in native Japanese and native Chinese people compared with white people.[1,5]

ETIOLOGY

Like many other chronic diseases, the etiology of RA is unknown. Current research into the causes of RA is based on a complex, but as yet incomplete, appreciation of the functions of the immune system that is beyond the scope of this chapter. To sum up briefly however, an **antigen** is a substance, usually foreign to the host, that provokes the immune system into action. The immune system may respond to the antigen directly (cellular immunity) or by the production of **antibodies** that circulate in the serum (humoral immunity). These responses involve two general kinds of lymphocytes: T cells, which are responsible for cellular immunity, and B cells, which produce circulating antibodies specific to the antigen. Antibodies are immunoglobulins, a type of serum protein.[1]

Based on the fact that individuals with RA produce antibodies to their own immunoglobulins, there is some reason to believe that RA is an *autoimmune* disorder. It is not clear, however, whether this antibody production is a primary event or is a response to a specific antigen from an external stimulus. Current theory and research on the cellular basis of autoimmunity suggest that aberrant functioning of cell-mediated immunity and defective T lymphocytes may trigger the autoimmune response that underlies RA.[6,7] A specific etiologic agent for RA has not been identified, even though investigators have been able to identify that specific external etiologic agents may produce an inflammatory arthritis (e.g., **Lyme disease**). The disease that is finally manifested may be more dependent on the host's manner of response than on the agent or the mechanism involved.[8]

Current evidence suggests that a variety of agents may initiate an arthritis through a number of different mechanisms. A number of bacterial organisms have been suggested, including streptococcus, clostridia, diptheroids, and mycoplasmas, but no connections have been definitively proven. There has also been discussion of a viral etiology for RA, particularly with regard to the evidence that the serum of patients with RA reacts with cells infected by the Epstein-Barr virus (EBV). The EBV can initiate lymphoid proliferation, which suggests that it has the ability to alter the regulation of the immune system. As with other investigations that seek to identify a viral etiology for RA, research in this area remains speculative.[8–10]

Rheumatoid factors (RF) have received considerable attention in the search for a causative agent in RA because they are found in the sera of approximately 70 percent of all patients with RA. Rheumatoid factors are antibodies specific to IgG. Current theory suggests that RF arise as antibodies to altered autologous (the patient's own) immunoglobulin G (IgG). Some modification of IgG changes its configuration and renders it an autoimmunogen, stimulating the production of RF. The first class of immunoglobulins formed after contact with an antigen is IgM and most RF are of this class, although RF may be of any immunoglobulin class.[1] The exact biological role of RF is unknown, and is given less weight in current theories on the pathogenesis of RA.[7] Rheumatoid arthritis occurs in the absence of RF in a substantial number of individuals. Individuals with RA, however, who do have RF, or seropositive disease, have increased frequency of subcutaneous nodules, vasculitis, and polyarticular involvement.[1,10]

Recent studies have also sought to establish a genetic predisposition to the development of RA. Human leukocyte antigens (HLA) are found on the cell surface of most human cells, and are capable of generating an **immune response** when genetically incompatible tissues are grafted to each other (e.g., during organ transplants). Genes controlling these HLA are found on the sixth chromosome. Four loci have been described: HLA-A, HLA-B, HLA-C, and HLA-D. Rheumatoid arthritis has been associated with increased HLA-D and HLA-DR (D-related) antigens, which suggests that certain genes determine whether a host is prone to an immunologic response that leads to RA.[5,8,10] HLA-DR4 is associated with more aggressive disease, especially among seronegative patients (i.e., individuals with RA but without RF).[1,11]

PATHOLOGY

Long-standing RA is characterized by the grossly edematous appearance of the **synovium** with slender villous or hairlike projections into the joint cavity. There are distinctive vascular changes, including venous distention, capillary obstruction, neutrophilic infiltration of the arterial walls, and areas of thrombosis and hemorrhage. Synovial proliferation of vascular granulation tissue, known as **pannus,** dissolves collagen as it extends over the joint cartilage. Eventually, if RA continues, the granulation tissue will result in adhesions and fibrous or bony ankylosis of the joint. Chronic inflammation can also weaken the joint capsule and its supporting ligamentous structures, altering joint structure and function. Tendon rupture and fraying tendon sheaths may produce imbalanced muscle pull on these pathologically altered joints, resulting in the characteristic musculoskeletal deformities seen in advanced RA.[1]

Pathogenesis

The key features that differentiate synovial joints from other kinds of joints are exactly those features that make them susceptible to persistent inflammation. Rapid changes may occur in the cellular content and volume of the synovial fluid following alterations in blood flow, due to low pressure in the joint space and the lack of a limiting membrane between the joint space and the synovial blood vessels. High molecular weight substances such as macroglobulins and fibrinogens can pass through the synovial capillaries during periods of inflammation and are not easily cleared.[1] Since the cartilage is avascular, antigen-antibody complexes may be sequestered within the joint cavity and may facilitate a process of phagocytosis and further development of pannus. Although it is accepted that sustained **synovitis** requires the proliferation of new blood vessels, the exact mechanism of capillary growth is not currently understood. One attractive hypothesis is that activated macrophages, responding to antigen-antibody complexes, may stimulate this development.

In established synovitis, polymorphonuclear (PMN) leukocytes are chemotactically drawn into the joint cavity and contribute to the inflammatory destruction of the synovium, although the exact mechanism of this destruction is unknown. It is known that the lysosomal enzymes that are released from these leukocytes can directly injure synovial tissues.[1,10,12]

CLINICAL DIAGNOSTIC CRITERIA

The clinical diagnosis of RA is based on careful consideration of three factors: the clinical presentation of the patient, which is elucidated through history-taking and physical examination; the corroborating evidence gathered through laboratory tests and radiography; and the exclusion of other possible diagnoses.[1,4]

Signs and Symptoms

SYSTEMIC MANIFESTATIONS

Morning stiffness lasting more than 3 minutes is a hallmark symptom of RA. Difficulty in moving after awakening and generalized stiffness despite morning activity help to differentiate this sign from the stiffness of a particular joint seen in DJD following inactivity.[2] Morning stiffness can be qualified in terms of its severity and duration, both of which are directly related to the degree of disease activity. As in other systemic diseases, anorexia, weight loss, and fatigue also may be present.[1,2,13]

JOINT INVOLVEMENT

Rheumatoid arthritis is marked by a bilateral and symmetrical pattern of joint involvement. Clinically the patient presents with immobility and the cardinal signs of inflammation: pain, redness, swelling, and heat.[1] The joint examination may also reveal **crepitus,** which is audible or palpable grating or crunching as the joint is moved through its range of motion (ROM). Crepitus is the result of uneven degeneration of the joint surface.

CERVICAL SPINE

The cervical spine is often involved in RA.[14,15] The atlantoaxial joint and the midcervical region are the most common sites of inflammation, which leads to decreased ROM, particularly in rotation, 50 percent of which takes place at the C-1 and C-2 levels. Involvement of these two vertebrae may produce life-threatening situations if the transverse ligament of the atlas should rupture or if the odontoid process should fracture or herniate through the foramen magnum. Cervical involvement may also produce radiating pain, and nerve and cord compression, which is most likely to be seen in the lower cervical spine where the cervical lordosis is greatest.[1] While neurologic involvement is not inevitable in individuals with cervical subluxations, it has been estimated that the 1-year mortality reaches 50 percent in patients who do have cord compression. Magnetic resonance imaging (MRI) is particularly useful for visualizing both the spinal column and the cord in these cases.[4]

TEMPOROMANDIBULAR JOINT

Involvement of this synovial joint results in an inability to open the mouth fully (approximately 2 in) with normal side to side gliding and protrusion. In a resting position, the normal approximation of the upper and lower teeth may be altered following persistent inflammation.[1,4]

SHOULDERS

Shoulder involvement may be seen in the glenohumeral, sternoclavicular, or acromioclavicular joints. These joints may demonstrate degeneration, pain, and loss of ROM. The scapulothoracic articulation may secondarily exhibit a loss of ROM as well. Chronic inflammation of the shoulders causes the capsule and the ligaments to become distended and thinned. Joint surfaces may be eroded until the shoulder eventually becomes unstable. Additionally, **tendinitis** and **bursitis** may complicate management.[1,13,16]

ELBOWS

Inflammation, capsular and ligamentous distension, and joint surface erosion may lead to elbow instability, and irregular or catching movements. Flexion contractures frequently develop, as the outcome of persistent spasm secondary to pain.[1,13]

WRISTS

Early synovitis between the eight carpal bones and the ulna leads to a fairly rapid development of a flexion contracture, which ultimately diminishes the individual's ability to execute power grasp. Chronic inflammation of the proximal row of carpals can lead to a volar **subluxation** of the wrist and hand on the radius, accentuating the normal 10 to 15 degrees of volar inclination of the carpus on the distal radius (Fig. 21-1). Chronic inflammation leads to the loss of radial ligamentous support, and destruction of the extensor carpi ulnaris and the fibrocartilage on the distal side of the ulna. The attenuation of these restraining structures allows the proximal carpals to slide down the distal radius toward the ulna, creating a radial deviation of the distal row of carpals in the wrist relative to the two bones of the forearm, where normally there are 5 to 10 degrees of ulnar deviation (Fig. 21-2).[13]

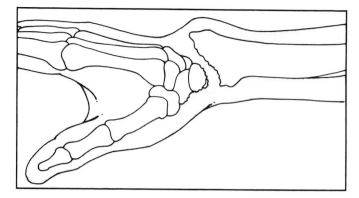

Figure 21-1. Volar subluxation of the carpus on the radius as a result of erosive synovitis of the radiocarpal joint. (From Melvin,[13] p 280, with permission.)

HAND JOINTS

Metacarpophalangeal (MCP)

Soft-tissue swelling around the MCP joints is very common. The volar subluxation and ulnar drift of the MCP joints frequently seen in RA are thought to result from accentuation of the normal structural shapes of these joints, which tilt the proximal phalanges in a ulnar direction. The anatomic placement and length of the collateral ligaments, which are most stretched during MCP flexion, and the insertions of the intrinsics, which also pull from an ulnar direction, also contribute to ulnar drift at the MCP joints during hand motion. Weakened

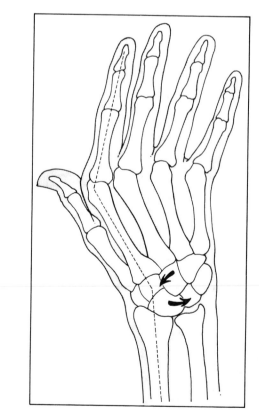

Figure 21-2. Relationship between wrist and metacarpophalangeal joint deformity. (From Melvin,[13] p 281, with permission.)

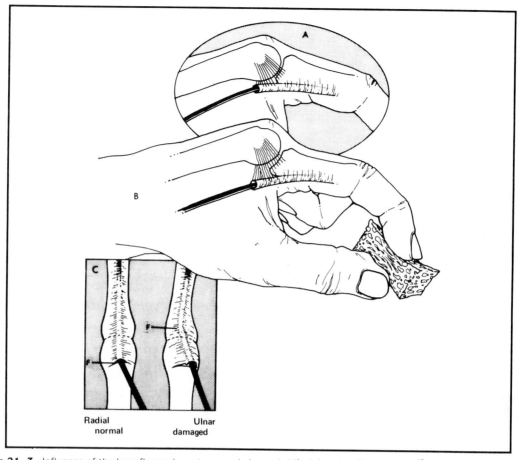

Figure 21–3. Influence of the long flexors in metacarpophalangeal drift deformity. (From Melvin,[13] p 283, with permission.)

ligaments cannot resist a pull toward volar subluxation, during power pinch or grasp, when flexor tendons bowstring across the MCP joints through frayed tendon sheaths damaged by long-term synovitis.[13] The bowstring effect results from moving the fulcrum of the flexor tendons distally, which places an ulnar and volar pull on the proximal phalanges (Fig. 21–3). Radial deviation of the carpals will further enhance MCP ulnar drift as the phalanges try to compensate for the loss of normal ulnar deviation at the wrist. This is known as the **zigzag effect,** where forces in the hand try to move the index finger back into its normal functional position in line with the radius (Fig. 21–2).[13,17–21]

Proximal Interphalangeal (PIP)

Swelling of these joints produces a fusiform or sausage-like appearance in the fingers. There are two characteristic deformities seen at the PIP joint in individuals with RA. The first of these is known as **swan neck deformity** and consists of PIP hyperextension and distal interphalangeal (DIP) flexion. Swan neck deformities arise in three distinct ways, depending on the site of initial involvement.[13,21] Most commonly, swan neck deformity follows from initial synovitis of the MCP, where the pain of chronic synovitis leads to reflex muscle spasm of the intrinsics (Fig. 21–4). The biomechanical force of the intrinsics then combines with the hyper-

mobility found in the chronically inflamed and structurally changed PIP to result in volar subluxation and PIP hyperextension. Swan neck deformity may also result when the volar capsule of the PIP is stretched; the lateral bands then move dorsally, and tension placed on the flexor digitorum profundis by the PIP flexes the DIP (Fig. 21–5). In these instances, a rupture of the flexor digitorum sublimus further predisposes an individual to swan neck deformity. A third mechanism for developing swan neck deformity involves a rupture of the extensor digitorum communis at its insertion on the DIP joint, resulting in DIP flexion and PIP hyperextension due to unrestrained pull by the flexor digitorum profundis (Fig. 21–6).[13]

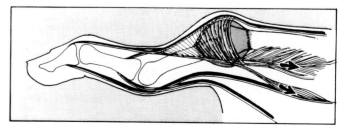

Figure 21–4. Swan neck deformity with initial synovitis at the metacarpophalangeal joint. (From Melvin,[13] p 285, with permission.)

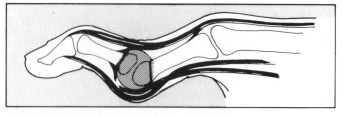

Figure 21–5. Swan neck deformity with initial synovitis at the proximal interphalangeal joint. (From Melvin,[13] p 286, with permission.)

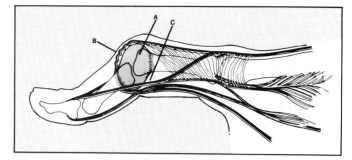

Figure 21–7. Boutonniere deformity. (From Melvin,[13] p 287, with permission.)

The other characteristic deformity of the PIP is known as **boutonniere deformity** and consists of DIP extension with PIP flexion (Fig. 21–7). As a result of chronic synovitis, the insertion of extensor digitorum communis into the middle phalanx (known as the central slip) lengthens, and the lateral bands slide volarly to force the PIP into flexion. Bony formations or outgrowths around the end of a joint are termed **osteophytes.** Those found at the PIP are known as **Bouchard's nodes,** and may be seen in OA. They are unrelated to RA, but an individual may have both kinds of arthritis at the same time.[13]

Distal Interphalangeal (DIP)

The DIP joint is most often uninvolved in RA. Osteophytes are, however, common in OA and are called **Heberden's nodes.** Occasionally the tendon of the extensor digitorum communis will rupture, and the unopposed pull of the flexor digitorum profundis will pull the DIP into flexion. This condition is known as **mallet finger** deformity.[13]

THUMB

As in the other digital joints, the primary cause of deformity in the thumb is synovial swelling. The fibers of the dorsal hood mechanism over the MCP joint, the joint capsule and collateral ligaments, and the tendons of the extensor pollicis brevis and extensor pollicis longus are particularly affected. The exact mechanism of thumb deformities depends on the particular combination of affected structures and may be classified according to the criteria elaborated by Nalebuff.[22] As in other hand deformities, the actual presentation depends on the site of initial synovitis, the direction of imbalanced muscle forces, and the integrity of the surrounding joint structures. A type I deformity, consisting of MCP flexion and interphalangeal (IP) hyperextension without involvement of the carpometacarpal (CMC) joint, is most commonly seen. The type II classification is assigned when the CMC joint is subluxed and the IP

joint is held in hyperextension. Carpometacarpal subluxation with MCP hyperextension is classified as a type III deformity, and is found more commonly in RA than a type II deformity.[13,22]

Mutilans Deformity (Opera-glass hand)

Grossly unstable thumbs and severely deformed phalanges are indicative of **mutilans type** deformity, also known as opera-glass hand. In this condition, the transverse folds of the skin of the thumb and fingers resemble a folded telescope. Radiographic study of the bones of the hand reveals severe bone resorption, erosion, and shortening, especially of the MCP, PIP, radiocarpal, and radioulnar joints. The negative impact of this deformity on hand function and ADL is significant.[13]

HIP

Although patients may present with complaints of pain in the groin, often due to trochanteric bursitis, the hip is less commonly involved in RA than in other kinds of arthritis. Radiographic hip disease is seen in about half of all patients with RA. Severe inflammatory destruction of the femoral head and the acetabulum may push the acetabulum into the pelvic cavity, a condition known as **protrusio acetabuli.**[1,4,13]

KNEES

Because of the relatively large amount of synovium in the knee, it is one of the most frequently affected joints in RA. Chronic synovitis results in distension of the joint capsule, attenuation of the collateral and cruciate ligaments, and destruction of the joint surfaces. Painful knees may be held in slightly flexed positions ultimately resulting in flexion contractures.[1,4,13]

ANKLES AND FEET

Chronic synovitis accentuates the natural tendency of the talus to glide medially and in a plantar direction, resulting in pressure on the calcaneus and leading to hind-foot pronation. The spring ligament is also stretched by these occurrences, flattening the medial longitudinal arch (Fig. 21–8). The calcaneus may erode or develop bony **exostoses** known as spurs. As synovitis weakens the transverse arch, the metatarsals spread and a splayed forefoot (**splayfoot**) may develop (Fig. 21–9). Synovitis of the metatarsophalangeal (MTP) joints is

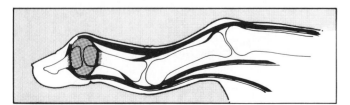

Figure 21–6. Swan neck deformity with initial synovitis at the distal interphalangeal joint. (From Melvin,[13] p 287, with permission.)

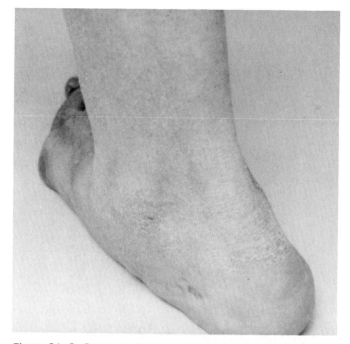

Figure 21-8. Posteromedial view of the foot and ankle showing calcaneal valgus, pes planus ("flatfoot") and hallux valgus. (Used by permission of the Arthritis Foundation.)

extremely common. A **hallux valgus** may also be present. When volar subluxation of the MTP joint combines with flexion of the PIP and hyperextension of the DIP joints, this condition is commonly referred to as **hammer toes** (Fig. 21-10). The MTP joints may also exhibit volar subluxation of the metatarsal head with flexion of the PIP and DIP joints, a condition known as **cock-up** or **claw toes** (Fig. 21-11). As the capsule and intertarsal ligaments are weakened and stretched, the proximal phalanges move dorsally on the metatarsal head (Fig. 21-12). As with conditions observed in the hand, the long toe extensors "bowstring" over the PIP joints, while the flexors are displaced into the intertarsal spaces.[1,4,13,23,24]

MUSCLE INVOLVEMENT

Muscle atrophy around affected joints may be present early. It is not definitively known, however, if this atrophy is the result simply of disuse or if there is selective attrition of muscles due to some unknown mechanism specifically related to the disease itself. Atrophy in the intrinsic muscles of the hand and the quadriceps are particularly evident in long-standing disease, although the mechanisms for these changes may not be the same. It appears that individuals with RA experience selective attrition of type II (phasic) muscle fibers through some unknown mechanism.[25,26] There is also some evidence that type I (tonic) muscle fibers of the quadriceps will undergo selectively atrophy following anterior cruciate damage.[27] Loss of muscle bulk may also be the result of a peripheral neuropathy, myositis, or steroid-induced myopathy. Muscle weakness may be due to either reflex inhibition secondary to pain, or atrophy.[25-27]

TENDONS

Inflammation of the synovial lining of the tendon sheaths results in a tenosynovitis that interferes with the smooth gliding of the tendon through the sheath and may directly damage the tendon itself. Eventually the tendon may rupture. A patient with tendon damage or muscle weakness may exhibit a **lag phenomenon** which refers to a substantial difference in passive versus active ROM. This is a nonspecific finding, which therapists need to evaluate carefully in order to determine its cause and design appropriate treatment.[4,13]

Laboratory Tests

Two concepts are essential to a full understanding of the use of laboratory tests in the detection of RA. The first is the concept of the *sensitivity* of a test, which indicates the proportion of truly diseased individuals who have a positive test. The clinical value of sensitive tests is particularly evident in those instances when a negative misdiagnosis would be deleterious to the health of the patient. In research terms, sensitivity is equivalent to the laboratory test's ability to avoid a false negative result. The concept of *specificity*, on the other hand, refers to the proportion of truly nondiseased individuals who have a negative test. In other words, the specificity of a laboratory test is a measure of its ability to avoid false positives. The clinical diagnostician will usually choose a mix of both sensitive and specific tests to confirm clinical impressions during the diagnostic process.

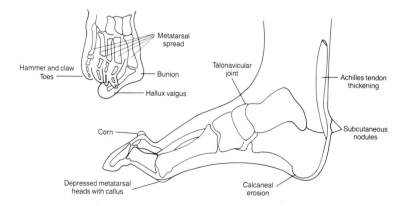

Figure 21-9. Major foot and ankle deformities seen in rheumatoid arthritis. (From Dimonte, P and Light, H, Pathomechanics and treatment of the rheumatoid foot. Phys Ther 62:1982 1148, with permission of the American Physical Therapy Association.)

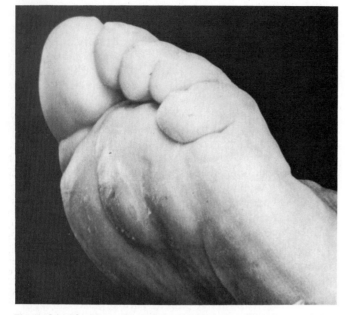

Figure 21-10. Metatarsophalangeal subluxation. (Used by permission of the American College of Rheumatology.)

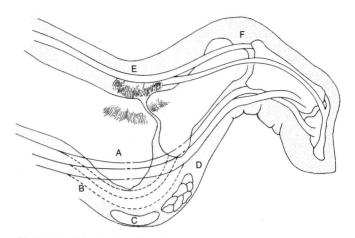

Figure 21-12. Relationship of structures to the metatarsal heads in metatarsalgia. (From Moncur, C and Shields, M, Clinical management of metatarsalgia in the patient with arthritis. Clin Manage Phys Ther 3:7, 1983, with permission.)

The erythrocyte sedimentation rate (ESR) is highly nonspecific but exceptionally sensitive to inflammatory processes. Therefore, it is a good test to choose when the clinician wishes to confirm the presence or absence of any inflammation, irrespective of the underlying pathology or disease. A normal ESR makes it unlikely that an inflammatory process underlies a patient's complaints. The ESR in individuals with RA is typically elevated and is a reasonable marker of overall disease activity. A return towards normal usually signals the success of medical management and can be used by physical therapists as an indication to commence more aggressive treatment.

There are two different tests to determine the presence of RF. The sheep cell agglutination test (SCAT) and the latex fixation test identify the proportion of RF in the sera following repetitive dilutions. The greatest dilution that produces a positive test is known as a *titer*. High titers after repeated dilutions indicate greater proportions of RF. In general, the SCAT is regarded as the more specific test, yielding fewer false positive results, while the latex fixation is thought to be more sensitive, yielding fewer false negatives. The SCAT is usually used as an initial screening test.

A complete blood count is also routinely ordered. Red blood cell counts are usually decreased. Anemia is found in approximately 20 percent of individuals with RA. The white blood cell count, by comparison, is usually normal. An increase in platelets, called thrombocytosis, is not unusual in active RA.

A synovial fluid analysis can greatly enhance the process of differential diagnosis. Normal synovial fluid is transparent, yellowish, viscous, and without clots. Synovial fluid from inflamed joints is cloudy, less viscous because of a change in hyaluronate proteins, and will clot. Significant inflammation will also increase the number of proteins in the fluid. A culture can be done to identify potential bacterial agents as the cause of the joint inflammation. If the joint is inflamed, there will be an elevation of white blood cells in the fluid, 90 percent of which may be polymorphonuclear (PMN) leukocytes. Normal fluid has a low cell count with only 25 percent PMN representation. The presence of crystals may confirm the diagnosis of gout (urate crystals) or pseudogout (calcium pyrophosphate crystals). A mucin clot is formed in synovial fluid on mixing it with acetic acid. If the synovial fluid is normal, a ropelike mass will form in a clear solution after mixing. Shredding indicates fair mucin clotting, while the formation of small masses with shreds is indicative of a poor mucin clot. Poor clotting accompanies acute infectious arthritis. Inflammatory arthritis, such as RA, produces fair mucin clotting. Good mucin clotting of the synovial fluid is found in a joint that presents with a noninflammatory arthritis.[1,4]

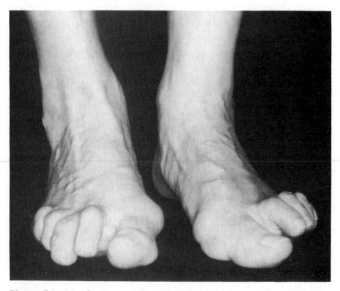

Figure 21-11. Common deformities of the rheumatoid foot. (Used by permission of the American College of Rheumatology.)

Radiography

Radiographic assessment is an essential component of the diagnostic workup for RA. Physical therapists working in rheumatology should be avid consumers of the radiographic information available in a patient's record. They should also develop a basic proficiency in identifying abnormalities in joint structure and the surrounding soft tissues that influence the course and outcome of rehabilitation. The ability to identify abnormalities assumes that the therapist has a firm notion of how a normal joint appears on a radiograph. Therapists can orient themselves to a radiograph by considering three parameters: alignment, bone density and surface, and cartilaginous spacing (Figs. 21–13 and 21–14). In assessing the alignment, the therapist should note whether the long axes of the proximal and distal bones of the joint are in their normal spatial relationships and whether the convex surface of one fits well with the concavity of the other. Normal bone density, in the absence of **osteoporosis,** is indicated by a uniform, somewhat opaque and milky appearance on radiographs. The cortices of each bone should be distinct, appropriately thick, and well defined. The soft tissues surrounding the joints should conform to known anatomic shape. The therapist

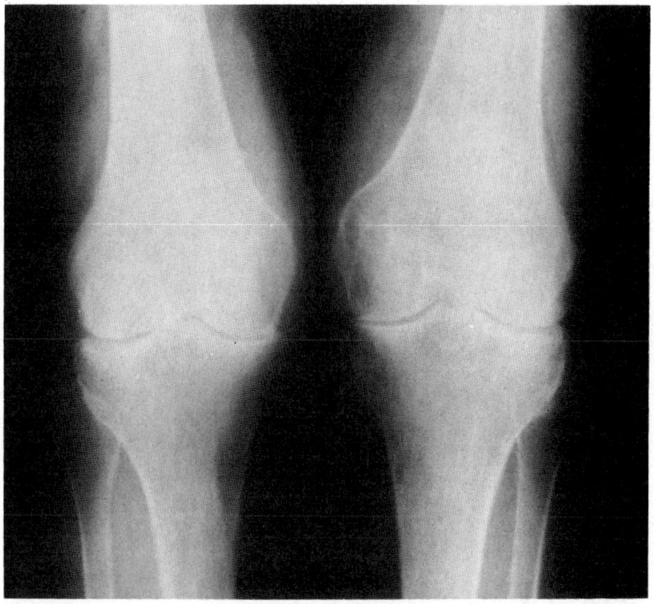

Figure 21–14. Frontal view of the knee with characteristics of rheumatoid arthritis. (Used with permission of the American College of Rheumatology.)

should note any soft-tissue swelling, evident on the radiograph, that might limit function. Finally, the therapist should note whether there is even spacing between the joint surfaces. Uneven, reduced, or absent spacing suggests loss of cartilage or erosion of the joint surfaces. Overall the joint surface should be smooth and conform to known anatomic shape without osteophytes. The progression of the disease can be characterized in four stages following periodic radiographic assessment (Table 21–2). The radiographic changes seen early in the disease are nonspecific, and usually limited to swelling in the surrounding soft tissues, joint effusions, and

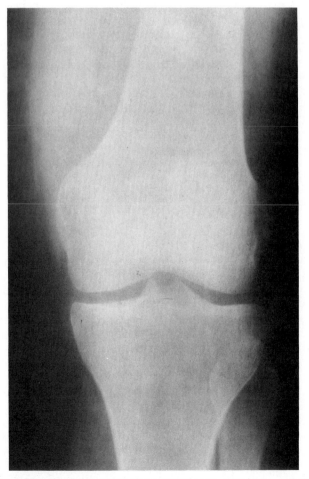

Figure 21–13. Frontal view of the normal knee. (Used by permission of the American College of Rheumatology.)

Table 21–2 CLASSIFICATION OF PROGRESSION OF RHEUMATOID ARTHRITIS

Stage 1, Early
*1. No destructive changes on radiographic examination.
2. Radiographic evidence of osteoporosis may be present.

Stage II, Moderate
*1. Radiographic evidence of osteoporosis, with or without slight subchondral bone destruction; slight cartilage destruction may be present.
*2. No joint deformities, although limitation of joint mobility may be present.
3. Adjacent muscle atrophy.
4. Extraarticular soft tissue lesions, such as nodules and tenosynovitis may be present.

Stage III, Severe
*1. Radiographic evidence of cartilage and bone destruction, in addition to osteoporosis.
*2. Joint deformity, such as subluxation, ulnar deviation, or hyperextension, without fibrous or bony ankylosis.
3. Extensive muscle atrophy.
4. Extraarticular soft tissue lesions, such as nodules and tenosynovitis may be present.

Stage IV, Terminal
*1. Fibrous or bony ankylosis
2. Criteria of stage III

From Schumacher, Klippel, and Robinson,[1] p 318, with permission.
*These criteria must be present to permit classification of a patient in any particular stage or grade.

periarticular demineralization. Diagnostic confirmation is available only later in the disease process when the typical joint space narrowing and erosions in the hands and feet are seen in the characteristic bilateral distribution.[28]

SECONDARY PROBLEMS AND COMPLICATIONS

Rheumatoid Nodules

Rheumatoid nodules are the most common extraarticular manifestations of RA and occur in approximately 25 percent of patients. They are most commonly found in the subcutaneous or deeper connective tissues, in areas subjected to repeated mechanical pressure such as the olecranon bursae, the extensor surfaces of the forearms, and the Achilles tendons. Nodules are usually asymptomatic, although they can be tender and may cause skin breakdown or become infected.[1,4]

Vascular Complications

Most forms of vascular lesions associated with RA are silent, although the fulminant form of rheumatoid arteritis can be life-threatening, and may be accompanied by malnutrition, infection, congestive heart failure, and gastrointestinal bleeding. Foot or wrist drop may occur as a result of vasculitis of the vasa arteriosum to the nerve supply of the radial or superficial peroneal nerves.[1,4]

Neurologic Manifestations

Mild peripheral neuropathies are often seen in RA, particularly in elderly patients, and are unrelated to vasculitis. Most neuropathies result from nerve compression or entrapment, for example, **carpal tunnel** or tarsal tunnel syndromes.[1,4]

Cardiopulmonary Complications

Pericarditis can be demonstrated during autopsy in about 4 percent of patients, but clinically detectable heart disease from RA is rare. Pleuropulmonary manifestations are also most commonly asymptomatic, although pleuritis is commonly found on autopsy.[1,4]

Ocular Manifestations

Ocular lesions are most usually associated with the dry eyes of **Sjogren's syndrome,** which is an inflammatory disorder of the lacrimal and salivary glands. Scleritis, and the relatively more benign episcleritis, can also be present and require careful medical treatment.[1,29]

CLINICAL MANIFESTATIONS OF RHEUMATOID ARTHRITIS

Disease Onset and Course

Disease onset in RA is most usually insidious with complaints of generalized joint pain and stiffness. Men who develop RA past the age of 60 typically present without stiffness and swelling in the upper extremities.[4] The question of whether elderly onset RA represents a distinct disease remains controversial. Comparisons of elderly onset RA with early onset RA have revealed that abrupt onset and large joint involvement, particularly of the shoulder girdle, were more common in the older group. The elderly onset group also more commonly had features of **polymyalgia rheumatica,** a distinct disease affecting the shoulder and pelvic girdles, with which elderly onset RA can be confused.[30] Older adolescent females may present with a chronic erosive arthritis of the knees without other joint involvement or systemic manifestations. It is not known whether this presentation is a variation of juvenile arthritis, adult onset RA, or a distinct form of arthritis involving only a few joints.[4]

Acute onset is seen in 8 to 15 percent of RA patients. Onset is intermediate in approximately 15 to 20 percent of patients. Most often, the onset is insidious, lasting weeks to months. Disease progression is highly variable. High titers of RF can indicate a more severe disease course. Spontaneous remissions can occur, although it often remains unclear if the individual had an accurately diagnosed case of RA or some other disease. Fifteen to 20 percent of patients experience an intermittent course characterized by partial to complete remissions longer than the periods of exacerbations. A third group of patients experiences the full destructive process of progressive RA.[1,4]

Prognosis

The question of mortality associated with RA is highly controversial. Previously it was widely believed that RA itself was not usually a cause of death, although conditions such as systemic vasculitis and atlantoaxial subluxation could be fatal. Now there is a growing body of evidence that individuals with RA may live less than their counterparts without disease, especially if the early years of RA were marked by aggressive disease and poor functional status.[30] Even in patients with milder forms of RA, long-term inflammation ultimately results in joint destruction and significant functional loss. Almost 50 percent of individuals with RA will eventually have marked restrictions in activities of daily living (ADL) or will be incapacitated.[1] Individuals with elderly onset RA appear to have a better functional outcome than those with early onset, but it is unclear whether this is the result of having the disease for a shorter period of time or of having a different form of the disease itself.[31] A broad classification of functional disability has been developed by the ARA to characterize the progressive

Table 21-3 AMERICAN COLLEGE OF RHEUMATOLOGY REVISED CRITERIA FOR CLASSIFICATION OF FUNCTIONAL STATUS IN RHEUMATOID ARTHRITIS*

Class I	Completely able to perform usual activities of daily living (self-care, vocational, and avocational)
Class II	Able to perform usual self-care and vocational activities, but limited in avocational activities
Class III	Able to perform usual self-care activities, but limited in vocational and avocational activities
Class IV	Limited in ability to perform usual self-care, vocational, and avocational activities

From Hochberg, MC, et al: The American College of Rheumatology 1991 revised criteria for the classification of global functional status in rheumatoid arthritis. Arthritis Rheum 35:498, 1992, with permission of the American College of Rheumatology.

*Usual self-care activities include dressing, feeding, bathing, grooming, and toileting. Avocational (recreational and/or leisure) and vocational (work, school, homemaking) activities are patient-desired and age- and sex-specific.

impacts of the disease (Table 21-3). The most severe social loss, income, is directly attributable to work disability secondary to loss of physical function.[32,33]

OSTEOARTHRITIS

Osteoarthritis is a condition marked by two features: the progressive destruction of articular cartilage and the formation of bone at the margins of the joint.[1,34]

Classification

Although joint inflammation is implied by the "-itis" in osteoarthritis, inflammation is typically found only after there has been substantial articular degeneration. The synovium of an osteoarthritic joint, however, can demonstrate marked changes in some joints, similar to those seen in RA.[35] In epidemiologic studies, OA is often graded on radiographs according to the criteria of Kellgren and Lawrence, which are based on an ordinal scale of 5 levels: grade 0 (normal radiograph); grade 1 (doubtful narrowing of the joint space and possible osteophytes); grade 2 (definite osteophytes and absent or questionable narrowing of the joint space); grade 3 (moderate osteophytes and joint space narrowing, some sclerosis, and possible deformity); and grade 4 (large osteophytes, marked narrowing of joint space, severe sclerosis, and definite deformity). Most studies have used grade 2 (the presence of definite osteophytes) as the criterion for defining disease, while a few others have required evidence of joint space narrowing (grade 3), corresponding to clinically identified disease, to designate osteoarthritis.[36] Patients with OA can be further differentiated in two ways. Some cases of OA are classified as idiopathic, when the etiology of the disease is unknown. Idiopathic OA may be localized to a specific joint, or generalized, affecting three or more joints. Osteoarthritis is classified as secondary, when an etiology (e.g., trauma, congenital malformation, or other musculoskeletal diseases) can be identified.[13]

Epidemiology

Osteoarthritis is an extremely common condition after 40 years of age, although it may not always be symptomatic when present. It is widespread in adults over 60, and affects men more than women.[37,38] It is likely that more than 60 million adults in the United States have OA.[35] Studies concerning racial predisposition to OA have yielded conflicting data, depending on the joint studied.

Etiology

As with RA, no single factor that predisposes an individual to OA has been identified. Although aging is indeed strongly associated with OA, it must be emphasized that aging in itself does not cause OA, nor should OA be considered a "normal" aging process.[34,39] Several factors related to aging may, however, contribute to its development. Trauma prior to adulthood may initiate a remodeling of bone that alters joint mechanics and nutrition in a way that becomes problematic only later in life. The role of repetitive "micro-trauma" in the etiology of OA has also received attention.[1,34] Specifically, occupational tasks such as repetitive knee-bending have been linked to the development of OA.[40] Finally, obesity has been shown to be a risk factor for the development of OA in later life.[1,41]

Pathology

Animal models involving knee trauma have provided much of the basis for what we now know about the earliest changes associated with OA in humans. Thus, it is possible that subtle, crucial, but as yet undiscovered, differences in humans may alter our understanding of OA in the future. The first osteoarthritic change in articular cartilage, which has been confirmed in humans, is an increase in water content. This increase suggests that the proteoglycans have been allowed to swell with water far beyond the normal extent, although the mechanism by which this occurs is unknown.[1,34] Additionally, there are changes in the composition of newly synthesized proteoglycan. In later stages of disease progression, proteoglycans are lost, with accompanying loss in the water content of cartilage. As proteoglycans are lost, articular cartilage loses its compressive stiffness and elasticity, and this, in turn, results in the transmission of compressive forces to underlying bone. Changes in cartilage proteoglycans will also negatively affect the ability of the cartilage to form a squeeze-film over its surface during joint loading. Collagen synthesis is increased initially, although there is a shift from type II collagen fibers to a larger proportion of type I collagen, which is the kind found in skin and fibrous tissue. As the articular cartilage is destroyed, the joint space narrows.[42]

One of the first noticeable changes in cartilage is the mild fraying or "flaking" of superficial collagen fibers. Deeper fraying or "fibrillation" of the upper third of the cartilage follows, and occurs in areas of greater weight bearing. The cartilage may degenerate to the point that subchondral bone is exposed. Subchondral bone in turn can then become sclerotic and stiffer than normal bone.[42]

The process of osteophyte formation in OA is not well understood. Current hypotheses have implicated increased vascularity in degenerated cartilage, venous congestion from subchondral cysts and thickened subchondral trabeculae, and the continued sloughing of articular cartilage. Each of these hypotheses may explain how this bony growth contributes to the pain and loss of motion that accompany OA.

Unlike the synovium in RA, the major pathologic changes of OA are found in the articular cartilage, particularly in the concentration of proteoglycan, which diminishes according to the severity of the disease. Furthermore, there are metabolic changes in the rate of enzyme production that facilitate the destruction of cartilage. Even though proteoglycan concentration decreases with OA, it is also true that proteoglycan and collagen synthesis increases until the later stages of the disease. This seeming paradox has given rise to several hypotheses concerning the pathogenesis of OA, which have yet to be proven. Given that proteoglycan synthesis increases with OA, it is possible that the quality of this newly synthesized product may not be equal to meeting the biomechanical load normally placed on an adult joint.[34]

Clinical Diagnostic Criteria

SIGNS AND SYMPTOMS

Clinically, a diagnosis is often made on the basis of symptoms and signs (e.g., pain and swelling, loss of ROM and bony deformity). Not all joints are equally affected by OA. In the upper extremity, the DIP and PIP joints, and the CMC joint of the thumb are commonly involved. The cervical and lumbar spine, hips, knees, and first MTP joint are also sites for OA. The MCP joints, wrists, elbows, and shoulders are usually spared in primary OA.[38] Unlike RA, OA does have not have a bilateral, symmetrical presentation. A single joint or any combination of joints in one individual may be affected.[37] Osteoarthritis is not a systemic disease, and is therefore not associated with systemic complaints such as generalized morning stiffness, fever, or loss of appetite. Individuals with OA may experience some stiffness in particular joints upon awakening that is similar to the stiffness felt when mobilizing the same joints after inactivity during the day, but this stiffness does not last nearly as long as in individuals with RA, nor is it generalized to the entire body.[38] Crepitus is a common clinical finding in OA as well as RA.[1,35,38]

Although cartilage degeneration is the primary manifestation of OA, cartilage is aneural, and therefore not the cause of a person's pain. Pain in OA may be attributed to incongruent articulations of joint surfaces, periosteal elevation secondary to bone proliferation at the joint margin, abnormal pressures on subchondral bone, trabecular microfractures, and distention of the joint capsule. Many patients will also experience secondary synovitis, especially when the knee is involved.[38] Symptoms do not always match the severity of the disease on radiographs. Some patients may magnify the pain they experience.[13] More important, unlike individuals with RA, who report pain on motion and at rest, persons with OA are likely to experience that their pain occurs or worsens only with motion, except in the later stages of the disease.[38] Patients with the most severe disease may not move their joints as frequently or in the ways that exacerbate their symptoms. Therefore, pain and disease severity in individuals with OA are potentially related to functional loss, although not in the same way. Among elders, it has been shown, for example, that the functional loss is more likely to be associated with severe radiographic OA without symptoms than is the loss associated with the presence of symptoms but milder disease.[43] One explanation of this finding is that individuals with OA limit their functional activities in order to avoid the movements that are painful. In the clinical evaluation of the patient with OA, one might assume that pain is a primary factor in limiting function as is the case in patients with RA. A clinical evaluation predicated on this assumption could lead to the hasty conclusion that the patient's functional status is normal if pain is absent. Given that individuals with OA may reduce or eliminate their symptoms by avoiding certain activities, clinicians should explore functional limitations in patients with OA separately from the evaluation of symptoms.

MEDICAL MANAGEMENT

Drug Therapy in Rheumatoid Arthritis

The overall goal of medical management in RA is to control inflammation and retard the long-term progression of the disease. Although a curative drug for RA does not exist, many of the available medications do reduce inflammation and some are believed to prevent the erosive effects of the disease. Drug therapy in the rheumatic diseases is currently under reconsideration.[44] Traditionally, drugs have been prescribed sequentially, beginning with aspirin, which has both an **analgesic** and an antiinflammatory effect. It is prescribed in a large dose, often 12 or more 325-mg tablets per day, that results in a serum salicylate level in the range of 20 to 25 mg/dl. **Tinnitus** is the major symptom of aspirin toxicity that may be reported by a patient to a physical therapist. In the traditional approach, if aspirin therapy failed to produce the desired therapeutic effects, or if the side effects of aspirin, such as gastrointestinal bleeding, became unmanageable, the patient was placed on one of the currently approved nonsteroidal antiinflammatory drugs (NSAIDs), which are differentiated according to their chemical derivation (Table 21–4). Although NSAIDs are more costly than aspirin, they require less frequent administration each day, and may have fewer side effects. There is no evidence, however, that they are more effective than aspirin in controlling inflammation.

Table 21–4 COMMON NONSTEROIDAL ANTIINFLAMMATORY DRUGS (NSAIDs)*

Agent	Strength (mg)	Dosing	Usual Daily Dose (mg)	Comments
Carboxylic acids				
Salicylates: aspirin	81	bid to qid	975–3600	Monitor salicylate levels
	325			
	400			
	500			
Timed-release	650			Variable half-life; lethal with overdose; major gastrointestinal toxicity
	800			
	975			
Effervescent	325			
	500			
Nonacetylated salicylates				
Salsalate	500	bid to qid	975–3600	Monitor salicylate levels
	750			
Choline magnesium salicylate	500			Less gastrointestinal toxicity
	750			
	1000			
Liquid	100 mg/ml			
Magnesium salicylate	325			
	500			
Fluorophenyl salicylate: diflunisal (Dolobid)	250	bid	500–1000	Not metabolized to salicylate; variable half-life
	500			
Propionic agents				
Propionic acids				
Ibuprofen (e.g., Motrin, Brufen)	200	tid to qid	600–2400	
	400			
	600			
	800			
Suspension	20 mg/ml			
Naproxen (Naprosyn)	250	bid	500–1000	
	375			
	500			
Suspension	25 mg/ml			
Fenoprofen (Nalfon)	200	tid or qid	800–2400	Interstitial nephritis
Ketoprofen (Orudis)	25	tid or qid	150–300	
	50			
	75			
Flurbiprofen (Ansaid)	50	bid or qid	200–300	
	100			
Indole/indene acetic acids				
Indomethacin (Indocin)	25	tid or qid	75–200	Effective, if tolerated
	50			
	75 SR†	qhs or bid	75–150	
Suspension	5 mg/ml			
Suppositories	50			
Sulindac (Clinoril)	150	bid	300–400	
	200			
Heteroaryl acetic acids: tolmetin (Tolectin)	200	tid or qid	600–1600	Short half-life; hypersensitivity
	400			
Arylacetic acids: diclofenac (Voltaren)	25	bid or tid	100–150	Enteric-coated; monitor liver enzymes
	50			
	75			
Fenamic acids: meclofenamate (Meclomen)	50	tid or qid	200–400	Laxative
	100			
Enolic acids				
Oxicams: piroxicam (Feldene)	10	qd	10–20	Very long half-life

From Batchlor and Paulus,[52] p 477, with permission.
*Approved for use in the United States.
†Sustained release.

Commonly, a physician considers using antimalarials, gold salts, or penicillamine if the patient fails to respond to either aspirin or NSAIDs. These drugs are sometimes referred to as DMARDs (disease-modifying antirheumatic drugs) on the basis of their presumed ability to alter the course of the disease. Positive effects from their administration, however, may not be noticed for 10 to 12 weeks. Therefore, in contrast to standard medical practice, it has been suggested that low doses of corticosteroids be administered as bridge therapy until the DMARD takes effect.[44] In choosing among these agents, a physician must weigh comparative efficacy against toxicity. A metaanalysis, which compared the data of many studies, indicated that all of the commonly used

DMARDs, with the exception of oral gold, were about as equally effective.[45] Antimalarials carry the remote risk of severe side effects to the retina and require that the patient receive periodic eye examinations. They are, however, the least toxic. Gold may be administered either orally or intramuscularly and is thought to prevent erosions. Injectable gold may be the most toxic of these agents.[45] Side effects from gold are not rare; the most common of these is skin rash. Penicillamine is a chelating agent that appears to have immunomodulating effects. Its major side effect is bone marrow depression. Other multiple side effects have led to its decreased usage.

If a patient fails to respond to all other drugs, the final step in the traditional sequence is to place the patient on cytotoxic or immunosuppressive drugs, azathioprine, cyclophosphamide, or most commonly, methotrexate (MTX). Low dose, pulsed MTX has the least serious side effects, and experience with its use in RA in the past 5 years has dramatically altered how patients with RA are medically managed.[46] Increasingly, physicians choose MTX earlier, either in place of gold therapy, or after gold therapy has failed and before penicillamine.[47] Cyclophosphamide has potentially the most serious side effects, including a predisposition to malignancy and leukopenia, and may additionally cause alopecia. Six months or more may be required in order to determine the effectiveness of one of these drugs.[1,48-50]

Drug Management in Osteoarthritis

The goals of drug therapy in patients with OA are to relieve pain and decrease inflammation when it is present. As our understanding of articular degeneration increases, it is expected that approaches to modifying the disease will be developed. The first line of defense in the medical management of OA is aspirin. Aspirin is used primarily for its analgesic effect at much lower doses than are required to achieve the antiinflammatory effect, which is obtained by using aspirin in higher doses in RA. Acetaminophen may also be used for analgesia, but it does not have a separate antiinflammatory effect as aspirin does. Many patients cannot tolerate long-term aspirin therapy and may be switched to an NSAID (Table 21–4). Although these drugs have side effects as well, they are much better tolerated by most individuals for long-term therapy. One of the important ways in which these drugs differ from each other is in their half-lives. A physician will take the ability to clear the drug rapidly into account if a certain side effect might be especially harmful to a particular patient.[1,51,52]

Surgical Management

Surgery represents one of the greatest advances in the management of RA in the last 30 years. It has also added to the armamentarium for treatment for OA. Surgery is not appropriate, however, for every individual with either RA or OA, and the careful selection of the patient and the timing of the procedure is critical. The primary indications for surgery are pain, loss of function and progression of deformity, although the last two are not always correlated. Surgical outcomes are greatly affected by the personal characteristics of the individual patient such as motivation and the quality of postoperative rehabilitation. The postoperative rehabilitation goals are to restore mobility to the affected joint, promote stability within the joint, and regain active control of joint motion.

In general there are three procedures that may be performed on soft tissues: synovectomy, soft tissue release, and tendon transfers. Similarly, there are three general bone and joint procedures: **osteotomy,** prosthetic **arthroplasty,** and **arthrodesis.** The choice of specific postoperative physical therapy procedures will depend upon the particular surgical intervention, the extent of joint involvement prior to surgery, and individual characteristics of the patient, including the disease. It is particularly important to remember that the patient with RA, compared to a peer with OA, will have multiple joint involvement, and that this will ultimately affect the functional outcome of the procedure. The patient with RA is also likely to be a surgical candidate at a much younger age than the patient with OA.[1,53]

REHABILITATIVE MANAGEMENT

Because arthritis is a chronic, progressive disease, care providers must always concern themselves with the long-range trajectory of the illness beyond the particular point in time that the care is provided. Rheumatoid arthritis is a systemic disease with multiple impacts on all facets of the individual's life. Osteoarthritis can significantly alter a person's function and quality of life. While each professional regards the individual as a whole person, the expertise of each professional addresses only certain aspects of the complex and interconnected problems faced by that individual. Without a broad range of expertise, none of these problems can be adequately solved. Therefore, the rehabilitation of the individual with arthritis requires the intense and coordinated efforts of a variety of health professionals, including physical therapists. While a therapist may provide services to assist a person in adjusting to the effects of a medical condition, it is the individual who must live within the constraints imposed by the illness each day and is the ultimate authority on the goals of therapy in whatever setting services are provided.

The objectives of treatment of OA and RA are similar: to maximize function and impede or remediate musculoskeletal impairment. Due to the global effects of RA on function, the remainder of this chapter will concentrate on the patient with RA, assuming that similar goals and treatment will apply to the individual with OA and can be adapted whenever it is appropriate.

The overall rehabilitation goals in RA are specific to the three stages of inflammation: acute, subacute, and chronic. During the acute stage, the primary goal is to reduce pain and inflammation by resting affected joints and applying pain relief modalities. Other goals are to maintain ROM, strength, and endurance, and assist independence in activities of daily living (ADLs). As the inflammation subsides and the individual enters the subacute stage, efforts should be directed towards increasing ROM, strength, and endurance and regaining independence in a broader range of ADLs. Affected joints should continue to be protected through proper positioning and reduced biomechanical stress. Once the inflammatory process has been controlled, the goals of rehabilitative management will change. Expanded goals will include the independent resumption of previous ADL levels, including work. The rehabilitation program will also seek to maintain optimal levels of physical, psychologic, and social functioning, with particular emphasis on patient education that enables the individual to reestablish a sense of control over his or her life despite chronic illness.[13,54]

Physical Therapy Assessment

The primary functional limitations of the individual with RA result from impairment of the musculoskeletal system. Therefore, an extensive and careful assessment of the musculoskeletal system as it contributes to the overall functional disability of the patient is imperative. Because quality care of the individual with RA involves an entire team of professionals, the physical therapist must carefully review the chart, if one is available in the setting in which the services will be provided, and consult with all other care-givers to ascertain their proposed plans and goals of treatment. The physical therapist should begin an evaluation by taking a patient history that will orient the therapist to the nature and extent of the current problem and relate that problem to the patient's past medical history. During the interview the therapist should elicit from the patient that individual's understanding of the disease and what is personally seen as the major problem at hand. In the acute and subacute stages, the patient is most often concerned with pain, which should be assessed in terms of its location, duration, and intensity; the therapist should also assess the other signs of inflammation: heat, **erythema,** and swelling. In the chronic stages, individuals are usually more concerned with loss of function, deformity, and the prevention of further deterioration. Specific information on joint symptoms, morning stiffness, previous level of activity, pattern and degree of fatigue, and current medication regimen should also be gathered. Although the majority of physical assessment procedures to be used in evaluating the individual with RA are generic to the practice of physical therapy, many of these procedures require particular adaptations due to the nature of joint involvement.

RANGE OF MOTION

Goniometric measurement of passive ROM is indicated at all affected joints, following a gross ROM assessment. Common wisdom suggests that a complete goniometric baseline is useful for documenting the progression of a chronic disease. Unless the method of measurement for each joint has been standardized in the clinical setting and used in every assessment, the potential variations in intra-rater and inter-rater reliability of goniometry call this practice into question, particularly given the considerable time that gathering such a database requires.[55] Although such a database may be useful in terms of a particular course of physical therapy, it is of questionable value when compared to data collected by another therapist using a different instrument and method of measurement. If joint pain or poor activity tolerance prohibit measurement of passive ROM, the therapist may consider substituting a functional ROM test by asking the patient to touch various body parts (e.g., the top of the head and small of the back) in order to determine the ROM available for performing self-care activities. During the ROM assessment, the therapist should note any tenderness, crepitus, or pain on movement.

STRENGTH

Application of standard manual muscle tests to assess strength in RA may be inappropriate because of pain at various points in the range. A patient may be strong in the pain-free portion of the range, but weak secondary to reflex inhibition in the very portion of the range that is essential to a functional activity. Joint effusions also inhibit muscle contraction.[56] Individuals with severe deformity and deranged joints are inappropriate candidates for traditional tests of strength. A functional test of strength, therefore, is a better indicator of rehabilitation needs and will identify the desired functional outcomes of strengthening programs prior to initiating treatment. An additional complicating factor in the application of conventional muscle tests is the frequent display of the lag phenomenon. Because the patient is able to move only partway through the available range, traditional grading systems are not sensitive to recording changes as the gap between active and passive ROM narrows in response to treatment. A therapist may want to comment specifically on the degrees of active motion and the grade of strength exhibited in that arc of motion. If a traditional testing method is used, therapists should also document the particular approach to testing used (e.g., break testing, isometric holding at the end of range, or resistance throughout the ROM), which will clarify the meaning of the grade assigned. Break testing generally yields higher grades than would be received if full range testing were done. It is also important to record whether the patient was receiving any medications that might alter performance or exercise tolerance. The therapist may also wish to document the time of day to take into account the effects of morning stiffness.

JOINT STABILITY

The ligamentous laxity of any affected joint should be fully investigated. Ligamentous instability of upper and lower extremity joints may be a significant deterrent to ADLs and ambulation. Improper loading of an unstable joint may also further contribute to its deformation.

ENDURANCE

Fatigue is one of the systemic manifestations of RA and should be carefully evaluated both during the course of a single day and over several days in order to obtain a full understanding of its pattern. The decreased cardiovascular fitness of individuals with RA demands specific attention.[57] Heart rate, respiratory rate, and blood pressure should all be measured during a functional activity that is reasonably stressful for the patient's current level of fitness. Excessive increases may indicate the need for more extensive and sophisticated testing. Because the costosternal and costovertebral articulations are synovial joints, chest expansion, breathing, and coughing may be compromised in the patient with RA and should be evaluated.

FUNCTIONAL ASSESSMENT

As with any long-term disease process, a number of different functional tests may be indicated. Functional assessments may include ADLs, work, and leisure activities. The choice of a functional assessment instrument is influenced by several factors, including the characteristics and needs of the individual patient, the level and depth of information required, and its predictive value in gauging the efficacy of treatment.[58-60] As with goniometric measurement, the reliability and validity of the instrument should be known if the data are to be used for comparative purposes. The Functional Status Index, which was designed expressly to be used in outpatient rheumatologic settings, is an instrument that is known to be reliable and valid, as well as to provide enough baseline data to be an effective screen of patient performance (see Appendix A).[61,62] This instrument is used to establish an individual's function in a representative sample of typical ADLs, along with the parameters of the pain, difficulty, and dependence experienced by the individual in performing these activities. Another arthritis-specific instrument, the Arthritis Impact Measurement Scales (AIMS), expands the concept of function to include performance in psychologic and social domains, as well as the physical. The AIMS also measures the patient's satisfaction with current functional status and individual preferences for outcome.[63]

FUNCTIONAL MOBILITY AND GAIT

A complete assessment of bed mobility and transfers is essential, particularly in the initial acute stage or in later recurrence of multiple joint inflammation. A complete and detailed gait evaluation is one of the most important contributions of the physical therapist to the rehabilitation team's understanding of the individual's functional abilities, and serves to identify additional areas for evaluation and treatment throughout the gait cycle (Table 24-5).[64] Substantial differences in knee ROM and gait velocity between patients with either OA or RA and their peers without arthritis have been demonstrated.[65]

SENSORY ASSESSMENT

Any indication of peripheral neuropathy or nerve involvement should be investigated using standard assessment procedures (see Chapter 6). Sensory changes that are concomitant with other conditions, such as diabetes, or normal processes, such as aging, should be considered when appropriate.

PSYCHOLOGIC STATUS

Despite folklore to the contrary, there is no personality type specific to individuals with RA or any other kind of arthritis that has been demonstrated in any scientifically acceptable way.[66-68] Reports of pain are, however, significantly correlated with self-reports of depression but are not correlated with functional level.[69] The overall psychologic status of the individual with RA is generally similar to those individuals with other chronic diseases that threaten a severe change in body image and disruption of social integration. Individuals respond to these threats with various coping strategies to maintain psychologic equilibrium. No single strategy is better than another, although some strategies ultimately facilitate the achievement of positive outcomes, while others will hinder an individual's progress toward self-chosen goals. Assessment of the patient's attitude toward rehabilitation as well as that of family members can assist the therapist in achieving the goals of treatment and instill a realistic, yet positive, orientation to future functional ability. The individual with RA is requested to implement a series of changes in daily life with respect to medications, exercise, and self-care. Failure to comply with professional recommendations is often interpreted as a rejection of the care-provider's assistance or psychologically maladaptive behavior. The physical therapist must avoid using professional authority as a reason to exert control over another person. Allowing the individual to set the direction of treatment and to use the expertise of the care-provider to attain these self-chosen goals offers the greatest opportunity for responsible and humane care.

ARCHITECTURAL BARRIERS

The therapist should be aware of physical barriers in the home and work environments that might require specific evaluation and recommendations for change (see Chapter 12). A discussion about the home and work environments may reveal conditions that impede regaining complete independence and can make the individual aware of the possibilities for altering these environments. The costs of such changes may be a limiting factor to implementing these recommendations.

TREATMENT

Specific goals of physical therapy treatment for the individual with arthritis include the following:
1. Decrease pain.
2. Increase or maintain the ROM of all joints sufficient for all functional activities.
3. Increase or maintain muscle strength sufficient for the patient's level of function.
4. Increase joint stability and decrease biomechanical stress on all affected joints.
5. Increase endurance for all functional activities.
6. Promote independence in all ADLs, including bed mobility and transfers.
7. Improve efficiency and safety of gait pattern.
8. Educate the patient, family, and other personnel to promote the individual's capacity for self-management.

The particular goal identified for each patient will depend on the type of arthritis, the clinical presentation, and individual circumstances. While programs for individuals with chronic diseases usually stress self-reliance, therapists must be accountable for their own professional actions. This includes determining the plan of care, implementing that plan safely and effectively, and delegating responsibility appropriately. One component of professional accountability is a documentation of treatment goals that allows an outside party to determine the purposes of treatment and the degree to which the therapist has realized these objectives. The therapist should also be able to ensure that these objectives are attained in the most expedient manner. Treatment goals should be specifically tailored to meet the needs of the patient and should be stated clearly in terms of measurable outcomes and the time period proposed for achievement: for example, increase ROM of the left shoulder in 3 weeks, and independent ambulation with platform crutches for at least 250 feet without fatigue within 1 month. Stating time frames for achievement of goals serves as a check for the therapist. Failure to achieve a certain outcome in a proposed period of time suggests that the therapist needs to reevaluate the nature of the problem or reformulate the treatment program along different lines to produce the desired effect. Goals should be revised to reflect changes in anticipated outcomes owing to other factors that may affect progress or alter the proposed time frames.

Treatment Procedures

MODALITIES FOR PAIN RELIEF

Therapists may choose from a variety of physical agents that provide superficial and deep heat, as well as superficial cold, to affected joints. The primary purpose of using any of these modalities is to suppress and to control the symptoms of inflammation. Superficial heat is used to produce localized analgesia and increase local circulation in the area to which it is applied. It penetrates only a few millimeters, however, and does not enter the depth of the synovial cavity. Superficial heat can be delivered through a number of means: moist hot pack, dry heating pads and lamps, paraffin, and hydrotherapy. There is no conclusive evidence that any method of application achieves a significantly better therapeutic effect, but patients often report clinically a greater tolerance for and comfort derived from moist heat. Paraffin is particularly useful in delivering superficial heat to irregularly shaped joints or to individuals who cannot tolerate the weight of a moist hot pack. Although paraffin mixtures can be concocted at home by the patient, instructions for its use should be provided cautiously because of the high flammability of the wax. Although hydrotherapy is one of the most expensive and time-consuming methods for delivering superficial heat, it does have the added advantage that the therapist can combine heat with exercise. It may also orient the patient to the value of a therapeutic swimming program that can be undertaken in conjunction with, or following, treatment.[70] Deep heating modalities may affect the

viscoelastic properties of collagen and increase the plastic stretch of ligaments. Their use in treating individuals with RA during the acute stage of inflammation is contraindicated in that they may stimulate collagenase activity within the joint and further its destruction.[71-73]

Local applications of cold will also produce local analgesia and increase superficial circulation at the site of application following an initial period of vasoconstriction. It is particularly useful around joints that are swollen, a condition that usually worsens with the application of superficial heat modalities. Therapists may use either wet or dry application techniques. Superficial cold is contraindicated in patients with Raynaud's phenomenon or cryoglobulinemia, the presence of an abnormal protein in the blood that forms gels at low temperatures. Both may be associated with RA.[54]

Therapists may also wish to consider using other modalities for pain relief in treating the individual with RA, including relaxation training and transcutaneous electrical nerve stimulation (TENS), although the value of the latter as reported in the literature is controversial.[74,75] Splints may be used to immobilize specific joints and help reduce pain and swelling by providing local rest. They may also negatively affect function during the times they are worn and should be used judiciously for this purpose.[13] Complete bed rest may similarly be beneficial but should be weighed against the deleterious systemic effects on the musculoskeletal and cardiopulmonary systems its overuse can produce.[54,76-78]

JOINT MOBILITY

A major factor affecting joint mobility in individuals with RA is the position in which they are kept when not in motion. Patients should be taught proper positioning when resting and should be encouraged to self-perform ROM to the extent possible, especially when any joint has been immobilized. In the acute stage, joint motion should be kept to a minimum as repetitive motion aggravates inflammation and delays recovery.[79] Therapists may apply neurophysiologic principles of therapeutic exercise to lengthen shortened muscles.[80] Patients should be given the opportunity to rest frequently when performing these exercises. Pain should be respected at all times and should be minimal after exercise. Common wisdom recommends that exercise-induced pain should subside within 1 hour. If the patient reports discomfort in excess of 1 hour, it is a good indicator that either the intensity or the duration of the exercise was too great and should be reduced at the next treatment session. Patients should be encouraged to exercise on their own during those times of the day when they feel best. Therapists should coordinate their treatment sessions with a patient's medication schedule so that treatment will be administered during a period of maximum analgesia. Local pain-relief modalities prior to or following treatment are important considerations and should be used as indicated. Splints and casts may be used to maintain newly gained ROM following treatment.[54]

STRENGTHENING

The role of isometric exercise in the treatment of individuals during the acute stage of inflammation is well accepted because of the low increase in intraarticular pressure and minimal joint movement involved.[81,82] It appears that as few as six maximal isometric contractions held for 6 seconds each will effectively increase isometric strength.[83] Isometrics should be done throughout the range, in order to ensure the ability of the muscle to hold isometrically through the range during functional activities.[84] There is little evidence, however, that isometric strength will carry over to isotonic function, which also requires endurance.[85] The literature has not expressly addressed the disease-specific problems of isotonic strengthening in RA. Can muscle really be strengthened in light of the known selective fiber atrophy that occurs with this disease, and which is unrelated to disuse? If a muscle must be fatigued in order to be strengthened, can the individual with systemic fatigue work at the appropriate intensity and duration? Muscle function is specific to its training and use. The most important consideration for the therapist, then, is the kind of contraction required by the patient's functional activity. Most functional activities require combinations of isotonic as well as isometric contractions. Isotonic and isokinetic exercise should be instituted as soon as the symptoms of inflammation subside.

JOINT STABILITY

Splints may be used to relieve pain, reduce inflammation, protect weak joints, preserve anatomic alignments, and enhance function. There is no conclusive evidence, however, that they prevent deformities beyond the fact that they help to relieve inflammation during acute periods.[13] Therapists should target functional activities that require specific techniques of joint protection.[86] Patients should be encouraged to incorporate joint care into all ADLs in order to minimize pain and conserve energy (see Appendix B).

Splinting of the lower extremity joints may also provide relief during periods of acute inflammation and pain.[87] When the patient is ready to resume functional activities and ambulation, foot orthotics can serve the dual purpose of relieving biomechanical stresses and enhancing function.[23,88] Finding the proper shoe can be a vexing problem for the individual with arthritic foot deformities, particularly as cosmesis evaporates with each additional recommendation for a shoe modification. The cost of special shoes may be formidable for some individuals and may not be reimbursable under many insurance programs. A good shoe will provide support and eliminate unnecessary joint motion in the talocalcaneal joint with a firm and wide heel counter. It should also help to maintain normal bony alignment and accommodate all existing foot deformities within a toe box of adequate dimensions. Pressure should be evenly distributed along the plantar surface of the foot during weight bearing. The latter goal may require the fabrication of orthotics.

ENDURANCE TRAINING

The cardiovascular fitness of individuals with RA or OA may be compromised. Several studies have attested to the ability to improve this impairment through regular cardiovascular conditioning, without aggravating

joints. Programs, similar to those designed for patients with cardiac conditions, can be instituted for individuals with arthritis by adapting the method of conditioning to a non-weight-bearing apparatus such as a bicycle ergometer. Furthermore, patients who have engaged in such a program often report an increase in self-esteem and psychological outlook.[89-95]

FUNCTIONAL TRAINING

Functional training for the individual with arthritis proceeds in the same fashion as for other individuals with similar deficits. Therapists may choose to reduce the functional demands of an activity either temporarily (for instance, under conditions of acute inflammation), or permanently, by incorporating into ADLs a variety of aids that substitute for lost ROM and strength. These modifications can include long-handled appliances, and devices with built-up handles for easier grasp. There are aids for dressing and grooming as well as personal hygiene.

Upper extremity involvement, particularly of the wrist and hands, may complicate the choice of an ambulation aid by barring any weight bearing on these affected joints. In these instances, platform attachments can be used to transform the forearm into a weight-bearing surface. Rearranging the home or work environment also can improve a person's functional abilities. Raising beds or chairs can reduce the effort needed to stand up. Railings placed around the bed and bath, and along stairways can also help increase an individual's independence.

GAIT TRAINING

Specific gait deviations will be evident throughout the gait cycle. These will include decreased velocity, cadence, and stride length; prolonged period of double support; inadequate heel strike and toe off; and diminished joint excursion through both swing and stance. Gait deviations in the patient with RA that are specifically due to progressive foot deformities will also be evident (Table 21–5).[65] Therapists should address the underlying joint and muscle impairments that contribute to these deviations prior to initiating gait training with persons with any type of arthritis.

The degree to which the gait of an individual with arthritis should, or can, approximate normal gait is one of the most difficult questions in designing a therapeutic program. Some "abnormalities" such as antalgic limping may in fact reduce joint loading. Joint destruction may necessitate the introduction of ambulation aids as cumbersome as platform crutches or rolling walkers with platform attachments. The gait of the individual with RA or OA should be safe, functional, and cosmetically acceptable to the patient rather than an unattainable idealized version of the norm.

EDUCATION

The goals for teaching will be as varied as the individuals who seek treatment. The Arthritis Foundation can supply the clinician or the individual with a variety of educational materials, pamphlets, and self-help courses that will increase cognitive understanding of the disease

Table 21–5 ANALYSIS OF GAIT DEVIATIONS, PHYSICAL EXAMINATION FINDINGS, AND TREATMENT GOALS

Gait Deviations	Physical Examination Findings	Treatment Goals
Pronated foot Shuffled progression Decreased step length Initial contact with medial border of foot Decreased single-limb balance Prolonged double-support phase Late heel rise Plantarflexion of ipsilateral ankle in swing Genu valgus with weight bearing	Tenderness over subtalar midtarsal area Limited inversion range Weak and painful posterior tibialis muscle Pronated weight-bearing posture of foot Lax medial collateral ligament of knee	Relieve subtalar and midtarsal joint stresses Increase ankle inversion Strengthen posterior tibialis muscle Stabilize hypermobile joints with rigid orthosis Maintain neutral alignment in stance by foot positioning
Hallux valgus Lateral and posterior weight shift Late heel rise Decreased single-limb balance	Lateral deviation of great toe Swelling of first MTP joint Shortening of flexor hallucis brevis muscle Tenderness of great toe Weakness of great toe abduction	Accommodate foot with wide toe box shoe Increase extension of great toe Relieve weight-bearing stresses
Metatarsophalangeal joint subluxation Diminished roll off Decreased single-limb stance Apropulsive progression Decreased single-limb balance	Painful MTP heads with weight bearing Callus formation over MTP heads Ulcerations over MTP heads Limited MTP flexion Prominent MTP heads	Redistribute pressure with metatarsal bar Relieve pressure with soft cutout shoe insert Increase flexion mobility of MTP joints Accommodate foot with extra-depth shoe
Hammer or claw toes Diminished roll off Decreased single-limb stance Apropulsive progression Decreased single-limb balance	Posture of MTP joint hyperextension with proximal and distal interphalangeal joint flexion Posture of MTP and distal interphalangeal joint hyperextension with proximal interphalangeal flexion Callus formation at plantar tips and dorsum of proximal interphalangeal joint Limited MTP flexion	Improve toe alignment with metatarsal bar Accommodate foot with extra-depth shoe Diminish pressure with soft insert Increase toe mobility
Painful heel Toe-heel pattern No heel contact in stance Decreased stride length Decreased velocity Plantar flexion of ankle in swing Increased hip flexion in swing Decreased step length of contralateral limb	Painful active plantar flexion Painful passive and active dorsiflexion Swelling and pain at Achilles insertion Tenderness over spur Decreased ankle dorsiflexion range	Decrease inflammation with steroid injection or modalities Relieve weight-bearing stress Decrease pressure over spur with soft shoe insert Maintain ankle mobility

From Dimonte and Light,[64] with permission.
MTP = metatarsal-phalangeal.

process and promote self-management skills. Many local chapters of the Foundation hold individual and family support groups to increase psychosocial adaptation as well. The Arthritis Health Professions Association, the professional section of the Arthritis Foundation, can provide the therapist with scientific and clinical enrichment for enhanced practice as well as a network of professional colleagues who work in rheumatology.

SUMMARY

Rheumatoid arthritis and OA are the two kinds of arthritis that a physical therapist is likely to see in clinical practice. The primary functional limitations of the individual with RA or OA result from musculoskeletal impairments. Irregularities on the bone surface, loss of joint mobility, muscle weakness, and atrophy contribute directly to limitations in ADLs and the ability to work. Pain, secondary to changes in normal joint structure and function, often limits function as well. Musculoskeletal impairments related to arthritis may also lead to impairments of other systems, such as decreased cardiovascular endurance for functional activities. The physical therapist is well suited to evaluate and treat these impairments and remediate the functional limitations they cause. Rehabilitation of the individual with arthritis is most often directed toward restoring or maintaining joint mobility and strength, and emphasizes functional retraining, especially patient education, which promotes the highest possible level of functional independence.

QUESTIONS FOR REVIEW

1. What epidemiologic factors are related to RA?
2. What are the major pathologic changes seen in RA?
3. State two hypotheses concerning the pathogenesis of RA.
4. Describe three factors that may predispose an individual to osteoarthritis.
5. Describe two changes in articular cartilage associated with osteoarthritis.
6. Name at least two laboratory tests used in the diagnosis of RA and state their purposes.
7. Explain three parameters for orienting to radiographs.
8. Describe the joint changes seen in each joint in the individual with RA.
9. Define ulnar drift, swan neck, boutonniere, hammer toes, claw toes, and hallux valgus.
10. Describe the overall goals of medical management in RA and OA.
11. What are the primary indications for surgery in RA?
12. Discuss the psychosocial impacts of arthritis and suggest how the physical therapist may assist the individual in coping with them.

13. Describe the key points to be covered in taking a history on the individual with arthritis.
14. What sort of adaptations of standard evaluation procedures should be made in evaluating the individual with RA?
15. What are the general goals of physical therapy in treating individuals with RA or OA?
16. Explain the progression of a strengthening program and the purpose of each kind of exercise.
17. Discuss treatment alternatives for increasing ROM.
18. Design a cardiovascular conditioning program for an individual with joint involvement.
19. State at least four principles of joint protection and give a practical application of each.
20. What criteria guide the selection of shoes for the individual with RA?
21. What are the purposes of splints?
22. Describe gait deviations commonly associated with RA.
23. Describe what kinds of assistive devices and ambulation aids are most suited to the individual with RA.

REFERENCES

1. Schumacher, HR, Klippel, JH, and Robinson, DR (eds): Primer on the Rheumatic Diseases, ed 9. Arthritis Foundation, Atlanta, 1988.
2. Arnett, FC, et al: The American Rheumatism Association 1987 revised criteria for the classification of rheumatoid arthritis. Arth Rheum 31:315, 1988.
3. O'Sullivan, JB and Cathcart, ES: The prevalence of rheumatoid arthritis. Followup evaluation of the effect of criteria on rates in Sudbury, Massachusetts. Ann Intern Med 76:573, 1972.
4. Harris, ED, Jr: The clinical features of rheumatoid arthritis. In Kelley, WN, et al (eds): Textbook of Rheumatology, ed 3. WB Saunders, Philadelphia, 1989.
5. Spector, TD: Rheumatoid arthritis. Rheum Dis Clin North Am 6 16:513, 1990.
6. Crow, MK and Friedman, SM: Microbial superantigens and autoimmune response. Bull Rheum Dis 41:1–4, 1992.
7. Panayi, GS, Lanchbury, JS, and Kingsley, GH: The importance of the T cell in initiating and maintaining the chronic synovitis of rheumatoid arthritis. Arthritis Rheum 35:729, 1992.
8. Bennett, JC: The etiology of rheumatic diseases. In Kelley, WN, et al (eds): Textbook of Rheumatology, ed 3. WB Saunders, Philadelphia, 1989.
9. Fox, RI, et al: Epstein Barr virus in rheumatoid arthritis. Clin Rheum Dis 11:665, 1985.
10. Harris, ED, Jr: Pathogenesis of rheumatoid arthritis. In Kelley, WN, et al (eds): Textbook of Rheumatology, ed 3. WB Saunders, Philadelphia, 1989.
11. Goldstein, R and Arnett, FC: The genetics of rheumatic disease in man. Rheum Dis Clin North Am 13:487, 1987.
12. Firestein, GS and Zvaifler, NJ: The pathogenesis of rheumatoid arthritis. Rheum Dis Clin North Am 13:447, 1987.
13. Melvin, JL: Rheumatic Disease: Occupational Therapy and Rehabilitation, ed 3. FA Davis, Philadelphia, 1989.
14. Moncur, C, and Williams, HJ: Cervical spine management in patients with rheumatoid arthritis. Phys Ther 68:509, 1988.
15. Kramer, J, Jolesz, F, and Kleefield, J: Rheumatoid arthritis of the cervical spine. Rheum Dis Clin North Am 17:757, 1991.
16. Gibson, KR: Rheumatoid arthritis of the shoulder. Phys Ther 66:1920, 1986.
17. Hakstian, RW and Tubiana, R: Ulnar deviation of the fingers. J Bone Joint Surg Am 49(A):299, 1967.
18. Pahle, JA and Raunio, P: The influence of wrist position on finger

deviation in the rheumatoid hand. J Bone Joint Surg Br 51(B):664, 1969.
19. Swezey, RL and Fiegenberg, DS: Inappropriate intrinsic muscle action in the rheumatoid hand. Ann Rheum Dis 30:619, 1971.
20. Smith, EM, et al: Role of the finger flexors in rheumatoid deformities of the metacarpophalangeal joints. Arthritis Rheum 7:467, 1964.
21. English, CB and Nalebuff, EA: Understanding the arthritic hand. Am J Occup Ther 7:352, 1971.
22. Nalebuff, EA: Diagnosis, classification and management of rheumatoid thumb deformities. Bull Hosp J Dis 24:119, 1968.
23. Moncur, C and Shields, M: Clinical management of metatarsalgia in the patient with arthritis. Clin Management Phys Ther 3:7, 1983.
24. Kirkup, JR, et al: The hallux and rheumatoid arthritis. Acta Orthop Scand 48:527, 1977.
25. Edstrom, L and Nordemar, R: Differential changes in Type I and Type II muscle fibers in rheumatoid arthritis. Scand J Rheumol 3:155, 1974.
26. Nordemar, R, et al: Changes in muscle fiber size and physical performance in patients with rheumatoid arthritis after 7 months physical training. Scand J Rheumol 5:233, 1976.
27. Edstrom, L: Selective atrophy of red muscle fibers in the quadriceps in longstanding knee-joint dysfunction. J Neurol Sci 11:551, 1970.
28. Forrester, DM and Brown, JC: The radiographic assessment of arthritis: the plain film. Clin Rheum Dis 9:291, 1983.
29. Tessler, HH: The eye in rheumatic disease. Bull Rheum Dis 35:1, 1985.
30. Pincus, T and Callahan, LF: Early mortality in RA predicted by poor clinical status. Bull Rheum Dis 41:1, 1992.
31. Deal, CL, et al: The clinical features of elderly-onset rheumatoid arthritis. Arthritis Rheum 28:987, 1985.
32. Yelin, EH, Henke, C, and Epstein, W: The work dynamics of the person with rheumatoid arthritis. Arthritis Rheum 30:507, 1987.
33. Yelin, E and Felts, WR: A summary of the impact of musculoskeletal conditions in the United States. Arthritis Rheum 33:750, 1990.
34. Mankin, HJ and Brandt, KD: Pathogenesis of osteoarthritis. In Kelley, WN, et al (eds): Textbook of Rheumatology, ed 3. WB Saunders, Philadelphia, 1989.
35. Mankin, HJ: Clinical features of osteoarthritis. In Kelley, WN, et al (eds): Textbook of Rheumatology, ed 3. WB Saunders, Philadelphia, 1989.

36. Kellgren, JH and Lawrence, JS: Atlas of Standard Radiographs: The Epidemiology of Chronic Rheumatism, vol 2. Blackwell Scientific, Oxford, 1963.

37. Felson, DT: Osteoarthritis. Rheum Dis Clin North Am 16:499, 1990.

38. Moskowitz, RW: Osteoarthritis—signs and symptoms. In Moskowitz, RW, et al (eds): Osteoarthritis: Diagnosis and Medical/Surgical Management, ed 2. Philadelphia, WB Saunders, 1992.

39. Brandt, KD and Fife, RS: Ageing in relation to the pathogenesis of osteoarthritis. Clin Rheum Dis 12:117, 1986.

40. Anderson, JJ and Felson, DT: Factors associated with knee osteoarthritis (OA) in the HANES I survey: evidence for an association with overweight, race and physical demands of work. Am J Epidemiol 128:179, 1988.

41. Felson, DT, et al: Obesity and knee osteoarthritis: the Framingham Study. Ann Intern Med 109:18, 1988.

42. Threlkeld, AJ and Currier, DP: Osteoarthritis: effects on synovial joint tissues. Phys Ther 68:364, 1988.

43. Guccione, AA, Felson, DT, and Anderson, JJ: Defining arthritis and measuring functional status in elders: methodological issues in the study of disease and disability. Am J Public Health 80:945, 1990.

44. Healey, LA and Wilske, KR: Reforming the pyramid: a plan for treating rheumatoid arthritis in the 1990s. Rheum Dis Clin North Am 15:615, 1989.

45. Felson, DT, Anderson, JJ, and Meenan, RF: The comparative efficacy and toxicity of second-line drugs in rheumatoid arthritis. Arthritis Rheum 33:1449, 1990.

46. Kremer, JM: Methotrexate therapy in the treatment of rheumatoid arthritis. Rheum Dis Clin North Am 15:533, 1989.

47. Harris, ED, Jr: Management of rheumatoid arthritis. In Kelley, WN, et al (eds): Textbook of Rheumatology, ed 3. WB Saunders, Philadelphia, 1989.

48. Roth, SR: Drug therapy and the rehabilitation process: a necessary interaction. In Ehrlich, GE (ed): Rehabilitation Management of Rheumatic Conditions. Williams & Wilkins, Baltimore, 1986.

49. Klinefelter, HF: Drug treatment of rheumatoid arthritis. Clin Rheumatol in Practice 3:100, 1985.

50. Goldenberg, DL and Cohen, AS: Drugs in the Rheumatic Diseases. Grune & Stratton, Orlando, FL, 1986.

51. Brandt, KD: Management of osteoarthritis. In Kelley, WN, et al (eds): Textbook of Rheumatology, ed 3. WB Saunders, Philadelphia, 1989.

52. Batchlor, EE and Paulus, HE: Principles of drug therapy. In Moskowitz, RW, et al (eds): Osteoarthritis: Diagnosis and Medical/Surgical Management, ed 2. Philadelphia, WB Saunders, 1992.

53. Sledge, CB: Reconstructive surgery in rheumatic diseases. In Kelley, WN, et al (eds): Textbook of Rheumatology, ed 3. WB Saunders, Philadelphia, 1989.

54. Gerber, LH: Rehabilitation of patients with rheumatic diseases. In Kelley, WN, et al (eds): Textbook of Rheumatology, ed 3. WB Saunders, Philadelphia, 1989.

55. Miller, PJ: Assessment of joint motion. In Rothstein, JM (ed): Measurement in Physical Therapy. Churchill Livingstone, New York, 1985.

56. Geborek, P, Moritz, U, and Wollheim, FA: Joint capsular stiffness in knee arthritis. Relationship to intraarticular volume, hydrostatic pressures, and extensor muscle function. J Rheumatol 16:1351, 1989.

57. Ekblom, B, et al: Physical performance in patients with rheumatoid arthritis. Scand J Rheumatol 3:121, 1974.

58. Liang, MH, et al: Comparative measurement efficiency and sensitivity of five health status instruments for arthritis research. Arthritis Rheum 28:542, 1985.

59. Guccione, AA and Jette, AM: Assessing limitations in physical function in patients. Arthritis Care Res 1:120, 1988.

60. Guccione, AA and Jette, AM: Multidimensional assessment of functional limitations in patients with arthritis. Arthritis Care Res 3:44, 1990.

61. Jette, AM: Functional capacity evaluation: an empirical approach. Arch Phys Med Rehabil 61:85, 1980.

62. Jette, AM: Functional Status Index: reliability of a chronic disease evaluation instrument. Arch Phys Med Rehabil 61:395, 1980.

63. Meenan, RF, et al: AIMS2: the content and properties of a revised and expanded Arthritis Impact Measurement Scales health status questionnaire. Arthritis Rheum 35:1, 1992.

64. Dimonte, P and Light, H: Pathomechanics, gait deviations, and treatment of the rheumatoid foot. Phys Ther 62:1148, 1982.

65. Brinkmann, JR and Perry, J: Rate and range of knee motion during ambulation in healthy and arthritic subjects. Phys Ther 65:1055, 1985.

66. Meyerowitz, S: The continuing investigation of psychosocial variables in rheumatoid arthritis. In Hill, AGS (ed): Modern Trends in Rheumatology. Appleton-Century-Crofts, New York, 1971.

67. Wolff, BB: Current psychosocial concepts in rheumatoid arthritis. Bull Rheum Dis 22:656, 1972.

68. Hoffman, AL: Psychological factors associated with rheumatoid arthritis. Nurs Res 23:218, 1974.

69. Bradley, LA: Psychological aspects of arthritis. Bull Rheum Dis 35:1, 1985.

70. Haralson, K: Therapeutic pool programs. Clin Management Phys Ther 2:10, 1985.

71. Harris, ED, Jr and McCroskery, PA: The influence of temperature and fibril stability on degradation of cartilage collagen by rheumatoid synovial collagenase. N Engl J Med 290:1, 1974.

72. Feibel, A and Fast, A: Deep heating of joints: a reconsideration. Arch Phys Med Rehabil 57:513, 1976.

73. Oosterveld, FGJ, et al: The effect of local heat and cold therapy on the intraarticular and skin surface temperature of the knee. Arthritis Rheum 35:146, 1992.

74. Griffin, JW and McClure, M: Adverse responses to transcutaneous electrical nerve stimulation in a patient with rheumatoid arthritis. Phys Ther 61:354, 1981.

75. Mannheimer, C and Carlsson, C: The analgesic effect of transcutaneous electrical nerve stimulation (TENS) in patients with rheumatoid arthritis. A comparative study of different pulse patterns. Pain 6:329, 1979.

76. Partridge, REH and Duthie, JJR: Controlled trial of the effects of complete immobilization of the joints in rheumatoid arthritis. Ann Rheum Dis 22:91, 1963.

77. Gault, SJ and Spyker, JM: Beneficial effects of immobilization of joints in rheumatoid arthritis and related arthritides. Arthritis Rheum 12:34, 1969.

78. Mills, JA, et al: The value of bedrest in patients with rheumatoid arthritis. N Engl J Med 284:453, 1971.

79. Michelsson, JE and Riska, EB: The effect of temporary exercising of a joint during an immobilization period: an experimental study on rabbits. Clin Orthop 144:321, 1979.

80. Cherry, DB: Review of physical therapy alternatives for reducing muscle contracture. Phys Ther 60:877, 1980.

81. Deusinger, RH: Biomechanics in clinical practice. Phys Ther 64:1860, 1984.

82. Jayson, MI and Dixon, AS: Intra-articular pressure in rheumatoid arthritis of the knee. Pressure changes during joint use. Ann Rheum Dis 29:401, 1970.

83. Muller, EA: Influence of training and of inactivity on muscle strength. Arch Phys Med Rehabil 51:449, 1970.

84. Lindh, M: Increase of muscle strength from isometric exercises at different knee angles. Scand J Rehabil Med 11:33, 1979.

85. Grimby, G, et al: Muscle strength and endurance after training with repeated maximal isometric contractions. Scand J Rehabil Med 5:118, 1973.

86. Cordery, JC: Joint protection, a responsibility of the occupational therapist. Am J Occup Ther 19:285, 1965.

87. Nicholas, JJ and Ziegler, G: Cylinder splints: their use in arthritis of the knee. Arch Phys Med Rehabil 58:264, 1977.

88. Locke, M, et al: Ankle and subtalar motion during gait in arthritic patients. Phys Ther 64:504, 1984.

89. Harkcom, TM, et al: Therapeutic value of graded aerobic exercise training in rheumatoid arthritis. Arthritis Rheum 28:32, 1985.

90. Ekblom, B, et al: Effect of short-term physical training on patients with rheumatoid arthritis, I. Scand J Rheumatol 4:80, 1975.

91. Ekblom, B, et al: Effect of short-term physical training on patients with rheumatoid arthritis, II. Scand J Rheumatol 4:87, 1975.

92. Nordemar, R, et al: Physical training in rheumatoid arthritis: a controlled longterm study, I. Scand J Rheumal 10:17, 1981.

93. Nordemar, R: Physical training in rheumatoid arthritis: a controlled longterm study. II. Functional capacity and general attitudes. Scand J Rheumatol 10:25, 1981.

94. Minor, MA, et al: Efficacy of physical conditioning exercise in patients with rheumatoid arthritis and osteoarthritis. Arthritis Rheum 32:1396, 1989.

95. Kovar, PA, et al: Supervised fitness walking in patients with osteoarthritis of the knee. Ann Intern Med 116:529, 1992.

GLOSSARY

Analgesic: Medication or modality used to relieve pain.

Ankylosing spondylitis: Chronic bone and joint disease in which the inflammatory process primarily affects the sacroiliac, spinal facet, and costovertebral joints.

Ankylosis: Immobility or fixation of a joint.

Antibody: A protein developed in response to an antigen, belonging to one of the immunoglobulin classes.

Antigen: Any substance that induces the formation of antibodies that will react specifically to that antigen.

Arthralgia: Pain in a joint.

Arthrodesis: Surgical procedure designed to produce fusion of a joint.

Arthroplasty: Any surgical reconstruction of a joint; may or may not involve prosthetic replacement.

Avascular necrosis: Necrosis of part of a bone secondary to ischemia; most commonly seen in the femoral or humeral head.

Baker's cyst: Cystic swelling behind the knee in the popliteal fossa.

Bouchard's nodes: Osteophyte formation around the proximal interphalangeal joints typical of degenerative joint disease; similar to Heberden's nodes.

Boutonniere deformity: Finger deformity with flexion of the proximal interphalangeal joint and hyperextension of the distal interphalangeal joint.

Bunion: Hallux valgus with a painful bursitis over the medial aspect of the first metatarsophalangeal joint.

Bursitis: Inflammation of a bursa, which can be due to frictional forces, trauma, or rheumatoid diseases.

Calcific tendinitis: Inflammatory involvement of a tendon associated with calcium deposits; commonly affects the supraspinatus and biceps tendons in the shoulder.

Carpal tunnel syndrome: Compression of the median nerve in the carpal flexor space; commonly seen in patients with flexor tenosynovitis.

Cock-up toe (claw toe): Deformity with hyperextension of the metatarsophalangeal joint and flexion of the proximal and distal interphalangeal joints.

Crepitation: A grating, crunching, or popping sensation (or sound) that occurs during joint or tendon motion.

Degenerative joint disease: A name sometimes used for osteoarthritis.

deQuervain's disease: Stenosing tenosynovitis of the first dorsal compartment of the wrist involving the abductor pollicis longus and the extensor pollicis brevis.

Edema: Perceptible accumulation of excess fluid in the tissues.

Effusion: Excess fluid in the joint indicating irritation or inflammation of the synovium; escape of fluid into a body cavity.

Erythema: Redness.

Exostosis: Ossification of muscular or ligamentous attachments.

Fibrosis: Abnormal formation of fibrous tissue.

Gout: Disease characterized by acute episodes of arthritis with the presence of sodium urate crystals in the synovial fluid or deposits of urate crystals in or about the joints and other tissues.

Hallux valgus: Valgus deformity at the first metatarsophalangeal joint.

Hammer toe: Deformity with hyperextension of the metatarsophalangeal joint, flexion of the proximal interphalangeal, and hyperextension of the distal interphalangeal joints.

Heberden's nodes: Bony enlargement of the distal interphalangeal joint; characteristic of primary degenerative joint disease.

Immune response: The reaction of the body to substances that are foreign or interpreted as foreign. A cell-mediated immune response involves the production of lymphocytes by the thymus (T cells) in response to an antigen. A humoral immune response involves the production of plasma lymphocytes (B cells) in response to an antigen and results in the formation of antibodies.

Lag phenomenon: Difference between active and passive range of motion.

Lyme disease: An epidemic, systemic inflammatory disorder transmitted by a tick bite and characterized by recurrent episodes of polyarthritis, skin lesions, and involvement of the cardiac and nervous systems. Named after the Connecticut town where it was first discovered in 1975.

Mallet finger deformity: Deformity involving only flexion of the distal interphalangeal joint; secondary to disruption of the insertion of the extensor tendon into the base of the distal phalanx.

Metatarsal bar: Ridge on the sole of the shoe to relieve metatarsal pressure and pain.

Metatarsal pad: Pad placed inside the shoe proximal to the metatarsal heads to relieve metatarsal pressure and pain.

Metatarsalgia: Pain over the metatarsal heads on the plantar aspect of the foot.

Morning stiffness: This term describes the prolonged generalized stiffness that is associated with the inflammatory arthritis upon awakening. The stiffness is indicative of systemic involvement. The duration of the stiffness correlates with the intensity of the disease. This generalized stiffness is in contrast to the localized stiffness, seen in osteoarthritis, that results from inactivity.

Morton's neuroma: A neuroma of the plantar digital nerve caused by trauma to the nerve as it passes between the metatarsal heads.

Mutilans deformity: Severe bony destruction and resorption in a synovial joint. In the fingers it results in a telescopic shortening (opera-glass hand).

Myalgia: Muscle pain.

Myositis: Inflammatory disease of striated muscle.

Osteoarthritis (DA): The most common rheumatic disease characterized by the progressive loss of articular cartilage and the formation of bone at the joint margin.

Osteophyte: Bone growth at joint margins.

Osteoporosis: Condition characterized by a loss of bone cells. It can be a primary condition or associated with other diseases, drug therapies (steroids), or disuse; can be improved or minimized with exercise.

Osteotomy: Surgical cutting of a bone.

Pannus: Excessive proliferation of synovial granulation tissue that invades the joint surfaces.

Polymyalgia rheumatica: Relatively common condition most typically found over the age of 50 and in females. Characterized by marked pain of the shoulder and pelvic girdle muscles, elevated sedimentation rate, and absence of muscle disease.

Protrusio acetabuli: Condition in which the head of the femur pushes the acetabulum into the pelvic cavity.

Pseudogout: Similar to gout clinically, but in this condition the synovitis is due to deposits of pyrophosphate crystals.

Raynaud's phenomenon: Intermittent attacks of pallor followed by cyanosis, then redness of digits, before return to normal.

Rheumatism: General term for acute and chronic conditions characterized by inflammation, muscle stiffness and soreness, and joint pain.

Rheumatoid arthritis (RA): A systemic disease characterized by a bilateral, symmetrical pattern of joint involvement and chronic inflammation of the synovium.

Rheumatoid factor: An immunoglobulin found in the blood of a high percentage of adults with rheumatoid arthritis. A person may be described as seronegative or seropositive. A latex fixation or sheep cell agglutination test is used to determine if the factor is present.

Rocker sole: Shoe sole, curved at the toe to facilitate push off for limited ankle motion.

Sjögren's syndrome: Disease of the lacrimal and parotid glands, resulting in dry eyes and mouth; frequently occurs with rheumatoid arthritis, systemic lupus erythematosus, and systemic sclerosis.

Splayfoot: Transverse spreading of the forefoot.

Subluxation: Incomplete or partial dislocation.

Swan neck deformity: Finger deformity involving hyperextension of the proximal interphalangeal joint and flexion of the distal interphalangeal joint.

Synovectomy: Surgical procedure to remove the synovial lining of joints or tendon sheaths.

Synovium: Tissue lining synovial joints, tendon sheaths, and bursa. In the joint it produces fluid to lubricate the joint and is the part of the joint that becomes inflamed in inflammatory joint disease.

Synovitis: Inflammation of the synovium.

Systemic: A condition that affects the body as a whole.

Systemic lupus erythematosus: Systemic inflammatory disease characterized by small vessel vasculitis and a diverse clinical picture.

Tendinitis: Inflammation of a tendon.

Tinnitus: Subjective ringing or buzzing sensations in the ear; used as an indicator of aspirin toxicity.

Tophi: Deposits of sodium biurate crystals near joints, in the ear, or in bone.

Zigzag effect: Ulnar drift at the metacarpophalangeal joints associated with radial deviation of the wrist.

APPENDIX A FUNCTIONAL STATUS INDEX

KEY: ASSISTANCE: 1 = independent; 2 = uses devices; 3 = uses human assistance; 4 = uses devices and human
assistance; 5 = unable or unsafe to do the activity

PAIN: 1 = no pain; 2 = mild pain; 3 = moderate pain; 4 = severe pain

DIFFICULTY: 1 = no difficulty; 2 = mild difficulty; 3 = moderate difficulty; 4 = severe difficulty

Time frame: On the average during the past 7 days

Activity	Assistance (1-5)	Pain (1-4)	Difficulty (1-4)	Comments
Mobility				
Walking inside	_____	_____	_____	
Climbing up stairs	_____	_____	_____	
Rising from a chair	_____	_____	_____	
Personal care				
Putting on pants	_____	_____	_____	
Buttoning a shirt/blouse	_____	_____	_____	
Washing all parts of the body	_____	_____	_____	
Putting on a shirt/blouse	_____	_____	_____	
Home chores				
Vacuuming a rug	_____	_____	_____	
Reaching into low cupboards	_____	_____	_____	
Doing laundry	_____	_____	_____	
Doing yardwork	_____	_____	_____	
Hand activities				
Writing	_____	_____	_____	
Opening container	_____	_____	_____	
Dialing a phone	_____	_____	_____	
Social activities				
Performing your job	_____	_____	_____	
Driving a car	_____	_____	_____	
Attending meetings/appointments	_____	_____	_____	
Visiting with friends and relatives	_____	_____	_____	

Used by permission of Alan M. Jette.

APPENDIX B JOINT PROTECTION, REST, AND ENERGY CONSERVATION

JOINT PROTECTION
Why Is Joint Protection Important?

Overuse and abuse of arthritic joints may lead to progressive deterioration of the joint and its surrounding tissues. Positive action is necessary to protect joints, to conserve energy, and to preserve function.

During activity, a normal joint is protected by the muscles around it that absorb the forces on the joint, preventing undue strain on the tendons, ligaments, and cartilage. A diseased joint is mechanically weak and poorly stabilized, which can contribute to the overstretching of the tendons and ligaments and damage to the cartilage. This increased stress can increase the destruction of the joint and cause increased pain.

How Can Joints Be Protected?

The main idea in joint protection is to minimize the strain on joints in daily activities. Joint protection techniques try to reduce the force on the joint, to slow down the joint damage. Good posture and positioning,

changing the method of an activity, and pacing all help to protect the joint.

Which Joints Need Protection?

People with a local type of arthritis, like osteoarthritis, need to pay close attention to the joints that are involved with the arthritis. People with a systemic or whole body type of arthritis, like rheumatoid arthritis, need to reduce the stress on all their joints. In addition to the joint protection principles and examples listed below, people with rheumatoid arthritis should look at the section below entitled Care of Rheumatoid Arthritis in the Hands.

In planning your joint protection, start by concentrating on the joints that are currently giving you the most trouble. Check off the principles that apply most strongly to you, and list several examples of how you can apply that principle to your problem joints.

JOINT PROTECTION PRINCIPLES

Your Examples

☐ 1. *Respect Pain*
   a. It is important to distinguish between discomfort and pain.
   b. Pain that lasts for more than 1 to 2 hours after an activity indicates that the activity is too stressful and needs to be modified.
   c. If there is a sharp increase in pain during activity, stop and rest, then modify the activity
   d. If there is unusual pain or stiffness the next day, look back at the previous day's activities to see if they were too strenuous.

☐ 2. *Avoid Positions of Deformity*
   The foremost position of deformity for most joints is flexion, bending of the joint. Maintaining a bent position increases the possibility of deformity.
   a. Stand erect, with weight evenly divided on both feet.
   b. Lay as flat as possible in bed, do not curl up or prop yourself up on several pillows.
   c. Work with your hands flat.
   d. Avoid tight grip or squeezing.

☐ 3. *Avoid Awkward Positions*
   Use each joint in its most stable and functional position: Extra strain is placed on a joint when it is twisted or rotated.
   a. Rise straight up from sitting, rather than leaning to one side for support.
   b. Reposition feet rather than twisting trunk or knees.
   c. Stand on stool to reach overhead.
   d. Reposition yourself closer to object rather than stretch your reach.
   e. Sit to clean or garden, rather than squatting or kneeling down.
   f. Use good posture when you stand, sit, and lie down.

☐ 4. *Use Strongest Joints or Distribute the Force over Several Joints*
   The stress on each individual joint is less if it is divided over several joints. The larger joints have greater muscles surrounding them to absorb the stress.
   a. Use two hands whenever possible.
   b. Carry packages in both arms rather than in one.
   c. Carry shoulder purse, or purse handle over forearm rather than in fingers.
   d. Use knapsack to carry packages on back.
   e. Lift objects from underneath, using wrist and elbow, rather than pinch gripping the sides.
   f. Lift objects with your knees bent, your back straight.
   g. Move large objects with body weight behind it, the push coming from the legs.
   h. Push with open palm or forearm rather than fingers.

☐ 5. *Use Adapted Equipment*
   Find equipment that will reduce the stress on the joint or make the job easier.
   The Self-Help Manual for People with Arthritis
   A catalog of adapted equipment is available from the local Arthritis Foundation.
   a. Equipment can be modified by
      1. Building up the handle so it is easier to grasp.
      2. Extending the handle so it is easier to reach.
   b. Equipment available:
      Walking aids
      Self-care aids
      Bathroom safety
      Homemaking equipment
      Job modification equipment

Joints that need protection: _____

_____

Activities to be modified: _____

_____

_____

_____

_____

_____

APPENDIX B   JOINT PROTECTION, REST, AND ENERGY CONSERVATION (Continued)

ADDITIONAL REMINDERS FOR THE PROTECTION OF THE RHEUMATOID HAND

1. Through exercise, maintain wrist extension (ability to pick hand up off table) to ensure power grip.
2. Through exercise, maintain supination (ability to turn palm up) to ensure ability to hold and to carry objects.
3. Avoid positions of deformity.
   a. Finger flexion
      1. Avoid making fist or tight grip—use built-up handles.
      2. Work with hand flat—use dust mitts, sponges.
      3. Avoid prolonged holding of objects: pen, book, pan, needle.
      4. Avoid putting any pressure on bent knuckles.
   b. Ulnar deviation (tendency of fingers to slide to little finger side)
      1. Avoid pressure toward little finger side of hand.
      2. Any twisting of hand, open door knobs, jars, etc., should be turned toward thumb.
      3. Grip objects parallel across palm, not diagonal; for example, hold utensil like dagger to cut food, stir with wooden spoon.
4. Avoid stress on small joints of hand.
   a. Use two hands whenever possible.
   b. Substitute larger stronger joints: for example, lift or carry with palms or forearm, not small finger joints; carry bag over elbow or shoulder, not in fingertips.
   c. Avoid activities involving pinching motions.
   d. Avoid twisting and squeezing motions with hands.

GETTING ADDITIONAL REST

Rest is important because it reduces the pain and fatigue that accompany arthritis. In addition, it aids the body's healing process and helps control the inflammation. Rest also may reduce the stress on joints and protect them from further damage. All of these benefits are important in managing arthritis.

Each day you need to make sure you get enough whole body rest, local joint rest, and emotional rest. There are many options: Mark off the options that may be possible for you.

☐ 1. *Plenty of Nightly Rest*
   Get the usual 8 to 10 hours of nightly rest. It is not as important that you sleep for that length of time, but make sure you stretch out with your joints supported, so that your body can rest.

☐ 2. *Daily Rest Periods*
   Ideally, several times a day you can stretch out for 15 to 60 minutes with your joints supported. Again, it is the body rest, not sleep, that is most important.

☐ 3. *Five-Minute "Breathers"*
   Partway through a task, sit back and take it easy for a few minutes. This will allow you to finish the task almost as quickly but more comfortably and with less fatigue.

☐ 4. *Local Joint Rest*
   When a joint hurts, stop and rest. If your hip or knee hurts while walking, sit down for a few minutes with your legs supported; if your hand hurts while writing, stop and lay it flat for a few minutes.

Splints can be used to rest painful wrists or fingers. If your neck hurts, lay down with just a small pillow supporting the curve of your neck. Any painful joint can be given extra rest.

☐ 5. *Take Time for Relaxing Activities*
   Listening to music, reading, playing cards, or other light leisure activities all can be a pleasant change of pace and can be restful and refreshing for you.

There are unlimited options for getting additional rest. It takes creativity to find ways to fit extra rest into your schedule; then it takes self-discipline to make sure you follow through, incorporating the additional rest in your activities. Making the effort to get more rest can pay off in a reduction of pain and fatigue.

Ways to get more rest:
Systemic, whole body rest _____
Local joint rest _____
Emotional rest _____

ENERGY CONSERVATION TO REDUCE FATIGUE

Why Is Energy Conservation Important?

One of the major symptoms of arthritis may be fatigue—getting tired very easily. In the inflammatory types of arthritis, fatigue may be part of the disease process. In all types of arthritis, pain and difficult movement may use up energy, so you tire more easily.

It is important to avoid getting overtired. Fatigue may increase the possibility of a flare-up in inflammatory types of arthritis like rheumatoid arthritis. In all types of arthritis, fatigue may make the pain and stiffness seem worse, and it will make activities more difficult. We hope to reduce this fatigue by conserving energy and using it carefully.

How Can You Reduce Fatigue?

Some people try to conserve energy and reduce fatigue by staying in bed all day. Others stop doing anything that is not absolutely necessary each day. Unfortunately, the activities that are usually cut out are the leisure activities—the enjoyable things people do for themselves or for fun. These are not good ideas.

You can conserve energy and reduce fatigue by modifying and simplifying your activities, pacing yourself, getting additional rest, and using adapted equipment.

Energy Conservation

By conserving your energy, you may be able to do as much or more activity with less pain and fatigue. We are trying to avoid both overactivity and underactivity. Conserving your energy and simplifying your work is *not* being lazy. It is not sensible to overtire yourself. Overwork will not keep your joints mobile, but it may damage your joints further.

It is not so much *what* you do, but *how* you do it that can help control your fatigue. An attempt should be made to modify any activities that leave you overly tired or cause pain that continues for more than 1 to 2 hours.

You will need to identify ways that your own daily activities can be simplified. As you read through the energy conservation strategies, check off strategies that may work for you, and list several of your own examples.

APPENDIX B JOINT PROTECTION, REST, AND ENERGY CONSERVATION (*Continued*)

☐ 1. *Plan the Task*   Your Examples
    a. Think the task through.
    b. Decide when and where the job is best done.
    c. Plan out the simplest approach to the job.
    d. Gather all supplies before you begin.
    e. Arrange step sequence so that it moves in one direction (usually left to right).
    f. Use fewer, more efficient movements to complete task.

☐ 2. *Eliminate Extra Trips*
    a. Organize your shopping list according to how the store is laid out.
    b. Stay in the laundry room until your laundry is finished.
    c. Clean one area at a time.

☐ 3. *Use Good Posture and Body Mechanics*
    a. Sit to work; you will be more stable and use your strength more efficiently.
    b. Use large strong muscle groups, rather than straining individual muscles and joints.
    c. Lift with your knees bent, your back straight.
    d. Carry objects close to your body.
    e. Push objects, with body weight behind it, rather than pulling or carrying.
    f. Avoid awkward bending, reaching, and twisting.

☐ 4. *Don't Fight Gravity*
    a. Slide, rather than lift objects.
    b. Use wheeled cart.
    c. Use lightweight equipment.
    d. Stabilize pitcher on surface and tilt to pour, rather than picking it up.

☐ 5. *Pace Yourself*
    a. Get plenty of nightly rest.
    b. Plan several rest periods during the day.
    c. Rest before you get tired.
    d. Avoid a rush.
    e. Work at a steady rate with rest period.
    f. Develop a rhythm to your movements.

☐ 6. *Use Energy-Saving Devices*
    a. Convenience foods.
    b. Adapted equipment.

Strategies to be tried: _____   Activities to be modified: _____

Excerpted from Brady, TJ: Home Management of Arthritis: Developing Your Own Plan. Arthritis Foundation, Minnesota Chapter, Minneapolis, 1983. Used by permission of the author.

CHAPTER
22

Multiple Sclerosis

Susan B. O'Sullivan

OBJECTIVES

1. Define the pathology, epidemiology, etiology, course, and clinical symptoms of multiple sclerosis.
2. Describe the diagnostic and evaluative procedures commonly used in the assessment of multiple sclerosis.
3. Describe the medical management of the patient with multiple sclerosis.
4. Describe the rehabilitative management of the patient with multiple sclerosis.
5. Value the role and contribution of the physical therapist in the long-term management of patients with multiple sclerosis.

Multiple sclerosis (MS) is a demyelinating disease of the central nervous system largely affecting young adults; it is often referred to as the "great crippler of young adults." It was described as early as 1822 in the diaries of an English nobleman and further depicted in an anatomy book in 1858 by a British medical illustrator. Dr. Jean Cruveibier, a French physician, first used the term *islands of sclerosis* to describe areas of hardened tissue discovered on autopsy. However it was Dr. Jean Charcot in 1868 who defined the disease by its characteristic clinical and pathologic findings. His findings included paralysis, and the cardinal symptoms of intention tremor, scanning speech, and nystagmus, that were later termed **Charcot's triad.** Using autopsy studies he identified areas of hardened plaques and termed the disease *sclerosis in plaques.*[1] Since this time, it has been the subject of intense study and investigation.

Multiple sclerosis is an unpredictable disease that varies greatly from one individual to another in terms of the problems presented and the severity of those problems. The onset of symptoms typically occurs between the ages of 15 and 45 years. The disease is rare in children, as is the onset of symptoms in adults over the age of 50 years. Women are affected more than men. Clinically MS is characterized by multiple signs and symptoms and by fluctuating periods of **exacerbation** and **remission.** An exacerbation involves a relapse or period of symptom flare-up, whereas a remission is a period free of evolving symptoms. The course of the disease is unpredictable. In the early stages relatively complete remission of initial symptoms may occur; however, as the disease progresses the remissions become less complete and neurologic dysfunction increases. Among the most common clinical features of multiple sclerosis are spasticity, decreased motor function, ataxia, intention tremor, impaired sensation, visual defects, speech problems, and bowel and bladder dysfunction.[2]

PATHOLOGY

The disease is characterized by demyelinating lesions known as **plaques** that are scattered throughout the central nervous system (CNS) white matter. Although the plaques are widely disseminated, there are certain areas of predilection, such as the periventricular areas of the cerebrum, cerebellar peduncles, brainstem, and dorsal spinal cord. Lesions tend to be symmetrical and have a perivenous distribution, containing lymphocytes, macrophages, and plasma cells. In the initial stages inflammation is accompanied by a reduction in the number of oligodendroglia (the myelin-producing cells). The **myelin** membrane breaks down with relative sparing of the axons themselves. Myelin serves as an insulator, speeding up the conduction along nerve fibers from one node of Ranvier to another (termed saltatory conduction). It also conserves energy for the axon because depolarization occurs only at the nodes.[3] **Demyelination** impairs neural transmission and causes nerves to fatigue rapidly. Marked infiltration of mononuclear cells, largely T cells and macrophages, has been found in the plaques and suggests an immunologically mediated pathogenesis. Infiltrates surround the acute lesion and further interfere with the conductivity of the nerve fiber. Conceivably, this infiltration (which gradually subsides) may, in part, account for the multiple remissions and exacerbations characteristic of this disease. The myelin sheath is ultimately replaced by the fibrous scarring produced by glial cells (**gliosis**). Because the sclerotic plaques may occur anywhere in the brain or spinal cord, symptoms will vary considerably among individual patients.[4,5]

EPIDEMIOLOGY

Epidemiologic studies have revealed a worldwide distribution of MS with areas of high, medium, and low frequency. High-frequency areas include the northern United States, Scandinavian countries, and northern Europe, southern Canada, New Zealand and southern Australia, with the incidence reported at rates of 30 to 80 (or more) per 100,000 population. Areas of medium frequency (southern United States and Europe, and the rest of Australia) have a reported incidence of 10 to 15 per 100,000. Low-frequency areas (Asia and Africa) have reported rates of under 5 per 100,000. Multiple sclerosis affects predominately white populations; blacks demonstrate approximately half the risk of acquiring the disease. Migration studies indicate the geographic risk of an individual's birthplace is retained if migration occurs after the age of 15 years. Individuals migrating before this age assume the risk of their new location. Two epidemics of MS have been reported in the literature, one in the Faroe Islands off the coast of Norway and one in Iceland following occupation by soldiers during World War II. These epidemiologic studies have lent support to a theory that environmental factors are involved in the pathogenesis of MS.[6,7]

ETIOLOGY

The cause of multiple sclerosis is unknown. Major causative theories currently focus on an infectious origin, on an immune-mediated pathogenesis, or a combination of the two. Geographic distributions, migrant data, and epidemic studies all suggest an infectious origin. Pathologic studies of inflammatory reactions in the CNS and serologic studies of antiviral antibodies in MS serum also lend support to this theory. The identification of increased **immunoglobulin** (IgG) and *oligoclonal bands* in the cerebrospinal fluid (CSF) of 65 to 95 percent of MS patients also provides convincing evidence of a persistent viral infection eliciting an autoimmune response. The causative agent most frequently suggested is a slow virus, although no specific agent has been identified. Numerous viruses have been linked to MS (canine distemper, rabies, measles, herpes simplex). It has been proposed that the virus may exist in a genomic or proviral form not currently recognizable by standard laboratory techniques. Population studies suggest that multiple sclerosis is acquired during the years of puberty and lies dormant for many years. Symptoms emerge an average of 12 years later (slow virus theory). Genetic predisposition and familial tendency have also been identified. Susceptibility to MS appears dependent on the genetically linked HLS antigen system.[7-9]

Immunopathogenesis of MS has also been long pro-posed as a theory. Evidence of active immune responses in immunoglobulin production in the CNS, serum and in the cerebrospinal fluid (IgG and oligoclonal bands) is abundant. Activated T cells have been found in the blood and CSF of MS patients in both clinically active and inactive stages of the disease. The exact role of these immune control mechanisms, however, remains unclear. They have been suggested as the direct cause of the demyelination or as the result of the disease process itself. Thus the viral infection may be the initial causative factor in producing demyelination. Inflammatory reactions and the production of antibodies then occur as the body's reaction to the primary infection. Alternately, the infection may institute an **autoimmune** reaction against the CNS itself, thereby initiating the demyelination process.[4,7,10]

DIAGNOSTIC CRITERIA

The diagnosis of multiple sclerosis is based on clinical findings, historical evidence, and supportive laboratory tests. Clinical criteria include multiple signs of neurologic dysfunction involving two or more parts of the CNS and reflecting predominant involvement of white matter (long tract damage). Two time patterns are identified: (1) two or more episodes of worsening, each lasting more than 24 hours and separated by no less than 1 month, or (2) slow or step-wise progression extending over at least 6 months. Thus the patient may present with blurred vision and tingling in the arms occurring sporadically over several months. A detailed neurologic exam is performed to confirm the symptoms and rule out other causes. A reliable patient history helps to pinpoint the episodic bouts.[11,12] Common symptoms are presented in Table 22–1).

Table 22–1 COMMON SYMPTOMS IN MULTIPLE SCLEROSIS

Clinical Symptoms
Blurred or double vision
Loss of vision in one eye
Slurred or slowed speech
Easy fatigability
Psychologic changes
Weakness or paralysis of limbs
Poor coordination
Shaking of limb
Staggering gait
Poor balance
Dragging feet
Numbness or pins-and-needles
Poor bladder or bowel control

Pattern of Symptoms
Vary greatly from person to person
Vary over time in each individual affected
First symptoms usually in young adults
Early symptoms are usually transient
Early symptoms usually include problems with vision
Problems develop in more than one nervous system function
Acute symptoms usually followed by months or years free of apparent disease

Various laboratory studies are used to assist in the diagnosis:

1. Lumbar puncture and cerebrospinal fluid evaluation. Typical changes seen in patients with MS include a reduced number of T suppressor lymphocytes, elevated IgG (seen in 70% of patients), and oligoclonal banding (seen in 90% of patients). These immunoglobin abnormalities are not unique to MS, however, and can be seen in other viral and occasionally in bacterial disorders. Elevated levels of myelin basic protein or myelin proteolytic fragments indicate active demyelination and are useful diagnostic indicators during acute episodes.[7]

2. Computed tomography (CT or CAT) scan. Computed tomography may be helpful in detecting large lesions but is limited in its ability to detect the smaller plaques that occur with MS. Contrast enhancement techniques are necessary to increase the detection sensitivity. Its principle use is in ruling out other neurologic conditions.

3. Magnetic resonance imaging (MRI). MRI is much more successful in identifying plaques of demyelination than CAT. The presence of scattered bright spots on an MRI is highly diagnostic of MS, a high rate (93% in some studies) of identification of MS lesions. Studies using MRI indicate that the lesion formation in the brain can be far greater than the presentation of symptoms and clinical exacerbation indicates.[9,11]

3. Myelography. A myelogram is used to investigate signs of spinal cord involvement. Contrast dye is injected by lumbar puncture and radiographs are made. A myelogram may be used to rule out other causes of spinal dysfunction. Demyelinating plaques are not evident with this test.

4. Electrophysiologic testing. The presence of lesions can also be confirmed by visual, auditory, and somatosensory evoked potentials. The rate of nerve impulse transmission is measured and compared with normal values. Slowed conduction time is evidence of demyelination (see Chapter 9). Electroencephalography (EEG) may be used to rule out other causes.

5. Blood. Changes in blood lymphocytes and in the distribution of T and B cells have been described in MS patients, particularly during acute exacerbations. Reports of increased numbers of activated T cells in blood indicate that abnormal immune activation is occurring outside the CNS.[4] Reduced numbers of T suppressor lymphocytes are also found.[7,13]

CLINICAL MANIFESTATIONS OF MULTIPLE SCLEROSIS

Course

The course the disease takes is quite variable. At one end of the continuum the course can be benign with mild symptoms and very little if any disability, while at the other end of the continuum it can be rapidly progressing, leading to severe disability or death from complications within a few years. Most individuals who develop severe disability do so within a few years of the appearance of initial symptoms of the disease.[14] Four main types of clinical courses have been recognized:[12]

1. Benign. The benign course affects approximately 20 percent of patients and is characterized by an abrupt onset with one or a few exacerbations and complete or nearly complete remissions. These individuals experience little or no permanent functional disability and remain relatively symptom-free.

2. Exacerbating-remitting. Approximately 20 to 30 percent of patients experience this type of course, which is characterized by a sudden onset of symptoms with partial or complete remissions. Patients remain relatively stable for long periods.

3. Remitting-progressive. Affecting 40 percent of patients, this course is similar to the exacerbating-remitting course but symptoms do not remit as completely, and progressive physical disability develops.

4. Progressive. The progressive course, which affects 10 to 20 percent of patients, progresses without remitting and leads to severe disability. The rate of onset is typically slow (gradual, insidious) resulting in progressive loss of function over a number of years. Rarely, it can be very rapid (acute, fulminating) resulting in early death. Men are more likely to demonstrate chronic progressive MS.

Because patients may alter their clinical presentation (e.g., going from a benign to a progressive course), clinicians must be alert to changes in symptoms, the rate of progression, and the frequency of relapses. This will also allow the clinician to better evaluate the effects of treatment, since it becomes extremely difficult to differentiate the effects of treatment from spontaneous neurologic recovery.

Clinical Signs and Symptoms

Symptoms vary considerably in character, intensity, and duration. The onset of symptoms can develop rapidly over a course of minutes or hours; less frequently the onset may be insidious, occurring over a period of weeks or months. Symptoms will depend on the location of lesions, and early symptoms often demonstrate involvement of the sensory, pyramidal, cerebellar, and visual pathways, or disruption of cranial nerves and their linkage to the brain stem (see Table 22–1).

SENSORY DISTURBANCES

Sensory symptoms are common and often unpredictable in MS patients. Altered sensations can include **paresthesias** (pins and needles sensation) or numbness in any area of the body. **Lhermitte's sign** (a sensation like an electric shock running down the spine and into the limbs and produced by flexing the neck) can be present and is indicative of posterior column damage in the spinal cord. Disturbances in position sense are also frequent, as are lower extremity impairments of vibratory sense. Complete loss of any single sensation (anesthesia) is rare.

Approximately 10 to 20 percent of the patients experience pain. **Hyperpathia,** a hypersensitivity to minor sensory stimuli, can occur. For example, a light touch or light pressure stimulus elicits a severe pain reaction. **Dysesthesias,** abnormal burning or pain sensations, are common. Burning can occur along the distribution of a nerve (pseudoradicular pain) and results from demyelinating lesions in spinothalamic tracts or in sensory roots. **Trigeminal neuralgia (tic douloureux)** results from demyelination of the sensory division of the trigeminal nerve and is characterized by short attacks of severe facial pain. Eating, shaving, or simply touching the face may trigger painful episodes. Pain may also result from involuntary spasms, spasticity, abnormal postures and contractures, and vertebral fractures. Increased frequency of headaches has also been reported in some patients.[14]

PARESIS

Signs of muscle weakness secondary to damage of the motor cortex or its pyramidal tracts may vary from mild paresis to total paralysis of the involved extremities. In patients with upper motor neuron (UMN) syndrome, loss of orderly recruitment and rate modulation of motoneurons contributes to signs of weakness, early loss of force, and the need for increased effort. Fast-twitch units are recruited early and are ineffective in sustaining muscle contraction. Muscle activation patterns and agonist-antagonist relationships are also disturbed. These problems result in a loss of orderly timing and ineffective or dyssynergic patterns of contraction. Stereotyped coactivation of muscles in primitive patterns can occur in UMN syndrome.[15] Weakness as secondary to disuse atrophy and prolonged inactivity must also be considered.

SPASTICITY

Spasticity results from demyelinating lesions in the descending pyramidal tracts and is characterized by increased excitability of spinal motoneurons and increased responsiveness of segmental reflexes. This is an extremely common problem in patients with MS, occurring in 90 percent of all cases. Spasticity may range from mild to severe in intensity, depending on the progression of the disease. As the stretch reflexes are velocity-dependent, muscle tone is greatly increased with rapid movements. Associated signs of upper motor neuron syndrome may also be present, including ankle clonus, spontaneous spasms, positive Babinski, and loss of precise autonomic control.[14,15]

MOVEMENT DISORDERS

Demyelinating lesions in the cerebellum and cerebellar tracts are common in MS. **Intention tremors** or action tremors occur when voluntary movement is attempted and result from the inability of the cerebellum to damp motor movements. Intention tremors vary in severity from slight quivering to massive involuntary oscillatory movements during purposeful activity. Severe tremors will impose significant limitations in performance of functional activities, particularly in such areas as personal hygiene, eating, and dressing. **Dysmetria, dysdiadochokinesia,** and **ataxia** are also classic findings of cerebellar disease. Dysmetria is an inability to fix the range of movement. Rapid movements are typically made with more force than necessary. Dysdiadochokinesia is the inability to perform rapidly alternating movements. Ataxia refers to incoordinated movement. Progressive ataxia of the trunk and lower limbs is often apparent. During gait activities ataxia is demonstrated by a staggering, wide-based pattern with poor foot placement and slow, uncoordinated progression of reciprocal lower extremity movement. Individuals may also develop severe limitations in functional skills (e.g., dressing or feeding), as a result of significant coordination deficits.[12,14]

Vestibular dysfunction and involvement of brain-stem vestibular white matter pathways is extremely common, affecting the majority of patients with MS. Symptoms range from difficulties with balance to dizziness, giddiness, and/or vertigo. Thus patients may experience general feelings of unsteadiness or the perception of imbalance, nausea, sweating, and even vomiting. True **vertigo** (the perception or illusion of movement) is less common. Symptoms are typically precipitated or made worse by movements of the head or eyes. Patients may also experience a **paroxysmal attack** or sudden onset of symptoms. This can be brought on by a period of hyperventilation.[16]

Lesions involving the basal ganglia are uncommon, affecting only 6.8 percent of patients. However, these patients may present with a wide spectrum of movement disorders including hemiballismus, generalized dystonia, focal dystonia (torticollis), chorea, athetosis, choreoathetosis, parkinsonian (resting) tremor, and/or dyskinesia.[17,18]

FATIGUE

Multiple sclerosis is characterized by a **fatigue pattern** that is one of the most commonly reported problems and it can be a significant cause of disability. The patient complains of persistent fatigue, loss of energy, and limited tolerance to exercise. A typical pattern often emerges in which the patient wakes relatively refreshed but by early afternoon gradually experiences fatigue and exhaustion. An increase in physical dysfunction is noted. Some recovery of energy may occur by early evening. Fatigue may also be brought on more frequently and more rapidly by excessive physical activity, muscle weakness and strain, underlying depression, or elevated body temperature.[14]

VISUAL DISTURBANCES

Visual symptoms are common with multiple sclerosis and are found in approximately 80 percent of the patients. Involvement of the optic and occulomotor nerves can produce loss of vision, field defects, **diplopia,** or blurred vision. **Optic neuritis** is a common symptom and can produce blurring or total loss of vision with pain on movement of the eyes. A large central **scotoma** (blind spot) can also develop, forcing the patient to rely on peripheral vision. Color perception is typically disrupted. **Nystagmus,** rapid involuntary oscillations of the eyes, is also common; it is more apparent when the eyes attempt to focus in a lateral or vertical direction. Visual disturbances frequently remit and are seldom the primary cause of disability, although reading and visual tracking activities may remain difficult for many patients.[14]

BLADDER AND BOWEL DISTURBANCES

Urinary bladder disturbances are present in 54 to 78 percent of MS patients. Common symptoms include urinary frequency, urgency, incontinence, retention or hesitancy. They may result from suprasacral neurologic lesions or from mechanical outlet obstruction. Neurogenic disorders may also impair bowel function, resulting in incontinence or constipation, and sexual function, producing impotence or retrograde ejaculation. These disturbances have tremendous functional and social implications for the patient and rehabilitation specialist.[14]

COGNITIVE AND BEHAVIORAL DISTURBANCES

The significant mental deterioration (global dementia) associated with extensive cerebral lesions in acute fulminating cases or in the later stages of progressive disease is relatively rare. Mild to moderate impairment of cognitive function is more common (seen in approximately 60% of patients) and is related to the specific distribution of the lesions rather than to the overall severity of the disease, its course, or the patient's disability status. Alterations in cognitive function can include deficits in recall, memory, attention and/or concentration, learning, conceptual reasoning, and visuospatial skills.[19,20]

Affective disorders in MS are common and include changes in mood, bodily feeling, and emotional expression and control. **Euphoria** is typical and consists of an exaggerated feeling of well-being, a sense of optimism incongruent with the patient's incapacitating disability. Pathologic laughing and weeping (**emotional dysregulation syndrome**), depression, and/or **bipolar affective disorders** (alternating periods of depression and mania) may also occur. The incidence of these symptoms is significantly higher in patients with MS than in patients with other chronic neurologic conditions and has been linked to disseminated disease and demyelinating lesions in the frontal lobes and diencephalic and limbic centers.[19,21]

Psychologic responses (anxiety, denial, anger, aggression, or dependency) can also occur in response to the stress of a chronic and unpredictable disease. Patients with MS face issues related to the ambiguity of their health status, the presence of borderline or nonvisible symptoms, the uncertainty of future status, and the loss of effective functioning during young adulthood. Moreover, many of the symptoms of MS (tremor, scanning speech, incontinence) are humiliating and embarrassing.

COMMUNICATION DISTURBANCES

Speech and swallowing defects secondary to demyelinating lesions of the cranial nerves are common in MS. Speech is typically slowed, with slurring of words, scanning of syllables, and low speech volume. Poor coordination of the tongue and other speech muscles results in dysarthria (difficult and defective speech). **Dysphagia** is characterized by swallowing difficulties and may result in impaired feeding, in choking, or aspiration. Poor coordination of breath control and poor posture can contribute to these difficulties.[22]

Secondary Impairments

Numerous secondary impairments can result from prolonged inactivity, bed rest, or static positioning in a wheelchair. These are summarized in Figure 22–1. Although the effects are not directly attributable to the disease itself, they may become primary limiting factors in the rehabilitation of patients.[23]

PSYCHOSOCIAL

Prolonged inactivity typically intensifies feelings of anxiety or depression and can lead to despondency or detachment. These feelings can then further compound the problems of inactivity by decreasing the patient's desire to move or interact with the environment. Withdrawn and detached individuals may also demonstrate deficits in intellectual functioning.

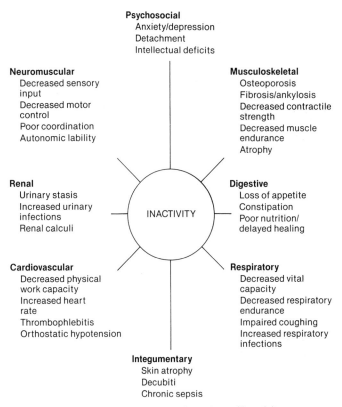

Figure 22–1. Clinical manifestations of inactivity.

NEUROMUSCULAR

Prolonged inactivity is concommitant with a decrease in the overall level of sensory input. Decreased motor activity results in neuromuscular disassociation and impaired processes of motor control and movement coordination. The autonomic nervous system may also demonstrate instability, rendering the individual unable to maintain a stable level of performance (homeostasis). Autonomic processes (sympathetic and parasympathetic functions) and somatic control interact in the reticular activating system and may be hypoactive or hyperactive.

MUSCULOSKELETAL

Significant functional limitations develop as MS symptomatology increases. The majority of patients experience a restriction in their mobility. Inactivity, poor positioning, and neglected spasticity will all contribute to progressive deformity. Typically, hip and knee flexion contractures and foot deformities develop if the patient is confined to bed or wheelchair and the limbs not regularly moved through their normal ranges. Progressive calcium loss in bones (osteoporosis) can lead to spontaneous fractures, hypercalciuria, and the deposition of calcium in soft tissues (heterotopic ossification). Joints may become fibrotic or ankylosed. The loss in contractile strength and endurance of muscles is often dramatic within a very short period, and muscle atrophy becomes visually apparent.

RENAL

Loss of calcium from bones can lead to the formation of renal calculi (kidney stones). Urinary stasis, urinary infection, and urinary obstruction are also serious problems for the inactive patient.

DIGESTIVE

Loss of appetite accompanied by a general decrease in gastrointestinal activity can lead to poor nutritional intake, delayed healing, and persistent problems with constipation.

CARDIOVASCULAR

Cardiovascular deconditioning results in a decrease in the overall physical work capacity, increased heart rate response to effort, orthostatic hypotension, decreased circulating blood volume, and increased likelihood of thrombophlebitis.

RESPIRATORY

Respiratory changes include a decrease in lung volume and vital capacity, a decrease in respiratory endurance, decreased efficiency of the coughing mechanism, and increased likelihood of respiratory infections. These changes may be life-threatening for the bedridden patient.

INTEGUMENTARY

With decreasing activity, skin atrophy and decubitus ulcers become a major concern. Changes in skin turgor, static posturing, and prolonged pressure over bony prominences increase the likelihood of skin breakdown. Complicating these problems are sensory impairments that decrease the patient's awareness of limb position and pressure sensation. Contractures, spasticity, and/or involuntary movements may cause friction effects between the patient's skin and supporting surfaces.

Exacerbating Factors

Exacerbations can occur at any time and without provocation. However several factors have been identified with worsening of symptoms in MS. They can result in full-blown exacerbations (episodes of demyelination) or can cause temporary effects that last for minutes or hours. The avoidance of these aggravating factors is important in ensuring the patient's optimal function.[14]

CHANGES IN HEALTH STATUS

An individual whose overall health deteriorates is more likely to have an exacerbation than one who remains healthy. Viral or bacterial infections (e.g., cold, flu, bladder infection) and diseases of major organ systems (e.g., hepatitis, pancreatitis, asthmatic attacks) are associated with exacerbations of disease.

Patients often identify trauma with the onset of MS or an exacerbation of symptoms. Unrelated physical injury or related diagnostic procedures (lumbar puncture) have been reported as precipitating factors. The first few months following pregnancy and birth have also been found to increase the risk of exacerbation, although the long-term outcome is generally considered nondeleterious.

Psychologic and emotional stress has frequently been implicated by patients in the worsening of their symptoms, although controlled studies are lacking. Major life stress events (divorce, death, losing a job) are cited.

CAUSES OF TRANSIENT DETERIORATION

Individuals with multiple sclerosis typically demonstrate an adverse reaction to heat. External heat, either in the form of climatic conditions (summer heat) or therapeutic modalities (hot baths, hot packs) may cause a temporary worsening of the clinical symptoms of MS. The effect is usually immediate and dramatic in terms of reduced function and increased fatigue. Internal heat (fever, increased body temperature following prolonged exercise) may also produce similar effects. The reduction in nerve conduction associated with the heating of impaired nerves is the probable cause.

Hyperventilation is associated with changes in the chemical composition of blood. These changes are sufficient to interfere with normal brain and spinal cord function and produce worsening of symptoms in the individual with MS. Additional factors that contribute to symptom worsening include exhaustion, dehydration, malnutrition, and sleep deprivation. All these changes provide additional stress on an already compromised nervous system.

Prognostic Indicators

The mean survival rate is 22 to 25 years with the cause of death typically being either respiratory or urinary infection. Several prognostic indicators have been identified in predicting the later course of the disease:

1. Onset with only one symptom. This is one of strongest indicators of a favorable prognosis.
2. An acute onset rather than a slow, insidious onset. A progressive course is generally considered ominous while benign and exacerbating-remitting courses are more favorable.
3. Onset before the age of 35. Onset after 35 is more frequently associated with a rapid progressive course and increased incidence of death.
4. Neurologic status at 5 years. Significant pyramidal and cerebellar signs and multiple system involvement at 5 years is associated with a poorer prognosis and more severe impairment.[23,24]

These remain general guidelines and do not necessarily fit the outcome of individual patients.

MEDICAL MANAGEMENT

Medical management of the patient with MS is directed at the overall disease process itself and at the specific symptoms that emerge. There is currently no treatment that can prevent or cure MS. The establishment of comprehensive care centers for patients with MS has enhanced ongoing treatment.[5] Acute exacerbations can be partially managed by instituting pharmacologic treatments aimed at suppressing immunologic reactions. Adrenocorticotrophic hormone (ACTH) or corticosteroids (prednisone, cortisone acetate) can shorten the duration of exacerbations and reduce inflammation but probably do not enhance the degree of recovery. Long-term steroid therapy is associated with numerous side effects (e.g., cataracts, osteoporosis and/or compression fractures, hypertension, infections, and so forth) and may not be tolerated. Other immunosuppressive drugs (azathioprine, cyclophosphamide, cyclosporine), either alone or in combination with ACTH, have been used with limited success to prevent disease progression in chronic progressive MS. Therapies found to be largely ineffective include the use of hyperbaric oxygen, dietary approaches, and plasmapheresis (plasma exchange).[25–28]

There are many effective treatments designed to ameliorate the problems that develop with MS. Careful assessment of multisystem function coupled with prompt treatment of infections and other problems are essential elements of care. Primary emphasis is on maintaining good health, normal weight, and regular daily exercise.[27] A variety of drugs are used in the treatment of MS symptoms (Table 22–2). The clinician should have a thorough understanding of the effects, side effects, and interactions of each of the drugs a patient is taking.

Urinary problems are almost universal and require a complete urodynamic evaluation to identify the specific cause of the problem and to arrive at the appropriate course for treatment. Treatment for a spastic bladder (uninhibited neurogenic bladder) typically involves pharmacologic management with anticholinergic drugs to regulate bladder emptying. Treatment of the flaccid bladder involves alternative techniques for emptying (e.g., intermittent self-catheterization, Crede maneuver). If the bladder problem cannot be controlled with medication and/or intermittent catheterization, continuous catheterization (Foley) or surgical urinary diversion (suprapubic catheter) may be necessary. Urinary

Table 22–2 MEDICATIONS USED IN SYMPTOMATIC THERAPY OF MULTIPLE SCLEROSIS

Symptom	Drug	Usual Dosage Range	Expected Benefit	Potential Adverse Effects
Spasticity	Baclofen	10 mg–20 mg tid or qid	Decreased hypertonus; improved movement	Weakness, liver dysfunction; sedation
	Clonopin	0.5 mg tid		
	Valium	5 mg–10 mg tid or qid		
	Dantrium	25 mg–50 mg tid or qid		
Cerebellar incoordination	INH	300 mg/day	Decreased tremor; improved truncal stability	Liver dysfunction (INH); cardiac effects (Inderal)
	Inderal	10 mg–20 mg tid or qid		
	Clonopin	0.5 mg–1 mg tid		
Urinary urgency	Ditropan	5 mg bid or tid	Improved bladder control; decreased urgency	Increased hesitancy of bladder; constipation
	Pro-Banthine	15 mg bid or tid		
Painful sensory disturbance	Tegretol	200 mg bid or tid	Decreased painful dysestheia	Bone marrow suppression
Depression	Tricyclic antidepressants (Aventyl, Elavil)	25 mg bid or tid	Decreased insomnia; improved mood	Dry mouth; constipation; urinary hesitancy; weight gain

From Maloney, F, Burks, J, and Ringel, S: Interdisciplinary Rehabilitation of Multiple Sclerosis and Neuromuscular Disorders, JB Lippincott, Philadelphia, 1985, with permission.

INH = isonicotinoylhydrazine.

tract infections result from retention of urine in the bladder and from catheterization procedures. Antibiotic therapy is the mainstay of treatment. Dietary modifications typically include reducing fluids that stress the bladder (e.g., caffeinated drinks, alcohol) and increasing agents that increase urine acidity (e.g., cranberry juice).[25,29] Constipation is a common problem and is typically managed with dietary changes (e.g., a high-fiber diet, increased fluid intake), manipulation of the patient's environment, and medications (e.g., use of stool softeners and suppositories and avoiding long-term use of laxatives and enemas).[14,30]

Medical management of spasticity and spasms includes pharmacologic, surgical, and selective regional management. Commonly used drugs are the antispasticity agents such as baclofen (Lioresal) and dantrolene sodium (Dantrium); and muscle relaxants such as diazepam (Valium). Numerous side effects including drowsiness, fatigue, weakness, and dizziness accompany the use of these drugs and usually necessitate frequent checks of blood chemistries and prescription modifications for long-term use. Intrathecal administration of baclofen and morphine via an implanted pump has been successful in controlling spasms and hypertonia by allowing the use of higher dosages of medications acting directly on the spinal cord. Functional implications must also be considered in the use of drugs. Many patients are able to use their spasticity to achieve stability and functional control (e.g., standing) or as an assist to lower extremity circulation. Without this hypertonus, muscle weakness may predominate, rendering function impossible. Tone and motor activity in antagonist muscles can be modified using functional electrical stimulation; for example, in ambulatory patients, excessive plantarflexion tone and ankle clonus can be blocked by stimulation of the peroneal nerve. An accurate assessment of an intact functional reflex arc is crucial to the success of this technique. Nerve and motor point blocks with injected phenol are effective in the temporary reduction of tone and are used to facilitate ranging of developing contractures. Surgical procedures (posterior rhizotomy, tendonotomy, myelotomy) may be indicated in cases of severe spasticity. A typical surgical candidate has had spastic paralysis for many years resulting in a nonfunctional limb and serious complications (e.g., contractures and skin breakdown).[25,31]

Pain associated with disturbed CNS function is managed according to the pathogenesis. Paresthetic pains are managed with low doses of tricyclic antidepressant drugs. The discomfort and pain associated with spasticity and spasms may be managed with over-the-counter (OTC) or prescription antiinflammatory drugs. Pain associated with optic neuritis can be successfully managed with steroids and trigeminal neuralgia is commonly treated with carbamazepine. Chronic pain occurs in about 50 percent of patients with MS and can be managed with behavioral approaches and mild painkillers. Narcotic analgesics are problematic and not typically prescribed.[25]

Symptomatic improvement of fatigue may result from the use of amantadine. Depression and anxiety can be managed with medications, counseling, and support groups. Patients with pathologic crying and laughing can benefit from the administration of low doses of tricyclic antidepressants.[25]

REHABILITATIVE MANAGEMENT

The chronicity and severity of this disease along with its unpredictable course may lead some to view patients with MS as poor rehabilitation candidates. This view is contradicted by available research, which demonstrates that patients with MS can make significant functional gains from a course of rehabilitation.[32-34] Gains are the combined result of spontaneous neurologic recovery, pharmacologic intervention, and rehabilitation programming. A coordinated interdisciplinary team approach is necessary to provide the comprehensive rehabilitation needed to address the patient's complex and multifaceted problems. A focus on long-range planning is critical for effective management. Professionals need to maintain a positive, caring attitude, providing ongoing support and guidance to patients and families. Effective management also requires an organized continuum of care from hospital-based, to home and community settings.[35,36]

The long-term goals of a physical therapy program include

1. Improve functional status and maximize independence.
2. Prevent or retard the development of secondary impairments.
3. Promote emotional, psychologic, and social adjustment of patient and family.
4. Educate patient and family to maximize retention of rehabilitation gains.

Assessment

Because many areas of the CNS may be affected, it is imperative that a careful assessment be performed to determine the extent of neurologic and functional involvement. Subsequent reassessment at specified intervals should attempt to distinguish a change in status as well as the effects of treatment. It may not always be possible to differentiate the treatment results from a remission of symptoms. Considering the variability of symptoms of any individual patient, it is often beneficial to perform assessment procedures over a period of several days in order to obtain a representative sample of baseline functioning. Fatigue patterns and exacerbating factors should be taken into account when testing.

Data can be gained from a review of the patient's chart and from a discussion with the patient and his family. In addition, there are a number of assessments that are appropriate:

1. Range of motion, assessment of deformity.
2. Sensation, including pain.
3. Muscle tone, including factors which influence tonal quality, such as positioning, stress, and so forth.

4. Muscle strength and control. If spasticity is severe, traditional manual muscle testing procedures will be inappropriate and strength should be assessed in terms of functional movement.
5. Coordination and balance.
6. Gait.
7. Fatigue patterns.
8. Skin integrity and condition.
9. Respiratory patterns.
10. Cognitive abilities.
11. Visual function.
12. Functional status, including functional mobility skills and activities of daily living.

Kurtzke[37] developed a scale for rating neurologic impairment in multiple sclerosis in 1955 (the Disability Status Scale or DSS). This scale was expanded in 1965 and again in 1982 (the **Expanded Disability Status Scale, EDSS**) and has been widely adopted.[38] Patients are graded on the basis of presenting symptoms in eight different functional systems (FS). They are then classified into one of 20 steps in the EDSS, based on the grades obtained in the FS evaluation. For example patients classified in EDSS step 2.5 (minimal disability) may have grade 2 involvement in two FS categories (Appendix A). Other scales frequently used to measure severity of disability include the Barthel Index (BI);[39] the Functional Independence Measure (FIM), which incorporates the BI;[40] and the **Minimum Record of Disability (MRD)** developed by the International Federation of Multiple Sclerosis Societies.[41] This latter scale includes two subscales, the Incapacity Status Scale (ISS) and the Environmental Status Scale (ESS). A comparison study of these functional assessment scales revealed that although all are predictive of the patient's physical care needs, the FIM was the most useful.[42] The use of a standardized test with established reliability and validity allows for comparison between similar groups of patients, and within a group, for monitoring the progression of disease and the effects of treatment. Because these instruments were developed as quantitative and not qualitative measures, their use must be augmented by other more qualitative assessments of function.

A sample physical therapy evaluation form is included in Appendix B.

Treatment

Whereas the individual needs of patients will vary considerably, the following generic short-term goals are often appropriate for physical therapy management of patients with multiple sclerosis:
1. Increase or maintain range of motion.
2. Improve sensory awareness.
3. Educate on skin care for the patient with sensory loss.
4. Diminish spasticity and tonal influences on movement.
5. Improve muscle strength.
6. Improve motor control.
7. Improve gait pattern.
8. Improve functional mobility and independence in activities of daily living.

a. Teach problem-solving skills.
b. Teach compensatory training.
c. Teach energy conservation.
d. Provide appropriate mobility aids and adaptive equipment.
9. Assist with psychologic adjustment of patient and family.
a. Promote understanding of the disease, its symptoms and management.
b. Emphasize realistic expectations while maintaining hope.
c. Focus on remaining abilities.
d. Educate patient about support groups, and the MS society

Each of these goals will not be appropriate for every patient or at every phase of the rehabilitation process. Goal setting and treatment selection should be carefully planned around the patient's individual abilities and needs. Full involvement of the patient in all stages of planning will help ensure the patient's cooperation, motivation, and self-reliance. At all times, specific attention should be given to fatigue patterns and exacerbating factors. Whereas optimizing function is a goal of treatment, overexertion must be carefully avoided.

REHABILITATION FOR RELATED IMPAIRMENTS
Sensory Deficits and Skin Care

Strategies should be instituted to compensate for sensory impairments. Patients with diminished sensation may respond favorably to sensory retraining. Stimulation techniques (vigorous rubbing or tapping) can be used to promote increased awareness of desensitized limbs. Patients with proprioceptive losses will demonstrate impaired motor learning and control. Effective strategies to compensate for these deficits include the use of alternate sensory systems for feedback and movement control, for example, a shift in focus to verbal or visual cues. Biofeedback also provides an augmented source of either visual or auditory feedback and may be effective for selected patients. Visual changes (e.g., blurred vision, double vision, moving images) may limit the use of visual information for control of movement. Blurred vision may be improved by the use of tinted glasses that reduce glare, or by increasing the contrast between items (e.g., stair markings). Eye patching is frequently used to reduce double vision, although some depth perception will be sacrificed. This requires a necessary adjustment in the performance of motor activities.[14,43]

Patients may not feel the discomfort of prolonged positioning or may be unable to shift position because of weakness or spasticity. Awareness, protection, and care of desensitized parts should be taught early in the rehabilitation process and consistently reinforced by all personnel. The patient should be educated in the cardinal rules of skin care:
1. Keep the skin clean and dry.
2. Follow a good diet and drink plenty of fluids.
3. Inspect skin regularly (at least once a day).
4. Provide regular pressure relief.
5. Prevention is the best strategy.

Decubitus ulcers are the result of pressure, time, and direction of forces.[44] Patients should be taught to inspect their skin carefully, paying particular attention to any persistent redness of the bony prominences. Soiled skin should be cleansed and dried promptly. Patients should change their position or be changed frequently, typically every 2 hours in bed and every 15 minutes when sitting in a wheelchair. Pressure-relieving mattresses (water, gel, air, or alternating pressure) may be helpful in distributing body weight and reducing shear and friction in bed. Pressure-relieving devices (sheepskins, air or foam cushions, cuffs, boots) may be necessary to protect areas prone to breakdown (shoulder blades, elbows, ischial tuberosities, sacrum, trochanters, knees, malleoli, or heels). Clothing should be comfortable, not too loose (wrinkled) or too tight. Seams, buttons and pockets should not press on the skin, particularly in weight-bearing areas. Clothing should be breathable and smooth or soft. The patient must be cautioned against activities that might traumatize the skin. Dragging, bumping, or scraping body parts during a transfer or bed mobility activities can produce a friction injury to the skin. Thermal injury may result from contact with ashes, hot water, or hot objects.

If skin redness develops (lasting longer than 30 minutes) patients should be instructed to stay off the area until the redness disappears. Blisters, blue areas, or open sores indicate more serious injury. The involved part must be protected from continued pressure and mechanical force injury. Cleansing and **debridement**, the removal of necrotic and devitalized tissue from a wound, is routinely done. Hydrotherapy is used to assist in debridement and removal of dressings and in the cleansing of wounds. Wounds are typically treated with any one of a number of different topical antibiotic agents and protective dressings.[44] An artificial type of skin (semipermeable film) may also be used to control and prevent wound dehydration. Systemic antibiotic therapy may be instituted if infection is extensive. Surgical intervention may be required (e.g., removal of necrotic tissue, skin grafts). Surgical sites must be similarly protected against irritation and pressure injury.[14,44,45]

Pain

The management of pain depends on an accurate assessment of the causes of pain. Musculoskeletal strain or joint malalignment from chronically weakened muscles are important considerations and are responsive to physical therapy intervention. Patients may experience relief of pain with stretching or exercise. Postural retraining and correction of faulty movement patterns along with orthotic and/or adaptive seating devices can reduce malalignment and pain. Low back pain secondary to spinal malalignment and disc impingement is a common complaint and may respond to physical therapy (e.g., modalities, exercise, and education). Hydrotherapy or pool therapy using lukewarm water may have a beneficial effect on painful paresthesias.[14,30,46] Patients with long-standing pain may benefit from a total management approach to chronic pain (see Chapter 27). The use of transcutaneous electrical nerve stimulation (TENS) to modulate pain in patients with MS has had conflicting results, with some patients experiencing a worsening of symptoms.[14]

Spasticity

Muscle tone, spasms, and the resultant abnormal movement patterns may be decreased using a variety of physical therapy treatment approaches. These include the use of modalities, therapeutic exercise, positioning, or any combination thereof.

Topical cold (ice packs, cold wraps, ice massage) or immersion in cold water reduces spasticity by decreasing tendon reflex excitability and clonus, and by slowing conduction of impulses in nerves and muscles. Improved function of antagonist muscles with improved range of motion may also result. The effects of cryotherapy are relatively short-lived, although some patients may experience enhanced ability to move that lasts for minutes or hours.[31]

Therapeutic exercises begun early in the course of the disease and continued through regularly scheduled exercise sessions can effectively help the patient maintain mobility function. A stretching program is an important part of treatment and serves to passively elongate chronically shortened spastic muscles. Patients should be taught self-stretching exercises. Typical lower extremity muscles involved in a stretching program are the hamstrings, quadriceps, adductors, and plantarflexors. When combined with low doses of baclofen, patients with MS who have minimal to moderate spasticity demonstrated significant improvements in overall levels of tone.[47] Stretching and range of motion (ROM) exercises can also be done in a pool, where the buoyancy of the water assists the movements and helps to conserve energy. Relaxation techniques (e.g., progressive contraction and relaxation of individual muscles) may also aid in tone reduction.[30]

Mat activities aimed at reducing tone should concentrate on trunk and proximal movement control, since many patterns of hypertonus seem to be fixed from the action of strong proximal muscles.[48,49] Trunk activities can begin with rotation patterns, practiced first in a sidelying position and then progressing to rolling from full supine to prone. Upper and/or lower trunk rotation can also be performed in additional postures such as hooklying, sitting, quadruped, modified plantigrade, and standing. A further progression might include rotation in combination with extremity patterns: for example, proprioceptive neuromuscular facilitation (PNF) chopping or lifting, in supine or sitting. Rotation in a reciprocal pattern (trunk counterrotation in sidelying) could also be used. Extensor tone seems to predominate, so activities which stress flexion with trunk rotation are generally the most effective. Specific exercise techniques that are effective in reducing tone include active assisted movement: for example, neurodevelopmental treatment (NDT) handling,[48-50] or PNF techniques of rhythmic initiation.[51-53] Finally, patterns of motion that encourage or utilize spasticity should be discouraged and antagonist actions should be promoted.

Positioning out of tone-dependent postures is an important adjunct to exercise. In general, prolonged or static positioning in any fixed posture can be deleterious to the patient with spasticity, and should be avoided. Mechanical aids (e.g., orthotics, splints, casts) can be helpful in perserving joint structures and improving ROM. They may also have an effect on reflex sensitivity and tone.[54,55] Abnormal reflex activity can be present in patients demonstrating upper motor neuron syndrome. Careful assessment and attention to positioning can modify their influence. Attention should be given to head position (full flexion or extension, or side head turning, may activate STNR or ATNR reflexes), body position (prone or supine positioning may activate TLR reflexes), and pressure on the ball of the foot, which can activate a positive support reaction.

Local facilitation techniques such as muscle tapping, vibration, or light touch may prove useful in facilitating the antagonist of a spastic muscle, thereby reducing tone in the spastic muscle. However, it should be noted that in the presence of strong spasticity, reciprocal relationships may not be normal.[49] The use of resistance to facilitate contraction in a weakened antagonist must be done cautiously since overflow or irradiation may result in an increase in tone in the spastic agonist muscle. Prolonged stretch or pressure on long tendons of spastic muscles also decreases tone due to the action of peripheral receptors. Therapeutically this can be achieved through the use of weight-bearing postures (e.g., quadruped, kneeling, sitting with extended arm support). A more generalized decrease in tone can be achieved through techniques aimed at decreasing CNS arousal mechanisms (slow stroking down the posterior primary rami, inverted or tonic labyrinthine postion, soothing verbal commands). Slow vestibular stimulation achieved through rolling or slow rocking movements has also been effective in reducing muscle tone. These techniques are reviewed more thoroughly in Chapter 13.

Functional electrical stimulation has been used to reduce spasticity and clonus by utilizing mechanisms of reciprocal inhibition.[56-58] Since ankle clonus is a common problem for ambulatory patients, peroneal stimulation can be an effective measure to improve function. An intact reflex arc and intersegmental reciprocal relationships are prerequisites for using this type of therapy. Biofeedback techniques have also been used to modulate the level of spasticity.[59,60]

Range of Motion Deficits

Passive ROM exercises for immobilized parts should be performed several times each day. This usually requires the involvement of nursing staff and family members in order to provide an effective prevention program. If possible, the patient should be instructed in ROM exercises and active limb movements to help maintain joint flexibility. Caution must be used to prevent overstretching of muscles. Some residual tightness may improve function (e.g., postural stability). Splinting or casting may be a necessary adjunct to treatment in order to maintain optimal position. If specific muscle tightness has developed, the PNF techniques of hold-relax and contract-relax are useful in gaining increased joint range. Capsular tightness should be addressed using manual techniques of joint mobilization. If spasticity is an apparent cause of joint tightness or limitation

in range, inhibitory techniques should be employed prior to exercise. Fixed contractures usually require more aggressive management including manual passive stretching or prolonged static stretching using weights or positioning. In one study of chronic immobilized patients, low-load prolonged stretch using modified Buck's skin traction and weights proved more effective in reducing contracture than a brief, manually applied high-load stretch.[61] Surgical releases may become necessary in situations unresponsive to more conservative treatment approaches.[62-64]

Paresis and Fatigue

Muscle weakness will vary considerably from patient to patient. Exercise techniques will therefore vary depending on the patient. Patients with cerebellar symptoms may demonstrate asthenia or generalized muscle weakness. Patients may also experience weakness secondary to inactivity and generalized deconditioning. Improving strength and endurance are therefore important goals of therapy. In cases of mild weakness, a resistive training sequence (progressive resistance exercise, isokinetics) may be appropriate. When spasticity is a major presenting symptom, strengthening can best be achieved using an exercise program designed to promote tone reduction while increasing functional mobility. Proprioceptive neuromuscular facilitation patterns are ideal because of their emphasis on diagonal movement (helpful in reducing tone) and on combining the action of major muscle groups (helpful when the patient fatigues easily). Since the patient typically has a limited amount of energy to expend, exercises must be chosen judiciously, achieving the greatest number of goals with the fewest exercises. Functional activities should always be stressed.

Scheduling the exercise session in the morning before fatigue sets in is an important consideration. Exercising to the point of fatigue is contraindicated and can result in increased internal temperatures and a transient increase in symptoms (e.g., paresis, ataxia). This may have additional adverse effects on motivation and induce stress-related relapses.[43] Environmental temperatures are another important consideration for the exercising patient. Exercise in a warm environment should be avoided and air-conditioning is a medical necessity in many climates. Cool baths and ice packs should be utilized if the patient becomes overheated.

A successful exercise program is dependent on a number of factors essential for motor learning, including practice, adequate feedback, and knowledge of results. The patient with MS is often restricted in practice by neuromuscular fatigue and by neurologic deficits that impair sensory feedback, attention, memory, and motivation. The successful therapist will need to carefully identify the patient's resources and abilities and capitalize on them to maximize the patient's chances for functional improvement. Concomitant with this is the ability to recognize treatment goals that are not realistic considering the patient's remaining abilities.

The use of group classes and self-paced, voluntary exercises can be a valuable component of a rehabilitation program. The therapist's primary role in this approach is one of educator. Successful management of group classes requires careful, individualized assessment of group members with specific predetermined goals. The therapist concentrates on effective use of verbal instructions instead of manual skills. Significant improvement in functional, balance, and daily living skills in a group of 40 patients with MS not in active exacerbations was obtained using this approach.[65]

Fatigue is a common problem in MS and can be quite debilitating. Patients need to be taught principles of *energy conservation.* Activity needs to be balanced with rest. Periodic rest periods need to be planned in advance when patients are considering their daily schedule. Time-outs should be instituted if an activity becomes exhaustive. Activities that are difficult or have high energy needs should be broken down into component parts. Priorities need to be set. Overall efficiency can be improved if patients learn to limit their activities, saving their strength for those activities that have the highest functional and most enjoyable gains. Assistive devices should be considered, since they help conserve energy and may mean the difference between independence and dependence. The occupational therapist can yield valuable advice on planning, work simplification, and energy-efficient activities.[30]

During an acute exacerbation of disease, the patient will fare better if he or she is allowed to rest for a few days. Pushing the patient to continue exercising or ambulating is not helpful. Therapy can be reinstituted when the deterioration has stabilized and no new symptoms are appearing. The pace of therapy must be adjusted according to the patient's specific abilities and needs at that time.[14]

Ataxia

Ataxia is present with cerebellar lesions. The patient typically presents with incoordination, disturbances of posture and balance, and static postural tremor. Therapy is directed at promoting postural stability, accuracy of limb movements, and functional gait. Postural stability can be achieved by focusing on holding in a number of different weight-bearing, antigravity postures (e.g., prone on elbows, sitting, quadruped, kneeling, plantigrade, and standing). Specific exercise techniques designed to facilitate stability include joint approximation through proximal joints or head and cervical spine, alternating isometrics, and rhythmic stabilization. Patients with significant ataxia will not be able to hold steady and may benefit from the application of the technique of slow reversal-hold, progressing through decrements of range.[51] As improvement occurs, dynamic postural responses can be challenged by incorporating controlled mobility activities (weight shifting or rocking, moving in and out of postures and/or movement transitions). The patient can practice such activities as supine-to-sit, sit-to-stand, or scooting on a mat. Distal extremity movements can be superimposed on proximal stability to further challenge control (e.g., PNF chopping or lifting patterns). Ataxic limb movements have sometimes been helped by the application of Velcro weight cuffs (wrist or ankle). Weighted cuffs increase the amount of proprioceptive feedback during activity and may also serve to decrease extraneous movement.

The last step in a progression should be to promote balance. Static balance can be challenged using gentle perturbations, while dynamic balance can be challenged using self-initiated dynamic movements or a moveable surface (e.g., sitting activities on a gymnastic ball or equilibrium board are excellent).[66]

Frenkel's exercises were originally developed in 1889 to treat patients with problems of incoordination and cerebellar ataxia due to a loss of proprioception from tabes dorsalis. They have also been widely applied in the treatment of MS to remediate similar problems. These exercises are designed to substitute the use of vision and hearing for the loss of proprioceptive sensation and require a high degree of mental concentration and visual control of movement. They are, therefore, not appropriate for all patients with MS. For those patients with the prerequisite abilities, they can be effective in reducing ataxia and regaining some control of functional movement. Patients with partial sensation may progress to practicing these exercises with eyes closed.[67] Frenkel's exercises are presented in Table 22–3.

Reciprocal limb movements can be promoted through the use of PNF patterns using slow reversals. Resistance should be carefully graded to promote balanced inter-

---

Table 22–3 FRENKEL'S EXERCISES

General instructions: Exercises can be performed with the part supported or unsupported, unilaterally or bilaterally. They should be practiced as smooth, timed movements, performed to a slow, even tempo by counting out loud. Consistency of performance is stressed and a specified target can be used to determine range. Four basic positions are used; they are lying, sitting, standing, and walking. The exercises progress from postures of greatest stability (lying, sitting) to postures of greatest challenge (standing, walking). As voluntary control improves, the exercises progress to stopping and starting on command, increasing the range, and performing the same exercises with eyes closed. Concentration and repetition are the keys to success. A similar progression of exercises can be developed for the upper extremities.

Examples:

1. Half-lying: hip and knee flexion and extension of each limb, foot flat on plinth.
2. Half-lying: hip abduction and adduction of each limb with the foot flat, knee flexed; then with knee extended.
3. Half-lying: hip and knee flexion and extension of each limb, heel lifted off plinth.
4. Half-lying: heel of one limb to opposite leg (toes, ankle, shin, patella).
5. Half-lying: heel of one limb to opposite knee, sliding down crest of tibia to ankle.
6. Half-lying: hip and knee flexion and extension of both limbs, legs together.
7. Half-lying: reciprocal movements of both limbs—flexion of one leg during extension of the other.
8. Sitting: knee extension and flexion of each limb; progress to marking time.
9. Sitting: hip abduction and adduction.
10. Sitting: alternate foot placing to a specified target (using floor markings or a grid).
11. Standing up and sitting down: to a specified count.
12. Standing: foot placing to a specified target (floor markings or grid).
13. Standing: weight shifting.
14. Walking: sideways or forward to a specified count. (A Frenkel mat, parallel lines or floor markings may be used as targets to control foot placement, stride length and step width.)
14. Walking: turning around to a specified count. (Floor markings can be helpful in maintaining a stable base of support.)

action between agonist and antagonist. A stationary bike and upper extremity cycle ergometer can also be used to promote reciprocal limb movements. Since endurance may be low and fatigue common, careful monitoring of ergometry work is essential.

The pool can be an important therapeutic modality. Swimming and shallow water calisthenics can be used to improve strength, decrease muscular fatigability, and increase endurance.[68] In addition, water provides a graded resistance that slows down the patient's ataxic movements, while the buoyancy aids in upright balance. Pool therapy allows for increased movements and with moderate pool temperatures will frequently lead to moderation of muscle tone.

In general, ataxic patients do better in a low-stimulus environment that allows them to concentrate more fully on control of movements. They require accurate feedback (knowledge of results, knowledge of performance) and high degrees of repetition in order to achieve learning of motor tasks.

Gait

Ambulation is frequently impaired. However at least 65 percent of patients who survive 25 years with MS are still able to walk.[14] Early gait problems often include poor balance and heaviness of one or more limbs. Patients frequently report difficulty lifting their legs (hip flexor weakness). Weakness in hamstrings and dorsiflexors is also common. Later problems center on developing clonus, spasticity, sensory loss and/or ataxia. Weakness generally extends to include the quadriceps and hip abductors. Problems with foot clearance may result in a circumducted gait. Quadriceps weakness typically results in hyperextension of the knee and forward flexion of the trunk with increased lumbar lordosis. A positive Trendelenburg and Trendelenburg gait pattern (hip abducter weakness) may also develop.[69] A well-designed mat program of tone reduction, using postural and preambulatory mat activities is essential. Standing and walking activities should stress safety, adequate weight transfer with trunk rotation, a stable base of support, and controlled progression.

Some patients with MS report the need for ambulatory assistance. In one study of 1145 patients with MS, 4 percent were using crutches, 6 percent leg braces, and 12 percent were using walkers or canes. Long-term function was more often maintained through the use of wheelchairs, seen in more than 40 percent of the patients.[70] Ankle-foot stability can be achieved by the addition of an ankle-foot orthosis (AFO). The presence or absence of spasticity will determine the type of device selected. Rocker shoes (modified Danish clogs) have also been successful with selected patients in compensating for lost ankle mobility. Gait patterns appeared more normal, with a significant savings in energy cost (150% over ambulation without rocker shoes).[71] Canes, crutches, or a walker may become necessary. The addition of weights to an ambulatory aid may help to stabilize the device and diminish the excursion of ataxia.[72]

Functional Impairments

Functional training should focus on the development of problem-solving skills, appropriate compensatory techniques, and energy conservation. Full participation of the patient in all phases of rehabilitation and problem solving will increase personal involvement and self-worth, while decreasing dependency and passivity.[36]

Because many patients will depend on the wheelchair as their primary means of mobility, appropriate prescription of the chair and its components is important (see Chapter 31). The stage and progression of the disease and presenting symptoms should be taken into consideration when deciding upon a wheelchair. For example, if the disease is rapidly progressing, a recliner wheelchair with elevating leg rests may be appropriate. An electric wheelchair or cart is indicated if the patient has insufficient strength in his or her arms to propel a standard wheelchair, or if fatigue problems are severe. Patients should be carefully instructed in wheelchair mobility skills and transfers. Attention to good posture and pressure relief are important considerations. Patients should be encouraged to balance time in the wheelchair with other activities such as walking or exercising and should be extra diligent in stretching muscles that tend to contract from prolonged sitting.

The majority of patients with MS use multiple devices.[73] This requires careful attention to the prescription of appropriate devices and to environmental modification. Adaptive equipment should assist the patient in conserving energy and maintaining function. Mobility aids may include the use of bed or toilet grab bars, an overhead trapeze, raised seats, sliding boards, or lifts. Adapted or weighted feeding utensils or ball-bearing feeders can assist the patient in feeding. Long-handled shoe horns, reachers, button hooks, sock aids, or other devices can assist in dressing. Effective communication may require built-up writing utensils, typewriter, or an electronic communication system. The clinician needs to recognize when a device is indicated and to assist the patient in learning how to use it before significant deterioration of function occurs. Assisting the patient in acceptance of the device also requires skill and understanding.[74]

A significant number of patients with MS (one out of every two patients) will also require the assistance of another person.[73] This places an extra burden on family members and/or on the financial resources of the patient if outside attendants must be utilized. The clinician will need to devote considerable time to an educational program aimed at instructing these individuals and coordinating home management with rehabilitation. An organized team approach to teaching with full active participation of the patient provides the best approach to this problem. A positive attitude and an honest, open presentation are important. Instruction should be kept appropriately brief, proceeding from simple to more complex procedures. The patient's abilities should be emphasized, stressing the need for optimal function while providing a realistic appraisal of the problems.[34,75]

Modifications in living and work environments are necessary to ensure continuing independence. Adjustments must take into account the patient's abilities and disabilities, as well as a consideration of disease progression and prognosis. Common housing barriers can be eliminated and the necessary adaptations instituted (see Chapter 12).

Respiratory Problems

Breathing exercises are an important consideration in treatment during all stages of the disease. Shallow respiratory patterns may contribute to speech difficulties and recurrent respiratory infections. Specific involvement of respiratory muscles should be ascertained. These muscles may be weak, ataxic, or spastic. Diaphragmatic breathing, resistive breathing, effective coughing, and postural training are all vital components of treatment. Segmental expansion should be facilitated through proper placement of manual contacts and resistance. When speech or feeding difficulties are apparent these efforts should be coordinated with a speech therapist.

Feeding and Nutritional Issues

Dysphagia is a common problem. Dietary counseling may be necessary to ensure that food is of the proper consistency. Feeding difficulties may be improved by focusing on sitting posture, head control, eye-hand coordination, and voluntary control of the muscles of mastication. Adaptive equipment may also be necessary. An upright posture and a slightly flexed head position is essential for good swallowing. Stretch and resistance can be used to facilitate and strengthen muscle action (jaw opening or closing, lip closure, tongue mobility). Sucking reflexes and saliva production can be stimulated by using an ice cube or a water popsicle. Resistive sucking through a straw can also be helpful. Brief icing of the tongue and laryngeal area of the neck may stimulate swallowing reflexes. Thicker liquids, which provide some resistance and therefore some facilitation of muscle action, are generally easier than thin liquids. Soft foods are easier than firm ones. Fatigue patterns also affect feeding, and patients may benefit from eating their main meal in the morning or from eating multiple small meals. Feeding tubes may be necessary in the more chronic stages of the disease.[29]

Psychosocial Issues

Patients with multiple sclerosis may show a variety of behavioral adaptations associated with the stress of a chronic disease. The primary role of clinicians is to assist the individual and family in their understanding of the disease and in their psychosocial adjustment. The unique feature of a disease with an exacerbating-remitting course is that it requires continual readjustment every time a new set of symptoms appears. Patients who appear well-adjusted at one stage may regress as the disease worsens. In addition, the unknown and unpredictable future creates a tremendous amount of stress for these individuals. Matson and Brooks point out that living with MS requires not only initial acceptance but also a tremendous flexibility to deal with this lack of closure.[76] Patients may also experience attitudes of "wait and see" or "nothing can be done." The longer they are exposed to these attitudes associated with chronicity the less likely they are to seek help. Personal and family counseling given early in the course of the disease, cou-

pled with timely referral to rehabilitation services, can best meet the needs of patients with MS.[77]

Patients also experience additional everyday stresses that are associated with inability to perform activities of daily living, dependency on others, architectural barriers, and so forth.[78] It is important to remember that emotional stressors can have a direct impact on the disease and can result in a temporary exacerbation of symptoms.

A positive, affirmative attitude can effectively influence patient attitudes. Clinicians should relay to their patients a strong belief that treatment can be beneficial. This maintenance of therapeutic hope is extremely important. Programs should focus on remaining abilities and should carefully build in successful experiences. As in any long-term care situation, a relationship of trust and caring is crucial in ensuring treatment success.[79]

A support group can also provide a necessary psychologic base for patients and their families. Within this environment individuals can gain accurate and useful information about the disease, can discuss common problems and methods of coping, and can share anxieties. Thus it provides the necessary forum to assist in the continual adjustment process. The National Multiple Sclerosis Society is a valuable resource for patients and their families.

SUMMARY

Multiple sclerosis is a chronic demyelinating disease of the central nervous system characterized by widespread lesions and multiple symptoms. Although the cause is unknown, major theories focus on an infectious viral origin, an immune-mediated pathogenesis, or a combination of the two. The diagnosis is usually based on clinical findings, including multiple signs of neurologic dysfunction occurring over time.

Multiple sclerosis is an unpredictable disease, typically presenting with an exacerbating-remitting course, although other clinical courses have been recognized. Common clinical findings include disturbances in sensation, muscle power, tone, fatigue, coordination, vision, communication, bladder and bowel function, and cognitive and behavioral function. Numerous secondary impairments can arise from prolonged inactivity and deconditioning. The prognosis is variable, although most patients survive 25 years with the disability.

Medical management is directed at the disease process itself or at amelioration of symptoms. There is no specific preventive or curative treatment. Interventions are typically pharmacologic, although in advanced disease surgical measures may be considered. Rehabilitation efforts are directed toward decreasing the effects of symptomatology and deconditioning on overall disability and handicap. Thus maximizing abilities, improving function, preventing secondary impairments, and promoting successful psychosocial adjustment become the central focus of care rather than altering underlying disease processes. The comprehensive efforts of an interdisciplinary team are needed to provide coordinated and continuing care.

QUESTIONS FOR REVIEW

1. What are the primary central nervous system impairments in multiple sclerosis? How is the function altered?

2. What are the most common signs and symptoms?

3. What are the two major causative theories? How might these two theories interact to explain the pathogenesis of MS?

4. What are the diagnostic measures used to confirm MS?

5. Differentiate between the four main types of clinical course recognized in MS.

6. What are the clinical effects of inactivity for the chronic, immobilized patient?

7. What are the major exacerbating factors in MS? What is the impact of these factors on the MS patient?

8. What components are included in a physical therapy evaluation? How might some of the standard evaluations have to be modified for the patient with MS?

9. What therapeutic exercises and techniques can be used to moderate spasticity?

10. What therapeutic exercises and techniques can be used to modify paresis? Ataxia?

11. Describe Frenkel's exercises. What motor learning principles do they incorporate?

12. What are the major functional devices likely to be used by the patient with MS? What are the major considerations in ordering this equipment?

13. What are the psychosocial issues in the adjustment of the patient to MS?

REFERENCES

1. Dean, G: The multiple sclerosis problem. Sci Am 223:40, 1970.
2. Gorelick, P: Clues to the mystery of multiple sclerosis. Postgrad Med 85:125, 1989.
3. Guyton, A: Basic Neuroscience. WB Saunders, Philadelphia, 1987.
4. Hafler, D, et al: In vivo activated T lymphocytes in the peripheral blood and cerebrospinal fluid of patients with multiple sclerosis. N Engl J Med 312:1405, 1985.
5. Ransohoff, R: Multiple sclerosis: new concepts of pathogenesis, diagnosis, and treatment. Compr Ther 15:39, 1989.
6. Kurtzke, J: Epidemiological contributions to multiple sclerosis: an overview. Neurology 30:61, 1980.
7. Dick, G and Gay, D: Multiple sclerosis—autoimmune or microbial? A critical review with additional observations. J Infect 16:25, 1988.
8. McFarlin, D and McFarland, H: Multiple sclerosis. N Engl J Med 307:1183, 1982.
9. Ellison, G: Multiple sclerosis: why? Biomed Pharmacother 43:327, 1989.
10. Chataway, S: What's new in the pathogenesis of multiple sclerosis? A review. J R Soc Med 82:159, 1989.
11. Kurtzke, J: Multiple sclerosis: what's in a name? Neurology 38:309, 1988.
12. Franklin, G and Burks, J: Diagnosis and medical management of multiple sclerosis. In Maloney, FP, Burks, J, and Ringel, S (eds): Interdisciplinary Rehabilitation of Multiple Sclerosis and Neuromuscular Disorders. JB Lippincott, Philadelphia, 1985.
13. Johnson, K: Cerebrospinal fluid and blood assays of diagnostic usefulness in multiple sclerosis. Neurology 30:106, 1980.
14. Lechtenberg, R: Multiple Sclerosis Fact Book. FA Davis, Philadelphia, 1988.
15. Katz, R and Rymer, Z: Spastic hypertonia: mechanisms and measurement. Arch Phys Med Rehabil 70:144, 1989.
16. Herrera, W: Vestibular and other balance disorders in multiple sclerosis. Neurol Clin 5:407, 1990.
17. Riley, D and Lang, A: Hemiballism in multiple sclerosis. Mov Disord 3:88, 1988.
18. Mao, C, Gancher, S, and Herndon, R: Movement disorders in multiple sclerosis. Mov Disord 3:109, 1988.
19. Petersen, R and Kokmen, E: Cognitive and psychiatric abnormalities in multiple sclerosis. Mayo Clin Proc 64:657, 1989.
20. Franklin, G, et al: Cognitive loss in multiple sclerosis. Arch Neurol 46:162, 1989.
21. Minden, S and Schiffer, R: Affective disorders in multiple sclerosis. Arch Neurol 47:98, 1990.
22. Ruttenberg, N: Assessment and treatment of speech and swallowing problems in patients with multiple sclerosis. In Maloney, F, Burks, J, and Ringel, S (eds): Interdisciplinary Rehabilitation of Multiple Sclerosis and Neuromuscular Disorders. JB Lippincott, Philadelphia, 1985.
23. Kurtzke, J, et al: Studies on the natural history of multiple sclerosis. J Chronic Dis 30:819, 1977.
24. Kraft, G, et al: Multiple sclerosis: early prognostic guidelines. Arch Phys Med Rehabil 62:54, 1981.
25. Noseworthy, J: Therapeutics of multiple sclerosis. Clin Neuropharmacol 14:49, 1991.
26. Goodin, D: The use of immunosuppressive agents in the treatment of multiple sclerosis: a critical review. Neurology 41:980, 1991.
27. Tindall, R: Therapy of acute and chronic multiple sclerosis. Compr Ther 17:18, 1991.
28. Carter, J and Rodriguez, M: Immunosuppressive treatment of multiple sclerosis. Mayo Clin Proc 64:664, 1989.
29. Blaivas, J: Management of bladder dysfunction in multiple sclerosis. Neurology 30:12, 1980.
30. Shapiro, R: Symptom Management in Multiple Sclerosis. Demos, New York, 1987.
31. Katz, R: Management of spasticity. Am J Phys Med Rehabil 67:108, 1988.
32. Feigenson, J, et al: The cost-effectiveness of multiple sclerosis rehabilitation: a model. Neurology 31:1316, 1981.
33. Greenspun, B, Stineman, M, and Agri, R: Multiple sclerosis and rehabilitation outcome. Arch Phys Med Rehabil 68:434, 1987.
34. Erickson, R, Lie, M, and Wineinger, M: Rehabilitation in multiple sclerosis. Mayo Clin Proc 64:818, 1989.
35. Slater, R: A model of care: Matching human services to patients' needs. Neurology 30:39, 1980.
36. Kottke, F: Philosophic consideration of quality of life for the disabled. Arch Phys Med Rehabil 63:60, 1982.
37. Kurtzke, J: On the evaluation of disability in multiple sclerosis. Neurology 11:686, 1961.
38. Kurtzke, J: Rating neurological impairment in multiple sclerosis: an expanded disability status scale (EDSS). Neurology 33:1444, 1983.
39. Mahoney, F and Barthel, D: Functional evaluation: the Barthel Index. Md State Med J 14:61, 1965.
40. Keith, R, et al: The functional independence measure: a new tool for rehabilitation. In Eisenberg, M and Grzesiak, R (eds): Advances in Clinical Rehabilitation. Springer-Verlag, New York, 1987.
41. Haber, A and LaRocca, N (eds): M.R.D. Minimal record of disability for multiple sclerosis. National Multiple Sclerosis Society, New York, 1985.
42. Granger, C, et al: Functional assessment scales: a study of persons with multiple sclerosis. Arch Phys Med Rehabil 71:870, 1990.
43. Pal Brar, S and Wangaard, C: Physical therapy for patients with multiple sclerosis. In Maloney, F, Burks, J, and Ringel, S (eds): Interdisciplinary Rehabilitation of Multiple Sclerosis and Neuromuscular Disorders. JB Lippincott, Philadelphia, 1985.
44. Kloth, L, McCuoolch, J and Feedar, J: Wound Healing: Alternatives in Management. FA Davis, Philadelphia, 1990.

45. Cardi, M: Skin Care for the Patient with Sensory Loss. Helen Hayes Hospital, West Haverstraw, NY, 1982.
46. Wells, P, Frampton, V, and Bowsher, D: Pain Management in Physical Therapy. Appleton & Lange, Norwalk, CT, 1988.
47. Brar, S, et al: Evaluation of treatment protocols on minimal to moderate spasticity in multiple sclerosis. Arch Phys Med Rehabil 72:186, 1991.
48. Bobath, K and Bobath, B: The facilitation of normal postural reactions and movements in the treatment of cerebral palsy. Physiotherapy 50:246, 1964.
49. Bobath, B: The treatment of neuromuscular disorders by improving patterns of co-ordination. Physiotherapy 55:18, 1969.
50. Davies, P. Right in the Middle. Springer-Verlag, New York, 1990.
51. Voss, D, Ionta, M, and Myers, B: Proprioceptive Neuromuscular Facilitation, ed 3. Harper & Row, Philadelphia, 1985.
52. Sullivan, P, Markos, P, and Minor, M: An Integrated Approach to Therapeutic Exercise. Reston, Reston, VA, 1982.
53. Sullivan, P and Markos, P: Clinical Procedures in Therapeutic Exercise. Appleton & Lange, Norwalk, CT, 1987.
54. Booth, B, Doyle, M, and Montgomery, J: Serial casting for the management of spasticity in the head-injured adult. Phys Ther 63:1960, 1983.
55. McPherson, J, Becker, A, and Franszczak, N: Dynamic splint to reduce the passive component of hypertonicity. Arch Phys Med Rehabil 66:249, 1985.
56. Levine, M, Knott, M, and Kabat, H: Relaxation of spasticity by electrical stimulation of antagonist muscles. Arch Phys Med Rehabil 11:668, 1952.
57. Bajd, T, et al: Electrical stimulation in treating spasticity resulting from spinal cord injury. Arch Phys Med Rehabil 66:515, 1985.
58. Baker, L: Clinical uses of neuromuscular electrical stimulation. In Nelson, R and Currier, D (eds): Clinical Electrotherapy. Appleton & Lange, Norwalk, CT, 1987.
59. Basmajian, J: Biofeedback in rehabilitation: a review of principles and practice. Arch Phys Med Rehabil 62:469, 1981.
60. Wolf, S and Segal, R: Conditioning of the spinal stretch reflex: implications for rehabilitation. Phys Ther 70:652, 1990.
61. Light, K, Nuzik, S, Personius, W, and Barstrom, A: Low-load prolonged stretch vs. high-load brief stretch in treating knee contractures. Phys Ther 64:330, 1984.
62. Cherry, D: Review of physical therapy alternatives for reducing muscle contracture. Phys Ther 60:877, 1980.

63. Sady, S, Wortman, M, and Blanke, D: Flexibility training: ballistic, static or proprioceptive neuromuscular facilitation? Arch Phys Med Rehabil 63:261, 1982.
64. Kaltenborn, F: Mobilization of the Extremity Joints: Examination and Basic Treatment Techniques. Olaf Norlis Bokhandel, Oslo, 1980.
65. DeSouza, L: A different approach to physiotherapy for multiple sclerosis patients. Physiotherapy 70:428, 1984.
66. Baer, G and Lewis, Y: The rehabilitation of a severely disabled multiple sclerosis patient. Physiotherapy 73:438, 1987.
67. Kottke, F: Therapeutic exercise to develop neuromuscular coordination. In Kottke, F, Stillwell, G, and Lehmann, J (eds): Krusen's Handbook of Physical Medicine and Rehabilitation. WB Saunders, Philadelphia, 1982.
68. Gehlsen, G, Grigsby, S, and Winant, D: Effects of an aquatic fitness program on muscular strength and endurance of patients with multiple sclerosis. Phys Ther 64:653, 1984.
69. Footh, W: Patterns of muscle weakness in patients with multiple sclerosis. Clinical Management 3:32, 1983.
70. Baum, H and Rothschild, B: Multiple sclerosis and mobility restriction. Arch Phys Med Rehabil 64:591, 1983.
71. Perry, J, Gronley, J, and Lunsford, T: Rocker shoe as walking aid in multiple sclerosis, I. Arch Phys Med Rehabil 62:59, 1981.
72. Kelly-Hayes, M: Guidelines for the rehabilitation of multiple sclerosis patients. Nurs Clin North Am 15:245, 1980.
73. Baum, H and Rothschild, B: Multiple sclerosis and mobility restriction. Arch Phys Med Rehabil 64:591, 1983.
74. Wolf, B: Occupational therapy for patients with multiple sclerosis. In Maloney, F, Burks, J, and Ringel, S (eds): Interdisciplinary Rehabilitation of Multiple Sclerosis and Neuromuscular Disorders. JB Lippincott, Philadelphia, 1985.
75. Price, G: The challenge to the family. Am J Nurs 80:283, 1980.
76. Matson, R and Brooks, N: Adjusting to multiple sclerosis: an exploratory study. Soc Sci Med 11:245, 1977.
77. Kraft, G, Freal, J, and Coryell, J: Disability, disease duration, and rehabilitation services needs in multiple sclerosis: patient perspective. Arch Phys Med Rehabil 67:164, 1986.
78. Pulton, T: Multiple sclerosis—a social psychological perspective. Phys Ther 57:170, 1977.
79. Scheinberg, L, et al: Comprehensive long-term care of patients with multiple sclerosis. Neurology 31:1121, 1981.

GLOSSARY

Ataxia: A general term used to describe uncoordinated movement; may influence gait, posture, and patterns of movement.

Autoimmune disease: A process in which the body's immune system causes illness by attacking body cells that are normal and essential for health.

Bipolar affective disorder: Alternating periods of depression and mania.

Charcot's triad: Cardinal symptoms of multiple sclerosis—intention tremor, scanning speech, and nystagmus.

Debridement: The removal of necrotic and devitalized tissue from a wound.

Demyelination: Destruction or removal of the myelin sheath of nerve tissue by a disease process.

Diplopia: Double vision.

Dyesthesias: Abnormal burning or pain sensations.

Dysdiadochokinesia: Impaired ability to perform rapid alternating movements.

Dysmetria: Impaired ability to judge the distance or range of a movement.

Dysphagia: Inability to swallow or difficulty in swallowing.

Emotional dysregulation syndrome: Pathologic laughing and weeping.

Energy conservation: Life-style suggestions and techniques designed to minimize fatigue and avoid exhaustion by conserving energy.

Euphoria: An exaggerated feeling of well-being.

Exacerbation: Acute worsening or flare-up of neurologic signs and symptoms, usually associated with inflammation and demyelination in the brain and spinal cord.

Expanded Disability Status Scale (EDDS; Kurtzke): A functional assessment scale used to measure the severity of functional impairment in multiple sclerosis.

Fatigue patterns: Characteristic pattern of afternoon exhaustion that occurs in multiple sclerosis.

Frenkel's exercises: Exercises designed to improve incoordination and cerebellar ataxia resulting from a loss of proprioception.

Gliosis: Proliferation of neuroglial tissue in the central nervous system.

Hyperpathia: A hypersensitivity to minor sensory stimuli.

Immunoglobulin: A general term for the various types of antibodies produced by the immune system.

Intention tremor: An involuntary oscillatory movement that occurs during voluntary movement.

Lhermitte's sign: A sensation like an electric shock running down the spinal cord and legs and produced by flexing the neck.

Minimum Record of Disability (MRD; National Multiple Sclerosis Society): A functional assessment scale that measures the physical incapacity (Incapacity Status Scale, ISS) and environmental handicaps (Environmental Status Scale, ESS) experienced by persons with MS.

Myelin: The fatty insulation of nerve fibers that is damaged in multiple sclerosis.

Neuralgia: Severe sharp pain along the course of a nerve.

> **Trigeminal neuralgia (tic douloureux):** Degeneration of the trigeminal nerve resulting in paroxysmal pain in the face.

Nystagmus: Rhythmic jerking movements of the eyes.

Optic neuritis: Inflammation of the optic nerve that causes transient or permanent loss of vision and is often associated with pain in the eye at the time vision deteriorates.

Paresthesias: Abnormal sensations such as numbness, prickling, or tingling without apparent cause.

Paroxysmal attack: A sudden onset of symptoms.

Plaque: A patch of demyelinated or inflamed central nervous system tissue.

Remission: A decrease in the signs and symptoms of a disease, seen in multiple sclerosis.

Scotoma: Islandlike blind gap in the visual field.

Vertigo: Sensation of movement of one's body or of objects moving about the body; usually accompanied by nausea and vomiting.

APPENDIX A AN EXPANDED DISABILITY STATUS SCALE (EDSS) FOR EVALUATING PATIENTS WITH MULTIPLE SCLEROSIS

Functional Systems.

Pyramidal Functions
0. Normal.
1. Abnormal signs without disability.
2. Minimal disability.
3. Mild or moderate paraparesis or hemiparesis; severe monoparesis.
4. Marked paraparesis or hemiparesis; moderate quadriparesis; or monoplegia.
5. Paraplegia, hemiplegia, or marked quadriparesis.
6. Quadriplegia.
V. Unknown.

Cerebellar Functions
0. Normal.
1. Abnormal signs without disability.
2. Mild ataxia.
3. Moderate truncal or limb ataxia.
4. Severe ataxia, all limbs.
5. Unable to perform coordinated movements due to ataxia.
V. Unknown.
X. Is used throughout after each number when weakness (grade 3 or more on pyramidal) interferes with testing.

Brain Stem Functions
0. Normal.
1. Signs only.
2. Moderate nystagmus or other mild disability.
3. Severe nystagmus, marked extraocular weakness, or moderate disability of other cranial nerves.
4. Marked dysarthria or other marked disability.
5. Inability to swallow or speak.
V. Unknown.

Sensory Functions (revised 1982)
0. Normal.
1. Vibration or figure-writing decrease only, in one or two limbs.
2. Mild decrease in touch or pain or position sense, and/or moderate decrease in vibration in one or two limbs; or vibratory (c/s figure writing) decrease alone in three or four limbs.
3. Moderate decrease in touch or pain or position sense, and/or essentially lost vibration in one or two limbs; or mild decrease in touch or pain and/or moderate decrease in all proprioceptive tests in three or four limbs.
4. Marked decrease in touch or pain or loss of proprioception, alone or combined, in one or two limbs; or moderate decrease in touch or pain and/or severe proprioceptive decrease in more than two limbs.
5. Loss (essentially) of sensation in one or two limbs; or moderate decrease in touch or pain and/or loss of proprioception for most of the body below the head.
6. Sensation essentially lost below the head.
V. Unknown.

Bowel and Bladder Functions (revised 1982)
0. Normal.
1. Mild urinary hesitancy, urgency, or retention.
2. Moderate hesitancy, urgency, retention of bowel or bladder, or rare urinary incontinence.
3. Frequent urinary incontinence.
4. In need of almost constant catheterization.
5. Loss of bladder function.
6. Loss of bowel and bladder function.
V. Unknown.

Visual (or Optic) Functions
0. Normal.
1. Scotoma with visual acuity (corrected) better than 20/30.
2. Worse eye with scotoma with maximal visual acuity (corrected) of 20/30 to 20/59.
3. Worse eye with large scotoma, or moderate decrease in fields, but with maximal visual acuity (corrected) of 20/60 to 20/99.
4. Worse eye with marked decrease of fields and maximal visual acuity (corrected) of 20/100 to 20/200; grade 3 plus maximal visual acuity of better eye of 20/60 or less.
5. Worse eye with maximal visual acuity (corrected) less than 20/200; grade 4 plus maximal acuity of better eye of 20/60 or less.
6. Grade 5 plus maximal visual acuity of better eye of 20/60 or less.
V. Unknown.
X. Is added to grades 0 to 6 for presence of temporal pallor.

Cerebral (or Mental) Functions
0. Normal.
1. Mood alteration only (does not affect DSS score).
2. Mild decrease in mentation.
3. Moderate decrease in mentation.
4. Marked decrease in mentation (chronic brain syndrome—moderate).
5. Dementia or chronic brain syndrome—severe or incompetent.
V. Unknown.

Other Functions.
0. None.
1. Any other neurologic findings attributed to MS (specify).
V. Unknown.

Expanded Disability Status Scale (EDSS)

0 = Normal neurologic exam (all grade 0 in functional systems [FS]; cerebral grade 1 acceptable).

1.0 = No disability, minimal signs in one FS (i.e., grade 1 excluding cerebral grade 1).

1.5 = No disability minimal signs in more than one FS (more than one grade 1 excluding cerebral grade 1).

2.0 = Minimal disability in one FS (one FS grade 2, others 0 or 1).

2.5 = Minimal disability in two FS (two FS grade 2, others 0 or 1).

3.0 = Moderate disability in one FS (one FS grade 3, others 0 or 1), or mild disability in three or four FS (three/four FS grade 2, others 0 or 1) though fully ambulatory.

3.5 = Fully ambulatory but with moderate disability in one FS (one grade 3) and one or two FS grade 2; or two FS grade 3; or five FS grade 2 (others 0 or 1).

4.0 = Fully ambulatory without aid, self-sufficient, up and about some 12 hours a day despite relatively severe disability consisting of one FS grade 4 (others 0 or 1), or combinations of lesser grades exceeding limits of previous steps. Able to walk without aid or rest some 500 meters.

4.5 = Fully ambulatory without aid, up and about much of the day, able to work a full day, may otherwise have some limitation of full activity or require minimal assistance; characterized by relatively severe disability, usually consisting of one FS grade 4 (others 0 or 1) or combinations of lesser grades exceeding limits of previous steps. Able to walk without aid or rest for some 300 meters.

5.0 = Ambulatory without aid or rest for about 200 meters; disability severe enough to impair full daily activities (e.g., to work full day without special provisions). (Usual FS equivalents are one grade 5 alone, others 0 or 1; or combinations of lesser grades usually exceeding specifications for step 4.0.)

5.5 = Ambulatory without aid or rest for about 100 meters; disability severe enough to preclude full daily activities.

APPENDIX A AN EXPANDED DISABILITY STATUS SCALE (EDSS) FOR
EVALUATING PATIENTS WITH MULTIPLE SCLEROSIS (Continued)

(Usual FS equivalents are one grade 5 alone, others 0 or 1; or combinations of lesser grades usually exceeding those for step 4.0.)

6.0 = Intermittent or unilateral constant assistance (cane, crutch, or brace) required to walk about 100 meters with or without resting. (Usual FS equivalents are combinations with more than two FS grade 3+.)

6.5 = Constant bilateral assistance (canes, crutches, or braces) required to walk about 20 meters without resting. (Usual FS equivalents are combinations with more than two FS grade 3+.)

7.0 = Unable to walk beyond about 5 meters even with aid, essentially restricted to wheelchair; wheels self in standard wheelchair and transfers alone; up and about in wheelchair some 12 hours a day. (Usual FS equivalents are combinations with more than one FS grade 4+; very rarely, pyramidal grade 5 alone.)

7.5 = Unable to take more than a few steps; restricted to wheelchair; may need aid in transfer; wheels self but cannot carry on in standard wheelchair a full day; may require motorized wheelchair. (Usual FS equivalents are combinations with more than one FS grade 4+.)

8.0 = Essentially restricted to bed or chair or perambulated in wheelchair, but may be out of bed itself much of the day; retains many self-care functions; generally has effective uses of arms. (Usual FS equivalents are combinations, generally grade 4+ in several systems.)

8.5 = Essentially restricted to bed much of the day; has some effective use of arm(s); retains some self-care functions. (Usual FS equivalents are combinations, generally 4+ in several systems.)

9.0 = Helpless bed patient; can communicate and eat. (Usual FS equivalents are combinations, mostly grade 4+.)

9.5 = Totally helpless bed patient; unable to communicate effectively or eat/swallow. (Usual FS equivalents are combinations, almost all grade 4+.)

10.0 = Death due to MS.

From Kurtzke,[38] with permission.

APPENDIX B RMMSC PHYSICAL THERAPY EVALUATION FORM
(AND EXPLANATIONS)

Hospital-number _____-___

Name _____
      (Last, First)

Date: Year 19___ Mo ___ Day ___

Sex: ___ (M = Male, F = Female)

Date of birth   Year 19___ Mo___ Day ___

Hand dominance ___ (R = Right, L = Left)

Age at first symptom ___   Year of diagnosis 19___

Physical status ___(R = remission, E = exacerbation, P = progression, S = stable, U = other)
   (Definitions below.)

Most involved extremity . . . UE ___ . . . LE ___ (R = Right, L = Left, E = Equal)

Have you ever received physical therapy before? ___ (Y = Yes, N = No)

Current sensory symptoms (check all that apply)

Paresthesia/numbness   Right UE ___   Left UE ___   Right LE ___   Left LE ___   Trunk ___

Dysesthesia/pain   Right UE ___   Left UE ___   Right LE ___   Left LE ___   Trunk ___

Definitions of Items Regarding Physical Status

Remission: Patient has recovered from an exacerbation and has resumed normal function.

Exacerbation: Patient is in an acute attack.

Progression: Patient is experiencing slowly or rapidly progressing MS.

Stable: Patient is in a stable condition with some residual symptoms of MS remaining.

Functional Movement Evaluation

(Use standard scale of 0 to 5. For + or −, use second box.) (If strength in an extremity is normal, record only for extremity as a whole. If not normal, record individual muscle groups.)

Right UE ___-___   Left UE ___-___   Right LE ___-___   Left LE ___-___

Right	Muscle Groups	Left	Right	Muscle Groups	Left
___-___	Shoulder flexors	___-___	___-___	Hip flexors	___-___
___-___	Shoulder extensors	___-___	___-___	Hip abductors	___-___
___-___	Shoulder abductors	___-___	___-___	Hip extensors	___-___
___-___	Elbow flexors	___-___	___-___	Knee extensors	___-___
___-___	Elbow extensors	___-___	___-___	Knee flexors	___-___
___-___	Wrist flexors	___-___	___-___	Ankle dorsiflexors	___-___
___-___	Wrist extensors	___-___	___-___	Ankle plantarflexors	___-___
___-___	Back extensors	___-___	___-___	Abdominals	___-___

APPENDIX B   RMMSC PHYSICAL THERAPY EVALUATION FORM
(AND EXPLANATIONS) *(Continued)*

Range of Motion
(Check functional range in each extremity below. 0 = Absent, 5 = Normal. If ROM is abnormal, check the appropriate range for the categories given.)
Right UE ___   Left UE ___   Right LE ___   Left LE ___
Shoulder abduction   Right UE ___   Left UE ___
   (A = 0–90, B = 90–180)
Ankle dorsiflexion/plantarflexion   Right LE ___   Left LE ___
   (A = 10–15 of dorsiflexion, B = neutral to +5 or −5, C = 10–20 plantarflexion, D = 25–35 plantarflexion)
List specific contractures (e.g., 20-degree hip flexion in contracture): _____

Sensation
Proprioceptive loss (1 = none, 2 = mild, 3 = severe. Explanation below.)
Right UE ___   Left UE ___   Right LE ___   Left LE ___
Definitions of Sensation Classifications
None: No loss of proprioception
Mild: Any loss at PIP joints in upper extremities and MP joint in toes.
Severe: Any loss at ankles or wrists

Muscle Tone

Tone Grade		Spasticity Grade	
(1 = normal, 2 = hypotonic, 3 = spastic)		(1 = mild, 2 = moderate, 3 = severe)	
Right UE. . . . ___	Left UE. . . . ___	Right UE. . . ___	Left UE. . . . ___
Right LE. . . . ___	Left LE. . . . ___	Right LE. . . ___	Left LE. . . . ___

(If spasticity exists, check appropriate categories to indicate amount of spasticity.)

Gait
Does vision affect your gait? ___ (Y = Yes, N = No)
   If Yes, check all that apply: Blurred vision ___ Double vision ___ Loss of vision ___
Patient ambulatory? ___ (Y = Yes, N = No)
Appliances used for ambulation (Check all that apply.)
   Shoes/braces ___   Crutches ___   Walker ___   Cane ___

(Check all listed items that definitely are present.)

	With Appliances and Shoes		Without Appliances or Shoes	
	Right	Left	Right	Left
Independent reciprocal gait	___	___	___	___
Recurvatum at mid stance	___	___	___	___
Toes in/out at mid stance	___	___	___	___
Circumduction on swing	___	___	___	___
Lack of reciprocal arm swing	___	___	___	___
Footdrop	___	___	___	___
Wide base	___	___	___	___
Ataxic	___	___	___	___
Additional comments: _____				

Explanation of Gait Evaluation

Most items of gait are evaluated by checking whether a type of gait, gait component, or structural change is present or absent. Gait is observed front, back, and side for all determinants. Patients are assessed with and without shoes, with and without aids, wearing clothing that permits easy view of the trunk, hips, and legs. Rather than setting up a several-point scale, the items that are used are assessed as definitely present, which means that mild tendencies on items that may cause disagreement among evaluators as to their presence would usually be termed absent. Also, for the item to be listed as present, it must be observed for at least 5 to 10 consecutive complete strides (heel strikes of the same foot).

Specifics of gait are as follows: Write "Y" if patient is ambulatory and "N" if nonambulatory. If nonambulatory, go on to "Balance." Check the appropriate numbers for appliances used. Please evaluate gait with shoes and appliances and without either.

1. Independent reciprocal gait is defined as the absence of all the factors evaluated.
2. Recurvatum is present when the knee is obviously thrown back on weight bearing or is curved more than 180 degrees visually at mid to late stance.
3. Toes in and out are judged from the front by watching the plane of the foot during stance as the foot strikes a line on the floor. A neutral

or greater adduction position is considered toe in, and an angle greater than 15 degrees of toe out is marked as toe out.
4. Circumduction is determined by obvious pattern of swing phase. Very mild and equivocal circumduction is termed as absent.
5. Person walks without reciprocal swing.
6. Foot drag assessment is either absent or present.
7. Wide base is present if the patient walks with greater than 9 in between feet. The 9 in is measured using the standard 9-in floor tile width. This may be due to mild limb ataxis or proprioceptive loss.
8. Ataxic—present if for any reason other than weakness the person cannot keep balance during gait especially during sharp turns, or base is wide because of balance impairments; equivocal assessments are listed as absent. This would indicate a more severe form of incoordination.

Balance
Sitting balance ___ (G = good, F = fair, P = poor, N = none)
Standing balance ___ (G = good, F = fair, P = poor, N = none)
   Standing on right foot ___ (A = 1 min, B = 10 sec, C = 1–9 sec, D = N/A or 0 sec)
   Standing on left foot ___ (A = 1 min, B = 10 sec, C = 1–9 sec, D = N/A or 0 sec)

APPENDIX B RMMSC PHYSICAL THERAPY EVALUATION FORM
(AND EXPLANATIONS) (Continued)

Multiple Sclerosis

Romberg Test (see definition below): Positive _____

Negative _____

Balance

Independent sitting and standing balance are evaluated:

Good—maintains balance in all directions even with moderate pushing from evaluator

Fair—cannot maintain balance with moderate push in any direction

Poor—cannot maintain balance with mild push in any direction

None—no balance

For evaluating one-leg standing balance choose one of the listed categories.

Romberg Test: Patient stands with comfortable stance with eyes open.

Positive Romberg is moderate to marked worsening of standing balance with eyes closed.

Negative Romberg is no change in patient's standing balance. The Romberg tests proprioceptive loss rather than cerebellar ataxis.

ADL Status

ADL status determined by ___ (D = demonstration, H = history) (use ADL scale below)

Roll side to side	___ 5 = independent and in optimal manner
Sit up in bed	___ 4 = independent, but less than optimal manner
Transfers	
Bed-W/C	___ 3 = independent, but impractical

W/C-Toilet	___ 2 = with standby attendant only
W/C-Car	___ 1 = with human assistance
Operate W/C	___ 0 = unable to perform

Functional mobility grade ___ (range 0–12, use scale below)

Functional Mobility Grade:

(Choose one or more items to signify present functional level. Use "Comments" space for further explanation of functional mobility level.)

1. No restrictions; minimal status
2. Definite impairment, but fully ambulatory without aids
3. Limited ability (distance) without aids; able to climb stairs
4. Needs cane and/or brace; stair-climbing equivocal
5. Requires crutches or walker
6. Uses wheelchair, but may use crutches or walker in the home
7. Wheelchair independent
8. Wheelchair independent, but cannot transfer
9. Requires motorized wheelchair (or could manage motorized chair)
10. Wheelchair dependent (specialized chairs)—cannot manage motorized
11. Bedridden, but still has arm and hand functions
12. Bedridden, helpless

Comments on functional mobility grade: _____

Additional comments: _____

Recommendations: _____

_____

From Maloney, F, Burks, J, and Ringel, S: Interdisciplinary Rehabilitation of Multiple Sclerosis and Neuromuscular Disorders. JB Lippincott, Philadelphia, 1985, p 99, with permission.

CHAPTER 23

Parkinson's Disease

Susan B. O'Sullivan

OBJECTIVES

1. Define terms associated with the pathology and management of Parkinson's disease.
2. Describe the etiology, pathophysiology, symptomatology, and sequelae of Parkinson's disease.
3. Describe the evaluative procedures commonly used in the assessment of Parkinson's disease.
4. Describe the rehabilitative management of the patient with Parkinson's disease.
5. Value the therapist's role in the management of patients with Parkinson's disease.

Parkinson's disease is a chronic, progressive disease of the nervous system. Patients typically exhibit classic clinical signs of rigidity, bradykinesia, resting tremor, and impaired postural reflexes. The clinical presentation and progression can be quite variable. Other common symptoms include episodes of "freezing," in which there is sudden difficulty in moving; dementia, depression, autonomic changes, poor posture, and masked face. The term **parkinsonism** is used to refer to changes in motor function that can result from a number of different causes, with Parkinson's disease or idiopathic parkinsonism being the most common cause.

EPIDEMIOLOGY

Parkinson's disease (PD) occurs in about 1 percent of the population older than 55 years of age and becomes increasingly common with advancing age, reaching proportions of 2.6 percent of the population by age 85 years. In the United States there are 1.5 million individuals afflicted, with 50,000 new cases appearing annually. This number is expected to rise with the aging of the population. The mean age of onset is between 58 and 62 years of age, with the majority of cases having their onset between the ages of 50 and 79. A small percentage, as many as 10 percent, develop young-onset PD, which is defined by the appearance of initial symptoms before the age of 40. These individuals usually have a more benign long-term course. The incidence in both sexes is approximately equal.[1,2]

ETIOLOGY

Several different causes of parkinsonism have been identified.

1. Idiopathic parkinsonism (Parkinson's disease). This term implies that the etiology is unknown. This group includes the true Parkinson's disease or paralysis agitans first described by James Parkinson in 1817, and is the most common form occurring in middle-aged or elderly persons. Distinct clinical subgroups have been identified. One group includes individuals whose dominant symptoms are postural instability and gait difficulties. Another includes individuals with tremor as the main feature.[3] The disease is slowly progressive, with a long subclinical period, estimated at 20 to 30 years. Once symptoms appear, the average life expectancy is 13 to 14 years for individuals on levodopa (L-dopa). Before L-dopa the average life expectancy was 9 to 10 years.[1,4]
2. Infectious parkinsonism. This type of parkinsonism results from infectious or postinfectious causes. The influenza epidemics of encephalitis lethargica that occurred from 1917 to 1926 produced large numbers of these patients. The onset of parkinsonian symptoms typically occurred after many years, giving rise to the theory that a slow virus was infecting the brain. There has been no recent reccurrence of this influenza and the incidence of this type of parkinsonism is slowly decreasing in frequency.[3] Moving case histories of these individuals are portrayed in the book *Awakenings* by Oliver Sacks.[5] The development of parkinsonism with other encephalitic conditions is rare.
3. Toxic parkinsonism. Parkinsonian symptoms occur in individuals exposed to certain industrial poisons and chemicals (manganese, carbon disulfide, carbon monoxide, cyanide, methanol). The most common of these toxins is manganese, which represents a serious occupational hazard to many miners.[3] Reports also describe severe and lasting parkinsonian symptoms in individuals who ingested a synthetic heroin containing the chemical MPTP.[6]

4. Pharmacologic parkinsonism. Various drugs can produce parkinsonian symptoms as a side effect—notably such neuroleptics and powerful tranquilizers as chlorpromazine, haloperidol, and thioridazine; blood pressure medications containing reserpine; and other miscellaneous agents. The severity of these effects may also be related to subclinical PD. Withdrawal of these agents usually reverses the parkinsonian symptoms within a few weeks, although in some cases the effects can be long-lasting.[3]

5. Atypical parkinsonism (multiple system atrophy). Degenerative diseases of the nervous system can affect the substantia nigra and produce parkinsonian signs and symptoms along with other neurologic signs. These diseases include striatonigral degeneration (SND), Shy-Drager syndrome, progressive supranuclear palsy (PSPO), olivopontocerebellar atrophy (OPCA), cortical-basal ganglionic degeneration, and diffuse Lewy body disease. Many of these conditions are rare and affect relatively small numbers of individuals. In addition, parkinsonian features can be exhibited in atherosclerosis, Alzheimer's disease, Pick's disease, Creutzfeld-Jacob disease, Parkinsonism-ALS-dementia complex, Wilson's disease, and Huntington's disease.[3,7]

6. Metabolic causes. Parkinsonism can be caused in rare cases by metabolic conditions, including disorders of calcium metabolism that result in basal ganglia calcification. Hypoparathyroidism is an example.[3]

PATHOPHYSIOLOGY

Parkinsonian signs are neurochemical in origin and are caused by a deficiency of the neurotransmitter **dopamine** within the corpus striatum. This deficiency is secondary to a degeneration of striatal neurons that terminate in the caudate nucleus and putamen. A depletion of 70 to 80 percent of striatal dopamine is estimated to occur before clinical signs of the disease are noted. Significant changes in striatal dopamine receptors may also occur and result in decreased binding of dopamine in the **basal ganglia.** Failure of dopaminergic synapses results in an imbalance in the basal ganglia's mutually antagonistic systems. The cholinergic system, acting through its neurotransmitter acetylcholine, is theorized to permit activity of the short-axon striatal interneurons, while the dopaminergic system provides tonic inhibition of these cholinergic interneurons. When dopamine is decreased and acetylcholine increased, the excessive excitatory output results in a generalized activation of skeletomotor and fusimotor systems by corticospinal, reticulospinal, and rubrospinal pathways.[8,9] These changes underlie the appearance of rigidity and bradykinesia. The production of tremor may be also related to the reduced levels of serotonin found in the basal ganglia. This explains why large doses of Sinemet, a form of L-dopa used to maintain striatal levels of dopamine in patients with parkinsonism, is more effective for alleviating rigidity and bradykinesia than tremor.[10–12] Figure

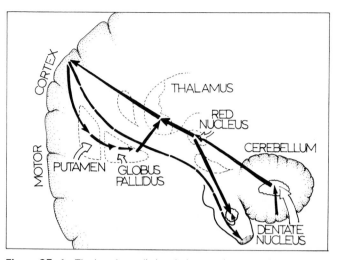

Figure 23–1. The basal ganglia in relation to other central nervous system structures.

23–1 diagrams the basal ganglia and its relationship to other central nervous system structures.

CLINICAL SIGNS

Rigidity

A major clinical sign of parkinsonism is **rigidity.** Patients frequently complain of "heaviness" and "stiffness" of their limbs. Rigidity may be defined as an increased resistance to passive motion and affects all striated muscle. It represents excessive supraspinal drive on a normal spinal mechanism (alpha and gamma motoneurons) and occurs in both agonist and antagonist muscle groups. Rigidity occurs throughout the range of motion. Rigidity may be unequal in distribution. It frequently begins in one limb or side, eventually spreading to involve the whole body. Loss of reciprocal arm swing during gait may be due to truncal rigidity. Active movement, mental concentration, or emotional tension may all increase the amount of rigidity present. Two variations are possible: cogwheel or leadpipe. **Cogwheel rigidity** is a jerky, rachetlike response to passive movement as muscles alternately tense and relax. **Leadpipe rigidity** is a constant, uniform resistance to passive movement, with no fluctuations. Prolonged rigidity can lead to serious secondary complications of contracture and postural deformity.[13]

Bradykinesia

Bradykinesia means slowness of movement. Patients with PD frequently have difficulty in initiating movement, and both voluntary and automatic movements are reduced in speed, range, and amplitude (**hypokinesia**). Often considerable time elapses between the patient's desire to move and the actual movement response (increased **reaction time**). Similarly, **movement time,** the time it takes to complete an activity, is also increased. Overall coordination is impaired, particularly in fine motor tasks such as writing or handling small objects. It is theorized that bradykinesia is due to failure of the basal ganglia to integrate sensory information so that motor planning and the facilitation of movement are altered.[14,15] The basal ganglia is responsible for the automatic execution of learned motor plans. Intact vision and kinesthesia allow the execution of slow movement patterns. Thus the patient with parkinsonism moves slowly and constantly checks his or her progress along the way. Fast ballistic movements may be difficult due to the patient's inability to initiate sufficient force of contraction.[16] Electromyography studies reveal that motor unit recruitment is delayed and that once initiated, it is characterized by pauses and an inability to increase firing rate as contraction continues.[17] Bradykinesia may or may not be associated with rigidity and oftentimes is among the most disabling of symptoms. When bradykinesia is severe, it is termed **akinesia,** which implies a complete state of immobility. This **freezing** of movement can last seconds, minutes, or hours.[13]

Tremor

Tremor is the initial manifestation of PD in about 50 percent of the patients. It is an involuntary oscillation of a body part occurring at a rate of about 4 to 7 oscillations per second. The parkinsonian tremor is described as a resting tremor, because it is typically present at rest and disappears with voluntary movement. This is usually manifest as a pill-rolling tremor of the hand, though resting tremors may also be seen in the feet, lips, tongue, and jaw. **Postural tremor** (action tremor) occurs when a limb is maintained against gravity. It is theorized that tremor results from nigrostriatal degeneration, which results in enhanced activity of the basal ganglia-thalamic-cortical circuit and the thalamic neurons.[11] Tremor tends to be less severe when the patient is relaxed and unoccupied; it is diminished by voluntary effort, and disappears completely during sleep. It is aggravated by emotional tension, excitement, or fatigue. In the early stages, tremor can be quite mild and occur for only short periods, whereas in later stages tremor can become severe, interfering with daily function. Fluctuations in frequency and intensity are common.[13,18]

Impaired Postural Reactions

Balance reactions are impaired or absent. Patients typically experience difficulty in maintaining upright balance, walking, or turning around. When balance is lost, patients fall easily due to loss of the reactive processes needed to adjust posture and regain equilibrium. Frequent injury is the result when protective extension responses are lacking. Anticipatory postural adjustments are also impaired or absent. Patients demonstrate difficulty in regulating feed-forward adjustments of postural muscles during voluntary movement.[19] Degeneration of the globus pallidus has been identified as the source of postural instability. Postural reactions are increasingly impaired if rigidity of the trunk is severe.[18] Some

patients are unable to perceive the upright or vertical position.[20] This may indicate an abnormality in processing the vestibular, visual, and proprioceptive information contributing to balance.

OTHER CLINICAL MANIFESTATIONS

Poverty of movement commonly affects patients with parkinsonism and involves an overall decrease in the total number of movements. Patients are often unable to perform two different movement tasks at the same time or to combine motor programs into complex sequences. Thus sequential motor tasks such as movement transitions from one position to another (e.g., a sit-to-stand transition) are problematic. As task complexity increases, reaction time increases. This also provides evidence of a central deficit in motor planning in patients with PD.[21] Automatic or unconscious movements are impaired or lost. An example of this is the loss of reciprocal arm swing during gait. The rotary component to movement is reduced, resulting in movement typically in one plane of motion. As a result of the loss of automatic movements, there are high cortical demands on the patient who is required to think about each aspect of movement in order to execute it successfully. Constantly combating the effects of bradykinesia, rigidity, and movement impoverishment can lead to mental fatigue and loss of motivation.

In patients with fully developed parkinsonism, fatigue is one of the commonest symptoms reported. The patient has difficulty in sustaining activity and experiences increasing weakness and lethargy as the day progresses. Repetitive motor acts may start out strong but decrease in strength as the activity progresses. Thus the first few words spoken may be loud and strong but diminish rapidly as speech progresses. Performance decreases dramatically after great physical effort or mental stress. Rest or sleep may restore mobility. When L-dopa therapy is initiated, the patient may notice a dramatic improvement and feel significantly less fatigued, but in long-standing drug therapy fatigue may reappear.[22]

The gait pattern of the patient with parkinsonism is highly stereotyped and characterized by an impoverishment of movement. Lower limb, hip, knee, and ankle motions are decreased, with a generalized lack of extension at all three joints. Trunk and pelvic motions are also diminished, resulting in a decrease in step length and reciprocal arm swing. Patients characteristically walk with a slow and shuffling gait. Persistent posturing of a forward head and trunk typically displaces the patient's center of gravity forward and may result in a **festination.** The patient takes multiple short steps in order to avoid falling forward and may eventually break into a run or trot. A *propulsive gait* has a forward accelerating quality, whereas a *retropulsive gait* has a backward accelerating one. Some patients are able to stop only when they come in contact with an object or a wall. Patients who are toe-walkers due to plantarflexion contractures exhibit an additional postural instability due to the narrowing of their base of support. Movements that involve turning or changing direction are particularly difficult to accomplish.[23]

Facial expression is described as **masklike** with infrequent blinking and lack of expression. Smiling may be possible only on command or with volitional effort. Impaired swallowing or **dysphagia** is present in 50 percent of patients and can lead to impaired nutrition and significant weight loss.[24,25]

Speech is typically disturbed. The predominant finding is **dysarthria. Hypophonia** or decreased volume of speech occurs and is secondary to rigidity and bradykinesia of the speech musculature, and decreased excursion of the chest. Speech is slurred and monotonous. In some advanced cases, the patient speaks in whispers or demonstrates **mutism.** Language function remains intact.[26]

Autonomic nervous system dysfunction also occurs. Common problems include excessive perspiration, greasy skin, increased salivation and drooling, thermoregulatory abnormalities (including uncomfortable sensations of heat or cold), and bladder dysfunction (urinary frequency and urgency). Patients have low appetites and decreased motility of the gastrointestinal (GI) tract, along with constipation. Cardiovascular abnormalities include orthostatic hypotension and low resting blood pressure (BP). Cardiac arrhythmias can occur as a result of L-dopa toxicity.[25]

Visual difficulties are often reported by patients with PD. These can include difficulty in reading; blurring with near vision, which can be made worse by **anticholinergic** medications; and, rarely, diplopia. In addition eye pursuit is altered and is characterized by a jerky and rachetlike movement termed "cogwheeling." Decreased blinking can produce bloodshot, irritated eyes that burn and itch. Pupillary abnormalities include decreased reflex responses to light and nociceptive stimuli.[27]

Mental changes (dementia and intellectual impairment) occur in 35 to 40 percent of the patients. This is associated with the imbalance of cholinergic metabolism. Coexisting Alzheimer's disease or multi-infarct atheriosclerotic disease may also be a factor in some of these patients. Consistent deficits have been reported in short-term memory. **Bradyphrenia,** a slowing of thought processes, with lack of concentration and attention also occurs.[26] Depression is common, being seen in 25 to 40 percent of the patients, and generally develops within 1 year of the onset of motor symptoms. A significant number of patients develop depression prior to the onset of their symptoms and diagnosis, suggesting an endogenous cause related to the dopamine depletion.[26,28,29] Patients may demonstrate apathy, passivity, loss of ambition or enthusiasm, and dependency. In severe cases, behavioral changes may also result from the sensory deprivation caused by the marked paucity of movement. Delusions and visual hallucinations are common complications due to L-dopa toxicity.[20,26]

Perceptual motor deficits are also present in this disease. Patients demonstrate significantly more errors than normal on visual perception tasks involving spatial organization. The basal ganglia, in association with the frontal lobe, appear to play an important role in the integration of sensory information. Deficits have been reported in vertical perception, topographic orientation, body scheme, and spatial relations. Motor tasks involving gestural movements, delayed double tasks, tracking, and construction are also impaired.[15,16,26,30]

Although patients with PD do not suffer from primary sensory loss, as many as 40 percent experience sensory symptoms. These can include numbness, tingling, abnormal temperature sensations, tightness, and pain that is cramplike and poorly localized. These symptoms are most commonly intermittent, and vary in intensity and location. While the cause is unknown, some of the discomfort these patients experience may result from lack of movement, muscle rigidity, faulty posture, or ligamentous strain. For example, low back pain may occur as a result of muscle rigidity and stooping posture. Some patients also experience extreme restlessness, "**akathisia,**" making it difficult for them to relax.[27,30]

SECONDARY IMPAIRMENTS

Most patients with parkinsonism are elderly and show the effects of generalized musculoskeletal deconditioning. The more severe the disease, the greater the inactivity and resultant deconditioning. Widespread rigidity and bradykinesia also add to the development of secondary or indirect impairments. These can include

1. Muscle atrophy and weakness secondary to disuse.
2. Loss of flexibility and contracture. Lack of movement in any body segment leads to loss of flexibility and length of both contractile and noncontractile tissue. Proximal segments are generally affected first, then more distal segments. Typically these changes first occur unilaterally, then bilaterally. Contractures commonly develop in rotators, hip and knee flexors; hip adductors; plantar flexors and toe flexors; upper chest, dorsal and lumbar spine, neck flexors; shoulder adductors and internal rotators; forearm pronators; and wrist and finger flexors. Function becomes progressively more limited by these musculoskeletal constraints.[31]
3. Deformity. **Kyphosis** is the most common postural deformity (Fig. 23–2). Some patients may develop a scoliosis, leaning consistently to one side with a C curve when walking or sitting. This generally results from unequal distribution of rigidity in the trunk.
4. Osteoporosis. This is often a serious problem because of prolonged inactivity and typical age. Poor diet may also contribute to the development of osteoporosis. Loss of automatic movement, poor balance reactions, and osteoporosis result in frequent falls and fractures. Fracture healing may also be delayed or disordered.
5. Cardiopulmonary changes. Deconditioning results from restriction of activity and sedentary life-style. Cardiac output is decreased and tachycardia and hyperpnea occur with activity. Vital capacity is usually markedly reduced as decreased thoracic expansion results from rigidity of the intercostals and kyphotic posture. These patients are in constant

Figure 23–2. Patients with Parkinson's disease develop a flexed or stooped posture that contributes to the problems of a festinating gait.

danger of respiratory complications such as pneumonia, which is one of the leading causes of death.

6. Circulatory changes. The lower extremities exhibit circulatory changes owing to venous pooling as a result of decreased mobility. These patients can present with mild to moderate edema of the feet and ankles, which usually subsides during sleep.

7. Nutritional changes. Patients with PD may have a loss of weight. Late in the disease, many of these patients become malnourished because of problems with appetite, eating, chewing, and swallowing. This contributes to the fatigue and exhaustion they often experience from ordinary activities of daily living.[32]

8. Decubitus ulcers. In advanced cases, prolonged inactivity and bed rest may lead to the development of decubitus ulcers. This is a serious complication, because healing is often delayed. If a prolonged infection occurs, it may become life-threatening.

9. Seborrheic dermatitis can result from the hyperac-

tivity of the sebaceous glands and excessive oily secretions. The skin becomes red, itchy, and scaly. The manifestations of Parkinson's disease are summarized in Table 23–1.

MEDICAL MANAGEMENT

There is no single definitive test or group of tests used to diagnose the disease. The diagnosis is usually made on the basis of history and clinical examination. Handwriting samples, speech analysis, and questions that focus on developing symptomatology can be used in the preclinical stage to detect early manifestations of the disease.[33] Laboratory tests, electroencephalography, and computerized axial tomography (CAT scan) can aid in the differential diagnosis by excluding other causes. An estimate of the stage and severity of the disease can be made using a staging scale. The most widely used is the **Hoehn-Yahr Classification of Disability Scale** (see Table 23–2).[34] It provides a useful measure for charting the progression of the disease among patients.

The physician prescribes a program of drug and nutritional therapy. Physical and occupational therapists institute an intensive exercise and activity program designed to keep the patient mobile and functionally independent. Counseling by all members of the multidisciplinary team assists the patient and family in the difficult adjustment to chronic disability. They should be helped to maintain realistic expectations about what therapy can and cannot achieve. In cases of marked depression and poor motivation, a psychiatric consult may be indicated. Therapy is symptomatic. A cure for PD is currently not available and the disease is progressive in nature. With early and vigorous treatment, the effects of the disease and secondary impairments are minimized.

Drug Management

Drugs are prescribed to control rigidity, bradykinesia, tremor, and depression. These drugs are summarized in

Table 23–1 MANIFESTATIONS OF PARKINSON'S DISEASE

Cardinal Manifestations of Parkinson's Disease
Tremor
Rigidity
Bradykinesia
Postural Instability

Secondary Manifestations of Parkinson's Disease

Incoordination	Edema
Micrographia	Scoliosis
Blurred vision	Kyphosis
Impaired upgaze	Pain and sensory symptoms
Blepharospasm	Seborrhea
Glabellar reflex	Constipation
Dysarthria	Urinary urgency, hesitancy, and frequency
Dysphagia reflex	Loss of libido
Sialorrhea	Impotence
Masked facies	Freezing
Hand and foot deformities	Dementia
Dystonia	Depression

From Stern and Hurtig,[4] p 4, with permission.

Table 23–2 HOEHN AND YAHR CLASSIFICATION OF DISABILITY

Stage	Character of Disability
I	Minimal or absent; unilateral if present.
II	Minimal bilateral or midline involvement. Balance not impaired.
III	Impaired righting reflexes. Unsteadiness when turning or rising from chair. Some activities are restricted, but patient can live independently and continue some forms of employment.
IV	All symptoms present and severe. Standing and walking possible only with assistance.
V	Confined to bed or wheelchair.

From Hoehn and Yahr,[34] p 433, with permission.

Table 23–3 ANTIPARKINSONISM DRUGS

Drug	Dosage	Precautions and Remarks
Anticholinergic drugs		
Trihexyphenidyl (Artane)	1–5 mg three times daily, starting at low dosage and slowly increasing. For oculogyric crisis use 10 mg three times daily.	May precipitate acute glaucoma in elderly persons and are contraindicated in patients with glaucoma. Blurred vision, dryness of mouth, vertigo, and tachycardia are early toxic symptoms; late symptoms are vomiting, dizziness, mental confusion, and hallucinations. The synthetic drugs are apt to cause more dizziness than the natural alkaloids and are somewhat less potent parasympatholytics.
Biperiden (Akineton)	2 mg three to four times daily.	
Procyclidine (Kemadrin)	2.5–5 mg three times daily after meals.	
Benztropine mesylate (Cogentin)	0.5 mg one to two times daily, increasing by 0.5 mg at intervals of several days to 5 mg daily or to toxicity. Often most effective as single dose at bedtime.	Side effects similar to those of trihexyphenidyl.
Dopaminergic drugs		
Levodopa (Dopar, Larodopa, etc.)	250 mg three times daily. Increase to tolerance (4–8 g daily).	Nausea, vomiting, postural hypotension, choreiform movements.
Levodopa and carbidopa (Sinemet)	3–6 tablets daily of Sinemet 25/250.	Nausea, vomiting, postural hypotension, dyskinesias.
Amantadine (Symmetrel)	100 mg twice daily.	Jitteriness, insomnia, depression, confusion, hallucinations, livedo reticularis.
Bromocriptine mesylate (Parlodel)	1.25 mg twice daily with food. Increase slowly as necessary by adding 2.5 mg daily at 2- to 4-week intervals.	Nausea, abnormal involuntary movement, hallucinations, confusion, drowsiness.

From Chusid, JG: Correlative Neuroanatomy and Functional Neurology, ed 19, Lange Medical Publications, Los Altos, CA, 1985, with permission.

Table 23–3. None is completely successful in alleviating all the symptoms, for these patients seem to develop a tolerance for drugs, necessitating a change in prescription from time to time. Oftentimes it is the therapist who first notices a change in the patient's status as the patient's system adapts to either the amount or type of drug prescribed. Accurate observation and reporting of these changes greatly assists the physician in modifying a drug prescription.

Patients in the early stages of PD may be given the drug deprenyl (Eldepryl), a monamine oxidase inhibitor. This drug appears to block a toxic reaction in the brain that has been linked to the destruction of brain cells. Clinically it has been found to delay the normal progression of the disease and to delay the point at which patients need to start taking L-dopa.[35,36]

Levodopa is the preferred treatment for PD and is administered orally with carbidopa, a decarboxylase inhibitor; the combination of L-dopa and carbidopa is marketed as Sinemet. Levodopa was first introduced in 1961 as an experimental drug and came into widespread clinical use in 1967. It is a metabolic precursor of dopamine that is able to cross the brain-blood barrier and raise the level of striatal dopamine in the basal ganglia; thus administration of the drug represents an attempt to correct the neurochemical imbalance. Carbidopa improves the action of L-dopa and decreases some of the side effects associated with the use of L-dopa alone. The primary benefit is in alleviating bradykinesia and rigidity; there is less effect on tremor. Often the initial functional improvement is dramatic. It is less effective in treating patients with long-standing disease, because there is a progressive loss of dopamine receptors in the striatal neurons as the disease progresses. There are numerous side effects to L-dopa therapy, but these usually do not present serious problems and can be controlled by adjusting the dosage or administering it in combination with other drugs. The most common side effects are (1) gastrointestinal disturbances (nausea and vomiting); (2) dyskinesias (facial grimacing with twitching of the lips, face and tongue protrusion, and choreoathetoid movements of the arms or legs); (3) mental disturbances (restlessness, general overactivity, anxiety or depression, disorientation, hallucinations or memory disturbance); and (4) occasional orthostatic hypotension (giddiness and fainting).[37] Patients may feel so much better while taking L-dopa that they may engage in sudden heavy physical activity, seriously overtaxing their musculoskeletal and/or cardiovascular systems. The therapist needs to watch for this and to pace the patient accordingly. Long-term use of L-dopa therapy may result in a deterioration of the drug's overall therapeutic effectiveness. This is most likely due to a progressive decrease in responsiveness of the dopamine receptors or to progressive loss of dopamine neurons. **End of dose deterioration** is a worsening of symptoms during the expected time frame of medication effectiveness. Off episodes (a sudden episode of immobility) may appear. Fluctuations in performance and drug response, "**on-off phenomenon**," occur in about 50 percent of the patients treated for more than 2 years.[38] After 3 to 5 years most patients gradually worsen. Dyskinesias and off episodes become more common and end-of-dose deterioration may occur earlier. An increase in parkinsonian fatigue or loss of sleep-benefit may also be noted.[39] Patients with decreased responsiveness to L-dopa therapy may be given a period of transient L-dopa withdrawal. This drug holiday averages 7 to 10 days and may enhance the responsiveness to the drug and decrease L-dopa-induced side effects. The beneficial effects of a drug holiday may last as long as 6 months to a year. Approximately 20 to 30 percent of patients do not benefit from a drug holiday.[40,41] Because there is a dramatic worsening of symptoms when drug therapy is halted, hospitalization is common to monitor the effects of the drug holiday and reinstitute drug therapy. During this time the secondary effects of immobility must be guarded against.

Patients with advanced PD may also benefit from administration of striatal dopaminergic agonist drugs such as bromocriptine (Parlodel). These drugs are thought to improve the function of dopamine receptors and are generally used in combination with carbidopa to prolong the effectiveness of L-dopa therapy.[36,42]

Another major group of drugs used, often in conjunction with L-dopa, is comprised of the anticholinergic drugs. These drugs block the action of acetylcholine in the basal ganglia and are most effective in moderating tremor. Trihexyphenidyl hydrochloride (Artane), benztropine (Cogentin), ethopropazine (Parsidol), and procyclidine (Kemadrin) are commonly prescribed drugs in this group. Side effects include dry mouth, constipation, urinary retention, and impairment of memory or judgment. Drugs to control tremor, depression, edema, and other secondary problems may also be prescribed.[36]

The therapist needs to be fully aware of each medication the patient is taking and of its potential side effects. New drugs are under development. Therapists may be also involved in the monitoring of patient performance during clinical drug trials.

Nutritional management consists of a high-calorie, low-protein diet. Research suggests that a high-protein diet can block the effectiveness of L-dopa and such a diet is therefore contraindicated in patients taking this medication.[43] Patients are advised to follow a diet that is restricted in total protein intake. Generally no more than 15 percent of calories should come from protein, and the intake of daily protein should be redistributed to the evening meal, when patients are less active. These dietary modifications minimize the fluctuations of motor function and maximize responsiveness to drug therapy. The patient is also encouraged to eat a variety of foods in order to ensure adequate intake of vitamins and minerals. A vitamin supplement may also be given. A vigorous activities of daily living training program to improve feeding and eating skills is also of considerable importance in helping to maintain the nutrition and general health of these patients. Patients are advised to increase their daily intake of dietary fiber and water to alleviate problems of constipation.[32,44]

Surgical Management

Stereotaxic surgery is used to alleviate the symptoms of parkinsonism in certain patients. This involves producing destructive lesions in the basal ganglia or thalamus by cryosurgery or chemosurgery. Advances in microelectrode techniques allow for precise subcortical localization of the lesions. The principal effects are to decrease or abolish tremor and to reduce rigidity. Surgery is effective in approximately 90 percent of the cases. The crippling effects of bradykinesia are not improved by stereotaxic surgery. The combined effects of surgery and L-dopa therapy may be beneficial for a few patients.[45,46]

Transplantation to the corpus striatum in patients with advanced PD is highly experimental and is currently under intense research investigation. Studies include the grafting of fetal cells or cells from the autologous adrenal medulla, either of which then produce dopamine. Clinical improvement in selective areas of function, along with numerous complications, have been reported. Only a very limited number of patients have undergone these procedures and they are not available for routine care.[47,48]

Rehabilitative Management

Physical therapy cannot alter the primary disease process or its direct impairments. Rehabilitative efforts can have an important effect on the secondary impairments and functional disability that ensue. The long-term goals of a physical therapy program appropriately include

1. Prevent and/or minimize the development of secondary impairments.
2. Teach compensatory strategies.
3. Maintain the functional abilities of the patient to the fullest extent.
4. Assist the patient and family in psychologic adjustment.

The attainment of these goals is dependent on a realistic understanding of the disease, its impairments, and resultant disability. An effective plan maximizes movement and engages the patient's full cooperation. It also requires a comprehensive team approach and the coordinated effort of all members of the rehabilitation team, including the patient and family.

ASSESSMENT

Evaluation begins with a thorough assessment of the motor signs and symptoms the patient exhibits and their impact on movement. The therapist needs to determine the degree of rigidity in response to passive movement, as well as the limitations imposed on active and automatic movements. Because the distribution of rigidity is very often unequal, it is important to determine which body segments are most affected. Close attention must be paid to the tone changes in the trunk; rigidity here can often be the most disabling in terms of loss of function. Musculoskeletal impairments can be determined using goniometric measurements for active and passive range of motion (ROM). Isokinetic dynamometry can be used to assess torque output at varying speeds during both eccentric and concentric contractions. It has also been suggested for documenting tremor, using slow speeds of movement (25 mm/s) and low torques.[49] Movement time is measured using a stopwatch and can be used to quantify the effects of bradykinesia. Motor planning ability can be assessed by requesting performance of movement sequences, for example, standing up from sitting. A thorough assessment of balance control is indicated. This includes an assessment of the sensory systems, interaction between the sensory systems, and postural synergies and reactions (see Chapter 8). A posture and gait evaluation is also important.

An assessment of the patient's functional abilities can be determined using a disability rating scale. The Unified Parkinson's Disease Rating Scale[4] was devised in the late 1980s and includes an assessment of the direct and indirect signs and symptoms of PD and drug-related fluctuations. It is divided into three parts: mental status, activities of daily living, and the motor scale. Items are graded on a scale of 0 to 4, with 0 being normal and 4 being the most severe. Scored performances on disability scales are frequently used to evaluate the patient's progression and responses to drug and rehabilitation therapy.

During the performance of functional tasks, each skill should be analyzed to determine the influence of direct and indirect impairments.[50] For example, a problem in gait may be due to a primary impairment of severe rigidity or it may be due to secondary impairments of decreased ROM and poor posture. The approach used in treatment to remediate the problem will be very different depending upon the source of the problem.[49] Difficulties will often be noted in those activities having a rotational component, such as rolling or turning in bed. Fine motor skills, such as feeding or dressing, will also be difficult. The time it takes to initiate and to complete an activity should be recorded. Because these patients experience increased fatigue with resultant fluctuations in performance, evaluations should be kept brief (i.e., 10 to 15 min) and repeat assessments should be taken at the same time of day. An accompanying videotape of functional performance can provide an objective record of dysfunction. Functional assessment in the home environment is also indicated.

More complicated and objective methods of studying movement have also been used to study patients with parkinsonism. Electromyography (EMG) has been used to quantify the effects of rigidity and bradykinesia on motor performance. Long latency responses (50 to 120 msec) have been observed in the EMG responses when muscles are subjected to sudden stretch. Abnormal patterns of motor unit recruitment are also present.[17,19] Tests for reaction time (RT, the interval between the presentation of a stimulus and the start of movement) and movement time (MT, the interval between the beginning and end of movement) have also been used to study motoric slowing. Patients with parkinsonism demonstrate prolonged times in both RT and MT, with larger increases in movement time. These results suggest that hypokinesia may represent a deficit of autoevoked arousal mechanisms (individual will) rather than exoevoked mechanisms (response to external stimuli).[19,51,52] Timed tests for rapidly alternating movements (alternate pronation-supination) and complex tasks (tapping tests, pegboards, and other coordination tests) have also been used.[53]

The therapist should also focus particular attention on evaluating the patient's cardiorespiratory status. Cardiovascular endurance is usually decreased from long-standing inactivity and poor respiratory function. Excessive fatigue, shortness of breath, and high heart rate response to exercise are all indices of marked deconditioning and exercise intolerance. Diaphragmatic movements, thoracic expansion, and chest wall mobility should also be evaluated. Respiratory function tests (vital capacity and forced expiratory volume) and screening for dysphagia should be routinely considered.

Finally, it is important to assess the patient's premorbid interests, abilities, and daily activities in order to translate them into a treatment program that will engage the patient's full cooperation. Identification of coping and adaptation strategies associated with psychosocial issues is also important. These patients typically experience loss of self-image, loss of self-esteem, role changes, and social isolation. They also experience the anxieties associated with chronic illness, fluctuations in performance, and an altered financial and/or employment picture.[54]

FORMULATING A TREATMENT PLAN

The following short-term goals are relevant to the treatment of the patient with parkinsonism:
1. Promote full functional range of motion in all joints.
2. Prevent contractures and correct faulty posture.
3. Prevent or minimize disuse atrophy and muscle weakness.
4. Enhance awareness of posture and balance reactions, and safety.
5. Promote functional gait.
6. Maintain or increase vital capacity, chest expansion, and speech.
7. Maintain or increase activity and functional independence.
8. Teach energy conservation techniques for patient and family.
9. Maintain or improve endurance.
10. Assist in psychologic adjustment to chronic disability and life-style modification.

Because each patient is unique and presents a different set of problems, these goals will vary accordingly. Early intervention for patients with mild disease is critical in preventing the devastating musculoskeletal impairments these patients are so prone to develop. In general, each treatment session should encourage as much activity and movement as possible. However, movement must be carefully balanced with adequate rest periods to ensure that the patient does not reach the point of fatigue and exhaustion. Thus frequent, short periods of physical activity are preferable.

RELAXATION EXERCISES

Gentle rocking and rhythmic techniques that emphasize slow vestibular stimulation can be used during therapy to produce generalized relaxation of the total body musculature. This effect was described almost 100 years ago in Paris by Professor Charcot, who noted dramatic improvement in patients with parkinsonism following rides in bumpy, horse-drawn carriages. Following this observation he constructed a vibrating chair to use with his patients.[55] The beneficial effects of repetitive vestibular stimulation on hypertonicity have been substantiated in the literature.[56,57] Clinically a rocking chair or rotating chair may provide an effective aid in reducing rigidity and improving mobility.[58] Slow rhythmical, rotational movements can also be accomplished in supported positions on a mat. The proprioceptive neuromuscular facilitation (PNF) technique of rhythmic initiation, in which movement progresses from passive to active-assistive to active, in small ranges, and progressing to full range of motion, was specifically designed to relax the patient with PD, and to overcome the crippling effects of bradykinesia.[59] Attention should be directed toward the trunk as well as the limbs. Activities such as hooklying, lower-trunk rotation; and sidelying, upper- and lower-trunk rotation are beneficial.

Patients should be taught techniques for self-relaxation. These can include the relaxation response of Benson,[60] and Jacobson's progressive relaxation techniques,[61] both of which emphasize relaxation and deep breathing. Relaxation tapes can be used at home to assist the patient. Stress management techniques are also important to assist the patient and family in modifying life-style. A daily schedule needs to be planned to accommodate the restrictions of the disease and the needs of the patient. Some positions of yoga can be effective for patients with parkinsonism because of the emphasis on combining relaxation with deep breathing and slow, steady stretching.[62] Additionally, some clinicians[31] have suggested that Feldenkrais' techniques,[63] which focus on relaxing specific spinal segments can be of value.[31]

RANGE OF MOTION EXERCISES

Both active and passive ROM exercises should ideally be completed several times a day. Active exercises should focus on strengthening the patient's weak, elongated extensor muscles, while stretching the shortened, tight flexor muscles. Specific muscle contractures may respond to autogenic inhibition techniques such as the PNF contract-relax technique, which combines inhibition from active movement with rotation of the limb.[59] Prolonged, passive stretching at the maximum tolerated length of muscle also increases range through autogenic inhibition and may be accomplished through manual or mechanical stretching (positioning, tilt table, and so on). The resistance to stretch in patients with PD is constant and present at all speeds of stretch, unlike spasticity where resistance is velocity dependent. The therapist should avoid excessive stretching and pain, which can stimulate pain receptors and cause a rebound muscle contraction. Excessive stretching can also cause tearing of the tissue, scar formation, and more shortening. These patients must be considered suspect with regard to osteoporosis and therefore must be ranged accordingly. Ideally, ROM exercises should be combined with other exercises, using functional patterns that stress total movements including trunk, scapula, and pelvic components. Prone-on-elbows and prone-extension activities can be used to improve thoracic extension. Patients with marked deformity and/or cardiorespiratory complications, however, may not be able to tolerate these positions. Standing with arms raised against a wall or in a corner can also be used to promote upper trunk extension. Joint mobilization techniques are helpful in patients with tightness of the joint capsule or of ligaments around a joint. By using selected grades of accessory movement, both improved ROM and decrease in pain can be achieved.[64] Home ROM exercise can oftentimes be accomplished by adaptive equipment such as wall pulleys, providing episodes of freezing are not common. Hanging from an overhead bar may also be used to provide a maintained stretch on the upper trunk and extremity flexors.

MOBILITY EXERCISES

An exercise program for patients with parkinsonism should be based on functional movement patterns that engage several body segments at once. Postural exercises and rotational activities should be stressed. Movements should be rhythmic and reciprocal, and should progress toward full ROM, beginning first in dependent positions and progressing to more upright, unsupported positions. The use of verbal, auditory, and tactile stimulation provides sensory reinforcement and helps increase patient awareness of movement. Verbal commands, music, clapping, marching, metronomes, mirrors, and floor markings are all examples of effective aids in promoting successful performance of an activity. These stimulation techniques are consistent with research findings describing an increased dependence on external stimuli for movement control.[51,65,66]

Proprioceptive neuromuscular facilitation[59] is an effective exercise approach for the treatment of the patient with PD. The use of diagonal limb and trunk PNF patterns achieves several exercise goals at once. Because these patients have a minimum of energy to expend, and multiple clinical problems, they benefit from exercising in total-body, physiologic patterns that combine several motions at once. Proprioceptive neuromuscular facilitation (PNF) patterns also emphasize rotation, a movement component that is typically lost early in PD. Extremity patterns should emphasize smooth, rhythmic movement, using the technique of slow reversals through increments of range. Particular emphasis should be placed on activating extensor muscles to counteract the tendency for a flexed, stooped posture. In the upper extremities, bilateral symmetrical diagonal 2 (D2) flexion patterns (shoulder flexion, abduction, external rotation) are useful in promoting upper trunk extension and in counteracting kyphosis. During this exercise, coordination with respiratory movements emphasizing increased chest expansion should be encouraged. In the lower extremities, hip and knee extension should be emphasized, ideally in a diagonal 1 (D1) extension pattern (hip extension, abduction, internal rotation) to counteract the typical flexed, adducted posture. As previously described, the PNF technique of choice is rhythmic initiation. As relaxation occurs and the movements are more easily accomplished, the patient is asked to participate in the movement first with assistance and then gradually against resistance. After several repetitions, the patient then moves actively through the pattern. This "pumping up" sequence can be used as an effective start to many activities. For example, in activities of daily living (ADL) tasks such as standing up, the patient can begin by swaying back and forth until a rhythm is set up and tone reduced. The active movement of standing up can then be superimposed on this relaxed state. Also helpful are PNF trunk and mat activities that emphasize mobility, rotational movements, and extensor, antigravity muscles. Upper trunk extension with rotation (lifting) is an example. This activity may become a useful component in teaching rolling or upright sitting. Rolling is a problematic activity that should receive early and intensive emphasis in treatment. Active rolling can be facilitated using rhythmic initiation and progressing first from segmental (either upper or lower trunk) rotation, to trunk counterrotation in the sidelying posture. Once control is achieved in sidelying, rolling from full prone to supine and reverse can be practiced.[67] Head and neck patterns, particularly extension with rotation may also be helpful. Standing balance may be improved with the use of rhythmic stabilization, a technique designed to improve imbalances in postural muscles through isometric reversals of antagonists and co-contraction. The grading of resistance is extremely important, for high levels of resistance are not appropriate for patients with hypertonia. Resistive techniques should provide minimal resistance and should be discontinued if they lead to an increase in rigidity.

The emphasis on rotational patterns, control of movement transitions, and balance training in the neurodevelopmental treatment approach (NDT)[68,69] also makes many of these treatment activities valuable for the patient with PD. Activities such as rolling, sitting and standing with active head and trunk rotation, and movement transitions (supine-to-sit, sidesitting-to-quadruped, and sit-to-stand) are useful. Effective handling by the therapist promotes relaxation and active postural adjustment with a minimum of assistance (handling).

Calisthenic exercises that emphasize active movements of the limbs in supine, sitting, and standing are helpful. The focus is on improving flexibility, strength, mobility, and posture. Use of a wand or bar can be effective during bilateral upper extremity exercises to stretch the arms overhead and maximize trunk rotation. Use of an Indian club can aid in achieving full rotation of the upper extremities, both with elbows extended and flexed. In standing, a chair or plinth can be used to assist in balancing during lower extremity static dynamic activities (e.g., lifting one leg while stabilizing on the other).[44,70-73] These exercises once learned can form the core of the home exercise program.

Facilitating movement of facial, hyoid, and tongue muscles is another important goal in exercise, since the patient may have limited social interaction and poor feeding skills in the presence of marked rigidity and bradykinesia. These factors can greatly influence the patient's overall psychologic state and motivation. Use of massage, stretch, manual contacts, resistance, and verbal commands may greatly enhance facial movement. Reciprocal motions should be stressed. In cases where eating is impaired by immobility, the movements of opening and closing the mouth and chewing, combined with neck control (stabilization in a neutral position) should be practiced. Icing to tongue, facial, and hyoid muscles may facilitate more normal function. The patient can also be instructed to practice lip pursing, movements of the tongue, swallowing, and facial movements such as smiling, frowning, and so forth, using a mirror for visual feedback. Verbal skills can be practiced in association with breath control.

Music therapy is a very effective modality with many patients. Episodes of freezing, locomotor difficulties, and problems in the flow of speech all can respond to the addition of music. Selection of the type of music and rhythm an individual patient responds to is an important consideration and can be greatly assisted by a certified music therapist. During therapy the patient can be instructed to sing or tap along with the music, march in time, or play a rhythm instrument.[74]

BALANCE ACTIVITIES

A number of positions and activities can be used for active balance training. Training should begin with low-velocity weight shifts in sitting and standing in order to help the patient develop an appreciation of his or her limits of stability. The therapist assists by promoting postural and safety awareness. Gradually the complexity of the activity can be increased by increasing the range of the weight shift or adding upper extremity tasks (cone stacking, picking up an object off the floor). Movement transitions such as sit-to-stand, stepping, and walking also increase the challenge on the postural system. An increase in the speed of the activity should be encouraged within the patient's abilities. Sitting activities on the gymnastic ball can be helpful in promoting postural reactions while encouraging pelvic and trunk mobility. Slow pelvic rolls, stepping or marching with reciprocal arm swings, and upper trunk rotation patterns with arm swings are examples of activities that can be performed on the ball.[69] Perturbations (gentle shifts of the patient's center of gravity) or use of a moveable surface (gymnastic ball) can also be added.

Practice of a variety of balance activities is essential to ensure motor learning and reproduction of the postural synergies needed for balance. It is important to remember that learning is task-specific. Practice should be expanded to include a variety of sensory and environmental conditions. Whenever possible the therapist should try to duplicate the conditions the patient will encounter in everyday life. The level of challenge is important. A therapist should know the limitations of the patient and the specific demands of the task. The more actively involved the patient is, the better the learning will be.

BREATHING EXERCISES

The patient is taught deep-breathing exercises that increase the mobility of the chest wall and improve vital capacity. Diaphragmatic breathing and basal chest expansion should be emphasized. Chest wall mobility can be increased by using stretch and resistance to the intercostals and by combining upper extremity patterns with breathing exercises (e.g., PNF upper extremity bilateral symmetrical D2 flexion and extension patterns). Pressure and manual contacts can be used to emphasize areas of poor chest expansion. Improving postural alignment in kyphotic patients is also important. Control of breathing can be greatly facilitated by using verbal and tactile stimuli. In order to prevent further respiratory complications from developing, these exercises should receive major emphasis in treatment.[75]

GAIT TRAINING

Gait training attempts to overcome the following primary deficits: a festinating and shuffling gait, poor postural alignment, and defective postural reflexes. Specific goals are to lengthen the stride, broaden the base of support, increase contralateral trunk movement and arm swing, improve heel-toe gait pattern, improve weight transference, and provide a program of regular walking. The patient can practice high-stepping and alternate ankle dorsiflexion while standing and holding on to a chair. Weight transference can be practiced with stepping movements forward and back. During gait, stride and width may be controlled through the use of floor markings (i.e., walking lanes, transverse lines, or footprints). Small blocks of about 5 cm (2 in) to 7.5 cm (3 in) may be used to encourage picking up the feet and avoiding a shuffling gait. Two wands or sticks (held by the patient and therapist, one in each hand) may facilitate reciprocal arm swing during gait. The therapist uses his or her arm swing to assist the patient's. Stopping, starting, changing direction, and turning, using small steps and a wide base, should be practiced. Walking sideways and braiding, a PNF activity of crossed-step side-walking, can be practiced holding on to the parallel bars. The overall rhythm of the gait pattern can be greatly improved by using voice commands (counting), music (e.g., Sousa's marches), or a metronome. Because these patients fall frequently, treatment should include instruction and practice in getting up from the floor.

For those problems that are not responsive to treatment, other measures may have to be employed. A neck collar can help control the forward head position but will inhibit active head movement and active postural responses. Carrying a bag in one arm may help to control listing of the trunk to the opposite side. If the patient demonstrates a shuffling gait, shoes should have leather or hard composition soles, as shoes with crepe or rubber soles will not slide easily. A festinating gait may sometimes be alleviated by the addition of small heels or shoe wedges. A flat heel or toe wedge may slow down a propulsive gait, while a slight heel or heel wedge may diminish a retropulsive gait pattern. Episodes of freezing during walking can sometimes be resolved with the use of visual cues to facilitate motor programming. Patients report success in unlocking these episodes with objects (e.g., dropping a tissue, throwing a cap down, use of an inverted cane) that provide a target to step over.[76]

FUNCTIONAL TRAINING

Activities of daily living generally require modification. Extra time will be required to accomplish many daily care activities. Patients and families should be assisted in planning and pacing these tasks. Energy conservation should be stressed and the patient should be advised to balance rest with activity. Activities with high energy demands should be planned for the morning when the patient is generally well rested. Activities used to promote relaxation and mobility should be incorporated into daily care routines. Positions that encourage abnormal posture or poor balance should be avoided.[77]

The patient should be carefully evaluated in terms of needs for adaptions and assistive devices that can improve function. Loose-fitting clothing with Velcro closures can be used to facilitate dressing. To promote bed mobility, the patient can be helped to assume a sitting position by elevating the head of the bed with blocks of approximately 10 cm (4 in), or by attaching a knotted rope to the end of the bed to pull on. The bed should be firm. If patients have problems in standing up, they should avoid soft, deep upholstered chairs. A firm chair with arm rests (captain's chair) should be used instead. The chair can be raised about 10 cm (4 in) with blocks, or tilted forward by elevating only the back legs about 2 in. Chairs that have spring-loaded seats that push the patient into standing are heavily marketed in the geriatric population and are not recommended as the patient would not have sufficient time to get his or her balance when reaching the standing position. Canes may be helpful with some patients, either to restrict a propulsive gait or to assist in balance. Patients with very poor balance or with a retropulsive gait would not benefit from the addition of a cane.[72]

Adequate nutrition and eating skills can be facilitated in a number of ways. The patient should be seated properly, close to the table, with good posture. Specially adapted utensils, plate guards, and enlarged handles can aid the patient's efforts. Because eating time will be prolonged, heated plates may help keep food warm and palatable. Extra time should be allowed and the patient should not be rushed. Drooling and/or spills should be anticipated and clothing protected.[42,77]

CONDITIONING

Cardiovascular conditioning can be achieved through moderate participation in regular aerobic exercise. Walking is an excellent form of exercise and should be encouraged on a daily basis. The duration, speed, and terrain covered can be modified, based on individual ability. In addition, cycling on a stationary ergometer (bicycle or seated device) can be used. Swimming, while an excellent aerobic activity, should not be done without supervision and may be too risky for the patient with moderate to severe disease and frequent episodes of freezing.[70]

GROUP TRAINING

Group exercise classes are often organized for patients with PD. Patients benefit from the positive support, camaraderie, and communication the group situation offers. Careful assessment of each patient prior to admission into a group is essential. Patients should be able to perform the therapeutic core of the class. Selecting patients with similar levels of disability is often advisable because the sense of competition can frequently be a key factor in motivating groups. The ratio of staff to patients should be kept small (ideally 1 to 8 or 10) and extra staff should be added if patients are unable to work on their own. A variety of activities can be used to stimulate and motivate patients. Warm-up activities or calisthenics involving large joints should be used to help patients limber up and get going. Exercise stations (e.g., stationary bicycle, mats, pulleys, and so on) are often used. Exercises done by the whole group together should focus on important exercise goals (e.g., improving ROM, mobility, and so on). Games or activities can follow the exercise portion, with such activities as dancing, singing or marching to recorded music, ball activities, bean-bag toss, and so forth. The activities selected should be interesting and varied. Relaxation training should also be incorporated. The class should then end on a quiet note with a discussion of home recommendations and everyday problems. The therapist's approach needs to be enthusiastic, energetic, and supportive. Teaching style should incorporate careful observation, gentle corrections, and a stimulating voice.[73,78,79]

Support groups for patients and families are available in many areas. They disseminate information and offer a chance to discuss common issues, problems, and management tips. They also provide a stabilizing influence, assisting patients and families to focus on "healthy behaviors," and on coping skills and acceptance. Information can be obtained through national Parkinson's disease associations:

1. National Parkinson Foundation, 1501 N.W. 9th Ave., Bob Hope Road, Miami, FL 33136
2. The American Parkinson Disease Association, 116 John Street, Suite 417, New York, NY 10038
3. United Parkinson Foundation, 360 W. Superior Street, Chicago, IL 60610

PATIENT AND FAMILY EDUCATION

Patients and their families should be assisted in learning about PD and about the goals of medical and rehabilitative care. They should be instructed in medications, including purpose, side effects, and dosage. A key element is stressing the importance of regular exercise and the avoidance of prolonged periods of inactivity. Regular stretching and mobility exercises should be incorporated into daily care at home. Patients and families can be taught compensatory techniques or triggering maneuvers to overcome the crippling effects of bradykinesia and freezing. Early morning warm-up calisthenics are helpful in reducing the increased stiffness patients may experience in the morning. Rocking movements can be used to initiate movement if the patient freezes. A rocking chair may also be helpful.[44,80]

Patients and families should be assisted in establishing a satisfactory time schedule to allow for completion of tasks. Patients cannot be hurried because performance will suffer. Care-givers should be encouraged not to provide too much assistance as this will foster dependence.[81]

MAINTENANCE THERAPY

Patients with mild to moderate parkinsonism are typically seen on an outpatient basis and are given a home program to attain the therapeutic goals of treatment. These should include exercises the patient can master, either alone or with the aid of a family member. They should be realistic and of moderate duration and intensity. The patient should be cautioned against overdoing activity, which could result in excessive fatigue. Exercises should be done daily and balanced with adequate rest periods. Patients successfully treated with L-dopa may exhibit a dramatic decrease in rigidity and bradykinesia. The alleviation of these symptoms does not always produce a similar amount of improvement in their function, however, for poor habits and faulty posture may persist. These patients will usually respond quite well to a rehabilitation program designed to facilitate mobility and independent function.

Patients with more advanced disease generally do not respond as well to medical management and experience increasing difficulties, fluctuations in performance, and side effects of chronic dopaminergic medication. These can be a source of great frustration to the patient and family. Goals and expectations need to be restructured. Generally these patients require increasing supervision in ADLs and mobility. These patients should be encouraged to move as much as possible and not let everything be done for them. Often, environmental adaptations may mean the difference between total dependence and partial independence. The entire rehabilitation team should be supportive of the patient's efforts no matter how small they may be. Families also suffer from the increasing demands of care and social isolation. Therapists need to be supportive and available for consultation.

Severely disabled patients are wheelchair-bound or bedridden and may require continual home health services or placement in a chronic care facility. This group of patients is one of the more debilitated populations seen in rehabilitation. They demonstrate limited skills to interact with their environment, with increasing social isolation and withdrawal. The needs of patient and family for ongoing psychosocial support are significant.[28]

SUMMARY

Parkinson's disease is a chronic, progressive disorder of the basal ganglia characterized by the classic signs of rigidity, bradykinesia, tremor, and loss of postural mechanisms. Clinical manifestations include the development of abnormal fixed postures, diminished automatic postural reactions, festinating gait pattern, fatigue, mask-like facial expression, and autonomic nervous system dysfunction. These patients are prone to develop any one of a number of secondary impairments due to their progressive inactivity. Pharmacologic management of the disease focuses on control of specific symptoms. Levodopa and its derivative remains the mainstay of drug therapy. Effective rehabilitation programs focus on maintaining the functional abilities of the patient within the limitations imposed by the disease. Programs also seek to delay or minimize the development of secondary impairments. A comprehensive team approach including active involvement of patient and family can provide optimal benefits. Team members need to maintain a realistic but positive outlook.

QUESTIONS FOR REVIEW

1. What are the major central nervous systems structures involved in PD? How is the function of these structures altered? What is the primary effect on the motor system?

2. What are the major clinical signs? Clinical manifestations?

3. How is PD evaluated? What are the key elements of such an assessment? What objective assessments are available?

4. Describe the drug therapy used in PD. How might a physical therapy program be influenced by drug management?

5. What are the major goals of an exercise program? Name three techniques that can be used to increase range of motion. Mobility.

6. What types of activities should a gait-training program stress? A home program?

7. What type of therapeutic program would you structure for the patient with advanced disease who is relatively unresponsive to drugs?

8. What are the major considerations in patient and family education?

REFERENCES

1. Marttila, R: Parkinson's disease: epidemiology. In Koller, W (ed): Handbook of Parkinson's Disease. Marcel Dekker, New York, 1987, p 35.
2. Stern, M, et al: The epidemiology of Parkinson's disease: a case control study of young onset and old onset patients. Arch Neurol 48:903, 1991.
3. Koller, W: Classification of parkinsonism. In Koller, W (ed): Handbook of Parkinson's Disease. Marcel Dekker, New York, 1987, p 51.
4. Stern, M and Hurtig, H: The Comprehensive Management of Parkinson's Disease. PMA, New York, 1988.
5. Sacks, O: Awakenings. HarperCollins, New York, 1990.
6. Langston, JW and Ballard, P: Chronic parkinsonism in humans due to a product of meperidine-analog synthesis. Science 219:976, 1983.
7. Burns, S: Atypical Parkinsonism: The Many Faces of Parkinsonism. Parkinson Report. National Parkinson Foundation, Miami, 1989.
8. Burke, D, Hagbarth, K and Wallin, G: Reflex mechanisms in parkinsonian rigidity. Scand J Rehabil Med 9:15, 1977.
9. Somjen, G: Neurophysiology: The Essentials. Williams & Wilkins, Baltimore, 1983.
10. Brooks, VB: Roles of cerebellum and basal ganglia in initiation and control of movements. Can J Neurol Sci 2:265, 1975.
11. Guyton, A: Basic Neuroscience. WB Saunders, Philadelphia, 1987.
12. Feldman, R: Parkinson disease individualizing therapy. Hosp Prac 20:80A, 1985.
13. Jankovic, J: Pathophysiology and clinical assessment of motor symptoms in Parkinson's disease. In Koller, W (ed): Handbook of Parkinson's Disease. Marcel Dekker, New York, 1987, p 99.
14. Denny-Brown, D and Yanagisawa, N: The role of the basal ganglia in the initiation of movement. In Yahr, MD (ed): The Basal Ganglia. Raven Press, New York, 1976.
15. Sharpe, M, Cermak, S, and Sax, D: Motor planning in parkinson patients. Neuropsychologia 21:455, 1983.
16. Marsden, C: The mysterious motor function of the basal ganglia: the Robert Wartenberg lecture. Neurology 32:514, 1982.
17. Milner-Brown, H, et al: Electrical properties of motor units in parkinsonism and a possible relationship with bradykinesia. J Neurol Neurosurg Psychiatry 42:35, 1979.
18. Cohen, A: Tremors and the Parkinson Patients. Parkinson Report. National Parkinson Foundation, Miami, 1991.
19. Rogers, M: Control of posture and balance during voluntary movements in Parkinson's disease. In Duncan, P (ed): Balance. American Physical Therapy Association, Alexandria, VA, 1990.
20. Bowen, FP: Behavioral alterations in patients with basal ganglia lesions. In Yahr, MD (ed): The Basal Ganglia. Raven Press, New York, 1976.
21. Rogers, M and Chan, C: Motor planning is impaired in Parkinson's disease. Brain Res 438:271, 1988.
22. Marsden, CD: "On-off phenomena" in Parkinson's disease. In Rinne, UK, Klinger, M, and Stamm, G (eds): Parkinson's Disease: Current Progress, Problems and Management. Elsevier/North-Holland Biomedical Press, New York, 1980.
23. Murray, P, Sepic, S, Gardner, G, and Downs, W: Walking patterns of men with Parkinsonism. Am J Phys Med 57:278, 1978.
24. Berger, J: Impaired swallowing and excessive drooling in Parkinson's disease. Parkinson Report. National Parkinson Foundation, Miami, 1985, p 1.
25. Tanner, C, Goetz, C, and Klawans, H: ANS disorders. In Koller, W (ed): Handbook of Parkinson's Disease. Marcel Dekker, New York, 1987, p 145.
26. Mayeux, R: Mental state. In Koller, W (ed): Handbook of Parkinson's Disease. Marcel Dekker, New York, 1987, p 127.
27. Weiner, W: Non-motor Symptoms in Parkinson's Disease. Parkinson Report. National Parkinson Foundation, Miami, 1989, 1990.
28. Levin, B and Reisman, S: The Psychological Aspects of Parkinson's Disease. Parkinson Report. National Parkinson Foundation, Miami, 1989.
29. Levin, B and Weiner, W: Psychosocial aspects. In Koller, W (ed): Handbook of Parkinson's Disease. Marcel Dekker, New York, 1987.
30. Koller, W: Sensory Symptoms in Parkinson's Disease. Parkinson Report. National Parkinson Foundation, Miami, 1985.
31. Schenkman, M, et al: Management of individuals with Parkinson's disease: rationale and case studies. Phys Ther 69:944, 1989.
32. Mantero-Atienza, E, et al: Nutritional Considerations of Parkinson's Disease. National Parkinson Foundation, Miami, 1990.
33. Tetraud, J: Preclinical detection of motor and nonmotor manifestations. Geriatrics 46:43, 1991.
34. Hoehn, M and Yahr, M: Parkinsonism: onset, progression and mortality. Neurology 17:427, 1967.
35. Marsden, C: The drug therapy of early Parkinson's disease. In Stern, M and Hurtig, H (eds): The Comprehensive Management of Parkinson's Disease. PMA, New York, 1988.
36. Weiner, W: Medications currently used to treat Parkinson's disease. Parkinson Report. National Parkinson Foundation, Miami, 1990, p 3.
37. Stern, PH, McDowell, F, Miller, J, and Robinson, M: Levodopa and physical therapy in the treatment of patients with Parkinson's disease. Arch Phys Med 51:273, 1970.
38. Lang, A: Motor fluctuations in Parkinson's disease. Parkinson Report. National Parkinson Foundation, Miami, 1985, p 1.
39. Greer, M: Recent developments in the treatment of Parkinson's disease. Geriatrics 40:34, 1985.
40. Koller, W, et al: Complications of chronic levodopa therapy: long-term efficacy of drug holiday. Neurology (Ny) 31:373, 1981.
41. Direnfeld, L, Spero, L, Marotta, J, and Seeman, S: The L-dopa on-off effect in Parkinson disease: treatment by transient drug withdrawal and dopamine receptor resensitization. Ann Neurol 4:573, 1978.
42. Weiner, W: Sinemet and Parlodel in the treatment of Parkinson's disease. Parkinson Report. National Parkinson Foundation, Miami, 1985, p 3.
43. Mantero-Atienza, E, et al: Nutritional Considerations of Parkinson's Disease. National Parkinson Foundation, Miami, 1990.

44. National Parkinson Foundation: The Parkinson Handbook. National Parkinson Foundation, Miami, 1990.
45. Cooper, I, et al: Bilateral parkinsonism: neurosurgical rehabilitation. J Am Geriatr Soc 16:11, 1968.
46. Kelly, P and Gillingham, F: The long-term results of stereotaxic surgery and L-dopa therapy in patients with Parkinson's disease. J Neurosurg 53:332, 1980.
47. Madrazo, I, et al: Open microsurgical autograft of adrenal medulla to the right caudate nucleus in two patients with intractable Parkinson's disease. N Engl J Med 316:831, 1987.
48. Goetz, C, et al: Multicenter study of autologous adrenal medullary transplantation to the corpus striatum in patients with advanced Parkinson's disease. N Engl J Med 320:337, 1989.
49. Bohannon, R: Documentation of tremor in patients with central nervous system lesions. Phys Ther 66:229, 1986.
50. Schenkman, M and Butler, R: A model for multisystem evaluation treatment of individuals with Parkinson's disease. Phys Ther 69:932, 1989.
51. Heilman, M, et al: Reaction times in Parkinson disease. Arch Neurol 33:139, 1976.
52. Terabavainen, H and Calne, DB: Assessment of hypokinesia in parkinsonism. J Neurol Transm Gen Sect 51:149, 1981.
53. Terabavainen, H and Calne, D: Quantitative assessment of parkinsonian deficits. In Rinne, UK, Klinger, M, and Stamm, G (eds): Parkinson's Disease Current Progress, Problems and Management. Elsevier/North-Holland Biomedical Press, New York, 1980.
54. Vemon, G and Stern, M: The comprehensive approach to Parkinson's disease. In Stern, M and Hurtig, H (eds): The Comprehensive Management of Parkinson's Disease. PMA, New York, 1988.
55. Tyler, W: History of Parkinson's disease. In Koller, W (ed): Handbook of Parkinson's Disease. Marcel Dekker, New York, 1987.
56. Pederson, D: The soothing effects of rocking as determined by the direction and frequency of movement. Can J Behav Sci 7:237, 1975.
57. Peterson, B, Franck, J, Pitts, N, and Daunton, N: Changes in response of medial pontomedullary reticular neurons during repetitive cutaneous, vestibular, cortical and fectal stimulation. J Neurophysiol 39:564, 1976.
58. Stockmeyer, S: An interpretation of the approach of Rood to the treatment of neuromuscular dysfunction. Am J Phys Med 46:900, 1967.
59. Voss, D, Ionta, M, and Myers, B: Proprioceptive Neuromuscular Facilitation, 3 ed. Harper & Row, New York, 1985.
60. Benson, H: The Relaxation Response. Avon, New York, 1975.
61. Jacobson, E: Progressive Relaxation. University of Chicago Press, Chicago, 1938.
62. Vishnudenananda, S: The Complete Illustrated Book of Yoga. Pocket Books, New York, 1972.
63. Feldenkrais, M: Awareness Through Movement: Health Exercises for Personal Growth. Harper & Row, New York, 1972.
64. Kaltenborn, F: Mobilization of the Extremity Joints: Examination and Basic Treatment Techniques. Olaf Norlis Bokhandel, 1980.
65. Cooke, J, Brown, J, and Brooks, V: Increased dependence on visual information for movement control in patients with Parkinson's disease. Can J Neurol Sci 5:413, 1978.
66. Stefaniwsky, L and Bilowit, D: Parkinsonism: facilitation of motion by sensory stimulation. Arch Phys Med Rehabil 54:75, 1973.
67. Sullivan, P, Markos, P, and Minor, M: An Integrated Approach to Therapeutic Exercise. Reston, Reston, VA, 1982.
68. Bobath, B: The treatment of neuromuscular disorders by improving patterns of coordination. Physiotherapy 55:18, 1969.
69. Davies, P: Right in the Middle. Springer-Verlag, New York, 1990.
70. Wroe, M and Greer, M: Parkinson's disease and physical therapy management. Phys Ther 53:631, 1973.
71. Palmer, S, et al: Exercise therapy in Parkinson's disease. Arch Phys Med Rehabil 67:741, 1986.
72. Duvoisin, R: Parkinson's Disease A Guide for Patient and Family. Raven Press, New York, 1984.
73. Davis, J: Team management of Parkinson's disease. Am J Occup Ther 31:300, 1977.
74. Michel, D: Music Therapy. Charles C Thomas, Springfield, IL, 1976.
75. Humbersone, N: Respiratory treatment. In Tecklin, I (ed): Cardiopulmonary Physical Therapy. CV Mosby, St Louis, 1985.
76. Dunne, J, Hankey, G, and Edis, R: Parkinsonism: upturned walking stick as an aid to locomotion. Arch Phys Med Rehabil 68:380, 1987.
77. Neustadt, G, Simon, M, and Spiegel, K: Managing the client with Parkinson's disease. Focus on Geriatric Care and Rehabilitation 2:1, 1988.
78. Hollis, M: Practical Exercise Therapy, 2 ed. Blackwell Scientific, Oxford, 1981.
79. Pedersen, S, et al: Group training in parkinsonism: quantitative measurements of treatment. Scand J Rehabil Med 22:207, 1990.
80. Hurwitz, A: The benefit of a home exercise regimen for ambulatory parkinson's disease patients. J Neurosci Nurs 21:180, 1989.
81. Kase, S and O'Riodan, C: Rehabilitation approach. In Koller, W (ed): Handbook of Parkinson's Disease. Marcel Dekker, New York, 1987.

GLOSSARY

Akathisia (acathisia): Extreme restlessness.

Akinesia: Inability to initiate or execute movement.

Anticholinergic agents: Drugs used to block excessive cholinergic activity in patients with Parkinson's disease. Commonly used drugs include artane, cogentin, or akineton.

Basal ganglia: Masses of gray matter located beneath the cerebral cortex and just lateral to the dorsal thalmus; included are the caudate nucleus and putamen (corpus striatum), globus pallidus, substantia nigra, and subthalmus.

Bradykinesia: Extreme slowness of movement.

Bradyphrenia: Slowness of thought processes, and lack of concentration and attention.

Dopamine: An inhibitory neurotransmitter secreted by neurons that are located in the substantia nigra and terminate in the striate region of the basal ganglia.

Dysarthria: Difficult and defective speech due to impairment of the tongue or other muscles essential to speech.

Dysphagia: Inability to swallow or difficulty in swallowing.

End-of-dose deterioration: Recurrence of symptoms before the expected time frame for therapeutic effectiveness of a drug; seen with long-term use of levodopa therapy.

Festination: Abnormal and involuntary increase in the speed of walking in an attempt to catch up with the displaced center of mass that results from the patient's leaning.

Propulsive gait: Gait that has a forward accelerating quality.

Retropulsive gait: Gait that has a backward accelerating quality.

Freezing: A sudden episode of immobility.

Hoehn-Yahr Classification of Disability Scale: A scale used to classify the stage and severity of Parkinson's disease.

Hypokinesia: Movements that are reduced in speed, amplitude, and range.

Hypophonia: Decreased volume of speech.

Kyphosis: Increased posterior curve of the spine; usually found in the dorsal spine.

L-Dopa (levodopa): A drug used in the treatment of

Parkinson's disease to raise the level of striatal dopamine in the basal ganglia.

Masklike face. A lack of facial expression and blinking.

Movement time (MT): The interval between initiation and completion of movement.

Mutism: Condition of being unable to speak.

On-off phenomenon: Fluctuations in performance and response seen with long-term use of levodopa therapy.

Parkinsonism: Changes in motor function that can result from a number of different causes, with Parkinson's disease or ideopathic parkinsonism being the most common.

Postural tremor (action tremor): Oscillation of a body part (usually proximal segments) that occur when a limb is maintained against gravity.

Reaction time (RT): The interval between the presentation of a stimulus and the start of movement.

Rigidity: Muscle stiffness or hypertonia; sustained contraction of muscle resulting in an inability to bend or be bent.

Cogwheel rigidity: A jerky, rachetlike resistance to passive movement.

Leadpipe rigidity: A smooth, uniform resistance to passive movement.

Sialorrhea: Increased drooling.

Stereotaxic surgery: The precise location and destruction of localized areas in the brain; lesions are produced in the basal ganglia or thalamus to reduce parkinsonian symptoms.

Tremor: An involuntary oscillation of a body part occurring at a rate of about 4 to 7 oscillations per second.

APPENDIX A UNIFIED RATING SCALE FOR PARKINSONISM VERSION 3.0: FEBRUARY 1987*

I. Mentation, behavior and mood
1. *Intellectual impairments:*
   0 = None.
   1 = Mild. Consistent forgetfulness with partial recollection of events and no other difficulties.
   2 = Moderate memory loss, with disorientation and moderate difficulty handling complex problems. Mild but definite impairment of function at home with need of occasional prompting.
   3 = Severe memory loss with disorientation for time and often to place. Severe impairment in handling problems.
   4 = Severe memory loss with orientation preserved to person only. Unable to make judgments or solve problems. Requires much help with personal care. Cannot be left alone at all.
2. *Thought disorder* (due to dementia or drug intoxication):
   0 = None.
   1 = Vivid dreaming.
   2 = "Benign" hallucinations with insight retained.
   3 = Occasional to frequent hallucinations or delusions; without insight; could interfere with daily activities.
   4 = Persistent hallucinations, delusions, or florid psychosis. Not able to care for self.
3. *Depression:*
   0 = Not present.
   1 = Periods of sadness or guilt greater than normal, never sustained for days or weeks.
   2 = Sustained depression (1 week or more).
   3 = Sustained depression with vegetative symptoms (insomnia, anorexia, weight loss, loss of interest).
   4 = Sustained depression with vegetative symptoms and suicidal thoughts or intent.
4. *Motivation/initiative:*
   0 = Normal.
   1 = Less assertive than usual; more passive.
   2 = Loss in initiative or disinterest in elective (nonroutine) activities.
   3 = Loss of initiative or disinterest in day-to-day (routine) activities.
   4 = Withdrawn, complete loss of motivation.
II. Activities of daily living (determine for "on/off")
5. *Speech:*
   0 = Normal.
   1 = Mildy affected. No difficulty being understood.
   2 = Moderately affected. Sometimes asked to repeat statements.
   3 = Severely affected. Sometimes asked to repeat statements.
   4 = Unintelligible most of the time.
6. *Salivation:*
   0 = Normal.
   1 = Slight but definite excess of saliva in mouth; may have nighttime drooling.
   2 = Moderately excessive saliva; may have minimal drooling.
   3 = Marked excess of saliva with some drooling.
   4 = Marked drooling, requires constant tissue or handkerchief.
7. *Swallowing:*
   0 = Normal.
   1 = Rare choking.
   2 = Occasional choking.
   3 = Requires soft food.
   4 = Requires nasogastric tube or gastrotomy feeding.
8. *Handwriting:*
   0 = Normal.
   1 = Slightly slow or small.
   2 = Moderately slow or small; all words are legible.
   3 = Severely affected; not all words are legible.
   4 = The majority of words are not legible.
9. *Cutting food and handling utensils:*
   0 = Normal.
   1 = Somewhat slow and clumsy, but no help needed.
   2 = Can cut most foods, although clumsy and slow; some help needed.
   3 = Food must be cut by someone, but can still feed slowly.
   4 = Needs to be fed.

10. *Dressing:*
    0 = Normal.
    1 = Somewhat slow, but no help needed.
    2 = Occasional assistance with buttoning, or with getting arms in sleeves.
    3 = Considerable help required, but can do some things alone.
    4 = Helpless.
11. *Hygiene:*
    0 = Normal.
    1 = Somewhat slow, but no help needed.
    2 = Needs help to shower or bathe; or very slow in hygienic care.
    3 = Requires assistance for washing, brushing teeth, combing hair, going to bathroom.
    4 = Foley catheter or other mechanical aids.
12. *Turning in bed and adjusting bed clothes:*
    0 = Normal.
    1 = Somewhat slow and clumsy, but no help needed.
    2 = Can turn alone or adjust sheets, but with great difficulty.
    3 = Can initiate, but not turn or adjust sheets alone.
    4 = Helpless.
13. *Falling (unrelated to freezing):*
    0 = None.
    1 = Rare falling.
    2 = Occasionally falls, less than once per day.
    3 = Falls on average of once daily.
    4 = Falls more than once daily.
14. *Freezing when walking:*
    0 = None.
    1 = Rare freezing when walking; may have start-hesitation.
    2 = Occasional freezing when walking.
    3 = Frequent freezing. Occasionally falls from freezing.
    4 = Frequent falls from freezing.
15. *Walking:*
    0 = Normal.
    1 = Mild difficulty; may not swing arms or may tend to drag leg.
    2 = Moderate difficulty, but requires little or no assistance.
    3 = Severe disturbance of walking, requiring assistance.
    4 = Cannot walk at all, even with assistance.
16. *Tremor:*
    0 = Absent.
    1 = Slight and infrequently present.
    2 = Moderate; bothersome to patient.
    3 = Severe; interferes with many activities.
    4 = Marked; interferes with most activities.
17. *Sensory complaints related to parkinsonism:*
    0 = None.
    1 = Occasionally has numbness, tingling, or mild aching.
    2 = Frequently has numbness, tingling, or aching; not distressing.
    3 = Frequent painful sensations.
    4 = Excruciating pain.
III. Motor examination
18. *Speech:*
    0 = Normal.
    1 = Slight loss of expression, diction, and/or volume.
    2 = Monotone, slurred but understandable; moderately impaired.
    3 = Marked impairment, difficult to understand.
    4 = Unintelligible.
19. *Facial expression:*
    0 = Normal.
    1 = Minimal hypomimia, could be normal "poker face".
    2 = Slight but definitely abnormal diminution of facial expression.
    3 = Moderate hypomimia; lips parted some of the time.
    4 = Masked or fixed facies with severe or complete loss of facial expression; lips parted ¼ in or more.
20. *Tremor at rest:*
    0 = Absent.
    1 = Slight and infrequently present.
    2 = Mild in amplitude and persistent; or moderate in amplitude, but only intermittently present.

3 = Moderate in amplitude and present most of the time.
4 = Marked in amplitude and present most of the time.

21. *Action or postural tremor of hands:*
    0 = Absent.
    1 = Slight; present with action.
    2 = Moderate in amplitude, present with action.
    3 = Moderate in amplitude with posture holding as well as action.
    4 = Marked in amplitude; interferes with feeding.

22. *Rigidity* (judged on passive movement of major joints with patient relaxed in sitting position; cogwheeling to be ignored):
    0 = Absent.
    1 = Slight or detectable only when activated by mirror or other movements.
    2 = Mild to moderate.
    3 = Marked; but full range of motion easily achieved.
    4 = Severe; range of motion achieved with difficulty.

23. *Finger taps* (patient taps thumb with index finger in rapid succession with widest amplitude possible, each hand separately):
    0 = Normal.
    1 = Mild slowing and/or reduction in amplitude.
    2 = Moderately impaired; definite and early fatiguing; may have occasional arrests in movement.
    3 = Severely impaired; frequent hesitation in initiating movements or arrests in ongoing movement.
    4 = Can barely perform the task.

24. *Hand movement* (patient opens and closes hands in rapid succession with widest amplitude possible, each hand separately):
    0 = Normal.
    1 = Mild slowing and/or reduction in amplitude.
    2 = Moderately impaired; definite and early fatiguing; may have occasional arrests in movement.
    3 = Severely impaired; frequent hesitation in initiating movements or arrests in ongoing movement.
    4 = Can barely perform the task.

25. *Rapid alternating movements of hands* (pronation-supination movements of hands, vertically or horizontally, with as large an amplitude as possible, both hands simultaneously):
    0 = Normal.
    1 = Mild slowing and/or reduction in amplitude.
    2 = Moderately impaired; definite and early fatiguing; may have occasional arrests in movement.
    3 = Severely impaired; frequent hesitation in initiating movements or arrests in ongoing movement.
    4 = Can barely perform the task.

26. *Leg agility* (patient taps heel on ground in rapid succession, picking up entire leg; amplitude should be about 3 inches):
    0 = Normal.
    1 = Mild slowing and/or reduction in amplitude.
    2 = Moderately impaired; definite and early fatiguing; may have occasional arrests in movement.
    3 = Severely impaired; frequent hesitation in initiating movements or arrests in ongoing movement.
    4 = Can barely perform the task.

27. *Arising from chair* (patient attempts to arise from a straight-backed wood or metal chair with arms folded across chest).
    0 = Normal.
    1 = Slow; or may need more than one attempt.
    2 = Pushes self up from arms of seat.
    3 = Tends to fall back and may have to try more than one time, but can get up without help.
    4 = Unable to arise without help.

28. *Posture:*
    0 = Normal erect.
    1 = Not quite erect, slightly stooped posture; could be normal for older person.
    2 = Moderately stooped posture, definitely abnormal; can be slightly leaning to one side.
    3 = Severely stooped posture with kyphosis; can be moderately leaning to one side.
    4 = Marked flexion with extreme abnormality of posture.

29. *Gait:*
    0 = Normal.
    1 = Walks slowly, may shuffle with short steps, but no festination or propulsion.
    2 = Walks with difficulty, but requires little or no assistance; may have some festination, short steps, or propulsion.
    3 = Severe disturbance of gait, requiring assistance.
    4 = Cannot walk at all, even with assistance.

30. *Postural stability* (response to sudden posterior displacement produced by pull on shoulders while patient is erect with eyes open and feet slightly apart; patient is prepared):
    0 = Normal.
    1 = Retropulsion, but recovers unaided.
    2 = Absence of postural response; would fall if not caught by examiner.
    3 = Very unstable, tends to lose balance spontaneously.
    4 = Unable to stand without assistance.

31. *Body bradykinesia and hypokinesia* (combining slowness, hesitancy, decreased armswing, small amplitude, and poverty of movement in general):
    0 = None.
    1 = Minimal slowness, giving movement a deliberate character; could be normal for some persons. Possibly reduced amplitude.
    2 = Mild degree of slowness and poverty of movement that is definitely abnormal. Alternatively, some reduced amplitude.
    3 = Moderate slowness, poverty, or small amplitude of movement.
    4 = Marked slowness, poverty, or small amplitude of movement.

IV. Complications of therapy (in the past week)
   A. Dyskinesias
32. *Duration: What proportion of the waking day are dyskinesias present?* (historical information)
    0 = None
    1 = 1–25% of day.
    2 = 26–50% of day.
    3 = 51–75% of day.
    4 = 76–100% of day.

33. *Disability: How disabling are the dyskinesias?* (historical information; may be modified by office examination)
    0 = Not disabling.
    1 = Mildly disabling.
    2 = Moderately disabling.
    3 = Severely disabling.
    4 = Completely disabled.

34. *Painful dyskinesia: How painful are the dyskinesias?*
    0 = No painful dyskinesias.
    1 = Slight.
    2 = Moderate.
    3 = Severe.
    4 = Marked.

35. *Presence of early morning dystonia* (Historical information):
    0 = No
    1 = Yes

   B. Clinical fluctuations
36. *Are any "off" periods predictable as to timing after a dose of medication?*
    0 = No
    1 = Yes

37. *Are any "off" periods unpredictable as to timing after a dose of medications?*
    0 = No
    1 = Yes

38. *Do any of the "off" periods come on suddenly, for example, over a few seconds?*
    0 = No
    1 = Yes

39. *What proportion of the waking day is the patient "off" on average?*
    0 = None
    1 = 1–25% of day.

APPENDIX A UNIFIED RATING SCALE FOR PARKINSONISM VERSION 3.0—FEBRUARY 1987 *(Continued)*

2 = 26–50% of day.
3 = 51–75% of day.
4 = 76–100% of day.
C. Other complications
40. *Does the patient have anorexia, nausea, or vomiting?*
0 = No
1 = Yes
41. *Does the patient have any sleep disturbances, for example, insomnia or hypersomnolence?*
0 = No
1 = Yes
42. *Does the patient have symptomatic orthostasis?*
0 = No
1 = Yes
Record the patient's blood pressure, pulse and weight on the scoring form.
V. Modified Hoehn and Yahr staging
Stage 0   = No signs of disease.
Stage 1   = Unilateral disease.
Stage 1.5 = Unilateral plus axial involvement.
Stage 2   = Bilateral disease, without impairment of balance.
Stage 2.5 = Mild bilateral disease, with recovery on pull test.
Stage 3   = Mild to moderate bilateral disease; some postural instability; physically independent.
Stage 4   = Severe disability; still able to walk or stand unassisted.
Stage 5   = Wheelchair bound or bedridden unless aided.

VI. Schwab and England activities of daily living scale
100%—Completely independent. Able to do all chores without slowness, difficulty, or impairment. Essentially normal. Unaware of any difficulty.
90%—Completely independent. Able to do all chores with some degree of slowness, difficulty, and impairment. Might take twice as long. Beginning to be aware of difficulty.
80%—Completely independent in most chores. Takes twice as long. Conscious of difficulty and slowness.
70%—Not completely independent. More difficulty with some chores. Three to four times as long in some. Must spend a large part of the day with chores.
60%—Some dependency. Can do most chores, but exceedingly slowly and with much effort. Errors; some impossible.
50%—More dependent. Help with half, slower, and so forth. Difficulty with everything.
40%—Very dependent. Can assist with some chores, but does few alone.
30%—With effort, now and then does a few chores alone, or begins alone. Much help needed.
20%—Nothing done alone. Can be a slight help with some chores. Severe invalid.
10%—Totally dependent, helpless. Complete invalid.
0%—Vegetative functions, such as swallowing, bladder and bowel functions, not functioning. Bedridden.

From Stern and Hurtig,[4] pp 36–41, with permission.
* Definitions of 0–4 scale.

Traumatic Head Injury

Patricia Leahy

OBJECTIVES

1. Describe the pathophysiology of traumatic head injury.
2. Describe three clinical rating scales and their usefulness.
3. Describe the role of a physical therapist in the acute care of a patient with traumatic head injury.
4. Describe commonly seen deficits that result from head trauma.
5. Explain the need for special consideration of a patient's cognitive status during physical therapy evaluation and treatment planning.
6. List the components of a physical therapy assessment for patients with head injury.
7. Describe the role of the physical therapist at various stages of rehabilitation for a patient with head injury.
8. Appreciate the need for a well-coordinated interdisciplinary team approach to the management of individuals with head injury.

Traumatic head injury is a common and devastating occurrence in American society. It is the number one killer of American children and young adults. On the average, one person is hospitalized with a head injury for every minute of every day, totalling more than 500,000 such hospitalizations per year. Of those, approximately 70,000 people will develop intellectual, behavioral, and/or physical disabilities that will prevent their return to a normal, independent life-style and 2000 people will exist in a persistent vegetative state. Motor vehicle accidents cause one half of all traumatic head injuries, with falls accounting for 21%, assaults and violence 12%, and sports and recreation 10%. Men are injured more often than women and the typical patient is between the ages of 15 and 24 years at the time of injury.[1] The goal of rehabilitation for individuals with head injury is to optimize function and minimize disability. This is a difficult process for all involved and demands a multifaceted approach that includes numerous professionals and a strong commitment from the patient's support system and, when feasible, from the patient themselves. This chapter will provide an overview of information related to the injury itself, clinical rating scales, diagnostic tests, and the rehabilitation process, from the time of injury until community reintegration.

No publication regarding head injury should neglect to mention prevention as the only truly successful "cure" for head injury. Rehabilitation professionals should become leaders in promoting preventative measures such as the use of passive restraints and helmets, responsible alcohol consumption, proper training in athletics, and so on. Our involvement in the promotion of these measures may help to decrease the staggering number of head injuries and the overwhelming loss that is felt by the patient, his family, and society as a whole.

CLASSIFICATION AND PATHOPHYSIOLOGY

Head injuries are classified as mild, moderate, or severe based on the Glasgow Coma Scale (Table 24–1). They may also be classified according to numerous other factors such as open or closed (depending on whether or not the skull is fractured); high-velocity or low-velocity (depending on whether it resulted from high speed trauma such as a motor vehicle accident or low speed trauma such as a blow from a blunt object or a fall from 6 ft or less); or as diffuse or focal (depending on the location of brain damage). To an experienced clinician, each of these factors provides information that can be used in predicting outcome and planning treatment. Given such information, it is possible to infer other meaningful information. Consider the following examples. Given that a patient has an open head injury, we know that there is much greater risk of infection than in a patient with a closed head injury. Given the initial severity of a patient's injury, we are able to make preliminary predictions about outcome. We know that high-velocity injuries are more likely to involve diffuse axonal injury than low-velocity injuries. Furthermore, the location of the brain injury provides a wealth of clues as to

Table 24-1 GLASGOW COMA SCALE

Activity	Score
EYE OPENING	
Spontaneous	4
To speech	3
To pain	2
No response	1
BEST MOTOR RESPONSE	
Follows motor commands	6
Localizes	5
Withdraws	4
Abnormal flexion	3
Extensor response	2
No response	1
VERBAL RESPONSE	
Oriented	5
Confused conversation	4
Inappropriate words	3
Incomprehensible sounds	2
No response	1

From Jennett and Teasdale,[5] p 78, with permission.

what specific deficits are likely to be encountered (for example, nondominant parietal lobe lesions are likely to result in spatial relation problems, frontal lobe damage is likely to produce deficits in executive functioning such as judgment and reasoning, and so forth). Much can be gleaned from information about the patient's injury. However, because traumatic head injury is often multifocal, and the effects are cumulative, it is very difficult, even for the most experienced clinician, to predict precisely what will follow. Following is a discussion of some of the most important factors to consider.

Factors That Influence Outcome

Three factors that influence the final outcome in patients with head injury are: the preinjury status of the patient, the amount of immediate damage to the brain from the impact of the head injury (the primary damage), and the cumulative effect of secondary brain damage produced by systemic and intracranial mechanisms that occur after the initial injury.

PREMORBID STATUS

When a head injury occurs in a person who has already lost a sizeable number of neurons because of previous brain disease or injury, the result of that head injury is usually much worse than it would have been in a person without prior brain damage. This is true even if the person has made a good recovery from the prior insult.[2] Thus, in a patient who has previously experienced stroke, hydrocephalus, or encephalitis, a relatively minor head injury can be very disabling. Similarly, older patients with some preexisting loss of neurons may do poorly after head injury. Therefore, when assessing potential for recovery, it is important to establish the preinjury status of the patient. This can be derived from academic records, previous medical records, job history, and information gathered from the patient's family.

PRIMARY DAMAGE

Depending on the nature, direction, and magnitude of the forces applied to the skull, brain, and body, primary damage to the brain may be of any or all of the following types.[3] **Local brain damage** is localized to the area of the brain that is under the site of impact on the skull. The damage may be in the form of contusion or laceration, or both. It may be mild, moderate, or severe. More severe damage may result in localizing neurologic signs, depending on the location of the injury. Sometimes the effects of the injury are not apparent until secondary damage results. For example, severe damage to one of the temporal lobes may result in no immediate effect, but may cause edema (a secondary effect), which may eventually produce signs of brain damage due to pressure.

A severe blow to the head may result in brain damage not only directly under the site of impact, but also directly opposite the site of impact. This results from the brain "bouncing" and making contact with the skull at a site opposite from the site of impact. Such injuries are referred to as "coup-contrecoup" injuries.

Polar brain damage results when the head is subjected to acceleration and deceleration, such as in a head-on collision. This damage results when the brain moves forward inside the skull and then suddenly stops due to impact with the skull. Damage to the tips (poles) and undersurface of the temporal and frontal lobes is most common. Damage to the occipital pole can also occur but is much less common. The damage may be in the form of contusion and/or laceration and often is not associated with abnormal neurologic signs until the **mass effect,** produced by edema, causes the brain to shift. This process may take 2 or 3 days and is one cause of delayed deterioration after head injury.

Diffuse brain injury (diffuse axonal injury, DAI) refers to widely scattered shearing of subcortical axons within their myelin sheaths that is not intense in any one location, but which causes a dramatic cumulative effect. Diffuse axonal injury may occur in isolation or may have local or polar damage superimposed on it; it is apparent in subcortical white matter in moderate injuries and with increasing severity, lesions extend downward and inward to include the midbrain and brain stem. With this type of injury, the patient is deeply comatose from the time of injury, usually with abnormal posturing of the extremities and autonomic dysfunction (p 24).[2]

SECONDARY INJURY

The energy requirements of the brain are extremely high. Following severe head injury, numerous conditions conspire to decrease the energy supply, causing secondary injury to the brain. A major pathologic process seen in patients with traumatic head injury is **hypoxic-ischemic injury** (HII). Such an injury may result in infarction of a particular vascular territory in the brain due to compromise of circulation secondary to shifting brain structures. A more diffuse form of HII, resulting in secondary brain injury, is caused by arterial hypoxemia (p 27).[2] The causes of arterial hypoxemia range from obstruction of the airway to trauma to the chest. These

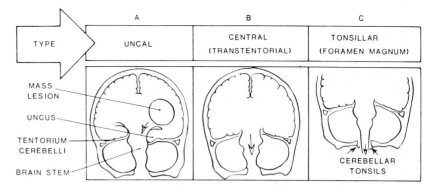

Figure 24–1. Herniations of the brain. (A) Herniation of uncus of temporal lobe through tentorial notch. (B) Herniation of midbrain and pons through tentorial notch. (C) Herniation of medulla and cerebellar tonsils through foramen magnum. (Adapted from Plum, F, et al: The Diagnosis of Stupor and Coma, ed 2, FA Davis, Philadelphia, 1972.)

systemic injuries may result in any number of respiratory impairments that deprive the brain of much needed oxygen. Arterial hypotension, often the result of massive blood loss, may also contribute to HII.

Late-occurring **intracranial hematomas** are another source of secondary brain damage. This complication can transform a seemingly mild injury into a life-threatening situation within hours. Intracranial hematomas are often associated with patients who "talk and die," that is those who are lucid for a period of time after the initial injury but who later lapse into coma and die. This late-appearing loss of consciousness is due to compression of the brain by the expanding hematoma. This "lucid interval" occurs in only a portion of patients with head injury. Many are in coma from the initial injury and the hematoma may go undetected and untreated, causing an avoidable death. These hematomas are usually classified according to their site (epidural, subdural, or intracerebral) and by the time after injury in which they develop: acute–within 3 days; subacute; or chronic—more than 2 to 3 weeks.

Because the brain is surrounded by the rigid skull, swelling of the damaged brain or abnormality of brain fluid dynamics often results in increased **intracranial pressure (ICP)**. Whereas even mildly increased ICP is associated with increased morbidity in survivors, severely increased ICP may result in **herniation** of the brain. Figure 24–1 and Table 24–2 explain various types of herniation syndromes and their effects. Other causes of secondary brain damage include intracranial infection, cerebral artery vasospasm, **obstructive hydrocephalus,** and **posttraumatic epilepsy.** Clearly, the early medical management of patients with traumatic head injury can have a major impact on the eventual outcome.

Recent research findings indicate that neurochemical changes also contribute to brain damage after trauma. Diffuse axonal injury is accompanied by **autodestructive cellular phenomena** that involve surges in levels of excitatory neurotransmitters.[4] These neurochemical changes set up a cascade of intracellular events that impede neuronal function and may go on to destroy neurons. These phenomena render cells extremely sensitive to other insults such as hypoxia. Several treatments to counter these neurochemical changes are currently under investigation.

Table 24–2 HERNIATIONS OF THE BRAIN

Type	Location	Cause	Anatomic Structures Involved	Clinical Effects
Uncal	Tentorial notch, midbrain	Mass lesion in temporal lobe or middle fossa	Hippocampal gyrus and uncus	
			Oculomotor nerve	
			Cerebral peduncle	Paresis of nerve III
			Midbrain ascending reticular activating system	Hemiparesis
				Coma
			Posterior cerebral artery	
				Homonymous hemianopia
Central (transtentorial)	Tentorial notch, midbrain	Mass lesion in frontal, parietal, or occipital lobe	Midbrain and pons	Decerebrate rigidity
		Progression of uncal herniation	Ascending reticular activating system	Coma
Tonsillar (foramen magnum)	Foramen magnum, medulla	Mass lesion in posterior fossa	Cerebellar tonsils	Neck pain and stiffness
		Progression of uncal or transtentorial herniation	Indirect activation pathways	Flaccidity
			Ascending reticular activating system	Coma
			Vasomotor centers	Alteration of pulse, respiration, blood pressure

From Daube, JR, et al: Medical Neurosciences, ed 2. Little, Brown, & Co, Boston, 1986, p 368, with permission.

Clinical Rating Scales

Clinical rating scales have been developed in an effort to standardize the description of patients who have sustained head injuries and to facilitate research in prognosticating outcome. Following, the most commonly used scales are briefly described and information regarding reliability is provided where it is available.

GLASGOW COMA SCALE (GCS)

This scale, developed by Jennett and Teasdale is used to document level of consciousness and define the severity of injury.[5] It relates consciousness to motor response, verbal response, and eye opening (Table 24-1). The GCS has been extensively tested for inter-rater reliability and shown to be reliable ($r = 0.92$).[6] Patients scoring a total of 8 or less are said to have severe head injuries. Patients with moderate head injuries score from 9 to 12, and those with mild head injuries score from 13 to the maximum of 15 points on the GCS.

RANCHO LOS AMIGOS LEVEL OF COGNITIVE FUNCTIONING

The Rancho Los Amigos Level of Cognitive Functioning (LOCF) is a descriptive scale that outlines a predictable sequence of cognitive and behavioral recovery seen in patients with traumatic brain injury (Table 24-3).[7] A patient may plateau at any level. This scale does not address specific cognitive deficits, but is useful for communicating general cognitive and/or behavioral status and using that information for treatment planning. Although this scale is used frequently, no published data are available regarding its reliability.

RAPPAPORT'S DISABILITY RATING SCALE (DRS)

This scale covers a wide range of functional areas and is used to classify levels of disability ranging from death to no disability (Table 24-4). It is used serially to document patient progress over time. The DRS has been demonstrated to have a high level of inter-rater reliability ($r = 0.97$).[8]

GLASGOW OUTCOME SCALE (GOS)

The Glasgow Outcome Scale has been expanded from its original three categories to eight. The categories are: dead, vegetative, and two levels each of severely and moderately disabled and good recovery (Table 24-5). This scale is used primarily for research purposes so that outcome can be quantified. In a reliability study with two raters and 150 patients, agreement was high ($r = 0.95$).[9]

Diagnostic Procedures

To aid in diagnosis and prognostication, patients with head injury often receive numerous special tests in addition to the standard neurologic examination. Following is a brief description of these tests.

Table 24-3 RANCHO LOS AMIGOS LEVELS OF COGNITIVE FUNCTIONING*

I. NO RESPONSE
Patient appears to be in a deep sleep and is completely unresponsive to any stimuli.

II. GENERALIZED RESPONSE
Patient reacts inconsistently and nonpurposefully to stimuli in a nonspecific manner. Responses are limited and often the same regardless of stimulus presented. Responses may be physiologic changes, gross body movements, and/or vocalization.

III. LOCALIZED RESPONSE
Patient reacts specifically but inconsistently to stimuli. Responses are directly related to the type of stimulus presented. May follow simple commands such as closing eyes or squeezing hand in an inconsistent, delayed manner.

IV. CONFUSED-AGITATED
Patient is in a heightened state of activity. Behavior is bizarre and nonpurposeful relative to immediate environment. Does not discriminate among persons or objects; is unable to cooperate directly with treatment efforts. Verbalizations frequently are incoherent and/or inappropriate to the environment; confabulation may be present. Gross attention to environment is very brief; selective attention is often nonexistent. Patient lacks short-term and long-term recall.

V. CONFUSED-INAPPROPRIATE
Patient is able to respond to simple commands fairly consistently. However, with increased complexity of commands or lack of any external structure, responses are nonpurposeful, random, or fragmented. Demonstrates gross attention to the environment but is highly distractible and lacks ability to focus attention on a specific task. With structure, may be able to converse on a social automatic level for short periods of time. Verbalization is often inappropriate and confabulatory. Memory is severely impaired; often shows inappropriate use of objects; may perform previously learned tasks with structure but is unable to learn new information.

VI. CONFUSED-APPROPRIATE
Patient shows goal-directed behavior but is dependent on external input or direction. Follows simple directions consistently and shows carryover for relearned tasks such as self-care. Responses may be incorrect due to memory problems, but they are appropriate to the situation. Past memories show more depth and detail than recent memory.

VII. AUTOMATIC-APPROPRIATE
Patient appears appropriate and oriented within the hospital and home settings; goes through daily routine automatically, but frequently robotlike. Patient shows minimal to no confusion and has shallow recall of activities. Shows carryover for new learning but at a decreased rate. With structure is able to initiate social or recreational activities; judgment remains impaired.

VIII. PURPOSEFUL-APPROPRIATE
Patient is able to recall and integrate past and recent events and is aware of and responsive to environment. Shows carryover for new learning and needs no supervision once activities are learned. May continue to show a decreased ability relative to premorbid abilities, abstract reasoning, tolerance for stress, and judgment in emergencies or unusual circumstances.

---

*Condensed form. From Professional Staff Association, Rancho Los Amigos Hospital,[7] pp 87–88, with permission.

ELECTROENCEPHALOGRAMS AND EVOKED POTENTIALS

Measures of central nervous system activity from electroencephalograms (EEGs) have been made for over 60 years, but advances in computer technologies are revolutionizing the ways in which EEGs are used. Electroencephalograms are easily obtained, noninvasive, and inexpensive. They can be repeated as often as needed. Information provided by EEG is both qualitative and

Table 24–4 DISABILITY RATING SCALE*

Category	Item
Arousability, awareness and responsivity	Eye opening[1] Verbalization[2] Motor response[3]
Cognitive ability for self-care	Feeding[4] Toileting[4] Grooming[4]
Dependence on others	Level of functioning[5]
Psychosocial adaptability	"Employability"[6]

[1]Eye Opening		[2]Best Verbal Response		[3]Best Motor Response		[4]Cognitive ability for self-care (Does patient know how and when? Ignore motor disability.)	
Spontaneous	0	Oriented	0	Obeying	0	Complex	0
To speech	1	Confused	1	Localizing	1	Partial	1
To pain	2	Inappropriate	2	Withdrawing	2	Minimal	2
None	3	Incomprehensible	3	Flexing	3	None	3
		None	4	Extending	4		
				None	5		

[5]Level of Functioning		[6]"Employability"		Total DR Score	Level of Disability
					Disability Categories
Completely independent	0	Not restricted	0	0	None
Independent in special environment	1	Selected jobs	1	1	Mild
Mildly dependent[a]	2	Sheltered workshop	2	2–3	Partial
Moderately dependent[b]	3	Not employable	3	4–6	Moderate
Markedly dependent[c]	4			7–11	Moderately severe
Totally dependent[d]	5			12–16	Severe
				17–21	Extremely severe
				22–24	Vegetative state
				25–29	Extreme veg. state
				30	Death

* Condensed form. From Rappaport,[8] p 119, with permission.
[a]Needs limited assistance (nonresident helper).
[b]Needs moderate assistance (person in home).
[c]Needs assistance with all major activities at all times.
[d]24-hour nursing care required.

Table 24–5 GLASGOW OUTCOME SCALE

Extended Scale	Original Scale	Contracted Scales			
Dead	Dead	Dead	Dead or Vegetative	Dead or Vegetative	Dead
Vegetative	Vegetative				
Degree of Disability: 5	Severely Disabled	Dependent	Severely Disabled		Survivors
4				Conscious	
3	Moderately Disabled				
2		Independent	Independent		
1					
0	Good Recovery				
Total Categories 8	5	3		2	

From Jennett and Teasdale,[5] p 306, with permission.

quantitative in nature. As new ways to quantify the information are developed, the usefulness of EEG increases. A particular form of quantified EEG activity is the evoked potential (EP). In EP testing, the EEG signals from subcortical and primary sensory areas of the cortex are averaged in response to repetitive presentations of sensory stimuli. This type of electrophysiologic evaluation has proven to be very useful in the evaluation of sensory function and has been used with some success to predict clinical outcome from the early stages of moderate to severe head injury.[10]

COMPUTED TOMOGRAPHY (CT)

Introduced in 1973, CT scanning revolutionized the acute management of head injury.[11] In particular, CT scans are most successful in identifying hematomas, ventricular enlargement, and atrophy. However, recent comparisons of CT and MRI confirm that CT is relatively insensitive to many of the lesions present after trauma. Professionals and family members should be warned that lack of significant abnormalities on CT does not rule out the presence of extensive brain damage.

MAGNETIC RESONANCE IMAGING (MRI)

Introduced in the early 1980s, MRI is more sensitive than CT to lesions after head injury, particularly to nonhemorrhagic lesions. Often, patients with normal CT scans will have evidence of abnormality on MRI.

CEREBRAL BLOOD FLOW MAPPING

The measurement of cerebral blood flow (CBF) is used in attempts to clarify dynamic relationships between physiology and behavior. Positron emission tomography (PET) is the method of choice for measurement of CBF, but is of limited clinical value due to the sparsity of PET centers (approximately 60 centers worldwide). Positron emission tomography clearly shows disturbances in cerebral metabolism beyond the structural abnormalities demonstrated by MRI or CT.[12,13] Another type of CBF mapping, called SPECT (single photon emission computed tomography) is available in the routine hospital nuclear medicine department. The major limitation of SPECT, in comparison with PET, is that it measures relative rather than absolute perfusion. This can lead to difficulties in interpreting results. For example, an area of high blood flow may truly be hyperemic, or may actually have normal blood flow that is only relatively high due to generally reduced flow in other regions.[14] In the future, SPECT and PET may be used to document the regional metabolism of specific neurotransmitters and receptors.

MANAGEMENT OF PATIENTS WITH TRAUMATIC HEAD INJURY

Management will be discussed in two sections. From a physical therapy perspective, early management is somewhat similar in most cases of moderate or severe head injury. It will be discussed briefly. Later management needs to be individualized according to the patient's cognitive and behavioral status, as well as his or her sensorimotor status. In the section about later management, an overview of deficits is presented, followed by management guidelines.

Acute Management

Early medical management focuses on determination of the severity of the injury, preservation of life, and prevention of further damage. Because it is impossible to make a valid assessment of neurologic function in a patient who is hypoxemic or shocked, the very first step is to ensure that the patient has an adequate airway, is adequately oxygenated, and has satisfactory arterial blood pressure and peripheral circulation. Level of consciousness is determined, using the GCS. Following a brief but thorough neurologic examination, the patient usually undergoes radiographic examination of the skull and cervical spine. If transportation is judged to be safe, the patient usually then undergoes more specialized tests, as previously described. Intracranial pressure is often monitored. This can be done via a catheter in the lateral ventricle, a screw in the skull inserted into the subarachnoid space, or a transducer placed directly in the epidural space. If the ICP becomes elevated over a mean value of 25 mmHg, measures are taken to reduce the pressure. If the ICP is consistently below 20 mmHg for 24 hours, the system can be discontinued.[15]

Currently there are a number of approaches to early medical management that are under investigation. Most of these involve pharmacologic intervention, though hypothermia is also being explored. The use of drugs, hypothermia, or a combination of both are being studied for their effectiveness in limiting the amount of secondary injury sustained by the brain.

Physical therapy is indicated in the early management of a patient with moderate or severe head injury. Initial therapy revolves around the prevention of complications such as respiratory distress, contracture development, and skin breakdown. Frequent position changes will assist with pulmonary hygiene and skin integrity. Postural drainage, percussion, and vibration are often used in attempts to keep the patient's lungs clear. This is usually carried out cooperatively by respiratory, physical therapy, and nursing staffs. Passive range of motion exercises should be performed regularly, but may not be enough to prevent the development of deformities. Other management options include the use of splints or prophylactic short leg casts, and passive standing on a tilt table. The importance of maintaining range of motion cannot be overemphasized, because deformities may lead to the need for additional therapy or even surgery during the rehabilitative phase.

Functional mobility training may begin when the patient's medical status is stable. Initial goals may include increasing the patient's tolerance of upright positioning and increasing the patient's active movement capabilities. For those patients who remain in a vegetative state, sensory stimulation is often provided.

Details of a sensory stimulation program and further discussion of range of motion will be presented later in this chapter. The physical therapist working in the intensive care unit must work closely with the nursing staff. Because a patient's status may change dramatically in a short period of time, it is helpful to check briefly with the nurse before each patient treatment. This will also alert the nurse that physical therapy is about to begin, which is important because treatment procedures may cause a change in status, such as a temporary increase in vital signs or ICP.

Rehabilitative Management

Assuming that the patient survives the immediate posttrauma stage, the arduous task of returning the patient to society at the highest possible level of function becomes the goal of rehabilitation. Patients who have sustained traumatic brain injury almost always display a complex array of deficits. The effects of brain injury are best pictured in a systems model, in which the whole is greater than the sum of its parts. In other words, the patient is often left with numerous and severe deficits that compound one another. For example, fractures of the lower extremities that render the patient non-weight-bearing are much more disabling if the patient is also too cognitively impaired to achieve independent wheelchair use. Similarly, functional training for the patient with hemiplegia is significantly more difficult if that patient also has marked memory deficits. It is the variety and complexity of deficits that makes head injury rehabilitation interesting and challenging for the therapist working with this population of patients. A highly skilled, specially trained interdisciplinary team offers the best hope for evaluating and treating the multiple physical, cognitive, perceptual, and emotional problems encountered by individuals with traumatic head injury.

DEFICITS RELATED TO HEAD INJURY

Before discussing the rehabilitation of patients with head injury, it is useful to provide an overview of the types of deficits usually encountered. Having an understanding of the deficits makes it easier to understand the cognitively based approach used in treating patients with head injury and why it is necessary to use such an approach.

Decreased Level of Consciousness

Altered level of consciousness occurs consistently with acceleration-deceleration type injuries and may occur with some focal injuries. Consistent use of terminology in dealing with altered consciousness is important. According to Jenett and Teasdale, **coma** is defined as "not obeying commands, not uttering words, and not opening the eyes."[16] Sometimes the GCS score is used to define coma, with a score of 8 or less defining coma. It is important to note that coma usually lasts only a few weeks at most. After that time, patients with a continuing decreased level of consciousness are usually referred to as being in a **persistent vegetative state (PVS).** (Some authors prefer the term postcomatose unawareness.)

Patients in this state have a wide range of responses, including eye opening with sleep-wake cycles, and sometimes the ability to follow with their eyes. However, these responses may occur at the subcortical level and do not necessarily indicate returning consciousness. Patients in a PVS do not speak or produce any type of behavior that is purposeful or psychologically meaningful (p 86).[16]

Even patients who appear to be fully conscious may be in a state of altered consciousness known as **post-traumatic amnesia (PTA).** This describes the time between the injury and the time when the patient is again able to remember ongoing events, such as what was for breakfast or what happened the day before. While the patient has PTA, it is as though each moment exists in isolation. There is no carryover of information from hour to hour or day to day. The implications of this on functional training are obvious. It is interesting to note, though, that there appears to be a difference between declarative and procedural memory. Whereas the patient with PTA is unable to describe memories (declarative memory), he or she may, at times, show carryover of skills that do not require verbal explanation (procedural memory). For example, a patient may improve in his or her ability to play a game without having any memory of having previously played the game. This is often seen in the patient's improvement in automatic activities such as gait.

Cognitive Deficits

Whereas most patients will eventually regain full consciousness, most will also be left with residual cognitive deficits. Using a variation of Prigatano's classification system, borrowed from Brooks, an overview will be presented of the types of cognitive problems most commonly encountered.[17] Often a neuropsychologist is instrumental in coordinating all of the cognitive and behavioral information and recommending intervention strategies. Each discipline's management of the patient can be strengthened by understanding the total array of deficits.

Disorders of learning, memory, and complex information processing. Although not fully understood, disorders of this type are extremely common after head injury. There are many reasons why a patient may have difficulty encoding, storing, and retrieving information. For example, attention deficits may interfere with a patient's ability to form and use memories. Another patient may not attach appropriate meaning to events and therefore have great difficulty in remembering them. Deficits such as these will have a great impact on many aspects of rehabilitation. Patients with head injury have deficits ranging from problems with selective attention (the ability to concentrate and ignore distraction) to problems understanding a task, to problems planning strategies for solution. The better understood the specific problems are, the more likely the therapist is to challenge the patient appropriately.

Deficits in communication. Numerous types of communication deficits are noted in patients following brain injury and these can have a significant impact on rehabilitation. Receptive and expressive communication should be evaluated, both formally by a speech and language pathologist (see Chapter 29), and informally by practitioners of all disciplines who come in contact with the patient. At times it is very difficult to differentiate between true language deficits and confused language that is reflective of marked cognitive deficits.

Behavioral Deficits

Research and clinical experience have established that behavioral disorders are the most enduring and socially disabling of any of the dysfunctions commonly seen after traumatic brain injury.[18] Long-term changes in behavior such as sexual disinhibition, apathy, aggression, low frustration tolerance, and depression often lead to a life of seclusion and loneliness. Factors to be considered in the evaluation and management of behavior are the person's premorbid personality; the physical, cognitive, and emotional effects of the injury; and the nature of the social environment. Typically, psychologists skilled in the evaluation and treatment of behavioral disorders play a leading role in determining behavioral programs. However, in order to achieve a successful outcome, behavior programs need to be generalized across all treatment settings.

Sensorimotor Deficits

This is the area where physical therapists are expected to complete a thorough evaluation, assess deficits and their causes, identify areas of strength, set appropriate short- and long-term goals, and develop a treatment program. To identify any of the following commonly seen movement deficits or any other sensorimotor deficits, a typical physical therapy evaluation should be conducted. (See Table 24–6 for an outline.) The extent of the evaluation will depend on the patient's ability to become involved in the assessment. Specific guidelines for assessing patients with varying degrees of cognitive ability will be discussed later in the chapter.

General deconditioning. Owing to the traumatic nature of their injuries, it is not uncommon for patients with traumatic head injuries to experience significant medical complications such as major blood loss, pulmonary distress, and so forth. The patient often comes to rehabilitation with generalized weakness and loss of flexibility. Even for those patients with relatively uncomplicated medical courses, the effects of coma, drastic changes in diet and activity level, and the additional energy requirements needed for healing, often produce significant deconditioning.

Hemiparesis. Hemiparesis is often the result of direct unilateral trauma to the cortex, but may also result from bleeding, hypoxia, or other secondary injury. The motor impairments are similar to those seen in patients with cerebral vascular disease, but the overall picture is often more complicated due to the severity of other types of deficits, especially those related to learning.

Bilateral hemiparesis. This indicates involvement of the trunk and all four extremities and results from bilateral brain damage. It may range from mild to severe and is often asymmetric. In the most involved patients, voluntary movement may be lacking entirely and movements may appear to be dominated by reflex activity.

Table 24–6 COMPONENTS OF THE PHYSICAL THERAPY ASSESSMENT

MEDICAL INFORMATION
History, onset, and etiology
Results of diagnostic tests (e.g., CAT scan, radiographs)
Precautions
Respiratory status
Dysphagia status
Bowel and bladder
Skin integrity
Medications
PSYCHOLOGIC INFORMATION
Previous function
Neuropsychologic or psychologic assessments
Educational and vocational status
SOCIAL INFORMATION
Family and supportive others
Economic and insurance information
Home or discharge environment
COGNITIVE/COMMUNICATIVE/BEHAVIORAL STATUS
Level of alertness
Attention
Orientation
Memory function
Communicative ability
Behavior status
Higher level cognitive abilities
SENSORIMOTOR FUNCTIONS
Visual and auditory ability
Visual—spatial ability
Sensation—kinesthesia, proprioception, light touch, pressure, pain
Muscle tone
Abnormal movement patterns
Abnormal reflexes
Equilibrium responses
Strength
Coordination
Praxis
Posture
Speed of movement
Quality of movement
Strategies of movement to maintain posture and balance
Functional movement (movement may be abnormal but compensates for deficit)
Endurance
FUNCTIONAL STATUS
Bed mobility
Transfers
Sitting and standing ability
Balance
Ambulation
Gait
Stairs
Outside terrain
Higher-level physical activities (may include sports)
Functional abilities in differing environments
Endurance
Work or school capacity

Adapted from Mills and Wusteney.[29]

Balance deficits. Almost all patients who have survived a moderate or severe head injury will experience some loss of balance. Some problems are subtle, so if no other sensorimotor deficits are seen, the evaluation should include high-level skills such as those needed for sports or other recreation activities. Figures 24–2 and 24–3 show a patient working on high-level balance activities.

Ataxia and incoordination. Due to damage of the cerebellum and basal ganglia, patients with head injury

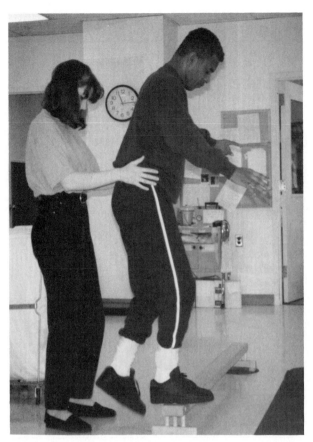

Figure 24–2. Patient in LOCF level VI working on high level balance activity.

Figure 24–3. Selection of activities is based on cognitive as well as physical demands. The progression of cognitive and physical demands can proceed at different rates.

may experience unilateral or bilateral ataxia, and problems with smooth execution of movement. Intention tremor may or may not be present.

Associated injuries. It is not uncommon for patients with head injuries resulting from trauma to have other injuries such as fractures, peripheral nerve injuries, or spinal cord injury.

MANAGEMENT BASED ON COGNITIVE LEVEL

Given the wide array of deficits that result from traumatic head injury, it is no wonder that treatment of patients with this diagnosis is challenging and multifaceted. Although treatment from a whole team of professionals is necessary, the remainder of this chapter will focus on the development and execution of physical therapy treatment programs. It is assumed that physical therapists will be working with other professionals and will consult with them regarding the coordination of treatment. Table 24–7 presents some of the more commonly prescribed pharmacologic agents for patients with head injury. The side effects of these drugs are important for physical therapists to consider.

Because the cognitive level of the patient determines the extent to which he or she can be actively involved in the treatment, the organization of physical therapy treatment information is built around the patient's cognitive level. Specific treatment considerations are discussed for patients in Rancho Los Amigos levels I–III;

IV; V–VI; and VII–VIII. One must remember that a patient may plateau at any level on the Rancho scale, and that any cognitive level can be paired with any level of physical functioning. That is, a patient may function at a high level physically and a low level cognitively or vice versa. Following the discussion of "management by level," a few specific treatments are discussed that cross all levels.

LOW-LEVEL MANAGEMENT

Patients in LOCF levels I–III have a decreased level of responsiveness, meaning they have little, if any, interaction with the environment. The goals of treatment are to prevent any complications such as contractures or decubitus ulcers and to increase the patient's level of interaction with the environment, by the encouragement of active movement and response to stimulation.

Evaluation

The patient should be evaluated in regard to passive range of motion, spontaneous activity, response to stimulation, muscle tone and reflexes, and the presence of gross motor skills such as postural reactions.

Treatment

1. **Intervention:** Passive range of motion.
Guidelines: Early passive range of motion exercises can be reasonably aggressive. Deficits that develop early will be difficult to correct later as the patient becomes more alert and agitated. Due to the patient's low level of consciousness, however, it is important to use caution in stretching. In particular, patients should be positioned in sidelying for shoulder range of motion to allow the scapula to move and prevent

Table 24–7 COMMON PHARMACOLOGIC AGENTS AND INTERACTIONS PERTINENT TO PATIENTS WITH HEAD INJURY

Name	Purpose	Contraindications	Side Effects	Comments
Elavil	Antidepressant Level II/III to heighten arousal; with higher levels to decrease agitation	Arrhythmias Urinary retention	Change in BP, change in blood sugar, sweating, dry mouth, weakness, fatigue, tingling, tremors, ataxia, arrhythmias, initial sedation, breast enlargement or testicular swelling	Is a central nervous system depressant that acts to decrease psychologic depression
Tofranil	Antidepressant	Myocardial infarction	Change in blood pressure, confusional states, numbness, tingling, ataxia, tremors, dry mouth, blurred vision, change in blood sugar	Stimulation of central nervous system
Ritalin	Stimulation to heighten alertness	Hypertension, history of drug dependency	Ataxia, insomnia, cardiac arrhythmia, nausea, anorexia, blurred vision, skin rash	Monitor blood pressure "tolerance" to drug effect
Phenobarbital	Anticonvulsant (seizure prevention)	Severe trauma, severe hypotension, uncontrolled diabetes, drug dependence	Lethargy/sedation, skin rash, ataxia, nystagmus, osteomalacia, habit-forming	Drug discontinuance should be done gradually
Thorazine	Tranquilization Management of psychotic disorders	Comatose states Presence of large amounts of CNS depressants	Drowsiness, jaundice, hypotension (usually transient), neuromuscular extrapyramidal reactions, dystonias, pseudoparkisonism, potential for hepatotoxicity	Precise mechanisms unknown
Haldol	Tranquilization Management of psychotic disorders	Severe toxic CNS depression or comatose states, Parkinson's disease	Neuromuscular extrapyramidal reactions, parkinsonian symptoms, restlessness, dystonia, akathisia, drowsiness	Dopamine blocker
Mellaril	Tranquilization Management of manifestations of psychotic disorders	Severe CNS depression or comatose strokes	Drowsiness (infrequently) Extrapyramidal symptoms	
Navane	Tranquilization Management of manifestations of psychotic disorders	Patients with circulatory collapse, comatose states, CNS depression, blood dyscrasias	Drowsiness, restlessness, agitation	May precipitate convulsions
Artane	Adjunct in treatment of all forms of parkinsonism Control of extrapyramidal disorders caused by CNS drugs	Cautious use for patients with cardiac, liver, or kidney disorders or with hypertension	Dryness of mouth, blurring of vision, dizziness, mild nausea, or nervousness	Size and frequency of dosage to control extrapyramidal reactions to tranquilizers must be determined empirically
Dilantin	Anticonvulsant	Previous hypersensitivity	Skin rash, hyperglycemia, osteomalacia, nystagmus, ataxia, gum hyperplasia	Drug discontinuance should be done gradually
Tegretol	Anticonvulsant temporal lobe	Liver abnormality	CBC abnormalities, rash, cardiac effects, (arrhythmia, edema, CHF) sedation	Long-term therapy is associated with hepatic complications
Dantrium	Control of spasticity	Liver abnormalities	Drowsiness, dizziness, weakness, fatigue, diarrhea Potential for hepatotoxicity (with greater than 800 mg daily)	Discontinue if no change in 45 days Directly interferes with the contractile mechanism of the muscle
Lioresal (Baclofen)	Control of spasticity General CNS depressant	Diabetes, epilepsy (should be monitored)	Transient drowsiness, dizziness, fatigue, frequent urge to urinate, constipation, nausea, impaired renal function	Should not exceed 80 mg/d Abrupt withdrawal can lead to hallucinations (interferes with the release of excitatory transmitters)

**Table 24–7 COMMON PHARMACOLOGIC AGENTS AND INTERACTIONS
PERTINENT TO PATIENTS WITH HEAD INJURY** (*Continued*)

Name	Purpose	Contraindications	Side Effects	Comments
Valium	Control of spasticity Skeletal muscle relaxant	Children under 6 months of age	Drowsiness, fatigue, ataxia, headaches, confusion, depression, blurred vision or double vision, skin rashes, urinary incontinence, constipation	May enhance effectiveness of Dilantin Physical/psychologic dependence Lowers blood pressure

Developed by Marion Miller, RPT, for New England Rehabilitation Hospital Brain Injury Unit Orientation Packet for Staff Physical Therapists. Orientation packet compiled by Marion Miller, RPT, and Mary Evens, RPT.

BP = blood pressure; CBC = complete blood count; CHF = congestive heart failure; CNS = central nervous system.

jamming the glenohumeral joint. Stretching should be done in a slow, controlled fashion. Rotation seems to be effective in relaxing patients with significant spasticity.

2. **Intervention:** Sensory stimulation.

Guidelines: Sensory stimulation is used for arousal and to elicit movement. The theory is that by providing stimulation in a controlled, multisensory manner, with a balance of stimulation and rest, the reticular activating system may be stimulated causing a general increase in arousal. Although the value of sensory stimulation for patients who are slow to recover remains unproven, theoretical support for such programs comes from research in four areas: (1) effects of sensory deprivation on neurologic recovery; (2) effects of "enriched" environments on behavior and nervous system structure and function; (3) nervous system plasticity; and (4) effects of environmental input during sensitive periods of neurodevelopment. For a thorough review of these findings, see Ansell.[19] Stimulation is most effectively administered for short treatment sessions (15 to 30 min), and it is important to present stimuli in an orderly manner via one or two modalities at a time, to prevent overstimulation. The importance of carefully structuring the sensory experiences has led one author to prefer the term "sensory regulation" to sensory stimulation.[20] One must allow sufficient time for processing delays that are likely to exist, and repetition of the same stimulus is necessary for the documentation of response consistency.

Although the treatment is referred to as sensory stimulation, it is actually the *response* that is of greatest interest. During this type of treatment, the patient must be closely monitored for subtle responses such as changes in heart rate, blood pressure, rate of respiration, or diaphoresis. Various motor responses, such as eye movements, facial grimacing, changes in posture, head turning, or vocalization should be recorded. In monitoring a response, it is important to note the following characteristics:

- **Latency:** the time delay between stimulus and response.
- **Consistency:** how many times out of a given number of stimulus presentations does the patient respond the same?
- **Intensity:** the response should be proportionate to the stimulation. For example, a gentle squeez-

ing of the Achilles tendon may normally cause a subtle withdrawal, but should not result in a massive movement of the entire lower extremity.
- **Duration:** brief forms of stimuli should result in brief forms of response.

Auditory stimulation is the most obvious place to begin. Normal conversational tones should be used and the therapist should begin by identifying him- or herself and explaining what is to be done. Discussion of topics that have meaning to the patient seem to be the most logical. Intermittent use of the radio or television may be therapeutic but constant background noise is undesirable. Habituation to background noise is likely to occur and it provides competition for meaningful stimuli.

Visual stimulation is provided by the use of familiar objects such as pictures of family and friends. It is important to systematically stimulate all areas of the visual field to compensate for visual field deficits that may exist and to document varying responses in different parts of the visual field. Visual attentiveness (how long the patient can maintain visual attention on an object) and visual tracking should also be documented.

Olfactory stimulation can be provided by placing scents under the patient's nose for 10 to 15 seconds during quiet breathing. Patients with a tracheostomy are not likely to respond because they do not breathe through their noses. Personal experience indicates that favorable results are most likely using patients' own favorite smells, such as freshly brewed coffee or a mate's favorite cologne.

Gustatory stimulation may involve the application of a cotton swab dipped in a flavored solution to the lips and gums, or may involve the use of flavored ice chips, popsicles, and so forth. A therapist skilled in dysphagia management should be involved in this treatment due to the increased risk of aspiration and the need to evaluate complex swallowing responses.

Tactile stimulation is provided during most functional activities such as turning, bathing, dressing, and so forth. Whereas most of us will note that different parts of our bodies are often in contact with one another (such as when crossing our legs, resting our head on our hands, crossing our arms) patients with head injuries are usually positioned in ways that prevent this. Tactile stimulation might include using the patient's own hands, for example by placing a washcloth in his hand and guiding him or her through the motions of face washing.

Vestibular stimulation can be provided by neck range of motion, rolling on a mat, rocking, or pushing the patient in a wheelchair.

A particularly important aspect of a sensory stimulation program is developing the patient's potential to perform a consistent, reliable response, with minimal latency, that can be applied to a simple yes/no communication system. Eye blinks or finger tapping may provide a viable yes/no system through which the patient can communicate. Of course, this requires the cognitive ability to interact meaningfully with the environment and is not feasible for all patients.

3. **Intervention:** Positioning.
Guidelines: The rate at which the patient is improving determines the amount of time, energy, and financial resources that should be expended toward positioning at this level. Many patients will progress rapidly through this stage of recovery and will require only temporary positioning. Others, such as those in a persistent vegetative state, may plateau at this level and providing appropriate, long-term positioning will become a primary focus of physical therapy.

The goals of positioning are to provide normal sensory experiences, thereby facilitating normal movement; to provide support for proper body alignment, thereby preventing deformities and skin breakdown; to allow mobility; and to improve cosmesis. It is beyond the scope of this chapter to provide a detailed description of full-body positioning systems but resources are provided in the supplemental readings. Positioning may also include simple measures such as strategic placement of towel rolls or pillows. Casting will be discussed later in the chapter.

In all circumstances, it is important to critically evaluate the effectiveness of positioning devices and make changes as needed. For example, footboards designed to prevent plantarflexion may actually increase the risk of equinus deformity if contact with the footboard elicits extension of the lower extremities. Ongoing evaluation is the key to effective positioning.

MID-LEVEL MANAGEMENT

Patients in LOCF levels IV–VI are considered to be mid-level. Because stage IV (confused-agitated) presents very specific challenges, it will be discussed separately.

Level IV

Patients in a confused and agitated state require a tremendous amount of structure to prevent overstimulation. Evaluation and treatment must be modified to include activities that are familiar and liked by the patient, and that will provide a high likelihood of success. Assessments that are needed at this stage include all of those previously listed for low-level patients with the addition of functional tasks such as basic transfers and ambulation. Creativity and an ability to estimate are important in the evaluation of agitated patients because they usually cannot tolerate formal evaluation. Goals include maintenance or improvement of joint range of motion, prevention of further physical deconditioning, improved response to simple commands, and prevention of agitated outbursts via the use of a highly structured environment. Tasks and activities include range of motion exercises to the patient's tolerance level and gross motor activities such as rolling, coming to sit, transfers, wheelchair propulsion, and gait. Generally, it is wise to work very near the patient's level of physical function and attempt to improve endurance rather than to attempt to progress to more challenging skills that would require new learning. Some agitated patients may not tolerate either of the above-mentioned types of treatment. It then becomes necessary to resort to other activities chosen simply because the patient is willing to be involved. For example, playing cards or listening to music can be made into a therapeutic activity. A patient who refuses to "take a walk" may be convinced to "come with me to get the cards." Because the early stages of head injury are characterized by profound attentional deficits,[21] any activity can be used to gradually increase the patient's attention span. When distractions occur, the therapist must redirect the patient's attention first back to the therapist, then back to the task at hand. It is crucial to provide a quiet environment and to limit the overall length of a session to within the patient's fatigue limits, gradually increasing as patient tolerance allows. Prompt and frequent praise should be provided when the patient does concentrate on a given task.

The following special considerations can lead to greater success in the management of patients in LOCF stage IV.

Remember, the patient is confused. To help decrease confusion, the patient should be seen by the same person at the same time and in the same place every day. Establishing a daily routine is very important. It is calming and reassuring to have a sense of familiarity. Additionally, orientation should be provided frequently in a nonthreatening manner. At this stage, it is often better to provide orientation information than to challenge the patient to provide it, particularly if the patient is not expected to succeed.

Expect no carryover. Teaching new skills in this stage is unrealistic. Return to previously overlearned skills, such as walking, may occur, but does not indicate general learning ability. The use of charts or graphs may be useful to help the patient progress each day. Without the use of such aids, the patient is likely to have no recall of the previous day's performance and therefore will be unable to build on it.

Model calm behavior. The patient is likely to perceive and reflect the demeanor of the care-giver. Therefore, it is important for the therapist to assume a calm and focused affect.

Be prepared with numerous activities. Because of limited attention span, the patient may not be able to concentrate on any given activity for a very long time. If the patient cannot be redirected to the selected task, it is appropriate to attempt to engage him or her in another.

Offer options. The patient can be given a sense of control, while maintaining therapeutic intervention by phrasing questions as "Would you rather play ball or go for a walk?" This prevents situations where the patient chooses an undesirable or unrealistic activity if asked "What would you like to do?" or the case where the patient simply answers "No" when asked "Would you like to . . . ?"

Expect egocentricity. At this point in recovery, the patient cannot be expected to see another's point of view. He or she will tend to think only of themselves and, at this point, it is unwise to stress the patient with attempts to do otherwise.

Levels V and VI

In LOCF levels V and VI, patients are confused but no longer agitated. They are able to follow simple commands fairly consistently, but if demands increase or structure decreases, the patient's performance may deteriorate. While carryover is now present, it is best for relearned activities. New learning is still very limited. It is usually possible to carry out a formal physical therapy evaluation at this point, but modifications will still be necessary. Instructions should be brief and simple, and the evaluation should be as concise as possible so as not to fatigue the patient unnecessarily. Goals at this level include increasing the patient's participation in the program, increasing or maintaining range of motion, increasing physical conditioning, and treating any focal motor deficits that exist such as hemiparesis, peripheral nerve injury, and so forth. Treatment should:

Maintain structure. Although internally driven agitation is decreased, the patient still requires structure to perform optimally. A patient who has been performing well may do poorly when a change in schedule occurs, or when something out of the ordinary takes place, such as family participation in therapy.

Emphasize safety. Because new learning is limited, those issues necessary for safety should receive priority.

Keep instructions to a minimum. Too much direction may confuse and irritate the patient. Speak slowly and allow time for processing delays. It is often useful to engage the patient in activities with which he or she is familiar so that the need for instruction is minimized (Figs. 24–3 and 24–4).

Use physical props to improve compliance. The use of a timer to make time more concrete is useful. For example, set a timer for 10 minutes and make an agreement with the patient that if he or she participates in a given activity for 10 minutes, they can then have a 2-minute rest period. If they act up during the 10-minute treatment time, the timer is reset. Continue to use charts or graphs to document progress. Figure 24–5 shows a patient using a notebook in which his schedule and a log of daily activities are recorded. Videotaping may be useful in helping the patient to view his or her performance realistically.

High-Level Management—Levels VII and VIII

It is usually in the late stages of level VI or early stages of level VII that patients are discharged from inpatient facilities. Prior to discharge, it is crucial to wean the patients from the structure that was so important in the early stages of recovery. As patients become better able to control themselves, control of environment should be

Figure 24–4. Patient motivation and success can be enhanced by using familiar, "real-life" tasks.

lessened. Because patients have some insight into their own strengths and weaknesses, it is important to involve patients in decision making as much as possible. Patients at this level are working to reintegrate into their homes and communities. Therefore, the focus of treatment is to maintain performance while decreasing structure and supervision. Independent work and cooperative work with others is encouraged.

At this level, the restoration of physical function is not significantly different than for patients without brain injury. Because carryover of new learning still takes place at a decreased rate, continued use of external memory aids is useful. The major goal of treatment at this stage is to assist the patient in integrating the cognitive, physical, and emotional skills that are necessary to function in the real world. Judgment, problem solving, and planning are emphasized. In order for the demands of treatment to approximate the demands of the real world, treatment focuses on advanced activities such as community skills, social skills, and daily living skills. For examples of these skills, see Table 24–8. These skills are usually taught by an interdisciplinary team that emphasizes the use of compensatory strategies and the need for the patient to assume responsibility. Honest feedback from the therapist and other patients is

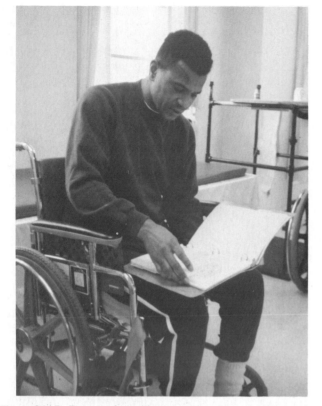

Figure 24–5. The use of cognitive "prostheses" can provide a patient with a source of information regarding what he or she has done, where he or she is expected to be next, and any other information that he or she is not able to remember.

crucial in order for the patient to learn how to function in society with his or her present abilities and limitations. Teaching the patient to give as well as receive feedback is an important aspect of therapy at this point.

Almost all patients who have incurred a moderate to severe brain injury will experience some degree of difficulty with sensorimotor integration. Even those without focal motor deficits will have subtle problems with activities that require speed, flexibility, interlimb coordination, rhythm, and timing. Therapists at Rancho Los Amigos coined the term *robot syndrome* to describe a characteristic set of problems they saw in patients 6 months to 1 year after brain injury.[22] The robot syndrome is characterized by robotlike motion, excessive eating, and sedentary avocational activities. No one factor is thought to cause the syndrome. Rather, residual senso-

Table 24–8 COMPONENTS OF COMMUNITY SKILLS, SOCIAL SKILLS, AND DAILY LIVING SKILLS PROGRAMS

Daily Living	Social Skills	Community Skills
Food preparation	Introductions	Shopping
Housekeeping	Nonverbal communication	Public transport
Money	Assertiveness	Map reading
management	Listening skills	Leisure planning
Meal planning	Giving/receiving feedback	Community
Telephone use		resources
Time management		

rimotor, cognitive, and psychosocial deficits contribute. Beginning around level VII, patients should be involved in a regularly scheduled program of physical activity that strives to expand their movement capabilities and make movement an enjoyable experience. The goal of such treatment is to encourage an active life-style to avoid future complications. It is important to help the patient develop a realistic fitness program that can be followed independently after contact with physical therapy is discontinued. Even for patients who do have significant focal motor deficits, a program designed to promote overall fitness is an important aspect of therapy and should not be neglected.

Patients fortunate enough to recover to level VIII will need vocational and driving services to ensure that they reach their optimal functional level. If physical therapy is needed at this level, it is usually for specific motor disorders and does not differ significantly from the types of therapy provided to individuals without cognitive dysfunction.

The most important thing to keep in mind when treating patients with brain injury is that the overall goal is for the patient to function optimally in society. Cognitive and emotional deficits are usually much more limiting in this regard than are physical deficits. The course of cognitive recovery is somewhat predictable and forms the basis for rehabilitation. In the early stages, increased interaction with the environment is the goal. In the middle stages, emphasis is placed on development of both physical and cognitive endurance. In the later stages, focus is placed on skills necessary for reentry into the community. Of course, the divisions between the stages are artificial and patients move gradually from one level to another. Patients may plateau at any level. Nevertheless, the use of these general guidelines can help to organize your approach to this very complex and challenging group of patients.

ISSUES THAT CROSS ALL LEVELS
Range of Motion

Patients with brain injury tend to lose range of motion (ROM) for numerous reasons, including decreased consciousness, prolonged bed rest, spasticity, **heterotopic ossification,** and lack of voluntary movement. Cognitive deficits may make it difficult for patients to understand and tolerate programs designed to improve ROM. Often, a combination of treatments is necessary. This might include oral medications for spasticity, **nerve** or **motor point blocks, serial casting,** and positioning systems for the bed and/or wheelchair. If all conservative measures fail to return ROM to functional limits, manipulation under general anaesthesia or surgical tendon release may be necessary. Areas of concern include the shoulders, elbows, wrist and hand, hips, and knees, but the most common, and perhaps most functionally disabling deformity, is equinus deformity at the ankle. It has significant functional implications in gait and transfers.

Despite aggressive passive ROM exercises, many patients with head injury develop deformities of the foot and ankle. Casting is often used to treat these deformities. Instead of waiting for the deformities to develop, the use of prophylactic short leg-casts to maintain the foot in a position of dorsiflexion may be warranted. Patients who remain unresponsive for more than 1 or 2 weeks should be considered for casting. Maintenance of dorsiflexion in rigid casts helps prevent secondary impairments associated with equinus deformities. Although the fear of skin breakdown is often cited as a reason to avoid casting unresponsive patients, it is unlikely to occur if the casts are well fabricated. The frequent use of casts for patients with associated lower extremity fractures provides evidence of the safety of casting patients with a low level of consciousness.

If deformities do develop, serial casts may be used to treat them. A typical regimen involves the application of a cast with the involved joint stretched to a near-maximal position. This cast is left on for 1 week, at which time the cast is removed, the joint is stretched and a new cast is applied with the joint in an improved position. This continues until satisfactory range of motion is achieved or until no further progress is made. The decision whether to use serial casts (or inhibitive casts, described below) involves many factors and should be made carefully. For a thorough discussion of the decision-making process, see Leahy.[23]

Casts are also used to improve functional skills. These casts have been referred to by some as "inhibitive" casts or "tone-reducing" casts because of a proposed method by which they affect function. Others prefer to call them simply "short-leg" casts and propose a biomechanical mechanism for their effect. While there is disagreement regarding the mechanism by which they affect the patient, there is significant agreement that such casts can be a valuable adjunct to treatment. Carlson[24] provides a discussion of the possible explanations for the effects of these casts and Cusick[25] provides specific guidelines for fabrication and use. Hands-on experience under the supervision of someone skilled in casting is recommended before attempting to cast patients.

Mobility

It is beyond the scope of this chapter to discuss general mobility issues at length. Physical therapists manage mobility issues such as hemiparesis, ataxia, and so forth for patients with traumatic brain injury much as they would mobility issues for other patients. Principles of learning are combined with neurophysiologic and biomechanical theory to provide opportunities for the patient to practice and problem solve the solution to movement problems. The main difference with patients with head injury is the need to take cognitive issues into consideration. However, it is also important to consider the converse perspective, that is, the effects of mobility on the return of cognitive and perceptual function. It is important to encourage active mobility as soon as possible so that the patient experiences the consequences of his or her attempts at movement. This may include early rolling for low-level patients, supervised wheelchair propulsion for mid-level patients, and assisted ambulation for any patient that appears to have the physical ability to walk. Power wheelchairs should be considered for patients with significant movement deficits. Although special modifications to the chair and exten-

sive training may be needed, the possibility of independent mobility, even if only indoors, may make a major difference in the patient's status (see Chapter 31). Patients with improved mobility have more opportunities to experience cognitive and perceptual challenges. This may result in improved function.

Documentation

Therapists working with patients with brain injury must be accurate and precise in recording findings so the patient's overall status (physical and cognitive) is documented. For example, some patients may be at a very high physical level, able to walk without physical assistance. However, if this same patient requires supervision because he or she is unable to find his or her way from place to place, or has poor safety awareness, then it is important that the documentation *not* reflect independent ambulation. Furthermore, the entire spectrum of physical activities that is typical for young adults should be considered. Independent ambulation on level surfaces and stairs does not fulfill the requirements for most young adults. Athletic activities, dancing, and other hobbies should be evaluated and practiced so that the patient can return to as full a life-style as possible.

Goal Setting and Outcome Prediction

This is probably the most difficult aspect of working with patients with traumatic brain injury. From the acute stage through rehabilitation, there are very few reliable indicators of eventual outcome. Nevertheless, it is important to attempt to set realistic goals, and to modify them as necessary. Hopefully, with experience, therapists learn to identify trends and make more accurate predictions. In order for this to occur, therapists need to make concentrated attempts to look for such trends and the likelihood of success is increased with interdisciplinary cooperation. Of particular interest is the possibility of combining the results of formal neuropsychologic testing with functional information gathered by physical, occupational, and speech therapists to predict learning potential and functional outcome. Efforts to set goals and plan treatments for a patient with head injury are strengthened by a thorough understanding of his or her learning capacity. Ideally, we want patients to be able to perform a wide variety of tasks consistently, automatically, and in a variety of situations. However, if it were determined that a particular patient had very little ability to generalize information from one situation to another, then it might be reasonable to practice very specific skills in the environment in which the patient would need to use them. Although this might be considered to be a very low level of functioning, it may optimize that particular patient's potential.

There is much to be learned about physical therapy for patients with head injury. Most studies examining motor learning have not included subjects with head injury. Most studies examining learning in patients with head injury have not focused on motor skills. Guidelines for the application of motor learning principles to patients with head injury are available but further research is needed.[26]

Issues related to outcome in head injury rehabilitation

are extremely complex. Although we are able to identify early recovery patterns in a very general sense, it is significantly more difficult to characterize long-term outcome. Researchers at the University of Virginia studied head injury survivors at 3 months postinjury and found that 4 percent were vegetative, 8 percent were severely disabled, 22 percent were moderately disabled, and 66 percent had made a good recovery.[27] It is important to note, however, that studies such as this one tend to look at recovery from a point of view that reflects a medical perspective of "recovery." A recent edition of the *Journal of Head Trauma Rehabilitation* was devoted to the very complex issue of "Quality, Outcome, and Value."[28] In this age of fierce competition for the health care dollar, the availability of lengthy and expensive rehabilitation can no longer be taken for granted, even for those with health insurance. A central question in the administration of head injury services today is "Who is the customer?" Payers, families, professionals, and head injury survivors may have different perceptions about what constitutes a successful outcome. Being able to live independently, have earned income, and manage daily activities and affairs are usually outcomes that survivors strive for. Many are able to reach this level of independence . . . and many are not. At this point, our ability to predict who will and who will not is limited. The field of head injury rehabilitation provides a wealth of challenging questions for researchers from many fields.

SUMMARY

Patients with moderate or severe head injury experience multiple and complex problems that significantly affect all aspects of their lives. An interdisciplinary team that emphasizes a functional approach provides the best chance for the patient's success. Physical therapists treating patients with head injury employ traditional physical therapy approaches to movement deficits but must make modifications and have flexible priorities due to the patients' cognitive, perceptual, and emotional deficits.

QUESTIONS FOR REVIEW

1. Discuss how premorbid status, primary brain injury, and secondary brain injury influence the final outcome in patients with traumatic head injury.

2. Describe local, polar, and diffuse brain injury in terms of areas commonly affected and the most common mechanisms of injury. Is it possible for one patient to have more than one type?

3. What is meant by "secondary injury?" Give three examples of secondary brain injury.

4. Describe how each of the following rating scales is utilized: Glasgow Coma Scale, Rancho Los Amigos Levels of Cognitive Functioning, Rappaport's Disability Rating Scale, Glasgow Outcome Scale.

5. List and describe three procedures that augment the standard neurologic examination in diagnosing and prognosticating patients with head injury.

6. Describe the role of the physical therapist in the acute management of patients with head injury.

7. How would a physical therapy treatment plan need to be modified for a patient in the stage of post-traumatic amnesia?

8. What is the significance of a patient's cognitive and behavioral status in relation to his or her physical therapy goals?

9. List and describe key features of physical therapy interventions designed for patients with low, middle, and high levels of function after head injury.

10. How does knowledge of a patient's ability or inability to learn new information affect a physical therapist's treatment plan?

REFERENCES

1. Interagency Head Injury Task Force Report, National Institute of Neurological Disorders and Stroke. National Institutes of Health, Bethesda, MD, 1989.
2. Miller, JD, Pentland, B, and Berrol, S: Early evaluation and management. In Rosenthal, M, et al. (eds): Rehabilitation of the Adult and Child with Traumatic Brain Injury, ed 2. FA Davis, Philadelphia, 1990.
3. Adams, JH: Head injury. In Adams, JH, Corsellis, JAN, and Duchen, LW (eds): Greenfield's Neuropathology, ed 4. Edward Arnold, London, 1984, p 85.
4. Katz, DI: Neuropathology and neurobehavioral recovery from closed head injury. Journal of Head Trauma Rehabilitation 7:1, 1992.
5. Jennett, B and Teasdale, G: Management of Head Injuries. FA Davis, Philadelphia, 1981, p 78.
6. Teasdale, G, Knill-Jones, K, and Vander Sande, JP: Observer variability in assessing impaired consciousness and coma. J Neurol Neurosurg Psychiatry 41:603, 1978.
7. Rehabilitation of the Head Injured Adult: Comprehensive Physical Management. Professional Staff Association, Rancho Los Amigos Hospital, Downey, CA, 1979.

8. Rappaport, M, et al: Disability rating scale for severe head trauma: coma to community. Arch Phys Med Rehabil 63:118, 1982.
9. Jennett, B, et al: Disability after severe head injury: observations on the use of the Glasgow Outcome Scale. J Neurol Neurosurg Psychiatry 44:285, 1981.
10. Thatcher, RW, et al: Comparisons between EEG, CT scan, and Glasgow Coma Scale predictors of recovery of function in neurotrauma patients. In Zappulla, RA (ed): Windows on the Brain: Neuropsychology's Technological Frontiers. New York Academy of Science, New York, 1991, p
11. French, BN and Dublin, AB: The value of computerized tomography in the management of 1000 consecutive head injuries. Surg Neurol 7:171, 1977.
12. Jenkins, A, et al: Brain lesions detected by magnetic resonance imaging in mild and severe head injury. Lancet ii:445, 1986.
13. Langfitt, TW, et al: Computerized tomography, magnetic resonance imaging, and positron emission tomography in the study of brain trauma: preliminary observations. J Neurosurg 64:760, 1986.
14. Wilson, JTL and Wyper, D: Neuroimaging and neuropsychological functioning following closed head injury: CT, MRI, and SPECT. Journal of Head Trauma Rehabilitation 7:29, 1992.

15. Miller, JD, Pentland, B, and Berrol, S: Early evaluation and management. In Rosenthal, M, et al (eds): Rehabilitation of the Adult and Child with Traumatic Brain Injury, ed 2. FA Davis, Philadelphia, 1990, p 45.
16. Jennett, B and Teasdale, G: Management of Head Injuries. FA Davis, Philadelphia, 1981, p 80.
17. Brooks, DN: Cognitive Deficits. In Rosenthal, M, et al (eds): Rehabilitation of the Adult and Child with Traumatic Brain Injury, ed 2. FA Davis, Philadelphia, 1990, p 163.
18. Rappaport, M, et al: Head injury outcome up to ten years later. Arch Phys Med Rehabil 70:885, 1989.
19. Ansell, BJ: Slow-to-recover brain-injured patients: rationale for treatment. J Speech Hear Res 34:1017, 1991.
20. Wood, RL: Critical analysis of the concept of sensory stimulation for patients in vegetative states. Brain Inj 5:401, 1991.
21. Howard, M: Behavior management in the acute care rehabilitation setting. Journal of Head Trauma Rehabilitation 3:14, 1988.
22. Mercer, L and Boch, M: Residual sensorimotor deficits in the adult head-injured patient. Phys Ther 63:1988, 1983.
23. Leahy, P: Precasting worksheet—an assessment tool. Phys Ther 68:72, 1988.
24. Carlson, SJ: A neurophysiological analysis of inhibitive casting. Physical and Occupational Therapy in Pediatrics 4:31, 1984.
25. Cusick, B: Serial Casts: Their Use in the Management of Spasticity Induced Foot Deformity. Words at Work, Lexington, KY, 1987.
26. Riolo-Quinn, L: Motor learning considerations in treating brain injured patients. Neurol Rep 14:12, 1990.
27. Rimel, RW, et al: Characteristics of the head-injured patient. In Rosenthal, M, et al. (eds): Rehabilitation of the Adult and Child with Traumatic Brain Injury, ed 2. FA Davis, Philadelphia, 1990, p 15.
28. Malkmus, DD and Evans, RW (eds): Quality, outcome, and value. Journal of Head Trauma Rehabilitation 7:4, 1992.
29. Mills, V and Wusteney, E: Physical therapy and the rehabilitation of patients with cerebrovascular accidents. In Kaplan, P, et al (eds): Stroke Rehabilitation. Butterworth, Stoneham, MA, 1986.

SUPPLEMENTAL READINGS

Bergen, A and Colangelo, C: Positioning the Client with Central Nervous System Dysfunction. Valhalla Rehab Publications, Valhalla, New York, 1985.
Eames, P (ed): Management of behavior disorders. Journal of Head Trauma Rehabilitation 3, 1988.
Friedman, WA: Head injuries. Ciba Clinical Symposia 35, 1983.
Finger, S, et al (eds): Brain Injury and Recovery. Plenum Press, New York, 1988.
Griffith, E and Lemberg, S: Sexuality and the Person with Traumatic Brain Injury. FA Davis, Philadelphia, 1993.
Horn, LJ and Cope, DN (eds): Traumatic brain injury. Phys Med Rehabil 3, 1989.

Katz, DI and Alexander, MP (eds): The neurology of head injury. Journal of Head Trauma Rehabilitation 7, 1992.
Kreutzer, JS and Wehman, P (eds): Community Integration Following Traumatic Brain Injury. Paul H Brookes, Baltimore, 1990.
Kreutzer, JS and Wehman, PH (eds): Cognitive Rehabilitation for Persons with Traumatic Brain Injury: A Functional Approach. Paul H Brookes, Baltimore, 1991.
Levin, HS, et al: Neurobehavioral Consequences of Closed Head Injury. Oxford University Press, New York, 1982.
Zasler, ND, et al: Coma stimulation and coma recovery: a critical review. NeuroRehabilitation 1:33–40, 1991.

GLOSSARY

Autodestructive cellular phenomenon: A series of events that occur in the brain due to trauma-induced changes in cellular membranes.

Coma: A state in which there is no eye opening (even to pain), failure to obey commands, and inability to utter recognizable words.

Diffuse brain injury: Widely scattered shearing of axons which, though not intense in any one location, causes dramatic disability as a result of its cumulative effect.

Herniation: Protrusion of an organ or part of an organ through a surrounding wall or cavity. In the brain, several types of herniation occur. The following herniations are listed in order of progressing severity.

Central herniation: Protrusion of the midbrain and pons through the tentorial notch.

Tonsillar herniation: Protrusion of the medulla and cerebellar tonsils through the foramen magnum.

Uncal herniation: Protrusion of the uncus and hippocampal gyrus of the brain through the tentorial notch.

Heterotopic ossification: Abnormal bone growth in soft tissue that may result in loss of range of motion. In patients with THI, the most common locations of heterotopic ossification are the shoulder, elbow, and hip.

Hypoxic-ischemic injury (HII): Brain damage that results from arterial hypotension and hypoxemia and is complicated by raised intracranial pressure, cerebral vasospasm, brain edema, and combinations of these, as well as an impaired ability of the vessels of the brain to autoregulate.

Intracranial hematoma: A collection of blood within the cranium that results from leakage from a blood vessel.

Epidural hematoma: Extravascular blood mass located between the dura and the skull.

Intracerebral hematoma: Extravascular blood mass located within the brain tissue.

Subdural hematoma: Extravascular blood mass located beneath the dura.

Intracranial pressure: Measure of pressure inside the cranium.

Local brain damage: Injury localized to the area of the brain underlying the site of impact. Produces predictable neurologic signs according to the specific location.

Mass effect: The effect of a space-occupying lesion within the closed environment of the cranium. Is often used to refer to tumors, but in the case of patients with head trauma, it refers to hematomas that result in further brain damage as a result of pressure and shifting of the brain.

Motor point block: Administration of a local anesthetic to a motor point within a muscle. Allows for more specificity than a nerve block.

Nerve block: Administration of a local anesthetic to a peripheral nerve for the purpose of decreasing spasticity.

Obstructive hydrocephalus: Enlargement of the ventricles of the brain caused by an impairment of flow and absorption of cerebrospinal fluid.

Persistent vegetative state: Long-lasting state of decreased consciousness characterized by eye opening and return of sleep-wake cycles, but without any purposeful or meaningful behavior.

Polar brain damage: Injury that results from contact between the surfaces of the brain and the cranium. Most commonly affects the frontal and temporal lobes.

Posttraumatic amnesia (PTA): State during the time between injury and when the patient is able to form memories of ongoing events.

Posttraumatic epilepsy: Seizure disorder that develops following head trauma.

Serial casting: Repeated application and removal of casts for the purpose of increasing passive range of motion.

CHAPTER

Burns 25

Marlys J. Staley
Reginald L. Richard
Jeffrey E. Falkel

OBJECTIVES

1. Describe the anatomy and physiology of the skin as an organ in a healthy state and in the damaged condition that occurs with a burn injury.
2. Describe the pathology, symptoms, and sequelae of burn injuries.
3. Explain the treatment for a patient with various depths and extent of burn injury in relation to medical, surgical, and rehabilitation management.
4. Describe the consequence of contracture formation following burn injury and the treatment of this condition.
5. List the guidelines for management of hypertrophic scars.
6. Outline the necessary skin care following burn wound healing.

Burn injuries are one of the major health problems of the industrial world, and the United States annually records the highest incidence of burn injury.[1] Survey data have indicated that more than 2 million persons are burned annually. One fourth of these require medical attention, and approximately 10,000 deaths are related to burn injury.[2,3] In addition, it has been estimated that there is a one in 70 chance of an American being burned in his or her lifetime seriously enough to require hospitalization.[1]

Although these data dramatically illustrate the extent of the health care problem caused by burn injury, recent medical advances have significantly reduced the number of deaths from burn injuries and have improved the prognosis and functional abilities of surviving patients.[3] The survival rate has improved annually due to improved resuscitation techniques, the acute medical and surgical care that are now available, and continued research into the management and care of the burned patient. As a result of improvement in care, treatment, and survival of burned patients, more physical therapists will become responsible for treating these patients, for a significant portion of their rehabilitation, in settings other than a hospital burn unit (e.g., outpatient clinics, community hospitals).

This chapter will introduce the problems that occur with the different depths of burn injury and the complications that can result from thermal destruction of the skin. Current techniques used in the medical, surgical, and rehabilitative management of the patient who has been burned will be described. For more in-depth information regarding the assessment and treatment of the patient with a burn injury, the reader is referred to additional sources.[1,4-7]

EPIDEMIOLOGY OF BURN INJURIES

Although the morbidity and mortality of patients with burns has dramatically decreased in recent years, the epidemiology of burns remains basically the same. There is a peak incidence of burn injury in children 1 to 5 years of age, primarily due to scalds from hot liquids.[3,8] The primary cause of burn injury in adolescents and adults is accidents with flammable liquids. Men between the ages of 17 and 30 years of age have the highest incidence of injury.[1,9] Fires that occur in homes and other structural dwellings are responsible for less than 5 percent of the hospital admissions for burn injuries, but account for nearly 45 percent of the burn-related deaths in this country.[1] Most of these deaths are due to smoke or inhalation injury. The number of burn-related accidents has decreased somewhat because of better preventative measures such as smoke detectors, education, and more stringent fire codes.

A major reason for the improved prognosis and survival of patients with severe burn injury is the increased number of specialized burn centers.[3] The advent of the burn center and the concentrated care and research that has been generated by these facilities has improved the prognosis and survival of the most severely burned patients, as well as reducing the average hospital stay in most cases.

The American Burn Association has established criteria for admission to a designated burn center:[10]

1. Partial- and full-thickness burns greater than 10 percent of total body surface area (TBSA) in patients under 10 or older than 50 years of age.
2. Partial- and full-thickness burns greater than 20 percent TBSA in other age groups.
3. Partial- and full-thickness burns involving the hands, feet, face, perineum, or skin overlying major joints.
4. Full-thickness burns greater than 5 percent TBSA in any age group.
5. Significant electrical burns, including lightning injury.
6. Significant chemical burns.
7. Inhalation injury.
8. Burn injury in patients with preexisting illness that could complicate management.
9. Burn injury in patients who will require special social and emotional or long-term rehabilitative support, including cases involving suspected child abuse.

The American Burn Association specifies that any burn patient in whom concomitant trauma poses an increased risk of morbidity or mortality may be treated initially in a trauma center until stable before transfer to a burn center.

There are 138 specialized centers for burn care consisting of approximately 1,700 burn-care beds in this country today.[11] Twenty years ago, there were only 12 specialized burn centers.

A burn center is staffed by specialists—physicians, nurses, physical therapists, occupational therapists, dieticians, psychiatrists, psychologists, social workers, child life and vocational rehabilitation specialists, and other support personnel—who direct all their energies toward the care, treatment, and rehabilitation of the burned patient. Each member is an integral part of the team, and the most effective burn centers are successful because of their team approach to the care of each patient.

SKIN ANATOMY AND BURN WOUND PATHOLOGY

The skin is the largest organ of the body, comprising approximately 15 percent of body weight. Anatomically, the skin consists of two distinct layers of tissue: the **epidermis,** which is the outermost layer exposed to the environment, and the deeper layer, termed the **dermis.** A third layer involved in the anatomic consideration of the skin is the subcutaneous fat cell layer directly under the dermis and above muscle fascial layers. These three layers can be seen in Figure 25–1. The epidermis performs several vital functions. The stratum corneum is responsible for the waterproof characteristic of the skin and serves to protect the body from infection. The stratum granulosum is the layer responsible for water retention and heat regulation. The stratum spinosum adds a layer of protection for the underlying basal layer. Cells

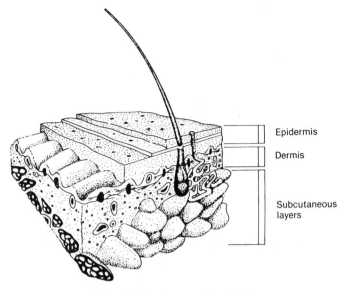

Figure 25–1. Cross section of skin.

in the basal layer enable the epidermis to regenerate. This layer also contains melanocytes, which determine the coloration of the epidermis. The undersurface of the epidermis that contacts the dermis consists of an extensive series of epidermal ridges that serve to increase the surface area between the epidermis and the dermis. These ridges are needed to overcome the frictional forces that skin is exposed to in daily activity. Lack of these ridges in the healed burn wound will result in abrasion and poor adherence of the new epidermal tissue when it comes in contact with clothing or other surfaces and thus is critical in the healing and recovery phases.

The dermis is the layer of skin that contains a network of blood vessels, lymphatics, nerve endings, collagen, and elastic fibers. It also encloses the epidermal appendages (sweat and sebaceous glands, and hair follicles), which provide a deeper source of epidermal cells. The dermis is 20 to 30 times thicker than the epidermis. It is comprised primarily of interwoven collagen and elastic fibers, which provide the skin with tensile strength and resistance to deformation. The predominantly parallel orientation of normal collagen in the dermis is different than the whorls of collagen typically seen in the scar tissue that results from burn injury.[12] The dermis is attached to the subcutaneous tissue by an irregular interlacing network of fibrous connective tissue.

In addition to the functions outlined above, the skin is important in the conservation of body fluids, temperature regulation, excretion of sweat and electrolytes, secretion of oils that lubricate the skin, vitamin D synthesis, sensation, and cosmetic appearance and identity. As a result of burn injury, some or all of these functions may be impaired and/or lost and the patient's defense mechanisms will be compromised.

One basic pathophysiologic consideration in the burn injury is the destruction of vascular integrity. This results in the formation of edema with the concomitant loss of protein-rich intravascular fluid into the interstitial spaces.[6] Edema formation occurs in the area of the burn as well as in adjacent tissues. One of the major concerns of the physical therapist on the burn team is that patients tend to protect the injured part by not moving, due to pain. This results in an even greater accumulation of fluid in the area and may lead to fibrosis of joints. From the protein-rich exudate, collagen fibers can form adhesions that will limit further range of motion (ROM) and movement of the involved tissues if physical therapy intervention is not implemented.[6]

The Burn Wound

The amount of skin destruction is based on the temperature to which the skin is exposed and the length of time the tissue is exposed to heat.[3,13] The type of insult (i.e., flame, liquid, chemical, or electrical) also will affect the amount of tissue destruction. A tremendous amount of heat is not required to cause damage. At temperatures below 44°C (111°F), local tissue damage will not occur unless the exposure is for prolonged periods. In the temperature range between 44°C and 51°C (111°F to 124°F), the rate of cellular death doubles with each degree rise in temperature, and short exposures will lead to cell destruction.[13] At temperatures in excess of 51°C (124°F), the exposure time needed to damage tissue is extremely brief.

The burn wound consists of three zones, shown in Figure 25–2.[13,14] In the zone of coagulation, cells are irreversibly damaged and skin death occurs. The zone of stasis contains injured cells that may die within 24 to 48 hours without specialized treatment. It is in this zone of stasis that infection and/or drying of the wound will result in conversion of potentially salvageable tissue to completely necrotic tissue, if satisfactory perfusion is not accomplished. Finally, the zone of hyperemia is the site of minimal cell damage, and the tissue here should recover within 7 days with no lasting ill-effects.[13,14]

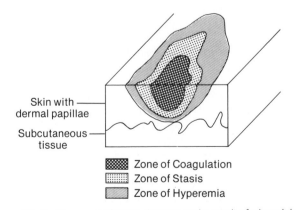

Figure 25–2. The zones of tissue damage as the result of a burn injury. The zone of coagulation is the site of irreversible skin death. The zone of hyperemia is the site of minimal cell involvement and early spontaneous recovery. The zone of stasis involves conversion of the wound from viable tissue to necrotic tissue due to infection. (From Artz, et al,[5] p 25, with permission.)

Classifications of Burn Injury

Until recently, burn injuries were classified according to their severity as first-, second-, and third-degree. Although these classifications still may be used by the lay public, most medical literature now classifies burn injuries by the depth of skin tissue destroyed.[3,13,15,16] The degree to which a burn causes skin damage depends on many factors, including the duration and intensity of heat, skin thickness and area exposed, vascularity, age, and a person's pigmentation.

The different classifications of burn wounds will present different clinical pictures and each can change dramatically during the course of treatment. In addition to the amount of direct tissue damage from a burn, a patient's metabolic, physiologic, and psychologic condition will greatly affect the patient's clinical status. This section will present the general clinical signs and symptoms seen in each of the burn wound classifications.

Superficial Burn

In this burn, cell damage occurs only to the epidermis. The classic sunburn is the best example of a **superficial burn.** Clinically, the skin appears red or erythematous. The erythema is a result of epidermal damage and dermal irritation but there is no injury to the dermal tissue. There is diffusion of inflammatory mediators from sites of epidermal damage and release of vasoactive substances from mast cells.[17–19] The surface of a superficial burn is dry. Blisters will be absent but slight edema may be apparent. Following a superficial burn there is usually a delay in the development of pain, at which point the area becomes tender to the touch.

In the absence of infection, the inflammatory reaction will cease and the injured epidermis will peel off or **desquamate** in 2 to 3 days.[20] Skin healing is spontaneous, that is, skin will heal on its own, and no scar will be present.

Superficial Partial-Thickness Burn

With a superficial, **partial-thickness burn,** as seen in Figure 25–3, damage occurs through the epidermis and into the upper layers of the dermis. The epidermal layer is destroyed completely but the dermal layer sustains only mild to moderate damage. The most common sign of a superficial, partial-thickness burn is the presence of intact blisters over the area that has been injured.

Although the internal environment of a blister is felt to be sterile, it has been shown that blister fluid contains substances that increase the inflammatory response and retard the healing process and it is recommended that blisters be evacuated.[21–23] Healing will occur more rapidly if the skin is removed and antibiotic agents applied.

Once blisters have been removed, the surface appearance of the burn area will be moist. The wound will be bright red because the dermis is inflamed. The wound will **blanch,** which means that if pressure is exerted

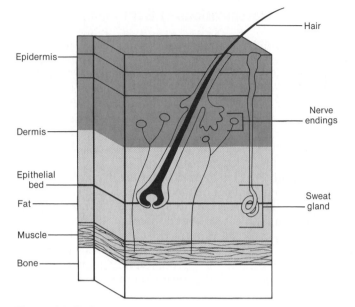

Figure 25–3. Superficial partial-thickness burn. (From Malick and Carr,[79] p 3, with permission.)

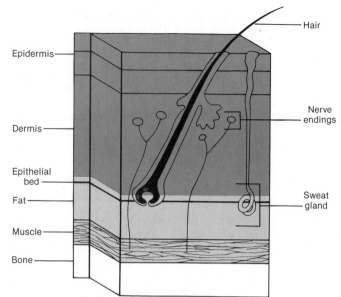

Figure 25–4. Deep partial-thickness burn. (From Malick and Carr,[79] p 4, with permission.)

against the tissue with a finger, a white spot appears due to displacement of blood in the capillaries under pressure. On release of pressure, the white area will demonstrate good capillary refill. Edema will be minimal.

This type of burn is extremely painful as a result of the irritation of the nerve endings contained in the dermis. When the wound is open, the patient will be highly sensitive to changes in air temperature, exposure to air, and light touch. In addition to pain, fever may be present if areas become infected.

As the burned tissue begins to heal, the area will develop a gelatin-like exudate that eventually will peel off, like the tissue that undergoes desquamation with a sunburn. This exudate is a coagulum of the topical antibiotic used to prevent infection and the serum that seeps from the wound as a result of the insult to the capillary integrity.

Superficial partial-thickness burns heal without surgical intervention, by means of epithelial cell production and migration from the wound's periphery and the surviving skin appendages. The new epithelium performs the barrier function of the skin and complete healing should occur in 7 to 21 days. There may be some residual skin color change due to destruction of melanocytes, but scarring is minimal.

Deep Partial-Thickness Burn

This burn injury, shown in Figure 25–4, involves destruction of the epidermis accompanied by severe damage to the dermal layer. Most of the nerve endings, hair follicles, and sweat glands will be injured, as most of the dermis is destroyed.

Deep partial-thickness burns appear as a mixed red or waxy white color. The red color is due to hemoglobin fixation within the damaged tissue. The deeper the injury, the more white it will appear. Capillary refill will

be sluggish following the application of pressure on the wound.

The surface usually is wet from broken blisters and alteration of the dermal vascular network, which leaks plasma fluid. Edema is moderate. There is a large amount of evaporative water loss through the area (15 to 20 times normal), because of tissue and vascular destruction.[3,13] The deep partial-thickness burn is a painful injury because not all the nerve endings have been destroyed. Sensation is intact to pressure but diminished to light touch or soft pinprick.

Healing occurs through scar formation and reepithelialization. By definition, in the partial-thickness burn the dermis is only partially destroyed; therefore, some epidermal cells remain viable within the surviving epidermal appendages and serve as a source of new skin growth.

The depth of a deep partial-thickness injury is difficult to determine, so allowing the wound to demarcate during the first few days is necessary. Demarcation becomes evident after several days as the dead tissue begins to loosen. Hair follicles that penetrate into the deeper dermal regions below the burn level remain viable. Preservation of hair follicles and new hair growth will indicate a deep partial-thickness burn rather than a deeper injury and there is a correspondingly greater potential for spontaneous healing. Factors that determine which epidermal structures survive and which die include the thickness of the skin in a particular location and/or the distance of the area from the source of heat.

Deep partial-thickness burns that are allowed to heal spontaneously will have a thin epithelium and may lack the usual number of sebaceous glands to keep the skin moist. New tissue usually appears dry and scaly, and is itchy and easily abraded. Creams are necessary to artificially lubricate the new surface. Sensation and the number of active sweat glands will be diminished and, depending on the depth of injury, may remain reduced.

A deep partial-thickness burn generally will heal in 3 to 5 weeks if it does not get infected. It is critical to keep the wound free of infection as infection can convert a deep partial-thickness burn into a deeper injury. The development of hypertrophic scars and keloids are a frequent consequence of a deep partial-thickness burn.

Full-Thickness Burn

In a **full-thickness burn,** as seen in Figure 25–5, all of the epidermal and dermal layers are destroyed completely. In addition, the subcutaneous fat layer may be damaged to some extent.

A full-thickness injury is characterized by a hard, parchmentlike **eschar.** Eschar is dead tissue that covers a full-thickness burn and is a coagulum of plasma and necrotic cells. Eschar feels dry and leathery to the touch, as well as rigid and nonpliable. The color of eschar can vary from black to white, the latter indicates total ischemia of the area. Frequently, thrombosis of superficial blood vessels is apparent and no blanching is observed.

Hair follicles are completely destroyed and so body hairs pull out easily. Likewise, all nerve endings in the dermal tissue are destroyed and the wound will be anesthetic. However, a patient may experience a significant amount of pain from areas of partial-thickness burn that normally surround a full-thickness injury.

Another major problem from deep burns is the damage to the peripheral vascular system. The full-thickness burn is characterized within 24 hours by having complete vascular occlusion and significantly marked edema. Due to the destruction of dermal and epidermal tissue, and the increased amount of fluid loss and edema, the extravascular spaces become filled with fluid that will restrict and even constrict deep vascular branches to the point of occlusion of blood flow. Because eschar does not have the elastic quality of normal skin, edema that forms in such an area can cause

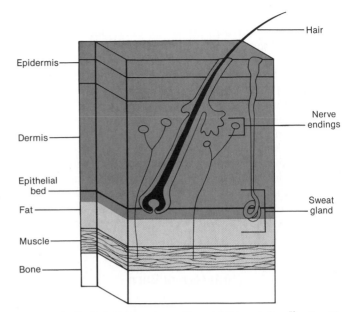

Figure 25–5. Full-thickness burn. (From Malick and Carr,[79] p 5, with permission.)

compression of underlying vasculature. If this compression is not relieved, it may lead to eventual occlusion with possible necrosis of the tissue.[3,24] To maintain vascular flow, an **escharotomy** may be necessary. An escharotomy is a midlateral incision of the eschar.[3,24] Figure 25–6 shows an escharotomy and the edema that forces the incision line open. Following an escharotomy, pulses are monitored frequently. If the escharotomy is successful, there will be an immediate improvement in the peripheral blood flow, as demonstrated by normal pulses distal to the wound, and by normal temperature, sensation, and movement in the distal extremity.

Because of the lack of viable tissue and the amount of the eschar, the risk of infection is increased. If infection

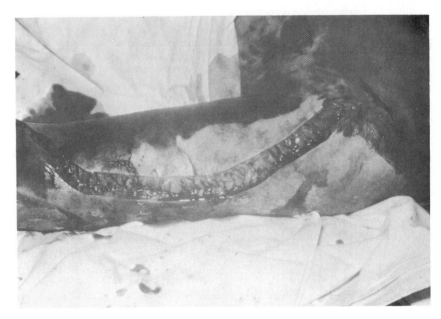

Figure 25–6. Escharotomy of the upper extremity. (From DiGregorio,[6] p 19, with permission.)

is not controlled, a full-thickness burn can convert to a deeper injury with additional cell death and necrosis of the underlying tissue. This potential complication emphasizes the need for careful monitoring of infection, the use of antibiotics, and the treatment of a burned patient in a specialized burn center.

While it may be difficult to differentiate a deep-partial from a full-thickness burn in the early postburn period, the differences will become evident after several days, as the eschar begins to loosen. With a full-thickness burn, there are no sites available for the reepithelialization of the wound. All epithelial cells have been destroyed and skin grafting of tissue over the wound will be necessary. Grafting will be discussed in detail in the section on surgical intervention in the treatment of burns.

Subdermal Burn

An additional category of burn, the subdermal burn, involves complete destruction of all tissue from the epidermis down to and including the subcutaneous tissue (Fig. 25–7). Muscle and bone may be damaged. This type of burn occurs through prolonged contact with a flame or hot liquid and routinely occurs as a result of contact with electricity. Extensive surgical and therapeutic management will be needed to return a patient to some degree of function.

ELECTRICAL BURN

The signs and symptoms of an electrical burn may vary according to the type of current, intensity of the current, and the area of the body the electric current passes through.[25] A burn results from the passage of an electric current through the body after the skin has made contact with an electrical source. Electric current follows the course of least resistance offered by various tissues.

Nerves, followed by blood vessels, offer the least resistance. Bone offers the most resistance.

Usually, there will be an entrance and an exit wound. The entrance wound is located where the current came in contact with the body. The entrance wound will be charred and depressed, and many times, will be smaller than the exit wound. The skin will appear yellow in coloration, and be ischemic. An exit wound typically will appear as if there has been an explosion out of the tissue at the site. It will be dry in appearance.[25] Tissues underlying the pathway of the current may be damaged due to the heat that has developed. An extremity or area that appears viable after an injury may become necrotic and gangrenous in a few days. Arteries may undergo spasm and there may be necrosis of the vascular wall. The blood supply to the surrounding tissues, including muscle, may be altered. Damaged muscle will feel soft. Because the course of tissue destruction is unpredictable, there may be unequal and uneven muscle damage.[25] Time will be required to determine which tissues will remain viable and which will not.

There are other consequences of electricity passing through the body. One of the cardiac effects is arrhythmia, and possible causes of death from electrical burns are ventricular fibrillation or respiratory arrest.[3,26]

There also may be renal consequences leading to renal failure as a result of excessive protein breakdown and the shock that follows a major trauma. One of the most severe complications of electric current damage to the kidney is acute tubular damage and eventual necrosis. Breakdown and catabolic activity of muscle myoglobin from the injured muscle tissue is the most likely cause of tubular failure.[3,25] Spinal cord damage occurs occasionally.[3] It is usually incomplete and is not necessarily associated with the path of the current or any particular vertebral fracture. Clinically, these patients will have spastic paresis but may or may not have any sensory pathway changes over concomitant areas of spasticity.[25] Many times the spinal cord and nervous system changes will not manifest themselves immediately, and may take months or years to become symptomatic.

EXTENT OF BURNED AREA

There are two major factors to consider when determining the seriousness and extent of a burn injury. The first is the percentage of the total body surface area that has been burned. In addition, the depth of the burned areas needs to be assessed. To allow for a rapid estimate of the percentage of total body surface area burned, Pulaski and Tennison developed the **rule of nines.**[27] The rule of nines divides the body surface area into segments that are approximately 9 percent of the total. Figure 25–8 shows the percentages using the rule of nines for adults. Lund and Browder altered the percentages of the body surface area for children to accommodate for growth of the different body segments and allow for a more accurate means of determining the extent of burn injury.[28] Figure 25–9 shows the relative percentages of burned areas for children and adults according to a mod-

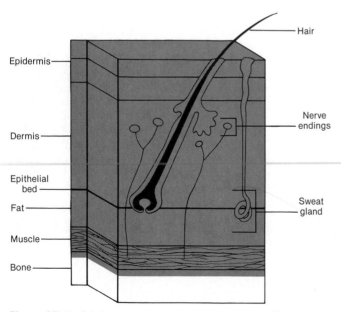

Figure 25–7. Subdermal burn. (From Malick and Carr,[79] p 6, with permission.)

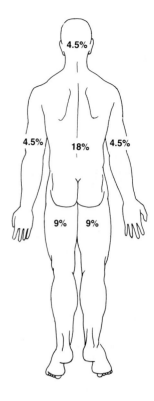
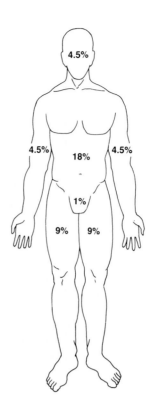

Figure 25–8. Rule of nines for determining percentage of body surface area burned in adults.

Burn Estimate and Diagram
Age vs Area

Initial Evaluation

Cause of burn_____

Date of Burn_____

Time of Burn_____

Age_____

Sex_____

Weight_____

Date of Admission_____

Signature_____

Date_____

Burn Diagram

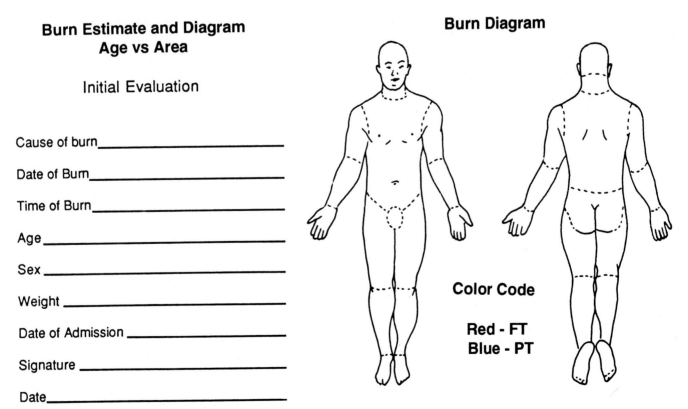

Color Code

Red - FT
Blue - PT

Figure 25–9. Modified Lund and Browder chart for determination of percentage of body surface area burned for various ages. (Courtesy Shriners Burns Institute, Cincinnati Unit.)

Area	Birth 1 yr.	1-4 yrs.	5-9 yrs.	10-14 yrs.	15 yrs.	Adult	PT	FT	Total	Donor Areas
Head	19	17	13	11	9	7				
Neck	2	2	2	2	2	2				
Ant. Trunk	13	13	13	13	13	13				
Post. Trunk	13	13	13	13	13	13				
R. Buttock	2 1/2	2 1/2	2 1/2	2 1/2	2 1/2	2 1/2				
L. Buttock	2 1/2	2 1/2	2 1/2	2 1/2	2 1/2	2 1/2				
Genitalia	1	1	1	1	1	1				
R.U. Arm	4	4	4	4	4	4				
L.U. Arm	4	4	4	4	4	4				
R.L. Arm	3	3	3	3	3	3				
L.L. Arm	3	3	3	3	3	3				
R. Hand	2 1/2	2 1/2	2 1/2	2 1/2	2 1/2	2 1/2				
L. Hand	2 1/2	2 1/2	2 1/2	2 1/2	2 1/2	2 1/2				
R. Thigh	5 1/2	6 1/2	8	8 1/2	9	9 1/2				
L. Thigh	5 1/2	6 1/2	8	8 1/2	9	9 1/2				
R. Leg	5	5	5 1/2	6	6 1/2	7				
L. Leg	5	5	5 1/2	6	6 1/2	7				
R. Foot	3 1/2	3 1/2	3 1/2	3 1/2	3 1/2	3 1/2				
L. Foot	3 1/2	3 1/2	3 1/2	3 1/2	3 1/2	3 1/2				
						Total				

Key: FT - Full Thickness
PT - Part Thickness

Figure 25–9. (Continued)

ified Lund and Browder formula. Although this formula provides an accurate assessment of TBSA, it may not be practical in the emergency triage of a burned patient and the rule of nines may be used in that situation.

SECONDARY COMPLICATIONS OF BURN INJURY

Depending on the extent of burn injury, the depth of the burn, and the type of burn, there may be secondary systemic complications. In addition, the health, age, and psychologic status of a patient who becomes burned will affect these complications. This section will highlight some systemic complications a patient may experience following a significant burn injury.

Infection

Infection, in conjunction with organ system failure, is a leading cause of mortality from burns.[29,30] The rich vascularity of the inflammatory phase of an acute burn, coupled with the vast amount of edema formed and the destruction of defense mechanisms against bacteria, make the wound very susceptible to infection. Even with the use of antibiotics, as one bacteria is destroyed, another organism, resistant to the medication used, infects the wound area. Some virulent strains of *pseudomonas aeruginosa* and *staphylococcus aureus* are resistant to antibiotics and have been responsible for epidemic infections in burn centers.[1] Systemic antibiotics are used to treat both burn and general system infections once they have been documented by analysis of a burn wound biopsy.[29] A bacterial count in excess of 10^5 per gram of tissue constitutes burn wound infection and levels of 10^7 to 10^9 are usually associated with lethal burns. In a patient treated with systemic antibiotics, the plasma levels of medication need to be assessed frequently due to the fluid losses from a burn and an increased metabolic rate of the patient.[31] Most wounds are treated with topical antibiotics and these will be discussed in the section on medical care of burns.

Pulmonary Complications

Any patient who has been burned in a closed space should be suspected of having an inhalation injury.[32] Among patients with burns, the incidence of smoke inhalation may be in excess of 33 percent,[33] and this rises to 66 percent in patients with facial burns.[34] Several studies have indicated that the incidence of pulmonary complications following severe burns ranges from 24 percent to over 84 percent of all burn accidents, and that death due to pneumonia alone may account for over one third of the deaths of burn patients.[3,35–37]

Signs of an inhalation injury include: any facial burns, singed nasal hairs, harsh cough, hoarseness, abnormal breath sounds, respiratory distress, and carbonaceous sputum and/or hypoxemia.[38] The primary complications associated with this injury are carbon monoxide poisoning, tracheal damage, upper airway obstruction, pulmonary edema, and pneumonia.[3,35] Lung damage from inhaling noxious gases and smoke may be lethal.[35] In order to determine the extent of inhalation injury, several diagnostic procedures should be performed. The most helpful diagnostic procedure is bronchoscopy.[39] Xenon lung scanning and serial pulmonary function tests also are performed to initially determine the extent of lung damage and status of pulmonary function, and then to monitor how successful interventions are in improving lung and pulmonary function.[3,35,40–42]

There are three primary complications of pulmonary origin: restrictive disease, inhalation injury, and late sequelae. Patients who have moderate-sized burns that involve the trunk may have some degree of restrictive lung disease as a result of a burn.[3] If these patients already have some form of restrictive lung disease from other causes, their condition will be more serious.[35] Vital capacity is significantly lower and pulmonary resistance is higher than in normal individuals. Patients with burns of the chest wall may have less chest movement with inspiration so that vital capacity and other pulmonary function parameters are decreased. The varying degrees of restrictive disease can lead to pulmonary complications such as pneumonia, atelectasis, and pulmonary edema.

Pulmonary edema results in part from an alteration in vascular permeability. Edema develops due to an efflux of vascular fluid from the intravascular to the interstitial space. This fluid shift causes a decrease in cardiac output and a simultaneous ventilation-perfusion imbalance. When patients are treated during resuscitation with large volumes of fluid, additional fluid may fill the lungs due to the imbalance in vascular permeability.[35]

Other problems associated with pulmonary conditions as a result of burns are those that occur later in the recovery phase.[43] A patient may develop either advanced restrictive disease or have additional pulmonary problems. A patient's relatively low level of activity may further complicate these conditions if pneumonia develops. To conclude, pulmonary complications can be life-threatening for a burn patient during the initial insult, or at any time during the recovery process. Active chest physical therapy procedures should be included as part of a burn patient's treatment plan to minimize these problems throughout the course of hospitalization.

Metabolic Complications

Thermal injury causes a great metabolic and catabolic challenge to the body. Most of the recent advances in burn treatment and rehabilitation have come directly from the increased understanding of the metabolic demands of a burn injury,[44,45] and from the ability to improve the patient's nutritional status to meet these demands.[46] The consequences of the increased metabolic and catabolic activity following a burn are a rapid decrease in body weight, negative nitrogen balance, and a decrease in energy stores that are vital to the healing process.[47] Figure 25–10 graphically shows the changes that occur in various metabolic processes following a

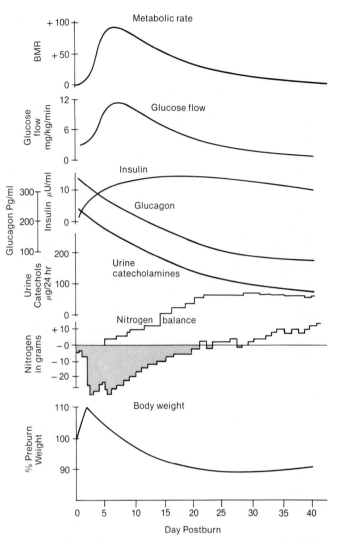

Figure 25–10. Metabolic changes that occur as a result of burn injuries. (From Artz, et al,[5] p 121, with permission.)

thermal injury. It should be noted that these metabolic changes occur for a prolonged period after a burn. One of the many ramifications of the altered metabolic state is the change in glucose kinetics, which results in hyperglycemia and the complications that it manifests.[47] An individual with diabetes who has been burned will be in a critical metabolic condition because of the altered metabolism of insulin and glucagon, and the development of hyperglycemia. Other hormonal imbalances in the catecholamines and regulatory hormones account for much of the altered metabolic state seen in the burn patient.[48,49]

As a result of the increased metabolic activity, there will be an increase of 1°C to 2°C (33.8°F to 35.6°F) in core temperature that seems to be due to a resetting of the hypothalamic temperature centers in the brain.[1] Wilmore et al.[50] have hypothesized that there is a significant relationship between the increased evaporative heat loss from the impaired skin barrier over a burn and the hypermetabolic state. In any event, if individuals with burns are placed in a room with normal ambient temperature, excessive heat loss will be exhibited and this will further exaggerate the stress response seen in these patients.[1,50] Therefore, it is recommended that room temperature for burn patients be kept at 30°C (86°F), which will lower significantly the metabolic rate.

Much of the improved management of burns has been attributed to the greater focus of research on the nutritional needs of patients. It is beyond the scope of this chapter to detail nutritional supplementation; the interested reader is referred to several excellent reviews of advances in burn nutrition.[46,51-54]

Cardiac Function and Circulatory Complications

There will be significant reductions in the plasma and intravascular fluid volume in a patient with a serious burn. Following these changes there will be a tremendous initial decrease in cardiac output; this may reach a 30 percent decrease in cardiac output within 30 minutes of injury.[55] Cardiac output will slowly return to normal levels and, in many patients, may rise to above nor-

Table 25–1 PHYSIOLOGIC AND BIOCHEMICAL CHANGES FOLLOWING BURN INJURY

Free fatty acids	Elevated proportional to burn size for short time.
Triglycerides	Elevated proportional to burn size for short time.
Cholesterol	Depressed proportional to burn size.
Phospholipids	Depressed proportional to burn size.
Fibrinogen	Initial fall, with subsequent prolonged rise. Consumption great but production greater.
Renin	Increase proportional to burn size, especially in children.
Angiotensin	Increase proportional to burn size, especially in children.
ACTH	Increase proportional to burn size, especially in children.
Protein	Rapid and persistent drop.
Albumin	Prompt and persistent drop persisting until wound closed. Production depressed and catabolism 2 to 3 times normal.
Globulin	Initial drop with rise to supranormal levels by 5 to 7 days. Catabolism 2 to 3 times normal, but production vastly increased.
IgG	Immediate depression followed by slow rise.
IgM	Altered little by burn in adults but in children follows pattern of IgG.
IgA	Altered little by burn in adults but in children follows pattern of IgG.
Red blood cells	Immediate loss proportional to burn size and depth. Life span 30% of normal due to plasma factor.
White blood cells	Initial and prolonged rise. May drop with sepsis.
Cardiac output	Precipitous drop to 20 to 40% of normal with slow spontaneous recovery in 24 to 36 hours. Myocardial depressant factor demonstrated.
Blood viscosity	Sharp rise proportional to hematocrit.
Carboxyhemoglobin	Not significant after 72 hours (<2%). Most prominent with inhalation injury (80%). Exists with or without surface burns.
Cortisol	Prompt rise to 2 to 4 times normal.
Aldosterone	Usually returns to normal by end of first week but may remain elevated for long periods. Varied response to ACTH often nil in early period.
Peripheral resistance	Rises sharply—slow fall.
Pulmonary vascular resistance	Rises sharply—slow fall.
Pulmonary artery pressure	Prompt rise and slow return.
Left arterial pressure	Normal or low. High with failure.
pO_2	Low with delay or inadequate therapy.
pH	Prompt response to therapy.
pCO_2	Initial alkalosis or hyperventilation promptly resolves.
Blood lactate	May rise to high levels with hyperventilation or poor perfusion.
Excess lactate	Mild elevations characteristic but may rise to high levels with inadequate or delayed resuscitation.
ALT	Prompt rise with peak at 2 to 3 days and persistence for several weeks owing to liver damage, not
AST	release of skin enzymes.
Alk. phos.	
Renal function	Renal plasma flow depressed more than glomerular filtration rates. Free water clearances down. All values promptly return to normal with adequate resuscitation.
Evaporative water loss	Donor sites and partial thickness burns have intermediate loss rates. Full thickness burns lose at same rate as open pan of water. Estimate (25 + % burn) × M² body surface. Fifteen to 20 times normal skin rates.
Pulmonary function (in absence of pneumonia)	Proportional to magnitude of burn. Independent of inhalation injury. Minute ventilation (V_e) increased up to 500%. Peak at 5 days. Static compliance (C_{stat}) usually normal but may change with onset of pneumonia. Lung clearance index (LCI) normal until terminal. Oxygen consumption greatly increased. Forced vital capacity (FVC) normal even with V_e increase. May drop with pneumonia.

ACTH = adrenocorticotropic hormone; ALT = alanine aminotransferase; AST = aspartate aminotransferase; IgA = immunoglobulin A; IgG = immunoglobulin G; IgM = immunoglobulin M.

mal levels and be maintained there for prolonged periods.

Hematologic and circulatory changes also occur following a severe burn injury. These changes include alterations in platelet concentration and function, clotting factors, white blood cell components, and red blood cell dysfunction.[56] These, coupled with cardiac changes and injured vascular beds, will significantly factor into initial treatment efforts, and if a patient survives, into how rapidly he or she will recover. Table 25–1 presents an overview of some of the physiologic and biochemical complications that lead to secondary problems in a burn injury.

BURN WOUND HEALING

The burn wound has been described and the causes and complications of burn injury have been reviewed. The remaining sections of this chapter will concentrate on the various types of therapeutic intervention and rehabilitation of the burned patient. However, before discussing the medical, surgical, and physical therapy aspects of burn treatment, knowledge of the healing process of a burn wound is needed.

The two layers of the skin, the epidermis and dermis, differ morphologically, and will heal by separate mechanisms. The physiology of each component will be described, along with an explanation of the clinical implications.

Dermal Healing

When an injury involves tissue deeper than the epidermis, dermal healing or scar formation takes place. Scar formation can be divided into three phases: inflammation, proliferation, and maturation. Although these phases will be described separately, they occur on a continuum and one phase often overlaps another.

INFLAMMATORY PHASE

The primary reaction of viable tissue to a burn wound is inflammation, which prepares the wound for healing through hemostatic, vascular, and cellular events. Inflammation begins at the time of injury, ends in about 3 to 5 days, and is characterized by redness, edema, warmth, pain, and decreased range of motion. Initially, when a blood vessel is ruptured, the wall of the vessel contracts to decrease blood flow. Platelets aggregate and fibrin is deposited to form a clot over the area. Fibrin serves a threefold function: it partially retains body fluids, protects the underlying cells from desiccation, and provides a firm coagulum substance from which cells can infiltrate. Therefore, fibrin can be thought of as forming a "ladder," from which cells can climb and work themselves into the healing structure.

Following a transient vasoconstriction of the vasculature, which lasts about 5 to 10 minutes, vessels vasodilate to increase blood flow to the area. There is increased permeability of the blood vessels, with leaking of plasma into the interstitial space and subsequent edema formation. Leukocytes infiltrate the area and begin to rid the site of contamination.

PROLIFERATIVE PHASE

During this phase, reepithelialization is occurring at the surface of the wound, while deep within the wound, fibroblasts are migrating and proliferating. *Fibroblasts* are the cells that synthesize scar tissue, which is composed of collagen and a viscous ground substance of protein polysaccharides. The collagen is deposited with a random alignment and no true architectural arrangement of fibers. Stresses, such as stretching forces, applied to the tissue cause the fibers to align along the path of these stresses. During this period of fibroplasia, the tensile strength of the wound increases at a rate proportional to the rate of collagen synthesis.

Along with collagen, granulation tissue is formed during this phase. Granulation tissue consists of macrophages, fibroblasts, and blood vessels. These newly formed blood vessels bring a rich blood supply to the area and encourage further wound healing. However, granulation tissue formation is not necessary for skin graft adherence and excess granulation tissue may lead to increased hypertrophic scarring.[57]

During the proliferative phase, wound contraction occurs. Wound contraction is an active process in which the body attempts to close a wound where a loss of tissue has occurred. The amount of contraction is determined by the amount of available mobile skin around the defect. It involves movement of existing tissue at a wound edge toward the center, not formation of new tissue. Two events that stop wound contraction are: the edges meet; or tension in the surrounding skin equals or exceeds the force of contraction. Skin grafting may decrease contraction, and the thicker a graft the less contraction there may be.

MATURATION PHASE

Although a wound is considered healed from the time epithelium covers the surface, remodeling of the scar tissue will continue for up to 2 years following a burn. The scar that forms during the proliferative phase is enlarged with many cells, blood vessels, and randomly oriented collagen fibers. During the maturation phase there is a reduction in the number of fibroblasts, vascularity decreases as a result of a lower metabolic demand, and collagen remodels, becoming more parallel in arrangement and forming stronger bonds. The ratio of collagen breakdown to production determines the type of scar that forms. If the rate of breakdown equals or slightly exceeds the rate of production, maturation results in a pale, flat, and pliable scar. If the rate of collagen production exceeds breakdown, then a **hypertrophic scar** may result. This scar is characterized by being red and raised in appearance, and firm in texture; it stays within the boundary of the original wound. A keloid is a large, firm scar that overflows the boundaries of the original wound; it is more common in blacks and Asians. Both of these scars take a prolonged period of time to mature and can lead to both functional and cosmetic deformities.

Epidermal Healing

When a burn injures just the epidermis, or if there are viable cells lining the skin appendages, epithelial healing can occur on the surface of a wound. The stimulus for epithelial growth is the presence of an open wound exposing subepithelial tissue of the body to the environment. The intact epithelium attempts to cover an exposed wound through the ameboid movement of cells from the basal layer of the surrounding epidermis into the wound. The epithelial cells stop migration when they are completely in contact with other epithelial cells. Following this "contact inhibition," the cells begin dividing and multiplying through mitosis. While epithelial cells move about the wound site, they maintain a connection with the normal epithelium at the wound margin. To continue migration and proliferation, a suitable base for the epithelial cells must be provided by adequate nutrition and blood supply, or the new cells will die.

Protection of new epithelial tissue is critical. If there are multiple occurrences of epithelial cell loss by any means over a long period of time, the available cells at the margin of the wound will become reduced in number so that continued outgrowth of the extending epithelium will be delayed or stopped.

The process of epithelialization is most evident clinically in the partial-thickness wound that has intact hair follicles and glands. The epithelial cells from skin appendages provide islands from which the wound may heal. The cells migrate peripherally from these **epithelial islands** into the wound. Skin growth and coverage can actually be seen over time from these epithelial islands.

Damage to sebaceous glands may cause dryness and itching of a healing wound. Lubrication can be a problem and the skin is characteristically dry and may crack. Dryness may continue for a long time as many of the sebaceous glands do not return to their normal function after a wound is epithelialized. The problem of dryness is further compounded by the poor absorption qualities of many topically applied moisturizing creams. Therapists need to educate patients about the types of creams to lubricate newly healed tissue, and about the frequency and techniques of application.

MEDICAL MANAGEMENT OF BURNS

Advances in the medical management of burns have resulted in the survival of thousands of patients who 10 or 15 years ago would have died. The research base and techniques available today at the modern burn center have enabled patients to receive better care through the use of more sophisticated techniques for the treatment of major burn injuries. This section will discuss the initial treatment of burned patients and the surgical procedures associated with debridement and grafting of new skin onto a burn wound.

Initial Management and Wound Care

The goal in initial management of a burned patient is to address the major life-threatening problems and stabilize the patient through procedures designed to: (1) establish and maintain an airway; (2) prevent cyanosis, shock, and hemorrhage; (3) establish baseline data on the patient and the amount of burned surface area; (4) prevent or reduce fluid losses; (5) clean the patient and wounds; (6) assess injuries; and (7) prevent pulmonary and cardiac complications. Triage using these procedures applies only to major burn trauma.

Initially, a patient must be transported from the site of injury to a treatment facility. If possible, transportation will be directly to a burn center rather than to a hospital emergency room. The goals of treatment in transit are to stabilize the patient and maintain an airway. Most burn patients are relatively stable immediately after injury. However, in circumstances where burns have occurred to the face or chest, a procedure may be necessary to establish an artificial airway.[3,58] During the initial transportation phase, patient history and personal data are gathered when possible. The type of agent causing the burn is noted, and initial assessment of the burn injury takes place. The emergency medical personnel may use the rule of nines to estimate the percentage of burn injury. They also will prepare the individual for triage at the burn center by removing all burned clothing and jewelry and initiating the administration of fluid through an intravenous (IV) line.

One of the major advances in burn care has been in fluid volume replacement initially and throughout a patient's treatment. Research has led to an improved understanding of the physiologic changes that occur in a patient following a burn injury and of the fluid volumes necessary to improve the chance for survival. Information about the physiologic changes responsible for the shifts in body fluids and protein has led to the use of intravenous solutions in the amount necessary to replace vital fluid and electrolytes.[3,58-60]

After a patient arrives at a burn center and adequate fluid therapy has been initiated, the burn team assesses the extent and depth of injury, and begins initial wound cleansing. Wound cleansing may be performed in a large hydrotherapy tank or whirlpool, where a patient can be totally immersed.[61] Water temperature should be between 37°C and 40°C (98.6°F and 104°F). The initial wound care session allows the team to establish body weight, examine a patient fully, remove hair where necessary and start the **debridement** process by removing any loose skin. The goals of wound cleansing and debridement are to remove dead tissue, prevent infection, and promote revascularization and/or reepithelialization of the area. A physical therapist may be involved in the tubbing procedure. A therapist should take extreme care during debridement and combine skilled care with compassion during the process.

Recently, some burn units have gone to the use of showers, spraying, or "bed baths" for the removal of dressings and daily cleansing of wounds, although the majority of burn centers still perform hydrotherapy in the care of patients.[62] The whirlpool tub usually will have some form of disinfectant in the water to assist in infection control.[63-65] While a patient is in the water, adherent dressings are removed. Care must be taken when removing the dressings to ensure minimal or no bleeding. The removal of dressings in water is less painful than dry removal; however, most patients require pain medication prior to wound cleansing.

After dressings are removed, the wound should be inspected carefully. The appearance, depth, size, exudate, and odor are noted. Infection is characterized by thick purulent drainage, odor, fever, a brownish-black discoloration, rapid separation of eschar, boils in adjacent tissue, or conversion of a deep partial-thickness burn to a full-thickness burn.

Wound care is carried out using clean or sterile technique. If **sharp debridement** (the use of surgical scissors and forceps to remove eschar) is performed, sloughed epidermis and loose eschar are removed and pockets of pus are drained, but bleeding should be minimized.

Active or passive ROM exercise may be performed while the patient is still in the water. It is critical to maintain as much ROM as possible during the wound healing phase, because the more range that can be maintained throughout the initial phases of recovery, the less difficult it will be to fully rehabilitate a patient once all wounds are closed.

When a patient has been removed from the tub, topical medications and/or dressings are reapplied. The patient is kept warm to reduce additional metabolic demands.

The technique of applying a topical cream or ointment without dressings is called the open technique and allows for ongoing inspection of the wound, and an assessment of the healing process. The topical medication must be reapplied throughout the day. The cream or ointment should be removed completely and reapplied, once or twice daily, normally during the tubbing procedure. Table 25–2 presents common topical medications used in the treatment of burns.

The closed technique consists of applying dressings over a topical agent. Dressings serve several purposes: (1) they hold topical antimicrobial agents on the wound; (2) they reduce fluid loss from the wound; and (3) they protect the wound. Dressings are changed once or twice a day, depending on the size and type of wound, and the type of topical antimicrobial used.

Dressings consist of several layers. The first layer is nonadherent to protect the fragile healing surface from disruption. This may be followed by cotton padding to absorb wound drainage. The final layer consists of roll gauze or elastic bandages, which hold the other layers in place but allow movement.

Surgical Management of the Burn Wound

Primary excision is removal of the eschar surgically. Much of the increased survival rate of patients with extensive burns has been due to the early primary excision of burn wounds. Normally, a patient will be taken to surgery following successful resuscitation and this is usually within 1 week of injury. As much of the eschar is removed at one time as possible. Proponents of early primary excision feel that this approach is easier on a patient than repeated debridement and that it promotes more rapid healing, reduces infection, and scarring and is more economical in terms of staff and hospital time.[66-68]

In many burn centers, a burn wound is closed with a graft at the time of primary excision. There are many types of grafts that can be used to close a wound. An **autograft** is a patient's own skin, taken from an unburned area and transplanted to cover a burned area. Autografts are desirable as they provide permanent coverage of the wound. An **allograft** or **homograft** is skin taken from an individual of the same species, usually cadaver skin. The skin can be kept frozen in skin banks for prolonged periods. Allografts are temporary grafts used to cover large burns when there is insufficient autograft available. A **xenograft,** also called a **heterograft,**

Table 25–2 COMMON TOPICAL MEDICATIONS USED IN TREATMENT OF BURNS

Medication	Description	Method of Application
Silver sulfadiazine	Most commonly used topical antibacterial agent effective against Pseudomonas infections.	White cream applied with sterile glove 2–4 mm thick directly to wound or impregnated into fine mesh gauze.
Sulfamylon (mafenide acetate)	Topical antibacterial agent effective against gram-negative or gram-positive organisms; diffuses easily through eschar.	White cream applied directly to wound with thin 1–2 mm layer twice daily; may be left undressed or covered with thin layer of gauze.
Silver nitrate	Antiseptic germicide and astringent; will penetrate only 1–2 mm of eschar; useful for surface bacteria; stains black.	Dressings or soaks used every 2 hours; also available as small sticks to cauterize small open areas.
Bacitracin/Polysporin	Bland ointment; effective against gram-positive organisms.	Thin layer of ointment applied directly to wound and left open.
Furacin (nitrofurazone)	Antibacterial cream used in less severe burns; indicated to decrease bacterial growth.	Applied directly to wound or impregnated into gauze dressing.
Garamycin (gentamycin)	Antibiotic used against gram-negative organism and staphylococcal and streptococcal bacteria.	Cream or ointment applied with sterile glove and covered with gauze.
Travase/Elase	Enzymatic debriding agent selectively debrides necrotic tissue; no antibacterial action.	Ointment applied to eschar and covered with moist occlusive dressing.

is skin from another species, usually a pig. Allografts or xenografts are used until there is sufficient normal skin available for an autograft. Reports have described success with allografts when primary excision and grafting were done within the first days of acute hospitalization and when a patient received the immunosuppressive drug **cyclosporine.**[69–71]

Perhaps the most exciting advance in the care of burn patients is the use of cultured epidermal autografts and dermal autografts for coverage of an excised wound.[72,73] Cultured skin is skin that is grown in a laboratory from biopsies of a patient's own tissue. Cultured skin is used when large areas of burn exist and coverage is necessary for a patient's survival. With this technique, both epidermal and dermal cells can be cultured from a patient's own skin and, after appropriate growth, can be grafted onto a burn wound.[72,73]

SKIN GRAFTING PROCEDURE

The removal of skin for use in grafting is done in surgery under anesthesia. The skin used for a graft usually is removed with a **dermatome.** This not only allows the surgeon to obtain a larger amount of skin, but a more consistent depth of skin can be obtained. The dermatome is adjusted to remove a predetermined thickness of skin for a **split-thickness skin graft (STSG).** A split-thickness skin graft contains epidermis and only the superficial layers of the dermis from the donor site, as opposed to a **full-thickness graft,** which consists of the full dermal thickness. The site from which a skin graft is taken is called the **donor site.** Common donor sites include the thighs, buttocks, and back. These wounds heal by reepithelialization, like a partial-thickness burn, and require appropriate care to prevent additional dermal damage with resultant scar formation. A full-thickness skin graft has the disadvantage of leaving a full-thickness wound that will require either primary closure or grafting with a split-thickness skin graft.

Generally, the thinner the graft, the better the adherence; the thicker the graft, the better the cosmetic result. Selection of depth depends on many factors, including whether or not the donor site needs to be used again for another skin graft. Taking a thicker graft adversely affects the possibility of taking another graft from the same site for a prolonged period of time. Harvesting from STSG sites may be repeated in 10 to 14 days, depending on the healing rate of the donor site.

A *sheet graft* is a skin graft that is applied to a recipient bed without alteration following harvesting from a donor site. The face, neck, and hands are covered with this type of graft for optimal cosmesis and function. When limited donor skin is available, most areas are covered with a **mesh graft.** The meshing of a graft consists of processing the sheet graft through a device that makes tiny parallel incisions in a linear arrangement. This process expands a graft before it is applied to the wound bed.[74] This allows coverage of a larger area and once the graft adheres, the interstices heal through reepithelialization. Figure 25–11 shows the transfer of a meshed graft to a burn wound.

A skin graft usually is held in place with sutures, staples, or steri-strips. Once a graft is fixed in position, any

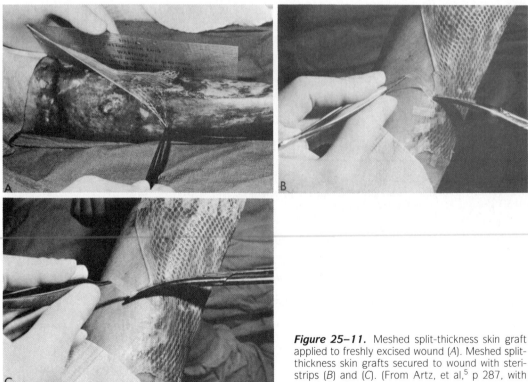

Figure 25–11. Meshed split-thickness skin graft applied to freshly excised wound (*A*). Meshed split-thickness skin grafts secured to wound with steri-strips (*B*) and (*C*). (From Artz, et al,[5] p 287, with permission.)

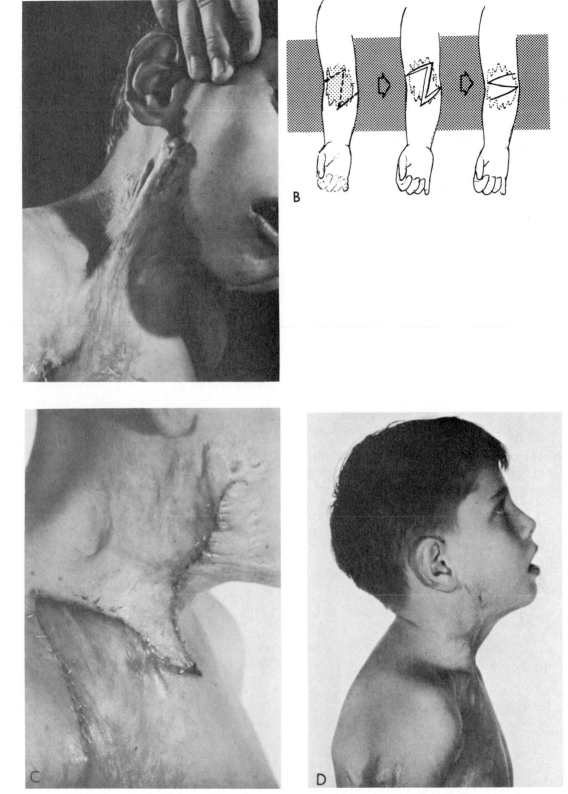

Figure 25–12. Scar formation and Z-plasty surgical correction. (From Artz, et al,[5] p 485, with permission.)

blood or serum that might have become located between the graft and the recipient site should be removed. Application of a pressure dressing facilitates total contact between a graft and recipient site, but does not necessarily hasten fibrin fixation of a graft. Fixation of a graft to the host bed by fibrin occurs spontaneously.

One of the basic necessities for successful adherence of a graft is sufficient vascularity within the wound bed. Grafts will not adhere to nonvascularized areas, such as tendon. Once a skin graft has been applied, separation of a graft from its bed must be prevented. Separation may be a result of excessive motion, mechanical trauma, or hematoma formation. Initially, an area is immobilized with a dressing that provides firm, even compression on the wound. Other reasons for graft failure include inadequate excision of necrotic tissue and infection.

Survival of a skin graft depends on several nutritive factors: (1) circulation, which provides a nutritive supply to the graft; (2) inosculation, or the process by which a direct connection is established between a graft and the host vessels; and (3) penetration of the host vessels into a graft site. Grafts that are commonly white and blanch at the time of transplantation, begin to show pinkish coloration within a matter of hours following their placement on an adequate vascular bed.

The reestablishment of circulation in a graft site will take place through the formation of direct anastomosis between respective vessels, with invasion from the host bed forming new channels, or by a combination of both. Twenty-four hours after grafting, numerous host vessels will have penetrated the graft.[57,75] The invasion of new capillaries seems to be the most important consideration in vascularization, as the pattern of ingrowing vessels generally differs radically from the original vascular pattern present in a graft. Initially, structural connections are fibrous. Precollagen material will be delivered via ingrowing capillaries. The collagen is then laid down to secure the attachment of a graft. Normally, within 72 hours, inosculation has proceeded so far that it is impossible to distinguish the graft from the host.

SURGICAL CORRECTION OF SCAR CONTRACTURE

If physical therapy interventions are not successful in averting scar contracture formation, and limitations are noted in ROM and function, surgery may be required. Surgery usually is not indicated in the active, immature phase of scar formation because the final results may be less than optimal due to the local response to the surgical trauma.[76] However, the successful release of scar contractures prior to scar maturation has been documented.[77] Each patient's scar will require individualized evaluation and treatment. Surgical treatment options are beyond the scope of this chapter, but common procedures to eliminate scar contractures are skin grafts and Z-plasties. A **Z-plasty** is shown in Figure 25–12. The Z-plasty serves to lengthen a scar by interposing normal tissue in the line of the scar. Skin grafts are used for more severe contractures. In the case of skin grafting, pressure dressings are required to prevent hypertrophic scarring.

PHYSICAL THERAPY MANAGEMENT

Rehabilitation of a burned patient begins the moment he or she arrives at the hospital and is an ever-changing process that may need to be modified daily. The previous sections of this chapter have discussed the pathophysiologic changes and alterations of the skin that occur in the burn wound and the closure of that wound with various types of graft materials. While the skin is healing, it is imperative that a patient's physical rehabilitation occurs concurrently. The physical rehabilitation consists of the prevention of scar contracture, maintenance of normal ROM, maintenance or improvement in muscular strength and cardiovascular endurance, return to function, and performance of activities of daily living.[4] The physical therapist interacts with other members of the burn team to assist patients in obtaining these goals. A patient can expect to return to a normal productive life provided he or she complies with the treatment plan. For most patients, the most difficult phase of rehabilitation occurs after the wounds have healed and the scar tissue begins to contract. If a therapist is actively involved in the burn team, and can establish a program of movement rehabilitation in conjunction with the wound healing process, rehabilitation after healing will be much less traumatic and more successful. The remainder of this chapter will address the physical therapist's role in a burned patient's rehabilitation program.

Physical Therapy Assessment

After the initial assessment of the depth of the burns and the total amount of body surface area involved, a physical therapist needs to assess a patient's ability to move. Active or passive ROM may be limited due to edema, restrictive eschar, or pain, but an initial baseline measure should be obtained. In addition, a therapist needs to obtain an accurate history from the patient and family members regarding any preexisting limitations or old injuries that may affect a patient's rehabilitation potential.

Other evaluation techniques can be included in the initial assessment and ongoing reassessments of a burned patient (e.g., strength, ambulation, functional activities). Because healing of a burn wound is a dynamic process, and changes may occur daily, the physical therapist needs to assess and monitor a patient for changes in skin integrity, ROM, and mobility routinely. Frequent assessment will keep the therapist and other members of the burn care team abreast of potential problems so that intervention can occur before a potential problem becomes a real one.

In addition to the physical damage a burn has on a patient, there also may be an enormous psychologic impact. The physical therapist should be cognizant of a potential problem during ongoing assessments, as psychologic trauma may affect the patient's progress and outlook toward his or her future and rehabilitation.

Referral to an appropriate professional for intervention may be necessary.

Goal Setting

Based on the assessment, extent and depth of the burn, a patient's current health status, age, and physical and mental condition, the prognosis for a patient can be estimated by the burn care team. The goals for rehabilitation and physical therapy management are contingent on a patient's prognosis and current medical status. It is difficult to list specific goals due to the varied nature of each burn injury; however, typical long-range goals might include:

1. Attaining a clean burn wound to enhance healing and graft adherence.
2. Full ROM.
3. Minimal or no scar contractures.
4. Minimal or no pulmonary complications.
5. Preinjury level of cardiovascular endurance.
6. Good to normal strength.
7. Independent ambulation.
8. Independent function in activities of daily living.
9. Minimal scarring.

The ultimate goal of rehabilitation is return of a patient to normal function and life as it was before the burn injury.

Physical Therapy Treatment

Patients with burns usually will begin physical therapy treatment on the day of admission, following an evaluation. The initial assessment of a patient will determine which areas need to be addressed first. Controlling edema formation and preventing contractures usually are the first priorities of physical therapy treatments. Elevating the extremities and encouraging active movement, especially of the hands and ankles, help to minimize edema formation. Preventing scar contractures can be accomplished through positioning, splinting, and exercise. Exercise and ambulation also will help mini-

mize the deleterious effects of bed rest on a patient. Following wound closure, massage and compression therapy will assist with minimizing contracture formation and management of burn scars.

The scar that forms across a joint while a burn wound is healing is comprised of immature collagen. A scar will shorten due to the contractile or pulling forces in scar tissue and limit ROM and function unless action is taken to prevent this process. While measures to prevent a contracture are undertaken in expectation of the best result, there will be patients who develop scar contractures. There are several methods available to the physical therapist to aid in the prevention and/or treatment of scar contracture.

As stated previously, positioning, splinting, and exercise are three relatively simple procedures effective in halting the scar contracture process. Active exercise and patient participation in functional activities are the best treatments to prevent or minimize contractures. However, owing to the relentless forces of scar tissue contraction and the pain associated with exercising a burned area, additional interventions may be necessary.

POSITIONING AND SPLINTING

Positioning should begin on the day of admission to assist in preventing contractures.[78,79] Unless supervised, a patient will not move the burned area because of pain, and this increases the likelihood of contracture development. General guidelines and some examples of proper positioning are provided in Table 25–3 and Figures 25–13 through 25–16. Burned areas should be positioned in an elongated or neutral position of function.

Although there are certain "antideformity" positions in which patients are generally splinted, the therapist needs to assess the location of the burn and which movements are difficult for the patient. With the exception of immobilizing a skin graft following surgery, splints should be fabricated for patients only if ROM or function would be lost without them. General indications for the use of splints include: (1) prevention of contractures; (2) maintenance of ROM achieved during an exercise session or surgical release; (3) correction of contractures; and (4) protection of a joint or tendon.[80]

Table 25–3 POSITIONING STRATEGIES FOR COMMON DEFORMITIES

Joint	Common Deformity	Motions to Be Stressed	Suggested Approaches
Anterior neck	Flexion	Hyperextension	Use double mattress—position neck in extension (Fig. 25–13); with healing—rigid cervical orthosis
Shoulder-axilla	Adduction and internal rotation	Abduction, flexion and external rotation	Position with shoulder flexed and abducted (Fig. 25–14) Airplane splint
Elbow	Flexion and pronation	Extension and supination	Splint in extension
Hand	Claw hand (also called intrinsic minus position)	Wrist extension; metacarpophalangeal flexion, proximal interphalangeal and distal interphalangeal extension; thumb palmar abduction	Wrap fingers separately (Fig. 25–15). Elevate to decrease edema. Position in *intrinsic plus* position, wrist in extension, metacarpophalangeal in flexion, proximal interphalangeal and distal interphalangeal in extension, thumb in palmar abduction with large web space (Fig. 25–16)
Hip and groin	Flexion and adduction	All motions, especially hip extension and abduction	Hip neutral (0°), extension with slight abduction
Knee	Flexion	Extension	Posterior knee splint
Ankle	Plantar flexion	All motions—especially dorsiflexion	Plastic ankle-foot orthosis with cutout at Achilles tendon and ankle positioned in 0° dorsiflexion

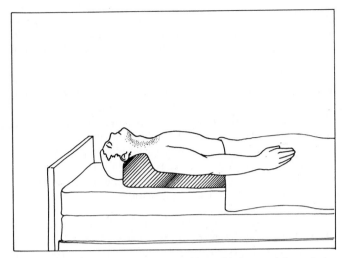

Figure 25–13. Position in bed of patient with burns of the anterior neck.

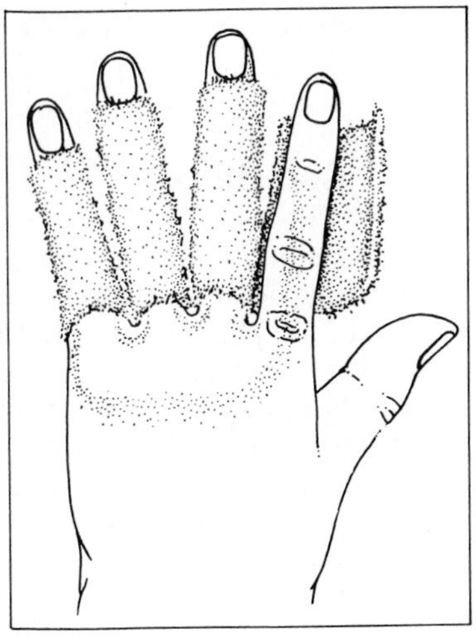

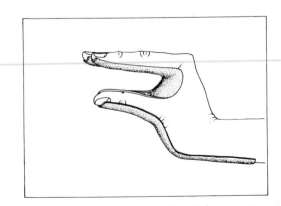

Figure 25–15. Dressing the hand by wrapping the fingers separately.

Splint design should be kept simple so that a splint is easy to apply, remove, and clean. Splints usually are worn at night, when a patient is resting, or continuously for several days following skin grafting. Splints should conform to the body part, and care must be taken to assure there are no pressure points that may cause a breakdown in the healing or normal skin. Splints should be checked routinely for proper fit and revised if necessary. Active motion is important, and splints and positioning are intended to serve as adjuncts to the therapy program until full active motion can be achieved.

Most splints used for burn patients are static. The splint has no moveable parts, and maintains position or immobilizes an area following skin grafting (Fig. 25–17). Recently, dynamic splints have been used in the care of burned patients (Fig. 25–18).[81,82] These splints have moveable parts that allow joint movement. Dynamic splints apply a low-load, prolonged stretch that can be adjusted to a patient's tolerance. They offer great potential for correcting a developing contracture and

the early return of active function in areas of extensive burn and grafting. The use of continuous passive motion devices also is appropriate for certain burned patients.[83–87]

ACTIVE AND PASSIVE EXERCISE

Active exercise of involved body parts is encouraged. Active exercise begins on the first day after admission.[88] Other forms of exercise should be used only if confusion, pain, limited ROM, or other complications prevent active exercise. A patient should perform active exercise of all joints, including the unburned areas. In most cases, active ROM should be done two to three times a day. Dressing changes are an opportune time for an exercise session because the burn wound will be visible and a therapist will be able to monitor the wound during the session. If a patient has just received a skin graft, active and passive exercise of the area may be discontinued for 3 to 5 days to allow the graft to adhere.[77,89,90] After the surgeon determines it is safe to begin exercise again, gentle ROM, first active, and then passive, if needed, is reinstituted.

Active-assistive and passive stretching exercise should be initiated if a patient cannot achieve full ROM actively.

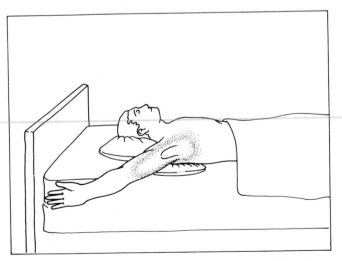

Figure 25–14. Position in bed of patient with burns of the axilla.

Figure 25–16. Intrinsic plus position of the burned hand.

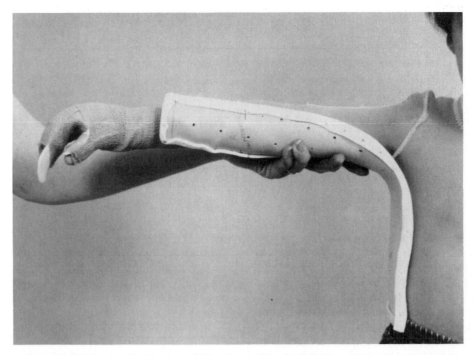

Figure 25–17. Static splint that immobilizes the shoulder in abduction and the elbow in extension.

Proprioceptive neuromuscular facilitation techniques of contract-relax and hold-relax can be used effectively to assist with stretching. The healed burned area should be lubricated prior to exercise to keep it moist. Care should be taken around areas of skin grafts and the stretch should be gentle, prolonged, and gradual. If the burns are well healed, heating modalities, such as paraffin or ultrasound, may be used to further increase the pliability of the tissue prior to stretching.[91]

Exercise in the area of unhealed burns will be extremely painful and most patients will indicate they would rather lose their motion than be subjected to the additional pain that occurs with movement. It usually is difficult and mentally draining on the physical therapist to push patients to exercise in and through pain, but it is critical that a therapist be persistent. Coordinating an exercise session with the administration of pain medication will lessen the problem.[88,92] There will be times when the physical therapist needs to accede to the

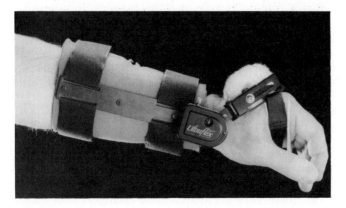

Figure 25–18. Dynamic splint providing a low-load, prolonged stretch.

wishes of a patient. However, a patient and his or her family need to be educated as to the consequences associated with *not* exercising. A physical therapist should elicit the assistance of the family in keeping the patient moving as much as possible. A patient must be encouraged and educated to accept an aggressive rehabilitation program.

RESISTIVE EXERCISE

As a patient continues the rehabilitation program, resistive and strengthening exercises are incorporated into the treatment plan.[88] Patients with major burns may lose body weight, and lean muscle mass can decrease rapidly. Exercise may consist of isokinetic, isotonic, or other resistive training devices. General principles of exercise training and strength improvement should be followed, but they may need to be modified on the basis of a patient's condition and the stage of wound healing. Resistive devices such as free weights, pull cords, and pulleys can be used to prevent loss of strength in the areas not burned.

When a patient initially begins strengthening or endurance exercise, the physical therapist may need to monitor vital signs (see Chapter 4) in order to assess cardiovascular and respiratory response to treatment. Insults to the respiratory system are common. In addition, the physiologic strain associated with the healing process is significant. When exercise is performed by a patient who may already be compromised in his or her respiratory and cardiovascular systems, overexertion may occur. Monitoring of pulse, blood pressure, and respiratory rate before, during, and after exercise, particularly in the recovery period following exercise, will yield valuable information as to the status of the cardiorespiratory system.

Patients should be encouraged to participate in exercises that will stress the cardiovascular system, such as walking from the burn unit to the physical therapy department. Cycle ergometry, rowing ergometry, or other forms of stationary aerobic exercise should be encouraged. These devices will not only work to increase cardiovascular endurance, but can have the added benefit of improving ROM of the extremities. In addition, they introduce variety into the rehabilitation program. The physical therapist needs to be creative and innovative to motivate patients to increase their exercise capacity.

AMBULATION

Ambulation should be initiated at the earliest appropriate time. If the legs are grafted, ambulation may be discontinued for 1 to 10 days until the physician indicates it is safe to resume.[93-96] When ambulation is initiated, the legs should be wrapped in elastic bandages in a figure-eight pattern to support the new grafts and promote venous return. If a patient cannot tolerate the upright position due to orthostatic intolerance, gradual increases in tilt-table treatment time will assist in preparing the patient for standing. Initially, a patient may require an assistive device to ambulate. However, independent ambulation without a device should be achieved as soon as possible.

MASSAGE

Massage is an intervention that may be useful in reducing scar contracture. Deep friction massage may loosen scar tissue by mobilizing cutaneous tissue from underlying tissue and act to break up adhesions.[97] When massage is used in conjunction with stretching and exercise, the immature scar tissue can be stretched, and contracture corrected.

The physical therapist will spend a great deal of time with each patient during each exercise session. The rewards of a successful treatment program are tremendous when a patient who has suffered a life-threatening burn is able to walk out of the hospital and return to productive community involvement.

Scar Management

Following wound closure, a skin graft or healed burn wound is vascular, flat, and soft. During the following 3 to 6 months, dramatic changes may occur. The newly healed areas may become raised and firm. Pressure has been used successfully to hasten scar maturation and minimize hypertrophic scar formation.[98] However, no one study validates the mechanism by which pressure alters scar tissue. Pressure may exert control over hypertrophic scarring by: (1) thinning the dermis, (2) altering the biochemical structure of scar tissue, (3) decreasing blood flow to the area, (4) reorganizing collagen bundles, or (5) decreasing tissue water content. Constant pressure dressings or garments exerting pressure exceeding 25 mmHg will decrease the vascularity, decrease the amount of mucopolysaccharides, decrease collagen deposition, and significantly lessen localized edema.[76] The early hypertrophic scar is readily influenced by compressive forces and thus will respond to pressure therapy. The earlier the scar tissue is exposed to pressure, the better the result.[99,100] Usually, if the scar is less than 6 months old, it will respond to pressure therapy by conforming to the pressure and remaining flat on the surface and not developing into a hypertrophic scar.[100] However, if the scar is still active or shows evidence of vascularity (red color), even if a year old, pressure therapy may still be successful.

In general, if a patient's wounds heal in less than 10 to 14 days, pressure may not be needed. If wound healing takes longer than 10 to 14 days, pressure usually is indicated.[101]

PRESSURE DRESSINGS

Elastic wraps can be used to provide vascular support of skin grafts and donor sites as well as to control edema and scarring. Elastic wraps should be used until a patient's skin or scars can tolerate the shearing force of pressure garment application, and open areas are minimal. Elastic wraps are applied in a figure-eight pattern on the lower extremities. A spiral wrap can be used on the upper extremities and a circular wrap on the trunk.[98]

A self-adherent elastic bandage can be used for the hand and toes. This bandage adheres only to itself and can be used over dressings prior to wound healing. It helps minimize edema and control scar formation. It may be used prior to application of a glove or as definitive pressure on an infant's hand.

Tubular support bandages come in various circumferences and garment styles. These provide a moderate amount of compression and may be used as interim garments before a custom-made garment is fitted. The tubular support bandage is especially useful for small children who grow rapidly and require frequent alterations in garment size.

Several companies manufacture pressure garments. Some are ready-made and of several sizes to fit all; others are custom-made for the individual patient. For the custom-made garments, a physical therapist uses specially designed tapes to measure the circumference of each limb every 1½ inches of its length in order to fit the garment exactly to the limb with the proper pressure. Garments are measured when a patient has only a few remaining open areas. The garments are very tight, and difficult to apply, but the pressure is necessary to prevent scar hypertrophy. Garments can be ordered for any or all body parts, including the face and head, and many styles, options, and colors exist (Fig. 25–19).[98] Garments can be worn when the skin or scars can tolerate the shearing force of application. Pantyhose may be used under waist height pants to assist with donning. Garments usually are worn 23 hours a day for as long as 12 to 18 months to prevent scar formation. Garments should be washed daily to prevent a buildup of perspiration and cream, which may lead to scar maceration. The patient usually receives two sets of garments, one to wear and one to wash.

Adequate pressure may not be obtained with elastic wraps or pressure garments over concave surfaces, such as the sternum or axilla, and an insert may be neces-

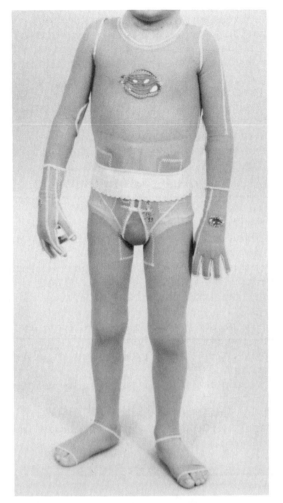

Figure 25–19. Pressure garments such as gloves, vest, and waist height pants are worn to minimize hypertrophic scar formation.

sary.[102] Inserts can be made of many materials including foam, silicone elastomer, elastomer putty, and dermal pads.[98,103,104] These items need to be removed and cleaned regularly to prevent maceration of the underlying tissue.

Early, consistent use of pressure will result in flat, pliable scars, desensitization and protection of scars, and relief of itching. Pressure is necessary until scar maturation, when the scars are pale, flat, and soft.

Follow-up Care

Prior to discharge from the hospital, a therapist should provide the patient with information regarding a home exercise program, a splinting and positioning program, and skin care.

A home exercise program should focus on stretching and massaging the areas involved in the burn injury, 2 to 3 times daily, to improve or maintain ROM. In addition, a patient should be encouraged to perform as many activities of daily living as independently as possible. Therapists can utilize videotaping of the patient's exercise program to provide the patient, family, and outpa-

tient therapist with the actual ROM and movement pattern used in each exercise. This facilitates education of those involved in the patient's rehabilitation program and helps to ensure consistency of treatment following discharge.[105]

The splinting schedule and pressure program that had been followed in the hospital just prior to a patient's discharge should be continued at home. A patient or a family member should be independent in applying and removing all splints and pressure appliances.

Proper skin care requires specifying the type of soap and cream a patient is to use. In general, soap should be mild without perfumes or other irritants. A moisturizing soap can be used after all open areas are healed. Creams should be applied three times a day and should not contain perfumes or have a significant alcohol content. Patients should be instructed to massage cream completly into their skin to avoid buildup on the surface. If a patient will be exposed to the sun, a sunscreen with a skin protection factor of at least 15 should be used and reapplied frequently.[106] Patients should be cautioned to avoid the sun if at all possible and to use hats or clothing to help protect their skin against the sun's rays.

Small, superficial open areas may plague a patient for many months following wound closure due to the fragility of a healed burn wound. A patient should be instructed to wash these areas twice daily, apply a small amount of antibiotic ointment and cover with a nonadherent dressing. Further maceration can be prevented by avoiding shearing forces, improper fit of clothing, brisk washing or soaking in water too long, or application of too much cream.

Itching may intensify when a patient is healed. A patient should be instructed to pat, rather than scratch, the irritated area. Application of cream may help decrease itching; however, some patients may require oral medication to help control this problem.

Some patients may require outpatient therapy to supplement the exercise regimen they are performing at home and to adjust their splinting and pressure program. Frequency of outpatient therapy is based on each individual patient's needs. Regardless of whether or not a patient receives outpatient therapy, he or she should be monitored at regular intervals through an outpatient clinic so burn team members can assess the patient's adjustment back into society and alter the rehabilitation program according to the patient's physical abilities and extent of scar maturation. When an adult patient's burns have matured and full ROM is achieved, further follow-up care is unnecessary. However, a child will need to be monitored until he or she is fully grown as burn scars will not grow with a child and surgical releases of scar tissue may be necessary.

SUMMARY

Burn injuries represent a major health problem in terms of management and care of surviving patients. Specific problems and complications vary according to the extent and depth of thermal destruction of the skin.

The classification of burn injuries is based on the depth of tissue destroyed and includes superficial burn, superficial partial-thickness burn, deep partial-thickness burn, full-thickness burn, and subdermal burn. The rule of nines and the Lund and Browder formula were developed to assist in the initial assessment of the extent of burn injury. The specific clinical signs and symptoms that result from a burn injury vary according to the different classifications. Secondary problems can include infection, pulmonary, metabolic, and cardiac and/or circulatory complications. Medical management addresses life-threatening problems and stabilization of the

patient. Dressings with topical medications, debridement, and surgical excision and skin grafting are primary treatment measures. Physical therapy management focuses on the prevention of scar contracture, maintenance of normal ROM, development of muscular strength and endurance, improvement of cardiovascular conditioning, independence in functional activities and prevention of hypertrophic scarring. Although burn trauma and subsequent recovery can be a devastating life occurrence, treatment facilities and medical professionals exist to assist burned patients and their families return to as normal a life-style as possible.

QUESTIONS FOR REVIEW

1. Describe the two layers of skin and their function.
2. Describe the differences between superficial, partial, and full-thickness burns.
3. Explain how a deep partial-thickness burn can convert to a full-thickness burn.
4. Compare the treatment for deep-partial and full-thickness burns.
5. Describe three primary complications of the pulmonary system due to extensive burns.
6. What are the major metabolic problems associated with burns and how are they treated?
7. List the events that occur in the healing of a burn wound.
8. What are the goals of the initial management and resuscitation of a patient with an acute burn injury?
9. Describe the various types of skin grafts.

10. Differentiate between a split-thickness and full-thickness skin graft.
11. List three essential factors for successful skin graft adherence.
12. List five goals for a burn patient's rehabilitation program.
13. Discuss the types of exercise that are useful in a patient's rehabilitation program.
14. What interventions can be used to prevent burn scar contractures?
15. What interventions can be used to prevent hypertrophic scar formation?
16. What information should be included in patient and family education prior to discharge from the hospital?

REFERENCES

1. Demling, RH: Medical progress: burns. N Engl J Med 313:1389, 1986.
2. Accident Facts. National Safety Council, Chicago, 1983.
3. Demling, RH and LaLonde, C: Burn Trauma. Thieme Medical, New York, 1989.
4. Richard, R and Staley, M (eds): Burn Care and Rehabilitation: Principles and Practice. FA Davis, Philadelphia, 1993.
5. Artz, CP, Moncrief, JA, and Pruitt, BA: Burns: A Team Approach. WB Saunders, Philadelphia, 1979.
6. DiGregorio, VR (ed): Clinics in Physical Therapy: Rehabilitation of the Burn Patient. Churchill Livingston, New York, 1984.
7. Fisher, SV and Helm, PA: Comprehensive Rehabilitation of Burns. Williams & Wilkins, Baltimore, 1984.
8. Baker, SP, O'Neill, B, and Karpf, RS: The Injury Fact Book. Lexington Books, MA, 1984, p 147.
9. MacKay, A, Halpren, J, Mcloughlin, E, et al: A comparison of age-specific burn injury rate in five Massachusetts communities. Am J Public Health 69:1146, 1979.
10. American Burn Association: Hospital and pre-hospital resources for optimal care of patients with burn injury: guidelines for development and operation of burn centers. J Burn Care Rehabil 11:97, 1990.
11. Burn Care Resources in North America 1993–1994. American Burn Association, Baltimore, 1993.
12. Lanir, Y: The fibrous structure of the skin and its relation to mechanical behavior. In Marks, R and Payne, PA (eds): Bioengineering and the Skin. MTP Press, MA, 1981, p 93.
13. Moncrief, JA: The body's response to heat. In Artz, CP, Moncrief, JA, and Pruitt, BA (eds): Burns: A Team Approach. WB Saunders Company, Philadelphia, 1979, pp 24–26.
14. Zawacki, BE: Reversal of capillary stasis and prevention of necrosis in burns. Ann Surg 180:98, 1974.
15. Hummel, RP: Triage and transfer procedures. In Hummel, RP

(ed): Burn Clinical Therapy. John Wright PSG, Boston, 1982, pp 26–27.
16. Johnson, CL, O'Shaughnessy, EJ, and Ostergren, G: Burn Management. Raven Press, New York, 1981, pp 7–8.
17. Gilchrest, BA, Sarter, NA, Staff, JS, et al: The human sunburn reaction: histologic and biochemical studies. J Am Acad Dermatol 5:411, 1981.
18. Johnson, BE and Daniels, F: Lysosome and the reaction of skin to ultraviolet radiation. J Invest Dermatol 53:85, 1969.
19. Sams, WM and Wendelman, RK: The effect of ultraviolet light on isolated cutaneous blood vessels. J Invest Dermatol 53:79, 1969.
20. Mochelle, AB, Pillsbury, RE, and Hurley, HH (eds): Dermatology. WB Saunders, Philadelphia, 1975, p 328.
21. Heggers, JP, et al: Evaluation of burn blister fluid. Plast Reconst Surg 65:798–804, 1980.
22. Rockwell, WB and Ehrlich, HP: Fibrinolysis inhibition in human burn blister fluid. J Burn Care Rehabil 11:1–6, 1990.
23. Garner, WL, et al: The effects of burn blister fluid on keratinocyte replication and differentiation. J Burn Care Rehabil 14:127–131, 1993.
24. Zane, LJ: Evaluation of the acutely ill burn patient. In DiGregorio, VR (ed): Clinics in Physical Therapy: Rehabilitation of the Burn Patient. Churchill Livingston, New York, 1984, p 5.
25. Artz, CP: Electrical injury. In Artz, CP, et al (eds): Burns: A Team Approach. WB Saunders, Philadelphia, 1979, p 351.
26. Hooshmand, H, Radfar, F, and Beckner, E: The neurophysiological aspects of electrical injuries. Clin Electroencephalogr 20:111, 1989.
27. Polaski, GR and Tennison, AC: Estimation of the amount of burned surface area. JAMA 103:34, 1948.
28. Lund, CC and Browder, NC: Estimation of area of burns. Surg Gynecol Obstet 79:352, 1955.
29. Marvin, JA, Heck, EL, Loebl, EC, et al: Usefulness of blood cul-

tures in confirming septic complications in burn patients: evaluation of a new culture method. J Trauma 15:657, 1975.

30. Alexander, JW: The body's response to infection. In Artz, CP, Moncrief, JA, and Pruitt, BA (eds): Burns: A Team Approach. WB Saunders, Philadelphia, 1979, p 107.

31. Zaski, DE, Sawchuck, RJ, Gerding, DN, et al: Increased dosage requirements of gentamycin in burn patients. J Trauma 16:824, 1976.

32. Moylan, JA: Smoke inhalation and burn injury. Surg Clin North Am 60:1530, 1980.

33. Greenberg, MI and Walter, J: Axioms on smoke inhalation. Hosp Med 19:13, 1983.

34. Chu, CS: New concepts of pulmonary burn injury. J Trauma 21:958, 1981.

35. Petroff, PA and Pruitt, BA: Pulmonary disease in the burn patient. In Artz, CP, Moncrief, JA, and Pruitt, BA (eds): Burns: A Team Approach. WB Saunders, Philadelphia, 1979, p 96.

36. Davies, LK, Poulton, TJ, and Modell, JH: Continuous positive airway pressure is beneficial in treatment of smoke inhalation. Crit Care Med 11:726, 1983.

37. Cahalane, M and Demling, RH: Early respiratory abnormalities from smoke inhalation. JAMA 251:771, 1984.

38. Scheulen, JJ and Munster, AM: The Parkland formula in patients with burns and inhalation injury. J Trauma 22:869, 1982.

39. Stephensen, BA: Smoke inhalation: the invisible injury. Registered Nurse 47:36, 1984.

40. Trunkey, DD: Inhalation injury. Surg Clin North Am 58:1133, 1978.

41. Moylan, JA: Smoke inhalation: diagnostic techniques and steroids. J Trauma 19:971, 1979.

42. Venus, B, Matsuda, T, Copiozo, JB, et al: Prophylactic intubation and continuous positive airway pressure in the management of the inhalation injury in burn victims. Crit Care Med 9:519, 1981.

43. Desai, MH, et al: Does inhalation injury limit exercise endurance in children convalescing from thermal injury. J Burn Care Rehabil 14:12, 1993.

44. Black, S, et al: Oxygen consumption for lower extremity exercises in normal subjects and burn patients. Phys Ther 60:1255–1258, 1980.

45. Leman, CJ, et al: Exercise physiology in the acute burn patient: Do we really know what we're doing? Proc Am Burn Assoc 24:91, 1992.

46. Mancusi-Ungaro, HR, VanWay, CW, and McCool, C: Caloric and nitrogen balances as predictors of nutritional outcome in patients with burns. J Burn Care Rehabil 13:695–702, 1992.

47. Wilmore, DW: Metabolic changes in burns. In Artz, CP, Moncrief, JA, and Pruitt, BA (eds): Burns: A Team Approach. WB Saunders, Philadelphia, 1979, p 120.

48. Wilmore, DW and Aulick, LH: Metabolic changes in burned patients. Surg Clin North Am 58:1173, 1978.

49. Shamoon, H, Hendler, R, and Sherwin, RS: Synergistic interactions among antiinsulin hormones in the pathogenesis of stress hyperglycemia in humans. J Clin Endocrinol Metab 52:1235, 1981.

50. Wilmore, DW, Mason, AD, Johnson, DW, et al: Effect of ambient temperature on heat production and heat loss in burn patients. J Appl Physiol 38:593, 1975.

51. Pelham, LD: Rational use of intravenous fat emulsions. Am J Hosp Pharm 38:198, 1981.

52. Alexander, JW, MacMillian, BG, Stinnett, JD, et al: Beneficial effects of aggressive protein feeding in severely burned children. Ann Surg 192:505, 1980.

53. Dominioni, L, Trocki, O, Mochizuki, H, et al: Prevention of severe postburn hypermetabolism and catabolism by immediate intragastric feeding. J Burn Care Rehabil 5:106, 1984.

54. Matsuda, T, Kagan, RJ, Hanumadass, M, et al: The importance of burn wound size in determining the optimal calorie:nitrogen ratio. Surgery 94:562, 1983.

55. Moncrief, JA: The body's response to heat. In Artz, CP, Moncrief, JA, and Pruitt, BA (eds): Burns: A Team Approach. WB Saunders, Philadelphia, 1979, p. 23.

56. Eurenius, K: Hematologic changes in burns. In Artz, CP, Moncrief, JA, and Pruitt, BA (eds): Burns: A Team Approach. WB Saunders, Philadelphia, 1979, p 132.

57. Greenhalgh, DG and Staley, M: Burn wound healing. In Richard, R and Staley, M (eds): Burn Care and Rehabilitation: Principles and Practice. FA Davis, Philadelphia, 1993.

58. Miller, SF, Richard, R, and Staley, M: Triage and resuscitation of the burn patient. In Richard, R and Staley, M (eds): Burn Care and Rehabilitation: Principles and Practice. FA Davis, Philadelphia, 1993.

59. Arturson, G: Microvascular permeability to macromolecules in thermal injury. Acta Physiol Scand (Suppl) 463:111, 1979.

60. Kramer, GC, Harms, BA, Bodai, BI, et al: Mechanisms for reduction of plasma protein following acute protein depletion. Am J Physiol 243:803, 1982.

61. Thomson, PD, et al: A survey of burn hydrotherapy in the United States. J Burn Care Rehabil 11:151–155, 1990.

62. Saffle, JR and Schnebly, WA: Burn wound care. In Richard, R and Staley, M (eds): Burn Care and Rehabilitation: Principles and Practice. FA Davis, Philadelphia, 1993.

63. Heggers, JP, et al: Bactericidal and wound-healing properties of sodium hypochlorite solutions. J Burn Care Rehabil 12:420–424, 1991.

64. Richard, RL: The use of chlorine bleach as a disinfectant and antiseptic in whirlpools. Physical Therapy Forum 7:7–8, 1988.

65. Richard, RL: Physical therapy topics. Physical Therapy Forum 9:6, 1990.

66. Burke, JF: Primary excision and prompt grafting as routine therapy for the treatment of thermal burns in children. Surg Clin North Am 56:477, 1976.

67. Heimbach, DM and Engrav, LH: Surgical Management of the Burn Wound. Raven Press, New York, 1984, pp 1–2.

68. Miller, SF, Staley, M, and Richard, R: Surgical management of the burn patient. In Richard, R and Staley, M (eds): Burn Care and Rehabilitation: Principles and Practice. FA Davis, Philadelphia, 1993.

69. Achauer, BA, Black, KS, Waxman, KS, et al: Long-term skin allograft survival after short-term cyclosporine treatment in a patient with massive burns. Lancet 1:14, 1986.

70. Black, KS, et al: Cyclosporine-induced long-term allograft survival and its potential in posttrauma tissue replacement. J Burn Care Rehabil 8:531–535, 1987.

71. Sakabu, SA, et al: Cyclosporine A for prolonging allograft survival in patients with massive burns. J Burn Care Rehabil 5:410–418, 1990.

72. Cuono, C, Langdon, R, and McGuire, J: Use of cultured epidermal autografts and dermal allografts as skin replacement after burn injury. Lancet 1:1123, 1986.

73. Munster, AM (ed): Cultured epidermal autografts in the management of burn patients. J Burn Care Rehabil 13:121, 1992.

74. Richard, R, et al: A comparison of the Tanner and Bioplasty mesher for maximal skin graft expansion. Proc Am Burn Assoc 25:120, 1993.

75. Bryant, WM: Wound healing. Clinical Symposia, CIBA Pharmaceutical Company 29:20–21, 1977.

76. Larson, D, Huang, T, Linares, H, et al: Prevention and treatment of burn scar contracture. In Artz, CP, Moncrief, JA, and Pruitt, BA (eds): Burns: A Team Approach. WB Saunders, Philadelphia, 1979, p. 466.

77. Greenhalgh, DG, Gaboury, T, and Warden, GD: The early release of axillary contractures in pediatric patients with burns. J Burn Care Rehabil 14:39–42, 1993.

78. Apfel, L, et al: Approaches to positioning the burn patient. In Richard, R and Staley, M (eds): Burn Care and Rehabilitation: Principles and Practice. FA Davis, Philadelphia, 1993.

79. Malick, MH and Carr, JA: Manual on Management of the Burn Patient. Harmarville Rehabilitation Center, Pittsburgh, 1982.

80. Daugherty, M and Carr-Collins, J: Splinting techniques for the burn patient. In Richard, R and Staley, M (eds): Burn Care and Rehabilitation: Principles and Practice. FA Davis, Philadelphia, 1993.

81. Richard, RL: Use of Dynasplint to correct elbow flexion burn contracture: a case report. J Burn Care 7:151, 1986.

82. Richard, R and Staley, M: Dynamic splinting—basic science + modern technology. Physical Therapy Forum, 11:21–22, 1992.

83. Covey, MH, et al: Efficacy of continuous passive motion (CPM) devices with hand burns. J Burn Care Rehabil 9:397–400, 1988.

84. McAllister, LP and Salazar, CA: Case report on the use of CPM on an electrical burn. J Burn Care Rehabil 9:401, 1988.

85. McGough, CE: Introduction to CPM. J Burn Care Rehabil 9:494–495, 1988.
86. Covey, MH: Application of CPM devices with burn patients. J Burn Care Rehabil 9:496–497, 1988.
87. Richard, RL, Miller, SF, and Staley, MJ: The physiologic response of a patient with critical burns to continuous passive motion. J Burn Care Rehabil 11:554–6, 1990.
88. Humphrey, C, Richard, R, and Staley, M: Soft tissue management and exercise. In Richard, R and Staley, M (eds): Burn Care and Rehabilitation: Principles and Practice. FA Davis, Philadelphia, 1993.
89. Herndon, DN, Rutan, RL, and Rutan, TC: Management of the pediatric patient with burns. J Burn Care Rehabil 14:3–8, 1993.
90. Schwanholt, C, Greenhalgh, DG, and Warden, GD: A comparison of full-thickness versus split-thickness autografts for the coverage of deep palm burns in the very young pediatric patient. J Burn Care Rehabil 14:29–33, 1993.
91. Ward, RS: The use of physical agents in burn care. In Richard, R and Staley, M (eds): Burn Care and Rehabilitation: Principles and Practice. FA Davis, Philadelphia, 1993.
92. Moss, BF, Everett, JJ, and Patterson, DR: Psychologic support and pain management of the burn patient. In Richard, R and Staley, M (eds): Burn Care and Rehabilitation: Principles and Practice. FA Davis, Philadelphia, 1993.
93. Schmitt, P, Richard, R, and Staley, M: Lower extremity burns and ambulation. In Richard, R and Staley, M (eds): Burn Care and Rehabilitation: Principles and Practice. FA Davis, Philadelphia, 1993.
94. Schmitt, MA, French, L, and Kalil, ET: How soon is safe? Ambulation of the patient with burns after lower extremity skin grafting. J Burn Care Rehabil 12:33–37, 1991.
95. Burnsworth, B, Krob, MJ, and Langer-Schnepp, M: Immediate ambulation of patients with lower-extremity grafts. J Burn Care Rehabil 13:89–92, 1992.
96. Grube, BJ, Engrav, LH, and Heimbach, DM: Early ambulation and discharge in 100 patients with burns of the foot treated by grafts. J Trauma 33:662–664, 1992.
97. Miles, WK and Grigsby, L: Remodeling of scar tissue in the burned hand. In Hunter, JM, et al (eds): Rehabilitation of the Hand, ed 2. CV Mosby, St. Louis, 1984, p 841.
98. Staley, M and Richard, R: Scar Management. In Richard, R and Staley, M (eds): Burn Care and Rehabilitation: Principles and Practice. FA Davis, Philadelphia, 1993.
99. Kischer, CW and Shetlar, MR: Microvasculature in hypertrophic scars and the effects of pressure. J Trauma 19:757–764, 1979.
100. Leung, PC and Ng, M: Pressure treatment for hypertrophic scars. Burns 6:224, 1980.
101. Deitch, EA, et al: Hypertrophic burn scars: analysis of variables. J Trauma 23:895, 1983.
102. Cheng, JCY, et al: Pressure therapy in the treatment of post burn hypertrophic scar—a critical look into its usefulness and fallacies by pressure monitoring. Burns 10:154, 1984.
103. Alston, DW, et al: Materials for pressure inserts in the control of hypertrophic scar tissue. J Burn Care Rehabil 2:40, 1981.
104. Perkins, K, Davey, RB, and Wallis, K: Current materials and techniques used in a burn scar management programme. Burns 13:406, 1987.
105. Gallagher, J, et al: Discharge videotaping—a means of augmenting occupational and physical therapy. J Burn Care Rehabil 11:470–471, 1990.
106. Braddom, RL, et al: The physical treatment and rehabilitation of burn patients. In Hummel, RP (ed): Clinical Burn Therapy. John Wright PSG, Boston, 1982, pp 297–298.

GLOSSARY

Allograft (homograft): Skin from the same species used to temporarily cover a burn wound. Usually cadaver skin.

Autograft: Skin taken from an unburned area of a patient and transplanted to cover a wound.

Blanch: A white spot seen in the skin when pressure is applied. This is an indication of the presence of viable capillary beds; the blanched area will become pink when pressure is released if the capillary bed is perfused.

Cyclosporine: A drug used to reduce the risk of rejection of transplanted organs (i.e., heart, kidney, liver, and now used with skin transplantation).

Debridement: The removal of eschar and/or any loose tissue from a burn wound.

Dermatome: Device used to harvest thin slices of skin for skin grafting.

Dermis: Deep layer of skin that contains blood vessels, lymphatics, nerve endings, collagen, and elastin; it encloses the sweat glands, sebaceous glands, and hair follicles.

Desquamation (desquamate): Peeling of the outer layers of the epidermis.

Donor site: Site from which a skin graft is taken.

Epidermis: The outermost layer of the skin, which provides the body with a barrier to the environment.

Epithelial islands: Surviving tissue from which new epithelial cell growth will originate.

Eschar: The dead, necrotic tissue from a burn wound.

Escharotomy: Midlateral incision of burned eschar used to relieve pressure in an extremity or on the trunk.

Full-thickness burn: Burn involving the entire dermis.

Full-thickness skin graft: Graft containing epidermis and full dermal thickness.

Hypertrophic scar: Raised scar that stays within the boundaries of the burn wound and is characteristically red, raised, and firm.

Keloid: Raised scar that extends beyond the boundaries of the original burn wound.

Mesh graft: Process in which the donor skin is passed through a device that increases the surface area of the graft.

Partial-thickness burn: Burn involving the epidermis and part of the dermis. Further specified as superficial partial-thickness or deep partial-thickness depending on the amount of dermis involved.

Rule of nines: A method of estimation used to determine the amount of total body surface area that has been burned. It divides the body into segments that are approximately 9 percent of the total.

Sharp debridement: Use of sterile scissors and forceps to remove eschar.

Split-thickness skin graft (STSG): Graft containing epidermis and only the superficial layers of the dermis.

Superficial burn: Burn involving only the epidermal layer, for example, sunburn.

Xenograft (heterograft): Skin used as a temporary wound cover and harvested from another species of animal, usually a pig.

Z-plasty: Procedure used to surgically lengthen a burn scar contracture to allow for greater range of motion.

CHAPTER
26

Traumatic Spinal Cord Injury

Thomas J. Schmitz

OBJECTIVES

1. Identify the major etiologic factors involved in traumatic spinal cord injury.
2. Describe the clinical features following damage to the spinal cord.
3. Describe the potential secondary complications associated with spinal cord injury.
4. Identify the anticipated functional expectations for patients with spinal cord injury at various lesion levels.
5. Identify and describe appropriate assessment and treatment procedures for both the acute and chronic phases of management.

Spinal cord injury (SCI) has been identified as a low-incidence, high-cost disability requiring tremendous changes in a patient's life-style.[1] It is estimated that approximately 11,000 new cases of spinal cord impairment occur in the United States annually. A gross estimate indicates that there are about 200,000 individuals with spinal cord dysfunction currently living in the United States.[2]

DEMOGRAPHICS

Statistics from the National Spinal Cord Injury Data Research Center (NSCIDRC) provide important demographic information about traumatic spinal cord injury.[3]
The NSCIDRC project was organized to determine the true incidence of traumatic SCI in the United States. The results of this project represent information obtained on over 6,000 patients collected between 1973 and 1981 from 17 regional SCI care systems located throughout the country. The sample is representative of approximately 10 percent of the annual incidence of SCI in the United States, for the years during which data were collected. According to J. S. Young (personal communication, June 1986), all the information obtained related to traumatic injuries. Data from this program are a frequently cited source of demographic information on SCI and will provide the statistical references reported in the following sections.

Etiology

Spinal cord injuries can be grossly divided into two broad etiologic categories: traumatic injuries and non-

traumatic damage. *Traumas* are by far the most frequent cause of injury in adult rehabilitation populations. They result from damage caused by a traumatic event such as a motor vehicle accident, fall, or gunshot wound. Because of their higher incidence, management of traumatic injuries will be described in this chapter; however, the treatment principles discussed will have direct application to nontraumatic lesions as well.

Statistics from the NSCIDRC indicate that accidents involving motor vehicles are the most frequent cause of traumatic SCI: automobile, 38 percent; motorcycle, 7 percent; and other vehicles, 1 percent. Jumps and falls ranked second (16 percent), followed by gunshot wounds (13 percent), diving accidents (9 percent), and injuries sustained from falling or flying objects (5 percent). The remaining injuries were largely related to other forms of sport activities and penetrating wounds (other than gunshot). Table 26–1 presents the type and incidence of all accidents reported to the NSCIDRC during the years of data collection.

Nontraumatic damage in adult populations generally result from a disease or pathologic influence. Several examples of nontraumatic conditions that may damage the spinal cord are vascular malfunctions (arterial venous malformation [AVM], thrombosis, embolus, or hemorrhage), vertebral subluxations secondary to rheumatoid arthritis or degenerative joint disease, infections such as syphilis or transverse myelitis, spinal neoplasms, syringomyelia, abscesses of the spinal cord, hysterical paralysis, and neurologic diseases such as multiple sclerosis and amyotrophic lateral sclerosis. Statistics are not currently available that detail the incidence of nontraumatic cord damage. However, it is estimated that nontraumatic etiologies account for 30 percent of all spinal cord injuries.[2]

Table 26–1 FREQUENCY DISTRIBUTION BY ETIOLOGY

Etiology	Cases n	%
Auto accident	2264	38
Motorcycle accident	397	7
Other vehicular accident	36	1
Boat accident	7	<1
Fixed wing aircraft	37	1
Helicopter	13	<1
Snowmobile	6	<1
Bicycle	43	1
Gunshot	782	13
Other penetrating wounds	41	1
Person-to-person	32	1
Explosion	3	<1
Diving	564	9
Football	63	1
Trampoline	32	1
Snow skiing	26	<1
Water skiing	11	<1
Other sports	16	<1
Wrestling	23	<1
Baseball	5	<1
Basketball	6	<1
Surfing	23	<1
Fall or jump	952	16
Falling/flying object	298	5
Pedestrian	100	2
Med./Surg. complication	76	1
Other	51	1
Horseback	16	<1
Gymnastics	18	<1
Rodeo	9	<1
Track/field	2	<1
Field sports	10	<1
Hang gliding	17	<1
Air sports	5	<1
Winter sports	19	<1
Skateboard	1	<1
Unknown	10	<1
TOTAL	6014	100

From Young, et al.,[3] p 26, with permission.

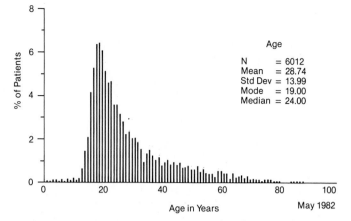

Figure 26–1. Frequency distribution at age of spinal cord injury demonstrating high concentrations in young adults. (From Young, et al.,[3] p 17, with permission.)

DISTRIBUTION BY NSCIDRC VARIABLES

The NSCIDRC project collected data on multiple preinjury and postinjury patient variables. The most salient statistics are presented here. Of the 6014 patients for whom data were collected, 82 percent were men and 18 percent were women. Almost one half of the population were between the ages of 15 and 24 years, with 80 percent of all injuries occurring under the age of 40 years (Fig. 26–1). Seventy-eight percent had only a high school education or less, and 54 percent were single at the time of injury. The data also indicated that a proportionately higher incidence of injuries (31.6%) occurred during the three summer months (June, 9.7%; July, 11.7%; and August, 10.2%) and that 38.6 percent of the injuries occurred on weekends (Saturday, 19.8%; and Sunday, 18.8%).

Cost

The financial impact of SCI is extremely high. The disability is characterized by extended periods of initial hospitalization, medical complications, extensive follow-up care, and recurrent hospitalizations. Medical cost analysis data were available on 6111 patients during the 1973 to 1981 period of the NSCIDRC project. It should be noted that this information is presented in 1981 dollars. Adjusting these data for inflation will provide estimates of charges for other calendar years. The mean hospital charges for the initial medical/rehabilitation period (defined as the period from initial onset of SCI until discharge to a living situation) were $75,300 for complete quadriplegia and $45,400 for complete paraplegia. Twenty percent of those with complete quadriplegia in this study had initial costs of over $100,000. Table 26–2 presents mean hospital charges, and mean and median numbers of days for the initial/rehabilitation period for patients with quadriplegia and those with paraplegia.

Follow-up hospitalization charges are also available

Table 26–2 NUMBER OF DAYS HOSPITALIZED AND HOSPITAL CHARGES DURING INITIAL MEDICAL/REHABILITATION PERIOD

Neurologic Category	Days Hospitalized			Hospital Charges, 1981 Dollars		
	Mean	Std. Dev.	Median	Mean	Std. Dev.	Median
Paraplegic						
Incomplete	110	54	101	$38,700	$21,818	$34,355
Complete	123	55	113	45,400	24,699	39,710
Quadriplegic						
Incomplete	149	78	139	$55,200	$33,161	$49,608
Complete	184	100	166	75,300	51,626	65,145

From Young, et al.,[3] p 123, with permission.

from this study. During follow-up years, individuals with complete quadriplegia spent between $9,100 and $14,000 annually on hospital care. Those with complete paraplegia spent between $8,500 and $11,800. These figures are not comprehensive estimates of follow-up costs, inasmuch as they include only hospital charges, without consideration of outpatient or in-home care, medications, supplies, equipment purchased after discharge, environmental modifications, and so forth.

This brief presentation of demographic information provides some important general perspectives on characteristics of SCI. It is a relatively low-incidence disability affecting a predominantly young population and is associated with lengthy and costly care. Spinal cord injury costs in the United States are estimated at 3 billion dollars annually.[3]

CLASSIFICATION OF CORD INJURIES

Functional Classification

Spinal cord injuries typically are divided into two broad functional categories: quadriplegia and paraplegia. **Quadriplegia** refers to partial or complete paralysis of all four extremities and trunk, including the respiratory muscles, and results from lesions of the cervical cord. **Paraplegia** refers to partial or complete paralysis of all or part of the trunk and both lower extremities, resulting from lesions of the thoracic or lumbar spinal cord or sacral roots.[4]

DESIGNATION OF LESION LEVEL
Several methods of identifying the specific level of lesion are used throughout the world.[5] The most commonly used method is to indicate the most distal uninvolved nerve root segment with *normal function* together with the skeletal level. The term normal function has a precise meaning used in this context.[6] The muscles innervated by the most distal nerve root segment must have at least a fair+ or 3+ grade on manual muscle testing. This grade generally indicates sufficient strength for functional use. For example, if the patient has an intact C-7 nerve root segment (with no sensory or motor function below C-7), the condition would be classified as a *C-7 complete quadriplegia.* However, if spotty sensation and some muscle function (with less than a fair+ muscle grade) were evident below the C-7 nerve root segment, the lesion would be classified as a *C-7 incomplete quadriplegia.*

Oblique injuries to the cord present asymmetric sensory and/or motor function. These lesions are classified in the same manner. However, they require designating the most distal nerve root segment with normal function *on each side* of the patient's body. For example, the designation for an oblique lesion would be recorded as C-6 complete on the right and C-7 complete on the left. This designation may be abbreviated to read *C-6(R) complete* and *C-7(L) complete.*

In considering designation of spinal cord lesions it is useful to review briefly the anatomic relationship of the spinal cord and nerve roots to the vertebral bodies (Fig. 26–2). There are 31 pairs of spinal nerves: eight cervical, 12 thoracic, five lumbar, five sacral, and one coccygeal. The upper cervical nerves are relatively horizontal as they exit the intervertebral foramina. However, the remaining nerves exit in a downward direction and do not emerge at the corresponding vertebral level. During fetal development the cord fills the entire length of the vertebral canal, and the spinal nerves run in a horizontal direction. As the vertebral column elongates with growth, the spinal cord, which does not elongate, is drawn upward. The roots assume an increasingly oblique and downward direction, running in an almost vertical direction in the lumbar area, giving the appearance of a "horse's tail" (cauda equina).

COMPLETE LESIONS
In a **complete lesion** there is no sensory or motor function below the level of the lesion. It is caused by a complete transection (severing), severe compression, or extensive vascular impairment to the cord.

INCOMPLETE LESIONS
Incomplete lesions are characterized by preservation of some sensory or motor function below the level of injury. This preservation of function indicates that some viable neural tissue is crossing the area of injury to more distal segments.[7] Incomplete lesions often result from **contusions** produced by pressure on the cord from displaced bone and/or soft tissues[8] or from swelling within the spinal canal. Some or even complete recovery from contusion is possible when the source of pressure is relieved. Incomplete lesions also may result from partial transection of the cord.

The clinical picture presented by incomplete lesions is unpredictable. There is a mixture of sensory and motor function below the level of lesion, with variable patterns of recovery. Early return of function is generally considered a good prognostic sign.

Despite the uncertainty associated with recovery of incomplete lesions, several syndromes have emerged with consistent clinical features. Information related to the anticipated sensory and motor functions of these syndromes is useful in establishing long-term goals and treatment planning. The area of cord damage of each syndrome is presented in Figure 26–3.

Brown-Sequard Syndrome
The **Brown-Sequard syndrome** occurs from hemisection of the spinal cord (damage to one side) and is typically caused by stab wounds.[7] Partial lesions occur more frequently; true hemisections are rare.[9] The clinical features of this syndrome are asymmetrical.[10,11] On the *ipsilateral (same)* side as the lesion, there is loss of sensation in the dermatome segment corresponding to the level of the lesion. Owing to lateral column damage, there are decreased reflexes, lack of superficial reflexes, clonus, and a positive Babinski's sign. As a result of dorsal column damage, there is loss of proprioception, kinesthesia, and vibratory sense. On the side *contralateral (opposite)* to the lesion, damage to the spinothalamic tracts results in loss of sense of pain and temperature. This loss begins several dermatome segments below the

FUNCTIONAL LEVEL   MUSCLES PRESENT

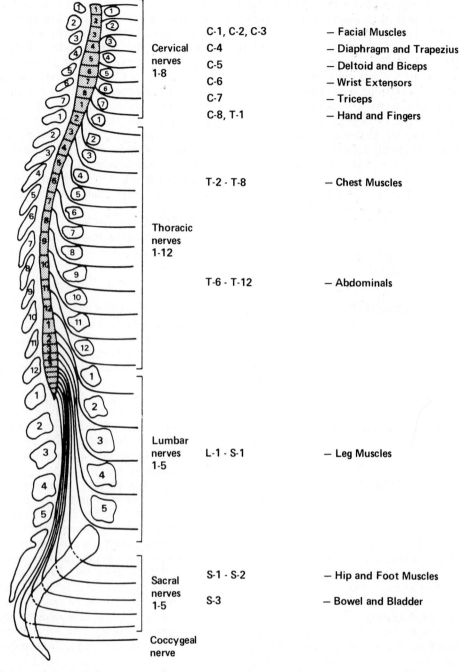

	C-1, C-2, C-3	— Facial Muscles
Cervical	C-4	— Diaphragm and Trapezius
nerves	C-5	— Deltoid and Biceps
1-8	C-6	— Wrist Extensors
	C-7	— Triceps
	C-8, T-1	— Hand and Fingers
	T-2 - T-8	— Chest Muscles
Thoracic nerves 1-12		
	T-6 - T-12	— Abdominals
Lumbar nerves 1-5	L-1 - S-1	— Leg Muscles
Sacral	S-1 - S-2	— Hip and Foot Muscles
nerves 1-5	S-3	— Bowel and Bladder
Coccygeal nerve		

Figure 26–2. Relationship between the spinal cord and nerve roots to vertebral bodies and innervation of major muscle groups. (From Coogler,[6] p 150, with permission.)

level of injury. This discrepancy in levels occurs because the lateral spinothalamic tracts ascend two to four segments on the same side before crossing.[12]

Anterior Cord Syndrome

The **anterior cord syndrome** is frequently related to flexion injuries of the cervical region with resultant damage to the anterior portion of the cord and/or its vascular supply from the anterior spinal artery. There is typically compression of the anterior cord from fracture dislocation or cervical disk protrusion.[12] This syndrome is characterized by loss of motor function (corticospinal tract

damage) and loss of the sense of pain and temperature (spinothalamic tract damage) below the level of the lesion.[11] Proprioception, kinesthesia, and vibratory sense are generally preserved, because they are mediated by the posterior columns with a separate vascular supply from the posterior spinal arteries.

Central Cord Syndrome

The **central cord syndrome** most commonly occurs from hyperextension injuries to the cervical region. It also has been associated with congenital or degenerative narrowing of the spinal canal.[7] The resultant com-

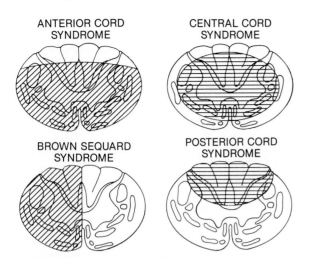

ANTERIOR CORD
SYNDROME

CENTRAL CORD
SYNDROME

BROWN SEQUARD
SYNDROME

POSTERIOR CORD
SYNDROME

Figure 26–3. Areas of spinal cord damage in incomplete cord syndromes. (From Rieser, et al.,[7] p 14, with permission.)

pressive forces give rise to hemorrhage and edema, producing damage to the most central aspects of the cord.[13] There is characteristically more severe neurologic involvement of the upper extremities (cervical tracts are more centrally located) than of the lower extremities (lumbar and sacral tracts are located more peripherally).

Varying degrees of sensory impairment occur[14] but tend to be less severe than motor deficits.[15] With complete preservation of sacral tracts, normal sexual, bowel, and bladder function will be retained.[16]

Patients with central cord syndrome typically recover the ability to ambulate with some remaining distal arm weakness. Surgical intervention to relieve the source of compression has produced significant improvement in some patients.[14]

Posterior Cord Syndrome

The **posterior cord syndrome** is an extremely rare syndrome resulting in deficits of function served by the posterior columns.[8] The clinical picture includes preservation of motor function, sense of pain, and light touch.[7] There is loss of proprioception and epicritic sensations (e.g., two-point discrimination, graphesthesia, stereognosis) below the level of lesion. A wide-based steppage gait pattern is typical. In the past, this syndrome was seen with tabes dorsalis, a condition found with late-stage syphilis.

Sacral Sparing

Sacral sparing refers to an incomplete lesion in which the most centrally located sacral tracts are spared. Varying levels of innervation from sacral segments remain intact. Clinical signs include perianal sensation, rectal sphincter contraction, cutaneous sensation in the "saddle area," and active contraction of the sacrally innervated toe flexors. These are important neurologic findings and often the first signs that a cervical lesion is incomplete.[7,12]

Cauda Equina Injuries

The spinal cord tapers distally to form the conus medullaris at the lower border of the first lumbar vertebra. Although some anatomic variations exist, this is the typ-

ical termination point of the spinal cord.[17] Below this level is the collection of long nerve roots known as the *cauda equina.* Complete transections in this area may occur. However, **cauda equina lesions** are frequently incomplete owing to the great number of nerve roots involved and the comparatively large surface area they encompass (i.e., it would be unlikely that an injury to this region would involve the entire surface area and all the nerve roots).

Cauda equina lesions are peripheral nerve injuries. As such, they have the same potential to regenerate as peripheral nerves elsewhere in the body.[18] However, full return of innervation is not common since (1) there is a large distance between the lesion and the point of innervation, (2) axonal regeneration may not occur along the original distribution of the nerve, (3) axonal regeneration may be blocked by glial-collagen scarring, (4) the end organ may no longer be functioning once reinnervation occurs, and (5) the rate of regeneration slows and finally stops after about 1 year.

Root Escape

Peripheral nerve roots at, or above, the lesion site may also be damaged following SCI. As with other peripheral nerve injuries, the potential for regeneration of nerve roots exists, and some improved function may be evident. The term **root escape** refers to the preservation or return of function of nerve roots at, or near, the level of the lesion. Although it is frequently associated with incomplete cauda equina injuries, root escape may occur at any lesion level.

MECHANISMS OF INJURY

Various mechanisms, often in combination, produce injuries to the spinal cord. Spinal cord injury most frequently occurs from indirect forces produced by movement of the head and trunk and less often from direct injury to a vertebra.[19] Common mechanisms operating in SCI include flexion, compression, hyperextension, and flexion-rotation. These forces result in either a fracture and/or dislocation. The intensity and combination of forces imposed have direct influence on the type and location of fracture(s), the amount of dislocation, and the extent of soft tissue damage.

The spine demonstrates various degrees of susceptibility to injury. Some areas are inherently more vulnerable owing to their high mobility and relative lack of stability as compared with other segments of the spine (e.g., the rigid thoracic region). The areas of the spine that demonstrate the highest frequency of injury are between C-5 and C-7 in the cervical region and between T-12 and L-2 in the thoracolumbar region.[20]

Table 26–3 presents a summary of the major mechanisms of injury involved in SCI.[21–23] Although these forces typically occur *in combination,* they are presented individually inasmuch as each has characteristic patterns of primary and associated injuries.

Two additional contributing mechanisms involved in SCI are **shearing** and **distraction.** Shearing occurs when a horizontal force is applied to the spine relative to the adjacent segment.[12] Shearing frequently disrupts ligaments and is associated with fracture dislocations of the thoracolumbar region.[19] Distraction involves a trac-

Table 26–3 MECHANISMS OF INJURY[19,21–23]

Force	Etiology	Associated Fractures	Potential Associated Injuries
Flexion	1. Head-on collision in which head strikes steering wheel or windshield. 2. Blow to back of head or trunk. 3. Most common mechanism of SCI.	1. Wedge fracture of anterior vertebral body (vertebral body compressed). 2. High percentage of injuries occur from C-4 to C-7 and from T-12 to L-2.	1. Tearing of posterior ligaments. 2. Fractures of posterior elements: spinous processes, laminae, or pedicles. 3. Disruption of disk. 4. Anterior dislocation of vertebral body.
Compression	1. Vertical or axial blow to head (diving, surfing, or falling objects). 2. Closely associated with flexion injuries.	1. Concave fracture of endplate. 2. Explosion or burst fracture (comminuted). 3. Teardrop fracture.	1. Bone fragments may lodge in cord. 2. Rupture of disk.
Hyperextension	1. Strong posterior force such as a rear-end collision. 2. Falls with chin hitting a stationary object (more commonly seen in elderly populations).	1. Fractures of posterior elements: spinous processes, laminae, and facets. 2. Avulsion fracture of anterior aspect of vertebrae.	1. Rupture of anterior longitudinal ligament. 2. Rupture of disk. 3. Associated with cervical lesions; only of minor influence in thoracolumbar injuries.
Flexion-rotation	Posterior to anterior force directed at rotated vertebral column (e.g., rear-end collision with passenger rotated toward driver).	Fracture of posterior pedicles, articular facets, and laminae (fracture is very unstable if posterior ligaments rupture).	1. Rupture of posterior and interspinous ligaments. 2. Subluxation or dislocation of facet joints. 3. In thoracic and lumbar regions, facets may "lock."

tion force and is the least common mechanism. It occurs when significant momentum of the head is created, as in whiplash injuries. This momentum creates a tensile force in the cervical spine as the head is pulled away from the body.[12,19]

CLINICAL PICTURE

Spinal Shock

Immediately following SCI there is a period of areflexia called **spinal shock.** This period of transient reflex depression is not clearly understood. It is believed to result from the very abrupt withdrawal of connections between higher centers and the spinal cord.[24] It is characterized by absence of all reflex activity, flaccidity, and loss of sensation below the level of the lesion. It may last for several hours to several weeks but typically subsides within 24 hours.[25] Early resolution of spinal shock is an important prognostic sign. One of the first indicators that spinal shock is resolving is the presence of a positive **bulbocavernosus reflex.** This test is part of the neurologist's examination. During a digital rectal examination, this reflex is elicited by pressure applied to the glans penis or glans clitoris or by intermittently "tugging" on an indwelling catheter. If positive, a reflex contraction of the anal sphincter around the examining digit will be evident.[26] A positive bulbocavernosus reflex indicates that spinal shock has terminated. This reflex may be present several weeks before deep tendon reflexes are apparent in the lower extremities.[25] However, if this reflex is positive without some evidence of accompanying sensory or motor return (par-

ticularly in the perianal region), spinal shock has subsided, and it usually indicates the presence of a complete lesion.[25]

MOTOR DEFICITS AND SENSORY LOSS

Following spinal cord injury there will be either complete or partial loss of muscle function below the level of the lesion. Disruption of the ascending sensory fibers following SCI results in impaired or absent sensation below the lesion level.

The clinical presentation of motor and sensory deficits is dependent on the specific features of the lesion. These include the neurologic level, the completeness of the lesion, the symmetry of the lesion (transverse or oblique), and the presence or absence of sacral sparing or root escape.

IMPAIRED TEMPERATURE CONTROL

After damage to the spinal cord the hypothalamus can no longer control cutaneous blood flow or level of sweating. This autonomic (sympathetic) dysfunction results in loss of internal thermoregulatory responses. The ability to shiver is lost; vasodilation does not occur in response to heat nor vasoconstriction in response to cold. There is absence of thermoregulatory sweating, which eliminates the normal evaporative cooling effects of perspiration in warm environments. This lack of sweating is often associated with excessive compensatory **diaphoresis** above the level of lesion. Patients with incomplete lesions may also demonstrate "spotty" areas of localized sweating below the lesion level.[27,28]

Changes in thermal regulation result in body temperature being significantly influenced by the external environment. This is a more frequent problem with cervical lesions than with thoracic or lumbar involvement. Patients must rely heavily on sensory input from the head and neck regions to assist in determining appropriate environmental temperatures. Although some improvement in thermoregulatory responses occurs over time, patients with quadriplegia typically experience long-term impairment of body temperature regulation, especially in response to extreme environmental changes.[12]

Respiratory Impairment

Respiratory function varies considerably, depending on the level of lesion. With high spinal cord lesions between C-1 and C-3, phrenic nerve innervation and spontaneous respiration are significantly impaired or lost. An artificial ventilator or phrenic nerve stimulator is required to sustain life. In contrast, lumbar lesions present with full innervation of both primary (diaphragm) and secondary (neck, intercostal, and abdominal) respiratory muscles.

All patients with quadriplegia and those with high-level paraplegia demonstrate some compromise in respiratory function. The level of respiratory impairment is directly related to the lesion level, residual respiratory muscle function, and additional trauma sustained at time of injury, as well as premorbid respiratory status. Respiratory involvement represents a particularly serious and life-threatening feature of SCI. Pulmonary complications (especially bronchopneumonia and pulmonary embolism) are responsible for a high mortality during the early stages of quadriplegia.[12]

There is a progressively greater loss of respiratory function with increasingly higher lesion levels. Multiple respiratory changes occur that are related to both the inspiratory and expiratory phases of ventilation. The primary muscles of *inspiration* are the diaphragm and external intercostals. As the diaphragm contracts and descends, the intercostals normally elevate the ribs and increase the lateral anteroposterior diameter of the thorax.[29] Paralysis of the intercostals results in decreased chest expansion and a lowered inspiratory volume. With progressively higher level lesions, increased involvement of the accessory muscles of respiration will be noted. These muscles assist with elevation of the ribs and include the sternocleidomastoid, trapezii, scaleni, pectoralis minor, and serratus anterior.

The primary muscles of *expiration* are the abdominals and internal intercostals. Normally, relaxed expiration is essentially a passive process which occurs through elastic recoil of the lungs and thorax. However, the abdominals and internal intercostals contribute several important functions related to movement of air out of the lungs. Loss of these muscles significantly decreases expiratory efficiency. When fully innervated, the abdominal muscles play an important role in maintaining intrathoracic pressure for effective respiration. They support the abdominal viscera[30,31] and assist in maintaining the position of the diaphragm. They also function to push the diaphragm upward during forced expiration.[12] With

paralysis of the abdominals this support is lost, causing the diaphragm to assume an unusually low position in the chest.[32] This lowered position and lack of abdominal pressure to move the diaphragm upward during forced expiration results in a decreased expiratory reserve volume.[12] This subsequently decreases cough effectiveness and the ability to expel secretions.

Paralysis of the external obliques also influences expiration. Their normal function is to depress the ribs and to compress the chest wall to assist with forceful expulsion of air.[30,33] With higher-level lesions this function becomes less efficient, with a further reduction in the patient's ability to cough and to expel secretions. These factors combine to make the patient with SCI particularly susceptible to retention of secretions, atelectasis, and pulmonary infections.[12]

Paralysis also results in the development of an altered breathing pattern.[29,34] This pattern (Fig. 26-4) is characterized by some flattening of the upper chest wall, decreased chest wall expansion, and a dominant epigastric rise during inspiration. With relaxation of the diaphragm a negative intrathoracic pressure gradient moves air into the lungs.[29,34] Over time, this breathing pattern will lead to permanent postural changes.

Two additional factors may further impair the respiratory status of the patient: *additional trauma* sustained at the time of injury, and *premorbid respiratory problems*. Fractures (e.g., ribs, sternum, or extremities), lung contusions, or soft tissue damage will also compound respiratory problems. These secondary injuries are particularly problematic if long periods of immobility are required for healing or if pain inhibits full lung expansion. Premorbid respiratory problems such as existing pulmonary disease, allergies, asthma, or a history of smoking will further compromise respiratory function.[12]

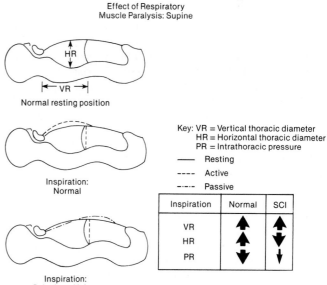

Effect of Respiratory
Muscle Paralysis: Supine

Normal resting position

Inspiration:
Normal

Inspiration:
Spinal cord injury

Key: VR = Vertical thoracic diameter
HR = Horizontal thoracic diameter
PR = Intrathoracic pressure

—— Resting
----- Active
-·--·- Passive

Inspiration	Normal	SCI
VR	↑	↑
HR	↑	↓
PR	↓	↓

Figure 26-4. Effect of paralysis on thoracic volume and breathing pattern. (From Alvarez, et al.,[29] p 1738, with permission.)

Spasticity

Spasticity results from release of intact reflex arcs from central nervous system control and is characterized by hypertonicity, hyperactive stretch reflexes, and clonus. It typically occurs below the level of lesion after spinal shock subsides. There is a gradual increase in spasticity during the first 6 months and a plateau is usually reached 1 year after injury.[25] Spasticity is increased by multiple internal and external stimuli, including positional changes, cutaneous stimuli, environmental temperatures, tight clothing, bladder or kidney stones, fecal impactions, catheter blockage, urinary tract infections, decubitus ulcers, and emotional stress.[12,35]

Spasticity varies in the degree of severity. Patients with minimal to moderate involvement may learn to trigger the spasticity at appropriate times to assist in functional activities. However, strong spasticity interferes with many aspects of rehabilitation and can be a deterrent to independent function. In these situations spasticity is often managed first through drug therapy. Drugs typically used include muscle relaxants and spasmolytic agents such as diazepam (Valium), baclofen (Lioresal), and dantrolene sodium (Dantrium).[36] Drug management is usually not completely successful in alleviating spasticity, and its benefits must be weighed against potentially harmful side effects. Additionally, patients often develop a tolerance to prolonged use of individual drugs.

Injected chemical agents also have been used to decrease spasticity. Generally, these are considered only if results obtained from drug management are deemed inadequate. The two approaches used are **peripheral nerve blocks** and **intrathecal injections.**

In nerve blocks, the chemical injection is used peripherally to selectively block transmission of the motor nerve to a spastic muscle and therefore to interrupt the intact reflex arc peripherally. This procedure provides a temporary reduction in spasticity. These procedures include (1) phenol peripheral nerve blocks, and (2) phenol motor point blocks.[25,36]

Intrathecal (within the spinal canal) injections are used to interrupt the reflex arc mechanism and subsequently to reduce spasticity. Intrathecal approaches provide a more permanent abatement of spasticity. These procedures include intrathecal phenol or alcohol injections.[25,36] Intrathecal injections are used only rarely because they interfere with bladder and sexual function.[4,36]

Surgical approaches also have been used to combat spasticity in more severe cases. They range from relatively simple orthopedic procedures to complex neurosurgery. Orthopedic surgical procedures used include **myotomy,** which is a sectioning or release of a muscle; **neurectomy,** a partial or complete severance of a nerve; or **tenotomy,** a sectioning of a tendon that allows subsequent lengthening (e.g., heel cords). Each of these procedures decreases spasticity by altering the contraction potential of the muscle.[4,25]

A number of more radical neurosurgical interventions are used to eliminate extremely severe spasticity. These destructive approaches (neural tissue is damaged) result in permanent and profound alterations in spasticity. These procedures are useful when spasticity is at an intolerable level and prohibits or significantly limits functional activities. Examples of these interventions include severance of nerve roots (**rhizotomy**) or of spinal cord nerve fibers (**myelotomy**).

Alterations in Bladder and Bowel Function

BLADDER DYSFUNCTION

The effects of bladder dysfunction following SCI pose a serious medical complication requiring consistent and long-term management. Data from the NSCIDRC project indicated that urinary tract infections (UTIs) are the most frequent medical complication during the initial medical-rehabilitation period. The incidence of UTI was 66 percent with paraplegia and 70 percent with quadriplegia.[3]

During the stage of spinal shock, the urinary bladder is flaccid. All muscle tone and bladder reflexes are absent. Medical considerations during this period are focused on establishing an effective system of drainage and prevention of urinary retention and infection.[3]

The spinal integration center for **micturition** is the conus medullaris. Primary reflex control originates from the sacral segments of S-2, S-3, and S-4. Following spinal shock, one of two types of bladder conditions will develop, depending on location of the lesion. Patients with lesions that occur within the spinal cord above the conus medullaris typically develop a *reflex* neurogenic bladder. Following a lesion of the conus medullaris or cauda equina, an *autonomous,* or *nonreflex,* neurogenic bladder develops.

Reflex (upper motor neuron) bladders contract and reflexly empty in response to a certain level of filling pressure. The reflex arc is intact. This reflex emptying may be triggered by manual stimulation techniques such as stroking, kneading, or tapping the suprapubic region[4] or thigh, and lower abdominal stroking, pinching, or hair pulling.[37]

Autonomous or nonreflex (lower motor neuron) bladders are essentially flaccid because there is no reflex action of the detrusor muscle. This type of bladder can be emptied by increasing intraabdominal pressure using a *Valsalva maneuver* or by manually compressing the lower abdomen using the **Crede maneuver.**[38]

Bladder Training Programs

The primary goal of bladder training programs is to allow the patient to be free of a catheter and to control bladder function.[39] Because urinary incontinence has very strong psychosocial implications for the patient, a coordinated approach to this problem is particularly important. Knowledge of and participation in the bladder training program is an important consideration for the physical therapist.

The bladder training program most frequently used with reflex bladders is *intermittent catheterization.* The purpose of this program is to establish reflex bladder emptying at regular and predictable intervals in response to a certain level of filling. Briefly, the program involves establishing a fluid intake pattern restricted to approximately 2000 ml per day. Fluid intake is monitored at 150 to 180 ml per hour from morning until early evening. Intake is stopped late in the day to reduce the need for catheterization during the night. Initially, the patient is catheterized every 4 hours. Prior to catheterization, the patient attempts to void in combination with one or more of the manual stimulation techniques. The catheter is then inserted and residual volume drained. A record is maintained of voided and residual urine. As bladder emptying becomes more effective, residual volumes will decrease and time intervals between catheterizations can be expanded.[39,40]

A *timed voiding program* is another method of bladder training and is indicated for autonomous or nonreflex bladders. This program involves first establishing the patient's pattern of incontinence. The residual urine volume is then checked to ensure that it is within safe limits. Once the pattern of incontinence has been established, it is compared with the patterns of intake. This information provides the basis for establishing a new intake and voiding schedule. The bladder gradually becomes accustomed or "trained" to empty at regular, predictable intervals. As incontinence decreases, the schedule is readjusted to expand the intervals between voiding. Fluid intake is avoided late in the day to decrease the risk of **nocturia**. Stimulation techniques are also incorporated into this type of training program.[39]

It should be noted that not all bladder training programs are successful. Some patients will require long-term use of either an external (condom) or indwelling catheter. For male patients, the condom catheter is preferred because it provides decreased risk of infection. For female patients, an indwelling catheter is currently the only option.

BOWEL DYSFUNCTION

As with the bladder, the neurogenic bowel conditions that develop after spinal shock subsides are of two types. In cord lesions above the conus medullaris there is a *reflex* bowel, and in conus medullaris or cauda equina lesions an *autonomous,* or *nonreflex,* bowel develops.[39]

Bowel Programs

Typically, reflex bowel management requires use of suppositories and digital stimulation techniques to initiate defecation.[41] Digital stimulation involves manual stretch of the anal sphincter, either with a gloved finger or an orthotic digital stimulator. This stretch stimulates peristalsis of the colon and evacuation of the rectum (mediated by S-2, S-3, and S-4).[36] Nonreflex bowel management relies heavily on straining with available musculature and manual evacuation techniques.

The major goal of a bowel program for the patient with a SCI is establishment of a regular pattern of evacuation. This is achieved through multiple interventions, including diet, fluid intake, stool softeners, suppositories, digital stimulation, and manual evacuation.

As with bladder programs, bowel management is an emotionally laden issue and an extremely high priority

for most patients. Lack of bowel control may negate other rehabilitation efforts because it will seriously limit the patient's involvement.[39]

Sexual Dysfunction

"Sexual information is as vital and as 'normal' a part of the rehabilitation process as is providing other information to enable the patient to better understand and adapt to his medical condition."[42] For many years physical disability was assumed to depress or to eliminate sex drives. This erroneous attitude fostered considerable neglect of sexual function as a component of the rehabilitation process.[1] Today, sexual disturbances are recognized as a complex rehabilitation issue. Characterized by physiologic dysfunction, and sensory and motor impairment, these disturbances are often accompanied by social and psychologic distress.[43] Greater numbers of SCI care centers now include a sexual counselor as a component team member. This individual may be a physician or a psychologist with a specialty in this area or a nonphysician specialist trained in sexual dysfunction.[43] Many rehabilitation centers also offer structured programs to assist patients with sexual adjustment.[42,44,45] Although the format of these programs varies, common shared goals include (1) direct patient care including assessment, prognosis, treatment, and counseling; (2) education of the patient and his or her partner; and (3) preparation of staff members to deal with sexual concerns.

THE MALE RESPONSE

Sexual response is directly related to level and completeness of injury. As with bowel and bladder function, sexual capabilities are broadly divided between upper motor neuron (UMN) lesions (damage to the cord above the conus medullaris) and lower motor neuron (LMN) lesions (damage to the conus medullaris or cauda equina).

A slowly expanding body of research is available on the male sexual response following SCI. Statistics related to sexual capacity provide important general information regarding anticipated function following a given type of injury. However, these statistics must be considered cautiously. Owing to the inherent methodologic difficulties in collecting these types of data and the close relationship between sexual activity and self-image, some discrepancy may exist between reported and actual sexual function.[1,46]

Erectile Capacity

In a review of the literature on sexual response after SCI, Higgins[46] presented two consistent findings: (1) erectile capacity is greater in UMN lesions than in LMN lesions, and (2) erectile capacity is greater in incomplete lesions than in complete lesions.

There are two types of erections: *reflexogenic* and *psychogenic*. Reflexogenic erections occur in response to external physical stimulation of the genitals or perineum. An intact reflex arc is required (mediated through S-2, S-3, and S-4). Psychogenic erections occur through cognitive activity such as erotic fantasy. They are mediated from the cerebral cortex either through the thoracolumbar or sacral cord centers.[47]

Comarr[16] reported on erectile capability in 525 patients with UMN lesions. His findings indicated that 93 percent of the patients with complete lesions and 98 percent of those with incomplete lesions had reflexogenic erections. Data were also collected on 154 patients with LMN lesions. In the group with complete LMN lesions, 74 percent had no erections and 26 percent had erections only by psychogenic stimuli. With incomplete LMN lesions, 83 percent had erections, but all by psychogenic means.

Ejaculation

Available data indicate that there is a higher incidence of ejaculation with (1) LMN lesions than with UMN lesions, (2) lower-level versus higher-level cord lesions, and (3) incomplete as compared with complete lesions.[16,46] Comarr[16] also presented data on ejaculation capability from the same total of 679 patients (525 UMN lesions and 154 LMN lesions). In the UMN group, 3 percent with complete and 28.5 percent with incomplete lesions were able to ejaculate. In the LMN group, 16.5 percent with complete and 60 percent with incomplete lesions achieved ejaculation.

Orgasm

Orgasm and ejaculation are two separate events. Orgasm is a cognitive, psychogenic event, whereas ejaculation is a physical occurrence. Relatively little information is available related to the effects of SCI on orgasm. This again relates to inherent difficulties in collecting such data. Higgins[46] also suggests that the few studies that have been done have demonstrated serious methodologic flaws. He identifies the major problems in these studies as a lack of criteria for defining orgasm, considering ejaculation and orgasm as identical events, and a lack of reported data on how subjects achieved orgasm. Currently, accurate data on the effects of SCI on male orgasm are not available.

Fertility

Relatively few patients with SCI are able to sire children. In a group of 529 patients followed to determine progeny, only 3 percent sired children, with patients in the LMN incomplete lesion group being most successful.[16] This low level of fertility results primarily from impaired spermatogenesis and secondarily from an inability to ejaculate.[47]

THE FEMALE RESPONSE

There is a scarcity of literature and systematic reports of data collection related to sexual dysfunction in women with SCI. This may be a function of women remaining capable of sexual intercourse following SCI. It also may be related to the fact that fertility is unaffected, or, perhaps, because of the proportionately lower number of female patients.[48] Trieschmann[1] also believes that this relates to the traditionally passive sexual roles ascribed to women. Consequently, sexual functions of women following SCI have been considered rel-

atively unimpaired and given comparatively little attention. Studies that have been completed have been criticized as lacking in a desired degree of sophistication.[46] The current available information does not clearly delineate the effects of SCI on female orgasm.

Female sexual responses also follow a pattern related to location of lesion. In patients with UMN lesions the reflex arc will remain intact. Therefore, components of sexual arousal (vaginal lubrication, engorgement of the labia, and clitoral erection) will occur through reflexogenic stimulation, but psychogenic response will be lost. Conversely, with LMN lesions, psychogenic responses will be preserved and reflex responses lost.[48,49]

Menstruation

The menstrual cycle typically is interrupted for a period of 1 to 3 months following injury. After this time normal menses return.

Fertility and Pregnancy

The potential for conception remains unimpaired. Pregnancy is possible under close medical supervision inasmuch as the patient is placed at high risk for impaired respiratory function. In addition, owing to impaired sensation the initiation of labor may not be perceived. Labor also may precipitate the onset of autonomic dysreflexia (see the following section on potential secondary complications). Consequently, patients are frequently hospitalized for a period of time prior to the expected delivery date to monitor cervical dilation.[48] Although uterine contractions are hormonally controlled and not affected by paralysis, patients with an inability to bear down during the final stages of delivery[48] or who experience prolonged or difficult labor may be candidates for cesarean section.[26]

A major consideration for the physical therapist regarding sexual dysfunction is that a patient will often direct questions to the individuals with whom he or she feels most comfortable. It is not uncommon for such a discussion to arise during a physical therapy session. These questions or issues should be addressed openly and honestly. In addition, the therapist must anticipate and be prepared for these situations by (1) obtaining accurate information about the patient's physiologic state and anticipated sexual function and (2) by having knowledge of referral options and support services available to the patient for appropriate assessment and counseling.[12]

POTENTIAL SECONDARY COMPLICATIONS

Pressure Sores

Pressure sores are ulcerations of soft tissue (skin or subcutaneous tissue) caused by unrelieved pressure and shearing forces. They are subject to infection, which can migrate to bone. Pressure sores are a serious medical complication, a major cause of delayed rehabilitation, and may even lead to death.[50] Pressures sores are among the most frequent medical complications following SCI[51,52] and were found in one study to be the single most important factor in increasing duration and subsequently cost of hospital stay.[3]

Impaired sensory function and the inability to make appropriate positional changes are the two most influential factors in the development of pressure sores. Other important factors are (1) loss of vasomotor control, which results in a lowering of tissue resistance to pressure; (2) spasticity, with resultant shearing forces between bony surfaces; (3) skin maceration from exposure to moisture (e.g., urine);[53] (4) trauma, such as adhesive tape or sheet burns; (5) nutritional deficiencies (low serum protein and anemia will reduce tissue resistance to pressure); (6) poor general skin condition; and (7) secondary infections.[54] Another primary factor in the development of pressure sores is the intensity and duration of the pressure. The higher the intensity of pressure, the shorter the time required for anoxia of the skin and soft tissues to occur.[53,55]

Pressure sores will develop over any bony prominence subjected to excessive pressure. Among the more common sites of involvement are the sacrum, heels, trochanters, and ischium. Other areas susceptible to skin breakdown are the scapula, elbows, anterior iliac spines, knees, and malleoli.

By far the most important intervention for eliminating the potential development of pressure sores is *prevention*. This will involve a coordinated approach, and it is a responsibility shared by each member of the rehabilitation team. Initially, the patient will be turned every 2 hours by the nursing staff on a 24-hour schedule. Skin condition should be monitored on a continual basis. If a reddened area occurs, the patient's position must be altered immediately to alleviate the pressure. As the rehabilitation program progresses, the patient gradually assumes responsibility for skin care. Preparation for assumption of this responsibility will include patient education as to the potential risks of pressure sores, and instruction in skin inspection techniques and the use of pressure relief equipment and procedures.

Autonomic Dysreflexia

Autonomic dysreflexia (or **hyperreflexia**) is a pathologic autonomic reflex that occurs in lesions above T-6 (above sympathetic splanchnic outflow). Reported incidence of this problem varies. One study[56] found a 48 percent occurrence in a group of 213 patients. Rosen[57] estimates that as many as 85 percent of those with quadriplegia and high-level paraplegia experience this problem during the course of rehabilitation. Episodes of autonomic dysreflexia gradually subside over time and are relatively uncommon, but not rare, 3 years following injury.[57]

This clinical syndrome produces an acute onset of autonomic activity from noxious stimuli below the level of the lesion. Afferent input from these stimuli reach the lower spinal cord (lower thoracic and sacral areas) and initiate a mass reflex response resulting in elevation of blood pressure. Normally, the impulses stimulate the receptors in the carotid sinus and aorta, which signal the vasomotor center to readjust peripheral resistance. Following SCI, however, impulses from the vasomotor center cannot pass the site of the lesion to counteract the hypertension by vasodilation.[57-59] This is a critical, emergency situation. Owing to the lack of inhibition from higher centers, hypertension will persist if not treated promptly. Death may result.

INITIATING STIMULI

The most common cause of this pathologic reflex is bladder distention. Other precipitating stimuli include rectal distention, pressure sores, urinary stones, bladder infections, noxious cutaneous stimuli, kidney malfunction, urethral or bladder irritation, and environmental temperature changes.[12,56] Episodes of autonomic dysreflexia also have been reported following passive stretching at the hip.[60]

SYMPTOMS

The symptoms of autonomic dysreflexia include hypertension, bradycardia, headache (often severe and pounding), profuse sweating, increased spasticity, restlessness, vasoconstriction below the level of lesion, vasodilation (flushing) above the level of the lesion, constricted pupils, nasal congestion, piloerection (goose bumps), and blurred vision.[12,56,61]

TREATMENT

The onset of symptoms should be treated as a *medical emergency*. Because bladder distention is a primary cause of autonomic dysreflexia, the drainage system should be assessed immediately. If the patient is wearing a clamped catheter, it should be released. The drainage tubes also should be checked for internal or external blockage or twisting. If lying flat, the patient should be brought to a sitting position, inasmuch as blood pressure will be lowered in this position. The patient's body should be checked for irritating stimuli such as tight clothing, restricting catheter straps, or abdominal binders.

If symptoms do not subside, or if the source of irritation cannot be located, medical and/or nursing assistance should be sought for possible bladder irrigation (a higher-level block may exist) and assessment for bowel impaction. Drug therapy (antihypertensives) may be indicated to control these episodes if more conservative approaches are unsuccessful.

The attending physician, nursing staff, and other team members should always be notified of occurrences of autonomic dysreflexia. This will allow careful monitoring of the patient for several days following the episode and will alert others to the risk of future occurrences. The individual patient's symptoms, precipitating stimuli, and methods of relief should be documented.

Postural Hypotension

Postural hypotension is a decrease in blood pressure that occurs when a patient is moved from a horizontal position to a vertical position. It is caused by a loss of sympathetic vasoconstriction control. The problem is enhanced by lack of muscle tone, causing peripheral venous and splanchnic bed pooling. Reduced cerebral flow and decreased venous return to the heart also may occur.[36]

Inasmuch as many patients are immobilized for up to 6 to 8 weeks, episodes of postural hypotension are a fairly common occurrence during early progression to a vertical position. They tend to occur more frequently with lesions of the cervical and upper thoracic regions. Patients will often describe the onset as feelings of "dizziness," "faintness," or impending "blackout." Although the exact mechanism is not clearly understood, the cardiovascular system, over time, gradually reestablishes sufficient vasomotor tone to allow assumption of the vertical position.[62]

A related problem is edema of the legs, ankles, and feet, which is usually symmetric and pitting in nature. It occurs secondary to the above problems and is complicated by decreased lymphatic return.[36]

To minimize these effects the cardiovascular system should be allowed to adapt gradually by a slow progression to the vertical position. This frequently begins with elevation of the head of the bed and progresses to a reclining wheelchair with elevating leg rests and use of a tilt-table. Vital signs should be monitored carefully, and the patient should always be moved very slowly. Use of compressive stockings and an abdominal binder will further minimize these effects. Drug therapy may be indicated: for example ephedrine to increase blood pressure[36,58] or low-dose diuretics to relieve persistent edema of legs, ankles, or feet.[36] As vasomotor stability returns, tolerance to the vertical position will gradually improve.

Heterotopic (Ectopic) Bone Formation

Heterotopic bone formation is osteogenesis in soft tissues below the level of the lesion.[55,63] The etiology of this abnormal bone growth is unknown. However, multiple theories have been proposed, including tissue hypoxia secondary to circulatory stasis,[64] abnormal calcium metabolism, local pressure,[65] and microtrauma related to overly aggressive range of motion exercises.[66,67]

Heterotopic bone formation is always extraarticular and extracapsular.[68] It may develop in tendons, in connective tissue between muscle, in aponeurotic tissue, or in the peripheral aspects of muscle.[55,66,68] It must be differentiated from *myositis ossificans,* which results from injury to a muscle and is characterized by bony deposits within muscle tissue. No relationships have been found between the development of heterotopic bone formation and level of injury, amount of exercise, or degree of spasticity or flaccidity.[64,69,70]

Heterotopic bone formation typically occurs adjacent to large joints, with the hips and knees most commonly involved.[63] Other joints that have demonstrated involvement include the elbows,[55] shoulders, and spine.[63] Early symptoms of heterotopic ossification resemble those of

thrombophlebitis, including swelling, decreased range of motion, erythema, and local warmth near a joint. Early onset is also characterized by elevated serum alkaline phosphatase levels and negative radiographic findings.[71] During later clinical stages, soft tissue swelling subsides and radiographic findings are positive.[71]

For many patients the development of heterotopic ossification will pose no significant functional limitations.[12] However, a serious complication affecting 20 percent of patients is joint ankylosis, with the hip most commonly affected.[55]

Management of ectopic bone formation utilizes several approaches, including drug therapy, physical therapy, and, with severe functional limitations, surgery.[12] Drug therapy (diphosphates) has been used to inhibit the formation of calcium phosphate and to prevent ectopic bone formation.[55] These drugs, however, have no effect on mature ectopic bone.[12] Physical therapy is important in maintaining range of motion and preventing deformity. Early research discouraged the use of range of motion, indicating that the exercise increased ectopic bone formation.[67,68] However, later studies have shown no increase in the formation of bone deposition with range of motion exercises.[63,64,70] A logical approach to maintaining functional range of motion appears to be a combination of drug therapy with regular exercises during the early formation stages of ectopic development.[12] Finally, surgery is used when extreme limitations in function impede rehabilitation. This generally involves resection of the ectopic bone.[55]

Contractures

Contractures develop secondary to prolonged shortening of structures across and around a joint, resulting in limitation in motion. Contractures initially produce alterations in muscle tissue but rapidly progress to involve capsular and pericapsular changes.[12] Once the tissue changes have occurred, the process is irreversible. A combination of factors places the patient with SCI at particularly high risk for developing joint contractures. Lack of *active muscle function* eliminates the normal reciprocal stretching of a muscle group and surrounding structures as the opposing muscle contracts.[55] *Spasticity* often results in prolonged unopposed muscle shortening in a static position. *Flaccidity* may result in gravitational forces maintaining a relatively consistent joint position. In addition, faulty positioning, ectopic bone formation, edema, and imbalances in muscle pull (either active or spastic) will contribute to the specific direction and location of contracture development.

Contractures are strongly influenced by the existing pattern of spasticity and the positioning methods used. The hip joint is particularly prone to flexion deformities and typically includes components of internal rotation and adduction. The shoulder may develop tightness in flexion or extension (depending on early positioning). Both patterns at the shoulder are associated with internal rotation and adduction. All joints of the body are at risk for contractures, including the elbows, wrist and fingers, knees, ankles, and toes.

The most important management consideration related to the potential development of contractures is *prevention.* Maintenance of joint motion is effectively achieved by a consistent and concurrent program of range of motion exercises, positioning, and, if appropriate, splinting.

Deep Venous Thrombosis (Thrombophlebitis)

Deep venous thrombosis (DVT) results from development of a *thrombus* (abnormal blood clot) within a vessel. The occurrence of such a clot is a dangerous medical complication. It has the potential to break free of its attachment and to float freely within the venous bloodstream. Such mobile clots are known as *emboli.* They are particularly likely to block pulmonary vessels (pulmonary emboli), which can result in death.[27]

The most important factor contributing to the development of DVT following SCI is loss of the normal "pumping" mechanism provided by active contraction of lower extremity musculature. This slows the flow of blood, allowing higher concentrations of procoagulants (e.g., thrombin) to develop in localized areas. This in turn results in a predisposition to thrombus formation. Normally, these procoagulants are rapidly mixed with large quantities of blood and removed in the liver.[27] The risks of DVT are heightened with age and prolonged pressure (e.g., extended contact against the bed or supporting surface).[53] Prolonged pressure can damage the vessel wall and precipitate initiation of the clotting process. In addition, loss of vasomotor tone and immobility further enhance the potential development of DVT.

The most frequent occurrence of DVT is within the first 2 months following injury.[53] The clinical features include local *swelling, erythema,* and *heat.* These signs are similar to those of early ectopic bone formation and long bone fractures.[55] Differential diagnosis is made on the basis of venous flow studies and venography.[55,72]

The clinical manifestations of DVT have been estimated to occur in approximately 15 percent of SCI patients.[72] However, one study reported an incidence as high as 40 percent.[73] Studies using iodine 125 fibrinogen scanning have yielded a much higher incidence. Fibrinogen scanning is sensitive to fibrin deposits and can detect the presence of an active thrombotic process in the absence of clinical manifestations.[74] Using this technique, incidence of DVT in patients with acute SCI has been reported at 90 percent in one group of 10 patients[75] and 100 percent in a group of 14 patients.[74]

Management of this secondary complication focuses on prevention. Prophylactic anticoagulant drug therapy is typically initiated following the acute onset of injury and routinely continued for 2 to 3 months[73] or for up to 6 months for patients at high risk.[76] Other preventative measures include (1) a turning program designed to avoid pressure over large vessels, (2) passive range of motion exercises, (3) elastic support stockings, and (4) positioning of the lower extremities to facilitate venous return.

Pain

Pain is a common occurrence following SCI.[77] Several classification systems have been developed to describe this pain.[12,78–80] These classifications are related to the source and type of pain as well as to the length of time since onset (acute versus chronic pain).

TRAUMATIC PAIN

Initially, pain experienced following acute traumatic injury is related to the extent and type of trauma sustained as well as to the structures involved. Pain may arise from fractures, ligamentous or soft tissue damage, muscle spasm, or from early surgical interventions. This acute pain generally subsides with healing in 1 to 3 months.[12] Typical management includes immobilization and use of analgesics.[36] Transcutaneous electrical nerve stimulation (TENS) also has been found effective in reducing this type of acute, postinjury pain.[81]

NERVE ROOT PAIN

Pain or irritation may arise from damage to nerve roots at or near the site of cord damage. Pain can be caused by acute compression or tearing of the nerve roots,[82] or it may arise secondary to spinal instability, periradicular scar tissue and adhesion formation, or improper reduction.[36,53] Nerve root pain is often described as sharp, stabbing, burning, or shooting and typically follows a dermatomal pattern.[12] It is most common in cauda equina injuries, in which a high distribution of nerve roots is present.[77]

Management of nerve root pain is a challenging clinical problem. Multiple approaches have been suggested, with varying degrees of success. Conservative management involves drug therapy[82] and transcutaneous electrical nerve stimulation.[80] Surgical interventions for more severe, debilitating pain include nerve root sections (neurectomy) and posterior rhizotomies.[36]

SPINAL CORD DYSESTHESIAS

It is not uncommon for patients to experience many peculiar, often painful sensations (**dysesthesias**) below the level of the lesion. The sensations tend to be diffuse and usually do not follow a dermatome distribution.[36] They occur in body parts that otherwise lack sensation and are often described by the patient as burning, numbness, pins and needles, or tingling feelings. Occasionally they involve abnormal proprioceptive sensations, causing the individual to perceive a limb in other than its actual position.[12,53] Dysesthesias have been described as "phantom" pains or sensations similar to those experienced following amputation.[83] The exact etiology of this pain is not well understood. However, it is theorized to be related to scarring at the distal end of the severed spinal cord.[28,36] These sensations are present following the acute onset of injury and typically subside over time. However, they tend to be more persistent and long-standing in cauda equina lesions.[53]

Dysesthesia pain is particularly resistant to treatment. It is important that the complaints be acknowledged as real and that the patient be educated as to the legitimacy of the pain. Gentle handling of the patient's limbs and careful positioning frequently make the pain more tolerable.[28] Drug management using carbamazepine (Tegretol) and phenytoin (Dilantin) has been found effective in reducing dysesthesia pain.[82] Narcotic analgesics are usually discouraged because of the danger of addiction.[28,37,78] Other forms of treatment have not been found effective in managing this type of pain.[82]

MUSCULOSKELETAL PAIN

Pain also may occur above the level of lesion and frequently involves the shoulder joint.[84,85] Pathologic changes at the shoulder often are related to faulty positioning and/or inadequate range of motion exercises, resulting in tightening of the joint capsule and surrounding soft tissue structures. In addition, the shoulder muscles are excessively challenged in their role as tonic stabilizers to substitute for lack of trunk innervation. This situation may be complicated by muscle imbalances around the joint, inflammation, or upper extremity fractures sustained at the time of injury.

Prevention of secondary shoulder involvement is critical, considering the importance of this joint in self-care and functional activities. Shoulder pain and limitation of range of motion will significantly delay the rehabilitation process. The most important preventative measures include a regular program of range of motion exercise and a positioning program designed to facilitate full motion at the shoulder. To achieve this latter goal, several useful additions to traditional positioning programs have been suggested for the acute patient.[84] The first involves use of arm boards, which can be slid under a mattress with pillows used to alter the height of the supporting surface. With the patient in a supine position, the side boards will allow positioning of the shoulders in 90 degrees of abduction with the elbows extended. A second suggestion, also with the patient in a supine position, is to place the arm above the patient's head for a short period of time. This will encourage external rotation and abduction beyond 90 degrees. The elbows should be in approximately 80 degrees of flexion. Finally, in sidelying, with the lower arm in 90 degrees of shoulder flexion, it is suggested that an axillary pillow be placed under the chest to help relieve pressure on the acromion process and head of the humerus. When the patient is in a sidelying position, the uppermost arm can be extended and abducted and supported on a pillow.

Osteoporosis and Renal Calculi

Changes in calcium metabolism following SCI lead to **osteoporosis** below the level of the lesion and development of renal calculi. Normally, there is a dynamic balance between the bone resorption activity of osteoclasts and the role of osteoblasts in laying down new bone. Following SCI there is a net loss of bone mass as the rate of resorption is greater than the rate of new bone formation.[55] Consequently, there is a greater susceptibility to fracture. As a result of this resorption there are large concentrations of calcium present in the urinary system (hypercalciuria), creating a predisposition to stone formation.

The highest incidence of bone mass changes and hypercalciuria occurs during the first 6 months following SCI.[86,87] After this period, changes gradually diminish and assume a constant low normal level after approximately 1 year.[86,88]

The exact mechanism causing bone mass changes following paralysis is not clearly understood. However, immobility and lack of stress placed on the skeletal system through dynamic weight-bearing activities are well accepted as major contributing factors.

Treatment consists primarily of dietary management and early mobility activities. Dietary considerations include calcium-restricted foods and vigorous hydration (especially increased amounts of water). Excessive intake of foods such as milk, ice cream, and other dairy products high in calcium is generally discouraged.[89,90] High-protein foods such as meats, whole-grain products, eggs, and vitamin-rich foods such as cranberries or dried fruit (e.g., prunes or plums) are encouraged.[40] In addition, the risk of calculi formation will be reduced by prevention of urinary tract infections and careful maintenance of bladder drainage to prevent urinary stasis.[40]

PROGNOSIS

The potential for recovery from SCI is directly related to the extent of damage to the spinal cord and/or nerve roots. Donovan and Bedbrook[21] have identified three primary influences on potential for recovery: (1) the degree of pathologic changes imposed by the trauma, (2) the precautions taken to prevent further damage during rescue, and (3) prevention of additional compromise of neural tissue from hypoxia and hypotension during acute management.

Formulation of a prognosis is initiated only after spinal shock has subsided and is guided by whether or not the lesion is complete. Following spinal shock, a lesion is generally considered *complete* in the absence of any sensory or motor function below the level of cord damage. Early appearance of reflex activity in these instances is considered a poor prognostic indicator.[23] In complete lesions, no motor improvement is expected other than that which may occur from nerve root return.

With *incomplete* lesions some evidence of sensory and/or motor function is noted below the level of the cord lesion after spinal shock subsides. Early signs of an incomplete lesion may be indicated by sacral sparing (perianal sensation, rectal sphincter tone, or active toe flexion). Incomplete lesions also may present with areas of spotty or scattered sensory and motor function throughout.

It is important to note that with most incomplete lesions improvement begins almost immediately following cessation of spinal shock. Many patients will have some progressive improvement of muscle return. It may be minimal or, less frequently, dramatic and usually becomes apparent during the first several months following injury. With a consistent progression of returning function (daily, weekly, or even monthly) further recovery can be expected at the same rate, or slightly slower. Meticulous and frequent assessment of sensory and motor functions during this period will provide important information about the progression of recovery.

In time, the rate of recovery will decrease, and a plateau will be reached. When the plateau is reached and no new muscle activity is observed for several weeks or months, no additional recovery can be expected in the future.

MANAGEMENT

The remainder of this chapter is divided into the acute and subacute phases of rehabilitation. The section on acute management addresses treatment interventions from the onset of injury until the fracture site is stable and upright activities can be initiated. The rehabilitation phase includes suggested treatment activities following initial orientation to the vertical position through preparation for discharge from the rehabilitation facility.

Acute Phase

EMERGENCY CARE

Ideally, management of SCI begins at the location of the accident. Techniques used in moving and managing the patient immediately following the trauma can influence prognosis significantly. Rescue personnel must be adept at questioning and assessing for signs of spinal injury before moving the individual.[12] When a spinal injury is suspected, efforts should be made to avoid both active and passive movements of the spine.[21] Movement of the spine can be averted by strapping the patient to a spinal back board or a full-body adjustable back board, use of a supporting cervical collar, and assistance from multiple personnel in moving the patient to safety. These measures will assist in maintaining the spine in a neutral, anatomic position and will prevent further neurologic damage.[21]

On arrival at the emergency room initial attention is focused on stabilizing the patient medically. A complete neurologic examination is performed. Radiographic studies, tomograms, and myelography assist in determining the extent of damage and plans for management.[21] Attention is directed toward preventing progression of neurologic impairment by restoration of vertebral alignment and early immobilization of the fracture site. A catheter typically is inserted, and secondary injuries are addressed. Unstable spinal fractures require early reduction and fixation. Symptoms of instability may include pain and tenderness at the fracture site, radiating pain, increasing neurologic signs, and decreasing motor function.

FRACTURE STABILIZATION
Cervical Injuries

Immobilization of unstable cervical fractures is achieved via skeletal traction. Traction can be applied by use of tongs attached to the outer skull (Fig. 26–5) or by a halo device (Figs. 26–6 and 26–7).

Tongs. Several types of tongs are available (e.g., Crutchfield, Barton, Vinke, Gardner-Wells), each with a

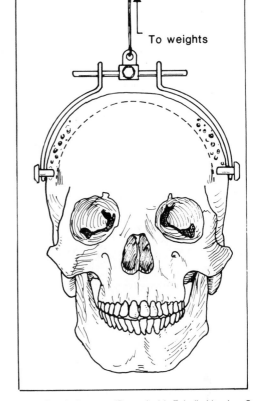

Figure 26–5. Cervical tongs. (From Judd, E (ed): Nursing Care of the Adult. FA Davis, Philadelphia, 1983, p 482, with permission.)

slightly different design. The tongs or calipers are inserted laterally on the outer table of the skull. Traction is accomplished by attachment of a traction rope to the skull fixation. With the patient in a supine position, this

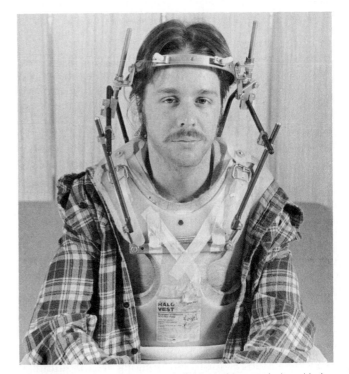

Figure 26–6. Halo device on an individual with a cervical cord lesion.

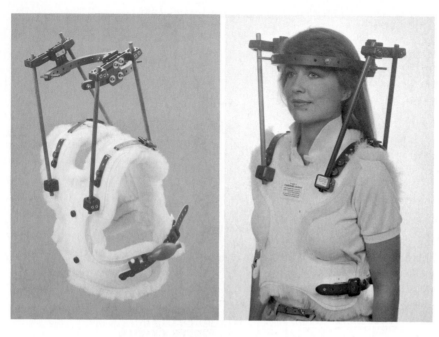

Figure 26–7. The PMT (Progress Mankind Technology) graphite halo system that is MRI compatible. (Courtesy PMT Corporation, Chanhassen, MN.)

rope is threaded through a pulley or traction collar with weights attached distally. The weights hang freely without touching the floor. With the use of tongs as the method of skeletal traction the patient is generally immobilized for about 12 weeks until healing occurs. Today, however, tongs are used primarily as a temporary mode of skeletal traction or for uncomplicated low cervical injuries.

Turning frames and beds. Several types of frames and beds are used during this period of immobilization. Each has different design characteristics and functions. Among the most commonly used turning frame is the Stryker frame. It consists of an anterior and posterior frame attached to a turning base (Fig. 26–8). In turning from a supine position, the anterior frame is placed on top of the patient. A circular ring clamps in place to secure the two frames during turning. Additional security is provided by safety straps. Rotation to the prone position is accomplished by manually turning the two frames as a unit. The uppermost frame is then removed. Return to the supine position is accomplished in the same manner. The primary benefit of these devices is that they allow positional changes while maintaining anatomic alignment of the spine. Turning can be accomplished without interruption of the cervical traction. A disadvantage of turning frames is that positioning is limited to prone and supine. This is particularly problematic for patients with a low tolerance for the prone position (e.g., cardiac or respiratory involvement). In addition, these frames cannot accommodate obese patients and are unsuitable for unconscious patients. Although once the norm for managing spinal fractures, frames are now used primarily as a temporary method of immobilization or for uncomplicated low-cervical, thoracic, or lumbar injuries.

The Roto Rest Kinetic Treatment Table (Roto Rest Bed) is an electronically operated unit that provides continuous side-to-side rotation along its longitudinal axis (Fig. 26–9). Its basic components include an oscillating base frame and a series of bolsters, pads, and supports for patient positioning. The primary advantage of this system for patients with SCI is the ability to maintain spinal alignment with reduction of the secondary complications of bed rest. The continuous oscillation provides the important advantages of improved pulmonary and kidney drainage as well as assisting with prevention of pressure sores via continual redistribution of tissue pressure.

It should be noted that some patients cannot tolerate the continuous oscillation provided by this unit and develop motion sickness. These symptoms may be successfully treated by drug intervention (e.g., Dramamine). If symptoms persist, it may be necessary to discontinue use of the bed. In addition, severe claustrophobia is generally considered a contraindication for use of this bed.

Historically, circular frame beds were also used for patients with SCI. These electronically powered units provided positional changes from supine to prone and reverse by a vertical (upright) turn. An anterior frame was placed on the patient before turning. This type of bed is no longer used for patients with acute SCI, because of the excessive loading of the spine in a vertical position.[91]

Finally, in some facilities standard hospital beds are used. Any of a variety of special mattresses (gel, sand, water, air, or foam) are used for pressure relief. Positional changes are accomplished by log rolling.

Halo devices. Currently, halo devices are used with much greater frequency to immobilize cervical fractures. They have replaced much of the earlier use of skeletal tongs and turning frames and radically altered management of cervical cord lesions. These traction devices (Figs. 26–6 and 26–7) consist of a halo ring with four steel screws that attach directly to the outer skull. The halo is attached to a body jacket or vest by four ver-

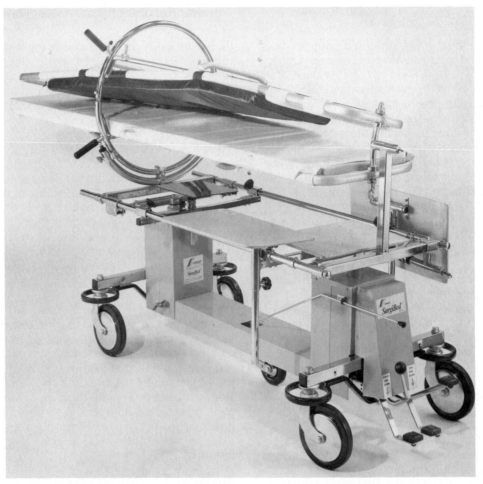

Figure 26–8. Stryker turning frame. (Courtesy Stryker Corporation, Kalamazoo, MI.)

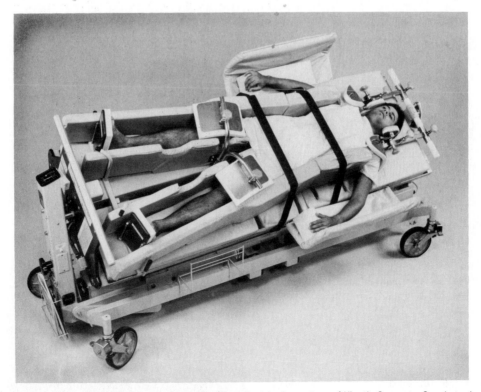

Figure 26–9. Roto Rest kinetic treatment table. (Roto Rest bed, courtesy of Kinetic Concepts, San Antonio, TX.)

tical steel posts. Owing to their structural configuration these devices are contraindicated with severe respiratory involvement.

The introduction of halo devices has generally been considered a major advance in managing cervical fractures. They provide several important advantages over use of tongs and prolonged confinement to a bed or turning frame. These devices reduce the secondary complications of prolonged bed rest, permit earlier progression to upright activities, allow earlier involvement in a rehabilitation program, and reduce the length and cost of hospital stay.[92] In addition, for patients without neurologic involvement, discharge from the hospital may occur several days after application of the halo device. These patients are then followed closely on an outpatient basis.[93]

Skeletal traction devices are left in place until radiographic findings indicate stability has been achieved (approximately 12 weeks). Following removal, a cervical orthotis is applied during a transitional period (approximately 4 to 6 weeks) until unrestricted movement is allowed. The SOMI (sterno-occipital-mandibular-immobilizer) cervical orthotis, Philadelphia collar, or custom-made plastic collars are frequently used during this period, with progression to a soft foam collar prior to resuming unsupported movement.

Thoracic and Lumbar Injuries

Fractures of the thoracic and lumbar area are typically managed by immobilization through bed rest or by application of a body cast or jacket. Bed rest is achieved by use of a turning frame or a standard bed, maintaining a logroll technique for positional changes. The expanded use of spinal orthotics also has allowed for earlier mobility activities following thoracic and lumbar injuries. Plaster or plastic body jackets (Fig. 26–10) function to immobilize the spine and allow earlier involvement in a rehabilitation program. Body jackets are typically bivalved to allow for removal during bathing and skin inspection.

SURGICAL INTERVENTION

Surgery may be indicated to restore bony anatomic alignment, to prevent further damage to the cord, and to stabilize the fracture site.[21] Compared with spontaneous healing times, surgical stabilization allows earlier initiation of rehabilitation activities.[21]

Surgical interventions for cervical fractures may include decompression (anterior or posterior) and fusion. Fusion is achieved by bone grafting and may be combined with posterior wiring of the spinous processes.[94]

Frequently, surgery for thoracic and lumbar fractures requires use of an internal fixation device, which may be used in combination with bone grafts. The three most common devices used for achieving spinal realignment, stability, and internal fixation are Harrington distraction rods, Harrington compression rods, and Weiss compression springs.[95] Following thoracic or lumbar surgery, the patient is placed in a spinal orthosis (e.g., Knight-Taylor orthosis, Jewett hyperextension orthosis; or a custom-made, plastic, bivalved body jacket) for a minimum of 3 months.[95]

PHYSICAL THERAPY ASSESSMENT DURING THE ACUTE PHASE

A general assessment of the patient is indicated, including respiratory function, muscle strength and

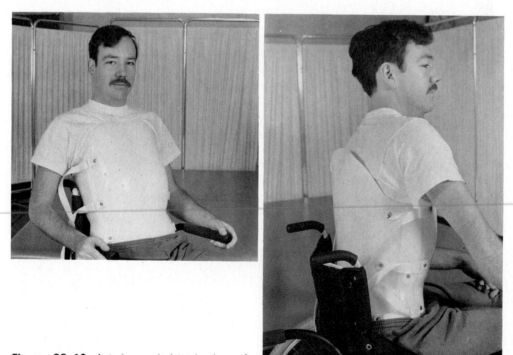

Figure 26–10. Anterior and lateral view of bivalved, plastic body jacket.

tone, and skin condition. Results will assist the therapist in determining the lesion level, identifying general functional expectations, and formulating appropriate treatment goals. As noted earlier, the lesion level is considered to be the lowest segmental level in which muscle strength is present at a fair+ grade. During the acute stage, spinal instability often precludes a complete and thorough physical therapy assessment. However, gross screening will provide important initial data until the patient is cleared for further activity.

1. Respiratory assessment. Details of respiratory status and function are essential. The areas listed below should be assessed:
   a. Function of respiratory muscles. Muscle strength and tone, and atrophy of the diaphragm, abdominals, and intercostals should be assessed; respiratory rate should be noted.
   b. Chest expansion. Circumferential measurements should be taken at the level of the axilla and xiphoid process using a cloth tape measure. Chest expansion is recorded as the difference in measurement between maximum exhalation and maximum inhalation. Normally, chest expansion is approximately 2.5 to 3 inches (6.4 to 7.6 cm) at the xiphoid process.[32]
   c. Breathing pattern. A determination should be made of muscles that are functioning and their contributions to respiration. This may be accomplished by manual palpation over the chest and abdominal region or by observation. Particular attention should be directed toward use of accessory neck muscles and alteration in breathing pattern when the patient is talking or moving.[29]
   d. Cough. Coughing allows the patient to remove secretions. Ineffective cough function will necessitate suctioning to avoid pulmonary complications. Alvarez and coworkers[29] have defined three cough classifications: (1) *functional:* strong enough to clear secretions; (2) *weak functional:* adequate force to clear upper-tract secretions in small quantities; assistance is required to clear mucus secondary to infection; and (3) *nonfunctional:* unable to produce any cough force.
   e. Vital capacity. Initial measures may be taken with a handheld spirometer.[29] Vital capacity measures also can be used as a baseline for defining respiratory muscle weakness.

2. Skin assessment. During the acute phase, meticulous and regular skin inspection is a shared responsibility of the patient and the entire subacute team. As management progresses into the rehabilitation phase, the patient will gradually assume greater responsibility for this activity. Patient education related to skin care is crucial and should be initiated early. Frequent position changes and skin inspection may be viewed by the patient as bothersome or as distracting from sleep if there is not adequate awareness of the importance and purpose of these activities.

   Skin inspection combines both visual *observation* and *palpation.*[96] The patient's entire body should be observed regularly with particular attention to areas most susceptible to pressure (Table 26–4). Palpation

Table 26–4 AREAS MOST SUSCEPTIBLE TO PRESSURE IN RECUMBENT POSITIONS

Supine	Prone	Sidelying
Occiput	Ears (head rotated)	Ears
Scapulae	—	Shoulders (lateral aspect)
Vertebrae	—	Greater trochanter
Elbows	Shoulders	Head of fibula
Sacrum	(anterior aspect)	Knees (medial aspect from contact between knees)
Coccyx	Illiac crest	
Heels	Male genital region	Lateral malleolus
	Patella	Medial malleolus (contact between malleoli)
	Dorsum of feet	

is useful for identifying skin temperature changes that may be indicative of a hyperemic reaction. This is particularly important in assessing dark-skinned individuals, since early skin responses to pressure may not be readily apparent. Skin reactions to excess pressure include redness, local warmth, local edema, and small open or cracked skin areas. Careful attention should be directed toward accidental skin abrasions or bruises, which increase the potential for skin breakdown.[96] If the patient is wearing a halo, vest, or other orthotic device, contact points between the body and the appliance must also be inspected.

3. Sensory assessment. A detailed assessment of superficial, deep, and combined sensations should be completed (see Chapter 6). It should be noted that the sensory level of injury may not correspond to the motor level of injury (i.e., incomplete lesions).

4. Tone and deep tendon reflexes. Muscle tone should be assessed (see Chapter 8) with reference to quality, muscle groups involved, and factors that appear to increase or to decrease tone. An assessment of deep tendon reflexes is indicated. The specific tendons selected for testing will be influenced by the lesion level. The deep tendon reflexes most commonly assessed and their levels of innervation are the biceps (C-6), triceps (C-7), quadriceps (L-3, L-4), and gastrocnemius (S-1).[48]

5. Manual muscle test (MMT) and range of motion (ROM) assessment. Standard techniques should be used for MMT[97] and ROM assessments.[98] Since mobility will be limited during the acute phase, deviations from standard positioning will be necessary and should be carefully documented. In cases of spinal instability, extreme caution should be used when performing gross muscle and ROM tests, because movements of this sort may place undue stress on the fracture site. Discretion should be used in applying resistance around the shoulders in quadriplegia and around the lower trunk and hips in paraplegia.

6. Functional assessment. Accurate and specific determination of functional skills usually must be delayed until the patient is cleared for activity. Once activity is allowed, a more detailed assessment of function can be made (see Chapter 11).

7. Sacral sparing. Periodic checks should be made for the presence of sacral sparing, which may not have been evident on admission (e.g., perianal sensation, rectal sphincter tone, or active toe flexion).

PHYSICAL THERAPY TREATMENT DURING THE ACUTE PHASE

During the acute phase of rehabilitation, emphasis is placed on respiratory management, prevention of secondary complications, maintaining range of motion, and facilitating active movement in available musculature. Pending orthopedic clearance, limited strengthening activities also may be initiated during this early phase.

1. Respiratory management. Respiratory care will vary according to the level of injury and individual respiratory status. Primary goals of management include improved ventilation, increased effectiveness of cough, and prevention of chest tightness and ineffective substitute breathing patterns.[29] Depending on the individual patient, the following treatment activities may be appropriate:

   a. Deep breathing exercises. Diaphragmatic breathing should be encouraged. To facilitate diaphragmatic movement and to increase vital capacity, the therapist can apply light pressure during both inspiration and expiration. Manual contacts can be made just below the sternum. This will assist the patient to concentrate on deep breathing patterns even in the absence of thoracic and abdominal sensation. To facilitate expiration, manual contacts are made over the thorax with the hands spread wide. This creates a compressive force on the thorax, resulting in a more forceful expiration followed by a more efficient inspiration.[4] Patients immobilized in traction devices or limited to recumbent positions may benefit from use of a mirror to provide visual feedback during these activities. Inflation hold and incentive spirometry are also useful adjuncts to deep breathing exercises.[99]

   b. Glossopharyngeal breathing. This activity is often appropriate for patients with high-level cervical lesions. The technique utilizes accessory muscles of respiration to improve vital capacity. The patient is instructed to inspire small amounts of air repeatedly, using a "sipping" or "gulping" pattern, thus utilizing available facial and neck muscles. By using this technique, enough air is gradually inspired to improve chest expansion despite paralysis of the primary muscles of respiration.

   c. Airshift maneuver. This technique provides the patient with an independent method of chest expansion. This maneuver is accomplished by closing the glottis after a maximum inhalation, relaxing the diaphragm and allowing air to shift from the lower to upper thorax. Airshifts can increase chest expansion by 0.5 to 2 inches (1.3 to 5.1 cm).

   d. Strengthening exercises. Progressive resistive exercises can be used to strengthen the diaphragm. This can be accomplished by manual contacts over the epigastric area below the xiphoid process or by use of weights. Strengthening exercises for innervated abdominal and accessory musculature are also indicated.

   e. Assisted coughing. To assist with coughing and movement of secretions, manual contacts are placed over the epigastric area. The therapist pushes quickly in an inward and upward direction as the patient attempts to cough.[4]

   f. Abdominal support. An abdominal corset or binder is indicated for patients whose abdomen protrudes, allowing the diaphragm to "sag" into a poor position for function. The corset will support the abdominal contents and improve the resting position of the diaphragm. In addition, abdominal supports provide the secondary benefits of maintaining intrathoracic pressure and decreasing postural hypotension.

   g. Stretching. Mobility and compliance of the thoracic wall can be facilitated by manual stretching of pectoral and other chest wall muscles.

   In addition to these respiratory approaches, intermittent positive pressure breathing may be utilized to assist in maintenance of lung compliance. Modified postural drainage and percussion techniques also may be indicated to assist with mobilizing and eliminating secretions.

2. Range of motion and positioning. While the patient is immobilized in bed or on a turning frame, full ROM exercises should be completed daily except for those areas that are contraindicated or require selective stretching. With paraplegia, motion of the trunk and some motions of the hip are contraindicated. Generally, straight leg raising more than 60 degrees and hip flexion beyond 90 degrees (during combined hip and knee flexion) should be avoided. This will avert strain on the lower thoracic and lumbar spine. If possible, ROM exercises should be completed in both the prone and supine positions (prone positioning may be contraindicated for some patients due to fracture and/or respiratory compromise in this position). In the prone position, attention should be directed toward shoulder and hip extension and knee flexion. With quadriplegia, motion of the head and neck is contraindicated pending orthopedic clearance. Stretching of the shoulders should be avoided during the acute period; however, the patient should be positioned out of the usual position of comfort, in which there is internal rotation, adduction and extension of the shoulders, elbow flexion, forearm pronation, and wrist flexion. Full ROM exercises are generally included for both lower extremities.

   Patients with spinal cord injuries do not require full ROM in all joints. In some instances, allowing tightness to develop in certain muscles will enhance function. For example, with quadriplegia, tightness of the lower trunk musculature will improve sitting posture by increasing trunk stability; tightness in the long finger flexors will provide an improved tenodesis grasp. Conversely, some muscles require a fully lengthened range. After the acute phase, the hamstrings will require stretching to achieve a straight leg raise of approximately 100 degrees. This ROM is required for many functional activities such as sitting, transfers, lower extremity dressing, and self-ROM exercises. This process of understretching some muscles and full stretching of others is referred to as *selective stretching.*

Positioning splints for the wrist, hands, and fingers are an important early consideration. Alignment of the fingers, thumb, and wrist must be maintained for functional activities or future dynamic splinting.[100] For high-level lesions the wrist is positioned in neutral, the web space is maintained, and the fingers are flexed.[100] If the wrist extensors are functional (fair muscle grade), a C-bar or short-opponens splint is usually sufficient.

Ankle boots or splints are indicated to maintain alignment and to prevent heel cord tightness and pressure sores. Sandbags or towel rolls also may be required to maintain a position of neutral hip rotation.

Following orthopedic clearance, the patient typically is placed on a schedule to increase tolerance to the prone position. For patients wearing a halo device, one or two pillows under the chest will allow assumption of the prone position. The ankles should be positioned at a 90-degree angle. Tolerance to the prone position should be increased gradually until the patient is able to sleep all, or at least part, of the night in this position. This routine will assist with prevention of pressure sores on posterior aspects of the body and development of flexor tightness at the hips and knees. Proning schedules also are considered to promote improved bladder drainage.

3. Selective strengthening. During the course of rehabilitation, all remaining musculature will be strengthened maximally. However, during the acute phase, certain muscles must be strengthened very cautiously to avoid stress at the fracture site. During the first few weeks following injury, application of resistance may be contraindicated to (1) musculature of the scapula and shoulders in quadriplegia, and (2) musculature of the hips and trunk in paraplegia.

An important consideration in planning exercise programs during the acute phase is to emphasize bilateral upper extremity activities because these will avoid asymmetric, rotational stresses on the spine. Several forms of strengthening exercises are appropriate during this early phase: bilateral manually resisted motions in straight planes; bilateral upper extremity proprioceptive neuromuscular facilitation (PNF) patterns; and progressive resistive exercises using cuff weights or dumbbells. Biofeedback training also may be a useful adjunct during early exercise programs. With quadriplegia, emphasis should be placed on strengthening the anterior deltoid, shoulder extensors, biceps, and lower trapezius. If present, the radial wrist extensors, triceps, and pectorals should also be emphasized because they will be of key importance in improving functional capacity. With paraplegia, all upper extremity musculature should be strengthened, with emphasis on shoulder depressors, triceps, and latissimus dorsi, which are required for transfers and ambulation.

Early involvement in functional activities should be stressed. In addition to their intrinsic value, many activities afford the important benefit of progressive strengthening. For example, self-feeding and involvement in limited personal care activities will assist with strengthening the shoulder and elbow flexors. Another example of a functional activity (although not appropriate during the acute phase) with important strengthening benefits is wheelchair propulsion (deltoids, biceps, and shoulder rotators).

4. Orientation to the vertical position. Once radiographic findings have established stability of the fracture site, or early fracture stabilization methods are complete, the patient is cleared for upright activities. As discussed earlier, the patient typically will experience symptoms of postural hypotension if approach to management has required some period of immobility. A *very gradual* acclimation to upright postures is most effective. The use of an abdominal binder and elastic stockings will retard venous pooling. During early upright positioning, elastic wraps are often used in combination with (placed over) the elastic stockings.

Initially, upright activities can be initiated by elevating the head of the bed and progressing to a reclining wheelchair with elevating leg rests. Use of the tilt-table provides another option for orienting the patient to a vertical position. Vital signs should be monitored carefully and documented during this acclimation period.

Patients who have been immobilized in halo devices or undergone surgical spine stabilization will not be confined to recumbent positions for prolonged periods. For these patients, the same progression is used, although a more rapid advance to the vertical position can be anticipated.

Subacute Phase

FUNCTIONAL EXPECTATIONS

A spinal cord injury will require that specific long-term functional goals be established as part of overall rehabilitation planning. Table 26–5 presents reasonable functional expectations, at various lesion levels, for a young, healthy patient unimpaired by secondary complications. This information may be a useful guide in establishing realistic goals. However, it is important not to adhere too closely to established "norms" and, hence, to limit the patient by your own expectations. Goals should be established individually for each patient on the basis of assessment findings in accordance with the level and extent of injury.

The term *key muscles* is a common expression in the management of these patients and is used in Table 26–5. Key muscles are those that add significantly to a patient's functional capability at each successive level of lesion. It is also important to note that the neurologic level of innervation may vary slightly from source to source.

PHYSICAL THERAPY ASSESSMENT DURING THE SUBACUTE PHASE

All the assessment procedures completed during the acute phase will be continued at regular intervals during the subacute phase of rehabilitation. Inasmuch as

Table 26–5 FUNCTIONAL EXPECTATIONS FOR PATIENTS WITH SPINAL CORD INJURY*

Most Distal Nerve Root Segments Innervated and Key Muscles	Available Movements	Functional Capabilities	Equipment and Assistance Required
C-1,C-2,C-3 Face and neck muscles (cranial innervation)	Talking Mastication Sipping Blowing	1. Total dependence in ADL	Respirator dependent: may use phrenic nerve stimulator during the day[101] Full-time attendant required
		Activation of light switches, page turners, call buttons, electrical appliances, and speaker phones	Environmental control units
		2. Locomotion	Electrical wheelchair (typical components include a high, electrically controlled reclining back, a seatbelt and trunk support); a portable respirator may be attached; microswitch or sip-and-puff controls may be used[99]
C-4 Diaphragm Trapezius	Respiration Scapular elevation	1. ADL a. Limited self-feeding	Mobile arm supports (possibly with powered elbow orthotic), powered flexor hinge hand splint Adapted eating equipment (long straws, built-up handles on utensils, plate guards, and so forth) Plexiglas lapboard[100]
		b. Typing	Electric typewriter using head or mouth stick or sip-and-puff controls; another option is a rubber-tipped stick held in hand by a splint (in combination with mobile arm supports and powered splints)
		c. Page turning	Head or mouth stick Environmental control unit for powered page turner
		d. Activation of light switches, call buttons, electrical appliances, and speaker phones	Environmental control units
		2. Locomotion	Electric wheelchair with mouth, chin, breath, or sip-and-puff controls
		3. Pressure relief	Electric reclining back on wheelchair
		4. Transfers and bed mobility	Dependent
		5. Skin inspection	Dependent
		6. Cough with glossopharangeal breathing	Dependent
		7. Recreation a. Table games such as cards or checkers	Head or mouth stick Built-up playing pieces
		b. Painting and drawing	Full-time attendant required
C-5 Biceps Brachialis Brachioradialis Deltoid Infraspinatus Rhomboid (major and minor) Supinator	Elbow flexion and supination Shoulder external rotation Shoulder abduction to 90 degrees Limited shoulder flexion	1. ADL: able to accomplish all activities of a C-4 quadriplegic with less adaptive equipment and more skill a. Self-feeding	Assistance is required in setting up patient with necessary equipment; patient can then accomplish activity independently Mobile arm supports Adapted utensils
		b. Typing	Electric typewriter Hand splints Adapted typing sticks Some patients may require mobile arm supports or slings
		c. Page turning	Same as above
		d. Limited upper extremity dressing	Assistance required
		e. Limited self-care (i.e., washing, brushing teeth, and grooming)	Hand splints Adapted equipment (wash mitt, adapted toothbrush, and so forth)
		2. Locomotion	Manual wheelchair with handrim projections Electric wheelchair with joystick or adapted upper extremity controls
		3. Transfer activities	Overhead swivel bar Sliding board Dependent
		4. Skin inspection and pressure relief	Dependent
		5. Cough with manual pressure to diaphragm	Assistance required
		6. Driving	Van with hand controls Part-time attendant required

Most Distal Nerve Root Segments Innervated and Key Muscles	Available Movements	Functional Capabilities	Equipment and Assistance Required

C-6
Extensor carpi radialis
Infraspinatus
Latissimus dorsi
Pectoralis major (clavicular portion)
Pronator teres
Serratus anterior
Teres minor
	Shoulder flexion, extension, internal rotation, and adduction
	Scapular abduction and upward rotation
	Forearm pronation
	Wrist extension (tenodesis grasp)
		1. ADL
		  a. Self-feeding
		
		  b. Dressing
		
		  c. Self-care
		
		  d. Bed mobility
		2. Locomotion
		
		3. Transfer activities
		4. Skin inspection and pressure relief
		5. Bowel and bladder care
		
		6. Cough with application of pressure to abdomen
		7. Driving
		
		8. Wheelchair sports
			Universal cuff
			Intertwine utensils in fingers
			Adapted utensils
			Utilizes momentum, button hooks, zipper pulls,[100] or other clothing adaptations; dependent on momentum to extend limbs
			Cannot tie shoes
			Flexor hinge splint
			Universal cuff
			Adaptive equipment
			Independent
			Manual wheelchair with projection or friction surface handrims
			Independent with sliding board
			Independent
			
			Can be independent, depending on bowel and bladder routine
			Independent
			
			Automobile with hand controls and U-shaped cuff attached to steering wheel
			Usually requires assistance in getting wheelchair into car
			Limited participation

C-7
Extensor pollicus longus and brevis
Extrinsic finger extensors
Flexor carpi radialis
Triceps
	Elbow extension
	Wrist flexion
	Finger extension
		1. ADL
		  a. Self-feeding
		  b. Dressing
		
		  c. Self-care
		
		2. Locomotion
		3. Transfers
		4. Bowel and bladder care
		
		5. Manual cough
		6. Housekeeping
		
		7. Driving
			Independent
			Independent
			Button hook may be required
			Shower chair
			Adapted hand shower nozzle
			Adapted handles on bathroom items may be required
			Manual wheelchair with friction surface handrims
			Independent (usually without sliding board)
			Independent with appropriate equipment (digital stimulator, suppositories, raised toilet seat, urinary drainage device, and so forth)
			Independent
			Light kitchen activities
			Requires wheelchair-accessible kitchen and living environment
			Adapted kitchen tools
			Automobile with hand controls
			Able to get wheelchair in and out of car

C-8 to T-1 Extrinsic finger flexors Flexor carpi ulnaris Flexor pollicis longus and brevis Intrinsic finger flexor	Full innervation of upper extremity muscles	1. ADL 2. Locomotion 3. Housekeeping 4. Driving 5. Employment	Independent in all self-care and personal hygiene Some adaptive equipment may be required (e.g., tub seat, grab bars, and so forth) Manual wheelchair with standard handrims Independent in light housekeeping and meal preparation Some adaptive equipment may be required (e.g., reachers) Requires a wheelchair-accessible living environment Automobile with hand controls Able to work in a building free of architectural barriers
T-4 to T-6 Top half of intercostals Long muscles of back (sacrospinalis and semispinalis)	Improved trunk control Increased respiratory reserve	1. ADL 2. Physiologic standing (not practical for functional ambulation) 3. Housekeeping 4. Curb climbing in wheelchair 5. Wheelchair sports	Independent in all areas Standing table Bilateral knee-ankle orthoses with spinal attachment Some patients may be able to ambulate for short distances with assistance Independent with routine activities Requires a wheelchair-accessible living environment Able to negotiate curbs using a ''wheelie'' technique Full participation
T-9 to T-12 Lower abdominals All intercostals	Improved trunk control Increased endurance	1. Household ambulation 2. Locomotion	Bilateral knee-ankle orthoses and crutches or walker (high energy consumption for ambulation) Wheelchair used for energy conservation

Table 26–5 FUNCTIONAL EXPECTATIONS FOR PATIENTS WITH SPINAL CORD INJURY* (Continued)

Most Distal Nerve Root Segments Innervated and Key Muscles	Available Movements	Functional Capabilities	Equipment and Assistance Required
L-2,L-3,L-4 Gracilis Iliopsoas Quadratus lumborum Rectus femoris Sartorius	Hip flexion Hip adduction Knee extension	1. Functional ambulation 2. Locomotion	Bilateral knee-ankle orthoses and crutches Wheelchair used for convenience and energy conservation
L-4,L-5 Extensor digitorum Low back muscles Medial hamstrings (weak) Posterior tibialis Quadriceps Tibialis anterior	Strong hip flexion Strong knee extension Weak knee flexion Improved trunk control	1. Functional ambulation 2. Locomotion	Bilateral ankle-foot orthoses and crutches or canes Wheelchair used for convenience and energy conservation

*This table presents general functional expectations at various lesion levels. Each progressively lower segment includes the muscle from the previous levels. Although the key muscles listed frequently receive innervation from several nerve root segments, they are listed here at the neurologic levels where they add to functional outcomes.

greater patient mobility is now allowed, more specific testing of muscle strength, ROM, and functional skills can be completed. A high level of skill in MMT is needed for the therapist to distinguish accurately between true voluntary contraction and movement associated with spasticity or substitution.

During this phase of management, the patient will be instructed gradually to assume responsibility for skin inspection. This will involve practice in use of long-handled (Fig. 26–11) or adapted mirrors to allow inspection of areas not easily visible. Wall mirrors adjacent to the bed may assist in achieving independence with this activity. Patients with high-level lesions may be incapa-

ble of skin inspection. It is important that these patients be instructed in how to direct others to complete this assessment. Continued emphasis by the therapist should be placed on the importance of skin inspection and the rationale for pressure relief. Skin inspection must become a regular and lifelong component of the patient's daily routine.

Once some wheelchair mobility has been achieved, assessment of cardiovascular endurance is indicated (see Chapter 16). The patient's age, sex, and cardiac history should be taken into account. Upper extremity stress testing or telemetry monitoring during wheelchair propulsion may be indicated for patients who are suspected of having impaired cardiovascular adaption to exercise.

PHYSICAL THERAPY TREATMENT DURING THE SUBACUTE PHASE
Continuing Activities

During this phase of management many of the treatment activities initiated during the acute period will be continued. Emphasis will remain on respiratory management, ROM, and positioning. The patient also will be involved in a continuing and expanded program of resistive exercises for all muscles that remain innervated (e.g., PNF, progressive resistance exercise (PRE) using manual resistance, weights, wall pulleys, sling suspension, group exercise classes). Development of motor control and muscle reeducation techniques directed at appropriate muscles (depending on lesion level) are indicated. Emphasis is also placed on regaining postural control and balance by substituting upper body control and vision (for lost proprioception). This phase of treatment will also focus on improved cardiovascular response to exercise. This can effectively be accomplished by use of interval training using an upper extremity aerobic activity (e.g., upper extremity ergometer).

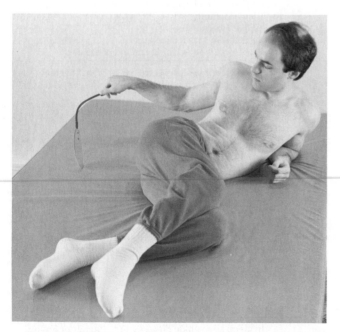

Figure 26–11. Skin inspection with use of long-handled mirror.

Mat programs. Mat activities constitute a major component of treatment during the rehabilitation phase. The sequence of activities typically progresses from achievement of stability within a posture and advances through controlled mobility to skill in functional use. Early activities are bilateral and symmetrical. A progression is then made to weight shifting and movement within the posture. A gradual emphasis is placed on improved timing and speed.

Mat activities are often individual components of more complex functional skills. They should be sequenced from easiest to most difficult so that the patient is performing activities within, or almost within, the sphere of mastery. As mastery of the various components of more complex and difficult activities is achieved, the patient should be asked to perform these tasks in the current living environment (i.e., hospital room, or eventually, home on weekends).

The therapist must determine the appropriate mat activities for each patient based on level of injury and medical status. It is important to note that complete mastery of an activity is not always necessary before moving on to the next. At some points in treatment, several components of the mat progression will be worked on concurrently.

Mat activities should be initiated as soon as the patient is cleared for activity. Progression through the sequence of mat activities develops improved strength and functional ROM, improves awareness of the new center of gravity, promotes postural stability, facilitates dynamic balance, and assists with determining the most efficient and functional methods for accomplishing specific tasks. It also provides the opportunity to develop functional patterns of movement (e.g., use of innervated musculature or momentum to move body parts that lack active movement).

The following section represents a sample progression of selected mat activities. The degree to which they can be performed independently and the time needed to learn them vary considerably with the level of lesion. Each component of the mat progression is presented with its functional implications and several suggested treatment activities to facilitate accomplishment of the activity. Chapter 13 should also be consulted for additional treatment suggestions.

1. Rolling. Rolling is of functional significance for improved bed mobility, preparation for independent positional changes in bed (for pressure relief), and lower extremity dressing.

   Rolling is a frequent starting point of mat programs for these patients and provides an early lesson in developing functional patterns of movement. It requires the patient to learn to use the head, neck, and upper extremities, as well as momentum, to move the trunk and/or lower extremities. It is usually easiest to begin rolling activities from the supine position, working toward the prone position. If asymmetric involvement exists, rolling should be initiated with movement *toward* the weaker side.

   The activity is initially taught on a mat. However, rolling must be mastered also on the surface of a bed, similar to the one that the patient will use at home. To develop maximum independence, bed rails, ropes, or overhead devices should be avoided, if possible. In addition, the patient should achieve independent rolling when covered by sheets and blankets.

   Mat activities. To begin training and to facilitate rolling, several approaches can be used.
   a. Flexion of the head and neck with rotation may be used to assist movement from supine to prone positions.
   b. Extension of the head and neck with rotation may be used to assist movement from prone to supine positions.
   c. Bilateral, symmetrical upper extremity rocking with outstretched arms produces a pendular motion when moving from supine to prone positions. The patient rhythmically rocks the outstretched arms and head from side to side and then forcefully "tosses" them to the side to which the patient is rolling. The trunk and hips will follow (Fig. 26–12). Use of wrist cuffweights (2 to 3 lbs) may be used initially to increase kinesthetic awareness and momentum.
   d. Crossing the ankles will also facilitate rolling (Fig. 26–12). The therapist crosses the patient's ankles so that the upper limb is toward the direction of the roll (e.g., the right ankle would be crossed over the left when rolling toward the left). Rolling can be promoted further by flexing the hip and knee of the top lower extremity and placing it over the opposite limb (e.g., the hip and knee of the right lower extremity would be flexed and placed over the left when rolling toward the left).
   e. In moving from the supine position to the prone position, pillows may be placed under one side of the pelvis (or scapula, if needed) to create initial rotation in the direction of the roll. The activity can be started with two pillows, progress to one, and then to rolling without the use of pillows. If difficulty is encountered in initiating the roll, the activity can be started from a sidelying position. To facilitate movement from prone to supine positions, pillows may be placed under one side of the chest and/or pelvis. Again, the number and height of pillows should be reduced gradually and eventually eliminated.
   f. Several PNF patterns are useful during early rolling activities. The upper extremity patterns of D1 flexion, D2 extension, and reverse chop will facilitate *rolling toward the prone position.* The upper extremity lifting pattern will facilitate *rolling toward the supine position* from sidelying.[102-104]

2. Prone-on-elbows position. The functional implications of this activity are improved bed mobility and preparation for assuming the quadruped and sitting positions.

   This component of the mat progression facilitates head and neck control as well as proximal stability of the glenohumeral and scapular musculature via cocontraction. Scapular strengthening exercises also can be accomplished in this position. At first, the patient may require the therapist's assistance in assuming the prone-on-elbows position. To assume

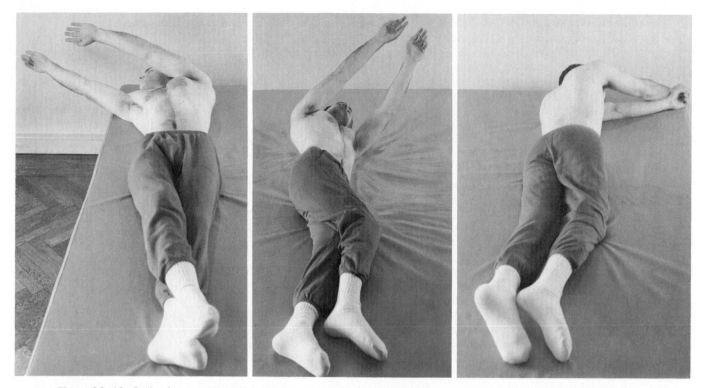

Figure 26–12. Rolling from supine position to prone position facilitated by upper extremity momentum and crossing of the ankles.

this position independently (from prone), the patient places the elbows close to the trunk and the hands near the shoulders and pushes the elbows down into the mat while lifting the head and upper trunk. From this position, one of two maneuvers can be used: (1) weight shifting from elbow to elbow will allow progressive movement of the elbows forward until they are under the shoulders; (2) or body weight can be shifted posteriorly until the elbows are under the shoulders.[32]

Mat activities. The prone-on-elbows position must be used with caution, particularly following thoracic and lumbar injuries. Some patients may find it difficult to tolerate the increased lordotic curve imposed by this position.

a. Weight bearing in the prone-on-elbows position will improve stability through increased joint approximation. Weight shifting assists with the development of controlled mobility and is usually easiest in a lateral direction with a progression to anterior or posterior movements.
b. Rhythmic stabilization may be used to increase stability of the head, neck, and scapula.[102]
c. Manually applied approximation can be used to facilitate tonic holding of proximal musculature.
d. Unilateral weight bearing on one elbow (static dynamic activity) can be achieved in the prone-on-elbows position by having the patient lift one arm. This further facilitates co-contraction in the weight-bearing limb.
e. Movement within this posture can be achieved by an on-elbows forward, backward, and side-to-side progression.

f. Strengthening of the serratus anterior and other scapular muscles can be completed in the prone-on-elbows position. This is accomplished by having the patient push the elbows down into the mat and tuck in the chin, while lifting and rounding out the shoulders and upper thorax (Fig. 26–13). This is similar to the "cat/camel" maneuver used in the quadruped position. The patient lowers the chin and upper chest to the mat again by allowing the scapula to adduct.

3. Prone-on-hands (with paraplegia). The functional carryover of this position (Fig. 26–14) includes devel-

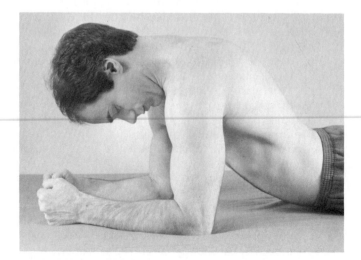

Figure 26–13. Prone-on-elbows position can be used for strengthening the serratus anterior and other scapular muscles.

Figure 26–14. Prone-on-hands position.

opment of the initial hyperextension of the hips and low back for patients who will require this postural alignment during ambulation, and standing from a wheelchair or rising from the floor with crutches and bilateral knee-ankle-foot orthoses (KAFOs).

Some patients may have difficulty assuming this position initially, and a gradual acclimation may be indicated (strong pectoralis major and deltoid muscles are required to accomplish this activity). A gradual progression can be made by supporting the patient's upper trunk with a wide, firm bolster or a sling suspension system. As the patient gradually becomes accustomed to the new position, the height of the support can be increased and eventually removed.

Hand placement for the prone-on-hands position is similar to a standard push-up position except that the hands are slightly more lateral and the arms are externally rotated.

Mat activities. It should be noted that this position will not be appropriate for every patient with paraplegia owing to the excessive lordosis required to assume and to maintain the position.
a. Lateral weight shifting with weight transfer between hands will increase joint approximation.
b. Additional approximation force can be applied through manual contacts to facilitate tonic holding of proximal musculature further.
c. Scapular depression and prone push-ups may be utilized as strengthening exercises.
4. Supine-on-elbows position. The purpose of this activity is to assist with bed mobility and to prepare the patient to assume a long sitting position (Fig. 26–15). There are several approaches to assuming the supine-on-elbows position.[32] If abdominal muscles are present, the patient may have sufficient strength to achieve

the position by pushing the elbows into the mat and lifting into the position.

A more common technique is for the patient to "wedge" the hands under the hips or to hook the thumbs into pants pockets or belt loops. By contracting the biceps and/or wrist extensors, the patient can pull up partially into the posture. By shifting weight from side to side, the elbows can then be positioned under the shoulders.

Finally, some patients may find it easiest to assume this position from sidelying. The lower elbow is first positioned and pushed into the mat. The patient then rolls toward the supine position and quickly extends the upper arm, landing on the elbow as close to the shoulder as possible. By weight shifting, placement of the elbows can then be adjusted.

Mat activities. Much of the inherent benefit of this activity is achieved in learning to assume the posture. In addition to its direct functional significance, this activity is also an important strengthening exercise for shoulder extensors and scapular adductors.
a. Lateral weight shifting can be practiced in this position.
b. Side-to-side movement in this posture will enhance the patient's ability to align the trunk over the lower extremities when in bed or in preparation for positional changes.
5. Pull-ups (with quadriplegia). The purpose of this activity is to strengthen the biceps and shoulder flexors in preparation for wheelchair propulsion.

Mat activity. The patient is positioned in the supine position. The therapist assumes the high-kneeling position with one lower extremity on each side of the patient's hips. The therapist grasps the patient's supinated forearms just above the wrists. The patient pulls to sitting and then lowers back to the mat.

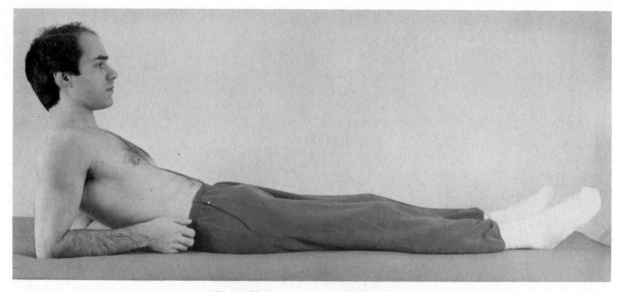

Figure 26–15. Supine-on-elbows position.

6. Sitting. Both long (Fig. 26–16) and short (Fig. 26–17) sitting positions are essential for many activities of daily living, such as dressing, self-ROM, transfers, and wheelchair mobility. Good sitting balance and the ability to move within this posture are also critical prerequisite skills to standing.

Patients with quadriplegia require at least 100 degrees of straight-leg ROM to assume a long sitting position. Without this available motion, hamstring tension will cause a posterior tilting of the pelvis. This will result in the patient's sitting on the sacrum, with resultant stretching of the lower-back musculature.

It is important to note that sitting posture will vary considerably with lesion level. Patients with low thoracic lesions can be expected to sit with a relatively erect trunk. Individuals with low cervical and high thoracic lesions will maintain sitting balance by forward head displacement and trunk flexion. Patients with high cervical lesions will demonstrate poor sitting posture.

For patients with triceps and abdominal musculature (paraplegia), the sitting position can generally be assumed without difficulty. Patients with quadriplegia initially are taught to assume a stable sitting position by placing the shoulders in hyperextension and external rotation, the elbows and wrists in extension with the fingers flexed (flexion of the fingers is particularly important to avoid overstretching, which will interfere with a functional tenodesis grasp). Weight is then borne on the base of the hand. Patients without triceps function can be taught to lock the elbows mechanically, using shoulder girdle musculature. The patient first tosses the shoulder into hyperextension with the forearm supinated. Once the base of the hand makes contact with the mat, the shoulder is quickly elevated to extend the elbow, followed by rapid shoulder depression to maintain elbow extension. This technique will stabilize the arm in hyperextension and external rotation.

There are two basic approaches to instructing the patient to assume the sitting position.[32] Starting in the supine-on-elbows position, the patient is instructed to shift weight from side to side. Once sufficient momentum is achieved, the patient tosses one arm behind and shifts the weight onto that extended arm. The opposite arm is then tossed behind into an extended position. From this point, the patient "walks" the arms forward until a stable sitting position is achieved.

From a prone-on-elbows position the patient creeps sideward, using the elbows and forearms. This will position the trunk in flexion and allow the patient to reach the lower extremities. The patient then hooks the uppermost forearm under the knee, pulls forward with this arm, using the biceps, and then quickly tosses the opposite extremity behind. The upper extremity originally placed under the knee is then also thrown into an extended position. The patient then "walks" forward until a stable sitting position is achieved.

Numerous patients have developed their own variations on these basic techniques. Often patient-devised approaches may be the most appropriate for the individual and should be assessed in terms of safety, function, and energy expenditure. In addition, during the early stages of rehabilitation, adaptive equipment such as an overhead trapeze, rope ladders, or graduated loops hanging from over-bed frames may be used to facilitate movement into sitting.

Mat activities. Several suggestions that can be utilized in a sitting position are listed below:

a. Initial activities will focus on practice in maintaining the position. During early sitting, a mirror may provide important visual feedback.

b. Manual approximation force may be used at the shoulders to promote co-contraction.

c. A variety of PNF techniques may be used. Specifically, alternating isometrics and rhythmic stabilization are important in promoting early stability in this posture.[103]

d. Balancing activities may be practiced in sitting. The base of support provided by the upper extremities can be gradually decreased, can progress to single limb support, or, with some patients, can be eliminated (Figs. 26–16 and 26–17). The patient's limits of stability can be challenged progressively in each position. Activities such as ball throwing or tapping a balloon between the patient and therapist (with or without cuff weights) also may be incorporated into a progression of sitting activities.

e. Sitting push-ups are an important preliminary activity for transfers and ambulation. For quadriplegia, the patient is positioned with the shoulders in extension, the elbows locked, and the hands posterior to the hips. The patient leans forward and depresses the shoulders to clear the buttocks. Initially this activity may be facilitated by manual assistance from the therapist and/or by use of sandbags or small, hard bolsters to provide a firmer weight-bearing surface for the upper extremities (Fig. 26–18). For paraplegia, a progression can be achieved by initiating the activity with weight bearing on the base of the hands placed directly on the mat and then using push-up blocks with graded increments in height.

f. Movement within this posture can be accomplished by using a sitting push-up in combination with momentum created by movement of the head and upper body. This momentum is created by throwing the head and shoulders forcefully in the direction opposite to the desired direction of motion.

For example, while performing a sitting push-up on the mat, simultaneous rapid and forceful extension of the head and shoulders will move the lower extremities forward; movement in a posterior direction can be achieved by use of a sitting push-up with simultaneous rapid and forceful flexion of the head and trunk. This same progression of movement is used with the swing-to and swing-through gait patterns. Early mobility activities in sitting should emphasize adequate clearance of the buttocks for skin protection.

7. Quadruped position (in paraplegia). The functional implication of this all-fours position is its importance as a lead-up activity to ambulation. It is the first position in the mat sequence that allows weight bearing through the hips and is useful for facilitating initial control of the available musculature of the lower trunk and hips.

Generally the patient is instructed to assume a quadruped position from the prone-on-elbows position. From this position the patient can "walk" backward on elbows, progressing to weight bearing on hands, one at a time. Forceful flexion of the head, neck, and upper trunk while pushing into the mat with the elbows or hands will assist with elevating the pelvis. The patient continues to "walk" backward until the hips are positioned over the knees.

A second technique is to assume the quadruped posture from long sitting. In this approach the patient rotates the trunk to allow weight bearing on the hands with the elbows extended. From this sidesitting posi-

Figure 26–16. Individual with a T-4 complete paraplegia in long sitting position without upper extremity support.

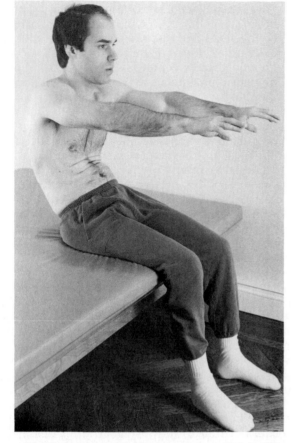

Figure 26–17. Individual with a T-4 complete paraplegia in sitting position without upper extremity support.

tion the patient then moves into the quadruped position by a combination of upper extremity and available trunk strength and momentum from the head and shoulders (moving opposite the direction of the hips).

Mat activities. Several suggested activities that can be utilized in the quadruped position are listed below:

a. Initial activities will involve practice in maintaining the position; rhythmic stabilization can be used to facilitate co-contraction.

b. Manual application of approximation force also can be used to facilitate co-contraction.

c. Weight shifting can be practiced in a forward, backward, and side-to-side direction.

d. Rocking through increments of range (forward, backward, side-to-side, and diagonally) will promote development of equilibrium responses.[102,103]

e. Alternately freeing one upper extremity from a weight-bearing position may be used in the quadruped position. This will provide greater joint approximation forces on the supporting extremity and increase tonic holding of the available postural muscles (e.g., moving the dynamic limb in a diagonal pattern).

f. Movement within the quadruped position (creeping) has important implications for ambulation. Creeping can be used to improve strength (resisted forward progression), to facilitate dynamic balance reactions, and to improve coordination and timing.

8. Kneeling (in paraplegia). This position is particularly important for establishing functional patterns of trunk and pelvic control and for further promoting upright balance control. It is an important lead-up activity to ambulation using crutches and bilateral knee-ankle orthoses.

It is usually easiest to assist the patient into the kneeling position from the quadruped position. From the quadruped position, the patient moves or "walks" the hands backward until the knees further flex and the pelvis drops toward the heels. The patient will be "sitting" on the heels. From this position the patient may be assisted to kneeling by using the upper extremities to climb stall bars while the therapist

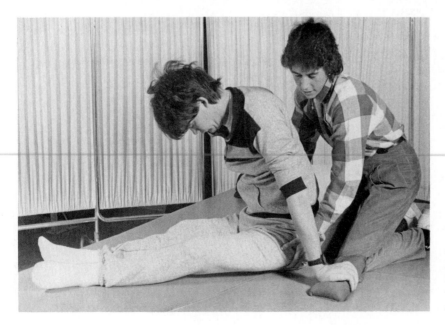

Figure 26–18. Individual with a C-5 incomplete quadriplegia in long sitting position. Pushups are initially facilitated by manual assistance from the therapist with use of sandbags for weight bearing. Note that hand placement maintains finger flexion during wrist extension to avoid stretching of the long finger flexors.

guides the pelvis. Another method is for the therapist to assume a heel-sitting position directly in front of the patient. The patient's upper extremities are supported on the therapist's shoulders while the therapist manually guides the pelvis. In time, the patient will be taught to assume a kneeling position using mat crutches (Fig. 26–19).

Mat activities. Several suggested activities that can be utilized during kneeling are listed below:

a. Initial activities will concentrate on maintaining the position using available musculature and postural alignment (hips fully extended with the pelvis slightly anterior to the knees).

b. The patient's balance may be challenged in this position. Balancing activities may progress from support with both upper extremities to support from only one.

c. A variety of mat crutch activities can be used in the kneeling position; examples include weight shifting anteriorly, posteriorly, and laterally, with emphasis on lower trunk and pelvic control; placing the crutches forward, backward, and to the side with weight shifts in each direction, alternately raising one crutch at a time and returning it to the mat; hip hiking; instruction in gait pattern and forward progression using crutches.

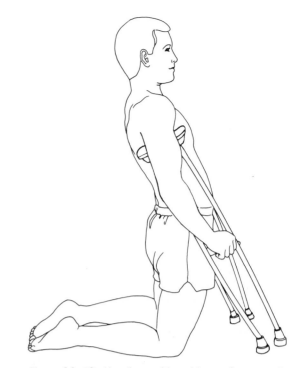

Figure 26–19. Kneeling position with use of mat crutches.

Transfers

Transfer training is generally initiated once the patient has achieved adequate sitting balance. It is a necessary prerequisite skill to many other functional activities, such as tub transfers, ambulation, and driving. Training is usually initiated on a firm mat surface and progresses to alternate surfaces such as a bed, toilet, bathtub, car, chair to floor (and reverse), and so forth. The technique most frequently used by patients with spinal cord injury is some variation of a sliding transfer (with or without the use of a sliding board) (Fig. 26–20). Some experimentation and problem solving between the patient and therapist is generally required

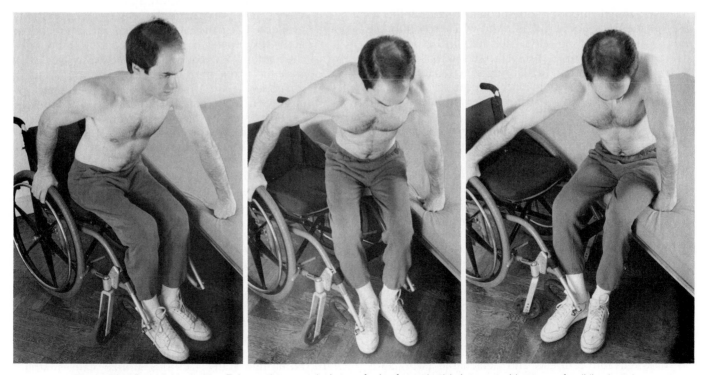

Figure 26–20. Individual with a T-4 complete paraplegia transferring from wheelchair to mat without use of a sliding board.

to determine the most efficient and safest method for an individual patient.

As with all functional skills, the patient is instructed in the component parts of the activity (e.g., locking the brakes, removing the armrests, placing the sliding board) before the entire sequence is attempted.

Wheelchair Prescription and Management

Most patients with spinal cord injuries will use a wheelchair as the primary means of mobility. Even the patient with paraplegia who has mastered ambulation with crutches and orthoses will choose to use a wheelchair on many occasions inasmuch as it provides a lower energy expenditure and greater speed and safety.

Prescription. Because most patients will be using a wheelchair extensively, it should be custom-ordered for each individual. A wheelchair prescription will vary according to the level and extent of injury. More specific information is presented in Chapter 31, however, some general considerations follow:

1. Seat depth should be as close as possible to 1 inch (2.5 cm) back from the popliteal space to allow an even weight distribution on the thighs and to prevent excessive pressure on the ischial tuberosities.
2. Floor-to-seat height is important. If a chair has a sling-type seat, a seat cushion will be required (some contoured, custom-designed seats eliminate the need for a seat cushion). The type and dimensions of the cushion or custom seat must be known so that seat height can be measured accurately, allowing adequate (2 inches [5.1 cm]) clearance from the floor to the foot pedals, and can provide 90-degree angles at the knees.
3. Back height is also a consideration. If the patient will not be pushing the wheelchair, a high back may be desired for added comfort and stability. A patient with quadriplegia who will be pushing the wheelchair requires a back height that is below the inferior angle of the scapula, so that the axilla is free of the handles during functional activities. Most patients with paraplegia prefer a lower back height, especially if they have intact abdominal muscles.
4. Seat width is variable. Wheelchairs come in narrow (16 inches [40.6 cm]) or adult (18 inches [46 cm]) sizes. The patient should be fitted in the narrowest chair possible as long as there is at least a hand's width between the hips and the sides of the chair. The patient's previous weight should be considered, especially if there has been a significant loss since the initial injury, and potential exists to regain the weight. If orthoses are worn, they must also be included in the consideration of width.
5. Patients with lower extremity spasticity may require heel loops and/or toe loops on the footrests to keep the feet in place. Elevating footrests may be necessary if circulatory problems are present.
6. Removable armrests and detachable swing-away legrests are important components of wheelchairs used by many patients with SCI. On some chairs (especially the newer models with tubular designs), the legrests do not detach and the armrests are of a "flip-up" design. The suitability of these features must be considered with respect to the transfer capabilities and techniques used by the individual patient.
7. For individuals who plan to transfer into a car, a lightweight chair is an important consideration. In addition, chairs designed without a below-seat crossbar further facilitate moving the chair into and out of a car. On these chairs the seat back folds down and the entire seating system lifts off. Each of the wheels can also be removed from the axle foundation. This design allows placement of the wheelchair into and out of the car in segmental components rather than as one large unit.
8. Additional wheelchair accessories may be required to meet specific patient needs. Several features that warrant consideration include enlarged release mechanisms on the legrests, a friction surface on the handrims (rubber tubing wrapped around the handrim is often effective), brake extensions, antitipping devices, and grade-aids (which decrease backward movement of the chair while ascending inclined surfaces).
9. Electric wheelchairs are indicated for all patients with C-4 lesions and above. Many patients with C-5 level lesions also elect to use electric wheelchairs, particularly for long-distance travel. Controls are usually either joystick or puff-and-sip types. Hydraulic reclining units are available to allow patients with quadriplegia or high thoracic lesions to manage independent reclining and pressure relief.
10. Some patients may require more than one wheelchair. Many standard lightweight chairs currently available are suitable for sport and recreational activities. However, depending on the interests of the patient, a second chair specifically designed for a particular sport may be required (e.g., racing chairs).

Management. The patient should be taught how to operate all the specific parts of the wheelchair. Management of the brakes, arms, and pedals is crucial for all transfer activities. Many patients with limited hand function are able to propel the wheelchair by using the base of the hand against the handrim. Some patients require assistive devices to aid in propulsion. Vertical or horizontal handrim projections (Fig. 26–21) are useful for patients with poor hand function. The use of leather hand cuffs (or cycling gloves) will protect the skin and also will improve the patient's grip on the handrims.

Wheelchair mobility activities should begin on level surfaces (including doorways and elevators) and progress to outdoor, uneven surfaces. Patients with sufficient upper extremity strength and upper trunk control also should be instructed in "wheelies," which involve balancing on the back wheels of the chair with the casters off the floor. Wheelies are required for independent curb climbing. Many facilities utilize canvas straps secured to the ceiling to assist with teaching this tech-

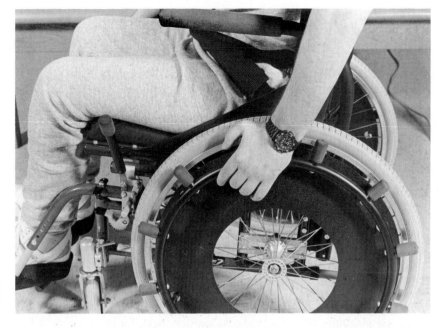

Figure 26–21. Handrim projections assist with forward propulsion of wheelchair for patients with limited grip.

nique. The distal end of each strap has a C-clamp, which attaches to the push handle of the wheelchair. This allows safe practice by eliminating the danger of a posterior fall.

The patient should be instructed in pressure relief techniques from a sitting position. Ten to 15 seconds of pressure relief (or tissue redistribution) for every 5 to 10 minutes of sitting should become part of the patient's daily routine. Although many patients will develop their own techniques, several common approaches to these activities include (1) wheelchair push-ups; (2) hooking an elbow or wrist around the push handle and leaning toward the opposite wheel (Fig. 26–22); and (3) hooking one elbow or wrist around the push handle and lean-

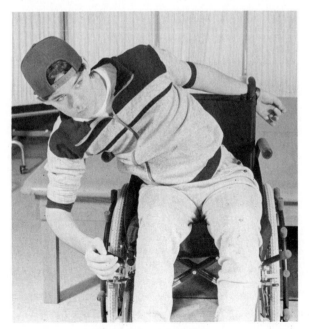

Figure 26–22. Lateral weight shift for pressure relief.

ing forward (if triceps are available, hooking the elbow or wrist will be unnecessary).

Those patients who will be driving a car must learn how to fold and/or disassemble the wheelchair and slide it in and out of the car as well as learn to drive with hand controls. Transfer techniques should be considered with respect to the type of car the patient will drive. Vans with self-contained lifting platforms are a great asset for patients with quadriplegia and can increase their functional independence significantly.

Ambulation for Patients with Paraplegia

After the patient has mastered bed, mat, and wheelchair activities, ambulation can be initiated. The goals of such training include (1) teaching functional ambulation, or (2) increasing physiologic standing tolerance. Initially, most patients expect that they will become functional ambulators.

A number of factors will influence the success or failure in attaining this goal. Patients must possess adequate muscle strength, postural alignment, range of motion, and sufficient cardiovascular endurance to be considered a candidate for ambulation. Patients who become functional ambulators are those whose trunk muscles (abdominals and erector spinae) grade fair or better. This usually excludes patients with high thoracic lesions (T-2 to T-8) who lack the ability to stabilize the trunk and pelvis and, in addition, who demonstrate poor respiratory reserve. Patients with incomplete lesions who demonstrate some residual strength in one or both hip flexors and/or quadriceps are more likely to achieve success in ambulating functionally.[105]

Inasmuch as spinal bracing is too restrictive, heavy, and impractical for functional ambulation, adequate range of motion and postural alignment are crucial in achieving stability of the trunk. Full ROM in hip extension is essential in attaining balance in the upright position. The patient learns to lean into the anterior ligaments of the hip in order to stabilize the trunk or pelvis. The absence of knee flexion and plantarflexion contractures is also important in attaining upright standing balance.

Adequate cardiovascular endurance also is a criterion for functional ambulation. Because the energy cost of ambulation for a patient with paraplegia is two to four times greater than normal walking, endurance becomes an important factor in determining success or failure as a functional ambulator.[106] Although some training effects can be attained with a program of endurance training for the upper extremities, the patient's age, body weight, and history of cardiovascular disease or respiratory problems can restrict the amount that can be achieved. Other factors that may restrict ambulation include severe spasticity, loss of proprioception (particularly at the hips and knees), pain, and the presence of secondary complications such as decubitus ulcers, heterotopic bone formation at the hips, or deformity. In addition, the patient's motivation plays a key role in determining success or failure in ambulation. A highly motivated patient can learn to ambulate with limited residual function. However, these patients may eventually find that the energy cost of ambulation is too great.

Follow-up studies of long-term continuation of ambulation have not been extensive. Mikelberg and Reid[107] surveyed 60 individuals with SCI for whom orthotics had been prescribed. They received a total of 35 replies. From this group, 60 percent used their wheelchairs as the primary means of mobility. Thirty-one percent completely discarded their orthoses. Those that did use their orthoses reserved them primarily for standing and exercise activities. Considering the high cost of orthoses and ambulatory training, the authors suggest careful individual consideration of each patient before orthoses are prescribed. They also suggest delaying decisions about ambulation; training might reasonably occur during a later, follow-up readmission.

Orthotic prescription and ambulation potential. The orthotic prescription varies according to the lesion level. Usually only ankle and/or knee control bracing is necessary. Patients with low thoracic lesions, T-9 to T-12, will require KAFOs. Conventional KAFOs include bilateral metal uprights, posterior thigh and calf bands, an anterior knee flexion pad, drop-ring or bail locks, adjustable locked ankle joints, a heavy-duty stirrup, and a cushion heel. The ankle joints are usually locked in 5 to 10 degrees of dorsiflexion to assist hip extension at heel strike. Orthotic hip control is not necessary, because the braces allow the patient to balance weight over the feet with the hips hyperextended (Fig. 26–23). The center of gravity is kept posterior to the hip joints but anterior to the ankles.

The Scott-Craig orthosis[108] is another type of KAFO that is frequently prescribed for patients with paraplegia (see Chapter 30). These orthoses consist of standard double uprights, an offset knee joint providing improved biomechanical alignment, bail locks, a posterior thigh band, an anterior tibial band, adjustable ankle joint, and a sole plate that extends beyond the metatarsal heads.[109] A modification of this orthosis (Fig. 26–24) includes a plastic solid ankle section in place of the metal ankle

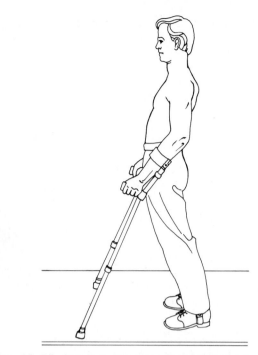

Figure 26–23. Standing alignment using bilateral knee-ankle-foot orthoses. Note that the upright position is maintained by leaning into the anterior Y ligaments, creating hyperextension at the hips.

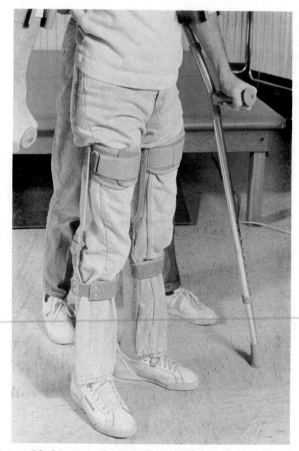

Figure 26–24. New England Regional Spinal Cord Injury Center (NERSCIC) orthosis (modification of the Craig-Scott orthosis). Note that patient is wearing orthoses over clothing for purposes of demonstration.

joint and sole plate.[110] This change decreases overall weight of the orthosis, improves cosmesis, and eliminates the need for custom-made shoes.[110]

Another type of orthotic device available to patients with SCI are the reciprocating gait orthoses (RGO) (see Chapter 30). The RGO is composed of two plastic KAFOs that are joined by a molded pelvic band with thoracic extensions. The RGO has a dual-cable system that runs posteriorly and attaches at the hip joints. These cable attachments transmit forces between lower extremities and provide reciprocal movement. Movement at the hip in one direction facilitates movement in the opposite direction on the contralateral hip. For example, as weight is shifted onto the left lower extremity the right is moved forward. The dual-cable system allows control of both flexion and extension. These cables function to "coordinate" action between the two extremities during ambulation. As the advancing leg is unloaded, it is assisted into flexion while the stance leg is simultaneously pushed into extension. Thus, the orthosis allows for unilateral leg advancement and a reciprocating gait pattern.[111] With this orthosis, a two- or four-point gait pattern can be used in combination with crutches or a reciprocating walker. Movement to a seated position is accomplished by unlocking the drop lock at the knee joint.

Pelvic bands and spinal attachments are rarely prescribed for use with conventional KAFOs. These attachments severely restrict dressing activities, movement from sitting to standing, and ambulation, by reducing trunk and pelvis flexibility and by adding extra weight (often as much as 4 lb). Furthermore, the use of these components makes gait slow, laborious, and usually nonfunctional. Patients who would require these attachments (T-2 to T-8 lesions) are usually not candidates for orthotic prescription. Instead, these patients can achieve physiologic standing with the use of posterior splints or a tilt-table.

Ankle-foot-orthoses (AFOs) are often appropriate for patients with lower-level lesions (e.g., L-3 and below). Either a conventional metal-upright or plastic AFO may be indicated. Patients with lesions of L-3 and below often demonstrate a maximus-medius gait pattern. The absence of gluteal muscles and hamstrings result in a sharp posterior movement of the trunk at heel strike. Lateral trunk flexion also will be noted at midstance. Crutches or canes are typically prescribed to improve the patient's gait pattern.

Functional electrical stimulation (FES). Functional electrical stimulation involves the use of electrical stimulation to elicit a muscle contraction that translates into a functional activity.[112-115] Within recent years this approach has become increasingly promising, for patients with SCI, as a mechanism to improve function and maintain muscle mass and bone density.[115] Most work in this area has focused on control of standing and stepping functions, exercise activities, and upper extremity activities of daily living (ADLs). It has also been used with cycle ergometry to improve endurance. The gait patterns achieved are somewhat unrefined and allow for only short-distance ambulation.

Electrical impulses for FES are provided via surface electrodes, surgically implanted electrodes, or percutaneous electrodes.[115] The electrical stimulation is interfaced with a computer, which controls the timing and onset of stimulation. The majority of systems in use are controlled by an *open loop* system. That is, the stimulus intensity and order of stimulation is preprogrammed for the individual. The problem with this system is lack of stimulus gradation and frequent overstimulation of the desired muscle. The current focus of research is directed toward a *closed loop* system in which movement is also initiated by the user but is modified without the user's input. For example, a movement could be modified without the user's knowledge by a feedback measure such as force or position.[115]

Although not yet in widespread clinical use, application of FES is expanding gradually. It has enabled some individuals to ambulate on level surfaces, on stairs, and on mild inclines, and to perform some upper extremity functional activities. Function has been further enhanced by combining FES with both upper and lower extremity orthoses. The RGO is frequently used in this capacity. Functional electrical stimulation appears to hold some future potential for achieving functional, cost-effective ambulation and improved upper extremity function for selected patients with SCI.

Preparation for ambulation. A swing-through type of gait pattern (Fig. 26–25) should be the ultimate goal for functional ambulators with KAFOs. In teaching this pattern, it is important to stress a smooth, even cadence. Crutches should be placed equidistant from both toes at toe-off and be equidistant from both heels at heel strike. It is important to establish an overall rhythm, as improved timing will result in improved energy efficiency and cosmesis. Relevant training activities include those described below.

1. Putting on and removing orthoses. The patient is first taught the correct way to apply the orthoses. The entire procedure is usually done in the supine or sitting position. The patient must be cautioned to check constantly for pressure areas, particularly after brace removal.

2. Sit-to-stand activities. These activities should be practiced in the parallel bars using a wheelchair. The patient must learn to slide to the edge of the chair and to lock and to unlock the orthoses. Initially the patient is taught to pull to standing, using the parallel bars (a progression is made to using the wheelchair armrests to push to standing). Once in an upright position, the patient pushes down on the hands and tilts the pelvis forward in front of the shoulders. Return to sitting is a reversal of this procedure.

3. Trunk balancing. The patient learns to balance the trunk in the hips-extended position, keeping the weight balanced over the feet, and learns to remove first one hand then both from the support. Placing hands forward and backward behind the hips while maintaining a stable position should also be practiced. Chapter 14 should be consulted for a more detailed description of suggestions for early parallel bar activities.

4. Push-ups. This includes lifting the body off the floor

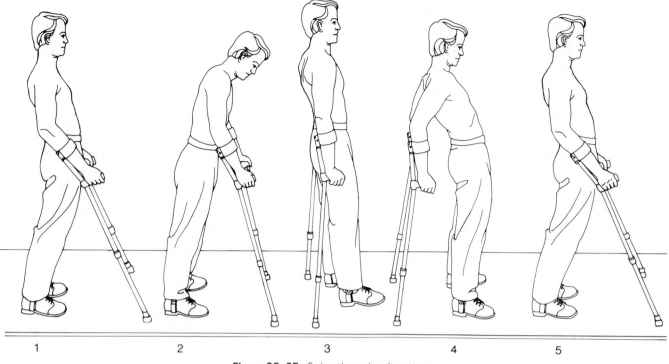

Figure 26–25. Swing-through gait pattern.

using shoulder depression, ducking the head to gain added height, and controlled lowering of the body.

5. Turning around. This involves lifting and lowering the body in 90-degree turns and changing hands from one bar to another.

6. Jackknifing. This entails controlling the pelvic position using upper extremity support and positioning the head and shoulders forward ahead of the pelvis. This is an unstable position, and the patient must be taught recovery in order to overcome and/or to prevent this from happening during ambulation.

7. Ambulation activities in the parallel bars. Four-point and two-point gaits require hip flexion or hip hiking. Patients with high lesions may learn this movement using the secondary hip-hikers (internal and external obliques and latissimus dorsi). Those with low lesions will have the quadratus lumborum intact. Trunk rotation on the swing side or lateral flexion toward the stance side will facilitate forward progression.

   Swing-to and swing-through gaits require varying degrees of body elevation and push-off. These gait patterns involve some jackknifing and recovery. At push-off, the head ducks to gain increased height, and at foot contact the head and back arch to help regain stability.

Crutch training. Forearm crutches are most often selected for patients with paraplegia. These crutches provide several advantages. They are lightweight; they allow use of the hand without the crutch becoming disengaged; they fit more easily into an automobile; and, most important, they improve function in ambulation and stair climbing by allowing unrestricted movement at the shoulders.

1. Standing from the wheelchair with crutches. To begin this activity the patient first places the crutches behind the chair, leaning against the push handle(s). To assume a standing position with crutches, the patient moves forward in the chair, locks both knee joints, crosses one leg over the other (Fig. 26–26), and then rotates the trunk and pelvis. Hand placements on the armrest are reversed and the patient pushes to standing by pivoting around to face the chair. The reverse of this technique is used to return to the chair.

2. Crutch balancing. Initially, the patient must learn to become secure in the tripod stance. This is best achieved by first balancing in the parallel bars or against a wall. Weight shifting, alternating lifting one crutch off the floor, and jackknifing should be practiced.

3. Ambulation activities. Four-point, two-point, swing-to, and swing-through gaits should be practiced. They demonstrate a progression from a slow, steady gait pattern to a faster, more unstable one. A gradual emphasis should be placed on improved timing and speed.

4. Travel activities. The patient should become proficient in walking sideward and backward, in turning, and in walking through doorways. Changes in floor surface (e.g., carpeting, tile) and terrain (sidewalks and grass) may present problems for the patient if they are not introduced during training. All patients will require proficiency in ambulation on level surfaces in order to master these more difficult activities successfully.

5. Elevation activities. The easiest pattern of ascent or descent of stairs is usually upstairs backward (Fig. 26–27) and downstairs forward (Fig. 26–28). Most

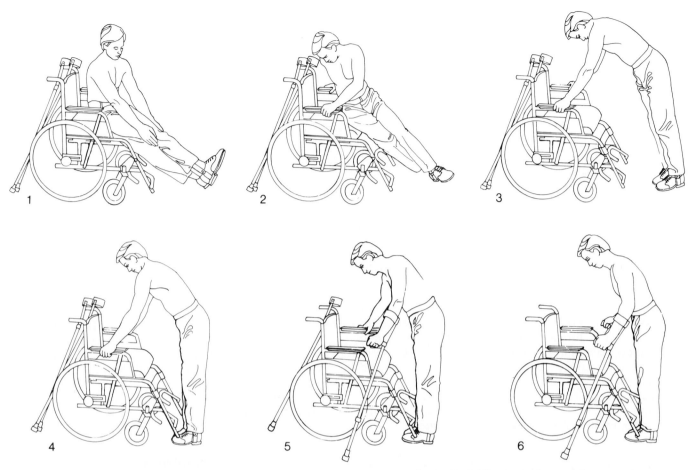

Figure 26–26. Standing from wheelchair using crutches and bilateral knee-ankle-foot orthoses. The reverse sequence is used to return to the chair.

patients will use a handrail, for it is only the very exceptional patient who can manage stairs without one. Once some degree of proficiency is attained, going upstairs forward and downstairs backward can be practiced as well. The use of graduated steps will help make the initial task of learning easier.

The therapist needs to guard and to support the patient adequately. The use of a properly fitting guarding belt is essential. Curbs should be attempted last, because this is usually the most difficult elevation activity. Using graduated platforms or curbs will assist the patient in mastery of this

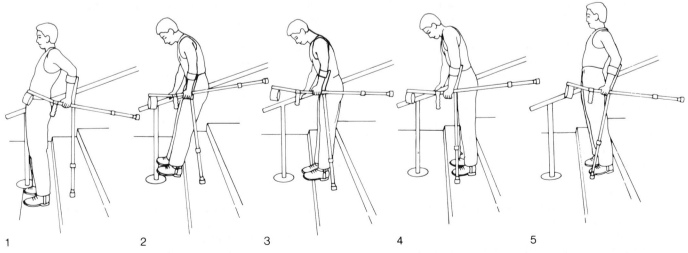

Figure 26–27. Ascending stairs backward. The crutch is placed on the step to which the patient is ascending. The head and trunk are forcefully flexed while depressing the shoulders and extending the elbows. This maneuver unweights the lower extremities and creates momentum for movement to the next higher step. Postural alignment is then regained.

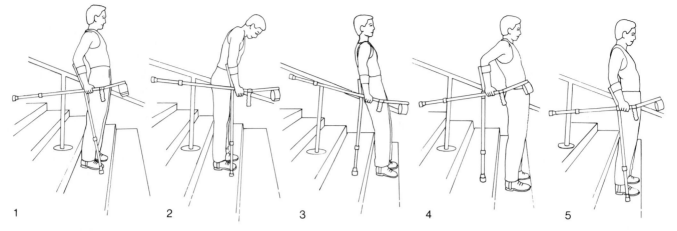

Figure 26–28. Descending stairs forward. To begin, the crutch remains on the step that the patient is leaving. Initial flexion of the head and trunk is immediately followed by forceful extension while depressing the shoulders and extending the elbow. This procedure unweights the lower extremities and creates momentum for the movement to the next lower step. The crutch is then lowered and postural alignment regained.

task. A four-point gait pattern, going up backward and down forward is the slower, more stable method. Swinging both legs up together takes considerable balance and is for the more advanced ambulator.

6. Falling. Controlled falling and getting up from the floor are important considerations for patients expected to become functional ambulators.

LONG-RANGE PLANNING

An important aspect of long-range rehabilitation planning involves educating the patient in lifelong management of the disability. This will focus on community reintegration and methods of maintaining the optimal state of health and function achieved during rehabilitation. Consideration must be given to multiple issues, including housing, nutrition, transportation, finances, maintaining functional skills and level of physical fitness, employment or further education, and methods for involvement in desired social or recreational activities. Each of these issues must be addressed early in the course of rehabilitation in consultation with the patient, the family, and appropriate team members. The patient also should be encouraged to contact and to explore the resources available through the local chapter of the National Spinal Cord Injury Association. Publications such as *Accent on Living, Paraplegia News, Sports'n Spokes,* and the National Spinal Cord Injury Association's *National Resource Directory* will provide the patient with current information on a variety of topics

such as research related to SCI, legislative activities, conferences, housing, transportation, new adaptive equipment, and sporting and recreational activities. Resource addresses for these publications are included in the appendix to this chapter. Finally, a coordinated plan must be developed for long-term periodic rehabilitation follow-up visits.

SUMMARY

This chapter has presented the principal clinical features and secondary complications of traumatic SCI. Emphasis has been placed on physical therapy intervention during both the acute and subacute phases of rehabilitation. Anticipated goals and treatment considerations have been addressed. These general goals and treatment suggestions must be tailored to meet the needs of an individual patient. This will be achieved through a process of careful assessment with specific attention to length of time since onset, lesion level, method(s) of fracture stabilization, premorbid interests, psychosocial factors, and presence of secondary complications.

Management of the patient with SCI is a complex and challenging task in which continuity of care is critical to achieving the overall goals of rehabilitation. Frequent and open communication among team members, patient, and family is vital to maintaining an organized and highly individualized approach to both rehabilitation and reintegration of the patient into the community.

QUESTIONS FOR REVIEW

1. Identify the clinical features of Brown-Sequard, anterior, central, and posterior cord syndromes.

2. Define spinal shock.

3. Describe the clinical picture associated with spinal cord injury. Your description should address altera-

tions that occur in each of the following areas:

   a. Motor function
   b. Sensory function
   c. Temperature control
   d. Respiratory function

e. Muscle tone

f. Bladder and bowel function

g. Sexual function

4. What is autonomic dysreflexia? Describe the initiating stimuli and symptoms of this syndrome. What action would you take if a patient experienced an onset of symptoms during a physical therapy treatment?

5. What is heterotopic bone formation? Describe the early symptoms. Where does it most commonly develop following SCI?

6. Describe the clinical features of deep venous thrombosis. Why are patients with SCI at risk for development of this secondary complication?

7. Suggest a positioning program to prevent limitations in ROM at the shoulders for a patient with quadriplegia during the acute phase of management.

8. Identify three primary influences affecting prognosis following spinal cord injury.

9. Describe the major advantages of halo devices as compared with tongs for immobilizing cervical fractures.

10. What is included in a physical therapy assessment during the acute phase of management? How might some of the standard assessment techniques have to be modified?

11. What is meant by the term selective stretching?

12. Identify the primary goals of respiratory care during the acute phase of management. Suggest potential treatment activities to meet these goals.

13. What forms of strengthening exercises are appropriate during the acute phase? Why are bilateral upper extremity activities emphasized?

14. Outline sample mat progressions for two patients, one with a C-6 quadriplegia and one with a T-12 paraplegia. Assume that both patients have complete lesions. Describe the specific mat sequence and activities you would include. Identify the functional significance of each. What type of progressive strengthening activities would you suggest for each patient as an adjunct to the mat progression?

REFERENCES

1. Trieschmann, RB: Spinal Injuries: Psychological, Social and Vocational Adjustment, ed 2. Demos Publications, New York, 1988.
2. Young, JS and Northrup, NE: Statistical information pertaining to some of the most commonly asked questions about SCI (monograph). National Spinal Cord Injury Data Research Center, Phoenix, 1979.
3. Young, JS, et al: Spinal Cord Injury Statistics: Experience of the Regional Spinal Cord Injury Systems. Good Samaritan Medical Center, Phoenix, 1982.
4. Bromley, I: Tetraplegia and Paraplegia: A Guide for Physiotherapists, ed 3. Churchill Livingstone, New York, 1985.
5. Michaelis, LS: International inquiry on neurological terminology and prognosis in paraplegia and tetraplegia. Paraplegia 7:1, 1969.
6. Coogler, CE: Clinical decision making among neurologic patients: spinal cord injury. In Wolf, SL (ed): Clinical Decision Making in Physical Therapy. FA Davis, Philadelphia, 1985, p 149.
7. Rieser, TV, Mudiyam, R, and Waters, RL: Orthopedic evaluation of spinal cord injury and management of vertebral fractures. In Adkins, HV (ed): Spinal Cord Injury. Churchill Livingstone, New York, 1985.
8. Hardy, AG and Rossier, AB: Spinal Cord Injuries: Orthopedic and Neurologic Aspects. Publishing Science Group, Acton, MA, 1975.
9. Ruge, D: Neurologic evaluation. In Ruge, D (ed): Spinal Cord Injuries. Charles C Thomas, Springfield, IL, 1969, p 51.
10. deGroot, J and Chusid, JG: Correlative Neuroanatomy and Functional Neurology, ed 20. Lange Medical Publications, Los Altos, CA, 1988.
11. Gilman, S and Newman, SW: Manter and Gatz's Essentials of Clinical Neuroanatomy and Neurophysiology, ed 8. FA Davis, Philadelphia, 1992.
12. Schneider, FJ: Traumatic spinal cord injury. In Umphred, DA (ed): Neurological Rehabilitation, ed 2. CV Mosby, St. Louis, 1990, p 423.
13. Bose, B, et al: Reanalysis of central cervical cord injury management. Neurosurgery 15:367, 1984.
14. Brodkey, JS, Miller, CF, and Harmody, RM: The syndrome of acute central cervical spinal cord injury revisited. Surg Neurol 14:251, 1980.
15. Raynor, RB and Koplik, B: Cervical cord trauma: the relationship between clinical syndromes and force of injury. Spine 10:193, 1985.
16. Comarr, AE: Sexual function in patients with spinal cord injury. In Pierce, DS and Nickel, VH (eds): The Total Care of Spinal Cord Injuries. Little, Brown, Boston, 1977, p 171.
17. Bedbrook, GM: Examination. In Bedbrook, G (ed): The Care and Management of Spinal Cord Injuries. Springer-Verlag, New York, 1981, p 8.
18. Pierce, DS: Acute treatment of spinal cord injuries. In Pierce, DS and Nickel, VH (eds): The Total Care of Spinal Cord Injuries. Little Brown, Boston, 1977, p 1.
19. Rogers, LF: Fractures and dislocations of the spine. In Calenoff, L (ed): Radiology of Spinal Cord Injury. CV Mosby, St. Louis, 1981.
20. Calenoff, L, et al: Multiple level spinal injuries: importance of early recognition. Am J Roentgenol 130:665, 1978.
21. Donovan, WH and Bedbrook, G: Comprehensive management of spinal cord injury. Ciba Clin Symp 34, Ciba Pharmaceutical, 1982.
22. English, E: Mechanisms of cervical spine injuries. In Tator, CH (ed): Early Management of Acute Spinal Cord Injury. Raven Press, New York, 1982, p 25.
23. Holdsworth, F: Fractures, dislocations, and fracture-dislocations of the spine. J Bone Joint Surg Am 52:1534, 1970.
24. Guttman, L: Spinal shock and reflex behaviour in man. Paraplegia 8:100, 1970.
25. Stauffer, ES: Long-term management of traumatic quadriplegia. In Pierce, DS and Nickel, VH (eds): The Total Care of Spinal Cord Injuries. Little, Brown, Boston, 1977, p 81.
26. Edibam, RC: Medical management. In Bedbrook, G (ed): The Care and Management of Spinal Cord Injuries. Springer-Verlag New York, 1981, p 109.
27. Guyton, AC: Human Physiology and Mechanisms of Disease, ed 5. WB Saunders, Philadelphia, 1992.
28. Thomas, EL: Nursing care of the patient with spinal cord injury. In Pierce, DS and Nickel, VH (eds): The Total Care of Spinal Cord Injuries. Little, Brown, Boston, 1977, p 249.
29. Alvarez, SE, Peterson, M, and Lunsford, BR: Respiratory treatment of the adult patient with spinal cord injury. Phys Ther 61:1737, 1981.
30. Romanes, GJ (ed): Cunningham's Textbook of Anatomy, ed 12. Oxford University Press, New York, 1981.
31. Moore, KL: Clinically Oriented Anatomy, ed 3. Williams & Wilkins, Baltimore, 1992.
32. Nixon, V: Spinal Cord Injury: A Guide to Functional Outcomes in Physical Therapy Management. Aspen, Rockville, MD, 1985.
33. Goss, CM: Gray's Anatomy of the Human Body. Lea & Febiger, Philadelphia, 1973.
34. Wetzel, J: Respiratory evaluation and treatment. In Adkins, HV: Spinal Cord Injury. Churchill Livingstone, New York, 1985, p 75.
35. Seidel, AC: Spinal cord injury. In Logigian, MK (ed): Adult Rehabilitation: A Team Approach for Therapists. Little, Brown, Boston, 1982, p 325.

36. Rosen, JS: Rehabilitation process. In Calenoff, L (ed): Radiology of Spinal Cord Injury. CV Mosby, St. Louis, 1981, p 309.

37. Cardenas, DD, Kelly, E, and Mayo, ME: Manual stimulation of reflex voiding after spinal cord injury. Arch Phys Med Rehabil 66:459, 1985.

38. Finkbeiner, AE, Bissada, NK, and Redman, JF: Urologic care of the patient with a spinal cord injury. J Arkansas Med Soc 74:30, 1978.

39. Pires, M and Kelly-Hayes, M: Collaborative nursing therapies for clients with neurological dysfunction. In Umphred, DA (ed): Neurological Rehabilitation, ed 2. CV Mosby, St. Louis, 1990, p 791.

40. Zejdlik, CP: Maintaining urinary function. In Zejdlik, CP (ed): Management of Spinal Cord Injury, ed 2. Jones and Bartlett, Boston, 1992, p 353.

41. Kiser, C and Herman, C: Nursing considerations: skin care, bowel and bladder training, autonomic dysreflexia. In Adkins, HV (ed): Spinal Cord Injury. Churchill Livingstone, New York, 1985, p 155.

42. Comarr, AE and Vigue, M: Sexual counseling among male and female patients with spinal cord and/or cauda equina injury, I. Am J Phys Med 57:107, 1978.

43. Miller, S, Szasz, G, and Anderson, L: Sexual health care clinician in an acute spinal cord injury unit. Arch Phys Med Rehabil 62:315, 1981.

44. Romano, MD and Lassiter, RE: Sexual counseling with the spinal cord injured. Arch Phys Med Rehabil 53:568, 1972.

45. Eisenberg, MG and Rustad, LC: Sex education and counseling program on a spinal cord injury service. Arch Phys Med Rehabil 57:135, 1976.

46. Higgins, GE: Sexual response in spinal cord injured adults: a review of the literature. Arch Sex Behav 8:173, 1979.

47. Gott, LJ: Anatomy and physiology of male sexual response and fertility as related to spinal cord injury. In Sha'ked, A (ed): Human Sexuality and Rehabilitation Medicine: Sexual Functioning Following Spinal Cord Injury. Williams & Wilkins, Baltimore, 1981, p 67.

48. Hanak, M and Scott, A: Spinal Cord Injury: An Illustrated Guide for Health Care Professionals. Springer-Verlag, New York, 1983.

49. Geiger, RC: Neurophysiology of female sexual response in spinal cord injury. In Sha'ked, A (ed): Human Sexuality and Rehabilitation Medicine: Sexual Functioning Following Spinal Cord Injury. Williams & Wilkins, Baltimore, 1981, p 74.

50. Thiyagarajan, C and Silver, JR: Aetiology of pressure sores in patients with spinal cord injury. Br Med J 289:1487, 1984.

51. Richardson, RR and Meyer, PR: Prevalence and incidence of pressure sores in acute spinal cord injuries. Paraplegia 19:235, 1981.

52. Seymour, RJ and Lacefield, WE: Wheelchair cushion effect on pressure and skin temperature. Arch Phys Med Rehabil 66:103, 1985.

53. Guttman, L: Spinal Cord Injuries: Comprehensive Management and Research, ed 2. Blackwell Scientific, London, 1976.

54. Constable, JD and Pierce, DS: Pressure sores. In Pierce, DS and Nickel, VH (eds): The Total Care of Spinal Cord Injuries. Little, Brown, Boston, 1977, p 187.

55. Hendrix, RW: Soft tissue changes after spinal cord injury. In Calenoff, L (ed): Radiology of Spinal Cord Injury. CV Mosby, St. Louis, 1981, p 438.

56. Lindan, R, et al: Incidence and clinical features of autonomic dysreflexia in patients with spinal cord injury. Paraplegia 18:285, 1980.

57. Rosen, JS: Autonomic dysreflexia. In Calenoff, L (ed): Radiology of Spinal Cord Injury. CV Mosby, St. Louis, 1981, p 554.

58. Comarr, AE: Autonomic dysreflexia. In Pierce, DS and Nickel, VH (eds): The Total Care of Spinal Cord Injuries. Little, Brown, Boston, 1977, p 181.

59. Yeo, JD: Recent research in spinal cord injuries. In Bedbrook, G (ed): The Care and Management of Spinal Cord Injuries. Springer-Verlag, New York, 1981, p 285.

60. McGarry, J, Woolsey, RM, and Thompson, CW: Autonomic hyperreflexia following passive stretching to the hip joint. Phys Ther 62:30, 1982.

61. Erickson, RP: Autonomic hyperreflexia: pathophysiology and medical management. Arch Phys Med Rehabil 61:431, 1980.

62. Belson, P: Autonomic nervous system dysfunction in recent spinal cord injured patients: a physical therapist's perspective. In Eisenberg, MG and Falconer, JA (eds): Treatment of the Spinal Cord Injured: An Interdisciplinary Perspective. Charles C Thomas, Springfield, MA, 1978, p 34.

63. Wharton, GW: Heterotopic ossification. Clin Orthop 112:142, 1975.

64. Stover, SL, Hataway, CJ, and Zeiger, HE: Heterotopic ossification in spinal cord-injured patients. Arch Phys Med Rehabil 56:199, 1975.

65. Abramson, AS: Bone disturbances in injuries to the spinal cord and cauda equina (paraplegia): their prevention by ambulation. J Bone Joint Surg Am 30-A:982, 1948.

66. Rossier, AB, et al: Current facts on para-osteo-arthropathy (POA). Paraplegia 11:36, 1973.

67. Silver, JR: Heterotopic ossification: a clinical study of its possible relationship to trauma. Paraplegia 7:220, 1969.

68. Damanski, M: Heterotopic ossification in paraplegia: a clinical study. J Bone Joint Surg Br 43-B:286, 1961.

69. Hardy, AG and Dickson, JW: Pathological ossification in traumatic paraplegia. J Bone Joint Surg Br 45-B:76, 1963.

70. Wharton, GW and Morgan, TH: Ankylosis in the paralyzed patient. J Bone Joint Surg Am 52-A:105, 1970.

71. Nicholas, JJ: Ectopic bone formation in patients with spinal cord injury. Arch Phys Med Rehabil 54:354, 1973.

72. Neiman, HL: Venography in acute spinal cord injury. In Calenoff, L (ed): Radiology of Spinal Cord Injury. CV Mosby, St. Louis, 1981, p 298.

73. van Hove, E: Prevention of thrombophlebitis in spinal injury patients. Paraplegia 16:332, 1978.

74. Todd, JW: Deep venous thrombosis in acute spinal cord injury: a comparison of ^{125}I fibrinogen leg scanning, impedance plethysmography and venography. Paraplegia 14:50, 1976.

75. Brach, BB, et al: Venous thrombosis in acute spinal cord paralysis. J Trauma 17:289, 1977.

76. El Masri, WS and Silver, JR: Prophylactic anticoagulant therapy in patients with spinal cord injury. Paraplegia 19:334, 1981.

77. Nepomuceno, C, et al: Pain in patients with spinal cord injury. Arch Phys Med Rehabil 60:605, 1979.

78. Burke, DC: Pain in paraplegia. Paraplegia 10:297, 1973.

79. Waisbrod, H, Hansen, D, and Gerbershagen, HG: Chronic pain in paraplegics. Neurosurgery 15:933, 1984.

80. Davis, R and Lentini, R: Transcutaneous nerve stimulation for treatment of pain in patients with spinal cord injury. Surg Neurol 4:100, 1975.

81. Richardson, RR, Meyer, PR, and Cerullo, LJ: Transcutaneous electrical neurostimulation in musculoskeletal pain of acute spinal cord injuries. Spine 5:42, 1980.

82. Davis, R: Pain and suffering following spinal cord injury. Clin Orthop 112:76, 1975.

83. Bors, E: Phantom limbs of patients with spinal cord injury. Arch Neurol Psychiatry 66:610, 1951.

84. Scott, JA and Donovan, WH: The prevention of shoulder pain and contracture in the acute tetraplegic patient. Paraplegia 19:313, 1981.

85. Ohry, A, et al: Shoulder complications as a cause of delay in rehabilitation of spinal cord injured patients: case reports and review of the literature. Paraplegia 16:310, 1978.

86. Claus-Walker, J, et al: Calcium excretion in quadriplegia. Arch Phys Med Rehabil 53:14, 1972.

87. Burr, RG: Urinary calculi composition in patients with spinal cord lesions. Arch Phys Med Rehabil 59:84, 1978.

88. Hancock, DA, Reed, GW, and Atkinson, PJ: Bone and soft tissue changes in paraplegic patients. Paraplegia 17:267, 1979.

89. Maynard, FM and Imai, K: Immobilization hypercalcemia in spinal cord injury. Arch Phys Med Rehabil 58:16, 1977.

90. Wilson, DR: Renal calculi: diagnosis and medical management. Primary Care 5:41, 1978.

91. Bohlman, HH: Complications and pitfalls in the treatment of acute cervical spinal cord injuries. In Tator, CH (ed): Early Management of Acute Spinal Cord Injury. Raven Press, New York, 1982, p 373.

92. Tator, CH, et al: Halo devices for the treatment of acute cervical spinal cord injury. In Tator, CH (ed): Early Management of Acute Spinal Cord Injury. Raven Press, New York, 1982, p 231.

93. Edmonds, VE and Tator, CH: Coordination of a halo program for an acute spinal cord injury unit. In Tator, CH (ed): Early Management of Acute Spinal Cord Injury. Raven Press, New York, 1982, p 263.

94. Cerullo, LJ: Surgical stabilization of spinal cord injury: section A: cervical spine. In Calenoff, L (ed): Radiology of Spinal Cord Injury. CV Mosby, St. Louis, 1982, p 202.

95. Meyer, PR: Surgical stabilization of spinal cord injury: section B: thoracic and lumbar spine. In Calenoff, L (ed): Radiology of Spinal Cord Injury. CV Mosby, St. Louis, 1981, p 202.

96. Zejdlik, CP: Maintaining protective functions of the skin. In Zejdlik, CP (ed): Management of Spinal Cord Injury. Jones and Bartlett, Boston, 1992, p 451.

97. Daniels, L and Worthingham, C: Muscle Testing: Techniques of Manual Examination, ed 5. WB Saunders, Philadelphia, 1986.

98. Norkin, CC and White, DJ: Measurement of Joint Motion: A Guide to Goniometry. FA Davis, Philadelphia, 1985.

99. Clough, P, et al: Guidelines for routine respiratory care of patients with spinal cord injury: a clinical report. Phys Ther 66:1395, 1986.

100. Trombly, CA: Spinal cord injury. In Trombly, CA (ed): Occupational Therapy for Physical Dysfunction, ed 3. Williams & Wilkins, Baltimore, 1989, p 555.

101. Van Steen, H: Treatment of a patient with a complete C1 quadriplegia. Phys Ther 55:35, 1975.

102. Sullivan, PE, Markos, PD, and Minor, MAD: An Integrated Approach to Therapeutic Exercise: Theory and Clinical Application. Reston, Reston, VA, 1982.

103. Voss, DE, Ionta, MK, and Myers, BJ: Proprioceptive Neuromuscular Facilitation: Patterns and Techniques, ed 3. Harper & Row, Philadelphia, 1985.

104. Voss, DE: Proprioceptive neuromuscular facilitation (NUSTEP Proceedings). Am J Phys Med 46:838, 1967.

105. Hussey, RW and Stauffer, ES: Spinal cord injury: requirements for ambulation. Arch Phys Med Rehabil 54:544, 1973.

106. Corcoran, PJ: Energy expenditure during ambulation. In Downey, J and Darling, R (eds): Physiological Basis of Rehabilitation Medicine. WB Saunders, Philadelphia, 1971, p 185.

107. Mikelberg, R and Reid, S: Spinal cord lesions and lower extremity bracing: an overview and follow-up study. Paraplegia 19:379, 1981.

108. Scott, BA: Engineering principles and fabrication techniques for the Scott-Craig long leg brace for paraplegics. Orth Pros 25:14, 1971.

109. Huang, CT: Energy cost of ambulation in paraplegic patients using Craig-Scott braces. Arch Phys Med Rehabil 60:595, 1979.

110. Lobley, S, et al: Orthotic design from the New England Regional Spinal Cord Injury Center: suggestion from the field. Phys Ther 65:492, 1985.

111. Durr-Fillauer Medical, Inc: LSU Reciprocating Gait Orthosis: A Pictoral Description and Application Manual. Durr-Fillauer Medical, Chattanooga, 1983.

112. Bajd, T, et al: Use of a two-channel functional electrical stimulator to stand paraplegic patients. Phys Ther 61:526, 1981.

113. Vodovnik, L, et al: Functional electrical stimulation for control of locomotor systems. Crit Rev Bioeng 6:63, 1981.

114. Brindley, GS, Polkey, CE, and Rushton, DN: Electrical splinting of the knee in paraplegia. Paraplegia 16:428, 1978.

115. Sipski, ML and DeLisa, JA: Functional electrical stimulation in spinal cord injury rehabilitation: a review of the literature. NeuroRehabilitation 1:46, 1991.

SUPPLEMENTAL READINGS

Bajd, T, et al: Electrical stimulation in treating spasticity resulting from spinal cord injury. Arch Phys Med Rehabil 66:515, 1985.

Barker, E and Higgins, R: Managing a suspected spinal cord injury. Nursing 19:52, 1989.

Bedbrook, GM (ed): Lifetime Care of the Paraplegic Patient. Churchill Livingstone, New York, 1985.

Becker, DM, Gonzalez, M, and Gentili, A: Prevention of deep vein thrombosis in patients with acute spinal cord injuries: Use of rotating treatment tables. Neurosurgery 20:675, 1987.

Benzel, E, Hadden, T, and Saulsbery, C: A comparison of the Minerva and halo jackets for stabilization of the cervical spine. J Neurosurg 70:411, 1989.

Berczeller, PH and Bezkor, MF (eds): Medical Complications of Quadriplegia. Year Book Medical, Chicago, 1986.

Brown, D, Judd, F, and Unger, G: Continuing care of the spinal cord injured. Paraplegia 25:296, 1987.

Brownlee, S and Williams, S: Physiotherapy in the respiratory care of patients with high spinal injury. Physiotherapy 73:148, 1987.

Buchanan, LE and Nawoczenski, DA (eds): Spinal Cord Injury: Concepts and Management Approaches. Williams & Wilkins, Baltimore, 1987.

Carter, ER: Respiratory aspects of spinal cord injury. Paraplegia 25:262, 1987.

Castillo, R and Bell, J: Cervical spine injury: stabilization and management. Postgrad Med 83:131, 1988.

Clough, P, et al: Guidelines for routine respiratory care of patients with spinal cord injury. Phys Ther 66:1395, 1986.

Corbet, B (ed): National Resource Directory: An Information Guide for Persons with Spinal Cord Injury and Other Physical Disabilities. National Spinal Cord Injury Association, 600 West Cummings Park, Suite 2000, Woburn, MA, 01801, 1985.

Curtis, KA: Physical therapist role satisfaction in the treatment of the spinal cord-injured person. Phys Ther 5:197, 1985.

Curtis, KA and Hall, KM: Spinal cord injury community follow-up: role of the physical therapist. Phys Ther 66:1370, 1986.

Davidoff, G, et al: Rehospitalization after rehabilitation of acute SCI: incidence and risk factors. Arch Phys Med Rehabil 71:121, 1990.

DeVivo, MJ and Fine, PR: Spinal cord injury: its short-term impact on marital status. Arch Phys Med Rehabil 66:501, 1985.

Dillingham, TR: Prevention of complications during acute management of the spinal cord-injured patient: first step in the rehabilitation process. Critical Care Nursing Quarterly 11:71, 1988.

Eriksson, P: Aerobic power during maximal exercise in untrained and well-trained quadri- and paraplegics. Scand J Rehabil Med 20:141, 1988.

Ford, JR and Duckworth, B: Physical Management for the Quadriplegic Patient, ed 2. FA Davis, Philadelphia, 1987.

Galli, R, Spaite, D, and Simon, R: Emergency Orthopedics: The Spine. Appleton & Lange, Norwalk, CT, 1989.

Hill, JP: A Guide to Functional Outcomes in Occupational Therapy. Aspen, Rockville, MD, 1986.

Holtzman, RNN and Stein, BM (eds): Surgery of the Spinal Cord: Potential for Regeneration and Recovery. Springer-Verlag, New York, 1992.

Hornstein, S and Ledsome, J: Ventilatory muscle training in acute quadriplegia. Physiotherapy Canada 38:145, 1986.

Kakulas, A: The applied neurobiology of human spinal cord injury: a review. Paraplegia 26:371, 1988.

Keene, JS: Thoracolumbar fractures in winter sports. Clin Orthop 216:39, 1987.

Keene, JS, et al: Significance of acute post-traumatic bony encroachment of the neural canal. Spine 14:799, 1989.

Kralj, A, Bajd, T, and Turk, R: Enhancement of gait restoration in spinal injured patients by functional electrical stimulation. Clin Orthop 233:34, 1988.

Lal, S, et al: Risk factors for heterotopic ossification in spinal cord injury. Arch Phys Med Rehabil 70:387, 1989.

Lindan, R, Leffler, E, and Freehafer, A: The team approach to urinary bladder management in SCI patients: a 26-year retrospective study. Paraplegia 28:314, 1990.

Lloyd, L: New trends in urologic management of SCI patients. Central Nervous System Trauma 3:3, 1986.

Marshall, S, et al: Neuroscience Critical Care: Pathophysiology and Patient Management. WB Saunders, Philadelphia, 1990.

Marsolias, E and Kobetic, R. Functional electrical stimulation for walking with paraplegia. J Bone Joint Surg Am 69:728, 1987.

Meyer, PR: Surgery of Spine Trauma. Churchill Livingstone, New York, 1989.

Mollinger, LA, et al: Daily energy expenditure and basal metabolic rates of patients with spinal cord injury. Arch Phys Med Rehabil 66:420, 1985.

Millington, PJ, et al: Thermoplastic minerva body jacket—a practical alternative to current methods of cervical spine stabilization: a clinical report. Phys Ther 67:223, 1987.

Novak, PP and Mitchell, MM: Professional involvement in sexuality counseling for patients with spinal cord injuries. Am J Occup Ther 42:105, 1988.

Nygaard, I, Bartscht, KD, and Cole, S: Sexuality and reproduction in spinal cord injured women. Obstet Gynecol Surv 45:727, 1990.

Oakes, D: Benefits of an early admission to a comprehensive trauma center for patients with SCI. Arch Phys Med Rehabil 72:637, 1990.

Ohry, A, Peleg, D, and Goldman, J: Sexual function, pregnancy, and delivery in spinal cord injured women. Gynecol Obstet Invest 9:281, 1988.

O'Neil, L and Seelye, R: Power wheelchair training for patients with marginal upper extremity function. Neurol Rep 14:19, 1990.

Ozer, MM: The Management of Persons with SCI. Demos, New York, 1988.

Parke, B and Penn, RD: Functional outcome after delivery of intrathecal baclofen. Arch Phys Med Rehabil 70:30, 1989.

Penn, RD and Kroin, JS: Long-term intrathecal baclofen infusion for treatment of spasticity. Neurosurg 66:181, 1987.

Phillips, CA: Functional electrical stimulation and lower extremity bracing for ambulation exercise of the spinal cord injured individual: a medically prescribed system. Phys Ther 60:842, 1989.

Phillips, CA: Medical criteria for active physical therapy. Physician guidelines for patient participation in a program of functional electrical stimulation. Arch Phys Med Rehabil 66:269, 1987.

Richards, J: Psychologic adjustment to spinal cord injury during first postdischarge year. Arch Phys Med Rehabil 67:362, 1986.

Santosh, L, et al: Risk factors for heterotopic ossification in spinal cord injury. Arch Phys Med Rehabil 70:387, 1989.

Sargent, C and Braun, MA: Occupational therapy management of the acute spinal cord injured patient. Am J Occup Ther 40:533, 1986.

Somers, MF: Spinal Cord Injury: Functional Rehabilitation. Appleton & Lange, Englewood Cliffs, NJ, 1992.

Sugarman, B: Medical complications of spinal cord injury. Q J Med 54:3, 1985.

Sullivan, PE and Markos, PD: Clinical Procedures in Therapeutic Exercise. Appleton & Lange, Norwalk, CT, 1987.

Urey, J and Henggler, S: Marital adjustment following spinal cord injury. Arch Phys Med Rehabil 68:69, 1987.

Verduyn, WH: Spinal cord injured women, pregnancy and delivery. Paraplegia 24:231, 1986.

Wanner, MB, Rageth, CJ, and Zach, GA: Pregnancy and autonomic dysreflexia in patients with spinal cord lesions. Paraplegia 25:482, 1987.

Welch, R, Lobley, S, O'Sullivan, S, and Freed, M: Functional independence in quadriplegia: Critical levels. Arch Phys Med Rehabil 67:235, 1986.

Whiteneck, G, et al: Management of High Quadriplegia. Demos, New York, 1989.

Woolsey, RM: Rehabilitation outcome following spinal cord injury. Arch Neurol 42:116, 1985.

Yarkony, GM, Roth, EJ, and Heinemann, A: Functional skills after spinal cord injury rehabilitation: three-year longitudinal follow-up. Arch Phys Med Rehabil 69:111, 1988.

Yarkony, GM, et al: Benefits of rehabilitation for traumatic spinal cord injury. Arch Neurol 44:93, 1987.

Zasler, N and Katz, G: Synergist erection system in the management of impotence secondary to spinal cord injury. Arch Phys Med Rehabil 70:712, 1989.

GLOSSARY

Anterior cord syndrome: Incomplete spinal cord lesion with primary damage in the anterior cord; loss of motor function, and sense of pain and temperature; perseveration of proprioception, kinesthesia, and vibration below the level of the lesion.

Autonomic dysreflexia (hyperreflexia): A pathologic autonomic reflex seen in patients with high-level spinal cord injuries. It is precipitated by a noxious stimulus below the level of the lesion and produces an acute onset of autonomic activity. It is considered an emergency situation; symptoms include hypertension, bradycardia, headache, and sweating.

Avulsion: Pulling or tearing of a piece of bone away from the main bone.

Brown-Sequard syndrome: Incomplete spinal cord lesion caused by hemisection of the cord; loss of motor function, proprioception, and kinesthesia on the side of the lesion; loss of sense of pain and temperature on the opposite side.

Bulbocavernous reflex (positive): Pressure on the glans penis or glans clitoris elicits a contraction of the external anal sphincter.

Burst (explosion) fracture: A comminuted vertebral fracture associated with pressure along the long axis of the vertebral column, also associated with flexion injuries, bone fragments are displaced centripetally.

Cauda equina lesion: Damage to peripheral nerve roots below the first lumbar vertebra; some regeneration is possible.

Central cord syndrome: Incomplete spinal cord lesion producing greater neurologic involvement in upper extremities (cervical tracts more centrally located) than in the lower extremities (lumbar and sacral tracts more peripheral).

Complete lesion (SCI): No sensory or motor function below the level of lesion.

Compression fracture: A vertebral fracture resulting from pressure along the long axis of the vertebral column and closely associated with flexion injuries.

Contusion (SCI): Damage to the spinal cord produced by pressure from displaced bone and/or soft tissues or swelling within the spinal canal.

Crede maneuver: Technique for emptying urine from a flaccid bladder; repeated pressure is placed between the umbilicus and symphysis pubis in a downward direction; manual pressure is also placed directly over bladder to further facilitate removal of urine.

Diaphoresis: Profuse sweating.

Dislocation: Displacement of a bone or vertebral body from its normal position.

Distraction: A traction force; separation of joint surfaces.

Dysesthesias (SCI): Bizarre, painful sensations experienced below the level of a lesion following spinal cord injury; often described as burning, numbness, pins and needles, or tingling sensations.

Heterotopic bone formation: Abnormal bone growth in soft tissues, a potential secondary complication following spinal cord injury; occurs below the level of the lesion (SYN: ectopic bone).

Incomplete lesion (SCI): Some preservation of sensory or motor function below the level of the lesion.

Intrathecal injection: A central (within the spinal canal) chemical injection that interrupts the reflex arc; used to decrease severe spasticity.

Maceration: Softening of a solid by exposure to water or other fluid; usually pertains to the skin.

Micturation: Voiding of urine (SYN: urination).

Myelotomy: Severance of nerve fibers of the spinal cord; used to reduce severe spasticity.

Myotomy: Surgical sectioning or release of a muscle; used to reduce spasticity.

Neurectomy: Partial or total excision or resection of a nerve; used to reduce severe spasticity.

Nocturia: Excessive urination during the night.

Osteoporosis: Decreased density or softening of bone.

Paraplegia: Partial or complete paralysis of all or part of the trunk and both lower extremities from lesions of the thoracic or lumbar spinal cord or sacral roots.

Peripheral nerve block: A local chemical injection (e.g., phenol) used to block transmission of a motor nerve selectively; used to decrease spasticity.

Posterior cord syndrome: A rare incomplete lesion with primary damage to the posterior cord; preservation of motor function, sense of pain, and light touch, with loss of proprioception and epicritic sensations below the level of the lesion.

Postural hypotension: A decrease in blood pressure that occurs when moving toward an upright posture. This occurs normally but may be severe following prolonged bed rest.

Pressure sore: Ulceration of soft tissue caused by unrelieved pressure and shearing forces (SYN: decubitus ulcer, bed sore).

Quadriplegia: Partial or complete paralysis of all four extremities and trunk, including the respiratory muscles from lesions of the cervical cord.

Rhizotomy: Division or severance of a nerve root; used to reduce severe spasticity.

Root escape: Preservation of peripheral nerve roots at the level of a spinal cord injury.

Sacral sparing: An incomplete lesion in which some sacral innervation remains intact; complete loss of motor function and sensation in other areas below the level of the lesion.

Shearing: Application of a horizontal or parallel force relative to adjacent structures; opposite to the force that is normally present; associated with fracture dislocations of the thoracolumbar region.

Spinal shock: Period immediately following injury to the spinal cord, characterized by absence of all reflex activity, flaccidity, and a loss of sensation below the level of the lesion; generally subsides within 24 hours.

Subluxation: Incomplete or partial dislocation.

Teardrop fracture: A bursting type fracture of the cervical region; produces a characteristic anterior-inferior bone chip. The fragment resembles a "teardrop" on radiographs and is associated with flexion and compression forces.

Tenotomy: Surgical section of a nerve; used to reduce spasticity.

APPENDIX A

Accent on Living (periodical)
PO Box 700
Bloomington, IL 61701
(309) 378-2961
(800) 787-8444

Paraplegia News and *Sports'n Spokes* (periodicals)
Paralyzed Veterans of America
801 18th Street, N.W.
Washington, D.C. 20006
(202) 872-1300

National Resource Directory: An Information Guide for Persons with Spinal Cord Injury and Other Physical Disabilities
National Spinal Cord Injury Association
600 West Cummings Park, Suite 2000
Woburn, MA 01801
(800) 962-9629

Chronic Pain Management

Barbara J. Headley

OBJECTIVES

1. Describe the physiology of pain and the mechanisms that contribute to chronic pain.
2. Identify the clinical manifestations of chronic pain.
3. Review the medical management for chronic pain.
4. Describe the assessment tools for identifying the factors contributing to a patient's pain experience.
5. Identify a treatment model for the chronic pain patient.
6. Describe the contributions of the members of a multidisciplinary pain management team.

Patients with chronic pain present with multiple complaints and problems, and they provide a unique challenge to the physical therapist. Because physical therapists often treat patients emerging from the acute pain stage into a chronic pain state, they must not only be able to recognize the patient with chronic pain, but also be able to modify a treatment plan accordingly. Although patients with acute pain respond well to the various therapeutic modalities within the armamentarium of physical therapy, patients with chronic pain present with a complex of psychologic, sociologic, and emotional states that affect the manner in which they experience and report their physical pain. All components of the pain experience must be addressed, and a multidisciplinary treatment program is in order. Restoration of function, not pain relief, is the primary goal with this patient population, and physical therapists play a primary role in the rehabilitation process.

HISTORICAL PERSPECTIVE

Throughout the ages, pain has had a variety of meanings to those experiencing it and those seeking to alleviate it. Our view of health, disease, and pain are a reflection of history. The introduction to the Hippocratic oath presupposes the sharing of power for health and illness by man and the gods and goddesses:

I swear by Apollo the physician, by Asclepius, by Hygeia and Panacea and by all the gods and goddesses making them my witnesses, that I will fulfill according to my ability and judgment this oath and this covenant.

In ancient Greece, sibyls and pythonesses held virtually exclusive power for exorcising the demons of illness and pain. Ancient Egyptians believed that either the spirits of the dead or the religious influences of their gods were responsible for painful afflictions, which generally entered the body in darkness. In ancient India, the universality of pain was attributed to unfulfilled desires. The ancient Chinese held that pain was a result of an imbalance of *yin* and *yang,* resulting in either excess or blocked *chi.*[2] Rebalancing the *chi,* or the flow of energy throughout the body, was believed necessary to restore physiologic balance and health.

Pain was subsequently removed from the realm of religion and placed into the realm of the emotions. Plato deduced that pain and pleasure, though opposite sensations, were linked together on a continuum, originating from the heart and representing passions of the soul. Aristotle, his student, held that the experience of pain was a hypersensitivity of every sensation and was caused by an excess of vital heat. Despite descriptions of pain related to inflammation by Celsus and Galens, the concept described by Aristotle prevailed for 23 centuries, attributing pain to a "passion of the soul."[2]

Significant changes in philosophy were not evident until after the Middle Ages and Renaissance when, in 1628, Harvey discovered the circulation of blood. Dissection of human bodies was still largely forbidden due to the strong religious convictions that had predominated for centuries. As long as the heart was considered the center of the soul and mind, the church forbid the study of the human body. To remove such strong prohibition by the church, Descartes conceptualized the separation of the mind and body. He described the pineal body as the connecting point, the center of the brain. Descartes proposed that for a person to be conscious of something, the experience had to go

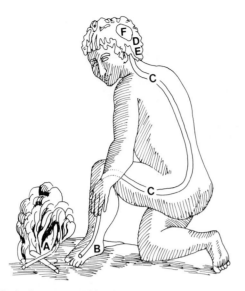

Figure 27–1. Descartes (1664) considered nerves to be tubes that contain a large number of fine threads, connecting the brain with the skin and other tissues. (From Melzack and Wall,[3] p 72, with permission.)

through this center. The pineal body was thus believed to be the point at which the physical transmission of information along the nervous system became transformed into conscious thoughts, feelings, and emotions.[2] Descartes considered nerves to be tubes containing a large number of fine threads that form the marrow of the nerves and connected the proper substance of the brain with the nerve endings in the skin and other tissues. Pain, experienced in the brain, was set off in the periphery by a stimulus that traveled up this hollow tube (Fig. 27–1).[3]

The next several hundred years saw rudimentary medicine grow to make complex discoveries of the nervous system and developing theories as to the nature and mechanism of pain.

THEORIES OF PAIN

Many theories concerning the mechanism of pain have been developed. At one time, pain was considered a problem of disease rather than a problem related to religion or the soul. Theories regarding the mechanisms by which pain occurs have evolved as science in general has evolved. These theories are instructive as they assist the health care professional to understand the basis for the many ways in which we have treated pain. For example, the specificity theory, which described pain as a specific physical sensation, led to many medical practices that were designed to "cut out" the pain, or the tissue from which the pain was believed to originate. Other theories, such as the fourth theory of pain, suggest that there is a one-to-one relationship between the intensity of the stimulus and pain experience. Such a theory would suggest that two individuals experiencing the same problem (e.g., a fractured leg) would have exactly the same amount of pain and exactly the same response to that pain. This contradicts what we now know regarding the influence of cultural, environmental, and personality factors on how an individual experiences pain. Yet, when examining two patients who have, in our minds, the same pain problem, we often evaluate one patient's response as being what we would expect from that experience while concluding that another individual's does not. Theories such as these continue to have a subtle impact on our perception of someone else's pain, and are worth exploring in detail. These theories are summarized in Table 27–1. The method by which we explain the origin of pain greatly influences how we rationalize and formulate treatment plans.

Livingston[4] described a central summation of impulses that evolve into a vicious cycle of pain. This theory has been expanded by many of the current theorists. Livingston proposed a "vicious cycle of reflexes:"

1. Chronic irritation of a peripheral sensory nerve gives rise to increased afferent impulses.
2. Increased afferent impulses result in abnormal activity in an "internuncial pool" of neurons in the lateral and anterior horn of the spinal cord.
3. The abnormal activity increases sympathetic reflex efferent activity.

This heightened sympathetic activity, including increased heart rate, vasoconstriction, and muscle spasm, produces further abnormal input, thereby creating a feedback loop that perpetuates the experience. The prolonged excitability of the internuncial pool is further maintained by fear and anxiety. Such pain is said to no longer be triggering an alarm of imminent danger, but to have become itself the pathology, residing within the nervous system. The pain pathways may be firing even though no noxious stimuli are present. The transmission of the signal is faulty, so that when a very minor, nonnoxious stimulus is present, the information is garbled and distorted and the pain pathways fire inappropriately.[5,6]

The gate control theory, originally presented in 1965, was modified in 1982 by its original authors, Melzack and Wall,[2] and continues to be the dominant theory influencing our approach to pain management. A schematic diagram of the theory is shown in Figure 27–2. The substantia gelatinosa appears to be the site of the "gate" control within the spinal cord. The noxious stimulus is transmitted to the spinal cord, where modification occurs as a result of either excitatory or inhibitory influences within the spinal cord cells and by descending influences from the brain. The final product, or pain experience, is a complex entity that results in significant individuality of both the experience and the response observed.[7]

Nociceptive afferents supply skin, subcutaneous tissue, periosteum, joints, muscles, and viscera. Some nociceptors respond only to noxious stimuli, while polymodal nociceptors respond to strong, long-lasting stimuli, including mechanical, thermal, and chemical stimuli, which may not initially be perceived as noxious. Most primary afferents, after entering the spinal cord, terminate in the ipsilateral dorsal horn, but some do extend across to the contralateral horn. Once in the spinal cord, the **C fibers** (small) appear to travel in the lateral portion of the dorsal white matter, and the large **A fibers** (large) travel more medially in the dorsal col-

Table 27–1 HISTORICAL THEORIES OF PAIN

Theory	Date/Author	Summary
Intensive (summation) theory	1874/Erb	This theory, built on Aristotle's concept that pain resulted from excessive stimulation of the sense of touch, was described by several authors in the 1840s. Erb maintained that every sensory stimulus was capable of producing pain if it reached sufficient intensity. The theory was further developed by Goldscheider, in 1894, who described both stimulus intensity and central summation as critical determinants of pain. It was implied that the summation occurred in the dorsal horn cells.
Specificity theory	1895/vonFrey	Based on the assumption that the free nerve endings are pain receptors and that the other three types of receptors are also specific to a sensory experience. The primary argument against this theory is that pain perception is not simply a function of the amount of physical damage alone; complex psychologic components are part of the pain experience.
Strong's theory	1895/Strong	As president of the American Psychological Association, Strong believed that pain was an experience based on both the noxious stimulus and the psychic reaction or displeasure provoked by the sensation.
Pattern theories	1934/Nafe	Early pattern theories suggested that all cutaneous qualities are produced by spatial and temporal patterns of nerve impulses rather than by separate modality-specific transmission routes.
Central summation theory	1943/Livingston	Proposal that the intense stimulation resulting from nerve and tissue damage activates fibers that project to internuncial neuron pools within the spinal cord. Abnormal reverberating circuits are created, with self-activating neurons. Prolonged abnormal activity bombards cells in the spinal cord, and information is projected to the brain for pain perception.
The fourth theory of pain	1940s/Hardy, Wolff, and Goodell	Theory developed to further expand Strong's theory. It stated that pain was comprised of two components: the perception of pain and the reaction one has to it. The reaction was described as a complex physiopsychologic process involving cognitive functions of the individual, influenced by past experiences, culture, and various psychologic factors that produce great variation in the "reaction pain threshold."
Sensory interaction theory	1959/Noordenbos	Description of two systems involving transmission of pain and other sensory information with a fast and slow system. The slow system, unmyelinated small diameter fibers, were presumed to conduct somatic and visceral afferents. The fast system, composed of large fibers, were said to inhibit transmission of the small fibers.
Gate control theory	1965/Melzack and Wall	Proposal that the neural mechanisms in the dorsal horns of the spinal cord act like a gate that can increase or decrease the flow of nerve impulses from peripheral fibers to the spinal cord cells that project to the brain. The somatic input is therefore subjected to the modulating influence of the gate before it evokes pain perception and response. It is suggested that large-fiber inputs tend to close the gate, whereas small-fiber inputs generally open it; descending controls from the brain also influence what is experienced.

umn. Collateral branches are given off at the same and nearby levels. The A and C fibers ending in the substantia gelatinosa are subject to excitatory and inhibitory influences; these influences may significantly affect the final pain experience. Wide dynamic range receptors in lamina V also have a major impact on pain. These receptors respond to a variety of inputs from low-threshold and high-threshold mechanical, thermal, and chemical stimuli by way of afferent fibers with a full range of diameters. These wide dynamic range receptors affect the threshold of neurons that subsequently project into ascending tracts. The "gating" action at this level, where the primary afferents enter the spinal cord, can either increase or decrease the amount of sensory information transmitted through this gate to the brain.

The gate control theory suggests that sensory information traveling on large fibers (e.g., comfortable, nonnoxious stimuli) tend to close the gate, while small-fiber inputs generally open it. Inhibitory systems come from higher centers via descending tracts, such as the reticulospinal (RST) and corticospinal (CST) tracts. The synaptic connections occurring as the information is transmitted to the brain also have an effect on the information through a variety of neurotransmitters.

Three ascending tracts subserve nociceptive information. These include the dorsal column postsynaptic (DCPS) system, the spinocervical (SCT) tract and the neospinothalamic (nSTT) tract. A nociceptive message ascending via one pathway may trigger different responses than the same message ascending via another pathway. When the system is functioning in another capacity, such as proprioception or light touch, it cannot

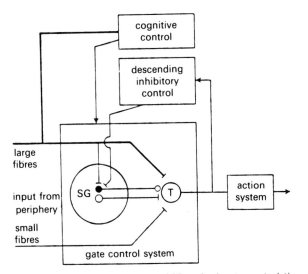

Figure 27–2. Melzack and Wall's 1983 revised gate control theory. (From Bonica,[2] p 10, with permission.)

transmit nociceptive stimuli. Another system, therefore, is used to transmit that information, assuring that the noxious input always has an available tract through which it can travel.

It is hypothesized that the slower conducting tracts, particularly the spinoreticular (SRT) tract and the paleospinothalmic (pSTT) tract, are likely to play a role in chronic, deeply unpleasant, diffuse pain. The stimulus characteristics of these tracts include response to innocuous stimuli that may be perceived as noxious if the stimulus continues and thresholds are lowered. Stimulation of portions of the SRT provides the sensation of diffuse pain, while surgical lesions including portions of the SRT result in relief of chronic pain. The pSTT provokes suprasegmental responses, which may include the motivational drive and unpleasant effect that triggers an organism's action.[8] These factors, described by Melzack and Casey,[7] led to an expansion of the gate control theory to include the motivational dimension of pain. They proposed that the rapidly conducting spinal tracts accounted for the majority of the sensory-discriminative dimension of pain and that the slowly conducting spinal systems were responsible for much of the motivational drive and unpleasant affect characteristics of pain, in conjunction with the reticular and limbic structures. Furthermore, they described neocortical or higher central nervous system (CNS) processes, such as evaluation of input in terms of past experience, as exerting control over activity in both the discriminative and motivational systems. The complex sequences of behavior which characterize pain are a composite of sensory, motivational, and cognitive processes that act on those brain areas that contribute to overt behavioral responses.

Another inhibitory pain mechanism involves the endorphin and opiate receptors. During early studies of stimulation-produced analgesia (SPA) it was found that analgesia induced by brain stimulation and that induced by opiate drugs appeared to share common receptor sites and modes of action. Further investigation suggested that opiate analgesia, like SPA, was an active process of pain inhibition. A receptor for morphine, a naturally occurring opium derivative and exogenous copy of endogenous beta-endorphins, was found to be abundant in central areas of pain control, including the periaqueductal gray matter, dorsal spinal cord, and limbic system.[9] It has been found that patients with chronic pain have a lower level of endorphins in their cerebrospinal fluid than healthy individuals, and this depletion of endorphins is positively correlated with pain intolerance. Bonica and Sternbach[5,10] suggest that this depletion, in conjunction with depletions of serotonin, may account for many of the physiologic and behavioral characteristics of chronic pain patients, such as poor quality of sleep, irritable depression, and withdrawal.

The motivational-affective dimension of pain is an additional, important component affecting how pain is perceived by the individual. Theories regarding the perpetuation of pain have further extended the gate control theory. The pattern-generating theory proposed by Melzack and Loeser[7] suggests the perpetuation of the pain is due to sustained activity in the neuron pools, including the dorsal horn (i.e., the entire gate system) and the homologous interacting systems associated with the cranial nerves. With reduction in the inhibitory influences, there is an abnormal bursting activity, which goes on unchecked and allows recruitment of additional neurons into the abnormally firing pools, leading to the spreading of the pain. This theory is helpful in that it emphasizes the independence of the pain transmission from the original precipitating stimulus.

Once the pattern-generating mechanisms become capable of producing patterns for pain, any input may act as a trigger. Such triggers may include gentle sensory input from distant areas, sympathetic activity, and psychoneural activities. The clinical support for this theory lies in the countless patients who continue to suffer severe phantom limb, neuralgic, and back pain after removal of neuromas, nerves and discs, oblative surgeries such as rhizotomies, cordotomies, and even total spinal cord resection.[7]

Summary

The evolving theories of pain have had important implications in the treatment interventions offered to patients. Early theories emphasizing a physical problem directly proportional to the pain encouraged attempts to cut out the pain. The gate control theory provided important concepts of pain modulation by internal and external systems, and treatment interventions were modified accordingly. As the motivational-affective and cognitive components of the pain experience were added to theories that expanded on the gate control theory, interventions involved more multidisciplinary approaches. The perpetuation of pain is now understood to include emotional, behavioral, and physiologic components, which offer treatment intervention possibilities targeting these multidimensional aspects of pain. The difference between acute and chronic pain mechanisms has encouraged treatment interventions for patients with chronic pain that take such mechanisms into account and emphasize the need to design, for patients with chronic pain, treatment that includes their additional needs.

PAIN CLASSIFICATION

Pain is something experienced by virtually all animals. Yet humans have difficulty with the definition of pain. Autonomic as well as emotional responses, including motivation, affective, and cognitive functions, contribute to the pain experience. The interpretation applied to the painful stimulus is ascribed on the basis of past and present experience.[11,12]

Acute Pain

Acute pain is a signal of real or impending tissue damage; it represents a signal of biological dysfunction. It appears concurrent with either tissue damage or stress

Table 27-2 PSYCHOLOGIC REACTIONS TO SPECIFIC CONDITIONS IN ACUTE PAIN SITUATIONS

Antecedent Conditions	Consequent Reactions
Lack of information (uncertainty)	Anxiety
Perceived loss of control	Helplessness, escape/avoidance
Social isolation	Anxiety, depression
Observation of another's pain behaviors	Increased pain behaviors

From Chapman, CR and Turner, JA: Psychologic and Psychosocial Aspects of Acute Pain, Lea & Febiger, Philadelphia, 1990, p 128, with permission.

and generally disappears with healing.[13,14] Acute pain is also a psychologic experience that is interpreted in the context of one's experience, one's environment, and one's cultural background. The psychologic responses to acute pain under specific conditions are summarized in Table 27-2. The characteristics described in Table 27-2, while most often associated with chronic pain, are also present in acute pain.

Patients with acute and chronic pain are differentiated by the degree to which these psychologic reactions to pain exist, the duration of psychologic reactions, and the duration and extent of physiologic adaptation responses. In the acute patient, removal of the physical cause of the pain eliminates these psychologic reactions to the pain. The patient is then able to return to a normal life-style without difficulty. In the patient with chronic pain these psychologic reactions to the pain become the problem, and the pathology of the original injury subsides. By addressing some of these factors early in treatment, the progression of some of these patients to the chronic state may be avoided.

Chronic Pain

Whereas acute pain is related to injury or damage to tissue, **chronic pain** is said to be the pain that persists after healing is completed. The taxonomy of the International Association for the Study of Pain has stipulated an arbitrary time (3 months) beyond which pain is said to be chronic; in practice this might be less than 1 month or more than 6 months.[5] Although acute pain generates sympathetic response mechanisms such as anxiety, patients with chronic pain often display few autonomic responses. Rather, these patients display increased preoccupation with somatic symptoms; disrupted interpersonal relationships; and disturbances in sleep, appetite, and libido.[15] Chronic pain is not an entity but a process; its neurophysiologic components are somewhat of a mystery.[16] Every practitioner must remember that chronic pain is no less "real" just because it is no longer a response triggered by a noxious stimulus, injury, or damage. The patient experiences pain, and that experience alone is sufficient to accept that the patient has pain. Following, mechanisms are described by which central pain may be perpetuated independent of any external or peripheral stimulus.

Central Pain

Central pain is characterized by the type of "vicious cycle of reflexes" originally described by Livingston.[4] The thalamic pain syndrome was first described by Dejerine and Roussy in 1906. A prominent feature of this disorder is contralateral pain that is continuous, and described as an ache, a boring, gnawing, burning, or crushing sensation. Autonomic and vasomotor dysfunction are commonly associated with this pain.[6] Patients may develop central pain immediately, as in a stroke that results in thalamic pain. In such a case, the lesion occurs in an area of the brain which elicits the central pain phenomenon from the time of the injury. In other cases, an acute type of pain becomes a centrally maintained pain due to such factors as those described in the pattern-generating theory. These patients have an intermediate period during which, if accurate diagnosis can be made, intervention can eliminate the development of the central pain phenomenon. Such patients often present with all, or many, of the characteristics of patients with chronic pain, but they continue to experience a very definitive, physically driven, pain. In contrast, the patient with chronic pain continues to have a peripheral pain complaint that is poorly localized, not related to the initial injury, and compounded by the motivational-affective, cognitive, and behavioral problems that characterize this group.

Central pain phenomena that begin as a peripheral injury include causalgia and reflex sympathetic dystrophy (RSD). Causalgia, first described in the mid-1800s, is the result of significant damage to a peripheral nerve, whereas the trauma from which RSD originates may be very insignificant. There are numerous local syndromes that fit into this continuum and have been described elsewhere.[17] A quote from the medical journals of S. Weir Mitchell,[18] a physician in the American Civil War, is eloquent:

> Its intensity varies from the most trival burning to a state of torment.... Exposure to the air is avoided by the patient with a care which seems absurd, and most of the bad cases keep the hand constantly wet, finding relief in the moisture rather than in the coolness of the application.... As the pain increases, the general sympathy becomes more marked. The temper changes and grows irritable, and the face becomes anxious, and has a look of weariness and suffering ... the rattling of a newspaper, a breath of air, the step of another across the ward, the vibrations caused by a military band, or the shock of the feet in walking, gives rise to an increase of pain. [p 221][18]

There are generally three stages associated with RSD:[17,18]

1. **Acute.** The patient experiences constant burning or aching pain, **hyperalgesia, hyperesthesia, hyperpathia,** localized edema, muscle spasm, and accelerated hair and nail growth. Skin temperature is often higher than normal by 2°F to 6°F, and movement is guarded and limited.
2. **Dystrophic.** Increased hypersensitivity and burning pain, lowered skin temperature, cessation of hair and nail growth, **hyperhidrosis,** pale cyanotic skin color, muscle atrophy, spotty osteoporosis and

emotional changes, including seclusion and marked protection of the extremity.

3. **Atrophic.** Decreased hypersensitivity, normalization of blood flow and temperature; skin is smooth, glossy and drawn; severe muscle atrophy, pericapsular fibrosis with diffuse osteoporosis, personality characteristics associated with a chronic pain syndrome.

Chronic pain and central pain are often used synonymously. The controversy is first one of terminology then one of pathophysiology. The patient with chronic pain cannot be treated by the modalities and interventions that are appropriate for the acute patient. The chronicity of pain itself imposes other components, including psychologic, emotional, and sociologic impact, which must become part of treatment. For this reason, the application of a modality to reduce the effects of injury or tissue damage is not sufficient. However, some patients with enormous psychosocial needs may not, as yet, experience a true central pain phenomenon. Compensatory responses to pain, such as an antalgic gait or a guarded stance, may become contributing factors to the chronicity of pain.[19] This dysfunctional movement adaptation results in abnormal shortening or lengthening of muscles and ligaments in addition to altered recruitment or movement strategies. If the acute injury is healed and the pain continues, the pain may be a result of dysfunctional movement patterns. Patients are often told they have central pain and they will "have to learn to live with it." These patients often make extraordinary progress with symptom reduction and increased function when the movement patterns are normalized. Failure to correct the dysfunctional movement may contribute to the eventual development of a true central pain phenomenon.

For the purposes of this chapter, the term **central pain** will be used for patients who suffer a true central pain phenomenon, and the term chronic pain will be used for patients for whom traditional, acute-care rehabilitation is no longer appropriate and who would benefit from the multidisciplinary approach.

CLINICAL MANIFESTATIONS OF CHRONIC PAIN

The clinical manifestations of a patient who is developing chronic pain, rather than recovering from acute pain, are initially subtle. When the acute-care physical therapist sees that the patient's response to treatment is slow or negligible it is important that the therapist begin to explore a bigger picture, and not simply the site, mechanism, and manifestation of the injury. By asking open-ended questions and waiting for answers, the therapist might learn that the patient has several significant stressors in his or her life; for example, the patient may mention a family crisis, or speak reluctantly of returning to work under a certain supervisor or coworker. The pain might also appear to spread to areas distant from the original site of the injury, confusing both the therapist and the patient.

Clinical Presentation

Leriche, in 1939, wrote eloquently of the ramifications of prolonged physical pain:

> In a very short time it will convert the brightest spirit into a being haunted, driven upon himself, thinking only of his disease, selfishly indifferent to everything and everybody, and constantly obsessed by the dread of recurrent spasms of pain.[5]

When a patient has experienced pain for several months, he or she will present for treatment with a composite of symptoms and complaints that need to be understood by the therapist. Painful experience is so intimately associated with affective distress that behavior without disagreeable emotional components is not reasonably described as pain. The longer the pain persists, the greater is the probability that the patient will become depressed, fearful, irritable, somatically preoccupied, and erratic in the search for relief.[12] It is common that as chronic pain persists both the physician and the patient become uncertain as to the most appropriate course of treatment, and both parties may develop a sense of helplessness. Over time, neither the patient nor the physician deals with their feelings directly, and it is rare for them to confront one another with their feelings. In the health care system, the more disappointed the patient and the physician are with each other, the less direct are their interactions.[20]

A patient will often interpret questions about other areas of his or her life as threatening, especially if some form of compensation is being awarded. The patient may perceive questions about family, work environment, and other stressors as an attempt by the health care provider to negate his or her pain complaints and terminate benefits. While this information is easily gathered and addressed in the acute phase, patients generally become very angry and threatened about addressing such issues when the pain is chronic. It is as if, in the patient's mind, the physician has given up looking for the physical problem and is trying to find another excuse for the patient's pain. The patient with chronic pain is committed to the belief that his or her pain has a physical cause (i.e., the body has been damaged) and that it is within the health care system that help will be found. To the patient who is suffering, it borders on absurdity to suggest that the discomfort being experienced is not real.[21] The communication breakdown, in conjunction with the frustration of not finding the relief sought from the health care provider, exacerbates the lack of trust and increases the difficulty of the patient when interacting within the health care model.[16]

Exclusive use of sensory formulations of pain neglect the major affective, cognitive, and behavioral components of the pain experience that are amenable to other forms of control. Discriminating between expressions of pain that originates in physical pathology and pain having major contributions from psychologic and social sources is a major problem when the patient is evaluated for treatment.[12] A patient whose primary complaint is chronic low-back pain often complains of fatigue, sleep disturbance, change in appetite, and decline in libido, all of which are common in clinical depression; the patient will often persist in attributing all of these symptoms to a physical pain problem.[22] Although many chronic pain conditions begin as a single treatable problem, with time the pain experience becomes enmeshed in a complex web of emotional, behavioral, and social interactions that defy simple solutions.[16] The social impact of the pain expression on a patient can be enormous, significantly influencing the role of the patient in the community, in the family, and among friends. What is crucial in the development of a treatment plan is the impact these changes have on the patient. A patient often undergoes an identity crisis because his or her role in society no longer satisfactorily meets the criteria of either a healthy person with a job or a sick person. Exempt from either role, the patient suffers loss of self-esteem and self-identity, and often describe an overwhelming sense of shame.[23]

A Case Presentation

How an individual experiences pain, and how that pain is reported to another person depends not only on a complex interaction among numerous physiologic, psychologic, social and cultural variables, but also on past pain experiences and how those pain experiences have been handled by health care providers.[16] These variables may best be appreciated in examining a case study. A 25-year-old woman is referred to a physical therapist for evaluation of a skiing injury. The diagnosis is a torn plantar fascia of the right foot. The patient is first seen 2 weeks after the injury, and enters the physical therapy clinic on crutches. The patient was instructed by the physician to begin weight bearing but finds this painful and difficult. During the initial evaluation, the therapist notes that there is a loss of dorsiflexion of the right ankle; otherwise, range of motion of the extremity is within normal limits. The strength of the right leg is normal, although attempts to test the dorsiflexors are limited by pain and decreased range of motion. The right foot appears slightly warmer than the opposite foot. The physician's orders request a whirlpool, active and passive range of motion of the right ankle, and progressive weight bearing. The treatment goals include restoring full range of motion and return to full weight bearing without assistive devices. The therapist anticipates that 2 to 3 weeks will be sufficient to accomplish the treatment goals.

At the end of 3 weeks, the therapist has not seen any significant progress. The patient is hypersensitive to touch on the dorsal and plantar surfaces of the right foot, and any attempt to move the ankle is reported as very painful. The patient is very reluctant to have the right foot touched, and passive range of motion has not been attempted in the last two sessions. The patient has also requested that the turbines on the whirlpool be turned down, and reports an increase in pain after the whirlpool treatment. The foot is noticeably warmer than the left foot. The therapist reports these findings to the physician. The physician sees the patient, agrees with the therapist's findings, and requests that the patient be pushed harder to become weight bearing. The patient

becomes more fearful, and reports that many common stimuli are now increasing the pain in the right foot. Vibrations, drafts, and sunlight are painful, and the pain when weight bearing is attempted elicits crying, refusal to cooperate, and anger from the patient.

The therapist notes that the patient is coming into each treatment session more withdrawn, and decides to spend time listening to the patient, and encouraging conversation about home and family. The patient reports not being able to work, living alone, and not being able to get around in her apartment. She reports that she has no family close enough to help, and that friends are less willing to spend time helping her. She reports that most of her day is spent alone, reading or trying to sleep. The patient is losing weight, and states that the medication is not helping her sleep. The pain medication given to her has been used up, and the prescription cannot be refilled. When the patient is asked by the therapist how much control she feels she has over her pain, the answer is "none." The therapist asks about pain experiences the patient had as a child, and how these incidences were dealt with by her family. The patient reports that she was encouraged to ignore pain, to "tough it out," and that her many sports injuries were often ignored. The patient states that she was always able to cope with these earlier injuries and that the pain was never much of a problem. The patient reports wanting to stop coming to therapy as she feels it is not helping.

The therapist reports to the physician that she sees several problems becoming evident with this patient. First, the pain is becoming worse, and shows signs of early RSD. Second, the patient reports changes in sleep and eating patterns. Third, there is a suggestion that the patient is becoming more isolated and withdrawn, possibly showing some signs of depression. Fourth, the patient reports that she feels she has no control over the pain and that this is very different from her past experiences with pain. The therapist has identified several important problems with this patient, who is not recovering from this injury as was first expected. An originally minor injury is showing several signs of early RSD and the original treatment plan is no longer considered sufficient. A multidisciplinary approach is necessary. The physician decides to consult an anesthesiologist specializing in RSD to assist in outlining future physical interventions, and to also request that the patient see a psychologist to determine the extent to which current coping skills can be enhanced to restore some sense of control. The physician reevaluates the medication needs and prescribes medication that may assist with sleep and address the anxiety the patient reports when being alone. The patient, 6 weeks after injury, has been identified as experiencing an increasing number of psychosocial, as well as physical problems, common among patients with chronic pain. A multidisciplinary approach is identified as being needed and a team is formed to develop new treatment interventions.

Because of the complexity of the problems that chronic pain patients represent, the need for a total evaluation has been recognized. The multidisciplinary team, including physician, physical therapist, psychologist, social worker, vocational counselor, and others, must evaluate the factors related to the person's level of function and impairment. The pain arising from the acute injury is no longer the problem. Factors influencing a person's pain experience may include financial difficulties, marital problems, lack of education and training, work stress, and an overall failure of the patient's coping skills to manage the experience. Information not revealed to one team member is often related to other team members. This sharing may reflect either the health practitioner's skill at addressing specific issues or the patient's expectations of who is the appropriate person to access certain information. The patient, for example, who often sees the physician as not wanting any information not directly related to symptoms may designate a physical therapist or psychologist as a person to whom other information will be revealed.

Sociological Perspective

The "sick role" has been studied extensively by medical sociologists. There are not only expectations regarding the physical condition, but also social expectations to be followed. These expectations, best defined by Talcott Parson,[24] can be enumerated as follows:
1. The sick person is exempt from "normal" social roles.
2. The sick person is not responsible for his or her condition.
3. The sick person should try to get well.
4. The sick person should seek technically competent help and cooperate with the physician.

The patient with chronic pain may be seen as assuming this role on an ongoing, or permanent, basis. Whereas the dependency and regression that is expected in the acute sick-role behavior is often expedient in allowing the physician in charge to make diagnostic and treatment recommendations, these attributes in patients with chronic pain become part of the problem. The patient with chronic pain is seen by some as not fulfilling his or her obligations within the sick role model.[6] Some patients with chronic pain are categorized as not wanting to get well, others may be seen as not being motivated to resume their normal roles related to family or work, and still others begin to feel they are being blamed by either the health provider or family members for failing to respond as expected to prescribed treatment.

Mechanic,[6] another sociologist, regards one's response to stress (or pain) as a product of the skills and abilities the person has that may be used to cope with the problem. Just as each individual possesses different coping skills, each also differs in his or her ability to manage certain problems effectively.[6] While we are often asked, as health care providers, whether we think the patient is motivated to get well, we must also ask whether or not the patient has the coping skills necessary to change his or her situation, and if not, what areas are lacking. By identifying the coping skills that the patient has acquired prior to the pain experience, one removes the patient's blame or lack of motivation as the primary issue. This allows for assessing what coping skills can be taught to enhance the patient's ability to function and resume a normal role in society.

Pain is regarded in our society not as a natural part of life but as something evil, something that one tries his or her best to eliminate. When the pain seems to become "all of who I am" the patient with chronic pain often sees the pain as evil and controlling. The entire universe of the patient with chronic pain is one that bears a similarity to a nightmare. The person may experience pain as a situation in which terrible things are happening, and feel that there is no certainty that worse will not happen; there is no sense of control and the sufferer is helpless to take action.[25]

Behavior Categories

Just as there are many factors that contribute to how a patient manifests his or her pain experience, there are many components within that presentation that we as health care providers can see as typical or atypical and to which we can then respond. Gildenberg and DeVaul[6] have defined four categories of patients with chronic pain. They include:
1. the need-to-suffer patient
2. the overwhelmed patient
3. the psychogenic patient, and
4. the assigned patient

The need-to-suffer group of patients with chronic pain represents only a small minority but is responsible for most of the frustration and disappointment associated with chronic pain management. For this group of patients, pain is a psychologic necessity, and sickness is used to fill a lifelong need to suffer. The patient who is overwhelmed best fits the case observed by Mechanic and mentioned previously where an individual may not have the necessary coping skills to handle a given stressor. The psychogenic category is one that has been studied for years and is characterized by preexisting psychologic problems, inadequate defense mechanisms, or other traumas, which then make it impossible for the patient to mobilize the necessary forces to deal with the current, chronic pain problem. The assigned patient is felt to have developed a chronic problem largely due to the actions of the primary health care provider. Identification of psychosocial stressors immediately after injury can have a significant impact on reducing the chronicity of the physical problem, but such issues are not often dealt with by the primary care physician or the physical therapist who sees the patient in the acute setting.

Some behaviors, if identified by the therapist in the acute stages, may indicate that the problems presented are no longer the type amenable to acute therapy. Such behavior may include any number of the following:
1. The patient no longer discusses return to work in relation to a specific time frame but rather in relation to a "cure."
2. A patient is unwilling to discuss family situations.
3. A patient maintains that it is the injury which has caused all his or her problems and that life was fine until then.

4. A patient directs excessive anger at a situation or an individual involved in his or her case (e.g., work, physician, insurance representative).
5. A patient demonstrates an "I'll show them attitude."
6. A patient is less interested in his or her home program than before.
7. A patient expresses comfort with role reversals in the home.

Any of these behaviors may indicate that a variety of problems are present rather than that a specific tissue damage exists. The behaviors are also representative of a patient who, to some degree, is entering a crisis state. The pain is perceived as something that has taken over control of the patient's life, and is meaningless. A perceived lack of meaning in one's environment weakens one's belief that any efforts he or she exerts the situation are meaningful. It therefore becomes harder to maintain these efforts.[25] There is no reason for the situation that the patient can comprehend, and in the situation's lack of meaning lies a need to defend pain's existence, for the pain is by this time the means by which money is obtained. In crisis, there is a loss of status, a regression if you will, which is reinforced by the medical model, either by the sociologist's concept of the sick role, or by the health practitioner's concept of providing a cure.

MEDICAL MANAGEMENT

When someone experiences an injury or sudden onset of pain, the involvement of the physician is appropriate and often necessary. Initial assessment may include taking a history, conducting tests, and dispersing medication. Also treatment such as physical therapy is often appropriate. The medical management of pain will be covered briefly here, and the rehabilitation aspect of pain management will follow in the next section. A primary role of the physician is to insure that care is comprehensive rather than segregated. As case manager, the physician insures that treatment is comprehensive and multidisciplinary, thereby maximizing the treatment outcomes.

Medication

The use of analgesics for acute pain management is common. Their function is not only to relieve pain but also the anxiety that accompanies the experience. In addition, nonsteroidal antiinflammatory medications and muscle relaxants may be prescribed. The goal of these medications is to minimize the damage to tissue and to maximize the ability of the tissue to heal. Reducing the anxiety and fear of the patient also reduces the sympathetic arousal level, allowing for increased blood flow and changes in pain perception.

Prolonged use of any medication may be problematic, although nonaddictive medications may be taken for a long time. Narcotic analgesics are often both physiologically and psychologically addicting, and their use

should be limited. Patients often experience their pain when using such medications, but "it no longer bothers them." The use of narcotics that fill the same receptor sites as the endorphins made within the body results in a decreased production of endorphins. Endorphin depletion occurs with prolonged use of narcotic medications, and with such depletion the need for the drug increases.

At the time the patient first seeks medical care, expectations are set up based on the physician's description of the patient's problem. Studies by Fordyce et al.[26] have shown that expectations have a significant effect on the duration, intensity, and problems associated with the pain. Fordyce et al. did a prospective study with two groups: One group was given medication and specific expectations were conveyed to them about how long they would need to take the medication; they were also assured that they would have no need to renew a prescription for pain medication, and that they would rapidly regain their level of function. The other group was handled in a more traditional manner. Patients were encouraged to call for more medication if needed, and were given no specific time frames in which they could expect to recover. Not only did the first group return to function faster, but they sustained higher levels of function after a year. The demographics and injuries were the same; the expectations of both physician and patient were not.

As the injury becomes chronic, the physician must be able to adjust the treatment regimen. Medications that were helpful in the acute phase are no longer helpful when the pain becomes chronic. Data from pain clinics, often the last stop for patients seeking help within the medical model, show that the single biggest factor in increasing the level of function and in successfully managing the pain program is the reduction of addictive medications.[6] Patients traditionally collect a wide array of medications, including pain medications, muscle relaxants, anxiety medication, and major tranquilizers. Such medication has often been prescribed initially in lieu of a psychologic assessment, and chronic use of such medication may contribute to the withdrawn, depressed appearance of patients with pain. Primary-care physicians have little experience in discussing with patients the advantages of having a psychologic assessment rather than prescribing antianxiety medications; moreover, they do not have time to do so. Although this practice in the short term may preserve the relationship of the physician as healer, it can be detrimental to the patient if continued over many months.

Anesthetic Nerve Blocks

For pain complaints, many different types of anesthetic nerve blocks can be administered to interrupt the transmission of impulses traveling via a specific nerve to or from the spinal column. Some blocks are used as a direct method of relieving pain; others are used as differential blocks to determine the type of pain, by altering only physiologic variables and observing the response. Peripheral nerve blocks interrupt the nociceptive input either at its source or along a peripheral nerve. Sympathetic blocks interrupt sympathetic input to a limb, again altering the nociceptive feedback loop in addition to increasing blood flow and allowing tissue homeostasis to return. Melzack,[7] in his pattern-generating theory, suggests that the interruption of nociceptive input for several hours stops the self-sustaining activity of neuron pools that may be responsible for some of the chronic pain states. By blocking afferent (nociceptive) or efferent (sympathetic) fibers for several hours, the return of abnormal activity may be avoided when the blockade wears off. In addition, during that time rehabilitation is facilitated and aggressive therapy can be performed that might otherwise not be tolerated. The restoration of normal movement patterns may enhance the perpetuation of relief after the block wears off.

Blocks that are diagnostic in nature may be indicated for the following reasons:

1. To determine the anatomic source of the pain.
2. To ascertain specific nociceptive pathways.
3. To differentiate between local and referred somatic pain.
4. To determine the role of the sympathetic nervous system in the pain experience.
5. To differentiate local pathology from reflex muscle spasm in such disorders as torticollis and the piriformis syndrome.

It may also be considered of primary interest to block the pain in order to determine the patient's response to the elimination of pain. Blocks may be used after surgery to reduce postoperative pain or used early in cases of RSD to reduce progression to a full RSD syndrome. Therapeutic blocks for RSD and causalgia interrupt the vicious cycle of continuous pain transmission and allow treatment to mobilize and restore function of the involved joints and tissue. The effect of this block may extend beyond the normal therapeutic duration of the drug used, and allow for normalization of sensory feedback loops. Additionally, patients who receive some relief from their physical pain are often more willing to work on the psychosocial aspects of their pain experience.[27]

Ablative Neurosurgery

Techniques such as rhizotomies and cordotomies were previously considered as techniques of last resort for patients with chronic pain. In many cases, the short-term results were excellent, but the long-term results were found to be poor; the pain found other tracts or neurons to travel on, and the pain returned after variable time periods of several months to years.[28–30] These techniques are now used for only a limited number of chronic pain problems.

Permanent **sympathectomy** for RSD or causalia may be very successful. Usually, multiple sympathetic nerve blocks are performed first to determine the effectiveness of the blockade. If the block relieves pain but the duration of the relief does not increase with several blocks, a permanent sympathectomy might be very beneficial. This technique works better in the earlier stages of the disorder as compared to the later stages.

REHABILITATION MANAGEMENT

Assessment

Patients needing chronic pain rehabilitation are a challenge for the health care practitioner. Several components are critical to patient assessment, as the intake information collected must be thorough and must identify all possible obstacles to successful completion of treatment. From this information the therapist is able to select appropriate modalities, plan functional restoration, and identify other necessary disciplines. It is uncommon that physical therapy alone will meet the needs of patients with chronic pain.

PATIENT INTERVIEW

It is generally helpful for patients to complete forms in regard to their past treatments, medications, and health care providers. The therapist will find it helpful to know the patient's thoughts about what treatment was beneficial in the past, what was felt to be not helpful, and why. It is also important to have the patient describe the original pain, its location, and the mechanism of onset. From this history, it is very often possible to identify the initial injury and the various compensatory mechanisms that have evolved into dysfunctional movement strategies, information that is helpful in planning treatment.

As previously mentioned, an individual's response to pain is a product of his or her unique life experiences. Each person brings into an injury a history (or no history) of pain, the environmental responses regarding pain, a cultural perspective, and a set of coping skills that may or may not have ever been applied previously to a pain experience. If one concedes that chronic pain is a stressor, then we can examine the methods by which someone may respond to pain as a stress-coping mechanism. Several responses have been outlined by Sternbach:[31]

1. Adaptive response. The individual may remain calm and optimistic and continue to function well despite adversity.
2. Behavior disorder. Addictive behavior, such as alcoholism, or shoplifting, may emerge; other forms of acting out may occur.
3. Thought disorder. Patients may respond by escaping into schizophrenic or paranoid disordered thinking.
4. Affective disorder. The sense of being overwhelmed may pervade, with the patient experiencing intolerable anxiety or depression.
5. Somatoform disorder. Physical dysfunction in excess of the original injury may develop, and symptoms such as nausea, dizziness, and fatigue emerge as a way to cope with an emotional distress of which the patient may be totally unaware.

It is helpful to think of these as possible responses to any significant stressor and not just to chronic pain. Chronic pain is unique in the degree to which the individual may become disabled as a result of the stressor, but the responses are similar to other major stressors.

The high levels of disability often encountered with chronic pain have been suggested to arise from the requirements for workers compensation, recompense through litigation following motor vehicle accident, or classification of disability as defined by the Social Security Administration.

Having a stress checklist[32] is also helpful to assist the therapist in evaluating the impact of the pain on the person's life. This list often identifies problems in family relationships, financial problems, or problems with intimacy. The patient is likely, at this chronic stage in his or her rehabilitation, to argue that these problems arose since the time of the injury and/or pain onset. What is important is the recognition that these problems also need to be dealt with during treatment, by appropriate professionals.

It is also informative to ask the patient for his or her perception of the cause of the continued pain. Patients often harbor fears of cancer and paralysis that, if alleviated, may significantly reduce symptom complaints. It is also helpful to ask patients how they will know that they are better. The answer should be related to function, not the elimination of pain. The answer may help lead to the other component of treatment planning, which includes obtaining input from the patient about treatment goals. Goals for patients with chronic pain should be functionally oriented, not dependent upon cessation of pain. To assess changes in function, use a detailed list of functional tasks that the patient does, no longer does, or has never done. This information is often an eye-opener for patients who may not realize the extent to which they have limited their activities.

BODY DIAGRAMS

Body diagrams are a useful tool for understanding the location of pain. Comparison with earlier records from other facilities is also very helpful. Body diagrams can be used in several ways. First, they can be used to determine whether the areas marked on the body diagram represent specific anatomic localization, or magnification of the pain, or extensive marking outside of the lines of the body. These indicators may be scored, and the score used to determine if extensive psychologic testing is in order.[33] Another use of pain drawings is to evaluate the extent to which compensatory movement patterns have developed. Particularly in patients with soft tissue injuries and myofascial pain syndrome, the development of satellite **trigger points,** altered movement strategies, and adaptive changes in the muscles and ligaments often have a significant impact on the body diagram. Figure 27–3 represents a patient who was perceived as having significant functional overlay with emotional issues. Treatment was based on identifying and treating each component of her body diagram; her diagram at discharge showed no complaints.

This patient, a 27-year-old woman, started with a low-back strain-sprain that was complicated by the presence of an extra cervical rib, which was asymptomatic until she developed postural dysfunction. Her remaining complaints were related to compensatory movement patterns that had developed as a result of the pain and trigger points. Addressing those problems as physical dysfunctional problems rather than indicators of psycho-logic problems allowed treatment to effect changes in level of function (she returned to work), but also in her level of pain and understanding of it. Although this was her third injury, all similar in nature and progression, this was the first time that she was able to understand and direct preventative measures toward the underlying problem of dysfunctional movement patterns.

PAIN EVALUATION: PSYCHOSOCIAL

The plethora of tests available for assessment of the patient with chronic pain are a testimony to the complexity of the problems with which these patients present. We can ask patients to provide us with information in a structured format about their pain, but this does not assure us that their reporting reflects any more than an interpretation of the pain at that time. Changes in function become increasingly important as the disability from pain with no objective findings increases. It is important also to keep in mind that disability is a legal problem, while functional impairment is a medical one. Many different factors are included in these tests in an attempt to find a protocol that will give us all the clues we might need in treating these patients. Many of these tests are available to therapists as part of a multidisciplinary program. Understanding our roles in the assessment process will help therapists treating patients for acute pain to recognize signs that the patients may be having problems that need to be dealt with but that are unrelated to their injuries.

The Sickness Impact Profile (SIP) is a test developed to measure health status and health-related dysfunction. It is not a specific test for patients with pain, although it has been used in evaluating patient populations with pain.[34] It covers physical and psychosocial factors, including information on home management and social interaction.

The Multi-Dimensional Pain Inventory (MPI) is a test designed to measure similar variables to the SIP, but it is targeted for patients with chronic pain. One of three profiles emerge, with characteristic scales elevated within each profile. The MPI provides helpful information in the area of support, perceived solicitous or punishing behavior by others, and levels of distress or lack of control.[35] A sample of the test is included in Appendix A. This test has also been used by the author to evaluate patients with acute pain who are seen for physical therapy, and it has provided some indicators for early involvement of a multidisciplinary intervention.

The McGill Pain Questionnaire is an assessment of the dimensions in which the patient perceives his pain. The categories include sensory, affective, and evaluative descriptors.[36] A sample of part of this questionnaire is located in Appendix B. Although it is a helpful tool in evaluating the quality and complexity of the patient's pain experience, one must keep in mind the factors that influence whether a patient fills a test out extensively or in a very brief fashion. That decision-making process has to do with the manner in which his or her reporting in the past has been accepted by previous health providers and with all the intrinsic factors related to the patient's experiences and coping skills.

Visual analog scales are also useful tools and can be used each session to assess present pain intensity. The

NAME:

Mark the area on your body where you feel the described sensations.
Use the appropriate symbol. Mark areas of radiation. Include all
affected areas. Just to complete the picture, draw your face.

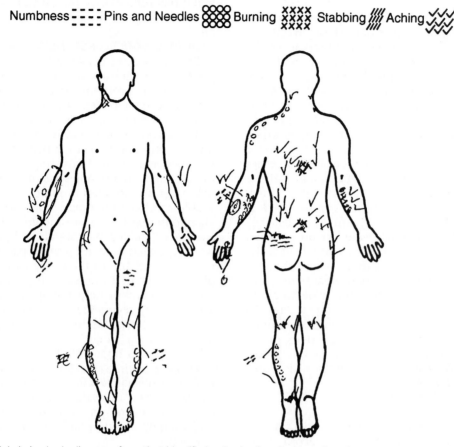

Figure 27–3. Admission body diagram of a patient identified as having functional overlay; diagram used during treatment to solve the patient's symptom complaints. The patient was asked to show where the pain was and what quality best described the pain.

patient is simply asked to rate his or her pain on a 1 to 10 scale, where 1 = no pain and 10 = worst possible pain. Some patients using this scale will report that the pain never changes (i.e., they continue to rate their pain with the same number). These patients may fall within a category of patients for whom pain is either on or off. That is, they either perceive themselves as having pain or they do not. For this subgroup of patients, the visual analog scale is not helpful unless someone on the team works with the patient and teaches him or her to be able to discriminate between the various levels of pain. The numbers on these scales may also have a meaning for the patient that is not the intended meaning of the staff. If, for example, a patient rates his pain high at one therapy session, he might be allowed to skip exercise that day. That patient might then continue to associate any pain experience rated that high as reason to stop all activity. Some practitioners using this scale have chosen to assign a meaning to the various numbers so that the ratings chosen by the patient are more meaningful. Visual analog scales have also been designed as pre- and posttreatment outcome measures, ranking a variety of

activities and situations. A sample can be found in Appendix C.

The Symptom Checklist-90 (SCL-90) is a test more detailed than the MPI but less involved and shorter than the Minnesota Multiphasic Personality Inventory (MMPI). The test contains nine symptom dimensions and an overscale of distress. It was not designed exclusively for use with chronic pain patients.[37] It does provide useful information regarding how the patient perceives his or her situation and relates to such distress behaviors as anxiety, depression, and disordered thinking. This information in turn is useful in designing appropriate treatment interventions.

The MMPI is a psychologic evaluation. It is common, when preparing a patient with chronic pain to take this test, to find that the patient is resistant to taking it. For many patients with chronic pain, the administration of this test is suggestive that health care providers do not believe the pain they are experiencing is real and that other reasons for the pain are being sought. The test is useful in assessing the coping styles and strengths of a patient and in structuring a program to fit his or her way of learning. The pattern of the scales is important; it conveys information regarding anxiety, depression, hypochondriasis, and somatic preoccupation, which is helpful in working with patients. While some patients can deal with the pain experience better if they are allowed to talk about it, for others this type of conversation is counterproductive and is best avoided. There is ample research on the use of the MMPI with patients having chronic pain.[38,39] Research has sought to define a pain profile and a pain personality, and to determine, of the patients with acute pain, who may develop chronic pain. So few of these tests have been done before injury that the profiles commonly seen as characterizing the patient with chronic pain can best be said to identify the response to chronic pain rather than to identify the underlying cause. Surveys done on military men before injury fail to demonstrate any predisposing psychogenic factors.[18] Research done by Sternbach and Timmermans[40] on patients before low-back surgeries and then at follow-up suggest, again, that the profiles seen so commonly on using the MMPI with patients having chronic problems may represent the effect of living with chronic pain. It is reasonable to infer that it is the marked decrease in pain that permits a return to previously normal levels of psychologic functioning.[40]

The information obtained from the tests described above can provide major input into the development of an effective treatment plan. Just as there is more than one chronic pain measurement tool there are a variety of multidisciplinary treatment options available to the therapist. It is a disservice to patients to assume that getting rid of all their pain is a realistic goal and that it can be done with physical interventions alone. Loeser[41] presents a graphic method of visualizing the complexity of chronic pain, and the multiple layers comprising the problem (Fig. 27–4).

As claims continue to be made regarding the ability of tests to detect malingering, it is imperative to keep in mind that chronic pain patients do have real pain. The incidence of true malingering (i.e., pretending to have pain when it does not exist) is extremely rare, and it is not considered professional for practitioners to describe pain as fake when objective ways to measure it have not been found. The fact that objective testing has not yet made pain quantifiable is our failure, not our patient's failure. Accepting that patients with chronic pain actually have pain is the first step in establishing the rapport necessary to work with them. Invalidation of a patient's symptoms by others is a common experience, and the patient must then devote more time to convincing the next health "helper" that the pain is real and that a physical reason for the pain exists.

Another disservice is to tell a patient that he or she will "have to learn to live with the pain." What that means on a psychologic level is that he or she will die if the pain goes away.[42] It also is unrealistic to tell a patient who is overwhelmed and to some degree out of control with a symptom such as pain (they would not be seeking treatment if this was not the case) that there is nothing you can do, and that he or she needs to accept living with the pain. The patient asking for help does not hear this message in terms of just the pain but rather in terms of the gestalt of the experience. So, in effect, you are saying that the pain will not change, and wrapped up in that pain is a composite of cognitive, affective, motivational, and emotional components that is interpreted as not changing. These are represented in the outer circles of Loeser's model (Fig. 27–4). If "no change" was tolerable, the patient would not be seeking treatment. If the patient is given the tools to feel in control, it will not matter if the pain remains the same.

PAIN EVALUATION: PHYSICAL

The physical therapist is presented with a complex challenge when asked to evaluate patients with chronic pain. These patients may be dysfunctional in the psychologic sense, as described in the above section, and this may make their physical assessments more difficult. Patients with chronic pain vary in the amount they communicate, from one extreme of wanting to tell you about everything that has happened since the onset of pain (characteristic of neuroticism) to saying almost nothing (when they are experiencing significant depression or lethargy). From patients with both styles of communication, the therapist must essentially obtain the same information. The assessment must often include more intensive appraisal of more systems than are necessary with other types of patients.

When a standard physical exam is performed on patients with chronic pain, the neurologic exam is often found to be normal, muscle strength testing is normal, and the posture may appear outwardly to be normal, although this is less common. The musculoskeletal examination results often leave the therapist overwhelmed with the extent to which the posture is asymmetrical and the extent to which patients lack awareness of the asymmetries. The movement patterns of patients with chronic pain are frequently rigid and guarded, often to compensate for balance disturbances. Joints distant from the original injury may be limited in range of motion (ROM). The patients may report virtually all

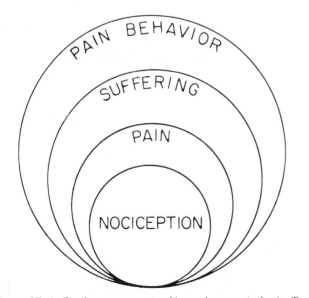

Figure 27–4. The four components of Loeser's concept of pain. (From Loeser,[41] with permission.)

movements to be painful. Movements may be limited by fear, by shortened soft tissue, or by the habit that drives the movement strategy. Testing these patients in another position often results in a marked increase in ROM. Such discrepancies may be less an attempt to fake limitations than real differences in movement strategies, which determine the range through which a movement occurs. This same phenomenon can be demonstrated in normal, healthy subjects as well.

The use of equipment may facilitate the identification of problems with endurance, motor firing patterns, or balance. Cardiovascular fitness is often poor in these patients, and low endurance combined with rapid muscle fatigue may result in inconsistent testing. Surface electromyography (SEMG) is invaluable in assessing these patients, because it can identify the movement strategies and the muscle firing patterns.[43-46] These components are generally not visible to the clinician, yet may be the most significant component in the perpetuation of pain.

Central pain is often presumed to be present if the patient appears to have sufficient healing of the injured tissues. It may be the responsibility of the therapist to determine if any adaptive changes of muscles or ligaments or any adhesions are contributing to the symptom complaints. Patients with dysfunctional movement patterns are thought to have central pain; however, adequate normalization of the movement patterns may result in a significant decrease in pain and increase in function. It is a disservice to identify these patients as having central pain that they have to learn to live with. Use of multiple channel SEMG is most helpful here in identifying the actual problems through the monitoring of multiple muscle groups during functional activities.

Patients with chronic pain often have autonomic and central nervous system dysfunctions such as myofascial pain syndrome, localized tissue problems, major movement strategy dysfunctions, and a sense that they are totally out of control. These problems are represented by Figure 27–5. Autonomic dysfunction can often be observed, at least in part, through multiple channel biofeedback recordings. These patients, for example, may show a discrepancy between objective and subjective thermal information (Fig. 27–6). Other examples are altered response patterning of two different factors such as temperature and sweat gland activity. For these autonomic factors, the temperature of the hand should increase and the sweat gland activity, measured as electrodermal activity, should decrease when the person is achieving a greater degree of relaxation. With dysfunctional autonomic states, these two parameters may both increase simultaneously.[47]

Treatment

Multiple treatment interventions may be applicable for any patient. The interventions may be done by several therapists on a rehabilitation team. The coordination of these interventions is necessary. The information and impressions gained by each member of the team are also important in the overall treatment planning. Meet-

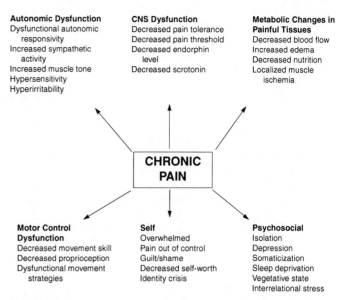

Figure 27–5. The assessment components for the complex psychophysiologic dimensions of chronic pain.

ings with a multidisciplinary team often reveal information that could not be obtained by any one member of the team. Figure 27–7 shows an overview of goals and interventions that may be appropriate to the problems identified in Figure 27–5.

Another reason for having multidisciplinary teams for these patients is that a problem arises when the medical model or team has identified a level of **impairment** that does not correlate with a higher level of **disability.** The former is a medical phenomenon and the latter is considered a legal or administrative one. The basic premise of the medical model is that symptoms are the expression of anatomic, physiologic, or biochemical abnormalities indicative of a disease process.[16] Patients with chronic pain often do not fit this model, as their level of disability far exceeds the known pathology. The medical and legal issues become inseparable because the health

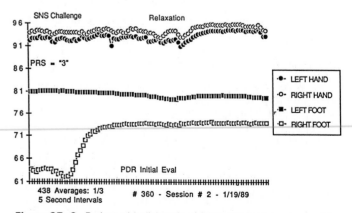

Figure 27–6. Patient with diagnosis of failed low-back syndrome subjectively experienced the left foot as slightly cooler than the right foot; objective measurement demonstrated a 20°F difference, with the left foot warmer than the right foot. Thermal recordings from hands and feet were collected over a 20-minute time period and plotted. SNS = sympathetic nervous system challenge; PRS = pain rating scale; PDR = physiologic dysregulation evaluation.

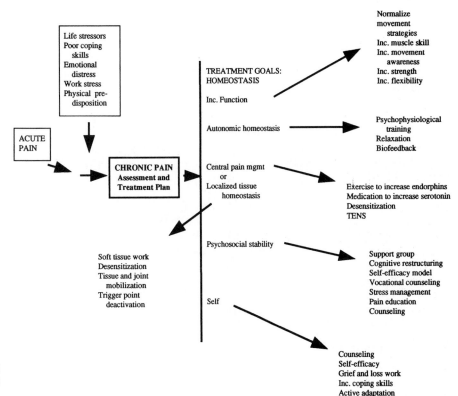

Figure 27–7. Use of the assessment model shown in Figure 27–5, with treatment interventions.

care providers are asked to determine if someone should receive compensation, such as social security, for his or her pain, which may exist without sufficient objective pathology to explain it.

The overall objective is to restore homeostasis, or internal stability and equilibrium, to the patient, to whatever extent this can be done. Full homeostasis is not often possible. The patient and clinicians must then come to terms with the issue that a cure is not the end goal of treatment and that the patient is going to need to adjust to permanent loss of function or continued pain. It is the confrontation of this adjustment issue that is often responsible for patients moving across the nebulous line from acute to chronic pain. Homeostasis can be approached by applying that term not just to autonomic factors but to the entire patient.

FUNCTION

Under the category of functional restoration the issues of normalization of movement strategies, skilled muscle recruitment, muscle strength, and flexibility are considered. Motor control has been discussed in Chapter 13 of this text; its importance cannot be overemphasized with many of these patients. Surface EMG is evolving into a useful tool for the normalization of motor control strategies. The compensatory patterns that developed immediately after the injury may have been useful then to protect structures and reduce pain, but these same patterns can become the source of the pain after the original injury has healed. Flor et al.[48] have described the difficulty patients with chronic pain have in the discrimination of muscle tension. This problem was evident when the discrimination involved the affected, painful area

and when the discrimination task involved nonaffected muscles. The delay or inability to respond to changes in muscle tension, which may be psychologic, postural, or myofascial in origin, may lead to significant changes in the muscle and muscle receptors. Muscle recruitment imbalances, shown in Figure 27–8 can be assessed with SEMG, and the same modality used for treatment.

Over time, SEMG has become most useful in understanding the effects of trigger points and myofascial pain syndrome. Not only can trigger points refer pain, as has been so well-documented by Travell and Simon,[49,50] but trigger points can also refer muscle spasm or inhibition[51,52] and other phenomena.[53] In reviewing the soft tissue problems of 45 patients with chronic low-back problems and assessing their muscle function with

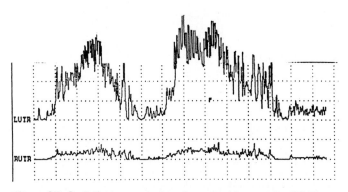

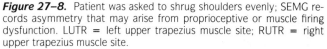

Figure 27–8. Patient was asked to shrug shoulders evenly; SEMG records asymmetry that may arise from proprioceptive or muscle firing dysfunction. LUTR = left upper trapezius muscle site; RUTR = right upper trapezius muscle site.

SEMG, Headley[54] showed that inhibition of the gluteal muscles by the quadratus lumborum may play a significant role in the chronicity of low-back pain. Release of the inhibition by deactivation of the trigger points in the quadratus lumborum (Fig. 27–9) results in rapid increases in strength and function of the gluteal mus-

cles. This phenomenon has also been described by Rosenmoff.[55] Mayer,[56] who does not propose strengthening until after the initial phases of comprehensive functional restoration, also reports that low strength levels are generally not a sign of severely advanced muscle atrophy but rather of deficits from factors such as fear of

SCAN 77

Patient's Name

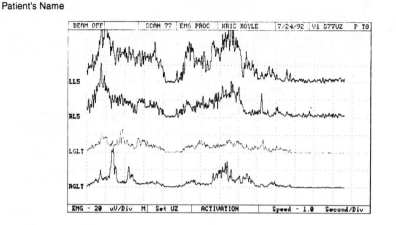

Seconds   SAMPLE - 13.6

LL5 Peak = 75.8 uV, Min.= 0.3 uV, Avg. = 20.4 uV, STD Dev. = 16.90, Area = 278
RL5 Peak = 62.3 uV, Min.= 0.3 uV, Avg. = 12.2 uV, STD Dev. = 10.49, Area = 166
LGLT Peak = 26.5 uV, Min.= 0.0 uV, Avg. = 5.6 uV, STD Dev. = 4.82, Area = 77
RGLT Peak = 44.3 uV, Min.= 0.0 uV, Avg. = 5.6 uV, STD Dev. = 6.51, Area = 77
   L5 Peak Difference = 13.5 uV, Peak % = 18%, Peak Total =138.0
   GLT Peak Difference = 17.8 uV, Peak % = 40%, Peak Total = 70.8

COMMENT:

Chair - waist lift - 20#

SCAN 57

Patient's Name

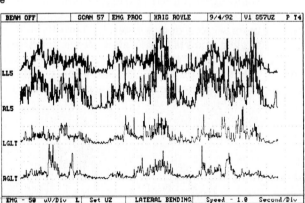

Seconds   SAMPLE - 13.6

LL5 Peak = 133.8 uV, Min.= 1.3 uV, Avg. = 36.0 uV, STD Dev. = 24.61, Area = 491
RL5 Peak = 217.3 uV, Min.= 1.5 uV, Avg. = 54.0 uV, STD Dev. = 37.31, Area = 738
LGLT Peak = 107.3 uV, Min.= 1.0 uV, Avg. = 23.5 uV, STD Dev. = 17.91, Area = 320
RGLT Peak = 99.3 uV, Min.= 0.8 uV, Avg. = 16.4 uV, STD Dev. = 15.37, Area = 224
   L5 Peak Difference = 83.5 uV, Peak % = 38%, Peak Total = 351.0
   GLT Peak Difference = 8.0 uV, Peak % =7%, Peak Total = 206.5

COMMENT:

35# W-C lift

Figure 27–9. Poor amplitude in the gluteal muscles, associated with trigger points in the quadratus lumborum (top). Retesting of the same patient, with an increase in gluteal amplitude following deactivation of quadratus lumborum trigger points (bottom). With proper gluteal recruitment the level of function of the patient has increased. Gluteal muscle site chosen was 3 inches below the middle of the illiac crest. LL5 = the left lumbar muscles adjacent to the fifth lumbar vertebra; RL5 = right lumbar muscles adjacent to the fifth lumbar vertebra; LGLT = left gluteal muscles; RGLT = right gluteal muscles.

reinjury, neuromuscular inhibition, and altered neural input to the muscle from higher centers (i.e., movement strategies).[56]

In repetitive motion disorder, which is the most rapidly increasing work-related problem faced by this country in the 1990s, muscle fatigue and overload is common. The pathophysiology of the muscle fatigue has been outlined by Simons[57] and the effect of muscle fatigue leading to overload, as measured with SEMG, can be seen in Figure 27-10. These problems are often not observable clinically, and they often yield test results that suggest the person is not putting forth maximal effort. This situation is another in which the use of SEMG has an advantage because it helps establish which muscles are being used to perform a task: the muscles considered to be the normal, prime movers, or the compensatory muscles that may be poorly equipped to perform such a service for any length of time.

Severe, chronic muscle fatigue has significant implications for rehabilitation. Normal muscles, when worked to fatigue, can recover to the preexercise state in 5 to 20 minutes.[45] This is measured with SEMG, using spectral analysis rather than amplitude. In patients with severe chronic repetitive motion disorder, several minutes of work can overload a muscle, and recovery of its spectral value can take 45 to 90 minutes. When tested over several days, these patients often do not recover overnight, so they present themselves for the second day of testing with lower spectral frequencies (more muscle fatigue) than they presented with the first day. These patients often report that they have increasing difficulty with their job over the course of a week, with pain higher at the end of the week than at the beginning. They often also report that they must spend the weekend resting in order to begin the next work week.

Many patients with chronic pain initially cannot tolerate the type of exercise program that is used during acute rehabilitation. These patients have fundamental problems with movement. They often cannot produce slow, smooth, controlled movements, even in body parts distant from the original injury. The misuse of muscles is significant, and is often more of a problem than actual loss of strength. Retraining these patients to move with slow, smooth, and controlled motions must precede any general strengthening program. Patients often cannot isolate a single joint movement, so retraining of this isolated joint movement is helpful as well. The first level of rehabilitation for these patients is often one of movement therapies. These can be based on Feldenkrais,[58] the Alexander technique,[59] Tai Chi, or any other techniques which increase awareness of how the movement is being performed and how corrections can be made.

Attempts to strengthen these patients invariably fail; they simply do not have the muscle endurance to sustain an activity. When accessory muscles are required to do a task for long periods, these muscles become fatigued, with poor recovery as well, and other muscles are forced to take over. Patients with chronic cumulative trauma often can present with a different movement strategy at several points during the same day because one set of compensatory patterns used to perform the required

task is subsequently replaced with other compensatory patterns. Restoration of muscle strength and endurance, once the muscles have reached this stage is long, costly (physiologically, emotionally, and financially), and not always successful.

Treatment of these patients must begin with soft tissue massage and manipulation. There are a variety of theories and techniques that have evolved in the field in the last 10 years. Techniques have been categorized under neuromuscular facilitation, muscle energy, myofascial release, strain and counterstrain, neuromuscular therapy, and trigger point release. The soft tissue work may include effleurage or deeper friction massage. The presence of trigger points, muscle spasm, and altered tone in muscle are treated to enhance the work targeted at restoring normal length, contractibility, and relaxation. Both physical and physiologic changes can have a significant impact on the ability of the muscle to function normally, and restoration of muscle function often begins with soft tissue work directed at muscle, ligaments, and the fascial layers. Such work must then be followed by muscle reeducation and movement training, before any strengthening program can be attempted. Many of the failures seen in the industrial rehabilitation area are with patients having problems in muscle tone or structure.

Once muscle recruitment has been normalized and efficiency of the muscle restored, strengthening is appropriate. Strengthening can be done either with minimal equipment or with sophisticated computerized equipment. It is important to remember that muscle strengthening is specific to the way the strengthening is done;[60] that is, a muscle strengthened isometrically at 45 degrees of extension will only use that increase of strength within that narrow range of joint motion and only when stressed isometrically. Functional strengthening of muscle is imperative, with monitoring of muscle activity to insure that the muscle is working as expected during the functional tasks.

Because these patients often demonstrate a level of disability greater than that attributable to their known pathology, pain management often must continue as a strong rehabilitation program gets underway. Patients' fears of reinjury, interpersonal conflicts at work, or family stress may all impair progress. Reassurance as to the difference between hurt and harm, with the development of strong internal coping skills, will increase the success of the physical rehabilitation component. The return to the full adult status means multiple psychophysiologic adjustments (e.g., reestablishing the responsibilities held within the family and at work), and the team must be ready to react to problems as they become evident, eliminating possible roadblocks to the success of the overall rehabilitation plan.

Exercise has other important advantages for these patients, in addition to strengthening muscles and restoring endurance. Both mental status and sleep have reportedly improved with increases in exercise.[61] Various measurement tools have shown that depression is lessened and self-esteem increased with an increase in cardiovascular fitness. McCain[61] also reports that the stages of sleep may be affected by exercise, with an

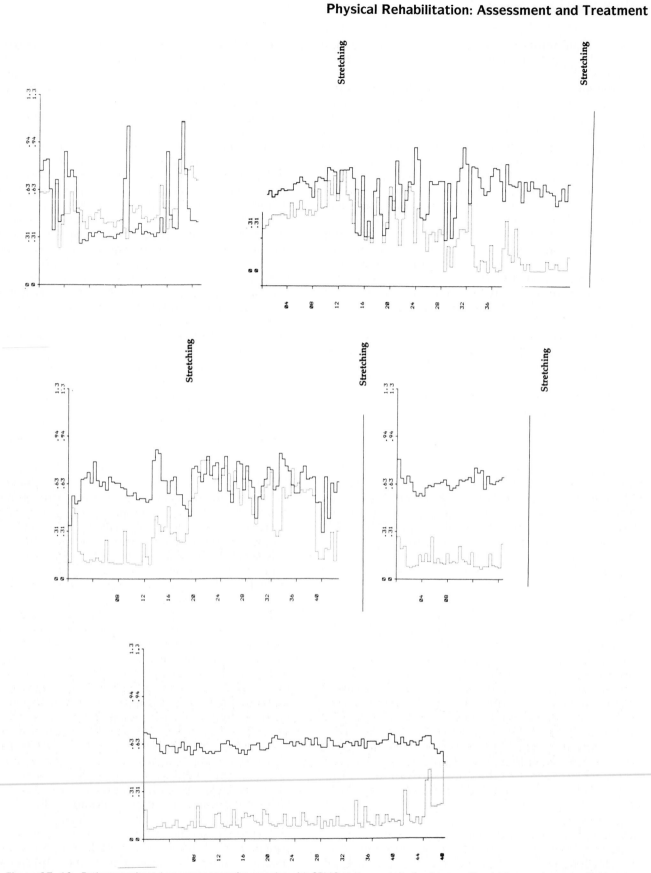

Figure 27–10. Patient monitored on upper trapezius muscles with SEMG at the worksite for 4 hours. The right upper trapezius (lighter line) experiences rapid fatigue as compared with the left upper trapezius (dark line). The patient continues to perform the symmetrical task with the SEMG showing overload on the right side after the first hour, despite stretching breaks. (Each panel is 45 minutes in duration; patient was instructed to stretch every 20–25 minutes throughout the recording period.)

increase in slow-wave sleep and a decrease in REM sleep.

Because the patient with chronic pain tends to evaluate his or her level of activity in terms of what could be done prior to the injury or onset of pain, it is important to present improvement in ways that are positive, even if the improvement is small. For example, when a patient is asked to compare the level at which he or she is functioning with that from 1, 2, or 3 weeks before, he or she is often able to see positive results. These are the changes that maintain motivation and build positive self-esteem, as well as develop coping skills that can be used by the patient after discharge from the program. As new skills develop, a patient's expectations of ultimate level of function may need to be clarified. A patient who has been disabled for over 5 years may expect to be restored to the same level of activity enjoyed prior to the injury. It is necessary, if these problems of unrealistic expectations arise, that the team members address the issues of grief and loss.

AUTONOMIC HOMEOSTASIS

The autonomic nervous system plays a significant role in the perpetuation of chronic pain states. Exercise is not the only intervention for which specificity of response applies. We cannot strengthen a patient in one posture and expect the results to generalize; neither can we train one aspect of the autonomic nervous system and expect that as it moves toward homeostasis, so will all other aspects. It is well known that individuals differ in the specificity of the autonomic nervous system and that specific situations may evoke different patterns.[47,62] Some autonomic parameters may be overactive, other reactions may be underreactive. Often autonomic parameters habituate as pain becomes more chronic.[63] A multimodal assessment and treatment plan may be necessary; such a plan can be carried out well with the new biofeedback technology. More than one autonomic parameter can be monitored (e.g., thermal and skin conductance, or blood pressure and heart rate) to allow for specificity training and normalization of autonomic nervous system activity.

CENTRAL PAIN MANAGEMENT

The central pain model presented by Melzack in his pattern-generating theory suggests several methods of intervention from a rehabilitation perspective. This theory describes the alteration of the central, self-perpetuating feedback loop with either hyperstimulation or hypostimulation. Hypostimulation can be achieved in deep states of relaxation, where physiologic elements have an environment in which homeostasis can be established more readily. Hyperstimulation can be achieved through rapid changes in an environment, such as one obtains from contrast baths, by alternating hot and cold water. The spray techniques of spray-and-stretch described by Travell and Simons[49,50] also may be used as a brief form of hyperstimulation. Frequently, the physician will perform a nerve block, allowing for temporary interruption of pain pathways, and then will ask the rehabilitation team to work with restoring normal movement and sensory input. This team approach may allow for more rapid progress than can be achieved in rehabilitation without pain interruption.

Central pain management may also address the areas of low endorphin levels and the use of TENS as a therapeutic modality. For the problem of a decrease in endorphin levels,[5] the treatment approach may be to use deep relaxation and imagery to assist in reversing endorphin depletion arising from the maintenance of a state of chronic stress.[64] Relaxation and imagery have been used with patients who have had chronic pain for approximately 15 years.[65] The rationale is based on the increased muscle tension and anxiety seen in these patients, and the need to reduce the sympathetic arousal level. Biofeedback training was seen by many as a method by which the stress of chronic pain could be reduced.[66,67] Chronic pain can be considered a chronic stressor, and increased sympathetic tone may be a persistent problem that in turn contributes to unbalanced or labored breathing patterns, chronic muscle tension and anxiety, and even a chronic low-grade level of panic. Reduction of this dysfunctional state, and return to a more homeostatic state, enhances normal neurochemistry.[47,62] A constant state of alert (e.g., Why is this pain getting worse? When am I going to be normal? Why can't someone find out what's wrong?) contributes to the negative effects of chronic stress on the organism. Biedermann[68] and others[69] attribute the success of relaxation enhanced with biofeedback to an increased sense of control over the problem rather than to specific physiologic changes.

The other method of increasing endorphin levels is exercise, because exercise will have a beneficial effect on the endorphin levels.[70] McCain[61] has reported that true modulation of pain sensitivity may depend on tissue levels of endogenous opioids, specifically on the level of beta-endorphin that is released, along with adenocorticotrophic hormone (ACTH), during exercise. Another problem is that serotonin levels also have been found to be low in many patients with chronic pain. Serotonergic antidepressants have been used for reduction of the clinical signs of vegetative behavior associated with such depletion.[71] These medications also have the added benefit of helping the patient sleep.

A modality that has been researched and explored at length has been the use of transcutaneous electrical stimulation (TENS). The gate control theory described by Melzack and Wall is the theoretical basis for the use of TENS. A small electrical stimulation is provided either near or distant from the area of pain and alters the information coming from the area of pain. The type of stimulation applied may differ with specific types of pain. Acute pain, which travels through fast ipsilateral tracts from the Aα fiber groups, responds to a different stimulation pattern than the pain carried through the C fibers, which are slower and more diffuse in their path. The use of TENS has been found to be effective in a number of acute pain syndromes and helpful in the immediate postoperative period.[72,73] The efficacy of TENS with chronic pain is more difficult to determine, as long-term follow-up is necessary. Choi and Tsay[74] critiqued many clinical studies of TENS with patients having chronic pain. They found an overall success rate of 60 percent initially, decreasing to 40 percent at 1 year and 30 percent at 2 years. Achterberg and Lawlis[75] cite a possible increase in endorphin production with TENS application, but stress the need to try various placements of the electrodes. Effective electrode placement may vary widely among patients. These authors report that the most successful placements were often those chosen by the patients themselves. The wide variance in electrode placement, combined with the options for wave forms used, complicate the ability to provide a straightforward protocol for TENS application.[74] Differences in stimulus frequencies also alter the neurophysiologic effects, and the wide variation in options now available with TENS units reflects the different approaches to pain modulation. Appropriate use of TENS for any condition requires an understanding of the neurophysiology underlying pain modulation, and a commitment to evaluating a wide variety of electrode sites and stimulus characteristics.

LOCALIZED TISSUE HOMEOSTASIS

Patients with chronic pain have adapted in dysfunctional patterns, both physical and psychologic. That adaptation has not only affected the motor strategies used, the adaptive length changes of numerous soft tissue components, but it has also habituated much of this behavior. The movement abnormalities are not only of motor strategy but also of speed, coordination, proprioception, and, often, slowing of the reversal of antagonists. The sensory feedback of these dysfunctional patterns will, over time, convince the central nervous system that these altered patterns are normal.[76] A model of the motor plan in governing coordination of posture and movement is shown in Figure 27–11. The reader is encouraged to refer to Chapter 13 in this text.

Soft tissue treatment, with reduction of adhesions and restoration of tissue homeostasis, may have a positive benefit on one's pain experience and on the functional level of activity. Muscle imbalances, existing for long periods or producing a multitude of dysfunctional patterns, have an influence on the joint alignment and tissue length. Pain may result when the muscle imbalance imposes abnormal forces upon the joint for a long period. Grieve[77] emphasizes the need to treat the entire arthrokinetic system—including the muscular imbalance, connective-tissue tightness or tethering, and the localized soft tissue changes—and, in effect, reduce the abnormalities of movement. Homeostasis of tissue length, tissue tension, and muscle firing patterns are as important to the overall well-being of the patient with chronic pain as is homeostasis of the autonomic nervous system.

PSYCHOSOCIAL AND SELF ISSUES

Many of the psychosocial issues and negative self-image issues will be addressed by several of the team members. Although these may be seen as the primary focus of the behavioral medicine, psychology, and social worker members of the team, the rehabilitation staff can do much as well. All team members can enhance the development of strong tools for self-responsibility and can address the fears and belief system that support the disability in these patients.

Virtually all patients who have chronic pain have difficulty in distinguishing between hurt and harm. They tend to identify any pain or discomfort as an increase in tissue damage and a signal to stop. They can learn with assistance to separate hurt from harm, and tolerate uncomfortable body sensations that accompany exercise. A patient with chronic pain may perceive any discomfort or increase in pain as causing harm or physical damage to tissue. This is seldom the case, and the hurt that is experienced is similar to the discomfort of anyone who increases their level of activity suddenly. Frequently, once patients have reduced their fears of harm, they experience a decrease in pain, and their progress is accelerated.

The psychobiology of changing a threat into a challenge has been well described by Rossi.[64] While threats are associated with the release of catecholamines and cortisol into the bloodstream, a challenge is associated only with release of catecholamine levels. As the self-responsibility of subjects increased, their levels of catecholamine levels decreased. Cognitive work to convert a negative stress of threat into a positive coping experience (i.e., a challenge) is associated with altered perception of one's pain.

This threat of pain has additional implications in rehabilitation. Often, in an attempt to increase the activity levels of patients with chronic pain, therapists have been encouraged to disregard all complaints. A patient who experiences a knifelike, stabbing pain in the back, for example, will be encouraged to continue to perform the task, with assurances that no harm is being done. Moreover, the image the person has of his or her pain, especially when the patient feels threatened, can have a significant impact on muscle recruitment patterns. In Figure 27–12 a subject was asked to perform a task that required the use of the muscles being monitored with SEMG. As the imagery of a "knife stabbing in the back" was introduced, muscle recruitment changed dramatically. Removal of the imagery allowed for normalization of the muscle recruitment pattern. Both the functional level of activity-exercise and the patient's perception of

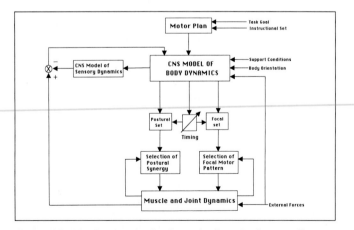

Figure 27–11. Sensory feedback mechanisms having an effect on altering posture and movement. (From Guymer,[76] p 58, with permission.)

SCAN 77

Patient's Name

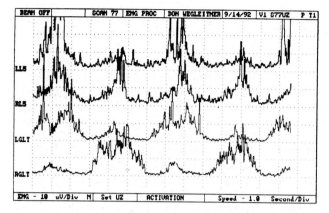

Seconds

SAMPLE - 13.6

LL5 Peak = 206.5 uV, Min.= 1.0 uV, Avg. = 12.1 uV, STD Dev. = 27.01, Area =166
RL5 Peak = 45.5 uV, Min.= 1.0 uV, Avg. = 7.6 uV, STD Dev. = 6.52, Area = 103
LGLT Peak = 48.8 uV, Min.= 0.5 uV, Avg. = 6.2 uV, STD Dev. = 5.94, Area = 85
RGLT Peak = 30.5 uV, Min.= 0.5 uV, Avg. = 6.5 uV, STD Dev. = 6.38, Area = 89
  L5 Peak Difference = 161.0 uV, Peak % = 78%, Peak Total = 252.0
  GLT Peak Difference = 18.3 uV, Peak % = 37%, Peak Total = 79.3

COMMENT:

pre - imagery, knee diagonals

SCAN 77

Patient's Name

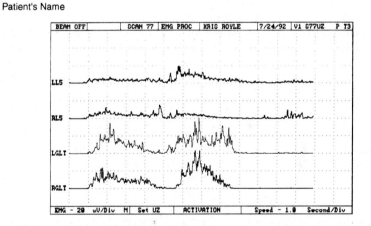

Seconds

SAMPLE - 13.0

LL5 Peak = 18.8 uV, Min.= 0.0 uV, Avg. = 3.1 uV, STD Dev. = 3.09, Area = 40
RL5 Peak = 15.0 uV, Min.= 0.0 uV, Avg. = 2.6 uV, STD Dev. = 2.45, Area = 34
LGLT Peak = 40.5 uV, Min.= 0.0 uV, Avg. = 6.9 uV, STD Dev. = 8.06, Area = 90
RGLT Peak = 42.8 uV, Min.= 0.0 uV, Avg. = 6.3 uV, STD Dev. = 8.36, Area = 82
  L5 Peak Difference = 3.8 uV, Peak % = 20%, Peak Total = 33.8
  GLT Peak Difference = 2.3 uV, Peak % =5%, Peak Total = 83.3

COMMENT:

QHA - hard to do with left/ some pain

Figure 27–12. Subject performing task requiring use of L3 paraspinal and gluteal muscles. Subject has history of low back pain but was not experiencing any at the time of the testing. Amplitude of muscles before imagery (top). Recruitment changes after stabbing back pain imagery imposed (bottom). The subject's movement pattern did not change during the imagery; recruitment returned to normal after the imagery was reversed. LL5 = left lumbar muscles 1 inch lateral to the fifth lumbar vertebra; RL5 = right lumbar muscles 1 inch lateral to the fifth lumbar vertebra; LGLT = left gluteal muscle group; RGLT = right gluteal muscle group.

pain are important. Using biofeedback techniques during imagery and cognitive restructuring, the behavioral medicine team members can assist patients and therapists in achieving more rapid gains in activity level.

Illness behavior is a component that can be addressed by the team as a whole, by recognizing what the behaviors represent and how positive coping skills can be implemented to reduce disability. Patients have, by and large, coped with some adversity in the past. Exploring past stressors and methods of coping may shed light on how a program can be tailored to maximize the use of such skills. A patient who has a sense of being able to effect a change in his or her own life has an internal locus of control. Such an individual has a strong conviction that what he does impacts his environment and the events in his life.

Patients who deal in very concrete details, rather than the abstract, will do better in a program that is very concrete. Patients who need to come to decisions on their own will succeed in a program that presents them with material that allows them to draw positive conclusions and effect their own change. Other patients will easily accept the decisions of others. Some patients like to feel that they are personally important and recognized every day, even in a group setting. To others, such individualized attention may have a negative impact. Every individual has his or her style of coping with life; understanding and enhancing the skills he or she has used well in the past increases the possibility of success in a pain management program. Just as we each have preferences in what we wear, what car we drive, and what we eat, so too we have preferences in the method by which we accept information, or reject it. Taking the time to understand an individual patient, and work within his or her armamentarium of coping skills, can go a long way to increasing the possibility of success.

Illness behaviors are summarized in Table 27–3. Increasing the level of function is more beneficial if patients have the confidence to proceed with the task, and if they actively make the choice to do so, than if they feel forced to do so. Allowing a patient to identify the discomfort from the activation of a trigger point, for example, can be beneficial if he or she has been encouraged to use the skills taught—to apply pressure, to stretch, and to eliminate the problem—rather than allowing the discomfort to become painful and subsequently lead to reduced activity. This problem solving becomes a positive coping mechanism.

Behavior modification techniques have been a vital component of pain management since Bonica introduced the concept in the early 1960s.[78] Fordyce introduced a program for elimination of chronic pain behaviors in the 1970s. Figures released by the University of Washington in Seattle, where Fordyce established his program, indicated that it was not uncommon for patients seen at this pain center to have experienced as many as 20 or more surgeries.[79] The focus of the new pain management programs was the modification of behavior and actions of both the patient and his or her family. The early pain programs focused on the excessive disability that was perpetuated by the behavior of the patient. Behaviors were categorized as behavior that did not occur often enough and needed reinforcement, behavior that occurred too often and needed to be reduced in frequency, or behavior that was missing from the patient's repertoire and was needed. Behavior was often learned from the environment, either the family or others in pain. The program stressed modification of the behaviors to reduce disability. The model was an operant one in that the staff was encouraged to provide positive feedback for well behaviors and to ignore pain behaviors. The patient increased his or her level of activity by decreasing pain behaviors and learning, often for the first time in years, that the pain did not increase with an increase in activity.[80] Unnecessary surgeries were avoided and the success rate at least equaled that of those patients who continued to be treated with surgery.

The contribution made by these early pain management programs cannot be overemphasized. Surgeries were no longer seen as the only treatment intervention. Disability was separated from pathology. Over time, pain management programs have evolved to include more cognitive-behavior interventions to enhance the coping skills of patients with chronic pain and to address covert pain behaviors amenable to operant treatment programs. The concept of multidisciplinary pain management evolved from these early programs.

Much of the illness behavior and the potential roadblocks to successful rehabilitation are a combination of inadequate coping skills, lack of education, and inappropriate labeling of sensation. All of these issues must be addressed during the active restoration phase of rehabilitation in order to insure that techniques taught in counseling sessions are generalized.

Changes to the sense of self must also be addressed. Some patients experienced the very boundaries of their bodies as changing as a result of the pain. The body image is distorted when one area of the body is the only area that one is conscious of, because this sensory information overrides other sensory input and overwhelms

Table 27–3 ELEMENTS OF ILLNESS BEHAVIOR

Symptom perception	For a change in an individual's function to be interpreted as a symptom, it must have evoked concern that the change is somehow not normal and is not readily accounted for except within the framework of illness. A cardinal characteristic of pain is that it has a unique ability to captivate one's attention and to hold that attention.
Meaning attribution	Meaning attribution is influenced by a host of psychosocial and cultural factors as well as by a person's prior experience with illness. Prior experience with pain in the same area will also have an influence on the meaning. A person's assessment of meaning may be as important to symptom formation as the original disturbances in functioning that initiated the concern.
Expression and communication	The outward expression—the observable illness behavior—of the patient in pain. This expression defines the severity of the problem for the health practitioner, family, and friends. It is often influenced in patients with chronic pain by how much the patients feel they need to prove to someone that they really have pain. Behaviors increase in many individuals when they experience pain as out of control or as not believed by others.
Help-seeking behavior and other coping responses	Coping responses may be more or less healthy and more or less consciously motivated. The abnormal functioning that occurs in chronic illness leads inevitably to compensatory behavior. This behavior, in turn, may have positive or negative effects on subsequent symptoms and levels of function.

the individual.[60] Children have eloquently demonstrated attacks to their body image through drawings of themselves during the rehabilitation phase.[81] A patient who has been in an occupation that has significantly contributed to his or her sense of self has great difficulty in describing that self in the absence of that occupation.[82] Inherent in these changes are the losses incurred in function. The losses must be acknowledged, and grieving must be allowed.

Educational groups have several benefits for patients with chronic pain. First, if the information is used to reduce the threat of a patient's experience, psychobiologic changes have been made. The neurotransmitters involved in the perception of pain have changed as the sense of threat is reduced.[64] Second, because the sense of support is often crucial in these patients, having an environment that can provide positive reinforcement is beneficial. Third, the group reinforces the realization, not only that the patients are not alone in their pain, but also that the issues and concerns that they have are common to individuals with chronic pain. This group process alone often reduces the self-defeating cognitive thinking that often prohibits patients from asking questions to allay their anxiety because they are fearful that they will be labeled as a "psych" case. Groups allowing for structured topics and dialogue are more beneficial than groups allowing for patients to tell their stories over and over and to dwell on the failure of health care providers to help them.

SUMMARY

Chronic pain management provides unique opportunities for the rehabilitation team. The opportunities lie in the challenge of identifying the factors that comprise the problems of patients with chronic pain and of selectively using therapeutic interventions to effect change. The role of physical therapists is unique in that they are often the treating practitioner during the patient's acute stage. This role offers the opportunity to identify these patients early and to assist in directing them to a multidisciplinary team for more effective intervention.

Chronic pain management is unique not only for its challenges in problem identification but also for the challenges to all health care providers to work with patients who expect a cure, but whose expections can no longer be met. The therapist must deal with their expections as well. By approaching these patients as individuals who are overcome by the complexity of chronic stressors and as individuals who need tools to assist themselves in dealing with those stressors, much of the stigma and blaming attitude directed toward these patients can be eliminated. Patients are a vital component of the team; they must work with the rest of the team, as valued and active participants, to effect the highest level of functional change possible.

Therapists have a number of modalities in their armamentarium that are useful for these patients; identification of the component parts of the individual's complaints will assist the therapist in determining specific interventions. The multitude of psychosocial, physiologic, and homeostatic problems necessitate an interactive team approach. The overall goals of treatment, including homeostasis, increased function, and self-responsibility cannot ignore the patient's perception of the problem as well as the solution.

Pain management is best done early. During acute care, therapists can determine what the pain means to the patients and which coping skills might be lacking in managing it. Early identification of psychosocial factors often reduces chronicity. The use of such tools as SEMG may identify physical factors perpetuating the symptoms and assist in treatment intervention.

Patients with chronic pain present with problems both unique and universal. Pain, one of the primary reasons for seeking health care, cannot be quantified or proven. It is an experience universal in the animal kingdom; it is unique in the solitary suffering it can cause in any given individual. The challenge to the therapist lies in altering a patient's perception of the experience and the enhancing sense of coping with it. The extent and costs of treatment can far exceed what would be expected from the known pathology or physical impairment, yet lack of pathology does not in itself disprove the existence of pain, which may be due to well-established central pain mechanisms or maladaptive compensatory movement strategies. Pain management takes the threat and the fearful mystery of pain and presents them to the patient as a challenge to be met with learned coping skills.

QUESTIONS FOR REVIEW

1. On what basis should a physical therapist consider referring a patient for a chronic pain evaluation?

2. Describe how the chronic pain from RSD differs from the chronic pain following a low back sprain.

3. List three ways SEMG may be helpful in evaluating a patient with chronic pain.

4. List the possible interventions for patients with chronic pain and the members of the team who would be expected to address those issues.

5. What is the benefit of a self-responsibility model over one that stresses "no pain, no gain"?

REFERENCES

1. Achterberg, J: Woman as Healer, Shambhala, Boston, 1990.
2. Bonica, JJ: History of pain concepts and therapies. In Bonica, JJ (ed): The Management of Pain. Lea & Febiger, Philadelphia, 1990, p 2.
3. Melzack, R and Wall, PD: Pain mechanisms: a new theory. Science 150:971, 1965.
4. Sternschein, MJ, Meyers, SJ, and Frewin, DB: Causalgia. Arch Phys Med Rehabil 56:58, 1975.

5. Bonica, JJ: General considerations of chronic pain. In Bonica, JJ (ed): The Management of Pain. Lea & Febiger, Philadelphia, 1990, p 180.

6. Gildenberg, PL and DeVaul, RA: The chronic pain patient. Evaluation and management. In Gildenberg, PL (ed): Pain and Headache. Karger, New York, 1985.

7. Melzack, R: Neurophysiological foundations of pain. In Sternbach, R (ed): The Psychology of Pain. Raven Press, New York, 1986.

8. Bonica, JJ: Anatomic and physiologic basis of nociception and pain. In Bonica, JJ (ed): The Management of Pain. Lea & Febiger, Philadelphia, 1990, p 28.

9. Bonica, JJ: Biochemistry and modulation of nociception and pain. In Bonica, JJ (ed): The Management of Pain. Lea & Febiger, Philadelphia, 1990, p 95.

10. Sternbach, RA: Pain Patients. Traits and Treatment, Academic Press, New York, 1974.

11. Casey, KL: The neurophysiologic basis of pain. Postgrad Med 53:58, 1973.

12. Craig, KD: Emotional aspects of pain. In Wall, P and Melzack, R (eds): Textbook of Pain. Churchill Livingstone, Edinburgh, 1984, p 153.

13. Bonica, JJ: Definitions and taxonomy of pain. In Bonica, JJ (ed): The Management of Pain. Lea & Febiger, Philadelphia, 1990, p 18.

14. Wu, W-H and Grzesiak, RC: Psychologic aspects of chronic pain. In Wu, W-H (ed): Pain Management. Assessment and Treatment of Chronic and Acute Syndromes. Human Sciences Press, New York, 1987, p 44.

15. Skevington, S: Social cognitions, personality and chronic pain. J Psychosom Res 5:421, 1983.

16. Osterweis, M, Kleinman, A, and Mechanic, D (eds): Pain and Disability. National Academy Press, Washington, DC, 1987.

17. Headley, BJ: Historical perspective of causalgia. Management of sympathetically maintained pain. Phys Ther 67:1370, 1987.

18. Bonica, JJ: Causalgia and other reflex sympathetic dystrophies. In Bonica, JJ (ed): The Management of Pain. Lea & Febiger, Philadelphia, 1990, p 220.

19. Headley, BJ: EMG and postural dysfunction. Clinical Management 10:14, 1990.

20. Aronoff, GM: The role of the pain center in the treatment for intractable suffering and disability resulting from chronic pain. Semin Neurol 3:377, 1983.

21. Fordyce, W: Learning processes in pain. In Sternbach, R (ed): The Psychology of Pain. Raven Press, New York, 1986, p 46.

22. Sternbach, RA, Wolf, SR, Murphy, RW, et al: Aspects of chronic low back pain. Psychosomatics 14:52, 1973.

23. Chapman, R: Psychological aspects of pain patient treatment. Arch Surg 112:767, 1977.

24. Cockerham, WC: Medical Sociology, ed 3. Prentice-Hall, Englewood Cliffs, NJ, 1986.

25. LeShan, L: The world of the patient in severe pain of long duration. In Garfield, CA (ed): Stress and Survival. The Emotional Realities of Life-Threatening Illness. CV Mosby, St. Louis, 1979, p 273.

26. Fordyce, WE, Brockway, JA, and Bergman, JA: Acute back pain: a control-group comparison of behavioral vs traditional management methods. J Behav Med 9:127, 1986.

27. Bonica, JJ and Buckley, FP: Regional analgesia with local anesthetics. In Bonica, JJ (ed): The Management of Pain. Lea & Febiger, Philadelphia, 1990, p 1883.

28. Hurt, R and Ballantine, H: Stereotactic anterior cingulate lesions for persistent pain. A report on 68 cases. Clin Neurosurg 21:334, 1973.

29. Nashold, BJ: Current status of the DREZ operation: 1984. Neurosurgery 15:942, 1984.

30. Spiegel, E and Wycis, H: Present status of stereoencephalotomies for pain relief. Confin. Neurol 27:7, 1966.

31. Sternbach, RA: Psychophysiologic pain syndrome. In Bonica, JJ (ed): The Management of Pain. Lea & Febiger, Philadelphia, 1990, p 287.

32. Lieberman, M and Lieberman, A: Psychosocial adjustment to physical disability. In O'Sullivan, S and Schmitz, T (eds): Physical Rehabilitation: Assessment and Treatment. FA Davis, Philadelphia, 1988, p 24.

33. Ransford, A, Cairns, D, and Mooney, V: The pain drawing as an aid to the psychologic evaluation of patients with low-back pain. Spine 1:127, 1976.

34. Turner, JA and Romano, JM: Psychologic and psychosocial evaluation. In Bonica, JJ (ed): The Management of Pain. Lea & Febiger, Philadelphia, 1990, p 595.

35. Kerns, RD, Turk, DC, and Rudy, TE: The West Haven-Yale Multidimensional Pain Inventory. Pain 23:345, 1985.

36. Melzack, R: The McGill Pain Questionnaire: major properties and scoring methods. Pain 1:277, 1975.

37. Derogatis, LR, Rickels, K, and Rock, AF: The SCL-90 and the MMPI: a step in the validation of a new self-report scale. Br J Psychiatry 128:280, 1976.

38. Cox, GB, Chapman, CR, and Black, RG: The MMPI and chronic pain: the diagnosis of psychogenic pain. J Behav Med 1:437, 1978.

39. Trief, PM and Yuan, HA: The use of the MMPI in a chronic back pain rehabilitation program. J Clin Psychol 39:46, 1983.

40. Sternbach, RA and Timmermans, G: Personality changes associated with reduction of pain. Pain 1:177, 1975.

41. Loeser, JD: Concepts of pain. In Stanton-Hicks, M and Boas, R (eds): Chronic Low Back Pain. Raven Press, New York, 1982.

42. Rossi, EL and Cheek, DB: Mind-Body Therapy. Methods of Ideodynamic Healing in Hypnosis. WW Norton, New York, 1988.

43. Kasman, G: Use of integrated electromyography for the assessment and treatment of musculoskeletal pain: guidelines for physical medicine practitioners. In Cram, J (ed): Clinical EMG for Surface Recordings, vol 2. Clinical Resources, Nevada City, 1990, p 255.

44. Khalil, T, Abdel-Moty, E, Diaz, E, et al: Electromyographic symmetry in patients with chronic low back pain and comparison to controls. Advances in Industrial Ergonomics and Safety III, p 483, Taylor & Francis, London, 1991.

45. Seidel, H, Beyer, H, and Brauer, D: Electromyographic evaluation of back muscle fatigue with repeated sustained contractions of different strengths. Eur J Appl Physiol 56:592, 1987.

46. Sihvonen, T, Partanen, J, Hanninen, O, et al.: Electric behavior of low back muscles during lumbar pelvic rhythm in low back pain patients and healthy controls. Arch Phys Med Rehabil 72:1080, 1991.

47. Schwartz, GE: Self-regulation of response patterning. Implications for psychophysiological research and therapy. Biofeedback Self-Regul 1:7, 1976.

48. Flor, H, Schugens, MM, and Birbaumer, N: Discrimination of muscle tension in chronic pain patients and healthy controls. Biofeedback Self-Regul 17:165, 1992.

49. Travell, J and Simons, D: Myofascial Pain and Dysfunction. The Trigger Point Manual, vol 1. Williams & Wilkins, Baltimore, 1983.

50. Travell, J and Simons, D: Myofascial Pain and Dysfunction. The Trigger Point Manual, vol. 2. Williams & Wilkins, Baltimore, 1992.

51. Headley, BJ: EMG and myofascial pain. Clinical Management 10:43, 1990.

52. Headley, BJ: Evaluation and treatment of myofascial pain syndrome utilizing biofeedback. In Cram, JR (ed): Clinical EMG for Surface Recordings. Clinical Resources, Nevada City, 1990.

53. Simons, DG: Referred phenomena of myofascial trigger points. In Vecchiet, L, Albe-Fessard, D, and Lindblom, U (eds): New Trends in Referred Pain and Hyperalgesia. In Pain Research and Clinical Management. Elsevier Science, Amsterdam, 1993, pp 341–357.

54. Headley, BJ: Use of SEMG in Discerning Myofascial Pain Syndrome in the Quadratus Lumborum. A Syndrome Common to Low Back Pain. Presented at the American Physical Therapy Association Conference; June 1992. Denver, CO.

55. Rosomoff, HL, Rishbain, D, Goldberg, M, et al: Myofascial findings in patients with "chronic intractable benign pain" of the back and neck. Pain Management 2:114, 1990.

56. Mayer, TG and Gatchel, RJ: Functional Restoration for Spinal Disorders: The Sports Medicine Approach. Lea & Febiger, Philadelphia, 1988.

57. Simons, DG: Myofascial pain syndrome due to trigger points. In Goodgold, J (ed): Rehabilitation Medicine. CV Mosby, St. Louis, 1988, p 686.

58. Feldenkrais, M: Awareness Through Movement. Health Exercises for Personal Growth. Harper & Row, New York, 1977.

59. Leibowitz, J and Connington, B: The Alexander Technique, HarperCollins, New York, 1990.

60. Sale, D and MacDougall, D: Specificity in strength training: a review for the coach and athlete. Can J Appl Sport Sci 6:87, 1981.

61. McCain, GA: Role of physical fitness training in the fibrositis/fibromyalgia syndrome. Am J Med 81(Suppl 3A):73, 1986.

62. Lacey, JI and Lacey, BC: Verification and extension of the principle of autonomic response-stereotypy. Am J Psychol 71:50, 1958.

63. Sternbach, RA: Clinical aspects of pain. In Sternbach, R (ed): The Psychology of Pain. Raven Press, New York, 1986.

64. Rossi, EL: The Psychobiology of Mind-Body Healing. New Concepts of Therapeutic Hypnosis, WW Norton, New York, 1986.

65. Hendler, N, Derogatis, L, and Avella J: EMG biofeedback in patients with chronic pain. Dis Nervous System 7:505, 1977.

66. Large, RG and Lamb, AM: Electromyographic (EMG) feedback in chronic musculoskeletal pain: a controlled study. Pain 17:167, 1983.

67. Peck, CL and Draft, GH: Electromyographic biofeedback for pain related to muscle tension. A study of tension headache, back and jaw pain. Arch Surg 112:889, 1977.

68. Biedermann, H-J: Mechanism of biofeedback in the treatment of chronic back pain. Psychol Rep 53:1103, 1983.

69. Holroyd, KA, et al: Change mechanisms in EMG biofeedback training: cognitive changes underlying improvements in tension headache. J Consult Clin Psychol 52:1039, 1984.

70. Achterberg, J: Shammanism and Modern Medicine. New Science Library, Boston, 1985.

71. Sternbach, RA: Effects of altering brain serotonin activity on human chronic pain. In Bonica, JJ and Albe-Fessard, D (eds): Advances in Pain Research and Therapy. Raven Press, New York, 1976, p 601.

72. Lampe, G: Transcutaneous electrical nerve stimulation. In O'Sullivan, SB and Schmitz, TJ (eds): Physical Rehabilitation: Assessment and Treatment. FA Davis, Philadelphia, 1988, p 647.

73. Sjolund, BH, Eriksson, M, and Loeser, JD: Transcutaneous and implanted electric stimulation of peripheral nerves. In Bonica, JJ (ed): The Management of Pain. Lea & Febiger, Philadelphia, 1990, p 1852.

74. Choi, J and Tsay, C: Technology of transcutaneous electrical nerve stimulation. In Wu, W (ed): Pain Management. Assessment and Treatment of Chronic and Acute Syndromes. Human Sciences Press, New York, 1987.

75. Achterberg, JA and Lawlis, GF: Bridges of the Bodymind. Behavioral Approaches to Health Care. Institute for Personality and Ability Testing, Champaign, IL, 1980.

76. Guymer, A: Neuromuscular facilitation of movement. In Wells, PE, Frampton, V, and Bowsher, D (eds): Pain Management in Physical Therapy. Appleton & Lange, Norwalk, 1988, p 55.

77. Grieve, GP: Common Vertebral Joint Problems, ed 2. Churchill Livingstone, New York, 1988.

78. Loeser, JD, Seres, J, and Newman, R: Interdisciplinary, multimodal management of chronic pain. In Bonica, JJ (ed): The Management of Pain. Lea & Febiger, Philadelphia, 1990.

79. Chapman, C, Turk, D, and Meichenbaum, D: Pain and Behavioral Medicine. A Cognitive-Behavioral Approach. Guilford Press, New York, 1983.

80. Fordyce, WE: Behavioral Methods for Chronic Pain and Illness. CV Mosby, St. Louis, 1976.

81. Headley, B: Effect of Burns on the Body Image of Children. Boston University, 1974.

82. Headley, B: Am I a Physical Therapist? Physical Therapy Forum, 1987.

SUPPLEMENTAL READINGS

Basmajian, J and DeLuca, C: Muscles Alive. Their Functions Revealed by Electromyography, ed 5. Williams & Wilkins, Baltimore, 1985.

Bonica, J (ed): The Management of Pain. vols 1 and 2, ed 2. Lea & Febiger, Philadelphia, 1990.

Caillet, R: Pain Mechanisms and Management. FA Davis, Philadelphia, 1993.

Soderberg, G (ed): Selected Topics in Surface Electromyography for Use in the Occupational Setting: Expert Perspectives, US Department of Health and Human Services, Publ. # 91–100, 1992.

Sternbach, R (ed): The Psychology of Pain, ed 2. New York, Raven Press, 1986.

Turk, D, Meichenbaum, D, and Genest, M: Pain and Behavioral Medicine. A Cognitive-Behavioral Perspective. New York, Guilford Press, 1983.

GLOSSARY

Acute pain: Pain provoked by noxious stimulation produced by injury and/or disease with unpleasant sensory and emotional experiences.

A fibers: Fibers innervating muscle spindles, mechanoreceptors, nociceptors, and thermoreceptors; larger in diameter and with faster pain conduction time than C fibers.

Central pain: Pain that is associated with a lesion of the central nervous system and that is independent of peripheral injury or tissue damage.

C fibers: Fibers innervating nociceptors, mechanoreceptors, and sympathetic postganglionic bodies; smaller in diameter and with slower conduction times than A fibers.

Chronic pain: Pain that persists beyond the usual course of healing of an acute disease or beyond a reasonable time for an injury to heal.

Disability: Disadvantage for a given individual that limits or prevents the fulfillment of a role that is normal for that individual.

Dystrophic: Related to abnormal nutrition, growth, or health; a reflex sympathetic dystrophy (stage of RSD).

Hyperalgesia: Increased response to a stimulus that is normally painful.

Hyperathia: Increased reaction to stimuli, especially when repetitive; increased threshold to stimuli.

Hyperhidrosis: Increased sweating response.

Impairment: Loss of abnormality of psychologic, physiologic, or anatomic structure or function. Functional impairment that results from an impairment is any restriction or lack of ability to perform an activity in the manner or within the range considered normal.

Nociceptive: System or receptor that is preferentially sensitive to a noxious stimulus or to a stimulus that would become noxious if prolonged.

Suffering: State of severe distress associated with events that threaten the intactness of the person. The state may or may not be associated with pain.

Sympathectomy: A severing of the sympathetic nervous system at either the cervical or lumbar ganglion. The area can also be blocked for a short time with drugs.

Trigger points: Palpable band or nodule within the muscle or connective tissue that refers pain and other phenomena, elicits a local twitch response when pressed, and is generally hypersensitive.

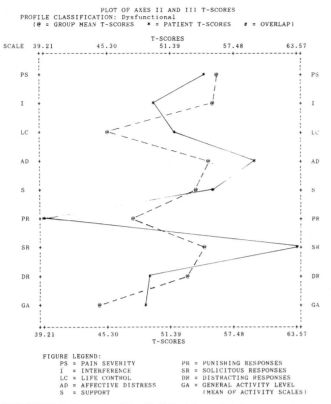

```
                    PLOT OF AXES II AND III T-SCORES
           PROFILE CLASSIFICATION: Dysfunctional
            (@ = GROUP MEAN T-SCORES   * = PATIENT T-SCORES   # = OVERLAP)

                                  T-SCORES
   SCALE  39.21       45.30       51.39       57.48       63.57
```

FIGURE LEGEND:
PS = PAIN SEVERITY   PR = PUNISHING RESPONSES
I = INTERFERENCE   SR = SOLICITOUS RESPONSES
LC = LIFE CONTROL   DR = DISTRACTING RESPONSES
AD = AFFECTIVE DISTRESS   GA = GENERAL ACTIVITY LEVEL
S = SUPPORT   (MEAN OF ACTIVITY SCALES)

APPENDIX 1 A sample of the Multidisciplinary Pain Inventory showing a dysfunctional profile. The solid line represents the patient's scores on each scale; the dotted line connects the mean scores for this profile against which the patient's answers are scored.

Pain Evaluation & Rehabilitation Center

Please mark an "X" along the line to show how your pain has effected your level of function.

1. At what level do you perceive your pain?
No Pain ─────────────────── Worst possible

2. At what level do you experience pain at night?
No Pain ─────────────────── Worst possible

3. Has the pain effected your level of activity?
No problem ─────────────────── Total change

4. How well does medication relieve your pain?
Complete relief ─────────────────── No relief

5. How stiff is your back/neck?
No stiffness ─────────────────── Totally stiff

6. Does your pain interfere with sitting?
No problem ─────────────────── Cannot sit

7. Is it painful for you to walk?
No pain ─────────────────── Cannot walk

8. Does your pain keep you from standing/sitting still?
No problem ─────────────────── Cannot do it

9. Does your pain interfere with your normal household chores?
No problem ─────────────────── Cannot do them

10. Does your pain effect your driving time in a car?
No problem ─────────────────── Cannot do it

11. Do you get relief from your pain by lying down?
Complete relief ─────────────────── No relief at all

12. How much have you had to change your job responsibilities?
No change ─────────────────── So much I can't work

13. How much control do you feel you have over the pain?
Total control ─────────────────── No control

14. How much control have you lost over other areas of your life due to the pain?
No control lost ─────────────────── Total loss of control

Name:_____ Date:_____

McGill Pain Questionnaire

What does your pain feel like?

Some of the words below describe your present pain. Circle ONLY those words that best describe it. Leave out any category that is not suitable. Use only a single word in each appropriate category - the one that applies best.

Sensory: 1-8   Evaluative: 16
Affective: 9-15   Miscellaneous: 17-20

1	2	3	4
Flickering	Jumping	Pricking	Sharp
Quivering	Flashing	Boring	Cutting
Pulsing	Shooting	Drilling	Lacerating
Throbbing		Stabbing	
Beating		Lancinating	
Pounding			

5	6	7	8
Pinching	Tugging	Hot	Tingling
Pressing	Pulling	Burning	Itchy
Gnawing	Wrenching	Scalding	Smarting
Cramping		Searing	Stinging
Crushing			

9	10	11	12
Dull	Tender	Tiring	Sickening
Sore	Taut	Exhausting	Suffocating
Hurting	Rasping		
Aching	Splitting		
Heavy			

13	14	15	16
Fearful	Punishing	Wretched	Annoying
Frightful	Gruelling	Blinding	Troublesome
Terrifying	Cruel		Miserable
	Vicious		Intense
	Killing		Unbearable

17	18	19	20
Spreading	Tight	Cool	Nagging
Radiating	Numb	Cold	Nauseating
Penetrating	Drawing	Freezing	Agonizing
Piercing	Squeezing		Dreadful
	Tearing		Torturing

APPENDIX 2 The McGill Pain Questionnaire asks patients to select the words that best describe how their pain feels. From their choices, scores are obtained in sensory, affective, evaluative, and miscellaneous categories.

APPENDIX 3 A sample visual analog scale developed by the author. Numerical scores can be obtained by measuring the placement of the mark along the line. Scores may be compared with repeat administration of the scale.

Assessment and Treatment Planning Strategies for Perceptual Deficits

Chaye Lamm Warburg

OBJECTIVES

1. Explain why it is essential for physical therapists to be familiar with the signs of perceptual dysfunction.
2. Describe how visual disturbances affect the ability of the patient to participate in rehabilitation.
3. Explain how a patient can be assisted to compensate for body scheme and/or body image disorders.
4. Describe how spatial relations can affect the patient's ability to follow directions.
5. Explain the effect of the various agnosias on the patient's ability to recognize stimuli in the environment.
6. Differentiate between ideomotor, ideational, and constructional apraxia. Describe how a patient with apraxia might behave in response to different instructional sets commonly employed in rehabilitation.
7. Describe how the psychologic, emotional, and cognitive status of a patient with perceptual impairment may affect participation in assessment and treatment sessions.

Perceptual and cognitive deficits are among the chief causes of confusion about and lack of progress in patients who have sustained a cerebral vascular accident (CVA), even among those whose motor skills have returned.[1] Thus, effective treatment of many patients with brain damage depends on understanding perception and cognition.

The perceptual motor process is a chain of events through which the individual selects, integrates, and interprets stimuli from the body and the surrounding environment. Cognition can be conceived of as the method used by the central nervous system (CNS) to process information.[2] Cognitive processes include knowing, understanding, awareness, judgment, and decision making.[1] The difficulty of separating perceptual from cognitive deficits is readily apparent, both in patient behavior and in contradictory conceptualizations of these two domains of function. For example, according to some authors cognition is conceived of as a general term that includes perception, attention, thinking, and memory.[3] According to other authors, perception is an umbrella term that encompasses both cognition and visual perception as subcomponents.[4] What is clear is that normally functioning perceptual and cognitive systems are a necessary key to successful interaction with the environment.

The patient who has sustained an initial CVA is thought to have focal or localized damage to discrete areas of the brain, often resulting in discrete perceptual problems. In contrast, patients who have sustained a traumatic brain injury are presumed to have generalized brain damage resulting in "cognitive impairment" with generalized deficits in attention, memory, learning, and so forth, rather than specific difficulties in discrete perceptual functions. However, elements of both perceptual and cognitive dysfunction may occur in brain damage due to either CVA or trauma. The distinctions between the two groups of patients become particularly blurred when one considers the patient who has suffered multiple strokes; this patient may in fact combine elements of focal and generalized brain damage.

Throughout this chapter, the patient with hemiplegia in whom brain damage has occurred as a result of a stroke will be the focus. The primary objective of this chapter is to introduce the reader to concepts relating to perceptual dysfunction following brain damage. Cognitive deficits and cognitive rehabilitation will be addressed in separate sections in this chapter, although the reader is cautioned again that perceptual and cognitive impairments often coexist within the same patient and may strongly influence each other and the patient's resulting behavior.

An important focus for the physical therapist should be on the understanding of how a particular perceptual disability might be manifested clinically, and how assessment and treatment of movement disorders might be adjusted to capitalize on the abilities and minimize the perceptual limitations of the patient. Disorders in the perceptual domain must be considered in order to assess fairly the patient's true residual abilities. Using sets of directions that would confuse an apraxic patient during a specific assessment may paint a picture of more or different motor disability than that which actually exists. Often the first clue to a perceptual problem appears during the initial sensorimotor assessment. Awareness of the possibility and nature of perceptual deficits will signal the therapist to redirect the method of assessment, particularly the instructional sets and cues.

RESPONSIBILITIES OF THE PHYSICAL AND OCCUPATIONAL THERAPISTS

Occupational therapists are the members of the rehabilitation team especially trained to assess and to treat perceptual dysfunction in relation to functional adaptation. They are responsible for the selection and administration of an appropriate constellation of assessment tools, accurate interpretation of results, and formulation of an overall program for perceptual rehabilitation.

In the hospital setting, the physical therapist is often the first member of the rehabilitation team to see a patient with brain injury. The physical therapist must understand the nature of perceptual dysfunction and recognize that individuals in certain diagnostic categories, such as stroke and traumatic head injury, are likely to behave in ways that indicate the presence of particular perceptual problems.[5] When this occurs, the physical therapist should be aware that it is appropriate to refer the patient to occupational therapy for assessment and remediation.

The assessment tools described in this chapter are included in order to assist the reader in understanding the nature of the different perceptual disabilities. They are not meant to be used as a substitute for an intensive assessment by a trained occupational therapist when it is deemed necessary.

An understanding of perceptual dysfunction may go a long way toward alleviating much of the potential frustration that often accompanies treatment of a patient with brain damage, most of which is the result of inappropriate expectations on the part of the therapist, the patient, and the family. Furthermore, by collaboration with the occupational therapist, with other members of the rehabilitation team, and with the family, consistent treatment strategies may be developed and carried out, with obvious benefits to the patient.

SENSATION AND PERCEPTION

The terms *perception* and *sensation* are often confused with each other. *Sensation* may be defined as the appreciation of stimuli through the organs of special sense (e.g., eyes, ears, nose, and so forth), the peripheral cutaneous sensory system (e.g., temperature, taste, touch, and so forth), or internal receptors (e.g., deep receptors in muscles and joints).[6] Perception cannot be viewed as independent of sensation. However, the quality of perception is far more complex than the recognition of the individual sensations.[6]

Perception is the ability to select those stimuli that require attention and action, to integrate those stimuli with each other and with prior information, and finally to interpret them. The resulting awareness of objects and experiences within the environment enables the individual to make sense out of a complex and constantly changing internal and external sensory environment, and forms the basis for cognition.[7] Perceptual ability is clearly a prerequisite for learning,[8] and rehabilitation is largely a learning process.[9] Thus, it is not surprising that patients with perceptual disorders are limited in the ability to learn self-care and activities of daily living (ADL) skills; hence, as a group, they are more limited in their potential for achieving independence.[10,11]

In any rehabilitation program geared toward achievement of maximum independence there is a compelling need for therapists to learn to recognize behavior related to perceptual deficits. While perceptual disorders should not be considered either a poor prognostic sign or a barrier to successful rehabilitation, they are a factor that must be considered in the design of the patient's therapy program.[12] The therapist's modification of a treatment approach in light of these deficits will ensure that patients receive the full benefit of both assessment and treatment.[8]

CLINICAL INDICATORS

A perceptual deficit ought to be ruled out as a cause of diminished functioning in all patients suffering from brain damage. It is a particularly likely culprit in cases in which the patient seems unable to participate fully in self-care tasks and has difficulty participating in physical therapy for reasons that cannot be accounted for by lack of motor ability, sensation, comprehension, or motivation. Perceptual dysfunction must be differentiated from premorbid cognitive perceptual deficits,[13] and from the general confusion and emotional sequelae that often accompany stroke and brain injury.

Often patients with perceptual difficulties will display the following characteristics: inability to do simple tasks independently or safely, difficulty in initiating or completing a task, difficulty in switching from one task to the next, and a diminished capacity to locate visually or to identify objects that seem obviously necessary for task completion. Additionally, they may be unable to follow simple one-stage instructions, despite apparently good comprehension. They may make the same mistakes over and over. Activities may take an inordinately long time to complete, or they may be done impulsively. Patients may hesitate many times, appear distracted and frustrated, and exhibit poor planning. They are frequently inattentive to one side of the body and extrapersonal space, and they may deny the presence or extent of the disability. These characteristics, all or some of which may be present, often make participation in ADL and active therapy seem an insurmountable problem. They will be explained and expanded upon throughout the remainder of this chapter.

Two typical scenarios will be presented to give the reader a concrete idea of when to suspect perceptual dysfunction. The first case involves a patient with a right-hemisphere stroke who presents clinically with a left hemiparesis and with good speech. Upon observation in the nursing unit, the patient appears to have functional strength in the unaffected right extremities and fair return on the affected left side. Yet the patient seems to have difficulty with simple range of motion (ROM) activities, even in the intact extremities, appearing confused and unable to move the arm up or down upon command. The patient cannot seem to follow instructions on walking with a quad cane, constantly confuses the proper step sequence, and is unable to maneuver a wheelchair around the corner without crashing into the wall.

This patient should not be dismissed as uncooperative, intellectually inferior, or confused. Rather, the therapist should have the patient assessed by the occupational therapist for perceptual dysfunction. In this instance, the patient is likely to be having difficulty in spatial relations, right-left discrimination, and vertical disorientation, or perhaps left-sided neglect and apraxia. Further observation and assessment should reveal the precise cause of the difficulties.

The second case involves a patient with left-hemisphere damage and a resulting right hemiparesis and mild aphasia. The patient can respond reliably to "yes/no" questions and is able to follow simple one-stage commands such as "put the pencil on the table" or "give me the cup." However, if asked to point to the arm, or asked to imitate the therapist's movements during an active ROM assessment even with the unaffected limbs, the patient does not respond and appears totally uncooperative. During therapy the same patient is on a mat table. The therapist explains and then demonstrates the proper techniques for rolling to one side. The patient does not move. However, a moment later when his wife arrives, the patient quickly initiates rolling in an attempt to sit up and to greet his wife. The astute therapist will realize that this patient may not be confused, stubborn, or uncooperative, as indeed he may appear. Rather, he may be suffering from a lack of awareness of body structure and relationship of body parts (**somatagnosia**), as evidenced by the assessment incident, and an inability to perform a task on command or to imitate gestures (**ideomotor apraxia**), as demonstrated in the rolling episode.

ALTERATIONS IN BRAIN INPUT FOLLOWING BRAIN DAMAGE AND HOSPITALIZATION

The brain that has been damaged functions as a whole, just as it does in individuals without brain damage. When one part is damaged, the behavior observed is not merely the result of the brain operating precisely as in the intact individual minus the "function" of the area that was subject to anoxia. Rather, it is an outward manifestation of the reorganization of the entire CNS, at multiple levels, working to compensate for the loss.[14]

Because of the brain damage, the patient must cope with a nervous system operating without normal sensory input at all levels, both cortical and subcortical.[14] Normal responses to environmental stimuli are difficult to obtain when the input on which they have to act is deranged or incomplete. Recovery of function can be attributed to structural reorganization of the CNS into a new dynamic system widely dispersed within the cerebral cortex and lower formations.[15]

A significant contributor to the clinical picture of a patient after a CVA is the response to hospitalization. From a perceptual perspective, when a patient is hospitalized (with or without brain damage), the inputs impinging on that patient's nervous system are radically different from the ones normally received. On the one hand, the environment is sensorially impoverished. There is no variation in temperature and lighting, and familiar background noises (e.g., familiar telephones, airplanes, dogs, and buses) are missing. On the other hand, an enormous array of unfamiliar noises are present: nurses talking, loudspeakers, and the whir of machines. Strange and different smells, and unfamiliar, unavoidable, and unpleasant sights abound. Often, because of motor impairment, the patient cannot move around to seek or to escape inputs; therefore, a multiplicity of sensory inputs bombards the nervous system. Even if orienting responses are preserved, there is a profound sense of loss of control. This sensory derangement compounds the problems faced by the patient with brain damage, because those very abilities that enable the individual to select, to filter out, and to integrate incoming sensations in order to organize the self for appropriate action often fail in this sensorially bizarre environment.

To gain insight into the experience of the patient under such circumstances, it is enlightening to browse through the biographic and autobiographic reports of some noted neurologists and neuropsychologists, themselves victims or relatives of victims of CVAs. Particularly instructive are the reports of Bach-y-Rita,[16] Brodal,[17] and Gardner.[18]

THE PURPOSE OF ASSESSMENT

The presence of perceptual dysfunction must be confirmed if it is suspected to be interfering with the patient's ability to carry out functional activities.[19] Perceptual performance is positively correlated with ability to perform ADLs; however, it is often difficult to correlate specific perceptual deficits gleaned from testing with specific elements of functional ability and loss.[1,11] Thus, formal testing is indicated only when there is a functional loss unexplained by motor deficit, sensory deficit, or deficient comprehension. It should be noted that not all areas of functional loss are typically detected within the hospital setting. It is not uncommon for the patient to perform adequately in self-care skills after therapy in the hospital but to fail on the same tasks in other environmental contexts, such as the home. Higher-level tasks, such as driving, banking, or planning a meal, may only emerge as areas of difficulty once the patient is discharged home. When appropriate, competence in these areas should be considered within the context of an ADL assessment.

The purpose of assessment is to determine which perceptual abilities are intact and which are limited. Understanding the manner in which a particular deficit influences task performance will foster the application of a therapeutic strategy in which intact capabilities may be used to compensate for or to overcome deficits.[11]

Failure in the performance of a task may result from any number of processes underlying perception. For example, a patient's inability to complete a jigsaw puzzle may result from an inability to see the picture (visual defect—**hemianopsia**) or difficulty in attending to one half of the picture (**unilateral spatial neglect**). The patient may be incapable of listening to the instructions (attentional deficit), unable to know what the pieces are for (organizational deficit), or unable to manipulate them (**apraxia**). Although it is often difficult to implicate reliably one or another of these problem areas, the therapist must be aware of the different deficits that may produce a similar pattern of behavior.[19,21]

A fascinating study conducted by Galski et al.[22] concerning the prediction of driving ability following brain injury (including stroke) in 35 patients underscores the critical nature of carefully selected perceptual and cognitive tests. In that study fully 64 percent of actual behind-the-wheel driving performance was predicted by performance on a selected battery of neuropsychologic tests that measured visual perception. Examination of individual test results uncovered the reasons for unsafe driving, enabling instructors to focus on remediating the specific deficits in preparation for safe driving.

Assessment is not an end in itself.[19] Careful assessment paves the way for realistic and cost-effective treatment.[11] Continuous monitoring of the patient's perceptual status will ensure the use of appropriate treatment regimens and their modification when necessary.

PSYCHOLOGIC AND EMOTIONAL CONSIDERATIONS AFFECTING RESPONSE TO ASSESSMENT AND TREATMENT

Psychologic and emotional considerations play an important role in the patient's ability to cope with disability and with the testing situation. The therapist needs to be aware of behaviors that reflect a patient's psychologic response to illness rather than particular perceptual abilities. Psychologic adjustment to disability depends on many factors, including age, vocational status, education, economic situation, attitude toward the reactions of others,[9] family support, and feelings of competence prior to the onset of disease.

When assessing psychologic status the following should be noted: whether the patient is confused; the level of comprehension for verbal instructions (written and spoken); whether communication is enhanced through the use of visual cues and demonstration; the ability to recognize errors; cooperation and initiative—whether the patient is realistic about capabilities and goals; and emotional stability.[9] Disturbances of emotional response are evidenced by rapid and frequent mood changes and low frustration tolerance. Difficult tasks may cause a catastrophic reaction.

The patient's ability to detect relevant cues from the environment, or to discriminate between relevant and irrelevant stimuli (necessary for perceptual competence) may be adversely influenced by poor judgment, fatigue, and prior expectations. Poor judgment is a major contributor to accidents in patients with hemiplegia. This is related in part to the diminished awareness by these patients as to their altered capabilities. The ambiguity of having one set of limbs that work normally and one set that is not functional may lead the patient to rely on solutions to the problems of daily living that are familiar but now inappropriate.[23]

Anxiety over capabilities may inhibit optimal performance during assessment and therapy. The patient's capacity to learn is enhanced if anxiety can be reduced.[9] Motivation is influenced by many factors, among them premorbid personality. It is of utmost importance for the therapist to structure the therapeutic environment so that the patient will be positively motivated to learn to the maximum ability.[9] To this end, therapeutic tasks should be structured to ensure success, thereby diminishing frustration.

The frontal lobes of both hemispheres are involved in planning, abstract reasoning, and foresight;[6] therefore, patients with frontal lobe involvement may present with additional symptoms. Family and hospital staff may complain of the patient's apparent apathy, poor or unreliable judgment, difficulty adapting to new situations, and/or lack of attention to the needs and feelings of others. In addition, a few of the symptoms experienced by patients with frontal lobe involvement may result in a diminished capacity for learning.[24] These are:

1. Problems in starting. There appears to be a decrease in spontaneity, slower rate of activity, and decreased initiation. This may cause the patient to appear "lazy."
2. Problems in stopping. There appears to be a disinhibition of inappropriate responses. Overreacting and impulsiveness are common. For example, impulsiveness is evidenced when a patient neglects to lock the wheelchair brakes before standing, attempts to walk unaided when assistance is clearly needed, or touches a hot stove. The patient may or may not have perceptual deficiencies that inhibit

the ability to lock a wheelchair, or to learn to walk, but the impulsive tendencies add a further complication: the patient does not take the time to use the information available through intact senses to generate an appropriate response. Rather, the patient acts in a habitual manner, failing to assess which is the most appropriate (safest) method for accomplishing the goal. The combination of perceptual deficits and poor judgment limits the ultimate degree of independence that a patient can attain.[6]

3. Difficulties in making mental or behavioral shifts. The patient may have difficulty shifting attention from one task or object to another, may perseverate both mentally and motorically, and appear inflexible.

4. Lack of self-awareness. The patient does not recognize errors, cannot project the effect behavior may have on others, and displays a general lack of social awareness.

5. Concrete thinking. The patient lacks insight and takes everything at face value. Typically, the patient displays a lack of ability to plan, to use foresight, and to sustain goal-directed behavior. Ability to use or to form abstract concepts is impaired. Patients who have difficulty solving problems in abstract ways tend to function more adequately in familiar surroundings.[6]

The combination of impulsiveness, poor judgment, poor planning ability, and lack of foresight, which is particularly problematic in patients with left hemiplegia, does not bode well for independent functioning. These disabilities may diminish somewhat with the passage of time.[6]

Cognitive and Intellectual Deficits

One of the difficulties in assessing the outcome of perceptual tests is clinically teasing apart perceptual problems from cognitive or intellectual deficits. Both perception and cognition rely on the recognition and interpretation of sensory information.[25] Cognition can be defined as the method used by the CNS to process information. This includes the ability to attend to, organize, and assimilate information.[2] Some of the most common cognitive subskills to be affected following a CVA are: attention, memory, initiation, judgment, insight, problem solving, abstract thinking, and mental flexibility.[1] Several are highlighted in the following section.

MEMORY

Memory can be defined as "a mental process that allows the individual to store experiences and perceptions for recall at a later time."[26] All memory is not localized in one particular place in the nervous system; rather, many and perhaps all regions of the brain may contain neurons with the adequate plasticity for memory storage.[27] There are three levels of memory storage. **Immediate recall** involves retention of information that has been stored for a few seconds. **Short-term memory** mediates retention of events or learning that has taken place within a few hours or days. **Long-term memory**

consists of early experiences and information acquired over a period of years.

The adequacy of memory functions can be assessed by having the patient recall lists or collections of objects that have just been presented (immediate recall), teaching the patient a new verbal or visual task and asking him or her to recall it a few hours or a day later (short-term memory), and requesting the patient to recall personal historical events (long-term memory). Frequently there is a loss of short-term memory following stroke, and this particularly interferes with the patient's ability to benefit from rehabilitation, especially from those activities involving the use of new and heretofore unfamiliar techniques.[19]

It is advisable to question the patient's family as to premorbid memory, as many patients in the stroke-prone age group have already begun to experience declining memory as part of the aging process.

ATTENTIONAL DEFICITS AND DISTRACTIBILITY

The inability of many patients with hemiplegia to maintain attention during therapy is a frequent complaint of therapists. Attention is the ability to select and to attend to a specific stimulus while simultaneously suppressing extraneous stimuli. A patient who is inattentive or distractible will have difficulty in processing and assimilating new information or techniques.[26] Often, patients who have suffered a CVA will have low arousal levels, and require a great deal of sensory input to be alerted to the environment. Low arousal thus must be considered as a cause for seeming inattention.

Diller and Weinberg[23] suggest that attention is not a unitary phenomenon. They have demonstrated that different aspects of attention seem to be impaired depending on the type of task and the side of the stroke. Tasks investigated required either scanning, searching the environment for clues; or spanning, retaining several bits of information at the same time. In addition, tasks could be divided into those requiring visual processing and those requiring verbal processing. As could be expected, in tasks that required auditory scanning, the performance of patients with right hemiplegia (generally language impaired) was inferior to that of those with left hemiplegia. And for tasks that required visual scanning, the performance of patients with left hemiplegia (generally impaired for visuospatial tasks) was inferior to that of those with right hemiplegia.

However, on spanning tasks, the findings were not as clear-cut. On verbal spanning tasks in which the stimuli were not present at all times (i.e., they required verbal rehearsal), the patients with right hemiplegia did poorly. On verbal spanning tasks in which the stimuli were present at all times, they performed adequately, because they could rely on the use of visual input to succeed in the task. Patients with left hemiplegia could not retain visual information long enough to succeed in the scan tasks but were able to use verbal rehearsal to improve their performance in the visual span tasks.

Clinically, the ability to attend to a task has implications for the therapeutic process. Diller and Weinberg[23] suggest that to improve the performance, the patient with left hemiplegia should be trained to scan the visual environment. A patient scanning too quickly should be advised to slow down. Patients with right hemiplegia should be spoken to more slowly to afford them the chance to process verbal information.[28] Additionally, patients with left hemiplegia should be encouraged to use verbalization to improve performance in visual tasks, and patients with right hemiplegia should be taught to use visualization techniques to facilitate attendance to verbal tasks.

For many patients, the inability to attend to significant stimuli is compounded by distraction due to extraneous stimuli in the environment. Often noise is the most distracting stimulus, causing irritability and diminished concentration. Ideally, distractible patients should be assessed in a noise-free, visually bland environment.

Some additional tools that may be used for the remediation of attentional deficits and distractibility are environmental restructuring, setting time limits or speed limits, amplification of critical stimuli, and making the crucial stimuli salient to the patient by various means.[29] The environment can be graded by having the patient initially perform some aspect of therapy in a nondistracting setting and then slowly increasing potentially distracting elements, both visual and auditory, as patient tolerance improves.[8] For patients who have difficulty reading as a result of diminished concentration abilities, a card with a slit large enough for only one line to appear at a time can be placed over the page while the patient reads. The slit is enlarged as the patient is able to tolerate more extraneous stimuli.[19]

ENVIRONMENT, CONTENT, AND LIMITATIONS OF THE FORMAL PERCEPTUAL ASSESSMENT

Environment

The patient should be sitting comfortably and wearing glasses and/or a hearing aid if needed. Ideally the room should be quiet and free of distraction. The therapist should be positioned opposite or next to the patient.

Content

Age, sex, and hand dominance should be noted.[30] Perceptual dysfunction needs to be differentiated from sensory loss, language impairment, hearing loss, motor loss (weakness, spasticity, incoordination), visual disturbances (poor eyesight, hemianopsia), disorientation, and lack of comprehension. The patient's behavior should not be misinterpreted because of a cultural bias, such as a lack of experience in taking tests. Premorbid intellectual ability should be ascertained from an interview with family or friends, as intellectual abilities may affect performance on some of the assessments and affect the patient's behavior in general. Premorbid memory should be determined as well. Specific assessment tools will be described following each deficit in the section on perceptual deficits that appears later in this chap-

ter. Scoring on a particular task is noted as intact, impaired, or absent.

The quality of the patient's response to the test media (e.g., how the task is approached, how and why the error is made) is as important to note as the success or failure in completing the task. Some aspects of response in the testing situation or during ADLs can be referred to as the patient's individual "perceptual style." Included under this rubric are the patient's perceptual strategy, response to various cues (such as auditory, visual, and tactile), rate of performance, and consistency of performance.[31]

Limitation of Formal Perceptual Assessment

The performance of a patient who has had a stroke may vary from day to day; a single assessment session is, therefore, usually unreliable.[11] A number of short sessions scheduled on successive days are preferable. To enhance its practical value, perceptual testing must be done in conjunction with observation in self-care and ADL skills, where the patient's judgment and discriminative abilities with regard to real-life tasks can be determined. It is not uncommon for patients to test poorly for visual perceptual skills but to perform adequately in ADLs with minimal effort or assistance.[29]

Technical issues surrounding formal assessment abound. There is little normative data on the sensory, motor, and perceptual abilities of the age group most prone to stroke. Few comprehensive test batteries or assessment tools have been examined experimentally in the adult poststroke population and found to be both reliable and valid. Ideally, a test instrument should be able to define perceptual dysfunction as an entity, to define its components, and to predict functional ability accurately. Perhaps the greatest challenge would be the development of an assessment battery in which the results would indicate specific avenues of therapeutic intervention.

Three promising instruments are under current investigation by occupational therapists. The Lowenstein Occupational Therapy Cognitive Assessment (LOTCA) for brain-injured patients is a battery lasting 35 to 40 minutes and composed of 20 subtests that evaluate four areas: orientation, visual and spatial perception, visuomotor organization, and thinking operations. However, direct relationship between test results and performance in ADLs has yet to be established.[3]

The perceptual component of the St. Mary's Evaluation is designed for use in an acute setting.[32] It is based on a high-factor analytic loading of measures of body scheme, figure-ground, position in space, spatial relations, and left-hand stereognosis. The validity of the instrument is in the process of being established.[33,34]

The Ontario Society of Occupational Therapists (OSOT) Perceptual Evaluation consists of 28 subtests that assess 6 functional areas: sensory function, scanning and spatial neglect, apraxia, body awareness, spatial relations, and visual agnosia. The battery was demonstrated to reliably differentiate between a neurologically impaired and neurologically normal population, and to be a reliable measure of perceptual dysfunction.[3,35]

The specific assessment tools that will be suggested below are used widely in the clinic. Most, however, are not standardized. The same holds true for treatment techniques. A few assessments are standardized on children but not adults. They are useful, however, for examining the quality of response to the test stimuli.

WALL'S ASSESSMENT AND TREATMENT PROCESS

It has been established that better functional results are achieved more quickly when patients are treated as soon as possible after the onset of any disability.[12,19] However, there is a lack of conclusive evidence supporting the efficacy of specific treatments of isolated perceptual deficits. The treatment techniques that are suggested here for each disability area are those that appear to be of value in current clinical practice.

Components of the treatment process for patients with cognitive-perceptual-motor dysfunction have been outlined by Wall[11] and are presented as a succinct way of summarizing the assessment and treatment process.

Part 1: Assessment

A thorough assessment of the patient in whom deficits are suspected is necessary in order to identify the specific perceptual problems. Assessment techniques will be included in the section describing individual perceptual deficits.

Part 2: Time

It must be recognized that natural progress in overcoming or compensating for perceptual deficits may be slow but will be forthcoming in the first few weeks and months following a CVA.

It is also necessary to recognize that it takes time for the patient, especially an elderly patient, to respond to instructional sets. Rushing either the assessment or the treatment will lead to frustration, which in turn will inhibit success. A great deal of patience is required on the part of both the therapist and the patient.

Part 3: Education

Education for the patient, family, and friends is essential for continuity of care. The family should understand why it is inadvisable or impossible for the patient to do some things safely or independently, and why other things must be done in a specific way. Explaining the reasons why the patient behaves in a particular way reduces the likelihood of inappropriate expectations from those without the background to know that brain damage affects not only how the patient moves but how he or she experiences and thus responds to the world.

Feedback is essential in the patient's own education.

Patients' feedback may be inaccurate owing to perceptual and cognitive dysfunctions. Thus, the individual may be unaware that a task has not been accomplished or that it has not been performed in the safest or most efficient manner. Feedback should be provided in the form of "knowledge of results" (KR), and "knowledge of performance" (KP). Knowledge of results is information regarding whether or not the patient attained the goal. Knowledge of performance is information regarding the manner in which the goal was accomplished.[36]

The form in which this feedback is delivered depends upon the specific limitations and strengths of the patient. For example, the physical therapy goal for a patient with left hemiplegia and visual perceptual involvement might be to walk to the end of the parallel bars. Knowledge of results would consist of a verbal confirmation by the therapist as to whether or not the patient reached the end of the parallel bars. Knowledge of performance might include comments by the therapist concerning the adequacy of the patient's visual scanning, positioning of the lower extremities, correct posture, and appropriate use of the upper limbs. For the verbally impaired patient the feedback would have to be visual. Tactile input also can be used effectively to cue patients with either right or left hemiplegia. A combination of inputs, using a number of sensory modalities, often facilitates patient success at a given task.

Part 4: The Art of Therapy

The patient must be addressed as a competent adult, and not patronized. He or she must be regarded as the principal participant in both the assessment and the treatment process. Conversation should be directed towards the patient when he or she is present. Open communication among the patient, staff, and family should be established early and maintained. In situations in which the perceptual deficit does not interfere with assimilation of information, the patient should have the major role in the decision-making process regarding the goals of therapy.

Part 5: The Therapeutic Program

Four major approaches to perceptual rehabilitation commonly employed by occupational therapists have been delineated and described by Zoltan, Siev, and Freishtat:[1] they are the transfer of training approach, the sensory integrative approach, the functional approach, and the neurodevelopmental approach.

Neistadt[37,38] characterized treatment approaches dichotomously as either "remedial" or "adaptive." The remedial approach encompasses the sensory integrative approach, neurodevelopmental treatment, and transfer-of-training approach, along with the cognitive retraining model.[2] They all focus on the patient's deficits and attempt to improve functional ability by retraining specific perceptual components of behavior.[38] The assumption uniting this set of tactics is that facilitation of or training in underlying skills will enhance the recovery or reorganization of deficient CNS functioning.[38,39] This,

Table 28–1 COMMON ASSUMPTIONS OF THE ADAPTIVE AND REMEDIAL TREATMENT APPROACHES

Adaptive Approach	Remedial Approach
The adult brain has limited potential to repair and reorganize itself after injury.	The adult brain can repair and reorganize itself after injury.
Intact behaviors can be used to compensate for impaired ones.	This repair and reorganization is influenced by environmental stimuli.
Adaptive retraining can facilitate the substitution of intact behaviors for impaired ones.	Perceptual and sensorimotor exercises can promote brain recovery and reorganization.
Adaptive activities of daily living provide training in functional behaviors.	Perceptual and sensorimotor exercises provide training in the perceptual skills needed for those exercises.
Training in specific, essential activities of daily living tasks is necessary because adults with brain injury have difficulty generalizing learning.	Remedial training in perceptual skills will be generalized across all activities requiring those perceptual skills.
Functional activities require perceptual skills.	Functional activities require perceptual skills.
Perceptual adaptation will improve functional performance.	Perceptual remediation will improve functional performance.

in turn, will automatically translate into improvement in functional skills.

The adaptive approach, analogous to the "functional approach" of Zoltan et al.,[38] mandates direct training in the functional skills that are deficient. It does not assume automatic carryover from tasks not obviously similar to the functional task to be learned, and thus minimizes the need for generalization. For a comparison of the assumptions underlying the remedial and adaptive approaches see Table 28–1.

While research directly comparing the efficacy of the various approaches has been sparse, attempts have been made recently to empirically define and test the methodologies.[37–40] Issues to consider in examining the techniques are: standardized measures of change in functional status and ADLs, length and frequency of treatment, group versus individual treatment, specific stimulus properties, format and frequency of feedback, and individual information processing styles.[39]

In order to provide the reader with more depth, the theoretical bases of the four approaches will be examined in this section. Specific applications will be offered in the treatment suggestions following the description of individual perceptual deficits. The four clinical models are not mutually exclusive. Many therapists use a combination of approaches, guiding their selection by their clinical expertise and the patient's response to the techniques. The functional approach will be emphasized because this is the most practical for the physical therapist. A fifth approach, termed cognitive rehabilitation, is a promising new area of research and will be discussed briefly.

THE TRANSFER-OF-TRAINING APPROACH

The premise underlying the transfer-of-training approach is that practice in one task with particular per-

ceptual requirements will enhance performance in other tasks with similar perceptual demands.[1,38] Thus, doing specifically selected perceptual exercises, such as pegboard activities, or parquetry blocks and puzzles will result in improved performance in ADLs and self-care activities by improving the perceptual skills required to perform those functional tasks. For example, Diller and coworkers[41] found that patients with left hemiplegia who received training in block design improved in their organization of eating behavior when compared with a control group. Similarly, Young and associates[42] demonstrated that training patients with left hemiplegia in block design, in addition to visual scanning and visual cancellation tasks, resulted in improvements in reading and writing, although no specific training in writing was offered. Because all tasks require the use of multiple perceptual skills it is difficult to ascertain precisely which perceptual skills are being trained during any one session.[38]

Thus far the research is so sparse that it is difficult to assess the efficacy of the transfer of training mode of treatment as a whole. The available research has not unequivocally demonstrated a generalization from perceptual-motor training to functional skills.[39] If it is believed that such exercises would be beneficial, they can be incorporated into other components of the treatment program, such as those aimed at maintaining sitting or standing balance, weight-bearing exercises, or functional use of the affected extremities.

THE SENSORY INTEGRATIVE APPROACH

The theory of sensory integration was developed by A. Jean Ayres in an effort to explain the relationship between neural functioning and the behavior of children with sensorimotor or learning problems.[43] The theory, strongly influenced by the neurobehavioral literature, describes normal sensory integrative development and functioning, defines patterns of sensory integrative dysfunction, and suggests treatment techniques.[43] Sensory integration can be defined as the organization of sensation for use.[44,45]

Integration of basic sensorimotor functions (tactile, proprioceptive, and vestibular) proceeds in a developmental sequence in the normal child within the context of goal-directed, meaningful activity. It is assumed that the production of an adaptive response facilitates sensory integration, which in turn enhances the ability to produce higher-level adaptive behaviors. Sensory integration is thought to occur at all levels of the nervous system.

The underlying assumption for treatment is that by offering opportunities for controlled sensory input the therapist can effect normal CNS processing of sensory information and thus elicit specific desired motor responses.[38] The performance of these "adaptive responses," in turn, influences the way in which the brain organizes and processes sensation, thus enhancing the ability to learn.

Some of the treatment modalities employed are rubbing or icing to provide sensory input, the use of resistance and weight bearing to impart proprioceptive input, and the use of spinning to provide vestibular input. Following the controlled sensory input, an adaptive motor response is required by the patient in order to integrate the sensations provided by the therapist. In young children, the use of compensatory or splinter skills (skills acquired in a manner inconsistent with, or incapable of being integrated with, those already present) is avoided in favor of remediating underlying deficits. For more detailed information the reader is referred to the work of Ayres.[43,44,45]

Zoltan et al.[1] argue that the elderly, who comprise the majority of the stroke population, experience sensory integrative dysfunction similar to that of children with learning disabilities, and that this is due to physiologic changes associated with aging, along with environmentally induced sensory deprivation. The limitations in mobility caused by a stroke further prevent the patient from receiving and thus processing adequate sensory input.

The application of this theory to the adult poststroke population, however, is open to serious debate. Fisher et al.[43] argue that the theory intends to explain mild to moderate learning and behavioral problems that are the result of a central deficit in processing sensations that are specifically *not* associated with frank brain damage. Further, there are a number of problems with the application of this approach to adult populations, even if it is theoretically tenable.

The treatment process is ordinarily quite lengthy. In addition, specific assessment and treatment regimens have been developed for and standardized on children, who presumably have sufficiently plastic nervous systems to be influenced by this form of therapy. The neurophysiologic literature is replete with examples of the ability of younger patients to compensate neurologically for abilities that would be completely lost in mature individuals with similar lesions.[15,46,47] Furthermore, a mature adult with diffuse cerebral damage may have other complicating medical concerns and deficits in mobility that actually contraindicate the use of the equipment that is essential to the treatment process.[43] It is likely that many of the treatment regimes described as "sensory integration" are best described as a sensorimotor approach, which utilizes handling or directed sensory stimulation to elicit a specific motor response.[43]

THE NEURODEVELOPMENTAL APPROACH

From a neurodevelopmental (Bobath) perspective, perception is facilitated during normal infant neuromotor development by the kinesthetic, proprioceptive, tactile, and vestibular feedback received through normal movement experience. The infant utilizes these sensations as he progresses from early physiologic flexion and comes up against gravity to sit, crawl, kneel, stand, and begin to walk. Sensorimotor development provides a sense of midline orientation, awareness of the two sides of the body, and total body awareness.[1]

For adults with neurologic impairment, perception is considered integral to the handling techniques that provide the patient with sensory input and to the subsequent feedback accompanying correct movement during movement retraining. For example, weight-bearing activities enhance proprioception, and bilateral activities enhance total body awareness and diminish unilateral neglect.[7]

THE FUNCTIONAL APPROACH

Probably the most widely used approach in dealing with perceptual dysfunction is the functional approach.[7] The basic assumption underlying the functional approach is that adults with brain trauma will have difficulty generalizing and learning from dissimilar tasks.[37] Direct repetitive practice of specific functional skills that are impaired is an efficient means of enhancing the patient's independence in those specific tasks. The proponents of this approach (this author included) favor addressing the functional problem over and above the treatment of its underlying cause when treating the adult poststroke population. For example, a patient with difficulty in depth and distance perception, who is therefore unable to navigate a flight of stairs, would be made aware of the deficit, provided with external cues to compensate for the perceptual disorder, and would repetitively practice adapted techniques for safe stair climbing. The more closely the therapeutic practice situation resembles the home situation in terms of stair depth and height, amount of traffic, lighting, and so forth, the less generalizing is required and the more success the patient is likely to have when he or she returns home. However, problems might still be displayed in depth and distance perception in other areas of daily function.

In the functional approach, therapy is viewed as a learning process that takes into consideration the unique strengths and limitations of the individual patient. It is composed of two complementary components: compensation and adaptation.[1] Compensation refers to the changes that need to be made in the patient's approach to tasks. Adaptation refers to the alterations that need to be made in the human and physical environment in order to facilitate relearning of skills.

To compensate for the disability, the patient first has to be made aware of deficiencies (**cognitive awareness**) and must then be taught how to circumvent them using intact sensations and perceptual skills. The patient should be instructed in specific techniques and assisted in developing successful functional habits. The patient will need to be taught to attend to cues from the environment to enhance skill performance. The therapist helps the patient identify and then call upon these new cues. For example, if the patient has a visual field cut, the therapist should explain that because of a visual problem, the patient is seeing only one half of the environment. The patient should then be shown how to turn his head to compensate for the deficit. Environmental scanning could be incorporated into general therapy sessions as well. A few general suggestions when teaching compensatory techniques are (1) use simple directions, (2) establish and carry out a routine, (3) do each activity in a consistent manner, and (4) employ repetition as much as necessary.

Adaptation refers to the alteration not of the patient's strategy, but of the environment. For example, if the patient cannot differentiate between right and left, or tends to neglect the left side of the body, a piece of red tape on the left shoe during gait training will allow the patient to attend more easily to the left side and thus to follow the therapist's instructions more accurately. The therapist can use the functional approach to assist patients in improving specific motor skills related to treatment goals.

There are several inherent benefits to the functional approach. First, the hospitalized patient will be involved in intense in-patient rehabilitation for an increasingly limited amount of time as new health care policies are put into effect. Therefore, it seems most efficacious to concentrate on goal-directed, real-life activities as independent performance of these activities at home is the ultimate goal of therapeutic intervention and will heavily influence discharge planning. Second, the activities are age-appropriate and concrete and are clearly relevant to the patient's concerns. For this reason they tend to be the most "motivating." Third, tasks can be incorporated into daily hospital routine. Dressing can be reinforced at bedside by the nursing staff, and eating skills can be reinforced at each mealtime.

The major limitation of this approach is that the methods learned in one task are not typically generalized to the performance of another task. The functional approach has been criticized as the teaching of "splinter skills," in which the causes of the dysfunction are not addressed.

COGNITIVE REHABILITATION

Cognitive rehabilitation focuses on training brain-injured individuals to structure and organize information.[31] It addresses memory, high language disorders, and perceptual dysfunction under one umbrella.[48] Information processing, problem solving, awareness, judgment, and decision making are among the areas addressed. The therapist using a cognitive remediation approach might be concerned with the patient's perceptual style, including perceptual strategy, response to different types of cues, and rate and consistency of task performance.[2] Diller and Gordon[49] provide a review of the literature pertaining to intervention strategies for cognitive deficits.

Cognitive strategies can be employed to facilitate the carryover from therapy to functional performance, since even in a non-brain-injured population, transfer of training does not automatically occur.[4] In her "multicontext treatment approach," to cognition Toglia[4] proposes that learning can be conceptualized as a dynamic interplay between characteristics of the patient, characteristics of the task, and the environment in which it is performed (Fig. 28–1). This has also been termed a "dynamic interactional approach."[51] Characteristics of the individual patient that might affect learning include information processing strategies, metacognition (including awareness of one's own cognitive abilities and ability to monitor one's own performance) and prior experience, attitudes, and emotions. Task-related variables that are proposed to affect learning include the nature of the task itself (familiarity with the task, spatial arrangements, instructional set, and movement and postural requirements), and the criteria that are used to assess the learner's abilities. Environmental variables include the social and cultural environment in which treatment occurs, as well as the physical context.

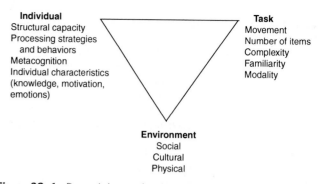

Figure 28–1. Dynamic interactional model of cognition. (From Toglia,[51] p 108, with permission.)

The cognitive treatment approach proposes a number of treatment strategies that may be relevant to the practice of physical therapy, a few of which will be related here.[4]

1. Use of multiple environments in which to carry out the training activity in order to enhance transfer of learning.
2. Analyzing the characteristics of the task in order to establish criteria to determine if transfer of learning in fact took place.
3. Providing training: making the patient aware of his abilities, and the level of difficulty of the task, and providing instruction in self-evaluation of performance.
4. Relating new information or skills to previously learned ones.

While these treatment strategies are well known within the field of cognitive-perceptual rehabilitation, the efficacy of the techniques remains to be established with the poststroke population. For a comprehensive understanding and practical guidelines to the evaluation and treatment of patients with cognitive impairments from a dynamic perspective see Toglia[51] and Abreu and Hinojosa.[25]

Part 6: Discharge Planning and Continuity of Care

Once areas of perceptual dysfunction have been identified and remediation techniques have been implemented, the therapist will be able to advise the family as to the patient's need for assistance and to recommend appropriate plans for discharge.

IMPLICATIONS FOR TREATMENT

Data Collection and Task Analysis

The use of systematic data collection provides the scientific basis for guiding treatment. Its importance cannot be overemphasized with respect to all facets of therapeutic intervention, including perceptual remediation. Task analysis is the breakdown of an activity or task into its component parts and a delineation of the specific motor, perceptual, and cognitive abilities necessary to perform each component. Task analysis is another tool that is critical to appropriate therapeutic intervention. For example, the strength, ROM, and balance abilities necessary to accomplish bed mobility and ambulation activities can be clearly defined by the physical therapist. However, the specific perceptual and cognitive requirements of each step needed to perform these two tasks may not be known. Without knowledge of the perceptual requirements for successful completion of a task, the therapist cannot simplify the task for the patient and progressively upgrade it.

VISUAL DISTURBANCES

Visual deficit is one of the most common forms of sensory loss affecting the patient with hemiplegia,[19] although it has previously received little attention in the therapy literature.[50] The lesion resulting from a stroke may affect the eye, the optic radiation, or the visual cortex, and thus correspondingly the reception, transmission, and appreciation of any visual array. Visual disturbances commonly encountered by patients with hemiplegia are poor eyesight, diplopia, homonymous hemianopsia, damage to the visual cortex, and retinal damage. It is important to be aware of the presence of these deficits so as not to confuse them with visual perceptual deficiencies, and in order that they be taken into account during the course of therapeutic intervention.

The critical nature of the basic visual skills (i.e., acuity, oculomotor control, and intact visual fields) in forming a basis for higher level visual perception is highlighted by Mary Warren[52,53] in a hierarchical model for treatment and evaluation of visual perceptual dysfunction. In this developmental model the basic visual skills enumerated above form the foundation for the next level of visual skills, which include visual attention, visual scanning, and pattern recognition. These skills, along with memory, are required to facilitate the highest level visual skill termed "visual cognition."[52,53] This model has implications for evaluation and treatment of visual perceptual disorders in a "bottom up" sequence (Fig. 28–2).[53]

Deficits in oculomotor control (control of eye movements) are a common occurrence following a CVA. Poor visual acuity is another frequent finding following stroke or head injury, even in the absence of other visual problems.[19] Therefore, it is recommended that the patient receive a comprehensive eye examination and have his or her eyeglass prescription checked.

Diplopia, or double vision, is often present following a stroke. The patient sees two of the entire environment. Diplopia is usually the result of decreased range of motion in one eye. Treatment usually consists of range of motion exercises for the eye muscles. In addition, the patient usually is instructed to wear a patch on alternate eyes until the condition clears. If the condition does not clear, the optometrist may recommend prisms.

Visual field deficit is probably the most common

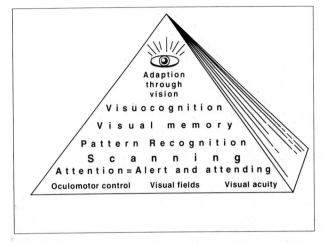

Figure 28–2. Hierarchy of visual perceptual skills in the central nervous system. Drawing courtesy of Josephine C. Moore PhD, OTR, DSc(HON)[2]. (From Warren,[52] p 43, with permission.)

visual deficit affecting patients with hemiplegia,[19] and occurs most frequently following damage to the middle cerebral artery near the internal capsule.[6] The diagnostic term for this deficit is **homonymous hemianopsia.** Recent studies indicate that the frequency of hemianopsia following a right-hemisphere stroke is as high as 46 percent,[54,55] and the relatively high frequency is probably related to the high incidence of CVA in this location. In addition, there is a significant correlation between the presence of visual field deficits and visual neglect.[56] Most important, the presence of a visual field deficit is a significant prognostic sign, predicting both a higher death rate following stroke and poorer performance in ADLs,[57] even following rehabilitation.[58]

Figure 28–3 demonstrates the normal functioning of the visual fields, in which the left side of the environ-

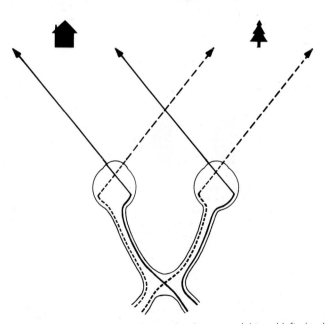

Figure 28–3. Normally functioning visual system; right and left visual fields. See text for explanation. (From Sharpless,[6] p 247, with permission.)

ment (the house) is perceived by the nasal retina of the left eye and the temporal retina of the right eye, and the right side of the environment (the tree) is perceived by the nasal retina of the right eye and the temporal retina of the left eye.[6]

The lesion producing homonymous hemianopsia interrupts inflow to the optic pathways on one side of the brain; this produces a loss of the outer half of the visual field from one eye and the inner half of the visual field of the other eye. The result is a loss of incoming information from half of the visual environment (left or right) contralateral to the side of the lesion. Thus the loss of the left half of the visual field accompanies left hemiplegia, and loss of the right visual field accompanies right hemiplegia. Figure 28–4 illustrates visual field deficits associated with a number of lesions to the visual system.

The presence of a visual field cut may inhibit performance in many daily activities. The patient is usually unaware of the condition and does not automatically compensate by turning the head unless specifically instructed. One of the dangers in this condition is street crossing, as illustrated in Figure 28–5. Another example of the effects of a visual field cut is illustrated in Figure 28–6. When presented with a tray of food, a patient with right homonymous hemianopsia may attend to the plate and fork on the left side and fail to "see" the knife, spoon, and cup on the right side of the plate. The patient might read only one half of the newspaper page—to the midline or from the midline.

Because of its prevalence, it is essential for the therapist to assess whether hemianopsia is present or not. A number of evaluation tools are currently employed. In the confrontation method, the patient sits opposite the

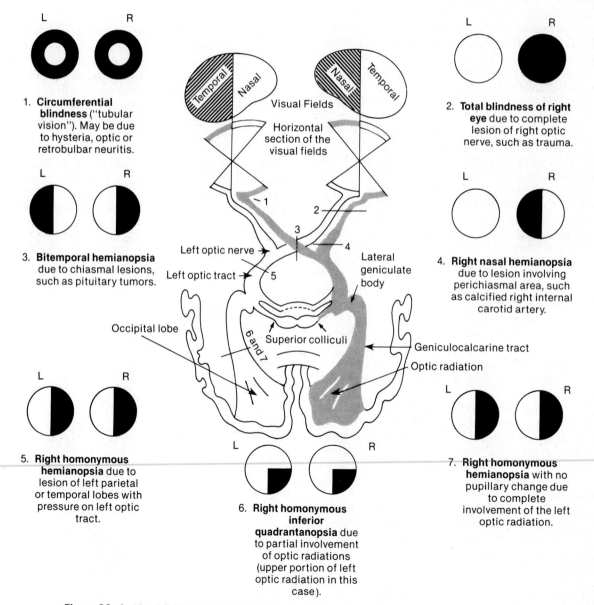

1. **Circumferential blindness** ("tubular vision"). May be due to hysteria, optic or retrobulbar neuritis.

2. **Total blindness of right eye** due to complete lesion of right optic nerve, such as trauma.

3. **Bitemporal hemianopsia** due to chiasmal lesions, such as pituitary tumors.

4. **Right nasal hemianopsia** due to lesion involving perichiasmal area, such as calcified right internal carotid artery.

5. **Right homonymous hemianopsia** due to lesion of left parietal or temporal lobes with pressure on left optic tract.

6. **Right homonymous inferior quadrantanopsia** due to partial involvement of optic radiations (upper portion of left optic radiation in this case).

7. **Right homonymous hemianopsia** with no pupillary change due to complete involvement of the left optic radiation.

Visual Fields

Horizontal section of the visual fields

Left optic nerve

Left optic tract

Lateral geniculate body

Occipital lobe

Superior colliculi

Geniculocalcarine tract

Optic radiation

Figure 28–4. Visual field deficits and associated lesion sites. (From Chusid,[59] p 114, with permission.)

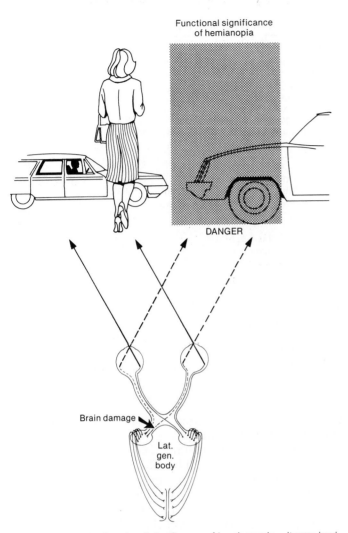

Functional significance
of hemianopia

DANGER

Brain damage

Lat.
gen.
body

Figure 28–5. The functional significance of hemianopsia—it may lead to accidents. (From Tobis and Lowenthal,[9] p 78, with permission.)

Figure 28–6. A table setting as it might appear to a patient with right homonymous hemianopsia following a stroke. The dotted lines indicate that she may be unable to locate her knife, spoon, cup, and so forth. (From Sharpless,[6] p 248, with permission.)

receives maximum stimulation. Of course, the patient will have to be reminded to turn the head at first. External cues can be employed as well. For reading, a red line can be drawn on the ignored side of the page. Red tape can be placed on the floor, mat, or parallel bars to attract the patient to the side of the environment that tends to be ignored. The patient should be taught to look for these cues. These external cues can be slowly tapered off over time. Patients can be instructed that they can devise their own cues to clue them into the neglected side of the environment in situations that have not been addressed per se in therapy. Exercises that require

therapist and is instructed to maintain his gaze on the therapist's nose (Fig. 28–7). The therapist slowly brings a target, such as a pen, into the patient's field of view alternately from the right or left. The patient is instructed to indicate when and where he or she sees the targets.[7]

To help the patient compensate for the visual field deficit the patient can first be made aware of the deficit and then be instructed to turn the head to the affected side. Patients usually require constant reminders at first. These may be tapered off with time and practice. Early in therapy, items (e.g., eating utensils, writing implements) should be placed where the patient is most apt to see them (on the intact side). They can be moved progressively to the midline and then to the affected side, if appropriate. The nursing staff should be made aware of the condition and requested to place the patient's essential bedside needs such as telephone, tissues, and so forth within the intact visual field. The therapist initially should sit on the patient's intact side when instructing or giving demonstrations and should alternate this with the affected side so that the patient

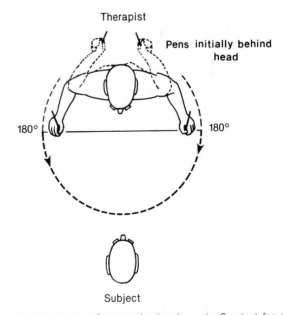

Therapist

Pens initially behind
head

180°   180°

Subject

Figure 28–7. Method for assessing hemianopsia. See text for explanation. (Modified from Pedretti, LW: Evaluation of sensation, perception and cognition. In Pedretti, LW (ed): Occupational Therapy: Practice Skills for Physical Dysfunction, ed 2. CV Mosby, St. Louis, 1985, p 99, with permission.)

motor crossing of the midline can be used to reinforce visual crossing of the midline and turning of the head.[30]

Oculomotor dysfunction is the third potential area of deficit in basic visual skills that is common in patients who have had a stroke. Eye movements, which are controlled by the extraocular muscles, are used to detect, to identify, and to derive meaning from objects and the environment. They allow a person to become oriented to and to explore the critical visual aspects of the environment.[14] Two types of eye movements are important to assess: (1) **fixation,** which allows the patient to maintain focus on an object as it is brought nearer or farther away; and (2) **ocular pursuits,** which enable the eyes to follow a moving object and visually scan the environment. Often the eyes will not follow a moving object visually, although the patient seems aware of the presence of that object and can locate it if asked. The patient is visually hypoactive. Oculomotor dysfunction often accompanies visual-perceptual dysfunction and is frequently related to attentional deficits.[29]

Visual scanning can be assessed as follows: Sit opposite the patient. Hold up a pencil with a colorful pencil-topper 18 inches in front of the patient's eyes. Slowly move the topper horizontally, then vertically, then diagonally. Repeat each direction two to three times. Note the smoothness of eye movements, the presence of a midline jerk or jump, and whether the eyes move together.[1]

Aside from the visual sensory deficits outlined above, many patients suffer from visual-perceptual dysfunction. Damage to areas of the cortex upon which visual information converges with information from other senses may interfere with the recognition and interpretation of visual information, even though the visual stimuli may have arrived at the visual cortex uninterrupted. A total failure to appreciate incoming visual sensory information due to a lesion in the cortex is referred to as **cortical blindness.** There is no statistical correspondence between the presence of visual field cuts and the presence of visual-perceptual disorders.[50] Similarly, there is no correspondence between **aphasia,** age, and time since infarct, and measures of visual-perceptual dysfunction.[50] However, within the realm of visual-perceptual disorders there is a significant difference between the performances of patients with right hemiplegia and those with left hemiplegia. Patients with left hemiplegia have frequently been found to perform more poorly on measures of visual-perceptual dysfunction than patients with right hemiplegia. Thus, therapists should be aware of the possibility of visual-perceptual deficits, particularly in the left hemiplegic population. Specific examples of visual-perceptual dysfunction are included within the four categories of perceptual disorders described in the following section.

Perceptual Deficits

This section is divided into four parts: disorders of body scheme and body image; spatial relations syndrome; agnosia; and apraxia, as outlined in Table 28–2. Each category encompasses a constellation of perceptual deficits, which are grouped together for ease of

Table 28–2 OUTLINE OF PERCEPTUAL DISABILITIES

I. Body scheme/body image disorders
   A. Body image disorder/simultagnosia
   B. Visual spatial neglect/unilateral spatial neglect
   C. Right/left discrimination
   D. Finger agnosia
   E. Anosognosia
II. Spatial relation syndrome
   A. Figure-ground discrimination
   B. Form constancy
   C. Spatial relations
   D. Position in space
   E. Topographic disorientation
   F. Additional visuospatial difficulties
     1. Depth and distance perception
     2. Vertical disorientation
III. Agnosias
   A. Visual object agnosias
     1. Simultagnosia
     2. Prosopagnosia
     3. Color agnosia
   B. Auditory agnosia
   C. Tactile agnosia/asteriognosis
IV. Apraxias
   A. Ideomotor apraxia
   B. Ideational apraxia
   C. Constructional apraxia
   D. Dressing apraxia

understanding. Information pertaining to each deficit will be organized identically:
1. Individual deficits will be defined.
2. Clinical examples will be offered.
3. An approximate lesion area will be identified, although for some disorders controversy exists as to the actual area of the cortex involved in producing a specific perceptual deficit, and to its laterality. When a cerebral hemisphere is designated it refers to the majority of cases cited in the literature. Exceptions do occur. Table 28–3 presents a compilation of perceptual disabilities associated with lesions of the right or left hemisphere of the brain.
4. Assessment methods in current use will be described.
5. Suggestions will be presented for the therapist to employ in treatment.

The value of dwelling on probable areas of cortical damage is controversial. The indication of cortical loci is an attempt to relate the study of neuroanatomy to actual patient behavior involving perceptual dysfunction. It does not imply that the author is a strict localizationist. An examination of cortical loci will give the reader a sense of which perceptual deficits are likely to be seen together.

As therapists, we are required to assist the patient to bridge the gap between maladaptive behavior and independent function in ADLs. Whether or not the area of the brain purported to produce a particular dysfunction appears damaged on a computerized axial tomography (CAT) scan or other neurologic or radiologic test is not a key determinant of the rehabilitative approach to therapy. The patient's approach to task performance and the relative strengths or weaknesses of the patient (motorically, cognitively, and perceptually), which the therapist ascertains through thorough observation and assess-

Table 28–3 PERCEPTUAL DISABILITIES: SITE AND SIDE OF LESION*

Lobe Vascular Supply[24,59,61]	Location of Lesion	
	Left Hemisphere Deficits (Dominant)	*Right Hemisphere Deficits (Nondominant)*

Temporal lobe
  Internal carotid artery
  Posterior cerebral artery
  Middle cerebral artery
	Somatagnosia[61]
	Auditory agnosia[61]
	Ideomotor apraxia[59]
	Ideational apraxia[61]
	Constructional apraxia[62]
	Disorders of speech[62]
	Acalculia[62]
		Unilateral neglect[62]
		Constructional apraxia[62]
		Difficulty recognizing complex or incomplete visual stimuli[24]

Occipital lobe Posterior cerebral artery	Visual object agnosia[59] Simultagnosia[61] Prosopagnosia[63] Color agnosia[62] Constructional apraxia[24] Right homonymous hemianopsia[59] Sensory aphasia[59] Alexia[24] Agraphia[24] Acalculia[24]	Visual object agnosia[59] Color agnosia[59] Topographical disorientation[62] Depth and distance perception[48] Prosopagnosia[63] Dressing apraxia[61] Left homonymous hemianopsia[24] Symbol agnosia[24] Complex visual hallucinations[24]

Parietal lobe
  Internal carotid artery
  Anterior cerebral artery
  Posterior cerebral artery
  Middle cerebral artery
	Somatagnosia[59]
	Right-left discrimination[65]
	Finger agnosia[66]
	Gerstmann's syndrome[62]
	Visual object agnosia[62]
	Visual spatial agnosia[62]
	Astereognosis[24]
	Ideomotor apraxia[68]
	Ideational apraxia[61]
	Constructional apraxia[69]
	
	Aphasia[24]
	Alexia[24]
	Agraphia[24]
	Acalculia[24]
	Diminished logic[5]
		Unilateral neglect[62]
		Right-left discrimination[66]
		Finger agnosia[66]
		Anosognosia[59]
		Spatial relations syndrome[67]
		Figure-ground discrimination[62]
		Form constancy[18]
		Position in space[18]
		Topographic disorientation[62]
		Vertical disorientation[24]
		Visual object agnosia[24]
		Visual spatial agnosia[24]
		Astereognosis[24]
		Dressing apraxia[61]
		Difficulty comprehending the emotional tone of language[27]

Frontal lobe[1,24,59]
  Internal carotid artery
  Middle cerebral artery
  Anterior cerebral artery
	Motor aphasia[1,24,59]
	Agraphia
	Verbal apraxia
	Motor apraxia
		Motor amusia
		Motor apraxia

*Superscript numbers in table refer to references at the end of the chapter.

ment, are much more pertinent to the selection of appropriate therapeutic strategies than the locus of the lesion.

Assessment tools are described for each perceptual disability in order to enhance the reader's awareness of the complexity of behavior ascribed to perceptual deficiencies. Familiarity with the tools used to assess perceptual dysfunction can serve as an aid in communication between physical and occupational therapists engaged in the treatment of the same patient.

The following section also includes specific treatment suggestions from the sensorimotor, transfer of training, and functional approaches described previously. The treatment techniques most relevant are those dealing with the functional approach and adaptation of the environment. In these sections, examples are given as to how to facilitate the patient's success within a treatment session. Information is provided on how the therapist might gear language, demonstrations, feedback, and the use of media and environment to the individual needs of the perceptually impaired patient.

BODY SCHEME AND BODY IMAGE DISORDERS

Body image is defined as a visual and mental image of one's body that includes feelings about one's body, especially in relation to health and disease.[1,11] The term **body scheme** refers to a postural model of the body, including the relationship of the body parts to each other and the relationship of the body to the environment. Body awareness is derived from the integration of tactile, proprioceptive, and interoceptive sensations, in addition to the individual's subjective feelings about the body.[60] An awareness of body scheme is considered one of the essential foundations for the performance of all purposeful motor behavior.[70] The two terms, body image and body scheme, are often used interchangeably.[65] Therefore, when researching this topic, close attention should be paid to the particular definition put forth by the author. Specific disturbances of body image and body scheme are **somatagnosia**, visual or unilateral spatial neglect, **right-left discrimination, finger agnosia**, and **anosognosia**.

Somatagnosia

1. Somatagnosia, or impairment in body scheme, is a lack of awareness of the body structure and the relationship of body parts in oneself or in others. Patients with this deficit may display difficulty following instructions that require distinguishing body parts and may be unable to imitate movements of the therapist.[11] Often patients report that the affected arm or leg feels unduly heavy.[30] Lack of proprioception may underlie or compound this disorder.[5] Body scheme impairment is also termed **autopagnosia**.[71]

2. Clinically, the patient may have difficulty performing transfer activities because he or she does not perceive the meaning of terms related to body parts, for example, "Pivot on your leg and reach for the armrest with your hand." Additionally, a patient with a body scheme disorder will have difficulty dressing. Patients may have a hard time participating in exercises that require some body parts to be moved in relation to other body parts; for example, "Bring your arm across your chest and touch your shoulder."

3. The lesion site is the dominant parietal lobe,[59] or posterior temporal lobe.[61] Thus, this disorder is seen primarily with right hemiplegia. However, impairment in body scheme may also occur with left hemiplegia.

4. Assessment techniques:

   a. The patient is requested to point to body parts named by the therapist, on himself or herself,[70,71] on the therapist, and on a picture or puzzle of a human figure. For example, "Show me your feet. Show me your chin. Point to your back." The words "right" and "left" should not be used because they may lead to an inaccurate diagnosis in the case of a patient who has difficulty with right-left discrimination. Aphasia should be ruled out as a cause of poor performance.

   b. The patient is asked to imitate movements of the therapist. For example, the therapist touches his or her cheek, arm, leg, and so forth. A mirror-image response is acceptable.[1,71]

   c. The patient is requested to answer questions about the relationship of body parts. For example, "Are your knees below your head? Which is on top of your head, your hair or your feet?" For patients with aphasia, questions should be phrased to require a yes-or-no or true-or-false response.[70] Patients with intact function in this area should respond correctly most of the time and within a reasonable period of time. Those patients with receptive aphasia are particularly likely to do poorly on tests for somatagnosia.[71]

5. Treatment suggestions:

   a. The sensorimotor approach attempts to associate sensory input with an adaptive motor response.[1] Facilitation of body awareness is accomplished through sensory stimulation to the body part affected. For example, the patient is asked to rub the appropriate body part with a rough cloth as the therapist names it or points to it.[30]

   b. With the transfer of training approach, the patient verbally identifies body parts, or points to pictures of them as the therapist touches them.[30]

Unilateral Visual or Spatial Neglect

1. Unilateral spatial neglect, sometimes termed visual hemi-inattention when referring to the visual component, is the inability to register and to integrate stimuli and perceptions from one side of the body and the environment. This usually, although not always, affects the left side of the body, and for purposes of this discussion, we will assume that it is the left. The patient ignores the left side of the body and stimuli occurring in the left personal space. This may occur despite intact visual fields, or concomitantly with right or left homonymous hemianopsia; however, it is not caused by hemianopsia.[64] Frequently the patient has sensory loss on the affected side, which compounds the problem. Although the patient with left-sided hemianopsia has actual loss of vision from the left visual field of both eyes, he or she may be aware of the problem and compensate automatically or learn to compensate by turning the head. The patient with visual neglect has intact vision but seems unaware of the problem and does not attempt to compensate spontaneously by turning the head. In extreme cases the patient appears totally indifferent to the left side of the body and environment, and may deny that the left extremities belong to him or her.[72] More time seems to be required in learning to compensate for this disability than with hemianopsia. There is great difficulty in integrating all stimuli from the left half of the body and personal space for use in ADLs. As with hemianopsia, the patient with visual spatial neglect often avoids crossing the midline visually or motorically.[30] Current theories consider spatial neglect a disturbance of attention.[72] It is important for the therapist to be familiar with this disorder as it is a frequent clinical finding following a right hemisphere stroke.[54]

2. Clinically, the patient ignores the left half of the body when dressing and forgets to put on the left sleeve or left pants leg. Often a male patient will forget to shave the left half of his face. A woman may neglect to put makeup on the left side of her face.[73] The patient may neglect to eat from the left half of a plate and will start reading a newspaper from the middle of the line. Typically, the patient bumps into objects on the left side or tends to veer towards the right when walking or propelling a wheelchair.

3. The lesion is located in the right nondominant hemisphere[64] in the parietooccipital association area.[24]

4. Assessment techniques: A variety of techniques will be presented because unilateral neglect may be manifested differently in individual patients, and no single task is adequate to identify the syndrome in all patients.

   a. The patient is asked to copy simple drawings of a house, a tree, a person, and/or a clock.[74] The drawings done by a patient with this deficit will have parts missing from the left half of the picture or be lacking in detail (Fig. 28–8). Differentiate these drawings from those likely to be produced by a patient suffering from constructional apraxia, in which most parts would be present but not in correct relation to each other. In addition, many patients with constructional apraxia (usually those with left-hemisphere damage) will improve when copying a model, but those with unilateral neglect (usually right-hemisphere damage) will not.

b. The patient is asked to read aloud. It should be noted if words are missed on the left half of the page or if there is hesitation at the beginning of a line.[75]

5. The purpose of therapy is to increase awareness of the left side of the body and space.

a. Restorative approach: Capitalizing on the rationale of the hemi-inattention theories, the following suggestions emerge. Use stimuli that are specialized for the right side of the brain, such as shapes and blocks, to enhance right brain activation. At the same time, minimize the presence of stimuli that are known to activate the left side of the brain, such as letters and numbers. Minimize the use of verbal instructions. Keep stimuli simple. Combine this with instructions to the patient to turn the head to the left, in order to anchor his or her attention to that side of space.[72]

b. Cognitive compensation (based on Weinberg and coworkers[76]): The patient is taught to be aware of the deficit through the method of visual scanning. This technique is used to help the patient become aware of the imbalance in perception of the two sides of space. The patient practices turning toward the left and shifting the eyes to the left (visual scanning). With experience, the patient will begin to

trust visual cues to guide action. For example, a patient does not shave properly on his left (affected) side. When asked to touch both sides of his face, or to look in the mirror, he will not notice that anything is amiss. However, after being trained to systematically scan the visual environment, starting with the left side of his face, the patient may notice the unshaven side in the mirror. At a later date, when asked to touch both sides of his face, he will confirm that one side is unshaven and take appropriate action.

A comprehensive and systematic training program for the treatment of right-brain-damaged patients, including the problem of left-sided neglect, has been developed over the past 15 years at the Department of Rehabilitation Medicine at New York University Medical Center in New York. For a detailed description of this program the reader is referred to Gordon and associates[73] and Weinberg and colleagues.[76,77]

c. Using the functional approach, repeated practice is used in particular areas of difficulty in ADLs, such as transferring from a wheelchair or eating. Visuospatial deficits may interfere extensively with performance of ADLs. Training in functional tasks in the hospital may not generalize to performance of the same functional skills at home, and may need to be learned anew.

The following steps are recommended by Stanton and associates:[78] Break down the activity into small components. Have the patient practice each one in sequence until a criterion level has been reached; then taper the cues. Finally, arrange the activity into larger components. Keeping ongoing records of progress will assist the therapist in guiding treatment appropriately. Encourage verbal self-cuing in verbally intact patients. It is worthwhile to refer to the aforementioned article for further details concerning the systematic implementation of therapeutic procedures.

d. Adapting the environment. The patient is addressed and given demonstrations from the unaffected side. The nursing staff should place the patient's call button, telephone, and other essential paraphernalia on the unaffected side. A bold red line may be drawn on the side of the page that is neglected.[79] A mirror may be placed in front of the patient while he or she is dressing or ambulating to draw attention to the neglected side.

e. Using the sensorimotor approach, the therapist stimulates the left side of the patient's body using a rough cloth, ice, or other material. The patient is reminded to watch what the therapist is doing. Next, the patient stimulates the affected side himself or herself while watching.[30]

f. In the transfer of training approach, the patient participates in tasks that make it necessary to look toward the affected side,[77] such as watching television. For example, the television can be placed initially at the midline and progressively moved toward the affected side. A brightly colored tape track may be placed along the floor and the patient

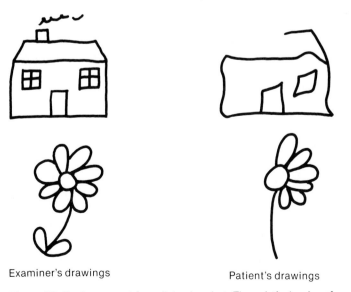

Examiner's drawings   Patient's drawings

Figure 28–8. Assessment for unilateral neglect. Therapist's drawing of a house and a flower (*Left*). Impaired copying by a patient with unilateral neglect following a stroke *(Right)*. (From Zoltan, Siev, and Freishtat,[1] p 61, with permission.)

may be instructed to walk or to guide the wheelchair along it.[1]

Right-Left Discrimination

1. A disorder in right-left discrimination is the inability to identify the right and left sides of one's own body or of that of the examiner.[65] This includes the inability to execute movements in response to verbal commands that include the terms "right" and "left." Patients are often unable to imitate movements.[65]
2. Clinically, the patient cannot tell the therapist which is the right arm and which is the left. The right shoe cannot be discerned from the left shoe, and the patient is unable to follow instructions using the concept of right-left, such as "turn right at the corner." The patient cannot discriminate the right from the left side of the therapist.
3. The lesion site is the parietal lobe of either hemisphere.[65] A close relationship between aphasia (usually owing to left hemisphere damage) and deficits in right-left discrimination has been reported. In nonaphasic patients (usually those with right hemisphere damage), a relationship has been reported between general mental impairment and right-left discrimination.[71]
4. The patient is asked to point to body parts upon command: right ear, left foot, right arm, and so forth.[7] Six responses should be elicited on the patient's own body, on that of the therapist, and on a model or picture of the human body.[71] To rule out somatagnosia, the patient should be tested first without the directional words.
5. Treatment techniques:
   a. In giving instructions to the patient the words "right" and "left" should be avoided. Instead, pointing or providing cues using distinguishing features of the limb are more effective (e.g., "the arm with the watch"). These guidelines are particularly salient for therapists teaching locomotion or transfers, where confusing instructions may have dangerous consequences.
   b. Adapt the environment. The right side of all common objects such as shoes and clothing should be marked with red tape or seam binding.[79]

Finger Agnosia

1. Finger agnosia can be defined as the inability to identify the fingers of one's own hands or of the hands of the examiner.[65] This includes difficulty in naming the fingers upon command, identifying which finger was touched, and, by some definitions, mimicking finger movements. This deficit usually occurs bilaterally and is more common on the middle three fingers.[80] Finger agnosia correlates highly with poor dexterity in tasks that require movements of individual fingers in relation to each other,[1] such as buttoning, tying laces, and typing.
2. Finger agnosia may be the result of a lesion located in either parietal lobe,[66] in the region of the angular gyrus, or in the supramarginal gyrus.[61] It is often found in conjunction with an aphasic disorder,[71] or with general mental impairment.[65,71] Bilateral finger

agnosia with right-left discrimination, agraphia, and acalculia is termed Gerstmann's syndrome.[65] Gerstmann's syndrome usually is associated with a focal lesion of the dominant hemisphere in the region of the angular gyrus.[59]

3. A portion of Sauguet's test assessment is recommended.
   a. The patient is asked to name the fingers touched by the therapist, with the eyes open (five times) and if successful, with vision occluded (five times).
   b. The patient is asked to point to the fingers named by the therapist on the patient's own hands (10 times), on the therapist's hands (10 times), and on a schematic model (10 times).
   c. The patient is asked to point to the equivalent finger on a life-sized picture when each finger is touched by the therapist (Fig. 28–9).
   d. The patient is asked to imitate finger movements; for example, curl the index finger, touch the thumb to the middle finger.
4. Treatment suggestions:
   a. To apply sensory integrative principles, the patient's discriminative tactile systems (touch and pressure) are stimulated. A rough cloth can be used to rub the dorsal surface of the affected arm, hand, and fingers, and the ventral surface of the affected fingers. Pressure can be applied to the ventral surface of the hand. For details, see Zoltan, Siev, and Freishtat.[1]
   b. To use the transfer of training approach, the patient is quizzed on finger identification.[1]

Anosognosia

1. **Anosognosia** is a severe condition including denial, neglect, and lack of awareness of the presence or severity of one's paralysis.[74,81,82] Presence of this disability may compromise rehabilitation potential greatly, because it limits the patient's ability to recognize the need for, and thus to use, compensation techniques.
2. Typically, the patient maintains that there is nothing wrong and may disown the paralyzed limbs and refuse to accept responsibility for them. The patient may claim that the limb has a mind of its own or that

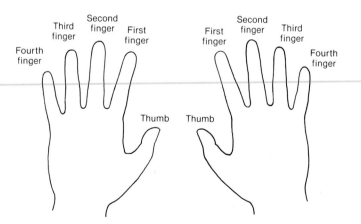

Figure 28–9. Hand chart for testing for finger agnosia (reduced from life size). (From Zoltan, Siev, and Freishtat,[1] p 68, with permission.)

it was left at home, or in a closet. It has been observed that patients suffering from anosognosia have a tendency to cover the paretic arm.[83]

3. The lesion is usually located in the nondominant parietal lobe,[61] in the region of the supramarginal gyrus.[59]

4. Anosognosia is assessed by talking to the patient. The patient is asked what happened to his arm or leg, whether he is paralyzed, how the limb feels, and why it cannot be moved. A patient with anosognosia may deny the paralysis, say that it is of no concern, and fabricate reasons why a limb does not move the way it should.

5. It is extremely difficult to compensate for this condition. Safety is of paramount importance in the treatment and discharge planning for patients suffering from anosognosia, because they typically do not acknowledge that they have a disability and will therefore refuse to be careful.[6]

SPATIAL RELATIONS DEFICITS

This group encompasses a constellation of deficits that have in common a difficulty in perceiving the relationship between objects in space or the relationship between the self and two or more objects.[1] Research suggests that the right parietal lobe has the primary role in space perception.[67] Thus a spatial relations deficit most frequently occurs in patients with right-sided lesions and resulting left hemiparesis.[61]

Spatial relations syndrome includes disorders of figure-ground discrimination, **form constancy,** spatial relations, **position in space,** and **topographical disorientation.** Additional visuospatial deficits, such as depth and distance perception, will be discussed in this section. **Constructional apraxia** and **dressing apraxia** are sometimes viewed as spatial relations problems.[1]

Figure-Ground Discrimination

1. A disorder in visual **figure-ground discrimination** is the inability to visually distinguish a figure from the background in which it is embedded. Functionally, it interferes with the patient's ability to locate important objects that are not prominent in a visual array. The patient has difficulty ignoring irrelevant visual stimuli and cannot select the appropriate cue to which to respond.[7] This may lead to distractibility, resulting in a shortened attention span,[60] frustration, and decreased independent and safe functioning.[11]

2. Clinically, the patient cannot locate items in a pocketbook or drawer, locate buttons on a shirt, or distinguish the armhole from the remainder of a solid colored shirt. The patient may not be able to tell when one step ends and another begins on a flight of stairs, especially when walking down.

3. The predominant lesion is generally in the nondominant parietal lobe[61] but may be located in any part of the brain.[44]

4. Assessment techniques:
   a. Ayres Figure Ground Test (subtest of the Southern California Sensory Integration Tests).[84] The subject must distinguish the three objects in an embedded test picture, from a possible selection of six items as in Figure 28–10. This test was standardized on children but may be useful as a clinical tool in identifying perceptual disorders in brain-damaged adults.[24] Normative data have been generated for normal adult males.[85]
   b. Functional tests. A white towel can be placed on a white sheet, and the patient is asked to find the towel. The patient can be asked to point out the sleeve, buttons, and collar of a white shirt, or to pick out a spoon from an unsorted array of eating utensils. It is necessary to rule out poor eyesight, hemianopsia, visual agnosia, and poor comprehension, to improve the validity of these assessment techniques.

5. Treatment techniques:
   a. Compensation through cognitive awareness. The patient is taught to become aware of the existence and nature of the deficit. The patient should be cautioned to examine groups of objects slowly and systematically and should be instructed to use other, intact senses (for example, touch) when searching for items such as clothing or silverware. When learning to lock a wheelchair, the patient should be advised to locate the brake levers by touch rather than by searching for them visually.
   b. Adaptation and simplification of the environment. Red tape may be placed over the Velcro strap of the shoe or orthosis to aid the patient in locating it.

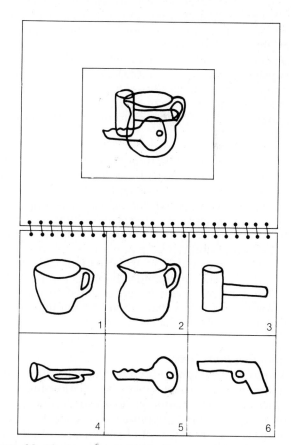

Figure 28–10. An example of the figure-ground perception test. (From Ayres,[84] Plate 2A, with permission.)

Few items should be placed in the patient's drawers or nightstand, and they should be replaced in the exact location each time. Brightly colored tape can be used to mark the edges on stairs.

c. With the functional approach, repeated practice is used in each specific area of difficulty. The same procedure should be employed during each practice session, incorporating verbal cues and touch as adjuncts to vision.

d. Using the transfer of training approach, the therapist should arrange for practice in visually locating objects in a simple array (such as three very different objects), and progress to more difficult ones (four or five dissimilar objects and three similar ones).

Form Constancy

1. Impairment in form constancy is the inability to perceive or to attend to subtle differences in form and shape. The patient is likely to confuse objects of similar shape or not to recognize an object placed in an unusual position.

2. Clinically, the patient may confuse a pen with a toothbrush, a vase with a water pitcher, a cane with a crutch, and so forth.

3. The lesion site is the parieto-temporo-occipital region (posterior association areas) of the nondominant lobe.[24]

4. Assessment techniques: A number of items similar in shape and different in size are gathered. The patient is asked to identify them. One set of items might be a pencil, pen, straw, toothbrush, watch, and the other might be a key, paper clip, coins, and a ring. Each object is presented several times in different positions (upside down, for example). Visual object agnosia must be ruled out as a cause for poor performance by first presenting objects separately and asking the patient to identify them or to demonstrate how they are used.

5. Treatment suggestions:

a. With the transfer of training approach, the patient should practice describing, identifying, and demonstrating the usage of similarly shaped and sized objects. The patient should sort like objects and should be assisted to focus on differentiating cues.

b. To achieve cognitive awareness and compensate for the disability, the patient must be made aware of the specific deficit. If the patient can read, frequently used and confused objects can be labeled. The patient should be encouraged to use vision, touch, and self-verbalization in combination when confused about objects.

Spatial Relations Deficit

1. A **spatial relations deficit**, or spatial disorientation, is the inability to perceive the relationship of one object in space to another object, or to oneself. This may lead to, or compound, problems in constructional tasks and dressing.[7] Crossing the midline may be a problem for patients with spatial relations deficits.[30]

2. Clinically, the patient might find it difficult to place the cutlery, plate, and spoon in the proper position when setting the table. The patient may be unable to tell the time from a clock because of difficulty in perceiving the relative positions of the hands, as illustrated in Figure 28–11. The patient may have difficulty learning to position his or her arms, legs, and trunk in relation to the wheelchair to prepare for transferring.

3. The lesion site is predominantly the nondominant parietal lobe.[24]

4. Assessment techniques:

a. The therapist draws a picture of a clock and then asks the patient to fill in the numbers and to draw in the hands to designate a particular time.[7] Responses indicative of impaired perception of spatial relations are illustrated in Figure 28–11. Patients with poor eye-hand coordination can be requested to place markers in the appropriate positions instead of drawing numbers.

b. Two or three objects (such as matchsticks or pencils) are placed on a piece of paper in a particular pattern. The patient is asked to duplicate the pattern.

c. To improve the validity of these assessments, unilateral neglect and hemianopsia should be ruled out as the causes of poor performance. If these are present, position the stimulus array appropriately.

5. Treatment suggestions:

a. Using the transfer of training approach to improve the ability to orient oneself to other objects, the patient can be given instructions on positioning himself or herself in relation to the therapist or another object; for example, "Sit next to me," "Go behind the table," "Step over the line." In addition, the therapist can set up a maze of furniture. Having the patient copy block or matchstick designs of increasing difficulty will increase awareness of the relationship between one object (block or matchstick) and the next.

b. With the sensorimotor approach, if the patient avoids crossing the midline, activities that require crossing the midline both motorically and visually can be incorporated into other therapeutic activities. One specific activity is to have the patient hold a dowel with both hands. The therapist guides it from the uninvolved side to the involved side. Later, the patient can progress to manipulating the dowel with only verbal or visual cues, and finally to guiding it independently.[30]

Figure 28–11. Responses to the draw-a-clock test, which may be indicative of defective perception of spatial relations. (From Pedretti,[7] p 109, with permission.)

Position in Space

1. A deficit in the perception of position in space is the inability to perceive and to interpret spatial concepts such as up, down, under, over, in, out, in front of, and behind.
2. Clinically, if a patient is asked to raise the arm "above" the head during a ROM assessment or is asked to place the feet "on" the footrests, the patient may behave as if he or she does not know what to do.
3. The lesion is located in the nondominant parietal lobe.[61]
4. Assessment techniques: To assess function, two objects are used, such as a shoe and a shoe box. The patient is asked to place the shoe in different positions in relation to the shoe box; for example, in the box, below the box, or next to the box. Alternatively, the patient is presented with two objects and asked to describe their relationship. For example, a toothbrush can be placed in a cup, under a cup, and so forth, and the patient is then asked to indicate the location of the toothbrush.

   Another mode of assessment is to have the patient copy the therapist's manipulations with an identical set of objects. For example, the therapist hands the patient a comb and a brush. The therapist then takes an identical set and places them in a particular relationship to each other, such as the comb on top of the brush. The patient is requested to arrange his or her comb and brush in the same way. Success in this task may represent sufficient ability to use position in space functionally.

   Figure-ground difficulty, apraxia, incoordination, and lack of comprehension should be ruled out when performing these assessments. Objects should be positioned to avoid compounding of results with hemianopsia and unilateral spatial neglect.
5. Treatment suggestions:
   a. To use the transfer of training approach, three or four identical objects are placed in the same orientation (wrist weights, combs, mugs, and so forth). An additional object is placed in a different orientation. The patient is asked to identify the odd one, and then to place it in the same orientation as the other objects.
   b. The sensorimotor approach used for treatment of spatial relations is similar to that used for treatment of disorders of position in space.

Topographic Disorientation

1. Topographic disorientation refers to difficulty in understanding and remembering the relationship of one location to another.[1] As a result, the patient is unable to get from one place to another, with or without a map.[70] This disorder is frequently seen in conjunction with other difficulties in spatial relations.[1]
2. Clinically, the patient cannot find the way from his or her room to the physical therapy clinic, despite being shown repeatedly. The patient cannot describe the spatial characteristics of familiar surroundings, such as the layout of his or her bedroom at home.[64]
3. The lesion site is the occipitoparietal lobe of the nondominant hemisphere.[19,62]

4. Assessment techniques: The patient is asked to describe or to draw a familiar route, such as the block on which he or she lives, the layout of his or her house, or a major neighborhood intersection.[64] The impaired patient will be unable to succeed in this task.
5. Treatment suggestions:
   a. Using the transfer of training approach, the patient practices going from one place to another, following verbal instructions. Initially, simple routes should be used, and then more complicated ones.[1]
   b. Using the functional approach, important routes in the hospital or in the patient's home are repeatedly practiced.
   c. Adapt the environment. Frequently traveled routes can be marked with colored dots. The spaces between the dots are gradually increased and eventually eliminated as improvement takes place.[1] This is an example of taking a normally right-hemisphere task and (because there is right-sided damage) converting it into a left-hemisphere task. In this instance we take the spatial task of remembering routes (right-hemisphere task) and substitute sequential landmarks (sequencing is typically a left-hemisphere strength) to accomplish the goal of getting from place to place.
   d. To reinforce cognitive awareness, the patient should be instructed not to leave the clinic, room, or home unattended, because he or she may get lost.

Additional Visuospatial Deficits

I. **Depth and distance perception.**
   A. The patient with deficits in these areas experiences inaccurate judgment of direction, distance, and depth. Spatial disorientation may be a contributing factor in faulty distance perception.
   B. Clinically, the patient may have difficulty navigating stairs, may miss the chair when attempting to sit, or may continue pouring juice once a glass is filled.[1,60]
   C. This may occur with a lesion in the right, nondominant hemisphere,[64] particularly in the occipital lobe.[24]
   D. Assessment techniques:
      1. For a functional assessment of distance perception, the patient is asked to take or to grasp an object that has been placed on a table. The object may be held in front of the patient, in the air, and the patient is again asked to grasp it. The impaired patient will overshoot or undershoot.[1]
      2. To assess depth perception functionally, the patient can be asked to fill a glass of water.[1] A patient with a depth perception deficit may continue pouring once the glass is filled.
   E. Treatment suggestions:
      1. Help the patient become aware of the deficit (cognitive awareness). Stress the importance of walking carefully on uneven surfaces, particularly the stairs.

2. With the transfer-of-training approach, the patient is requested to place the feet on designated spots during gait training.[30] Also, blocks can be arranged in piles 2 to 8 inches high. The patient is asked to touch the top of the piles with the foot. This is done to reestablish a sense of depth and distance.[30]

3. With the functional approach, practice in compensating for disturbances in depth and distance perception occurs intrinsically in many ADLs, both those involving moving through space and those that involve manipulation.

II. Vertical disorientation.

A. Vertical disorientation refers to a distorted perception of what is vertical. Displacement of the vertical position can contribute to disturbance of motor performance, both in posture and in gait. Early on in recovery most post-CVA patients demonstrate some impairment in the sense of verticality.[86] This is not influenced by the presence or absence of homonymous hemianopsia.[11] Scores on one test for visual perception of the vertical position were found to correlate with differences in walking ability.[50]

B. An example of the way in which a person with distorted verticality views the world and the way this may affect posture is depicted in Figure 28–12.

C. The lesion site is in the nondominant parietal lobe.

D. Assessment techniques: The therapist holds a cane vertically and then turns it sideways to a horizontal plane. The patient is handed the cane and asked to turn it back to the original position. If the patient's perception of the vertical position is distorted, the cane will most likely be placed at an angle, representing the patient's conception of the world around him- or herself.[19]

E. Treatment suggestions: The patient must be made aware of the disability. The patient should be instructed to compensate by using touch for proper self-orientation, especially when going through doorways, in elevators, and on the stairs.

AGNOSIA

Agnosia is the inability to recognize familiar objects using one or more of the sensory modalities, while often retaining the ability to recognize the same object using other sensory modalities.[59] All types of agnosia represent an impairment in the transmission of the sensory signal to the conceptual level.

Visual Object Agnosia

1. **Visual object agnosia** is the most common form of agnosia.[75] It is defined as the inability to recognize familiar objects despite normal function of the eyes and optic tracts.[87] One remarkable aspect of this disorder is the readiness with which the patient can identify an object once it is handled (i.e., information is received from another sensory modality).[75] Visual object agnosia may occur with or without hemianopsia.[59] The patient may not recognize people, possessions, and common objects. Specific types of visual agnosia are described below.

    Simultagnosia, also known as Balint's syndrome,[24] is the inability to perceive a visual stimulus as a whole. The patient perceives an entire array one part at a time. The lesion is in the dominant occipital lobe.[61]

    Prosopagnosia was traditionally considered to be the inability to recognize faces as being familiar. This phenomenon is now thought to be related to any visually ambiguous stimulus, the recognition of which depends on evoking a memory context, such as different species of birds or different makes of cars. Prosopagnosia is usually accompanied by visual field defects. Bilaterally symmetric occipital lesions are thought to be responsible for this deficit.[63]

    Color agnosia is the inability to recognize colors; it is not color blindness. The patient is unable to name colors or to identify them on command, although the ability to name objects is retained.[64] Color agnosia is frequently associated with facial or other visual object agnosias.[24,64] It is usually the result of a dominant hemisphere lesion.[62] The simultaneous occurrence of left-sided hemianopsia, alexia, and color agnosia is a classic occipital lobe syndrome.[62]

2. The lesions associated with visual object agnosias are thought to occur in the occipito-temporo-parietal association areas of either hemisphere; these areas are responsible for the integration of visual stimuli with respect to memory.[59] The exact nature of the disability may be determined by the laterality of the lesion.[61] Color agnosia frequently accompanies diffuse dementia.[62]

Degree of verticality

Figure 28–12. Vertical disorientation may contribute to disturbances of posture and gait. (From Tobis and Lowenthal,[9] p 37, with permission.)

3. To assess this disorder, several common objects are placed in front of the patient. The patient is asked to name the objects, to point to an object named by the therapist, or to demonstrate its usage. It is important to rule out aphasia and apraxia, although this is not easily done.
4. Treatment suggestions:
   a. Using the transfer of training approach, drills can be used to practice discrimination between faces that are important to the patient (using photographs), in discrimination between colors, and common objects. The therapist should assist the patient in picking out salient visual cues for relating names to faces.
   b. With compensation techniques, the patient is instructed to use intact sensory modalities such as touch or audition to distinguish people and objects.

Auditory Agnosia

1. Auditory agnosia refers to the inability to recognize nonspeech sounds or to discriminate between them. This rarely occurs in the absence of other communication disorders.[24]
2. The patient with auditory agnosia cannot tell, for example, the difference between the ring of a doorbell and that of a telephone, or between a dog barking and thunder.
3. The lesion is located in the dominant temporal lobe.[61]
4. Assessment techniques: Assessment is usually carried out by a speech therapist. The patient is asked to close the eyes and to identify the source of various sounds. The therapist rings a bell, honks a horn, rings a telephone, and so forth, and asks the patient to identify the sound (verbally or by pointing to a picture).
5. Treatment suggestions: Treatment generally consists of drilling the patient on sounds, but this has not been found to be particularly effective.[1]

Tactile Agnosia or Astereognosis

1. **Tactile agnosia,** or **astereognosis,** is the inability to recognize forms by handling them, although tactile, proprioceptive, and thermal sensations may be intact. This condition commonly causes difficulties in ADLs, inasmuch as many self-care activities that are normally done in the absence of constant visual monitoring require the manipulation of objects. If tactile agnosia is present in combination with unilateral neglect or sensory loss, performance in ADLs may be severely hampered.[11]
2. If a patient is handed an object (key, comb, safety pin) with vision occluded, the patient will fail to recognize it.
3. The lesion is in the parieto-temporo-occipital lobe (posterior association areas) of either hemisphere.[24]
4. Assessment techniques: The patient is asked to identify objects placed in the hand by examining them manually without visual cues.
5. Treatment suggestions:
   a. With the transfer of training approach, the patient practices feeling various common objects, shapes,

and textures with vision occluded. The patient is instructed to immediately look at the object for visual feedback and note special characteristics of the object.
   b. To achieve cognitive awareness, the patient is made aware of the deficit and is instructed in visual compensation.

APRAXIA

Apraxia is a disorder of voluntary learned movement. It is characterized by an inability to perform purposeful movements, which cannot be accounted for by inadequate strength, loss of coordination,[88] impaired sensation,[6,59] attentional difficulties,[89] abnormal tone, movement disorders, intellectual deterioration, poor comprehension, or uncooperativeness.[90] The patient is unable to accomplish the task even though the instructions are understood.[59,90] Many patients with apraxia also present with aphasia, and the two disorders are sometimes difficult to distinguish.[90]

Ideomotor and **ideational apraxias** are generally thought to be the result of dominant hemisphere lesions and may be particularly difficult to assess in the patient with aphasia. Although aphasia and apraxia often occur together, there is not a strong correlation between the severity of the aphasia and the severity of the apraxia. Apraxia is a disorder of skilled movement and not a language disorder.[90] Dressing apraxia and constructional apraxia occur with lesions in either hemisphere.

Ideomotor Apraxia

1. Ideomotor apraxia refers to a breakdown between concept and performance.[6] There is a disconnection between the idea of a movement and its motor execution. It appears that information cannot be transferred from the areas of the brain that conceptualize to the centers for motor execution. Thus the patient with ideomotor apraxia is able to carry out habitual tasks automatically and describe how they are done but is unable to perform a task upon command and is unable to imitate gestures.[5] Patients with this form of apraxia often perseverate;[59] that is, they repeat an activity or a segment of a task over and over, even if it is no longer necessary or appropriate. This makes it difficult for them to finish one task and then to go on to the next.[6] Patients with ideomotor apraxia appear most handicapped when requested to perform tasks that require use of many implements and that have many steps. This form of apraxia can be demonstrated separately in the facial areas, upper extremity, lower extremity, and for total body movements.[88] Patients with apraxia are often observed to be clumsy in their actual handling of objects.[89] Impairment is often suspected when observing the patient in ADLs or during a routine motor assessment.
2. Several examples of ideomotor apraxia follow: The patient is unable to ''blow'' on command. However, if presented with a bubble wand, the patient will spontaneously blow bubbles. The patient may fail to walk if requested to in the traditional manner. However, if a cup of coffee is placed on a table at the other end of the room and the patient is told, ''Please have some

coffee," the patient is likely to traverse the room to get it.[5]

A male patient is asked to comb his hair. He may be able to identify the comb and even tell you what it is used for; however, he will not actually use the comb appropriately when it is handed to him. Despite this observation in the clinic, his wife reports that he combs his hair spontaneously every morning.

A female patient is asked to squeeze a dynamometer. She appears not to know what to do with it, although her comprehension is adequate, the task has just been demonstrated, and it is clear that she has adequate strength.

3. The lesion is generally found in the dominant supramarginal gyrus.[59,68]

4. Assessment techniques:
   a. The Goodglass and Kaplan[88] test for apraxia is comprised of universally known movements, such as blowing, brushing teeth, hammering, shaving, and so forth. It is based on what the authors consider a hierarchy of difficulty for patients with apraxia. First the patient is told, "Show me how you would bang a nail with a hammer." If the patient fails to do this or uses his or her fist as if it were a hammer, the patient is asked, "Pretend to hold the hammer." If the patient fails following this instruction, the therapist demonstrates the act and asks the patient to imitate it. The patient with apraxia typically will not improve after demonstration but will improve with use of the actual implements.[90] Ability to correct oneself on following verbal suggestions is considered to be counterindicative of apraxia.
   b. The therapist sits opposite the patient. The patient is asked to imitate different postures or limb movements.[84] The patient with apraxia is unable to imitate postures.
      Additional apraxia tests may be found in *Clinical Neurophysiology* by Heilman and Roth.[90]

5. Treatment suggestions:
   a. Anderson and Choy[30] suggest the modification of instructional sets as follows: Speak slowly and use the shortest possible sentences. One command should be given at a time, and the second command should not be given until the first task is completed. When teaching a new task, it should be broken down into its component parts. One component is taught at a time, physically guiding the patient through the task if necessary. It should be completed in precisely the same manner each time. When all the individual units are mastered, an attempt to combine them should be made. A great deal of repetition may be necessary.[11] Family members must be advised to use the exact approach found to be successful in the clinic. Performing activities in as normal an environment as possible is also helpful.
   b. Using the sensorimotor approach, multiple sensory inputs are used on the affected body parts in order to enhance the production of appropriate motor responses.[91] The reader is referred to the work of Okoye[91] for additional details on this approach.

Ideational Apraxia

1. Ideational apraxia is a failure in the conceptualization of the task.[6] It is an inability to perform a purposeful motor act, either automatically or on command, because the patient no longer understands the overall concept of the act,[11] cannot retain the idea of the task,[59] and cannot formulate the motor patterns required.[6] Often the patient can perform isolated components of a task but cannot combine them into a complete act. Furthermore, the patient cannot verbally describe the process of performing an activity, describe the function of objects, or use them appropriately.

   Sharpless[6] claims that ideational apraxia is an unusual complication of stroke and is often present concomitantly with agnosias.

2. Ideational apraxia is typified by the following behavior: When presented in the clinic with a toothbrush and toothpaste and told to brush the teeth, the patient may put the tube of toothpaste in the mouth, or try to put toothpaste on the toothbrush without removing the cap. Furthermore, the patient may be unable to describe verbally how toothbrushing is done. Similar phenomena may be evident in all aspects of ADL (washing, meal preparation, and so forth) and so may limit the safety and potential independence of the patient.[11] It has been shown that patients with ideational apraxia test poorly in the clinical situation and appear more able to perform ADLs at the appropriate time and in a familiar setting.[91]

3. The lesion causing ideational apraxia is thought to be in the dominant parietal lobe.[61] This deficit also may be seen in conjunction with diffuse brain damage, such as cerebral arteriosclerosis.[59,61]

4. Assessment techniques:
   a. The tests for ideational apraxia are essentially the same as those for ideomotor apraxia. The major difference to be expected in response is that the patient with ideomotor apraxia can perform a motor act spontaneously and automatically at the appropriate time, but the patient with ideational apraxia is unable to do so.

5. Treatment suggestions: The treatment techniques used are the same as those for ideomotor apraxia.

Constructional Apraxia

1. Constructional apraxia is characterized by faulty spatial analysis and conceptualization of the task.[6] Normal constructional skills encompass the capacity to understand the relationship of parts to a whole.[65] This ability is critical in activities such as drawing, dressing, building from a model, copying block designs, and the like. Performance of these complex tasks requires a combination of visual perception, motor planning, and motor performance.[38]

   Thus, constructional apraxia is most evident in the inability to produce two- or three-dimensional forms by drawing, constructing, or arranging blocks or objects spontaneously or upon command.[92] It hampers the patient's ability to manipulate the environment effectively because of an inability to construct things from component parts. Although able to understand and to identify the individual components, the patient cannot place them into a correct, meaningful relationship.[6]

This deficit is found in patients with lesions to either hemisphere, but upon testing there is a difference in the quality of their responses.[69,93] Patients with right-sided lesions appear to be more severely affected than those with left brain involvement.[93] They clearly lack the visuospatial ability to succeed in a task. Additionally, they lack perspective, are unable to place a figure in the appropriate position in space, and seem unable to analyze parts in relationship to each other.[93,94]

Patients with left-hemisphere damage seem to lack the analytic or planning ability necessary to initiate and perform movements in sequence to complete a constructional task. In a study by McFie and Zangwill,[69] the left-lesioned group (in contrast to the right-lesioned group) rarely presented with unilateral neglect or topographic disorientation but often demonstrated an impairment in constructional tasks in conjunction with general intellectual impairment.

The presence of constructional apraxia is thought to be related to body scheme disorders, and often results in difficulty in dressing and diminished performance in other ADL skills.[95,96]

2. Constructional apraxia is demonstrated, for example, by a patient who understands all about sandwiches and what they are for but is unable to assemble one, even with all ingredients laid out in front of them.

3. Lesions are located in the posterior parietal lobe of either hemisphere.[69] Constructional apraxia is more common and more severe in patients with right-hemisphere lesions. Right-sided lesions that result in constructional apraxia tend to be less diffuse than left-sided lesions.[93]

4. Assessment techniques:
   a. The patient is asked to copy a drawing of a house, a flower, or a clock face. Figure 28–13 depicts typical drawings of a house done by patients with left- and right-hemisphere lesions, respectively.
   b. The patient is requested to copy geometric designs (e.g., circle, square, or T shape).
   c. The patient is instructed to copy block bridges, matchstick designs, or pegboard configurations.

A Left hemisphere lesion   B Right hemisphere lesion

Figure 28–13. Impaired responses to the draw-a-house test for constructional apraxia. Note the differences in response between the patient with a left hemisphere lesion (*A*) compared with a right (*B*) hemisphere lesion. (From Zoltan, Siev, and Freishtat,[1] p 39, with permission.)

Initially only three pieces are used and a progression is made to use more.

Visuoconstructive difficulties found with right- and left-sided lesions demonstrate qualitative differences, as described above. In response to the assessment materials, patients with right-sided damage tend to draw on the diagonal and neglect the left side of the page.[93] They draw pieces of the picture without any coherent relationship to each other. Thus their drawings tend to be complex, yet unrecognizable.[69] They have immense difficulty with copying or constructing anything in three dimensions, are not helped by the presence of a model or by landmarks in a picture, and do not generally improve with practice.[94]

In contrast, the drawings of patients with left-hemisphere damage are usually more recognizable.[93] They are characterized by great simplicity.[69] Patients with left-side lesions draw slowly and hesitatingly,[69] are often unable to draw angles, and have general difficulty in execution.[97] In contrast to that of right-hemisphere stroke victims, their performance often improves with the aid of a model,[93] the use of landmarks in drawing, and with repeated trials.[94] Short-term visual memory impairment is thought to be associated with constructional apraxia in patients with right-sided lesions.[67] The reader is encouraged to consult Warrington and coworkers,[67,92] who provide a comprehensive review of constructional apraxia, including many examples of the drawings of patients with right and left hemiplegia.

Verbal and comprehension difficulties, poor manual dexterity, and the presence of homonymous hemianopsia must be ruled out during assessment for this disorder.

5. With the transfer of training approach, the patient is asked to practice copying geometric designs, both by drawing and by building. Initially, simple patterns are used, progressing to the more complex.[1] Patients with left-hemisphere lesions may benefit from the use of landmarks, and then their gradual withdrawal as skill improves.[94] The remedial approach has been criticized by Niestadt[38] for its use of pediatric materials, an underlying assumption that the sequence of recovery from brain injury follows the sequence of normal child development, and the use of treatment materials that closely resemble evaluation tools.

Dressing Apraxia

1. Dressing apraxia is the inability to dress oneself properly owing to a disorder in body scheme or spatial relations[24] rather than difficulty in motor performance or incoordination.

2. For example, the patient puts on clothes upside down, inside out, or backward; does not align buttons properly; puts both legs into one pant leg; neglects to dress one side of the body. Geometric patterns may add to the confusion.[6]

3. The lesion site is the nondominant occipital or parietal lobe.[61]

4. Assessment techniques: Clinical observation is the most effective method of assessment. The patient should be asked to dress and to undress. The patient is observed for the problems described above.

Because dressing apraxia and constructional apraxia exhibit a high degree of correlation, tests for constructional apraxia are sometimes performed.[95,96]

5. Treatment suggestions: Using the functional approach, the therapist develops a set sequence and pattern for dressing and has the patient practice the exact same routine daily. A key to successful performance is proper positioning of garments. One suggestion, for example, is to have the patient drape his or her shirt or blouse over the back of a chair and slide into it. Other guides are to start always from the bottom button, to mark the right side of all garments and shoes, and to color code the inside and the outside of garments.

SUMMARY

Perception—the process by which an individual selects, integrates, and interprets stimuli from the body and surrounding environment—is critical to the normal functioning of each human being. The patient with brain damage may be lacking in those abilities that allow one to make sense of and to respond appropriately to the outside world. It is essential for the physical therapist to be able to recognize when a patient is suffering from some type of perceptual dysfunction and to have the requisite tools to understand the causes of the behavior.

This chapter has attempted to provide an overview of perceptual dysfunctions that may occur following brain damage, particularly that resulting from a stroke, and how such dysfunctions can affect the functioning of the patient, especially within the context of the rehabilitation setting. The importance of differentiating perceptual dysfunction from problems related to lack of motor ability, inadequate sensation, poor language skills, and simple uncooperativeness has been emphasized. Treatment in the form of adaptation of the physical environment and instructional sets and the teaching of compensatory techniques has been singled out as the most effective avenue for intervention. Although alluded to in a very abbreviated fashion, activity analysis and systematic data collection remain two of the most powerful tools at the disposal of the therapist attempting to develop a firm rationale for, and empirically to justify the efficacy of any treatment regimen selected.

QUESTIONS FOR REVIEW

1. Describe the relationship between sensation and perception. How does perceptual impairment interfere with rehabilitation?

2. Differentiate between the roles of the occupational therapist and the physical therapist in the treatment of perceptual dysfunction following stroke.

3. What behaviors should prompt the therapist to suspect that a patient may have perceptual difficulties?

4. How does the hospital setting compound the difficulties faced by the patient who is attempting to make sense out of the environment following a stroke?

5. Describe some of the psychologic and emotional consequences of stroke that may affect the patient's performance during assessment and treatment sessions.

6. What behaviors are found following frontal lobe damage that may interfere with the ability to participate in rehabilitation?

7. Describe three stages of memory and assessment methods for each.

8. Explain how attentional deficits and distractibility interfere with task performance. Under what circumstances would patients with left hemiplegia typically appear more handicapped? Under what circumstances would patients with right hemiplegia appear more handicapped? Suggest appropriate cues to facilitate improved performance.

9. Describe and differentiate between the two components of feedback: KR and KP. How should feedback for patients with right hemiplegia differ from that for patients with left hemiplegia?

10. Describe the theories underlying the transfer of training, the sensory integrative, the neurodevelopmental, and the functional approaches to the treatment of individuals with perceptual deficits. Define and give clinical examples of compensation, adaptation, and cognitive awareness.

11. Define task analysis. Describe how this technique can be used to improve therapy.

12. Define and diagram homonymous hemianopsia. Give examples of how this disorder can interfere with the patient's success in ADL and therapeutic tasks. Describe ways in which the physical therapist can assist the patient to compensate.

13. Define body scheme and body image. Enumerate and describe five disorders that can be grouped in this category. Are they commonly found in patients with right or left hemiplegia?

14. Describe unilateral neglect. Give clinical examples of its manifestation. Describe how this disorder is assessed, and how it is differentiated from homonymous hemianopsia and constructional apraxia. Describe how the physical therapist can structure treatment sessions to help the patient compensate for this disability.

15. What is anosognosia? Why are safety considerations of paramount importance in dealing with the patient with anosognosia?

16. Describe spatial relations syndrome. Does it usually occur in patients with right hemiplegia or left hemiplegia? Describe disorders in figure-ground discrimination, form constancy, spatial relations, and position-in-space and topographic disorientation. Give a clinical example of each.

17. Describe how the physical therapist might structure assessment and treatment sessions to facilitate suc-

cessful participation of the patient with deficits in spatial relations and position in space.

18. Describe how faulty depth and distance perception and vertical disorientation affect ambulation, posture, and participation in other ADLs. How can the physical therapist assist in the remediation of these conditions?

19. Define agnosia. Differentiate between the agnosias affecting vision, audition, and touch.

20. Differentiate between ideomotor and ideational apraxias, and offer clinical examples for each. Describe how the therapist can modify instructional sets to facilitate more successful participation of the patient in various tasks.

21. Define constructional apraxia and give clinical examples. Describe how patients with right versus left hemiplegia respond differently to drawing tasks.

REFERENCES

1. Zoltan, B, Siev, E, and Freishtat, B: The Adult Stroke Patient: A Manual for Evaluation and Treatment of Perceptual and Cognitive Dysfunction, ed 2 rev. Charles B Slack, Thorofare, NJ, 1986.
2. Abreu, BC and Toglia, JP: Cognitive rehabilitation: a model for occupational therapy. Am J Occup Ther 41:439, 1987.
3. Katz, N, et al: Lowenstein Occupational Therapy Cognitive Assessment (LOTCA) battery for brain injured patients: reliability and validity. Am J Occup Ther 43:184, 1989.
4. Toglia, JP: Generalization of treatment: a multicontext approach to cognitive perceptual impairment in adults with brain injury. Am J Occup Ther 45:505, 1991
5. Johnstone, M: Restoration of Motor Function in the Stroke Patient, ed 2. Churchill Livingstone, New York, 1983.
6. Sharpless, JW: Mossman's A Problem Oriented Approach to Stroke Rehabilitation, ed 2. Charles C Thomas, Springfield, IL, 1982.
7. Pedretti, LW: Evaluation of sensation, perception and cognition. In Pedretti, LW and Zoltan, B (eds): Occupational Therapy: Practice Skills for Physical Dysfunction, ed 3. CV Mosby, St Louis, 1990.
8. Spencer, EA: Functional restoration. In Hopkins, HL and Smith, HD (eds): Willard and Spackman's Occupational Therapy, ed 8. JB Lippincott, Philadelphia, 1993.
9. Tobis, JS and Lowenthal, M: Evaluation and Management of the Brain-Damaged Patient. Charles C Thomas, Springfield, IL, 1960.
10. Lehmann, JF, et al: Stroke rehabilitation: outcome and prediction. Arch Phys Med Rehab 56:383–389, 1975.
11. Wall, N: Stroke rehabilitation. In Logigian, MK (ed): Adult Rehabilitation: A Team Approach for Therapists. Little, Brown, Boston, 1982, p 225.
12. Carr, JH and Shepherd, RB. A Motor Relearning Programme for Stroke. Heineman Physiotherapy, London, 1987.
13. Adams, GF: Capacity after stroke. Br Med J 1:91, 1973.
14. Luria, AR: Higher Cortical Functions in Man. Basic Books, New York, 1966.
15. Moore, J: Neuroanatomical considerations relating to recovery of function following brain injury. In Bach-y-Rita, P (ed): Recovery of Function: Theoretical Considerations for Brain Injury Rehabilitation. University Park Press, Baltimore, 1980, p 9.
16. Bach-y-Rita, P: Brain plasticity as a basis for therapeutic procedures. In Bach-y-Rita, P (ed): Recovery of Function: Theoretical Considerations for Brain Injury Rehabilitation. University Park Press, Baltimore, 1980, p 225.
17. Brodal, A: Self-observations and neuroanatomical considerations after a stroke. Brain 76:675, 1973.
18. Gardner, H: The Shattered Mind: The Person After Brain Damage. Alfred A Knopf, New York, 1975.
19. Jones, M: Approach to Occupational Therapy, ed 3. Butterworths, London, 1977.
20. Titus, MND, et al: Correlation of perceptual performance and activities of daily living in stroke patients. Am J Occup Ther 45:410, 1991.
21. Sahs, AL, Hanman, EC, and Aronson, SM (eds): Guidelines for Stroke Care. DHEW Pub (HRA) 76-14017. US Department of Health, Education, and Welfare, Washington, DC, 1976.
22. Galski, T, et al: Driving after cerebral damage: a model with implications for evaluation. Am J Occup Ther 46:324, 1992.
23. Diller, L and Weinberg, J: Evidence for accident prone behavior in hemiplegic patients. Arch Phys Med Rehabil 51:358, 1970.
24. Lezak, MD: Neuropsychological Assessment, ed 2. Oxford University Press, New York, 1983.
25. Abreu, BC and Hinojosa, J: The process approach for cognitive-perceptual and postural control dysfunction for adults with brain injuries. In Katz, N (ed): Cognitive Rehabilitation: Models for Intervention in Occupational Therapy. Andover Medical, Boston, 1992.
26. Strub, RL and Black, FW: The Mental Status Examination in Neurology, ed 2. FA Davis, Philadelphia, 1985.
27. Kupferman, I: Learning and memory. In Kandel, ER, Schwartz, JH, and Jessel, TM (eds): Principles of Neuroscience, ed 3. Elsevier, New York, 1991, p 996.
28. Diller, L and Weinberg, J: Differential aspects of attention in brain-damaged persons. Perceptual and Motor Skills 35:71, 1972.
29. Abreu, BC: Interdisciplinary approach to the adult visual perceptual function-dysfunction continuum. In Abreu, BC (ed): Physical Disabilities Manual. Raven Press, New York, 1981, p 151.
30. Anderson, E and Choy, E: Parietal lobe syndromes in hemiplegia: a program for treatment. Am J Occup Ther 24:13, 1970.
31. Toglia, J and Abreu, BC: Cognitive Rehabilitation. Supplement to Workshop: Management of Cognitive-Perceptual Dysfunction in the Brain-Damaged Adult. Sponsored by Braintree Hospital, Braintree, MA, and Cognitive Rehabilitation Associates, New York, NY, May, 1987.
32. Harlowe, D and Deusen, JV: Construct validation of the St. Marys CVA evaluation: perceptual measures. Am J Occup Ther 38:184, 1984.
33. Van Deusen, J and Harlowe, D: Continued construct validation of the St. Marys CVA evaluation: Brunnstrom arm and hand stage ratings. Am J Occup Ther 40:561, 1986.
34. Van Deusen, J and Harlowe, D: Continued construct validation of the St. Marys CVA evaluation: bilateral awareness scale. Am J Occup Ther 41:242, 1987.
35. Boys, M, et al: The OSOT Perceptual Evaluation: A research perspective. Am J Occup Ther 42:92, 1988.
36. Gentile, AM: A working model of skill acquisition with special reference to teaching. Quest Monograph 17:61, 1972.
37. Neistadt, ME: Occupational therapy treatment for constructional deficits. Am J Occup Ther 46:141, 1992.
38. Neistadt, ME: A critical analysis of occupational therapy approaches for perceptual deficits in adults with brain injury. Am J Occup Ther 44:299, 1990.
39. Neistadt, ME: Occupational therapy for adults with perceptual deficits. Am J Occup Ther 42:434, 1988.
40. Jongbloed, L, Stacey S, and Brighton, C: Stroke rehabilitation: sensory integrative treatment versus functional treatment. Am J Occup Ther 43:391, 1989.
41. Diller, L, Ben-Yishay, Y, and Gerstman, L: Rehabilitation, Monograph 50: Studies in cognition and rehabilitation in hemiplegia. New York University Medical Center, New York, 1974.
42. Young, GC, Collins, D, and Hren, M: Efficacy of pairing scanning training with block design training in the remediation of perceptual problems in left hemiplegics. J Clin Neuropsychol 42:312, 1983.
43. Fisher AG, Murray, EA, and Bundy, AC: Sensory Integration: Theory and Practice. FA Davis, Philadelphia, 1991.
44. Ayres, JA: Sensory Integration and Learning Disorders. Western Psychological Services, Los Angeles, 1972.
45. Ayres, JA: Sensory Integration and the Child. Western Psychological Services, Los Angeles, 1980.
46. Finger, S and Stein, DG: Brain Damage and Recovery: Research and Clinical Perspectives. Academic Press, New York, 1982.
47. Laurence, S and Stein, DG: Recovery after brain damage and the concept of localization of function. In Finger, S (ed): Recovery

from Brain Damage: Research and Theory. Plenum Press, New York, 1978, p 369.

48. Giantusos, R: What is cognitive rehabilitation? J Rehabil 46:36, 1980.

49. Diller, L and Gordon, WA: Intervention strategies for cognitive deficits in brain-injured adults. J Consult Clin Psychol 49:822, 1981.

50. Van Ravensberg, CD, et al: Visual perception in hemiplegic patients. Arch Phys Med Rehabil 65:304, 1984.

51. Toglia, JP: A dynamic interactional approach to cognitive rehabilitation. In Katz, N (ed): Cognitive Rehabilitation: Models for Intervention in Occupational Therapy. Andover Medical, Boston, 1992.

52. Warren, M: A hierarchical model for evaluation and treatment of visual perceptual dysfunction in adult acquired brain injury, I. Am J Occup Ther 47:42, 1993.

53. Warren, M: A hierarchical model for evaluation and treatment of visual perceptual dysfunction in adult acquired brain injury, II. Am J Occup Ther 47:55, 1993.

54. Hier, DB, Mondlock, J, and Caplan, LR: Behavioral abnormalities after right hemisphere stroke. Neurology 33:337, 1983.

55. Kertesz, A and Dobrowolski, S: Right hemisphere deficits: lesion size and location. J Clin Neuropsychol 3:283, 1981.

56. Hier, DB, Mondlock, J, and Caplan, LR: Recovery of behavioral abnormalities after right hemisphere stroke. Neurology 33:345, 1983.

57. Haerer, AF: Visual field defects and the prognosis of stroke patients. Stroke 4:163, 1977.

58. Feigenson, JS, et al: Factors influencing outcome and length of stay in a stroke rehabilitation unit, I. Stroke 8:651, 1977.

59. Chusid, JG: Correlative Neuroanatomy and Functional Neurology, ed 19. Lange Medical Publications, Los Altos, CA, 1985.

60. Halperin, E and Cohen, BS: Perceptual-motor dysfunction. Stumbling block to rehabilitation. Md Med J 20:139, 1971.

61. McFie, J: The diagnostic significance of disorders of higher nervous activity. In Vinken, PJ and Bruyn, GW (eds): Handbook of Clinical Neurology, vol 4. Disorders of Speech, Perception, and Symbolic Behavior. American Elsevier, New York, 1969, p 1.

62. Hecaen, H: Aphasic, apraxic, and agnostic syndromes. In Vinken, PJ and Bruyn, GW (eds): Handbook of Clinical Neurology, vol 4. Disorders of Speech, Perception, and Symbolic Behavior. American Elsevier, New York, 1969.

63. Damasio, AR, Damasio, HD, van Hoesen, GW: Prosopagnosia: anatomical basis and behavioral mechanism. Neurology 32:331, 1982.

64. Benton, A: Visuoperceptual, visuospatial, and visuoconstructive disorders. In Heilman, KM and Valenstein, E (eds): Clinical Neuropsychology, ed 2. Oxford University Press, New York, 1985.

65. Benton, A: Body scheme disturbances: finger agnosia and right-left discrimination. In Heilman, KM and Valenstein, E (eds): Clinical Neuropsychology, ed 2. Oxford University Press, New York, 1985, p 115.

66. Gainotti, G: Emotional behaviour and hemispheric side of the lesion. Cortex 8:41, 1972.

67. Warrington, EK and James, M: Disorders in visual perception in patients with localized cerebral lesions. Neuropsychologia 5:253, 1967.

68. Hecaen, H and Sauguet, J: Cerebral dominance in left-handed subjects. Cortex 7:19, 1971.

69. McFie, J and Zangwill, OL: Visual-constructive disabilities associated with lesions of the left cerebral hemisphere. Brain 83:243, 1960.

70. Macdonald, J: An investigation of body scheme in adults with cerebral vascular accident. Am J Occup Ther 14:72, 1960.

71. Sauguet, J, Benton, AL, and Hecaen, H: Disturbances of the body scheme in relation to language impairment and hemispheric locus of lesion. J Neurol Neurosurg Psychiatry 34:496, 1971.

72. Herman, EWM: Spatial neglect: new issues and their implications for occupational therapy practice. Am J Occup Ther 46:207, 1992.

73. Gordon, WA, et al: Perceptual remediation in patients with right brain damage: a comprehensive program. Arch Phys Med Rehabil 66:353, 1985.

74. Gregory, ME and Aitkin, JA: Assessment of parietal lobe function in hemiplegia. Occup Ther 34:9, 1971.

75. Wode, DT, et al: Stroke: A Critical Approach to Diagnosis, Treatment, and Management. Yearbook Medical, Chicago, 1986.

76. Weinberg, J, et al: Training sensory awareness and spatial organization in people with right brain damage. Arch Phys Med Rehabil 60:491, 1979.

77. Weinberg, J, et al: Visual scanning training effect in reading-related tasks in acquired right brain damage. Arch Phys Med Rehab 58:479, 1977.

78. Stanton, KM, et al: Wheelchair transfer training for right cerebral dysfunctions: an interdisciplinary approach. Arch Phys Med Rehabil 64:276, 1983.

79. Burt, MM: Perceptual deficits in hemiplegia. Am J Nurs 70:1026, 1970.

80. Hecaen, H, et al: The syndrome of apractagnosia due to lesions of the minor cerebral hemisphere. Arch Neurol Psychiatry 75:400, 1956.

81. Friedlander, WJ: Anosognosia and perception. Am J Phys Med 46:1394, 1967.

82. Ullman, M: Disorders of body image after stroke. Am J Nursing 64:89, 1964.

83. Zankie, HT: Stroke Rehabilitation. Charles C Thomas, Springfield, IL, 1971.

84. Ayres, JA: Southern California Sensory Integration Tests. Western Psychological Services, Los Angeles, 1972.

85. Peterson, P and Wikoff, RL: The performance of adult males on the Southern California figure-ground visual perception test. Am J Occup Ther 37:554, 1983.

86. Anderson, TP: Rehabilitation of patients with a completed stroke. In Kottke, FJ and Ellwood, PM (eds): Krusen's Handbook of Physical Medicine and Rehabilitation, ed 4. WB Saunders, Philadelphia, 1990, p 666.

87. Dicmonas, E: Sensory system structure and function. In Abreu, BC (ed): Physical Disabilities Manual. Raven Press, New York, 1981.

88. Goodglass, H and Kaplan, E: The Assessment of Aphasia and Related Disorders, ed 2. Lea & Febiger, Philadelphia, 1983.

89. Geschwind, N: The apraxias: neural mechanisms of disorders of learned movement. American Scientist 63:188, 1975.

90. Heilman, KM and Rothi, LJG: Apraxia. In Heilman, KM and Valenstein, E (eds): Clinical Neuropsychology. Oxford University Press, ed 2, New York, 1985, p 131.

91. Okoye, R: The apraxias. In Abreu, BC (ed): Physical Disabilities Manual. Raven Press, New York, 1981, p 241.

92. Warrington, EK: Constructional apraxia. In Vinken, PJ and Bruyn, GW (eds): Handbook of Clinical Neurology, vol 4. Disorders of Speech, Perception, and Symbolic Behavior. American Elsevier, New York, 1969, p 67.

93. Piercy, M, Hecaen, H, and de Ajuriaguerra, J: Constructional apraxia associated with unilateral cerebral lesions—left and right sided cases compared. Brain 83:225 1960.

94. Hecaen, H and Assal, G: A comparison of constructive deficits following right and left hemisphere lesions. Neuropsychologia 8:289, 1970.

95. Lorenze, EJ and Cranco, R: Dysfunction in visual perception with hemiplegia—its relation to activities of daily living. Arch Phys Med Rehabil 43:514, 1962.

96. Williams, N: Correlation between copying ability and dressing activities in hemiplegia. Am J Phys Med 46:1332, 1967.

97. Gainotti, G and Taicci, G: Patterns of drawing ability in right and left hemisphere patients. Neuropsychologia 8:379, 1970.

SUPPLEMENTAL READINGS

Carter, LT, et al: The relationship of cognitive skills performance to activities of daily living in stroke patients. Am J Occup Ther 42:449, 1988.

Cohen, H (ed): Neuroscience for Rehabilitation. JB Lippincott, Philadelphia, 1993.

Finger S, et al: Brain Injury and Recovery: Theoretical and Controversial Issues. Plenum Press, New York, 1988.

Goldstein, G and Ruthven, L: Rehabilitation of the Brain-Damaged Adult. Plenum Press, New York, 1983.

Kandel, ER, Schwartz, JH, and Jessell, TM (eds): Principles of Neuroscience, ed 3. Elsevier, New York, 1991.

Kovitch, KM and Bermann, DE: Head Injury: A Guide to Functional Outcomes in Occupational Therapy. Aspen, Rockville, MD, 1988.

Malkmus, D: Integrating cognitive strategies into the physical therapy setting. Phys Ther 63:1952, 1983.

Rosenthal, M, et al: Rehabilitation of the Adult and Child with Traumatic Brain Injury, ed 2. FA Davis, Philadelphia, 1990.

Sabari, JS: Motor learning concepts applied to activity based interventions with adults with hemiplegia. Am J Occup Ther 45:523, 1991.

Sacks, O: The Man Who Mistook His Wife for a Hat. Harper & Row, New York, 1985.

Smith, GW: Care of the Patient with a Stroke: A Handbook for the Patient's Family and the Nurse, ed 2. Singer, New York, 1976.

Toglia, JP: Visual perception of objects: an approach to assessment and intervention. Am J Occup Ther 43:587, 1989.

Umphred, DA (ed): Neurological Rehabilitation, ed 2. CV Mosby, St. Louis, 1990.

Van Deusen, J: Unilateral neglect: suggestions for research by occupational therapists. Am J Occup Ther 42:391 1988.

GLOSSARY

Adaptation: Alteration of the environment in order to compensate for perceptual dysfunction.

Agnosia: The inability to recognize familiar objects with one sensory modality, while retaining the ability to recognize the same object with other sensory modalities.

Anosognosia: A perceptual disability including denial, neglect, and lack of awareness of the presence or severity of one's paralysis.

Aphasia: Absence or impairment of the ability to communicate through speech, writing, or signs owing to dysfunctions of brain centers.

Apraxia: A disorder of voluntary learned movement that is characterized by an inability to perform purposeful movements and which cannot be accounted for by inadequate strength, loss of coordination, impaired sensation, attentional deficits, or lack of comprehension.

Association areas: Areas of the cerebral cortex that border on and are connected to the primary sensory areas; analyzes and synthesizes incoming isolated sensations into a whole or gestalt, so that complex environmental displays can be perceived and acted upon.

Astereognosis: The inability to recognize objects by handling them, although tactile, proprioceptive, and thermal sensations may be intact.

Attention: The ability to select and to attend to a specific stimulus while simultaneously suppressing extraneous stimuli.

Autopagnosia: Impairment of body scheme.

Body image: A visual and mental image of one's body that includes feelings about one's body, especially in relation to health and disease.

Body scheme: A postural model of one's body, including the relationship of the body parts to each other and the relationship of the body to the environment.

Cognitive awareness: The knowledge that one has a deficit.

Cognitive rehabilitation: An approach to the remediation of cognitive-perceptual skills that focuses on how the individual acquires and uses knowledge, and seeks overall strategies for the brain-damaged patient to approach task performance.

Color agnosia: An inability to recognize colors.

Compensation: An approach to the treatment of the perceptually disabled that advocates use of intact abilities and alternate methods for solution to functional problems.

Constructional apraxia: Faulty spatial analysis and conceptualization of a task. It is most evident in the inability to produce two- or three-dimensional forms by drawing, constructing, or arranging blocks or objects, spontaneously or upon command.

Cortical blindness: A total failure to appreciate incoming visual sensory information owing to a lesion in the cortex, rather than injury to the eyes.

Dressing apraxia: An inability to dress oneself properly owing to a disorder in body scheme or spatial relations, rather than difficulty in motor performance or incoordination.

Figure-ground discrimination: The ability to distinguish a figure from the background in which it is embedded.

Finger agnosia: The inability to identify the fingers on one's own hands or on the hands of the examiner, including difficulty in naming the fingers upon command, identifying which finger was touched, and mimicking finger movements.

Fixation: The ability to maintain focus on an object as it is brought closer to and farther away from the eyes.

Form constancy: The ability to perceive or to attend to subtle differences in form and shape. The perceptually impaired patient is likely to confuse objects of similar shape or to fail to recognize an object placed in an unusual position.

Functional approach: An approach to the treatment of perceptually impaired individuals that advocates practice in the specific functional tasks in which the patient is deficient, in order to enhance independence.

Hemianopsia: Inability to see half the field of vision in one or both eyes.

Homonymous hemianopsia: Blindness in the outer half of the visual field of one eye and the inner half of the visual field of the other eye, producing an inability to receive information from either the right or the left half of the visual environment.

Ideational apraxia: An inability to perform a purposeful motor act, either automatically or upon command; an inability to retain the idea of the task and to formulate the necessary motor patterns. The patient no longer understands the overall concept of the act.

Ideomotor apraxia: The inability to perform a task upon command and to imitate gestures, even though the patient understands the concept of the task and is able to carry out habitual tasks automatically.

Immediate recall: The ability to remember information that has been stored for a few seconds.

Long-term memory: A compilation of early experiences and information acquired over a period of years.

Memory: A mental process that allows the individual to store experiences and perceptions for recall at a later time.

Ocular pursuits: The ability of the eyes to follow a moving object.

Perception: The process of selection, integration, and

interpretation of stimuli from one's own body and the surrounding environment.

Position-in-space disorder: The inability to perceive and to interpret spatial concepts such as up, down, under, over, in, out, in front of, and behind.

Prosopagnosia: An inability to recognize faces or other visually ambiguous stimuli as being familiar and distinct from one another.

Right-left discrimination disorder: The inability to identify the right and left sides of one's own body or of that of the examiner.

Sensorimotor approach: An approach to perceptual remediation that posits that by offering specific sensory stimulation and carefully controlling the subsequent motor output, one can influence the way in which the brain organizes and processes sensations.

Short-term memory: The retention of events or learning that has taken place within a few hours or days.

Simultagnosia: The inability to perceive a visual stimulus as a whole; also known as Balint's syndrome.

Somatagnosia: Impairment in body scheme; a lack of awareness of the body structure and the relationship of body parts of oneself or of others.

Spatial relations deficit: The inability to perceive the relationship of one object in space to another object or to oneself.

Spatial relations syndrome: A constellation of deficits that have in common a difficulty in perceiving the relationship between objects in space, or the relationship between the self and two or more objects. Included are disorders of figure-ground discrimination, form constancy, spatial relations, position-in-space perception, and topographic disorientation.

Splinter skill: A trained or learned skill that is acquired in a manner inconsistent with, or incapable of being integrated with, skills the individual already possesses.

Tactile agnosia: The inability to recognize forms by handling them, although tactile, proprioceptive, and thermal sensations may be intact; also known as astereognosis.

Task analysis: The breakdown of an activity or task into its component parts and a delineation of the specific motoric, perceptual, and cognitive abilities that are necessary to perform each component.

Topographic disorientation: Difficulty in understanding and remembering the relationship of one place to another.

Transfer of training approach: Remediation that posits that practice in tasks with particular perceptual requirements will enhance performance in tasks with similar perceptual demands.

Unilateral spatial neglect: The inability to register and to integrate stimuli and perceptions from one side of the body and the environment (usually the left). As a result, the patient ignores that side of the body and stimuli occurring on that side of personal space.

Unilateral visual neglect: The inability to register and to integrate visual stimuli and perceptions from one side of the environment (usually the left). As a result, the patient ignores stimuli occurring in that side of personal space.

Vertical disorientation: A distorted perception of the upright (vertical) position.

Visual object agnosia: The inability to recognize familiar objects despite normal function of the eyes and optic tracts.

CHAPTER 29

Neurogenic Disorders of Speech and Language*

Martha Taylor Sarno

OBJECTIVES

1. Explain the organization of language with respect to the role of phonologic, lexical, syntactic, and semantic systems.
2. Gain an understanding of the role of the motor speech system in the speech production process.
3. Explain and characterize the classic aphasic syndromes.
4. Identify and explain the critical factors in the evaluation of the recovery and rehabilitation of aphasia.
5. Identify and describe general approaches to aphasia rehabilitation and some specific treatment methods.
6. Describe the primary types of dysarthria and rationales for dysarthria treatment.
7. Describe speech apraxia and its treatment.
8. Gain an understanding of neurogenic swallowing disorder.
9. Describe the goals and rationales for the use of augmentative communication systems.

Most human beings take the ability to produce and understand speech for granted and pay little attention to the nature and function of the processes involved in communication. Yet speech, like tool making, sets us apart from animals and is one of the most human of our behaviors. Even in its most primitive societies, the human race has used the oral-motor speech code to share experiences, ideas, and feelings. Not all human communities have developed writing and reading systems.

The term **communication** encompasses all of the behaviors, including speech, which human beings use to transmit information. It consists of a delicate and rapid sequence of sensory and motor events requiring the coordinated activity of several parts of the body. The use of oral-motor speech for communication involves many levels of human activity, ranging from the purely anatomic, mechanical functions of fine motor coordination to the subtle shades of meaning that take place at the cognitive-semantic level. Gestures, pantomime, and other nonverbal pragmatic behaviors such as turn taking are also essential components of communication.

Among unimpaired speakers, speech behavior varies greatly, yet it is an efficient system for the exchange of

even complicated information. In fact, individuals usually produce different sound waves with varying characteristics when they produce the same word. But listeners do not usually rely only on information derived from speech waves. We also depend on many cues that are components of what is referred to as **context.** Context includes aspects of a communicative exchange such as the purpose of the activity, the location of the exchange, the knowledge of the participants, the roles of each participant, and the level of formality required by the situation.

Our use of speech for communication contributes to our identity as human beings and to the perception of "self." As a result, disruptions in the ability to communicate, whether on the basis of structural abnormalities (e.g., cleft palate), neurologic conditions (e.g., Parkinson's disease), or nonorganic conditions (e.g., nonorganic articulatory disorders) may affect an individual's daily life in important ways. For some people, the acquisition of a communication disorder may have an impact great enough to cause an individual to withdraw from the work force. In other cases, the disorder may not impede an individual's vocational life, but may draw sufficient attention to itself that it interferes with socialization. For others, whose communication disorders began in childhood and have persisted into adult life, the disorder can represent a considerable vocational handicap. Communication disorders, then, are complex, multifaceted behavioral impairments that compromise an aspect of human behavior that is closely associated with one's

* The preparation of this chapter was supported in part by the National Institute of Deafness and Other Communication Disorders (NIDCD) grant RO1NS25367-01A1, of which the author is Principal Investigator, and the National Institute of Disability and Rehabilitation Research (NIDRR) grant G00830000.

personhood and may negatively affect all aspects of life.

This chapter addresses the neurogenic disorders of communication, a category of communication disorders represented by the majority of patients receiving speech-language pathology services in rehabilitation medicine programs. The most common of these disorders are **aphasia,** a language disorder, and **dysarthria,** a motor-speech disorder.

The field of speech-language pathology, which came into being in 1925 with the establishment of the American Speech-Language-Hearing Association, is dedicated to the diagnosis and treatment of individuals with congenital or acquired disorders of speech and language. Communication disorders exact a large economic toll, costing the United States economy an estimated $30 billion a year in lost productivity, special education costs, and medical costs. The National Institute on Deafness and Other Communication Disorders (NIDCD) estimates the number of cases of language disorders at 6 to 8 million, and of speech impairment at 10 million.[1] Nearly 2 million Americans are either totally deaf or suffer such significant loss of hearing in both ears that they cannot hear conversations. Another 14 to 15 million are moderately to severely impaired. Of the population older than 65 years of age, 9.6 million individuals are hearing impaired. More than 1.4 million children younger than 18 years of age have a hearing impairment.[1]

In the population older than 65 years of age, 10.8 percent have speech and language disorders, whereas those younger than 45 years of age, 9.9 percent have speech and language disorders. The largest population with impaired communication consists of children with language disorders (43.7%) and articulation disorders (32.1%).[1] Of adults with speech-language impairment approximately 15 percent have acquired aphasia.[2]

The field of speech pathology has grown rapidly. Affiliates (members and certificate holders) in the American Speech-Language-Hearing Association (ASHA) increased from 1623 to 35,000 in the period from 1950 to 1980. Today, there are over 62,000 speech-language pathologists certified by the ASHA (24.4 per 100,000 residents in the United States), of whom more than 95 percent are women.[3] Speech-language pathology is a master's degree entry field and more than 80 percent of all states require licensure in order to practice. The ASHA awards the Certificate of Clinical Competence (CCC) to speech-language pathologists who meet specified academic and clinical experience requirements, which include a clinical fellowship year (CFY). Only slightly more than 15 percent of certified speech-language pathologists work in hospital settings.[4] The CCC and licensure are usually required for hospital employment. The term speech-language pathologist is the official designation of professionals in this field who hold the CCC. The term speech therapist, although no longer considered professionally appropriate, is a term that is often used informally.

In order that the presence and degree of speech or language pathology manifest by a given person can be identified and measured, his or her performance must be compared with a standard of "normal." One may choose as the standard (1) the language common to the cultural community of unimpaired persons in which the patient lives, in which case an individual's verbal function would be compared with that of others in the same community of similar age, sex, education, and achievement; or (2) the patient's verbal behavior prior to the onset of illness or trauma. The latter will vary from individual to individual and is based on premorbid educational achievement, specific cultural characteristics, personality, and other factors. A patient is verbally impaired when he or she deviates in any parameter of language and/or speech processing from the "normal" communication behavior of the community in which he or she functioned premorbidly.

A "normal" standard is implied in the terms **impairment, disability,** and **handicap.** In 1980, the World Health Organization (WHO)[5] presented a classification schema that distinguished among these terms: impairment refers to the pathology itself (its location, measured size and so forth); disability, to the consequences of an impairment and its impact on everyday personal, social, and vocational life; and handicap, to the value the individual, family, and community place on the disability and the degree to which the individual is disadvantaged.

THE ORGANIZATION OF LANGUAGE

When an individual generates an idea that he or she wants to say, it is systematically transformed into words and sentences, calling into play certain physiologic and acoustic events. The message is converted into linguistic form at the listener's end. The listener, in turn, fits the auditory information into a sequence of words and sentences that are ultimately understood.

We refer to the system of symbols strung together into sentences expressing our thoughts, and the understanding of those messages, as *language.* In the first few years of life, infants and children gain a great deal of practice and experience in the use of language, until it becomes habitual and is used without conscious awareness.

Words are made up of speech sounds or **phonemes.** Phonemes in and of themselves do not symbolize ideas or objects, but when put together they are the basic linguistic units that make words. Words comprise the **lexicon,** or vocabulary of a language. Phonemes are generally divided into **vowels** and **consonants.** In English, there are 16 vowels and 22 consonants, which are combined into larger units called **syllables.**

There are between 1000 and 2000 syllables in English; these are usually comprised of a vowel as a central phoneme surrounded by one or more consonants. Most languages have their own rules about how phonemes may be combined into larger units. For example, in English, syllables never start with the *ng* phoneme. The most frequently used words in English are sequences of between two and five phonemes. Some have as many as ten phonemes or as few as one. Generally, however, the most frequently used words have few phonemes. New words are added to the English language every day, even though only a small number of phoneme combinations are possible. Though there are several hundred thousand English words, we use a repertoire of only about 5000 to 10,000 words 95 percent of the time.

The grammar, or **syntax,** of a language determines the sequence of words that are acceptable to form sentences. In English, for example, it is possible to say "the black box on the table," but unacceptable to say "box black table on the." Another example, "The old radio played well," is syntactically correct, but "Old the well played radio" is not. The sentence, "The boy walked to the store," is meaningful, but the sentence, "The book walked to the store," is not. The language system that refers to the meanings of words is called **semantics.**

In addition to the **phonologic** (sounds), lexical (vocabulary), syntactical (grammar), and semantic (meaning) systems of a language, we also utilize **prosody** (stress and intonation) to help make distinctions among questions, statements, expressions of emotional feelings, shock, exclamations, and so forth.

SPEECH PRODUCTION

The organs of speech production consist of the lungs, the trachea, the larynx (which contains the vocal cords), the pharynx, nose, and mouth. When considered together, these organs comprise the "tube" referred to as the **vocal tract,** which extends from the lungs to the lips. Vocal tract shape is varied by moving the tongue, lips, and any other part of the tract. These changes in the configuration of the vocal tract act to modify the aerodynamic qualities of the air stream during speech (Fig. 29–1).

The primary function of the vocal organs involves basic life-sustaining functions such as breathing and swallowing. These organs not only take on different roles for speech, but function differently when engaged in speech production. For example, breathing for life-sustaining purposes is far more rapid than for speech production. A full-cycle inhalation and exhalation takes approximately 5 seconds, whereas during speech we control the breathing rate according to the demands of the words and sentences we are producing, sometimes reducing the rate of breathing to as little as 15 percent of that devoted to inhalation. This is the result of the fact that, when speaking, we generally take in air and exhale it gradually during the production of a complete thought.

The steady stream of air exhaled from the lungs is the source of energy for speech production, which is made audible by the rapid vibration of the vocal cords. During speech, we continuously alter the shape of the vocal tract by moving the tongue, lips, and other parts of the system. By moving the vocal tract, thereby modifying its acoustic properties, we are able to produce the different sounds. That is, by altering the shape of the vocal tract on phonation, we transform the air stream into a resonance chamber (Figs. 29–2 and 29–3).

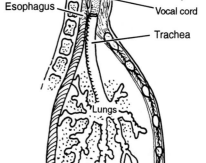

Figure 29–1. The human vocal organ

The *larynx* acts as a barrier to prevent food from entering the trachea and lungs by closing automatically during the act of swallowing, which is also helped by the action of the epiglottis. By opening and closing the flow of air from the lungs, the larynx acts as a valve between the lungs and the mouth. The laryngeal valve also acts to lock air into the lungs, which we do automatically when we perform heavy work with our upper extremities. The larynx is not a fixed, rigid organ; because of its cartilaginous construction and its corresponding con-

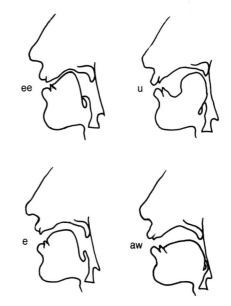

Figure 29–2. Outlines of the vocal tract during articulation of various vowels.

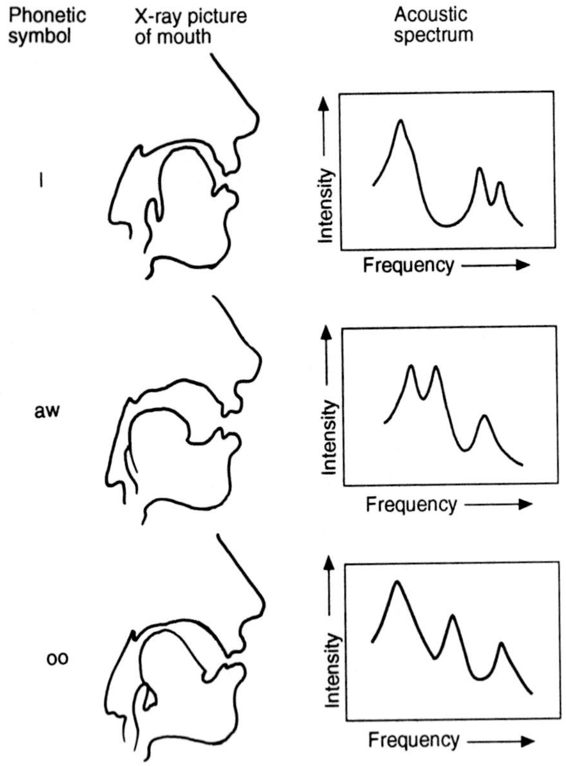

Phonetic symbol   X-ray picture of mouth   Acoustic spectrum

I

aw

oo

Figure 29–3. Vocal tract configuration and corresponding spectra for three different vowels. The peaks of the spectra represent vocal tract resonances. The vertical lines for individual harmonics are not shown.

necting muscles and ligaments, it is able to move up and down during both swallowing and speaking.

The *vocal cords* extend on either side of the larynx from the Adam's apple at the front to the arytenoid cartilages at the back. We refer to the space between the vocal cords as the **glottis.** When the cords are pressed together, the passage of air is sealed off and the valve is shut. Since the cords are held together at the front where they articulate with the Adam's apple, the open glottis is V-shaped, opening only at the back. When we speak, we vibrate the vocal cords in a rhythmic fashion, opening and closing the air passage from the lungs to the oral and/or nasal cavities.

The frequency of sound produced by the vocal cords is directly related to their mass, tension, and length. We alter the tension and length of the vocal cords continuously while speaking. In normal speech, the range of

vocal cord frequencies is from about 60 cycles per second to 350 cycles per second. Most people use a vocal cord frequency range that covers about one-and-a-half octaves.

The **pharynx** is the area of the vocal tract connecting the larynx with the nose and mouth. We isolate the nasal cavity from the pharynx and back of the mouth by raising the soft palate. The most adjustable component of the vocal tract is the mouth, whose shape and size can be modified more than any other organ of the oral-motor system by changing the relative positions of the palate, tongue, lips, and teeth. The lips are rounded, spread, or closed to alter the shape and length of the vocal tract or to stop air flow. The teeth and their relationship to the lips or tongue tip change the air flow. An important component of the teeth ridge is the *alveolus,* which is the area covered by the gums.

The term *articulation* refers to the articulating, or "meeting" of the various organs of the oral-pharyngeal cavity to produce the sounds of speech. Speech **intelligibility** refers to how a person "sounds" when speaking. A number of factors can influence judgments of intelligibility, such as the presence or absence of visual cues or of extraneous movements (e.g., tremor). The precision of the production of consonant sounds is one of the primary factors that contribute to speech intelligibility. Consonants are described by specifying their place and manner of articulation and whether they are voiced or unvoiced (Table 29–1). The "places" of articulation are the lips (labial), teeth, gums (alveolar), palate, and glottis. The manner of **articulation** refers to the plosive, fricative, nasal, liquid, and semi-vowel categories.

Plosive sounds, sometimes referred to as "stop" sounds, are those produced by building up air pressure in the oral cavity and suddenly releasing it (e.g., *p, t*). The blockage can occur by pressing the lips together or by pressing the tongue against either the gums or soft palate. There are plosive consonants that are labial, alveolar, or **velar.**

Fricatives are produced by making the air turbulent (e.g., *f, v*). Most consonants are produced with the soft palate raised, thereby closing off the flow of air to the nasal cavity, except for the **nasals** (e.g., *m, n, ng*), which are made by lowering the soft palate and blocking the oral cavity somewhere along its length. **Liquids** are sounds made with the soft palate raised (e.g., *r, l*).

Semi-vowels refer to those sounds produced by maintaining the vocal tract in a vowel-like position, then

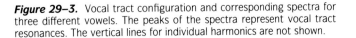

Table 29–1 CLASSIFICATION OF ENGLISH CONSONANTS BY PLACE ARTICULATED AND MANNER OF ARTICULATION

Place of Articulation	Manner of Articulation				
	Plosive	*Fricative*	*Semivowel*	*Liquids (including laterals)*	*Nasal*
Labial	p b	—	w	—	m
Labio-dental	—	f v	—	—	—
Dental	—	θ th	—	—	—
Alveolar	t d	s z	y	l r	n
Palatal	—	sh zh	—	—	—
Velar	k g	—	—	—	ng
Glottal	—	h	—	—	—

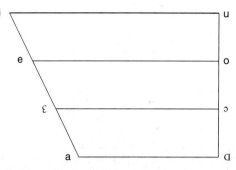

Figure 29–4. The cardinal vowels represented as a vowel quadrilateral. The cardinal vowels are extremely placed reference points for vowel articulation. Vowels on the same horizontal line were believed to have an equally high tongue height, while vowels in the left-right position were assumed to be equally backed and fronted. (Adapted from Ladefoged, P: A Course in Phonetics. Harcourt Brace Jovanovich, New York, 1975, with permission.)

changing the position rapidly for the vowel that follows (e.g., *w, y*).

Speech sounds are affected by their context, that is, the sounds that immediately precede or follow. A speech sound wave is a continuous event rather than a sequence of discrete segments. The identification of a speech sound depends on relating acoustic features of the sound wave at different points in time.

A standard reference for the quality of vowels are the eight cardinal vowels (Fig. 29–4). This schema of the positions of the tongue for the production of the vowels of the language help us to visualize the tongue's movements during speech. It is, in a sense, a map of the tongue positions for vowel production. Tongue placement is described by specifying where the main body of the tongue at its highest point is located. For example, for the vowel /i/ as in the word *beat,* the tongue tip is pointed in a high frontal configuration, whereas for the (a) as in the word *father* the highest point of the tongue is low and posterior in the oral cavity.

All vowel sounds and some consonant sounds are **voiced.** That is, the vocal cords vibrate during their production. When a sound is produced without vocal cord vibration, we say that it is **unvoiced** (e.g., *p, s*). Table 29–1 shows that many consonant sounds are articulated in the same manner, and differ only in the voicing dimension (e.g., *p–b; s–z; f–v; k–g*).

Speech behavior comprises a complex motor event that goes well beyond the skilled movements required of the oral-motor system; yet we are capable of producing speech without thinking about it, even while involved in other activities simultaneously. However, to transform thought into speech takes some voluntary, conscious behavior that allows us to take information stored in memory and translate it into a coherent production of words and utterances that follow certain grammatical rules.

The importance of the communication process and its underlying systems becomes apparent when we consider the two most common neurogenic communication disorders: aphasia and dysarthria. This chapter will focus primarily on aphasia and will also consider dysarthria, **verbal apraxia,** dysphagia, and the use of augmentative and alternate systems of communication.

APHASIA

Epidemiology

It is predicted that by the year 2000 there will be 31 million people over the age of 65 years in the United States.[6] In the past two decades the over-65 population has increased by 56 percent while the under-65 population has grown by only 19 percent.[7] The proportion of persons over 65 is projected to reach 21 to 22 percent of the total population by the year 2030.[8] It is estimated that there are over 1 million individuals with aphasia in the United States[9] and that there are about 84,000 new patients with aphasia in the United States each year, most of whom desire treatment.[10] A great number of these people fall into the over-65 category. The majority of cases are the result of strokes, but a substantial number are the consequence of head trauma and neoplasms. The onset of aphasia can also reflect the early stages of Alzheimer's disease. In 1969, the cost of speech-language rehabilitation for aphasia was estimated at $13.2 million per year.[11] The number has probably tripled in the intervening years.

History

Language disturbances were recorded as early as 3500 B.C.E.[23] and attempts to "retrain" individuals with aphasia have been recorded throughout history. Some of the first documented cases of both natural recovery and intervention were the patients of Nicolo Massa and Francisco Arceo in 1558.[24] In Mettler's classic text, *History of Medicine,* cashew (anacardium) is mentioned as having been "recommended for virtually all psychiatric and neurological afflictions, especially aphasia."[25] In 1783, Samuel Johnson attributed the beginning of his recovery from aphasia to the fact that his doctor had pressed blisters into his back and from his ear to his throat.[26]

In his landmark paper, "Du siège de la faculté du langage articulé," Paul Broca[27] was one of the first to discuss the feasibility of retraining in aphasia. He cited some anecdotal experiences with retraining and theorized that patients with aphasia could be taught language in the same way one teaches a child.

In 1904, Charles K. Mills[28,29] was the first to address recovery and rehabilitation in aphasia in an English-language publication. He reported the training of a patient with poststroke aphasia whom he and Donald Broadbent treated using methods largely determined by the patient, who began by systematically repeating letters, words, and phrases. Even though they were published over a century ago, Mills' observations and approach to aphasia rehabilitation are remarkably similar to much present-day practice and thought. His paper discusses the possible influence of semantic, lexical, and cognitive factors in recovery and suggested that different methods were appropriate for different patients and syndromes. He also noted that not all patients benefit from retraining to the same degree and acknowledged that spontaneous recovery might have an influence on the course and extent of recovery.

In the wake of World War I and its brain-damaged combat survivors, centers were established where patients with posttraumatic aphasia were treated, especially in Europe.[30-34] A two-volume treatise on aphasia based on an experience in England with 26 soldiers who had suffered gunshot wounds during World War I was published in 1926.[35] Nielsen[36] reported residual language impairments in 16 of 200 head-injured patients who were treated at Hospital No. 1 in Cape May, New Jersey, from 1918 to 1919. One of the most comprehensive descriptions of the systematic treatment of a large number of head-injured patients, of whom 90 to 100 were followed for a 10-year period was provided by Kurt Goldstein in Frankfurt during World War II.[37]

Until World War II, reports of retraining civilians with poststroke aphasia were rare. The aphasia literature was based almost exclusively on posttraumatic aphasia. In 1933, Singer and Low[38] reported the case of a 39-year-old woman who developed aphasia as a result of an apparent vascular infarct after a full-term delivery. The woman showed continuous language improvement with consistent training over a 10-year period.

In a landmark 5-year study supported by the Commonwealth Fund, Weisenburg and McBride[39] addressed the general topic of aphasia, without special reference to recovery, and commented on the effectiveness of reeducation in a study of 60 patients of less than 60 years of age, a majority of whom had suffered strokes. They concluded that reeducation increased the rate of recovery, assisted in facilitating the use of compensatory means of communication, and improved morale. Their work also documented the psychotherapeutic benefits of treatment.

Aphasia and its concomitant neurologic deficits in the stroke patient were generally viewed as natural and necessary components of the aging process in the period before World War II. The treatment of aphasia in the civilian population was not considered an option.

Wepman[40] was one of the first to draw attention to the large population of untreated civilians who, like the war veterans, could benefit from therapy. Based on data obtained at the Aphasia Center of DeWitt General Hospital in Auburn, California, Wepman[40] described the language retraining, based on a pedagogic model, of 68 patients with aphasia, with a mean age of 25.8 years, who began treatment 6 months after trauma.

In Moscow, at the Institute of Neurology, Academy of Medical Sciences, Luria[41] reported on a large series of patients with traumatic aphasia, and concluded that systematic retraining based on a careful psycholinguistic analysis and aimed at developing compensatory function provides the foundation for the successful restoration of verbal skills.

Many variables had an influence on making the treatment of aphasia the common practice that it is today. The advent of speech pathology as a health profession, the emergence of rehabilitation medicine as a medical specialty, the mass media explosion, a larger and more affluent middle class, an increased life span, a larger percentage of stroke and head trauma survivors, and increased public expectations of medicine in the age of technology are among them. The latter has been particularly important in the industrialized world, where it is widely believed that there is a treatment for every human ill.

Journals devoted to brain and/or language issues have become indispensable information sources for aphasiologists (e.g., *Aphasiology, Brain and Language,* and *Cortex*). The Academy of Aphasia, a scholarly society dedicated to the study of aphasia, was established in 1962. The National Aphasia Association (NAA) was founded in the United States in 1987 for the purpose of providing information to the public about aphasia, advocating for the aphasic community, and encouraging the establishment of support groups called Aphasia Community Groups (ACGs).

Several informational publications designed for use by the families and friends of patients with aphasia also appeared in the post–World War II period.[42-47] One of these, "Understanding Aphasia,"[48] is still widely read and has been published in 11 languages.

Classification and Nomenclature

In this chapter the term *aphasia* refers to the acquired communication disorder that is manifest in individuals who were previously capable of using language appropriately. It does not refer to those developmental language disorders that may be observed in individuals who never developed language normally in the first place and for whom the ability to use language will never reach age-appropriate performance levels.

In acquired aphasia, central nervous system disease or trauma compromises certain structures in a focal rather than generalized fashion. The study of the neuro-anatomic correlates of the aphasias has engaged neurologists since the late nineteenth century and the correlation between aphasic syndromes and cerebral localization is extremely consistent. However, the introduction of new neuroradiographic tools such as the various types of brain scans, especially computerized axial tomography (CAT), has made localization in aphasia a subject of much research in the past two decades.

Aphasiologists generally agree that there are distinct major aphasic syndromes that adhere to specific profiles of impairment. This is not surprising since the lesions that produce aphasia, particularly following cerebral vascular accident, tend to be located in brain loci that are especially vulnerable to infarct. It is not always possible, however, to classify patients according to these syndromes. Estimates of the proportion of cases that can be unambiguously classified range from 30 percent to 80 percent.[12]

The characteristics of a patient's speech production are used to determine aphasia classification. Speech output that is characterized as hesitant, awkward, interrupted, and produced with effort is referred to as *nonfluent;* in contrast, speech output that is facile in articulation, and produced at a normal rate, with preserved flow and melody, is referred to as **fluent aphasia.** Fluency judgments are made during extended conversation with a patient.

Fluent aphasia is characterized by impaired auditory

comprehension and fluent speech that is of normal rate and melody. Fluent aphasia is usually associated with a lesion in the vicinity of the posterior portion of the first temporal gyrus of the left hemisphere. When fluent aphasia is severe, word and sound substitutions may be of such magnitude and frequency that speech may be rendered meaningless. Patients with fluent aphasia tend to have greatest difficulty in retrieving those words that are substantive (i.e., nouns and verbs). They also tend to have some degree of impaired awareness and are rarely physically disabled, since their lesions are located in the posterior portion of the brain, distant from motor areas. There are several types of syndromes subsumed under the fluent aphasia classification (Table 29–2).

Nonfluent aphasia is characterized by limited vocabulary, slow, hesitant speech, some awkward articulation, and restricted use of grammar, in the presence of relatively preserved auditory comprehension. Nonfluent aphasia is associated with anterior lesions, usually involving the third frontal convolution of the left hemisphere. Patients with nonfluent aphasia tend to express themselves in vocabulary that is substantive (i.e., nouns), and lack the ability to retrieve less substantive parts of speech (i.e., prepositions, conjunctions, pronouns). Patients with nonfluent aphasia tend to have good awareness of their deficit and usually have impaired motor function on the right side (i.e., right hemiplegia or paresis).

A severe aphasia with marked dysfunction across all language modalities and with severely limited residual use of all communication modes for oral-aural interactions is referred to as **global aphasia.** Global aphasia is not a type of aphasia but rather a designation of severity. The patient with global aphasia generally has extensive damage, which may be anywhere in the left hemisphere, and is sometimes bilateral.[13] Global aphasia has been cited as the most common type of aphasia in patients referred for speech rehabilitation services.[14,15]

The most common category of fluent aphasia is *Wernicke's aphasia* (also referred to as sensory aphasia and/or receptive aphasia). Wernicke's aphasia is usually the result of a lesion in the posterior portion of the first temporal gyrus of the left hemisphere. It is characterized by impaired auditory comprehension and fluently articulated speech marked by word substitutions. Reading and writing are usually severely impaired as well. Although these patients may produce what seem like complete utterances and use complex verb tenses, they often add a word or phrase and "augment" speech production. They may also speak at a rate greater than normal. Although their production of speech sounds is generally precise, patients with Wernicke's aphasia may reverse phonemes and/or syllables (e.g., hopspipal, trevilision) and may produce *neologisms* (nonsense words).

Wernicke's aphasia, during the early stages, may evolve into *anomic aphasia* in the course of recovery. Anomic aphasia is characterized by a significant word-finding difficulty in the context of fluent, grammatically well-formed speech. Auditory comprehension is relatively preserved for most speaking situations. Speech output may be somewhat vague and the patient may be facile in producing circumlocutions to skirt the lack of specificity of language use.

Broca's aphasia is the most common type of aphasia found in patients receiving comprehensive rehabilitation services. This syndrome is also referred to as expressive aphasia, motor aphasia, and/or verbal aphasia. Broca's aphasia is the result of a lesion involving the third frontal convolution of the left hemisphere, the subcortical white matter, and extending posteriorly to the inferior portion of the motor strip (precentral gyrus). It is characterized by awkward articulation, restricted

Table 29–2 CLASSIFICATION BY APHASIA SYMPTOMS

	Wernicke's Aphasia	Broca's Aphasia	Global Aphasia	Conduction Aphasia	Anomic Aphasia	Transcortical Motor Aphasia	Pure Word Deafness
Area of infarction	Posterior portion of temporal gyrus	Third frontal convolution	Third frontal convolution and posterior portion of superior temporal gyrus	Parietal operculum or posterior superior temporal gyrus	Angular gyrus	Supplementary motor areas	Both Heschl's gyri or connection between Heschl's gyrus and posterior superior temporal gyrus
Spontaneous speech	Fluent	Nonfluent	Nonfluent	Fluent or nonfluent	Fluent	Nonfluent	Fluent
Comprehension	Poor	Good	Poor	Good	Good	Good	Poor
Repetition	Poor	Poor (but may be better than spontaneous speech)	Poor	Very poor	Good	Excellent	Poor
Naming	Poor	Poor (but may be better than spontaneous speech)	Poor	Poor	Very poor	Poor	Good
Reading comprehension	Poor	Good	Poor	Good to poor	Good to poor	Good	Good
Writing	Poor	Poor	Poor	Poor	Good to poor	Poor	Good

vocabulary, and restriction to simple grammatical forms, in the presence of a relative preservation of auditory comprehension. Writing skills generally mirror the pattern of speech. Reading may be less impaired than speech and writing. The patient may be limited to one- and two-word productions for expression and find it impossible to combine words into sentences. Articulation may be awkward and arduous (see section on verbal apraxia). Nonfluent Broca's aphasia is rarely found in aphasia after closed head injury (CHI). Anomic disturbances predominate in aphasia secondary to CHI. In children, aphasia after closed head injury is generally characterized by a reduction of output with hesitancy, difficulty initiating speech, and sometimes mutism.[16]

Many measures of aphasia and related disorders have been developed for use in both clinical and research settings. Aphasia assessment tools were beginning to appear in the early part of the twentieth century and their number has increased over the past two decades. In an inpatient setting, patients with aphasia are generally screened by means of a bedside clinical evaluation, which aims to obtain a general idea of a patient's profile of deficits and preserved areas of language function as a basis for recommendations for more comprehensive testing and possible rehabilitation. Obviously, such screening tests have limited value since they offer few details about the type and severity of aphasic deficits, which lead to a syndrome classification. An important purpose of a comprehensive examination is to provide a baseline measure against which to gauge progress in the course of rehabilitation.

Comprehensive language tests designed to measure aphasic impairment generally contain specific domains of performance assessment. In addition to the general requirements for the construction of tests, such as reliability, standardization, and demonstrated validity, certain factors are considered important in the design of tests intended to identify and measure aphasia. These include the range of item difficulty, use in measuring recovery, and ability to contribute to diagnostic classification.[17] Aphasia tests are generally based on assessments of linguistic task performance and include, minimally, tasks of visual confrontation *naming;* a spontaneous or conversational speech sample, which is analyzed for fluency of output, effort, articulation, phrase length, prosody, word substitutions, and omissions; *repetition* of digits, single words, multisyllable words and sentences of increasing length and complexity; *comprehension of spoken language* for single words, and for sentences that require only yes or no responses and pointing on command; *word retrieval* (word finding), which measures the ability to generate words beginning with a particular letter of the alphabet or in a particular semantic category (animals); *reading;* and *writing,* from dictation and spontaneously.

Some widely used aphasia measures include the Boston Diagnostic Aphasia Examination (BDAE),[12] the Neurosensory Center Comprehensive Examination for Aphasia (NCCEA),[18] and the Western Aphasia Battery.[19]

In addition to the measurement of performance on specific linguistic tasks, an aphasia assessment also requires some supplementary "functional communica-

tion" measures. This is necessary because an individual's actual use of language in everyday life may not correspond to the degree of pathology measured by linguistic task performance. Functional communication measures are usually in the form of rating scales with high inter-rater reliability. The Functional Communication Profile (FCP)[20,21] and Communicative Activities of Daily Living (CADL)[22] are widely used for this purpose.

Evaluation of Recovery and Treatment

If complete recovery from aphasia is to occur, it usually happens within a matter of hours or days following onset. Once aphasia has persisted for several weeks or months, a complete return to a premorbid state is usually the exception.

Most patients do not consider themselves "recovered" unless they have fully returned to previous levels of language performance.[49] When unrecovered patients are satisfied with their level of competence and consider themselves "recovered," this is a psychologic perception and must not be confused with an objective evaluation of communication abilities. The true test of aphasia rehabilitation outcome is best assessed by patients' perceptions of the quality of their lives.

In aphasia, it is desirable to distinguish between two separate recovery dimensions: one that is objective and attempts to identify to what extent the patient has regained previous language abilities; and a second, which in humanistic terms may be more important, that measures the degree of recovery of **functional communication.**

The concept of a "functional" dimension of communication behavior emerged logically from the experience of treating patients with aphasia in the rehabilitation medicine setting.[19,50] Historically, rehabilitation medicine has acknowledged that the ability of patients to function in their daily lives, to perform the so-called activities of daily living (ADL), does not necessarily correlate directly with the extent of physical disability. Improvement in quantitative measures of language performance does not necessarily represent improvement in functional communication.[51]

The Efficacy of Therapy in the Patient with Aphasia Due to Stroke

It is generally believed that many methodologic problems have limited the number of studies that examine the efficacy of aphasia rehabilitation.[52-57] Nevertheless, treatment accountability issues are compelling and are the focus of professional concern. Studies that investigate treatment effects, specific techniques, and approaches have been reported since the late 1950s.[58] Vignolo,[59] Hagen,[60] and Basso et al.[61,62] have used untreated control and treated groups and shown a treatment effect. The more recent work of Shewan and Kertesz[63] and Poeck et al.[64] with treated and untreated groups has also yielded positive treatment effects. Variables such as spontaneous recovery,[65-67] age,[68] duration and intensity of treatment,[55] and specific treatment techniques[69,70] have been studied. Although studies to date have varied methodologically and by research focus, the net result provides a strong indication for positive treatment effects.

Factors in Recovery

SPONTANEOUS RECOVERY

It is acknowledged that in the period immediately following onset, some degree of natural recovery takes place in the majority of patients with or without intervention. There is, however, a lack of consensus about the duration of the spontaneous recovery period.[71-73] Luria[41] referred to a period of 6 to 7 months after onset as the time when spontaneous restitution takes place, and Culton[74] reported rapid spontaneous language recovery in the first month following the onset of aphasia. A number of studies have concluded that the greatest improvement occurs in the first 2 to 3 months after onset.[59,61,65,75,76] Butfield and Zangwill,[77] Sands et al.,[78] and Vignolo[59] found that the recovery rate dropped significantly after 6 months. Others have reported that spontaneous recovery does not occur after 1 year[61,74] and Sarno and Levita[79] reported that a greater change took place in the first 3 months than in the second 3 months in a sample of patients with severe aphasia seen up to 6 months after a stroke.

In a survey of 850 acute patients, aphasia was present in 177 patients during the acute phase (up to 1 month after stroke). In the 4- to 12-week poststroke period, aphasia improved in 74 percent of the patients and cleared in 44 percent.[10]

AGE

In the healthy aged, language performance is not static. Naming skills decline significantly between the seventh and eighth decades,[80,81] and it has been noted that performance decreases on comprehension tasks commencing in the sixth decade and continuing through the eighth decade.[82,83]

Aphasiologists generally consider age an important variable in recovery outcome;[52,84] yet the effects of age on recovery are reported as both a strong[59,63] and a weak variable.[68] This wide discrepancy in the aphasia recovery literature regarding the influence of age on recovery is probably directly related to differences in sampling and the methodology employed.

GENDER

It has been suggested that language in men is more discretely lateralized than in women[85] and, as a result, that left hemisphere strokes result in aphasia more often in men than in women.[86] In general, however, the literature does not support the idea that gender is a significant factor in recovery from aphasia.[63,65,87-90] One of the few studies that found gender a significant factor in recovery from aphasia was conducted by Basso et al.,[91] who reported that women recovered significantly more

in oral expression than men, but did not show significant differences in recovery of auditory verbal comprehension ability.

TYPE AND SEVERITY OF APHASIA

Many investigators have concluded that patients with different aphasia syndromes recover differently. For example, in the Kertesz and McCabe study,[65] Broca's (nonfluent) aphasics had the highest degree of recovery. There were no qualitative or quantitative differences between groups (fluent, mixed, nonfluent, severely nonfluent), despite differences in severity, in the study done by Prins et al.[15]

Sarno and Levita[92] reported that people with fluent aphasia reached the highest level of functional communication, whereas nonfluent and global aphasic patients made smaller gains in the 8- to 52-week poststroke period.

The majority of investigators report that patients with severe aphasia do not recover as well as those with mild aphasia.[65,78,93,94]

ETIOLOGY

It is generally agreed that posttraumatic aphasia has a better prognosis than aphasia due to vascular lesions.[59,77] In fact, some cases of aphasia after closed head injury have been reported to recover completely.[65,95] In another study, patients who recovered normal levels of language performance at 6 months after closed head injury had mild diffuse brain injury. Those with global cognitive deficit, including language impairment, had suffered more severe diffuse damage.[16]

NEURORADIOLOGIC CORRELATES OF RECOVERY

Yarnell et al.[49] reported that CAT scans showed a high degree of correlation between the size, location, and number of lesions and recovery from aphasia. Those patients with extensive dominant hemisphere lesions, either one large or many small ones, fared poorly, whereas those with lesser lesions did better. Bilateral lesions, at times unrecognized clinically, helped to account for significant aphasia residuals.

Similar CAT scan correlations for global aphasia were reported by Kertesz.[95] Patients initially classified as having global aphasia and reclassified as having Broca's aphasia at 3 to 6 months after a stroke showed the greatest amount of temporoparietal damage on CAT scans.[95] Yarnell and his coworkers[49] reported little prognostic value in angiographic and radioscintigram findings. Similarly, in a Norwegian study, CAT scans did not help in predicting who might profit from language retraining.[72]

In a report on the relationship between hemispheric asymmetries seen on CAT scans and recovery from stroke in right-handed patients with global aphasia more than 7 months poststroke, Pieniadz et al.[96] found a significant correlation between auditory comprehension recovery and the presence of atypical CT occipital asymmetries.

Selnes et al.[97] identified changes on CAT scans that correlated with recovery of auditory comprehension. Two specific sites of lesion were implicated, the left posterior superior temporal and left infrasylvan supramarginal regions. In a later analysis of the same data, recovery of single-word comprehension was correlated with CAT scans. Lesions in Wernicke's area did not necessarily imply a persistent impairment of single-word comprehension, but at the sentence level there was a strong relationship between recovery of comprehension and sparing of Wernicke's area.[94,97]

RECOVERY PATTERNS

A number of studies have supported the conclusion that comprehension improves more than expression.[15,59,98,99] Prins et al.[15] found no overall clinical improvement in spontaneous speech in any aphasia type in the first year after stroke. Sentence comprehension improved significantly in all types of aphasia patients. In a study of individuals with nonfluent aphasia, Kenin and Swisher[98] found the greatest improvement on imitative tasks, and auditory comprehension improved more than expressive language.

Equal improvement was found on all language tasks for patients with good comprehension, and more selective improvement, largely in comprehension and imitative tasks, for those with severely impaired auditory comprehension.[75] In a study by Reinvang and Engvik, the profile of linguistic impairment tended to be maintained during the 2- to 6-month period.[72] In a study assessing the recovery of connected language across a 1-year period, Shewan[67] found that verbal output increased significantly for a majority of the classical types of aphasia, regardless of severity. In general, patients made the greatest changes on those variables in which they were initially most impaired.

TIME SINCE ONSET

Time since onset emerged as an important prognostic factor in a retrospective study conducted in Milan:[59] 2 and 6 months from onset seemed to be important milestones. Patients who were treated for more than 6 months were compared with those who received training for less than 6 months, and the findings showed that those in training longer improved to a greater degree.

Greater improvement was noted in a group of patients who began treatment up to 2 months after stroke than a group that started treatment after 4 months.[78] The deferment of treatment for 12 weeks did not influence outcome in another study.[55] Basso et al.[61] found the least recovery in patients with the longest duration of symptoms.

Reinvang and Engvik[72] reported a significant degree of improvement in the period 2 to 6 months after onset. Prins et al.[15] noted significant time changes in spontaneous speech variables in the first year after stroke. Changes after the first year poststroke were noted by Marks et al.[58] and Sands et al.[78] On the other hand, Kertesz and McCabe[65] reported little or no change after the first year.

In the Sarno and Levita study,[92] little change was observed on any of the measures administered in the 4- to 8-weeks poststroke period. However, in the 12- to 26-week poststroke period, all diagnostic groups, particularly those designated as fluent, made gains on all measures.

PSYCHOSOCIAL AND RELATED FACTORS

Psychologic factors such as depression, anxiety, premorbid personality, fatigue, and paranoia are often cited as having an adverse effect on recovery. The social isolation experienced by people with aphasia and their families has a profound impact on their quality of life.[57,100] The effect of aphasia on the individual's sense of "self" is often extremely negative, leading to a loss of self-esteem and feelings of helplessness. The opportunity for "healing conversation," so essential to individuals who have suffered losses, is often unavailable to those with aphasia. Deep depression is frequently the result of this combination. The influence of these psychosocial variables on recovery is usually negative and is believed to be considerable.

In summary, until the early 1950s, aphasia rehabilitation was essentially limited to patients with aphasia secondary to trauma due to missile wounds. Since then, patients with poststroke aphasia, who are generally older than posttraumatic patients, have been the primary aphasic population receiving therapy. Reports of the efficacy of aphasia rehabilitation are generally positive. However, conclusions regarding the limits of spontaneous recovery and the relative influence of many variables on outcome are still not definitive.

APPROACHES TO THE TREATMENT OF APHASIA

Literally hundreds of specific techniques are cited in the aphasia rehabilitation literature. Aphasia therapy is rarely the same in any two treatment settings. The lack of therapeutic uniformity has undoubtedly impeded carefully controlled studies on the effects of language retraining.[44] Most methods derive essentially from traditional pedagogic practices, relying heavily on repetition.[101-104]

The primary assumption in aphasia rehabilitation is that language in the brain is not "erased," but that retrieval of its individual units has been impaired. Approaches to aphasia therapy have generally followed one of two models: a *substitute skill model* or a *direct treatment model,* both of which are based on the assumption that the processes that subserve normal performance need to be understood if rehabilitation is to succeed.[105] An example of the substitute skill model can be found in deaf individuals, some of whom use speech reading, a visual input rather than an auditory input, as an aid to comprehend spoken language. If a direct treatment model is followed, specific exercises individually designed to ameliorate specific linguistic deficits are the basis of treatment.

In general, treatment methods can be categorized as those that are largely indirect stimulation-facilitation, that is, the provision of assistive cueing when indicated and the encouragement of verbalization; and those that are direct-structured pedagogic, that is, treatment based on an educational plan.[44,95,101,104,106,107] The two principles that underlie these categories of treatment methods reflect contrasting views of aphasia as either impaired access to language or a "loss" of language. The stimulation methods generally follow an impaired access theory, and pedagogic approaches are based on a theory of aphasia as a language loss.

In practice, however, much of aphasia therapy addresses the "performance" aspect of language, in which repeated practice and "teaching" strategies are assumed to help restore impaired skills through a "task-oriented" approach (e.g., naming practice). One of the commonly used techniques involves self-cueing and repetition exercises that manipulate components of grammar and vocabulary. Another approach involves "stimulating" the patient to use residual language by encouraging conversation in a permissive setting, where a patient's responses are unconditionally accepted and topics are of personal interest.[108]

Some Innovative Treatment Methods

VISUAL COMMUNICATION THERAPY

Visual communication therapy (VIC) is an experimental technique designed for global aphasia.[109] It employs an index card system of arbitrary symbols representing syntactic and lexical components that patients learn to manipulate so as to (1) respond to a command and (2) express needs, wishes, or other emotions. The system attempts to circumvent the use of natural oral language, which is severely impaired and often unavailable to the patient with global aphasia. An adaptation and application of the VIC system, called Computer-Aided Visual Communication system (C-VIC), was developed by Steele and coworkers.[110-113]

Investigators conclude that the evidence supports the view that some patients who have severe aphasia can master the basics of an artificial language and that some of the cognitive operations entailed in natural language are preserved despite the severity of their condition.

VISUAL ACTION THERAPY

A technique developed at the Boston Veterans Administration Medical Center by Helm-Estabrooks and her associates, visual action therapy (VAT) is designed to train people with global aphasia to use symbolic gestures representing visually absent objects.[114,115] The tasks leading to this goal include associating pictured forms with specific objects, manipulating real objects appropriately, and finally producing symbolic gestures that represent the objects used (e.g., cup, hammer, razor).

AMERIND AND OTHER GESTURE SYSTEMS

In an attempt to utilize systematized gestural language to facilitate oral production, American Indian sign language has been modified in a method that combines common gestural sign with oral speech production (Amerind) for selected patients.[116-118]

FUNCTIONAL COMMUNICATION PRAGMATIC THERAPY

In the functional communication treatment (FCT) method developed by Aten, Caliguri, and Holland,[119] emphasis is placed on restoration of communication in the broadest sense. Therapy is designed to improve patients' information processing in the activities necessary to conducting ADLs, social interactions, and self-expression of both physical and psychologic needs.[120]

Promoting aphasics' communicative effectiveness (PACE), a technique intended to reshape structured interaction between clinicians and patients into more natural communicative exchanges, includes several pragmatic components common to natural conversation.[121]

Toward a Comprehensive Approach to Aphasia Rehabilitation

The unfortunate reality is that once the condition of aphasia has stabilized, very few patients recover normal communication function, with or without speech therapy. Accordingly, aphasia rehabilitation should be viewed as a process of patient management in the broadest sense of the term. That is, the task is primarily one of helping the patient and his or her intimates adjust to the alterations and limitations imposed by the disability. Effective aphasia rehabilitation management requires the participation of a variety of disciplines, including medicine, psychology, physical and occupational therapy, social work, vocational counseling, and, most critically, aphasia therapy.

The Patient with Aphasia

Ullman[122] observed that the variability of patients' psychologic reactions is rarely determined by the type or location of their lesions but is an expression of the whole life experience of the person who has had a stroke.

In a study of patients with aphasia participating in a group psychotherapy program, Friedman[123] investigated the nature of psychologic regression where the patient was impaired in his or her awareness of the reality of his or her disability. Beyond the communication difficulties posed by aphasia, he observed that patients remained psychologically isolated. They did not maintain a consistent level of group participation and expressed intense feelings that they were very different from other people. Both withdrawal and projection were apparent as each patient acted in isolation and yet complained of this characteristic withdrawal in others.

The selective and discriminating use of speech therapy to stimulate and support the patient through the various stages of recovery is an effective management tool.[73,124,125] Experienced aphasia therapists recognize that while working on aphasic deficits, they are simultaneously dealing psychotherapeutically with a readjusting personality.[40] Speech therapy, therefore, serves different purposes at different points along the way. Sometimes it allows patients to "borrow time," as Baretz and Stephenson[126] have aptly stated. Occasionally depression lifts after speech therapy has been initiated, reflecting the supportive and nurturing nature of the therapeutic relationship rather than an objective improvement in recovery of speech and/or language.[122]

Aphasia rehabilitation can be viewed as a dynamic process consisting of a series of stages like the stages of mourning described by Elizabeth Kübler-Ross,[127] through which the majority of patients evolve. Some, of course, never emerge from a state of severe depression.[128] Kübler-Ross[127] and other authors have suggested that the stages through which someone with aphasia passes could be characterized as attempts to overcome the sense of loss; the stages include denial, rage, and bargaining, awareness of the loss, and acceptance of the loss.

By directly addressing a patient's linguistic deficits and channeling attention and energies toward constructive ends, speech therapy may produce a noticeable reduction in depression. Therapy tasks, in this instance, act as an equivalent for work, which has long been recognized as an antidote for depression.

There is a great tendency to overestimate the capacity of individuals with aphasia to return to work, particularly if the verbal deficits are mild. Premature attempts to return to work can have a negative psychologic impact. Professional rehabilitation counselors are best equipped to explore and evaluate a patient's vocational potential and carry out the long and arduous process of evaluating work performance and job requirements.

Experienced aphasia clinicians stress the importance of the patient's family in the rehabilitation process. Some of the potentially negative reactions of the family include overprotectiveness, hostility, anger, unrealistic expectations, overzealousness, lack of knowledge of the dimensions of the disorder, and inability to cope with practical difficulties. The apparently natural tendency of family members to minimize the patient's communication impairment, particularly in the early stages of recovery, requires understanding and tactful management.

The quality of premorbid relationships generally tends to be intensified after a catastrophic event; those that were problematic may deteriorate further, whereas the bond between a loving couple may become stronger. The reversal of roles, changes in levels of dependency, and a changed economic situation, so often a consequence of chronic disability, can have a critical, negative impact on the patient and family.

In a positive family milieu, patients are encouraged to develop regular daily routines as close to premorbid patterns as possible and are treated as contributing members of the family. Patients need to be allowed some sense of control. Including the patient in rehabilitation planning helps to restore feelings of self-worth. In this regard, the emphasis on function rather than complete recovery, pointing up success rather than performance failure, adds to a patient's sense of self. It is essential to listen to patients, particularly to their expressions of loss. Commiseration is often more comforting than optimistic prognostic statements.

Group speech therapy, stroke clubs, and other social groups are frequently used resources that can be effective tools in the management of some patients with chronic aphasia. The National Aphasia Association (NAA) was founded in the United States in 1987, following the lead of existing organizations established in Finland in 1971, Germany in 1978, the United Kingdom in 1980, Sweden in 1981. Knowledge that one is not alone often helps to reduce depression and loneliness.[73,106]

Group therapy with peers also provides a comfortable atmosphere in which patients can meet new friends and ventilate feelings, though not all individuals with aphasia find it beneficial. A positive effect seems related to such personality factors as adaptability, outgoing style of socialization, optimistic attitude, and drive for restoration. While group therapy generally plays an important role in aphasia rehabilitation, it should be noted that much of its effectiveness depends on the skill of the group leader.

In our present state of knowledge, aphasia rehabilitation remains eclectic and specifically tailored to the individual patient. Fundamental to this therapeutic philosophy is the acknowledgment and appreciation of the uniqueness of the individual. No two persons with aphasia are exactly alike in pathology, personality, linguistic deficits, reactions to catastrophic illness, life experience, spiritual values, and a host of other factors. The influence of these factors carries different weight and strength at different stages of recovery, and they are all related to recovery outcome.

Experience suggests that, except for severely depressed individuals with aphasia, patients generally produce everything they are capable of producing. Therapists must not allow their expectations to contaminate the therapeutic interaction; this is not uncommon, and is usually motivated by laudatory aspirations—therapists want to see their patients improve—but is nonetheless counterproductive. Patients with involvement of subcortical areas may have low levels of activation, a purely physiologic process independent of psychologic motivation. The distinction between these two processes must be understood.

Many ethical-moral dilemmas face those who manage the rehabilitation of patients with aphasia. One of the principal issues is a result of the need to select which individuals will receive treatment. Rehabilitation medicine services are not only "scarce" in many situations but they are also not a right or entitlement. Services are usually provided on a selective basis to those individuals believed to have the potential to "benefit." This process assumes that we know who can "benefit."[100,129–131] Many who are experienced in aphasia rehabilitation management hold the view that all people should be given a trial treatment period to determine their candidacy for further treatment and that trials should be provided at different points in the recovery course. Goal setting, the patient's right to self-determination, and the criteria appropriate in determining the termination of therapy are also important ethical issues.[100,108]

Summary

In spite of the reality of anatomic and physiologic pathology in aphasia, those who engage in this work have not been deterred. New knowledge and research have opened promising areas for exploring and developing more sophisticated rehabilitation techniques. Contemporary studies on language processing, new applications of microcomputer technology, the development of alternative communication systems, and research in the management of the psychosocial reactions offer hope for improving the treatment management of patients with acquired aphasia. The study of human brain mechanisms is one of the last frontiers of biology and as such will continue to be an irresistible challenge.

DYSARTHRIA

The term dysarthria refers to an impairment of speech production, resulting from damage to the central or peripheral nervous system that causes weakness, paralysis, or incoordination of the motor-speech system. Any one or all of the components of the motor-speech system—respiration, phonation, articulation, resonance, and prosody—may be compromised by neural damage. The type and degree of dysarthria depends on the underlying etiology, degree of neuropathology, coexistence of other disabilities, and the individual response of the patient to the condition. It is not unusual for dysarthria to coexist with aphasia in patients who have suffered cerebral vascular accidents or traumatic head injury. The severity of dysarthria may range from the production of occasional imprecisely articulated consonant sounds to speech that is rendered totally unintelligible by the degree of impairment to the underlying systems. When patients are totally unintelligible as the result of severe motor-speech system impairment, they are referred to as **anarthric.**

Dysarthria is generally reflected in deficits occurring in multiple motor-speech systems, but may sometimes occur in a single system (e.g., an impairment of soft palate movement resulting in hypernasality). It is most notably prevalent in cerebral palsy, traumatic brain injury (TBI), cerebral vascular accidents, demyelinating diseases (e.g., multiple sclerosis, Parkinson's disease, amyotrophic lateral sclerosis), and neoplasm.

Types of Dysarthria

There are five primary types of dysarthria: **spastic, flaccid, ataxic,** *hypokinetic,* and *hyperkinetic.* When two or more types coexist, the term **mixed dysarthria** is used.

SPASTIC DYSARTHRIA

Spastic dysarthria is characterized by imprecise articulation, slow labored articulation, hypernasality, harsh to strained phonation, and monotonous pitch. Syllables may be given equal stress and inflection. There is often reduced exhalatory control, with shallow inhalations and slow breaths. The spastic dysarthrias are the result of bilateral pyramidal system damage involving the corticobulbar tracts (upper motor neurons). The pathology may cause weakness and paresis of the face and tongue musculature on the side opposite the lesion.

FLACCID DYSARTHRIA

Flaccid dysarthria is characterized by slow and/or labored articulation, hypernasality, and hoarse, breathy phonation. Phrases may be short, inhalation is shallow, and the control of exhalation may be reduced. There is often a reduction in the variation of pitch and loudness with audible inspirations.

ATAXIC DYSARTHRIA

Ataxic dysarthria is characterized by disturbances of timing, speech, movement, range, control, and coordination of the muscles of speech and respiration. Speech is imprecise, slow, and irregular. There may be intermittent periods of explosive inflection, syllable stress, and loudness patterns. Phonemes may be prolonged, pitch and loudness are monotonous. The lesions producing ataxic dysarthria are bilateral, generalized lesions involving the deep midline nuclei and pathways of the cerebellum.

HYPOKINETIC DYSARTHRIA

Hypokinetic dysarthria is characterized by variable articulatory precision, slow rate of speech, harsh, hoarse voice quality, excessive and overly long pauses, prolonged syllables, and reduced phonation. Patients with Parkinson's disease or parkinsonian symptoms often manifest hypokinetic dysarthria that is caused by lesions of the substantia nigra.

HYPERKINETIC DYSARTHRIA

Hyperkinetic dysarthria is characterized by variable articulatory precision, vocal harshness, prolonged sounds and intervals between words, monotonous pitch, and loudness. Patients with Huntington's disease manifest hyperkinetic dysarthria, which is caused by lesions of the basal ganglia and/or their extrapyramidal projections.

Dysarthria Rehabilitation

Speech rehabilitation for the patient with dysarthria must be individually designed and must take into account the profile of impairment and the variability of its disability effects. The successful performance of components of the motor-speech system does not necessarily result in changes in the disabling effects of the dysarthria;[132] that is, the intelligibility of speech. Goals that relate to the level of disability rather than normal speech are generally more realistic, for they do not focus on normalcy, which is usually an unachievable goal, or improvement in the performance of a single component of the motor speech system, which may not, in the overall picture, be functionally important.

The focus of speech rehabilitation for the patient with dysarthria is sometimes based on an approach to treatment that stresses compensatory skills. These techniques tend to encourage the patient to minimize the overall disability by strategies that may actually deviate from the normal (e.g., slowing down the rate of speech production to increase intelligibility of consonant production).

The primary objective of speech rehabilitation with dysarthric patients is to improve the intelligibility of speech. Though exercises are generally administered that are intended to increase the precision, strength, and coordination of movements of the motor-speech system and the coordinated action of various components of the system, the general focus of dysarthria rehabilitation is phonetic, since it is articulatory precision that contributes most to overall intelligibility. Clearly, as a patient's overall physical coordination and precision of movement are increased, there are corresponding improvements noted in the control of the motor-speech system, hence improved speech intelligibility.

approaches, designed to improve phonetic placement accuracy, typically depend on imitation, stress, and progressive approximation. Patients are rehearsed in these drills using kinesthetic, visual, and auditory cues. Generally, the stimuli used as the bases for these exercises are selected in a presumed order of difficulty, beginning with nonoral imitation, followed by sounds, words, phrases, and finally utterances.

Treatment techniques for speech dyspraxia have been described by many clinicians.[133-141] Dworkin et al.[142] reported an effective treatment regimen in a study of a single subject. Various rhythmic techniques in which the patient generates the rhythm have also been reported as facilitory methods to increase articulation accuracy.[93,143] In contrast, Shane and Darley[144] found that articulation precision tended to deteriorate under externally imposed rhythmic stimulation. Melodic intonation therapy has also been employed as a facilitory technique in the treatment of the patient with speech dyspraxia.

The long-term nature of the recovery of phonemic production in patients with verbal apraxia was confirmed in a study of a patient with aphasia who received speech therapy for 10 years. The errors that prevailed in the first poststroke year were compared with his performance at 10 years. The features of place and manner of production had improved, and though voicing and addition errors persisted, omission errors were virtually eliminated.[145]

VERBAL APRAXIA

Some patients with nonfluent (Broca's) aphasia present with articulatory difficulty manifest in imprecise and awkward articulation, distortion of phoneme production, and some literal *paraphasic* (sound substitution) errors in the absence of impaired strength or coordination of the motor speech system. This characteristic, which may be so severe that the patient is hardly intelligible, can appear to be independent of any difficulty in language processing and is referred to as verbal apraxia (or speech dyspraxia, apraxia of speech, cortical dysarthria, phonetic disintegration). Unlike dysarthric speakers, apraxic speakers do not generally have deficits in performing nonspeech movements of the oral musculature. The possible independence of this deficit from the language disorder of Broca's aphasia remains controversial.

Treatment of the Patient with Verbal Dyspraxia

The disorder of articulation referred to as verbal dyspraxia seldom, if ever, is manifest in the absence of a coexisting Broca's aphasia, however mild. The verbal dyspraxia component of this multifaceted communication disorder appears to be especially amenable to direct therapeutic intervention, using approaches adapted primarily from traditional articulation therapy techniques, including stress, and intonation drills. These

DYSPHAGIA

Many patients with neurogenic communication disorders also manifest deficits in swallowing (**dysphagia**). Because dysphagia is frequently associated with neurologic conditions, it rarely exists independent of other disabilities (e.g., facial palsy, speech deficit). An estimated 13 percent of individuals who have suffered strokes comprise a significant proportion of those with swallowing deficits.[146] Dysphagia is often present in patients with Parkinson's disease, Huntington's disease, the dystonias and dyskinesias, amyotrophic lateral sclerosis, multiple sclerosis, neoplasm, and other degenerative neurologic conditions, as well as cerebral palsy. In the poststroke patient, dysphagia may be mild or severe, and in some cases is only present in the acute phase immediately after the stroke. Swallowing deficits in poststroke patients usually involve pharyngeal dysfunction, reduced elevation of the larynx and closure of the laryngeal inlet, and insufficient muscular control of the pharyngeal wall and tongue base to propel a bolus.

The assessment of dysphagia is generally accomplished by administering modified barium swallow examinations and videoendoscopy.[147,148]

Rehabilitation of Dysphagia

Many compensatory treatment techniques designed to redirect food with less risk and greater efficiency are employed in the management of patients with swallowing disorders. Postural techniques are introduced to reduce the possibility of aspiration.[149] Exercises to increase the coordination and range of motion of the muscles involved in the pharyngeal swallow, such as laryngeal elevation and tongue retraction, are also employed.[150]

ALTERNATIVE AND AUGMENTATIVE COMMUNICATION SYSTEMS AND DEVICES

New technology, especially that employing synthetic speech generators and microcomputers, has been adapted for use as either a compensatory means of communication or a facilitatory technique to enhance or substitute for impaired speech (i.e., aphasia, dysarthria). Since the advent of microcomputers, they have been adapted for use in the treatment of aphasia.

Microcomputers were the basis for an approach that Seron et al.[151] found effective in treating patients with writing disorders associated with aphasia. With continued exposure to training, an improvement in accuracy and recognition time in reading commonly used words,[152] and improvement in auditory comprehension were noted in a patient with aphasia who, when followed at a later date, showed additional gains.[153,154] Computer-generated phonemic cues were effective in improving naming in five patients with Broca's aphasia.[155] An augmentative system was developed for a Broca's aphasia patient;[156] a word retrieval facilitation program was developed for individuals with aphasia;[157] and Steele et al.[112] and Weinrich et al.[158] replicated and extended the findings of Gardner et al.[109] and Baker et al.[159] by training those with aphasia to use a computerized version of the VIC system.

If an individual who is unable to make him- or herself understood has residual writing and/or spelling skills, aids which utilize the alphabet can provide a means of communication (e.g., an alphabet board). A communication book may consist of pictures or words arranged according to topics (e.g., foods, family members) in a notebook for easy access. The same type of material has also been adapted for computerized access in the form of portable or table-top devices. Alternative and **augmentative communication devices** can be divided into "high-tech" and "low-tech" categories. Typewriters, telephones, communication books, and other similar devices are in the low-tech category, requiring only batteries or electricity. The high-tech category includes specially adapted computers and switching systems.

Thus far, only a small proportion of the aphasia population has benefited from alternative and augmentative applications. A larger number of motor-speech impaired persons (i.e., those with cerebral palsy) have been able to increase their communicative effectiveness with technical aids. The complex interaction of language, the motor-speech system, and cognition in aphasia pose a challenge to current and future technology.[160]

THE PHYSICAL THERAPIST AND THE COMMUNICATION-IMPAIRED PATIENT

In some settings, especially the acute hospital situation, the physical therapist may be the first to become aware of a patient's communication disorder. The patient should be referred to a speech-language pathologist for evaluation. The physical therapist can contribute to the patient's improvement in communication function in two important ways: by providing physiologic support for speech functions, and by stimulating and facilitating communication through successful, fulfilling interaction with the patient. In either case, the physical therapist will want to work closely with the speech-language pathologist to ensure that they agree as to the treatment goals, and that their respective roles are not in conflict.

The provision of physiologic support for speech functions is especially relevant to the patient with pathology of the oral-motor system (e.g., dysarthria). The physical therapist will want to explore the influence of physiologic support on the patient's speech when planning the appropriate physical therapy intervention. Proper posture, for example, can help to inhibit reflexes that may trigger primitive movements. When a patient's speech function is influenced by overflow movements, stabilization techniques may be indicated.

Control of respiration is essential to the improvement of vocalization and the phrasing of speech. The muscles of respiration can be strengthened with exercises designed to increase head control, (trunk) stability, and sitting balance. It goes without saying that proper posture and eye contact enhance the possibility that speech will be audible and clear.

Muscle-strengthening exercises to increase the speed and range of motion of the tongue, lips, and general facial musculature, and to improve coordination of the oral-motor system also increase the probability of intelligible speech and help the patient with dysphagia. Postural techniques are especially important for patients with dysphagia. Such patients require individually tailored treatment programs designed to facilitate swallowing and prevent aspiration. When communication-impaired patients are prescribed a communication board, physical therapists contribute by determining a patient's sitting balance and tolerance, upper extremity motor control, and the best method for responding (e.g., pointing).

Because communication is a social activity, the physical therapy setting is a natural context for social interaction. The setting can be supportive by providing an atmosphere that is conducive to conversation and allows the patient to engage in a successful verbal interaction.

Neurologically compromised patients often have difficulty processing information in a distracting setting. Excessive noise, competing voices, and the presence of other multiple stimuli can make communication particularly difficult. When possible, the physical therapist should strive to work with the communicatively impaired patient in a setting that is free of these distractions. Patients with communication disabilities do best when they are positioned in such a way that face-to-face communication is possible, including the visualization of gestures and facial expressions. In this regard, room lighting needs to be sufficient.

The physical therapist can be confused and frustrated by patients who manifest neurogenic speech-language disorders, especially those with aphasia. The individual nature of each aphasia argues for a close working relationship between physical therapist and speech-language pathologist. It is desirable that the physical therapist discuss individual cases with the speech-language pathologist and request guidelines on the most effective communication strategies.

One of the greatest difficulties in managing patients with acquired aphasia is the assessment and acknowledgment of a patient's level of auditory comprehension. Virtually all patients with aphasia have some degree of difficulty in comprehending spoken language. Physical therapists need to become skilled at recognizing and dealing with auditory comprehension deficits since they can comprise a major deterrent to successful therapy management.

Misconceptions of auditory comprehension level for a patient with aphasia can range from the assumption that a patient understands everything to the assumption that the patient comprehends nothing and must be excluded from conversation. A guiding principle to keep in mind is that auditory comprehension can vary greatly, depending on the context and complexity of the task at hand. Switching topics quickly, speaking too quickly, background noises, talking while a patient is engaged in physical activity, and conversing with more than one person at a time can impede the individual's ability to process information in the auditory mode. Sentences should be short and simple, and the patient should be given sufficient time to process the information and formulate a response. Directives or questions that require elaborate answers, such as "Tell me about your vacation," or "What do you think about the latest news?" are generally difficult for patients with aphasia to answer. It is best to ask questions that can be answered with "yes" or "no" or another single word. Physical assistive cues to comprehension such as gestures, facial expression, and voice inflection can facilitate and enhance a patient's understanding. It is also important for the physical therapist to know that patients with aphasia often find it easier to respond to whole body or axial commands ("stand up," "sit down") than distal commands ("point," "pick up").

It can be tempting to try to remedy a laborious communication situation by "talking down" to a patient with aphasia, as if speaking to a child, or raising one's voice as if speaking to someone with impaired hearing. The best strategy is to endeavor to speak a little more slowly, using language that is not too complex, and remaining consistent in giving instructions. This can be particularly important in the physical therapy setting, where verbal commands are a fundamental element in the patient-therapist interaction. At times it may be necessary to repeat oneself in order to be understood.

It is almost universal that rehabilitation team members overestimate the degree to which a person with aphasia understands spoken language. Physical therapists, when possible, should turn to the speech-language pathologist for an indication of the patient's preserved auditory comprehension. It may be necessary to rephrase questions and supplement speech with body language in order to ensure comprehension.

The use of accompanying visual cues, such as gestures and facial expressions, can be extremely helpful for some patients. Others may understand best if a message is supplemented by written cues. Sometimes one can assist by asking questions that can be answered by "yes" or "no" in a "twenty questions" format. When those with aphasia are having trouble expressing themselves, it usually helps to allow them extra time to speak. If a patient becomes visibly frustrated, it is desirable to remain calm and to suggest that the patient wait and try again later.

In carrying out physical therapy techniques, patients with aphasia can be encouraged to produce single-word, repetitive speech that coincides with physical movements as a means of providing supplemental speech practice. Such activities as counting movements in series 1–10; using words like up and down, left and right, and so forth while performing physical movements are examples. The physical therapist, however, should always remain sensitive to the possibility of making speech demands that are beyond a patient's level of preserved communicative skill.

CONCLUSION

Ever since World War II, speech-language pathologists have played an important role on the rehabilitation medicine team in the management of patients with neurogenic speech-language disorders, especially aphasia and dysarthria. For the physical therapist, an understanding of normal and pathological communication behavior can not only make this population of patients more interesting to work with, but can also enhance the quality of treatment provided for them.

Communication using the speech code is a complex, species-specific behavior that consists of the coordinated interaction of cognitive, motor, sensory, psychologic, and social skills. The neurogenic disorders of speech and language, specifically aphasia and dysarthria, dominate the population of communication-impaired patients in the rehabilitation medicine setting. Viewed as a group, patients with neurogenic communication disorders comprise a relatively severely impaired segment of the disabled population.

The impact of neurogenic speech-language disorders on the "self," the family, community life, and vocational options makes these disorders especially challenging. The close relationship of one's verbal characteristics to personality and identity may cause even the mildest neurogenic communication disorder to affect the psychosocial domain. Current research is investigating the interaction of linguistic, cognitive, and psychosocial variables and their influence on the outcome of recovery and rehabilitation.

QUESTIONS FOR REVIEW

1. Define aphasia.
2. Describe the differences that distinguish nonfluent from fluent aphasic syndromes and give clinical examples.
3. Discuss the components of a comprehensive language test designed to measure aphasic impairment.
4. Describe some critical factors in the evaluation of recovery in aphasia.
5. Describe psychologic sequelae that may have a negative effect on the outcome of aphasia rehabilitation.

6. Discuss the importance of time since onset as it relates to recovery from aphasia.
7. Define dysarthria.
8. What neurologic conditions are generally associated with dysphagia?
9. Describe augmentative communication systems and some specific techniques and/or devices that may enhance the treatment of aphasia.

REFERENCES

1. Adams, PF and Benson, V: Current estimates from the National Health Survey, 1990. National Center for Health Statistics. Vital Health Statistics 10:181, 1991.
2. Slater, SC: Portrait of the professions. 1992 Omnibus Survey. ASHA 34:61, 1992.
3. Shewan, CM and Slater, SC: ASHA Data: ASHA's speech-language pathologists and audiologists across the United States. ASHA 64, 1992.
4. Bender, M: ASHA Data: roots and wings: ASHA's membership 1925 to 1989. ASHA 31:76, 1989.
5. World Health Organization (WHO): International Classification of Impairment, Disabilities and Handicap. World Health Organization, Geneva, Switzerland, 1980.
6. US Census Bureau: Current Population Report. Publication No. 541. Government Printing Office, Washington, DC, 1975.
7. US Department of Health and Human Services: Aging America: Trends and Projections, 1987-88 Edition. Government Printing Office, Washington, DC, 1988.
8. Spencer, G: Projects of the Population of the United States by Age, Sex, and Race: 1983 to 2080. Current Population Reports, Series P-25, No. 952. US Bureau of the Census, Washington, DC, 1984.
9. National Institutes of Health (NIH): Aphasia: Hope Through Research. NIH Publication No. 80-391, Bethesda, MD, 1979.
10. Brust, JC, et al: Aphasia in acute stroke. Stroke 7:167-174, 1976.
11. National Institutes of Health (NIH): Decade of research: answers through scientific research. The National Advisory Neurological and Communicative Disorders and Stroke Council. The National Institutes of Health, Bethesda, MD, 1989.
12. Goodglass, H and Kaplan, E: The Assessment of Aphasia and Related Disorders, ed 2. Lea & Febiger, Philadelphia, 1983.
13. Damasio, A: Signs of aphasia. In Sarno, MT (ed): Acquired Aphasia, ed 2. Academic Press, New York, 1991, pp 27-43.
14. Sarno, MT: A survey of 100 aphasic Medicare patients in a speech pathology program. J Am Geriatr Soc 18:471-480, 1970.
15. Prins, R, Snow, C, and Wagenaar, E: Recovery from aphasia: spontaneous speech versus language comprehension. Brain Lang 6:192-211, 1978.
16. Levin, HS, et al: Linguistic recovery after aphasia closed head injury. Brain Lang 12:360-374, 1981.
17. Spreen, O and Risser, A: Assessment of aphasia. In Sarno, MT (ed): Acquired Aphasia, ed 2. Academic Press, New York, 1991, pp 73-150.
18. Spreen, O and Benton, AL: Neurosensory Center Comprehensive Examination for Aphasia, ed 2. University of Victoria, Department of Psychology, Neuropsychology Laboratory, Victoria, BC, 1977.
19. Kertesz, A: Western Aphasia Battery. Grune & Stratton, New York, 1982.
20. Taylor Sarno, M: A measurement of functional communication in aphasia. Arch Phys Med Rehabil 46:101-107, 1965.
21. Sarno, MT: The Functional Communication Profile: Manual of Directions. Rehabilitation Monograph No. 42. New York University Medical Center, Rusk Institute of Rehabilitation Medicine, New York, 1969.
22. Holland, AL: Communicative abilities in daily living. University Park Press, Baltimore, 1980.
23. Benton, AL: Contributions to aphasia before Broca. Cortex 1:314-327, 1964.
24. Benton, AL and Joynt, RJ: Early descriptions of aphasia. Arch Neurol 3:109-126, 1960.
25. Mettler, CC: History of Medicine. Blakiston, Philadelphia, 1947.
26. Critchley, M: Aphasiology and Other Aspects of Language. Edward Arnold, London, 1970.
27. Broca, P: Du siège de la faculté du langage articulé. Bulletin de la Societe d'Anthropologie 6:377-399, 1885.
28. Broadbent, D: A case of peculiar affection of speech, with commentary. Brain 1:484-503, 1879.
29. Mills, CK: Treatment of aphasia by training. JAMA 43:1940-1949, 1904.
30. Poppelreuter, W: Ueber psychische ausfall sercheinungen nach hirverletzungen. Munchener Medizinische Wochenschrift 62:489-491, 1915.
31. Isserlin, M: Die pathologische physiologie der sprache. Ergebnisse der Physiologie, Biologischene Chemie und Experimentellen Pharmakologie 29:129, 1929.
32. Frazier, C and Ingham, S: A review of the effects of gunshot wounds of the head. Arch Neurol Psychiatry 3:17-40, 1920.
33. Gopfert, H: Beitrage zur Frage der Restitution nach Hirnverletzung. Zeitschrift fur die Gesamte Neurologie und Psychiatrie 75:411-459, 1922.
34. Franz, S: Studies in re-education: the aphasics. J Comp Psychol 4:349-429, 1924.
35. Head, H: Aphasia and kindred disorders of speech, vols 1 and 2. Cambridge University Press, London, 1926.
36. Nielsen, J: Agnosia, apraxia, aphasia: their value in cerebral localization. Hoeber, New York, 1946.
37. Goldstein, K: After effects of brain injuries in war: their evaluation and treatment. Grune & Stratton, New York, 1942.
38. Singer, H and Low, A: The brain in a case of motor aphasia in which improvement occurred with training. Arch Neurol Psychiatry 29:162-165, 1933.
39. Weisenburg, T and McBride, K: Aphasia: a clinical and psychological study. Commonwealth Fund, New York, 1935.
40. Wepman, JM: Recovery from aphasia. Ronald Press, New York, 1951.
41. Luria, AR: Rehabilitation of brain functioning after war traumas. Academy of Sciences Press, Moscow, 1948.
42. Aphasia and the family. Publication EM 359. American Heart Association, Dallas, 1969.
43. Backus, O, et al: Aphasia in adults. University of Michigan Press, Ann Arbor, 1947.
44. Taylor Sarno, M: Language therapy. In Burr, HG (ed): The Aphasic Adult: Evaluation and Rehabilitation. Proceedings of the Short Course in Aphasia. Wayside Press, Charlottesville, VA, 1964.
45. Boone, D: An Adult Has Aphasia: For the Family, ed 2. Interstate Printers and Publishers, Danville, IL, 1984.
46. Sarno, JE and Sarno, MT: Stroke: A Guide for Patients and Their Families, ed 3. McGraw-Hill, New York, 1991.
47. Simonson, J: According to the Aphasic Adult. University of Texas (Southwestern) Medical School, Dallas, 1971.
48. Taylor-Sarno, M: Understanding Aphasia: A Guide for Family and Friends. Monograph No. 2. Rusk Institute of Rehabilitation Medicine, New York University Medical Center, New York, 1958.
49. Yarnell, P, Monroe, P, and Sobel, L: Aphasia outcome in stroke: a clinical neuroradiological correlation. Stroke 7:514-522, 1976.
50. Sarno, MT: The functional assessment of verbal impairment. In

Grimby, G. (ed): Recent Advances in Rehabilitation Medicine. Almquist & Wiksell, Stockholm, 1983, pp 75–81.

51. Sarno, JE, Sarno, MT, and Levita, E: The functional life scale. Arch Phys Med Rehabil 54:214–220, 1973.

52. Darley, F: The efficacy of language rehabilitation in aphasia. J Speech Hear Disord 37:3–21, 1972.

53. Prins, R, Schoonen, R, and Vermeulen, J: Efficacy of two different types of speech therapy for aphasic stroke patients. Applied Psycholinguistics 10:85–123, 1989.

54. Wertz, RT, et al: VA cooperative study on aphasia: a comparison of individual and group treatment. J Speech Hear Disord 24:580–594, 1981.

55. Wertz, RT, et al: Comparison of clinic, home, and deferred language treatment for aphasia: a VA cooperative study. Arch Neurol 43:653–658, 1986.

56. Wertz, RT: Language treatment for aphasia is efficacious, but for whom? Top Lang Disord 8:1–10, 1987.

57. Sarno, MT: Recovery and rehabilitation in aphasia. In Sarno, MT (ed): Acquired Aphasia, ed 2. Academic Press, San Diego, 1991.

58. Marks, M, Taylor Sarno, ML, and Rusk, H: Rehabilitation of the aphasic patient: a survey of three years experience in a rehabilitation setting. Neurology 7:837–843, 1957.

59. Vignolo, LA: Evolution of aphasia and language rehabilitation: a retrospective exploratory study. Cortex 1:344–367, 1964.

60. Hagen, C: Communication abilities in hemiplegia: effect of speech therapy. Arch Phys Med Rehabil 54:545–463, 1973.

61. Basso, A, Faglioni, P, and Vignolo, L: Étude controlée de la reeducation du langage dans l'aphasie: comparaison entre aphasiques traites et non-traites. Revue Neurologique 131:607–614, 1975.

62. Basso, A, Capitani, E, and Vignolo, LA: Influence of rehabilitation on language skills in aphasic patients. Arch Neurol 36:190–196, 1979.

63. Shewan, C and Kertesz, A: Effects of speech and language treatment on recovery from aphasia. Brain Lang 23:272–299, 1984.

64. Poeck, K, Huber, W, and Willmes, K: Outcome of intensive language treatment in aphasia. J Speech Hear Disord 54:471–479, 1989.

65. Kertesz, A and McCabe, P: Recovery patterns and prognosis in aphasia. Brain Lang 100:1–18, 1977.

66. Levita, E: Effects of speech therapy on aphasics' responses to the Functional Communication Profile. Percept Motor Skills 47:151–154, 1978.

67. Shewan, CM: Expressive language recovery in aphasia using the Shewan Spontaneous Language Analysis (SSLA) System. J Commun Disord 17:175–187, 1988.

68. Wertz, RT and Dronkers, N: Effects of age on aphasia. Paper presented at the American Speech-Language-Hearing Association Research Symposium on Communication Sciences and Disorders and Aging, Washington, DC, 1988.

69. Helm-Estabrooks, N and Ramsberger, G: Treatment of agrammatism in long-term Broca's aphasia. Br J Disord Commun 21:39–45, 1986.

70. Glindemann, R, et al: The efficacy of modelling in PACE-therapy. Aphasiology 5:425–429, 1991.

71. Darley, F: Language rehabilitation: presentation 8. In Benton, A (ed): Behavioral Change in Cerebrovascular Disease. Harper, New York, 1970.

72. Reinvang, I and Engvik, E: Language recovery in aphasia from 3–6 months after stroke. In Sarno, MT and Hook, O (eds): Aphasia: Assessment and Treatment. Almquist & Wiksell, Stockholm, Masson, New York, 1980.

73. Sarno, MT: Review of research in aphasia: recovery and rehabilitation. In Sarno, MT and Hook, O (eds): Aphasia: Assessment and Treatment. Almquist & Wiksell, Stockholm, 1980.

74. Culton, G: Spontaneous recovery from aphasia. J Speech Hear Res 12:825–832, 1969.

75. Lomas, A and Kertesz, A: Patterns of spontaneous recovery in aphasic groups: a study of adult stroke patients. Brain Lang 5:388–401, 1978.

76. Demeurisse, G, et al: Quantitative study of the rate of recovery from aphasia due to ischemic stroke. Stroke 11:455–458, 1980.

77. Butfield, E and Zangwill, O: Re-education in aphasia: a review of 70 cases. J Neurol Neurosurg Psychiatry 9:75–79, 1946.

78. Sands, E, Sarno, MT, and Shankweiler, D: Long-term assessment of language function in aphasia due to stroke. Arch Phys Med Rehabil 50:203–207, 1969.

79. Sarno, MT and Levita, E: Natural course of recovery in severe aphasia. Arch Phys Med Rehabil 52:175–179, 1971.

80. Nicholas, M, et al: Empty speech in Alzheimer's disease and fluent aphasia. J Speech Hear Res 28:405–410, 1985.

81. Bayles, KA and Kaszniak, AW: Communication and cognition in normal aging and dementia. Little, Brown, Boston, 1987.

82. Obler, LK, et al: On comprehension across the adult life span. Cortex 21:273–280, 1985.

83. Bloom, R, et al: Impact of emotional content on discourse production in patients with unilateral brain damage. Brain Lang 42:153–164, 1992.

84. Sarno, MT: The status of research in recovery from aphasia. In Lebrun, Y and Hoops, R (eds): Recovery in Aphasics. Swets & Zeitlinger, Amsterdam, 1976, pp 13–30.

85. McGlone, J: Sex differences in human brain asymmetry: a critical survey. Behav Brain Sci 3:215–263, 1980.

86. McGlone, J: Sex differences in the cerebral organization of verbal functions in patients with unilateral brain lesions. Brain 100:775–793, 1977.

87. Gloning, K, et al: Prognosis and speech therapy in aphasia. In Lebrun, Y and Hoops, R (eds): Recovery in Aphasics. Swets & Zeitlinger, Amsterdam, 1976, pp 57–64.

88. Rose, C, Boby, V, and Capildeo, R: A retrospective survey of speech disorders following stroke, with particular reference to the value of speech therapy. In Lebrun, Y and Hoops, R (eds): Recovery in Aphasics. Swets & Zeitlinger, Amsterdam, 1976, pp 189–197.

89. Wade, DT, Hewer, RL, and Wood, VA: Stroke: influence of patients' sex and side of weakness on outcome. Arch Phys Med Rehabil 65:513–516, 1984.

90. Sarno, MT, Buonaguro, A, and Levita, E: Gender and recovery from aphasia after stroke. J Nerv Ment Dis 173:605–609, 1985.

91. Basso, A, Capitani, E, and Moraschini, S: Sex differences in recovery from aphasia. Cortex 18:469–475, 1982.

92. Sarno, MT and Levita, E: Recovery in treated aphasia in the first year post stroke. Stroke 10:663–670, 1979.

93. Schuell, H, Jenkins, J, and Jimenez-Pabon, E: Aphasia in Adults. Harper, New York, 1964.

94. Selnes, OA, et al: Recovery of single-word comprehension CT scan correlates. Brain Lang 21:72–84, 1984.

95. Kertesz, A: Aphasia and associated disorders: taxonomy, localization and recovery. Grune & Stratton, New York, 1979.

96. Pieniadz, JM, et al: CT scan cerebral hemisphere asymmetries—measurements in stroke patients with global aphasia: atypical asymmetries. Cortex 19:371–391, 1983.

97. Selnes, OA, et al: Computed tomographic scan correlates of auditory comprehension deficits in aphasia. A prospective recovery study. Ann Neurol 13:558–566, 1983.

98. Kenin, M and Swisher, L: A study of pattern of recovery in aphasia. Cortex 8:56–68, 1972.

99. Lebrun, Y: Recovery in polyglot aphasics. In Lebrun, Y and Hoops, R (eds): Recovery in Aphasics. Neurolinguistics, vol 4. Swets & Zeitlinger, BV, Amsterdam, 1976.

100. Sarno, MT: The silent minority: the patient with aphasia. Hemphill Lecture. Rehabilitation Institute of Chicago, Chicago, 1986.

101. Darley, FL, Aronson, AE, and Brown, JR: Motor speech disorders. WB Saunders, Philadelphia, 1975.

102. Sarno, MT: Aphasia rehabilitation. In Dickson, S (ed): Communication Disorders: Remedial Principles and Practices. Scott Foresman, Glenview, IL, 1974.

103. Sarno, MT: Disorders of communication in stroke. In Licht, S (ed): Stroke and Its Rehabilitation. Williams & Wilkins, Baltimore, 1975, pp 380–408.

104. Sarno, MT: Language rehabilitation outcome in the elderly aphasic patient. In Obler, LK and Albert, ML (eds): Language and Communication in the Elderly: Clinical, Therapeutic and Experimental Issues. DC Heath, Lexington, MA, 1980, pp 191–204.

105. Goodglass, H: Neurolinguistic principles and aphasia therapy. In Meier, M, Benton, A, and Diller, L (eds): Neuropsychological Rehabilitation. Guilford, New York, 1987.

106. Benson, DF: Aphasia, Alexia, and Agraphia. Churchill Livingstone, New York, 1979.

107. Burns, MS and Halper, AS: Speech/Language Treatment of the Aphasias: An Integrated Clinical Approach. Aspen, Rockville, MD, 1988.

108. Sarno, MT: Management of aphasia. In Bornstein, RA and Brown,

GG (eds): Neurobehavioral Aspects of Cerebrovascular Disease. Oxford University Press, New York, 1990.

109. Gardner, H, et al: Visual communication in aphasia. Neuropsychologia 14:275, 1976.

110. Weinrich, MP, Steele, RD, and Illes, J: Implementation of a visual communicative system for aphasic patients on a microcomputer. Ann Neurol 18:148, 1985.

111. Steele, RD, et al: Evaluating performance of severely aphasic patients on a computer-aided visual communication system. In Brookshire, RH (ed): Clinical Aphasiology: Conference Proceedings. BRK Publications, Minneapolis, 1987.

112. Steele, RD: Computer-based visual communication in aphasia. Neuropsychologia 27:409–426, 1993.

113. Weinrich, MP: Computerized visual communication (C-VIC) therapy. Paper presented at the Academy of Aphasia, Phoenix, Arizona, 1987.

114. Helm-Estabrooks, N and Benson, DF: Visual action therapy for global aphasia. Presentation at the 16th Annual Meeting of the Academy of Aphasia, Chicago, 1978.

115. Helm-Estabrooks, N, Fitzpatrick, PM, and Barresi, B: Visual action therapy for aphasia. J Speech Hear Disord 47:385–389, 1982.

116. Skelly, M, et al: American Indian sign (AMERIND) as a facilitator of verbalization for the oral verbal apraxic. J Speech Hear Dis 39:445–456, 1974.

117. Rao, P and Horner, J: Gesture as a deblocking modality in a severe aphasic patient. In Brookshire, RH (ed): Clinical Aphasiology: Conference Proceedings. BRK Publications, Minneapolis, 1978.

118. Rao, P, et al: The use of American-Indian Code by severe aphasic adults. In Burns, M and Andrews, J (eds): Neuropathologies of Speech and Language Diagnosis and Treatment: Selected Papers. Institute for Continuing Education, Evanston, IL, 1980.

119. Aten, JL, Caliguri, MP, and Holland, AL: The efficacy of functional communication therapy for chronic aphasic patients. J Speech Hear Disord 47:93–96, 1982.

120. Aten, JL: Function communication treatment. In Chapey, R (ed): Language Intervention Strategies in Adult Aphasia, ed 2. Williams & Wilkins, Baltimore, 1986.

121. Wilcox, M and Davis, G: Promoting aphasics' communicative effectiveness. Paper presented to the American Speech-Language-Hearing Association, San Francisco, 1978.

122. Ullman, M: Behavioral Changes in Patients Following Strokes. Charles C Thomas, Springfield, IL, 1962.

123. Friedman, M: On the nature of regression. Arch Gen Psychiatry 3:17–40, 1961.

124. Brumfitt, S and Clarke, P: An application of psychotherapeutic techniques to the management of aphasia. Paper presented at Summer Conference: Aphasia Therapy, Cardiff, UK, July 19, 1980.

125. Tanner, D: Loss and grief: implications for the speech-language pathologist and audiologist. J Am Speech Hear Assoc 22:916–928, 1980.

126. Baretz, R and Stephenson, G: Unrealistic patient. N Y State J Med 76:54–57, 1976.

127. Kübler-Ross, E: On Death and Dying. Macmillan, New York, 1969.

128. Espmark, S: Stroke before fifty: a follow-up study of vocational and psychological adjustment. Scand J Rehabil Med Suppl 2:1–107, 1973.

129. Caplan, AL, Callahan, D, and Haas, J: Ethical and Policy Issues in Rehabilitation Medicine. A Hastings Center Report, Special Supplement. The Hastings Center, Briarcliff Manor, NY, 1987.

130. Hass, J, Caplan, AL, and Callahan, DJ: Case Studies in Ethics and Rehabilitation. The Hastings Center, Briarcliff Manor, NY, 1988.

131. Sarno, MT: The Case of Mr. M: The Selection and Treatment of Aphasic Patients. Case Studies in Ethics and Rehabilitation Medicine. The Hastings Center, Briarcliff Manor, NY, 1988, pp 24–28.

132. Yorkston, KM, Beukelman, DR, and Bell, KR (eds): Clinical Management of Dysarthric Speakers. Little, Brown, New York, 1988.

133. Deal, J and Florance, C: Modification of the eight-step continuum for treatment of apraxia of speech in adults. J Speech Hear Disord 43:89–95, 1978.

134. Halpern, H: Therapy for agnosia, apraxia, and dysarthria. In Chapey, R (ed): Language Intervention Strategies in Adult Aphasia. Williams & Wilkins, Baltimore, 1981.

135. Rosenbek, JC: Treating apraxia of speech. In Johns, DF (ed): Clinical Management of Neurogenic Communication Disorders. Little, Brown, Boston, 1978.

136. Rosenbek, JC, et al: A treatment for apraxia of speech in adults. J Speech Hear Disord 38:462–472, 1973.

137. Wiedel, IMH: The basic foundation approach for decreasing aphasia and verbal apraxia in adults (BFA). In Brookshire, RH (ed): Clinical Aphasiology: Conference Proceedings. BRK Publications, Minneapolis, 1976.

138. Rosenbek, JC: Advances in the evaluation and treatment of speech apraxia. In Rose, FC (ed): Advances in Neurology. Progress in Aphasiology, vol 42. Raven Press, New York, 1984, pp 327–335.

139. Wertz, RT, LaPointe, L, and Rosenbek, JC: Apraxia of Speech in Adults: The Disorder and Its Management. Grune & Stratton, New York, 1984.

140. Wertz, RT: Language disorders in adults: state of the clinical art. In Holland, AL (ed): Language Disorders in Adults. College Hill, San Diego, 1984.

141. Rubow, R, et al: Vibrotactile stimulation for intersystemic reorganization in the treatment of apraxia of speech. Arch Phys Med Rehabil 63:97–105, 1982.

142. Dworkin, JP, Abharion, GG, and Johns, DF: Dyspraxia of speech: the effectiveness of a treatment regimen. J Speech Hear Disord 53:289–294, 1988.

143. Rosenbek, JC, et al: Treatment of developmental apraxia of speech: a case study. Language, Speech and Hearing Services in the Schools 5:13–22, 1974.

144. Shane, H and Darley, FL: The effect of auditory rhythmic stimulation on articulatory accuracy in apraxia of speech. Cortex 14:444–450, 1978.

145. Sands, E, Freeman, F, and Harris, K: Progressive changes in articulatory patterns in verbal apraxia: a longitudinal case study. Brain Lang 6:97–105, 1978.

146. Frattali, CM: Statement on Post Stroke Rehabilitation presented to the Agency for Healthcare Policy and Research, Washington, DC, 1992.

147. Logemann, JA: A Manual for the Videofluoroscope Evaluation of Swallowing. College Hill, San Diego, 1986.

148. Langmore, SE, Schatz, K, and Olsen, N: Fiberoptic endoscopic examination of swallowing safety: a new procedure. Dysphagia 2:216–219, 1988.

149. Horner, J, et al: Aspiration following stroke: clinical correlates and outcomes. Neurology 38:1359–1362, 1988.

150. Logemann, JA and Kahrilas, P: Relearning to swallow post CVA: application of maneuvers and indirect biofeedback: a case study. Neurology 40:1136–1138, 1990.

151. Seron, X, et al: A computer-based therapy for the treatment of aphasic subjects with writing disorders. J Speech Hear Disord 45:45–58, 1980.

152. Katz, RC and Nagy, V: A computerized approach for improving word recognition in chronic aphasic patients. In Brookshire, RH (ed): Clinical Aphasiology: Conference Proceedings. BRK Publications, Minneapolis, 1983.

153. Mills, RH: Microcomputerized auditory comprehension training. In Brookshire, RH (ed): Clinical Aphasiology: Conference Proceedings. BRK Publications, Minneapolis, 1982.

154. Mills, RH and Hoffer, P: Computers and caring: an integrative approach to the treatment of aphasia and head injury. In Marshall, RC (ed): Case studies in Aphasia Rehabilitation. University Park Press, Baltimore, 1985.

155. Bruce, C and Howard, D: Computer-generated phonemic cues: an effective aid for naming in aphasia. Br J Disord Commun 22:191–201, 1987.

156. Garrett, K, Beukelman, D, and Low-Morrow, D: A comprehensive augmentative communication system for an adult with Broca's aphasia. Augmentative and Alternative Communication 5:55–61, 1989.

157. Hunnicutt, S: Access: A lexical access program. Proceedings of RESNA 12th Annual Conference, New Orleans, LA, 1989, pp 284–335.

158. Weinrich, MP, et al.: Processing of visual syntax in a globally aphasic patient. Brain Lang 36:391–405, 1989.

159. Baker, E, et al: Can linguistic competence be dissociated from natural language functions? Nature 254:609–619, 1975.

160. Kratt, AW: Augmentative and alternative communication (AAC): Does it have a future in aphasia rehabilitation? Aphasiology 4:321–328, 1990.

SUPPLEMENTAL READINGS

Albert, ML, Goodglass, H, Helm, N, Rubens, AB, and Alexander, MP: Clinical Aspects of Dysphasia. Springer-Verlag, New York, 1981.

Albert, ML and Helm-Estabrooks, N: Manual of Aphasia Therapy. Pro-Ed, Austin, 1991.

Chapey, R: Language Intervention Strategies in Adult Aphasia, ed 2. Williams & Wilkins, Baltimore, 1986.

Code, C (ed): The Characteristics of Aphasia. Taylor & Francis, London, 1989.

Davis, GA: A Survey of Adult Aphasia. Prentice-Hall, Englewood Cliffs, NJ, 1983.

Goldstein, K: Language and Language Disturbances. Grune & Stratton, New York, 1948.

Goodglass, H and Kaplan, E: The Assessment of Aphasia and Related Disorders, ed 2. Lea & Febiger, Philadelphia, 1983.

Levin, H, Benton, AL, and Grossman, R: Neurobehavioral Consequences of Closed Head Injury. Oxford University Press, New York, 1982.

Obler, LK and Albert, ML (eds): Language and Communication in the Elderly. DC Heath, Lexington, MA, 1980.

Ponzio, J, LaFond, D, Degiovani, R, Joanette, Y, and Sarno, MT (eds): Living with Aphasia. Singh, San Francisco, 1993.

Reinvang, I: Aphasia and Brain Organization. Plenum Press, New York, 1985.

Sarno, MT and Hook, O (eds): Aphasia: Assessment and Treatment. Almquist & Wiksell, Stockholm; and Masson, New York, 1980.

Sarno, MT (ed): Acquired Aphasia, ed 2. Academic Press, San Diego, 1991.

GLOSSARY

Anarthria (anarthric): Unintelligible speech resulting from a brain lesion, particularly in the brain stem, causing severe impairment of the motor-speech system (SYN: dysarthria).

Aphasia: A communication disorder caused by brain damage and characterized by an impairment of language comprehension, formulation, and use; excludes disorders associated with primary sensory deficits, general mental deterioration, or psychiatric disorders. Partial impairment is often referred to as dysphasia.

Fluent aphasia: A type of aphasia in which speech flows smoothly, with a variety of grammatical constructions and preserved melody of speech; paraphasias and circumlocutions may be present. Auditory comprehension is impaired. Wernicke's aphasia and anomic conduction aphasia are the most common types of fluent aphasia.

Global aphasia. Severe aphasia characterized by marked impairments of the production and comprehension of language; all sensory modalities may be impaired. The individual may be unable to use any expressive speech and may use some gestures or pantomime instead. Gestural language may also be impaired. Responses are not necessarily relevant to context.

Nonfluent aphasia: A type of aphasia in which the flow of speech is slow and hesitant, vocabulary is limited, and syntax is impaired. Articulation may be labored. Broca's aphasia is the most frequently occurring type of nonfluent aphasia.

Apraxia: See verbal apraxia.

Articulation: In speech, the vocal tract movements responsible for speech and sound production; these involve accuracy in placement of the articulators: lips, tongue, velum, or pharynx. Also involved are timing, direction of movements, speed of response, and neural integration of all events.

Articulation disorder: Omission or incorrect production of speech sounds due to faulty placement, timing, direction, pressure, speed, or interaction of the lips, teeth, tongue, velum, or pharynx.

Augmentative communication device: A device used by a person impaired by a communication disorder to provide a compensatory means of communication or to enhance the individual's residual communication skills; for example, manual or electronic communication boards.

Communication: Any means by which an individual relates experiences, ideas, knowledge, and feelings to another; includes speech, sign language, body language, gestures, writing; the process by which meanings are exchanged between individuals through a system of symbols.

Consonant: A speech sound made with (voiced) or without (unvoiced) vocal fold vibration, by certain successive movements of the vocal tract, including the interaction of the articulators (lips, tongue, teeth, velum), which modify, interrupt, or obstruct the exhaled air stream.

Fricative. A category of speech sounds using friction formed by directing the breath stream with adequate pressure against one or more surfaces, principally, the hard palate, gum ridge behind the upper teeth, and lips. The breath stream is continuously flowing but restricted: for example, /f/, /v/.

Liquid: A category of speech sounds made with the soft palate raised: /l/, /r/.

Nasal: A category of speech sounds resulting from the closing of the oral cavity to prevent air from escaping through the mouth, and from a lowered position of the velum or soft palate with a free passage of air through the nose. Nasal sounds are usually voiced but may lose their voicing in combination with voiceless consonants: /n/, /m/, /ng/.

Plosive: A category of speech sounds produced when the impounded air pressure in the portion of the vocal tract behind the constriction is released through the oral cavity: for example, /t/ in short. Plosive sounds are often referred to as "stop" sounds.

Semi-vowel: A category of speech sounds produced by keeping the vocal tract briefly in the vowel-like position, and then changing to the position required for the following vowel in the syllable. Semi-vowel sounds are usually followed by a vowel in whatever syllable they are used: /w/, /y/, /r/.

Context: Aspects of communicative exchange, such as its purpose, environment, location, knowledge of the participants and their various roles, and the level of formality required by the situation.

Disability: The consequences of an impairment and its impact on everyday personal, social, and vocational life.

Dysarthria: A category of motor-speech disorders caused by impairment in parts of the central or peripheral nervous system that mediate speech production. Respiration, articulation, phonation, resonance, and/or prosody may be affected; volitional and automatic actions (e.g., chewing and swallowing), and movement of the jaw and tongue may also be deviant. It excludes apraxia of speech, and functional or central language disorders.

Ataxic dysarthria: Dysarthria associated with damage to the cerebellar system is characterized by speech errors relating primarily to timing, so that equal stress is given to each syllable; articulation problems are typically characterized by intermittent errors ranging from mild to severe; vocal quality is harsh, with monotonous pitch and volume; prosody may range from reduced to unnatural stress.

Flaccid dysarthria: Dysarthria associated with disorders of the lower motor neurons is characterized by mild to marked hypernasality, coupled with nasal emission; continuous breathiness may be present during phonation, with audible inspiration of air; consonant production is imprecise.

Mixed dysarthria: When two or more types of dysarthria coexist, the term mixed dysarthria is used.

Spastic dysarthria: Dysarthria associated with a bilateral upper motor lesion and characterized by imprecise articulation, monotonous pitch and loudness, and poor prosody; muscles are stiff and move sluggishly through a limited range; speech is labored and words may be prolonged; it is often accompanied by facial distortions and short phrasing.

Dysphagia: A swallowing disorder.

Dysphasia: See aphasia.

Functional communication: An individual's communicative effectiveness in everyday life; specifically, the ability to communicate needs, desires, and reactions.

Glottis: The vocal apparatus of the larynx, consisting of the true vocal folds and the opening between them.

Handicap: The value an individual, family, and community place on a disability and the degree to which an individual is disadvantaged because of it.

Impairment: The nature of the pathology itself, including its location and measured size.

Intelligibility: The degree of clarity with which one's utterances are understood by the average listener; influenced by articulation, rate, fluency, vocal quality, and intensity.

Lexicon: 1. The vocabulary or list of all the words in a language. 2. The repertoire of linguistic signs, words, and morphemes in a given language.

Pharynx: An irregular tubular space, considered part of the respiratory and alimentary tracts, which extends from the nasal cavities to the esophagus and is also continuous with the eustachian tubes, mouth, and larynx; in its lower two-thirds it is capable of considerable change of dimension from front to back and from side to side, a factor that contributes to the act of swallowing and influences vocal resonance. It is considered the principal resonator of the human voice.

Phoneme: A sound; the basic linguistic units with which words are formed.

Phonology (phonologic): The study of the sound system of a language.

Pragmatic language: Those nonverbal components of communication that influence the transmission of information (e.g., initiating, turn-taking, maintaining a topic).

Prosody: The melody of speech; determined primarily by modifications of pitch, quality, strength, and duration, which are perceived primarily as stress and intonational patterns.

Semantics (semantic): The study of meaning in language; includes the relationships of language, thought, and behavior.

Spontaneous recovery: In aphasia, the return, complete or incomplete, of impaired communication skills, usually in the first few months after onset.

Syllable: A unit of speech whose central phoneme is a vowel, which may stand alone or be surrounded by one or more consonants: for example, I, in, me, men.

Syntax (syntactical): The internal structure of language, including the order in which the parts of speech of a language are put together to form phrases, clauses, or sentences; sometimes referred to as grammar.

Velar: Sounds formed with the back of the tongue on or near the soft palate. Velar sounds are referred to as gutteral.

Verbal apraxia: Impairment of volitional articulatory movement secondary to cortical, dominant hemisphere lesion. It is manifested in imprecise and awkward articulation, and distortion of phoneme production, without commensurate pathology to the motor-speech system; sometimes referred to as speech dyspraxia, apraxia of speech, cortical dysarthria, or phonetic disintegration.

Vocal tract: That part of the speech mechanism above the level of the vocal folds capable of modifying speech sounds generated by the vocal folds, including the pharyngeal, oral, and nasal cavities.

Voiced sounds: Sounds produced with simultaneous vibration of the vocal folds; includes all vowels, semivowels, diphthongs, and voiced consonants.

Voiceless sounds (unvoiced sounds): Sounds produced without vibration of the vocal folds.

Vowel: A voiced speech sound resulting from the unrestricted passage of the air stream through the mouth or nasal cavity without audible friction or stoppage. It is described in terms of (1) relative position of the tongue in the mouth; (2) relative height of the tongue in the mouth; and (3) relative shape of the lips.

Orthotic Assessment and Management

Joan E. Edelstein

OBJECTIVES

1. Relate the major parts of the shoe to the requirements of individuals fitted with lower-limb orthoses.
2. Compare the characteristics of plastics, metals, and other materials used in orthoses.
3. Describe the main components of foot, ankle-foot, knee-ankle-foot, hip-knee-ankle-foot, trunk-hip-knee-ankle-foot, and trunk orthoses.
4. List the orthotic options available for clients with paraplegia.
5. Identify the principal features of lower-limb and trunk orthoses that are assessed during the evaluation process.
6. Recognize the physical therapist's role in management of clients fitted with lower-limb and trunk orthoses.

An *orthosis* is an external appliance worn to restrict or assist motion or to transfer load from one area to another. The older term, *brace,* can be used synonymously. A *splint* connotes an orthosis intended for temporary use. Alternative designations, such as *walking irons* and *calipers,* give insight into orthotic materials and designs. An *orthotist* is the health care professional who designs, fabricates, and fits orthoses. *Orthotic* is an adjective, although some use the word as a noun. Archaeologic evidence indicates that orthoses have been used at least since the fifth Egyptian dynasty, 2750–2625 B.C.E. The term orthosis appears to have been coined soon after World War II.

This chapter presents contemporary orthoses for the lower limb and the trunk, and includes descriptions of the most frequently prescribed orthoses, together with key elements in training patients in their use. The focus is on orthotic design characteristics, their biomechanical rationale, merits of specific materials, and criteria for judging the adequacy of orthotic fit, function, and construction.

TERMINOLOGY

Generic terminology is superseding the traditional use of eponyms. Naming orthoses by the joints they encompass and the type of motion control facilitates communication among clinicians and consumers. Thus, foot orthoses (FO) are appliances applied to the foot and placed inside or outside the shoe, such as metatarsal pads and heel lifts. Ankle-foot orthoses (AFO) encom-

pass the shoe and terminate at some point below the knee. The term replaces the older nomenclature, short leg brace and below-knee orthosis. The knee-ankle-foot orthosis (KAFO) extends from the shoe to the thigh; the term is preferable to long leg brace or above-knee orthosis. A hip-knee-ankle-foot orthosis (HKAFO) is a KAFO with a pelvic band that surrounds the lower trunk. A trunk-hip-knee-ankle-foot orthosis (THKAFO) covers the thorax as well as the lower limbs. A knee orthosis (KO) and a hip orthosis (HO) are other applications of the same terminology system.

TYPES OF ORTHOSES

Characteristics and functions of the principal FOs, AFOs, KAFOs, HKAFOs, and THKAFOs, and trunk orthoses, together with the clinically important attributes of shoes, will be described. Although physical therapists also encounter KOs, HOs, and orthoses for special purposes, such as management of Legg Calve Perthes' disease, these orthoses are not included because they are used less frequently than the appliances that appear in this chapter.

LOWER-LIMB ORTHOSES

Lower-limb orthoses range from shoes used for clinical purposes to trunk-hip-knee-ankle-foot orthoses.

Shoes

The shoe is the foundation for most lower-limb orthoses. Each part of the shoe contributes to the efficacy of orthotic management and offers many options for selection.[1] Shoes transfer body weight to the ground and protect the wearer from the bearing surface and the weather. The ideal shoe should distribute bearing forces so as to preserve optimum comfort, function, and appearance of the foot. For the individual with an orthopedic disorder, footwear serves two additional purposes: (1) it reduces pressure on sensitive deformed structures by redistributing weight toward pain-free areas and (2) it serves as the foundation of AFOs and more extensive bracing. Unless the shoe is correctly fitted and appropriately modified, the alignment of the orthosis will not provide the designed pattern of weight bearing. The major parts of the shoe are the upper, sole, heel, reinforcements (Fig. 30–1), and the last. These features are found in both the traditional leather shoe and the contemporary athletic sneaker.

UPPER

The portion of the shoe over the dorsum of the foot is the *upper* (Fig. 30–2). It consists of an anterior component called the *vamp* and the posterior part, the *quarter.* If the shoe is to be used with an ankle-foot orthosis having an insert as its distal attachment, then the vamp should extend to the proximal portion of the dorsum to secure the shoe and the rest of the orthosis high onto the foot. The vamp contains the lace stays, which have eyelets for shoe laces. Laces provide more precise adjustment over the entire opening than do pressure closures. The latter, however, enable some individuals with manual impairment to manage the shoe more easily. For most orthotic purposes, a lace stay in the *Blucher* pattern is preferable; it is distinguished by the separation between the anterior margin of the lace stay and the vamp. The alternate design is the Bal, or Balmoral, lace stay, in which the lace stay is continuous with the vamp. The Blucher opening permits substantial adjustability, an important feature for the patient with edema. It also offers a large inlet into the shoe, so that one can determine that paralyzed toes lie flat within the shoe. An *extra depth shoe* is one having an upper contoured with additional vertical space. The shoe is manufactured with

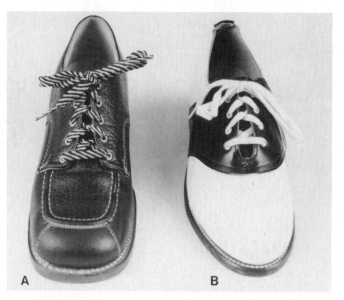

Figure 30–2. Low quarter shoes: (A) Blucher and (B) Bal (Balmoral).

a second inner sole that can be removed to accommodate an insert or thick surgical dressing.

Quarter height is another consideration in shoe prescription. The low quarter terminates below the malleoli and is satisfactory for most orthotic purposes. This style does not restrict foot or ankle motion and is faster to don. If the patient will be wearing a plastic orthosis molded about the ankle, it should not be necessary to go to the additional expense of providing a high-quarter shoe for ankle support. A high-quarter shoe, covering the malleoli, is indicated to cover the foot having rigid pes equinus. It is also appropriate to augment foot stability in the absence of an ankle-foot orthosis. The high-quarter shoe, however, is more difficult to don and more expensive than a comparable low-quarter one.

SOLE

The sole is the bottom portion of the shoe. For use with a riveted metal attachment between shoe and orthosis, the sole should have two parts, the outer and the inner sole, both made of leather. Between the two lies a metal reinforcement that receives the rivets. This type of shoe, however, is heavier than an athletic shoe with a single sole. Leather soles absorb little impact shock and provide minimal traction.

Regardless of material, the outer sole should not contact the floor at the distal end; the slight rise of the sole is known as *toe spring* (Fig. 30–3), which allows a rocker effect at late stance. If a lift is added to the sole to compensate for leg length discrepancy, the lift should be beveled to achieve toe spring.

HEEL

The heel is the portion of the shoe adjacent to the outer sole, under the anatomic heel. A broad, low heel provides greatest stability and distributes force between the back and front of the foot. For adults, a heel 2.5 cm (1 in) tilts the center of gravity slightly forward to aid transition through stance phase, but does not disturb

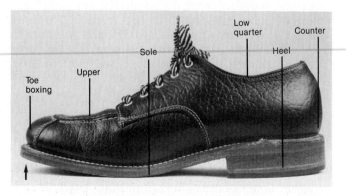

Figure 30–1. Low quarter Blucher shoe.

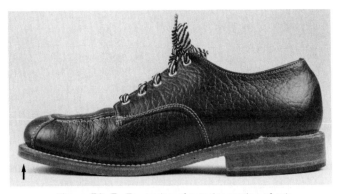

Figure 30–3. Toe spring of anterior portion of sole.

normal knee and hip alignment significantly. A higher heel places the ankle in its extreme plantarflexion range and forces the tibia forward. The wearer compensates either by retaining slight knee and hip flexion or by extending the knee and exaggerating lumbar lordosis. The high heel transmits more stress to the metatarsals. Nevertheless, transferring load anteriorly may be desirable if the patient has heel pain. The higher heel also reduces tension on the Achilles tendon and other posterior structures and accommodates rigid pes equinus. Although most heels are made of firm material with a rubber plantar surface, a low resilient heel is indicated to permit slight plantar flexion if the ankle cannot move because of orthotic or anatomic limitation.

REINFORCEMENTS
Reinforcements located at strategic points preserve the shape of the shoe. *Toe boxing* in the vamp protects the toes from stubbing and vertical trauma; it should be high enough to accommodate hammer toes or similar deformity. The *shank* piece is a longitudinal plate that reinforces the sole between the anterior border of the heel and the widest part of the sole at the metatarsal heads. A corrugated steel shank is necessary if an orthotic attachment is to be riveted to the shoe. The **counter** stiffens the quarter and generally terminates at the anterior border of the heel. The patient with pes valgus, however, should have a shoe with a long medial counter that provides reinforcement along the medial border of the foot to the head of the first metatarsal, thus resisting the tendency of the foot to collapse medially.

Because reinforcements are not visible in the finished shoe, it is important that the physical therapist become familiar with details of construction of the shoes that are being considered for orthotic wearers.

LAST
The **last** is the model over which the shoe is made. The last, whether of traditional wood, custom-made plaster, or computer-generated design, remains with the manufacturer; the shoe shape duplicates the last's contour. A given shoe size may be achieved with many lasts, each transmitting different forces to the foot. Consequently, the physical therapist should ascertain that the shoe shape fits the foot satisfactorily, rather than relying on a particular shoe size. The patient with a markedly

deformed foot requires a shoe made over a special last, either factory- or custom-made.

Foot Orthoses

Foot orthoses are appliances that apply forces to the foot. These may be an **insert** placed in the shoe, an **internal modification** affixed inside the shoe, or an **external modification** attached to the sole or heel of the shoe. They can enhance function by relieving pain and improving the wearer's transition during stance phase. Pain may be lessened by transferring weight-bearing stresses to pressure-tolerant sites, and by protecting painful areas from contact with the shoe and with adjacent portions of the foot. Shoes also may improve gait by modifications to equalize foot and leg lengths on both limbs and by altering the rollover point in late stance. Comfort and mobility can be improved by *correcting alignment of a flexible segment,* or by *accommodating fixed deformity* by altering the contour of the shoe. In many instances, a particular therapeutic aim can be achieved by various devices.

INTERNAL MODIFICATIONS
Generally, the closer the modification is to the foot, the more effective it is. Consequently, inserts and internal modifications are widely used. Biomechanically, both are identical. The insert permits the patient to transfer the orthosis from shoe to shoe, if the shoes have the same heel height; otherwise, a rigid insert may rock in the shoe. Most inserts terminate anteriorly just behind the metatarsal heads; thus, they may slip forward, particularly if the shoe has a relatively high heel. Some inserts extend the full length of the sole, preventing slippage, but occupying the often limited space in the anterior portion of the shoe. Internal modifications are fixed to the shoe's interior, guaranteeing the desired placement, but limiting the patient to the single pair of modified shoes. Both inserts and internal modifications reduce shoe volume, so proper shoe fit must be judged with these components in place.

Inserts made of soft materials, such as the **viscoelastic** plastics PPT, Sorbothane, and Viscolas, reduce shear and impact shock, thus protecting painful or sensitive feet.[2] Inserts are also constructed of semirigid or rigid plastics, rubber, or metal, often with a resilient overlay.

A heel-spur insert orthosis (Fig. 30–4), for example, may be made of viscoelastic plastic or rubber. In either

Figure 30–4. Plastic heel spur pad inferior aspect. Note the depression for spur.

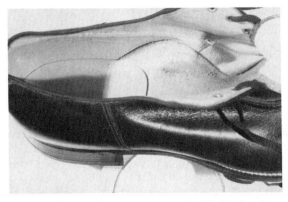

Figure 30–5. Leather scaphoid pad glued inside the shoe.

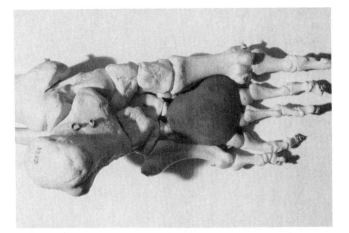

Figure 30–7. Rubber metatarsal pad. Whether used as an internal modification or as part of an insert, the pad should be oriented as shown on the skeleton.

case, the orthosis will slope anteriorly to reduce load on the painful heel. In addition, the orthosis will have a concave relief to minimize pressure on the tender area.

Longitudinal arch supports are intended to prevent depression of the subtalar joint. The orthosis may include a wedge (post) to alter foot alignment. The minimum support is a rubber **scaphoid pad** (Fig. 30–5) positioned at the medial border of the insole with the apex between the sustentaculum tali and the navicular tuberosity. The long-term efficacy of such an orthosis has been challenged.[3] Flexible flat foot can be realigned with a semirigid plastic **University of California Biomechanics Laboratory (UCBL) insert** (Fig. 30–6).[4,5] It is molded over a plaster model of the foot, taken with the foot in maximum correction. It encompasses the heel and midfoot, applying medialward force to the calcaneus, and lateral and upward force to the medial portion of the midfoot. Inserts are used successfully by runners, who benefit from improved foot alignment.[6]

The **metatarsal pad** (Fig. 30–7) is a convexity that may be incorporated in an insert or may be a resilient domed component glued to the inner sole so that its apex is under the metatarsal shafts. The pad transfers stress from the metatarsal heads to the metatarsal shafts.

Occasionally, modifications are sandwiched between the inner and outer soles; for example, the patient with marked arthritic changes in the front of the foot probably will be more comfortable if the shoe has a long steel

spring between the soles to eliminate motion at the painful joints. The same effect can be achieved with a rigid insert.

EXTERNAL MODIFICATIONS

An external modification ensures that the patient wears the appropriate shoes and does not reduce shoe volume, but will erode as the patient walks and is somewhat conspicuous. In addition, the client is limited to wearing the modified shoe, rather than being able to choose from a wide selection of shoes.

A heel wedge (Fig. 30–8) is a frequently prescribed external modification. It alters alignment of the calcaneus. A medial heel wedge, by applying laterally directed force, can aid in realigning flexible pes valgus or can accommodate rigid pes varus by filling the void between the sole and the floor on the medial side. A medial wedge is incorporated in a **Thomas heel,** intended for flexible pes valgus. The anterior border of the Thomas heel extends forward on the medial side to augment the effect of the medial wedge in supporting the longitudinal arch. A *cushion heel* is made of resilient material to absorb shock at heel contact. Because it provides slight plantarflexion, the cushion heel is indicated

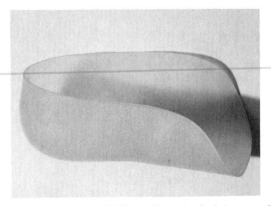

Figure 30–6. University of California Biomechanics Laboratory (UCBL) insert.

Figure 30–8. Medial heel wedge.

Figure 30–9. Leather outer sole with metatarsal bar.

when the patient wears an orthosis with a rigid ankle. *Sole wedges* alter mediolateral metatarsal alignment. A lateral wedge shifts weight bearing to the medial side of the front of the foot. It compensates for fixed forefoot valgus, allowing the entire front of the foot to contact the floor.

A **metatarsal bar** (Fig. 30–9) is a flat strip of leather or other firm material placed posterior to the metatarsal heads. At late stance, the bar transfers stress from the metatarsophalangeal joints to the metatarsal shafts. A **rocker bar** is a convex strip affixed to the sole proximal to the metatarsal heads. It reduces the distance the wearer must travel during stance phase, improving late stance,[7] as well as shifting load from the metatarsophalangeal joints to the metatarsal shafts.

The patient with leg length discrepancy of more than 1 cm (½ in) will probably walk better with a shoe lift made of cork or lightweight plastic. Approximately 0.8 cm (⅜ in) of the elevation can be accommodated inside a low-quarter shoe at the heel.

Ankle-Foot Orthoses

The AFO is composed of a foundation, ankle control, foot control, and a superstructure.

FOUNDATION
The foundation of the orthosis consists of the shoe and a plastic or metal component.

Foot Plate
An insert or foot plate foundation (Fig. 30–10) is often used; it provides the best control of the foot, because internal modifications can be incorporated. To use an insert, the shoe must close high on the dorsum of the foot to retain the orthosis. The foot plate facilitates donning the orthosis as the shoe can be separated from the

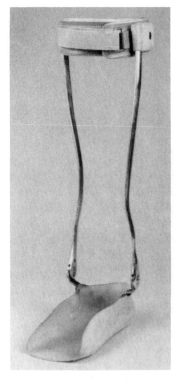

Figure 30–10. Ankle-foot orthosis with plastic shoe insert.

rest of the brace. The insert also permits interchanging shoes, assuming that all shoes have been made on the same last, so that the orthosis can exert the intended effect on the lower limb. Less expensive shoes, such as sneakers, can be worn, for the foundation does not need to be riveted to the shoe. The orthosis with an insert is relatively lightweight because the insert is usually made of a thermoplastic, such as polyethylene or polypropylene. These materials are heated, then molded over a plaster model of the patient's limb. The orthotist modifies the model, removing some plaster in areas where the orthosis is to apply substantial pressure, and adding plaster where pressure relief is required.

A foot plate foundation is inappropriate if the patient cannot be relied upon to wear the orthosis with a shoe of proper heel height. If the orthosis is placed in a shoe with too low a heel, the uprights would incline posteriorly, increasing the tendency of the wearer's knee to extend.[8] Conversely, if the orthosis is worn with a higher heeled shoe, the patient might experience knee instability. The insert reduces interior shoe volume, and thus must be used with suitably spacious shoes. Custom-molded foot plates may be more expensive than other types of foundation. If the orthosis is to be used by a very obese or exceptionally active individual, a plastic foot plate may not provide adequate support. Some insurance programs insist that the shoe be physically attached to the remainder of the brace in order that the cost of the shoes be reimbursed.

Stirrup
The traditional foundation for the AFO is a steel **stirrup,** a U-shaped fixture, the center portion of which is riveted to the shoe through the shank. The arms of the

Figure 30–11. Solid stirrup.

stirrup join the brace uprights at the level of the anatomic ankle, providing congruency between orthotic and anatomic joints. The **solid stirrup** (Fig. 30–11) is a one-piece attachment that provides maximum stability of the orthosis on the shoe. The **split stirrup** (Fig. 30–12) has three segments. The central portion has a transverse rectangular opening. Medial and lateral angled side pieces fit into the opening. The split stirrup simplifies donning the orthosis because the wearer can detach the uprights from the shoe. If a central piece is riveted to other shoes, then shoes can be interchanged. The extremely active client may dislodge a side piece from its receptacle unintentionally. The split stirrup is bulkier and heavier than a solid stirrup or foot plate.

ANKLE CONTROL

Most AFOs are prescribed to control ankle motion by limiting plantarflexion and/or dorsiflexion, or by assisting motion. The patient with dorsiflexor weakness or

paralysis risks dragging the toe during swing phase. Dorsiflexion assistance can be provided by a **posterior leaf spring** that arises from a plastic insert (Fig. 30–13). The upright is bent backward slightly during early stance. When the patient progresses into swing phase, the plastic recoils to lift the foot.[9] Thin, narrow plastic permits relatively greater motion.[9] Motion assistance can also be achieved with a steel **dorsiflexion spring assist** (Klenzak joint) (Fig. 30–14) incorporated into each stirrup. The coil spring is compressed in stance and rebounds during swing. The tightness of the coil can be adjusted, but the orthosis is noticeably bulkier than the posterior leaf spring model. Both types of spring assist will yield slightly into plantarflexion at heel contact, affording the wearer protection against inadvertent knee flexion.

The alternate approach to prevent toe drag is plantarflexion resistance, which prevents the foot from plantarflexing so that the patient with drop foot will not catch the toe and stumble during swing phase. A *plastic overlap joint* in a hinged solid ankle AFO or a metal *posterior stop* (Fig. 30–15) can be incorporated in the stirrup. The stop tends to impose flexion force at the knee during early stance.

An *anterior stop* limits dorsiflexion, aiding the individual with paralysis of the triceps surae to achieve late stance. A flexible alternative is a plastic *anterior spring* extending from the mid dorsum of the foot to the proximal margin of the orthosis.[10]

A *limited motion stop* is a metal joint that resists both plantarflexion and dorsiflexion. *Bichannel adjustable ankle locks (BiCAALs)* (Fig. 30–16) consist of a pair of joints, each of which has an anterior and a posterior spring. Ordinarily, the springs are replaced by metal pins, the lengths of which determine the amount of motion and thus the alignment of the orthosis. The plastic **solid ankle-foot orthosis** (Fig. 30–17) also limits all foot and ankle motion. Its trimline is anterior to the malleoli. To compensate for lack of plantarflexion in early stance, the shoe used with the solid ankle-foot orthosis or the orthosis with a limited motion stop should have a resilient heel. Similarly, to facilitate early rollover in late stance, the shoe sole should have a rocker bar. The solid ankle orthosis may be divided

Figure 30–12. Split stirrup.

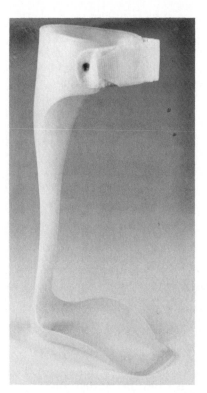

Figure 30–13. Plastic foot plate on posterior leaf spring ankle-foot orthosis.

Figure 30–15. Steel stirrup with posterior stop at its proximal end. Stop is to the left.

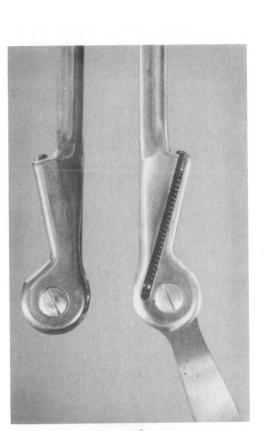

Figure 30–14. Steel dorsiflexion spring assist. (From Fishman, S, et al: Lower-limb orthoses. In American Academy of Orthopaedic Surgeons: Atlas of Orthotics, ed. 2. CV Mosby, St Louis, 1985, p 203, with permission.)

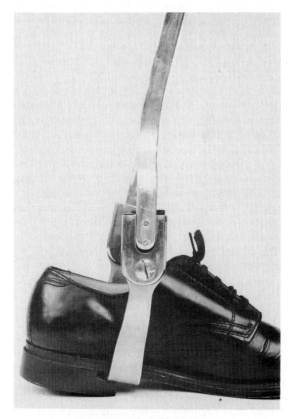

Figure 30–16. BiCAAL joints.

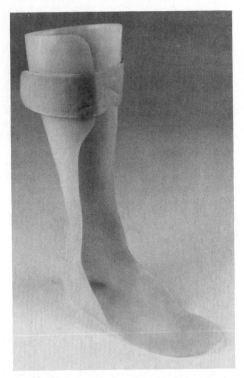

Figure 30–17. Plastic solid ankle-foot orthosis.

Figure 30–18. Valgus correction strap incorporated in metal and leather ankle-foot orthosis. (From Fishman, S, et al: Lower-limb orthoses. In American Academy of Orthopaedic Surgeons: Atlas of Orthotics, ed. 2. CV Mosby, St Louis, 1985, p 200, with permission.)

transversely at the ankle, with the two sections hinged. The **hinged solid ankle-foot orthosis** provides slight sagittal motion, fostering achievement of the foot-flat position in early stance. The joint at the hinge may be a plastic overlap or a plastic rod. A versatile option is a pair of metal hinges that can be adjusted to alter the excursion of ankle motion.

FOOT CONTROL

Mediolateral motion can be controlled with a solid ankle-foot orthosis. The rigidity of the orthosis can be increased by using thicker or stiffer plastic, corrugating the plastic, forming the edges with a rolled contour, or embedding carbon fiber reinforcements. A solid ankle AFO or a hinged solid ankle AFO also controls frontal and transverse plane foot motion. Less effective is a metal and leather orthosis to which a leather *valgus (varus) correction strap* (Fig. 30–18) is attached. The valgus correction strap is sewn to the medial portion of the shoe upper near the sole, and buckles around the lateral upright, exerting a laterally directed force to restrain pronation. The varus correction strap has opposite attachments and force application. Either strap, although adjustable, complicates donning.

SUPERSTRUCTURE

The proximal portion of the orthosis, the superstructure, consists of uprights, and a shell, band, or brim. Plastic AFOs usually have a single upright or shell. The solid ankle and hinged solid ankle AFO have a posterior shell extending from the medial to the lateral midline of the leg, thus providing excellent mediolateral control and a broad surface to minimize pressure. The posterior leaf spring AFO has a single posterior upright and thus does not contribute to frontal or transverse plane con-

trol. The *spiral* AFO (Fig. 30–19) is a design made of nylon acrylic or polypropylene, in which the single upright spirals from the medial aspect of the foot plate around the leg, terminating medially in a proximal band.[11] The spiral orthosis controls, but does not eliminate, motion in all planes. Orthoses with plastic shells or uprights are molded over a cast of the patient's leg and are designed to fit snugly for maximal control and minimal conspicuousness. Such AFOs are contraindicated for the individual whose ankle and leg volume

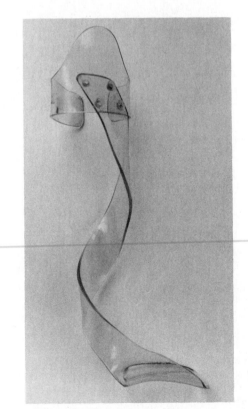

Figure 30–19. Spiral ankle-foot orthosis.

fluctuates markedly, since the orthoses cannot be adjusted readily.

Metal and leather orthoses usually have medial and lateral uprights to maximize structural stability. Occasionally, a single side upright will suffice when a less conspicuous orthosis is required and the wearer is not expected to exert undue force. Aluminum uprights are of lighter weight than steel; to increase the rigidity of the orthosis, a broader bar of aluminum can be used. Carbon graphite uprights weigh appreciably less than aluminum and rival the strength of steel; however, orthoses made of the newer material are more expensive.

Most orthoses have a posterior *calf band* made of plastic or leather-upholstered metal. The band has an anterior buckled or pressure closure strap (Fig. 30–20). The farther the band is from the ankle joint, the more effective the leverage of the orthosis; however, the band must not impinge on the peroneal nerve. An *anterior band* that is part of a solid ankle AFO imposes posteriorly directed force near the knee, enabling the AFO to resist knee flexion.[12] Such an orthosis is sometimes known as a **floor reaction orthosis.** In fact, all orthoses are influenced by the floor reaction when the wearer stands or is in the stance phase of gait. If the AFO is to reduce the amount of weight transmitted through the foot, it may have a **patellar-tendon-bearing brim** (Fig. 30–21), resembling a below-knee prosthetic socket. The plastic brim has a slight indentation over the patellar ligament (tendon), and is hinged to facilitate donning. The brim must be used with a plastic solid ankle or a metal limited-motion ankle joint.

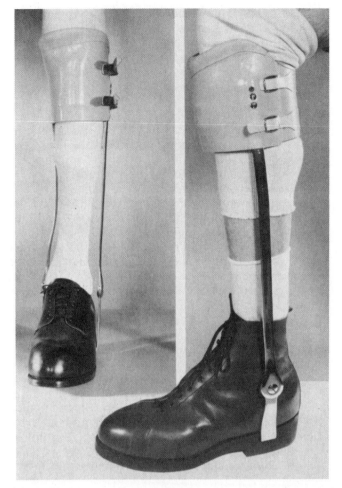

Figure 30–21. Ankle-foot orthosis with stirrup, steel uprights, and plastic patellar-tendon-bearing brim. (From Fishman, S, et al: Lower-limb orthoses. In American Academy of Orthopaedic Surgeons: Atlas of Orthotics, ed. 2. CV Mosby, St Louis, 1985, p 208, with permission.)

Tone-reducing orthoses are plastic AFOs designed for children with spastic cerebral palsy and adults with spastic hemiplegia. The foot plate and broad upright are designed to modify reflex hypertonicity by applying constant pressure to the plantarflexors and invertors. They are particularly useful for individuals who have moderate spasticity with varus instability, but do not have fixed deformity. They control the tendency of the foot to assume an equinovarus posture; in addition, some versions have a foot plate that maintains the toes in an extended or hyperextended position, thus assisting children who have spasticity to walk with better foot and knee control.[13–15] Similar versions have proved successful with adults who have sustained cerebral vascular accident.[16] Before a custom-made plastic orthosis is ordered, however, the patient should be assessed in a tone-reducing cast that subjects the limb to the same pressures as will the orthosis.

Knee-Ankle-Foot Orthoses

Individuals with more extensive paralysis or limb deformity may benefit from KAFOs, which consist of a shoe, foundation, ankle control, knee control, and

Figure 30–20. Ankle-foot orthosis with stirrup attachment, limited motion ankle joints, bilateral uprights, and upholstered metal calf band.

superstructure. Knee-ankle-foot orthoses often include a foot control. The shoe, foundation, ankle control, and foot control of the KAFO may be selected from the components already described. Donning a plastic and metal KAFO is appreciably faster than putting on a metal and leather orthosis.[17]

KNEE CONTROL

The simplest knee joint is a hinge. Because most KAFOs include a pair of uprights, the orthosis has a pair of knee hinges that provide mediolateral and hyperextension restriction while permitting knee flexion.

The **offset joint** (Fig. 30–22) is a hinge placed posterior to the midline of the leg. The patient's weight line falls anterior to the offset joint, stabilizing the knee during the early stance phase of gait when the wearer is on a level surface. The offset joint does not hamper knee flexion during swing or sitting. The joint may, however, flex inadvertently when the wearer walks on ramps. The joint is contraindicated in the presence of knee flexion contracture.

The most common knee control is the *drop ring lock* (Fig. 30–23). When the client stands with the knee fully extended, the ring drops, preventing the uprights from bending. Both medial and lateral joints should be locked for maximum stability. A pair of drop ring locks is thus inconvenient, unless each upright is equipped with a spring-loaded **retention button.** The button permits the wearer to unlock one upright, then attend to the other one without having the first lock drop. The buttons also enable the physical therapist to give the patient a trial period of walking with the knee joints unlocked.

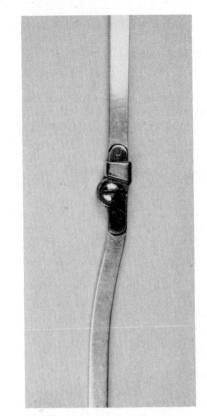

Figure 30–23. Hinge with drop ring lock.

The **pawl lock with bail release** (Fig. 30–24) also provides simultaneous locking of both uprights. The pawl is a spring-loaded projection that fits into a notched disk. The patient unlocks the brace by pulling upward on the posterior bail. Some people are agile enough to be able to nudge the bail by pressing it against a chair. The bail is bulky and may release the locks unexpectedly if the wearer is jostled against a rigid object.

The offset joint and the basic drop ring and pawl locks are contraindicated in the presence of knee flexion contracture. If one cannot achieve full passive knee extension, an adjustable knee joint (Fig. 30–25) is required. Such joints have a drop ring lock for stability in the partially flexed attitude.

Sagittal stability is augmented by a *knee cap* (Fig. 30–26) or *anterior band or strap* (Fig. 30–27) that completes the three-point pressure system necessary for stability. The cap or band applies a posteriorly directed force to complement the anteriorly directed forces from the back of the shoe and the thigh band. The leather knee cap is the traditional component. It has four straps buckled to both uprights above and below the knee and applies a posteriorly directed force to oppose any tendency of the knee to flex. The knee cap requires the patient to buckle two straps when donning the orthosis. When the straps are tight enough to stabilize the knee, the pad is likely to restrict flexion when the wearer sits. A more practical alternative is a rigid *anterior band,* either a *pretibial band* or a *suprapatellar band,* both of which apply posteriorly directed force but do not interfere with sitting and are easier to don. The bands generally are molded of plastic and are not readily adjustable. The prepatellar band rests over the bony proximal

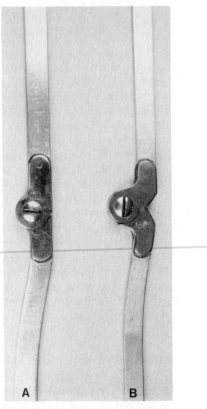

Figure 30–22. Knee joint-offset hinge.

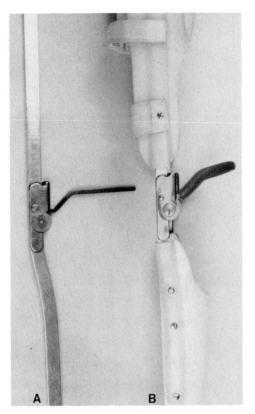

Figure 30–24. Pawl lock: basic component (A) and pawl lock installed in knee-ankle-foot orthosis with bail shaped to curve posteriorly (B).

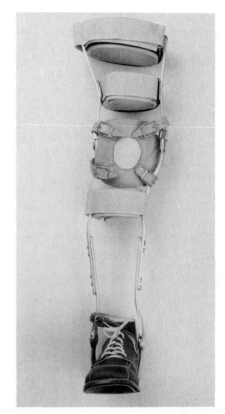

Figure 30–26. Knee-ankle-foot orthosis with knee cap.

portion of the leg and requires careful contouring to be comfortable. The suprapatellar band fits over the fleshy anterodistal thigh.

Frontal plane control may be achieved with plastic calf shells shaped to apply corrective force for genu valgum or genu varum. To reduce genu valgum, the medial

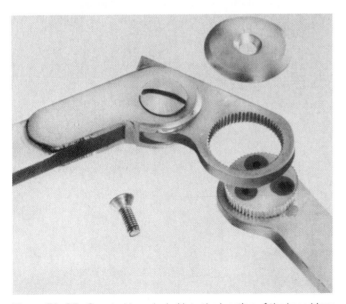

Figure 30–25. Serrated knee lock. Note the location of the knee hinge and the serrated disk. (From Fishman, S, et al: Lower-limb orthoses. In American Academy of Orthopaedic Surgeons: Atlas of Orthotics, ed. 2. CV Mosby, St Louis, 1985, p 213, with permission.)

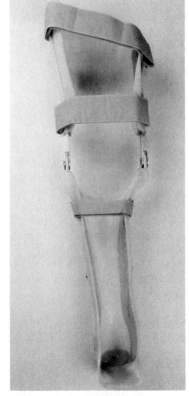

Figure 30–27. Knee-ankle-foot orthosis with Velcro webbing anterior prepatellar and supracondylar bands.

portion of the shell extends proximally in order to apply laterally directed force at the knee. The semirigid shell is more effective than a valgum correction strap, which is a knee cap with a fifth strap designed to be buckled around the lateral upright. The opposite force application is indicated for the patient who has genu varum. The shell does not require time in donning and applies force over a broad area without impinging on the popliteal fossa.

When control in the transverse plane, as well as the frontal and sagittal planes, is required, the *Oregon Orthotic System* incorporating rigid plastic AFOs or KAFOs may be effective. The AFO version includes a foot plate, BiCAAL ankle joints, bilateral uprights, and an anterior band over the proximal leg. The KAFO model adds thigh uprights and thigh bands. The orthoses are aligned to establish triplanar control at the foot, ankle, and knee joints by strategic placement of the ankle and knee joint axes.

SUPERSTRUCTURE

Thigh bands provide structural stability to the orthosis. If the distal portion of the limb cannot tolerate full weight bearing, then the proximal thigh band may be shaped to form a weight-bearing brim. Either the quadrilateral or the ischial containment design can be used. To eliminate all weight bearing through the entire leg, the orthosis must include a weight-bearing brim, a locked knee joint, and a **patten** bottom. The patten is a distal extension that keeps the shoe on the braced side of the floor. To maintain a level pelvis the patient must also wear a lift on the opposite shoe; the height of the lift should equal the height of the patten.

Hip-Knee-Ankle-Foot Orthoses

Addition of a pelvic band and hip joints converts the KAFO to an HKAFO.

HIP JOINT

The usual hip joint is a metal hinge (Fig. 30–28) that connects the lateral upright of the KAFO to a pelvic band. The joint prevents abduction and adduction, as well as hip rotation. If the patient requires only control of hip rotation, a simpler alternative to the hip joint and pelvic band is a webbing strap. To reduce internal rotation, the strap resembles a prosthetic Silesian bandage. To reduce external rotation, the strap joins the lateral uprights of the KAFOs and passes anteriorly at the level of the groin. If flexion control is required, a drop ring lock is added to the hip joint. A two-position lock stabilizes the patient in hip extension for standing and walking, and at 90 degrees of hip flexion for sitting.

PELVIC BAND

An upholstered metal band (Fig. 30–29) will anchor the HKAFO to the trunk. The band is designed to lodge between the greater trochanter and the iliac crest on each side. Hip-knee-ankle-foot orthoses are not used very often because they are much more awkward to don than KAFOs, and, if the hip joints are locked, they

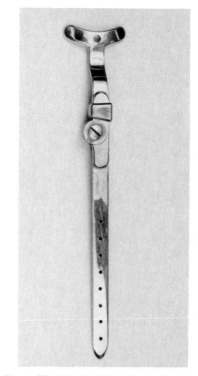

Figure 30–28. Hip joint with drop ring lock.

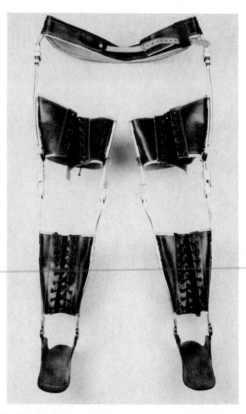

Figure 30–29. Hip-knee-ankle-foot orthoses. Laced thigh cuffs and leg cuffs are seldom prescribed.

restrict gait to the swing-to or swing-through pattern. The pelvic band is likely to be uncomfortable when the wearer sits.

Trunk-Hip-Knee-Ankle-Foot Orthoses

Patients who require more stability than provided by HKAFOs may be fitted with THKAFOs (Fig. 30–30), which incorporate a lumbosacral orthosis attached to KAFOs. The pelvic band of the trunk orthosis serves as the pelvic band used on HKAFOs. Because the THKAFO is very difficult to don and is heavy and cumbersome, it is seldom worn after the client is discharged from the rehabilitation program. Alternative orthoses providing standing stability, with or without provision for walking, are available for individuals with paraplegia.

Orthotic Options for Paraplegia

Orthoses are often prescribed for patients with spina bifida, spinal cord injury, or other disorders resulting in paraplegia. The functional goals for such people include standing to maintain skeletal, renal, respiratory, circulatory, and gastrointestinal function and some form of ambulation. Upright posture also affords the individual important psychologic benefits.

MASS-PRODUCED ORTHOSES

Several appliances are readily available for children with spina bifida or other disorders resulting in paraplegia. The appliances provide the youngster with considerable function and are less expensive and easier to don than are custom-made orthoses.

Standing Frame and Swivel Walker

Designed for children, the **standing frame** (Fig. 30–31) consists of a broad base, posterior nonarticulated uprights extending from a flat base to a midtorso chest band, and a posterior thoracolumbar band. Anterior leg bands contribute to stability. The child wears ordinary shoes without any special attachments. The shoes are strapped to the base of the frame.

A similar orthosis is the **swivel walker,**[18] made in child and adult sizes. The major difference is the base, which has two distal plates that rock slightly to enable a swiveling gait.

The mass-produced frame and walker are less expensive than custom-made orthoses. They permit the wearer to stand without crutch support, freeing the hands for play or vocational activities. With either device, the user can move from place to place by rotating the upper torso to shift weight, causing the frame to rock and rotate alternately on one edge then the other.

Parapodium

The **parapodium** (Fig. 30–32) differs from the standing frame by virtue of joints that permit the wearer to sit.

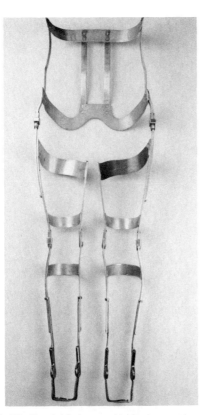

Figure 30–30. Trunk-hip-knee-ankle-foot orthoses without upholstery.

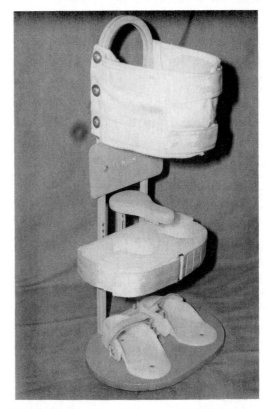

Figure 30–31. Standing frame. (Courtesy of Variety Village, Electro Limb Production Centre, Scarborough [Toronto], Ontario, Canada.)

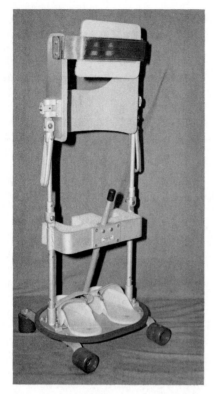

Figure 30–32. Parapodium. (Courtesy of Variety Village, Electro Limb Production Centre, Scarborough [Toronto], Ontario, Canada.)

The base is flat. The stabilizing points on the standing frame, swivel walker, and the parapodium are the same. One version of parapodium has provision for keeping the knees locked while the child unlocks the hips for leaning forward to pick up objects from the floor.[19] Crutchless ambulation in the parapodium is achieved by using the same technique as with the standing frame. For walking longer distances, the youngster uses crutches or a walker in the swing-to or swing-through pattern. Both the standing frame and the parapodium are worn on the outside of trousers, which school-age children eventually find cosmetically objectionable.

CUSTOM-MADE ORTHOSES

Whereas the mass-produced devices afford considerable function to their users, many individuals seek more streamlined orthoses. Custom-made AFOs, KAFOs, and THKAFOs provide sufficient rigidity, either by metal joints or anatomic alignment, to enable selected patients to stand. Ambulation requires crutches or similar aids, together with well-coordinated use of the upper trunk and upper limbs. Some patients may not realize the extent of the physical conditioning program required to prepare them for ambulation. Consequently, a trial period is advisable using temporary orthoses that can be assembled easily, such as lightweight nonarticulating KAFOs made of extruded plastic frames.[20]

Stabilizing Boots

Ankle-foot orthoses designed for adults with paraplegia include a pair of plastic orthoses molded to conform to the patient's legs and feet. The foot plate is angled at

approximately 15 degrees plantarflexion to shift the wearer's center of gravity anterior to the ankles.[21,22] The plastic component is inserted into leather boots with flat soles. The legs are thus inclined posteriorly, to keep the knees extended. The patient maintains standing stability by leaning backward, with the iliofemoral ligaments resisting a backward fall. Crutches, a walker, or a pair of canes are needed for two- or four-point gait. Ambulation requires shifting the upper torso diagonally forward to allow one leg to swing ahead. The orthoses are easy to don and do not restrict sitting. The candidate must not have any hip or knee flexion contractures, and must be able to extend the hips and lumbar trunk fully.

Craig-Scott KAFOs

A pair of **Craig-Scott KAFOs** (Fig. 30–33) are often prescribed for adults with paraplegia. The original design of each orthosis included a shoe reinforced with transverse and longitudinal plates, BiCAAL ankle joints set in slight dorsiflexion, a pretibial band, a pawl lock with bail release, and a single thigh band.[23] An alternate version substitutes a plastic solid ankle section for the reinforced shoe and metal ankle joints.[24] The orthosis enables the patient to stand with sufficient backward lean so as to prevent untoward hip or trunk flexion. The gait pattern usually is swing-to or swing-through, with the aid of crutches or a walker. Although the orthoses do not restrict hip motion, the patient with thoracic spinal injury cannot flex the hips voluntarily, and the orthosis has no mechanism to aid single-leg progression. Some individuals perform a two- or four-point gait by shifting

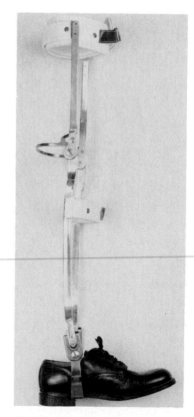

Figure 30–33. Craig-Scott knee-ankle-foot orthosis.

the trunk enough to allow the leg to swing forward in a pendular manner.

Reciprocating Gait Orthosis

Both children and adults can be fitted with a **reciprocating gait orthosis (RGO)** (Fig. 30–34), a THKAFO in which the hips are joined by one or two metal cables.[25] The knees are stabilized with knee locks, offset knee joints, or pretibial bands, and the feet are encased in solid ankle orthoses. The latest version has no thigh shells. To walk, the wearer uses a four-stage procedure: (1) shift weight to the right leg; (2) tuck the pelvis by extending the upper thorax; (3) press on the crutches; and (4) allow the left leg to swing through. The procedure is reversed for the next step. The steel cable(s) prevent inadvertent hip flexion on the supporting leg. Reciprocal, four- or two-point gait is stable, since one foot is always on the floor, but the pace is slow. For sitting, the wearer releases the cable(s) to enable the hips to flex.

ParaWalker

The **ParaWalker**[26] is a THKAFO that has exceptionally sturdy hip joints; these limit the excursion of hip flexion and resist hip abduction and adduction as the wearer shifts weight from side to side during ambula-

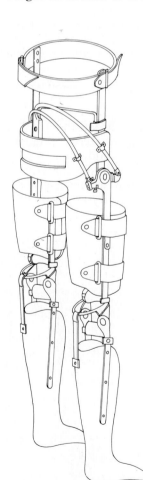

Figure 30–34. Reciprocating gait orthosis. (From *LSU* Reciprocating Gait Orthosis: A Pictorial Description and Application Manual. Durr-Fillauer Medical, Chattanooga, TN, 1983, p 14, with permission.)

tion. The shoes fit into loops on flat foot plates. The gait maneuver is the same as used with the RGO.

Functional Electrical Stimulation

Orthoses may be combined with *functional electrical stimulation (FES)*[27] to enable selected patients to achieve household, or in rare cases, community ambulation. This technique involves the use of electrical current to produce muscular contractions. Typically, stimulation is provided to the quadriceps and gluteus maximus. If the ankles are not supported by AFOs, then the system also includes surface electrodes over the peroneal nerves to initiate dorsiflexion, as well as reflex hip flexion. The candidate should have full passive mobility in all joints and should be able to use a control system that regulates the timing and amount of current needed to transfer from the chair to the standing position and to walk in various directions. Functional electrical stimulation is occasionally used to foster lower-limb exercise, thereby maintaining muscle bulk and reducing the risk of pressure ulcers.

TRUNK ORTHOSES

Trunk orthoses may be used in association with lower-limb orthoses or may be worn to reduce the disability caused by low-back pain, neck sprain, scoliosis, or other skeletal or neuromuscular disorders. Although the traditional name for an orthosis that encompasses the torso is *spinal orthosis,* in fact, such an appliance does not contact the spine directly. By supporting the trunk, the orthosis assists in controlling spinal motion; however, forces that the orthosis exerts are modified by the skin, subcutaneous tissue, and musculature that surround the vertebral column, and, in the case of higher orthoses, by the thoracic cage. Patients with spinal cord injury benefit from trunk orthoses in two ways: (1) the orthoses impart control of motion of the lumbar region, with or without thoracic control, and (2) they compress the abdomen to improve respiration. Individuals with cervical lesions may need to wear an orthosis that restrains neck motion until stability is achieved by surgery or other means. A special group of trunk orthoses are designed for children and adolescents with scoliosis.

Corset

If abdominal compression is the sole goal, a **corset** (Fig. 30–35) will suffice. It is a fabric orthosis that has no horizontal rigid structures, although frequently it has vertical rigid reinforcements. The corset may cover only the lumbar and sacral regions, or may extend superiorly as a thoracolumbosacral corset. The primary effect of a corset is to increase intraabdominal pressure.

Some individuals with low-back disorders find that corsets relieve pain.[28,29] The increase in intraabdominal pressure reduces stress on posterior spinal musculature, thus diminishing the load on the lumbar intervertebral disks. Although temporary reduction of abdominal and

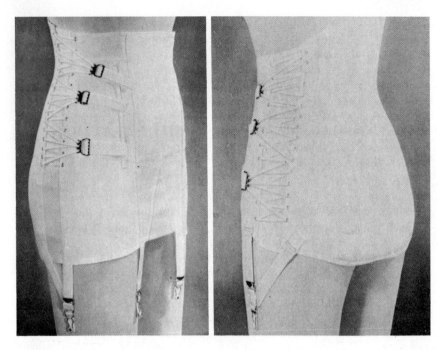

Figure 30–35. Women's model of a canvas lumbo-sacral corset. (This corset is provided exclusively by Camp International 1991 BISSELL Healthcare Corporation.)

erector spinae muscular activity is therapeutic, long-term reliance on a corset can promote muscular atrophy and contracture, as well as psychologic dependence on the appliance.

Rigid Orthoses

Most lumbosacral and thoracolumbosacral orthoses include a corset or a fabric abdominal front to compress the abdomen. Rigid orthoses are distinguished by the presence of horizontal, as well as vertical, rigid plastic or metal components. Motion limitation is accomplished by a series of three-point pressure systems, in which force in one direction is counteracted by two forces in the opposite direction.

LUMBOSACRAL FLEXION, EXTENSION, LATERAL CONTROL ORTHOSIS (LS FEL)

A typical example of a rigid trunk orthosis is the LS FEL orthosis (Fig. 30–36), also known as a *Knight spinal orthosis.* This appliance includes a *pelvic band,* which should provide firm anchorage over the midsection of the buttocks, and a *thoracic band,* intended to lie horizontally over the lower thorax without impinging on the scapulae. The bands, which may be foam-lined rigid plastic or leather-upholstered metal, are joined by a pair of *posterior uprights,* which lie on either side of the vertebral spines, and a pair of *lateral uprights* placed at the lateral midline of the torso. A corset or abdominal front completes the LS FEL orthosis. The orthosis restrains flexion by a three-point system consisting of posteriorly directed force from the top and bottom of the abdominal front or corset and an anteriorly directed force from the midportion of the posterior uprights. Extension is controlled by posteriorly directed force from the midsec-

tion of the abdominal front or corset and anteriorly directed force from the thoracic and pelvic bands. The lateral uprights resist lateral flexion.

A plastic *lumbosacral jacket* restricts motion in all directions, and is effective in the management of selected patients who complain of low-back pain.[30]

THORACOLUMBOSACRAL FLEXION, EXTENSION CONTROL ORTHOSIS (TLS FE)

Also called a *Taylor brace,* the TLS FE orthosis consists of a pelvic band, posterior uprights terminating at midscapular level, an abdominal front or corset, and axillary straps attached to an interscapular band. This orthosis reduces flexion by a three-point system consisting of posteriorly directed force from the axillary straps

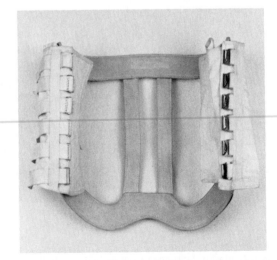

Figure 30–36. Lumbosacral flexion-extension-lateral control orthosis.

and the bottom of the abdominal front or corset, and anteriorly directed force from the midportion of the posterior uprights. Extension resistance is provided by posteriorly directed force from the midsection of the abdominal front or corset and anteriorly directed force from the pelvic and interscapular bands. Addition of lateral uprights converts the orthosis to a TLS FEL orthosis (Fig. 30–37). A plastic *thoracolumbosacral jacket* limits trunk motion in the frontal, sagittal, and transverse planes, and provides maximum support.

Cervical Orthoses

Cervical orthoses are classified according to design characteristics.[31] Minimal motion control is provided by *collars* (Fig. 30–38) that encircle the neck with fabric, resilient material, or rigid plastic. A few collars encompass the chin and posterior head (Fig. 30–39) for slightly greater restraint. For moderate control a *four-post* orthosis (Fig. 30–40) is used. Usually it has two anterior adjustable posts joining a sternal plate to a mandibular plate and two posterior uprights connecting a thoracic plate to an occipital plate. The sternal plate is strapped to the thoracic plate and the occipital plate is strapped to the mandibular plate.

Maximum orthotic control of the neck may be achieved either with a **Minerva**[32] or a **halo**[33,34] orthosis (Fig. 30–41). The Minerva orthosis is a noninvasive appliance that has a rigid plastic posterior section extending from the head to the mid trunk; the superior portion is held in place by a forehead band. The halo orthosis has a circular band of metal that is fixed to the skull by four tiny screws. Uprights connect the halo to a thoracic orthosis.

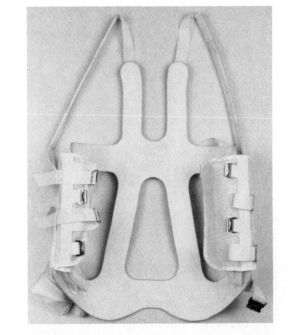

Figure 30–37. Thoracolumbosacral flexion-extension-lateral control orthosis.

Scoliosis Orthoses

Children and adolescents with thoracic, thoracolumbar, or lumbar scolioses or kyphoses may be fitted with a TLS orthosis that applies forces to realign the vertebral column and thoracic cage. While substantial improvement is evident when the orthosis is worn, long-term follow-up indicates that the major achievement is that the orthosis prevents the curve from increasing beyond its original contour. The **Milwaukee** orthosis[35,36] (Fig. 30–42) is often prescribed. The orthosis consists of a

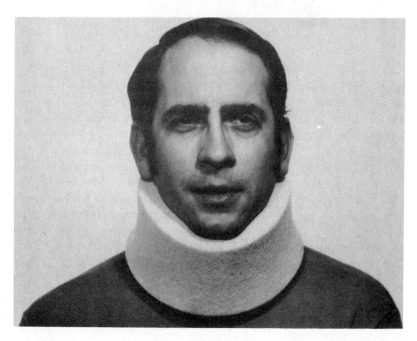

Figure 30–38. Soft foam rubber collar. (This collar is provided exclusively by Camp International 1991 BISSELL Healthcare Corporation.)

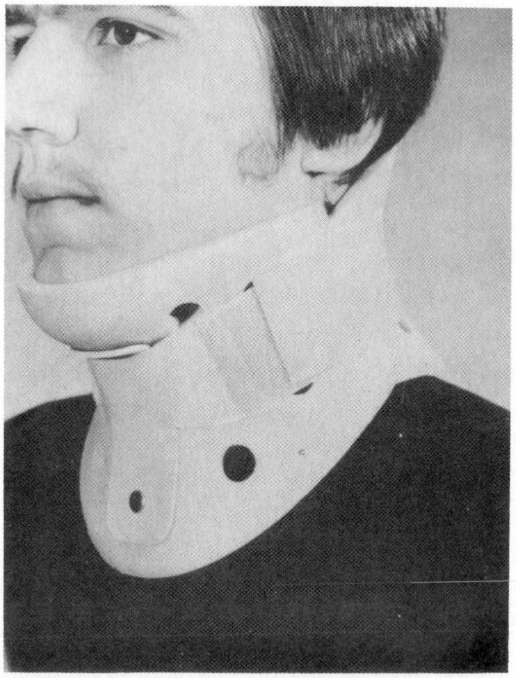

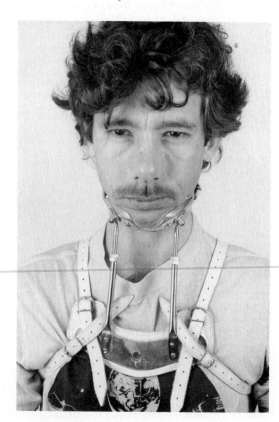

Figure 30–39. Philadelphia collar. (The Philadelphia collar is provided exclusively by Camp International 1991 BISSELL Healthcare Corporation.)

Figure 30–41. Halo-vest orthosis. (Courtesy Durr-Fillauer Medical, Chattanooga, TN.)

Figure 30–40. Four-poster cervical orthosis.

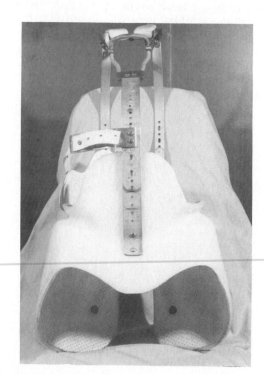

Figure 30–42. Anterior view of the plastic and metal Milwaukee orthosis.

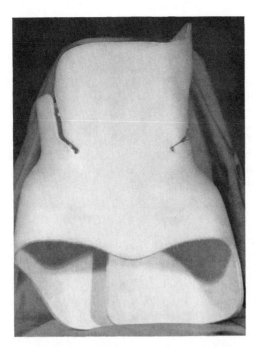

Figure 30–43. Plastic Boston orthosis.

frame composed of a pelvic girdle, two posterior uprights, an anterior upright, and a superior ring. Unlike the original Milwaukee orthosis, the current version features a superior ring that lies on the upper chest and can be hidden by most clothing. Various pads are strapped to the frame to apply corrective forces. The **Boston** orthosis[37,38] (Fig. 30–43) usually does not extend as high as the Milwaukee orthosis; its foundation is a mass-produced plastic module that the orthotist alters to meet the needs of the individual patient. The **Wilmington** orthosis[39] is another design that is in current use. It consists of a custom-made thoracolumbosacral jacket intended to guide the trunk to straighter alignment. These and most other scoliosis orthoses are most effective on patients who have immature spines and moderate vertebral curves in the midthoracic or more inferior portions of the trunk. The classic protocol required the youngster to wear the orthosis 23 hours each day; however, evidence suggests that part-time wearing is almost as effective in terms of maintaining trunk alignment and is better tolerated by patients.[40]

ORTHOTIC MAINTENANCE

To obtain the best service from orthoses, the patient should observe basic routine inspection and care procedures. Written instructions help reinforce the recommendations of the orthotist and therapist.

Shoes

Whether or not the shoe is attached directly to the orthosis, it is important that footwear be kept in good condition, with replacement of the sole and heel as soon as moderate wear is evident. The replacements should include whatever wedges, bars, or elevations were originally prescribed. The patient who tends to strike on the toe may need metal toe plates to preserve the sole. Shoes that are outgrown or distorted will not afford the wearer optimal function from the orthosis. If a stirrup is attached to the shoe, the patient should inspect the rivets to make certain that none have separated; if so, the shoe should be returned to the orthotist for repair.

Clean hose without holes or repairs should be worn. In addition, long hosiery or cotton leggings shield the leg from pressure at the edges of the brace uprights, bands, and shells.

Shells, Bands, and Straps

Plastic bands and shells should be wiped with a damp cloth to remove any surface soil. One should not try to hasten drying by using a hair dryer or other heat source that might soften the plastic. The patient should check the plastic periodically for any cracking; if any is noted, the orthosis should be brought to the orthotist for immediate repair. Pressure straps eventually become infiltrated with lint, which interferes with the hook and loop closing action; one should inspect straps to determine when they should be replaced. Leather bands require periodic cleaning and can be washed with mild saddle soap. If the original leather deteriorates to the point that portions of the underlying metal are exposed, new leatherwork is required. Leather straps eventually become brittle and may break. One should watch for loss of flexibility and replace the straps before they break.

Uprights

In a plastic and metal KAFO for a child, the metal upright is screwed or riveted to the plastic shell. The orthosis can be lengthened by removing the fasteners and inserting them in new holes drilled farther up on the calf shell and farther down on the thigh shell. In a metal and leather AFO or KAFO for a child, the uprights are overlapped and secured with screws. The screws tend to work loose, reducing the stability of the orthosis. This problem should be reported to the orthotist. The orthosis is lengthened by removing all screws, setting the uprights at the appropriate distance, and reinserting the screws.

Joints and Locks

Metal components should be kept away from sand, liquids, and other foreign substances. If the joints do not articulate smoothly or become noisy, if the locks do not engage properly, then cleaning and lubrication may remedy the problem. Otherwise, professional attention is required.

PHYSICAL THERAPY MANAGEMENT

Physical therapists participate in management of the wearer of an orthosis (1) prior to orthotic prescription, (2) at orthotic prescription, (3) upon delivery of the orthosis, and (4) during training to facilitate proper use and care of the orthosis.

In the best situation, the therapist is a member of an orthotic clinic team, working directly with the physician and orthotist to develop the orthotic prescription and to assess the patient and orthosis before and after training. The physical therapist is also responsible for training the patient.

Whether or not the hospital or rehabilitation center has a clinic team, the physical therapist is expected to accomplish the following:
1. Perform the preorthotic assessment.
2. Contribute to the orthotic prescription.
3. Assess the prescribed orthosis.
4. Facilitate orthotic acceptance.
5. Train the patient to don, to use, and to maintain the orthosis.

Preprescription Assessment

Matching the patient's biomechanical requirements to the appropriate orthosis requires careful assessment.

JOINT MOBILITY

A thorough goniometric examination, including both active and passive ranges of motion, is a prerequisite to orthotic prescription. If the patient has a fixed foot deformity, either the shoe will have to be modified to accommodate the foot, or an insert will have to be fabricated. In either instance, the goal is to achieve comfortable contact of the entire plantar surface of the foot on the inner sole of the shoe. Knee flexion contracture necessitates prescription of accommodative joints, because the regular drop ring and pawl locks can be used only with a knee that can be brought to the fully extended position. Hip flexion contracture precludes the prescription of orthoses that depend on alignment for stability, such as the offset knee joint, stabilizing boots, or Craig-Scott KAFOs.

LIMB LENGTH

The therapist should ascertain whether there is a discrepancy in leg length. If the patient can stand, one can check the pelvis to determine if it is level. For the recumbent individual, one can measure each leg from the anterior superior iliac spine to the medial malleolus. With a difference of more than 1 cm (½ in) there should be compensation by a shoe elevation. For the patient with weakness in one limb, a 1-cm (½-in) lift on the contralateral shoe will aid clearance of the paralyzed leg during swing phase.

MOTOR FUNCTION

The manual muscle test should be augmented by a functional activities assessment to determine what sub- stitutions the patient is able to make to accomplish standing and walking. Although the muscle test may reveal marked weakness, if the patient can manage without an orthosis, it is unlikely that it will be accepted. For example, the person with dorsiflexor paralysis who can ambulate by exaggerating hip flexion during swing phase may not agree to an AFO with a posterior stop. An important consideration in assessment of motor function is that traditional manual muscle tests are inappropriate in the presence of marked spasticity. In such instances, functional tests of motor performance are essential.

SENSATION

The clinician should record the extent of any sensory loss. Intimately fitted plastic orthoses are satisfactory for individuals with sensory loss if the edges of the orthosis are smooth and the orthosis does not pinch the patient's flesh. Proprioceptive loss may indicate the need for orthotic stabilization, such as a solid ankle AFO to control a Charcot neuropathic ankle.

UPPER LIMBS

Although the patient is being considered as a candidate for lower-limb or trunk orthoses, the therapist must determine the mobility and motor power of the upper limbs. Significant weakness, stiffness, or deformity will interfere with donning the orthosis. Substitution of pressure closures for leather buckles may suffice. If the individual cannot ambulate without canes or crutches, the therapist should determine whether standard aids will be satisfactory or whether modification of the handpieces is required. If the upper limbs are very weak, the patient will not be able to use the lower-limb orthoses for walking. Alternate standing arrangements may be preferable, such as the use of a standing frame, standing table, or standing wheelchair to provide weight-bearing stress.

PSYCHOLOGIC STATUS

Realistic orthotic prescription requires ascertaining that the patient is willing to wear the orthotic device. The patient with a recent spinal cord injury may still deny the permanence of paralysis and thus be adverse to wearing orthoses that are visible reminders of disability. The adolescent with spina bifida may prefer to sit unbraced in a wheelchair rather than struggle with donning orthoses and walking slowly, in a manner very different from the individual's peers. The patient with spinal cord injury must be prepared to work vigorously to increase upper limb and trunk strength and aerobic capacity. The person who has sustained a cerebral vascular accident resulting in severe perceptual deficiency may not be able to walk, even with orthotic assistance because the environment now seems unfamiliar. An orthosis for prevention of deformity may be prescribed, rather than one that is designed to aid gait.

The therapist should judge the extent to which the patient is likely to comply with instructions pertaining to orthotic use and care. For example, if it is doubtful that the individual will wear appropriate shoes with an insert orthosis, then the prescription should specify stirrup attachment to suitable shoes.

Orthotic Prescription

Lower-limb orthoses benefit individuals with a wide variety of musculoskeletal and neurologic disorders. The particular diagnosis is less important in formulating the prescription than consideration of the patient's disability. Prognosis also influences prescription. The person who is likely to recover partial or full function should have an orthosis that can be adjusted to accommodate the changing status. An individual with recent hemiplegia, for example, may exhibit marked spasticity, indicating a need for a limitation in motion at the ankle. As the person regains voluntary control, the ankle can be adjusted to permit more movement.

Life-style has a bearing on orthotic selection. One who is very active requires an orthosis made of exceptionally sturdy materials. Split stirrups, for example, may not be appropriate because they can spring loose from the receptacle on the shoe if excessive mediolateral stress is applied. The client's concern with appearance is another practical consideration; it may dictate use of a shoe insert so that reasonably fashionable shoes may be worn. Similarly, plastic shells are less bulky than metal uprights and calf bands, and do not present a shiny metal appearance. Although most people want the orthosis to be as inconspicuous as possible, some children and adults opt for bright colors, which can be achieved with various plastics.

ANKLE-FOOT ORTHOSES

The primary candidates for AFOs are those with peripheral neuropathy, especially peroneal lesions, and hemiplegia. Those with foot drag can be fitted with an AFO with a posterior stop; this design, however, tends to cause the knee to flex excessively in early stance when controlled plantarflexion is normally achieved. In the absence of plantarflexion, the patient may flex the knee to effect a foot-flat position. The alternative is a resilient shoe heel, or an AFO with a plastic posterior leaf spring or a metal dorsiflexion spring assist, both of which permit controlled plantarflexion early in stance to prevent knee stress.

Orthotic management of hemiplegia depends on the extent of spasticity and paralysis. If the motor loss is confined to poor dorsiflexion, the posterior leaf spring AFO suffices. An even simpler and less expensive option is a 1-cm (⅛-in) lift on the heel and sole of the contralateral shoe to provide clearance for the paretic limb during swing phase. Those with mediolateral and sagittal plane instability require an AFO with limited-motion ankle joints or a plastic spiral AFO. With pain or severe instability, a solid ankle AFO is required. In the presence of severe spasticity, a spring assist for joint motion is contraindicated because the spring action may serve to increase spasticity.

KNEE-ANKLE-FOOT AND OTHER LOWER-LIMB ORTHOSES

A KAFO may be used to compensate for paralysis of the entire leg. The physical therapist should assess the patient with a temporary orthosis in order to proceed more confidently with prescription of an expensive, custom-made orthosis. Several versions of temporary ortho-

ses are manufactured and prove exceedingly useful in demonstrating whether the patient is likely to benefit from orthotic knee control.

Stabilizing AFOs, Craig-Scott KAFOs, HKAFOs, the reciprocating gait orthosis, and the ParaWalker are options for patients with paraplegia. For the child, the orthotic program should start with a simple standing frame and progress to the parapodium before involving the child in the greater expense and donning difficulty of form-fitting bracing. Children and adults may begin with a swivel walker or lightweight modular frames.

TRUNK ORTHOSES

A corset may be adequate to increase intraabdominal pressure and thereby reduce the discomfort of low-back pain. Where greater motion restriction is indicated, such as for the individual with trunk paralysis, the LS FEL, TLS FE, or TLS FEL orthosis will provide substantial support. Plastic lumbosacral or thoracolumbosacral jackets offer maximum support. Cervical orthoses, whether collars or post devices, restrain motion and remind the wearer not to move the head in an abrupt manner. Collars also retain body heat, which may prove therapeutic. For maximum neck control, a Minerva or halo orthosis is required.

An array of orthoses has been designed for management of patients with scoliosis. These include the Milwaukee orthosis, which is the most extensive, as well as the Boston and Wilmington orthoses, which do not terminate quite so high on the trunk.

Orthotic Assessment

Evaluation is an essential element of orthotic management. The physical therapist should be certain that the orthosis fits and functions properly before attempting to train the patient to use it. Evaluation may be conducted under the aegis of a formal orthotic clinic team. If so, when the orthosis is delivered, the team should assess the adequacy of the orthosis as *pass, provisional pass,* or *fail*. Pass indicates that the orthosis is altogether satisfactory and the patient is ready for training. Provisional pass means that minor faults exist, generally having to do with the cosmetic finishing of the appliance; the patient can wear the orthosis in the training program without harmful effect. Failure signifies that the orthosis has a major defect that would interfere with training; for example, shoes that are too tight for the patient. The problem must be resolved before training can begin. If the orthosis is not prescribed by a clinic team, then the therapist should use the assessment procedure to assure that the orthosis meets the patient's needs. Final assessment is performed at the conclusion of training to reassess the fit and function of the orthosis and the patient's skill in using it.

LOWER-LIMB ORTHOTIC STATIC EVALUATION

Evaluation involves both static assessment of the orthosis on the patient while standing and sitting, as well as examination of the device off the individual.

Dynamic assessment refers to analysis of the wearer's gait.

The orthosis is assessed as the wearer stands and sits. The patient's skin and the construction of the orthosis are checked with the orthosis off the patient. The orthosis should be compared with the prescription. Departures from the original specifications must be approved by the individual(s) who developed the prescription.

The patient should stand in parallel bars, or other secure environment, and should attempt to bear equal weight on both feet. The shoe should fit satisfactorily, particularly in length, width, and snugness of the counters. Whether or not wedges or lifts have been added to the shoe, the sole and heel should rest flat on the floor, except for the distal portion, which should curve upward slightly to aid in late stance. The ankle joint should be at the distal tip of the medial malleolus, in order to be congruent with the anatomic ankle and to avoid vertical motion of the orthosis on the leg during gait.

The calf band should terminate below the fibular head to avoid impingement on the peroneal nerve. If a patellar-tendon-bearing brim is used, it should have a concave relief to limit pressure on the fibular head. This component does not eliminate distal weight bearing; however, one should judge to see that the shoe heel is somewhat unloaded. This can be estimated by placing a ribbon in the shoe before the patient dons the shoe. One end of the ribbon hangs out the back of the shoe. When the patient stands with the shoe and orthosis on, the therapist should be able to pull the ribbon out of the shoe. The calf shell or band or patellar-tendon-bearing brim should not intrude on the popliteal fossa so that the patient has difficulty flexing the knee when sitting. Donning ease is affected by the type of closure of both the shoe and band.

The mechanical knee joints should be congruent with the anatomic knee; for the adult, the usual placement is approximately 2 cm (¾ in) above the medial tibial plateau. The knee lock should function properly, for use of a lock is often the major reason for wearing a KAFO. The medial upright should terminate approximately 4 cm (1½ in) below the perineum. The calf and distal thigh shells or bands should be equidistant so that when the orthosis is flexed, as in sitting, the plastic or metal parts will contact one another, rather than pinch the back of the wearer's leg.

If the KAFO has a quadrilateral brim to reduce weight bearing through the bony skeleton, the brim should have adequate provision for the sensitive adductor longus tendon and should provide a sufficient seat for the ischial tuberosity.

The pelvic joint is set above the greater trochanter to compensate for the usual angulation of the femoral neck; setting the joint anterior to the trochanter takes into account the medial rotation of the femur. The pelvic band should conform to the contours of the wearer's torso, without edge pressure.

When the brace is off, the therapist should inspect the patient's skin to detect any irritations attributable to the orthosis. One should move the joints slowly to check the range of motion. *Binding* refers to tilting of the distal portion of the joint in relation to the proximal member so as to interfere with movement. If the medial and lateral stops do not contact their respective stops at the same time, the stop that contacts first will erode rapidly and may contribute to twisting of the orthosis.

DYNAMIC ASSESSMENT

The gait pattern exhibited by the person who wears an orthosis reflects both the contribution of the wearer's physique and the orthotic motion control and assistance. Table 30–1 relates orthotic and anatomic causes of the most commonly observed gait deviations. It should be noted that observational gait analysis is a moderately reliable assessment; sagittal plane deviations are easier to judge than are those that occur in the frontal or transverse plane.[41]

During early stance the patient may exhibit foot slap, striking with toes first, or flat-foot contact, indicating inability to restrain plantarflexion or failure of the orthosis to support the foot and ankle. Excessive medial or lateral contact may indicate that the orthosis does not track the way the patient's limb does. Knee hyperextension or excessive flexion indicates that the orthosis is not applying adequate control. A posterior stop on the AFO should prevent the lax knee from hyperextending. If the patient wears a KAFO and has knee hyperextension, the stops in the knee joint are set improperly or have eroded, or the calf and thigh shells or bands are too deep. Anterior and posterior trunk bending are seen at early stance when the patient attempts to control a weak knee or hip. If the quadriceps are weak, the patient will bend forward. The person who fears that the knee may collapse may benefit from an AFO with a solid ankle and an anterior band, or a KAFO with a knee lock. If the gluteus maximus is weak, the individual is apt to lean backward. Lordosis indicates hip flexion contracture or a KAFO that does not fit properly. Lateral trunk bending in early stance phase may result from hip abductor weakness or hip instability; however, uncompensated shortness of the limb will also give rise to this problem, as will a medial upright on a KAFO that is too high, or an abducted pelvic joint on an HKAFO. A wide walking base may be the patient's compensation for a medial upright or shell that impinges into the perineum.

The client may have difficulty during late stance—either delaying weight transfer or being unable to transfer weight over the paralyzed foot. The problem can be mitigated with an anterior stop and a rocker bar. One should be certain that the trimlines of the solid ankle AFO or the stops on the stirrup function properly.

During swing phase the patient must be able to clear the floor with the braced leg. Hip hiking occurs when the hip flexors are weak, as well as when the limb is functionally longer than the contralateral limb. Increased length may be produced by a faulty posterior stop that no longer limits plantarflexion, or by a locked knee joint. The problem should be anticipated and, for the unilateral KAFO wearer, can be prevented by adding a 1-cm (½-in) lift to the contralateral shoe. Internal or external hip rotation may be caused by motor imbalance between medial and lateral musculature; the orthotic causes relate to malalignment of the brace. Similarly, excessive medial or lateral foot contact may indicate that

Table 30-1 ORTHOTIC GAIT ANALYSIS

Deviation	Orthotic Causes	Anatomic Causes
Early Stance		
1. Foot slap: forefront slaps the ground	Inadequate dorsiflexion assist Inadequate plantarflexion stop	Weak dorsiflexors
2. Toes first: tiptoe posture may or may not be maintained throughout stance	Inadequate heel lift Inadequate dorsiflexion assist Inadequate plantarflexion stop Inadequate relief of heel pain	Short leg Pes equinus Extensor spasticity Heel pain
3. Flat foot contact: entire foot contacts ground initially	Inadequate traction from sole Requires walking aid, e.g., cane Inadequate dorsiflexion stop	Poor balance Pes calcaneus
4. Excessive medial (lateral) foot contact: medial (lateral) border contacts floor	Transverse plane malalignment	Weak invertors (evertors) Pes valgus (varus) Genu valgum (varum)
5. Excessive knee flexion: knee collapses when foot contacts ground	Inadequate knee lock Inadequate dorsiflexion stop Plantarflexion stop Inadequate contralateral shoe lift	Weak quadriceps Short contralateral leg Knee pain Knee and/or hip flexion contracture Flexor synergy Pes calcaneus
6. Hyperextended knee: knee hyperextends as weight is transferred to leg	Genu recurvatum inadequately controlled by plantarflexion stop Excessively concave calf band Pes equinus uncompensated by contralateral shoe lift Inadequate knee lock	Weak quadriceps Lax knee ligaments Extensor synergy Pes equinus Short contralateral leg Contralateral knee and/or hip flexion contracture
7. Anterior trunk bending: patient leans forward as weight is transferred to leg	Inadequate knee lock	Weak quadriceps Hip flexion contracture Knee flexion contracture
8. Posterior trunk bending: patient leans backward as weight is transferred to leg	Inadequate hip lock Knee lock	Weak gluteus maximus Knee ankylosis
9. Lateral trunk bending: patient leans toward stance leg as weight is transferred to leg	Excessive height of medial upright of KAFO Excessive abduction of hip joint of HKAFO Insufficient shoe lift Requires walking aid, e.g., cane	Weak gluteus medius Abduction contracture Dislocated hip Hip pain Poor balance Short leg
10. Wide walking base: heel centers more than 10 cm (4 in) apart	Excessive height of medial upright of KAFO Excessive abduction of hip joint of HKAFO Insufficient lift on contralateral shoe Knee lock Requires walking aid, e.g., cane	Abduction contracture Poor balance Short contralateral leg
11. Internal (external) rotation: limb internally (externally) rotated	Uprights incorrectly aligned in transverse plane Requires orthotic control, e.g., rotation control straps, pelvic band	Internal (external) hip rotators spastic External (internal) hip rotators weak Anteversion (retroversion) Weak quadriceps: external rotation
Late Stance		
1. Inadequate transition: delayed or absent transfer of weight over the forefoot	Plantarflexion stop Inadequate dorsiflexion stop	Weak plantarflexors Achilles tendon sprain or rupture Pes calcaneus Forefoot pain
Swing		
1. Toe drag: toes maintain contact with ground	Inadequate dorsiflexion assist Inadequate plantarflexion stop	Weak dorsiflexors Plantarflexor spasticity Pes equinus Weak hip flexors
2. Circumduction: leg swings outward in a semicircular arc	Knee lock Inadequate dorsiflexion assist Inadequate plantarflexion stop	Weak hip flexors Extensor synergy Knee and/or ankle ankylosis Weak dorsiflexors Pes equinus

677

Table 30–1 ORTHOTIC GAIT ANALYSIS (Continued)

Deviation	Orthotic Causes	Anatomic Causes
3. Hip hiking: leg elevated at pelvis to enable the limb to swing forward	Knee lock Inadequate dorsiflexion assist Inadequate plantarflexion stop	Short contralateral leg Contralateral knee and/or hip flexion contracture Weak hip flexors Extensor synergy Knee and/or ankle ankylosis Weak dorsiflexors Pes equinus
4. Vaulting: exaggerated plantarflexion of contralateral leg to enable the limb to swing forward	Knee lock Inadequate dorsiflexion assist Inadequate plantarflexion stop	Weak hip flexors Extensor spasticity Pes equinus Short contralateral leg Contralateral knee and/or hip flexion contracture Knee and/or ankle ankylosis Weak dorsiflexors

the orthosis does not track the way the patient's limb does. A walking base that is abnormally wide can be caused by a limb that is longer than that on the opposite side. *Vaulting* refers to exaggerated plantarflexion on the contralateral limb during swing phase of the affected side. Vaulting occurs because the braced leg is functionally too long, possibly because the posterior ankle stop has eroded or a knee lock is used. The less agile patient may obtain foot clearance by *hip hiking*, that is, elevating the pelvis on the swing side.

TRUNK ORTHOSIS STATIC ASSESSMENT

Lumbosacral and thoracolumbosacral orthoses usually include thoracic and pelvic bands, which should fit flat against the trunk, without edge pressure. Uprights should not press against bony prominences, particularly when the patient sits. The abdominal front should extend from just below the xiphoid process to just above the pubic symphysis. The cervical orthosis should hold the head in the best tolerated position. Rigid components, such as a mandibular plate, occipital plate, sternal plate, or thoracic plate should be shaped to apply maximum area to the body segment.

Facilitating Orthotic Acceptance

Clinic team management is valuable to foster acceptance of the orthosis by the patient. The team also enables clinicians to join efforts to help the client achieve the maximum benefit from orthotic rehabilitation. Bringing the new wearer of an orthosis in contact with other users in the physical therapy department can help the new patient recognize that orthotic use is not a strange occurrence. Peer support groups for patients and their families are helpful for sharing concerns and anxieties and reaching workable solutions to common problems. Support groups usually are organized for people having particular disabilities, such as paraplegia or hemiplegia; many clients will have orthoses as part of their rehabilitation. The physical therapist can guide

some meetings of the group. The therapist works most closely with the patient, usually on a daily basis, and thus is able to identify those individuals whose response to disability is sufficiently aberrant as to require psychologic attention.

Orthotic Training

Orthoses are designed to provide the individual with a maximum of function with a minimum of discomfort and effort. No single training program suits every orthosis wearer because of the wide range of disorders for which orthotic management is indicated. To the extent possible, however, the physical therapist should instruct the patient in the correct manner of donning the orthosis, developing standing balance, walking safely, and performing other ambulatory activities.

Optimal performance depends on the favorable interaction of many factors. Foremost is the extent of skeletal and neuromuscular involvement. The mobility, strength, and coordination of all body segments, especially in the lower limbs and trunk, are important, as is the individual's muscle tone, cardiovascular and pulmonary health, body weight, psychologic status, and chronologic age. The quality of the orthosis also influences the client's achievements.

Most orthosis wearers have chronic conditions, such as rheumatoid arthritis, or permanent sequelae from trauma, such as paraplegia following spinal cord injury. Orthotic management enhances function without necessarily influencing the underlying pathology. Training prepares the patient for lifelong activity with a brace. Persons with reversible disorders, such as peroneal neuropathy, often benefit from temporary use of an orthosis. Such individuals should learn proper use of the orthosis to prevent secondary disorders and should receive reassessment so that the orthosis may be altered as the condition changes. Patients with progressive disorders, such as muscular dystrophy and multiple sclerosis, require vigilant reassessment so that the extent of physical deterioration may be reflected in orthotic changes, as well as continual training to cope with altered functional abilities. For all situations, a carefully devised exercise and activity program should enable the patient to manage efficiently for maximum independence.

DONNING ORTHOSES

Regardless of type of orthosis, the patient should wear clean, properly fitting hose. The AFO with shoe insert is most easily donned by applying the orthosis to the foot and leg, prior to placing the braced limb in the shoe. If the AFO has a split stirrup, the shoe should be donned first; then the orthosis should be fitted into the box caliper on the shoe. If the AFO has a solid stirrup, the patient will have to insert the foot into the shoe, then fasten the calf band.

The same general procedures are useful with KAFOs. The patient may find donning easier if the brace is applied while lying on a bed or a mat table. If the KAFO is donned while the patient sits, the therapist should check the tightness of the knee cap, if this component is part of the orthosis. A knee cap that is comfortable for sitting will probably be too loose for effective knee control when the wearer stands. Donning HKAFOs and THKAFOs is much more arduous. The beginner should lie on a mat table alongside the orthosis. By rolling to one side, the patient should be able to pull the brace under the legs so as to permit lying in it. Then the patient dons the shoes and fastens the various straps.

Lumbosacral and thoracolumbosacral corsets and rigid orthoses should be donned while the patient is supine in order to achieve maximum compression of the abdomen. The orthosis should be fastened from the bottom upward.

STANDING BALANCE

The problem of standing safely is most difficult for the individual who wears a pair of KAFOs or more extensive bracing. In ordinary standing, all weight passes through the feet, whereas when standing and walking with orthoses and crutches, the patient must learn to distribute weight partly on the hands and partly on the feet. The line of gravity falls within a tripod bounded by the hands and feet. The tripod is a compromise between leaning too far forward on the hands, to increase stability at the price of fatiguing the arms, and leaning too far backward, which reduces arm strain but makes balance precarious. As balance improves, the patient uses the hands only for balance, rather than for substantial weight bearing.

The person who wears bilateral KAFOs will need crutches or other aids for independent gait. A prerequisite for crutch ambulation is the ability to shift weight. Shifting weight to the heels takes pressure off the hands so they can be moved. The beginner shifts all weight to the feet and raises and lowers one hand, then the other hand. The goal is to be able to lift both hands simultaneously, as may be done with crutches when performing a drag-to or similar gait. Once the patient is able to shift weight from the feet to the hands and back to the feet confidently, the same exercise should be done with crutches. Advanced skills, such as moving the hands and eventually the crutches, behind the body, should be practiced. Those who will walk in reciprocal fashion, alternating foot steps, need to practice diagonal weight shifting.

GAIT TRAINING

The various crutch gaits differ in the sequence of crutch and foot steps. Patterns vary in speed, safety, and amount of energy required. The patient should learn as many gaits as possible, so as to modify walking in crowds, over long distances, and in situations in which speed is desired. In addition to walking forward, the client needs to be able to walk sideward, to turn corners, and to maneuver on different surfaces, such as rugs, gravel, grass, and through doors. A repertoire of gaits permits the client to adjust to environmental requirements.

Gait selection depends on the individual's functional ability, including:

1. Step ability. Can the patient take steps with either or both lower limbs?
2. Weight-bearing and balance ability. Can the patient bear weight and remain balanced on one or both lower limbs?
3. Upper-limb power. Can the patient push the body off the floor by pressing down on the hands?

Reciprocal Gaits

The *four-point* and *two-point gaits* require that one move the lower limbs alternately by hip flexion or pelvic elevation. The patient shifts weight as each limb is moved. The four-point sequence is (1) right hand, (2) left foot, (3) left hand, and (4) right foot. The two-point sequence requires greater balance and coordination, but is a faster mode of walking: (1) right hand and left leg; (2) left hand and right leg.

The patterns also are useful when one is confronted with crowds or slippery surfaces. These gaits are also suited to persons who lack the coordination and balance needed for simultaneous gaits.

Simultaneous Gaits

If both lower limbs are moved simultaneously, the patient places considerable stress on the upper limbs. The series includes the *drag-to, swing-to,* and *swing-through* patterns. Although the swing-through gait can be performed rapidly, simultaneous gaits generally are slow and very fatiguing, for the upper limbs are poorly adapted for ambulatory function; a sizable amount of nonfunctioning bodily structure must be controlled by a smaller muscular apparatus. The weight of the orthoses, and in the case of a patient with spinal cord lesion, absence of peripheral sensation, aggravate the problem of using a simultaneous gait pattern.

The drag-to gait is the most elementary of the group, but it is very slow. The sequence is (1) advance both hands, then (2) push on the crutches enough to drag the feet forward. The feet do not pass ahead of the hands. The swing-to pattern is more rapid, for the patient swings rather than drags the lower limbs. Swinging is accomplished by extending the elbows and depressing the shoulder girdle to elevate the trunk and lower limbs. The swing-through gait is the most advanced pattern, requiring much balance, strength, and coordination of the upper limbs, because the patient swings the legs beyond the hands, or crutch tips. The sequence is (1) advance both hands, (2) swing both legs to a point in front of the hands to reverse the basic tripod position, and (3) advance both hands to the starting position. The swing-through gait requires extensive preliminary training, including push-ups to strengthen the arms. The gait is rapid but requires more floor space than the other patterns, to permit alternate swinging of legs and crutches. Detailed instructions in gait training are provided in Chapters 14 and 26.

The ultimate test of walking proficiency is the ability to conduct a conversation while ambulating, an activity pattern that indicates some degree of automatic functioning. Practice in the clinical setting should be extended to walking on varied terrain, indoors and outdoors.

ACTIVITIES

The patient should learn as many activities of daily living as the physical condition permits. Daily life often involves negotiating stairs, curbs, and ramps, as well as transferring from the chair to the upright position, and into an automobile. Instruction in driving a suitably equipped automobile is an important part of rehabilitation. Not all individuals who wear orthoses achieve the full range of ambulatory activities, yet they benefit from partial independence in accomplishing tasks, at least from the psychologic and physiologic values attendant to ambulation.

FINAL ASSESSMENT AND FOLLOW-UP CARE

Prior to discharge, the orthosis wearer and the brace should be reassessed to make certain that fit, function, appearance, and use are acceptable.

The client should return to the hospital or rehabilitation center at regular intervals so that the clinic team can monitor the individual's function and the orthosis, and can spot incipient abrasions or other signs of misfit or disrepair. The follow-up visit also enables the physical therapist to reinforce skills taught in the intensive program and to address any new problems the patient may present.

Functional Capacities

The patient's ambulatory ability and capacity for other physical activities reflect both orthotic and anatomic factors. Energy measurement is a valuable guide to functional capacity. Energy cost is calculated from the amount of oxygen consumed as the subject performs. Consumption may be determined either per unit of distance traversed or per unit of time. One tends to select a walking speed that requires the least energy per unit of distance. If the energy cost is too high, the patient will realize that ambulation is not a practical mode of locomotion. Sometimes, high energy cost is tolerable for short distances, as in household ambulation. Community ambulation, however, demands sustained effort for longer distances, plus the ability to maneuver over curbs and other irregularities in the walking surface. Many energy studies have been conducted with the two largest groups of individuals who wear orthoses, namely those with paraplegia and those with hemiplegia.

PARAPLEGIA

The level of spinal cord damage is a critical determinant of functional capacity. Investigators generally conclude that functional ambulation is not feasible for those with lesions above the T-11 segment of the spinal cord. Patients with thoracic injuries consume nine times the energy expended by nondisabled individuals per meter, while those with lumbar lesions require triple the normal amount of oxygen, when walking at self-selected speeds. Those with high-level paraplegia use three times their own basal oxygen rate ambulating with Craig-Scott KAFOs; they choose a very slow walking pace. Subjects with lesions between T-11 and L-2 wearing bilateral KAFOs select walking speeds less than half that of nondisabled persons, with oxygen uptake six times normal. Wheelchair propulsion by the same group increases oxygen uptake less than 10 percent more than normal, at a considerably faster speed.[42] The very high energy cost may be accounted for by the fact that the lower-limb paralysis requires that the individual move by upper limb and thoracic action, usually in a swing-to or swing-through gait. This pattern is extremely strenuous, taxing nondisabled adults by at least 75 percent more energy than normal walking.

Of less significance in determining functional capacity is the type of orthosis. Restraining both plantarflexion and dorsiflexion, as provided by Craig-Scott KAFOs, reduces energy demand very slightly.[43] Ankle restraint, however, makes no appreciable difference in the energy required to negotiate stairs and ramps. Performance is somewhat more efficient with molded plastic KAFOs, which weigh slightly less than traditional metal and leather braces. Most subjects fitted with both the ParaWalker and the reciprocating gait orthosis preferred the latter primarily because of its appearance and perception of stability.[44]

One should not lose sight of the principal purpose of ambulation, namely to get from one place to another, rather than to execute an exhausting physical stunt. The near universal abandonment of orthoses by individuals with thoracic spinal cord injury upon discharge from the rehabilitation center attests to the fact that most decide that accomplishing vocational and recreational tasks is more important than struggling with brace donning and awkward ambulation.

HEMIPLEGIA

Although the increased energy demand occasioned by hemiplegic ambulation is not nearly as dramatic as that for paraplegic gait, the cost should be considered in planning reasonable goals. Energy cost rises in proportion to the amount of spasticity. The increase ranges from no appreciable difference for persons with hemiplegia to a 100 percent increase for relatively inexperienced walkers. On average, comfortable gait is approximately half the speed of that for nondisabled individuals.

The type of orthosis does not appear to make much difference in functional capacity, although patients with hemiplegia perform more efficiently with some form of AFO than without any bracing. Investigation of the factors that influence energy expenditure, especially physical status, help the clinician plan the most appropriate rehabilitation program and forecast long-term performance.

SUMMARY

This chapter has focused on lower-limb and trunk orthotics. The most frequently prescribed orthoses and orthotic components have been presented. In addition, the responsibilities of the physical therapist in orthotic management have been emphasized.

Ideally, an orthosis is prescribed by an orthotic clinic team composed of a physician, physical therapist, and orthotist. The prescription should be based on a thorough assessment, with particular attention to the specific factors discussed in this chapter. Input from the patient and all team members during the decision-making process is critical. This approach will ensure an optimum match between the patient's biomechanical and psychologic requirements and an appropriate orthosis capable of performing its intended function. Once the orthosis has been prescribed, it should be evaluated to ensure satisfactory fit, function, and construction, and the patient should have the benefit of a suitable training program for donning the orthosis and using it effectively.

QUESTIONS FOR REVIEW

1. What is meant by the terms ankle-foot orthosis and knee-ankle-foot orthosis?

2. Describe the major parts of the shoe. What is the advantage of the Blucher opening? A low quarter?

3. Specify the purpose and placement of a metatarsal bar.

4. What are the advantages and disadvantages of the shoe insert as compared with the solid stirrup?

5. Indicate the clinical use of a posterior leg band, an anterior leg band, and a patellar-tendon-bearing brim.

6. How do tone-inhibiting AFOs improve the patient's function?

7. What orthotic knee joint is indicated for the patient with knee flexion contracture?

8. How do stabilizing AFOs or Craig-Scott KAFOs support a client with paraplegia?

9. What orthoses permit the child with paraplegia to stand without the aid of crutches?

10. Describe the three-point system in a lumbosacral flexion extension control orthosis that controls flexion.

11. Outline a maintenance program for a plastic and metal KAFO with solid ankle and pawl lock.

12. What facts should be assessed prior to formulating an orthotic prescription?

13. What features of the AFO are considered in static assessment?

14. Delineate the training program for a person with paraplegia who has been fitted with bilateral KAFOs.

15. List the orthotic options for a patient with hemiplegia.

16. What are the anatomic and orthotic causes of vaulting?

REFERENCES

1. Edelstein, JE: Foot care for the aging. Phys Ther 68:1882, 1988.
2. Pratt, DJ: Long-term comparison of some shock absorbing insoles. Prosthet Orthot Int 14:59, 1990.
3. Wenger, DR, et al: Corrective shoes and inserts as treatment for flexible flatfoot in infants and children. J Bone Joint Surg [Am] 71:800, 1989.
4. Mereday, C, Dolan, CME, and Lusskin, R: Evaluation of the University of California Biomechanics Laboratory shoe insert in "flexible" pes planus. Clin Orthop 82:45, 1972.
5. McCulloch, MU, Brunt, D, and Vander Linden, D: The effect of foot orthotics and gait velocity on lower limb kinematics and temporal events of stance. J Orthop Sports Phys Ther 17:2, 1993.
6. Gross, ML, Davlin, LB, and Evanski, PM: Effectiveness of orthotic shoe inserts in the long-distance runner. Am J Sports Med 19:409, 1991.
7. Richardson, JK: Rocker-soled shoes and walking distance in patients with calf claudication. Arch Phys Med Rehabil 72:554, 1991.
8. Cook, TM and Cozzens, B: The effects of heel height and ankle-foot-orthosis configuration on weight line location: a demonstration of principles. Orthot Prosthet 30:43, 1976.
9. Lehmann, JR, et al: Plastic ankle-foot orthoses: evaluation of function. Arch Phys Med Rehabil 64:402, 1983.
10. Yamamoto, S, et al: Comparative study of mechanical characteristics of plastic AFOs. J Prosthet Orthot 5:59, 1993.
11. Lehneis, HR: Plastic spiral ankle-foot orthoses. Orthot Prosthet 28:3, 1974.
12. Yang, GW, et al: Floor reaction orthosis: clinical experience. Orthot Prosthet 40:33, 1986.
13. Middleton, EA, Hurley, GRB, and McIlwain, JS: The role of rigid and hinged polypropylene ankle-foot-orthoses in the management of cerebral palsy: a case study. Prosthet Orthot Int 12:129, 1988.
14. Embrey, DG, Yates, L, and Mott, DH: Effects of neuro-developmental treatment and orthoses on knee flexion during gait: a single-subject design. Phys Ther 701:626, 1990.
15. Shamp, JK: Neurophysiologic orthotic designs in the treatment of central nervous system disorders. J Prosthet Orthot 2:14, 1989.
16. Diamond, MF and Ottenbacher, KJ: Effect of a tone-inhibiting dynamic ankle-foot orthosis on stride characteristics of an adult with hemiparesis. Phys Ther 70:423, 1990.
17. Krebs, DE, Edelstein, JE, and Fishman, S: Comparison of plastic/metal and leather/metal knee-ankle-foot orthoses. Am J Phys Med Rehabil 67:175, 1988.
18. Stallard, J, et al: The ORLAU VCG (variable center of gravity) swivel walker for muscular dystrophy patients. Prosthet Orthot Int 16:46, 1992.
19. Gram, M: Using the Parapodium: A Manual of Training Techniques. Eterna Press, Rochester, NY, 1984.
20. Engen, T: Lightweight modular orthosis. Prosthet Orthot Int 13:125, 1989.

21. Kent, HO: Vannini-Rizzoli stabilizing orthosis (boot): preliminary report on a new ambulatory aid for spinal cord injury. Arch Phys Med Rehabil 73:302, 1992.

22. Lyles, M and Munday, J: Report on the evaluation of the Vannini-Rizzoli stabilizing limb orthosis. J Rehabil Res Dev 29:77, 1992.

23. Scott, BA: Engineering principles and fabrication techniques for the Scott-Craig long leg brace for paraplegics. Orthot Prosthet 25:14, 1971.

24. Lobley, S: Orthotic design from the New England Regional Spinal Cord Injury Center. Phys Ther 65:492, 1985.

25. Douglas, R and Solomonow, M: The LSU reciprocating gait orthosis. J Rehabil Res Dev 25:57, 1987.

26. Summers, BN, McClelland, JR, and El Masri, WS: A clinical review of the adult hip guidance orthosis (ParaWalker) in traumatic paraplegics. Paraplegia 26:19, 1988.

27. Jaeger, RJ: Lower extremity applications of functional neuromuscular stimulation. Assist Technol 4:19, 1992.

28. Alaranta, H and Hurri, H: Compliance and subjective relief by corset treatment in chronic low back pain. Scand J Rehabil Med 20:133, 1988.

29. Stillo, JV, Stein, AB, and Ragnarsson, KT: Low-back orthoses. Phys Med Rehabil Clin North Am 3:57, 1992.

30. Micheli, LJ: The use of the modified Boston brace system (B.O.B.) for back pain: clinical indications. Orthot Prosthet 39:41, 1985.

31. Beavis, A: Cervical orthoses. Prosthet Orthot Int 13:6, 1989.

32. Millington, P, et al: Thermoplastic Minerva body jacket: a practical alternative to current methods of cervical spine stabilization. Phys Ther 67:223, 1987.

33. Wang, GJ, et al: The effect of halo-vest length on stability of the cervical spine: a study in normal subjects. J Bone Joint Surg [Am] 70A:357, 1988.

34. Pringle, RG: Review article: halo versus Minerva: Which orthosis? Paraplegia 28:281, 1990.

35. Blount, WP and Moe, JH: The Milwaukee Brace, ed 2. Williams & Wilkins, Baltimore, 1980.

36. Andrews, G and MacEwen, GD: Idiopathic scoliosis: an 11-year follow-up study of the role of the Milwaukee brace in curve control and trunco-pelvic alignment. Orthopedics 12:809, 1989.

37. Emans, JB, et al: The Boston bracing system for idiopathic scoliosis: follow-up results in 295 patients. Spine 11:792, 1986.

38. Montgomery, F and Willner, ST: Prognosis of brace-treated scoliosis: comparison of the Boston and Milwaukee methods in 244 girls. Acta Orthop Scand 60:383, 1989.

39. Bassett, GS, Bunnell, WP, and MacEwen, GD: Treatment of idiopathic scoliosis with the Wilmington brace. J Bone Joint Surg [Am] 68:602, 1986.

40. Green, N: Part-time bracing of adolescent idiopathic scoliosis. J Bone Joint Surg [Am] 68:738, 1986.

41. Krebs, DE, Edelstein, JE, and Fishman, S: Reliability of observational kinematic gait analysis. Phys Ther 65:1027, 1985.

42. Cerny, K, et al: Walking and wheelchair energetics in persons with paraplegia. Phys Ther 60:1133, 1980.

43. Merkel, KD, Miller, NE, and Merritt, JL: Energy expenditure in patients with low-, mid-, or high-thoracic paraplegic using Scott-Craig knee-ankle-foot orthoses. Mayo Clin Proc 60:165, 1985.

44. Whittle, MW, et al: A comparative trial of two walking systems for paralysed people. Paraplegia 29:97, 1991.

SUPPLEMENTAL READINGS

Aisen, ML: Orthotics in Neurologic Rehabilitation. Demos, New York, 1992.

American Academy of Orthopaedic Surgeons: Atlas of Orthotics, ed 3. CV Mosby, St. Louis, 1994.

Bunch, WH and Keagy, RD: Principles of Orthotic Treatment. CV Mosby, St. Louis, 1976.

Bunch, WH and Patwardhan, AG: Scoliosis: Making Clinical Decisions. CV Mosby, St. Louis, 1989.

Campbell, JM and Meadows, PM: Therapeutic FES: from rehabilitation to neural prosthetics. Assist Technol 4:4, 1992.

Edelstein, JE: Prosthetic and orthotic gait. In Smidt, GL (ed): Gait in Rehabilitation. Churchill Livingstone, New York, 1990.

Fisher, SV: Cervical orthotics. Phys Med Rehabil Clinics North Am 3:29, 1992.

Halar, E and Cardenas, D: Ankle-foot orthoses: clinical implications. Phys Med Rehabil State Art Rev 1:45, 1987.

King, HA: Orthotic management of idiopathic scoliosis. Phys Med Rehabil Clinics North Am 3:45, 1992.

Lantz, SA and Schultz, AB: Lumbar spine orthosis wearing, I. Restriction of gross body motions. Spine 11:834, 1986.

Lantz, SA and Schultz, AB: Lumbar spine orthosis wearing, II. Effect on trunk muscle myoelectric activity. Spine 11:838, 1986.

Lehmann, JF, de Lateur, BJ, and Price, R: Knee-ankle-foot orthoses for paresis and paralysis. Phys Med Rehabil Clinics North Am 3:161, 1992.

Lockard, MA: Foot orthoses. Phys Ther 68:1866, 1988.

McHugh, B and Campbell, J: Below-knee orthoses. Physiotherapy 73:380, 1987.

Nixon, V: Spinal Cord Injury: A Guide to Functional Outcomes in Physical Therapy Management. Aspen, Gaithersburg, MD, 1985.

Redford, JB (ed): Orthotics Etcetera, ed 3. Williams & Wilkins, Baltimore, 1986.

Rose, GK: Orthotics: Principles and Practice. William Heinemann, London, 1986.

Schwartz, RS: Foot orthoses and materials. In Jahss, ML (ed): Disorders of the Foot. WB Saunders, Philadelphia, 1982.

Sypert, GW. External spinal orthotics. Neurosurgery 20:642, 1987.

Winter, RB: The Milwaukee brace: 1992. J Assoc Child Prosthet-Orthot Clinics 27:16, 1992.

GLOSSARY

Bail: Posteriorly protruding semicircular handle of a pair of knee locks, usually pawl locks. Moving the bail upward releases the locks.

Bichannel adjustable ankle lock (BiCAAL): Ankle joint having posterior and anterior receptacles with springs that can be compressed to assist motion or can be replaced by pins to alter the alignment of the joint and thus the uprights attached to the joint.

Boston orthosis: Thoracolumbosacral orthosis intended for correction of scoliosis; its foundation is a mass-produced plastic module which is custom-altered.

Corset: Lumbosacral or thoracolumbosacral fabric orthosis that may have vertical reinforcements, but does not have rigid horizontal components.

Counter: Shoe component consisting of stiff material placed in the posterior aspect of the shoe to reinforce the quarter and increase stability of the back of the shoe.

Craig-Scott knee-ankle-foot orthosis: Knee-ankle-foot orthosis (KAFO) intended for persons with paraplegia and invented by Bruce Scott, an orthotist at the Craig Rehabilitation Center, Denver, Colorado. Each of the pair of orthoses consists of a reinforced shoe, stirrup, BiCAAL ankle joints, anterior leg band, pawl locks with bail release, and a single thigh band. A solid ankle may be substituted for the reinforced shoe, stirrup, and BiCAAL ankle joints.

Floor reaction orthosis: Any lower-limb orthosis; the term is usually applied to an ankle-foot orthosis (AFO) that has an anterior band and a solid ankle.

Halo: Cervical orthosis that includes a metal ring

secured to the skull, four vertical posts, and a thoracic vest.

Insert: Removable component placed in the shoe, extending from the posterior margin of the inner sole to a point immediately posterior to the point corresponding to the metatarsophalangeal joints, or farther anterior.

University of California Biomechanics Laboratory (UCBL) insert: Custom-made plastic insert intended to maintain correction of a flexible pes valgus; it includes a wall covering the medial, posterior, and lateral margins of the foot; the wall is continuous with a plantar plate.

Knight spinal orthosis: Lumbosacral flexion, extension, lateral control orthosis.

Last: Foot-shaped form over which a shoe is made.

Metatarsal bar: Strip of firm material attached transversely to the outer sole immediately posterior to a point corresponding to the metatarsophalangeal joints; intended to relieve weight bearing on those joints.

Metatarsal pad: Resilient dome-shaped material placed on the inner sole or in an insert, with the apex immediately posterior to one or more metatarsophalangeal joints; intended to relieve weight bearing on those joints.

Milwaukee orthosis: Thoracolumbosacral orthosis intended for correction of scoliosis that consists of a frame composed of a pelvic girdle, one anterior and two posterior uprights, and a thoracic ring, to which various corrective pads may be strapped.

Minerva orthosis: Cervical orthosis consisting of a rigid posterior section extending from the head to the thorax, and an anterior section extending from the mandible to the thorax. The orthosis is held in place by a forehead band.

Offset joint: Knee joint in which the axis is located posterior to the midline of the leg; intended to increase knee stability.

Parapodium: Mass-produced frame intended to enable children to stand and sit. Consists of a base connected to a thoracolumbar band by lateral uprights that are hinged and locked at the knees and hips. Chest and anterior leg bands stabilize the device.

ParaWalker: Trunk-hip-knee-ankle-foot orthosis, originally known as the hip guidance orthosis. Includes sturdy hip joints that permit a limited flexion excursion, but block frontal and transverse plane motion; also includes foot plates to which shoes are strapped.

Patellar-tendon-bearing brim: Plastic proximal portion of an AFO, intended to support part of the client's weight proximally, especially on the patellar ligament (tendon).

Patten: Distal termination of a knee-ankle-foot orthosis (KAFO) intended to relieve the braced limb of all weight bearing.

Pawl lock: Knee lock consisting of a proximal segment having a pivoted bar that lodges in a notch on the distal segment.

Posterior leaf spring orthosis: Plastic ankle-foot orthosis (AFO) which has a posterior upright continuous with an insert; intended to assist dorsiflexion.

The upright does not extend anteriorly beyond the malleoli.

Reciprocating gait orthosis: Trunk-hip-knee-ankle-foot orthosis (THKAFO) intended for clients with paraplegia. Consists of a pair of KAFOs to which is attached a mechanism having steel cables passing from the right to the left proximal margin of the thigh shell. The mechanism is secured to the torso with a thoracic strap.

Retention button: Spring-loaded projection on a drop ring knee lock.

Rocker bar: A convex strip affixed to the sole proximal to the metatarsal heads.

Scaphoid pad: Resilient dome-shaped material placed at the junction of the inner sole and medial quarter of the shoe, with the apex located between the navicular tuberosity and the sustentaculum tali of the calcaneus; intended to support the longitudinal arch.

Solid ankle-foot orthosis: Plastic ankle-foot orthosis (AFO) that has a posterior shell continuous with an insert. The shell extends anteriorly beyond the malleoli.

Hinged solid ankle-foot orthosis: Plastic orthosis with similar trimlines that has a transverse separation between the shell and the insert to provide sagittal plane motion.

Stabilizing boot orthosis: Also known as the Vannini-Rizzoli boot. Ankle-foot orthosis (AFO) that includes an inner plastic foot plate and shell that maintains the foot in plantarflexion. The plastic component is worn in a flat-bottomed boot. This orthosis is intended for clients with paraplegia.

Standing frame: Mass-produced trunk-hip-knee-ankle-foot orthosis (THKAFO) that supports the wearer with a nonarticulated posterior frame equipped with a thoracolumbar pad, and an anterior chest band and knee band. The base of the frame is flat and has loops to secure the shoes.

Stirrup: Steel U-shaped shoe attachment that connects the uprights to the shoe.

Solid stirrup: One-piece attachment, the central portion of which is riveted to the shoe shank; the shoe cannot be detached from the uprights.

Split stirrup: Three-piece attachment, the central portion of which is riveted to the shoe shank; the shoe can be detached from the uprights.

Swivel walker: Mass-produced trunk-hip-knee-ankle-foot orthosis (THKAFO) that supports the wearer with a nonarticulated posterior frame equipped with a thoracolumbar pad, and an anterior chest band and knee band. The base of the frame has two plates that pivot slightly enabling the wearer to achieve a swiveling gait.

Taylor orthosis: Thoracolumbosacral flexion extension control orthosis.

Thomas heel: Heel designed in the nineteenth century by Hugh Owen Thomas in which the anterior margin is curved, such that its medial border extends anteriorly, usually with a slight medial wedge; intended to support flexible pes valgus.

Tone-reducing orthosis: Ankle-foot orthoses (AFOs) designed to inhibit spasticity by maintaining a neutral foot position; some tone-reducing orthoses position the toes in hyperextension and have pads that apply constant pressure to the Achilles tendon.

Viscoelastic: Having both viscous and elastic properties; exhibited by various polyurethane plastics, such as Sorbothane, Viscolas, and PPT which are used in shoe inserts to absorb shock.

Wilmington orthosis: Thoracolumbosacral orthosis intended for correction of scoliosis; its foundation is a custom-made plastic jacket.

APPENDIX A   LOWER-LIMB ORTHOTIC EVALUATION

1. Is the orthosis as prescribed?
2. Can the client don the orthosis easily?

Standing

3. Is the shoe satisfactory and does it fit properly?
4. Are the sole and heel of the shoe flat on the floor?
5. If a shoe insert is used, is there minimal rocking between insert and shoe?

Ankle

6. Do the mechanical ankle joints coincide with the anatomic ankle?
7. Is there adequate clearance between the anatomic ankle and the mechanical ankle joints?
8. Does the valgus or varus correction strap control the foot position?

Knee

9. Do the mechanical knee joints coincide with the anatomic knee?
10. Is there adequate clearance between the anatomic knee and the mechanical knee joint?
11. Is the knee lock secure and easy to operate?

Shells, Bands, Cuffs, and Uprights

12. Do the shells, bands, cuffs, and uprights conform to the contours of the leg and thigh?
13. Is there adequate clearance between the top of the calf shell or band and the head of the fibula?
14. Is there adequate clearance between the orthosis and the perineum?
15. Is the orthosis below the greater trochanter but at least 2.5 cm higher than the medial shell or upright?
16. Are the uprights at the midline of the leg and thigh?
17. Do the shells, bands, and cuffs conform to the contours of the leg and thigh?
18. Is any flesh roll above the shell or band minimal?
19. Are the bottom of the thigh shell or distal thigh band and the top of the calf shell or band equidistant from the knee?
20. In a child's orthosis, is there adequate provision for lengthening the orthosis?

Weight-Relieving Components

21. In a patellar-tendon-bearing brim, is there adequate relief for the head of the fibula?
22. With a quadrilateral brim, is the client free from excessive pressure in the anteromedial and medial aspect of the brim?
23. With a quadrilateral brim, does the ischial tuberosity rest on the ischial seat?
24. With a patellar-tendon-bearing or proximal thigh brim, is there adequate reduction in weight bearing through the orthosis?

Hip

25. Is the center of the pelvic joint slightly above and ahead of the greater trochanter?
26. Is the hip lock secure and easy to operate?
27. Does the pelvic band fit the torso accurately?

Stability

28. Does the orthosis provide adequate stability to the client?

Sitting

29. Can the client sit comfortably with hips and knees flexed 90 degrees?
30. Can the client lean forward to touch the shoes?

Walking

31. Is the client's performance in level walking satisfactory?
32. Is the client's performance on stairs and ramps satisfactory?
33. Is the orthosis sufficiently rigid?
34. Does the varus or valgus correction strap provide adequate support?
35. Does the orthosis operate quietly?
36. Does the client consider the orthosis satisfactory as to comfort, function, and appearance?

Orthosis off the Client

37. Is the skin free of abrasions or other discolorations attributable to the orthosis?
38. Is the construction satisfactory?
39. Do all components function satisfactorily?

APPENDIX B   TRUNK ORTHOTIC EVALUATION

1. Is the orthosis as prescribed?
2. Can the client don the orthosis easily?

Standing

Pelvic Band

3. Does the pelvic band lie flat on the trunk below the posterior superior iliac spines?
4. Does the pelvic band pass between the trochanters and iliac crests?

Thoracic Band

5. Does the thoracic band lie flat on the trunk below the scapulae?
6. Does the thoracic band lie horizontally on the trunk?

Uprights

7. Do the posterior uprights avoid pressure on bony prominences, such as the vertebral spines or scapulae?
8. Do the lateral uprights extend along the lateral midlines of the trunk?

Abdominal Front

9. Is the abdominal front of adequate size?

Cervical Orthosis

10. Is the head in the prescribed position?
11. Do all rigid components fit properly?

Sitting

12. Can the client sit comfortably with the hips and knees flexed 90 degrees?
13. Does the client consider the orthosis satisfactory as to comfort, function, and appearance?

Orthosis off the Client

14. Is the skin free of abrasions or other discolorations attributable to the orthosis?
15. Is the construction satisfactory?
16. Do all components function satisfactorily?

The Prescriptive Wheelchair: An Orthotic Device

Adrienne Falk Bergen

OBJECTIVES

1. Identify the postural support components of a wheelchair seating system.
2. Identify the components that make up a wheeled mobility base.
3. Identify the components of the assessment process.
4. Identify the measurements that are needed for correct wheelchair fitting.
5. Describe some of the wheelchair features needed for sports use.
6. Describe the process of supply and support.

Physical therapists are often called on to assist with the prescription of wheelchairs. A properly prescribed wheelchair can be a useful device in reintegrating a person with a disability into the mainstream, whereas a poorly prescribed one can actually exacerbate the problems associated with a disability. This chapter presents a systematic approach to providing a prescriptive wheelchair. First, attention will be directed toward the seating system required to provide the proper support for the individual user. Second, the features available to create a proper mobility base for the seating system will be described. The seating system and mobility base combine to create a prescriptive wheelchair, a seated environment from which the client can function comfortably to his or her greatest potential.

A wheelchair is truly a mobility orthosis. An *orthosis* is a device used to provide support or to straighten or to correct a deformity. It is typically some type of brace made of metal or plastic that increases or maintains a person's level of function. If properly prescribed, a wheelchair will provide sufficient support to help deter the effect of deforming forces or weakened structures on function of the system. In simpler terms, it should support the user as needed to allow functioning to maximum potential. Inasmuch as it is on wheels, the system can be called a *mobility orthosis,* providing appropriate support to allow maximum functional mobility.

Like a well-made orthosis, the wheelchair should fit correctly. It should be reasonably cosmetic to the user. It should also be as lightweight and yet as strong as possible. It can be obtained from a stock supply when that type of device works, but most often individual modifications for the client's special needs are required.

Like a well-made orthosis, a well-fitted wheelchair should be prescribed by a qualified professional(s). The decision making concerning a prescriptive wheelchair should be done by the entire team. It is important that all those concerned with the person's present and future function be a part of this team. This includes the wheelchair user, therapists, family members, nurses, physicians, vocational counselors, and a qualified rehabilitation technology supplier. To ensure that the most suitable device is obtained the team must have a clear idea of where this chair will be used and who will be using it. Once the chair is supplied, the team is responsible for adjusting and fitting the final device, as well as teaching the client how to use and maintain the device to ensure continued optimal performance.

A prescriptive wheelchair is a combination of a **postural support system** and a **mobility base** that are joined to create a dynamic seated environment (Fig. 31–1). The *support system* is made up of the surfaces that contact the user's body directly. This includes the seat and back as well as any additional components needed to maintain postural alignment. Maintenance of postural alignment may require such additions as head support; lateral supports for the trunk, hips, and knees; medial support for the knees; foot supports; and upper extremity support surfaces, as well as straps or bands (such as anterior chest and pelvic controls) needed to keep the user interfaced with the support surfaces. The *mobility base* consists of the tubular frame, armrests, foot sup-

Figure 31–1. A prescriptive wheelchair consists of a seating system and a mobility base.

ports, and wheels. Once the decisions are made about the type of support system needed, the team must then decide what type of mobility base best suits the user's functional level and environmental and care-giver needs. Clear information will be needed to ensure that the postural support system and the mobility base interface properly. For users who utilize more than one mobility base (for example, power and manual), the most cost-effective approach is to have one support system interface with all the mobility bases. This is not always practical, and sometimes it is best to have the individual use the full-support system in the chair used most frequently, and forgo optimal postural support in the backup system in order to facilitate transport for short trips.

PLANNING THE SYSTEM

Creating a dynamic seating environment involves three steps: assessment, goal setting, and intervention. This process will allow appropriate recommendations and product choices. As noted above, the overall goal is to create a dynamic seating environment that is a comfortable base from which the user can attain a maximum functional level. Before the physical assessment is begun, information must be gathered from the entire team (client, care-givers or significant others, counselors, and clinicians) regarding their expectations. A great deal can be learned at this point about what the various players hope the system will be able to do for the client. It is extremely important to bring all the obvious and hidden issues out into full view before the process is begun. Team members often come into the process with a hidden agenda that can sabotage the result before the process begins. Team members may assume that the

wheelchair and seating system can achieve unrealistic goals (normalize posture, provide total pain relief, facilitate independent transfers). When these hidden goals are not met, the "wishing" members are often so disappointed that they cannot see the other benefits of the system, and may become depressed or angry.

Assessment

During the initial assessment information must be gathered from the entire team to determine the person's present level of function and the targeted goals. Complete assessments in physical, psychosocial, and cognitive perceptual areas are imperative to the process. The assessments should be completed by the appropriate professionals and submitted to the seating team for review. The team must be totally informed about the client's medical and surgical history and plans, neurologic status, postural control, skeletal factors, sensory status, functional skill level, cognitive-behavioral status, and communication level. Accurate information about the client's home, work, educational, and recreational environments must be considered, along with the method the client will use to transport the wheelchair. Funding sources should be listed so that the team is aware of any possible problems and advanced planning can begin.

PHYSICAL ASSESSMENT

The first component is the physical assessment. This physical assessment will be used to create an orthosis made of rigid and semirigid materials. Although it may be time-consuming, it is absolutely critical that this component of the assessment be complete and accurate, as changes may be difficult to make later. Accurate recording provides a permanent record of why certain decisions were made. During the ordering or manufacturing process, additional decisions concerning modifications may be needed. If accurate measurements are on file, decisions can often be made without recalling the person to the clinic.

The purpose of the physical assessment is to learn as much as possible about the person's range of available movement and about how movement of one body part affects tone, comfort, position, control, and performance in other body segments. The goal is to preserve spinal alignment whenever possible, maintaining the natural lumbar curve whenever it can be produced. The person should be assessed in a gravity-eliminated position (supine or sidelying), as well as a gravity-included (sitting) position, whenever possible. To create a properly fitted system, accurate measurements will be needed of hip flexion, abduction, adduction and rotation, underthigh length, leg length; distance from the seat to the lower scapula, mid scapula, and shoulder; distance from hanging elbow to seat surface; and width across the hips, the shoulders, and from outside knee to outside knee.

Supine Assessment

The supine assessment usually requires more than one examiner. The client should be supine on a firm surface (a mat or carpeted floor works well; a bed is not firm enough.) The careful range of motion in supine should assess available hip flexion range as it relates to spinal and pelvic alignment. The legs must be well supported by the examiner, with the knees flexed 95 to 100 degrees or as much as is needed to eliminate the influence of the hamstring muscle group (Fig. 31–2) Care should be taken to neutralize the pelvic tilt if at all possible. This can be accomplished by using tone reduction techniques while the examiner palpates the anterior superior iliac crests of the pelvis. Both hips can then be flexed at the same time to obtain an initial impression. This can be followed by more detailed examination of each limb individually. In addition to hip flexion, the assessment should include abduction, adduction, internal and external rotation, and their affect on pelvic position, as well as general body alignment. If the pelvis is asymmetric when the knees are pointed upright, this may indicate limited range of hip abduction or adduction. In some cases it will be necessary to allow the legs to rotate off to one side (**windblown position**) to achieve good pelvic alignment and minimize any negative effect on spinal alignment. If movement through the hip range, and/or opening of the knee angle (introducing hamstring influence) in one or both legs negatively affects pelvic alignment and the lumbar curve, decisions must be made about eliminating this influence in the seating unit (therapeutic interventions, chemical blocks, surgery, positional accommodations).

Once range of motion is documented, linear measurements should be recorded. From a supine position, the examiner should support the limb(s) in an optimal position and neutralize the pelvis. A second person measures the undersurface of the thigh from the popliteal fossa to the support surface. This should be done for each leg individually, obtaining a left and right measurement of sitting depth (Fig. 31–3).

Seated Assessment

Once the supine assessment is recorded the client should be placed in a supported sitting position such that the knees can be flexed to 100 degrees or more to eliminate the influence of the hamstring muscle group. One examiner should be in front of the person and another behind, offering support (Fig. 31–4). The examiner in front should now assess pelvic position and

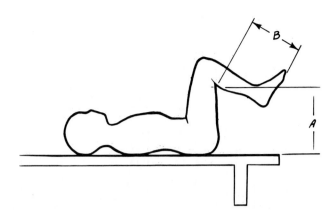

Figure 31–3. In the supine position with the hips and knees flexed the examiner can measure the undersurface of the thigh from the popliteal fossa to a firm support surface (A) and the length from the popliteal fossa to the heel (B).

mobility with the hips in flexion, by using pressure at the front of the knees counterbalanced by manipulation of the pelvis, to achieve a neutral posture with good lumbar and trunk alignment. The examiner in this position is able to determine the degree of flexibility and the influence of gravity on the person, as well as to begin to formulate some ideas about where control may be needed to achieve postural goals.

In the supported sitting position the examiner should remeasure (Fig. 31–5) the sitting depth (Asit) from behind the buttocks into the popliteal fossa. This may differ from the supine measurement, and careful assessment should reveal whether the difference is secondary to correctable postural difficulties or simply variable flesh distribution in sitting versus supine. Leg measurement (B), from the popliteal fossa to the heel with customary footwear in place, will be needed to decide footrest length on the wheelchair.

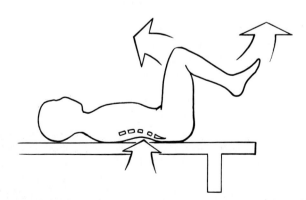

Figure 31–2. The examiner must monitor the lumbar curve as the hips are flexed and the knees extended.

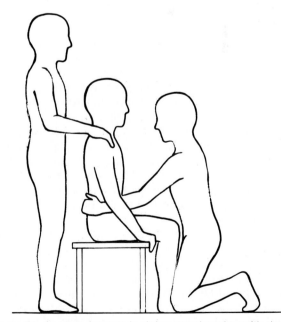

Figure 31–4. Measurements in sitting must be taken with the client sitting on a surface with a thin top. This will allow the knees to flex as needed.

Goal Setting

During goal setting, information must be compiled from the entire team to determine the person's present level of function and the target goals. Using the information gathered from the assessment, and honest conversation, all of the important data must be explored. It is often necessary to compromise and set priorities if all of the goals cannot be met. It is important that all of the goals brought to the table are discussed adequately to avoid system failure due to poor planning, poor communication, and/or unrealistic expectations from any of the team members.

A well-planned seating system may be able to normalize tone, decrease pathologic reflex activity, improve postural symmetry, enhance range of movement, maintain and/or improve skin condition, increase comfort and sitting tolerance, decrease fatigue, and improve function of the autonomic nervous system. A properly prescribed mobility base will provide the user with access to the macroenvironment outside the wheelchair base (home and community), whether alone or with a care-giver. It should work for all daily goals at home, school, work, and recreation and, where necessary, assist the care-giver with management of the client. The base supports the seating system and can provide the user with changes in orientation in space (recline and tilt, both manual and power activated).

When setting priorities it is important that clinical team members do not override the client with their "professional opinions." Hospital-based clinical teams are often not fully aware of the barriers facing wheelchair users in the outside environment. Clinicians may observe a client ambulating in the clinic and feel that with added practice he or she could ambulate full-time. This clinician will recommend crutches and a simple manual wheelchair. In the real environment, the client may face traversing long distances to independently shop, attend community activities, and function at school or work. Walking to these activities would require extraordinary effort. Propelling a standard manual wheelchair may not offer very much additional assistance. A motorized scooter would probably better serve this user as a supplement to short-distance ambulation.

Planning the Intervention

Once all of the information is gathered and recorded, the team must begin planning the intervention. The postural goal is to achieve good trunk position, because all function, both central (control, alignment, internal organ function) and distal (gross and fine motor control in the head and arms), is based on the position and control in the trunk and limb girdles. The mobility goal is to provide efficient ease of movement from the user's and care-giver's perspectives. The system goal is to provide comfort and maximal functional independence. The intervention consists of the features of the seating system and the mobility base and how they work together.

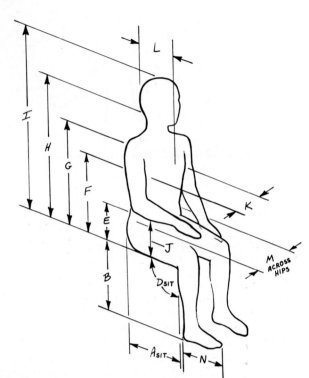

Figure 31–5. The following measurements are added to those taken in the supine position.
Asit (right and left side): behind hips/popliteal fossa
B (right and left side): popliteal fossa/heel
D: knee flexion angle
E: sitting surface/pelvic crest
F: sitting surface/lower scapula
G: sitting surface/shoulder
H: sitting surface/occiput
I: sitting surface/crown of head
J: sitting surface/hanging elbow
K: width across trunk
L: depth of trunk
M: width across hips
N: heel/toe

Measurement of back height should be taken from the sitting surface to the posterior superior pelvic crests (E), lower scapula (F), mid scapula, and to the top of the shoulder (G). These measurements will provide a detailed record should decisions regarding wheelchair back height be needed once the assessment is completed. Measurement of the "hanging elbow" (J) is needed to determine proper armrest height. With the person in a corrected sitting position, the upper extremity is positioned at the side of the body with 90 degrees of elbow flexion, and the shoulder in a neutral position. A measurement is taken from the bottom of the elbow to the sitting surface.

During this seated assessment, measurements should be taken across the shoulders, trunk (K), hips (M), and knees (for decisions regarding support accessories), as well as width of the seating system and the mobility base. To ensure accurate recommendations it is important to consider orthoses, clothing, and recent weight loss or gain, and the client's potential for growth when recording these measurements.

The assessment information can now be used in determining whether the person is functioning to his or her highest potential, or whether additional support would be helpful in freeing distal body parts to improve function. It will also help to assess the consequences of poor posture on skin condition, respiratory function, speech, and general functioning. It is usually helpful at this point to simulate various interventions. This can be accomplished using a simulator chair, which has various adjustments for surface dimensions (seat depth, back height, calf length), as well as angles between seat and back, seat and calf, and calf and foot; and tilt-in-space and postural supports.[2] If one is not available, the team can use various available chairs and/or support systems set up in different configurations. The mode of propulsion, method of transfer, and interaction with the environment can be observed. Performance in each of these areas will be influenced by the individual's strength, posture, and tone and can be modified by support system intervention. Proper intervention may enhance function (e.g., respiratory or motor), whereas improper intervention (e.g., insufficient support, poorly placed wheels, or excessive chair width) may interfere with function.

In choosing chair properties, careful attention must be given to possible secondary problems that may be created. For example, if the intervention includes a high seat cushion for pressure relief, will the user be able to get under tables and desks, transfer, or reach the wheels for self-propulsion? If the recommendation includes a custom support system, will the weight preclude easy self-propulsion or care-giver management? Will the bulk make automobile transport difficult or impossible? Attention to these issues can produce modifications that will create workable systems. Inattention to them can produce increased disability.

The components of the system that will directly affect comfort and maintenance of posture are the seat surface, back surface, pelvic belt, and upper extremity and foot supports. These areas should be addressed together as the postural support system.

POSTURAL SUPPORT SYSTEM

Features such as the makeup of the support surfaces, their relationship to each other, and their orientation in space, will affect the user. Increased contact between the user and the support surfaces increases comfort and control, and decreases pressure over bony prominences.[3-10] The continuum of available support surfaces runs from firm planar (wood, firm foam) (Fig. 31–6), through deformable surfaces (knit covered foam) (Figs. 31–7, 31–8), and contoured surfaces (Fig. 31–9), up to and including custom-molded surfaces (Fig. 31–10).

Angular relationships between the surfaces at the hip and knee joints (seat and back surfaces, seat and calf surfaces) must be determined by the range of motion results obtained in the physical assessment. These angles must respect and accommodate limitations in

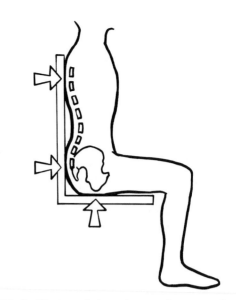

Figure 31–6. Clients seated on planar surfaces may show increased pressures over boney prominences.

range of motion, in order to allow for deformity, assure proper alignment of body segments, and minimize pressure distal to the joint. Changes of orientation in space (fixed or dynamic) affect the user's comfort level, pressure over skin surfaces, fatigue, and ability to work in gravity-minimized and gravity-influenced positions. Attention to these features will help ensure the success of the seating intervention.

Seat Surface

Most wheelchairs come with a sling seat. This type of surface reinforces a poor pelvic position since the hips tend to slide forward, creating a posterior pelvic tilt. The

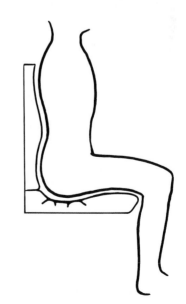

Figure 31–7. Some types of foam will contour as a response to body weight.

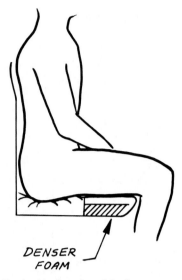

Figure 31–8. Varying the firmness of the foams can create a more contoured seat.

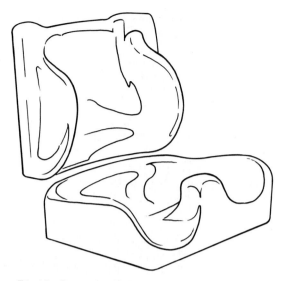

Figure 31–10. Custom-molded cushions match the client's body contours.

thighs typically move toward adduction and internal rotation, and the client tends to sit asymmetrically (Fig. 31–11). Most wheelchair users can benefit from a firm sitting surface (Fig. 31–12). Total contact between the undersurface of the thigh and the seating surface will enhance sitting ability by providing a stable base of support on which to mount upper body function.[3] The front of the seat can actually extend into the popliteal fossa, provided that the front edge is well padded and contoured to provide relief for hamstring tendons, calf bulk, and/or bracing. This surface many require specialized foam in one or varying firmnesses, or a specific contour. The person also may require a special cushion for comfort, control, and/or pressure relief. Cushions are generally made of foam, gel, liquid, pockets of air, or a combination of these elements.

The depth of the seat should be measured carefully, because an overly deep seat will encourage a posterior pelvic tilt and a resultant tendency toward **kyphotic posturing.** A seat that is too shallow will not provide enough support, making maintenance of lower extremity alignment more difficult.

For persons with neuromuscular problems (e.g., multiple sclerosis, muscular dystrophy, cerebral palsy, traumatic head injury), the seat may require lateral hip, or

medial or lateral knee positioners to maintain alignment of the lower extremities. The chair must be prepared for these additions before being upholstered. The seat also may require a change in orientation, or increased contour, to affect tone at the hips. This can be done with varying foam firmnesses, contouring, hardware changes, or properties built into the chosen mobility base.

Back Surface

Wheelchair users who have fair to good trunk control usually require only back support to the mid scapula. Many prefer it lower; however, evidence exists that

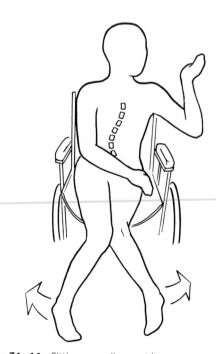

Figure 31–11. Sitting on a sling seat increases asymmetries.

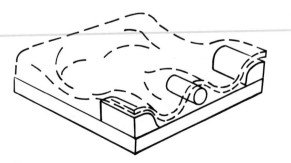

Figure 31–9. Firmer foam shapes can be placed under a more flexible foam to create a contoured cushion.

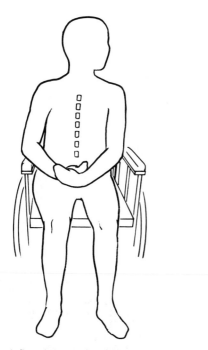

Figure 31–12. A firm sitting surface offers a good support base.

although some lower back supports work well in the short run, they may cause problems over longer periods of use, with users experiencing fatigue and back pain.[11] For persons who have poor trunk control and those who tend to push into extension, the back height should be to the shoulders (approximately to the level of the acromium process). This is especially critical if any type of shoulder support is to be used. This higher back may make it more difficult for care-givers to adjust the person's posture, but the added control offered will decrease the need for frequent postural adjustments.

Many individuals will not be provided adequate support from the standard fabric back that comes with a wheelchair. Some wheelchair backs are available with reinforcing straps that can be adjusted to provide contoured support. This type of support may be sufficient for some clients, but others will require a solid panel or insert placed into a pocket in the upholstery, or strapped or Velcroed on in front of the upholstery, or installed on hardware instead of upholstery.

The insert is fabricated from a firm base such as very firm foam, wood, plastic, or Triwall cardboard padded with foam. If placed in front of the upholstery, the foam can vary in thickness and firmness allowing more or less control at the pelvis or across the scapular and shoulder areas. The team must assess the person's response to a back insert and vary the surface consistency, shape, and/or angle to the seat surface, according to postural needs and comfort level. A very firm foam may work well for individuals with low central tone by encouraging more extension, but those with prominent bony protuberances may not tolerate this type of surface. Others may achieve good extension following alignment, but lose lateral stability and require additional lateral contour and/or lateral supports.

Pelvic Positioner

A belt or more rigid pelvic positioner may be needed for safety and for assistance with postural control.[8,12] When using a belt, attention must be given to style, size, direction of pull, and placement to achieve maximum effectiveness.[13] Generally, the belt should form a 45-degree angle with the sitting surface (Fig. 31–13). For some people, a 90-degree angle of pull may be more effective in providing postural control and alignment, while leaving the pelvis free for anterior or posterior movement (Fig. 31–14).

Upper Extremity Supports

ARMRESTS

Wheelchair armrests have many important functions. They provide assistance for pushing up to standing, a support surface for arms and upper extremity support surfaces such as lapboards, a mechanism for relief of ischial pressure (sitting push-up), and some small amount of lateral stability. Attention should be directed to the height of the armrests, and the length and size of the support surface. It may be necessary for the client to use the armrests to support the upper extremities and thus to decrease pull on the shoulders and trunk. This approach is often used with very weak individuals, such as those with high spinal cord injuries or muscular dystrophy. Individuals who lean on their armrests or upper extremity support surface (UESS) for postural assistance will have decreased functional use of the upper extremities. For many individuals, the armrests will be used to mount an upper extremity support surface (UESS) (tray, trough).

UPPER EXTREMITY SUPPORT SURFACE

Upper extremity support surfaces provide several important functions. They can be used to achieve sym-

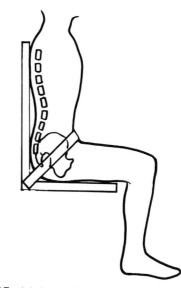

Figure 31–13. A belt crossing the pelvic-femoral junction works well for most clients.

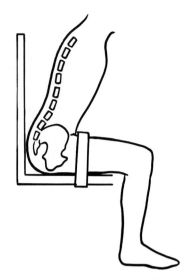

Figure 31–14. A belt placed over the upper thigh will free the pelvis for natural anterior tilting.

metric positioning of the upper extremities, to maintain corrected alignment of the glenohumeral joint and scapula, and to serve as a work or communication surface. They also can act as an adjunct to the postural control system by supporting the weight of the arms and decreasing pull on the shoulders and trunk. In addition, in special cases, high (elevated) UESSs can be used to inhibit tone around the shoulders and neck. In extreme cases, the arms of individuals with athetosis may be purposely anchored beneath the UESS to decrease interference from involuntary movement when using a head pointer or during feeding activities.

Foot Supports

Style and position are important considerations when selecting wheelchair foot support systems. Placement of

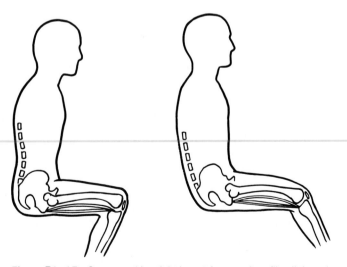

Figure 31–15. Overstretching tight hamstring muscles will pull the pelvis into a posterior pelvic tilt.

the foot support system will directly affect the position of the entire lower body, affecting tone and posture in the trunk, head, and arms. Good hip flexion will help keep the pelvis well positioned on the sitting surface. Good foot support height and style is required for maintenance of this position. Foot supports that are too low will result in lower knees, placing the hips in a more open angle and encouraging sliding forward of the pelvis. Foot supports that are too high may unload the thighs, placing increased weight on the ischial tuberosities. Elevating leg rests even in their lowered position may place excessive stretch on tight hamstrings, pulling the pelvis into a posterior tilt (Fig. 31–15). Any limitation of motion imposed by the hamstrings will directly influence the choice of foot positioners. In order to achieve maximum comfortable hip flexion it may be necessary to flex the knees more than 90 degrees, requiring special intervention on the foot supports. Decisions on straps and foot positioners must be made early, based on the range of motion assessment, in order to ensure clearance for placement on the final unit.

THE WHEELED MOBILITY BASE: WHEELCHAIR FEATURES AND ACCESSORIES

The wheeled base forms the mobility structure for the seating system. Mobility bases include dependent systems, independent systems activated manually, and independent systems activated under battery power.

Dependent systems include strollers, pushchairs, and many of the elaborate postural support systems used with individuals who are severely physically and mentally impaired. These systems may have small wheels not intended for self-propulsion. When considering a dependent mobility system it is important to determine the function of the unit. Is this a primary mobility system or a backup for the person who has a powered mobility unit? If the ability to use any independent movement exists, the person should be assessed for either a manual or powered wheelchair as the primary mobility system. Sophisticated technology now allows even the most severely physically impaired individual to achieve independent mobility. This should be encouraged and assisted by the proper wheeled mobility base. If at all possible, even very young children (12 months or older) and the elderly should be provided with a means of independent mobility that allows them to extend beyond the boundary of their physical impairment. Research supports the beneficial impact of independent functioning on all aspects of cognitive and psychosocial well-being.

When preparing the specifications for a wheeled mobility base, many features have to be carefully studied. There are dozens of bases available. Each have subtly different features. The team will be challenged in their effort to make the correct user–product match (Fig. 31–16).

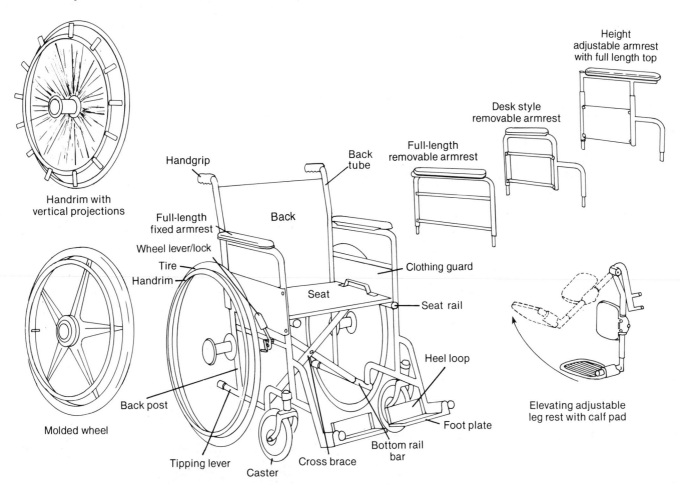

Figure 31–16. Multiple options are available in creating a prescriptive wheelchair.

The Seat

SEAT DEPTH

Correct seat depth is particularly important to achieve maximum postural support and tone control. Wheelchairs are readily available from manufacturers in various seat depths. The depth measurements given in the catalog usually correspond to the depth of the upholstery itself from the back to the front edge. Depending on the manufacturer, the upholstery depth may be equal to, less than, or greater than that of the metal seat rail. The team must be aware of different manufacturers' features. If the client does not fit a listed size, modifications can be made incorporating one or more of the following methods: a back insert, frame construction, or upholstery modifications.

Back Insert

To alter the overall depth of the sitting surface, a back insert can be used to increase or decrease the available sitting surface. This back insert, or cushion, can be ordered with any specified overall thickness, and usually consists of a piece of wood or plastic, and foam padding. Inserts can be placed in front of the wheelchair's upholstery, or the upholstery can be removed and the back insert can be mounted with specialized hardware (Fig. 31–17).

When ordering back inserts it is imperative to know the manufacturer's standard thickness and type of foam. With most styles of wheelchairs one can specify whether the insert is to be positioned between the back tubes or in front of them. This choice will affect the impact of the back insert on overall available sitting surface. If the upholstery is to remain in place, it is important to note whether it is mounted in front of the back tubes, between the back tubes, or half and half, inasmuch as this will directly affect the placement of the back insert. It is also critical to note whether the back tube has a bend, which will affect the vertical orientation of the back insert. Putting the insert in front of the back tubes will push the user forward, and may affect the client's ability to reach the wheels for self-propulsion.

Frame Construction

Seat depth also can be modified (increased or decreased) by frame construction. Modifications by construction should be considered with short and wide, or very tall persons, or long-legged individuals who have slowed or completed their growth cycle. An important factor to consider is that lengthening the chair frame

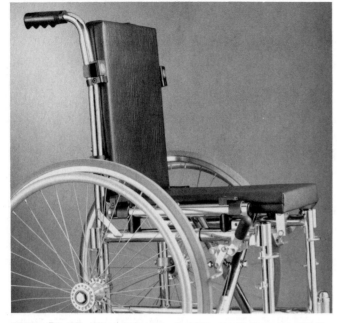

Figure 31–17. Wheelchair seat upholstery can be replaced with firm inserts held to the frame by specialized hardware. Usually the seat, or a cushion with a seat board inside, can safely extend approximately 2 in beyond the end of the seat rail.

will increase the turning radius and may prevent the user from maneuvering the chair in small spaces. A few manufacturers supply seat extension kits or special rear frame designs that extend the seat rail a few inches without changing the overall length of the frame. Seat rail extension kits work well on many frames, but on others they may extend over the top of the footrest and prevent removal of the footrest when the wheelchair is in the open position.

Upholstery Modifications

Wheelchair seat depth may also be altered by upholstery changes. This can be achieved symmetrically if leg length is equal, or asymmetrically if leg length is unequal. Seat depth can be increased or decreased within specific dimensions set by the manufacturer. Generally, a seat insert or a seat cushion with a board inside its cover can be extended 1 to 2 inches beyond the front end of the seat rail without creating an unstable sitting surface (Fig. 31–17). The seat upholstery, insert, or cushion can be cut back several inches to shorten the seat surface. Inserts can be fabricated with "growth" tails that fit between the back tubes as unused sitting surface; more seat depth can be exposed by pulling the seat forward along the seat rail as needed. The effects on foot placement of any of these modifications must be assessed. Subsequent foot-plate adjustments may be required.

Working on the upholstery of the chair requires detailed knowledge of what each manufacturer considers standard. For instance, is upholstery depth as listed in the catalog the same as seat rail length, 1 inch shorter or 1 inch longer? If the chair is offered with a seating system, are the measurements supplied taken from the seating system or the wheelchair frame? Are standard

foot plates a large or small size, and how close are they to the front end of the frame? Can they be ordered closer to the frame to minimize effect on overall length, so that the seat can be deepened without affecting turning radius? Careful assessment of various wheelchairs will reveal differences in available parts and interfaces depending on wheelchair style and manufacturer.

SEAT WIDTH

The width of the sitting surface, as well as the overall width of the wheelchair, is important to functional use. For individuals who wear orthoses, require control blocks at the hip, wear bulky clothing, or experience weight fluctuations, special considerations will be needed. The natural tendency is to increase the width of the seat. Such a solution must be approached cautiously, however, inasmuch as this will also increase the overall width of the chair and may create difficulty for those needing to reach the wheels for self-propulsion (Figs. 31–18, 31–19), or for those who must maneuver in tight places.

The goal is to create a chair that fits as close to the user's body as possible. This will make the chair easy to wheel and easier to maneuver. It also will make the chair seem, visually, more congruent with the user's body lines.

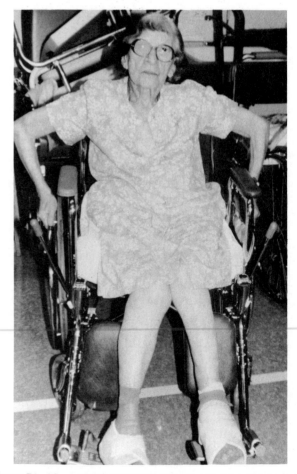

Figure 31–18. A wheelchair that is too wide will make wheel approach more difficult for the client.

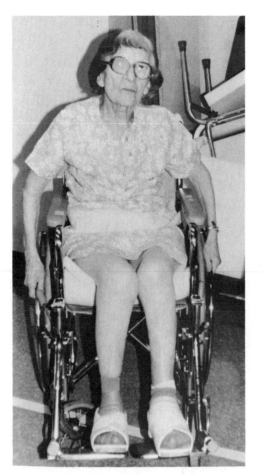

Figure 31–19. A narrower wheelchair with the armpads turned to the inside allows easier wheel approach.

Seat width can be changed in several ways. Widening can be accomplished by use of fixed offset or removable arms; in the course of construction, on a new chair; or by changing the cross braces, on an existing chair. Seat narrowing can be achieved by upholstery or by construction. Narrowing a chair by upholstery essentially creates a "growing" chair out of any size chair. The chair is simply folded a bit. A limiter strap and/or narrower upholstery is mounted, preventing full-width opening. This will raise the seat height. This should not be done on chairs where the top seat rail must clip to the bottom rail for stability.

The overall outside width of the chair should be as narrow as possible for optimal function. Excessive width makes the chair difficult to maneuver through doorways and in small areas. It is also more difficult to propel the chair if the user must widely abduct his or her arms to reach the wheels. This wide abduction requires the client to use available muscular strength around the shoulder girdle for stability and posture, leaving less to use for functional push (Figs. 31–18 and 31–19). The width can be modified by several means. The modifications include various hand rims and armrest options, internal mounting of the wheel axle plate on some ultralight wheelchairs, and wheelchair narrowing devices (which can be used to move the chair through a narrow space for a short distance). The narrowing devices are useful

only for individuals who have sufficient coordination to rock the chair forward and back while turning the crank handle of the device. The device will not work with solid seat inserts, or with reclining wheelchairs that have spreader bars to reinforce the back. If there is enough room to use the wheelchair-narrowing device comfortably, perhaps the wheelchair should have been narrower in the first place.

SEAT HEIGHT

The height of the wheelchair sitting surface is important for optimal independent functioning in foot-assisted, self-propulsion transfers (especially reentering the chair using a standing or stand pivot approach), approaching working surfaces, interacting with peers, and transfer into a van via lift or ramp. Seat height must be assessed with respect to the entire chair, inasmuch as it may alter the user's position relative to the armrests, back height, wheel locks, wheels, and footrests.

Seat height can be altered by one or more methods, including altering the frame construction when ordering the chair, changing the wheel size, altering the rear axle and front caster placement on frames that allow this, altering the thickness of the seat inserts or cushions, removing the seat upholstery, and using solid hook-out seat boards with varying depth hardware to raise or drop the seat on the frame.

SEAT SURFACE

A firm sitting surface will provide a more symmetric sitting base. The firm surface will provide the person with a more stable base of support for the upper body, usually resulting in improved function. A firm sitting surface can be achieved in a variety of ways, with or without specialized cushions.

Prior to deciding on a nonstandard seat surface, the team should inspect what the manufacturer considers a standard seat. Some manufacturers use extremely taut fabric for their seat slings (notably some of the ultralight wheelchairs). In combination with a firm foam cushion, no other support may be needed. Others use a fabric design that allows the sling component to be adjusted. This works adequately for some users, allowing them to adjust the tension as the sling becomes slack with extended use.

If a firmer seat is needed, there are several ways this can be achieved (Fig. 31–20). The simplest is to incorporate a homemade or commercially fabricated board into the foam cushion that comes with the chair; or into an off-the-chair foam cushion (purchased separately from the chair) that comes with a removable cover. It is possible that this lightweight unit may slide about in the chair, producing an asymmetric sitting surface. Many cushions do have special nonslip fabric or Velcro strips on the underside that discourage slippage.

A second option for a firm seat is to order the wheelchair with a standard hammock seat and a solid seat insert on top. This type of insert adds a slight additional weight to the wheelchair system. The insert is usually made of foam and wood, and is covered with vinyl to match the chair. The standard thickness and firmness of the foam varies with each manufacturer. The individual

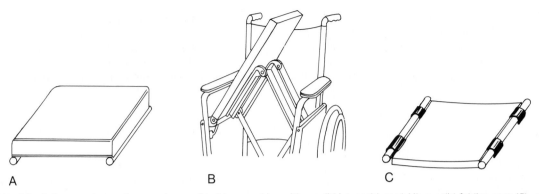

Figure 31–20. A firm seating surface can be provided by a cushion with a solid internal board (A), a solid folding seat (B), or a solid hook-on seat (C).

rehabilitation technology supplier will provide information on standard foam characteristics so that alterations can be made as needed. Custom thicknesses and firmnesses are available if requested, either directly from the primary manufacturer or from a manufacturer of wheelchair component parts.

The solid seat insert has several drawbacks. The insert may slip about in the seat, especially when the armrests are spaced away from the seat, creating an asymmetric sitting surface. The insert must be removed to fold the chair, which may result in loss after several foldings. Some users may eventually discard this extra piece.

Another option for firm seating is a solid folding seat. This type of seat is an integral part of the frame. It is permanently hinged to one seat rail, folding up when the chair is folded and dropping down into place as it is opened. When the chair is folded, this style of seat alters the shape of the chair. It is important to determine whether this shape will fit into the family car. When this folding seat is in the opened position, it rests between the seat rails, leaving the rails exposed. If it is 1 inch thick overall, its top surface will be level with the seat rails. If it is fabricated with thicker foam, the solid folding seat surface will be above the seat rails. In a 16-inch wide wheelchair, for instance, there will be 14 inches of upholstered and padded seating surface and 1 inch of rail exposed on each side. Some users find this uncomfortable if they are using the full seat width as a sitting surface.

The advantage of a solid folding seat is that it cannot get lost, or be eliminated from the seating system for convenience. The Everest and Jennings (E&J) hardware for solid folding seats actually adds some strength to the frame but will also add 7 to 10 pounds to the weight of the chair. This style of seat on other manufacturer's wheelchairs has a simpler mechanism, which adds neither weight nor additional strength to the frame of the chair.

A fourth option for providing a solid seating surface is the solid hook-on seat. This is a separate seat board that has hook-type hardware along both sides. These hooks clip onto the seat rail, securing the seat in the chair. The seat can hook on at the level of the seat rails, or below or above them. With this variability, and with the different thicknesses of foam available for the insert, and/or separate seat cushions, it is possible to change the height of the sitting surface without altering the frame.

When the seat is removed to fold the chair, there is no sitting surface on the chair frame and there is no extra hardware. The hook-on seat does not add weight to the folded frame, but will add weight to the open frame. Care should be taken in providing this alternative to users who drive, as frequently the wheelchair's seat upholstery is used as a handle for pulling the chair into the car.

In addition to the standard bent hooks, the solid hook-on seat can be equipped with specialized hardware that allows the seat surface to be angled. Many styles of hardware are available from different manufacturers. Several wheelchair manufacturers include angle-adjustable seats in their catalogs.

The Back

To determine the height of the back, the degree of back support needed to achieve optimal function must be ascertained. The wheelchair back can be ordered to specification. Until the person's medical status is stable, consideration should be given to ordering add-on or removable parts, such as a headrest extension, a sectional-height back that can be removed and replaced later with lower upholstery and back tubes, or an adjustable-height back.

The additional back height may make the chair too large to fit into a car, or may not allow adequate clearance for entering a van. In such cases, or in cases in which a custom chair is not possible or an existing chair is in good condition, a removable back insert in a custom height might suffice.

When increasing or decreasing the back height, attention should be directed to the level of the push handles. On many chairs these can be mounted at a height most useful for the care-givers. An extra reinforcement cap of upholstery may provide additional strength to the upper edge of the upholstery. A few wheelchairs are upholstered with the top edge of the back upholstery wrapped around the front of the back tubes; on other chairs, the upholstery forms a sleeve around the back tubes.

On standard wheelchairs, the back tubes rise straight to midback level and then angle backward. When a user leans on these for support, they tend to facilitate shoulder retraction and back extension. Clients often need this leeway to feel comfortable. If a solid back insert is used, the user may push the top edge until it rests on the tubes, forcing the bottom edge to push the pelvis forward on the wheelchair seat. If this problem is anticipated, it is possible to order the chair with straight tubes instead of the standard angled ones. It is also possible to brace the insert to maintain the designated angle for good posture.

The Pelvic Positioner

The pelvic belt is one of the simplest features on a prescription wheelchair. Most clinicians know that the pelvic belt should cross the pelvis at a 45-degree angle to the sitting surface, and many understand that the closure style is often critical. There is more than this involved, however, in deciding on a proper pelvic belt.

The style of closure is important in facilitating independent use. Many clients can manage only Velcro, but others can manage only buckles. If the user is not able to use the belt independently, and/or significant postural control is required, the style of belt is limited. Some Velcro belts are not strong enough for use by persons with severe extensor tone. For these, and for others who require a great deal of control, a Velcro and D-ring style belt, or a belt with a cinching-style buckle arrangement, is the most suitable. Cinching-style buckles similar to those on automobile seat belts are available in push-button and flipper styles. The critical feature desired on all styles is that once the initial contact has been made with the fastener, the belt can be adjusted further to increase tightness.

The direction and angle of pull of the belt is important. For example, if one hip tends to pull forward consistently, it may be useful to have the belt tighten by pulling it down toward that hip. The angle of pull to the seating surface should normally be 45 degrees. Some clients respond well to belts that form a 90-degree angle with the sitting surface. This pull discourages clients who tend to "stand" in their wheelchairs as a result of tone increases. This 90-degree placement also leaves the pelvis free for anterior tilting, an assist for those clients who can use this mobility for added function.

Mounting the belt to the seat rail is common. Caution should be used with clients who push into excessive extension. This type of belt placement may cause the wheelchair to fold as the rider pushes upward on the belt. In such situations, a custom-made piece of hardware may be needed to mount the belt at a specific point on the lower wheelchair rail (Fig. 31–21).

The width of the belt and size of the buckle will affect the level of control offered. The belt and buckle must be correctly proportioned to the user's body. Small children should have belts 1 inch wide; larger children, belts 1½ inches wide; and adults, belts 2 inches wide. The buckles should be comfortable. Plastic buckles may be more comfortable for some users. Padding may increase comfort and allow for tighter control.

The Lower Extremity Support

The footrest (swing-away) and legrest (elevating and swing-away) lengths are determined by measuring the leg length from the popliteal fossa to the heel and subtracting 1 inch. The corresponding measurement on the wheelchair is called the minimum footboard extension (MinFBX). This measurement is the distance from the seat rail to the foot plate. If separate cushions or an insert with or without special foam thickness has been added, or if the seat itself must be angled, the MinFBX measurement must be modified accordingly when the chair is ordered from the manufacturer. For example, if the distance from the popliteal fossa to the heel is 16 inches, and the client is to sit on a cushion 2 inches thick, a MinFBX of approximately 14 inches will be needed if the seat is firm, or 15 inches if the seat is of soft foam.

Optimal foot placement may be difficult to achieve in the presence of postural control problems or abnormal tone. Proper sitting posture for maximum control may call for a 90-degree knee flexion angle with a neutral ankle position. Many times this knee-foot alignment is imperative for maintaining total body alignment, especially for people with tightness in the hamstring muscle group. For small individuals this is rather simple. When dealing with larger clients it may be necessary to raise them on cushions, order special, smaller casters (with or without special-length stem bolts or forks), use a special extended wheelchair frame, or order a chair with the large fixed wheels in the front to allow the knees to be flexed to 90 degrees without the feet interfering with caster movement.

There are several styles of foot support: a one-piece footboard, tubular foot supports, or two individual foot plates. These supports can be mounted directly to the frame, on clip-off hangers, on swing-away hangers, or on elevating hangers. The style of hardware the particular manufacturer uses will change the orientation of the foot support to the frame of the chair and to the user's body. Swing-away hangers, for example, may place the foot plates parallel to the floor, or at an angle, and may locate them close to the chair frame or as much as 3 to 4 inches anterior to the front upright. Many manufacturers offer hangers with standard options at various angles (90, 70, 75, 60, and 65 degrees being the most common), and still others will make custom hangers on request. These can be ordered on the original wheelchair, or as a later addition.

The mounting hardware should be chosen for function as well as posture. For individuals with edema, detachable elevating legrests may be required. For clients with increased hamstring tone or tightness (as in cerebral palsy, multiple sclerosis, or muscular dystrophy), elevating legrests are usually not recommended

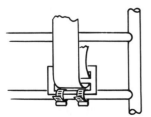

Figure 31–21. Specialized hardware can be used to clamp a lapbelt to the wheelchair rail.

because opening the knee angle will stretch the hamstrings and may pull the pelvis out of alignment. Detachable swing-away footrests do not elevate but do swing away to assist in transfers and in a better approach to the front of the wheelchair. When ordering front-rigging styles, consideration must be given to both present and future function so that the user will be able to continue to improve within the chair and not have a chair that actually exacerbates problems of management.

The size of the foot-plate surface can vary. A few manufacturers offer three different sizes, others offer only one or two. The ultralight wheelchairs are often available with open or filled-in foot plates. The foot plate should accommodate the length of the foot, as well as the width of orthoses, or oversized shoes. Narrowing a chair for a better fit around the hips and better hand placement on the rims also decreases the available space between the front tubes for the foot plates. Some of the flip-up style foot plates have additional hardware, which further limits the available space in this area.

Calf straps or pads can be used to help keep the feet on the foot plates. Heel loops and/or ankle straps may be needed to control the feet on the foot plate. Heel loops are available in webbing, vinyl, and plastic in various heights. Although plastic and extra high heel loops offer more control, they can prevent the foot plates from being flipped up, interfering with some transfer styles.

Ankle straps control the heel position on the foot plate. The straps should make a 45-degree angle with the foot-plate surface, causing weight to be placed into the heel. These straps can be simple Velcro, Velcro with D rings, or straps with buckles. Crossed ankle straps or figure-eight strapping also can be effective.

A few users also may benefit from toe loops (or straps). Toe loops are generally fabricated from leather webbing and attach in a half-circle pattern to the anterior portion of the foot plate. Many toe loops are solid; others have Velcro or buckle openings. Toe loops are used to help control severe involuntary movements or spasticity (especially extensor spasms).

The Upper Extremity Support

Nonremovable armrests offer no specific benefits for a wheelchair user unless it is likely that removable armrests will be lost. They are often ordered in an attempt to reduce the overall width of the chair. This can be achieved with wraparound or "space saver" armrests that are removable and that allow for transfers, sitting without armrests, use of special adapted inserts, changing from fixed-height to adjustable-height armrests, and so forth. Although adjustable and wraparound armrest styles may be more costly on the initial frame, they provide for a more flexible system that can be altered as the client's functional needs change.

Wraparound armrests reduce the overall outside width of the chair by 1½ inches as they bring the wheels in closer. This is accomplished by structural placement of the posterior upright of the armrest behind (wrapped around) the back tube (Fig. 31–22). This narrows the chair for easier maneuverability and places the wheels

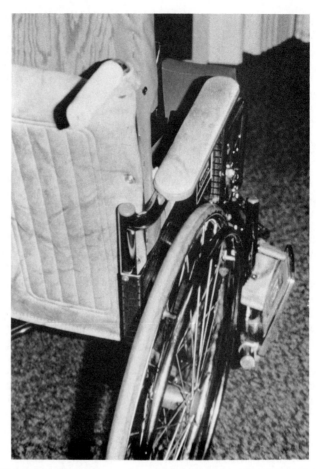

Figure 31–22. Wraparound or space saver armrests insert behind the wheelchair's back tube.

closer for better hand approach. Removal and repositioning of this style armrest may be difficult for some individuals, and a careful assessment is needed.

Height-adjustable armrests (Fig. 31–23) are important for children, especially those whose chair frames have been ordered with built-in growth allowance. This type of adjustability also is useful for users who need more or less support depending on the time of day or activity. They permit placement of an upper extremity support surface without extensive custom modifications.

Full-length arm pads give more room for a UESS to be secured. They also afford the user a larger surface to grasp for push-ups and transfers. Standard full-length armrests, however, may prevent the user from getting close to tables or work surfaces. Shorter-length, desk arms can be ordered to allow for this function. Alternately, full-length height-adjustable armrests allow the user to remove the armrest top or to raise it above the table surface; the front jog feature can then be used in a manner similar to a desk arm, while providing the longer top surface of a full-length pad.

Many of the wheelchairs in use today have nontraditional armrest styles. Some armrests are tubular, with rounded tops rather than flat armrest pads. Several of these styles have only one point of mounting on the chair. Although they may appear unstable, most of these work well for weight bearing (e.g., for pressure relief or

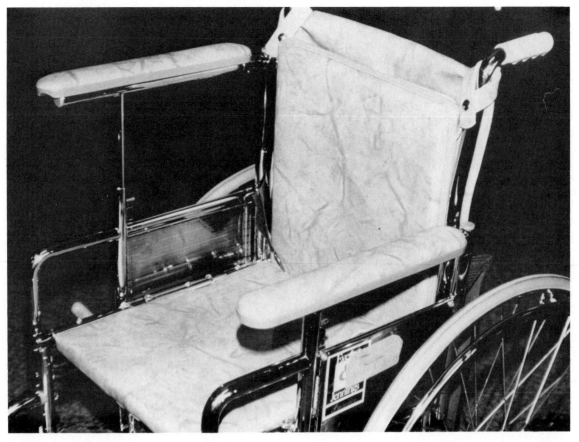

Figure 31–23. Height adjustable arms are available in desk or full length. They allow variable arm heights with a simple adjustment.

depression transfers). A few of the newer styles flip up but do not remove, and others swing out to the side. Some have clothing guards, and others do not. It is important to examine all available options with function in mind to be certain which product will best suit the consumer's need.

When ordering a specific armrest style, the height of the armrest from the seat rail should be checked. After comparing this to the measurement obtained for the hanging elbow, a custom-ordered armrest height may be required. Wheelchair armrest height is determined by adding 1 inch to the hanging-elbow measure. Armrests that are too high will cause shoulder elevation, and those that are too short may encourage leaning. Those spaced too far apart may interfere with the person's ability to wheel the chair.

Wheels, Handrims, and Tires

Wheels are available in 12-, 16-, 20-, 22-, 24-, and 26-inch diameters and are available through wheelchair manufacturers, as well as through specialty companies. They are available with standard or heavy-duty spokes, and in spokeless or molded styles. The spokeless styles are growing in popularity because they are easier to maintain, but they do add some extra weight to the frame. When quick-release axles are available as an option, they may be desirable because removing the rear

wheels can reduce the folded size as well as reduce the weight of the chair by 8 pounds, making it more readily lifted or stored.

Wheel size and location may be critical to the client's ability to self-propel.[1,5,14,15] The rule of thumb is to achieve hand to wheel-crest touch with the elbow in at least 30 degrees of flexion. This will allow the user to produce an efficient stroke. Weak users may require a greater angle at stroke initiation and will tend to lean forward or to the side to increase the elbow angle and achieve a stronger push. Generally, the 24-inch wheel is adequate. This size may need to be specially ordered on small chairs. Although these large wheels often look strange on small chairs, they can add significantly to function because of their proximity to the user's hands. Clients who are weak or poorly coordinated may be able to self-propel if a choice of axle position allows for a personalized wheel placement. This is often a justification for ordering an ultralight wheelchair with a multi-position axle plate.

For clients who are unable to manage dual-wheel propulsion, one-arm drive systems are available (Fig. 31–24). These units use a double handrim on one wheel to drive both wheels. Operation can be confusing and difficult to coordinate for those with limited cognitive or perceptual ability. Clients with increased tone may demonstrate spastic overflow and asymmetry when using one hand to propel the chair. When supplying this type of chair, attempts should be made to use one of the units

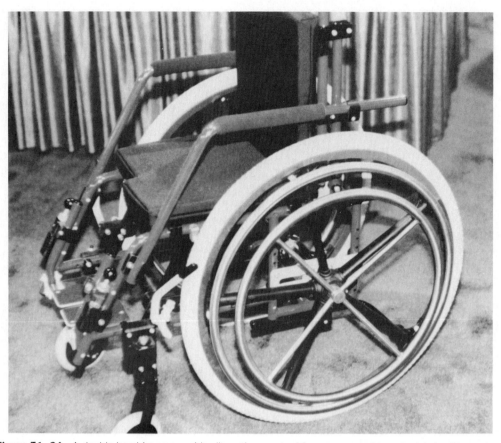

Figure 31–24. A double handrim on one side allows the user to drive a one-arm drive wheelchair with one hand.

with a very lightweight frame, multiple axle positions, and precision wheel bearings, which decrease rolling resistance.

Separate metal handrims are standard on most wheels. They can be spaced further from the wheel if requested, but this will add width to the chair. Some users have difficulty propelling the wheelchair because of poor hand control or a weak grip. A leather glove or coated handrim will add friction between the hand and rim, making wheeling easier. At higher speeds this friction on an ungloved hand may be uncomfortable when trying to slow or stop the wheelchair. Special handrims can be ordered in increased diameter, with sponge coatings, and with knobs or projections.

Tires affect performance in both forward and turning movements, since they interface with the environmental surface. The goal is minimal resistance between the tire and the floor surface. This allows the user to achieve the maximum result from each push. This is especially critical for clients who are weak or uncoordinated, and for those who are using the chair in athletic competition. Standard hard-rubber tires are useful for most individuals. They are durable and easily maintained. Their narrow footprint offers minimal resistance to wheeling on most surfaces. Pneumatic (air-filled) tires are standard on some models and are available as a special order on others. These require more maintenance but provide a smoother ride and improved traction in some instances. Special high-pressure pneumatics offer the minimal resistance of the narrow, hard tire with the ride and performance of a pneumatic. In most pneumatic tires, zero

pressure tubes or flat-proof liners can be substituted for the tube to create a flat-proof tire with the appearance of a pneumatic. The ride with these liners is not as smooth, and in some cases the life of the tire may be shortened.

The Frame

Most people who use wheelchairs utilize outdoor frames (Fig. 31–25). This means that the large wheels are in the back and the casters are in the front. Chairs with large wheels in the front are called indoor chairs (Fig. 31–26). They are sometimes ordered for individuals with severe knee flexion contractures, and for those whose upper extremity range of motion is limited. Although access to the wheels may be easier with the indoor model, overall maneuverability may be more difficult, and transfers may present a problem. Use of these chairs outdoors is difficult as it is almost impossible to pull them up curbs or steps. (Front-wheel drive, "outdoor," power wheelchairs have their larger wheel in the front. They are usually powerful enough to climb small curbs, but the wheel configuration precludes a care-giver's pulling them up larger curbs and steps.)

Chair frames are available in rigid or folding styles. Most rigid frames offer fold-down backs and removable wheels to allow some breakdown for stowage in vehicles. Rigid frames are tighter, and each of the user's pushes are translated into chair motion. However, on uneven terrain the user of a rigid frame may be uncomfortable, as the frame transfers rather than absorbs shock.

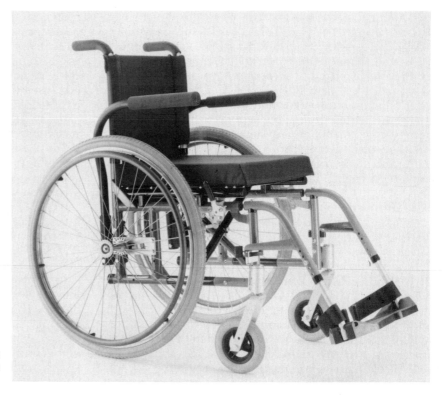

Figure 31–25. Traditional wheelchairs have the large wheel in the rear and a smaller wheel, or caster, in the front. (Photo courtesy of Quickie Designs.)

Rigid frames are the lightest available, with some weighing 20 pounds or less with the wheels in place.

Chair frames are available in heavy-duty, standard, lightweight, active-duty lightweight, and ultra-light-weight construction. Clients and their care-givers who are functioning in the community should be offered the lightest, strongest possible frame whenever feasible. The lighter frames are easier for the user to propel and easier for care-givers to manage. For individuals in institutions, or when care-givers do not have to lift and carry the unit, the issue of weight may be secondary to the issue of price. To justify the added expense of an active-duty lightweight or ultra-lightweight chair, explanation for its necessity must be provided to the third party payer as a medical need.

Accessories

Many accessories are available to personalize the chair for functional and aesthetic reasons. Crutch holders, antitippers, utility bags, and upper extremity support surfaces all may serve a functional purpose. A choice of frame and upholstery color, usually at no extra cost, will help to personalize the chair.

Making the perfect match between consumer and product will require a careful determination of the user's needs and a matching of these to the product features. Something as simple as the style of arm lock or the type of push handle may have important long-term functional or care-giving implications.

Specialized Wheelchairs

POSITIONING

Clients with poor postural control, abnormal tone, muscle shortening, or skeletal deformities often require wheeled chairs that offer varied positioning possibili-

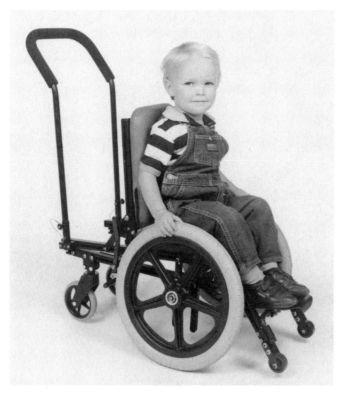

Figure 31–26. Wheelchairs with large front wheels and small rear casters may be easier for some patients to push, but are more difficult to use outdoors. (Photo courtesy of Mulholland Positioning Systems.)

ties. A frame may be needed that offers a fixed or adjustable posterior tilt-in-space (Fig. 31–27). This frame may need to be combined with a reclinable back or an angle-adjustable seating surface or both. Some chairs allow care-givers to change the seat position, while others afford the rider this control. Some offer components for positioning, such as head and torso supports.

Several manufacturers offer systems that include positioning components on a mobility base. Others do not offer the components and it is necessary to interface more than one manufacturer's products in order to have a complete chair.

POWER

For clients over the age of approximately 16 months who are not capable of using one or more upper and/or lower extremities for functional self-propulsion, consideration should be given to some form of powered mobility (Fig. 31–28).[10,16-24] Motorized toys (2-, 3-, and 4-wheeled vehicles) and wheelchairs are available in many styles with varying degrees of portability, power, and electronic sophistication. In all cases it would be ideal if a proportional drive system could be used. **Proportional drives** respond to pressure like an automobile accelerator; the more pressure, the more speed. Because the speed and degree of acceleration are controlled by the rider's movement of the joystick, this type of system gives the user the greatest degree of control. With the advent of microprocessor-controlled wheel-

chairs, the performance parameters of the joystick can be altered to adapt to the user's ability. Such systems allow individuals with severe spasticity and those who are extremely weak to continue with a proportional system. Alternate access spots for users who cannot use their hands should be considered. This might include the head, foot, chin, tongue, or extensions of body parts, and using pointers or similar adapted accessors.

For clients who cannot use a proportional controller the team may want to consider using a microswitching system. A **microswitching system** is an all-or-none drive system. The speed is preset. The operator applies any degree of pressure, and as soon as the switch is activated the system runs at the preset speed. Individual switches are provided for the four directions (forward, reverse, right, left), and a series of individual movements are required to maneuver in tight spaces. Individual switches can be operated through a puff-n-sip tube, they can be arranged around a joystick in a control box, or they can be placed anywhere around the body in order to allow the user to drive the chair. For example, there might be two switches on a UESS for gross pressing with the hand, and additional switches at the head, knees, or feet to allow mobility in all four directions. For clients with less than four or five movements, chairs with dual- and single-switch accessing systems are available; however, such systems make the chair progressively more tedious to operate.

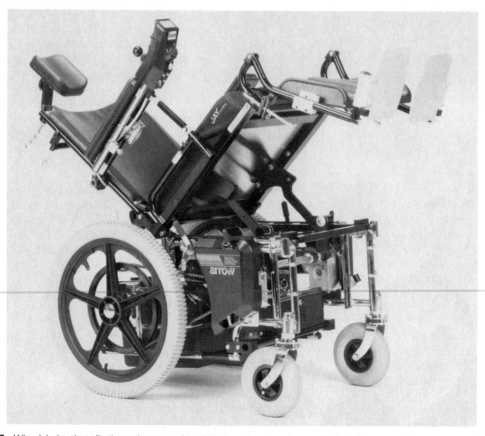

Figure 31–27. Wheelchairs that tilt through space with all their angles preset are called tilt-in-space wheelchairs. They are available in manual and motorized models. (Photo courtesy of La Bac.)

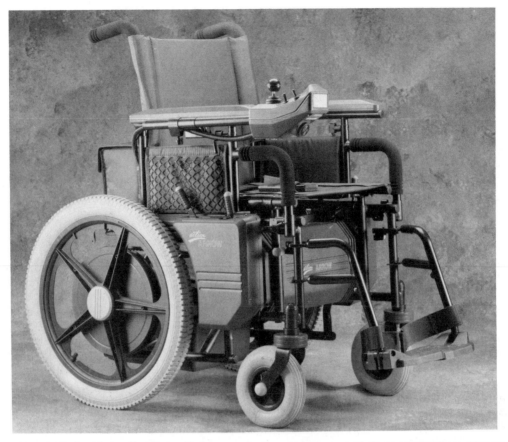

Figure 31–28. Motorized wheelchairs offer clients with poor coordination, weakness or paralysis, an opportunity to move around in their environment. (Photo courtesy of Invacare Corp.)

SPORTS AND RECREATION

Many users are active in recreational and competitive sports, some of which are done from the wheelchair. These clients may need more than one wheelchair: a "street" or "everyday" chair, and a finely tuned competition chair or recreational chair (Fig. 31–29). It is even possible to have a chair personally built for the user from a computer design based on the user's body parameters and the specific use the chair will have. For some sports such as archery, discus, shotput, and precision javelin a more stable chair is an advantage. A wide wheel camber can achieve this even on a lightweight frame. For basketball, tennis, and dancing the chair's responsiveness is critical. Competition chairs (Fig. 31–30) are usually of rigid construction, and made of very strong lightweight materials (the newest units are made of carbon). Wheel and caster placement, tiring, axles, and bearings can make a radical difference in chair performance when matched with the user's body weight and configuration. Users who participate in more than one activity may want a chair with a great deal of adjustability, to allow parameter changes for various activities.

Wheelchair users who hike off-road, on more challenging trails will require knobby tires, as the tread of normal wheelchair tires will tend to get stuck in softer ground. Those who compete in road racing will need competition chairs that have taken many of their design features from racing bicycles: narrow, hard tires; frames made of lightweight alloys or carbon; low seats for min-

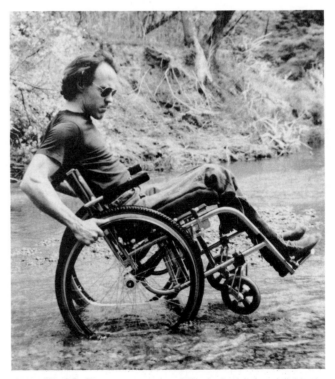

Figure 31–29. There are many specialized wheelchairs available that allow clients full access to their environment. (Photo courtesy of Iron Horse Productions.)

Figure 31–30. Wheelchairs that are designed for sports have special features specific to the intended use of the chair. (Photo courtesy of Quickie Designs.)

imum air resistance; and small pushrims for higher "gearing." Racers sit in a tucked position, with approximately 120 degrees of hip flexion and knees and legs strapped together, to present a very sleek line and minimal wind resistance as the unit (wheelchair and user) moves quickly along the track. For tennis and dance the chair is trimmed down to its sleekest configuration with all accessories, even wheel locks, removed. Wheel hubs and spoke configurations are designed to hold a tennis ball during competition. The backs are as low as possible to leave the user's upper body free for movement.

Supply and Support

Once the assessment is complete, the client's and care-givers' needs have been determined, and clinical goals have been outlined, it is time for trials and decision making. Before selecting a chair, many first-time wheelchair users will require a training period. During this time the client will learn how to move the chair in all directions, using both arms, one or two arms in combination with one or two legs, or one arm using a dual-wheel drive system. He or she must also learn how to operate the wheel locks, foot supports, and armrests; and to use the locking mechanisms safely without tipping forward or sideways out of the chair seat. He or she will learn how to transfer in and out of the chair, with the least possible assistance. Some users will always require maximal assistance for transfer activities, but others will be able to achieve some level of independence based on chair features such as removable or swing-away arm and foot supports, and lowered seat heights. For clients who do standing transfers (independent or assisted), special attention should be given to the user's ability to get back into the chair, as the seat height may prove problematic. Most chairs with a cushion allow a user to slide forward and come to standing, but transferring back up onto a standard height seat may be almost impossible.

Clients who are capable of independent community mobility must learn to "pop wheelies," in order to negotiate curbs by balancing the chair on the rear wheels while allowing the front casters to mount the curb. Clients who drive may need to transfer from the wheelchair to the car seat and then pull the chair frame into the vehicle either behind the seat, or across his or her body into the passenger seat. Either method is very dependent on the chair's folded size and weight, the user's upper body skill and strength, and the internal configuration of the car.

Power chair training is slightly different, and usually concentrates primarily on driving skill and safety. The initial challenge is to locate a reliable access site and method (hand control with a joystick, head control with individual switches). Training then involves working with the user on consistent responses (especially to STOP commands, or the recognized need to stop based on the user's awareness), and accurate maneuverability. Although switch activation can be judged using a computer program, actual "road time" is necessary for training and assessment in order to be sure how the driver will respond to distractions and obstacles.

Some rehabilitation facilities have large fleets of sample chairs that can be used with clients for assessment and training. If this option is not available it is time to locate a qualified supplier. Traditional home care and/or durable medical equipment companies are well qualified to accept prescriptive information over the phone. They keep standard-sized items in stock, and can get them to the end user quickly, often within 24 hours. More specialized equipment usually requires input to the team from a rehabilitation technology supplier. He or she is a specialist and can work with the team to design a system that fits the client's unique needs. Once the team's goals are explained to the rehabilitation technology supplier, he or she will be able to provide a list of available products that match the user's needs. The rehabilitation technology supplier should be able to explain the pros and cons and prices of various options to everyone involved. It may be advisable for the user to actually try several chairs before a decision is made. The supplier can work with the team to arrange this opportunity.

Once a system has been selected, the clinical team's generic needs assessment (including physical, psychosocial, and cognitive factors if applicable), physician's prescription, and the price estimate should be forwarded to the third party payer(s). The "justification" package should explain the medical need for each feature requested, along with an expected outcome from the intervention. Providing measurable outcomes will help the payer to make an informed decision.

The rehabilitation technology supplier should keep all of the team members apprised as the process moves along from submission through approval, ordering, and receiving of the chair and its components. Once the system is complete, the supplier must deliver it as instructed by the prescriber (to the clinic, school, or home of the user). At delivery those involved with formulating the prescription should have an opportunity to inspect the system and be sure that it meets the specifications, as well as to observe and assist as the supplier makes final adjustments. The process may require more than one or two visits for complex systems that require interim fittings.

On final delivery the rehabilitation technology supplier (RTS) explains to the user and/or care-givers how to use the chair, including use of all safety features (straps, wheel locks, antitippers), assembly and disassembly for folding, and normal maintenance (including battery maintenance on power wheelchairs and scooters). Once the chair is delivered, the user and/or care-givers should carefully read any manuals provided and mail in all warranty and registration materials. The user and/or care-givers are responsible for all normal cleaning and maintenance. The supplier and the company he or she works for should be located close enough to the user to provide emergency repairs as needed. Warranty repairs are the responsibility of the supplier who provided the chair.

SUMMARY

A systematic approach to providing a prescriptive wheelchair has been presented. The individual components of both the postural support and the wheeled mobility base have been described. The primary goal in developing any prescriptive wheelchair is maximum function and independence. It must be the result of a thorough assessment using a problem-solving approach, with attention to the specific factors discussed in this chapter. Input from the user and all team members during the decision-making phase is critical. This process will result in an optimally designed chair capable of achieving its intended purpose. This problem-solving approach, with open communication among team members, user, family, rehabilitation technology supplier, and manufacturer will ensure that each prescriptive wheelchair is designed to meet the needs of the individual.

QUESTIONS FOR REVIEW

1. Describe the following seating components and give two reasons why each is needed.
   a. Firm seat
   b. Firm back
   c. Lapboard
   d. Lapbelt
2. Describe the following wheelchair components; compare and contrast their functional benefits:
   a. Detachable swing-away footrests/elevating legrests.
   b. Fixed-height armrests/adjustable-height armrests.
   c. Single-axle placement/multiple-axle placement.
   d. Proportional drive/microswitching system.
3. When measuring seat depth, what two positions would you place the client in and why?
4. Identify landmarks and measurements needed to help determine the size of the following parts of a wheeled mobility system:
   a. Seat width.
   b. Seat depth.
   c. Seat back height.
   d. Armrest height.
   e. Minimum footrest extension (MinFBX).

REFERENCES

1. Vaeger, H, et al: The effect of rear wheel camber in manual wheelchair propulsion. J Rehabil Res Dev 26:37–46, 1989.
2. Saftler, F, et al: Use of a positioning chair in conjunction with proper seating principles for a seating evaluation. Proceedings from ICCART, 1988.
3. Sprigle, S, et al: Reduction of sitting pressures with custom contoured cushions. J Rehabil Res Dev 27:135–140, 1990.
4. Sprigle, S, et al: Factors affecting seat contour characteristics. J Rehabil Res Dev 27:127–134, 1990.
5. van der Woude, L, et al: Seat height in handrim wheelchair propulsion. J Rehabil Res Dev 26:31–50, 1989.
6. Hobson, D: The contributions of posture and deformity to the body-seat interface variables. Proceedings of the 5th International Seating Symposium, Memphis, TN, February 19, 1989. RESNA Press, Washington, DC, 1989.
7. Chung, K: Comparative evaluation of pressure distribution on flat foams and contoured cushions. Proceedings of the 10th annual conference of RESNA, San Jose, CA, June 19–23, 1987. RESNA Press, Washington, DC, 1987.
8. Hobson, D: Comparative effects of posture and pressure distribution at the body-seat interface. Proceedings of the 12th Annual Conference of RESNA, New Orleans, LA, June 25–30, 1989. RESNA Press, Washington, DC, 1989.
9. Sprigle, S and Chung, K: The use of contoured foam to reduce seat interface pressures. Proceedings of the 12th Annual Conference of RESNA, New Orleans, LA, June 25–30, 1989. RESNA Press, Washington, DC, 1989.
10. Sprigle, S and Chung, K: The influence of physical characteristics on seat contours. Proceedings of the 12th Annual Conference of RESNA. New Orleans, LA, June 25–30, 1989. RESNA Press, Washington, DC, 1989.
11. Phillips, L, et al: Spinal Cord Injury. Raven Press, New York, 1987.
12. Margolis, S, et al: The sub-ASIS bar: an effective approach to pelvic stabilization in seated position. Proceedings of the 8th Annual Conference of RESNA, Memphis, TN, June 24–28, 1985. RESNA Press, Washington, DC, 1985.
13. Bergen, AF: A seat belt is a seat belt is a . . . Assistive Technology 1:7–9, 1989.
14. Ball, M: It's not just a wheelchair anymore. Homecare 12:176–178, 1990.
15. Brubaker, C: Wheelchair prescription: an analysis of factors that affect mobility and performance. J Rehabil Res Dev 23:19–26, 1986.
16. Breed, A and Igler, I: The motorized wheelchair: new freedom new responsibility and new problems. Dev Med Child Neurol 24:366–371, 1982.
17. Butler, C: Effects of powered mobility on self-initiated behaviors of very young children with locomotor disability. Dev Med Child Neurol 28:325–332, 1986.
18. Butler, C, Okamoto, G, and McKay, T: Powered mobility for very young disabled children. Dev Med Child Neurol 25:472–474, 1983.
19. Chiulli, C, et al: Powered mobility vehicles as aids in independent locomotion for young children. Phys Ther 68:997–999, 1988.
20. Douglass, J and Ryan, M: A preschool severely disabled boy and his powered wheelchair: a case study. Child Care Health Dev 13:303–309, 1987.

21. Lotto, W and Milner, M: Evaluations and Development of Powered Mobility Aids for 2–5-Year-Olds With Neuromuscular Disorders. Ontario Crippled Child Centre, 350 Rumsey Rd, Toronto, Ontario CN M4G 1R8, 1983.
22. Trefler, E, Kozole, M, and Snell, E: Selected Readings on Powered Mobility for Children and Adults with Severe Physical Disabilities. RESNA Press, Washington, DC, 1986.
23. McEntyre, L and Neal, R: Successful power mobility by blending technology with therapeutic programming. Proceedings of the 12th Annual Conference of RESNA, New Orleans, LA, June 25–30, 1989. RESNA Press, Washington, DC, 1989.
24. Scott, J and Elder, S: An integrated approach to power mobility and communication freedom. Proceedings of the 12th Annual Conference of RESNA, New Orleans, LA, June 25–30, 1989. RESNA Press, Washington, DC, 1989.

SUPPLEMENTAL READINGS

Bergen, AF, et al: Positioning for Function: Wheelchairs and Other Assistive Technologies. Valhalla Rehab, Valhalla, NY, 1990.

Bergen, AF: The Rehabilitation Team: Members and Roles, I. Homecare July: 78–80, 1985.

Bergen, AF: The Rehabilitation Team: Members and Roles, II. Homecare Aug: 34–40, 1985.

Brubaker, C: Wheelchair prescription: an analysis of factors that affect mobility and performance. J Rehabil Res Dev 223:19–26, 1986.

Butler, C: Effects of powered mobility on self-initiated behaviors of very young children with locomotor disability. Dev Med Child Neurol 28:325–332, 1986.

Enders, A and Hall, M (eds): Assistive Technology Source Book. RESNA Press, Washington, DC, 1990.

Hedman, G (ed): Seating Systems: The Therapist and Rehabilitation Engineering Team. Physical Therapy and Occupational Therapy in Pediatrics. American Physical Therapy Association 10:11–45, 1990.

Henderson, B (ed): Seating in Review: Current Trends for the Disabled. Otto Bock Orthopedic Industry of Canada, 1989.

Hill, J and Presperin, J: Orthotic Management and Positioning. Spinal Cord Injury: A Guide to Functional Outcomes in Occupational Therapy. Aspen, Rockville, MD, 1986.

Padula, W: A Behavioral Vision Approach for Persons with Physical Disabilities. Optometric Extension Program, Santa Ana, CA, 1988.

Presperin, J: Seating systems: the therapist and rehabilitation engineering team. J Phys Ther Occup Ther Pediatrics. Spring 1990.

Trefler, E, et al: Selected Readings on Powered Mobility for Children and Adults with Severe Physical Disabilities. RESNA Press, Washington, DC, 1986.

Wilson, A Jr and McFarland, S: Wheelchairs: A Prescriptive Guide. Rehabilitation Press, Charlottesville, VA, 1986.

Zacharkow, D: Wheelchair Posture and Pressure Sores. Charles C Thomas, Springfield, IL, 1984.

Zacharkow, D: Posture: Sitting, Standing, Chair Design and Exercise. Charles C Thomas, Springfield, IL, 1988.

GLOSSARY

Abductor pommel (abductor, medial knee block): An upholstered block or wedge placed on the front of the wheelchair seating surface; used to maintain abduction of the lower extremities.

Adductor cushion (lateral knee block): An upholstered block or pad placed on the lateral aspect of the wheelchair seating surface; used to control excessive adduction of the lower extremities.

Contoured seating: Custom molded seating surface created by carving foam, building up the surface with pads and blocks, or preforming, based on research about human contours.

Control blocks (blocking): Use of upholstered supports or pads attached to the seating system to enhance postural alignment.

Kyphotic posturing (kyphosis): Excessive convex curvature of the thoracic spine as viewed laterally.

Microswitching: Power wheelchair activation system that produces an all-or-none response; the switch is preset to respond to a specific degree of pressure; when the right amount of pressure is applied the switch activates the system at a preset speed.

Mobility base: A wheelchair support and movement system; consists of the tubular frame, the legrests and armrests, foot supports, and wheels.

Molded seating: Seated environment created from a casted shape taken of the person's body contours. Foam is carved or poured to create an exact duplicate of the person's shape.

Planar seating: A seated environment created from the interfacing of flat support surfaces arranged as needed to create postural alignment and/or stability.

Postural support system: A wheelchair seating, support, and postural alignment system; consists of the seat surface, seat back, and any additional components such as a torso support, lateral and medial knee cushions, and/or pelvic belt needed to maintain alignment.

Proportional drive: Power wheelchair activation system that is tiller-controlled and responds to movement through an arc. The further the tiller is moved the faster the chair moves.

Windblown position: Positioning of the lower extremities to the side with one limb adducted and the other abducted.

David E. Krebs
Donna Wolf Behr

OBJECTIVES

1. Describe the purposes of biofeedback techniques.
2. Describe the motor learning principles underlying biofeedback techniques.
3. Describe biofeedback equipment technical requirements and limitations.
4. Identify differences in EMG biofeedback techniques used for spastic versus paretic muscle groups.
5. Describe the application of kinematic and kinetic biofeedback techniques to gait training.

Biofeedback has matured from its early cult cure-all days to its current status as a legitimate adjunctive technique for specific neuromuscular and behavioral disorders. Biofeedback can be used to inform the patient about movement, muscle activity, whole-body balance, force, joint displacement, skin temperature, heart rate, blood pressure, or other physiologic information by amplifying and displaying this information so that the patient can learn to control these. To quote John Basmajian,[1] biofeedback is a "technique to reveal to human beings some of their internal physiological events, normal and abnormal, in the form of visual and auditory signals in order to teach them to manipulate these otherwise involuntary or unfelt events by manipulating the displayed signals." Most often, biofeedback techniques are used for the patient who has difficulty accessing the information through normal physiologic mechanisms such as proprioception or visual cues (Table 32–1).

Muscle activity or electromyographic (EMG) biofeedback is most frequently employed in clinical physical therapy settings, so this chapter will focus primarily on EMG feedback. Joint position and force feedback will be considered less comprehensively.

GENERAL PRINCIPLES

The goal of **biofeedback** in physical therapy is to improve motor performance by facilitating motor learning. To use biofeedback correctly and effectively, therapists must understand the principles of motor learning and the technical limitations of biofeedback machines.

Motor Learning

Excellent reviews of normal motor control are available to the student, many of them substantial and comprehensive (e.g., Herman et al.[2] and Brooks[3]), so the field will be considered here only briefly. The motor control literature, however, has few unifying theories, and the limited work that has been done on abnormal populations tends to contradict the remaining areas of agreement. Thus, although it is accepted that motor control requires information from the external world as well as proprioception, how that information is processed is presently unknown. Attempts to dogmatically view biofeedback as a substitute for proprioceptive pathways are therefore, at best, a naive misunderstanding of the extremely sophisticated human control systems that have evolved.

A behavioral positive reinforcement or reward model is usually employed with biofeedback techniques. Simply stated, when patients generate appropriate motor behaviors, they are positively reinforced. The audio and visual feedback stimuli, and other nonverbal information is usually much faster and more accurate than the therapist's comments. In contrast to other therapies, the benefits of accomplishing small changes in motor behavior in the desired direction can be reinforced, a process that should speed the rehabilitation process. In behavioral learning terminology, the therapist uses the biofeedback signal to shape the motor behavior by reinforcing the patient's successive approximations to the goal behavior or functional outcome.[4]

When the patient succeeds in controlling the signal, the therapist must relate it to the underlying motor behavior and then reset the goals. Reinforcing already learned behaviors is, of course, futile, so the machine's threshold should be monitored frequently, increasing the task's difficulty as motor skills progress.

PHYSIOLOGIC FEEDBACK

The fastest cortical feedback circuits, (i.e., those which could take into account changes in environmental conditions) have at least 100- to 200-msec latencies. For

Table 32–1 SCHEMATIC RELATIONSHIP OF BIOFEEDBACK DEVICE TO PATIENT.

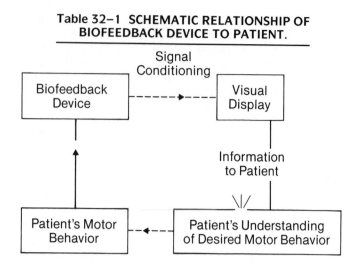

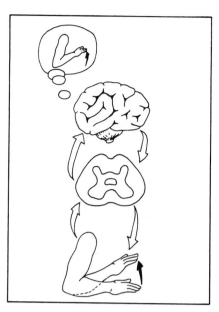

Figure 32–1. Schematic representation of closed-loop motor learning theory.

example, a pianist performing a fast "run" cannot possibly rely on visual or auditory feedback during the "run." The performance is therefore "open-loop": if a mistake is made, several notes will be played before the performer is even aware that the mistake has occurred and several more notes will be played (i.e., about 0.2 sec of music) before any adjustments to the motor plan can be made.

Ambulation also requires a series of preplanned motor events. If a disruption occurs, feedback of the "mistake" can only be acted upon and built into the plan for *ensuing* steps. Normal walking cadence is about 1 cycle per second. Ankle dorsiflexors, for example, must resist foot slap from heel strike to foot-flat for about 60 msec. Therapists attempting to encourage normal gait in patients with hemiplegia by using feedback from dorsiflexor EMG should not, therefore, ask a patient to correct inadequate dorsiflexor motor unit activity *within* each gait cycle. At best, patients will use that information during the next gait cycle; the information to be given is merely that EMG activity was inadequate during the past gait cycle. The therapist and patient must determine the correct neurophysiologic strategy to increase dorsiflexor motor unit activity in anticipation of ensuing heel strikes.

BIOFEEDBACK IN REHABILITATION

When using biofeedback, the patient must (1) understand the relationship of the electronic signal to the desired functional task, (2) practice controlling the biofeedback signal, and (3) perform the functional task until it is mastered and the patient no longer needs the biofeedback. Biofeedback techniques thus require that patients engage in "closed-loop" learning, using ongoing feedback (Fig. 32–1), until motor skills develop sufficiently so that "open-loop" movements (where no feedback is required) can be accomplished.*

---

*The reader should be aware that this oversimplified dichotomy of open- and closed-loop movements is included here for its heuristic value, not because it is a physiologically validated motor control paradigm.

Winstein[5] and others have shown that a combination of open- and closed-loop learning, called scheduled feedback, can be more effective than closed-loop, classic biofeedback. In scheduled feedback paradigms, subjects practice the task initially with feedback following each trial, then spend increasingly long practice periods without feedback following each trial. Apparently, scheduled feedback encourages subjects to rely upon normal, internal feedback mechanisms and decreases their dependence on relatively "unnatural" biofeedback.

Conventional neuromuscular reeducation is based heavily upon providing patients with helpful comments (feedback) to assist their recovery of previously acquired skills. The therapist's job, often, is to focus the patient's attention on the underlying motor programs and biomechanical schema required to recoup those skills. If a postmeniscectomy patient cannot execute a straight-leg raise, for example, then gait rehabilitation will be impeded, and the therapist usually prescribes quadriceps-setting exercise. Biofeedback-assisted quad-setting, however, might improve that patient's information processing and result in more rapid rehabilitation by augmenting knee joint or quadriceps proprioception with electronic feedback and supplementing the normal feedback inhibited by the meniscectomy.[6,7] As shown schematically in Figure 32–2, if the patient's normal proprioception and other physiologic mechanisms are disrupted, normal movement control and relearning of motor skills is restricted.

Biofeedback is simply one technique that therapists may employ to help convey their message about motor programs and biomechanical schema to the patient. Biofeedback can assist the rehabilitation process by:

1. Providing a clear goal (motor behavior or outcome) that the patient should achieve.
2. Permitting the therapist and patient to experiment

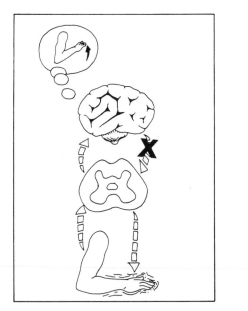

Figure 32–2. Abnormal feedback loop impedes normal movement control.

with various strategies (processes) that generate motor patterns to achieve the goal.

3. Reinforcing appropriate motor behavior.
4. Providing a process-oriented, timely, and accurate knowledge of results of the patient's efforts.

By attending to the biofeedback signal, the patient can "close the loop," as shown in Figure 32–3. Some patients become more motivated when biofeedback is employed because they know the machine will not be falsely encouraging. Both the therapist and the patient must therefore understand the meaning of the feedback signal and appropriate goals must be agreed upon.

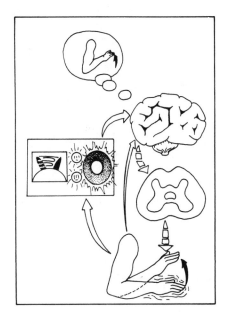

Figure 32–3. Abnormal feedback loop augmented by biofeedback signal.

The therapist must explain what the machine's signals mean to the patient, and what constitutes success. The machine should be set to give auditory or visual feedback that corresponds to the motor behavior desired. For example, if spastic antagonist muscles are monitored, the patient should be instructed to decrease the EMG activity; the biofeedback device is set to flash a light to signal accomplishment of this goal. Alternatively, an **electrogoniometer** might be employed that changes the pitch of a buzzer as the joint is moved in the proper direction.

MOTOR LEARNING SUMMARY

Biofeedback techniques are used to augment the patient's sensory feedback mechanisms through precise information about body processes that might otherwise be inaccessible. Positive reinforcement is the operative learning model.

Technical Limitations

Feedback must be relevant, accurate, and rapid in order to enhance motor learning. If any of these three elements is missing, traditional verbal feedback is probably just as useful, and is certainly more convenient.

RELEVANCE

Useful information is pertinent to the desired motor outcome: neither too much nor too little information should be given, and the information should be immediately applicable to the behavior. Although therapists may verbally describe the location of agonist and antagonist muscles, and even make attempts to describe the "feelings" patients should experience if the muscles are used appropriately, there is no way to communicate which motor units to activate. Electromyographic biofeedback can provide relevant information regarding motor unit activity that patients do not otherwise have available.

ACCURACY

It should come as no surprise that disagreement exists regarding the utility of biofeedback, because today's technology is quite crude and most forms of feedback (especially EMG feedback) merely communicate "more" or "less" activity. The information provided to patients via current technology is decidedly unsophisticated and incomplete compared to that which intact nervous systems can provide during normal movement. Many therapists prefer to work with devices that directly measure force or joint range of motion (ROM). These therapists feel that EMG signals are not sufficiently informative nor sophisticated to be true "process" feedback, and that EMG does not reflect actual outcome adequately (e.g., limb displacement or torque) to provide accurate knowledge of results. In order to maximize the utility of biofeedback, it is necessary to be certain that the type of device and the way in which it is attached provide accurate information.

Feedback must be timely to be useful. While feedback is employed, the movements necessarily are "closed-loop," as previously described.

In addition to endogenous, physiologic latencies, most EMG biofeedback instruments have built-in integrators or averagers, which further slow the signal output. In addition, all EMG processors delay electrical events during signal amplification and conversion to the audio speaker and visual meter, due to inherent delays from the electrical circuits. Most commercial EMG feedback instruments introduce 50- to 100-msec delays before the signal can even reach the ears and eyes of patients, and further delays ensue within the patient's neural "circuits."

TECHNICAL SUMMARY

Information to be fed back to patients must be accurate, relevant, and timely in order to be of any therapeutic use. Therapists must choose the instrument or device that provides the most meaningful information to patients. Commercially available EMG instruments, for example, can provide timely feedback if the motor behavior being monitored is at least 0.5 second in duration. Thus, for feedback during a 5-second isometric contraction, adequate time may be available for patients to adjust the motor program and change the motor strategy being employed. During most functional activities, therefore, the "feedback" acts as an error signal to provide knowledge of results, which is used in planning future movements.

USING ELECTROMYOGRAPHIC FEEDBACK FOR NEUROMUSCULAR REEDUCATION

General Introduction

The basic EMG biofeedback device includes one ground and two active surface electrodes, an amplifier, an audio speaker, and a video display. The EMG signal (which is on the order of millionths of a volt, or microvolts) is transmitted from the muscle through the skin, through the electrode paste, through the electrodes, wires, and thence to the amplifier.

Surface electrodes are metal discs, which should be ½ in or less in diameter (Fig. 32–4). Electrode paste is a gel that reduces the resistance between the electrodes and the skin. Some modern biofeedback units do not require the use of electrode paste or gel because they have very high input impedance (more on impedance later in this section). Those that do, however, require the user to carefully apply the paste so that it "just covers" the electrode. Use of excess paste is not only sloppy, it will affect the apparent amplitude of the EMG signal, perhaps even short-circuiting the two active electrodes. Therapists should generally place one electrode on the motor point, where most of the endplates are

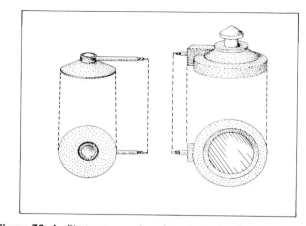

Figure 32–4. Electromyograph surface electrodes. Center area is concave and should be filled flush to its surface with electrode paste.

located, and the other electrode distal to it, and parallel to the direction of the fibers.

The rest of the equipment is somewhat more complex, and requires a fairly thorough understanding of the EMG signal's characteristics.

In this section, the origins of the EMG signal will be briefly reviewed and its progress followed from the patient (starting with the intention to move) through the monitoring instrumentation, and back to the patient for error correction.

Muscle Physiology: Where Does the Electromyographic Signal Come From?

After the central nervous system (CNS) signals its intention to move, and the signal travels down the spinal cord, the anterior horn cell discharges. The motor nerve then depolarizes, conducting its electrical current toward the muscle at 40 to 60 m/s. Because a motor unit consists, by definition, of the anterior horn cell, its nerve, and all the muscle fibers it innervates, the amount of muscle that is activated depends upon the size of the motor unit field (i.e., the number of muscle fibers innervated by each anterior horn cell and its axon).

After all motor nerve terminal branches have discharged, the action potential hits the neuromuscular junction. The most distal end of the nerve contains acetylcholine, which diffuses across the synaptic cleft. The acetylcholine receptors cause a second action potential to occur, this time in the sarcolemma, or jacket, surrounding the muscle (from the Greek, sarcos = flesh, and lemma = sheath). The sarcolemmal depolarization, or action potential, travels more slowly than the nerve action potential propagation. The EMG device registers this sarcolemmal depolarization; it does not register muscle tension. After the electrical excitation travels through the muscle, the action potential reaches a storage area for calcium ions. Only after the electrical depolarization reaches this storage area and causes calcium to be released does the mechanical event, muscle contraction, occur. The muscle's electrical action potential normally, although not always, results in tension (force) production by the muscle.[8,9]

In EMG feedback, surface electrodes are most often used. Surface electrodes summate all potentials beneath their surfaces. Therefore, an increase in observed EMG activity may result from more muscle cells discharging, or from changes in electrode placement. The surface electrodes' summation masks the precise source of the signal. Electromyographic activity may be from a muscle immediately below the electrodes or from a distant source. Furthermore, the EMG signal will increase whether patients are developing increased activation of small motor units more rapidly and synchronously, or if a greater number of units are being recruited.

It should be understood from the preceding paragraphs that measuring a muscle's electrical activity, as is done with EMG, is not the same as measuring muscle tension. The important point for understanding biofeedback is that the EMG signal arises prior to and occasionally independent of, muscle mechanical activity, so blind reliance on EMG output can be deceiving.

Electromyographic Biofeedback Equipment and Technical Specifications

The EMG biofeedback device is at heart a very sensitive **voltmeter** with a speaker and meter attached. Like any "differential" voltmeter, an EMG instrument can only sense electrical signals if one pole experiences a different voltage than the other: one pole of the instrument must be negative with respect to the other pole to register any activity. After the electrical signal is detected, most biofeedback instruments condition the signals so that positive and negative impulses are "rectified" (the machine finds the signal's absolute amplitude); then the device "smooths" (filters) the signal, prior to display to decrease the normal fluctuations present in the muscle's electrical output. (See Chapter 9 for further details on signal conditioning.) Thus, although the muscle's electrical event occurs prior to its mechanical contraction, by the time the EMG machine produces the feedback signal, the mechanical event is over. The quality of the machine, and therefore its output, are chiefly indicated by its input **impedance, common mode rejection ratio** (CMRR), frequency response, **noise** level, and ability to cope with non-EMG **artifacts.**

INPUT IMPEDANCE

Ohm's Law indicates that resistance (impedance) is inversely related to voltage. At the muscle fiber level, muscle action potentials have a magnitude of several thousandths of a volt. The summated current passes through the resistive subcutaneous tissues and skin where the voltage is reduced, sometimes by 100-fold. Therefore, EMG signals from obese patients or from limb sites with above-average amounts of adipose tissue, will appear smaller than normal, even if the signals at the muscle fiber level are equivalent to that from other muscles with less intervening tissue. In fact, all intervening tissues, including bone, and atrophic, necrotic, or especially oily skin resist the muscles' electrical signals. Because skin resistance varies but internal resistance from fat and other tissues probably remains constant, only skin resistance is typically a concern.

If the EMG machine's impedance is much greater than skin impedance, skin resistance becomes trivial in comparison, and the biofeedback signal reflects more valid muscle EMG activity. As a rule of thumb, EMG instruments should have at least 1000 times as much input impedance as that measured between the two active electrodes. One can easily measure skin electrode impedance by attaching an **ohmmeter** to the surface electrode after they are attached to the skin. Generally, a standard, careful skin preparation to remove dead surface skin and excess oil will decrease resistance to 1,000 Ω or less, a level which can be accommodated by contemporary instruments with high (at least 100 MΩ) input impedance.

Electrode size also alters the effective resistance seen by the amplifier. Larger electrodes have lower resistances. The greatest resistance occurs with needle electrodes, because their surface area is so small. Changing electrodes may cause an ostensible change in the EMG signal, and the therapist must realize that this is an artifact.

COMMON MODE REJECTION RATIO

Contemporary EMG instruments almost always utilize a differential amplifier, comparing the voltage at one active electrode to the other active electrode. The ground electrode in a good EMG machine may be placed almost anywhere on the patient. If the voltage travels down the muscle and arrives at both electrodes simultaneously, no difference between the electrodes is registered and the instrument reflects no change of activity. Therefore, therapists must choose electrode placements that maximize the likelihood that EMG signals will first reach one active electrode and later reach the other active electrode.

The advantage of the differential recording system is its "rejection" of extraneous voltages. Although we may not be aware of it, patients' skin receives a great many voltages, from lights, motors, and other hospital appliances that produce currents that travel through the air and can affect the recordings on the skin. Other muscles (e.g., the heart) also produce voltages. If the electricity from these other sources reaches the two active electrodes simultaneously, a differential amplifier with a high CMRR will "reject" these artifactual signals.

The voltage from lights and other exogenous generators nearly always reach the two skin electrodes simultaneously, so room current (60 Hz) interference is often minimal. Myocardial activity, however, is often a problem when electrodes are on the chest or upper back, near the heart. The presence of a regularly alternating signal in the "feedback" signal, unrelated to the muscle(s) being monitored, indicates that the electrodes should be repositioned perpendicular to the progression of the electrocardiogram (ECG) wave, so that the ECG signal arrives at both electrodes concurrently.

Electronic common mode rejection is not perfect. If a signal of 60 Hz interferes with a therapy session, the therapist should turn off the room lights or look for a nearby whirlpool or diathermy machine as the culprit. An ungrounded appliance operating from the same electrical circuit as the EMG feedback instrument will occasionally interfere with EMG recordings. If the EMG instrument cannot operate by batteries, then disconnect the ungrounded appliance, or install an outlet for the EMG that is isolated from other appliances.

As with input impedance, higher is better. Common mode rejection ratios (CMRRs) should be at least 200,000:1. If the muscles being monitored are especially paretic and generate only a few microvolts, then large amplifier gains are required. Large gains, unfortunately, also amplify the artifacts; therefore, a high CMRR is especially desirable when using biofeedback for the low myoelectric signals common in neuromuscular reeducation.

FREQUENCY RESPONSE (BANDWIDTH)

Bandwidth is the difference between the lowest and highest frequency response of an EMG instrument. Most of the power at surface kinesiologic EMG recordings is between 20 and 200 Hz, so manufacturers often dictate that their EMG instruments need no more than 200 Hz as its highest cut-off frequency. However, instrument responsiveness relates not only to the frequency of the monitored signal but also to how quickly the signal changes. Optimally, the high end of the machine's bandwidth should exceed 500 Hz to enable the machine to respond to all components of the signal. In general, a frequency response of 32 to 500 Hz is adequate for surface kinesiologic EMG feedback.

NOISE LEVEL

In general, the lower the noise, the better. If the noise level of the device is, say, 5 μV, a muscle contraction of 4 μV would be lost within the machine. Modern devices, using high-quality electronic components typically result in acceptable noise levels of 2 μV or less.

OTHER ARTIFACTS

False readings can be traced to many sources, but the most common artifacts in EMG biofeedback are volume-conduction and movement.

Volume-conducted artifacts result when signals from nearby muscles are inadvertently sampled by the surface electrodes. The easiest solution is to bring the active electrodes closer to one another. The therapist might also palpate the suspected muscle during the movement, but must be aware that tendons and muscle bellies become palpably tense from simply being passively stretched. A better solution is to use a second set of electrodes to monitor the offending muscle's activity on another channel.[10]

For example, when treating a patient with hemiplegia to increase elbow extension by increasing triceps EMG amplitude, the therapist should realize that spastic elbow flexors may be contracting. Although the EMG signal may appear to increase, the elbow still does not extend. The increase in EMG registered by the biofeedback device in this case might result from spastic biceps muscle activity, which in turn explains why the elbow does not extend. The solution therefore would be to attempt first to relax the biceps brachii, then to facilitate triceps motor activity using the EMG biofeedback.

Patients with paretic muscles from lower motor neuron disorders sometimes use similarly incorrect strategies. Because paretic muscles, for example those resulting from peroneal palsy, have too few active motor units, the low EMG signals must be amplified greatly, perhaps by using an EMG scale of 0 to 10 μV. By using the biofeedback machine at such high gains, therapists can discern practically any amount of motor unit activity. Unfortunately, patients often try to please their therapists and to show themselves "there is life in my muscle," so they clench their teeth and co-contract throughout the limb. In so doing, they are successful in increasing the response of the biofeedback instrument, but in this case, biofeedback reinforces functionally inappropriate motor behavior. Therefore, it is the therapist's responsibility to ensure that the feedback is valid.

This author has had many patients referred for biofeedback because, according to the referring clinician, "The patient can increase the muscle's EMG, but can't achieve any functional gains." The problem is virtually always volume-conduction EMG artifact. As indicated above, multichannel biofeedback is employed to monitor all the muscles in the limb, to allow the examiner to understand the strategy the patient is employing to increase the EMG signal. The goal of therapy becomes inhibition of the antagonists and facilitation of the agonists. Some patients require as many as three or more sessions to reverse the effects of previous "biofeedback" (which was in fact artifact feedback).

Movement artifacts are one of the most vexing problems in EMG biofeedback. Particularly where muscles are weak and amplification perforce is high, movement artifacts, whose greatest power is below 20 Hz, can be easily mistaken for EMG signals. Whenever movement occurs, the cables move and signals are fed back, even if the muscles are not generating electrical activity. Of course, a high CMRR can decrease this problem, but the best solution is to eliminate the cables altogether by putting the preamplifier at the electrode site. To date, only Motion Control, of Salt Lake City, currently provides this electrode/preamplifier combination in a commercially available biofeedback instrument for neuromuscular reeducation (Fig. 32–5).

A Typical Treatment Session

In the most general terms, EMG feedback can be used only to help the patient increase or decrease muscle activity.[11,12] Thus, for paretic muscles the goal is usually to increase the EMG signal, and for spastic muscles the goal is to decrease the EMG signal. Note that the etiology of paresis or spasticity is not mentioned: biofeedback techniques to date make no distinction among the various diagnostic categories. Biofeedback applications distinguish only between paresis and spasticity, that is,

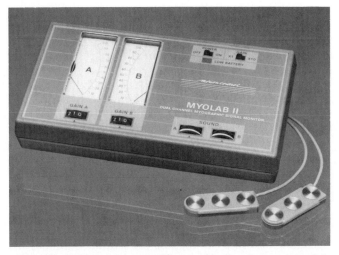

Figure 32–5. Electrode/preamplifier combination in a commercially available biofeedback instrument for neuromuscular reeducation. (Courtesy of Motion Control, Salt Lake City, UT.)

functional classifications. As a result, a typical treatment session should include: (1) patient functional assessment, (2) problem identification and setting of treatment goals, and (3) therapeutic intervention.

Patient functional assessment is performed in the usual way: tests and measurements are conducted to determine the status of motor, psychologic, and other relevant factors. The therapist should be especially observant of cooperation and attention because they are critical to successful implementation of biofeedback techniques.

Problem identification flows from functional status assessment, and setting of treatment goals follows from the problem list thus generated. After determining the functional deficit, the therapist performs a kinesiologic assessment to identify the muscle(s) that require(s) intervention. The EMG device can be connected to further enhance the information gathered at this time, which can be particularly helpful in identifying goals of initial treatment sessions. If the therapist's kinesiologic assessment is correct, then therapeutic interventions to augment control of the muscle group(s) should lead directly to enhanced function.

Therapeutic interventions in EMG feedback typically require the therapist to:

1. Select the muscle(s) to be monitored.
2. Prepare the skin at the surface electrode site.
3. Prepare the electrodes and apply them to the skin.
4. Determine the maximum and minimum EMG readings *without* patient feedback, to determine baseline readings. At this time, the therapist must be sure that the signal reaching the patient is artifact-free and valid.
5. Set the goals for the session and be sure the patient understands them. Typically, goal setting at each session requires the audio and visual thresholds to be set.
6. Teach the patient to manipulate the controls of the machinery, to maximally involve patient participation in the intervention. The more responsibility

the patient assumes for the treatment, the greater the chances of a successful intervention.
7. Use facilitation or other neuromuscular reeducation techniques. In so doing, both the therapist and the patient react to the EMG feedback to monitor their success.
8. Remove and clean the device and the patient's skin after the session's end.

The initial session is structured to permit *the therapist* to understand the motor dysfunction, and to permit *the patient* to understand the equipment. Therefore, simple tasks are given to the patient, and following mastery, more difficult tasks are given. After explaining to the patient the purpose of biofeedback techniques and after choosing the appropriate muscle, the therapist will demonstrate what the patient should make the biofeedback device do by placing the electrodes on the patient's sound, contralateral limb. If both limbs are affected, the therapist will use his or her own limb for the demonstration.

The therapist should prepare the skin according to the recommendations indicated above, using alcohol or other skin abrasives if the device's input impedance is not optimal.

Choice of electrode size is essentially a decision based upon the quality of the equipment to be used. In general, smaller electrodes are better: they are less likely to transmit volume-conducted artifact, and permit wider choice in electrode site selection, because few sites are too small to seat them well. The therapist should be aware, however, that impedance varies inversely with electrode size, so that unless the amplifier has a high input impedance, small electrodes may induce signal artifacts. The preferred electrode size is about 10 mm in diameter, as shown in Figure 32–4.

Prepare the electrodes as shown in Figure 32–6. The adhesive collars shown are only one way of attaching the electrodes to the skin; one may also use adhesive tape,

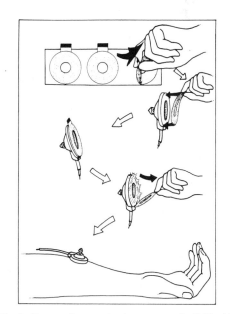

Figure 32–6. Preparation and placement of EMG biofeedback electrodes.

rubber or elastic bands, nonelastic Velcro-fastening bands, spring-loaded clips, or adhesive electrode-paste—in any combination—so long as the electrodes remain securely attached to the skin. When applying the electrode paste, it is most important to fill the concave well, but only to the point that the gel is level with its surface. Too little gel leaves gaps between the electrode and the skin, decreasing the effective electrode size; too much gel oozes out onto the surrounding skin, increasing the effective electrode size and possibly even creating a short circuit if the gel from both electrodes touch.

The closer the electrodes are to one another, the more confidence the therapist has that the signal is coming from the target muscle. Wider electrode spacing yields greater signal amplitude (more apparent voltage), but today's electronic amplifiers do not need assistance from widely spaced electrodes. For the same reason, if the signal amplitude recordings are made to help chronicle the patient's progress, the therapist should also register the electrode locations and separation distance.

When treating inpatients, the therapist can mark the patient's skin, tracing the electrode locations for replication on ensuing days. Otherwise, the therapist can specify in the treatment record the electrode locations according to anatomic markers on that patient: a mole, blemish, or any other permanent skin marker is best. The closer the reference point to the electrode site the easier the replication will be at the next visit.

PATIENT CONSIDERATIONS

After the equipment is in place and the therapist is satisfied that the feedback signal is accurate, the patient should be taught to master the movement. Generally, the therapist should begin by requesting a simple isometric contraction, setting the amplification gains so that the patient achieves the criterion for feedback (the audio or video threshold) on about two out of three contractions. Thus, the gains are set quite high for paretic muscles and low for spastic muscles.

Use of imagery, proprioceptive neuromuscular facilitation, ice, vibration, indeed even electrical stimulation, in conjunction with biofeedback can enhance the patient's motor performance—so long as the adjunctive treatment (e.g., melting ice) does not induce artifactual feedback. Probably the most useful technique is to have the patient imagine the motor activity, and while the electrodes monitor the muscle and the therapist gives verbal reinforcement and manual assistance such as tapping, tendon pressure, or putting the muscle on stretch—the patient attempts to perform that activity.[13]

EXAMPLE

Consider the typical patient with hemiplegia who has a classic foot-drop gait. Initial sessions should concentrate on recruiting more dorsiflexor activity (and/or less plantar flexor spasticity, if present) until the patient can reliably isolate dorsiflexion. Positional differences are important: Most patients will be able to dorsiflex most easily in sitting, with the knee at about 70 to 80 degrees of flexion and the foot flat on the floor. The task should be advanced by increments so as to require the patient

to dorsiflex with the knee flexed to 90 degrees and then with the knee in progressively less flexion—until dorsiflexion is possible in sitting with the knee at full extension. The patient should now be able to dorsiflex while standing, so the next task is to introduce this skill during walking. As indicated previously, dorsiflexion must be rapid to be helpful in clearing the foot, so the patient should be trained from the outset to explosively contract the dorsiflexors—while keeping the plantarflexors relatively quiet.

To help relax spastic muscles, the therapist should use the EMG device to monitor muscle activity during slow passive stretch, then increase the challenge by more rapid stretch. Finally, there should be progress to active-assisted movement and then to independent movement. The patient must keep the EMG levels below a certain threshold, say 20 μV at first. As the patient improves his or her ability to control spastic muscle activity during passive or active stretch, there should be a gradual increase in the task difficulty as the detection threshold is lowered to, say 17 or 15 μV.

During gait training, the patient should walk with the dorsiflexor EMG feedback acting as an error signal, telling him or her which strategies have been successful in eliciting the appropriate motor activity. The therapist should of course continue to treat the entire patient, including the "nonaffected limb," whether or not these muscles participated directly in the feedback session.

Note that little clinical research has been done to delineate the usefulness of providing EMG feedback for spasticity, so the above example should be considered only as a guide.[1,14,15] Furthermore, there is no agreement among gait analysis experts on what constitutes normal EMG activity for a given muscle group,[16,17] nor even of the best way to analyze and present the EMG signal.[18] Therefore, use and interpretation of EMG biofeedback signals for gait training in general should be undertaken with circumspection. The therapist should not rely upon the EMG signal alone for signs of functional progress, particularly for patients with spastic muscles.

Patients with paretic muscles present a different challenge. The challenge is to recruit more motor units or to use the motor units more effectively, rather than to find strategies for controlling the muscle or its antagonist. Patients with weak muscles whose manual muscle test (MMT) values are F+ or less are good candidates for EMG feedback. If some resistance can be accommodated (i.e., G− or greater MMT value) then resistive exercises should be given. Biofeedback can enhance muscle control, but no research to date has shown that EMG feedback plus resistive exercises are better than the latter alone. Experimental research has, however, shown that EMG feedback plus isometric quad-setting is substantially more effective than the quad-setting exercises alone, in increasing muscle power following knee arthrotomy.[5]

GENERAL RELAXATION

Relaxation therapy techniques sometimes combine EMG feedback with Jacobson's progressive relaxation,[19] Schultz's autogenic imagery,[20] and other psychologic techniques.[21] In these sessions, the EMG is typically monitored from frontalis or forearm muscle sites. The patient sits quietly while passively attempting to decrease the EMG signal, attending to the psychologic and behavioral correlates of relaxation.[22] Very deep relaxation can be induced, so nonpsychologists must be wary of their comments and actions around patients whose defenses are so relaxed.

Relaxation sessions may also include finger temperature, skin impedance, blood pressure, or heart rate feedback. Particularly with respect to skin temperature feedback, the therapist's knowledge of physiology is an important determinant of whether or not the patient's experience can be successful. Most important, however, is the therapist's personality. Support of the patient's goals, warmth, compassion, and belief in the techniques have been demonstrated to be as important as technical capabilities, in relaxation therapies.

Patients who find it difficult to relax, or those with stress-related disorders, may benefit from relaxation biofeedback techniques. Temperature feedback for Raynaud's disease is now the treatment of choice.[23] Occasionally, patients with spasticity recalcitrant to the interventions described above will benefit from a session or two of general relaxation. It is frequently amazing to realize the general population's ignorance of tension-related stigmata: some patients literally do not realize that when they clench their fists, grind their teeth or otherwise tense their muscles, they are increasing their muscle tension. These patients find it quite difficult to relax their spastic muscles because they do not know how to relax their normal muscles!

TREATMENT SESSION SUMMARY

No matter what the diagnosis, the biofeedback technique treatment approach is similar: (1) Select a muscle whose EMG signal is relevant to the functional activity, (2) have the patient practice controlling the signal, and (3) withdraw the feedback as function is gained.

Electromyograph Biofeedback Summary

Electromyographic biofeedback has probably been employed since the first diagnostic electromyographic examination was performed, with the examiner asking the patient to watch the oscilloscope and listen to the speaker to relax or increase muscle activity. At present, EMG biofeedback is the treatment of choice or has been found to be of greatest benefit in treating patients with dystonic or idiopathic torticollis,[24] and patients with neurogenic or orthopedic muscle paresis.[10,25,26] Patients with hemiplegia, spinal cord injuries, ataxia and other movement disorders are more difficult to help with EMG biofeedback, but at a minimum the addition of EMG information provides the clinician with greater insight.[27] The following is a list of neuromuscular disorders "for which there exists sufficient evidence to justify the use of biofeedback."[28] It is not intended to be exhaustive, but is provided merely to give the reader an idea of the breadth of diagnoses and disabilities currently considered amenable to biofeedback interventions.

1. Foot drop due to stroke
2. Muscle tendon transfer
3. Hemiplegia and/or hemiparesis
4. Pain, chronic (due to muscle spasm)
5. Peripheral nerve injury
6. Bell's palsy
7. Lower motor neuron lesions
8. Paretic muscles
9. Spastic muscles
10. Torticollis
11. Immobilization (following orthopedic trauma)
12. Low back pain (due to muscle spasm)
13. Spinal cord lesion, incomplete
14. Joint repair
15. Paralysis, residual (due to polio)
16. Blepharospasm
17. Cerebral palsy
18. Parkinson's disease
19. Writers cramp

KINEMATIC (JOINT MOTION) FEEDBACK

Joint motions are commonly measured by using a goniometer. An electrogoniometer, or el-gon (Fig. 32-7) is an electronic version of the manual goniometer that employs a **potentiometer** (i.e., a variable resistor, or **rheostat**) attached to the "movable" and "stationary" arms. The arms move just as they do in a conventional goniometer—they correspond to the position of the limb segments.[29]

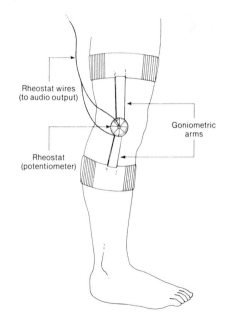

Rheostat wires (to audio output)

Goniometric arms

Rheostat (potentiometer)

Figure 32-7. Electrogoniometer. Note that its arms attach to patient's limb segments.

How Electrogoniometers Work

Rheostats are commonly used as the volume control knob on stereos or as room light dimmers. Rotating the rheostat changes its resistance, which in turn increases or decreases the current from the feedback device's signal. If a volume control knob or room light dimmer were connected to an el-gon on a knee, for example, each step would cause the audio signal or lights to fluctuate.

It is important to be sure that the feedback is indeed linearly related to joint motion. For the same reason that a 20-degree turn of a stereo's volume control knob should always result in the same audio volume change, so should a 20-degree knee flexion always result in the same electrogoniometer feedback change. The voltage through the electrogoniometer is provided by a battery. Joint movement causes the rheostat's pitch or volume to change proportionately.[30,31]

Clinical Applications

As in all biofeedback techniques, the therapist should first demonstrate the desired behavior by attaching the electrogoniometer to the patient's uninvolved limb or to the therapist's own corresponding limb segments.[32] The other "principles" of biofeedback techniques also apply to kinematic feedback, such as positive reinforcement and the "two-thirds" criterion for success described above. The therapist should begin by setting the "error" signal range to be quite forgiving during the early stages of training and then gradually increase the task's difficulty as mastery is achieved.[33] The baseline position on the el-gon is generally set for silence (no feedback), but movement in the desired direction is reinforced with sound.

Children with orthopedic disorders can be especially easy to treat. By making the volume of the TV or radio contingent upon movement in the proper direction, for example, louder volume can be used to indicate increased knee flexion, and the child's postsurgical recovery can be hastened by allowing cartoons to be watched and heard as long as knee flexion is above a criterion level.

Recently, the "stiff-legged" (insufficient knee flexion) gait of hemiplegia has been successfully treated by el-gon biofeedback. Subjects with hemiplegia learned to reduce knee stance-phase hyperextension and to increase swing-phase flexion.[34]

Patients with above-knee amputations need to learn to keep their prosthetic knee extended during stance. Fernie and colleagues[35] and Wooldridge et al.[36] described the use of an el-gon to facilitate this learning by providing audio feedback that indicated when the knee was safe for weight bearing.

The therapist must, however, have a good working knowledge of normal **kinematics** and of the kinematics expected of patients with that particular diagnosis (Fig. 32–8). It is, for example, inappropriate to ask a patient with hemiplegia to dorsiflex beyond neutral during the swing phase, or to ask a patient with above-knee amputation to employ normal knee kinematics during prosthetic stance phase (Fig. 32–9).[37]

The same logic applies to orthotic rehabilitation. Orthoses are frequently prescribed to support or restrict joint motions quite distant from the device itself. For example, setting the orthotic ankle joint in slight plantarflexion encourages knee extension during stance. Patients using such devices should not be expected to attain normal knee motions, and kinematic biofeedback should not be used to encourage flexion when such "ground reaction" orthoses are being employed.

Construction

DeBacher[28] provides detailed instructions on the use and construction of electrogoniometers. Therapists can easily and inexpensively fabricate a simple el-gon. The electrical parts are available from the local electronics store, and the rest of the device consists essentially of a manual goniometer.[27] The potentiometer should have at least 90 percent linearity, but almost all commercially available rheostats today satisfy that requirement. Finally, it should be noted that most isokinetic devices have a built-in electrogoniometer. Asking the patient to monitor the printed goniometric channel is often a good method of encouraging joint mobility through kinematic biofeedback techniques.

STANDING (BALANCE) FEEDBACK

Somewhere between kinematic and **kinetic** feedback lies standing balance or posturography feedback. Balance feedback has become increasingly popular as therapists are asked to treat elderly patients, and others at risk of falling. Such posturography feedback devices usually consist of force-measuring scales on which the subject is requested to stand as still as possible. Although they are typically marketed as measuring center of gravity or center of mass sway, balance platforms such as Balance Master only measure the center of pressure under the feet. Center of pressure (CP) displacement is loosely associated with whole-body center of mass (CM) sway such that the CP acts to push the CM back if one sways forward too far;[28] the CP pushes the CM forward if one sways backward too far. Hence, CP excursion always exceeds CM sway if any movement is occurring.

Biofeedback of "postural sway" (whether the CP or CM or other variables are actually measured) to patients with balance impairment is a promising but unproven application. It seems reasonable that subjects who sway excessively could be taught to decrease their sway using balance feedback, but research results to date are equivocal. Balance control in the past has been defined as the ability to maintain an upright position by attaining equilibrium between the forces of gravity, muscles, and iner-

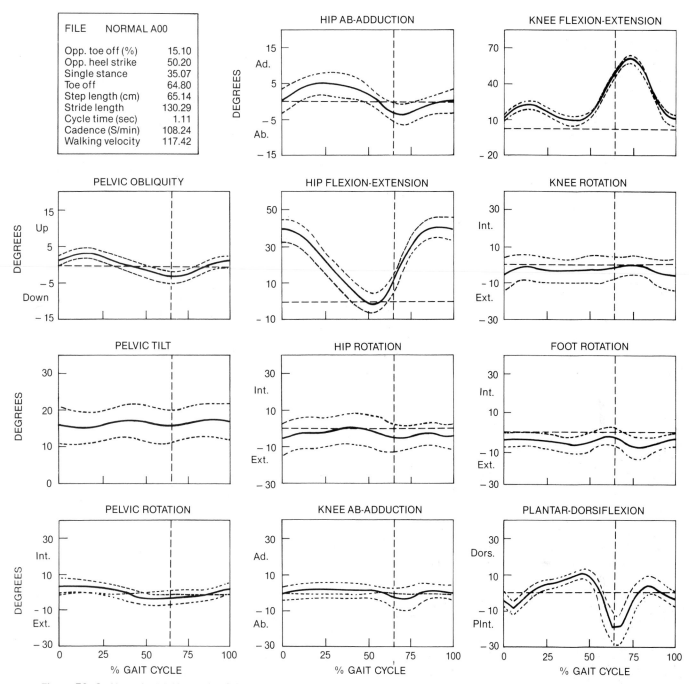

FILE	NORMAL A00
Opp. toe off (%)	15.10
Opp. heel strike	50.20
Single stance	35.07
Toe off	64.80
Step length (cm)	65.14
Stride length	130.29
Cycle time (sec)	1.11
Cadence (S/min)	108.24
Walking velocity	117.42

Figure 32–8. Normal adult kinematics. Solid line is average joint angle; dashed line represents mean plus or minus 1 standard deviation. Note particularly the dorsiflexion angle. (Data collected at Newington Children's Hospital Gait Analysis Laboratory, Newington, CT.)

tia acting on the body's center of gravity (CG); the ground reaction forces' center of pressure (CP) is thus maintained within the base of support (Fig. 32–10).[39] For example, Shumway-Cook et al.[40] determined that standing balance feedback improved balance control (measured by CP) in 14 subjects with hemiplegia from cerebral vascular accident (CVA). Winstein et al.,[41] however, reported that although a controlled trial of standing balance training improves static standing measures, no specific improvement on locomotor parameters could be demonstrated. Indeed, two decades ago

Sheldon[42] found that older subjects can be confused by sway biofeedback, and may perform better with their eyes closed than while receiving postural sway biofeedback!

One limitation of using the CP to measure postural sway is that CP motion maintains a close relationship to CG motion only during relatively normal "ankle strategy" motions, where the subject moves like a pendulum, or a rigid body, about his or her ankles.[43] When upper body motion becomes significant as in a "hip strategy," or when postural sway cannot be assumed to

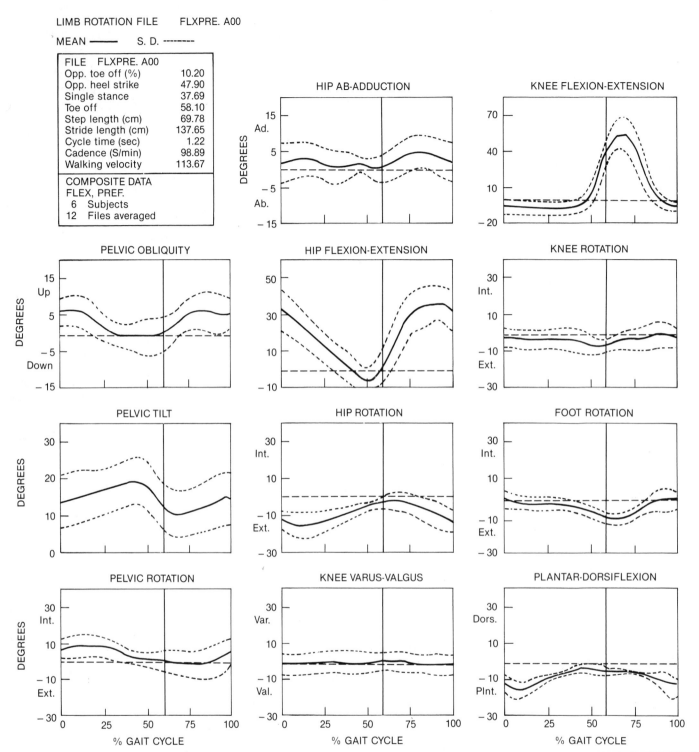

LIMB ROTATION FILE   FLXPRE. A00

MEAN ——— S. D. --------

FILE FLXPRE. A00	
Opp. toe off (%)	10.20
Opp. heel strike	47.90
Single stance	37.69
Toe off	58.10
Step length (cm)	69.78
Stride length (cm)	137.65
Cycle time (sec)	1.22
Cadence (S/min)	98.89
Walking velocity	113.67

COMPOSITE DATA
FLEX, PREF.
  6   Subjects
 12   Files averaged

Figure 32–9. Above-knee amputation kinematics, preferred walking speed. Note that the knee remains fully extended throughout stance. (Data collected at Newington Children's Hospital Gait Analysis Laboratory, Newington, CT.)

stem from ankle motion alone, the CP–CG relationship becomes distorted, so that the CP does not adequately reflect the CM sway.[44]

A second limitation is that during dynamic activities such as locomotion the body's mass *must* be displaced outside its support base (Fig. 32–11). This fundamental difference between static and dynamic stability may account for the reported poor ability of static balance

tests to explain or predict locomotor instability, such as falling, among elders.[45] Most falls occur during dynamic body displacements such as walking, climbing stairs, or arising from a seated position.[46] Indeed, the relationship between the results of standing "posturography" balance tests, such as the Equitest popularized by Nashner and colleagues, and dynamic stability during activities of daily living (ADL) including gait, stair climbing, and

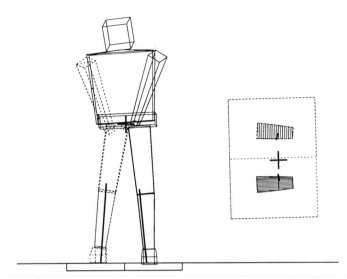

Figure 32–10. During stable, quiet standing, the whole body center of gravity (CG, dark plus sign shown between feet) remains within the base of support, as bounded by the feet (right). Individual center of pressure (CP) positions from each foot can be combined to create a whole body CP. A front view of a whole body model of the same subject in the same quiet standing task (left). The ground reaction vectors (heavy lines from each foot) have, by definition, the CP as their point of application at the ground. Here again the whole body CG is shown as a dark plus sign at waist height.

transferring from sitting to standing, are unknown for *any* balance-disabled humans—despite the growing clinical use of standing posturography to assess patients with balance disorders[43] as well as the elderly.[47]

Clearly, balance rehabilitation will be increasingly important in the next decade (and perhaps throughout the next century) but it is not clear that biofeedback will play a leading role.

In summary, available literature supports the assertion that elderly subjects at risk for falling, and those with neurologic disorders including parkinsonism and hemiplegia, improve their standing balance as a result of standing balance training. Insufficient data exists to assert that standing balance biofeedback confers any benefit upon dynamic locomotor control. Better conceptual definitions of static and dynamic stability are needed,[48] as well as more empirical research.

KINETIC (DYNAMIC FORCE) FEEDBACK

Kinetic or dynamic force feedback renders information regarding the amount or rate of loading through the limbs. As in other types of biofeedback, an audio or visual feedback signal is used. In kinetic feedback, the goal is usually one of informing the patient that weight bearing is correct, or excessive, or insufficient.

Force feedback requires the therapist to be familiar with the same general motor learning strategies (the time sequence, positive reinforcement, and the "two-thirds" success ratio) as discussed previously under EMG and kinematic biofeedback. Understanding the overall goals of kinetic feedback and the equipment limitations is also required.

Types of Kinetic Feedback Devices

The most familiar type of kinetic feedback is a bathroom scale, which can be used to habituate patients to the weight-bearing requirements of their fracture, prosthesis, or orthosis during static standing. The bathroom scale, however, is not useful for dynamic force feedback, in part because it will register artifactually high forces during the loading phase, as in the stance phase of gait. Another familiar but little-appreciated kinetic feedback device is the force reading from isokinetic devices like the Cybex machine.

FOOT SWITCHES

A simple foot switch can be used for kinetic feedback. It is easily fabricated in the physical therapy clinic. A buzzer and a battery connected to a foot switch can warn the patient not to bear weight on a fractured limb, or help to encourage heel-strike gait from a patient with hemiplegia or cerebral palsy. When the metal parts of the foot switch come into contact during the stance phase, the buzzer sounds and gives audible biofeedback. Two foot switches could be used bilaterally to provide stance time symmetry biofeedback. Of course, the

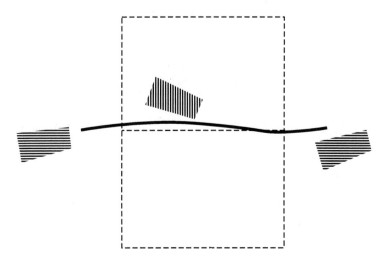

Figure 32–11. Top view of subject walking. The sinusoidal line shows the route taken by the center of gravity (CG) (see Fig. 32–10). Note that the CG never comes within the foot perimeter and so cannot be within the base of support during single limb support (midstance).

weight-bearing force is unknowable using this simple system, but foot switches have the benefit of convenience.

One advantage of foot switches is that they can be used to record the patient's progress in achieving heel contact by attaching them to a strip-chart recorder. This technique was previously used in gait laboratories before more sophisticated methods were devised.

LIMB LOAD MONITOR

A **limb load monitor** (LLM) is most frequently used to provide kinetic feedback in the clinic, because it gives feedback concerning the *amount* of weight born on a limb.[49] Limb load monitors generally have a strain gauge built into an insole or the sole of a sandal. The strain gauge works by decreasing its electrical resistance as the force on the foot increases.[50] Less resistance, in turn, permits more electricity to reach the audio speaker, which beeps faster or at a higher pitch as greater loads are applied.

The feedback threshold is set according to the amount of weight required to be applied on the limb. For example, if an absence of weight bearing is required, the therapist might set the audio signal to respond as soon as 2 pounds or more is sensed by the LLM. When weight bearing exceeds the threshold, an audible tone warns the patient and informs the therapist or orthopedist that the protocol is being violated.[51,52]

In other applications, the therapist may want to encourage weight bearing. Patients with amputation, hemiplegia, and other weight-bearing disorders can use the LLM to inform them when they have achieved the weight-bearing criterion set by the therapist.[53] Again, modest goals are set initially, and then gradually increased as success is achieved consistently. When the patient achieves full weight bearing on the limb, feedback is withdrawn and the patient attempts to maintain the treatment effect without supervision. The LLM can then be used to monitor the patient's success surreptitiously.

Technical Limitations

Only the vertical ground reaction component is registered by LLMs: fore-aft, torsional, and horizontal sheer forces are not monitored separately in present devices. Therefore, limb load monitors may feed back invalid signals, especially if the patient uses a pathologic gait pattern, as is typically true in lower limb disability. The greatest danger of artifact occurs during heel strike, particularly during fast walking.

Until technology improves, the prudent therapist employs limb load feedback only as an indication of gross errors in timing and weight bearing.

Clinical Applications

Gait training is tiring. And gait training with kinetic feedback is probably more tiring, since there is another cognitive demand to cope with. The patient must not only exercise, but must also concentrate on the feedback signal. The therapist must therefore provide frequent rest periods, and occasionally reassess the patient's progress to ensure that treatment goals are accomplished. Fatigue interferes with learning no less in biofeedback than in other neuromuscular reeducation.

The therapist will usually start a treatment session by reviewing the goals for that day with the patient. If it is the patient's first exposure to balance biofeedback or the LLM, the therapist demonstrates the task on him- or herself and then on the patient's "uninvolved" limb.

The first session usually consists of static weight shifting. Next, the patient practices walking in place, usually in the parallel bars. If the patient cannot understand the LLM feedback, the therapist can use bathroom scales combined with the LLM to show the LLM feedback's relationship to a familiar "load monitor."[54]

After consistently successful static performance, the patient is asked to "walk in place" while generating the appropriate biofeedback signal. Weight shifting and balance should be encouraged by stance- and swing-phase biofeedback. After roughly two-thirds or more of the trials are successful, short-distance ambulation with biofeedback can be introduced.

After several sessions, reassess the patient's progress. Are the therapy goals appropriate? Is biofeedback enhancing or interfering with progress in other areas of therapy? Review sessions should occasionally be provided, including static weight shifting and dynamic gait activities, to ensure that the basic skills are not forgotten.

Most important is the need to assess the patient's performance without biofeedback. Normal gait is a smooth, automatic, and subconsciously controlled activity; that goal should remain preeminent. In contrast, biofeedback compels voluntary attention to the tasks to be practiced. Hesitation or slow gait may indicate excessive reliance on the biofeedback, which in fact detracts from normal gait. Some therapists have patients with reasonable cognitive levels recite the pledge of allegiance, or perform mental arithmetic, to allay excessive cognitive control and elicit more automatic control.

To develop normal locomotor skills, the therapist must encourage normal walking speed. Many patients with hemiplegia, for example, can look fairly normal while using biofeedback during slow walking, but when asked to walk at a normal pace, about 1 cycle per second, their control disintegrates. Biofeedback is only a tool; the therapist retains responsibility for the correct timing and speed of movement training.

To summarize, effective kinematic and kinetic biofeedback depends on appropriate goal setting. Patients with hemiplegia should generally be encouraged to flex the affected knee during stance, but patients with above-knee amputations should not. The patient's diagnosis and prosthetic and/or orthotic appliances will give rise to differences in gait requirements, which modify treatment goals and functional expectations. Any therapeutic technique, including biofeedback, should achieve the most efficient gait possible, consistent with safety and stability.

Figure 32–12. Example of computer-assisted biofeedback device. Note that cartridges in foreground supply movement templates or computer games to facilitate patient participation in therapy. (Courtesy of Self-Regulations Systems, Redmond, WA.)

NEW CONCEPTS AND AREAS FOR FURTHER RESEARCH

The necessity for further research in biofeedback cannot be overemphasized. The great potential of biofeedback techniques is that they put the responsibility for healthy behavior squarely upon the patient. The paradigm of therapist or doctor as healer becomes a paternal relic if the patient takes the role of healer. To realize this potential, however, self-regulation techniques such as biofeedback need to be subjected to the scrutiny of critical thinkers and tested empirically through clinical research.

Perhaps the chief impediment to giving patients more direct control of their rehabilitation is our current inability to understand deeply the rules and mechanisms governing human orthopedic and neurologic recovery. We can hardly translate to layman's terms that which scientists do not understand. The challenge to the therapist, then, is to better understand the rules of human behavior. Biofeedback techniques can be used to monitor physiologic results and to help patients gain access to these otherwise unfelt concomitants of recovery. Until the underlying physiology is better understood, technical applications may be futile.

One recent area of excitement is adaptation of computers to rehabilitation. The addition of microcomputers to biofeedback-assisted therapy may improve information processing (Fig. 32–12). Storing normal movement templates in the microcomputer, with its enormous memory, and subsequently requesting patients to approximate those movement patterns has been widely advertised to be effective in teaching neuromuscular skills. However, excess information can overwhelm patients and therapists with its sheer volume.

Perhaps the most pressing deficiency in the rehabilitation biofeedback literature is the lack of controlled studies involving patients. Most of the evidence that supports the utility of biofeedback techniques is based on normal subjects or small samples of patients.

It is abundantly clear that electronic advances should be exploited clinically to the advantage of disabled populations. The therapist must assume the responsibility for exploring its potential, and validating biofeedback techniques through clinical research, particularly on patient populations.

QUESTIONS FOR REVIEW

1. What is the primary psychologic and/or motor learning model employed in biofeedback?

2. What event during muscle activation does EMG biofeedback record?

3. What is the most likely source of an artifactual, rhythmically repeating EMG interference when the EMG electrodes are on the patient's back?

4. Why is input impedance important to therapists using EMG feedback?

5. What is an el-gon? How can it be made in the clinic?

6. What type of biofeedback, kinetic or kinematic, is represented by a bathroom scale?

REFERENCES

1. Basmajian, JV: Introduction: principles and background. In Basmajian, JV (ed): Biofeedback: Principles and Practice for Clinicians. Williams & Wilkins, Baltimore, MD, 1983.

2. Herman, RM, Grillner, S, Stein, PSG, and Stuart, DG (eds): Neural Control of Locomotion. Plenum, New York, 1976.

3. Brooks, VB (ed): Handbook of Physiology. Section 1: The Nervous System, vol 2: Motor Control (Part 1). American Physiological Society, Bethesda, MD, 1981.

4. Mulder, T and Hulstyn, W: Sensory feedback therapy and theoretical knowledge of motor control and learning. Am J Phys Med 63:226, 1984.

5. Winstein, CJ: Knowledge of results and motor learning—implications for physical therapy. Phys Ther 71:140, 1991.

6. Krebs, DE: Clinical electromyographic feedback following meniscectomy: a multiple regression experimental analysis. Phys Ther 61:1017, 1981.

7. Krebs, DE, Staples, WH, Cuttita, D, and Zickel, RE: Knee joint angle: its relationship to quadriceps femoris activity in normal and postarthrotomy limbs. Arch Phys Med Rehabil 64:441, 1983.

8. Lenman, JAE: Quantitative electromyographic changes associated with muscular weakness. J Neurol Neurosurg Psychiatry 22:306, 1959.

9. Lippold, OCJ: Relation between integrated action potentials in human muscle and its isometric tension. J Physiol 117:492, 1952.

10. Wolf, SL: Essential considerations in the use of EMG biofeedback. Phys Ther 58:25, 1978.

11. Inglis, J, Campbell, D, and Donald, MW: Electromyographic biofeedback and neuromuscular rehabilitation. Can J Behav Sci 8:299, 1976.

12. Keefe, FJ, and Surwit, RS: Electromyographic feedback: behavioral treatment of neuromuscular disorders. J Behav Med 1:13, 1978.

13. Cataldo, ME, Bird, BL, and Cunningham, CE: Experimental analysis of EMG feedback in treating cerebral palsy. J Behav Med 1:311, 1978.

14. Wolf, SL: Electromyographic feedback for spinal cord injured patients: a realistic perspective. In Basmajian, JV (ed): Biofeedback: Principles and Practice for Clinicians. Williams & Wilkins, Baltimore, MD, 1983.

15. Balliet, R, Levy, B, and Blood, KMT: Upper extremity sensory feedback therapy in chronic cerebrovascular accident patients with impaired expressive aphasia and auditory comprehension. Arch Phys Med Rehabil 67:304, 1986.

16. Shiavi, R, Champion, S, Freeman, F, and Griffin, P: Variability of electromyographic patterns for level-surface walking through a range of self-selected speeds. Bull Prosthet Res 10:5, 1981.

17. Winter, DA: Pathologic gait diagnosis with computer-averaged electromyographic profiles. Arch Phys Med Rehabil 65:393, 1984.

18. Yang, JF and Winter, DA: Electromyographic amplitude normalization methods: improving their sensitivity as diagnostic tools in gait analysis. Arch Phys Med Rehabil 65:517, 1984.

19. Jacobson, E: Progressive Relaxation, ed 2. University of Chicago Press, Chicago, 1938.

20. Schultz, JH: Das Autogene Training: Konzentrative Selbstent-spannung. Georg Thieme Verlag, Stuttgart, 1932.

21. Stoyva, JM: Guidelines in cultivating general relaxation: biofeedback autogenic training combined. In Basmajian, JV (ed): Biofeedback: Principles and Practice for Clinicians. Williams & Wilkins, Baltimore, MD, 1983.

22. Collins, GA, Cohen, MJ, Naliboff, BD, and Schandler, SL: Comparative analysis of paraspinal and frontalis EMG, heart rate and skin conductance in chronic low back pain patients and normals to various postures and stress. Scand J Rehabil Med 14:39, 1982.

23. Sedlacek, K: Biofeedback for Raynaud's disease. Psychosomatics 20:537, 1979.

24. Korein, J and Brudny, J: Integrated EMG feedback in the management of spasmodic torticollis and focal dystonia: a prospective study of 80 patients. In Yahr, MD (ed): The Basal Ganglia. Raven Press, New York, 1976.

25. Draper, V and Ballard, L: Electrical stimulation versus electromyographic biofeedback in the recovery of quadriceps femoris muscle function following anterior cruciate ligament surgery. Phys Ther 71:455, 1991.

26. Shelton, GL and Thigpen, LK: Rehabilitation of patellofemoral dys-

function: a review of the literature. Journal of Orthopedic and Sports Physical Therapy 14:243, 1991.

27. Health and Public Policy Committee, American College of Physicians: Biofeedback for neuromuscular disorders. Ann Intern Med 102:854, 1985.

28. Biofeedback Society of America, Committee on Legislation and Public Policy: The Efficacy of Biofeedback in the Treatment of Specified Medical Disorders. Biofeedback Society of America, Wheat Ridge, CO, 1982.

29. Binder, SA: Assessing the effectiveness of positional feedback to treat an ataxic patient: application of a single-subject design. Phys Ther 61:735, 1981.

30. Gilbert, JA, Maxwell, GM, George, RT Jr, and McElhaney, JH: Technical note—auditory feedback of knee angle for amputees. Prosthet Orthot Int 6:103, 1982.

31. DeBacher, G: Feedback goniometers for rehabilitation. In Basmajian, JV (ed): Biofeedback: Principles and Practice for Clinicians. Williams & Wilkins, Baltimore, MD, 1983.

32. Koheil, R and Mandel, AR: Joint position biofeedback facilitation of physical therapy in gait training. Am J Phys Med 59:288, 1980.

33. Colborne, CR and, Onley, SJ: Feedback of joint angle and EMG in gait of able-bodied subjects. Arch Phys Med Rehabil 71:478, 1990.

34. Morris, ME, Matyas, TA, Bach, TM, and Goldie, PA: Electrogoniometric feedback: its effect on genu recurvatum in stroke. Arch Phys Med Rehabil 73:1147, 1992.

35. Fernie, G, Holden, J, and Soto, M: Biofeedback training of knee control in the above-knee amputee. Am J Phys Med 57:161, 1978.

36. Wooldridge, CP, Leiper, C, and Ogston, DG: Biofeedback training of knee joint position of the cerebral palsied child. Physiotherapy Canada 28:138, 1976.

37. Krebs, DE: Effect of Variations in Residuum Environment and Walking Rate on Residual Limb Muscle Activity of Selected Above-Knee Amputees. PhD Dissertation; University Microfilms International, Ann Arbor, MI, 1986.

38. Murray, MP, Wood, A, Seireg, A, and Sepic, S: Normal postural stability and steadiness: quantitative assessment. J Bone Joint Surg Am 57A:510, 1975.

39. Horak, FB: Clinical measurement of postural control in adults. Phys Ther 67:1881, 1987.

40. Shumway-Cook, A, Anson, D, and Haller, S: Postural sway biofeedback: its effect on reestablishing stance stability in hemiplegic patients. Arch Phys Med Rehabil 69:395, 1988.

41. Winstein, CJ, Gardner, ER, McNeal, DR, et al: Standing balance training: effect on balance and locomotion in hemiparetic adults. Arch Phys Med Rehabil 70:755, 1989.

42. Sheldon, JH: The effect of age on the control of sway. Gerontol Clin 5:129, 1963.

43. Nashner, LM and McCollum, G: The organization of human postural movements: a formal basis and experimental synthesis. Behav Brain Sciences 8:135, 1985.

44. Benda, BJ, Riley, PO, and Krebs, DE: Biomechanical relationship between center of gravity and center of pressure during standing. IEEE Trans BME, Rehabilitation Engineering, submitted.

45. Fernie, GR, Gryfe, CI, Holliday, PJ, and Llewellyn, A: The relationship of postural sway in standing to the incidence of falls in geriatric subjects. Age Ageing 11:11, 1982.

46. Tinetti, ME, Speechley, M, and Ginter, SF: Risk factors for falls among elderly persons living in the community. N Engl J Med 319:1701, 1988.

47. Peterka, RJ and Black, FO: Age-related changes in human posture control: sensory organization tests. Journal of Vestibular Research 1:73, 1990.

48. Krebs, DE: Biofeedback in therapeutic exercise. In: Basmajian, JV and Wolf, SL (eds): Therapeutic Exercise, ed 5. Williams & Wilkins, Baltimore, 1990, p 109.

49. Gapsis, JJ, Grabois, M, Borrell, RM, et al: Limb load monitor: evaluation of a sensory feedback device for controlled weight bearing. Arch Phys Med Rehabil 63:38, 1982.

50. Wolf, SL and Binder-Macleod, SA: Use of the Krusen limb load monitor to quantify temporal and loading measurements of gait. Phys Ther 62:976, 1982.

51. Craik, RL and Wannstedt, GT: The limb load monitor: an augmented sensory feedback device. In Proceedings of a Conference

on Devices and Systems for the Disabled. Krusen Research Center, Philadelphia, PA, 1975, p 19.

52. Wannstedt, GT and Herman, RM: Use of augmented sensory feedback to achieve symmetrical standing. Phys Ther 58:553, 1978.

53. Kegel, B and Moore, AJ: Load cell: a device to monitor weight bearing for lower extremity amputees. Phys Ther 57:652, 1977.

54. Peper, E and Robertson, J: Biofeedback use of common objects: the bathroom scale in physical therapy. Biofeedback Self-Regul 1:237, 1976.

SUPPLEMENTAL READINGS

Azrin, N, et al: Behavioral engineering: Postural control by a portable apparatus. J Appl Behav Anal 1:99, 1968.

Ball, T, McCrady, R, and Hart, A: Automated reinforcement of head posture in two cerebral palsied, retarded children. Percept Mot Skills 40:619, 1975.

Basmajian, JV, et al: Biofeedback treatment of foot-drop after stroke compared with standard rehabilitation technique: Effects on voluntary control and strength. Arch Phys Med Rehabil 56:231, 1975.

Bjork, L and Wetzel, A: A positional biofeedback device for sitting balance. Phys Ther 63:1460, 1983.

Block, JD, et al: Hemiplegic hand spasticity: Amelioration by assisted extension practice with augmented feedback. Arch Phys Med Rehabil 52:573, 1971.

Bohannon, RW and Short, D: Compact device for positional biofeedback. Phys Ther 64:1235, 1984.

Bowman, BR, Baker, LL, and Waters, RL: Positional feedback and electrical stimulation: An automated treatment for the hemiplegic wrist. Arch Phys Med Rehabil 60:497, 1979.

Brown, DM, DeBacher, GA, and Basmajian, JV: Feedback goniometers for hand rehabilitation. Am J Occup Ther 33(7):458, 1979.

Catanese, AA and Sandford DA: Head-position training through biofeedback: Prosthetic or cure? Dev Med Child Neurol 26:369, 1984.

Driscoll, B: Creative technological aids for the learning-disabled child. Am J Occup Ther 29:102, 1975.

Dworkin, B: Instrumental learning for the treatment of disease. Health Psychol 1:45, 1982.

Greenberg, S and Fowler, RS: Kinesthetic biofeedback: A treatment modality for elbow range of motion in hemiplegia. Am J Occup Ther 34:738, 1980.

Hallum, A: Subject-induced reinforcement of head lifting in the prone position. Phys Ther 64:1390, 1984.

Hallum, A: How to build simple, inexpensive biofeedback systems. Phys Ther 64:1235, 1984.

Harris F, Spelman, F, and Hymer, J: Electronic sensory aids as treatment for cerebral palsied children. Phys Ther 54:354, 1974.

Harris, FA: Treatment with a position feedback-controlled head stabilizer. Am J Phys Med 58:169, 1979.

Huggins, M and Gallen, D: A training program for operation of a head-controlled electric wheelchair. Physiotherapy (Canada) 36:204, 1984.

Hurd, WW, Pegram, V, and Nepomuceno, C: Comparison of actual and simulated EMG biofeedback in the treatment of hemiplegic patients. Am J Phys Med 59:73, 1980.

Ince, LP, Leon, MS, and Christidis, D: Experimental foundations of EMG biofeedback with the upper extremity: A review of the literature. Biofeedback Self Regul 9:371, 1984.

Ince, LP, Leon, MS, and Christidis, D: EMG biofeedback for improvement of upper extremity function: A critical review of the literature. Physiotherapy (Canada) 37:12, 1985.

Inglis, J, et al: Electromyographic biofeedback and physical therapy of the hemiplegic upper limb. Arch Phys Med Rehabil 65:755, 1984.

Lee, K-H, et al: Myofeedback for muscle retraining in hemiplegic patients. Arch Phys Med Rehabil 57:588, 1976.

Leiper, CI, et al: Sensory feedback for head control in cerebral palsy. Phys Ther 61:512, 1981.

Maloney, FP: A simplified mercury switch head-control biofeedback device. Biofeedback Self Regul 5:257, 1980.

Middaugh, SJ: EMG feedback as a muscle re-education technique: A controlled study. Phys Ther 58:11, 1978.

Middaugh, SJ and Miller, MC: Electromyographic feedback: effects on voluntary muscle contractions in paretic subjects. Arch Phys Med Rehabil 61:24, 1980.

Morris, A and Brown, M: Electronic training devices for hand rehabilitation. Am J. Occup Ther 30:376, 1976.

Mroczek, N, Halpern, D, and McHugh, R: Electromyographic feedback and physical therapy for neuromuscular retraining in hemiplegia. Arch Phys Med Rehabil 59:258, 1978.

O'Brien, F and Azrin, N: Control of posture by informational feedback. J Appl Behav Anal 3:235, 1970.

Prevo, AJH, Visser, SL, and Vogelaar, TW: Effect of EMG feedback on paretic muscles and abnormal co-contraction in the hemiplegic arm, compared with conventional physical therapy. Scand J Rehabil 14:121, 1982.

Tiller, J, et al: Treatment of functional chronic stooped posture using a training device and behavior therapy. Phys Ther 62:1597, 1982.

Turczynski, B, Hartje, W, and Sturm, W: Electromyographic feedback treatment of chronic hemiparesis: An attempt to quantify treatment effects. Arch Phys Med Rehabil 65:526, 1984.

Walmsley, RP, Crichton, L, and Droog, D: Music as a feedback mechanism for teaching head control to severely handicapped children: a pilot study. Develop Med Child Neurol 23:739, 1981.

Wolf, SL: Electromyographic biofeedback applications to stroke patients: A critical review. Phys Ther 63:1448, 1983.

Wolf, SL and Binder-MacLeod, SA: Electromyographic biofeedback applications to the hemiplegic patient: Changes in lower extremity neuromuscular and functional status. Phys Ther 63:1404, 1983.

Wolf, SL and Binder-MacLeod, SA: Electromyographic biofeedback applications to the hemiplegic patient: Changes in upper extremity neuromuscular and functional status. Phys Ther 63:1393, 1983.

Wooldridge, CP and Russel, G: Head position training with the cerebral palsied child: An application of biofeedback techniques. Arch Phys Med Rehabil 57:407, 1976.

Zimnicki, BZ and Fernie, GR: Biofeedback and the lower amputee: A new training aid. Physiotherapy (Canada) 28:7,

GLOSSARY

Artifact: A voltage signal generated by a source other than the one of interest.

Biofeedback: "A technique to reveal to human beings some of their internal physiological events, normal and abnormal, in the form of visual and auditory signals in order to teach them to manipulate these otherwise involuntary or unfelt events by manipulating the displayed signals."[1]

Common mode rejection ratio (CMRR): A proportion expressing an amplifier's ability to reject unwanted noise while amplifying the wanted signal.

Electrogoniometer: A rheostat, or variable resistor, with extended attachments for limb segments. Joint rotation changes the "el-gon's" resistance to a current passing to a recorder or speaker for kinesiologic recording or biofeedback, respectively.

Endogenous: Produced or caused by factors within a cell or organism.

Impedance: The property of a substance that offers resistance to current flow in an alternating current.

Kinematics: The description of the movement and displacement of objects (usually limb segments) in motion without reference to the forces that cause motion.

Kinetics: The description of the forces applied to objects (usually limb segments) in motion.

Limb load monitor: A device to measure and report the forces experienced by the lower limbs during walking or other weight-bearing activities.

Noise: An unwanted electrical signal that is detected along with the desired signal.

Ohmmeter: A device that measures electrical resistance; measured in ohms.

Ohm's Law: The strength of an electrical current is equal to the voltage divided by the resistance.

Potentiometer: An instrument used to measure voltage.

Rheostat: A mechanism for regulating the resistance in an electrical circuit; controls the amount of electrical current entering a circuit; variable resistor.

Voltmeter: An instrument for measuring electromotive force (in volts).

Index

Note: Page numbers followed by *f* indicate figures; those followed by *t* indicate tables.